Y0-CRM-492

# WORLD COMMUNISM

# A HANDBOOK

# 1918-1965

# WORLD COMMUNISM

# A HANDBOOK

# 1918-1965

Edited
by
Witold S. Sworakowski

HOOVER INSTITUTION PRESS
Stanford University
Stanford, California
1973

The Hoover Institution on War, Revolution and Peace, founded at Stanford University in 1919 by the late President Herbert Hoover, is a center for advanced study and research on public and international affairs in the twentieth century. The views expressed in its publications are entirely those of the authors and do not necessarily reflect the views of the Hoover Institution.

Hoover Institution Publications 108
International Standard Book Number 0-8179-1081-3
Library of Congress Card Number 70-149798
Printed in the United States of America
© 1973 by the Board of Trustees of the
  Leland Stanford Junior University
All rights reserved

# TABLE OF CONTENTS

| | |
|---|---|
| Preface | ix |
| Contributors | xiii |
| Albania   *Nicholas C. Pano* | 3 |
| Algeria   *Claude Harmel* | 7 |
| Argentina   *Rollie E. Poppino* | 13 |
| Armenia   *Louise Nalbandian* | 15 |
| Australia   *Alastair Davidson* | 18 |
| Austria   *Witold S. Sworakowski* | 22 |
| The Balkan Communist Federation   *Witold S. Sworakowski* | 29 |
| Belgium   *Branko Lazitch* | 31 |
| Belorussia   *John S. Reshetar, Jr.* | 36 |
| Bolivia   *Rollie E. Poppino* | 39 |
| Brazil   *Rollie E. Poppino* | 40 |
| Bulgaria   *L. A. D. Dellin* | 42 |
| Burma   *Frank N. Trager* | 47 |
| Cambodia   *Branko Lazitch* | 51 |
| Cameroon   *Claude Harmel* | 54 |
| Canada   *Ivan Avakumovic* | 56 |
| Ceylon   *George J. Lerski* | 59 |
| Chile   *Rollie E. Poppino* | 64 |
| China   *Dennis J. Doolin and John E. Rue* | 66 |
| Colombia   *Rollie E. Poppino* | 74 |
| The Communist Information Bureau   *Witold S. Sworakowski* | 76 |
| The Communist International   *Witold S. Sworakowski* | 78 |
| The Communist Youth International   *Witold S. Sworakowski* | 92 |
| Costa Rica   *Rollie E. Poppino* | 95 |
| The Council for Mutual Economic Assistance   *Witold S. Sworakowski* | 96 |
| Cuba   *Theodore Draper* | 98 |
| Cyprus   *Georges Georgalas* | 105 |
| Czechoslovakia   *Richard F. Staar* | 108 |
| Denmark   *Bjarne Nørretranders* | 115 |
| Dominican Republic   *Rollie E. Poppino* | 118 |
| Ecuador   *Rollie E. Poppino* | 119 |
| El Salvador   *Rollie E. Poppino* | 121 |
| Estonia   *Elmar Lipping and Edgar Anderson* | 122 |
| Finland   *Jack L. Kangas* | 125 |
| The Fourth International   *Witold S. Sworakowski* | 131 |
| France   *Claude Harmel* | 136 |
| Georgia   *Peter P. Kruschin* | 148 |
| Germany   *Ossip K. Flechtheim* | 151 |

| | |
|---|---|
| Great Britain *Walter Kendall* | 163 |
| Greece *Georges Georgalas* | 170 |
| Guadeloupe *Claude Harmel* | 174 |
| Guatemala *Rollie E. Poppino* | 177 |
| Guyana *Kenneth M. Glazier* | 179 |
| Haiti *Rollie E. Poppino* | 182 |
| Honduras *Rollie E. Poppino* | 184 |
| Hungary *Rudolf L. Tőkés* | 185 |
| Iceland *Witold S. Sworakowski* | 192 |
| India *Morton Schwartz* | 194 |
| Indonesia *Guy Pauker and Ewa Pauker* | 200 |
| The International Association of Democratic Lawyers *Milorad Popov* | 206 |
| International Communist Front Organizations *Witold S. Sworakowski* | 210 |
| The International Federation of Resistance Fighters *Milorad Popov* | 213 |
| The International Organization for Aid to Revolutionaries *Witold S. Sworakowski* | 216 |
| The International Organization of Journalists *Milorad Popov* | 217 |
| The International Peasants' Council *Witold S. Sworakowski* | 219 |
| The International Union of Students *Milorad Popov* | 221 |
| Iran *George Lenczowski* | 225 |
| Iraq *George Rentz* | 229 |
| Ireland *Witold S. Sworakowski* | 232 |
| Israel *Jacob M. Landau* | 235 |
| Italy *Charles F. Delzell* | 238 |
| Japan *Robert A. Scalapino* | 243 |
| Jordan *George Rentz* | 251 |
| Kazakhstan *Richard A. Pierce* | 253 |
| Kirgizia *Richard A. Pierce* | 255 |
| Korea *Chong-Sik Lee* | 257 |
| Laos *Branko Lazitch* | 263 |
| Latin America *Rollie E. Poppino* | 266 |
| Latvia *Edgar Anderson* | 297 |
| Lebanon and Syria *Michel G. Nabti* | 300 |
| Lesotho *Lewis H. Gann* | 306 |
| Lithuania *Alfred Erich Senn* | 308 |
| Luxembourg *Nicholas Lang* | 312 |
| Malagasy Republic *Claude Harmel* | 314 |
| Malaysia and Singapore *Frances L. Starner* | 316 |
| Martinique *Claude Harmel* | 321 |
| Mexico *Rollie E. Poppino* | 324 |
| Morocco *Claude Harmel* | 326 |
| Nepal *Leo E. Rose* | 330 |

The Netherlands   *Branko Lazitch* .................................... 333
New Zealand   *Herbert Roth* ........................................ 337
Nicaragua   *Rollie E. Poppino* ...................................... 340
Niger Republic   *Claude Harmel* .................................... 341
Nigeria   *Lewis H. Gann* ............................................ 343
Norway   *Jahn Otto Johansen* ...................................... 345
Outer Mongolia   *Tamotsu Takase* .................................. 348
Pakistan   *Branko Lazitch* .......................................... 351
Panama   *Rollie E. Poppino* ........................................ 354
Paraguay   *Rollie E. Poppino* ...................................... 355
Peru   *Rollie E. Poppino* .......................................... 356
The Philippines   *Claude A. Buss* .................................. 358
Poland   *Witold S. Sworakowski* .................................... 361
Portugal   *Ronald H. Chilcote* ...................................... 370
The Red International of Labor Unions   *Witold S. Sworakowski* ........ 375
The Red Sport International   *Witold S. Sworakowski* ................ 377
Réunion   *Claude Harmel* .......................................... 379
Rumania   *Stephen Fischer-Galati* .................................. 380
San Marino   *Branko Lazitch* ...................................... 384
Senegal   *Lewis H. Gann* .......................................... 385
South Africa   *Lewis H. Gann* ...................................... 388
Spain   *Ronald H. Chilcote* ........................................ 395
Subsaharan Africa   *Peter Duignan* ................................ 402
The Sudan   *Lewis H. Gann* ........................................ 412
Sweden   *Bruno Kalnins* .......................................... 414
Switzerland   *Witold S. Sworakowski* .............................. 418
Tadzhikistan   *Richard A. Pierce* .................................. 425
Thailand   *Branko Lazitch* ........................................ 427
Tunisia   *Claude Harmel* .......................................... 429
Turkey   *George S. Harris* ........................................ 434
Turkmenistan   *Richard A. Pierce* .................................. 439
The Ukraine   *John S. Reshetar, Jr.* ................................ 440
Union of Soviet Socialist Republics   *John S. Reshetar, Jr.* .......... 445
United Arab Republic   *George Rentz* .............................. 458
United States of America   *Theodore Draper* ........................ 462
Uruguay   *Rollie E. Poppino* ...................................... 472
Uzbekistan   *Richard A. Pierce* .................................... 474
Venezuela   *Rollie E. Poppino* .................................... 476
Vietnam   *Frank N. Trager* ........................................ 477
The Warsaw Treaty Organization   *Witold S. Sworakowski* .......... 484
The Women's International Democratic Federation   *Milorad Popov* ...... 485
The World Council of Peace   *Milorad Popov* ........................ 488

The World Federation of Democratic Youth  *Milorad Popov* ..............492
The World Federation of Scientific Workers  *Milorad Popov* ..............496
The World Federation of Trade Unions  *Milorad Popov* ................498
Yugoslavia  *Milorad M. Drachkovitch* ...........................503

Appendix: List of Communist Parties by Country, with Name
   Changes, 1918-1965  *Witold S. Sworakowski* .......................515
Index of Persons....................................................537
Index of Subjects ..................................................553

# PREFACE

This *Handbook*, limited in coverage to the years 1918 to 1965, provides the background information for the Hoover Institution's *Yearbook on International Communist Affairs*, which began publication in 1967 with coverage of the year 1966. Seven *Yearbooks* are now available. The user of the much more detailed *Yearbook* will find in the *Handbook* an encyclopedic treatment of past events in the international communist movement. Conversely, the user of this *Handbook* will find in the *Yearbook* information on the movement and the individual communist parties since the beginning of 1966.

Ever since communism become a subject of interest to scholars, librarians, students, publicists, and the broad public, there has been a need for a concise reference book on the international movement and its composite parts, the communist parties of the world. The *Handbook* attempts to meet this need. It provides a succinct historical background for every communist party that existed anywhere in the world up to the end of 1965, and it covers the developments leading to the founding of each party and the most important activities of each.

The chief difficulty in preparing such a volume was the fact that communist parties have always operated on two levels—openly wherever political conditions permitted, and clandestinely where the parties were illegal and even in some countries where open activities were allowed. As a result, factual information on organization, membership, and the full range of activities of communist parties was not easy to obtain. In most cases the only available public source was the communist press, whose information was, under the circumstances, incomplete and of limited reliability. Each of the articles in this volume, however, was prepared by a specialist on the affairs of the country discussed. Thus fifty-three scholars from all over the world have contributed articles which in many instances are based on firsthand knowledge. A full list of the contributors and their affiliations follows the Preface.

A related problem was the identification of a particular party as a communist party. For those parties active before World War II, membership in the Communist International, or Comintern, was considered sufficient evidence of communist character. The conditions of admission to the Comintern clearly stipulated that only communist parties were eligible. During and after World War II, however, when many parties operated under names intended to disguise their true orientation, some other objective criterion was needed. In this case participation of party representatives in the international meetings of communist parties in Moscow in 1957 and 1960 and attendance at congresses of the Communist Party of the Soviet Union were considered sufficient evidence of a party's communist nature. The branch of the international communist movement organized by Trotskyist groups and known as the Fourth International is surveyed in a separate article, rather than being systematically covered in its national manifestations.

Many parties have changed their names since 1918, in some cases several times. Most of these changes are noted in the text, and the index facilitates their location. Furthermore, a list of all parties, arranged alphabetically by country, with changed party names given in chronological order, has been added as an appendix. Thus any communist party may be readily identified as such regardless of numerous name changes, and regardless of whether its name actually includes the term "communist."

The *Handbook* is organized alphabetically by country, and there is an article on each of the 106 countries in which a communist party was or is active. There are also articles on two large geographical units, Latin America and Subsaharan Africa. These overviews of the development of organized communism in those two areas as a whole shed a great deal of light on developments in the individual countries. In addition, articles on the international communist organizations operating before and after World War II—the prewar Comintern and the postwar Cominform—have been included. But the picture of the international communist movement would still be incomplete if the many communist front organizations functioning on an international scale were to be omitted. Therefore an overview of these organizations is presented, along with articles on the six auxiliary organizations of the Comintern and the nine major post-World War II front organizations. Furthermore, short articles on the Council for Mutual Economic Assistance and the Warsaw Treaty Organization also have been added in order to explain to the reader the nature of those organizations created after World War II by communist-dominated states. Cross references in individual articles refer the reader to pertinent related events in the general area or the international movement.

Those communist leaders who used party pseudonyms are generally referred to throughout the text by those pseudonyms. In many instances the real name is given in parentheses at the first mention of the pseudonym. For each individual, the real name is indicated in the index, along with the known pseudonyms he or she used in different times and countries.

For convenient reference, most articles are followed by a paragraph on important party records or documents and on party press organs, a list of party congresses, and a short bibliography. The older, larger parties have published quite detailed information on their activities at various times, and there is ample literature on them. However, the dozens of newer, smaller parties in all parts of the world have published scant information. Bibliographies on some of the recently founded parties in Africa, for example, consist almost exclusively of journal articles simply because usually no books on them are yet available.

The footnotes documenting important events and facts refer to the original sources of information. As might be expected, few of these works are in English, and hence they are available only at a few specialized libraries. Most of them may be found in the library of the Hoover Institution on War, Revolution and Peace at Stanford University.

Although the writing style of each contributor has been retained in so far as possible, as an aid to the reader certain editorial points have been made consistent throughout. The *Handbook* deals with communist parties that use some forty different languages. In general the names of all political parties are given in the original language and in English translation, and are then referred to within the article by abbreviation; thus the French Communist Party (Parti Communiste Français, PCF) is referred to in the article on France as the PCF and in other articles as the French Communist Party. Exceptions are party names which customarily appear in some other form, such as the Communist Party of the Soviet Union (CPSU), the Chinese Communist Party (CCP), the League for the Independence of Vietnam (Viet Minh), and a very few others. Temporary coalitions and electoral blocs and labor and youth groups (with a few well-known exceptions) are referred to in English after their first mention in an article; the names of the numerous international mass and front organizations are given in English.

Each of the fifty-three scholars who contributed to the *Handbook* was asked to discuss certain general topics as well as any pertinent matters peculiar to the country, party, or front organization under discussion. Unfortunately, some articles had to be shortened to fit the available space; each shortened version was checked by its author to ensure that no critical information had been omitted. In many instances the writers were asked for further specific details. Articles submitted in French, German, or Russian were translated; the English versions were then checked by the writers. Some articles by writers for whom English was not a first tongue required clarification of language; again, any questions of meaning were referred to the writer. Thus, while the time required in preparing this extensive work was lengthened by these checking procedures, each contributor has retained full responsibility for the content of his article.

As editor of and contributor to this collective work, I should like to express my warmest thanks to each of the fifty-two other contributors to this volume. I am grateful to them for the time and effort they devoted to preparing the material, their friendly cooperation in adjusting their articles to the space available, and finally, their patience in awaiting publication of this work. Most of them have undoubtedly participated in collective works, but perhaps not in one that had fifty-three contributors and was prepared by a team of only four people. I undertook this work with the help of my trustworthy secretary and research assistant, Mrs. Laverne Marcotte Klebofski, whose aid extended from tracking down minute details to the translation of a number of the contributions from French into English. Without her devoted help, this volume would not have been completed. A free-lance editor assisted in preparing the work of so many writers for publication in a single volume. Miss Liselotte Hofmann, an editor for the Hoover Institution Press, reviewed the entire manuscript and supervised its proofreading and indexing; and Mrs. Carole H. Norton, editor-in-chief at the press, gave generous support in preparing the manuscript for print. I am greatly indebted to them.

But this *Handbook* owes its appearance first of all to the Director of the Hoover Institution, Dr. W. Glenn Campbell, who recognized the great need for such a reference work and made Institution funds available for the project.

WITOLD S. SWORAKOWSKI

Stanford, California

# CONTRIBUTORS

Witold S. Sworakowski, Professor Emeritus, Stanford University, and Consultant to the Director, Hoover Institution, Stanford, California; editor of *Handbook*

Edgar Anderson, Professor of History, San Jose State College, San Jose, California

Ivan Avakumovic, Professor of History, University of British Columbia, Vancouver, British Columbia

Claude A. Buss, Professor of History Emeritus, Stanford University, Stanford, California

Ronald H. Chilcote, Associate Professor of Political Science, University of California, Riverside, California

Alastair Davidson, Lecturer in Politics, Monash University, Clayton, Australia

L. A. D. Dellin, Professor of Economics and Political Science and Director of the Center for Area Studies, The University of Vermont, Burlington, Vermont

Charles F. Delzell, Professor of History, Vanderbilt University, Nashville, Tennessee

Dennis J. Doolin, Research Curator of East Asian Collection, Hoover Institution, Stanford, California

Milorad M. Drachkovitch, Senior Fellow, Hoover Institution, Stanford, California

Theodore Draper, Research Fellow, Hoover Institution, Stanford, California; and Member, Institute of Advanced Study, Princeton, New Jersey

Peter Duignan, Senior Fellow and Curator of African Collection, Hoover Institution, Stanford, California

Stephen Fischer-Galati, Professor of History, University of Colorado, Boulder, Colorado

Ossip K. Flechtheim, Professor of Political Science, Otto-Suhr-Institut, Free University of Berlin, Berlin

Lewis H. Gann, Senior Fellow and Deputy Curator of African Collection, Hoover Institution, Stanford, California

Georges Georgalas, Editor, *Sovietology*, Athens

Kenneth M. Glazier, Chief Librarian, University of Calgary, Calgary, Alberta

Claude Harmel, Editor, *Est & ouest*, Paris

George S. Harris, Visiting Associate Professor, School of Advanced International Studies, The Johns Hopkins University, Washington, D.C.

Jahn Otto Johansen, Norsk Rikskringkasting, Oslo

Bruno Kalnins, Slaviska Institutionen, University of Stockholm, Stockholm

Jack L. Kangas, Instructor in Political Science, Purdue University, Lafayette, Indiana

Walter Kendall, Senior Research Fellow, Nuffield College, Oxford University, Oxford, England

xiv  CONTRIBUTORS

Peter P. Kruschin, Assistant Chief Editor, *Bulletin*, Institute for the Study of the USSR, Munich, Germany

Jacob M. Landau, Professor of Political Science, The Hebrew University, Jerusalem

Nicolas Lang, Editor, *Est & ouest*, Paris

Branko Lazitch, Editor, *Est & ouest*, Paris

Chong-Sik Lee, Associate Professor of Political Science, University of Pennsylvania, Philadelphia, Pennsylvania

George Lenczowski, Professor of Political Science, University of California, Berkeley, California

George J. Lerski, Professor of Political Science, University of San Francisco, San Francisco, California

Elmar Lipping, Brooklyn, New York

Michel G. Nabti, Assistant Curator of Middle East Collection, Hoover Institution, Stanford, California

Louise Nalbandian, Professor of History, California State University, Fresno, California

Bjarne Nørretranders, Professor of East European History, University of Copenhagen, Copenhagen

Nicholas C. Pano, Assistant Professor of History, Western Illinois University, Macomb, Illinois

Ewa Pauker, Santa Monica, California

Guy Pauker, The Rand Corporation, Santa Monica, California

Richard A. Pierce, Professor of History, Queen's University, Kingston, Ontario

Milorad Popov, Research Associate, Hoover Institution, Stanford, California

Rollie E. Poppino, Professor of History, University of California, Davis, California

George Rentz, Curator of Middle East Collection, Hoover Institution, Stanford, California

John S. Reshetar, Jr., Professor of Political Science, University of Washington, Seattle, Washington

Leo E. Rose, Lecturer in Political Science and Associate Editor of *Asian Survey*, University of California, Berkeley, California

Herbert Roth, Deputy Librarian, University of Auckland, Auckland, New Zealand

John E. Rue, Professor of Political Science, Oakland University, Rochester, Michigan

Robert A. Scalapino, Professor of Political Science, University of California, Berkeley, California

Morton Schwartz, Associate Professor of Political Science, University of California, Riverside, California

Alfred Erich Senn, Professor of History, University of Wisconsin, Madison, Wisconsin

Richard F. Staar, Senior Fellow and Associate Director, Hoover Institution, Stanford, California

Frances L. Starner, Associate Professor of Political Science, The University of North Carolina, Charlotte, North Carolina

Tamotsu Takase, Professor of Political Science, Kyoto Sangyo University, Kyoto, Japan

Rudolf L. Tőkés, Associate Professor of Political Science, University of Connecticut, Storrs, Connecticut

Frank N. Trager, Professor of International Affairs and Director of National Security Program, New York University, New York

# WORLD COMMUNISM

# A HANDBOOK

# 1918-1965

# AFRICA

*See* Subsaharan Africa *and individual countries*

# ALBANIA

The Albanian Communist Party (Partia Komuniste e Shqipërisë, PKSH) was founded on November 8, 1941, and in 1948 was renamed the Albanian Party of Labor (Partia e Punës së Shqipërisë, PPSH). Enver Hoxha, a former schoolteacher, was appointed leader of the PKSH at its founding conference; in 1965 Hoxha was still party leader and the only surviving member of the original Albanian central committee.

## HISTORY

Prior to 1941 the communists played only a minor role in Albanian political life. During the first days of the bolshevik revolution a handful of Albanians were swayed toward the Soviet regime by the bolsheviks' exposé of the 1915 London treaty providing for the partition of Albania. In December 1920 the Kosovo committee, which advocated the formation of an enlarged ethnic Albanian state, sought to enlist Soviet support for this venture.

Meanwhile the Soviets, through their agent in Albania, the Russian-educated Kostandin Boshnjaku, had been attempting to build a following among Albanian students and youth. The procommunist elements in Albania unanimously supported the short-lived liberal Fan Noli government (June-December 1924), and when Ahmed Zogu returned to power, most communist sympathizers fled the country. One group, based in Vienna, established the National Liberation Committee (Komiteti Nacional Clirimtar), known as Konare. This organization maintained close ties with the Balkan Communist Federation and the Comintern. A second group, which numbered about two dozen, went to the Soviet Union for ideological and political indoctrination. In August 1928 they formed the Albanian Communist Group (Grupi Komunist Shqiptar, GKSH) in Moscow, chiefly for the purpose of preparing cadres for service in Albania.

By 1928 the first communist cell in Albania had been formed in Koritsa (Korçë); and in 1930 the GKSH sent several agents into Albania to strengthen the communist movement there. With the exception of Ali Kelmendi, who worked closely with the Koritsa group until his imprisonment in 1932, the Soviet-trained organizers met with little success. During the 1930s the few converts to communism in Albania were mostly students and laborers.

On the eve of the Italian invasion in April 1939, there were four major Albanian communist groups, two centered in Tirana and the others in Koritsa and Skutari (Shkodër). Of these, only the Koritsa group had ties with the Comintern.

During 1940 and 1941, the Albanian communist factions had made several unsuccessful attempts to forge a common front. It was not until the intervention during the summer and fall of 1941 of two Yugoslav communists, Miladin Popović and Dušan Mugoša, members of the Kosovo-Metohija (Kosmet) regional committee, that the Albanian groups were brought together as a party. After the PKSH was founded in November 1941, Popović and Mugoša remained in Albania. By 1944 with the aid of other Yugoslav advisors, they had succeeded in transforming the Albanian party into an appendage of the Yugoslav communist party.

The new PKSH resorted initially to the strategem of the antifascist popular front to enhance its position. On September 16, 1942, the communists succeeded in forming the National Liberation Movement (Levizja Nacional-Clirimtar) at Pezë. This organization assumed the major responsibility for coordinating military and political action against the Axis forces in Albania. By July 1943 the Albanian National Liberation Army, also under communist control, had been formed.

In August 1943, however, a split developed in the National Liberation Movement. Under pressure from their Yugoslav advisors, the Albanian communists had repudiated that section of the Mukaj agreement calling for the incorporation of Kosovo and Metohija into Albania after the war. As a result, during the last months of 1943 and most of 1944 the communists were waging a two-front war through the National Liberation Movement—on one hand against the Germans and on the other against their domestic political opponents, the moderates in the National Front (Balli Kombëtar) and the promonarchists in the Legality (Legaliteti) organization. The communists were successful on both fronts. By late November they had expelled the Germans from Albania and had defeated their internal rivals militarily and politically.

To solidify their position the communists convoked a national congress at Përmet on May 24, 1944. The congress repudiated the regime of the exiled King Zogu, elected an Antifascist Council of National Liberation (Këshilli Antifashist Nacional-Çlirimtar), headed by Hoxha, to serve as the "supreme executive and legislative organ" for Albania, and appointed Hoxha commander in chief of the National Liberation Army. On October 20, 1944, a congress in Berat proclaimed the establishment of the Provisional Democratic Government of Albania, with Enver Hoxha as prime minister.

The communist seizure of power was accompanied by a serious split within the PKSH. This cleavage stemmed primarily from Yugoslavia's desire to dominate the Albanian party and Albania itself. Between 1944 and 1948 the PKSH was torn by a struggle between the "intellectuals," comprising Enver Hoxha, Sejfulla Maleshova, Nako Spiru, and Mehmet Shehu, and the pro-Yugoslav "proletarians," led by Koçi Xoxe and Pandi Kristo. By the beginning of 1948 it appeared as if the Xoxe faction would emerge victorious. Hoxha was on the verge of being removed as party leader, Albania had been closely tied militarily and economically to Yugoslavia by a series of bilateral treaties, and Yugoslavia's commanding position in Albania had been recognized when Tirana was not granted membership in the Cominform.

At this juncture the Soviet-Yugoslav rupture occurred. Hoxha took advantage of this development to break the Yugoslav stranglehold on Albania. Albania now became a full-fledged Soviet satellite, and at the first congress of the Albanian party, in November 1948, Hoxha initiated a purge of all pro-Xoxe, pro-Yugoslav elements. By the time the purge had run its course in late 1951 some 12,000 Albanian communists, one-fourth of the party's membership, had been dropped from the rolls. In the ensuing reorganization Mehmet Shehu emerged as the second-ranking member of the party hierarchy.

There were no serious problems in Soviet-Albanian relations until Stalin's death in March 1953. The Albanians became increasingly uneasy over the subsequent policy of de-Stalinization and Soviet moves to effect a reconciliation with Yugoslavia. The Stalinist Albanian party leaders regarded both these policies as a threat to themselves and to Albanian independence. In April 1955 Hoxha indicated his displeasure with the Kremlin by purging central committee members Tuk Jakova and Bedri Spahiu, both known for their pro-Yugoslav and anti-Stalinist views.

By March 1956 Hoxha was clearly disturbed by the strongly anti-Stalinist line approved by the Soviet party's twentieth congress. On the eve of the third congress of the PPSH a meeting of the Tirana city party organization was unsuccessful in challenging Hoxha's stand on Yugoslavia and de-Stalinization. The Albanian leadership was also able to resist a Soviet request to rehabilitate Xoxe as a gesture of good will toward Tito.

The outbreak of the Polish and Hungarian rebellions during 1956 and Moscow's subsequent retreat from its Yugoslav and de-Stalinization policies resulted in a Soviet-Albanian truce that lasted until 1959. By 1960, however, serious political and doctrinal differences had developed between the Albanians and Russians. In addition to the Yugoslav and de-Stalinization issues, Tirana resented Moscow's efforts to inhibit the development of Albanian industry and to create a strong anti-Hoxha faction within the Albanian party.

At the outbreak of Sino-Soviet polemics in April 1960, the Albanians allied themselves with the Chinese. Both at the Rumanian party congress in June and at the Moscow conference of world communist parties in November the Albanians attacked the Soviet leadership and its policies. Moscow sought to bring Tirana into line by reducing drastically its exports of food and technical equipment to Albania and encouraging pro-Soviet elements in the Albanian party, military, and civil service to topple the Hoxha-Shehu regime. Albania was able to obtain sufficient supplies of food and other commodities from China to survive, and the Soviet-inspired plots against the regime were crushed. In September 1960 politburo member Liri Belishova and central committee member Koço Tashko were ousted from the party for pro-Soviet activities. A group of civil servants and officers were convicted of conspiring to overthrow the regime by force after a show trial in May 1961.

At the fourth congress of the PPSH in February 1961 the Albanians made clear their determination to go their own way. With the aid of a $125 million Chinese loan, they were able to underwrite their third Five-Year Plan (1961 to 1965). At the twenty-second congress of the Soviet party in October Khrushchev for all practical purposes expelled the Albanians from the world communist movement, and in early December Moscow severed diplomatic ties with Tirana. In 1962 the Albanians were excluded from the activities of the Warsaw Pact and Comecon. During the mid-1960s Albania continued its drift into the Chinese camp.

## ORGANIZATION AND MEMBERSHIP

The organization of the PPSH, from the cell to the top leadership, is based essentially on the Soviet model. In theory the highest party organ is the party congress, which ordinarily meets once every four years. In practice, however, the politburo and central committee are the major decision-making bodies within the party.

The fourth party congress in 1961 announced that party membership was 53,659 (50,802 members and 2,857 candidates), or 5,015 more than in 1956. The percentage breakdown of the party membership by social group in January 1961 and April 1956 was as follows:

|  | April 1956 | January 1961 |
|---|---|---|
| Laborers | 19.76 | 29.66 |
| Peasants (collective farmers) | 10.02 | 23.62 |
| Individual farmers | 21.42 | 3.15 |
| Office workers, intellectuals, etc. | 45.20 | 41.94 |
| Others (students, housewives, etc.) | 3.58 | 1.62 |

SOURCE: *Kongressi IV i Partisë së Punës së Shqipërisë* (The Fourth Congress of the Albanian Party of Labor), Tirana, 1961, p. 121.

The large increase of laborers in party membership between 1956 and 1961 stems from the growth of industry in Albania, while the accelerating tempo of collectivization accounts for the decline of individual peasants and the rise of collective farmers.

A comparison of the party membership statistics and census data for 1961 reveals that the farmers (both collectivized and independent) are grossly underrepresented, while the laborers and white-collar workers are overrepresented. Although approximately 69 percent of the Albanian people lived in rural areas in 1961, less than one-third of the party membership was drawn from these regions.[1]

## PARTY PRESS ORGANS AND RECORDS

The party press organs are *Zëri i Popullit* (Voice of the People), the PPSH daily, and *Rruga e Partisë* (Road of the Party), its monthly theoretical journal.

For party records see *Dokumenta Kryesore të Partisë së Punës së Shqipërisë* (Principal Documents of the Albanian Party of Labor), vols. 1 and 2, Tirana, 1960, 1961; *Kongresi IV i Partisë së Punës së Shqipërisë* (The Fourth Congress of the Albanian Party of Labor), Tirana, 1961; and *Statuti i Partisë së Punës së Shqipërisë* (The Statute of the Albanian Party of Labor), Tirana, 1961.

## PARTY CONGRESSES

1st congress, PKSH, November 8-22, 1948, Tirana
2d congress, PPSH, March 31-April 7, 1952, Tirana
3d congress, PPSH, May 25-June 3, 1956, Tirana
4th congress, PPSH, February 13-20, 1961, Tirana

## BIBLIOGRAPHY

Amery, Julian: *Sons of the Eagle*, London, Macmillan, 1948.
Frasheri, Kristo: *The History of Albania: A Brief Survey*, Tirana, 1964.
Griffith, William E.: *Albania and the Sino-Soviet Rift*, Cambridge, Mass.: MIT Press, 1963.
Hamm, Harry: *Albania: China's Beachhead in Europe,* trans. by Victor Anderson, New York, Praeger, 1963.
*Historia e Partisë së Punës të Shqipërisë* (History of the Albania Party of Labor), Tirana, "Naim Frashëri," 1968.
Pano, Nicholas C.: *The People's Republic of Albania*, Baltimore, Johns Hopkins Press, 1968.
Skendi, Stavro: *Albania*, New York, Praeger, 1956.
*Twenty Years of Socialism in Albania*, Tirana, "Naim Frashëri," 1964.

NICHOLAS C. PANO

1. *Anuari Statistikor i RPSH, 1961*, Tirana, 1962, p. 53.

# ALGERIA

At the congress of Tours on December 25-30, 1920, which brought about the split in the French Socialist Party and the birth of the French Communist Party, the socialist federations of Algeria, Oran, and Constantine (1,500 members strong) came out by a majority of thirty-four votes out of forty-one in favor of joining the Comintern. Their spokesman, Charles André Julien, announced that this constituted, on the part of the communist party, a "pledge to give colonial questions the importance they deserve."[1]

As a matter of fact, this adherence to the Comintern was accomplished in confusion, and even if the "overseas socialists" did not want to be treated as "poor relatives," they were far from espousing the Comintern's theses regarding the colonial issue. From 1921 on, the Algerian sections of the French Communist Party made it known that they were opposed to any policy based on alleged Arab nationalism. When the Comintern issued its call "for the liberation of Algeria and Tunisia" on May 20, 1922, the Sidi-bel-Abbès section (the first to join the Comintern) denounced this plan for a revolt of the Muslim masses as "dangerous folly" for which the Algerian communists would not take responsibility.

## HISTORY

It took several years and the effects of French communist activity during the Moroccan war of 1924-1925 to defeat the "French nationalist spirit" in the Algerian federation of the party, as noted with satisfaction at the fifth congress of the French Communist Party at Lille on June 20-26, 1926. This victory was won at the price of a considerable decline in membership, which decreased by perhaps as much as three-fourths (800 members in 1926, according to Schiavro, secretary of the Algerian federation)—a decline which resulted from the fact that "the national question had been posed with such extreme acuteness, as it had never been posed before in Algeria."[2] This nationalist agitation became a good reason for repression by the colonial authorities, and Governor General Viollette imprisoned all the communist delegates from France. Moreover, the communists ordered some of their militant members in the French Unity General Confederation of Labor (CGTU) to reorganize the party under the cover of the CGTU trade-union organizations. This produced temporary successes for the French communists. In the Algerian railwaymen's union elections in 1926 the CGTU candidates received 31,000 out of 35,000 votes.

In the years that followed, however, the communists concentrated principally on the Algerian workers employed in metropolitan France, through the newspaper *L'Etoile nord-africaine*, founded in March 1926 with the help of Hadj Ali Abd el-Kader, a member of the French party's central committee and communist candidate in the department of Seine in the 1924 elections. At this point the communists were campaigning in favor of "complete independence for Algeria and complete evacuation of the troops of imperialism." They spread this propaganda especially during the centennial celebrations of the French conquest of Algeria (in 1930). The campaign was accompanied by a violent denunciation of the Algerian "reformist nationalists," who were demanding reforms without questioning French sovereignty.

This development led to the transformation of the Algerian federation of the French party into an apparently autonomous organization, the Communist Party of Algeria (Parti Communiste d'Algérie) and later the Algerian Communist Party (Parti Communiste Algérien, PCA). The transformation was carried out gradually in 1935 under the leadership of the Frenchman Jean Chaintron (also known as Barthel), and was made official at the French party's congress at Villeurbanne in January 1936. The objective of this transformation was to accelerate the recruitment of members by giving the party a certain national character; it was to be composed essentially of the avant-garde of the Algerian proletariat.

The metropolitan French communist leaders (and those in Moscow) had thought that in granting autonomy to the Algerian federation they would be giving more strength to their propaganda favoring national independence of Algeria. At the moment that this gradual transformation became effective, however, the French communists changed positions on the national question, and, eager to profit from French nationalism, they abandoned their demand for the right of separation for the Algerians. The PCA was invited not only to join the popular front with the "reformist nationalists" who had so recently been denounced, but also to relegate to the background the slogan of "national independence."

At the same time the PCA broke with Messali Hadj (since 1927 editor of *L'Etoile nord-africaine*), who upheld the demand for independence. Since 1934 Messali, who had come under the influence of Jacques Doriot, had been in disagreement with the French leadership, and it was perhaps to forestall him that the PCA had been founded. Nevertheless, the French communists did not delay in embarking on a vigorous campaign in Algerian circles in France against the "fascists" of *L'Etoile nord-africaine*, which had been Messali's press organ since 1927. Ben Ali Boukhort attacked the Messali group in an address before the Villeurbanne congress of the French party. On January 26, 1937, the popular-front government of France decided to close the paper. In March Messali founded the resolutely anticommunist Algerian People's Party (Parti du Peuple Algérien, PPA).

The communist policy on Algerian matters was defined by Maurice Thorez at a public meeting in Algiers on January 9, 1939. He did not reject the right of the Algerians to independence, but he opposed the groups pushing for division of Algeria into national parts. The reorganization of the movement on these new bases, the presence of Muslims such as Amar Ouzegane and Ben Ali Boukhort at the head of the movement, the use of less revolutionary slogans, and the formation of the popular-front government in Paris all assured rapid growth for the PCA. In 1937 it had twenty-nine sections, 192 local cells, thirty-six shop cells, and 7,500 members. In the legislative elections of May 1936 it offered its own candidates in nine out of ten electoral districts and received 15,068 votes (or 9.4 percent of the total vote in these districts, and 19.2 percent in the first district of Algiers). In addition, the party began publication of a daily newspaper, *Alger républicain.*

The PCA was dissolved by government decree on September 26, 1939, along with the French Communist Party. It continued to exist undergound, although its activity did not have much importance. However, the arrested Algerian militants were joined in prison by the French communists who had been convicted and transferred to Algeria and were thus able to continue their ideological and political education in prison. All were liberated in early 1943. In June the French Committee for National Liberation repealed the decree of September 1939, restoring legal existence to the French party and the PCA. On July 1, 1943, the first issue of the weekly PCA organ *Liberté* appeared in Algiers. This newspaper was immediately successful; by the end of 1944 its circulation had exceeded 120,000.

Profiting from the discredit into which the prominent Algerians who had followed Marshal Pètain had fallen, the Algerian communists succeeded in penetrating a great number of official organizations and thereby extending their influence. They had, moreover, adopted a very moderate policy, advocating economic and social reforms and the granting of full political rights to the Muslims. They denounced as tools of imperialism those who advocated a federalist statute (Ferhat Abbas) or independence (the PPA). They approved the ordinance of March 7, 1944, which constituted an important step toward assimilation and was for that reason rejected by the nationalists.

The riots of May 8, 1945, in the Sétif region led the communists to express their unequivocal opposition to independence. They approved of the repression and denounced the nationalists, whom they accused of having fomented the revolt, as nazi agents. At the tenth congress of the French party in June 1945 Paul Caballero, secretary of the PCA, declared: "The Algerian people have the same enemies as the French people, and they do not want to be separated from France.... On the contrary, the PCA is fighting for the strengthening of the union of the Algerian people with the people of France."[3]

This policy bore fruit. In the October 21, 1945, elections to the French constituent assembly the PCA candidates received 82,669 votes in the French-Muslim constituency (16.4 percent of the registered voters and 24.4 percent of the votes cast) and won four seats out of thirteen (Pierre Fayet and Paul Tubert in Algiers and Alice Sportisse and Camille Larribere in Oran). In the second constituency (Muslims) the results were not quite as good: 136,293 votes, or 10.1 percent of the registered voters and 19.2 percent of the votes cast, and two seats (Amar Ouzegane in Algiers and Mohammed Chouadria in Constantine). The PCA had also tripled its membership since 1939. At the third party congress on March 21-24, 1946, at which André Marty presided, the PCA leadership confirmed the political orientation which had brought these successes.

In the elections of June 2, 1946, the PCA lost considerable ground to the Democratic Union for the Algerian Manifesto (Union Démocratique du Manifeste Algérien, UDMA), the former Friends of the Manifesto, legalized by the amnesty of March 16, 1946. In the second constituency the communist candidates received only 57,566 votes (4.3 percent of the registered voters and 9.1 percent of the votes cast), and none were elected. In the first constituency, however, the PCA held its position with two successful candidates, Fayet and Sportisse, and 83,592 votes (15.8 and 23.2 percent). The PCA was decidedly still a party which attracted predominantly the European (French) population; its influence was greater in European circles than among the Muslims.

Alarmed by these results, on July 20-21, 1946, the PCA central committee modified its political line and demanded "the immediate creation of an assembly and Algerian government which would handle all Algerian affairs." Foreign affairs and military questions would remain in the jurisdiction of the French Republic, and the Algerian Democratic Republic would remain "united [to France] by federative ties freely decided upon within the French Union."[4]

It is possible that this switch in policy was responsible for the sudden new gain of influence for the PCA. In the elections of November 10, 1946, it won 82,895 votes (6.8 percent of the registered voters and 16.9 percent of the votes cast) and two seats (Djemard Abd er-Rahmane and Moktari Mohammed) in the second constituency. It kept its position in the first constituency with the same two successful candidates (Fayet and Sportisse).

Nevertheless, even though the communists had outbid the UDMA with regard to Algerian nationalism, they remained at a distance from the position adopted by Messali Hadj's PPA, now called the Movement for the Triumph of Democratic Liberties (Mouvement pour le Triomphe des Libertés Démocratiques, MTLD). After his return to Algeria in October 1946 Messali demanded total independence, while still remaining solidly anticommunist. The communists did not attempt to overtake the MTLD, either because they would not have been able to keep their European following, or because the French communists, who had not given up their hope of soon taking power in France, were still counting on leading the French empire in one bloc into the communist camp. During the debate in the French chamber of deputies on the status of Algeria, put to a vote on September 20, 1947, they defined their position by demanding the transformation of Algeria into a state associated with France, within the framework of the French Union, and opposed the demands of the MTLD.

From that time on, even though the PCA and the nationalist organizations did not completely break off collaboration, the nationalists were plainly distrustful of the communists. In the legislative elections of June 17, 1951, falsified by the maneuvers of the administration, the PCA held its position in the first constituency, where Fayet and Sportisse were reelected, with 14.7 percent of the registered voters and 21.03 percent of the votes cast, but received only 2.9 percent of the vote in the second constituency. The party made some efforts to come out of its isolation, and on August 5, 1951, it succeeded in forming an Algerian Front for the Defense and Respect of Liberties with the MTLD (Messali Hadj), the UDMA (Ferhat Abbas), and the Oulemas. The PCA's partners quickly realized, however, that the communists were little concerned with the prime objective of this alliance—the annulment of the elections—but were more interested in using the front to mobilize the Algerian masses and place them at the service of the policy of the international communist movement (the fight against NATO, the American bases in North Africa, and the war in Indochina). This resulted in a break, after which the front kept up only a nominal existence. In fact, during the next three years the PCA, disappointed over the failure of its Algerian policy, confined itself to "broad international policy"—indoctrinating militants, spreading its interpretation of Marxism among the students, and retaining some influence through the communist trade unions (dockers' strike in Oran against the Vietnam war).

Thus cut off from the nationalist organizations, the communists were surprised by the outbreak of an insurrection on November 1, 1954. They denounced it at first and cast suspicion on the movement. On November 8 the French party declared that it disapproved of acts of individual terrorism against the French colonists, particularly if they were not to be blamed for the motives of the disturbance. The central committee of the PCA adopted the same position.

As soon as the communists recovered from the unexpected start of the revolt, however, they came out in support of the rebels by creating "peoples' committees for struggle against the repression and for amnesty," spreading social unrest, and finally engaging in terrorist activities. As a result, the PCA was dissolved by government decree on September 12, 1955, but its activities continued. The outstanding events were the desertion of the aspirant Henri Maillot (in civilian life a member of the editorial staff of *Alger républicain*) and the creation of underground fighter squads, the Fighters for the Liberation (Combattants de la Libération).

At the same time the communists began lengthy negotiations with the National Liberation Front (Front de Libération Nationale, FLN). The negotiations dragged on and ended in a compromise in July 1956. The communists wanted to join the FLN but still retain the autonomy of their party. The

FLN leaders, however, demanded that the PCA be dissolved and that its members join individually. The communists would not accept this proposal and pledged only to support the action of the FLN and to order their Fighters for the Liberation to join its armed groups. In November 1957 the PCA also decided to abandon the CGT-affiliated General Union of Algerian Trade Unions (Union Générale des Syndicats Algériens) in favor of the General Union of Algerian Workers (Union Générale des Travailleurs Algériens), formed in February 1956 by militants who had left the CGT on orders from the FLN. Messali's party had, in the meantime, formed the Union of Trade Unions of Algerian Workers (Union des Syndicats des Travailleurs Algériens).

Among the reasons given to justify the continuation of the PCA, the communists declared that Algeria's working class and poor peasantry would strive more willingly for national liberation if they were assured, through the PCA's existence, that their class interests would be defended after the victory, and that the existence of the PCA would strengthen the sympathy the Algerian cause enjoyed among the international working classes.

Until the end of the rebellion the PCA cooperated with the FLN and supported its struggle against the French army and against the Messali group. However, it never gave up its autonomy and did not cease to try to infiltrate the FLN organizations—efforts which had few results, except in the General Union of Algerian Workers and the General Union of Algerian Muslim Students. The communist Fighters for the Liberation, in particular, were not trusted by the FLN groups, and nearly all fell into the hands of the French troops.

The communists played only an insignificant role in the guerrilla war as long as the terrorist activities were individual in character. Starting at the end of 1961, however, they took an important part in the mass demonstrations launched in the cities, particularly in Algiers. With the signing of the Evian agreement on March 19, 1962, and the proclamation of Algeria's independence, the PCA was openly revived. Meetings of the political bureau and central committee were held in Algiers, and its newspapers reappeared—the daily *Alger républicain* (with no mention that it was the PCA organ) and the review *el-Houriya (Liberté)*, which apparently supported the government, but not without exploiting the discontent and gaining its own following. Aware of the danger, on November 7, 1962, the government informed Larbi Bouhali, general secretary of the PCA, that "the PCA must cease all activity." It seized *el-Houriya*, banned communist meetings, and removed the communists from the leadership of the General Union of Algerian Workers (January 1963). However, members of the party were not arrested.

The communist reaction was weak. Even while demanding "the PCA's return to legality," the communists declared that they would continue to support the FLN and Ahmed ben Bella. Then, after the decrees of March 1963 on the land question and Ben Bella's speech putting Algeria "on the road to socialism" (April 1963), they agreed to recognize the National Liberation Front as the only party in the country (December 1963). During the April 1964 congress of the FLN the editorial staff of *Alger républicain* stated that it was ready to put the newspaper at the disposition "of the avant-garde party which will be formed by the congress." Bachir Hadj Ali, the PCA's ideologist and one of its secretaries, wrote that an Algerian revolutionary in 1964 was "one who supports by virtue of the very positive and decisive role that Ben Bella plays in the revolution, the general secretary of the National Liberation Front."[5] The PCA was not officially dissolved, but it disintegrated. It was not invited to attend the seventeenth congress of the French Communist Party in May 1964; the FLN was invited in its stead.

In response to this tactic the Algerian communists tried to seize leadership of the FLN, which all the militants were ordered to join. Despite obstacles to their entrance in its directing bodies, especially the central committee, communists appeared in ever-growing numbers in Ben Bella's entourage. Under Soviet pressure (the Soviet Union was the only supplier of arms to the Algerian government), Ben Bella concluded an agreement with the French communists in October 1964. It was decided at the beginning of June 1965 to merge the FLN press organ *Le Peuple* with the communist *Alger républicain* in order to give the FLN only one organ, *el-Mouajahid*. Its editorial staff remained principally communist.

The *coup d'état* in Algiers of June 19, 1965, and Ben Bella's demise put an end to this "Cuban method" of conquering the only and ruling party by infiltration. The European communists in Ben Bella's entourage (the *pieds rouges*) were expelled. The Algerian communists, who had immediately formed a clandestine body, the Organization of Algerian Resistance (Organisation de la Résistance Algérienne), were arrested in large numbers; among them was Bachir Hadj Ali. The French communist press began an intense campaign against the new Algerian government.

## RELATION TO SOVIET LEADERSHIP

The PCA was represented at the two conferences of the international communist movement in Moscow in 1957 and 1960, as well as at the twenty-second congress of the Communist Party of the Soviet Union in October 1961, where Larbi Bouhali was its delegate. In the Sino-Soviet conflict, it has aligned itself with the Soviet party.

## PARTY PRESS ORGANS

After World War II the PCA published, with some interruptions, the daily *Alger républicain* and the weekly *el-Houriya (Liberté)*, which ceased to appear in 1964 and 1965, respectively.

## CONGRESSES OF THE PCA

1st congress, October 1936
2d congress, December 1938
3d congress, March 1946
6th congress, February 1952

The PCA has not met in a congress since 1952.

## BIBLIOGRAPHY

*Est & ouest*, no. 222, 1959; no. 302, 1963; nos. 349 and 351, 1965.
Julien, Charles-André: *L'Afrique du nord en marche*, Paris, Julliard, 1952.
Le Tourneau, Robert: *Evolution politique de l'Afrique du nord musulmane, 1920-1961*, Paris, Armand Colin, 1962.

CLAUDE HARMEL

1. *Parti socialiste, SFIO, 18e Congrès national tenu à Tours, les 25, 26, 27, 28, 29, 30 décembre 1920: Compte rendu sténographique*, Paris, 1921, p. 69.

2. *Ve Congrès national du Parti communiste français tenu à Lille du 20 au 26 juin 1926: Compte rendu sténographique*, Paris, Bureau d'Editions, 1927, pp. 10, 252, 255, 695.

3. *L'Humanité*, June 30, 1945.

4. André Marty, in *Cahiers du communisme*, August 1946.

5. *La Nouvelle revue internationale*, August 1964.

# ARGENTINA

The communist movement in Argentina originated in 1917, before the outbreak of the Russian revolution, among dissidents expelled from the Socialist Party of Argentina (Partido Socialista de la Argentina, PSA) because they objected to the pro-Allied sentiments of the socialist leaders. On January 6, 1918, this bloc of several hundred members created the International Socialist Party (Partido Socialista Internacional, PSI), under the leadership of Juan Ferlini, Victorio Codovilla, Rodolfo Ghioldi, J. F. Penelón, and others, From the outset the new party identified itself with the cause of the bolsheviks in Russia. It claims to have been a charter member of the Comintern, represented at the founding congress by the Italian Socialist Party (although the Italian delegation never reached the congress), and in December 1920 it accepted Lenin's Twenty-one Conditions and adopted its present name, Communist Party of Argentina (Partido Comunista de la Argentina, PCA).

## HISTORY

The Argentine party has never exerted a decisive influence on national politics, even though it has usually been able to attract a fairly substantial urban labor and student following. The party was legal until the mid-1920s and enjoyed freedom of operation until 1930. It took part in electoral campaigns with modest success in Buenos Aires and competed at a disadvantage with the socialists for control of organized labor. Factionalism kept the leadership divided and party membership low during these years. Early in the 1920s Victorio Codovilla emerged as the outstanding figure in the party, largely because of his personal contacts within the Comintern. With the coup of September 1930 the party was driven underground, where it was isolated as a result of its refusal to cooperate with other opposition groups.

The adoption of the popular-front line in 1935 permitted the party to achieve an informal understanding with other left-wing elements, to increase its strength in the labor movement, and to win considerable popular sympathy for its protests against authoritarian rule at home and fascism abroad. Membership rose to several thousand. The party was briefly isolated again by the Hitler-Stalin pact of 1939, but its fortunes soared when it adopted a strong pro-Allied position after June 1941.

The military coup of June 1943 and the subsequent rise of Juan D. Perón resulted in immediate repression of party activities and destruction of much of the communist base in the trade unions. This situation was reversed in 1945, with the Allied victory in Europe and the restoration of political liberties in Argentina. The party regained legal status and was able to operate without restraint for the first time in twenty years. Expanding rapidly to about 30,000 members, the PCA polled over 150,000 votes in the national elections of 1946. Membership remained at this level, but the party's political influence declined sharply during the decade of the Perón administration (1946 to 1955).

With the overthrow of Perón in 1955, the communists recruited vigorously, seeking now to win the allegiance of members of the outlawed Peronist party. The PCA polled more than 200,000 votes in the elections of 1957 and 1958 but placed no candidates in the federal or provincial legislatures. Its close cooperation with Peronists, a virulent propaganda campaign against President Frondizi, and exposure of clandestine communist paramilitary training led in 1959 to the first of a series of measures to restrict the party's freedom of operation.

At the party's twelfth congress in 1963 Codovilla was elected president of the party and A. Alvarez was elected first secretary. The party was formally outlawed, however, by decree laws of May and July 1963. These laws were repealed in 1964, but early in 1965 the party was declared ineligible to present its own candidates for election to public office. In 1965 the communists controlled a few trade unions and were represented in the majority faction of the student organization at the University of Buenos Aires.

## ORGANIZATION AND MEMBERSHIP

Numerically, the Argentine party has always been one of the stronger communist organizations in Latin America, and since the mid-1950s it has consistently been the largest of the nonruling Latin American parties. In 1963 the PCA claimed to have exceeded 100,000 members. United States sources estimate the party's membership in 1965 as 65,000.[1] The communists are concentrated heavily in the greater Buenos Aires area and in the larger provincial capitals.

The Argentine communists have made little use of front parties, but have consistently maintained a broad array of ostensibly nonpolitical front organizations. For a full discussion see *Latin America*.

## RELATION TO SOVIET LEADERSHIP

The Argentine party was one of two Latin American communist parties to request Soviet explanations after the fall of Khrushchev. For a discussion of the relations of the Argentine party, and particularly of Victorio Codovilla, with the Moscow-directed international communist movement, see *Latin America*.

The PCA strongly endorsed Khrushchev's thesis of the "peaceful road to socialism" and has consistently supported the Soviet position in the ideological dispute with Communist China.

## PARTY PRESS ORGANS AND RECORDS

The PCA newspaper for national circulation is the weekly *Nuestra palabra*; the newspaper for Buenos Aires province is *Frente unido*. The monthly theoretical journal is *Nueva era*. The party also publishes monthly cultural and economic reviews for general circulation, *Cuadernos de cultura* and *Revista económica*. In addition to publishing separate newspapers and magazines for the communist women's, youth, and student organizations, the party also reprints the Spanish edition of *Problems of Peace and Socialism* for distribution in South America.

The PCA has one of the most active press and publications programs of any communist party in Latin America. The communist publishing house, Editorial Anteo, regularly releases pamphlets, documents, and monographs containing current pronouncements by party leaders and committees on the political and propaganda issues of the day, as well as revisions of the statutes and the party program. These are seldom available outside the country.

## PARTY CONGRESSES

1st congress, PSI, January 1918
2d congress, PSI, April 1919
3d congress, PSI, April 1920
Extraordinary congress, PCA, December 1920
4th congress, PCA, January 1922
5th congress, PCA, July 1923
6th congress, PCA, July 1924
7th congress, PCA, Decmeber 1925
8th congress, PCA, November 1928
9th congress, PCA, January 1938
10th congress, PCA, November 1941
11th congress, PCA, August 1946
12th congress, PCA, February-March 1963

## BIBLIOGRAPHY

Codovilla, Victor: *Statii i rechi, 1926-1956* (Articles and Speeches, 1926-1956), Moscow, 1957.

Codovilla, Victor: *Una Trayectoria consecuente en la lucha por la liberación nacional y social del pueblo argentino*, Codovilla's selected works, Buenos Aires, Anteo, 1964. 4 vols.

Communist Party of Argentina: *Esbozo de historia del Partido comunista de la Argentina*, Buenos Aires, Anteo, 1947.

Ramos, Jorge Abelardo: *El Partido comunista en la política argentina: Su historia y su crítica*, Buenos Aires, Coyoacán, 1962.

Ravines, Eudocio: *The Yenan Way*, New York, Scribner, 1951.

Resio Trejo, Alvaro: *Historia de las relaciones ruso-argentinas*, Buenos Aires, 1946.

See also *Latin America*, refs. 1, 2, 6, 13, 24.

ROLLIE E. POPPINO

---

1. U.S. Department of State, Bureau of Intelligence and Research, *World Strength of the Communist Party Organizations*, Eighteenth Annual Report, Washington, January 1966, p. 166.

# ARMENIA

In January 1920 the Communist Party of Armenia (Hayastani Komunistakan Partia, HKP) was officially established in Yerevan after a series of meetings starting in 1919. The principal organizers were Sarkis Kasian and Askanaz Meravian, both of whom had been active bolsheviks since 1905 and members of the Caucasian committee of the Russian Social Democratic Labor Party. Other important founders included Stepan Alaverdian, chief of the communist committee of Yerevan, and Ghukas Ghukasian, leader of the Armenian communist youth organization Spardak, which he had founded with the aid of Aghasi Khandjian in Armenia in April 1919.

## HISTORY

The HKP had its beginnings as early as 1902 in Tiflis (Georgia). A group of Tiflis Armenians affiliated with the Russian Social Democratic Labor Party of Tiflis founded the Union of Armenian Social Democrats (Hai Sotsial Demokratneri Miuthiun) in 1902. Its organ *Proletariat* was published in the Armenian language and was officially welcomed by Lenin in his *Iskra*. In the same year the new party merged with the Tiflis committee of the Russian Social Democratic Labor Party, which published a new organ, *Proletariati Kriv* (Fight of the Proletariat), in Armenian, Georgian, and Russian. In the meantime branches of the Russian party were formed in various cities of Armenia, and in 1906 and 1907 these organizations sent delegates to the fourth and fifth congresses of the Russian party.

During these formative years Armenian newspapers were published and bolshevik literature was disseminated through the efforts of such leading bolsheviks and followers of Lenin as Stepan Shaumian, Suren Spandarian, and Bogdan Kenuniants. In June 1917 the bolsheviks published *Banvori Kriv* (Fight of the Worker). By 1918 bolshevik newspapers had multiplied, and a new group of leaders emerged to attack the ideology and policies of other political groups and parties in Armenia. Attacks were directed against the "specifics," or Armenian Social Democratic Workers' Organization (Hai Sotsial Demokratneri Banvorakan Kazmakerputhiun), led by Ananun; the mensheviks, or Armenian Social Democratic Party (Hai Sotsial Demokratneri Kusaktsuthiun), led by Erzenkian; the constitutional democrats, or Armenian People's Party (Hai Zhoghovurdakan Kusaktsuthiun), led by S. Haruthiunian; the Armenian Social Revolutionary Party (Hai Sotsialist Heghapokhakan Kusaktsuthiun), led by Atabegian; the hunchaks,[1] or Social Democratic Hunchakian Party (Sotsial Demokrat Hunchakian Kusaktsuthiun); and particularly the dashnaks,[2] or Armenian Revolutionary Federation (Hai Heghapokhakan Dashnaktsuthiun). The dashnaks, the controlling political party of the Armenian republic from 1918 to 1920, were the prime target of the bolsheviks.

During 1919 two major events took place which led to the official founding of the HKP. In May 1919 in Baku a group of fifteen or twenty communists from Armenia, Georgia, and Azerbaidzhan met to discuss the feasibility of forming separate parties for each of the three areas of Transcaucasia. The group did not come to a formal agreement, but the issue was considered by the central committee of the Russian Communist Party, which decided in favor of separate parties. In September 1919 the first consultation of representatives of all communist organizations in the Armenian republic took place in Yerevan. This was the first step in bringing together the leaders of these various groups. They elected a central committee, known as the Armenkom, which started the coordination of all the communist organizations in Armenia. The May and September 1919 meetings led to the first (illegal) conference of representatives of twenty-two communist organizations, with a membership of 1,200. This conference held in Yerevan on January 18-19, 1920, officially founded the HKP, elected a new Armenkom, and resolved to overthrow dashnak control in the Armenian republic and to sovietize the country. On November 29, 1920, the Red Army occupied an area in the northeastern part of the Armenian republic, and the revolutionary committee of the Armenian bolsheviks proclaimed sovietization of the country. A few days later, on December 2, the dashnak government and the bolsheviks signed an agreement in Yerevan which proclaimed Armenia an autonomous socialist republic, thus ending dashnak control.

By April 1920 party membership had grown to 3,000. After communist control of Armenia was secured, party membership grew to 8,251 (3,046 members and 5,205 candidates). At the end of 1921 purges of the membership started. Elements accused of prodashnak leanings were eliminated first, followed by Trotskyists and Zinovievists. During the period from 1927 to 1936 "counterrevolutionary nationalists" were driven from the party, and repressions were started against noncommunist intellectuals. The party secretary, Aghasi Khandjian, and the entire party leadership became victims of this continuous purge. During these years the number of party members fluctuated greatly.

In January 1922 the first congress of the HKP was held in Yerevan. Closer ties with the Russian party were established, and as time went on the Armenian party became a pseudo-autonomous part of the Russian party. Anastas I. Mikoyan, one of the early activists of the HKP, rose to high offices in the Russian party and in the state organization of the Soviet Union. He has apparently had little influence on Armenian party affairs in recent years.

After World War II Malenkov was accused by Khrushchev of purging the party apparatus in Armenia in past years, and there were renewed tensions in the area of ethnic solidarity and national aspirations. Of particular concern to recent critics within the HKP have been the historic Armenian lands remaining under Turkish and Azerbaidzhani rule and retribution for the 1.5 million Armenians massacred by the Turks in 1915.

## ORGANIZATION AND MEMBERSHIP

The HKP is an integral part of the Communist Party of the Soviet Union and is bound by the directives of its central committee. It is the official party of the Armenian Soviet Socialist Republic, with its capital at Yerevan. Its members are nearly all of Armenian origin, since the republic's population of 2,134,000 (as estimated in 1965) is nearly 90 percent Armenian.

According to the report of the twenty-fourth congress of the HKP, the party had 105,062 members and 5,296 candidates, an increase of 12,013 persons since 1964-1965. Of this number, 65,736, or 59.6 percent of the party membership, are workers; of these, 35,439 work in industry, construction, transportation, and communication, and 25,203 work in agriculture and cattle raising. The remaining members are white-collar workers, of which the greatest portion are engineers and technicians.

The Armenian republic is divided into four municipalities, five municipal districts, and thirty-three counties, each with a controlling party committee. Of a total of 3,963 primary party organizations subordinated to these territorial committees, 859 are in industrial, construction, and transportaition enterprises and 745 are in collective and state farms. Party members receive their ideological training in thirty-three party schools and in party-directed seminars and conferences. Of the 3,963 secretaries of the primary party organizations, 1,602 were university graduates, 361 had some university education, 1,614 had completed high school; 221 were laborers and 462 were peasants.

Party members are recruited from the Communist Youth Union (Komyeritmiutium), which has branches throughout the republic.

## PARTY PRESS ORGANS AND RECORDS

The party press organs are *Sovetakan Hayastan* (Soviet Armenia), a daily in Armenian, *Kommunist*, a daily in Russian, and *Soviet Ermanistani* (Soviet Armenia), a daily in Azerbaidzhani. *Rea Taza* (New Life) is published three or four times a week in Kurdish. *Leninian Ughiov* (Lenin's Path) is a monthly journal in Armenian, and *Agitatori Bloknot* (Agitator's Notebook) is a bimonthly journal in Armenian.

Party records appear in the Armenian publication *Sovetakan Miutian Komunistakan Kusagtsutian Kanonatrutiune* (Bylaws of the Communist Party of the Soviet Union), Yerevan, 1966, and A. Y. Kotchinian, *Hayastani Komunistakan Partiai Kentronakan Komitei Hashvetu Zekutsume Hayastani Kompartiai XXIV Hamagumarin* (Report of the Central Committee of the Communist Party of Armenia at the Twenty-fourth Congress of the Communist Party of Armenia), Yerevan, 1966.

## BIBLIOGRAPHY

Arzumanian, M. V.: *Bolshevikneri Gordzuneutiune Yev Revolutsion Sharjumnere Hayastanum, 1907-1917, Tevakannerin* (Activities and Revolutionary Movements of the Bolsheviks in Armenia during the Years 1907-1917), Yerevan, 1959.

Karapetian, H. N.: *Hayastani Komyeritmiutian Dzenunde* (Birth of the Communist Youth Union in Armenia), Yerevan, 1956.

Margarian, H. Kh., A. N. Menatsakanian, and Kh. H. Barseghian (eds.): *Hayastani Komunistakan Partiai Patmutian Urvagdzer* (Historical Outline of the Communist Party of Armenia), Yerevan, 1958.

Nersisian, M., and V. Parsamian (eds.): *Hai Djoghovurdi Patmutiun* (History of the Armenian People), vol. II, Yerevan, 1958.

Hakobian, A. M., and A. N. Menatsakanian (eds.): *Hai Djoghovurdi Patmutiun* (History of the Armenian People), vol. III, Yerevan, 1958.

Vratzian, S.: *Hayastani Hanrapetutiun* (The Armenian Republic), Paris, 1928.

1. The word *hunchak* means "bell" in English. Members of the party are referred to as hunchaks or hunchakists.

2. *Dashnaktsuthiun* means "federation," and members of the party are referred to as dashnaks or dashnakists.

LOUISE NALBANDIAN

# AUSTRALIA

The Communist Party of Australia (CPA) was formed in Sydney on October 30, 1920, by twenty-six people, members of small socialist and left-wing groups. The most influential groups present were members of the Australian Socialist Party (ASP), which had called the meeting, and former members of the Socialist Party of Australia (SPA). Both groups had proclaimed themselves "communist" before the conference, the former in December 1919 and the latter in September 1920. The motives for the formation of the CPA were inspiration by the Russian revolution and a desire to find some basis for unifying Australia's socialists. The theories of the bolsheviks or the Comintern were not a motive, as nobody in Australia had a clear understanding of Leninism at that time; nor was there any revolutionary situation, as described by the Comintern, although working-class militancy was high after the war and strikes were frequent in 1919 and 1920.

The ASP members withdrew on December 14, 1920, after quarreling over leadership, and control of the party passed to the former members of the SPA, who created a new executive on March 26, 1921, of J. S. Garden, H. L. Denford, P. Larkin, C. Baker, W. P. Earsman, N. Jeffrey, A. Thomas, H. Ross, C. Smith, and Bowman. Garden and Earsman went on to play important roles in the party. None are now CPA members. Garden was expelled in 1926 and Denford in 1927; Larkin left the party around 1922 and Baker in 1924; Earsman went to the Soviet Union and became part of Trotsky's entourage; the remaining five are dead (Jeffrey, Ross, and Smith evidently remained communists; there is no record of continued association of the other two with the CPA).

Although the CPA was formed by Australians, the bolshevik consul, Peter Simonoff, a member of the Russian Association of Brisbane from 1912, encouraged its formation. He claimed to have been associated with the Russian revolutionary movement before 1911, but with which wing or party is not known.

The CPA has been known variously as the Communist Party of Australia (1920 to February 1922), United Communist Party of Australia (to July 1922), Communist Party of Australia, Section of the Communist International (from 1922 to 1944), Australian Communist Party (1944 to 1951), and again the Communist Party of Australia (since 1951).

## HISTORY

Even before the Comintern introduced the united-front policy in 1921 the CPA had started to cooperate, according to traditional socialist policy, with the Australian Labor Party (ALP). CPA members also joined the ALP, and for four months in 1923 the CPA was an affiliate of the ALP in New South Wales. In other states the communist branches had died out. Communists Garden, J. Graves, and J. Beasley were elected to the ALP executive, but the hostility of parliamentarians and moderate unionists soon caused the expulsion of the communists, and known communists have never since been admitted to the ALP. As a result, the CPA dwindled from 900 members in 1922 to 249 in 1928. Garden and his followers left the party in 1926. The new party leader, J. Kavanagh, favored a passive propaganda policy, and his opposition to the social-fascist theory led to his replacement in 1929 by J. B. Miles (general secretary from 1921 to 1948), L. L. Sharkey (general secretary from 1948 to 1965), and H. Moxon.

The expulsion of Kavanagh and his followers was engineered by Comintern representative Herbert Moore (H. M. Wicks), a member of the communist party of the United States. Moore's organizational innovations, the onset of the depression, and the aggressive policies of the new leaders led to the first real CPA successes. By 1937, under the auspices of the front Militant Minority Movement, which had been set up in 1928, the communists had won control of the traditionally militant Miners' Federation, Waterside Workers' Federation, Federated Ironworkers' Association, New South Wales Sheetmetal Workers' Union, and New South Wales branch of the Australian Railways Union. They continued to increase their influence in the unions until the end of the war. In 1948 there were 300 top communist union leaders, and a conservative estimate of the membership of communist-controlled unions in 1945 was 275,000, or 25 percent of the Australian workers organized in trade unions. This success resulted chiefly from the fact that in traditionally militant unions there were openings after 1929 for new militant leaders, and in other unions a combination of excellent communist organizational work and the "incompetence, dishonesty, and inertness" of the existing leadership allowed their replacement by communists.

From 1937 to 1947 communists had a strong position in the Australian Council of Trade Unions congresses. After 1947, however, the activity of the anticommunists, especially the Roman Catholics, who had formed their own unions attached to the ALP and opposed affiliation with the communists, made inroads in the CPA's influence in the trade unions. In addition, the belief that the CPA had fostered a series of strikes after the war, culminating in the coal strike of 1949, led to strong anticommunist measures and resulted in a decline of support for the party. Nevertheless, the communists still have great influence in militant unions and have lost only the top positions in some others.

After the war the CPA's adoption of the Cominform line resulted in a decline in the party from 22,052 members in December 1944 to 12,108 in 1947 and 5,580 in 1958. Votes in elections also declined, and the only communist member of parliament, Fred Paterson in the Queensland state legislature, lost his seat in 1950. The party was further isolated by legislation to prevent misuse of union ballots, the proposal of a narrowly defeated bill to dissolve the communist party, and the exposure of communist complicity in the Petrov spy affair in 1954-1955. A temporary revival from 1954 to 1957 in the unions by means of unity tickets with ALP union leaders (CPA and ALP candidates were listed together on the same how-to-vote union election card) did not last after the ALP condemned unity tickets in 1957.

## ORGANIZATION AND MEMBERSHIP

The CPA's organizational form is democratic centralism, first established by the 1927 bylaws but not applied until after 1931. The lowest unit is the branch, based on place of residence or work and responsible for recruiting, propaganda, and party education. Branches are grouped in sections and directed by section committees. Sections are groups in districts and directed by district committees. The districts are controlled by the state committee in each state, controlled in turn by the central committee, divided into a political committee of forty-two members, a disputes committee of about twelve, and the four-man national secretariat, in effect the directing body of the party.

The district and state committees are elected by a conference of delegates from the two lower divisions and the outgoing committee. Conferences are held annually in the sections, not less than twice in any three years in districts and states, and the national congress is held every three years. Eligibility for election to a committee is membership of one year for the section, four years for district and state, and seven years for the central committee.

Factional activity, formerly condemned in all democratic centralist parties, is openly permitted, but there are rumors that this form of organization will soon be formally discarded.

The party members have always been nearly all from the industrial proletariat. There are few communist women, agricultural workers, intellectuals, or youths under eighteen. The main influx of intellectuals came during World War II, often via student labor clubs at Sydney and Melbourne universities, which were controlled by very able communist students. Most intellectuals remained in lower cadres, however, as the proletarian leaders were suspicious of them. Many were expelled in the decade after the war, when their gradual disillusionment was focused on such specific issues as the refusal of the leadership to allow discussion of Khrushchev's "secret speech" denouncing Stalin and the 1956 Hungarian uprising.

There are no important communist front organizations in Australia. Except for the years 1940 to 1942, the CPA has always been legal. The party has considerable influence in the peace movement, especially through the Australian and New Zealand Congress for International Cooperation and Disarmament. However, the small Realist Writers' Group, the Australia-China Friendship Society (which is splitting because the CPA has split), and the Australian-Soviet Friendship Society have all declined with the CPA, especially after the expulsion of intellectuals from 1956 to 1958.

The student labor clubs are no longer controlled by communists. The communist youth front, the Eureka Youth League, is not very strong and is not growing significantly. The party has about 5,300 members and has not grown, despite a recruiting drive in 1965.[1]

## RELATION TO SOVIET LEADERSHIP

After 1930 the CPA followed the line of the Comintern, and then the Cominform until that body was also dissolved. No Australian became prominent in either body.

The first reaction of the CPA to the Sino-Soviet dispute was to support the Chinese, possibly because of the "leftism" of secretariat members E. Hill, Sharkey, and R. Dixon, but at the Moscow conference of communist parties in 1960 fear of a split forced Sharkey and Dixon to support the Soviet Union, with the consequent expulsion of Hill and his followers in 1963 when they refused to follow suit. In 1964 a rival Communist Party of Australia (Marxist-Leninist), which supported the Chinese position, was established in Melbourne, with Hill as chairman, P. Malone and C. O'Shea as vice chairmen, and F. Johnson as secretary. The new party is small (about 200 members), but it controls some Melbourne unions. It publishes a monthly journal, *Australian Communist*, and a weekly newspaper, *Vanguard*. The extreme Stalinist position it originally adopted is weakening slightly and it is growing outside Victoria. Its violent attacks on the CPA for revisionism have increased with the CPA's establishment of a new "Italian-line" secretariat of L. Aarons and C. Jones, with Sharkey and Dixon, the former Stalinists, playing lesser roles.

## FUTURE PROSPECTS

The objective of the CPA is to return to the traditional policy of a fringe group on the left of the ALP. It envisages a parliamentary road to socialism in which it does not even see itself taking the leading role, but rather playing an inspirational one. The line of the Italian Communist Party certainly inspires the present CPA leaders. So far nothing has come of the new line, because the Stalinist lower cadres are refusing to implement the new policy. The hostility of the ALP is still very high. However, informal contact with the Trotskyists and the more radical socialists in the ALP has increased, and the independent left is no longer so set on being independent of the CPA. The attractiveness of the new policy, once the CPA has shown that it means what it says, could result in an increase in party membership.

## PARTY PRESS ORGANS AND RECORDS

The CPA's daily is the *Tribune* (formerly *Workers' Weekly, Communist, Australian Communist*); its monthly journal is *Australian Left Review* (formerly *Communist Review, Communist, Proletarian, Proletarian Review*).

Statutes of the CPA are covered in *Rules and Constitution of the Communist Party of Australia*, adopted by the twentieth national congress, held in Sydney in June 1964. For the party program see *Resolution, Twentieth Congress Communist Party of Australia*, June 1964.

The original reports for conferences before 1922 are in the W. Hancock Collection, Mitchell Library, Sydney. Before 1935 the party congresses were sometimes reported in the party press; after that date they were reported in the press and in pamphlet form. Some of the pamphlets published by the party are *For the Unity of the Working Class*, Sydney, Forward Press, 1936; *Communists in Congress*, Sydney, 1946; *The Way Forward*, Sydney, 1948; *Australia's Path to Socialism*, Sydney, 1952, 1955, 1958; and *The People Against Monopoly*, Sydney, 1961.

## CONGRESSES AND CONFERENCES OF THE CPA

Founding congress, October 1920
Conference, March 1921
1st annual conference, December 1921
2d annual conference, December 1922
3d annual conference, December 1923
4th annual conference, December 1924
5th annual conference, December 1925
6th annual conference, December 1926
7th annual conference, December 1927
8th annual conference, December 1928
9th annual conference, December 1929
10th congress, April 1931
11th congress, December 1935
12th congress, December 1938
13th congress, March 1943
14th national congress, August 1945
15th national congress, May 1948
16th national congress, August 1951
17th national congress, May 1955
18th national congress, April 1958
19th national congress, June 1961
20th national congress, June 1964

## BIBLIOGRAPHY

Bacon, E. A.: *Outline of the Post-war History of the Communist Party of Australia*, draft for discussion, Forest Lodge, 1966.

Campbell, E. W.: *History of the Australian Labor Movement: A Marxist Interpretation*, Sydney, 1945.

Davidson, Alastair: *The Communist Party of Australia: A Short History*, Stanford, Calif., Hoover Institution Press, 1969.

Ellis, M. H.: *The Red Road*, Sydney, Sydney and Melbourne Publishing Company, n.d.

Ellis, M. H.: *The Garden Path*, Sydney, Land, 1949.

*Report of the Royal Commission* inquiring into the origins, aims, objects and funds of the communist party in Victoria and other related matters, Melbourne, Government Printer, 1950.

Sharkey, L. L.: *An Outline History of the Australian Communist Party*, Sydney, 1944.

ALASTAIR DAVIDSON

1. *Tribune*, July 28, 1965.

# AUSTRIA

Syndicalism, anarchism, Marxism, and related radical movements started in Austria in the nineteenth century, and by 1914 Marxism had a strong following. The Social Democratic Workers' Party (Sozialdemokratische Arbeiterpartei, SDAP) was prominent in Austrian politics, and Austrian socialist leaders (Otto Bauer, Karl Renner, and others) played an important part in the development of the international socialist movement. During World War I the SDAP drifted far to the left and played a decisive role in the revolutionary transformation of the Hapsburg monarchy into a democratic republic. Meanwhile, in bolshevized Russia, Austrian prisoners of war who had undergone communist indoctrination had formed an Austrian Soviet of Workers' and Soldiers' Deputies in which young Austrian leftists obtained revolutionary experience.

During the days when the Austro-Hungarian empire was disintegrating a small group of radical leftists founded the Communist Party of German Austria (Kommunistische Partei Deutsch-Oesterreichs, KPDO) on November 3, 1918, in Vienna. This was in essence an enlarged discussion group, which went over to revolutionary propaganda only after a steady flow of returning prisoners of war from Russia provided a fast-growing number of experienced revolutionaries. Both Karl Tomann and Johann Koplenig, the party's early leaders (the latter from 1927 until recently), were former prisoners of war who had served their revolutionary apprenticeship in the ranks of bolshevik organizations in Russia.

The first convention of the KPDO, held in Vienna on February 9, 1919, adopted a party statute and elected an executive committee, with Tomann as its head. In September, following the change of German Austria to the Republic of Austria, the party changed its name accordingly to Communist Party of Austria (Kommunistische Partei Oesterreichs, KPO). In addition to the well-indoctrinated and disciplined group of former war prisoners, the new party attracted syndicalist and anarchist elements who had considered the SDAP insufficiently radical; hence the new membership tended from the very beginning toward factionalism.

## HISTORY

*1918 to 1927*  The SDAP had had a strong party organization since the campaigns that preceded the prewar elections. It was kept intact through the war years and grew considerably stronger during the revolutionary days of October and November 1918. Moreover, the SDAP leaders, Renner and Bauer, who had opposed Lenin's disruptive activities in the Second International, were quite familiar with bolshevik methods and splitting tactics. Finally, the social and economic program of the SDAP was itself sufficiently radical that the communists were unable to outbid it. These circumstances all portended difficulties for the development of a strong communist movement in Austria.

During the turbulent November-December 1918 events in Austria the KPDO was able to gain some influence in the Soviet-modeled workers' councils set up in many Austrian factories and localities, and by February 1919, the time of the party's first convention, membership was about 3,000, mostly concentrated in Vienna and its industrialized surroundings. Encouraged by the establishment of communist governments in Hungary (March 21) and Bavaria (April 4), the Austrian communists staged a revolt in Vienna on June

5, which, owing to complete lack of preparation and lack of support by the workers' masses, collapsed on the second day. Nevertheless, at the second all-Austrian conference of workers' councils on June 30 the communists attempted to proclaim Austria a soviet republic; a strong majority of social democratic delegates thwarted this attempt.

Confused by the failure of the June 1919 uprising, discredited by the cruelties of the defunct communist regime in Hungary, faced with the progressive stabilization of political and economic conditions in Austria and torn by internal factional strife, the party declined rapidly. By early 1927 its membership had shrunk to about 2,000 hard-core militants.

*1927 to 1933* At this low point, in June 1927, the ninth convention voted a complete reorganization of the party, purged it of both leftist and rightist deviationists, and installed the Soviet-trained Koplenig as secretary general. Under his astute leadership the party regained influence and strength among the workers and their labor unions. The simultaneous decline of the SDAP contributed further to the general growth of communism. The SDAP-inspired workers' demonstration in Vienna on July 15, 1927, caught the communists by surprise. The riots started as a mass demonstration against a court verdict absolving the nationalist assassins of two troopers of the Schutzbund, a semi-military organization of the SDAP, but the SDAP lost control of the mob and the communists incited it to violence; the outcome was the famous burning of the Vienna Palace of Justice and five deaths. The communists found their way to the dissatisfied workers, and by the end of 1927 the party claimed a membership of over 5,000.

During the next five years the KPO copied the actions and tactics of the quite successful Communist Party of Germany. In 1931 it issued a "program for the national and social liberation of the people," containing promises to attract workers' support. An elaborate scheme to transform the KPO into a mass party was implemented with funds from Moscow. Defections from the SDAP became numerous, and the communist membership began to grow. In the 1932 elections the KPO polled over 60,000 votes. In the fall of that year it organized over 100 meetings commemorating the fifteenth anniversary of the Russian revolution which attracted well over 100,000 participants. Under the guise of an antifascist front, the KPO was able to attract at that time not only social democrats, but also Christian democratic elements.

*1933 to 1945* Hitler's rise to power in Germany produced nazi disturbances in Austria, and in March 1933 the government suspended the Austrian parliament. This act was followed by socialist, communist, and nazi demonstrations against the government, which led to further repressions. The government struck first against the weakest link in this left-to-right opposition. On May 23, 1933, the KPO was dissolved by decree and went underground, but owing to a lenient attitude of the Austrian government (which saw the nazis as the real danger), the illegal KPO was able to develop quite a lively activity and to gain strength. It offered the SDAP a plan of a united front against the government, which was rejected because communist strength seemed negligible to the SDAP.

Still strong in Vienna and several provincial industrial centers, the SDAP intended to settle accounts with the weak government by a revolt which would result in a comeback of a socialist government. The communists, who had by this time infiltrated the Schutzbund and local socialist organizations, started preparations of their own. In order to placate Mussolini (who at that time supported Austrian opposition to the nazi *Anschluss* plans), the government planned to liquidate the socialist organizations. The nazis, aware of the government's preparations, decided to use the occasion for their own purposes. When the Austrian authorities raided provincial socialist headquarters during the night of February 11-12, 1934, the nazis joined them with their own raids. The next day Vienna reacted with a general strike, which the government answered with an armed assault on a large workers' housing development in the Vienna suburbs that was considered a socialist stronghold. The Schutzbund offered strong resistance, in which the communists played a considerable role. The socialist leadership lost control of the situation, and the communists stepped into their place. When the government finally put down the uprising after several days of fighting, the communists had become the heroes of the Austrian workers.

The SDAP, which had also been dissolved by the government, was less prepared for underground work than the communists. Their activities against the government and the growing nazi movement were often parallel, but the communists had the advantage of broader illegal experience and steady moral and financial support from Moscow. A social democratic group which called itself the Revolutionary Socialists also developed during this period and reappeared after the defeat of Nazi Germany. A large number of Schutzbund troopers and other socialists and communists fled to Czechoslovakia, where the local communist party organized aid and helped emigration to the Soviet Union. It is apparent in retrospect that the Austrian government's harassment of the socialists contributed to the growth of both nazism and communism in Austria.

After Hitler's occupation of Austria persecution of the socialists and communists became more intensive and harsh. Although no major acts of sabotage or proof of other resistance activities during World War II can be attributed to the communist underground, many socialist and communist leaders and militants were thrown into concentration camps. A large number survived both the occupation and the concentration camps. The Schutzbund troopers and February combatants who had fled to the Soviet Union fared much worse; most were executed in the Soviet purges of the late 1930s or disappeared in Siberian forced-labor camps.

*1945 to 1965* The occupation of Vienna by the Soviet army on April 13, 1945, created a completely new situation for the KPO. It reemerged into legality, disposed of a hard-core membership of allegedly 20,000, and for the first time in its existence was able to operate not only unopposed by the governing authorities, but with their full support. On the day after the Soviet occupation the surviving leaders of the Christian democrats, the old SDAP, and the KPO held a consultation. All present agreed on the demands to be presented to the Soviet occupation authorities: annulment of the *Anschluss*, restoration of Austria's independence, and creation of a provisional government. On April 29 the Soviet command announced the formation of a provisional government comprising representatives of these three parties and some nonparty persons. The old SDAP leader Karl Renner became head of this government. In this phase of Allied relations the Soviet government was not willing to establish a single-party communist government in Austria and could not avoid legalizing the two prominent noncommunist parties of the prewar period. However, Soviet insistence that the ministries of the interior (with control of the police) and information (control of the press) be assigned to communists foreboded Soviet intentions to maneuver the KPO into a dominant position. In June 1945 Austria was divided into four occupation zones, with a four-power control commission. The Soviet zone included half the country (over 16,000 square miles), with one-third of the population (2.4 million).

Looting, rape, and murder by Soviet soldiers during the first weeks of occupation were a bad introduction of communist rule to the Austrian population. Although Soviet support for the KPO was broad and lavish during the next ten years, plans to transform Austria into a "people's republic" in the East European-satellite fashion did not appeal to the Austrians. Furthermore, the rigorously correct behavior of the other three occupation powers encouraged the population of the

Soviet zone to resist all attempts to sovietize the country.

The carrot-and-stick tactics of the Soviet occupation authorities did produce some initial results, and both Moscow and the KPO expected a 25 to 30 percent communist vote in the first elections to the national assembly (November 25, 1945). When the votes were counted, however, the KPO had polled only 174,257 votes (5.4 percent) and won four seats out of 165. Delegates to the first postwar (thirteenth) convention of the KPO in Vienna in April 1946, obviously embarrassed by these meager election results, adopted a new plan of action; Soviet aid was secured in forcing the workers of Soviet-controlled state industries to join the party. Chicanery by the occupation authorities against the two noncommunist parties had to do the rest. These joint efforts produced some increase in membership, but the results were far below expectations. In the next elections (October 9, 1949) the KPO increased its total vote to 213,000 and five seats in the parliament, but because of a marked increase in the total vote, the percentage fell to 4.8.

The failure of all efforts to increase communist strength in Austria, and particularly in Vienna, convinced the KPO and its Soviet sponsors that more direct action for the establishment of a Soviet Austria had to be taken. A plan for a communist coup was carefully worked out, and the full logistic support of Soviet military units was secured. The first communist attempt to overthrow the Austrian government took place September 25-29, 1950, and was frustrated by the spontaneous resistance of the general populace and the workers in particular. This was followed by a second, more violent attack, well prepared by local Soviet commanders, who immobilized the Austrian police. From October 4 to 6 well over 100 communist attempts to occupy local and provincial government offices, communication centers, power stations, factories, and labor union offices were liquidated by a concerted action of workers, police, and citizens at large. This well-planned attempt to sovietize Austria failed mainly because of a deep-rooted opposition to communism on the part of the great majority of the population and its willingness to express these feelings in deeds.

Although the failure of the September-October coup resulted in a further loss of communist prestige in Austria, incessant pressure on the steadily growing number of workers employed by Soviet-controlled industries kept communism on the march. In the presidential elections of May 6, 1951, the communist candidate Gottlieb Fiala was able to poll 220,000 votes, or about 5 percent of the total vote. At the last parliamentary elections under Soviet occupation, in May 1953, the communist list received 228,000 votes (5 percent) and three seats, the highest following communism has been able to claim in Austria. Later election results showed a fast decline in communist votes:

|  | *Votes* | *%* | *Seats* |
| --- | --- | --- | --- |
| May 1956 | 192,000 | 4.1 | 3 |
| May 1959 | 142,000 | 3.0 | 0 |
| November 1962 | 135,000 | 2.8 | 0 |
| March 1966 | 18,638* | - | 0 |

*The KPO ran candidates in only one electoral district of Vienna, which has traditionally produced the largest communist vote. Here they polled 2,000 fewer votes than in 1962. In all other districts the KPO asked its followers to vote for the Socialist Party of Austria candidates. It is doubtful that this request was followed, because the socialist party suffered a decided loss of votes.

SOURCE: All election results are from *Archive der Gegenwart*, March 9, 1966, p. 12371.

The communists had obtained three portfolios in the provisional government appointed by Soviet authorities shortly after the nazis left Vienna, but after the small communist vote in the November 1945 elections the Figl government included only one communist. Since the communist vote in 1949 showed a slight percentage drop and the political situation of Austria improved, no communist was included in the governments that followed these and later elections. A similar development took place in the provincial diets, where the communists at first had some weak representation but later, particularly after the Hungarian uprising of 1956, lost all their seats.

After the termination of the Soviet occupation of Austria in September 1955 the KPO met with growing difficulties in continuing its activities. In many localities party quarters which had been assigned by the occupation authorities had to be vacated. All assistance to local cells and groups, as well as sinecures given to party activists, ceased. The party retrenched to defensive positions behind slogans of Austrian patriotism and promises of new benefits for "the working people." The KPO now became the staunchest defender of Austrian neutralism. The de-Stalinization period did not influence internal developments in the party. The old party apparatus, painfully constructed during the Stalin regime, remained untouched. Koplenig and his close collaborators in the leadership adjusted themselves to Khrushchev's line and made another adjustment after his sudden demise as Soviet leader. The "new way to Austrian socialism," inaugurated during the Khrushchev period and based on "peaceful coexistence," prevailed until the end of 1965. All these developments were accompanied by a steady decline both in party membership and in the KPO's influence on Austrian political affairs. The old party members started to die out rapidly, young candidates have become increasingly scarce, and Austrian communism is vanishing from day to day.[1]

## ORGANIZATION AND MEMBERSHIP

The internal organization of the KPO is based on the Soviet model of democratic centralism, with local or factory cells grouped into county organizations. These in turn form provincial committees, which are controlled by the politburo. The highest authority is the party convention, which now meets every four years. The convention (about 400 to 450 delegates) elects a central committee (eighty-five members), a control commission (five members), and an arbitration commission (ten members). The central committee elects from its members the party chairman (now Franz Muhri), the all-powerful politburo (eleven members, including Muhri), and two secretaries (now Friedl Fürnberg and Erwin Scharf, both members of the politburo).

No official figures are available concerning the social and educational structure of the membership. The number of votes for communist candidates in various elections is only an indirect reflection of membership strength. The published reports and minutes of the last six conventions (1948 to 1965) contain discrepant figures on the number of new members. Moreover, although they contain the names of those who were purged and expelled, there is no mention of members who left the party voluntarily. A careful analysis of the financial data in the last three reports, however, permits the extraction of a few interesting conclusions. First of all, the number of employed members is steadily decreasing; from 1961 to 1965 it fell from 60 to 52 percent of dues-paying members. The remainder were emeriti and old-age pensionists, and the party has regularly complained that the enrollment of young members is not satisfactory. A recent report indicated that party membership had dropped from more than 42,000 in 1961 to 36,000 in 1964.[2] Thus the KPO probably had about 35,000 members in 1965.

The strongest party organizations are in Vienna and its industrial suburbs, where more than half the entire membership is concentrated. The second largest group is in the city and suburbs of Steyer, where there are large industrial plants. It is estimated that about 65 percent of the members are industrial workers, whereas the remainder are clerks in commercial and other enterprises and self-employed craftsmen, with a thin sprinkling of intellectuals. According to the report on the nineteenth convention in 1965, of the 430 delegates, 87 percent were workers and employees, 10 percent were pensionists, craftsmen, and others, and only 3 percent (a total of twelve persons) were classified as intellectuals. It is not clear where the party functionaries (*apparatchiks*), who formed a large group among the delegates, were included. Their presence produced some criticism during the discussion, indicating a growing discontent among the membership.

The financial reports of the central committee provide some insight into the party's operations. During the four years from April 1961 to May 1965 the total income of the central committee was 24.9 million schillings (almost $1 million), of which 38 percent derived from membership dues and donations, with the remainder from other donors and various sources. The KPO owns the Globus-Verlag in Vienna, a modern printing enterprise employing 1,000 persons, and its income from commercial printing finances all party publications.

Before World War II the KPO was able to initiate or infiltrate existing pacifist and antinazi organizations. During the period of Soviet occupation the party concentrated chiefly on increasing its numerical strength. Attempts to create procommunist, and implicitly pro-Soviet, fronts failed. However, the party developed three youth organizations which are communist controlled. The Children's World Young Guard (Kinderland-Junge Garde), which concentrates on youth under sixteen, is strongest in workers' districts of Vienna. The Free Austrian Youth (Freie Oesterreichische Jugend), which corresponds to the Soviet Komsomol, and serves as the recruiting ground for party members, had strong appeal in the early years of the Soviet occupation but has recently showed a steady decline in membership and activities. The Association of Democratic Students (Vereinigung Demokratischer Studenten) is the most active of the three youth organizations, but because of its constant opposition to the predominance of party *apparatchiks* in the leadership, it is not fully trusted. It depends heavily on a hard core of "eternal students" and on scholarships from party sources. Attempts of the KPO to infiltrate pacifist organizations dominated by the socialists have failed several times.

## RELATION TO SOVIET LEADERSHIP

Bolshevized Austrian prisoners of war participated in the Russian revolution of November 1917 and in the following civil war, particularly in the struggle against Kolchak and the Czechs. A representative of the Austrian Soviet of Workers and Soldiers Deputies (Horn) participated in the international meeting in Petrograd on December 19, 1918, held to discuss the founding of the Comintern. Representatives of the KPO were present at all later Comintern congresses and plenums. First Karl Tomann and later Johann Koplenig were the main delegates; Koplenig also served several times as member of the Comintern Presidium.

Shortly after its founding, when the KPO boycotted the elections to the first national assembly in 1919, Lenin issued an open letter to the Austrian communists condemning this attitude as a "leftist disease" and appealing to the membership for ideological and organizational unity. Until 1927, when Koplenig assumed leadership of the party, its internal quarrels were a continual subject of discussions and decisions by the Comintern. Koplenig followed Stalin's line faithfully, survived all purges, and continued as party leader well past the Khrushchev period.

When the Soviet army occupied Austria in 1945, only a few of the Austrian communists and procommunist Schutzbund members who had survived the purges in the Soviet Union returned to Austria with the Soviet troops and became the backbone of the revived KPO. The KPO was also a member of the Cominform in 1947; it did not play a prominent role there but faithfully followed Moscow's desires. After Stalin's death the party accepted the Khrushchev leadership and became an ardent advocate of his peaceful-coexistence slogan and the peaceful-road-to-socialism program. The KPO was represented at the two meetings of communist parties in Moscow, in November 1957 and November 1960, and endorsed their resolutions.

In the Sino-Soviet dispute the KPO has consistently supported the Moscow leadership, although this has been challenged by a two-pronged opposition among the membership. Some older members, remembering the disastrous consequences of taking sides in the Soviet party wrangles during the Stalin period, advocated neutrality of the party in this new strife. They did not form a group and were easily silenced by the leadership loyal to Moscow. However, the pro-Chinese group in the party became a real challenge to the leadership. According to party publications, Albanian and Chinese influences were able to bring about the formation of a pro-Peking faction, which has published *Rote Fahne* since October 1963. Its publisher, Franz Strobl, and a dozen other "splitters" were expelled from the party by the nineteenth convention in 1965. This group is active in Vienna, Linz, and Steyer and has led to scattered investigations of "political jaundice" among the party membership. The strength of this opposition is difficult to establish.

## FUTURE PROSPECTS

Austria was the only country to have experienced Soviet occupation and escaped a communist takeover. The KPO missed its only chance to increase its strength and maneuver itself into power when it failed to do so during the ten years of Soviet occupation. After the withdrawal of the Red Army this chance was lost; the behavior of the communist occupants has left a strong feeling against communism among the Austrian population. Recent party enrollment and election results show a steady decline in whatever appeal the party has had. The failure to enroll young members has resulted in a progressive aging of its membership. At the May 1965 party convention the tone of most of the speeches and discussions was quite pessimistic. Franz Marek, a member of the politburo, properly defined the situation of the party when he complained that the appeals and actions of its leadership were being crushed against "a wall of indifference" among the membership.

## PARTY PRESS ORGANS AND RECORDS

The first official press organ of the party was the daily *Rote Fahne*, started in September 1919. Its largest circulation in the 1920s was 30,000. When the party was outlawed in 1932 the paper was banned, but it appeared sporadically as an underground sheet. During the Soviet occupation eight communist dailies and six weeklies appeared in Austria. At present the party publishes one daily, *Die Volksstimme*, and a theoretical organ of the central committee, *Weg und Ziel*. Both have a circulation of less than 20,000.

The party has published the proceedings of all nineteen of its conventions, with the exception of the twelfth convention in Prague in 1934. These publications contain all resolutions concerning the party's program and the statutes.

## PARTY CONVENTIONS AND CONFERENCES

With the exception of the 1934 convention and the 1937 conference in Prague, all meetings were held in Vienna.

Founding conference, November 1918
1st convention, KPDO, February 1919
2d convention, KPDO, July 1919
3d convention, KPO (conference), December 1919
4th convention, KPO, January 1921
5th convention, KPO, March 1922
6th convention, KPO, March 1923
7th convention, KPO, March 1924
Conference, November 1924
8th convention, KPO, September 1925
9th convention, KPO, June 1927
10th convention, KPO, February 1929
11th convention, KPO, June 1931
12th convention, KPO, September 1934
Conference, August 1937

13th convention, KPO, April 1946
14th convention, KPO, October-November 1948
15th convention, KPO, November 1951
16th convention, KPO, May 1954
17th convention, KPO, March 1957
Conference, February 1958
18th convention, KPO, April 1961
19th convention, KPO, May 1965

BIBLIOGRAPHY

*Anschlag auf Oesterreich: Ein Tatsachenbericht über den kommunistischen Putschversuch im September-Oktober 1950,* Vienna 1950.

*Aus der Vergangenheit der KPO: Aufzeichnungen und Erinnerungen zur Geschichte der Partei,* Vienna, 1961.

*Die Kommunisten im Kampf für die Unabhängigkeit Oesterreichs: Sammelband,* Vienna, 1955.

*Kommunisticheskaia partiia Avstrii, v borbe za massy: Rechi tt. Kopleniga, Videna, Dopplera, Germana, delegatov Avstriiskoi kompartii* (The Communist Party of Austria in the Struggle for the Masses: Speeches by Comrades Koplenig, Widen, Doppler, German, Delegates of the Austrian Communist Party), Moscow, Partizdat, 1935.

Koplenig, J.: *Reden und Aufsätze, 1924-1950,* Vienna, 1951.

Mochalin, D. N.: *Vena na barrikadakh* (Vienna on the Barricades), Moscow, 1964.

Schönau, Alexander: *The February Insurrection of the Austrian Proletariat,* Moscow, 1934.

Stearman, William Lloyd: *The Soviet Union and the Occupation of Austria,* Bonn, Vienna, Zurich, n.d.

*40 [Vierzig] Jahre Kommunistische Partei Oesterreichs,* Vienna, 1958.

*Von 1934 bis 1946: 12 Jahre Kampf für Freiheit und Demokratie,* Referat von Friedl Fürnberg auf dem 13. Parteitag der KPO, Vienna, 1946.

WITOLD S. SWORAKOWSKI

1. For further developments see *Yearbook on International Communist Affairs,* 1966 and following years, Stanford, Calif., Hoover Institution.

2. *World Marxist Review,* July 1965, p. 66.

# THE BALKAN COMMUNIST FEDERATION

The Balkan Communist Federation (BCF) is in fact a continuation of the Balkan Socialist Federation (BSF), formed at a conference in Belgrade in 1910. Members of the BSF were the socialist parties of Bulgaria, Greece, Rumania, and Serbia. Owing to the agricultural character of these countries, their socialist parties were weak and insignificant; so, too, was the BSF. A second conference was held in July 1915 in Bucharest, but the BSF was inactive until the end of World War I. After the war, when the member parties of the BSF adopted the name communist, they met at a conference in Sofia in 1920, renamed themselves the Balkan Communist Federation, and joined the Comintern. Bulgarian communists V. Kolarov and Georgi Dimitrov played a leading role in this organization. The BCF office (after 1924) was located in Vienna. Between its founding in 1920 and its dissolution in 1932 the BCF held seven conferences.

This federation of four communist parties came into being, not as a result of Moscow's initiative, but as a continuation of an earlier Marxist attempt to create a larger, supranational economic unit. In joining the Comintern the BCF secured Moscow's approval for its final aims. At its second conference, held in May 1921, the BCF defined its aims as promotion of proletarian revolutions in the Balkan countries, abolition of monarchical governments in all countries, and the formation of a Balkan Socialist Soviet Federal Republic comprising Bulgaria, Greece, Rumania, and Yugoslavia; this future Balkan republic was to "unite its efforts to the efforts of the Soviet Union . . . for the broadening and strengthening of the front of the international revolution, aiming toward the acceleration of its final victory." These aims were to be reached by supporting all dissatisfied national minorities, particularly the Macedonians, in the struggle against the governments of their homelands. The unstable and explosive nationality and minority situations in all four countries were to be used for the promotion of permanent unrest and subversion in these countries. According to the BCF's expectations, these countries would be kept busy with internal difficulties and thus prevented from joining "the bourgeois counterrevolutionary forces working against the Soviet Union." The fifth congress of the Comintern in 1924 fully approved and supported this program.

Government repression of the communist parties in all four countries after 1923 considerably hampered their activities. Factional strife in the Greek and Yugoslav parties and a complete standstill in the Rumanian party in the mid-1920s reduced the federation to a mere paper organization. However, under Comintern prodding the September 1928 conference of the BCF moved to reorganize and revitalize the federation; it was to become the "unified directing center" of all four Balkan parties. Despite initial support from Moscow, this attempt failed before it materialized, since the member parties refused to submit to this decision.

In 1932, when the purges in the Soviet Union were extended to the communist parties abroad, Moscow decided to liquidate the federation. The obvious method of accomplishing this was withdrawal of Comintern financial support of the BCF's office and its press organ, *Fédération balkanique*. Soviet sources claim that the danger of fascism and war had created a new situation in which the Balkan parties had to concentrate on the creation of united fronts in their countries. It is apparent, however, that Moscow never subscribed to the concept of a unified communist state in the Balkans. When Georgi Dimitrov, a former leader of the BCF and prime minister of communist-dominated Bulgaria, voiced new plans for a Balkan federation of communist-dominated states in 1948, he was severely rebuked by Moscow.

PARTY PRESS ORGANS AND RECORDS

The only comprehensive source for information on the aims and activities of the BCF is its press organ *Fédération balkanique*, which appeared in Vienna from July 15, 1924, until 1932. It also contains sporadic information on the conferences and their resolutions. Additional information can be found in the Comintern periodicals *Communist International*, and *International Press Correspondence*.

CONFERENCES OF THE BCF

1st conference, 1920, Sofia
2d conference, May 1921
3d conference, 1922
4th conference, 1923, Sofia
5th conference, 1924, Vienna
6th conference, 1925, Moscow
7th conference, September 1928

BIBLIOGRAPHY

Dimitrov, G.: "Polozhenie na Balkanakh i zadachi Balkanskoi kommunisticheskoi federatsii (The Situation in the Balkans and the Problems of the Balkan Communist Federation)," *Izbranye proizvedeniia* (Selected Works), vol. I, Moscow, 1957, pp. 242-266.

Kabakchiev, Kh.: "Balkanskaia kommunisticheskaia federatsiia (Balkan Communist Federation)," in Kh. Kabakchiev, B. Boshkovich, and Kh. Batis, *Kommunisticheskie partii balkanskikh stran* (Communist Parties of the Balkan Countries), preface by V. Kolarov, Moscow, Gosizdat RSFSR, 1930.

WITOLD S. SWORAKOWSKI

# BASUTOLAND
*See* Lesotho

# BELGIUM

The communist party was founded in Belgium following a split brought about by the far left in the socialist Belgian Workers' Party (Parti Ouvrier Belge, POB). Two groups on the far left broke away from the party. In August 1920 several militants of the Belgian Socialist Youth (Jeunesse Socialiste Belge), including Edouard van Overstraeten, left the POB and formed a communist group whose organ became the newspaper *L'Ouvrier communiste*. In addition, the minority socialists of the left set up a group within the POB, but in open opposition to the party majority, with the newspaper *L'Exploité* as their press organ; they held three consecutive congresses and then, in May 1921, broke with the POB and formed the Communist Party of Belgium (Parti Communiste de Belgique, PCB), with Joseph Jacquemotte as leader.

As the Comintern stipulated that there could be only one communist party in each country, the two Belgian communist groups were invited to send two delegates each to Moscow to negotiate with the Comintern Executive with a view toward their union. Negotiations began in the summer of 1921 during the third congress of the Comintern, with van Overstraeten and Jacquemotte taking part, and unification was achieved at the congress of Brussels on September 3-4, 1921.

## HISTORY

*Between the Two World Wars* The party's beginnings were difficult; nearly all the workers had remained loyal to the old POB and the reformist trade unions. The party's total membership was very low. According to official figures, shortly after its founding it could count 517 members; in 1924 there were 590, and in 1927, 1,500.

As for political trade-union action, it was not until 1923 that the party was able to emerge from its tight circle, thanks to two important events—the occupation of the Ruhr, against which the communist group organized an act of protest, and the miners' strike in 1923, which pointed to the communists as being active militants. These events led to the arrest of about fifty communists, of which some fifteen, including van Overstraeten and Jacquemotte, were brought before a tribunal in July 1923, tried, and acquitted. In 1925 Jacquemotte was elected as the first communist deputy; the following year van Overstraeten also was elected to the parliament.

The PCB was shaken by a serious crisis following the conflict between Stalin and Trotsky and Zinoviev in Moscow. In November 1927 van Overstraeten got the central committee to adopt (by a vote of fifteen to three) a resolution protesting the exclusion of Trotsky and Zinoviev from the Russian party. The machinery of the Comintern reacted vigorously: it set Jacquemotte up against van Overstraeten, published an open letter to the party members, and in March 1928 sent secret emissaries to Brussels empowered to apply pressure, so that in the end van Overstraeten lost the majority. A party conference in March 1928 decided on his exclusion, but the split which followed brought about a spectacular drop in membership. The party counted no more than 500 members in 1928; although it reached the 1,000 figure in 1929 and 1930, the party organ *Le Drapeau rouge,* a daily since its founding in 1921, dropped to a circulation of 3,500 and even ceased to appear as a daily for a time.

The party did not begin to recover until several years later, at first by exploitation of the economic crisis (the general strike of miners in the summer of 1932), and then by exploitation of the antifascist tactics of the popular front. Membership climbed to 2,500 in 1935, to reach a high of 7,000 to 9,000 from 1936 to 1939. Voting strength increased in an even more striking manner. In 1932 the party had received 65,000 votes (with three deputies), but in 1936 it had already increased to 143,000 (with nine deputies), representing 6.06 percent of the total votes cast (as opposed to 757,000 socialist votes representing 32 percent of the total vote).

Throughout this period Joseph Jacquemotte remained at the head of the party. He had been elected a member of the Comintern Executive at the Comintern's fifth and sixth congresses and reelected a deputy member at its seventh congress in the summer of 1935.

*World War II* In the first phase of the war, from 1939 to 1941, the PCB switched tactics from one extreme to the other—from defeatism to ultrapatriotism, from an anti-Allied position to an anti-Axis position. These sudden changes were not caused by the German attack on Belgium in May 1940, but by the Soviet-German war in June 1941. Following the attack on the Soviet Union, the German occupying forces in Belgium, as in other occupied European countries, proceeded to arrest the leaders of the party, including Xavier Relecom, general secretary since Jacquemotte's disappearance in 1936. These arrests did not prevent the party from continuing its clandestine activities; in preparation for the arrests, the party had provided for a replacement leadership, several members of which were former combatants in the International Brigades in the Spanish Civil War.

The party managed to organize two resistance groups, which became more and more important as the German defeat approached. One group, the Armed Partisans (Les Partisans Armés), was purely communist; the other, the Independence Front (Le Front de l'Indépendance), claimed to have a vast national representation, but the key positions remained in the hands of the communists.

Military action alone was too weak to sway the course of the war in Belgium, which was settled by the intervention of Allied troops; however, under cover of the resistance movement the communists succeeded in setting up a political-military organization capable of affecting the evolution of the country. In November-December 1944, profiting from a ministerial crisis, the communists set the resistance movements in motion and organized a "march to parliament." The police intervened and shots were exchanged, leaving some victims. The capital was not restored to order until the Allied high command issued a declaration that the disorders would not be tolerated. In April 1945 the communists once more attempted to provoke a mass movement, in Brussels and elsewhere—with the slowness of the trials of the collaborators as a pretext— but order was rapidly reestablished.

Although the use of violence had been ineffective, the PCB had recourse to legal and parliamentary channels after this point. As a consequence, in the two-year period immediately following the liberation, the communist movement in Belgium reached its highest development. In November 1945 Edgar Lalmand, the new general secretary, proudly announced that party membership had passed the 100,000 mark for the first time. In December 1945 the party became part of a government coalition (socialist, communist, and liberal), to which it contributed three ministers (Lalmand was named food minister).

In the first parliamentary elections after the war, in February 1946, the communists recorded considerable progress. Although it did not get the results expected by party leaders, the PCB elected twenty-three deputies, with 300,000 votes (12 percent of the total votes cast, whereas the POB received 31 percent). The party also made considerable gains in the trade-union field. After long negotiations at the beginning of 1946 the socialist and communist trade unionists joined in a General Federation of Belgian Labor (Fédération Générale du Travail Belge), which had two general secretaries, one of whom, Dejaze, was a communist.

This advantageous situation for the PCB came to a sudden end in 1947, when the cold war began to set in over Europe, bringing the departure of communists from all the European governments in which they had held positions. In March 1947 the communist ministers, laying the blame for their disagreement on a secondary point, resigned from the Belgian government. In December of the same year Dejaze also resigned from his post as general secretary of the General Federation of Belgian Labor.

*The Cold War*  From 1947 on the PCB found itself cut off from all the other political and trade-union forces of the country, and its blind following of the meanderings of Stalin's policies produced catastrophic results. The party ceased to issue membership figures, but in January 1949 it counted scarcely 35,000 members. The parliamentary elections of June 1947 reflected its declining power: from 12 percent of the vote in 1946, it fell to 7 percent, and from twenty-three deputies it fell to twelve. The decline continued in subsequent elections; in 1950 the party polled 4.74 percent of the votes cast and elected seven deputies and in 1954 only 3.5 percent of the votes and four deputies. The circulation of two party dailies, *Le Drapeau rouge* and *De Rode Vaan*, fell in the same proportions. In 1946 the two newspapers together printed more than 100,000 copies, but total circulation fell in 1949 and 1950 to 60,000 and in 1955 to a maximum of 10,000.

This loss in the PCB's political influence was compounded by some serious conflicts and major purges of the leadership. After Jacquemotte's disappearance in 1936 two titular leaders of the party were Julien Lahaut, named president, and Relecom, promoted to general secretary. After the war Edgar Lalmand replaced Relecom, who had been criticized for his behavior in the German concentration camps. Relecom was censured by the central committee and finally expelled from the party in July 1949. Lahaut was killed in August 1950 by unknown assassins.

There were further purges among the remaining leadership. At the eleventh congress, held at Vilvorde in December 1954, the entire political bureau was eliminated, with the sole exception of Henri Glineur, deputy from Charleroi (who passed into the Chinese camp several years later). Among those eliminated were Lalmand, former minister Jean Terfve (who managed to reinstate the political bureau several years later), and former minister Jean Borreman. Direction of the party now was entrusted to a new, younger team, whose two responsible leaders were René Beelen, first secretary of the central committee and a former worker who had gone through the Comintern school at Moscow from 1930 to 1932, and Ernest Burnelle, second secretary and a former schoolteacher.

These changes in leadership were accompanied by a change in tactics as a result of the policy ushered in by Stalin's successors in Moscow. This policy, which abandoned the out-and-out war against the socialist parties and trade unions and returned to the tactics of a united front and unity of action, was adopted by a resolution of the December 1954 congress: "Unity of action of the socialist and communist workers is an element essential for the assembling of the entire working class, all the democratic forces—an essential condition for winning the battle for peace, independence, and social progress." These principles also specified that this unity of action was to apply not only to the political domain, but to the trade unions as well: "Trade-union work in the General Federation of Belgian Labor is the principal link permitting the communists to associate themselves closely with the working masses in view of the defense of their demands."

*The Khrushchev Era* Once the new general line was drawn and the new team had been installed in the leadership, it remained for the party to act on this policy. However, obstacles were encountered on both the political and the labor planes. There were difficulties first of all with some of the militant communists themselves. Since the rupture between the socialists and the communists in 1947, the communists had grouped their trade unions into an autonomous organization, Les Syndicats Uniques, but the weakening of its membership meant that this organization was no longer recognized as representative of the workers by either the government or the employers. However, when the PCB decided to dissolve Les Syndicats Uniques and have its militant members rejoin the General Federation of Belgian Labor, the only two communist trade unions that still had any supporters, those of the miners and the quarrymen, refused to submit to this decision. It was not for another year that they finally yielded and requested their members to join.

Once in the General Federation, the militant communist trade unionists succeeded in getting themselves elected to minor offices and in leading some important strikes (the dockers' strike at Antwerp in June-July 1955), in directing certain campaigns for their demands (the one in favor of nationalization of coal mines), and in bringing certain resolutions to a vote (peaceful coexistence, recognition of Communist China, etc.).

In internal politics the PCB was able to record several successes in its efforts for a united front with socialist youth and in unity on the aims formulated by both the socialist and communist peace movements. On the whole, however, the reaction of the socialists was negative, a fact acknowledged in the draft platform of the PCB for its twelfth congress in April 1957: "To forge indispensable unity between the socialist and communist workers, it is necessary to know how to make a criticism of the POB and its directors on the right." The lack of an audience for the PCB was confirmed in the legislative elections of June 1, 1958. While the PCB had received 184,000 votes and 3.5 percent of the votes cast in the elections of 1954, in 1958 it received only 111,000 votes and 1.89 percent, with only two deputies elected (as opposed to four in 1954, seven in 1950, and twelve in 1947).

The events of 1956 in the communist world did not leave the PCB unaffected. De-Stalinization, inaugurated by the twentieth congress of the Soviet party in February, did not produce any great backwash. The PCB's delegation to the congress, led by Ernest Burnelle, was very quiet after its return, and when the first rumors of Khrushchev's "secret speech" began to spread, a national conference, held during Easter, rapidly settled the Stalin question by this resolution: "We have looked into the facts for which Stalin has been reproached with a spirit of responsibility, being careful to defend the Soviet Union, not to allow the adversary to disorient our comrades, to express forcefully all that the Soviet Union's announcement promises, in the way of power, democracy, and growth. This is not the first time that we are being induced to close ranks around the Soviet Union before the adversary's campaigns."

The Hungarian revolution, however, provoked defections in the party at all levels—in communist electoral strength, in party membership, and even in its leadership (two members of the central committee, one a former communist deputy and the other a professor at the University of Brussels, resigned from the PCB to join the POB).

The split in the party over the Sino-Soviet dispute did not bring about a decline in membership in the PCB or a loss in votes analogous to the continual decline that the party had been experiencing since 1947. In fact, the tactic of a united front with the socialists and the trade-union left in general, which the party had followed since the end of 1954 with no notable results for several years, finally began to bear fruit in the early 1960s. Party membership began to rise for the first time in fifteen years. According to official figures, from the beginning of 1959 to the end of 1962 the number of members rose from 11,345 to 14,533 and was continuing to climb.

In the parliamentary elections the same progress was recorded. In 1961 the PCB collected 162,238 votes, with 3.8 percent of the total vote and six deputies, already an improvement over the 1958 returns; even this was surpassed in the following elections, on May 23, 1965. For the first time, in most of the Walloon districts the communists offered united-front lists with the left socialists who had abandoned the POB and with some progressive social Christians; they received 236,333 votes, or 4.56 percent of the votes cast, and six seats in the parliament (while the POB lost 460,000 votes and twenty seats). Thus the Belgian party is one of the very few communist parties in Europe which has showed a consistent recovery of strength in recent years.

## ORGANIZATION AND MEMBERSHIP

The PCB has a pyramidal organization patterned after the Soviet model. When the Comintern ordered its member parties to make political bureaus their supreme organs, the Belgian communists complied; they did the same when, according to the Soviet model, the general secretary became leader of the party. After Stalin's death the post of party president was introduced in numerous Western communist parties, and in 1965 the PCB had a president (Ernest Burnelle), a vice president (René Beelen), a national secretary (Albert de Coninck), and a political bureau of several members.

There is a clear difference in the roots of the party among the Walloons and among the Flemish. The PCB has a greater following and greater electoral strength in the Walloon provinces than in the Flemish provinces, and the major part of its successful municipal and parliamentary candidates come from the Walloon regions, particularly the two industrial and mining provinces Hainaut and Liège. The party enjoys a certain degree of support in Brussels, and as far as the Flemish part of the country is concerned, it has recorded noticeable progress only in the great port of Antwerp in the municipal elections of October 1964.

In the 1950s the party tried to act through various peace movements, particularly the International Movement for Peace, the Belgian Union for the Defense of Peace, and the Committee for the Solution of the German Problem. In recent times the party has strived to revive pacifist sentiment through exploitation of the "German revanchist danger" on the one hand and "American aggression in Vietnam" on the other.

## RELATION TO SOVIET LEADERSHIP

At the conference of the eighty-one communist parties held in Moscow in November 1960 the PCB was represented by a delegation led by Ernest Burnelle, who had become party president. Upon its return the delegation informed the central committee of the difficult aspects of the debates in Moscow, marked by Sino-Soviet antagonism, but *Le Drapeau rouge* did not report it. A year later, at the twenty-second congress of the Soviet party, the Belgian delegation was again led by Burnelle, but this time a member of the central committee, Jacques Grippa, opposed the PCB's alignment with the Soviet position and defended the Sino-Albanian point of view. The debate was published in part in the party's daily in January 1962. Grippa and his adherents left the PCB in December 1963 and founded the Belgian Communist Party, Marxist-Leninist (Parti Communiste Belge, Marxiste-Léniniste, PCB-ML). Its members are most numerous in Brussels and Liège. This splinter party, obviously well financed from China, developed an intensive propaganda and publications activity. Thus the PCB became the first party in Europe in which a member of the central committee sided with the Chinese party and undertook to form a pro-Chinese communist movement.

The municipal elections of October 1964, in which both the PCB and the PCB-ML presented candidates, disclosed the weakness of the pro-Chinese party. Whereas the PCB increased the number of its municipal councillors in the country from ninety-one in 1958 to 176 in 1964, the PCB-ML obtained only one municipal mandate.

## PARTY PRESS ORGANS

In earlier years the PCB published several newspapers and journals. In 1965 its press was limited to the daily *Le Drapeau rouge*, a four-page bulletin, *PCB Information*, and a weekly in Flemish, *De Rode Vaan* (The Red Flag). The PCB-ML publishes the weekly *La Voix du peuple*.

## CONGRESSES OF THE PCB

1st congress, September 1921
2d congress, January 1923
3d congress, January 1925
4th congress, January 1927
5th congress, March 1929
6th congress, November 1936
7th congress, August 1939
8th congress, May-June 1946
9th congress, May 1948
10th congress, March 1951
11th congress, December 1954
12th congress, April 1957
13th congress, April 1960
14th congress, April 1963
15th congress, November 1964

## BIBLIOGRAPHY

Demany, Fernand: *Si c'était à refaire*, Brussels, Editions Est & Ouest, 1952.

Jacquemotte, Joseph: *Articles et interpellations parlementaires, 1912-1936,* Brussels, 1961.

Liebman, Marcel: "Origine et signification idéologiques de la scission communiste dans le POB (1921)," doctoral dissertation, Brussels, Free University of Brussels, 1963.

Massart, Ch.: *La Belgique socialiste et communiste*, preface by Amédée Dunois, Paris, Librairie de l'Humanité, 1922.

BRANKO LAZITCH

# BELORUSSIA

The Communist Party of Belorussia (Kamunistychnaia Partyia Belarusi, KPB) can be said to have descended indirectly from small social democratic groups that emerged during the late 1890s in several Belorussian cities. These groups had little to do with the Belorussian peasantry, and peasant unrest was not prompted by their activities. Belorussians played no role in the founding congress of the Russian Social Democratic Labor Party, held in March 1898. Lenin's movement had to compete with the Jewish Social Democratic Bund, the Belorussian Socialist Hromada, and the Polish Socialist Party. Small social democratic groups were organized in Minsk, Gomel, Bobruisk, Vitebsk, Mogilev, Mozyr, and Polotsk, but many came under menshevik influence soon after the 1905 revolution.

The proximity of Belorussia to the eastern front in World War I provided opportunities for bolshevik agitation designed to promote the disaffection of troops. In late June 1917 the bolsheviks in Minsk began to publish the newspaper *Zvezda*, with financial support and direction from Lenin's central committee. The bolsheviks waged campaigns against the Belorussian Socialist Hromada and the Jewish Bund. Prominent bolsheviks active at this time in Belorussia were such non-Belorussians as M. V. Frunze, A. F. Miasnikov, V. G. Knorin, K. I. Lander, and V. V. Fomin.

## HISTORY

Initially no Belorussian communist organization existed under that name. A northwestern committee of the Russian Social Democratic Labor Party had been formed in 1904. This unit became the northwestern regional (*oblast*) organization of the Russian party in September 1917; it claimed more than 7,100 members, most of whom were from military units stationed in the area. A regional committee was elected and claimed 60,000 members, but this was a temporary swelling caused by the disintegration of the Russian army. By February 1918 German occupation and a developing Belorussian nationalism had created unfavorable conditions for bolshevik activity. It was only after the Red Army seized Minsk in December 1918, following the German withdrawal, that the Belorussian Soviet Socialist Republic and the KPB were formed. The sixth conference of the northwestern regional party, held in Smolensk, became the first congress of the KPB, with 206 delegates representing 17,771 members. The KPB remained a part of the Russian Communist Party (Bolshevik), but with a new name. Knorin became the first secretary of its central bureau, and Miasnikov was its chairman; both were Russians.

Lenin proceeded to merge the new republic and party with the abortive communist regime in Lithuania. In late January 1919 a Lithuanian-Belorussian Soviet Socialist Republic (Litbel) was formed, and in March the two parties merged at a meeting in Vilna, later known as the second congress of the KPB. The new party had 17,636 members and was still a part of the Russian Communist Party (Bolshevik); it was headed by the Lithuanian V. S. Mickevičius-Kapsukas. The new party published newspapers in Russian, Lithuanian, Polish, and Yiddish, but not in Belorussian. Polish forces held most of Belorussia from mid-1919 until July 1920. Reestablishment of Soviet rule in Belorussia and its collapse in Lithuania led to the dissolution of Litbel. Belorussian "independence" was proclaimed on July 31, 1920. In November of that year the KPB had only 1,700 members.

The impact of Belorussian nationalism and the fact that this nationalism also persisted in areas under Polish rule necessitated the commitment of Moscow and of the KPB to a policy of Belorussification. Russia also felt it advisable to cede the Mogilev, Vitebsk, and Gomel regions to the Belorussian republic. In 1922 only 21 percent of the KPB membership was Belorussian, but by 1927 it had increased to 46.7 percent and was accompanied by an unprecedented flowering of the national culture.

By 1932 the Belorussian membership in the KPB had risen to 60.4 percent, but this further increase was offset by Stalin's determination to impede and control the Belorussification process. The Russian language was hastily imposed in the late 1930s. The KPB was first purged in 1922, and later Trotskyists and nationalists were excluded. During the 1930s the purges were very severe and claimed party secretaries Gikalo and Sharangovich and Premier Haladzed as victims. As the purges ended, P. K. Ponomarenko, a Soviet apparatus official from Moscow, was appointed KPB first secretary in late 1938. Ponomarenko and his aides soon had to flee before the invading nazis; he returned in 1944 to head the KPB until 1950 and was succeeded by N. S. Patolichev, a Russian, who served until July 1956. K. T. Mazurov, a native of Belorussia, served from 1956 to March 1965 and was succeeded by P. M. Masherov.

The KPB is faced with the difficult task of

determining its role in the preservation of the ethnic identity of the Belorussian people. It has had only limited success in developing and retraining native cadres; its future will hinge on its ability to cope with this problem.

## ORGANIZATION AND MEMBERSHIP

The KPB is a subordinate part of the Communist Party of the Soviet Union but has its own central committee, presidium (bureau), and secretariat. Its congresses are supposed to be held every four years. It is divided into six regional (*oblast*) organizations and has 10,600 primary party units. As of January 1, 1965, party membership was 319,196, of whom 290,752 were full members and 28,444 were candidate members.[1]

## PARTY PRESS ORGANS

The central committee publishes the daily newspapers *Zviazda* (The Star) and *Sovetskaia Belorussia* (Soviet Belorussia), the latter in Russian. The KPB journal *Kamunist Belarusi* (The Communist of Belorussia) is published in separate Belorussian and Russian editions.

## CONGRESSES OF THE KPB

1st congress, December 1918, Smolensk
2d congress, March 1919, Vilna
3d congress, November 1920, Minsk
4th congress, February-March 1921
5th congress, October 1921
6th congress, March 1922
7th congress, March 1923
8th congress, May 1924
9th congress, December 1925
10th congress, January 1927
11th congress, November 1927
12th congress, February 1929
13th congress, May-June 1930
14th congress, January 1932
15th congress, January 1934
16th congress, June 1937
17th congress, June 1938
18th congress, May 1940
19th congress, February 1949
20th congress, September 1952
21st congress, February 1954
22d congress, January 1956
23d (extraordinary) congress, January 1959
24th congress, February 1960
25th congress, September 1961

## BIBLIOGRAPHY

Kraŭchanka, I. S., and N. V. Kamenskaia (eds.): *Historyia Belaruskai SSR* (History of the Belorussian Soviet Socialist Republic), vol. II, Minsk, Vyd-va AN BSSR, 1958.

Meshkov, N. M., and N. A. Khalipov (eds.): *Ocherki istorii Kommunisticheskoi partii Belorussii, 1883-1920* (Outlines of the History of the Communist Party of Belorussia, 1883-1920), vol. I of projected history, Minsk, Gosizdat, 1961.

Vakar, Nicholas P.: *Belorussia: The Making of a Nation*, Cambridge, Mass. Harvard University Press, 1956.

Vakar, Nicholas P.: *Bibliographical Guide to Belorussia*, Cambridge, Mass., Harvard University Press, 1956.

JOHN S. RESHETAR, JR.

1. "KPSS v tsifrakh, 1961-1964 gody," *Partiinaia zhizn*, no. 10, May 1965, p. 8.

# BOLIVIA

Little is known about the individuals who organized the communist movement in Bolivia. This movement comprises three parties: the Trotskyist Revolutionary Workers' Party (Partido Obrero Revolucionario, POR), founded in 1938; the intellectual Marxist Party of the Revolutionary Left (Partido de la Izquierda Revolucionaria, PIR), formed in 1940 and recreated in 1955; and the Communist Party of Bolivia (Partido Comunista de Bolivia, PCB), founded in early 1950 by dissidents from the youth wing of the PIR. In the 1960s Mario Monje Molina was secretary general of the PCB. For a discussion of the circumstances in which these parties emerged see *Latin America*.

## HISTORY

The PCB was illegal during its first two years. It attracted some support among students and urban workers in La Paz but was not yet well established when the 1952 revolution brought the noncommunist leftist National Revolutionary Movement (Movimiento Nacional Revolucionario, MNR) to power. The communists acquired legal status but could not compete in a climate of social revolution with the MNR for the allegiance of the large population of tin miners and the peasantry. The PCB participated in the quadrennial elections with minimal results. It exerted some influence on labor matters by working through MNR organizations from 1952 to 1964 and through other noncommunist leftist parties formed by MNR dissidents after 1958. It retained its legal status following the military coup that toppled the MNR regime in 1964. In spite of bolder tactics, however, it had still failed to attract meaningful mass support by the end of 1965.

## ORGANIZATION AND MEMBERSHIP

United States sources estimated membership in the Bolivian Marxist parties in 1965 as 4,000 to 5,000 in the PCB, 1,500 in the POR, and 1,000 in the PIR.[1] For a full discussion of communist strength in Bolivia see *Latin America*.

## RELATION TO SOVIET LEADERSHIP

None of the elements of the communist movement in Bolivia appear to have been seriously affected by the Sino-Soviet dispute. The PCB remained loyal to Moscow; the POR adopted a strong pro-China position; and the PIR issued no public declaration on the subject.

## PARTY PRESS ORGANS AND RECORDS

The Bolivian communist movement has meager press and publication facilities. Since 1953 the PCB has issued an irregular newspaper, *Unidad*. The POR publishes *Lucha obrera* and *Masas* from time to time. Records of the first and second congresses of the PCB are contained in the party's *Documentos*, published in La Paz in 1959 and 1964, respectively.

## PARTY CONGRESSES

Between February 1951 and June 1954 the PCB held six conferences. They were followed by its first congress in April 1959 and its second in March-April 1964. The PIR held its sixth congress in July 1956.

## BIBLIOGRAPHY

*Estudios sobre el comunismo*, vols. I-V, Santiago, 1952-1956.
Party of the Revolutionary Left: *P.I.R. y*

*desarrollo nacional: Soluciones para los problemas nacionales*, La Paz, 1961.

See also *Latin America*, refs. 2, 6, 13, 24.

ROLLIE E. POPPINO

1. U.S. Department of State, Bureau of Intelligence and Research, *World Strength of the Communist Party Organizations*, Eighteenth Annual Report, Washington, January 1966, p. 168.

# BRAZIL

Of the founding members of the communist party in Brazil, only two, Astrogildo Pereira and Octávio Brandao, had long or distinguished careers in the party and the international communist movement. For a discussion of the circumstances in which the party was formed in Brazil see *Latin America*.

## HISTORY

The original Communist Party of Brazil (Partido Comunista do Brasil, PCdB) was founded in March 1922 by a small group of men who had broken away from the anarchist movement. Inspired by the accomplishments of the Soviet regime in Russia, they immediately adhered to the Comintern and set out to win control of the urban workers. The PCdB was outlawed within a few months in the wake of a rash of politicomilitary revolts in which it was not involved. Despite sporadic repression and the extralegal status of the incipient labor movement, the communists seized the chief labor federation in the 1920s, but factionalism and repercussions from the Stalin-Trotsky feud kept the party politically impotent in the first decade. The communists boycotted the 1930 revolution that initiated the fifteen-year reign of Getulio Vargas and remained politically isolated until 1934. In that year, perhaps anticipating the popular-front line, they helped to form the democratic-leftist National Liberation Alliance (Aliança Nacional Libertadora) of anti-Vargas, antifascist parties.

In 1935 Luiz Carlos Prestes, the revolutionary hero of the 1920s, returned to Brazil after four years of training in the Soviet Union, publicly to take over the National Liberation Alliance and clandestinely to assume leadership of the communist party. Throughout the next three decades he remained the top communist in the country. Failing to gain power by peaceful means, Prestes launched a revolt in November 1935 which led to his imprisonment and to the suppression of the communist party for a decade. Communist prisoners were released and the party was legalized in 1945, when democratic practices were resumed in Brazil.

Capitalizing on Prestes' popularity and on its association with the victorious Allied cause in World War II, the PCdB grew within two years to become the largest communist organization in the western hemisphere. By 1947 it had about 150,000 members. The communists polled half a million votes in both 1945 and 1947, campaigning on a moderately nationalistic reform program. With the cold war in 1947, the party program was altered to fit the militant Soviet line. The PCdB was again outlawed, and it suffered a drastic loss of membership. The anticommunist laws were not rigidly enforced, however, with the result that the party continued to operate an effective and virulent propaganda campaign. The communists identified themselves with virtually the entire range of noncommunist parties. It was commonly believed that communist support was essential for political victory in Brazil.

By 1958 Prestes and other prominent communist personalities emerged from hiding to work openly for various political and propaganda objectives, including legalization of the party. As part of this campaign the party name was changed in 1960 to Brazilian Communist Party (Partido Comunista Brasileiro, PCB) to give it a more "nationalist" flavor. During the Goulart regime after 1961 the communists operated with increasing boldness, seizing control of key labor and student organizations, infiltrating the bureaucracy, and achieving a significant influence on the formation of national policies. This position was destroyed by the revolution of 1964. The Castello Branco administration broke the party's hold on the labor movement and brought its overt activities to a halt.

After 1950 Prestes' dominant position within the party was periodically but unsuccessfully challenged, each time in response to developments in the Soviet Union. The rigid revolutionary line imposed on the party by Stalin in the early 1950s provoked criticism by dissidents led by Pedro Pomar, who was expelled in 1952. Following the denunciation of Stalin by Khrushchev, a group headed by Agildo Barata left the party after failing to secure a change in leadership. A more serious test arose at the party's fifth congress in 1960. Several high-level communists, including Mauricio Grabois and João Amazonas, who demanded an active revolutionary strategy along Chinese lines, were removed from the central committee. In 1961 they broke away to form their own organization, reviving the old name Communist Party of Brazil (Partido Comunista do Brasil, PCdB). This body provided a rallying ground for some of the earlier dissidents and, after 1964, for other communists disillusioned by the failure of Prestes' nonviolent policies. The dissidents remained numerically weak, however, and even less able than the parent party to affect the course of events in Brazil.

## ORGANIZATION AND MEMBERSHIP

United States sources in 1965 estimated the membership of the PCB as 20,000 and that of the dissident (pro-Chinese) PCdB as under 3,000.[1] The Brazilian communists have consistently maintained an active propaganda apparatus employing interlocking front groups. For a full discussion see *Latin America*.

## RELATION TO SOVIET LEADERSHIP

Ever since he became a communist in the 1930s Luiz Carlos Prestes has been a loyal follower of the Soviet line. He was elected to full membership in the Executive Committee of the Comintern in 1935. For a full discussion of the Brazilian party's relationship to the international communist movement see *Latin America*.

The PCB is firmly pro-Soviet, while the dissident PCdB advocates the Chinese line.

## PARTY PRESS ORGANS AND RECORDS

The communist press was not permitted to circulate regularly after April 1964. However, the two parties attempted to continue issuing their principal newspapers and journals; these were the PCB's newspaper *Novos rumos* and bimonthly *Estudos sociais* and the splinter PCdB's newspaper *A Classe operária*.

Prior to the revolution of 1964 the Brazilian communists maintained an active press. Party documents were published for circulation among the members and occasionally for sale to the public as well. The current version of the party program and statutes was usually published in the monthly theoretical journal *Problemas* before 1958 and in the bimonthly *Estudos sociais* thereafter.

## PARTY CONGRESSES

1st congress, PCdB, March 1922
2d congress, PCdB, May 1925

3d congress, PCdB, December 1928-January 1929
4th congress, PCdB, November 1954
5th congress, PCB, September 1960

A sixth congress scheduled for 1964, had not been held by the end of 1965.

There is no indication that the dissident PCdB had held a congress by the end of 1965.

BIBLIOGRAPHY

Amado, Jorge: *O cavalheiro da esperança: Vida de Luiz Carlos Prestes*, 10th ed., Rio de Janeiro, Editorial Vitória, 1956.

Barata, Agildo: *Vida de um revolucionário (Memórias)*, Rio de Janeiro, Editôra Melso, n.d.

Dias, Everardo: *História das lutas sociais no Brasil*, São Paulo, Editôra Edaglit, 1962.

Pereira, Astrojildo: *Formação do PCB, 1922-1928*, Rio de Janeiro, Editorial Vitória, 1962.

See also *Latin America*, refs. 1, 2, 6, 8, 13, 24.

ROLLIE E. POPPINO

1. U.S. Department of State, Bureau of Intelligence and Research, *World Strength of the Communist Party Organizations,* Eighteenth Annual Report, Washington, January 1966, p. 169.

# BRITISH GUIANA
*See* Guyana

# BULGARIA

The Bulgarian Communist Party (Bulgarska Komunisticheska Partiya, BKP) had its origin in the Bulgarian Social Democratic Party (Bulgarska Sotsialdemokraticheska Partiya, BSDP), formed in 1891 under the leadership of Dimitŭr Blagoev and Yanko Sakŭzov and the influence of Russian and German Marxism. A split in 1903 resulted in the formation of the Workers' Social Democratic Party (Narrow Socialists) [Rabotnicheska Sotsialdemokraticheska Partiya (Tesni Sotsialisti)], led by Blagoev, which renamed itself Bulgarian Communist Party (Narrow Socialists) in 1919.

The party was ordered disbanded by the courts in April 1924, and in 1927 it reappeared as the legal Workers' Party (Rabotnicheska Partiya, RP). After the dissolution of all political parties by the Military League-Zveno government in 1934 it continued illegally as the Bulgarian Workers' Party (Communist) [Bulgarska Rabotnicheska Partiya (Komunisti), BRP(K)], and in December 1948, after the seizure of power, changed its name to Bulgarian Communist Party.

Blagoev, the "grandfather" of Bulgarian socialism, participated as a student in the establishment of the first Marxist circles in Russia in 1883 and 1884, and as founder of the Bulgarian party embued it with a doctrinaire and exclusivist approach. Also among the founders were Vasil Kolarov, who had been introduced to Marxism by Plekhanov at Geneva and later became a leading official of the Comintern, and Georgi Dimitrov, who rose from the labor movement to become secretary general of the Comintern in 1934. Dimitrov and Kolarov directed the party's policies from Moscow between 1923 and 1945.

HISTORY

The traditional, industrially underdeveloped, and overwhelmingly small-land-owning Bulgarian peasant society presented generally adverse conditions for an unsupported communist movement. Nevertheless, the Bulgarian party was the strongest communist organization in the Balkans, drawing support primarily from intellectuals, disgruntled peasants, and segments of the incipient labor movement, usually after national debacles. Thus the party claimed its largest membership (21,577 in 1919 and 38,686 in 1920) of the interwar period immediately after Bulgaria's defeat in World War I. In the March 1920 elections it polled one-fourth (184,616) of the votes cast and took fifty of the 229 seats in the national assembly, becoming the second in strength only to the Bulgarian National Agrarian Union (Bulgarski Zemledelski Naroden Sŭiuz, BZNS), led by Alexandŭr Stambolyiski.

The communists failed to capitalize on these successes, however, not only because of the strength of the radical agrarians and the competition of the social democrats in the trade unions, but also because of their refusal to collaborate with any of these groups. Only after Stambolyiski's violent overthrow in 1923, by a nationalist coalition which was just as antiagrarian as anticommunist, did the communists belatedly join the agrarians and stage the armed uprising of September 1923. This was a fiasco, as was the bomb explosion in the Sofia Cathedral in April 1925, aimed at the life of the king and high government officials and organized in alliance with agrarians, with whom the communists had finally formed a "united front" in 1924. As a result, communist leaders Georgi Dimitrov, Vasil Kolarov, Vŭlko Chervenkov, and others fled the country, the party was outlawed, and its membership was decimated.

Reorganized as the legal RP in 1927, the party recuperated substantially in the early 1930s. In 1931, aided by the agricultural depression, the RP claimed 30,000 members, gathered 166,000 votes, elected thirty-one out of 274 deputies, and won the Sofia municipal elections in 1932. However, by and large it continued its ultraleft, uncompromising policies until the dissolution of all political parties in 1934.

An ostensible turnabout occurred in 1935, when the seventh Comintern congress, through its secretary general, the Bulgarian Georgi Dimitrov, proclaimed the antifascist popular-front line. The party, now operating illegally as the BRP(K), complied, encouraging the formation of a popular front with the left-wing agrarian splinter group Pladne in 1936 and appealing to other groups, although with little success. It succeeded only in forming temporary election coalitions and infiltrating trade unions for strike purposes. The pendulum had swung first toward the traditional democratic parties, and after the coup of 1934 toward royal authoritarianism. Economic conditions had also improved, as had the international atmosphere in the Balkans.

The party leaders remained united in its support of the Moscow line, regardless of its many switches in policy. With the Nazi-Soviet war they reversed their stand once more, exposing the party's subservience to Moscow and jeopardizing potential support during World War II.

During the war the party called for armed resistance against the Germans and their Bulgarian allies, but because of its numerical weakness and the fact that Bulgaria was not militarily engaged and benefited territorially from the Axis victory in the Balkans, it could not generate much support. Only when the war turned against the Axis did the BRP(K) start partisan activities, still on a limited scale. On the political front, Dimitrov's call for the formation of a Fatherland Front (Otechestven Front) in 1942 bore limited fruit in August 1943, when the communists were joined in a coalition by left-wing agrarians, left-wing socialists, the Military League-Zveno, and other sympathizers. The party claimed that at this point it had a People's Liberation Army of 30,000 and an additional 50,000 underground supporters, although a recent source revealed that party membership was no more than 13,700.[1]

In 1944, through the Fatherland Front, the communists openly pressed the government for Bulgaria's disengagement, at the same time preparing secretly for a takeover. In the midst of the armistice negotiations between the antinazi, democratic coalition government of Konstantin Muraviev and the Western Allies, the Fatherland Front suddenly refused to continue participating. Instead, it temporized until the Red Army reached the Bulgarian frontier and the Soviet Union unexpectedly declared war on Bulgaria, refused immediate Bulgarian offers for an armistice, and ordered its forces to cross the frontier. In the ensuing confusion, through its secret adherents in Muraviev's government, War Minister Ivan Marinov and his aide Captain Petŭr Iliev, the Fatherland Front engineered a bloodless coup and seized power on September 9, 1944.

The communists filled the key positions in the new government, most notably the ministries of the interior (police) and justice (courts), and although they were numerically in the minority, they consolidated their hold under the umbrella of the occupying Soviet armed forces. The party immediately started a wholesale purge of actual and potential enemies (some estimates place the number of persons killed as high as 100,000), gave unlimited power to the Fatherland Front's local committees, created a people's militia of trusted adherents, and sent the Bulgarian army out of the country in pursuit of the Germans. Gradually they also eliminated their allies, and by 1949 the country was under formal communist control.

Moscow's heavy-handed domination and the example of Marshal Tito led eventually to resentment by "native" communist leaders, most notably Traycho Kostov, first in line as Dimitrov's successor. Dimitrov himself, who assumed the premiership in 1947, showed vacillations, as exemplified by his rapprochement with Tito and his proposal for a Balkan Federation. Yet he returned quickly to the Soviet fold and initiated the purge of native Bulgarians which was completed by his successor and brother-in-law, Vŭlko Chervenkov, an ardent Moscow-educated Stalinist. Kostov was executed in 1949, and his wide following was thoroughly purged. The worst period of Stalinist purges, identified with Chervenkov's rule (1950 to 1953), brought about Bulgaria's external and internal alignment with the Soviet Union.

Stalin's death found Bulgaria one of the most obedient and Sovietized satellites in Eastern Europe. Following the Soviet example, Chervenkov gave up his party general secretaryship to Todor Zhivkov in 1954 and tried to initiate at least a nominal "thaw" and a reconciliation with the surviving former opponents. However, Khrushchev's accession to power and his personal antipathy toward Chervenkov, an ideologue and a power politician in his own right, shifted Moscow's support away from Chervenkov. The shock of Khrushchev's denunciation of Stalin and the Hungarian revolt of 1956 threatened the very survival of the Bulgarian communist regime, so that extreme caution and unity among all factions was imperative, as Zhivkov himself admitted in 1962. Thus Chervenkov's demotion was gradual, starting openly at the April plenum of 1956, continuing at the November 1961 plenum, and ending at the eighth party congress in November 1962.

In the meantime, Zhivkov, a former protégé of Chervenkov's, consolidated his position, ostensibly with strong backing by Khrushchev. He aped every Soviet move and purged rivals after having shared power with them. A group of heterogeneous native communists (Chankov, Terpeshev, Panov) who insisted on deemphasis of industrialization and a more independent policy was purged in 1957, Chervenkov himself and Prime Minister Anton Yugov and his group of "careerists" were purged in 1962, and in April 1965 former partisans and military men (General Anev) who attempted a coup, possibly with the goal of a Rumanian-like policy for Bulgaria, suffered a similar fate.

It is interesting to note that the dismissal of Khrushchev, who was considered Zhivkov's benefactor, did not generate any response at all from the beneficiary, and in fact seems to have made Zhivkov more self-assured.

ORGANIZATION AND MEMBERSHIP

The party follows the familiar organizational pattern of the Soviet prototype, based on democratic centralism and the territorial-production principle. The primary organization, or lowest unit, exists in economic enterprises, government offices, the armed forces, educational institutions, neighborhoods, and other places in which at least three party members are present. The hierarchical ladder ascends to the municipality, the city or district and the province levels and ends with the national party organization. The latter is represented by a congress, which elects a central committee and a central revision commission. The central committee, consisting since 1962 of 168 members, elects a politburo of eleven members, a secretariat of seven members, and a control commission.[2] The party first secretary since 1954 has been Todor Zhivkov.

Before World War II party membership averaged 4,000 to 5,000, only occasionally reaching 30,000 to 40,000, and included primarily intellectuals and some peasants and workers. It swelled to 495,658 after the communist takeover in 1948 and then dropped to 455,251 in 1954 as a result of mass expulsions in the wake of the Titoist-Kostovist purges, when close to 100,000 members, including about 25,000 peasants, were expelled. Subsequent purges—in 1957, 1962, and 1965—were limited primarily to higher party officials belonging, respectively, to the "revisionist," "dogmatist," and "army-plotter" groups.

At the 1962 party congress total party membership was 528,674 (506,261 full members) out of a population of 8 million, although the Dimitrov Communist Youth Union (Dimitrovskiǔ Komunisticheski Mladezhki Sŭiuz) had 1 million members in 1963. The percentage share of social groups was workers 37.16, peasants 34.16, and employees 23.52. Comparison with the corresponding percentages of 26.50, 44.74, and 16.28 for 1948 shows a considerable decline in peasant membership by 1962, owing to industrialization and urbanization, but also to peasant opposition to collectivization, an increased number of industrial workers, and a most rapid relative increase in employees (bureaucrats, intellectuals, and technocrats). Since the peasantry still constitutes two-thirds of the Bulgarian population, their underrepresentation in the party is noteworthy. Youth and women are also seriously underrepresented. Zhivkov reported that in 1962 the proportion of members under thirty had dropped from 21.26 to 15.58 percent, with peasant youth admissions practically at a standstill, and the share of women members was only 17 percent, although women slightly outnumber men in the total population. All this suggests large numbers of adverse peasants, apathetic youth, and unreceptive families. Zhivkov also made reference to the privileged position of party members and to a "certain frigidity between leaders and masses." This estrangement seems due to the exceedingly pro-Soviet attitude of the leadership, its resistance to internal relaxation, and its attachment to vested interests and favoritisms.[3]

Of the political parties existing at the time of the communist takeover only the BZNS now coexists with the BKP, albeit in a completely subordinate position. The present BZNS, with a current membership of about 120,000,[4] is a remnant of what was once the strongest political organization and has been purged many times by the communists since 1944. It officially recognizes the supremacy of the BKP and thus does not compete for power. A possible reason for its formal existence is the communist desire both to exploit its heritage and former popularity among the peasants and to propagandize the semblance of a two-party system for foreign consumption. In fact, however, the BZNS is a communist appendage, without personality or policy of its own.

Other front organizations include the Fatherland Front itself. Termed a "mass nonpolitical organization" and embracing 3.4 million members (63 percent of the voting population) in 1963, it too has lost all resemblance to the original coalition of war and immediate postwar years. Completely dominated by the communists, it serves their goals of mass indoctrination and participation.

The trade unions, with a membership of 1,600,000 in 1963, are also communist controlled.

## RELATION TO SOVIET LEADERSHIP

The BKP claims to have been among the founders of both the Comintern and the Cominform. Its early leaders, Dimitrov, Kolarov, and Chervenkov, played a major role in the international communist movement, especially in the Balkans, often propounding Bulgarian interests at the expense of other Balkan parties. In the last analysis, however, they devoutly followed Moscow's lead and quickly adjusted their policies at the slightest hint of any deviation. Especially after 1935, from a doctrinaire and militant group, the party became thoroughly Leninist-Stalinist. The most notable leadership purges initiated by Moscow occurred in the postwar Stalinist period, when Kostov and his followers were liquidated as Titoists.

With the possible exception of a brief deviation in favor of the Chinese, especially by Chervenkov in 1958, the Bulgarian leadership has backed Moscow unequivocally. Chervenkov's praise of the "communes," quickly recanted, was a possible rebuff to Khrushchev and a manifestation of sympathy with the hard-line Soviet leaders, rather than support of China against the Soviet Union. Shortly thereafter Zhivkov himself borrowed Mao's "great-leap-forward" slogan in connection with the stepped-up development plan of 1958 to 1960, but this too had no anti-Soviet implications. In fact, the Bulgarian leadership has been among the staunchest supporters of the Moscow line—on Comecon and the Warsaw Pact, on the war in Vietnam, and on all international and domestic issues, as well as on the Sino-Soviet rift. In 1965 Zhivkov went so far as to characterize the attempted military coup against his regime as having been inspired by China, which, though hardly plausible, seems to indicate his desire to link China with conspiratorial activities in Bulgaria.

## PARTY PRESS ORGANS AND RECORDS

The press organs of the BKP are the daily *Rabotnichesko delo* (Workers' Cause), and the monthly *Novo vreme* (New Times).

The newest text of the party's bylaws is contained in *Ustav na Bulgarskata komunisticheska partiya* (Statute of the Bulgarian Communist Party), adopted by the eighth party congress on November 13, 1962, and reported in *Rabotnichesko delo*, November 14, 1962. No party program has been adopted since the 1920s; the closest approximation is *Direktivi na osmiya kongres na Bulgarskata komunisticheska partiya za razvitieto na Narodna Republika Bulgaria prez perioda 1961-1980* (Directives of the Eighth Congress of the Bulgarian Communist Party on the Development of the People's Republic of Bulgaria during 1961-1980), adopted on November 13, 1962, and reported in *Rabotnichesko delo*, November 17, 1962.

Records of party congresses are contained in *Bulgarskata komunisticheska partiya v rezolyutsii i resheniya na kongresite, konferentsiite i plenumite na TsK* (The Bulgarian

Communist Party in Resolutions and Decisions of the Congresses, Conferences, and Plenums of the Central Committee), vols. I-IV, Sofia, 1947-1955; *Materiali po istoriyata na Bulgarskata komunisticheska partiya* (Materials on the History of the Bulgarian Communist Party), Sofia, 1955; *Bulgarska komunisticheska partiya: Kongresi: Stenograficheski protokol* (Bulgarian Communist Party: Congresses: Minutes), vols. I-IV, Sofia, 1948-1962; and *Proceedings of the Eighth Party Congress.*

CONGRESSES OF THE BKP

1st congress, May 1919
2d congress, May-June 1920
3d congress, May 1921
4th congress, June 1922
5th congress, December 1948
6th congress, February-March 1954
7th congress, June 1958
8th congress, November 1962

BIBLIOGRAPHY

Dellin, L. A. D.: "Bulgaria," in Stephen D. Kertesz (ed.), *East Central Europe and the World: Developments in the Post-Stalin Era*, South Bend, Ind., Notre Dame University Press, 1962.

Dellin, L. A. D.: *Trade Unions and Labor Legislation in Bulgaria: 1878-1953,* New York, Mid-European Studies Center, 1953.
Dellin, L. A. D. (ed.): *Bulgaria*, New York, Praeger, 1957.
Newman, Bernard: *Bulgarian Background*, London, Hale, 1961.
Padev, Michael: *Dimitrov Wastes No Bullets*, London, Eyre & Spottiswoode, 1948.
Rothschild, Joseph: *The Communist Party of Bulgaria: Origins and Development, 1883-1936*, New York, Columbia University Press, 1949.
Sanders, Irwin T.: *Balkan Village*, Lexington, Ky., University of Kentucky Press, 1949.

L. A. D. DELLIN

1. *Istoricheski pregled*, no. 2, 1965.

2. *Ustav na Bulgarskata komunisticheska partiya*, adopted on November 13, 1962, reported in *Rabotnichesko delo*, November 14, 1962.

3. Todor Zhivkov, *Doklad na tsentralniya komitet na Bulgarskata komunisticheska partiya pred osmiya kongress*, reported in *Rabotnichesko delo*, November 6-8, 1962.

4. Bulgarian Academy of Sciences, *Istoriya na Bulgaria*, vol. III, Sofia, 1964.

# BURMA

In 1959 the illegalized Burma Communist Party (BCP), led by Thakin Than Tun,[1] announced that it had been organized in 1939, thereby providing itself with a history of twenty years. This starting date was also used (in a 1943 publication) by Thein Pe, now known as Thein Pe Myint, a journalist, a Marxist, and an ardent supporter of the revolutionary council government headed by General Ne Win. Thein Pe, who left the BCP in 1948, claimed that he had become a communist while attending the University of Calcutta and had organized the BCP on his return to Burma in 1939.

The BCP is opposed by another illegalized communist splinter group known as the Communist Party of Burma (CPB). This group, headed by Thakin Soe, almost captured the apparatus of the BCP in 1946. Following its defeat, and in opposition to the policy of the majority of thakins who led the aboveground nationalist struggle against the restoration of British imperial power in Burma, Soe and his CPB went underground and have since conducted an almost ceaseless struggle against any government in power in Burma.

## HISTORY

Some authorities[2] accept the 1939 date as the origin of a communist party in Burma. There are indications, however, that there were both some socialists and some communists in the thakin nationalist group at the end of the 1930s, although there was no party of either name before World War II. A Burma (sometimes called National or People's) Revolutionary Party, in which most of the leading nationalists, including General Aung San, held membership, was organized in 1939 and headed by Thakin Mya, the leading socialist. Because of its opposition to British rule, it came to have both aboveground and underground sections. Most, if not all, nationalists at this time were vaguely identified with the We Burmans Association (Dohbama Asiayone), founded in the early 1930s, which in 1939 decided on noncooperation with the British as a tactic to win Burma's freedom (it must be recalled in this connection that the Soviet Union did not enter the war in Europe until June 1941).

In late 1942 or early in 1943,[3] while Than Tun was a minister in the Japanese-sponsored Ba Maw government, he and communists Thakin Soe (an oil worker), Thein Pe (initially a self-appointed antifascist representative to and later an employee of the British Forces in India), Ba Hein, and others, formally organized the Burma Communist Party for the first time. With the confused state of Burmese nationalist politics in the early war years, most of the nationalists who had formed the BCP also retained membership in a relatively undifferentiated nationalist-Marxist amalgam organized by Ba Maw and called the We Burmans Poor Man's Association (Dohbama Sinyetha Asiayone). However, although the BCP had no quarrel with the nationalists who had not joined their party, the non-BCP thakins apparently decided to give renewed emphasis to a party label which most of them, including those who now considered themselves communists, had taken in 1939, the Burma (or National or People's) Revolutionary Party. This group in the fall of 1945 renamed itself the Burmese Socialist Party. As in 1939, it was headed by Thakin Mya.

In 1943 the communist and socialist thakins, working together, with the full knowledge of Ba Maw's puppet government and with the participation of General Aung San, his deputy Colonel Ne Win, and a group of key officers in the renamed Burma Defense Army, began organizing what came to be called the resistance. They established military contact with the British behind the lines in Burma at the end of 1943 and with the British in India in 1944. In August and September 1944 "underground" meetings were held at Dedaye in the delta, and at Thakin (later Prime Minister) Nu's home. Out of these meetings[4] came the Pasabala, a coalition of all resistance-dedicated groups, including the BCP, led by Aung San. First called in English the Antifascist Organization, on August 19, 1945, at a famous mass meeting held at Nathuyein Hall in Rangoon, the Pasabala was given its full translation of Antifascist People's Freedom League to emphasize that its task was not only to fight fascism, but to achieve Burma's freedom.

Within a year, however, the BCP split into two still unreconciled factions, the "red flags" of Thakin Soe and the "white flags" of Thakin Than Tun. The former went underground to fight against the Pasabala, and the latter was later voted out of the coalition.

A series of separate events between 1936 and 1939 had resulted in the popular bases for the communist and socialist parties and for the Pasabala coalition. The All-Burma Peasants' Organization, formed in 1938-1939, remained under socialist leadership. The All-Burma Trade Union Congress, formed in 1940, was captured by the communists and later gave way to the socialist Trade Union

Congress of Burma. Through these organizations the thakins achieved what no one else had been able to effect in modern Burmese history, a viable anti-British political instrument with its roots in something resembling a unified mass base of students, trade unionists, and peasants. The leaders of these organizations comprised a wide spectrum of nationalist and socialist leaders for independent Burma, including the later communist leaders.

In 1943-1944, when the communists and socialists had agreed to form the Pasabala, the communists were prepared to make concessions to the British as allies of the Soviet Union. The socialists rejected this posture as damaging to their overall strategy for independence after the war. The issue between them was papered over by a joint resolution of August 1944 which brought the Pasabala into being, but it was not resolved until the Pasabala, by vote of the executive committee in October and the council in November 1946, removed the BCP from its membership. In the interim Thakin Soe, at a plenum of the BCP in March 1946, had attacked Than Tun's leadership of the BCP on the charge of "Browderism," that is, compromising with imperialists and opportunists. Than Tun had admitted his guilt and promised to "go left." However, by vote he was able to retain control of the BCP apparatus, and at this point Soe and his followers split off to form the CPB, where he has remained.

At the time of its expulsion from the Pasabala the BCP was accused of engaging in subversive activities both within the coalition and in the country at large. It was also charged with following Moscow's directives. In 1947 the Pasabala went on to its constituent assembly and constitution drafting, preparatory to Burma's independence. In July of that year Aung San was assassinated during an attack organized by a right-wing ex-premier. U Nu succeeded him as leader of the Pasabala and on January 4, 1948, became the first prime minister of independent Burma.

Although the communists opposed the 1947 Aung San-Nu-Attlee agreement leading to independence, they put up a momentary show of cooperation after Aung San's assassination. U Nu made a series of attempts at this point to reforge the wartime unity of the socialists, communists, and other factions within the Pasabala, but his efforts were doomed to failure by the directions of the Cominform for a series of blows at southern Asia. In order to bring about an understanding of its new leftist strategy Moscow had dispatched to Asia various couriers and indigenous communist party leaders who had been residents in the Soviet Union during the previous years (S. Dange to India, Musso to Indonesia). Between November 1947 and March 1948 a series of meetings were held in Bombay and Calcutta, with the Communist Party of India serving as the vehicle through which Moscow's new "left" line was transmitted throughout southern Asia. Than Tun and Ba Tin (H. Goshal), the "theoretician" of the BCP, attended these meetings and dutifully adopted the new Cominform line of revolution, armed struggle, and "national liberation," even in those countries that had already won their independence.

In accordance with Moscow's directives, on March 30, 1948, the BCP began its rebellion against U Nu's independent anti-imperialist socialist government. Than Tun's BCP, Soe's CPB, and other Marxist rebels were joined by dissident groups of army mutineers, military police, and ex-soldiers from an organization known as the People's Volunteer Organization. Thus the communists and related Marxist groups—as distinguished from the Karens, a major ethnic group also in rebellion—began their uprising with a hard core of approximately 13,000 armed men with some military training. In one way or another insurrectionary activity has continued since then. Thein Pe Myint, who refused to support the BCP's rebellion, left the party and later formed his own aboveground People's Unity Party. He has remained an independent "Marxist" ever since. In December 1950 another group headed by Ba Nyein, Chit Maung, Lwin, and Hla Kyway, split off from the Pasabala to form the cryptocommunist Burma Workers' and Peasants' Party, later called the Burma Workers' Party (BWP). The Chinese communists provided training facilities for the BCP at Kunming, and until 1953 *Pravda* kept up a series of articles on the "right-wing socialist traitors" in Burma.

As late as 1963, when General Ne Win, who had assumed power the year before, offered to negotiate an end of the rebellion with all insurgents, one of the two main cadre groups who had come to negotiate was provided with safe passage from Kunming, and later, when these negotiations failed, he returned to Kunming.

## ORGANIZATION AND MEMBERSHIP

When the BCP began its rebellion in 1948, according to September 1950 minutes of its central committee it had 3,000 members. A government source gave them "25,000 active followers and sympathizers." Than Tun boasted in a speech to the Communist Party of India that "we have more than a *lakh* [100,000] class-conscious militants.... We also have *lakhs* of workers, peasants and common people behind us." It is probable that at that time Soe's CPB could muster close to 2,000 members and followers.

The most recent estimates of communist strength in Burma indicate that the BCP has approximately 1,200 members, the CPB has between 300 and 500 members, and there are some 2,500 to 3,000 unaffiliated communists scattered throughout the country. Although nearly all the leaders of the Burmese political parties have had secondary-school education and many have had university training, at least 80 percent of Burma's population of 26 million is rural, and it must be assumed that the composition of the party membership bears a general relationship to this distribution.

## THE SINO-SOVIET DISPUTE

The BCP relationship with the Chinese communists, begun with Moscow's consent in 1949, has gradually deepened. Between 1954 and 1967 both Moscow and Peking maintained "friendly" government-to-government relations with all Burmese governments. Relations between Moscow and Rangoon have continued in this vein. Just before Ne Win's coup in March 1962, communist-oriented students at the University of Rangoon burned effigies of Khrushchev and Mikoyan as "reactionaries." In 1965 both the BCP and CPB were on record in support of Peking's position in the Sino-Soviet dispute; so too was the aboveground communist daily *Ludu*, published in Burmese in Mandalay. However, Thein Pe Myint and the *Botatung*, published in Burmese in Rangoon, are pro-Moscow.

## FUTURE PROSPECTS

The illegal insurrectionary BCP and CPB are doomed in Burma unless Communist China intervenes even more directly than it has in the past. Than Tun and most of the established BCP leadership in Burma are dead. Soe will die or be killed unless he surrenders without any further offer of amnesty. There are no discernible replacements in Burma for their leadership in what is left of their organization.

## PARTY PRESS ORGANS

There is no regular communist party press in Burma. The cryptocommunist BWP publishes the daily *Ludu* (Masses), which is pro-Peking, and some communist writers make regular contributions to the daily *Botatung* (Vanguard), which is pro-Moscow.

## PARTY CONGRESSES

No exact information is available on congresses of the BCP. The CPB held its first congress in 1943 and its second congress in July 1945, but there is no information on later congresses.

## BIBLIOGRAPHY

Kaznacheev, Aleksandr: *Inside a Soviet Embassy: Experiences of a Russian Diplomat in Burma*, Philadelphia, Lippincott, 1962.
McLane, Charles B.: *Soviet Strategies in*

*Southeast Asia*, Princeton, N.J., Princeton University Press, 1966, pp. 316-338, 371-385.

Thomson, John S.: "Marxism in Burma," in Frank N. Trager (ed.), *Marxism in Southeast Asia: A Study of Four Countries*, Stanford, Calif., Stanford University Press, 1959.

Trager, Frank N.: *Burma from Kingdom to Republic: A Historical and Political Analysis*, New York, Praeger, 1966.

Trager, Frank N.: "Nationalism and Communism in Burma," in Jeane J. Kirkpatrick (ed.), *The Strategy of Deception: A Study in World-wide Communist Tactics*, New York, Farrar, Straus, 1963, pp. 135-164.

Trager, Frank N. (ed.): *Burma*, vol. III, New Haven, Conn., Human Relations Area Files, Inc., 1956, chaps. 18-21.

U.S. Department of State, Bureau of Intelligence and Research: *World Strength of the Communist Party Organizations*, annual reports, Washington, 1948-1966.

FRANK N. TRAGER

1. *Thakin*, a Burmese word meaning "master," was a means of address commonly demanded by the British and was adopted by the young nationalists to indicate that they intended to become masters in their own country.

2. For example, Saul Rose, *Socialism in Southern Asia*, New York, Oxford University Press, 1959, and J. H. Brimmell, *Communism in Southeast Asia*, New York, Oxford University Press, 1959.

3. A Chinese source, quoted in Shen-yu Dai, *Peking, Moscow and the Communist Parties of Colonial Asia*, MIT China Project, E/54-3, Cambridge, Mass., MIT Center for International Studies, 1954, pp. 19 and 143, flatly gives 1943 as the date.

4. *People's Age*, March 14, 1948.

# CAMBODIA

Communist activity in Cambodia first developed within the ranks of the Communist Party of Indochina (Dong Duong Cong San Dang), which was founded in 1930 by Ho Chi Minh and was active over the entire Indochinese peninsula. It was based in the area now known as Vietnam, with few extensions into Cambodia itself. After the official dissolution of this party in 1945 and France's recognition in 1946 of three states associated within the French Union—Vietnam, Laos, and Cambodia—the communists organized a separate Cambodian party. However, actual leadership by the Vietnamese communists continued. In 1951 the secret directives of Ho Chi Minh's Vietnam Workers' Party specified that it was to play the directing role, adding that "later on, when conditions permit this to be carried out, the three revolutionary parties of Vietnam, Cambodia, and Laos will be reunited to form a single party."[1]

## HISTORY

The first foundations of the autonomous communist organization in Cambodia were laid in 1951 in the form of the People's Party of Khmer (Parti Populaire du Khmer, PPK), but its permanent and official creation was not completed until 1955. In 1951 the Cambodian communists were still acting as a branch of the Vietnamese party, which made no attempt to conceal its aims in the neighboring regions. In April 1953, for example, a Viet Minh (North Vietnamese) mission to Cambodia declared: "The mission of the [Vietnam Workers' Party] and the Vietnamese people is to make a revolution in Cambodia and Laos. We Viet Minh militants have been sent to serve the revolution and build a union of Vietnam, Cambodia, and Laos."[2]

At the time of the offensive action against French forces in 1953 and 1954, before the Geneva accords, the Viet Minh included Cambodia in their insurrectionary activities. The country was invaded twice by military formations of the Viet Minh, first in December 1953 in southern Battambang province, and again in April 1954 in the provinces of Stung-Treng and Kratié. The presence of these insurgent units enabled the communists to install their first infrastructure in these areas, both communist cells and the first elements of a People's Khmer Army of Liberation, commanded by Son Ngoc Minh, whose obvious objective was to prepare for the conquest of Cambodia.

Under the Geneva accords of July 1954, the new People's Republic of North Vietnam was obliged to evacuate its troops from Cambodia, while the communist units which the Viet Minh forces had helped to organize in Cambodia were transformed into a true political movement. After July 1955 the PPK was recognized as a communist grouping by both Hanoi and Moscow, and that year it began to seek a legal cover which would permit it to carry on its activities within the framework of the constitution of the Cambodian state. Under cover of the legal opposition Masses party (Prachéachon) the communists took over both its organization and its four newspapers, *Mitr Phéap* (Friendship), *Ek Phéap* (Independence), *Prachéachon* (Masses), and *L'Observateur* (published in French).

Also in 1955, Prince Norodom Sihanouk founded a new political party, the Popular Socialist Community (Sangkum Reastr Niyum), generally known as Sangkum. Sangkum entered a full slate of candidates in the elections of September 11, 1955, and received 82 percent of the votes cast as well as every one of the ninety-one seats in the national assembly. No Prachéachon candidates were elected, and they received only 3 percent of the vote. In the elections of March 23, 1958, Prince Sihanouk's movement once again won all sixty-one seats; four of the five communist candidates withdrew on the eve of the balloting, and the lone communist candidate to confront the electoral competition received only 396 votes, as opposed to 13,542 for the opposing candidate from Sihanouk's party.

In the years following their formation conflicts between Sihanouk's Sangkum, now in power, and the Prachéachon opposition shaped up as no more than a political struggle. The communists attacked the regime on numerous points, such as corruption, and Sihanouk in turn was ever ready to polemicize against the communists. At a press conference held March 29, 1959, he declared: "The Khmer Party is naturally antimonarchist and anti-Sangkum. Nevertheless, it has enjoyed every freedom to campaign during the last two legislative elections and to enter its candidates. Its newspapers appear regularly, despite the fact that I do not approve this ideology."

However, the accommodation that Sihanouk claimed to grant in 1959 was seriously endangered the following year. In February 1960, in the Cambodian-language weekly *Neak Cheat Niyum* (Nationalist) founded and edited by Sihanouk, the prince revealed that a communist assassination attempt against his person had just failed. Another revelation immediately followed: a secret committee of "free Khmers" had been founded in the Svay-Rieng province by a Khmer Vietnamese, Kol-Sy; when Kol-Sy was arrested and executed by the provincial guard during an attempted escape, the police found in his possession a copy of a letter to Ho Chi Minh establishing that he had met the emissaries of the Viet Minh in January in the Svay-Rieng province. Signing themselves the Popular Groups (Groupes Populaires), the communists published an open letter to Prince Sihanouk in *Prachéachon* expressing their loyalty to the throne and Sihanouk's regime and declaring that they knew nothing of the plot he had uncovered. Nevertheless, Sihanouk's attitude toward the "free Khmers" stiffened from that point, and legal communist activity was no longer tolerated as easily as before.

In August 1960 the Cambodian police announced that a "communist plot" had been discovered in Phnom Penh. Fifteen known communist militants were arrested, including several of the editors of *L'Observateur* and *Prachéachon*. The government banned *Prachéachon*, and several days later all other communist-oriented newspapers ceased to appear. A month later Sihanouk freed most of the arrested communists, but the communist press was not permitted to resume legal publication.

In January 1962 the police announced the liquidation of another communist net; fourteen communists were arrested, including several of the PPK leaders. Documents taken from the prisoners revealed that they had been assigned with the gathering of information on the police and the Cambodian army in the border regions. Sihanouk affirmed that the PPK was "a revolutionary organization, therefore anticonstitutional, directed from abroad by the Viet Minh.... All the red Khmers have only been carrying out the orders of the Vietnamese communist organization."[3] Son Suan, the head of the communist net, and several of his accomplices were sentenced to death, but their penalty was commuted by Sihanouk.

These repressive measures seem to have brought about a change in tactics for the Cambodian communists. Instead of working in open political struggle against Sihanouk's Sangkum, they attempted to infiltrate it and give it a leftist tendency—judging, at least, from the declarations of Prince Sihanouk, who was quick to accuse certain influential members of his party and government of being communist agents: "Hou Yuon, Hu Nim, Khieu Samphan, whom their red allies from Kompong Cham and Kratié designate by name as their inspirers and their chiefs after Son Suan, have never been worried. The Sangkum has made them deputies and members of the government."[4]

## RELATION TO SOVIET LEADERSHIP

The PPK was not one of the signatories of the manifesto issued by the world communist conference held in Moscow in November 1957. It was not on the list of parties present at the conference of eighty-one communist parties in November 1960. The PPK has not attended the congresses of the Communist Party of the Soviet Union, including the twenty-second congress, which was attended not only by communist parties, but also by the delegations of various national-liberation and progressive movements.

Inasmuch as neither the Moscow nor the Peking press speaks of the activities of the Cambodian communists, and as they do not make themselves known abroad through written or radio propaganda, the exact state of affairs of the communist movement in Cambodia is very difficult to establish. It is clear, however, that the future of the movement will be closely linked to the eventual advance of communism in Southeast Asia, particularly in Indochina.

## PARTY PRESS ORGANS

In 1955 the PPK began publication, through Prachéachon, of the periodicals *Mitr Phéap* (Friendship), *Ek Phéap* (Independence), *Prachéachon* (Masses), and *L'Observateur*. In 1960 the communist press organs were banned and have not since resumed legal publication.

BRANKO LAZITCH

1. "Top-secret" directive dated November 1, 1951, reprinted in P. J. Honey, *Communism in North Vietnam: Its Role in the Sino-Soviet Dispute*, Cambridge, Mass., MIT Press, 1963, p. 170.

2. *Est & ouest*, no. 386, 1967, p. 23.

3. "Arrestations de dirigeants communistes au Cambodge," *Est & ouest*, no. 278, May 1-15, 1962, p. 20.

4. *Est & ouest*, no. 386, 1967, p. 23.

# CAMEROON

The first attempt to establish a communist movement in Cameroon was on the trade-union level. In 1945 the Union of Confederated Trade Unions of Cameroon (Union des Syndicats Confédérés du Cameroun), a provincial branch of the French General Confederation of Labor (CGT), was founded by two French communists, Gaston Donnat and Ernest Fines. Both were soon joined by Cameroons Charles Assalé and Ruben Um Nyobé. Um Nyobé, born in 1913, became general secretary of the Cameroon trade-union organization in April 1947. However, this organization achieved little success with the trade unions themselves, and even less success politically; none of the communist candidates was elected to the French national assembly in November 1946 or to the Cameroon representative assembly in December 1946. Also, in November 1947, at the instigation of the French Communist Party, with Gaston Donnat (who had returned to France) as intermediary, it was decided to form a mass political movement, the Cameroon Peoples' Union (Union des Populations Camerounaises, UPC), with Um Nyobé taking over the leadership. Thus, although the Union of Confederated Trade Unions continued to exist, it lost its best militants.

## HISTORY

To avoid disclosing its communist character, the new UPC did not affiliate directly with the French Communist Party, but instead with the African Democratic Rally (Rassemblement Démocratique Africain, RDA), then connected with the French party. The UPC's statutes, set down on April 10, 1948, made the UPC the Cameroon section of the RDA. In January 1949 Um Nyobé was elected vice president of the RDA, a position he held until the UPC's exclusion from the RDA in July 1955.

In 1949 Um Nyobé had Félix Moumié, a young African doctor known for his relations with d'Arboussier, who was leader of the left wing of the RDA, named president of the UPC. At that time the UPC vice presidents were Abel Kingué and Ernest Ouandié, and its general secretary was Ruben Um Nyobé. The party adopted the slogans "unification" and "independence" and soon decided to resume the spelling "Kamerun," not out of nostalgia for the German influence, but to call to mind the time when the two Cameroons, French and English, were one. The new party won much sympathy, particularly among the civil servants, and recruited a fairly large number of members. By 1955 it claimed to have 80,000 members (its opponents gave it 20,000) and 400 local cells.

The party's rather tumultuous activity invited government repression, but its first major action was the publication on April 22, 1956, of a "joint declaraction" signed by the UPC, its satellite organizations the Democratic Union of Cameroon Women and the Democratic Youth of Cameroon, and the Cameroon General Confederation of Labor (Confédération Générale du Travail du Kamerun), the new name of the communist Trade-Union Confederation. The declaration called for an end to the mandate government, establishment of Cameroon as a sovereign state, a provisional government, and general elections. Shortly afterward Um Nyobé presented the flag that the party proposed as the national emblem, a black crab on a red field.

On May 22, on the occasion of a lecture by Moumié and Ouandié that was heckled by defectors from the party who wanted to form a "national anticommunist front," riots began which resulted in vigorous intervention by the authorities. The party was dissolved by decree on July 13, 1955, but communist activity continued, both secretly and in exile—at first in western Cameroon, then, after the party was also banned by the Nigerian authorities, in Cairo and Accra, and from 1958 on in Conakry, Guinea. The exiles were led by Félix Moumié. Within Cameroon, the communists reorganized along military lines at the end of 1956 under the leadership of a National Organizational Committee (Comité National d'Organisation) and launched guerrilla operations under the direction of Um Nyobé.

On May 15, 1957, Cameroon set up its first government. The guerrillas continued their struggle, and Um Nyobé was killed in combat in September 1958. Finally the party began to fall apart. Certain militant members founded the unsuccessful Cameroon People's Party (Parti Populaire Kamerunais, PPK), whose proclamation on May 1, 1957, denounced "the tragic folly" of the armed struggle and the personality cult raging in the UPC. On January 1, 1960, Cameroon became independent. After the amnesty of February 1959 and the decree of February 25, 1960, repealing dissolution of the UPC, its remnants in Cameroon rallied under the leadership of Mayi Matip and reestablished the party as a legal opposition. In the elections of April 10, 1960, the new UPC came up with its own candidates and won eighteen mandates. However, the old party leadership in exile condemned the new offshoot in Cameroon, denied its right to speak for the party, and remained firmly resolved to continue its own guerrilla struggle. On December 29, 1959, the exile leadership had issued the slogan "for a total revolution." An attempt to bring the two factions together—undoubtedly encouraged by the government, which was anxious to end the guerrilla war which was ravaging the country, especially in the Bamileke regions—was unsuccessful.

Moumié died in Geneva on November 3, 1960, apparently from poison. This loss, together with the internal conflicts in the international communist movement and the effectiveness of the Cameroon government's military action against the guerrillas, brought on a further split in the communist organization. In December 1960, at the close of a conference held in Accra, the exile party issued a new joint declaration, signed by the women's and youth organizations, but not by the Cameroon General Confederation of Labor. The declaraction denounced both Jacques Ngom, the labor confederation general secretary, and Mayi Matip as renegades. After a condemnation of American imperialism, in conformity with the theses adopted by the conference of the eighty-one communist parties in Moscow in November 1960, the declaration noted the successes of the guerrilla army (particularly the economic paralysis of the country) and called for intensification of the armed struggle to make 1961 the year of victory.

This declaration was the last joint action of the revolutionary old guard. Abel Kingué, one of the party vice presidents, after managing to get back the party treasury from Moumié's heirs, began to recommend an end to revolutionary activity and a return to legality. Then, following a visit to Peking, he created (or rallied) the pro-Chinese faction which appeared in the party as soon as the Sino-Soviet conflict broke out in 1961.

Since 1961 the Cameroon party has been divided into two groups. The Revolutionary Committee of the UPC (Comité Révolutionnaire de l'UPC), loyal to the Soviet Union, is headed by Second Vice President Ernest Ouandié and maintains close relations with the French Communist Party, with which it had had at least two secret official meetings resulting in joint declarations.[1] Its program calls for the establishing of a united national front, but it is no longer in a position to influence or lead other political groups in Cameroon; its only organizations are abroad, and its main center is in Accra.

After the death of Abel Kingué a group which calls itself the Directing Committee of the UPC (Comité Directeur de l'UPC) developed an increasingly pro-Chinese orientation. This group, led by Osende Afana and centered in Congo (Brazzaville), held its first plenary session on May 20-27, 1965 (probably in Congo), at which it decided to "form an armed detachment of partisans and to engage in revolutionary struggle with a view toward creation of the first revolutionary support base in a rural area of Cameroon." On September 1, 1965, this detachment, commanded by Osende Afana in person, penetrated "the great equatorial forest situated in the southeast of Cameroon."[2]

By 1965 the strength of the combined UPC factions was at most several hundred. Guerrilla activities within Cameroon have been liquidated over the years, and nearly all of the party membership is now in exile, chiefly in Ghana.

PARTY PRESS ORGANS

In 1955 the UPC was publishing a weekly, *L'Etoile*, and a bimonthly, *Lumière*.

BIBLIOGRAPHY

Zang-Atangana, Joseph Marie: "Les Forces politiques du Cameroun réunifié," doctoral dissertation, University of Paris, 1962.

CLAUDE HARMEL

1. *L'Humanité*, August 20, 1962; February 1, 1965.

2. Report of activities presented on May 2, 1966, to the general assembly of the first communist group of Cameroon, *La Voix du peuple*, June 17, 1966.

# CANADA

The first probolshevik groups in Canada formed part of the illegal Communist Party of America and United Communist Party of America. The decision to form the Communist Party of Canada (CPC) was reached at a convention at Guelph, Ontario, in May 1921. In February 1922 the still illegal CPC created the Workers' Party of Canada (WPC), which operated legally for two years. From 1943 to 1959 the CPC was known as the Labor Progressive Party (LPP).

The founders of the CPC included Maurice Spector, who was the party chairman until his expulsion in 1928; Jack Macdonald, party secretary in the 1920s, who was expelled in 1930; Florence A. Custance, who died in 1929; W. Moriarty, who remained in the CPC until his death in 1936; and T. Buck, who led the CPC for three decades.

HISTORY

Founded by a group of young British or anglicized skilled workers and intellectuals, the CPC recruited its staunchest supporters among left-wing immigrants of East European extraction, mainly Finns and Ukrainians. Its membership fluctuated from 2,500 to 5,000 throughout the 1920s and declined in the early stages of the Depression. Government repression, including the arrest of eight party leaders in August 1931, drove the CPC underground from 1931 to 1934.

During the popular-front period the CPC abandoned its policy of dual unionism and advocated cooperation with the more numerous democratic socialists organized in the Cooperative Commonwealth Federation. The rapid increase in party membership and communist influence in the late 1930s was cut short by the defeatist attitude the CPC adopted in the early stages of World War II. The Liberal Party government of Mackenzie King banned the CPC in June 1940 and interned over 100 party leaders and militants. The arrested communists were set free in 1942.

In 1943 the communists reorganized as the Labor Progressive Party and supported the war effort against the Axis powers. Once again party membership rose, and in August 1943 the first and only communist was elected to the federal parliament. However, in 1945 the disclosures of Igor Guzenko, a cypher clerk who had defected from the Soviet embassy in Ottawa, implicated a number of communists, several of whom were sentenced to imprisonment. The impact of these revelations, coupled with the public reaction to communist policies in Europe and Asia, resulted in measures against communists holding positions of responsibility in the Canadian trade-union movement, reducing the party to a small and ineffective political organization on the fringe of Canadian politics.

Khrushchev's denunciation of Stalin in 1956 and news about the mistreatment of Jews in the communist world contributed to major differences in the leadership of the party and thinned the ranks of party members even further. It was only in the early 1960s that the party, now known again as the CPC, began to recover some of its influence by exploiting Canadian anxieties over various aspects of United States foreign and economic policies. Despite these renewed efforts, there is little evidence that the CPC has made significant headway in expanding its membership and organization in a society that is essentially conservative.

## ORGANIZATION AND MEMBERSHIP

The party organization follows the usual pyramidal order, starting at the bottom with the party club and ending with the national convention of the CPC, which elects the national committee.

The Young Communist League of Canada and communist clubs at a number of Canadian universities are responsible for most of the communist agitation among the young.

Industrial and white-collar workers and a sprinkling of intellectuals provide the bulk of the party members. In 1964, according to an official communist source, the average age of the rank and file was in "the fifties." The CPC is extremely weak in the Maritimes and among French-speaking Canadians in the province of Quebec. Whatever strength it possesses lies in the industrial and mining centers of Ontario, British Columbia, and the Prairies, in particular the city of Winnipeg. The estimates for the membership of the CPC in the mid-1960s ranged from 4,000 to 8,000.

The CPC has dozens of front organizations and still exercises considerable influence in several small trade unions, especially the United Electrical, Radio and Machine Workers of America; the United Fishermen and Allied Workers' Union; and the International Union of Mine, Mill and Smelter Workers. Party members and sympathizers are also active in a number of peace groups run by noncommunist critics of the foreign policies of the United States and Canada.

## RELATION TO SOVIET LEADERSHIP

The CPC was affiliated with the Comintern until 1940. Periodic purges of leaders and militants who were unwilling to carry out Soviet directives had little effect on its fortunes until 1956. In that year a group of CPC leaders, many of whom were of Jewish extraction, called for a new type of relationship between the Communist Party of the Soviet Union and the CPC and for the resignation of T. Buck, the party leader who was closely associated with Stalinist policies. At one stage of the struggle the revisionists, led by J.B. Salsberg, were in a majority in the CPC's national committee. However, the failure of the revisionists to consolidate their position, coupled with the antirevisionist drive throughout the international communist movement, enabled the pro-Stalinist elements to make a comeback and led to Salsberg's departure from the CPC in 1957.

The CPC has given strong support to Moscow in the Sino-Soviet quarrel, and a number of militants, mostly in the Vancouver region, were expelled for refusing to accept the official CPC version of the dispute. In the autumn of 1964 this group formed the Progressive Workers' Movement (PWM) under the leadership of Jack Scott and started publication of a monthly, *The Progressive Worker*.

## PARTY PRESS ORGANS AND RECORDS

The CPC press organs are *The Canadian Tribune*, a weekly, and *The Marxist Quarterly*, both published in Toronto. The pro-Chinese PWM publishes *The Progressive Worker*, a monthly.

The CPC's bylaws may be found in *Constitution of the Communist Party of Canada* (as amended at the seventeenth national convention of the Communist Party of Canada, 19-21 January 1962), Toronto, Communist Party of Canada, 1962. For the program of the CPC see *The Road to Socialism in Canada: Program of the Communist Party of Canada*, Toronto, Communist Party of Canada, 1960; for amendments to this program see *Documents of the Seventeenth National Convention, January 19, 20, 21, 1962,* Toronto, Communist Party of Canada, 1962, pp. 26-27.

## PARTY CONVENTIONS

1st (unity) convention, May 23, 1921
2d convention, CPC, and 1st convention, WPC, February 22-23, 1922
2d convention, WPC, February 22, 1923
3d convention, WPC, April 18-19, 1924
4th convention, CPC, September 11-13, 1925
5th convention, CPC, June 17-20, 1927
6th convention, CPC May 31-June 1, 1929
7th convention, CPC, July 23-28, 1934
8th convention, CPC, October 8-12, 1937
Constituent convention, LPP, August 21-22, 1943
2d convention, LPP, June 1-5, 1946
3d convention, LPP, February 4-8, 1949
4th convention, LPP, January 25-28, 1951
5th convention, LPP, March 25-28, 1954
6th convention, LPP, April 19-22, 1957
16th convention, CPC, October 9-12, 1959
17th convention, CPC, January 19-21, 1962
18th convention, CPC, March 27-30, 1964

## BIBLIOGRAPHY

Avakumovic, I.: "The Communist Party of Canada and the Sino-Soviet Dispute," *Pacific Affairs* (Vancouver), vol. 37, no. 4, winter 1964-1965, pp. 426-435.

Buck, T.: *Canada: The Communist Viewpoint*, Toronto, Progress Books, 1948.

Buck, T.: *Our Fight for Canada: Selected Writings, 1923-1959,* Toronto, Progress Books, 1959.

Buck, T.: *Thirty Years, 1922-1952: The Story of the Communist Movement in Canada*, Toronto, Progress Books, 1952.

Canada, Government of: *Report of the Royal Commission Appointed under Order in Council P.C. 411 of February 5, 1946,* to investigate the facts relating to and the circumstances surrounding the communication, by public officials and other persons of trust, of secret and confidential information to agents of a foreign power, Ottawa, Cloutier, 1946.

Communist Party of Canada: *Questions for Today: Documents and Commentary of the Communist Party of Canada, 1952-1964,* Toronto, Progress Books, 1964.

Morris, L.: *Challenge of the '60s,* Toronto, Progress Books, 1964.

Sullivan, J. A.: *Red Sails on the Great Lakes*, Toronto, Macmillan, 1955.

IVAN AVAKUMOVIC

# CEYLON

The first socialist movement was launched in Ceylon on December 18, 1935, as the Ceylon Equality Party (Lanka Sama Samaja Pakshaya, LSSP). It was founded by British-educated radicals who had been active for several years in the youth leagues and were responsible for organization of the Sunflower (Suriya Mal) anti-imperialist protest movement against the traditional Armistice Day poppy sale for the benefit of British ex-servicemen.

The founders of the LSSP, the first Ceylonese political party worthy of the name, were A. S. Wickremasinghe, a popular physician and member of the first state council; N. M. Perera, a pupil of Harold Laski; Colvin R. de Silva, a brilliant lawyer; and Leslie Goonewardena, a militant Marxist organizer. All were from wealthy Sinhalese families and were introduced during their studies in London to scientific socialism, with its explosive Hobson-Lenin corollary of "the inevitable collapse of colonial imperialism as the last stage of decaying monopoly capitalism." An exception was D. P. R. Gunawardena (nicknamed Philip), who received his training in Marxism from Scott Nearing at the University of Wisconsin.

## HISTORY

The 1935 manifesto of the LSSP emphasized first the attainment of complete national independence and second that of socialism. Advocating the gradual Fabian approach rather than the Marxist class struggle, the LSSP proposed to implement social reforms through socialization of the means of production, distribution, and exchange and through abolition of social and economic inequality and oppression arising from differences of class, caste, race, creed, or sex. These broad objectives, aimed at the complete transformation of Ceylon's caste-ridden society into an egalitarian welfare state, were to be achieved not by violent revolution, but by peaceful means enumerated in twenty-two specific down-to-earth demands. De Silva was elected president of the LSSP, and militant proctor Vernon Gunasekera became secretary general. The young party met with considerable success, particularly among intellectuals and college students gradually indoctrinated in Marxist theory, although its active membership failed to pass the 1,000 mark. A "T" (for Trotsky) conspiracy within the LSSP leadership dominated the movement. It became partisan to Trotsky's views, and was particularly impressed with his exposure of Soviet Russia's growing deviation from Marxism-Leninism and protested the zigzag popular front tactics of the Comintern as applied in China, Spain, and France. Comintern agents in the British party attempted to swing the left movement in Ceylon to Stalinism through influence on the Ceylonese group in London, led by Wickremasinghe, the official LSSP representative. However, in 1939 the Ceylonese Marxists openly revolted against Stalin's leadership, primarily over the issue of the Comintern's opportunistic switch of tactics regarding British colonialism. Until 1956, when the last British bases disappeared from Ceylon, the LSSP considered British imperialism the main enemy. Hence it could hardly approve the Comintern's instructions following the Ribbentrop-Molotov agreement and the subsequent partition of East Central Europe between Nazi Germany and Soviet Russia.

When the Comintern's abrupt change of line called for a showdown, with the minority group blindly supporting Stalin's instructions, the LSSP executive committee resolved that "since the Third International has not acted in the interests of the international revolutionary working-class movement, while expressing its solidarity with the Soviet Union, the first workers' state, the Lanka Sama Samaja Party declares that it has no faith in the Third International."

Twenty-nine voted for the resolution; of the five who voted against it, Wickremasinghe, M. G. W. Ariyaratne, A. Gunasekara, and K. Ramanathan, editor of the party's Tamil-language weekly *Samatharmam,* were subsequently expelled. In November 1940, together with one-tenth of the LSSP membership, this group formed the United Socialist Party, the precursor of the official communist party. Pieter Keuneman, ex-president of the Cambridge Union and an accomplished Marxist, was elected general secretary, a position he still holds.

Until the nazi invasion of Russia both the LSSP and the expelled Stalinists were preaching some sort of "revolutionary defeatism" and publicly renouncing any "loyal support" for the prosecution of what they termed the typical imperialist war. However, the Trotskyists in the LSSP could not refrain from some vindictiveness in attacking the Stalinist popular-front concept of expedient alliance with the national bourgeoisie in the anti-imperialist coalition. Their new publication *Straight Left* declared that the Stalinists would "go down to history as the first group of Stalinists to be expelled from a revolutionary party. In every other country Russian money enabled the Stalinists to expel the Marxists (dubbed by them Trotskyists). In Ceylon alone it happened otherwise."[1]

The LSSP was the only active group fighting for the liberation of Ceylon from colonial rule. Following Trotsky's appeal in his July 1939 open letter to the Workers of India, it claimed that, like World War I, "this war too is for the division and re-division of the colonies and semi-colonies. We refuse to be a Party to any Imperialist War.... We refuse to consider that the people of this country are at war with any people anywhere else in the world, and therefore we refuse to participate in any Imperialist War...."[2]

The LSSP decided to intensify its attempts to organize strikes throughout tea and rubber plantations. Some party leaders felt that the almost 1 million stateless Tamil laborers imported from south India by the planters should be considered the true epicenter of the future revolution in Ceylon. The strike wave reached its dramatic zenith in the upcountry on January 19, 1940, when the first of the Trotskyist hero martyrs, the worker Govidnan, was killed by the police in the Mool Oya estate dispute, led by Veluchamy, secretary of the All-Ceylon Estate Workers' Union.

To prevent the class struggle instigated by the LSSP from becoming a definite hindrance to the British war effort, the Churchill government decided after the fall of Paris to strike at the Ceylonese revolutionaries. De Silva, Edmund Samarakkody, Perera, and Philip Gunawardena were detained on June 17, 1940, under the defense regulations. On the party's prior instructions, Leslie Goonewardena evaded arrest and went underground. Although the party press was raided and sealed, work continued in a semiclandestine way. On April 20, 1941, a secret conference, attended by forty-two delegates, adopted a new revolutionary program and formalized the LSSP's association with the Fourth International (see *The Fourth International*). The Stalinists were also harassed by police until June 1941, and some of them, including Wickremasinghe, U. Sarankara Thero, and D. P. Yasodis, were imprisoned under the defense regulations.

The gap between the Trotskyists and the Stalinists widened further with Hitler's invasion of the Soviet Union. The Stalinists switched their policy overnight to help Russia's new allies, whereas the Trotskyists firmly stuck to the view that the imperialist character of the war was not changed, and any postponement of the struggle for national independence would constitute a betrayal of Marxist-Leninist principles. Such an adamant stand made the LSSP the most seditious enemy of the Allied war effort in Ceylon. A card of revolutionary heroism was written by the Trotskyists on April 7, 1942, when the four main LSSP prisoners escaped from prison, along with their guard, Comrade Solomon. As they were being hunted in Ceylon, most of the LSSP leaders decided to take refuge in India, on the premise that the revolution in Ceylon could develop successfully only as part of the Indian revolution. Another wave of arrests took place after the jail break, and the Trotskyist movement was suspended in Ceylon until after the war when a new wave of workers' unrest culminated in the general strikes of October 1946 and May-June 1947.

In striking contrast, the Stalinists, officially recognized in July 1943 as the Ceylon Communist Party (Lanka Kommunist Pakshaya, LKP), applied a "united-front-from-above" tactical line, urging greater productivity and discouraging strikes. This was a matter of no mean strategic importance since the loss of Malaya and the Dutch East Indies to Japan had left Ceylon as the only large producer of natural rubber. The LKP took full advantage of its wartime opportunities to develop a party organization and take over the transport unions, which had been organized by the LSSP. In April 1945 the first congress of the LKP, attended by some 100 delegates, endorsed the report of the central committee, presented by Keuneman, including association with the Ceylon National Congress, which the communists had joined in 1943 over the protest resignation of its founder, D. S. Senanayake. A central committee of twelve was elected, with Keuneman in the key position of general secretary.

The Trotskyists had also been plagued by a series of organizational differences and personal animosities between the Ceylonese leaders of the Bolshevik-Leninist Party of India and those of the exiled LSSP. They were reunited in 1950, except for a small group led by Philip Gunawardena and his brother Robert, who had formed a revolutionary splinter group.[3]

Independence from Britain after protracted negotiations following World War II brought the three Marxist parties into an electoral contest with the almost *ad hoc*-created United National Party (UNP). In the August-September 1947 elections the Marxists secured 18 percent of the seats, four for the LKP and seventeen for the two Trotskyist factions, which contested the election separately. The March 1960 elections gave the leftist parties the greatest parliamentary strength they were ever able to secure. The combined left vote was almost one-fourth of the total, with twenty-six Marxists elected, five of whom were LKP members. The UNP government of Dudley Senanayake was defeated in its first vote in the parliament, and new elections were held in July 1960. A no-contest pact was concluded by the LSSP and the Ceylon Freedom Party (Sri Lanka Nidahas Pakshaya), generally known as the Sri Lanka Freedom Party (SLFP). As a result, the SLFP, led by Sirimavo Bandaranaike, the widow of the assassinated prime minister, came to power with the tacit approval of the communists, always eager to prevent the anti-Marxist UNP from acquiring power.

Praising the nonalignment policy of both Bandaranaikes, the communists officially announced their joy at the defeat of the UNP in the 1956 and 1960 elections. At the sixth party congress, held in December 1960, they emphasized the paramount importance of pro-Soviet orientation in foreign policy, the main task of the party being "to strengthen still further Ceylon's contribution to the fight for peace and against colonialism and to develop and consolidate its relations with the socialist and anti-imperialist countries."

The LKP took the initiative in organizing mass demonstrations in support of communist causes in Cuba, the Congo, Algeria, and Vietnam. They were also able to secure some Soviet-bloc economic aid for the troubled Bandaranaike government, starting with the symbolic Soviet steel factory. Planning skillfully and taking advantage of communal hatreds and contradictions within the new establishment, they managed to penetrate and infiltrate the government apparatus to a substantial degree.

The Trotskyists were much more confused. Ever since the successful August 1953 *hartal*, or concerted cessation of work, they had been protesting the increased prices of consumer goods and the cut in the rice ration. They were striving for a united left front against the national bourgeoisie. The abrupt withdrawal of American aid over the nationalization of foreign oil companies actually helped to call into being a short-lived United Left Front of the Marxist parties, inaugurated in 1963 by jointly organized May Day celebrations. A common platform worked out by the leaders of the LSSP, the People's United Front (Mahajana Eksath Peramuna, MEP), and the LKP not only emphasized the nationalization of large foreign-owned and Ceylonese-owned enterprises, but also accepted the controversial policy of making Sinhalese the only official language, with regional concessions only to Tamil. This issue of communalism, or cultural groupings, versus national unification inevitably created a crisis second only to the growing division between the followers of Moscow and those of Peking within the three groups. Indeed, the United Left Front was soon ridiculed as being actually composed of six groups fighting in pairs.

Moreover, the crypto-Marxists in the ruling SLFP approached the reformist-inclined leaders of the LSSP with a coalition idea to help Mrs. Bandaranaike's government, in view of the SLFP's dwindling parliamentary strength and mounting labor unrest. Weary from years of unsuccessful opposition and eager to implement at last some of their socialist concepts, most of the LSSP members abandoned their leftist partners and joined forces with the middle-class SLFP. Thus in June 1964 Perera became finance minister in the coalition government, with four other ex-Trotskyists joining the cabinet as full or junior ministers. This switch of ideological allegiance may be assessed as the most critical development in the postwar history of this unique Trotskyist formation. Fourteen members of the central committee, led by the militant revolutionary Edmund Samarakkody and Bela Tampoe, one of Ceylon's principal trade-union leaders, established the Revolutionary Ceylon Equality Party (Viplavakari Lanka Sama Samaja Pakshaya, VLSSP), recognized in July 1964 as the only Ceylon Unit of the Fourth International.

One of the principal ideological attractions of the LSSP, its anticommunalist stand, was now abandoned by the pragmatic mainstream of the party in order to woo the Sinhalese majority, and as a result most of the Tamil Trotskyists joined the VLSSP. Similar realignment occurred in the LKP over the same issue, with the pro-Chinese faction led by Nagalingam N. Sanmugathasan, veteran member of the LKP's politburo and general secretary of the communist-sponsored Trade Union Federation of Ceylon. In 1964 the two factions held separate party congresses, and the pro-Peking members of the LKP central committee, followed by some 100 party members, then decided to create a separate pro-Chinese communist party.

## ORGANIZATION AND MEMBERSHIP

Although it is small, the pro-Soviet LKP is distinguished by strict discipline based on the practice of democratic centralism, closely supervised by Moscow's representatives in Colombo. In 1962 the party claimed a membership of about 19,000, but other estimates indicate a membership of 3,000 to 5,000.[4] In view of the 1964 split, the active membership could probably be placed just below the 3,000 mark. Since the LKP is much more pragmatic than its principled ultrarevolutionary Trotskyist or pro-Peking competitors, it stands a good chance of increasing its support among the rural and urban masses of the Sinhalese majority, particularly at the expense of other Marxist groups, which have been losing members to the LKP since 1953.

## RELATION TO SOVIET LEADERSHIP

Until 1962 both Russia and China seemed to support the neutralist posture of the Bandaranaike government. In September 1957

Communist China gave Ceylon a grant of approximately $16 million, with no strings attached, to be drawn on from 1958 to 1962, primarily for the improvement of rubber plantations; China needed Ceylon's natural rubber to exchange for Burmese rice. However, the Russians displayed greater shrewdness in handling the Sinhalese majority, and the Chinese were left with the choice of exploiting the frustrations of the Tamil minority—actually not such a bad choice in view of the fact that there are some 30 million Tamils in nearby southern India.

The LKP, led by Keuneman and Wickremasinghe, was still able in early 1963 to combine its pro-Soviet line with support of Chinese policy on the question of India. In September 1963, however, it switched to complete support of the Moscow policy on all issues of the Sino-Soviet dispute. After Wickremasinghe's return from Moscow the two pro-Chinese leaders, Sanmugathasan and Premalal Kumarasiri, were expelled from the party and accused of distributing Chinese propaganda material against the Soviet Union.

China's leading spokesman in Ceylon is Mrs. Theja Gunawardhena, chairman of the Afro-Asian Solidarity Movement. Indeed, the main strength of the Chinese faction consists of the support it finds in a number of ancillary front organizations such as the Ceylon Trade Union Federation and the youth leagues. Moscow and Peking accuse each other of bribing and financing the competing communist groups.

## PARTY PRESS ORGANS

The LKP publishes *Forward* in English, with a circulation of 7,000, and *Mavimba* (Mother Earth) in Sinhalese, with a circulation of 18,000. It also publishes a Tamil-language organ, *Desabhimani* (The Patriot), with a circulation of 10,000, and one in the Malayalam language, *Nevasakthi* (New Force), with a circulation of 4,500.

## CONGRESSES OF THE LKP

1st congress, April 1945, Colombo
2d congress, January 1948, Velavatta
3d congress, September 1948
4th congress, September 1950, Matara
5th congress, 1955
6th congress, December 1960, Colombo
7th congress, April 1964, Colombo

## BIBLIOGRAPHY

Abhayavardhana, Hector: *Categories of Left Thinking in Ceylon*, Colombo, Communist Institute, n.d.

Barnett, A. Doak: *Communist China and Asia: Challenge to American Policy*, New York, Harper, 1960.

Goonewardena, Leslie S.: *The Third International Condemned*, Colombo, Ceylon Equality Party, March 1940.

Hansard: *Debates in the State Council of Ceylon*, 1939.

Kearney, Robert N.: "The Ceylon Communist Party: Competition for Marxist Supremacy," in Robert A. Scalapino (ed.), *The Communist Revolution in Asia: Tactics, Goals, and Achievements*, Englewood Cliffs, N.J., Prentice-Hall, 1965.

Mendis, G. C.: *Ceylon Today and Yesterday: Main Currents of Ceylon History*, Colombo, Associated Newspapers of Ceylon, 1952.

Pakeman, S. A.: *Ceylon*, New York, Praeger, 1964.

*A Short History of the Lanka Sama Samaja Party*, Colombo, Ceylon Equality Party, 1960.

Singer, Marshall K.: *The Emerging Elite: A Study of Political Leadership in Ceylon*, Cambridge, Mass., MIT Press, 1964.

Wriggins, W. Howard: *Ceylon: Dilemmas of a New Nation*, Princeton, N.J., Princeton University Press, 1960.

GEORGE J. LERSKI

1. "The United Socialist Party: A Fifth Column for Stalin," *Straight Left: Paper of Views and News*, vol. I, no. 1, February 1, 1941.

2. Hansard, *Debates in the State Council of Ceylon*, 1939, p. 3480.

3. Robert N. Kearney, "The Ceylon Communist Party: Competition for Marxist Supremacy," in Robert A. Scalapino (ed.), *The Communist Revolution in Asia: Tactics, Goals, and Achievements*, Englewood Cliffs, N.J., Prentice-Hall, 1965, pp. 373-398.

4. Kearney, *op. cit.*, p. 394.

# CHILE

The Communist Party of Chile (Partido Comunista de Chile, PCCh) began as the Socialist Workers' Party (Partido Obrero Socialista, POS) founded by Luis Emilio Recabarren in July 1912. At the fifth congress of the POS during December 1921-January 1922 Recabarren led his party intact into the world communist movement as the PCCh. For a discussion of the circumstances surrounding this event see *Latin America*.

### HISTORY

The Chilean party has more consistently followed a nonviolent approach in its quest for political power than any other communist organization in Latin America. At its inception the PCCh inherited a large enfranchised labor following, control of the Federation of Chilean Workers, an established nationwide electoral machinery, and several public offices held by party members. It continued to use these assets, regularly presenting candidates for local, state, and national office; it never willingly jeopardized its position in the labor movement, usually employing persuasion rather than force to extend its influence among white-collar workers, students, and the lower middle class.

The PCCh lost some of its more effective leaders when the Comintern's third-period line prohibited cooperation with other political groups after 1928 (see *The Communist International*), and it was notoriously unsuccessful when it sought to promote violence in the late 1920s and exploit the revolutionary ferment of 1932. However, it made striking gains in membership and political influence after 1935, when the new popular-front policy was implemented in Chile, under the direction of Comintern agents. In alliance with socialists, small democratic parties, and the large, center Radical Party (Partido Radical), the communists contributed to the electoral victories in 1936 and 1937, winning a degree of respectability that survived the negative impact of the Hitler-Stalin pact from 1939 to 1941. The high point was reached between November 1946 and April 1947, when three communists were included in the cabinet of President González Videla. The communists overreached themselves and were dismissed after five months in office, but during that time the party grew to 50,000 members and attained a dominant position in the labor movement.

With the onset of the cold war the communist position deteriorated. The PCCh was outlawed in 1948, and some 40,000 registered communist voters were denied the franchise. It was rescued from this position in 1952 with the formation of a so-called People's Front, with the socialists, which led in 1958 to restoration of its legal status and a revival of the popular front, now known as the Popular Action Front (Frente de Acción Popular). Even before their formal admission to the Popular Action Front the communists regained much of their influence at the polls, contributing to the near victory of the front candidate in the 1958 presidential elections.

Since 1960 they have consistently run ahead of their socialist allies in nationwide elections, but behind the rival Christian democrats.

## ORGANIZATION AND MEMBERSHIP

United States sources estimated the strength of the PCCh as 30,000 in 1965.[1] The party was supported by the full range of Latin American front organizations. For a full discussion see *Latin America*.

## RELATION TO SOVIET LEADERSHIP

From the outset the Chilean party was associated with the Comintern, which intervened through its South American Bureau in party matters and decided among rivals for party leadership on numerous occasions in the 1920s and 1930s. In 1935 the Comintern sent agents to Chile to test the popular-front experiment in Latin America.

The PCCh firmly endorsed Khrushchev's policy of a "peaceful road to socialism" and has supported the Soviet position in the ideological controversy with China. In 1964 the Chilean party was one of two in Latin America to request a Soviet explanation of the fall of Khrushchev. For a discussion of other aspects of the relations between the PCCh and the Soviet-directed world communist movement see *Latin America*.

## PARTY PRESS ORGANS AND RECORDS

The leading party publications are the daily *El Siglo*, the weekly *Vistazo*, and the monthly theoretical journal *Principios*. The Chilean communists operate an active publications program, issuing formal party documents and a larger number of biographies and memoirs of party leaders than any other Latin American communist organization. The recent statutes and programs of the party are included in *Documentos e informes emanados de plenos y congresos del Partido comunista de Chile*, published by the party in 1964.

## CONGRESSES OF THE PCCH

The Chilean communists met seventeen times in party congresses between May 1915 and October 1965. The POS, forerunner of the PCCh, held five national congresses between 1915 and 1922; the final one appears in the PCCh listing as its first congress. Accounts of these congresses are inconsistent.

1st congress, December 1921-January 1922, Rancagua
2d congress, December 1923, Chillán
3d congress, September 1924, Viña del Mar
4th congress, September 1925
5th congress, December 1926-January 1927, Santiago
6th congress, May 1933 (?)
7th congress, April 1938, Santiago
8th congress, December 1939, Santiago
9th congress, December 1945, Santiago
10th congress, April 1956, Santiago
11th congress, November 1958, Santiago
12th congress, March 1962, Santiago
13th congress, October 1965, Santiago

## BIBLIOGRAPHY

*Estudios sobre el comunismo*, vols. I-V, Santiago, 1952-1956.
Halperin, Ernst: *Sino-Cuban Trends: The Case of Chile*, Cambridge, Mass., MIT Center for International Studies, March 1964.
Lafertte, Elías: *Vida de un comunista: Páginas autobiográficas*, Santiago, Talleres Gráficos Horizonte, 1961.
*Ricardo Fonseca: Combatiente ejemplar*, Santiago, Communist Party of Chile, 1952.
Stevenson, John R.: *The Popular Front in Chile*, Philadelphia, University of Pennsylvania Press, 1942.
Teitelboim, Volodia: *La semilla en la arena*, Santiago, Editora Austral, 1957.
Vergara, Marta: *Memorias de una mujer irreverente*, Santiago, Editora Zig-Zag, 1963.

See also *Latin America*, refs. 1, 2, 13, 15, 24.

ROLLIE E. POPPINO

1. U.S. Department of State, Bureau of Intelligence and Research, *World Strength of the Communist Party Organizations*, Eighteenth Annual Report, Washington, January 1966, p. 171.

# CHINA

Organization of the Chinese Communist Party (Chung-kuo Kung-ch'an-tang, CCP) began early in 1920, when G. Voitinsky, secretary of the Far Eastern Bureau of the Comintern, arrived in China with Wang Ming-chai and contacted Li Ta-chao and Ch'en Tu-hsiu. Li, librarian of Peking's national university, Peita, had organized Marxist study groups there in 1918. Ch'en, former dean of Peita, was editor of *Hsin Ch'ing-nien* (New Youth), the most influential radical journal in China. In August 1920 this group formed the Chinese Socialist Youth Corps (Chung-kuo She-hui Chu-i Ch'ing-nien T'uan) and soon established ten communist or youth groups, six in China and one each in Japan, Moscow, Berlin, and Paris. Chou En-lai and Ch'en Yi, currently premier and foreign minister, respectively, of the People's Republic of China, founded the Western European branches; Ch'ü Ch'iu-pai and Liu Shao-ch'i founded the Moscow branch.

The CCP was officially founded in Shanghai in July 1921. Twelve delegates attended this first "congress," representing fifty-seven members. Mao Tse-tung, born in 1893, current chairman of the party's central committee, was among the delegates, although his role at this meeting is much exaggerated today by CCP propagandists. Neither Ch'en Tu-hsiu nor Li Ta-chao attended, but Ch'en was elected chairman in absentia. Ch'en, regarded by Western observers as the founder, is not so acknowledged by Peking; Li is implicitly accorded that honor. The key second congress in 1922 accepted Lenin's Twenty-one Conditions for Comintern membership.

Ch'en Tu-hsiu was dismissed as chairman in 1927 for a "right deviation" and expelled from the CCP in November 1929 as a "Trotskyist." Li was captured in a raid on the Soviet Embassy in Peking; he was executed by the warlord Chang Tso-lin in April 1927 and is considered to have died a martyr's death. Other party members prominent during the 1920s were later purged. Ch'ü Ch'iu-pai, who replaced Ch'en Tu-hsiu, was condemned for "putschism" in 1928 and "factionalism" in 1930 and was executed by the Nationalist Party (Kuomintang) in June 1935. Li Li-san, who assumed real power after Ch'ü's removal in 1928, was condemned by the party in 1930. Ho Meng-hsiung, prominent labor organizer and outspoken critic of the Li Li-san line, was expelled by Li and executed by Kuomintang police after being informed against by Wang Ming (Ch'en Shao-yü), a protégé of Pavel Mif and acting secretary general after Hsiang Chung-fa's death. Chang Kuo-t'ao, delegate to the first congress, was expelled in 1938 by Mao as the result of a dispute over united-front tactics (Chang now resides in Hong Kong). Wang Ming was purged by Mao for "deviations" in 1942.

With few exceptions, purges within the elite levels of the CCP have not been accompanied by imprisonments and executions, as was the case under Stalin. Rather, high-ranking members have been "publicly exposed," ruthlessly "struggled against" in meetings, and stripped of real power. Many of them, however, have been permitted to retain their central committee membership. As institutionalized disgraces, they serve as living examples of the cost paid for error. Notable cases are Li Li-san, who was reelected to the eighth central committee in 1956 and ranks eighty-ninth among ninety-seven full members, but has appeared only rarely in the last decade, and Wang Ming, lowest-ranking full member of the eighth central committee, who apparently holds no party or government post aside from central committee membership and resided in Moscow from 1951 through 1965.

## HISTORY

From 1923 to 1927 most Chinese communists were also members of the Kuomintang. The first united front (against the warlords) was based on a declaration signed on January 1, 1923, by Sun Yat-sen and Adolf Joffe, the Soviet envoy to China. The CCP adopted the declaration, under Comintern pressure, at its third congress in June. The Kuomintang accepted the principle of dual membership at its first congress in January 1924. At this time the goal of Comintern policy was to create a "bloc within," rather than a two-party alliance, or "bloc without."

After Sun's death in 1925 real power in the Kuomintang, as well as command of the northern expedition to overthrow the Peking government, passed to Chiang Kai-shek. In April 1927 the united front began to fall apart as a result of the massacre in Shanghai of communists and workers who had attempted to take over the city in anticipation of assistance by Chiang's advancing army. Chiang's troops did not intervene, however, until warlord forces had annihilated the insurrectionists. The united front with the left wing of the Kuomintang continued until July 1927. Communist-led insurrections followed (such as Mao's famous Autumn Harvest uprising in Hunan, the Nanchang uprising, and the Canton commune), but they were unsuccessful. Mao, Chu Teh, and others retreated to Chingkangshan, a remote mountainous area on the Hunan-Kiangsi border.

After a series of abortive insurrections culminating in the capture and loss of Changsha in 1930, the strategy of urban insurrection was dropped, and in 1931 a Chinese Soviet Republic was established in Juichin, Kiangsi province, with Mao as its chairman. The Kuomintang launched a series of campaigns against the Soviet areas in late 1930, and with German officers as advisors, it finally forced the Red Army to evacuate its Kiangsi base in October 1934. Thus began the Long March covering some 6,000 miles, and terminating in late 1935, when the survivors reached northern Shensi province. During the Long March, as the result of conferences at Tsunyi and Maoerhkai, Mao defeated his major opponents in the CCP and became party chairman, a post he has held to this day.

During this period the Chinese Red Army was established, and Mao developed his theories concerning guerrilla warfare and base areas, as well as his emphasis on maintaining a viable tax base to support the army. This latter emphasis led to conflicts with the Comintern from 1929 to 1935.

In effect, the Sino-Japanese war of 1937 saved the CCP from possible annihilation at the hands of the Kuomintang. During the first years of the war the communist base areas were not subjected to major assaults by the Japanese (who were content to garrison strong points and control rail lines), leaving the CCP relatively free to consolidate and expand its control in such rural areas as Shensi, Chahar, and Hopei. With the entrance of the United States into the war in 1941, both the CCP and the Kuomintang began to preserve their remaining forces in anticipation of a resumption of hostilities between the two antagonists after the defeat of Japan.

The Kuomintang emerged from World War II victorious on the international scene but on the verge of civil defeat. Chinese communist forces, taking advantage of the presence of Russian troops in Manchuria, expanded their control to that strategic industrial region. General George C. Marshall, U.S. Army chief of staff during World War II, was appointed special envoy to China by President Truman to mediate the Kuomintang-CCP conflict and obtained a short-lived cease-fire agreement in early 1946. The nationalists committed their crack units to Manchuria, where they were surrounded in the urban centers by communist forces who held the countryside. By the end of 1948 the communists controlled Manchuria.

The great cities of the Yangtze Valley fell in mid-1949, and in early 1950 Chiang Kai-shek and the remnants of his forces took refuge on the strategic offshore islands of Quemoy and Matsu, the Pescadores, and the island of Taiwan (Formosa). The communists proceeded with the task of eliminating isolated pockets of resistance and securing control to the frontiers (including Tibet). On June 25, 1950, the Korean War began, and the Chinese communists intervened in the conflict in late October. Two days after the outbreak of hostilities, the United States Seventh Fleet was dispatched to interdict the Taiwan Strait, thus placing Taiwan and the Pescadores beyond the reach of Chinese communist forces. This situation still obtains.

From 1951 to 1953 the People's Liberation Army was modernized, inflation was checked, and economic output was restored to the pre-1949 high. The "three-anti" (*san-fan*) campaign of 1951 and 1952 was followed by the "five-anti" (*wu-fan*) campaign of early 1952 (directed against the bourgeoisie in an urban equivalent of land reform), which netted the regime over $2 billion through fines and confiscations. A massive land redistribution was also carried out, accompanied by much bloodshed and violence. This redistribution paved the way for future collectivization. During this period the foreign policy of the People's Republic of China was essentially hard line, directed against "imperialism" in general and the United States in particular.

The CCP leadership apparently viewed Stalin's death in 1953 as the beginning of a new era in that the passing of the Soviet dictator eased Chinese fears of subordination to the Soviet Union. Moreover, party control over the mainland was nearly complete, and party leaders judged 1953 a propitious year for initiating the "transition to socialism." This drive, beginning with the first Five-Year Plan (1953 to 1957), paralleled significant changes in the pattern of Communist China's foreign relations. Thus in China's case the period of intensive socialist development and the period of the "thaw" were the same.

A constitution for the People's Republic of China, drafted by the party central committee, was unanimously ratified by the national people's congress on September 20, 1954. This document was to be applicable only for the transition period before socialism was achieved. The united front continued to operate, but it was to be progressively narrowed (eliminating the nationalists and petite bourgeoisie) through restrictions directed against the private sector of the economy. The new constitution designated the national people's congress the highest organ of state power, but all real power continued to reside in the CCP, with party rule constitutionally sanctioned by a party-dominated governmental structure.

Chinese communist influence abroad increased markedly during this period. The 1954 Geneva conference on Indochina allowed China to deal directly with the "imperialist" powers, and party leaders perceived such intercourse as tantamount to ratification of China's great-power status. The zenith of Chinese diplomacy in this period was Chou En-lai's triumph at the 1955 Bandung Conference, at which he not only approved of Asian neutralism, but also identified the People's Republic of China with the foreign-policy objectives of neutral Asian states.

Within China this period also saw the famous and short-lived explosion of discontent on the part of noncommunist as well as some communist intellectuals and officials in the "hundred-flowers" movement. As a result of severe criticism leveled against the CCP during May and early June 1957, the party launched an "antirightist" campaign to punish the dissidents. This campaign heralded the return to a domestic hard line.

In 1958, by means of the radical "great leap forward" and the people's commune movement, the CCP attempted to catapult China into the modern age literally overnight. In this period the party emphasized the sending of young people from the urban centers to the countryside and barren border areas such as Sinkiang and Tibet (the *hsia-fang* and *tun-tien* movements), and increased indoctrination ("socialist education") among key sectors of the population. Both the leap and the communes were failures, and 1960 to 1963 were grim years. The second Five-Year Plan (1958 to 1962) was never published, and the third Five-Year Plan was not scheduled to begin until 1966, three years later. It is generally agreed that China has only recently regained the level of "prosperity" that existed in 1957 (with a population increase since then of some 100 million).

Major events on China's periphery included the Quemoy crisis in 1958, suppression of the Tibetan revolt in 1959, the Sino-Indian border war of 1962, repeated armed clashes along the Russian Turkestan-Sinkiang border after 1963, the Vietnam conflict beginning in 1961, and the abortive coup by pro-Peking communists in Indonesia in 1965. As a result of such events and policies, the People's Republic of China has become increasingly isolated from the rest of the world.

ORGANIZATION AND MEMBERSHIP

The Chinese party is organized on the usual pyramidal basis of "democratic centralism." At the base are the lowest party units, the cells, which are grouped in local branch committees, and then in county (*hsien*) committees, which in turn are organized in provincial committees at the next level (including special municipalities, autonomous regions, and autonomous districts [*chou*]. The provincial committees are organized by region (north, east, northeast, northwest, southwest, and central south) and are headed by the national party congress, the highest party authority. The party congress elects a central committee (nearly 200 members at full strength), and from this body are drawn a military-affairs committee, a control commission, and the party secretariat, which governs the various departments of party work. The eighth party congress, which reelected the incumbent central committee, was held in 1956; the ninth congress had not yet met by the end of 1965, although the party statute calls for a congress at least every five years. On the basis of this delay Khrushchev before his ouster criticized Mao Tse-tung for continuing to hold his post as party chairman in contravention of the CCP statute.

Real power in the CCP rests in the twenty-one-member political bureau of the central committee, which in 1966 was made up of Mao Tse-tung, Lin Piao, Chou En-lai, T'ao Chu, Ch'en Po-ta, K'ang Sheng, Li Fu-ch'un, Teng Hsiao-p'ing, Liu Shao-ch'i, Chu Teh, Ch'en Yün, Tung Pi-wu, Ch'en Yi, Liu Po-ch'eng, Ho Lung, Li Hsien-nien, Li Ching-ch'üan, T'an Chen-lin, Hsü Hsiang-ch'ien, Nieh Jung-chen, and Yeh Chien-ying. Absolute authority, however, is wielded by an elite group of old-guard party leaders who form a seven-member "standing committee of the political bureau." Thus in 1966 the party was in fact rigidly controlled by Mao Tse-tung, party chairman; Lin Piao, minister of defense; Chou En-lai, premier of the state council; T'ao Chu, party propaganda chief; Ch'en Po-ta, head of the "cultural-revolution" group; K'ang Sheng, advisor to the "cultural-revolution" group; and Li Fu-ch'un, economic planner.

The most significant large-scale party purge since the founding of the People's Republic of China in October 1949 was the "three-anti" campaign of 1951 and 1952, a massive operation aimed at eliminating the "three evils" of corruption, waste, and bureaucratism in party and state agencies. Notable figures purged included Kao Kang, party boss of Manchuria (reportedly a suicide in prison); Jao Shu-shih, party boss of East China (fate unknown); P'eng Te-huai, minister of defense (stripped of power); and Huang K'o-ch'eng and others purged along with P'eng. Both Huang and P'eng remain on the central committee. Purges notwithstanding, the party elite has remained remarkably stable and cohesive over the last three decades. Twenty-odd years of civil war, together with experience in governing various areas with populations ranging from 100,000 to 100 million, has tempered and strengthened this already tightly knit group.

Other noteworthy features of the leadership of the Chinese party have been Mao Tse-tung's formulations of "new democracy" (a united-front "democracy" of national and petite bourgeoisie, peasants, and workers in which the CCP struggles for hegemony) and of "people's democratic dictatorship" (democracy for the "people" and dictatorship over the "nonpeople," who include such class enemies as counterrevolutionaries, revisionists, "feudal remnants," "wreckers of the socialist cause"), together with his obsession concerning contradictions in society and nature and his attempt to establish a cult of his "thought," as distinguished from Stalin's cult of "personality." In addition, the CCP leaders have emphasized both the cadre system and thought reform and have insisted that cadres, students, and even major officials at the various levels must engage in physical labor with the "masses."

At present the CCP is the largest communist party in the world. In 1961 Liu Shao-ch'i, chairman of the People's Republic of China, reported that the party had over 17 million members. Estimated membership in 1965 was 18 to 19 million. These figures do not include the tens of millions who belong to the Young Communist League (Ch'ing-nien Kung-ch'an Chu-i T'uan) and the Young Pioneers (Shao-nien Hsien-feng Tui). Over 80 percent of the present party members joined after the regime was established. The highly centralized nature of party authority, together with the continuity of the top elite, has facilitated control over the state as well as the party. However, Mao and the "old guard" have expressed concern over the resulting lack of dedication, confidence, and militance among the younger party members as well as among the the population at large.

According to the 1956 statute, party membership is open to any citizen eighteen or older who "works and does not exploit the labor of others, accepts the program and constitution of the party, joins and works in one of the party organizations, carries out the party's decisions, and pays membership dues." New members are admitted through a party branch on recommendation of two full members, acceptance by the local branch, and approval by the next higher party committee. If approved, the applicant is admitted to the party as a candidate and becomes a full member after a one-year probationary period.

As many urban workers as possible have been recruited into the CCP, but since China remains a predominantly agrarian state, the vast majority of members have always been peasants (once called the "rural proletariat," to meet objections that the CCP was a party without a proletariat). Little effort has been made in recent years to recruit intellectuals. Although the CCP was in fact founded by intellectuals, the current leadership has evinced suspicion and hostility toward them for over two decades.

A concerted, steady effort is made to interest youngsters in party activities (and more important, to infuse them with "the thought of Mao Tse-tung") from an early age. Over 50 million Chinese youngsters between the ages of nine and fifteen belong to the Young Pioneers. The Young Pioneers is under the direct leadership of the Young Communist League, for those between fifteen and twenty-five years of age, and this organization is directly controlled by the CCP. This system allows the party to effect maximum dissemination of propaganda and policy statements, to inculcate "correct" attitudes and habits into the next generation, to extend control and observation into home, school, and place of work, and to select only the proven and "politically pure" for elevation to the next rung on the party ladder. Also worthy of note is the Chinese communist cadre apprenticeship system, whereby a veteran cadre selects his eventual successor and proceeds to train him himself under close personal, as well as party, supervision.[1]

In the 1920s most CCP members worked in the Kuomintang, but a few joined other organizations which became fronts. Among them were the Practical Society, the Soul of Hainan, the New Army Society, the Ch'iung-yai Association, the New China Study Association, the New Yunnan Society, the Szechwan Revolutionary Youth, and the Reform Society. The most important fronts in the

1930s were the League of Left-Wing Writers (Left League), and the leagues of left-wing social scientists, playwrights, and artists.

In the 1940s the communists sponsored or infiltrated several minor political parties which continued under the control of the CCP's united-front-work departments. Seven such parties still exist:

The Kuomintang Revolutionary Committee, organized in 1948 in Hong Kong; the chairman is Mme. Ho Hsiang-ning.
The China Democratic League, organized in 1941; the chairman is Yang Ming-hsüan.
The China Democratic National Construction Association, organized in 1945, made up of industrialists and intellectuals working in industry; it has no chairman at present.
The China Association for Promoting Democracy, organized in 1946, with members drawn from educational and cultural circles; the present chairman is Ma Hsü-lun.
The Chinese Peasants' and Workers Democratic Party, originally formed in 1927 by T'an P'ing-shan under the name Third Party, with members drawn from medical circles; the present chairman is Chi Fang.
The China Devotion to Justice Party (Chih Kung Tang), established in 1947 from elements of a party founded in 1926 (this name was one used by Chinese Masons supporting Sun Yat-sen's efforts to overthrow the Ch'ing dynasty); the present chairman is Ch'en Ch'i-yu.
The September Third Society (Chiu-san Hsüeh-she), organized in 1945 and made up of intellectuals in scientific and technical work; the chairman is Hsü Te-hung.

Chinese communist friendship associations (some thirty in number) have been especially active recently in Cambodia, Pakistan, Congo (Brazzaville), Syria, Afghanistan, Nepal, Tanzania, and Mali. The CCP controls front organizations operating overseas through such groups as the Afro-Asian Solidarity Committee, under central committee member Liao Ch'eng-chih; the Asia-Africa Society, under central committee member Chou Yang; the Committee for the Promotion of International Trade, under Nan Han-chen; the Chinese People's Association for Cultural Relations with Foreign Countries, under Ch'u T'u-nan; and the Chinese People's Committee for World Peace, under Kuo Mo-jo.

## RELATION TO SOVIET LEADERSHIP

The CCP was organized by a representative from the Comintern's Far Eastern Bureau in Irkutsk. In 1922 this bureau moved to Khabarovsk, then to Vladivostok, and had a branch in Shanghai. It received instructions and funds through the West European Bureau in Berlin. A democratic-centralist structure was not established until 1927, since most CCP members were working semipublicly as a faction in the Kuomintang. However, Comintern representatives worked in Shanghai with the central committee, Soviet military and political advisors controlled communist factions in the Kuomintang, and the Soviet ambassador, L. Karakhan, attempted to control and coordinate activities of both Soviet advisors and CCP members in North China.

The major Comintern representatives sent to China were G. Voitinsky (1920-1927, purged in 1938), H. Sneevliet (Maring) (1921-1923, left the Comintern in 1924 to become leader of Left Socialist Party in the Netherlands), M. N. Roy (January-July 1927, expelled in 1929 with Brandler and Thalheimer), B. Lominadze (July-November 1927, led a move to depose Stalin in late 1930 and was purged in the mid-1930s), Heinz Neumann (September-December 1927, purged in the mid-1930s), Earl Browder (1928-1930, expelled in the late 1950s), Gerhart Eisler (1929-1930, now living in East Germany), Pavel Mif (Mikhail Firman) (1930-1931, purged in 1938), Hilaire Noulens (Paul Ruegg) (1930-1932, executed by the Kuomintang in 1932), and Li T'e (Albert Wagner, Otto Braun) (1933-1937, now living in East Germany). No Comintern representatives have been identified for the period 1937 to 1943. Several persons with similar functions under the control of the Soviet foreign affairs ministry worked in the Soviet embassy in Chungking and in Sinkiang. Among them were Apresoff (purged as a Trotskyist), Ouyanjak, Latoff, Bakulin, Karpov, and Dekanozov (purged with Beriia).

The two most prominent Soviet advisors to the Kuomintang were Borodin (Grusenberg) (died in 1952, perhaps a victim of the Jewish purge) and Galen (Blücher), commander of the Soviet Far Eastern Army (purged in 1938).

Chinese who attained prominence in the Comintern included Ch'en Tu-hsiu (elected to the first Comintern Executive Committee), T'an P'ing-shan (member of the Presidium during the seventh plenum), Hsiang Chung-fa (member of the Presidium during the ninth plenum and of the Executive Committee after the sixth congress), Ch'ü Ch'iu-pai (member of the Political Secretariat and the Executive Committee after the sixth congress), Li Kwang (member of the Executive Committee after the sixth congress), and Hsiu Yen and Cheng Chen (members of the International Control Commission after the sixth congress). Mao Tse-tung (in absentia), Chang Kuo-t'ao (in absentia), and Wang Ming were elected to full membership on the Executive Committee of the Comintern at the seventh congress; Po Ku (in absentia) and K'ang Sheng were elected candidates. Tu Ho-hsin became a member of the International Control Commission. Wang Ming was elected member of the Presidium and candidate in the Secretariat at the seventh congress.

Major figures in the Moscow leadership who were associated with the Comintern's Far Eastern Bureau were Otto Kuusinen, Palmiro Togliatti, and L. Magyar.

The CCP did not join the Cominform.

## THE SINO-SOVIET DISPUTE

Conflict between the Chinese and Soviet parties dates back to the early 1920s, but it was crystallized by Khrushchev's "de-Stalinization" speech to the twentieth party congress in 1956, which destroyed the myth of the infallibility of Soviet leadership. The Hungarian revolt, which brought the CCP into East European politics for the first time, was a direct consequence of de-Stalinization. In the same period the CCP supported Polish demands for greater autonomy within the communist bloc. These interventions, coupled with Mao's seniority in the communist movement, led the CCP to expect coequality with the Soviet party in determining international communist policy.

With the advent of Sputnik, the CCP demanded a militant policy against the West, while the Soviets did not share the Chinese belief that the military balance of power had shifted fundamentally in their favor. For a time these differences were contained. Although the jointly sponsored Moscow declaration of late 1957 was worded more strongly than Khrushchev's political report to the twentieth party congress, his three principles (peaceful coexistence, noninevitability of war, and peaceful transition to socialism) remained intact. The CCP's cosponsorship of this declaration in fact weakened the force of its later attacks on Soviet "revisionism."

In 1958 the CCP attempted to force the Soviet hand (as well as to probe the extent of the United States commitment in Taiwan) by renewed attacks on the offshore islands. The Soviet Union, however, stated that it would not intervene in the "continuing civil war," and when Khrushchev stopped in Peking on his return to the Soviet Union, after a state visit to the United States, he was given an extremely cool reception. This coolness probably also stemmed from P'eng Te-huai's alleged intrigue with Khrushchev against Mao's policies and leadership.

In mid-1960 all Soviet advisors and technicians were withdrawn from China on Khrushchev's orders. In addition, Moscow reneged on its earlier promise to provide China with a sample atomic bomb. Khrushchev had his final opportunity to take a stand in 1962, when the Chinese attacked India; he responded by supplying military aid to India and denouncing Chinese aggression. By the end of that year the polemic was in the open, and the

CCP began to pursue "splittist" tactics in other parties. At the end of 1965 the communist parties of ten countries were generally pro-Chinese: Albania, Indonesia, Japan, North Korea, Laos, Malaysia, New Zealand, Thailand, North Vietnam, and South Vietnam. Open splits occurred in Australia, Belgium, Brazil, Burma, Ceylon, Colombia, France, India, Lebanon, Mexico, Paraguay, Spain, and Switzerland. In addition, there were pro-Chinese factions in the communist parties of Austria, Ecuador, Nepal, and Peru.

Khrushchev's ouster allowed only a short hiatus in the polemics. Fundamental disagreements remained unresolved, and the CCP considers the present Soviet leadership to be of Khrushchev's identical persuasion, but infinitely more cunning. The Soviet party up to the end of 1965 had not replied in kind to Chinese charges, but neither had it made any concessions on matters of fundamental principle.

## FUTURE PROSPECTS

A distinction must be made between the prospects for the CCP and the prospects for China. With regard to the party, there is little likelihood that the CCP will be deposed in the foreseeable future, barring such unexpected developments as a major war. However, there is the possibility of serious intraparty conflict after Mao and the anticipated Liu Shao-ch'i interregnum pass from the scene. The successors to Mao and Liu may in fact follow an even harder line than their predecessors. The present aging elite perceives a loss of revolutionary élan on the part of many younger Chinese, who see an unsatisfactory present but have few if any memories of the Kuomintang era. In time this may turn the party away from its present militancy, but the short-run prospects for such a development are slight.

In the international arena the CCP has suffered a series of staggering setbacks, including the Indonesian debacle, anti-Peking coups in Africa, and Viet Cong defeats in South Vietnam. Moreover, there are indications of a growing awareness among noncommunist Asian states that mutual cooperation in military, economic, and political programs would be very useful in meeting the threat from the People's Republic of China. Finally, the CCP has been unable to "liberate" Taiwan, shake United States opposition to Chinese expansion, or to come to an agreement with the Soviet Union and her allies in the dispute.

Aside from these problems of the CCP, there are monumental problems that would have to be faced by any Chinese government, irrespective of political orientation. These include a population of some 730 million, which will reach 1 billion by 1985 if present trends continue, a lack of arable virgin territories that can be put under the plow, and insufficient capital for simultaneous development in agriculture and industry. Maoist dogmatism works against the formulation of flexible, pragmatic policies to deal with these problems. Although this dogmatism permits the CCP to maintain tight control, barring essential modifications in policy, the future bodes ill for the Chinese people.

## PARTY PRESS ORGANS AND RECORDS

The official newspaper of the CCP is the *Jen-min Kih-pao* (People's Daily). *Hung-ch'i* (Red Flag) is the theoretical journal of the central committee.

For laws, party and government directives and regulations, treaties, lists of party and governmental personnel, and major policy statements, see *Jen-min Shou-ts'e* (People's Handbook), Peking, Tak-kung Pao-she, 1950.

## CONGRESSES OF THE CCP

1st congress, July 1921, Shanghai
2d congress, July 1922, Shanghai
3d congress, June 1923, Kwangchow (or Canton)
4th congress, January 1925, Shanghai
5th congress, April-May 1927, Hankow
6th congress, June-July 1928, Moscow
7th congress, April-June 1945, Yenan
8th congress, September 1956, Peking

8th congress (second session), May 1958, Peking

## BIBLIOGRAPHY

Berton, Peter, and Eugene Wu: *Contemporary China: A Research Guide,* Stanford, Calif., Hoover Institution, 1967.

Brandt, Conrad, et al.: *A Documentary History of Chinese Communism,* Cambridge, Mass., Harvard University Press, 1952.

Compton, Boyd: *Mao's China: Party Reform Documents, 1942-1944,* Seattle, Wash., Washington University Press, 1952.

*Constitution of the Communist Party of China,* Peking, Foreign Languages Press, 1956.

*Constitution of the People's Republic of China,* Peking, Foreign Languages Press, 1954.

Mao Tse-tung: *Selected Works,* vols. I-IV, Peking, Foreign Languages Press, 1961-1965.

*The Polemic on the General Line of the International Communist Movement,* Peking, Foreign Languages Press, 1965.

Wilbur, C. Martin, and Julie Lien-ying How: *Documents on Communism, Nationalism, and Soviet Advisers in China, 1918-1927,* New York, Columbia University Press, 1956.

DENNIS J. DOOLIN
JOHN E. RUE

[1]. A cadre in China is not necessarily a party member, but is a party activist, the "transmission belt between the party and the masses," and is often more zealous and militant than a CCP member.

# COLOMBIA

The communist movement in Colombia originated in the mid-1920s with the formation of an informal "communist group" of young intellectuals and labor leaders. Its members were influential in creating the Socialist Revolutionary Party (Partido Socialista Revolucionario, PSR) in 1926 and in promoting its affiliation as a member of the Comintern two years later. Relatively few Colombian communists of the 1920s remained active in the movement for long. Most of the leaders of the new party deserted to the Liberal Party (Partido Liberal, PL) in 1929 and 1930, greatly reducing the effectiveness of the PSR. Charter member Guillermo Hernández Rodríguez, who obeyed Comintern instructions to transform the remnants of the PSR into the Communist Party of Colombia (Partido Comunista de Colombia, PCC) in July 1930, was expelled in 1932. Another founder of the PSR, Ignacio Torres Giraldo, was removed from office as secretary general of the party in 1939. For further discussion of the origins of the PCC, and of the dissident Communist Party of Colombia, Marxist-Leninist (Partido Comunista de Colombia, Marxista-Leninista, PCC-ML), founded in 1964, see *Latin America*.

## HISTORY

The Colombian party has seldom exerted significant influence in national affairs. It remained obscure and ineffectual until the mid-1930's, when the election of a reformist administration in Colombia and the Comintern's popular-front policy permitted it to cooperate with stronger political forces. The communists endorsed the government's program and were allowed to share in the leadership of the Workers' Confederation of Colombia (Confederación de Trabajadores de Colombia), which in 1938 became a founding member of the Workers Confederation of Latin America (Confederación de Trabajadores de America Latina). With the Hitler-Stalin pact of 1939, the party lost much of its labor base and its political respectability until the adoption of the Soviet wartime policy after the nazi attack again permitted communists to work closely with the dominant PL.

The high point of communist fortune in Colombia was reached in 1944. In that year the party adopted a new name, Social Democratic Party (Partido Social Democrático, PSD), polled some 30,000 votes to place about seventy-five candidates in office across the nation, and assisted in the communist takeover of the Workers' Confederation of Latin America. Within two years, however, the spectacular rise of the charismatic liberal politician Jorge Gaitán and a series of inept decisions by communist political leaders virtually destroyed the effectiveness and appeal of the communist movement in Colombia. In adversity, it split into squabbling factions. Eduardo Vieira White emerged as head of the largest group, which restored the original name of the party in 1947 but was subsequently unable to turn the bitter civil strife (known as *la violencia*) from 1948 to 1958 to its advantage, or after 1959 to apply the lessons of the Cuban revolution to the Colombian situation. In 1965 the party controlled a portion of the labor movement but lacked a popular following adequate either to make it effective at the polls or to win power by violence.

## ORGANIZATION AND MEMBERSHIP

According to United States estimates, the membership of the PCC in 1965 was 10,000 and that of the dissident PCC-ML was 2,000.[1] The Colombian communists maintain a substantial number of interlocking front groups. For a full discussion see *Latin America*.

## RELATION TO SOVIET LEADERSHIP

The PCC was represented at recent meetings of the international communist movement in Moscow and the last congresses of the Soviet party. For a discussion of the relations of the Colombian communists with the Soviet-directed international communist movement see *Latin America*. The PCC has endorsed the Soviet position, while the PCC-ML supports China in the ideological dispute.

## PARTY PRESS ORGANS AND RECORDS

The leading organs of the PCC are the irregular weekly *Voz proletaria* and the quarterly theoretical journal *Documentos políticos*. In the early 1960s the party was also responsible for printing the Spanish version of *Problems of Peace and Socialism* for distribution within Colombia.

The Colombian party maintains a modest publications program. Reports of the secretary general and of members of the executive committee usually appear in *Documentos políticos* and are occasionally issued separately as well. The party statutes and similar documents are ordinarily mimeographed for distribution only among the membership.

## CONGRESSES AND CONFERENCE OF THE PCC

The Colombian communists include congresses of the PSR in their numerical listing of party congresses. Information about the dates and frequency of the party congresses is incomplete and contradictory. They are listed below on the basis of Colombian and Soviet sources:

1st congress, August 1941
2d congress, August 1944
3d congress, December 1945
4th congress, May 1946
5th congress, July 1947
6th congress, August 1949
7th congress, April 1952
8th congress, December 1958
9th congress, June 1961
National conference, February 1963

BIBLIOGRAPHY

Communist Party of Colombia: *Treinta años de lucha del Partido comunista de Colombia*, Bogotá, 1961.

Vieira White, Gilberto: *Organicemos la revolución colombiana: Informe político al IX congreso del Partido comunista de Colombia*, Bogotá, 1961.

See also *Latin America*, refs. 1, 2, 13, 24.

ROLLIE E. POPPINO

1. U.S. Department of State, Bureau of Intelligence and Research, *World Strength of the Communist Party Organizations*, Eighteenth Annual Report, Washington, January 1966, p. 173.

# THE COMECON
*See* The Council for Mutual Economic Assistance

# THE COMINFORM
*See* The Communist Information Bureau

# THE COMINTERN
*See* The Communist International

# THE COMMUNIST INFORMATION BUREAU

The Communist Information Bureau (Informatsionnoe Biuro Kommunisticheskikh Partii), generally known as the Cominform, was set up in September 1947 at a secret meeting in Szklarska Poręba, Poland, attended by representatives of the communist parties of the Soviet Union, Bulgaria, Czechoslovakia, France, Hungary, Italy, Poland, Rumania, and Yugoslavia. A press release issued by the conference stated that "in view of the negative effect caused by the absence of contracts among the parties represented ... and taking into account the need for mutual exchange of experience, [they decided] to set up an Information Bureau.... The task of the Information Bureau will be to organize interchange of experience among the parties, and if need be, to coordinate their activities on the basis of mutual agreement."[1] Andrei Zhdanov, a close associate of Stalin, headed the Soviet delegation and did the most to promote formation of the new organization.

Although the Cominform was at first considered to be a revival of the defunct Communist International, in reality it proved to be quite different. Whereas the Comintern had been set up as a worldwide political party and operated under tight statutory rules, the Cominform did not claim to be a party and had no statute at all. In retrospect it appears that its main purpose was to oppose the spreading influence of the United States, and in particular to prevent the Eastern European countries that had recently come under communist domination from participating in the American-sponsored European Recovery Program. Poland and Czechoslovakia, who had intended to join this program, had to be persuaded to drop these plans.

According to the resolutions based on reports by Zhdanov and Władysław Gomułka (Poland), in the six Eastern European countries in which communist parties occupied the dominant or most important role in government, the primary task was to consolidate communist strength and leadership. The French and Italian parties were scolded for neglecting to seize power immediately after the war, when their strength and position would have permitted them to do so. The fact that in 1944 and 1945 the Soviet government had advised them against this step, in order not to expose its expansionist intentions too soon, was somehow forgotten.

The founding of the Cominform was the first step in the new Soviet "hard line" that led to the cold war. The United States, a wartime ally of the Soviet Union, now became the main enemy. Although the Cominform had no power to issue orders to its affiliated parties, its bimonthly *For a Lasting Peace, for a People's Democracy* was closely followed by all communists and regarded as an instruction sheet.

A second meeting of the Cominform parties, held in Yugoslavia in January 1948, continued the harangue against the United States and appointed the Soviet journalist P. F. Iudin as editor of the press organ.

By the time the third meeting convened, in June 1948, Yugoslavia was under Soviet attack because of Tito's refusal to submit the country to complete political and economic control by the Soviet Union. Accused of having taken "the road to nationalism," Yugoslavia was excluded from the Cominform. A Cominform statement appealed to the members of the Yugoslav party to get rid of "nationalist elements" in the party leadership (Tito) and to replace them with "internationalist" (pro-Soviet) leaders. However, these efforts to split the Yugoslav party and unseat Tito were defeated by the public outcry against Moscow's methods.

The seat of the Cominform was moved from Belgrade to Bucharest, and in November 1949 the Cominform held its last meeting. Its chief goal was to continue the fight against the "Tito-Ranković clique" in Belgrade. Stalin had intended this break with Yugoslavia as a punitive measure against the "nationalist deviationist" Tito and was convinced that the Yugoslav party would expel Tito and return to the Moscow fold. This did not happen, however, and Yugoslavia's defection became the first real crack in the communist monolith.

Stalin now embarked on the purge and execution of alleged Tito supporters in other communist-dominated countries, branding even the slightest opposition to his political and economic demands as "Titoism." Traycho Kostov in Bulgaria, Rudolf Slánský and Vlado Clementis in Czechoslovakia, László Rajk in Hungary, and many other prominent communists in these countries were tried for "Titoism" and executed. Only Gomułka in Poland managed to ride out the storm in prison.

In the April 17, 1956, issue of its press organ the Cominform announced its dissolution, stating that neither its composition nor its line of activities corresponded to the "new situation." Stalin's death in March 1953 had indeed created a new situation. In addition, the creation in 1949 of the Council for Mutual Economic Assistance (Comecon) and in 1955 of the Warsaw Pact, the Soviet counterpart of NATO, offered better opportunities for Moscow's control of its satellites. Khrushchev, the new ruler of the Soviet Union, considered the enlistment of Yugoslavia into these two organizations particularly important, and the Cominform was dissolved to prepare for the Soviet-Yugoslav rapprochement that had been begun by Khrushchev's visit to Tito in May 1955. Thus, like its predecessor, the Comintern, the Cominform was created and liquidated by *fiat* from Moscow.

See also *The Council for Economic Assistance* and *The Warsaw Treaty Organization*.

## PRESS ORGAN

The bimonthly *For a Lasting Peace, for a People's Democracy*, issued in several languages, began publication in Belgrade on November 10, 1947. After Yugoslavia was excluded from the Cominform in June 1948 it was moved to Bucharest. Its last issue appeared on April 17, 1956.

## MEETINGS OF THE COMINFORM

Founding meeting, September 22-27, 1947, Szklarska Poręba (Poland)
2d meeting, January 1948 (Yugoslavia)
3d meeting, June 1948
4th meeting, November 1949

## BIBLIOGRAPHY

Blanco, Tobio M.: *El Kominform, quinta columna del comunismo*, Madrid, 1948.

Hutton, J. Bernard: *Danger from Moscow*, London, 1960.

Nerman, Ture: *Kommunisterna: Fron Komintern till Kominform* (The Communists: From Comintern to Cominform), Stockholm, 1949.

Reale, Eugenio: *Nascita del Cominform*, Milan, 1958.

*The Soviet-Yugoslav Dispute: Text of the Published Correspondence*, London, Royal Institute of International Affairs, 1948.

Ulam, Adam B.: *Titoism and the Cominform*, Cambridge, Mass., 1952.

WITOLD S. SWORAKOWSKI

1. *For a Lasting Peace, for a People's Democracy*, no. 1, November 10, 1947, p. 1.

# THE COMMUNIST INTERNATIONAL

The Communist International (Kommunisticheskii Internatsional), or Third International, generally known as the Comintern, was founded by Lenin in March 1919 to promote world revolution. It was ostensibly an international organization of all communist parties and was to serve as the "general staff of world revolution," with the ultimate goal an "international soviet republic." In actuality, the Comintern's intended function was to break the complete isolation in which Lenin's new Soviet state found itself in the first stage of its existence.

## ORIGINS

Shortly after the outbreak of war in 1914, the Second (Socialist) International, in effect, disintegrated. The socialist parties in the countries at war patriotically supported the war efforts of their homelands. The old resolutions of socialist congresses that in case of war organized socialists must oppose credits for its continuation lost validity. The socialist parties in the neutral countries, without German, French, or British leadership, remained inactive.

Lenin, leader of the bolshevik wing of the Russian Social Democratic Labor Party, in exile in Switzerland, took advantage of the Second International's collapse and late in 1914 started to advocate the creation of a third International. It was to be based on "parties of a new type," meaning well-disciplined parties of professional revolutionaries that would play the role of "the vanguard of the proletariat." His attempt to impose this concept at an international conference of socialists at Zimmerwald (Switzerland) in September 1915 and at similar meetings failed. His ill fame as the "splitter" of socialist organizations prevented him from gaining wider influence in the international socialist movement during the war.

## HISTORY

The Russian revolution that overthrew the imperial government, and Lenin's return to Russia in April 1917, gave him occasion to renew his initiative for the creation of a third International. In the same month a conference of the bolshevik splinter of the Russian Social Democratic Labor Party passed a resolution directing its central committee "to proceed immediately toward the founding of the Third International."[1]

On December 26, 1917, six weeks after the bolsheviks assumed power, the new Soviet government issued a decree granting "two million rubles for the needs of the revolutionary international movement.... In consideration of the fact ... that the struggle against war and imperialism can lead toward complete victory only if waged on an international scale, the Soviet of People's Commissars considers it necessary to offer assistance by all possible means, including money, to the left international wing of the labor movement of all countries...."[2] The decree was signed by Lenin and by Trotsky as commissar of foreign affairs. On January 23, 1918, Yakov Sverdlov opened the third congress of soviets in Petrograd with the assurance that "there is no doubt that our socialist republic will start a revolutionary conflagration in every country of the world."

Early in 1918 supervision of the revolutionary activities in other countries was transferred to the Commissariat of Nationality Affairs, under the direction of Joseph Stalin. The presence in Russia of 2 million demoralized prisoners of war awaiting repatriation to all parts of Eastern and Central Europe, plus a few British, American, and Japanese prisoners and deserters and over 1 million refugees from Poland, the Baltic states, Bessarabia, and the Caucasus, provided Stalin with an unusual opportunity. Through extensive propaganda and lavish material aid bolshevik sympathizers were recruited in all the nationality groups. Within the framework of Stalin's commissariat, various "national commissariats" were set up to train communists who would be returning to their homelands to lead future communist movements there. Corresponding "red regiments" were created to "carry at the tips of their bayonets the liberation of the working class." Stalin's national commissariats did in fact form the nuclei of short-lived communist governments in Finland, Latvia, Estonia, Lithuania, Poland, Hungary, Slovakia, and some other countries. They also formed a number of the "parties" that founded and became members of the Comintern.

On December 19, 1918, an "international meeting" was held in Petrograd to prepare for a founding congress of the Communist International. Maxim Gorky, then an ardent supporter of bolshevism, chaired the meeting, and Grigorii Zinoviev (Apfelbaum) was the keynote speaker. He assured the audience: "I consider our present meeting as only a small prelude to the future great congress of the true Third International, which, I am convinced, will also meet in Petrograd."[3] However, an appeal issued at the same time for a revival of the Second (Socialist) International forced Lenin to act quickly. In January 1919 "representatives" of communist and socialist parties of Russia, Poland, Hungary, Austria, Latvia, Finland, the United States, and the Balkan Revolutionary Social Democratic Federation issued an invitation to communist and socialist parties and workers' organizations in thirty-nine countries to attend a founding congress of the Communist International in Moscow on March 2. Despite the international appearance of the invitation, of the nine signatories, two were Russian; three (Poland, Hungary, and Austria) signed in the name of "foreign bureaus" of their parties located in Russia; one signed as representative of the Bureau Abroad of the Latvian party; Reinstein, signing for the Socialist Workers Party of America, was a permanent resident of Russia; Rakovskii, who signed for the Balkan Socialist Federation, had once belonged to that federation, but at the time he was an official of the Soviet Commissariat of Foreign Affairs; and Sirola, in exile from Finland, was employed by Stalin's Finnish commissariat.

Thus the international appearance of the invitation was a hoax, with the deliberate misrepresentation of the identity of its signers intended to deceive the invited parties as well as world opinion. A socialist conference that met in Bern in February denounced the bolshevik attempt to create a third International as a further effort by Lenin to split the international labor movement and mislead the working class.

*Founding Congress*  The first congress of the Comintern, held in Petrograd on March 2-6, 1919, was attended by fifty-one delegates from thirty countries.[4] Only thirty-three of these delegates had voting rights, and of these thirty-three, thirteen were members of various communist parties inside Russia and eight were officials of Stalin's national commissariats and hence of the Soviet state. In addition, Lenin was assured of the votes of five "delegates from Finland," who were in fact residents of Russia after their unsuccessful attempt to impose communism in Finland. Thus only seven delegates arrived from abroad: two from Austria and one each from France, Germany, Norway, Sweden, and Switzerland. Although the delegate from Germany, Hugo Eberlein, had come to the congress with instructions to oppose the creation of a new international, under pressure from Lenin he abstained from voting when the congress passed the resolution founding the Communist International.[5] The Swiss delegate, Fritz Platten, had gone to Moscow without permission from his socialist party, and on his return his party expelled him. Thus Lenin's new international was far from a success. It was an extension of the international hoax started with the invitation. Nevertheless, heavily financed propaganda misrepresented the founding of the Communist International as a great achievement.

The first congress, chaired by Zinoviev, passed twenty-seven resolutions, including a verbose manifesto to the workers of the world, condemnation of the League of Nations as a "capitalist conspiracy," and a political platform opposing social democracy and advocating "dictatorship of the proletariat," expropriation of the bourgeoisie, and the "socialization" of industry. The congress also established an Executive Committee (sometimes referred to as the ECCI) which was to include several Russian members and one representative from each of seven major communist parties. Zinoviev became chairman and Karl Radek became secretary of the Executive Committee. In closing the congress Lenin assured the delegates that "the victory of the proletarian revolution in the entire world is certain. The founding of the International Soviet Republic will materialize."[6]

*Second Congress*  The second congress opened with a festival session in Petrograd on July 19, 1920, and closed in Moscow on August 7 in a joint session with the All-Russian central executive committee of soviets (the Soviet state parliament), the Moscow soviet, the All-Russian Council of Trade Unions, and the Moscow Factory Committee. Lenin and the Russian leadership had good cause to celebrate. Although three soviet republics had risen and fallen in Europe (Hungary, March 22-August 1, 1919; Bavaria, April 1-May 1, 1919; Slovakia, June 20-July 2, 1919) since the first Comintern congress, the Allies had withdrawn from northern Russia and Kolchak and Denikin had been defeated. The Red Army continued its advance toward Warsaw, with Germany its next objective. The economic crisis, social breakdown, and political upheavals in Central and Western Europe following World War I promised communist success. All this prompted Zinoviev to state at the opening of the congress that in the past year "the idea of 'democracy' has withered before our eyes and at the present moment is living its last days.... I assert with confidence that one year sooner or later, a little more patience, and we shall finally possess an International Soviet Republic, which will be guided by our Communist International."[7]

According to official figures and lists of delegates, forty-one countries were represented. Of the 169 delegates with voting rights, sixty-four represented Russia, the Ukraine, and other parts of the Russian Socialist Federal Soviet Republic and at least twenty-eight were members of various national commissariats, refugees, and other residents of Russia who aspired to represent communist parties that did not exist in their homelands. Only seventy-seven delegates—a minority—were actually from other countries.[8] This predominance of Russian communists and non-Russian residents of Russia both at the congress and in its Executive Committee made the "international," in effect, an adjunct of the Soviet government.

The first paragraph of the Comintern's statute adopted by the congress clearly formulated its purpose as "the overthrow of capitalism, the establishment of the dictatorship of the proletariat and of the International Soviet Republic." There was considerable controversy, however, over Lenin's Twenty-one Conditions for Admission, which imposed "democratic centralism" and strict party discipline on the member parties. The subordination of member parties, as "sections of the Communist International," to the Comintern Executive, whose majority of Russian members were Soviet government officials, produced such dissension in some parties that several prominent leaders and their contingents withdrew. The net result, however, was that all elements opposed to communist party discipline were eliminated from the international communist movement. Trotsky rightly said after the adoption of the Twenty-one Conditions that "we have created one solid International Party of Communists which has its branches in various countries."[9]

The congress devoted much attention to the labor-union movement. Following a report by Karl Radek, it decided to support the creation of the Red International of Labor Unions (Profintern), a new labor organization intended to challenge the old socialist labor organization, which had been revived the year before.

Less than two weeks after the congress closed, the Red Army was decisively defeated at the gates of Warsaw, and a few days later Budennyi's army, whose political commissar was Stalin, was defeated in the south of Poland, bringing to an end the great hope that "over the dead body of Poland leads the road to world revolution." In Russia economic difficulties, the collapse of the transportation system, and finally the Kronstadt uprising forced Lenin to abandon "war communism" and inaugurate the New Economic Policy, a return to limited capitalism, and a semifree market—measures which failed to stave off a calamitous famine in parts of Russia in the second half of 1921.

These developments were no encouragement for other nations to follow the Soviet example, and by the end of 1920 the communists were having considerably less success in recruiting new members. Nationalist sentiment was increasing in many countries, and despite growing unemployment and labor riots in a number of Western and Central European industrial centers, the communists lost ground to the social democrats. In March 1921 an uprising encouraged by Comintern representatives in Germany failed because of lack of support from the workers. In Italy

Mussolini's fascists began to have greater appeal to the workers than the communists.

*Third Congress*   The third congress met on June 22-July 12, 1921. The title of Trotsky's report, *The International Situation: A Study of Capitalism in Collapse*, obviously expressed communist wishful thinking. Lenin, however, evaluating the situation more realistically, felt that it was time for the parties to "go to the masses." Explaining that the Comintern must apply "flexible tactics," he urged all communists to cooperate with the socialist parties at the membership level, bypassing leadership of these "enemy parties," and subvert their organizations by infiltration. This tactic, known as the "united front from below," was to be abandoned and readopted at frequent intervals throughout the Comintern's history.

At the end of December the Comintern and the Profintern, whose first congress had been held in July, issued a joint appeal containing detailed instructions on united-front-from-below strategy. At the same time the Comintern Executive Committee also recommended a first step toward a "united front from above." This was in response to the Vienna Socialist Union (also known as the Second-and-a-Half International), which had been founded in February 1921 by a group of Austrian and German "socialists of the center" who—for the sake of "proletarian unity"—sought a merger of the Second and Third Internationals. The Comintern Executive reluctantly agreed to meet in Berlin in April 1922 to negotiate with the leaders of the Vienna Union and the Second International, but, in line with Leninist "flexibility," continued to denounce them in united-front-from-below propaganda as "social patriots," "traitors of the working class," and "lackeys of the bourgeoisie."

This April conference resulted in the creation of a "committee of nine," which was to continue negotiations for unification. However, after the trial and conviction of a group of Russian social revolutionaries in Moscow in June 1922 the representatives of the Second International withdrew from the committee, putting an end to the negotiations. The socialist organizations of the Vienna Union, also alienated by the Soviet government's harsh measures against dissenting socialists, returned to the social democratic parties of their respective countries, and by May 1923 the Vienna Union had ceased to exist.[10]

Before the fourth congress convened, the Comintern Executive had to hold two plenums to deal with organizational questions, internal strife in several member parties, and opposition to Comintern tactics. The first meeting of the "enlarged" Executive, which included representatives from each of the member parties not represented in the Executive Committee, was held on February 24-March 4, 1922, and approved the previous decisions concerning united-front-from-below tactics. Such "plenums" were later held between congresses, and during the Stalin period they actually replaced the congresses.

*Fourth Congress*   The fourth congress met on November 5-December 5, 1922. Of the twenty commissions appointed, eleven were to deal with internal difficulties and the quarrels of member parties with the Comintern. The Comintern had by now developed a sizable apparatus, including several "regional bureaus" and front organizations, and its high-handed relations with the member parties were producing increasing difficulties and opposition. The "federal" basis of selecting the Executive, whereby each member was designated by the party he represented, was changed to direct election by the congress of a twenty-four-member Executive Committee and a Chairman (Zinoviev). In response to the demands for broader representation of the non-Russian parties, the new Executive was to include only three Russians instead of five.

This was the last Comintern congress that Lenin attended. Shortly afterward he became ill and was unable to continue his personal participation. The triumvirate that emerged to replace him—Stalin, Zinoviev, and Lev Kamenev—became involved in internal Russian party fights and left Zinoviev a relatively free hand in running Comintern affairs. However, the international situation was becoming increasingly unfavorable for communism. The economic crisis in most countries had been brought under control; in Italy a fascist government had forced the communists underground; in Germany and France there was a political swing to the center; in the Balkans communism was outlawed and lost ground. "Democratic pacifist" tendencies in the member parties became steadily stronger, and the Comintern apparatus applied all its force to stem this tide of "rightist deviations." Although the resolutions of the third plenum, held a year later, dealt with a definition of the "workers' and peasants' government," the struggle against religion, and similar less important subjects, the matter of rightist deviations in individual parties was dealt with extensively in private sessions, the Comintern's first moves toward secrecy.

In September 1923 the communists in Bulgaria attempted an uprising in Sofia, which was put down by the government with great losses for the communists. In October a Comintern-inspired rising in Hamburg turned into a costly defeat for the communists. Both these local uprisings were from their very inception doomed to failure, but as both had been approved by the Comintern leadership, they resulted in a strong controversy with Moscow.

*Fifth Congress* The fifth congress met in Moscow on June 17-July 8, 1924. Although the number of non-Russian delegates with voting rights was considerably greater than at previous congresses, the 108 votes of the Russian party plus the votes of the Ukraine, Belorussia, Armenia, Azerbaidzhan, Georgia, the Communist Youth International, and several illegal parties whose delegates had become permanent residents in Russia placed a handsome majority at Stalin's disposal.

Lenin had died on January 21, and Stalin lost no time in imposing his own brand of "democratic centralism" on the member parties. All parties were instructed to adopt "everything in Russian bolshevism that has international significance." This started the "bolshevization" of all member parties. Nineteen commissions were appointed to draft "theses" and resolutions and to "resolve" internal differences in eight parties. The Comintern representatives sent to individual parties as advisors were now to participate in sessions of the party leadership and express their own (the Comintern's) views, opening the way to widespread accusations within member parties of rightist and leftist "deviations" from Stalin's "new line."

Until Lenin's death Stalin had been only a minor figure in the Comintern, and his views had been discounted by the older leaders of other parties. His election to the Presidium now enabled him to participate in all meetings of the Comintern and its commissions. For the first time a Comintern commission acted as a party court, and its verdict, upheld by the congress, expelled a prominent leader of the French party, Boris Souvarine, from the Comintern Executive Committee. In the next few years, with or without Stalin's personal participation, various "territorial commissions" deposed the leaders of many parties for "deviations" and replaced them by Stalin's choices, who often commanded only the slimmest minority in the parties in which they were installed. "Bolshevization" of the member parties was continued, and by the end of 1926 the Comintern had "corrected" the party leadership in China, Czechoslovakia, England, France, Germany, Norway, and the United States, and such old-line communists as Arkade Maslow and Ruth Fischer of Germany, David Wijnkoop of Holland, and Boris Souvarine of France had been excluded from their parties.

According to its statutes the Comintern was to have a congress every year. However, the next congress was not held until 1928, and in the interim Stalin availed himself of 116 meetings of the Presidium, ninety-four meetings of the Secretariat, sixteen meetings and six plenums of the Executive Committee, and an unknown number of *ad hoc* commissions to maneuver against Trotsky, oust the leaders of Trotskyist factions in the member parties, and install his own supporters in the Comintern. At the seventh plenum, late in 1926, Zinoviev was removed from the chairmanship and all other Comintern functions on charges of Trotskyism and was replaced by Nikolai Bukharin in the new capacity of general secretary; Viacheslav Molotov became an alternate member of the Presidium. Less than a year later Trotsky and Voja Vujovich of Yugoslavia were expelled from their positions as alternate members of the Comintern Executive.

In the meantime Soviet and Comintern leaders had been expressing increasing concern about the danger of war and of an "imperialist attack against the Soviet Union, the fatherland of the proletariat." After the failure in the labor field of the Anglo-Russian Trade Union Committee and the failure in the political field of the Chinese party's attempted cooperation with the Kuomintang, the Comintern denounced the united front from above as a right deviationist compromise with social democracy and returned to the united front from below, which it had abandoned at the fourth congress for lack of results. Social democracy and the left bourgeoisie were branded the chief enemies of the working class, a policy that was to have unfortunate ramifications in Germany and Italy.

In France the united-front-from-below practice came to an end because socialist and leftist bourgeois parties refused further cooperation with the communists in parliamentary elections. The French Communist Party was divided, with the followers of Trotsky on the "right," the old guard in the center, and a growing group of young leaders on the left. This last group had Stalin's support. The crisis was resolved by the party's central committee, which decided to enter its own candidates in the first round of the approaching elections and to seek cooperation with socialist and other leftist parties only in the runoff. This new device became known as the "class-against-class" tactic. The ninth plenum of the Comintern, held in February 1928, approved this new political line and confirmed the expulsion from the French party of the Trotskyist leaders Albert Treint, Suzanne Girault, and their associates (see *France*).

*Sixth Congress* At the sixth congress, which held forty-eight sessions from July 17 to September 1, 1928, Bukharin, reporting on the international situation and the tasks of the Comintern, outlined three periods in the world communist movement. The "first period," characterized by a sharp crisis in the capitalist system and direct revolutionary action of the proletariat, culminated in communist strength in 1921 and ended with the defeat of the proletarian uprising in Germany in October 1923. During the "second period," which lasted until early 1928, capitalism recovered, developed considerably through innovations, and reached partial stabilization. At the same time the Soviet Union was able to recover from the civil-war depression and make great progress in socialist reconstruction, and although the international proletariat had been weakened by previous defeats, some communist parties had grown in strength and increased their influence on the masses. The start of the "third period"—in Bukharin's view—was marked by emerging conflicts among the imperialist powers and new internal tensions in the capitalist states as the outcome of their economic and industrial development; this period heralded new wars among the imperialists and increased the danger of imperialist attack against the Soviet Union. In the resolution that resulted from Bukharin's report all communist parties were instructed to oppose any preparation for an "imperialist war" and in the event of an attack on the Soviet Union to provide "revolutionary support" by starting civil wars in their own countries.

The congress also adopted a new program— over which a special program commission had labored for almost three years—expressing the communist view of the world situation and setting forth new plans for a world revolution. The class-against-class tactic, confirmed by the congress as the new political line for all Comintern members, meant that the struggle against social democracy and the bourgeois left would be stepped up. These two groups again were pointed out as the "main enemies of the working class," with both "black" fascism (Italian) and "brown" fascism (German) considered the lesser dangers. Later, with the aid of hindsight, Moscow confessed this evaluation to have been a gross mistake.[11] In Germany, for example, the communist struggle against the social democrats created a diversion that certainly helped Hitler to come to power.

A lengthy resolution defined "bourgeois-democratic revolutions" in colonial and semicolonial countries as the first step in a socialist revolution and instructed communists in these areas to assist in throwing off imperialist domination and establishing independent republics in preparation for the second step, a dictatorship of the proletariat. This resolution remained in effect even after the dissolution of the Comintern as a basic directive on communist activities in Asia, Africa, and Latin America.

The congress elected a fifty-nine-member Executive Committee, with Stalin, Molotov, Dmitrii Manuilskii, Aleksei Rykov, and Solomon Lozovskii as the Russian representatives. Bukharin was reelected general secretary, but a few months later, as a result of his complaint that Stalin's purges were damaging to the international communist movement, he was replaced by Molotov. Trotsky, Ruth Fischer, Albert Treint, Suzanne Girault, David Wijnkoop, and several other old communists who had appealed expulsion from their parties were branded traitors to the "proletarian cause." (See *France, Germany, The Netherlands*.)

In making Trotskyism an international issue Stalin provided a specific rallying point for dissenting factions in nearly every party; moreover, by depriving most parties of their old and experienced leaders, he severely impaired the efficiency of communist efforts on the international scene. Nevertheless, in the period following the sixth congress the charge of "Trotskyism" became a catchword for all who opposed Stalin. In May 1929 the Comintern Presidium deposed Jay Lovestone and Benjamin Gitlow from the leadership of the Communist Party of the United States and replaced them with Stalin's choices, Earl Browder and William Foster (see *United States of America*). Supported in the Comintern by Molotov, Stalin now gained even tighter control of the international communist movement. He could count on the faithful support of certain exiled foreign communists who permanently resided in Moscow: Wilhelm Pieck and Walter Ulbricht from Germany (since early 1933), Otto Kuusinen from Finland, Palmiro Togliatti from Italy, and Georgi Dimitrov from Bulgaria (after his exchange return from Germany following the famous Reichstag fire trial in Leipzig in the fall of 1933). Earl Browder and William Foster from the United States, Dolores Ibarruri from Spain, Maurice Thorez from France, William Gallacher and Harry Pollitt from England, and Klement Gottwald from Czechoslovakia were also champions of the "Stalin line" in the international communist movement. They remained faithful to Stalin until his death in 1953, and with the exception of Ibarruri, they all played leading roles in the communist parties of their homelands after 1945, some of them (Pieck, Ulbricht, Togliatti) until the 1960s.

After the July 1929 plenum official Comintern records were selectively "abridged," but the published reports and resolutions that did appear indicate that subsequent meetings and plenums were concerned primarily with the "imminent danger" of an armed attack on the Soviet Union by the Western European powers and the struggle against the social democratic parties in all countries. Germany was given particular attention as the most likely place for a new communist victory. However, a resolution of February 1930 charging the German social democrats with increased cooperation with the "fascists" did not even mention Hitler's National Socialist Workers' Party as a danger.

The Comintern was in fact confronted with a dilemma concerning Germany. In April 1922 in Rapallo, the Soviet Union and Germany had concluded a political alliance which was later extended to clandestine military cooperation, and Germany was producing arms and training soldiers on Soviet soil, for the Soviet Union as well as for herself. Collaborating closely with the German army brass, the Soviet leaders could not afford to attack Hitler's national socialists, who were supported by the German generals. In this situation the Comintern, echoing official Soviet policy, avoided the subject of national socialism in Germany. In August 1931 the German communists, faithfully following the Comintern's class-against-class policy, voted with the nazis in a referendum to defeat the socialist government of Prussia. The same year they succeeded in creating a leftist faction in the socialist party which split away and joined them. Under these circumstances the German party's proposals to the socialists for a joint strike in July 1932 were met with distrust and refusal. The last opportunity to stop Hitler—by forming a "grand coalition" of antinazi forces in the November 1932 elections—was passed up. The German and Soviet party leaders made no secret of their intended political game: by letting Hitler come to power at a time when his party was still a minority party, a "revolutionary situation" would be created in Germany, and in a future anti-Hitler revolution the strong Communist Party of Germany would take the lead and be victorious. Hence, now that Hitler's victory was clearly in sight, it was time to start the campaign for a "soviet socialist Germany."[12]

By the end of August 1932, demonstrating remarkable agility in following this oblique reasoning, Kuusinen broke the Comintern's silence on the national socialists and for the first time labeled them a danger. In a report that occupied the first three sessions of the twelfth plenum, he conceded that "for some time the Communist Party of Germany underestimated the national socialist movement and partly neglected the struggle against it; certainly, it would be incorrect to assert that this neglect by the Communist Party of Germany created the possibilities for the growth of fascism, because this growth had its objective causes."[13] However, even this cautious charge of "neglect" on the part of the German communists was belied by the fact that no German communist leaders were purged, and Georgi Dimitrov, the Comintern representative in Berlin during this period (and later one of Stalin's staunchest supporters), was given a hero's reception by the Kremlin after his conviction by the nazis and subsequent exchange to the Soviet Union.

By March 1933, after Hitler's rise to power, the Communist Party of Germany had been practically decimated: 4,000 party functionaries had been arrested after the Reichstag fire on February 27, and although the communists had polled 4,700,000 votes in the March 5 elections, the eighty-one deputies elected were either arrested or fled the country. Eight months later, again adroitly following Stalin's zigzag policy, Kuusinen claimed at the thirteenth plenum that it was the socialists who were to blame for Hitler's rise to power. A year earlier he had assured the twelfth plenum that the full economic crisis and growing ranks of unemployed in Germany made a communist victory certain; now he assured the thirteenth plenum that several capitalist countries were approaching catastrophic economic collapse and that this "revolutionary crisis" must be exploited. A resolution recommended continuation of the struggle against the social democrats, again bypassing the "social-fascist" party leaders, with a return to the united-front-from-below policy.

During the next two years of worldwide economic depression there were strikes and workers' demonstrations in England, the United States, Poland, Czechoslovakia, and even fascist Italy. Separate socialist and communist counterdemonstrations provoked in February 1934 by profascist organizations in Paris had led a few months later to a "popular front" of the French communists, socialists, and left bourgeoisie to combat the far right. However, the Schutzbund uprising in Austria (February 1934) and the brutally suppressed insurrections in Spain (October 1934) had resulted in heavy losses for both the socialists and the communists, and by the summer of 1935 only twenty-six communist parties were still in legal operation.

*Seventh Congress* The seventh congress, which did not meet until July 25-August 21, 1935, was obviously influenced by the recent defeat of communism in Germany and by reports of the first successes of the popular front in France. Dimitrov delivered a seven-hour report on "the fascist offensive and the tasks of the Communist International in the fight for the unity of the working class against fascism," and Wilhelm Pieck, in a report supporting past Comintern policies, admitted that the German communists had "underrated the Hitler movement" and had labored under the "absolutely false conception that all bourgeois parties are fascist, that there are no two methods of bourgeois rule." Regardless of the fact that the Comintern had not only initiated this "absolutely false conception," but had enforced its application by all parties, such bashful admission of gross political error was unprecedented in Comintern proceedings.

During the discussion of Pieck's report several delegates demanded that the Comintern stop interfering in the internal affairs of member parties, and according to the ensuing resolution, the Comintern was now "to proceed, in deciding any question, from the concrete situation and specific conditions obtaining in each particular country, and as a rule to avoid direct intervention in internal organizational matters of the Communist Parties."[14] After more than ten years of Stalin's strong-hand rule this was a remarkable development. However, it was somehow lost afterward in the loud popular-front propaganda, and it was not until almost twenty years later that Togliatti returned to this concept of "polycentrism."

The congress stressed the need for a "united front on a national as well as an international scale," that is, a return to the previously condemned united front from above. The long-denounced social democrats were now presented as welcome allies in the struggle against fascism, although the instruction for cooperation included only those "organizations that fight against the reformist policy" and did not extend to the "reactionary sections" of the social democratic parties. In the final sections of the resolution based on Dimitrov's report, however, the real purpose of the popular-front tactic was disclosed as preparation for "the second round of proletarian revolutions," which, after the popular front had served its purpose, were to be directed against those who were allies in the popular front.

The popular front was successful for some time in France, and similar coalitions in other countries produced some temporary results (see *Latin America*). However, owing to the Comintern's conspicuous secrecy after the seventh congress, contact with all but the few parties that were still in legal operation was seriously hampered.

The apparent reversal of Moscow's attitude toward Nazi Germany and the conclusion of the Ribbentrop-Molotov pact in August 1939 took all the communist parties by surprise. Stalin, eager to show his friendship toward Hitler, returned to him German communists who had been given asylum in the Soviet Union but were critical of the Stalin regime and policies; from "the fatherland of the proletariat" they went straight to execution or nazi concentration camps. Walter Ulbricht, praising the Hitler-Stalin collaboration and the new Soviet line, concluded in the Comintern's new organ *Die Welt* that "whoever makes intrigues against the friendship of the German and Soviet peoples is an enemy of the German people and will be branded as an accomplice of English imperialism."[15]

This change in Comintern policy, imposed for Moscow's benefit, resulted in disillusionment in both the upper and lower echelons of all communist parties. Wholesale resignations reduced some parties to skeleton organizations. After the outbreak of World War II, acts of sabotage and defeatist propaganda by the remnants of the communist parties in the Western democracies, in accordance with the Comintern's instructions to oppose the "imperialist war," were of material assistance to Germany, which was unhampered by an active communist party. As a result, public opinion drove the communists even further underground in the Allied countries and most of the neutral countries, and cost them still more members and nearly all their remaining influence.

Hitler's attack on the Soviet Union in June 1941 and the overnight transformation of the Soviet Union into a member of the Allied powers saved many parties from complete liquidation. Communists everywhere immediately rallied to support the Allied war effort in aid of the Soviet Union. However, the Comintern's role as "general staff of world revolution" and the odium of past Comintern interference in the affairs of other countries had become a burden to Soviet foreign policy. As a demonstration to the United States and England that he intended no further interference in the affairs of other states, Stalin closed down the Comintern. In May 1943, in violation of its statute, the Presidium voted to dissolve the Communist International. The member parties dutifully ratified this decision, and some changed their names and took on the guise of cultural or political societies. The Communist International disappeared as an institution directing the world communist movement. However, world revolution has remained as much an aim of the Soviet Union as when it was first advocated by Lenin.[16]

## ORGANIZATION AND MEMBERSHIP

According to the principle of "democratic centralism" outlined by Lenin's Twenty-one Conditions for Admission to the Comintern, all member parties were to submit to the decisions of the Comintern congresses and, between congresses, to the decisions of the Comintern's Executive Committee. The Executive was at first elected on a federal basis, with each party elected to participate in the Executive designating its own representative. In 1922 this was changed to direct election by the congress. After the first congress, for more efficient operation, the Executive Committee elected a "small bureau" of five members, later increased to nine. In 1921 this bureau was renamed the Presidium; by 1928 it had increased to twenty-nine members and had become the policy-making body of the Comintern.

The current business of the Comintern was first conducted by its chairman and secretary. In 1922 the fourth congress established a Secretariat, consisting of five members of the Executive. In 1926 this body was increased to nine members, renamed the Political Secretariat, and given broader powers. From 1922 to 1928, the period of the Comintern's broadest activities, there was also an Organizational Bureau, composed of seven members of the Executive. The Comintern's Control Commission, which supervised the financial operations of the organizations and dealt with disciplinary matters, became quite important after the fifth congress, when Stalin started his purges in the Comintern and its member parties.

In addition to these subdivisions of the Executive Committee, the Comintern developed a large bureaucracy in Moscow and abroad. To assist policy-making bodies of the Executive in handling the complicated affairs of communist parties all over the world, so-called *Ländersekretariats* (country secretariats) were established in Moscow. They dealt with the day-to-day matters of the individual member-parties and were composed of nationals from the respective countries and Russians. Some of these country secretariats were set up on a regional basis (for example, for the Anglo-Saxon countries, Far Eastern countries, Latin American countries, etc.). In some cases corresponding regional "bureaus" abroad were created. Among the most important and active of these were the Western European Bureau, based first in Vienna and later in Berlin, the Latin American Bureau in Buenos Aires, and the Far Eastern Bureau at first in Irkutsk and later in Khabarovsk and Vladivostok, with a very active branch in Shanghai. The activities of these bureaus were kept quite secret; some of the special Comintern emissaries who directed them were also Soviet intelligence agents.[17] Liaison between the Comintern and the more important parties was handled by Comintern representatives, who were assigned whenever and wherever the need arose to "advise" on policy.

The composition of its founding congress was in large measure typical of the "international" representation at all Comintern congresses. The published membership figures for 1935 indicate the difficulty of assessing actual membership in the Comintern at any point. According to the official minutes of the seventh congress, there were seventy-six affiliated parties, nineteen of which were "sympathizing parties." This term is not defined in Comintern publications, but according to the *Soviet Encyclopedia of History*, the seventy-six parties had a total membership of 3,141,000 of which 785,000 lived in "capitalist countries"; moreover, fifty of these parties had been "chased underground" and hence may not have been operative in their own countries. The official minutes of the seventh congress do not list the delegates but state that sixty-five parties were represented. The *Soviet Encyclopedia of History* mentions "fifty-seven communist parties and also several international organizations, such as the Red Aid, the Communist Youth International, the Red International of Labor Unions, and others."[18] These "international organizations," which include the Comintern's International Control Commission and the Comintern Executive itself, do bring the total to sixty-five, but even the "fifty-seven communist parties" include such minor parties as the People's Revolutionary Party of Tuva.[19]

After the seventh congress a number of new communist parties were founded, especially in Latin America, and joined the Comintern. At the time of its dissolution in 1943 the Comintern supposedly had sixty-six member parties.

## PRESS ORGANS AND RECORDS

Immediately after its founding the Comintern developed very active information and propaganda work through its own information office, which was reorganized on several occasions and adjusted to the need of Comintern activities. In addition, the agitation and propaganda (*agitprop*) agencies of the member parties reproduced and distributed Comintern material in their respective countries. The larger parties (such as those of Germany, France, Britain, Italy, the United States, and Mexico) had their own publishing houses, which were charged with producing and distributing materials originating in the Soviet Union as well as their own material.

The main ideological organ of the Executive Committee, *Communist International*, began publication in 1919 in Petrograd, in Russian, German, French, and English; short-lived editions in Czech, Spanish, Chinese, and Danish-Norwegian were added later. Each of these editions was designed for its own prospective audience. For example, of the two English-language versions published from 1935 to 1940, the London edition was designed for Britain and the English-speaking colonies in Asia and Africa and the New York edition was designed primarily for the United States and Canada.

For the communist and procommunist press in Europe and in some British and French colonies *International Press Correspondence*, also known as *Inprecorr*, was published in English, German, and French (and in 1925 and 1926 in Italian). After Hitler's rise to power the German edition had to be relocated and appeared at different times under different names (*Rundschau* [Basel] from 1932 to 1939 and *Die Welt* [Stockholm] from 1931 to 1941). After 1938 the English edition changed its title to *World News and Views*. This press service, delivered gratis to noncommunist newspapers and journalists, was intended particularly to provide communist staff members on noncommunist newspapers with the opportunity to slip communist views and information into the "bourgeois" press.

The Comintern also issued a large number of bulletins. During the second to fifth congresses and the fourth enlarged plenum of the Executive such bulletins appeared daily, some in as many as four languages, and contained detailed information on the sessions.

The periodical publications of the Comintern's affiliated mass organizations, such as the Profintern, the Communist Youth International, and the Peasants' International, are listed in the articles on these organizations in this *Handbook*.

Until the summer of 1929 the stenographic records of all Comintern congresses and plenums were published in Russian, and most also appeared in official translations into German, French, English, and Spanish. After 1929 only abridged records were issued. A full record of the seventh congress was to be published in Russian, but it never appeared. For a list of all known records of congresses and meetings of the Comintern and its front organizations in twenty-two languages see Witold S. Sworakowski, *The Communist International and Its Front Organizations: A Research Guide and Checklist of Holdings in American and European Libraries*, Stanford, Calif., Hoover Institution, 1965.

## CONGRESSES, PLENUMS, AND MEETINGS

Not all Executive Committee meetings were publicly announced, and the following list includes only those brought to public attention by publication of their decisions or resolutions. "Enlarged" Executive Committee plenums included representatives of member parties which were not otherwise represented in the Executive Committee.

1st (founding) congress, March 2-6, 1919, Petrograd
2d congress, July 19, 1920, Petrograd; July 23-August 7, 1920, Moscow
3d congress, June 22-July 12, 1921, Moscow
Executive Committee meeting, December 27-28, 1921, Moscow
1st plenum, February 24-March 4, 1922, Moscow
Executive Committee meeting, May 19, 1922, Moscow
2d plenum, June 7-11, 1922, Moscow
4th congress, November 5-December 5, 1922, Petrograd-Moscow
3d plenum, June 12-23, 1923
4th plenum, July 12-13, 1924
5th congress, June 17-July 8, 1924
5th plenum, March 21-April 6, 1925
6th plenum, February 17-March 15, 1926
7th plenum, November 22-December 16, 1926
8th plenum, May 18-30, 1927
9th plenum, February 9-25, 1928
6th congress, July 17-September 1, 1928
10th plenum, July 3-19, 1929
11th plenum, March 26-April 11, 1931
12th plenum, August 27-September 15, 1932
13th plenum, November 28-December 12, 1933
7th congress, July 25-August 21, 1935
Executive Committee meeting, November 6, 1939

## BIBLIOGRAPHY

Borkenau, Franz: *The Communist International*, London, Faber & Faber, 1938; also published as *World Communism: A History of the Communist International*, Ann Arbor, Mich., University of Michigan Press, 1962.

Borkenau, Franz: *European Communism*, London, Faber & Faber, 1953.

Hulse, James W.: *The Forming of the Communist International*, Stanford, Calif., Stanford University Press, 1964.

James, Cyril B.: *World Revolution, 1917-1936: The Rise and Fall of the Communist International*, London, Secker & Warburg, 1937.

*Kommunisticheskii Internatsional: Kratkii istoricheskii ocherk* (The Communist International: A Short Historical Outline), Moscow, Institut Marksizma-Leninizma pri TsK KPSS, 1969.

Kun, Bela (ed.): *Kommunisticheskii Internatsional v dokumentakh: Resheniia, tezisy i vozzvaniia kongressov i plenumov IKKI, 1919-1932* (The Communist International in Documents: Resolutions, Theses and Appeals of the Congresses and Plenums of the ECCI [Executive Committee], 1919-1932), Moscow, Partiinoe Izd-vo, 1933.

Lazić, Branko M.: *Lénine et la IIIe Internationale*, Neuchâtel, Bacconière, 1951.

Lozovskii, A. (ed.): *Istoriia Kommunisticheskogo Internatsionala v kongressakh* (The History of the Communist International by Congresses), parts 1-6, Moscow, "Proletarii," 1929-1930.

Nollau, Günther: *International Communism and World Revolution: History and Methods*, London, Hollis & Carter, 1961.

Sworakowski, Witold S.: *The Communist International and Its Front Organizations: A Research Guide and Checklist of Holdings in American and European Libraries*, Stanford, Calif., Hoover Institution, 1965.

Tivel, A., and K. Kheimo (comps.): *10 [desiat] let Kominterna v resheniakh i tsifrakh: Spravochnik po istorii Kominterna* (Ten Years of the Comintern in Resolutions and Figures: A Reference Book on the History of the Comintern), Moscow, Gosizdat, 1929.

Trotsky, Leon: *The Third International after Lenin*, New York, Pioneer, 1936.

Ypsilon (Johann Rindle and Julian Gumperz): *Pattern for World Revolution*, Chicago, Ziff-Davis, 1947.

WITOLD S. SWORAKOWSKI

1. A. Tivel and K. Kheimo (comps.), *10 let Kominterna v resheniiakh i tsifrakh: Spravochnik po istorii Kominterna*, Moscow, 1929, p. 9. This volume is based on the official records of the Comintern; its introduction is signed by the Propaganda and Publications Office of the Comintern, which gives the information contained in the volume the official approval of the Comintern. The Soviet party's recent "short historical outline" (*Kommunisticheskii Internatsional: Kratkii istoricheskii ocherk*, Moscow, Institut Marksizma–Leninizma pri TsK KPSS, 1969) makes no mention of this volume; in fact, it contains only a few references to Stalin, with the apparent intent of minimizing his role in the international communist movement between the two wars.

2. *Sobranie uzakonenii i rasporiazhenii rabochego i krestianskogo pravitalstva*, no. 8, 1917, p. 119 (official gazette of the Soviet government); for an English translation see James Bunyan and H. H. Fisher, *The Bolshevik Revolution, 1917-1918*, Hoover War Library Publication no. 3, Stanford, Calif., 1934, p. 285.

3. *Sovetskaia Rossiia i narody mira*, with a preface by Maxim Gorky, Petrograd, Gosizdat, 1919, p. 11. This pamphlet, which also appeared in German and French translations, has been overlooked in most writings about the founding of the Comintern. It is noteworthy that Lenin and Trotsky did not attend, and this meeting is not mentioned in Soviet writings about the Comintern.

4. Tivel and Kheimo, *op. cit.*, pp. 26-27.

5. Ossip K. Flechtheim, *Die Kommunistische Partei Deutschlands in der Weimarer Republik*, Offenbach a.M., 1948, p. 57.

6. *Der erste Kongress der Kommunistischen Internationale: Protokoll der Verhandlungen in Moskau vom 2. bis zum 19. März 1919*, Petrograd, Kommunistische Internationale, 1920, p. 311.

7. *The Second Congress of the Communist International: Proceedings...*, Moscow, Communist International, 1920, p. 16.

8. Figures are from Tivel and Kheimo, *op. cit.*, pp. 49-51. Tivel, who had access to official Comintern records, published more reliable lists of delegates than those contained in the proceedings of the congress, which contained no mention of the parties that were illegal at that time in their home countries.

9. *The Second Congress of the Communist International: Proceedings...*, p. 444.

10. For details see G. D. Cole, *A History of Socialist Thought*, vol. IV, New York, St. Martin's Press, 1958, pp. 680ff.

11. *Sovetskaia istoricheskaia entsiklopedia*, vol. VII, Moscow, 1961, col. 759.

12. *Kommunisticheskii Internatsional*, pp. 329-331, 347-348, 359.

13. *XII plenum IKKI: Stenograficheskii otchet*, vol. I, Moscow, 1933, p. 34.

14. *Seventh Congress of the Communist International: Abridged Stenographic Report*, Moscow, 1939, p. 566.

15. *Die Welt* (Stockholm), February 2, 1940.

16. For information on the international communist movement after 1965 see the *Yearbook on International Communist Affairs*, for 1966 and the following years, Stanford, Calif., Hoover Institution.

17. Walter G. Krivitsky, *In Stalin's Secret Service: An Exposé of Russia's Secret Policies by the Former Chief of the Soviet Intelligence in Western Europe*, New York, Harper, 1939.

18. *Sovetskaia istoricheskaia entsiklopediia*, vol. VII, col. 762.

19. Tuva, also called Tannu Tuva, is an area of about 75,000 square miles bordering Outer Mongolia. The *Great Soviet Encyclopedia* does not give the population. In 1914 the Imperial Russian government detached the area from Outer Mongolia and created a separate protectorate. During the civil war in Russia from 1918 to 1921 it was occupied by the Red Army. In August 1921 the area declared itself the Tannu Tuva People's Republic, and in 1922 the People's Revolutionary Party was created and became the ruling party of the republic. In August 1944, at the request of the "small khural," a kind of "people's representation," the republic was incorporated into the Soviet Union as the Tuva Autonomous Region.

# THE COMMUNIST YOUTH INTERNATIONAL

The Communist Youth International[1] (Kommunistische Jugend-Internationale) was founded at a youth meeting in Berlin on November 20-26, 1919, as a continuation of the pre-1914 International Union of Socialist Youth Organizations (Internationale Verbindung Sozialistischer Jugendorganisationen). During the war most member organizations of this union had become inactive, but its directing body, the International Bureau in Zurich, carried on limited pacifist activity influenced by Lenin, then residing in Zurich.

Local socialist youth organizations had sprung up before the turn of the century in the Netherlands, Belgium, Austria, and France, but the first national associations were founded only after 1900. On August 24-26, 1907, during the Stuttgart congress of the Second (Socialist) International, twenty delegates of youth associations from thirteen countries founded the International Union of Socialist Youth Organizations, generally known as the Socialist Youth International.

The establishment of a soviet government in Russia in 1917 had great influence on the leftist elements of youth organizations in other countries. The bolshevik promises and slogans sounded very attractive, and the creation in Russia of a large youth organization following bolshevik ideology swayed some of the revived youth organizations to similar ideas.

In December 1918 the International Bureau of the Socialist Youth International, under the leadership of Willy Münzenberg, moved from Zurich to Berlin. Following Münzenberg's arrest by German authorities, the reactivated Zurich group initiated the calling of an international socialist youth congress. On May 29, 1919, the Executive Committee of the Comintern, which had been founded two months earlier, issued an appeal to all "proletarian" youth organizations, asking for their cooperation in creating a Communist Youth International. In addition, the Comintern appointed a commission to prepare for a founding congress. Georgii Chicherin, an official of the Soviet Commissariat of Foreign Affairs, and Lazar Shatskin, an official of the Comintern Secretariat—both well over the age of thirty, and hence hardly "youth" representatives—played the leading roles in this commission.

A congress of communist youth organizations was called for August 1919 in Budapest, where the communist regime of Béla Kun was in power. Before the delegates could reach Budapest, however, the Béla Kun regime was ousted. The congress was held instead in Vienna on August 25-26, with youth representatives from Russia, Germany, Poland, Italy, and Hungary. On August 26 all participants were arrested, and the conference was not concluded. However, it had managed to elect a "provisional committee," which called a congress of communist youth representatives for November in Berlin. The congress finally convened on November 20, with twenty delegates representing Russia, Germany, Austria, Switzerland, Sweden, Poland, Denmark, Norway, Hungary, and Rumania. Delegates from Italy, Spain, and Czechoslovakia arrived later. Thus, despite great difficulties, the Communist Youth International was created, with the purpose of promoting the revolutionary movement among the youth of all countries, in close cooperation with the Comintern and the local communist parties. The destruction of the bourgeois society and state was indicated as the path to victory for communism. The Berlin congress adopted a statute and program, and an executive committee was elected, with its seat in Berlin. Willy Münzenberg became general secretary.

During its first year the Communist Youth International conducted extensive organizational activities. Communist youth organizations were created in several countries. In other countries, the socialist youth associations which remained under strong social-democratic influence were split by communist factions, and new communist associations were created. Special attention was given to strengthening youth organizations in those countries where the communists had to operate illegally. At first Berlin was headquarters, and subsecretariats were created in Vienna, Basel, Stockholm, and Moscow. In 1921 headquarters were moved to Moscow. In addition, regional conferences of communist youth leaders were arranged in several countries.

Thus the first year was perhaps the most successful. With this expansive activity, however, came the first misunderstanding with the Comintern. The first session of the Youth International executive committee in June 1920 defined the relationship of the Youth International to the Comintern as follows: "The Communist Youth International, while keeping its organizational independence, is a part of the Communist International."[2] The Comintern Executive Committee obviously disagreed with this formulation; at its own meeting on August 17, 1920, it adopted a resolution establishing quite a different relationship between the two organizations: "The Communist Youth International is a part of the Communist International, and as such subordinates itself to the decisions of the congresses of the Communist International and to the political directives of its Executive Committee, and at the same time independently conducts its work in directing, organizing, strengthening, and expanding the Youth International."[3]

Nevertheless, Münzenberg, who directed this work from Germany, to a large degree considered himself strong enough—with the support of German youth militants—to disregard the advice of the Moscow subsecretariat to call the second congress of the Youth International in Moscow. Instead he announced that it would be held in Jena, Germany, on April 7, 1921. The Comintern Executive insisted that the congress be moved to Moscow, where it could meet under better conditions. The congress convened in Jena, and despite protests from the majority of the participants, the Comintern declared it to be unofficial. Just as the local police were about to disband the meeting, the congress was suspended, and a new one (still the second) was called for July 9, 1921, in Moscow. The failure of this attempt to remove the Youth International from the Comintern's direct influence assured Moscow's control of its future activities.

Between its founding in November 1919 and its dissolution by the Comintern in May 1943, the Communist Youth International held six congresses, and its executive committee, presidium, and bureau met in more than thirty sessions. It faithfully followed the bizarre political line of its parent organization, cooperating on the ever-changing united-front tactic, adopting bolshevization of its membership, participating in the struggle against Trotsky and "Trotskyism," adapting itself to the popular-front tactic, and accepting the Hitler-Stalin pact. But it did not escape the vicissitudes of the Stalin purges. Its founders and most active members, including V. T. Chemodanov and R. M. Khitarov, were purged and executed during the "period of Stalin's cult of personality."[4] Many foreign youth leaders were also liquidated during these purges. Münzenberg survived these years as a political exile in France, but he too died under mysterious circumstances.

## PRESS ORGANS

In 1919 the former socialist monthly *Jugend-Internationale* became the official organ of the Communist Youth International. Another publication, *Internationale Jugend-Korrespondenz*, which was started at the same time as a hectographed instruction sheet, developed into a printed periodical, issued three times monthly, from which communist youth publications in various countries reprinted desired items.

For a listing of over 200 books and pamphlets published by and about the Communist Youth International see Witold S. Sworakowski, *The Communist International and Its Front Organizations: A Research Guide and Checklist of Holdings in American and European Libraries*, Stanford, Calif., Hoover Institution, 1965, pp. 402-434.

## CONGRESSES

1st congress, November 20-26, 1919, Berlin
2d congress, April 7-10, 1921, Jena, Berlin; July 9, 14-24, 1921, Moscow
3d congress, December 4-16, 1922, Moscow
4th congress, July 15-24, Moscow
5th congress, August 20-September 18, 1928, Moscow
6th congress, September 25-October 10, 1935, Moscow

## BIBLIOGRAPHY

*Geschichte der Kommunistischen Jugend-Internationale*, vol. I, *Von den Anfängen der proletarischen Jugendbewegung bis zur Gründung der KJI*; vol. II, *Gründung und Aufbau der Kommunistischen Jugend-Internationale*; vol. III, *Der Kampf um die Massen, vom 2. zum 5. Weltkongress der KJI*, Berlin, Jugend-Internationale, 1929-1930; vol. II also appeared in Russian as Alfred Kurella, *Ot Berlina do Moskvy, 1919-1921* (From Berlin to Moscow, 1919-1921), Moscow, 1931.

Nasonov, I.: *Istoriia KIM, v kratkom izlozhenii* (The History of the CYI, in Summary), Moscow, 1930.

Tschitscherin [Chicherin], Georgij: *Skizzen aus der Geschichte der Jugend-Internationale*, Berlin, 1921.

WITOLD S. SWORAKOWSKI

1. The name Young Communist International, often used for this organization, stems from an incorrect translation of the German name. For an explanation of this error see W. S. Sworakowski, *The Communist International and Its Front Organizations: A Research Guide and Checklist of Holdings in American and European Libraries*, Stanford, Calif., Hoover, Institution, 1965, pp. 42-43.

2. Alfred Kurella, *Geschichte der Kommunistischen Jugend-Internationale*, vol. II, *Gründung und Aufbau der Kommunistischen Jugend-Internationale*, Berlin, Jugend-Internationale, 1929, p. 224.

3. *Ibid.*, p. 226.

4. *Sovetskaia istoricheskaia entsiklopediia*, vol. VII, Moscow, Gosizdat, 1961, col. 779.

# COSTA RICA

The communist movement in Costa Rica originated in 1929, when a young intellectual, Manuel Mora Valverde, formed the Communist Party of Costa Rica (Partido Comunista de Costa Rica, PCCR). Another prominent figure in the party during its early years was the Venezuelan exile Rómulo Betancourt. Manuel Mora was still head of the party in 1965. For further discussion of the circumstances in which the PCCR was formed see *Latin America*.

## HISTORY

The PCCR, which enjoyed legal status and complete freedom of action during the first nineteen years of its existence, was unique among Latin American communist organizations in the early 1930s in the mildness of its political program. It was also unique in Costa Rica in its interest in the working class. Until the late 1940s no other party sought to build a strong labor following. For a few years during and after World War II the communists collaborated with the national administration, exerting considerable influence on the government and gaining control of much of the labor movement.

In keeping with the wartime trend toward "national" communist parties, the Costa Rican communists changed the name of their organization to Popular Vanguard Party (Partido Vanguardia Popular, PVP) in June 1943. By 1948 the PVP had grown to some 3,000 members and had seven deputies in the national congress. With the revolution of that year, however, the party's ties with the regime were severed, its legal status was cancelled, and its influence and following declined rapidly. Many Costa Ricans who might otherwise have supported the PVP were now drawn to José Figueres' noncommunist leftist National Liberation Party (Partido Liberación Nacional). The communists continued after 1948 to operate with comparative freedom but were never able to regain their lost prestige or influence in national politics.

## ORGANIZATION AND MEMBERSHIP

In 1965 United States sources estimated PVP membership as 400.[1] After losing its legal status in 1948, the PVP attempted to participate in elections through a succession of front parties, with limited success. It also operates a range of propaganda front groups. For a full discussion see *Latin America*.

## RELATION TO SOVIET LEADERSHIP

The Costa Rican party affiliated with the Comintern about 1934 and became a full member in 1935. It has been represented at recent meetings of the international communist movement in Moscow and at the congresses of the Communist Party of the Soviet Union. For a discussion of other aspects of the PVP's relation to the international communist movement see *Latin America*.

The Costa Rican party has been militantly pro-Soviet in the ideological controversy with Communist China.

## PARTY PRESS ORGANS

The Costa Rican communists have limited press facilities. The only party publication to appear with reasonable frequency is the weekly long known as *Adelante* and renamed *Libertad* in 1963.

## PARTY CONGRESSES

There is little information on the congresses of the Costa Rican party, which appears to have met quietly and at fairly regular intervals in the postwar period. The ninth congress was held in 1962. A tenth congress was scheduled for 1964 but had apparently not met by 1965.

## BIBLIOGRAPHY

See *Latin America*, refs. 1, 2, 13, 24.

ROLLIE E. POPPINO

1. U.S. Department of State, Bureau of Intelligence and Research, *World Strength of the Communist Party Organizations*, Eighteenth Annual Report, Washington, January 1966, p. 150.

# THE COUNCIL FOR MUTUAL ECONOMIC ASSISTANCE

When the United States launched the Marshall Plan for economic assistance to wartorn European countries in 1948, the Soviet government forbade Czechoslovakia and Poland from accepting American aid. Instead, Moscow promised to provide her satellites with all necessary assistance. For this purpose an economic conference in Moscow in January 1948 created the Council for Mutual Economic Aid, more widely known as CMEA or Comecon. The founding members of the council were Bulgaria, Czechoslovakia, Hungary, Poland, Rumania, and the Soviet Union; soon after, Albania and the German Democratic Republic joined. During its first ten years the council was little more than a discussion forum at which future reforms and policies were considered. In those years Soviet aid took the form of credits to some of the member states for purchases in the Soviet Union.

Events in Poland and Hungary in October and November 1956 persuaded the Moscow leadership that more positive economic measures had to be taken if the communist bloc was to survive its economic crises and internal pressures. In December 1959, at a council meeting in Sofia, the first statute of the organization was adopted. Surprisingly, this organization of countries, each of which observed the principle of majority rule, incorporated into its bylaws veto rights which entitled any individual member state to abstain from implementing council decisions that were deemed harmful to its interest. In recent years Poland and particularly Rumania have made frequent use of this veto right. At the Sofia meeting the member states also signed an additional treaty authorizing the Comecon to conclude agreements, to acquire, lease, and lend property, and to be represented in court as a juridical person. In addition, offices and officials of Comecon agencies in the several member states were accorded diplomatic immunity.

On the basis of the 1959 statute and later agreements, the organizational structure of the Comecon has grown to sizable proportions. The highest authority of the organization is the Council, composed of representatives of the associated states. The Council is supposed to meet twice yearly; up to the end of 1965 there had been nineteen sessions. The Council appoints a secretary who is its top executive. Representatives of the member countries can be called to attend meetings as needed. All members have permanent representatives at the seat of the organization who may act on their behalf. A Bureau of Economic Planning and some twenty permanent commissions analyze all aspects of the economies of member states and on the basis of their analyses make recommendations to the Council. Six semi-autonomous organizations direct current transnational operations in the fields of electric power, freight and transportation, nuclear research, and product standardization. The most important of these organizations is the International Bank for Economic Cooperation in Moscow, which had a founding capital of 30 million gold rubles. Since it began operation in 1964 the International Bank has issued short-term credits and served as a clearinghouse for trade payments among member states.

The major controversy confronting the Comecon has revolved around the Marxian principle of "socialist division of labor," by which designated member states have been assigned to manufacture certain products which other members are then obliged to cease manufacturing. Since all of the Soviet satellites are far from self-sufficient in raw materials and all are lacking to some degree in plant capacity and skilled-labor resources, the Moscow promoters of this policy insist that specialization by each country in a limited field of production (for example, Czechoslovakia, automobiles; Poland, tractors; East Germany, tools) will yield better results for the entire economic community than would the manufacture of all products by all members. Only the Soviet Union is considered fully self-sufficient and thus able to manufacture all products. It is obvious that this plan makes the communist-dominated states economically interdependent and integrates them into the "socialist economy" under Soviet leadership. It also deters the satellites from economic relations with the West and makes them increasingly economically dependent on the Soviet Union. The policy has met with resistance from certain member states (particularly from Rumania) which want to retain their economic independence.

Since 1960 the Comecon has developed rapidly into an organization similar in some respects to the Common Market of Western Europe. But whereas the Common Market concentrates most of its efforts on removing customs barriers and improving the methods and channels of marketing, the Comecon has emphasized the expansion and allocation of industrialization, production, and distribution. In its early years the Comecon attracted the cooperation of the communist-ruled Asian states—China, Outer Mongolia, North Korea, and North Vietnam. However, after the Sino-Soviet rift came out into the open during the twenty-second congress of the Communist Party of the Soviet Union in October 1961, Albania declined to participate further in Comecon meetings and activities, and China, North Vietnam, and North Korea ceased to participate as "observers." At the beginning of 1965 only Outer Mongolia, a Soviet satellite since the 1920s, retained status as an "associate member" of the Comecon; later that year Yugoslavia was accorded the same status in the organization. In spite of its defiance of Soviet leadership and its refusal to pay annual dues, Albania has not been expelled: formally it is still a full member of the Comecon.

An English translation of the Comecon's statute is contained in Michael Kaser's *Comecon: Integration Problems of the Planned Economies*, London, Oxford University Press, 1965, pp. 181-187. For more detailed information on the Comecon see also:

Faddeev, Nikolai V.: *Sovet Ekonomicheskoi Vzaimopomoshchi* (The Council of Mutual Economic Assistance), Moscow, Ekonomika, 1964.

Staar, Richard F.: *The Communist Regimes in Eastern Europe: An Introduction*, Stanford, Calif., Hoover Institution, 1967. (Chapter on the Comecon.)

Uschakow, Alexander: *Der Rat für gegenseitige Wirtschaftshilfe Comecon*, Cologne, Wirtschaft und Politik, 1962. (Includes a broad collection of documents.)

WITOLD S. SWORAKOWSKI

1. The Council for Mutual Economic Assistance is

mentioned in several articles of this *Handbook*. Because it is an important conduit of Soviet economic policy, supported by communist parties, this brief summary of its organization and functions has been added for the convenience of the reader.

# CUBA

The pioneer popularizer of Marxist thought in Cuba in the first half of the 1880s was Enrique Roig y San Martín, but he apparently gained his knowledge mainly from anarchist sources. Until the end of the nineteenth century the names Karl Marx and Friedrich Engels were hardly known in Cuba; the great revolutionary heroes and teachers were Mikhail Bakunin, Enrico Malatesta, Petr Kropotkin, and other anarchist leaders and writers. In 1885 the anarchists founded a workers' circle in Havana. By 1892 a labor congress in Havana had been captured by the anarchists, who remained the dominating influence in the labor movement until the late 1920s.

Cuban reformist socialism was founded in the early 1890s by a noted intellectual, Diego Vicente Tejera. He formed a short-lived Cuban Socialist Party (Partido Socialista Cubano) in 1899, the year after the collapse of Spanish rule, and an equally short-lived Popular Party (Partido Popular) the following year, but he died in 1903 with little to show for his efforts. After several more false starts, the Workers' Party of Cuba (Partido Obrero de Cuba) was formed in 1904 as an independent labor party; it came out in 1905 for a full socialist program and changed its name to Socialist Workers' Party (Partido Obrero Socialista). This is generally considered the first Cuban socialist party in the direct line of communist ancestry. Its leading figure, Carlos Baliño, was also one of the founders of Cuban communism twenty years later.

The socialists fought a losing battle against the anarchists; only small, isolated socialist groups survived World War I. After the bolshevik revolution of October 1917 in Russia the Socialist Group of Havana (Agrupación Socialista de La Habana) was split into "left" and "right" wings, corresponding to their sympathy for the new communist doctrine. In 1923 the left wing, headed by Carlos Baliño, broke away to form the Communist Group of Havana (Agrupación Comunista de La Habana). Other communist groups sprang up in Guanacaboa, San Antonio de los Baños, Manzanillo, and one or two other places. A student leader, Julio Antonio Mella, joined the Havana communist group in 1924.

## HISTORY

The first congress of the Communist Party of Cuba (Partido Comunista de Cuba, PCC) was held in August 1925, a month after the inauguration of President Gerardo Machado y Morales. It was attended by only thirteen delegates, among them Carlos Baliño, Julio Antonio Mella, and Yunger Semjovich, a delegate from the Hebrew section of the Havana group, later better known as Fabio Grobart. Since the largest single group in Havana numbered only twenty-seven at this time, at its founding the party was still very small. A leading role seems to have been played by a Mexican representative, Enrique Flores Magon. The first congress elected José Miguel Pérez was quickly deported to the Canary Vilaboa as organization secretary. The Communist Youth League (Liga Juvenil Comunista) was not formed until 1929.

*The Machado Regime: 1925 to 1934* The Machado regime immediately cracked down on both the anarchist-dominated labor movement and the newborn communist party. Pérez was quickly deported to the Canary Islands, his birthplace, and was replaced as general secretary by José Peña Vilaboa, who lasted about a year. Mella was arrested and went on a famous nineteen-day hunger strike in prison. After his release in December 1925 he went into exile. His assassination in Mexico City three years later, when he was twenty-six, made him the movement's legendary martyr. Baliño, the oldest of the founding fathers, died in 1926 at the age of seventy-seven. Another outstanding intellectual, Rubén Martínez Villena, joined the party in 1927 but was forced by illness to go to Moscow in 1930. The general secretary from 1927 to 1932 was apparently Jorge Vivó, later a professor of social sciences at the University of Mexico.

In general the period from 1925 to 1930 was one of relentless persecution and extremely slow growth. The leadership passed from one hand to another as Machado's police caught up with the more prominent communists. Nevertheless, since the anarchist labor leaders were equally persecuted, a communist trade-union leader, César Vilar, succeeded the anarchist Alfredo López, who was assassinated in 1927, as general secretary of the outlawed trade-union center, the Cuban National Labor Federation (Confederación Nacional Obrera Cubana).

A communist-led one-day general strike in March 1930 and a student demonstration in September 1930 signaled the opening of a new stage in the anti-Machado struggle. In the next three years, as this struggle intensified, the communists succeeded in breaking out of their isolation and achieving a much wider influence. Accepted by all the other anti-Machado groups as loyal allies, they concentrated on organizing industrial enterprises, especially the sugar mills, and on forming "peasant leagues." After returning from Russia in May 1933, Martinez Villena took over effective leadership of the party. Machado was overthrown in August 1933 as a result of a general strike which brought increasing United States pressure for his removal. Because the communist leadership could not believe that the United States would really permit Machado to fall, it accepted a bid from the government to call off the general strike in return for Machado's belated capitulation to the workers' economic demands. To the communists' surprise, however, the strike went on without them, and Machado was forced to flee the country. The victorious anti-Machado forces regarded the communist efforts to call off the general strike as treason, and the communists were never again able to regain their confidence. This split decisively influenced communist policy and prospects for years to come.

The Comintern soon condemned the ill-fated deal with Machado and blamed the Martínez Villena leadership for the "error." Francisco Calderío, a communist trade-union leader from Manzanillo in Oriente province, was brought to Havana to take over the top leadership. Calderío, who took the name Blas Roca, was elected party general secretary at the second congress in April 1934. The new leadership that accompanied him maintained its control of the party for over a quarter of a century. Among its outstanding members were the brothers Aníbal and César Escalante; the trade-union leaders César Vilar, Lázaro Peña, and Ursinio Rojas; Joaquín Ordoqui, a former railroad worker; Salvador García Agüero, a former teacher; as well as Manuel Luzardo Severo Aguirre and Carlos Rafael Rodríguez, a rising young intellectual. In the background as the party's *éminence grise* hovered the only party founder to survive in the top leadership, Fabio Grobart.

*The First Batista Regime: 1934 to 1944* In September 1933 an army coup led by sergeant-typist Fulgencio Batista, soon promoted to colonel, put in office a short-lived government headed by Ramón Grau San Martín. Though the new regime was radically nationalistic and put through drastic social and economic reforms, it was violently opposed by the communists. In line with the Comintern's third-period policy in the early 1930s (see *The Communist International*), the Cuban communists demanded nothing less than "a workers' and peasants' government." In imitation of Russian practice, "soviets" were set up in outlying agrarian districts, the most famous of which was at Realengo 18. Opposed by the United States, beset by the communists, and weakened by internal divisions, Grau San Martín's government fell in January 1934. Grau was replaced as president by Colonel Carlos Mendieta, though the real power was held by the head of the armed forces, Colonel Batista. In March 1935 a general strike to overthrow the Mendieta-Batista regime was forcibly suppressed. Although the communists had originally opposed the strike as premature, they were caught up in it, and in the general repression which followed its failure they were again driven underground.

At just this point, however, the Comintern instituted its new popular-front policy. The communists first made overtures for a popular front to the exiled Grau San Martín, who had formed the nationalist-reformist Cuban Revolutionary Party (Authentics) [Partido Revolucionario Cubano (Auténticos)], but they were rejected. They then turned to Batista as their partner, and here they were more successful. The first sign of a Batista-communist alliance came in 1937 with the open appearance of an ostensibly popular-front party, the Revolutionary Union Party (Partido Unión Revolucionaria, PUR), headed by a well-known communist intellectual, Juan Marinello. On May 1, 1938, Batista permitted the publication of a communist newspaper, *Hoy*, edited by Aníbal Escalante. The PCC itself was legalized on September 25, 1938. Batista also enabled the communists to reorganize the trade-union movement, which had been outlawed as a result of the 1935 general strike, and the Workers' Confederation of Cuba (Confederación de Trabajadores de Cuba) was formed in January 1939, with Lázaro Peña as its secretary general. In return, as early as 1938 the communists recognized Batista as the national leader and extolled him as "no longer the focal point of reaction, but the defender of democracy."

The alliance with the communists enabled Batista to make the transition from a virtual military dictator to a constitutionally elected president. A constitutional convention early in 1940 wrote a new constitution, and elections were held in July 1940. The communists formed part of the socialist-democratic coalition which supported Batista's candidacy and elected ten members to the chamber of deputies and more than a hundred municipal councillors. The PUR and the PCC merged in 1940 as the Revolutionary Union Communist Party (Partido Unión Revolucionaria Comunista, PURC). When the noncommunist group which had originally joined the PUR withdrew from the PURC in January 1941, the PURC became a purely communist party.

World War II brought Batista and the communists into the closest community of interests. In March 1943 President Batista took a communist, Juan Marinello, into his cabinet as minister without portfolio. When Marinello decided to run for senator in the 1944 elections, he was replaced by another communist, Carlos Rafael Rodríguez. Thus Lázaro Peña was the first Latin American communist to head a national trade-union movement, and Marinello and Rodríguez were the first Latin American communists to become cabinet ministers. The communists gratefully repaid their patron Fulgencio Batista with extravagant praise and homage. The party organ *Hoy* on January 16, 1944, eulogized Batista as "the people's idol, the great man of our national politics, the man who incarnates the sacred ideals of a new Cuba."

*The Grau Regime: 1944 to 1948* In 1944 the communists backed Batista's candidate for the presidency, Carlos Saladrigas, against the Auténticos candidate, who was again Grau San Martín. This time, however, Grau scored an overwhelming victory, sufficient proof that the election, under Batista's auspices, was the fairest in Cuban history. Although they had suffered a setback in the presidency, the communists continued to improve their political position. Three communists (César Vilar, Juan Marinello, and Salvador García Agüero) were elected to the senate and eight were elected to the chamber of deputies. Since Grau had not won a majority in the Cuban congress, the strength of the communists in both houses gave them an important bargaining position and enabled them to remain a major factor in Cuban politics.

The Communist Party of the United States had long acted on behalf of the Comintern as mediator in Cuban communist affairs. The Cuban communists had been accustomed to coming to New York to settle their major internal disputes and discuss important changes of policy. Blas Roca faithfully followed the lead of the United States communist leader, Earl Browder. Both the United States and Cuban parties changed their names in 1944; in January the PCC was transformed into the Popular Socialist Party (Partido Socialista Popular, PSP), anticipating the United States party's change of name by four months. In April 1945 an article by Jacques Duclos in the French communist organ *Cahiers du communisme* set in motion Browder's downfall and also caused a temporary crisis in the Cuban party leadership. Duclos named the Cuban party as one of the two Latin American parties (the other was the Colombian) most guilty of "Browderism." Unlike Browder, however, Blas Roca managed to ride out the storm and hold on to his leadership.

Always opportunistic, the PSP managed to establish a *modus vivendi* with the Grau San Martín regime. Juan Marinello was elected vice president of the senate, the first Latin American communist to hold such a high post. However, in 1946 Grau's party succeeded in winning a majority in both houses of congress, thereby making it less dependent on communist support. In May 1947 an open split at the fifth congress of the Workers' Confederation temporarily resulted in two trade-union federations claiming the same name, one pro-Auténticos and the other pro-communist. Grau's minister of labor, Carlos Prío Socarrás, recognized the former, and the communists were unable to hold out against government pressure. Thus 1947 marked the end of almost a decade of communist influence based on alliances with the person or party in power. Open political warfare broke out between the ruling Auténticos and the PSP in the last year of Grau's regime.

*The Prío Regime: 1948 to 1952* In the 1948 presidential election the communists made overtures to the newly formed Party of the Cuban People (Orthodox) [Partido del Pueblo Cubano (Orthodoxos)], headed by Eduardo Chibás, who had split away from the Auténticos. Chibás repulsed them, and the communists were unable to prevent the election of the Auténticos candidate Prío Socarrás, whom they now considered their chief enemy.

For the next four years, the PSP faced the open hostility of the Prío regime. In August 1950 Prime Minister Antonio de Varona, who served as acting minister of labor for only four days for this purpose, closed down both *Hoy* and the communist radio station, popularly known as "Mil Diez" (1,010). The Cuban courts ruled in favor of the newspaper, but the radio station was sold to private interests. Deprived of their long-time control of the Workers' Confederation and hampered by government restrictions, the communists lost ground steadily during the Prío regime.

*Batista's Comeback: 1952 to 1958* On March 10, 1952, a successful military coup was staged by former president Fulgencio Batista. The PSP issued a statement the following day condemning the coup but putting the blame on the "Yankee imperialists" rather than on its former ally. Batista's new regime permitted the party press and organization to function largely as before. The big change in communist-Batista relations came after the abortive attack headed by Fidel Castro on the Moncada barracks in Santiago de Cuba on July 26, 1953. The PSP publicly denounced this attack, stating: "We repudiate the putschist methods, peculiar to bourgeois political factions, of the action in Santiago de Cuba and Bayamo, which was an adventuristic attempt to take both military headquarters. The heroism displayed by the participants in this action is false and sterile, as it is guided by mistaken bourgeois conceptions." Nevertheless, Batista closed down *Hoy* the day after the attack, raided PSP headquarters, and later that year outlawed the PSP altogether. However, the party leaders were not touched by Batista's crackdown, and a communist weekly, *Carta semanal*, was easily obtainable although not openly sold.

Batista tolerated the communists to this extent because they did not advocate the violent overthrow of his regime. As late as October 10, 1956, *Carta semanal* still criticized the Moncada attack as "dangerous and sterile." Castro has said that "contact and collaboration" with the "old communists" took place in Mexico in 1955 and 1956, when he was preparing his invasion of Cuba, but the basic communist policy of resisting Batista "with every peaceful expression of the popular will" had not yet changed. In February 1958 it appears that the PSP partially changed its tactics and adopted a dual policy of simultaneously supporting both "the armed struggle in the countryside and the unarmed, civil struggle in the cities." The first communist emissary was sent to the Sierra Maestra, where Castro had been fighting for over a year. Nevertheless, Castro's representatives in Havana did not invite the communists to take part in the ill-fated general strike of April 9, 1958. The available evidence suggests that Castro and the communists did not reach some kind of working agreement until the second half of 1958.[2]

*The Castro-Communist Fusion* Castro's exact relationship to the PSP in the first two years of his rule has not yet been determined. After Batista's flight at the end of 1958 the new government which came into power was headed by President Manuel Urrutia and Prime Minister José Miro Cardona. The real power, however, was vested in Fidel Castro, who at first was satisfied to become chief of the general staff in control of the armed forces. Castro replaced Miro Cardona as prime minister on February 13, 1959, and drove Urrutia out of office on July 17, 1959, by which time he had taken complete control of the government. The Twenty-sixth of July movement (Veinte-seis de Julio), with which Castro had won power, was still nominally the leading political force, although it did not function as a traditional political party.

The PSP, as the official communist party was still called, set itself up in business again in the first days of January 1959, taking the position that it supported Castro's regime but differed with him on ideological grounds.[3] In the first six months of 1959 what the PSP publicly advocated and what Castro chose to do were not always the same, as in the case of the "agrarian reform" of May 1959, but the PSP always ended by enthusiastically backing whatever Castro did. In April and May 1959 Castro made several unfavorable allusions to communism as a system of government. Nevertheless, whatever differences may have existed at this time were not permitted to stand in the way of ever closer relations. The turning point seems to have come in the fall of 1959. The arrest of Major Hubert Matos in October and his twenty-year prison sentence in December made anticommunism a state crime. In November 1959 Castro personally intervened to save the communists from total rout at the trade-union congress.

In any case, Castro undoubtedly decided on "fusion" with the old-time communists by the end of 1960, a decision manifested by a meeting on December 2, 1960, setting up a school to train cadres of the future "united party." In the spring of 1961 this party began to take shape in the preliminary form of the Integrated Revolutionary Organizations (Organizaciones Revolucionarias Integradas,

ORI), in which Aníbal Escalante was given a key position. On December 2, 1961, Castro declared: "I am a Marxist-Leninist, and I will be one until the last day of my life." The twenty-five-member ORI directorate set up in March 1962 contained ten old-time communists and twelve or thirteen "Castroists."[4] In a sensational speech on March 26, 1962, Castro denounced the old-time communist leader Aníbal Escalante for "errors" and "crimes" which included his partisan control of the ORI. He admitted past communist domination of the organization and demanded that the "old" and "new" communists bury their differences.

Escalante's downfall signified the end of the old-time communist organizational predominance, but other old-time communists continued to serve in high positions of Castro's government. The main economic organization, the National Institute of Agrarian Reform, was entrusted in 1962 to Carlos Rafael Rodríguez, former editor of *Hoy*, and Joaquín Ordoqui was made vice minister of the armed forces. However, economic deterioration and political antagonisms continued to plague the old-time communists. A particularly humiliating experience was the trial in March 1964 of a former communist informer, Marcos Rodríguez. As a result of his implication in the Marcos Rodríguez case, Ordoqui was suspended from all his posts in November 1964. Carlos Rafael Rodríguez was removed as head of the National Institute in February 1965. Meanwhile, between 1962 and 1964 the ORI was transformed into the United Party of the Socialist Revolution (Partido Unido de la Revolución Socialista); in October 1965 the party returned to its original name, Communist Party of Cuba.

## ORGANIZATION AND MEMBERSHIP

The present PCC is headed by Fidel Castro as general secretary. It is governed by a central committee of 104 members, only about one-quarter of them old-time communists. The political bureau is made up of eight members, none of them old-time communists: Fidel Castro, Raúl Castro, Sergio del Valle, Ramiro Valdés, Juan Almeida, Guillermo García, Osvaldo Dorticós, and Armando Hart. The secretariat of six is made up of Fidel Castro, Raúl Castro, Osvaldo Dorticós, Armando Hart, Blas Roca, and Carlos Rafael Rodríguez, the last two of whom were old-time communists. Armando Hart is party secretary.

Membership figures for the party's illegal period from 1925 to 1938 were once given by Blas Roca as 80 in 1925, about 500 in 1930, about 3,000 in 1933, 5,000 in 1937, and 10,000 in 1938.[5] By 1944, as a result of the alliance with Batista, membership had increased to 23,000, with about 100,000 *afiliados*, those who registered their electoral identification with the party but were not actual members.[6] The membership apparently stabilized at 15,000 to 20,000 from 1945 to 1950 but began to decline in the spring of 1950. By late 1951 "a grave financial situation" in the party was reported,[7] but no further figures seem to be available.

The communists first participated in an election in 1939 for delegates to the constitutional convention to meet the following year. In this election they polled 97,000 votes. In the 1946 elections the communist vote reached a high of 196,000 and during the next four held at about 150,000. The last election in Cuba was in 1950, but results are not available.

## RELATION TO SOVIET LEADERSHIP

Official Cuban-Soviet relations were inaugurated in February 1960 with the visit to Havana by Soviet Deputy Premier Anastas Mikoyan. On February 13 the first Soviet-Cuban trade agreement was signed, the most important provisions of which obligated the Soviets to purchase Cuban sugar over a five-year period and to lend the Cuban government $100 million. Soviet-Cuban diplomatic relations were formally resumed in May 1960. Major Ernesto Che Guevara, then a leading proponent of Cuban collaboration with the Soviet bloc, toured Eastern Europe early in 1960 and lined up credits from other members of the bloc. Cuba recognized Communist China in September 1960, and the latter promised to purchase 1 million tons of Cuban sugar in 1961 and to give Cuba an interest-free loan of $60 million. Thereafter the Cubans made an effort to treat the Soviet Union and China with equal consideration, although Cuban relations with the Soviet Union were far more intimate and extensive. The "missiles crisis" of October 1962 brought on a decided strain in Cuban-Soviet relations, but after his first trip to the Soviet Union in April-May 1963 Castro extolled Soviet leader Nikita Khrushchev as "a great leader and a formidable adversary of imperialism."

As the Sino-Soviet conflict intensified publicly in 1962 and 1963 the Cuban leaders took the position that they wished to stay out of the conflict and hoped to serve as a bridge for reuniting the world communist movement. By 1965, however, this "neutralism" in the Sino-Soviet struggle had become harder and harder to maintain, even as a public posture. In February Major Raúl Castro, minister of the armed forces, was sent to Moscow to attend a meeting of nineteen pro-Soviet communist parties. Another straw in the wind may have been Guevara's mysterious "disappearance" after his visit to Peking in the same month. By September, Castro later revealed, the Cuban authorities had become disturbed about an apparent increase in Chinese communist propaganda aimed at the Cuban armed forces. On September 14 Premier Castro and President Dorticós informed the Chinese chargé d'affaires in Havana that this propaganda had to cease, and they also protested what they called an anti-Cuban "slander campaign" by pro-Chinese groups throughout the world. The Chinese struck back in November by refusing to go through with an exchange of rice for sugar to which Castro claimed they had already agreed.

## PARTY PRESS ORGANS AND RECORDS

The daily publication *Noticias de hoy*, usually called *Hoy*, was first issued on May 16, 1938, and appeared (with the exception of a short period in 1950 and 1951) until July 27, 1953, when it was suppressed by the Batista regime. Its reappearance began on January 6, 1959, after the fall of Batista. *Hoy* and *Revolución*, the organ of the Twenty-sixth of July movement, were merged in favor of a new daily, *Granma*, which first appeared on October 4, 1965. A theoretical organ, *El Comunista*, appeared in 1939 and 1940 and was succeeded in April 1941 by the monthly *Fundamentos*, which was suppressed in 1952, reappeared in February 1959, and was replaced by *Cuba socialista* in September 1961.

Statutes for the PSP of 1960 may be found in Partido Socialista Popular, *VIII Asamblea Nacional: Informes, resoluciones, programa, estatutos*, Havana, Ediciónes Populares, 1960, pp. 727-749. The last program of the PSP also appears in this work, on pp. 655-725. These statutes and program are no longer operative, but none have been issued since then.

## PARTY CONGRESSES

1st (founding) congress, PCC, August 1925, Havana
2d congress, PCC, April 1934, Havana
3d congress, PCC, January 1939, Santa Clara
1st congress, PSP, January 1944, Havana
2d congress, PSP, September 1944, Havana
5th congress, PSP, November 1948
6th congress, PSP, February 1950
7th congress, PSP, February 1952
8th congress, PSP, August 1960, Havana

Dates of the third and fourth congresses are unknown. No further party congresses had been held by 1965.

## BIBLIOGRAPHY

Draper, Theodore: *Castroism: Theory and Practice*, New York, Praeger, 1965.
Goldenberg, Boris: *The Cuban Revolution and Latin America*, New York, Praeger, 1965.
Grobart, Fabio: *XV [quinze] años de lucha*, Havana, Ediciónes Sociales, 1940.
Marinello, Juan: *Rubén Martínez Villena*, Havana, Ediciónes Sociales, 1941.
Rito, Esteban: *Sobre el movimiento obrero de*

*América y Europa*, Havana, 1946.

Roca, Blas: *Los fundamentos del socialismo en Cuba,* rev. ed., Havana, Ediciónes Populares, 1960.

Roca, Blas: *Vida de Julio Antonio Mella*, Havana, Ediciónes Sociales, 1947.

Serviat, Pedro: *40 [quarento] aniversario de la fundación del Partido comunista*, Havana, Editorial EIR, 1965.

Wilkerson, Loree: *Fidel Castro's Political Programs from Reformism to "Marxism-Leninism,"* Gainesville, Fla., University of Florida Press, 1965.

Zapata, Felipe: "Esquema y notas para una historia de la organización obrera en Cuba," *Unidad gastronómica* (Havana), June-November 1948.

THEODORE DRAPER

1. Some sources incorrectly name Mella as first general secretary.

2. See Theodore Draper, *Castroism: Theory and Practice*, New York, Praeger, 1965, pp. 26-34.

3. "It is not that we approve each one of Fidel Castro's statements. There are many doctrinal problems, from which many sharp differences arise, precisely because the movement which he heads is not communist." Carlos Rafael Rodríguez, in *Hoy*, May 10, 1959, p. 1.

4. Draper, *op. cit.*, pp. 34-39, 82-83, 200 n.

5. Blas Roca, in *Fundamentos*, September-October 1946, p. 106.

6. Fabio Grobart, in *Fundamentos*, February 1944, p. 102.

7. Blas Roca, in *Fundamentos*, October 1951, p. 925.

# CYPRUS

The Communist Party of Cyprus (Kommunistikon Komma Kiprou, KKK) was founded in 1926, when Cyprus was still a British colony. Its first congress, meeting that year, determined to struggle "for an independent Cyprus in the framework of a Socialist Balkan Federation" (see *The Balkan Communist Federation*). However, this position was poorly received by the Greek population of Cyprus, which was demanding unification with Greece. The following year the KKK called an extraordinary congress to correct its political line, but the change took place more on paper than in action. The KKK launched the slogan of a "national front for the struggle against colonialism" without taking any stand on unification with Greece, in line with Moscow's policy to oppose unification but to avoid openly condemning it.

In 1929 a Cypriot delegation traveled to London to ask the Labour Party government to grant union of Cyprus with Greece. At this point the communist parties of Greece and Cyprus openly went on record against unification, and when the KKK went to the polls in June 1930 with the slogan of "autonomy," it was defeated.

In October 1931 the Greeks in Cyprus rebelled against British domination in favor of unification with Greece. Although it did not participate in this "chauvinist" revolution, the KKK found itself outlawed by the British authorities along with the other political parties and political organizations of the Greek population. After the seventh congress of the Comintern in 1935, in an attempt to promote the new popular-front line, the outlawed KKK adopted a program of unification with

Greece. However, the switch came too late; there was no popular response, and the party in Cyprus ceased to exist. Only a KKK organization in London, with some membership from Cypriots living in England, remained active.

HISTORY

The KKK reappeared in Cyprus in 1941 under the new name Reform Party of the Working People (Anorthotikon Komma Ergazomenu Lau, AKEL). At its founding congress in April 1941 it was defined as a progressive, legal, and antifascist national party and did not claim to be the successor to the KKK. After the German attack on the Soviet Union the AKEL appealed to its members to enter the British army to combat the Axis. Its second congress, in January 1943, took a position for unification of Cyprus with Greece. These attitudes contributed greatly to the AKEL's popularity. Other factors were the lack of political experience in Cyprus, the absence of organized opponents, the anticolonial policy of the Soviet Union, the indulgence of the British authorities, and the anti-Western spirit caused by British domination. As a result, the AKEL succeeded in dominating the majority of the trade unions and becoming the greatest political force in Cyprus. In the municipal elections of 1946 it was victorious in the capital of Nicosia and in all the other large cities, and by 1947 it represented 40 percent of the Greek population of the island. Its support contributed to the victory of Leontios as archbishop of Cyprus.

In 1947 the British offered self-government to the Cypriots, who rejected it and demanded unification with Greece. The AKEL, however, accepted and participated in the parliament convoked by the British governor Winster in 1948. This stand lessened its strength, with the result that opponents of the AKEL and the British plan succeeded in electing Makarios III as archbishop.

At its sixth congress in August 1949 the AKEL again switched tactics and took a position for unification. At the same time it decided to purge the party of the petite bourgeoisie and transform it into a true "proletarian" party. This provoked an internal crisis which reached its apogee in 1952 and divided the party into two opposing factions. The victors accused the others of all the "faults" of the party, calling them "agents of the British." By 1954 the party's influence was sufficiently diminished that it received only 25 percent of the Greek population's vote.

In April 1955 the armed struggle of the Greek Cypriots against British domination began. Although the AKEL took a position against this struggle, which it characterized as "adventurist" and "terroristic,"[1] the British authorities outlawed it along with all the other Greek organizations. The AKEL remained "illegal" until 1959, but this illegality was unusual; at first the six members of the party's political bureau remained free, along with nearly all the party rank and file. In December 1955 the party newspaper, *Neos Democratis*, closed, but it reappeared on February 17, 1956, as the daily *Haravgi*. Although Ezekias Papaioannou, general secretary of the AKEL, was arrested, he escaped to work against the National Association of Cypriot Fighters, which was directing the armed strife. Later Papaioannou appeared in London, where, with the other party secretary, Ziartides, he held press conferences and worked against the nationalists among the 100,000 Cypriots who were living in London.

In May 1956 the AKEL central committee officially called for the end of the armed battle against the British. *Haravgi* led a systematic campaign against the Cypriot Fighters and its head, General George Grivas, as well as against Archbishop Makarios, and AKEL cadres collaborated with the British authorities against the terrorists. The Cypriot Fighters denounced this as treason. In 1958 they began the execution of communists who had collaborated with the colonial authorities, whereupon the AKEL organized demonstrations against the terrorists. In May, however, when the Cypriot Fighters published a "black book" on the AKEL treason, the party was obliged to make an about-face and declare that its position against the nationalist movement had been "erroneous." The tolerance of the British authorities toward the AKEL was probably a result of its opposition to the Cypriot Fighters, a position based on the consistent opposition of Moscow to the unification of Cyprus with Greece.

The AKEL became legal again in December 1959, after the proclamation of Cyprus' independence. Its prestige and influence had suffered considerably, and in a settlement reached in 1960 by all parties the AKEL accepted five of the fifty seats in the parliament. However, through exploitation of the faults, divergences, and lack of experience of its adversaries, the Greco-Turkish controversy, "Soviet aid" to the new state, the support of the neutral countries, and the anti-Western spirit that resulted from the struggle for independence and from opposition of the Western powers to unification with Greece, the party was able to win back the ground it had lost and more besides. Its membership of 2,500 in 1955 had more than quadrupled by 1962.

The AKEL's tactics are flexible. In 1965 it was supporting its old enemy Makarios III. It presents itself as a "patriotic-progressive and anti-imperialist" party. It has called for a "national front" to complete the independence of the island, remove the British bases, and declare Cyprus' neutrality. Its goal is not unification with Greece, but "complete independence without restrictions on the island," in the hope that an independent Cyprus can gradually be transformed into a communist state. With its slogans for independence, the AKEL is attracting those who, for varying reasons, do not want unification. At the same time it presents independence, vaguely, as a necessary step toward self-determination of the Cypriots, who would then be able to express themselves for or against unification. Thus the AKEL has maintained the public image of a Greek organization, and by supporting Makarios it is advancing its position in the machinery of the new state.

## ORGANIZATION AND MEMBERSHIP

The AKEL is organized along the Soviet pattern of democratic centralism. For many years its membership was exclusively Greek; only recently have a few Turks joined the party. In 1962 the AKEL had 10,432 members. Its youth branch, the United Democratic Youth Organization (Eniea Democratiki Organossis Neoleas), is 18,000 strong, with 12,000 men and 6,000 women between the ages of fifteen and thirty. Its organization for children under fifteen has 4,000 members.[2]

The AKEL has at its disposal a whole series of front organizations; the most important is the organization of communist trade unions, the Cypriot Workers' Confederation (Pankipria Ergatiki Omospondia), with 40,000 members. An important role is also played by the U.S.S.R.-Cyprus Association.

## RELATION TO SOVIET LEADERSHIP

The Cypriot party, both as the KKK and as the AKEL, has always been loyal to Moscow. In the Sino-Soviet conflict the AKEL supports Moscow.

## PARTY PRESS ORGANS

The AKEL publishes the daily *Haravgi* (Dawn), with a circulation of 16,000, edited by Chrysis O. Demetriades. It also publishes a theoretical review, *Democratis* (Democrat).

## PARTY CONGRESSES

1st congress, KKK, 1926
Extraordinary congress, KKK, 1927
Constituent conference, AKEL, April 14, 1941, Skarinou
1st congress, AKEL, October 5, 1941, Limassol
2d congress, AKEL, January 30-31, 1943, Famagusta
3d congress, AKEL, April 23, 1944, Larnaca
4th congress, AKEL, August 18-20, 1945, Nicosia
5th congress, AKEL, September 13-15, 1947, Nicosia

6th congress, AKEL, August 27-28, 1949, Nicosia

7th congress, AKEL, December 1-2, 1951, Nicosia

8th congress, AKEL, March 5-7, 1954, Nicosia

9th congress, AKEL, September 9, 1959, near Famagusta

10th congress, AKEL, March 8-11, 1962, Nicosia

11th congress, AKEL, March 3-6, 1966, Nicosia

BIBLIOGRAPHY

Adams, T. W., and Alvin J. Cottrell: "Communism in Cyprus," *Problems of Communism*, v. 15, May-June 1966, pp. 22-30.

"Cypriot Communists in London," *Sovietology*, no. 5, 1963, p. 309.

"The Cyprus Battle for Freedom and the Communists," *Sovietology*, no. 7, 1962, p. 422.

Georgalas, Georges: "The 10th Congress of AKEL and Communism in Cyprus," *Sovietology*, no. 4, 1962, p. 243.

"Moscow and the Problem of Cyprus," *Sovietology*, nos. 7-8, 1964, p. 273.

"The Underground Activity of Communism in Cyprus," *Sovietology*, no. 5, 1963, p. 308.

GEORGES GEORGALAS

1. Resolution of the central committee of the AKEL, April 1, 1955.

2. Statistics from a report to the tenth congress of the AKEL. March 8-11, 1962. No newer figures are available. It should be noted that the island has a population of over 500,000, of which a majority are Greeks and a minority are Turks.

# CZECHOSLOVAKIA

The communist party has ruled Czechoslovakia since February 1948, when it seized power in a bloodless coup and immediately reorganized the government, without benefit of parliamentary elections. These circumstances, unusual for Eastern Europe, where other communist parties had assumed control as a result of direct or indirect Red Army pressure, led to the paradoxical claim of "a parliamentary road to power."

The first attempt to establish a communist movement took place immediately after World War I, when eighty former Czech prisoners of war and workers in Russia gathered in Moscow on May 25-28, 1918, to found a party. They called for a social revolution, rejecting the bourgeois republic of Thomas Masaryk. Headed by Alois Muna, a former Viennese tailor and left-wing social democrat, the group organized a Red Guard which fought on the communist side in the Russian civil war.

Muna returned to Czechoslovakia and appears to have played a role in the formation on May 14-15, 1921, of a communist group, subsequently announced at the fourteenth congress of the Czechoslovak Social Democratic Party. Active in this enterprise were Bohumil Šmeral; Břetislav Hůla, Alois Muna, and Antonín Zápotocký (all three imprisoned at the time); and Karl Kreibich. The new political movement soon claimed 300,000 members, However, it was not until October 30-November 4, 1921, that the several communist groups were unified, when the Communist Party of Czechoslovakia (Komunisticka Strana Československa, KSC) held its own constituent congress at Prague and accepted the Twenty-one Conditions for Admission to the Comintern. The new party embraced Czechs, Slovaks, Germans, Hungarians, Carpatho-Ruthenians, Poles, and the Jewish Poale-Zion group.[1]

In Slovakia communism developed in a different manner. The Austro-Hungarian war prisoners repatriated in early 1919 from Soviet Russia included a score of Slovaks who had joined the Russian Communist Party, received revolutionary training in Russia, and even fought in Soviet military units in that country's civil war. They found Slovakia a fertile ground for propaganda. This region still belonged formally to Hungary, and its incorporation by the Czecho-Slovak Republic still awaited a final decision of the Paris peace conference. Various "councils" were established in Slovak towns and villages, and some of them were dominated by these repatriated communists. After the proclamation of a "soviet republic" in Hungary (March 21, 1919) some military units in Slovakia placed themselves under communist command from Budapest. Encouraged by the Hungarian events, the Slovak communists organized local mass meetings to protest annexation by "imperialist" Czechoslovakia and to call for union with Hungary. A meeting in Prešov (Pressburg) on June 16, 1919, proclaimed the Slovak Soviet Republic and elected a revolutionary executive committee. Similar events followed in other cities and towns. The revolutionary committee from Prešov met in Košice on June 20 and established a revolutionary government, with A. Janoušek as its head.

The Soviet Russian government and the Comintern sent congratulatory telegrams to this Slovak regime, thus giving it implied recognition. The Košice government asked the soviet regime in Hungary for support, and Hungarian red regiments were dispatched to Slovakia. However, the Slovak Soviet Republic was short lived. On July 31, 1919, the Hungarian government collapsed. Its leaders (Béla Kun and others) escaped before the Rumanian army units, which had been sent by the Paris peace conference to reestablish order, could reach Budapest. Before the fall of the Béla Kun regime an allied mission had negotiated the withdrawal of Hungarian army units from Slovakia, and Prague ordered its military to enter the country. Without broader support among the local population, the Slovak revolutionary government disintegrated. On July 1 it abandoned Košice, and by July 7 all of Slovakia was under Czechoslovak control. Thus another little-known "soviet republic" created in 1919 collapsed after fifteen days of existence.[2]

## HISTORY

During the second congress held in Prague in October-November 1924, the KSC remained subservient to the Moscow line and attacked the Czech majority in the government for allegedly exploiting the minorities throughout the country. A Comintern-ordered purge of nationalists from the party brought it down to fewer than 100,000 members in 1925, and an independent communist splinter party was formed under Josef Bubnik. However, during the November elections that year the KSC won almost 1 million votes and forty-one seats in parliament. It became the second largest party in the country. Successive elections in 1929 witnessed a drop to thirty seats, owing to the party's internationalist position and weakness among the trade unions.

Šmeral, who had stood for a more independent stance vis-à-vis Moscow, was replaced by Josef Haken as KSC chairman, and the rather strong-minded Bohumil Jílek became general secretary. Both were in turn ousted at the important fifth party congress in February 1929 by Stalin's protégé Klement Gottwald, who had become the first Czech member of the Comintern Executive Committee the year before. Rudolf Slánský, Antonín Zápotocký, Viliam Široký, Jaromír Dolanský, and Václav

Kopecký, who became prominent later, entered the central committee at this same time. Muna, Jílek, and many others were purged from the party in mid-1929.

Violent opposition to the government in connection with the sudden world economic crisis is evidenced in speeches before the parliament, where in December 1929 Gottwald declared "a war of violence" by the KSC against Czechoslovakia, which he described as "a nation's jail." In November 1930 Kopecký said, in reference to the Sudeten area, that communists would fight "for the right of unification for all parts of the German nation into one entirety." In February 1931 Zápotocký described Czechoslovakia as a "rotten country."[3] The class struggle was sharpened by demonstrations of unemployed, organized by the KSC. There were numerous workers' strikes with casualties, and communist membership in trade unions doubled from 1930 to 1932. A so-called Left Front of communist intellectuals was founded in 1930.

In 1934 the KSC refused to vote for Masaryk and entered its own presidential candidate, Klement Gottwald. This attitude changed overnight on May 16, 1935, when Moscow signed a treaty of alliance with Prague. The KSC immediately began to call for a popular front and announced its support of the government. In the 1935 elections it gained 100,000 more votes than it had in 1929. This coincided with attempts by the Soviet Union to create an antinazi coalition among the major powers, a policy which had been pursued vigorously in the League of Nations. At the seventh Comintern congress, held in Moscow in 1935, Antonín Novotný, as a member of the KSC delegation, called for a popular front. This was repeated at the seventh party congress in 1936, and later the KSC dispatched a brigade to fight in the Spanish civil war.

Following the agreement at Munich and detachment of the Sudeten area, on October 20, 1938, the KSC found itself outlawed. The rest of Czechoslovakia fell under German occupation on March 15, 1939, and communist leaders fled to Moscow, Paris, or London.[4] Several of them (Dolanský, Hendrych, Novotný, and Zápotocký) were caught and spent the war in a nazi concentration camp. Not much is known about KSC activities during this period, although the party was run clandestinely inside the Bohemia-Moravia protectorate by lesser functionaries such as Július Fucik. After being shot by the nazis, Fucik became the official KSC martyr.

Slovak independence was recognized by the Soviet Union in September 1939, and in December Zdeněk Fierlinger, the ambassador of the Czechoslovak exile government in London, was told by the Russians that his diplomatic status would no longer be recognized. Gottwald made radio broadcasts from Moscow during the period of the Hitler-Stalin pact (August 23, 1939, to June 22, 1941), and various underground KSC leaflets attacked the Eduard Beneš government in London as well as the British and French "aggressors."

The December 1943 Moscow treaty signed by Beneš and Stalin strengthened the prestige of the KSC leadership in the Soviet Union. It supplied the basis for the Eastern Czechoslovak Liberation Army, which operated under Red Army command in and around Slovakia during 1944 and 1945. Many opportunists joined the reactivated KSC as Soviet troops advanced westward.

Meanwhile, ever since the ban on the KSC in October 1938 by the independent Slovak government a separate Communist Party of Slovakia (Komunisticka Strana Slovenska, KSS) had been operating under the leadership of Július Ďuriš. The communists in Slovakia enjoyed considerable autonomy, owing to lack of contact with their comrades in the so-called Protectorate of Bohemia and Moravia. The KSS program of May 1, 1941, even proclaimed a future communist Slovakia that would be completely free and independent from Prague.

During World War II the communists had 3,000 to 5,000 members in Slovakia. The party leaders included Jan Osoha (arrested in June 1942), Viliam Široký, Karol Bacílek,

Gustav Husák, Karol Šmidke, and Laco Novomeský. The one great achievement claimed by the Slovak communists in the resistance movement against the Germans is that they spearheaded the uprising which broke out in eastern Slovakia on August 29, 1944. Although the uprising failed, the KSS was able to unify various Marxist groups, and after the war it attained half the positions in all government agencies.

On September 17, 1944, during the anti-German uprising in Slovakia, the social democrats there decided to fuse with the KSS (the same thing occurred in the rest of Czechoslovakia on June 27, 1948, after "liberation" of the whole country). The Slovak communists held their first postwar congress on August 11-12, 1945, and in a telegram to the KSC they stated: "The Communist Party of Slovakia is proud to represent a part of the unbreakable unity within the Communist Party of Czechoslovakia." This status has continued, with a separate central committee and presidium for the KSS.[5]

The Gestapo had functioned so efficiently in Bohemia and Moravia that it was not until the fall of 1944, about the same time as the uprising in Slovakia, that the underground KSC was able to perform any important sabotage operations. In Košice a national front was formed which established the so-called "Košice program" as a basis for the postwar state. This program was greatly influenced by the KSC. When the Red Army entered Prague on May 9, 1945, the KSC had only 25,000 members in all of Czechoslovakia. Less than a year later, as a result of massive recruitment and patronage dispensed from key posts held by communists in the coalition government, the eighth congress claimed a party membership of just over 1 million, making the KSC the largest party in the country.

National elections on May 26, 1946, gave the KSC some 38 percent (2.7 million votes) of the ballots and 114 deputies in the 300-seat parliament. The communists were able to infiltrate the trade unions and national committees at the local and intermediate levels of government. They also spearheaded confiscation and socialization of property from ethnic minorities and "enemies of the state." In 1947 they purged 180,000 "unreliable elements" from their own ranks. Gottwald became premier under President Beneš, and communists took half of the eighteen ministerial portfolios (of these the KSS held three) in the coalition government; the defense minister, Ludvík Svoboda, joined the KSC later. Following a coup in February 1948, elections under pressure on May 30 gave the communists 214 of the 300 parliamentary mandates on a national-front unity list. The new constitution of May 9, 1948, made Czechoslovakia a "people's democracy," and on June 14, after Beneš' resignation, Gottwald became president of the country.

At the ninth party congress in May 1949 Gottwald proclaimed "the building of socialism" as the general line. According to the program resolution, "the final goal of the KSC is communism, for the victory of which the socialist order in society provides all conditions." In view of its new official status as the ruling party, the KSC now issued specific instructions to establish control over all factory, army, national-security, rural (collectivization), and other enterprises. The communists also began their struggle against the Catholic church and replaced many independent priests with "peace partisans."

Another KSC purge began with the arrest in December 1949 of Vilém Nový, chief editor of *Rudé Právo*, and Evžen Löbl, deputy foreign-trade minister. During 1950 about 9 percent of the total membership was expelled from the party. An alleged "bourgeois-nationalist conspiracy of Westerners and Zionists in Slovakia" led to a further wave of arrests which claimed KSC General Secretary Rudolf Slánský in the fall of 1951. Political trials from 1952 to 1954 resulted in the execution of Slánský, ex-foreign minister Vladimír Clementis, and other Slovak communists. The more fortunate received prison sentences.

Gottwald died on March 14, 1953, in Prague, after returning from Stalin's funeral in

Moscow. A week later Antonín Novotný was named to direct the work of the secretariat and on September 14 he was confirmed by the central committee as first secretary. In the summer of 1953 the first open anticommunist demonstration occurred after a KSC-decreed currency reform had deprived the population of its savings. Peasants also began to leave the newly established collective farms, until in 1955 the countryside was in chaos. The collective-leadership principle, introduced after Stalin's death by the Communist Party of the Soviet Union, does not seem to have affected Czechoslovakia to any great extent. However, the KSC did pay lip service to this principle at its tenth congress by inserting a new phrase into the party statutes and by separating the top government and KSC positions. Zápotocký became chief of state (president) and Novotný remained first secretary of the party.

Gottwald's death so soon after Stalin's gave the KSC an opportunity to project an image of divesting itself from the "cult of the individual" (a euphemism for one-man rule). The Soviet line did not become absolutely clear until February 1956, when Khrushchev delivered his secret address denigrating Stalin. Alexei Čepička, Gottwald's son-in-law, became the scapegoat and two months later lost his positions as first deputy premier, defense minister, and member of the political bureau, allegedly because of serious shortcomings in the armed forces. However, in general de-Stalinization in the KSC was mild.

The country remained relatively quiet in 1956 during the "Polish October" and the Hungarian revolution. In July 1957, when Khrushchev visited Prague after ousting "antiparty" opponents from his own central committee, he could declare: "We are leaving you with the conviction that the cause of Leninism in Czechoslovakia is in good hands." The KSC had become the model child of the Soviet Union. Another 99 percent electoral victory in 1957 "confirmed" its authority. At the eleventh party congress in June 1958 attention focused on the "struggle against revisionism" and condemnation of Yugoslavia. In accordance with Soviet directives, Novotný placed further emphasis on expanding the machine-tool industry which supplied the Soviet Union.

Two years later, on July 11, 1960, a new constitution proclaimed the attainment of socialism in the form of the Czechoslovak Socialist Republic. According to the preamble of this document, the KSC promised to strive for establishment of the "material and moral prerequisites for transition of our society to communism." The new constitution also specifically established the communist party as "the leading force in society and in the state." Emphasis was placed on ideology and the education of youth along Marxist-Leninist lines. Local elections in 1960 were again won by a 99 percent margin.

At a plenary session of the KSC central committee in mid-November 1961 Novotný stated that the program adopted by the Soviet party the month before also represented the program of the Czechoslovak party. However, at the twelfth KSC congress toward the end of 1962 a new party statute was promulgated, the preamble to which comprises an abbreviated program, with the party defined as "the leading and guiding force in society, according to the will of the working people." The need for change in the economy, as a result of failure, was recognized.

After fifteen years of communist power the cumbersome Czechoslovak administrative machinery began to break down. During 1963 the gross national product dropped 3.2 percent. By September widespread discontent had forced Novotný to dismiss Premier Viliam Široký and remove two more old Stalinists, Karol Bacílek and Július Ďuriš, from high positions. Two other Slovaks, Josef Lenárt and Alexander Dubček, assumed the posts of national premier and party first secretary, respectively. However, superficial reorganization of the government was not considered sufficient by the liberals, especially those in Slovakia, and they continued to press for reforms. During 1964 and 1965 the KSC central committee rehabilitated juridically (but not politically) a number of prominent Slovak writers and former government officials who had been convicted of "bourgeois nationalism" and other "political mistakes."

In January 1965 a new economic management system was adopted, to be put into effect the following year. The goals included creating incentive to uncover reserves in enterprises and plans to solve investment and development problems. Also, foreign aid to the less developed countries, hitherto given on Moscow's orders, was cut back, with an explanation about the "limited possibilities of Czechoslovakia." Obviously the country stood at a crossroads, awaiting the thirteenth party congress scheduled for May-June 1966.

## ORGANIZATION AND MEMBERSHIP

The structure of the KSC is the usual pyramid, with final authority in the hands of a small group at the top. In reality, of course, as in the Soviet party, the operating procedures and focus of power are entirely different from those presented in the formal structure.

The KSC presidium (previously called the political bureau) of the central committee determines policies. A self-perpetuating elite of eleven to twenty-five members, formally elected by the central committee of about 110 members and insulated from the rank and file by several layers at regional, district, and local levels, the presidium exercises supreme authority. The secretariat is officially restricted to implementation of policy. It transmits KSC directives from top to bottom and supervises the secretaries at lower party levels. Several members of the national secretariat are also members of the presidium, thus providing an interlocking directorate.

Connecting the top party organs with the broad base of primary units are the territorially graduated levels that correspond to those within the state administrative structure. Below the national level are the regional organizations, each of which is broken down into districts. The primary party units at local levels form the base of the organizational pyramid, and most of them operate in the individual city block, plant, office, or collective farm. A minimum of three members is necessary to constitute such a basic unit.

The KSC has difficulty in recruiting youth, and the average age of party members is forty-five, with the number of older persons increasing. In two-thirds of the primary units for the capital city of Prague the average age is sixty.[6] About 90 percent of the total membership joined the party between 1945 and 1948, during the coalition period, when it was expedient to do so.

A problem *sui generis* involves KSC social composition. The party has attempted to attain a ratio of 60 percent from the industrial proletariat, some 20 percent from collectivized farmers, and the remainder from other categories including the intellectuals. At the end of 1965, however, only 30.2 percent of the membership came from among factory workers and 5.4 percent from the *kolkhoz* peasantry.[7] In Slovakia recruitment is even more difficult because of the strength of the Catholic church and resentment against the traditional centralism emanating from Prague.

The total party membership was only about 75,000 during the late 1930s. At the end of World War II membership had dropped by two-thirds. A year later it had grown to over 1 million, and it more than doubled again after the 1948 coup. A subsequent purge reduced membership to just under 1.7 million, where it has remained since 1951. Of this total, Slovak communists number about 300,000, or 17.5 percent, compared with a population ratio of 30 percent in the country as a whole.

Several organizations, including the KSC and the KSS, comprise the National Front (Narodni Fronta), which is promoted as the main political organization. It actually represents a coalition of four KSC-dominated puppet parties, several quasi-political groups, and the mass organizations. This has proved useful in preserving the fiction of a multiparty system. Some of the mass organizations also operate as links to population segments that reject communism.

The Czechoslovak Youth League (Československý Svaz Mládeže) claims 1 million members between the ages of fifteen and twenty-six. The Revolutionary Trade Union Movement (Revolucni Odborové Hnutí), which has about 5 million workers on the rolls, is concerned almost exclusively with party goals rather than workers' interests. The Union for Cooperation with the Army (Svaz pro Spolupráci s Armádou), which claims about 800,000 members, supervises paramilitary training.

## FUTURE PROSPECTS

In view of its position of control, it is difficult to envisage any circumstances under which the KSC might be overthrown. Czechoslovakia's vulnerable geographic position, with its longest borders on East Germany, Poland, the Soviet Union, and Hungary—all communist-ruled states—makes this even less likely. It is possible that the continuing ferment among intellectuals and students may lead to more concessions by the KSC leadership. Novotný, however, cannot afford to let de-Stalinization run its course, because he himself provided the perjured evidence which resulted in the execution of Slánský, Clementis, and other Slovaks. Only a post-Novotný regime might bring with it some degree of true liberalization.

## PARTY PRESS ORGANS AND RECORDS

The KSC publishes the daily *Rudé Právo* (Red Justice) in Czech in Prague and in Slovak in Bratislava, as well as the theoretical journal *Život Strany* (Party Life) in Prague. The KSS has its own daily, *Pravda* (Truth), which appears in Bratislava. The Youth League publishes *Mladá Fronta* (Youth Front) in Prague. The trade-union organ is *Prace* (Labor), published in both Prague and Bratislava.

The KSC has been a legal party except from 1938 to 1945 and has regularly published transcripts of all congresses. The proceedings of the 1962 congress appear under the title *XII sjezd Kommunistické Strany Československa, Praha, 4.-8. prosince 1962* (Twelfth Congress of the KSC, Prague, December 4-8, 1962), Prague, 1963. Proceedings of the previous congresses have similar titles.

## CONGRESSES OF THE KSC

Constituent congress, October 30-November 4, 1921
1st congress, February 2-3, 1923
2d congress, October 31-November 4, 1924
3d congress, September 26-28, 1925
4th congress, May 25-28, 1927
5th congress, February 18-23, 1929
6th congress, May 7-11, 1931
7th congress, April 11-14, 1936
8th congress, March 28-31, 1946
9th congress, May 25-29, 1949
10th congress, June 11-15, 1954
11th congress, June 18-21, 1958
12th congress, December 4-8, 1962

## BIBLIOGRAPHY

Korbel, Josef: *The Communist Subversion of Czechoslovakia, 1938-1948: The Failure of Coexistence*, Princeton, N.J., Princeton University Press, 1959.

Krechler, Vladimir (ed.): *Příruční slovník k dějinám KSC* (Handbook Dictionary on KSC History), vol. I-II, Prague, Nakladatelství Politické Literatúry, 1964.

Kuhn, Heinrich: *Der Kommunismus in der Tschechoslowakei*, Cologne, Verlag Wissenschaft und Politik, 1965.

Reisky de Dubnic, Vladimir: *Communist Propaganda Methods: A Case Study on Czechoslovakia*, New York, Praeger, 1960.

Staar, Richard F.: *The Communist Regimes in Eastern Europe: An Introduction*, Stanford, Calif., Hoover Institution, 1967.

Taborsky, Edward: *Communism in Czechoslovakia, 1948-1960*, Princeton, N.J., Princeton University Press, 1961.

Tomasic, Dinko A.: *The Communist Leadership and Nationalism in Czechoslovakia*, Washington, Institute of Ethnic Studies at Georgetown University, 1960.

Vietor, Martin: *Slovenska Sovietska Republika v r. 1919* (The Slovak Soviet Republic in 1919), Bratislava, Slovenské Vydavatelstvo Politickej Literatúry, 1955.

Zinner, Paul E.: *Communist Strategy and Tactics in Czechoslovakia*, New York, Praeger, 1963.

RICHARD F. STAAR

1. H. Gordon Skilling, "The Formation of a Communist Party in Czechoslovakia," *The American Slavic and East European Review*, vol. 14, no. 3, October 1955, pp. 346-358.

2. An objective discussion of these events appears in Martin Vietor, *Slovenská Sovietska Republika v r. 1919* (The Slovak Soviet Republic in 1919), Bratislava, 1955.

3. Quotations from these speeches appear in Josef Korbel, *The Communist Subversion of Czechoslovakia*, Princeton, N.J., Princeton University Press, 1959, pp. 29-30.

4. Gottwald, Slánský, Kopecký, and Zdeněk Nejedlý spent the war in Moscow; Jan Šverma and Vladimír Clementis fled initially to Paris; Václav Nosek, Anežka Hodinová, and Kreibich reached London. Korbel, *op. cit.*, p. 35.

5. The KSS central committee decided at a plenum on November 17-18, 1948, to fuse with the KSC as a single unified party; since then the KSS has functioned as a territorial branch of the KSC. This was confirmed at the ninth KSC congress in May 1949 upon elimination of a separate Slovak organizational statute. Heinrich Kuhn, *Der Kommunismus in der Tschechoslowakei*, Cologne, Verlag Wissenschaft und Politik, 1965, p. 56.

6. Radio Prague, December 9, 1965.

7. *Život Strany*, September 1966.

# DENMARK

The Danish Communist Party (Danmarks Kommunistiske Parti, DKP) originated as a splinter group of the Danish Social Democratic Party (Danmarks Socialdemokratiske Parti, DSP) shortly after the bolshevik revolution in Russia in 1917. Several opposition groups within the DSP found their common center in its youth group, the Social Democratic Youth Organization (Socialdemokratiske Ungdomsforbund), which eventually established itself in 1919 as the independent Danish Left Socialist Party (Venstresocialistisk Parti). It became the Danish Communist Party after joining the Comintern on November 9, 1920. The DKP's founding leaders, Ernst Christiansen, Sigvald Hellberg, and Einar Nielsen, returned to the DSP after 1930.

## HISTORY

During the first decade of its existence the DKP was occupied primarily with internal struggles among various factions representing such diverse ideas as syndicalism, pacifism, and the idea of permanent revolution. The party was confined to an isolated position in Danish politics and in the working class. The Comintern showed much concern about this situation, and on December 17, 1929, its Executive sent an open letter to the members of the DKP which initiated a thorough discussion of the DKP's policies. The founding leaders of the party resigned, and leadership was taken over by Aksel Larsen, a young worker who enjoyed the full confidence of the Comintern and much prestige in the Danish industrial proletariat owing to his skilled and ardent propaganda activity among the growing mass of unemployed.

This realignment of the party, added to the effects of the economic crisis, resulted in growing support for the communists. At the parliamentary elections of November 16, 1932, they made their political breakthrough and obtained two seats. Larsen, who quickly developed into an able and efficient parliamentarian, adroitly utilized the situation to secure more political influence for his party than would be indicated by the amount of votes it had obtained. His position was further reinforced by the growth of fascism during the 1930s. However, his unequivocal support of Stalinist terror in the Soviet Union, and later of the Stalin-Hitler pact of 1939, prevented many radical groups from joining or supporting his party.

The Soviet-Finnish war and the German occupation of Denmark on April 9, 1940, caused a short period of paralysis. Following Germany's attack on the Soviet Union, however, the communists began underground activities. The DKP was one of the initiators of the Danish resistance movement and participated astutely and energetically in all branches of its activity, from clandestine information service to industrial and transportation sabotage. Several communists were members of the executive committee of the resistance movement, and since the DKP was the only political party that had become involved in active resistance against the German occupation, it enjoyed considerable prestige with the Danish population after the liberation in May 1945.

The coalition government formed immediately after the liberation included two communists, Aksel Larsen as minister without portfolio and Alfred Jensen as minister of transport. In the parliamentary elections of October 1945 the DKP reached its peak influence, with 10.7 percent of the total vote and eighteen seats. Although the new government was formed without communist participation, the DKP made substantial contributions to certain aspects of legislation, especially social legislation. Nevertheless, as a result of its foreign policy, which unalterably followed the Soviet line, it began to decline in influence. In 1947 the party lost half its seats in the parliament, and after the communist putsch in Prague in 1948 it also lost a considerable number of members, many of whom made their decision public.

The communists gained no strength from their campaign against Danish participation in NATO and lost further prestige by their advocacy of all things Russian. The turning point was reached in 1956. Soviet intervention in Hungary shocked the party membership, perhaps more than it should have. Moreover, the Soviet de-Stalinization policy had forced Larsen to publicly confess his reservations about much that he had been supporting during the preceding years. Taking the consequences of his painful reevaluation, he decided that the party line should now be adjusted to the wishes of the membership. This decision isolated him in the party leadership, and finally, in November 1958, the party congress decided against the Larsen line in the presence of Piotr Pospelov, the Soviet party delegate. Under the new leadership of Knud Jespersen, a young trade unionist, the DKP continued its line of absolute loyalty to Moscow, and in 1960 it lost its last seat in the parliament, with no immediate prospects of regaining it.

Larsen immediately founded a new, uncommitted socialist party, the Socialist People's Party (Socialistisk Folkeparti), which achieved considerable success at the expense of the DKP and the DSP. Larsen's party is declared to be a socialist, but not a communist or a revolutionary party.

## ORGANIZATION AND MEMBERSHIP

The DKP is organized in the usual pyramidal structure. The local party cell elects a chairman, a secretary, and a treasurer. Cells are coordinated locally in a district organization, which elects an executive committee. The party cells of Copenhagen are coordinated, through several district organizations, in a superstructure, the capital organization, which holds a conference. The highest authority is the party congress, which elects a central committee; the central committee elects an executive committee, which appoints the party secretaries. The party congress also elects a control commission. The party has a youth organization, the Danish Communist Youth (Danmarks Kommunistiske Ungdom).

The DKP does not publish membership statistics, and any evaluation of its social composition and political strength must be based on such secondary evidence as election figures, personal knowledge, and occasional opportunities of checking communist influence in trade unions. A general estimate of social composition indicates two main groups: a core of skilled workers in larger industrial cities and a small group of intellectuals, scattered all over the country. The party is bound by its statute to operate entirely legally; consequently, the very fact that since 1960 it has been unable to obtain parliamentary representation through elections defines its potential as insignificant in Danish political life.

## RELATION TO SOVIET LEADERSHIP

After its readjustment in 1929 and 1930 the DKP showed absolute loyalty to the Comintern. Party leaders traveled regularly to Moscow for consultation, and it seems that the relative weakness of the party at home bound them to a corresponding dependence on the international superstructure; the Comintern's directives were followed without reservation and without regard for their effects in Denmark. During the Cominform period the DKP continued this policy, with no formal possibilities, of course, of influencing Cominform policy, but also with no possibilities of making the Cominform policy popular in Denmark. The party has, in fact, shown little or no inclination to avail itself of opportunities to form its own independent policy. During recent years the only officially disclosed concern about the Moscow line was over the degradation of Khrushchev in 1964, which was accepted, however, after a few days' hesitation and hurried consultations in Moscow. Even in this case the vacillation seems to have been inspired by fear of lack of leadership from Moscow, rather than by fear of excessive Moscow leadership.

The weak position of the DKP in Denmark seems to have inspired the party leadership to deny, or at least ignore, any major disputes between stronger communist parties in the world. The Sino-Soviet dispute was disregarded as long as possible. At the Moscow conference of eighty-one parties in November 1960 the Danish representatives supported the Soviet view but avoided specific mention of the Chinese. Finally, in August 1963 the DKP central committee took a clear stand against the Peking line. In consequence, a tiny group of intellectuals broke away from the party in June 1964 and formed its own organization, the Communist Working Circle (Kommunistisk Arbejdskreds), led by Gotfred Appel and Benito Scocozza. This group has published a few pamphlets and a small mimeographed bulletin, *Kommunistisk Orientering* (Communist Orientation), reproducing Chinese views. The group has not been trying to assume the role of a political party and will probably have no immediate chance to do so.

## PARTY PRESS ORGANS AND RECORDS

Party press organs are *Land og Folk* (Land and People), a daily, *Tiden* (The Times), a periodical, and *Fremad* (Forward), the monthly of the Danish Communist Youth.

The official edition of the DKP statutes as of 1958, with minor amendments from 1962, is *Danmarks Kommunistiske Parti: Love* (Danish Communist Party: Statutes), Copenhagen, 1962. The latest political manifesto of the party, issued by the twenty-second congress in November 1965, is *Nye Veje for Danmark: Danmarks Kommunistiske Parti, Politisk Manifest* (New Ways for Denmark: Danish Communist Party, Political Manifesto), Copenhagen, 1965. Records of party congresses are not published separately, but are only mentioned in party press organs.

## CONGRESSES OF THE DKP

Data on congresses held before 1930 are unobtainable. All congresses on record have been held in Copenhagen.

13th congress, 1932

14th congress, December 1936
15th congress, May 1946
16th congress, May 1949
17th congress, May 1952
18th congress, October 1955
19th congress, January 1957
20th congress, October-November 1958
21st congress, May-June 1962
22d congress, November 1965

BIBLIOGRAPHY

Holmgaard, Bergholt: "Danmarks Kommunistiska Parti," in Ake Sparring (ed.), *Kommunismen i Norden* (Communism in the Nordic Countries), Stockholm, 1965.

BJARNE NØRRETRANDERS

# DOMINICAN REPUBLIC

The first communists in the Dominican Republic were refugees from the Spanish civil war who set up their own organizations in exile after 1939. Inspired by their example, a few Dominicans who had become communists as students elsewhere in Latin America formed the Dominican Communist Party (Partido Comunista Dominicano, PCD) among university students in the capital in 1942. Among the leaders of the new party were Pericles Franco Ornes, Francisco Henríquez, and Juan and Felix Doucoudray.

## HISTORY

The PCD has been an ineffectual exile organization during most of its existence. Established clandestinely in 1942, it was tolerated by the Trujillo dictatorship during the remaining years of the war. In 1945 the party was repressed and its leaders were exiled. The following year the exiles were invited to return to register the party and take part in the 1947 elections; to improve his international standing Trujillo wanted the communists as a conspicuous, impotent opposition. The invitation was accepted, and the party was established openly as the Dominican Popular Socialist Party (Partido Socialista Popular Dominicano, PSPD) on August 27, 1946. Within a few months the PSPD had grown to about 2,000 members and had begun to attract a following among trade-union leaders. On June 14, 1947, it was proscribed, and its leaders were jailed or exiled.

For the next fourteen years the communist movement virtually disappeared from the Dominican Republic, while its spokesmen took refuge successively in Guatemala, Mexico, and Cuba. After the assassination of Trujillo in May 1961 some communists returned, but they sought to operate through a front party, the Dominican Popular Movement (Movimiento Popular Dominicano, MPD). The PSPD was again outlawed in July 1961, and the MPD was banned in October of that year. The Bosch administration, inaugurated in February 1963, did not enforce the anticommunist laws, but in October 1963 the military regime prohibited all communist activities. In April 1965, when communists attempted to seize the leadership of the military-civilian revolt, they again identified their organization as the Dominican Communist Party.

## ORGANIZATION AND MEMBERSHIP

United States sources estimated that there

were about 1,000 members in the PCD in 1965. In addition, the MPD, with about 700 members, was heavily infiltrated by communists.[1] As an exile organization the Dominican party was not able to sustain the usual communist front groups within the homeland. After 1961 the communists made frequent use of front parties in their attempts to gain a voice in national politics; their principal front party was the MPD. They also infiltrated and sought to manipulate the Castroist Fourteenth of June Political Grouping (Agrupación Política Catorce de Junio), named in commemoration of Cuba's attack on the country in 1959, and the Nationalist Revolutionary Party (Partido Nacionalista Revolucionario).

### RELATION TO SOVIET LEADERSHIP

The Dominican communists have been too preoccupied with domestic questions to concern themselves deeply with the ideological dispute between the Soviet Union and Communist China. The PCD has expressed *pro forma* approval of the Soviet position, while the front parties, which follow the Cuban model, have taken no public stand on the issue.

### PARTY PRESS ORGANS

The party has never been sufficiently well established to develop a regular or effective publications apparatus. An irregular weekly, *El Popular*, appeared for a time during 1962 and 1963.

### PARTY CONGRESSES

There is no evidence that the Dominican communists had held a party congress by the end of 1965.

### BIBLIOGRAPHY

See *Latin America*, refs. 2, 6, 13.

ROLLIE E. POPPINO

1. U.S. Department of State, Bureau of Intelligence and Research, *World Strength of the Communist Party Organizations*, Eighteenth Annual Report, Washington, January 1966, p. 153.

# ECUADOR

The communist movement in Ecuador started among left-wing intellectuals in Quito, who founded the Ecuadorean Socialist Party (Partido Socialista Ecuatoriano, PSE) in 1926. In the beginning the party leadership was divided between socialists, who left the organization after a few years, and self-styled communists. The outstanding figure among the latter was a physician, Ricardo Paredes, who represented the party in Moscow on the tenth anniversary of the Russian revolution, secured its admission to the Comintern in 1928, and converted it into the Communist Party of Ecuador (Partido Comunista del Ecuador, PCE), in 1931.

### HISTORY

The clandestine PCE led a marginal existence until the 1940s, gradually extending its influence among students and intellectuals and competing with socialists for a following among organized workers in Quito and Guayaquil. The revolution of May 1944, in which the communists took part as allies of the socialists and liberals, catapulted the party into national prominence, bringing it both legal status and a direct voice in the new administration. A communist, Gustavo Becerra, was included as a member of the junta which held power briefly before transferring executive authority to President Velasco Ibarra, while in August the communist poet Alfredo Vera y Vera became Velasco's minister of education, a post he held for five months. Meanwhile, the communists had won fifteen seats—one-sixth of the total—in the constituent assembly, and helped to draft the new national constitution.

After January 1945, when Velasco broke with the communists, their fortunes rapidly declined, even though the party remained legal and was regularly represented in the senate by Pedro Saad, secretary general of the PCE, until 1960. The new military regime outlawed the party and jailed its most prominent leaders in July 1963, effectively undermining the communist position in the student movement. In 1965, however, the communists still shared control of the small labor confederation with the Castroist revolutionary socialists.

## ORGANIZATION AND MEMBERSHIP

United States sources estimated party membership in 1965 as 2,000 to 3,000.[1] For a full discussion of communist strength in Ecuador see *Latin America*.

## RELATION TO SOVIET LEADERSHIP

The PCE has been represented at recent meetings of the international communist movement in Moscow and at the congresses of the Soviet party. For a discussion of the ties between the Ecuadorean party and the Soviet-directed international communist movement see *Latin America*.

## PARTY PRESS ORGANS AND RECORDS

The PCE did not maintain a strong publications program even when it enjoyed full freedom of operation. Prior to July 1963 it issued the weekly *El Pueblo* and published a second weekly, *Revolución*, jointly with the Castroist party.

Declarations of the executive committee are occasionally distributed as flysheets, and the current party program may be discussed in general terms in the international communist press, but statutes and other internal party documents are usually circulated only among the membership.

## PARTY CONGRESSES

1st congress, PSE, May 1926, Quito
2d congress, PCE, 1931
3d congress, PCE, 1946
4th congress, PCE, July 1949, Guayaquil
5th congress, PCE, July 1952, Ambato
6th congress, PCE, May 1947, Quito
7th congress, PCE, March 1962, Guayaquil

## BIBLIOGRAPHY

Crespo Toral, Jorge: *El comunismo en el Ecuador*, Quito, 1958.

See also *Latin America*, refs. 1, 2, 6, 13, 24.

ROLLIE E. POPPINO

1. U.S. Department of State, Bureau of Intelligence and Research, *World Strength of the Communist Party Organizations*, Eighteenth Annual Report, Washington, January 1966, p. 175.

# EGYPT
*See* United Arab Republic

# EL SALVADOR

The communist movement in El Salvador began in the mid-1920s, when agents from the Mexican and Guatemalan communist parties organized a few students into a branch of the proposed Communist Party of Central America (see *Latin America*). The organization functioned in and inseparably from the Salvadoran branch of the world communist front group International Red Aid. Salvadoran communists in the 1960s claimed that the Communist Party of El Salvador (Partido Comunista de El Salvador, PCS) was formed in 1930. Many of the founding members, including Augustín P. Martí, the leader of the party, became victims of the 1932 revolution. Miguel Mármol and Abel Cuenca were the most prominent of the founders who survived the years of repression.

## HISTORY

The PCS has never enjoyed full legal status, although it has experienced occasional short periods of *de facto* freedom of operation. It is distinguished as one of the first communist parties in Latin America to seek a peasant following, and the first in the western hemisphere to try to seize power by revolution. This attempt, in January 1932, was brutally repressed, and the party was practically destroyed for a dozen years.

A handful of Salvadoran communists who had been jailed in Guatemala were released when the Ubico dictatorship was overthrown in July 1944. The fall of the Martínez regime in El Salvador two months earlier left a temporary political vacuum in which they were able to reestablish the party and build a firm base in the newly organized labor movement. The communists subsequently managed to preserve their organizational structure through alternating periods of repression and political turmoil but never developed a large following or a significant influence in national politics. Their best opportunity came in late 1960, with the fall of the Lemus regime. During a three-month period of open political activity they tried to foment a Cuban-type agrarian revolt, which provoked the armed forces to seize the government. The party was again repressed, and at the end of 1965 its activities were still closely circumscribed.

## ORGANIZATION AND MEMBERSHIP

The Salvadoran party is one of the smallest in Latin America. Its membership was estimated by United States sources as 200 in 1965.[1] During the 1950s and after, the communists attempted to participate in politics through a front party, the Revolutionary Party of April and May (Partido Revolucionario de Abril y Mayo), but with minimal results. For a full discussion see *Latin America*.

## RELATION TO SOVIET LEADERSHIP

The Salvadoran communists appear to have affiliated with the Comintern in about 1930, when the party was formally established. Their relations with the Moscow-directed world communist movement follow the general Latin American pattern (see *Latin America*). The PCS leadership has publicly endorsed the Soviet position in the ideological controversy with Communist China.

## PARTY PRESS ORGANS

The Salvadoran communists have limited press and publications resources. One of the few irregular, clandestine periodicals issued by the party is *La Verdad*, an internal publication of the central committee.

## CONGRESSES OF THE PCS

According to communist sources, the PCS held five congresses; official records of these congress have not been published.

1st congress (constituent assembly), March 1930
2d (1st) congress, August 1946
3d (2d) congress, 1948
4th (3d) congress, August 1950
5th (4th) congress, February 1964

## BIBLIOGRAPHY

See *Latin America*, refs. 1, 2, 6, 13, 16, 24.

ROLLIE E. POPPINO

1. U.S. Department of State, Bureau of Intelligence and Research, *World Strength of the Communist Party Organizations*, Eighteenth Annual Report, Washington, January 1966, p. 155.

# ENGLAND
*See* Great Britain

# ESTONIA

The Marxist movement in Estonia dates back to the close of the nineteenth century. In 1902 and 1903 Mikhail I. Kalinin, a close collaborator of Lenin, agitated in the capital city of Tallinn and was instrumental in organizing the Tallinn Committee of the Russian Social Democratic Labor Party (Vene Sotsiaaldemokraatliku Tööliste Partei, VSDTP) at the end of 1904. Dmitri Ulianov, Lenin's younger brother, was active among the students at the University of Tartu.

Following the directives of the third congress of the VSDTP, the Estonian social democrats organized a revolution in Estonia in 1905. During the next years the Estonian socialists were split between the mensheviks and the bolsheviks. The latter began to publish their organ *Kiir* (Ray) in Narva on June 12, 1912.

After the March 1917 revolution in Russia

the first congress of the Northern Baltic Russian Social Democratic Organization (VSDTP Põhja-Balti Komitee) met in Tallinn. At that time there were 1,300 bolsheviks in Tallinn, 400 in Narva, and 180 in Tartu, led by Jaan Anvelt and Ivan Rabchinskii. The second congress was held on August 26-29, 1917.

## HISTORY

In October 1917 the Estonian Social Democratic Labor Party (Eesti Sotsiaaldemokraatlik Tööliste Partei, ESTP) formally came into existence. Its left wing, headed by Mihkel Martna, for a while favored cooperation with the bolsheviks. The Estonian bolsheviks preferred to remain in an Estonian section of the Russian bolshevik party. Their leading members included Viktor Kingisepp and Hans Pöögelmann.

After the bolshevik revolution in Russia in November 1917, the Estonian bolsheviks, cooperating with bolshevized units of the Russian army, were able to impose a Soviet regime in Estonia, but it was weak because the Estonian masses favored separation from Russia and independence. When peace negotiations between the Central Powers and Soviet Russia broke down in mid-February 1918, the German army occupied Estonia and put an end to bolshevik domination. The Estonians proclaimed their independence on February 24, 1918, but the German occupants had their own plans: Estonia and Latvia were to form a Baltic duchy under German rule. Not until after the collapse of Imperial Germany on November 11, 1918, was an independent Estonian republic established.

Between February and November 1918, however, the Estonian bolsheviks who had fled to Russia became very active and received much attention from the Soviet government, which had not given up its hope of recapturing Estonia. On May 11, 1918, an Estonian commissariat was created in the Soviet government's Commissariat of Nationality Affairs, and the recruitment of Estonian "red regiments" was begun. Hans Pöögelmann headed the Estonian commissariat, and Jaan Anvelt became the commander of the Estonian red regiments. The Estonian bolsheviks still remained organizationally bound to the Russian party and prepared for new bolshevization of the country.

After the collapse of Germany, the Soviet army, together with its Estonian units, began its march into Estonia with the announced aim of "liberating the country and transforming it into another soviet republic." The military forces of the independent Estonian republic, organized in haste by Johan Laidoner, were very weak and poorly armed. The Soviet forces were able to occupy the northern and eastern parts of Estonia (Narva on November 29 and Tartu on December 22). On November 16, only four days after the Red Army entered Estonia, a clandestine conference of Estonian bolsheviks was held in Tallinn to create the Estonian Organization of the Communist Party (Vene Kommunistliku Eesti Osakondade Keskkomitee). Viktor Kingisepp and Richard Vakman, who had entered the country illegally from Russia for this purpose, became its leaders. On November 29, in captured Narva, the Estonian commissariat proclaimed the Estonian Soviet Republic (also called the Estonian Workers' Commune), with Pöögelmann as head of the new Soviet government and Anvelt as commander of its military forces. On December 15 Soviet Russia recognized this new republic by decree, and the Red Army now claimed that its advance into Estonia was justified as aid to the Estonian comrades. For a few days it seemed that bolshevik planning was producing the desired results.

The Estonian government in Tallinn and its military leader Laidoner now made an effort to rally the Estonian masses for defense of the country against bolshevism. In early January 1919 the Estonian army, aided by some anti-bolshevik Russian units and a few volunteers from Finland, was able to start a counteroffensive. By the end of the month the Red Army and its Estonian units were defeated and forced to withdraw from Estonia. The front was stabilized outside Estonian territory, and some fighting by antibolshevik Russian units continued until December 1919, when an armistice was signed. In Tartu, on February 2, 1920, Soviet Russia signed a peace treaty with Estonia, recognizing its territorial integrity as an independent republic.

The "executive" power of the Estonian soviet government, which had been disbanded on June 5, 1919, was transferred to a Bureau Abroad of the Estonian Organization of the Communist Party in Russia. The communist organization was decreed illegal in Estonia. At its first congress, in November 1920, following the recommendation of the Comintern, the organization changed its name to Estonian Communist Party (Eestimaa Kommunistlik Partei, EKP). At the time the underground party had only 500 members, active in Tallinn, Narva, Tartu, Pärnu, Valga, Viljandi, Rakvere, Paide, and Tapa. As a result of revolutionary agitation in various youth organizations, athletic clubs, trade unions, and cultural associations, by March 1921 the EKP had 73 cells, with 1,100 members (365 in Tallinn alone). A year later membership had increased to 1,320 in a country of 1 million inhabitants. The party's central committee had nine members, including Kingisepp, Anvelt, Pöögelmann, Vakman, and Otto Rästas, and was publishing the illegal organ *Kommunist*.

In May 1922 Kingisepp was captured, tried, and executed. On December 1, 1924, the Estonian communists, openly assisted by Soviet Russian agencies, started an ill-fated coup while the Soviet armed forces waited at the borders. The Estonian authorities crushed the communist revolt by the end of the same day. A number of party leaders, including Jaan Tomp, Hans Heidemann, Jaan Kreuks, and Arnold Sommerling, were captured and sentenced to death, others were imprisoned, and still others escaped to Soviet Russia. As a result of recriminations in the communist camp, Pöögelmann was removed from the party leadership and replaced by A. Rürman. In 1927 Rürman was replaced by Aleksander Leiner, and after 1930 the party was led by Johannes Jürma.

Despite the fact that it had been greatly decimated, the EKP continued its illegal activities in Estonia. The Estonian communists had boycotted the elections to the constituent assembly and to the first parliament. In the elections to the second and third parliaments they participated under the name United Front of Working People (Töörahva Uhine Väerind) and captured 3.8 and 13 percent of the vote, respectively. In the second parliament they had ten deputies, including Jaan Tomp and Hans Heidemann. In July 1935 the EKP made an agreement with the left-wing socialists, some of whom (Aleksander Jõeäär, Nigol Andressen) became spokesmen for the communists in the parliament.

Following a general amnesty in 1938, many of the communists who had been imprisoned in 1925 were released. Neeme Ruus, Kristjan Jalak, and Aleksander Jõeäär participated in the new parliament as representatives of the Working People's United Group (Töötava Rahva Uhtlusrühm). Nevertheless, the EKP had been weakened by Stalin's purges, when such prominent Estonian communists as Anvelt and Pöögelmann had disappeared in the Soviet Union. When Estonia was invaded by the Soviet army on June 17, 1940, the EKP became a section of the All-Union Communist Party (Bolshevik).

## ORGANIZATION AND MEMBERSHIP

As early as 1921 the communists had managed to infiltrate the Estonian Trade Association (Eestimaa Ametiühing) in Tallinn, and within a year its membership increased from 10,000 to 20,000. The leading communists in this movement were Tomp and Paul Keerdo. The association was dissolved by the Estonian government because of its subversive activities.

An All-Estonian Proletarian Youth Association (Üle-Eestimaaline Noorproletaarlaste Ühing) was active from the end of 1920 to April 1921 and had 1,200 members in its twelve chapters. Its legal publication was *Noor tööline* (Young Worker), and it illegally published *Noor proletaarlane* (Youth Proletarian). The association was organized by Arnold Sommerling; Jaan Kreuks and Johannes Lauristin organized its successor, the Estonian Communist Youth Organization (Eestimaa Kommunistlik Noorsooühing), which had 300 members.

## RELATION TO SOVIET LEADERSHIP

The EKP was accepted in 1919 as a section of the Comintern, in which Pöögelmann played some role. The abortive revolt of December 1, 1924, although it had been inspired by the Comintern, was followed by mutual recriminations by the Comintern and the party leadership, resulting in Pöögelmann's removal from the party leadership.

## PARTY PRESS ORGANS

The Estonian communists had an illegal publication, *Rahva hääl* (People's Voice), in Estonia, and a legal publication, *Edasi* (Forward), in Leningrad.

## CONGRESSES AND CONFERENCES OF THE EKP

1st congress, November 1920 (underground in Estonia)
2d congress, October 1921 (underground in Estonia)
1st conference, November 13, 1926
2d conference, January 1, 1929
3d conference, August 1934
4th conference, April 1940

## BIBLIOGRAPHY

Laaman, Eduard: *Eesti iseseisvuse sünd* (The Birth of Estonian Independence), Tartu, Loodus, 1936.
Naan, G. I. (ed.): *Eesti NSV ajalugu (koige vanemast ajast tänapäevani)* (History of the Estonian SSR from Ancient Times to the Present), Tallinn, Eesti Riiklik Kirjastus, 1957.
Naan, G. I. (ed.): *Istoriia Estonskoi SSR* (History of the Estonian Soviet Socialist Republic), Tallinn, Estonskoe Gosizdat, 1958.

ELMAR LIPPING
EDGAR ANDERSON

# FINLAND

During the Finnish civil war which broke out early in 1918 a "red government" was set up by members of the Finnish Social Democratic Party (Sosialidemokraattinen Puolue, SDP), supported by Russian soldiers garrisoned In Finland. When the Red Guard, the paramilitary arm of the SDP, was defeated by volunteer units led by Carl Mannerheim and supported by military help from Germany, this government fled to Moscow. There, in an abandoned seminary building, they founded the Finnish Communist Party (Suomen Kommunistinen Puolue, SKP) in the last week of August 1918. The central committee elected at this founding congress included Otto Wille Kuusinen, Yrjö Sirola, K. M. Evä, Lauri Letonmäki, and Jukka Rahja.

Kuusinen and Sirola were to play especially prominent roles. Both had been leading figures in the executive committee of the SDP and had represented the SDP in the Finnish parliament. Kuusinen had been commissar of education in the 1918 red government, and in 1921 he was elected to the Executive Committee of the Comintern. One of his early posts was head of the policy section of the West European Bureau, where he was responsible for the Scandinavian and Finnish communist parties. In the ill-famed Terijoki government set up in Finland by the Soviets in 1939, Kuusinen served the dual role of prime and foreign minister, and when the Finnish-Soviet conflict ended in 1944 he remained in Moscow. By 1957 he was a ranking member of the presidium of the Communist Party of the Soviet Union. The senior author of *Fundamentals of Marxism-Leninism*, Kuusinen was one of the major ideologists of the Soviet party and until his death on May 17, 1964, a forceful proponent of the Soviet position in the Sino-Soviet schism.

Yrjö Sirola, who held the foreign-affairs portfolio in the 1918 red government, was one of the signatories of the invitation to the founding congress of the Comintern in 1919. He functioned both as an instructor in socialist theory in the Comintern and as a member of the SKP central committee. He died in Moscow in 1936.

## HISTORY

*1918 to 1922* In the period of "revolutionary crisis" following the Finnish civil war the SKP, which existed only in Russia, was at first totally opposed to any association with the Finnish social democrats. In an open letter to Lenin the party labeled parliamentary and trade-union activity as useless "Sisyphus work," and Kuusinen attacked the "middle-of-the-road" Finnish social democrats for failure to prove their Marxism. The SKP adopted a militant program and issued instructions on how to conduct an armed revolution.[1]

In May 1920 a Socialist Workers' Party (Sosialistinen Työväenpuolue) was established in Finland, primarily on Kuusinen's initiative. Although this party was not approved by the extreme left wing of the SKP, Lenin apparently intended it to serve as a model for the international movement. The party was dissolved by the Finnish authorities when it joined the Comintern. A month later, however, its platform was rewritten without the clause which formally affirmed its commitment to Comintern principles, and its name was changed to Finnish Socialist Workers' Party (Suomen Sosialistinen Työväenpuolue, SSTP). In addition to this success in forming a legal electoral party within Finland, in the spring of 1920 the communists gained control of the Finnish trade-union organization.

*1922 to 1928* During the 1920s, a period of relative political and economic stability in Finland, the communists enjoyed a certain degree of toleration and began to build an organizational network of various front organizations. In the 1922 general election the SSTP was able to send twenty-seven representatives to the 200-seat parliament. In the 1924 election the number was eighteen, and in the 1927 election twenty. Although the communists were outdistanced in all three elections by the social democrats, the agrarians, and the conservative national coalitionists, the SSTP had become a contender for the vote of the Finnish left.

In the trade-union field the communists concentrated on moving the focus of union activity to the work sites and local industrial councils. In 1922 the trade unionists voted to join the Profintern, but it was decided that formal adherence might alienate the social democrats in the organization and bring reprisals from the Finnish authorities. A Finnish Red Trade Union Federation (Suomen Punainen Ammattijärjestö) was formed, but it was limited in size and inconsequential.

In 1923 the Finnish Socialist Youth League (Suomen Sosialistinen Nuorisoliitto) was founded (and shortly afterward renamed Socialist Youth League). A part of this organization—the part that at the same time belonged to the underground Finnish Communist Youth League (Suomen Kommunistinen Nuorisoliitto)—joined the Communist Youth International. The Socialist Youth League was dissolved by the Finnish authorities in

1925 but continued to carry on its work until the middle 1930s.

*1928 to 1939* With the onset of economic crisis in 1928 communists throughout Europe were confronted with the rise of a reactionary right-wing movement intent on eliminating the left as an active political force. In Finland this was the Lapuan movement, named for the town where the conservatives first touched off an altercation with the communists. The Lapuan movement had originated coincidentally with continental fascism, but its roots were deep in the Finnish civil-war period and the ideological cleavages of the nineteenth century. In accordance with Comintern policy, the SKP now reviled the Finnish social democrats as "social fascists," and proclaimed opportunism as the main danger to the international communist movement. This rigid and militant policy was reflected in the communist involvement in the longshoremen's labor strike in 1928-1929 and the creation in 1930 of the Finnish Red League of the Men at the Front.

Anticommunist laws in effect by November 1930 drove the communists even further underground. In the 1929 general election the SSTP had managed to send twenty-three representatives to the parliament, but in the 1930 election it received a mere 11,504 valid ballots and was unble to obtain any parliamentary representation. The SSTP was never able to recuperate from these losses, and communist influence within Finland was almost completely eliminated.

The 1933 plenum of the SKP central committee still advocated the policy of a "united front from below," but in line with the Comintern's switch, the 1934 plenum reversed this stand. The Comintern had begun to push its new popular-front policy and in the spring of 1934 was directing its sections to negotiate with the socialist parties. The SKP offered to join the Finnish social democrats in a united front, but its offer was rejected. The sixth congress of the SKP in 1935 drew up resolutions outlining a modified united-front policy. Front activity was to be concerned primarily with the "economic struggle" and trade unions, and special emphasis was to be given to extending the work of youth organizations, cooperatives, and women's groups.

The anticommunist laws made it impossible for any communist front party to participate in the 1936 elections. The SKP central committee did, however, issue a public statement that the supporters of the Lapuan movement should be rejected at the polls and that everything possible should be done to check the "war-adventure politics" of the "fascists." The statement also protested the indictment of the SKP as a "criminal" organization.

*1939 to 1944* In November 1939 the Soviet Union invaded Finland, and the "winter war" began. The SKP's underground activity was even more strictly curtailed because collaboration with the Soviet party was synonymous with treason. In spite of this situation, the party did manage to maintain an organizational structure and to make pronouncements on the war situation. Many Finnish communists spent time in prison during the war and were apparently active in the ranks of prison inmates. However, the SKP's capacity to propagandize and to recruit in this period was minimal, and its success was limited.

During the winter war a puppet government was set up by the Soviets in the Finnish town of Terijoki. The response of the Finnish people to this maneuver was hostile, and the project was abandoned before the armistice in March 1940. With the renewal of hostilities in June 1941 and Finland's cobelligerency status with Nazi Germany, the SKP spent most of its time attacking the fascists in Germany and their sympathizers in Finland. A party pronouncement issued in September 1941 called for "peace, food, and freedom" and blamed Finland's involvement with the Soviet Union on the Finnish leaders (particularly Ryti, Tanner, and Mannerheim). With the termination of the Finnish-Soviet conflict in 1944 and the legalization of the SKP in the same year, the communists were instrumental in prosecuting the Finnish "war-guilt trials."

*1944 to 1965* Immediately after its legalization in September 1944 the SKP set up another electoral front party, the Finnish People's Democratic League (Suomen Kansan Demokraattinen Liitto, SKDL). In April 1945 the three largest parliamentary parties, the social democrats, the agrarians, and the SKDL, announced a plan to cooperate on certain legislative proposals. In March 1946 a cabinet was formed by Mauno Pekkala, a member of the Socialist Unity Party (Sosialistinen Yhtenäisyyspuolue), a minor left-wing group in sympathy with the SKDL program. The Pekkala cabinet included Matti Janhunen and Yrjö Murto (respectively, the minister of social affairs and the minister of supply), two members of the SKP who had participated in the illegal activity of the party during its underground period. In addition, the critical ministry of the interior was in the hands of Yrjö Leino, an active communist since the 1930s.

However, Leino became involved in a power struggle within the party, and by 1948 he was on the brink of defeat and in danger of being purged from the party. Despite the fact that he was married to Hertta Kuusinen, the daughter of Otto Kuusinen, who was by then a high-ranking official of the Soviet party, his principal opponent, Aimo Aaltonen, had the support of the Soviet party. Leino apparently represented the less radical wing of the SKP and was considered too nationalistic. Whatever his motives, he was instrumental in preventing a communist coup by alerting the Finnish authorities to possible "disturbances from the left." Soon afterward he lost both his cabinet position and his membership in the SKP. Since then the party has been controlled primarily by Aaltonen as party chairman, Wille Pessi as party secretary, and Hertta Kuusinen as chairman of SKDL's parliamentary group.

A treaty of friendship, cooperation, and mutual assistance signed by Finland and the Soviet Union in 1948 allayed fears that Finland would be drawn behind the Iron Curtain. Since then no communists have participated in the cabinet, and the SKP's influence at this level has been minimal. However, the communists have had striking success on the electoral front, where they have operated through the SKDL. From 1945 to 1962 they consistently captured 20 to 25 percent of the parliamentary seats. The SKDL has also been successful at the local level. In the 1964 municipal elections it received 22.0 percent of the valid ballots, approaching the socialist vote of 27.7 percent. This means that 19.6 percent of the councillors represented the SKDL, and 23.2 percent represented the socialists.

Through their numerous front organizations the communits have managed to penetrate virtually every sector of Finnish political and social life. The SKP's current program identifies it as a working-class party, with socialism as its goal. In October 1965 the SKP published a document[2] proclaiming that Marxist theory outlined no inflexible plan for attaining socialism, and that both Marx and Lenin had recognized the legitimacy of the nonviolent approach to effecting the socialist revolution. The current party program, adopted in 1957, also points out that the SKP desires to attain socialism through peaceful means, but both documents make it clear that nonviolent methods are not always possible in a capitalist society.

## ORGANIZATION AND MEMBERSHIP

The organizational network of the SKP extends throughout the country and has the structure common to Marxist-Leninist parties. The lowest units, the cells, are grouped in sections, regions, and then city organizations. These are further grouped by district, and representatives from the district units elect delegates to the party congress. The party congress, which since 1945 has been held every third year, elects a central committee, which in turn forms numerous functional committees with overlapping membership.

Precise membership figures of the SKP are available for the period 1955 through June 1965:

| | | | |
|---|---|---|---|
| 1955 | 48,722 | 1961 | 52,018 |
| 1956 | 48,345 | 1962 | 52,197 |
| 1957 | 47,138 | 1963 | 52,233 |
| 1958 | 48,482 | 1964 | 47,396 |
| 1959 | 42,893 | 1965 | 47,451 |
| 1960 | 48,016 | | |

A Finnish communist source in 1961 indicated that 83.4 percent of the SKP membership were workers.[3] The proceedings of the thirteenth party congress in 1963 gave this percentage as 84 percent. In the postwar period the communist vote in Finland was concentrated in two diverse geographical settings, the heavily industrialized areas in the southern and western parts of the country and the rapidly developing rural areas in the north and east.

The more important and influential of the front organizations of the SKP are the Finnish People's Democratic League, the Finnish Women's Democratic League, the Finnish Democratic Youth League, the Finnish Defenders of Peace, and the Finnish-Soviet Society.

## RELATION TO SOVIET LEADERSHIP

During most of its history the SKP was an underground party and to a great extent was dependent on the support of Moscow. Moreover, the SKP leadership was physically located in the Soviet Union, primarily in Moscow, Leningrad, and Petroskoi. This situation left little room for challenging directives of the Soviet party or the Comintern. The fact that during this period Otto Kuusinen was both a member of the SKP central committee and a ranking functionary of the Comintern further contributed to the SKP's subordination to Comintern policy.

During the postwar era the SKP made its contribution to Stalin's image and the "cult of personality." Even after Stalin's death this hero worship continued. With the revelations of Khrushchev's 1956 "secret speech," the SKP managed to make the required change in attitude: one of the first party articles to deal explicitly with this speech maintained that the principles of the SKP were in no way affected and that Stalin's misdeeds were an internal affair of the Soviet party.[4]

The SKP congresses held during Khrushchev's tenure endorsed without qualification his handling of the communist movement and the principle of "peaceful coexistence." With his fall in October 1964 the SKP was able to accept the transition to the new Soviet leadership without much difficulty. At a meeting between delegates of the SKP (Aaltonen, Pessi, Kuusinen, Saarinen, and Tuominen) and the Soviet party (Brezhnev, Suslov, and Ponomarev) both delegations affirmed "the *complete* coincidence of their parties' positions on urgent questions of the international communist movement" and that "both parties in *all* their activity *invariably* are guided by the propositions of the 1957 declaration and the 1960 statement, the program documents of the world communist movement."[5] The SKP had subscribed to these two documents prior to the deposition of Khrushchev, and the meeting simply served as evidence for anyone concerned that the change in Soviet leadership meant no change in the relations between the two parties.

Even though the SKP as a party has basically conformed to the directives of the Moscow leadership, there have been occasional deep cleavages within its ranks. The record indicates factions from the formative years of the party to the present, such as the early split between Kuusinen and Kullervo Manner over the issue of "ultrabolshevism," the divisive events surrounding the so-called "Kuusinen Club murders," the Stalinist purges in the 1930s, when many of the top SKP leaders (including Manner and E. Gylling, who had been one of the political bosses of Soviet Karelia) were eliminated, the defection of Arvo Tuominen, first secretary of the party between 1935 and 1940, primarily over the issue of the Terijoki government, and more recently, the appearance of the journal

*Tilanne* (The Situation), with its indictment of Stalinism within the party ranks.[6] Reports of a party purge against non-Stalinist elements appeared in the press in early 1964.[7]

At the twenty-second congress of the Soviet party the SKP delegation made some anti-Albanian statements which were published in *Pravda*.[8] The published proceedings of the SKP's thirteenth congress, held in April 1963, noted that the Albanians and the Chinese had "unfortunately" failed to carry on discussions in a "comradely spirit" after the November 1960 Moscow meeting. The SKP in addition found the Chinese and Albanian reaction to Soviet behavior in the Cuban missile crisis "incomprehensible." The SKP's restraint may be attributed to the fact that at that point the Soviet party was trying to bring about a meeting with the Chinese, and the polemics were being deescalated. At the 1960 congress of the SKP the Chinese had been represented by U Tze-pu, who was listed second only to the Soviet delegation, headed by Brezhnev. At the 1963 congress the Chinese were not represented, and the Soviet delegation was headed by a second stringer, V. S. Tolstikov.

It was not until the summer of 1963 that the position of the SKP on the Chinese question was made explicit. In an editorial entitled "The Attitude of the Chinese Communist Leaders,"[9] the SKP severely criticized the behavior of the Chinese and gave full support to the Soviet handling of the international communist movement. This position was reiterated at a February 1965 meeting of the Finnish and Soviet party leaders.

## FUTURE PROSPECTS

Even as an underground party the SKP has always been an active element in Finnish politics and was represented in the institutional structure of the international communist movement. Since its legalization in 1944 the party has continued to express its ambition to attain a proletarian internationalism but has at the same time been anxious to cultivate a role within the framework of the Finnish multiparty system. The SKP can probably be expected to become increasingly more integrated into the structure and political system of the Finnish state.

## PARTY PRESS ORGANS AND RECORDS

*Kansan Uutiset* (People's Voice) is the leading party newspaper, and *Kommunisti* is the theoretical journal of the party.

For the current bylaws of the SKP, adopted at the eleventh congress in 1957, see *Suomen Kommunistinen Puolueen säännöt* (Statutes of the Finnish Communist Party), Helsinki, 1957. The present program, also adopted at the 1957 congress, is contained in *Suomen Kommunistinen Puolueen ohjelma* (Program of the Finnish Communist Party), Helsinki, 1957.

## CONGRESSES OF THE SKP

1st congress, August 1918, Moscow
2d congress, 1919, Moscow
3d congress, 1920, Moscow
4th congress, 1921, Moscow
5th congress, 1925, Moscow
6th congress, 1935, Moscow
7th congress, October 1945, Helsinki
8th congress, August 1948, Helsinki
9th congress, November 1951, Helsinki
10th congress, October 1954, Helsinki
11th congress, May-June 1957, Helsinki
12th congress, April 1960, Helsinki
13th congress, April 1963, Helsinki

## BIBLIOGRAPHY

Allardt, Erik: *Social Sources of Finnish Communism: Traditional and Emerging Radicalism*, Helsinki, University of Helsinki Institute of Sociology, 1963 (mimeographed).

Borg, Olavi: *Suomen puolueet ja puolueohjelmat, 1880-1964* (Finnish Parties and Party Programs, 1880-1964), Helsinki, Werner Söderström Osakeyhtiö, 1965.

Hakalehto, Ilkka: *SKP ja sen vaikutus poliittiseen ja ammatilliseen työväenliikkeeseen, 1918-1928* (The SKP and Its Influence on the Political and Trade Workers' Movement, 1918-1928), Porvoo, Werner Söderström Osakeyhtiö, 1966.

Hyvämäki, Lauri: *Vaaran vuodet, 1944-1948* (Years of Danger, 1944-1948), Helsinki, Kustannusosakeyhtiö Otava, 1955.

Kuusinen, O. W.: *Bibliothek der Kommunistischen Internationale*, vol. XV, *Die Revolution in Finnland*, Hamburg, 1921.

Matti, Bengt: "Finlands Kommunistiska Parti" (Finnish Communist Party), in Åke Sparring (ed.), *Kommunismen i Norden* (Communism in the Nordic Countries), Lund, Utrikespolitiska Institutet, 1965; published in English as William E. Griffith (ed.), *Communism in Europe: Continuity, Change, and the Sino-Soviet Dispute*, Cambridge, Mass., MIT Press, 1965.

Rintala, Marvin: *Three Generations: The Extreme Right Wing in Finnish Politics*, Bloomington, Ind., Indiana University Press, 1962.

Sirola, Yrjö: *Muistelmia suomalaisesta demokratian esitaistelijasta* (Memories of a Finnish Champion of Democracy), Helsinki, Kansankultturi Oy., 1946.

*SKP taistelujen tiellä* (The SKP on the Path of Struggle), vols. I-XII, Helsinki, Puoluetoimikunnan Valistusjaosto, 1945-1956.

Tuominen, Arvo: *Kremlin kellot* (Kremlin Bells), Helsinki, Kustannusosakeyhtiö Tammi, 1957.

JACK L. KANGAS

1. *Kiireellisiä toimintaohjeita: Suomen vallankumoukselliselle työväelle ja sotaväelle*, Pietari, Central Committee of the Finnish Communist Party, 1919.

2. "On the Marxist Thoery of the State and the Finnish Path to Socialism," reprinted in *Kommunisti*, no. 10, 1965.

3. *Kommunisti*, no. 6, 1961, pp. 218-219.

4. *Kommunisti*, nos. 7-8, 1956, p. 382.

5. *Pravda*, February 20, 1965, pp. 1-2 (italics added).

6. See especially the issue of February-March 1962 and, in the same connection, the counterindictment of *Tilanne*'s editor in *Literaturnaia gazeta*, March 26, 1964.

7. *Helsingin Sanomat*, January 10 and February 9, and *Kansan Lehti*, February 3.

8. *Pravda*, November 14, 1961.

9. *Kansan Uutiset*, July 2, 1963.

# THE FOURTH INTERNATIONAL

Late in 1923 a group of members of the Moscow organization of the Russian Communist Party (Bolshevik), led by Leon Trotsky, started a left opposition which later spread to other party organizations. Some of the old bolshevik party leaders, such as Lev Kamenev and Grigorii Zinoviev, who at first supported Stalin's action against this opposition, in 1926 went over to Trotsky's "Left Opposition." By that time the main cause for dissent was Stalin's implementation of his theory of "socialism in one country," which in Trotsky's view destroyed the revolutionary impetus of bolshevism outside Soviet Russia. Trotsky continued to preach his theory of the "permanent revolution" on a worldwide scale. The Stalin-Trotsky struggle slowly spread to other communist parties where Zinoviev, through his leading role in the Comintern (see *The Communist International*), had many personal friends and followers.

Through his domination of the party apparatus Stalin was able to eliminate Trotsky from the Soviet party and have him deported in 1929 to Turkey. Trotsky immediately began to organize the opposition leaders in other parties, and in 1930 the Trotskyists, most of whom had been expelled from their own communist parties, called a "world conference" of the Left Opposition in Paris and founded the International Communist League. The purpose of this league was to spread Trotsky's theoretical and practical opposition to Stalinism and to divert communist support from the Comintern.

Stalin's ruthless suppression of Trotskyists in other communist parties as well as in his own had the effect of polarizing the left opposition. Prominent communists expelled from their parties on charges of "Trotskyism" (James P. Cannon and Max Shachtman in the United States, Boris Souvarine in France, and many others) contributed greatly to the anti-Stalinist campaign led by Trotsky, whose prolific writings, circulated in several languages, were an important factor in the growth of this leftist-radical communist movement.

In July 1936 a conference organized by the International Communist League met in Geneva. Among the most prominent delegates were the representatives of Trotskyist organizations in France, Belgium, Italy, Switzerland, and the Netherlands; representatives from the United States (Workers Party) participated as observers. The conference established a General Council, an International Secretariat, and a Bureau and resolved to call a founding congress of the Fourth International. The political line adopted, which was continued with little change, was based on Trotsky's interpretation of Marxist ideology during the early bolshevik stage in Russia. Perhaps most characteristic of the movement was its attitude toward the Soviet regime:

> The proletarian vanguard of the entire world will support the USSR in war, in spite of the parasitic bureaucracy of the uncrowned Negus in the Kremlin, because the social regime of the USSR, despite all its deformations and ulcers, represents an enormous historical step forward in comparison with putrified capitalism.... The defeat of the Soviet Union would not only signify the collapse of the Soviet bureaucracy, but also the replacement of the state and collective property by capitalist chaos.[1]

In 1936 this expressed Trotsky's hopes that the left opposition would return to power in Russia after Stalin's expected demise. Even after Trotsky was assassinated in Mexico City in 1940 by Jacques Mornard, an agent of the Soviet secret police, and after the start of the German-Soviet war, as well as after its victorious outcome, the Trotskyists continued to defend and support the Soviet Union.

The founding congress of the Fourth International, held in Switzerland in September 1938, met in secrecy; shortly before, Soviet secret police had kidnapped and killed Rudolf Klement, the secretary of the League's Bureau. The thirty delegates represented organizations in the Untied States, France, Great Britain, Germany, the Soviet Union, Italy, Poland, Belgium, Greece, the Netherlands, and Latin America. Delegates from several other states were allegedly unable to attend because of difficulties in leaving their own countries.

The goal of the Fourth International was a "world party of the socialist revolution," as distinguished from a "world communist party," which was the goal of the Third (Communist) International. The program and organizational scheme of the League were retained. Trotsky provided the basic theoretical and strategic outlook for the entire movement which, in a permanently changing interpretation, was used as policy and tactics by organizations of his followers. The founding congress adopted a "program of transition," a vague and elastic document that was accepted by all delegates but was soon interpreted in a divergent manner by many member sections and their components. Growing international tension provided the nourishment for these divergencies that produced factional strife in most sections after the outbreak of World War II.

In 1939, before World War II began, the International Secretariat of the Fourth International moved secretly to the United States, operating with the support of the Socialist Workers Party (SWP), the strongest section of the International. But early in 1940, as an outcome of a quarrel within the SWP over the

Soviet aggression against Finland, a group led by Max Shachtman left the SWP and this weakened the party. In order to establish smoother cooperation with its sections in the western hemisphere, the International Secretariat called an extraordinary international conference "somewhere in America" in May 1940 with participation of prominent Trotskyists, refugees from Europe. A situation report prepared by Trotsky and entitled "The Proletarian Revolution and the Second Imperialist War" formulated the new policy of the Trotskyists.

A few weeks after this conference Trotsky was assassinated, and the movement suffered a setback from which it never recovered. Without the support of "the prophet," permanent quarrels and splits in the Trotskyist groups and parties often turned into factional struggles in which a party leader might be praised as a hero one day, only to be branded an "opportunist," "revisionist," or outright traitor a month later.

Late in 1940, to escape prosecution under the Voorhis act's ban on political parties with headquarters abroad, the SWP dropped formal membership in the Fourth International in favor of "fraternal affiliation" with it. This, however, did not affect the prominent role of the SWP in the movement.

Despite German occupation the Trotskyist underground organizations in Western Europe managed to hold a European conference in February 1944 which reestablished a European Secretariat and revived the movement in the occupied countries. After the collapse of Nazi Germany the Trotskyists in the liberated countries shared in the gains made by all leftist parties and increased their membership and activities. In the spring of 1946 the American and European secretariats called an international conference which promoted itself to be a congress. Twelve sections participated in this meeting and a new Executive Committee and International Secretariat with the seat in Paris were elected. The conference recommended that sections with various organizational forms create political parties with mass appeal. The new leadership was entrusted with the preparation and calling of a second world congress.

This next congress was held in Paris in April-May 1948. A total of twenty-two delegations from nineteen countries participated. The new political line adopted by this meeting rehashed Trotsky's old theses: Stalin and his bureaucracy were condemned as enemies of the proletariat but all his conquests and institutions belonging to "the first proletarian state" were praised as great achievements which Trotskyists must defend at all costs. Unconfirmed rumors at the time of the congress pointed out that acceptance of this line by both the Fourth International and the Kremlin leadership was negotiated by Isaac Deutscher in exchange for a promise by Moscow that assassinations of Trotskyist leaders by the NKVD would stop.

The 1951 congress emphasized this line again, and at the same time shifted the movement still further to the left. At the congress an ideological and tactical difference emerged between the British Trotskyists and Michel Pablo (Michael Raptis, of Greek origin), the leader of the French Trotskyists and head of the Fourth International. This conflict led to a split at the fourth congress, held in Paris in 1953. The "Pabloists" retained command of the International but the SWP and the British Socialist Labour League (SLL) accused Pablo of opportunism and revisionism and left the International. In September 1953 the SLL called a conference in London which created the International Committee of the Fourth International. The SWP as well as other anti-Pabloist sections or their splinter parties joined this new organization.

The congresses of the old Fourth International in 1957 and 1961 showed the weakness resulting from splits in the sections and their components, and from the division into Paris and London centers. But by 1961 the need for unity and joint action had become apparent to leaders of both centers. Negotiations between both groups, initiated by the SWP, gave partial results. The strongest opposition was raised by the British SLL, which was supported by a small American group that later split away from the SWP and founded the Workers League. A campaign for a "unification congress" found positive response in most sections of the International. But before this congress was held, Juan Posadas, leading a Latin American faction with some followers in Great Britain, France, Belgium, and Italy, seceded from the International in 1962 and established his own International Secretariat in Argentina. Early in 1963 the SWP left the London Committee and joined in the efforts for unification.

The Rome unification congress was held in 1963, with delegates from twenty-six countries participating, and it accomplished the unification of the great majority of Trotskyist parties and organizations from around the world. The congress adopted a sixteen-point program which was first drafted and accepted by the SWP. Several political resolutions dealt with the Sino-Soviet split, with de-Stalinization, with the revolutionary movement in Africa, with recent developments in Yugoslavia, and with other current problems.

Although Pablo presided over this widely advertised unification, it obviously did not satisfy his own plans. Shortly after the congress, in 1964, he left the International and formed his own organization with followers mostly in France and former French Africa.

Another important development after the unification congress concerned the Trotskyist Lanka Sama Samaja Party (LSSP) in Ceylon. (See *Ceylon*.) After 1948 it grew to be the second strongest political party on the island and secured strong worker support (notably lacking in all other Trotskyist parties). It gained some stature in the International and some influence among leftists in Southeast Asia. Its united front with the local communists and other leftist "bourgeois" parties led to electoral success and a strong position in a coalition government. But the leaders of the Fourth International criticized the Ceylonese party, demanding adjustment to orthodox Trotskyist theories and tactics. At the Rome congress the party was censured and ordered to comply with the International's demands for political amendments. It is noteworthy that the Trotskyists, who in the past had strongly objected to interference by the Comintern in the internal party affairs of their members, now repeated this themselves, but without desired results. In June 1964 the United Secretariat expelled the LSSP from the Fourth International.

The eighth congress, held in Paris in December 1965 with the participation of sixty delegates from twenty-five countries, proceeded in an atmosphere of unity and harmony. Its resolutions dealt with the defense of Vietnam, with the need for leadership in the revolutionary movement in Africa, and with an analysis of the "new left" in the United States. The sections were urged to take an active part in these developments.

Thus at the end of 1965 there were four active Trotskyist international centers. The old Fourth International, with its United Secretariat in Paris, was headed by Pierre Frank from the French Party of Communist Internationalists, Joseph Hansen from the SWP, Livio Maitan from Italy, and Hugo Blanco from Peru. The International Committee in London was headed by Cliff Slaughter and Gerry Healy (both from the SLL), Tim Wohlforth (Workers League, USA), Pierre Lambert and Stephen Just (France), M. Ratos and M. Varga. The International Secretariat headed by Posadas in Argentina was the third center that made efforts to have an international following. The insignificant Pablo group in Paris included some dissenters from the above three groups. The old Fourth International definitely had by far the largest following among Trotskyists active throughout the world.

Despite its organizational fragmentation and small formal membership, the Trotskyist movement has considerable influence in some circles. In addition to its local chapters around the world, its doctrinaire radicalism has many unaffiliated followers, particularly among middle-class intellectuals and revolutionary youth. In strikes and mass demonstrations Trotskyist militants usually join the communists of both the Moscow and Peking camps.

## THE SINO-SOVIET DISPUTE

All three Trotskyist groups have evidenced great concern about the Sino-Soviet split, which they see as a danger to the survival of the communist regimes. The old Fourth International has attempted to maintain a neutral stand; it criticizes both sides and advocates a common front of all communist-dominated states. The British International Committee keeps its criticism of Soviet bureaucracy in moderate terms but defends "Peking's achievements" against Soviet attack. Posadas attacks with equal violence Soviet bureaucracy and Yugoslav revisionism, showing sympathy for Maoist China.

## PRESS ORGANS

Since 1936 the Paris Bureau of the Fourth International has issued the quarterly *Quatrième Internationale*, which carries the subtitle "Organ of the Executive Committee of the Fourth International." A biweekly press service, *World Outlook—Perspective mondiale*, with Joseph Hansen and Pierre Frank as editors, appears in New York in English and in Paris in French. In the United States the Socialist Workers Party began publication in 1940 of *The Fourth International*, a quarterly that changed its name in 1956 to *International Socialist Review* (New York) and is the semiofficial organ of the party.

In 1964 the International Committee of the Fourth International in London began publication of an irregular periodical entitled *Fourth International*; it replaced *Labour Review*, which was published for twelve years.

The Posadas group publishes *Cuarta Internacional* as the official organ of the International Secretariat of the Fourth International. *Revista marxista latinoamericana* and *Red Flag* are published by its Latin American and European bureaus, respectively.

## CONFERENCES AND CONGRESSES OF THE FOURTH INTERNATIONAL

International conference for the Fourth International, July 1936, Geneva
1st (founding) congress, September 1938 (Switzerland)
International conference (congress), spring 1946
2d congress, April-May 1948, Paris
3d congress, 1951, Paris
4th congress, 1953, Paris
5th congress, 1957
6th congress, 1961
7th (reunification) congress, 1963, Rome
8th congress, December 1965, Paris

## BIBLIOGRAPHY

Cannon, James P.: *The End of the Comintern, with the Manifesto of the 4th International*, New York, Pioneer Publishers, 1943.

Cannon, James P.: *The History of American Trotskyism: Report of a Participant*, New York, Pioneer Publishers, 1944.

Frank, Pierre: *La Quatriéme Internationale* Paris, F. Maspero, 1969.

Posadas, Juan: *The Intellectuals and the Professional Workers: The Development of the Socialist Revolution and the IVth International*, "Red Flag" supplement, n.p., 1968.

Shachtman, Max: *Ten Years: History and Principles of the Left Opposition*, New York, Pioneer Publishers. 1933.

*Theses, Resolutions, and Appeals of the First International Conference for the Fourth International*, published by the International Secretariat for the Fourth International, Toronto, Workers Party of Canada [1936] (mimeographed).

Tilak, K.: *Rise and Fall of the Comintern: From the First to the Fourth International*, Bombay, Spark Syndicate, 1947.

WITOLD S. SWORAKOWSKI

1. *Theses, Resolutions, and Appeals of the First International Conference for the Fourth International*, Toronto, Workers Party of Canada [1936] (mimeographed), p. 19.

# FRANCE

The French Communist Party (Parti Communiste Français, PCF) was born at the eighteenth national congress of the Socialist Party, French Section of the Workers' International[1] (Parti Socialiste, Section Française de l'Internationale Ouvrière, SFIO), held at Tours on December 25-30, 1920. Those who advocated affiliation with the Comintern managed to get their point of view adopted by a majority of 3,208 to 1,022 on a motion of the Committee for the Reconstruction of the International. The motion was presented by Jean Longuet, a grandson of Karl Marx, and Paul Faure, who later became general secretary of the SFIO. At the time of the vote Léon Blum had withdrawn the motion of his Committee for Socialist Resistance and urged his colleagues not to take part in the vote; thus there were 397 abstentions, the votes of Blum's faction.

The majority, soon to rename itself Communist Party, French Section of the Communist International (Parti Communiste, Section Française de l'Internationale Communiste, PCF), retained only thirteen deputies out of sixty-eight and one daily newspaper out of six, but this daily was the only one with national distribution, *L'Humanité*, founded by Jean Jaurès in 1904. This group also retained the party headquarters, two-thirds of its assets, and a majority of its membership (109,000 out of 178,000). Thus the PCF began with real estate, money, resources, a party apparatus, a daily newspaper, a following, and a place in French society.

## HISTORY

After the congress at Tours the new party was far from being homogeneous, and equally far from constituting a bolshevik type of party. The resolution which had won the majority of the votes had been presented jointly by the Committee for the Reconstruction of the International and the Cachin-Frossard faction. Thus, officially, the majority at Tours embraced two groups: those who had advocated for a long period of time and in all sincerity "adherence to Moscow," and the "centrists," won over with much reluctance and many reservations.

Even the Committee for the Reconstruction of the International included some militants who refused to accept unreservedly the Moscow theses, particularly with regard to the relations between the party and the trade unions, or who were mistaken about the true nature of bolshevism, to which they had rallied principally out of hatred for war. Nevertheless, the militants who were devoted to Moscow formed the solid nucleus on which Grigorii Zinoviev, chairman of the Comintern, and Leon Trotsky, specialist on French questions, depended to give the party the structure, composition, and spirit which would make it a "new kind of party," the organization of professional revolutionaries of which Lenin had spoken.

Conflicts between the two factions developed during 1921. At first the communists and their allies were not successful in ousting the leadership of the General Confederation of Labor (Confédération Générale du Travail, CGT) and getting it to join the Red International of Labor Unions. A communist minority, led by Gaston Monmousseau and Pierre Monatte, left the CGT and in 1922 founded the Unity CGT (CGT Unitaire, CGTU), in which the numerous revolutionary trade unionists and anarchosyndicalists were to struggle for several years against total domination by the communists.

Within the party the centrists and their anarchist allies did their utmost to resist the injunctions and summonses they received from Moscow. At the first party congress, held in Marseilles in December 1921, a violent debate began on the "question of the delegate to the Executive Committee of the International," Boris Souvarine, who suddenly became the target for criticism of the Comintern leadership. When the congress chose a new directing committee, Souvarine was not reelected, and Fernand Loriot, Amedée Dunois, and Paul Vaillant-Couturier resigned in protest.

This crisis was complicated by the fact that in the same month the Comintern had launched the slogan of a "united front"—an alliance with the same socialists from whom the French communists had been ordered to separate one year earlier. The great majority of the party leaders protested this reversal, and the delegation which they sent in February 1922 to the meeting of the enlarged Executive Committee of the Comintern was composed mainly of militants hostile to the new line. They gave in only after being ordered to do so, but the party continued to act as it pleased, with the result that it was accused by Zinoviev of sabotaging the decisions of the Comintern.

At the second congress of the PCF (Paris, October 1922), attended by Dmitrii Manuilskii as Comintern representative, the party was divided into three factions. The motion of the center (Cachin-Frossard) won 1,698 votes; that of the left, which carried the Comintern's approval, received 1,516 votes; there were 814 abstentions because the rightist faction did not risk a vote. Marcel Cachin announced, in the name of his faction, that the center would assume leadership of the party. In the face of a threatened split by the left, however, the majority accepted Manuilskii's arbitration.

The fourth congress of the Comintern in 1922 passed a "resolution on the French question" which fixed the composition of the PCF's governing bodies, particularly its secretariat (André Louis Frossard and Albert Treint, general secretaries, and Louis Sellier, Frossard's deputy), as well as the "program of work and action" which the party was to follow. The resolution implicitly excluded from membership those who belonged to the Freemasons and any who contributed to papers which were not party organs. On January 1, 1923, Frossard resigned. About 100 militants, at whom the Comintern resolution was aimed, formed a resistance committee and were immediately excluded from the party. Many followers, including some workers, also left. Party membership fell to approximately 45,000.[2]

This crisis would certainly have been more serious had the party not suddenly found itself engaged in a revolutionary situation. In December 1922, in conformance with the directives of the Comintern, the PCF and the CGTU had formed a joint action committee charged with organizing agitation against the occupation of the Ruhr by French troops. On their return from an international meeting at Essen on January 6, 1923, the eight committee delegates—including Treint, the party's general secretary, and Cachin, who had lost his parliamentary immunity—were arrested. This was the party's first great clash with the government; although the communists had not succeeded in arousing the French working masses, their action among the French occupation troops had been effective enough to warrant retaliation by the French government.

*Bolshevization: 1924 to 1927* The third congress of the PCF, meeting in Lyons on January 20-24, 1924, initiated a transformation of the party structure, increasing the importance of the shop cells, and of the composition of its cadres, with workers replacing the intellectuals. It defined the communist position on the legislative elections of May 11, 1924, where it presented its candidates under the aegis of a "worker and peasant bloc." The PCF won 877,000 votes and twenty-six seats, sixteen of which were in the Paris area.

Action against the "Rif war," inaugurated in September 1924 by the famous

Doriot-Sémard telegram to Abd el-Krim, continued during 1925 under the leadership of a central action committee. Although Maurice Thorez, member of the PCF central committee since January 1924, chaired this committee, Jacques Doriot played the leading role. The activities of the committee brought on an intensification of antimilitarist action and the organization of anticolonialist agitation.

Even while pursuing this violent course of action, in compliance with the directives of the fifth congress of the Comintern (June-July 1924), the party proceeded with "bolshevization": reorganization from the shop cells up, creation of a centralized leadership apparatus, substitution of regional organizations for the former federations of loose groups, creation of communist factions in the trade unions, increased emphasis on workers in the party ranks, and emphasis on the antimilitarist struggle. In August 1924 the party leadership approved the directives on bolshevization and ruled that reorganization should be accomplished by December 31. The fourth party congress at Clichy in January 1925 postponed this deadline until April.

A new crisis arose when Boris Sourvarine was excluded from the Comintern Executive Committee for "Trotskyism" in July 1924, a measure which was also to affect unionists Alfred Rosmer and Pierre Monatte, allies of Souvarine, the following December.

At the party's fifth congress, held at Lille in June 1926, Souvarine was expelled from the PCF, Treint and Suzanne Girault were dropped from the political bureau and replaced by Jacques Doriot, Maurice Thorez, and Henri Barbé, the secretary of the Communist Youth (Jeunesses Communistes). Treint and Suzanne Girault, accused of forming a Trotskyist faction, were expelled from the party at the national conference in January 1928 (although Suzanne Girault was reinstated several years later).

*Class against Class: 1927 to 1933* In the period that followed, the Comintern's directives tended on one hand to render the PCF's external action more revolutionary, in compliance with the Moscow thesis on "radicalization of the masses," and on the other hand to push into the leadership of the party the militants of the younger generation who had held no positions in the SFIO and had come chiefly from the communist youth organization.

On April 2, 1927, a letter from the Presidium of the Comintern ordered the PCF to "adjust" its party line and to "bring parliamentary political life out of its traditional rut by dominating the political struggle and the electoral struggle of the following year, with great movements of class struggle." After long discussions, a majority broke away from the central committee and in November 1927 adopted the "class-against-class" tactic. Before the legislative elections of April 1928 the PCF proposed to the SFIO that a worker-peasant bloc be formed in the runoff to unite against the bourgeois candidates (including a Radical Party[3] candidate) in support of the socialist or communist candidate who received the most votes in the first balloting. In the event that agreement could not be reached (and the communists knew that this would be the case, for the SFIO would be obliged to break completely with the Radicals to make such an arrangement), the communist candidate would remain in the runoff, even against the socialist candidate. The result of this tactic was that although the number of votes received climbed to 1,070,000, the number of communist seats dropped from twenty-five to fourteen. Despite this defeat, the tactic was upheld. In the May 1932 elections the PCF polled no more than 783,000 votes and won only twelve seats.

At the same time, in the name of the "radicalization of the masses," the party organized tumultuous street demonstrations which resulted in repression of both the party and the CGTU. The demonstration most damaging for the communists occurred on August 1, 1929; it was organized on instructions from the Comintern under the slogan of "defense of the Soviet Union against imperialist aggression." In the aftermath of this failure a large number of PCF leaders were arrested, and for the first time the party was reduced to near illegality. Membership dropped (52,000 members in 1928, 38,000 in 1930, 28,000 in 1933), and internal conflicts provoked new purges, such as the exclusion of Louis Sellier, former general secretary, and his group in November 1929.

It was in this period that the matter of the Barbé-Célor group developed. In 1928 Manuilskii, then secretary of the Comintern, had ordered the Communist Youth militants to take over leadership of the party in order to eliminate the old socialists from the higher positions. At the congress of Saint-Denis, in March-April 1929, the post of general secretary, occupied by Pierre Sémard since Treint's liquidation, was replaced by a "collectively responsible political secretariat" comprising Henri Barbé, Pierre Célor, Benoît Frachon, and Maurice Thorez, who was charged with propaganda and organization. At first this "youth group" worked in perfect harmony according to the directives of the Comintern Secretariat. Suddenly, in July 1931, Manuilskii condemned the group; Raymond Guyot was charged with the task of denouncing the "youth group," of which he was a member, at a meeting of the PCF political bureau. The investigation was entrusted to André Marty. The group was dissolved, but amicably so: Célor alone was excluded (at the end of 1932); Barbé was demoted, and Lozeray and François Billoux were reprimanded. Barbé left the party for other reasons in 1934.

*The Popular Front: 1934 to 1939* With Hitler's rise to power in Germany on January 30, 1933, rightist organizations in Paris called for a street demonstration for February 6, 1934, to show their strength. This developed into a riot with socialist counterdemonstrators, who were joined by communist militants, and sixteen persons were killed. The PCF at that time called for common action of the working class and for a "united front from below" with the socialist rank and file, bypassing any cooperation with the socialist leadership. In fact the communist press attacked the SFIO leaders as "lackeys of the bourgeoisie" and "social patriots" cooperating with the government. On February 9, the PCF called for a counterdemonstration, again appealing for support from the socialist ranks while abusing the socialist leadership; another six victims were the result. The SFIO then called for a mass demonstration in Vincennes on February 12, the date the CGT had announced for a general strike. Under pressure of public opinion the communists agreed to join. This was the first demonstration organized jointly by the SFIO, the PCF, the CGT, and the CGTU, and the first harbinger of the common action by the two parties of the French left which led to the formation of the so-called "popular front"[4] (see *The Communist International*).

After long haggling, on July 27, 1934, the PCF and the SFIO signed a pact for unity of action in the struggle against fascism and the economic and social policy of the government. A coordinating committee was formed to direct the common action. On October 9 Thorez proposed to the committee that the unity pact be extended to the Radical Party, to seal "the alliance of the middle classes with the working class," and the PCF immediately began campaigning for a popular front. Despite some protest from both revolutionary militants and some socialists, on July 14, 1935, a huge popular demonstration celebrated the creation of the Popular Front (Rassemblement Populaire), composed of the PCF, the SFIO, the Radical Party, the CGT, the CGTU, and the League for the Rights of Man. The CGT and CGTU were unified several months later.

The hostility of the PCF to national defense, in accordance with the Comintern policy of opposition to the "imperialist war," lasted until May 1935—or, more specifically, until the Laval-Stalin communiqué of May 15, 1935. The communiqué stated: "Mr. Stalin understands and approves fully the policy of national defense set by France to maintain her armed forces at a security level." Thorez then declared: "If, for whatever reasons, there would be on the side of the Soviet Union [as an ally] an imperialist state, the war would not be a war of two imperialist camps.... We would no longer have to apply our slogan of transformation of the imperialist war into a civil war, because in such a war it is not a question of an imperialist war. We are not judging the war as petit bourgeois pacifists. We have always supported Stalin and we shall always support him in the future."[5]

The seventh congress of the Comintern, meeting in Moscow in July-August 1935, recommended that all communist parties adopt this new popular-front policy. Dimitrov publicly gave credit for this tactic to the PCF, which apparently now ranked second only to the Soviet party in the Comintern, a position hitherto belonging to the Communist Party of Germany. Under this official policy the PCF emphasized its reconciliation with the center. On October 17, 1935, Thorez, who officially became the general secretary of the PCF at the eighth congress held in January 1936, declared that the communists were "ready to assume their responsibility in a popular-front government." In January 1936 the PCF did not seem opposed to the formation of a government under leadership of the Radicals; its deputies voted for this government at the time of the ratification of the Franco-Soviet mutual-assistance pact on February 27. On April 17 Thorez appealed to the Catholics: "We offer you our hand, Catholic worker, employee, artisan, peasant, we who are laymen, because you are our brothers."

In the May 1936 elections the PCF won seventy-two seats out of 618 and polled 1,468,949 votes (or 12.45 percent of the total registered electorate and 14.76 percent of the total vote). Although the communists refused to participate in the government headed by Léon Blum, they refrained from any exploitation of the great strike movement and the occupation of factories in June 1936. On June 11, following the Matignon agreements, Thorez came out against the continuation of social unrest: "It is necessary to know how to end a strike." In compliance with the directives of the Comintern, the PCF now made efforts to sway French foreign policy to an anti-Hitler stand. With social unrest barely subsided, the PCF adopted a nationalist orientation, advocated a "French front," and undertook a campaign of "excitation to patriotism." This policy was pursued for the next three years with the objective of compelling the succeeding governments to transform the Franco-Soviet pact into a military alliance.

The second major objective from 1936 to 1939 was the strengthening of the PCF, at the expense of the SFIO. In the CGT the communists profited from the considerable number of unskilled workers (membership of the CGT had increased from 1 million to 5 million) and gradually took over all the command posts. Party membership grew steadily, increasing from 30,000 by January 1934, to 74,000 by January 1936, and to 341,000 by December 1937, when the party held its ninth congress.

*World War II* The German-Soviet pact of August 23, 1939, surprised the communists in the midst of their all-out anti-Hitler campaign. They approved the pact, declaring that it served to "reaffirm the general peace,"[6] and for three weeks (even after the outbreak of World War II) declared that they would take part in national defense. In the middle of September, however, in compliance with the directives brought back from Moscow by Raymond Guyot, the party entered the "struggle against the imperialist war" and advocated "revolutionary defeatism." Outlawed by government decree on September 29, the PCF did not lessen its pursuit of this subversive action. This period was marked by the desertion of Thorez in October (he finally turned up in the Soviet Union), by the trial of the communist deputies in March and April 1940, and by a certain amount of sabotage of arms manufacture which led to the execution in May 1940 of several militants.

After the French defeat in May-June 1940 the PCF tried to resume a legal existence. It sought to obtain authorization from the Germans to begin publishing *L'Humanité* again. It lay responsibility for the war on the Vichy politicians, called for a "government of the people," with Thorez in the government, encouraged fraternization with the German soldiers, and attacked General de Gaulle. A large number of communists now came out of hiding, thus facilitating the task of the French police, who proceeded with numerous arrests at the end of 1940. This policy provoked dissatisfaction in some organizations which had escaped party control; thus the anti-German turn taken by the miners' strike in May 1941 was the achievement of communists acting contrary to party directives.

German aggression against the Soviet Union on June 22, 1941, brought a radical switch in policy: the PCF now took part in the resistance and, on French territory, organized the essential forces within the movement. Although there is still some confusion concerning the PCF's dealings with the resistance, Fernand Grenier arrived in London on January 12, 1943, to bring to General de Gaulle the PCF's allegiance to Free France; on February 5, 1943, the communist deputies imprisoned in Algeria since 1940 were released; first Grenier and then Marty, who had returned from Moscow, arrived in Algiers; communist parliamentarians entered the Free French consultative assembly; and the communists François Billoux and Grenier were included in de Gaulle's provisional government in London in April 1944.

At home the PCF created its own underground armed force, the French Free Shooters and Partisans (Francs Tireurs et Partisans Français), directed by Charles Tillon and Marcel Prenant, and drew closer to other resistance formations. The Le Perreux agreements of April 17, 1943, provided for the communists' return to the CGT, and the foundation of the National Council of the Resistance on May 27, 1943. At the same time the PCF maintained the autonomy of its organizations, reinforced them, and created a National Front of Struggle for the Independence of France (Front National de Lutte pour l'Indépendance de la France), which permitted it to take part under another name in many of the joint resistance organizations. This action cost the party numerous militants (although the figure of 75,000 executed by the Germans is considerably exaggerated), but it recruited, especially in 1944, new followers who were attracted by its patriotic action rather than by its doctrine. By the time Paris was liberated in August 1944 the PCF was the best organized party in France, both politically and militarily.

*The PCF in the Government: 1945 to 1947* It is likely that several leaders of the PCF, then in France, may have thought of seizing power during August and September 1944 by exploiting the "patriotic insurrection." However, directives from Moscow indicated that the communists were to proceed by legal, parliamentary tactics. The most outstanding act to this effect was the dissolution of the patriotic militias, decreed by the government on October 25, 1944, and accepted by Thorez on January 21, 1945.

In application of this new tactic the PCF participated in the government, at the outset giving its propaganda a nationalist character which facilitated collaboration with de Gaulle (who granted amnesty to Thorez and allowed him to return to France). In June 1945 the communists proposed to the socialists the formation of a French Labor Party which would absorb the two parties. The socialists declined this offer, but in the October 21 elections to the constituent assembly the communists received 5,004,121 votes, or 26 percent of the votes cast, and 152 seats out of 545. The PCF was now the "first party of France."

This success encouraged the communists to increase their demands. The government formed on November 21, 1945, contained five communists: Thorez (minister of state without portfolio), Charles Tillon (armaments), Marcel Paul (industrial production), Ambroise Croizat (labor), and François Billoux (national economy). However, de Gaulle refused to grant them any of the key ministries they asked for—war, interior, and foreign affairs. Léon Blum similarly succeeded in pushing aside the communist-proposed merger with the socialists in August 1945. In addition, the CGT, by then completely dominated by the communists, failed in its efforts to absorb the French Confederation of Christian Workers.

Despite these secondary defeats, the PCF continued to grow. In the elections of November 10, 1946, it received 5,475,355 votes (28.2 percent of the total vote) and 166 seats out of 544. It was now in a position to claim the presidency of the council of ministers. Thorez announced his candidacy on December 4, 1946, but received only 259 of the 310 votes necessary. Nevertheless, the PCF participated in the government formed on January 22, 1947, by socialist Paul Ramadier. Thorez was named vice premier, François Billoux minister of national defense, Ambroise Croizat minister of labor, Georges Marrane minister of public health and population, and Charles Tillon minister of reconstruction.

The military operations which were begun in Indochina in November 1946, however, created some disagreement within the majority group, and the communists refused to support the government. At the end of April 1947 strikes broke out, and the communists upheld the demands of the unions. On May 5 Ramadier removed the communists from his cabinet, thus ending communist hopes of winning power within the bounds of legality.

*The PCF until the Death of Stalin: 1947 to 1953* The communists had anticipated regaining some portfolios in the event of a new ministerial crisis, but on June 27, 1947, the Soviet Union refused to be a beneficiary of American aid to Europe (the Marshall Plan), and in September, at the founding meeting of the Cominform in Poland, the PCF found itself reproached for its lack of revolutionary daring. On November 11 the PCF and the CGT launched a strong wave of strikes which were not only political, but insurrectional as well. This attempt failed, primarily because of the split in the CGT provoked by the unionists who refused to obey the PCF. The same operation was attempted in connection with the miners' strikes in October 1948 with no more success. On February 25, 1949, Thorez declared that the French people would never make war against the Soviet Union even if Soviet armies penetrated France itself in pursuit of "imperialist aggressors."

For six years the PCF conducted fierce campaigns against "imperialism," against the American atom bomb (the Stockholm peace appeal in March 1950), the "American occupation of Europe," the "dirty war in Indochina," and the "revanchists of Bonn," thus mixing the traditional nationalist slogans with their antimilitarism. This policy, rather incoherent at times (especially during the absence of Thorez, who suffered a stroke in October 1950 and was taken to the Soviet Union in November for treatment), culminated on May 28, 1952, in a violent demonstration organized on the occasion of American General Matthew Ridgway's arrival in Paris. In accordance with the instructions brought back by Billoux in March 1952 from Thorez in Moscow, the guiding principle was that the party should "work for the defeat of the French army wherever it is fighting."[7]

This return to a policy of violent opposition, closely linked with Soviet policy, provoked some clashes within the party. Many militants who had joined the PCF during the war or after the liberation because of its national-republican orientation gradually left its ranks. As a consequence, the party membership, which had reached 804,229 in 1946, fell to less than 300,000 in 1953. The PCF's electoral strength, however, did not decline in the same proportions. In the June 17, 1951, elections it received 4,910,000 votes (25.67 percent) and 103 seats. At the same time Thorez removed from the directing bodies the militants who had won their posts as a result of their activity in the resistance. Some of the more spectacular of these "liquidations" were the "Guingouin affair" (1951-1952), the "Marty-Tillon affair" (1952-1953), and the "Lecoeur affair" (1954).

*From the Death of Stalin to the Death of Thorez: 1953 to 1964* Stalin's death in 1953, the ensuing "thaw" in the Soviet Union, and the new tactics of the Soviets in international politics (the détente) enabled the PCF to adopt an attitude calculated to break its isolation. In June 1953 the communists offered to uphold Pierre Mendès-France's demand for investiture as premier if he would agree to make peace in Vietnam when he took office. This gesture marked a change in policy. In October the PCF announced that it was ready to form an alliance with all those who opposed the projected European army. As a result, it endorsed Mendès-France's selection as premier on June 7, 1954, and contributed to the rejection of the proposed army on August 30 by adding its vote to that of the nationalist opposition.

The communists were at odds with the socialists on this issue, but after April 1955, in response to Soviet directives, the PCF increased its offers for common action with the socialists. After the legislative elections of January 2, 1956, in which the PCF received 5,406,803 votes (25.6 percent of the total) and 144 seats—indicating a revival of its influence—the party supported the government of socialist Guy Mollet (who agreed to visit the Soviet Union), including the passage of special powers for the continuation of the war in Algeria. This caused some trouble among party militants and sympathizers, who were disappointed that the PCF did not give more open support to the Algerian National Liberation Front.

The twentieth congress of the Communist Party of the Soviet Union in February 1956 raised further problems. Thorez sought to limit the consequences of de-Stalinization for the PCF. When Khrushchev's report was published the PCF political bureau sent a delegation to Moscow to demand explanations—something that had not happened in thirty years. Despite this demonstration, the party leadership remained unshakably loyal to the Soviet Union, even during the events in Poland and Hungary. As early as November 4, 1956, the political bureau approved the entry of Soviet troops into Hungary. However, the official attitude concerning support of the government on the Algerian issue, de-Stalinization, and approval of the repression in Hungary brought on a new crisis within the party, especially among the intellectuals and those on the fringe, who began to pull away. On November 8, 1956, during a powerful popular demonstration in Paris, the demonstrators tried to sack PCF headquarters. This was the first time such an assault had been made. The PCF was once again isolated.

In 1957, after campaigns against the "tortures in Algeria," the PCF regained support from one part of public opinion, but the advent of the Fifth Republic showed that the communists had lost much of their influence. In May 1958 they failed in their attempt to stir the masses against the return of Charles de Gaulle to power. Attempts to form a coalition for defeat of the referendum were also unsuccessful. In the legislative elections of November 23, 1958, the PCF received 3,882,204 votes (18.9 percent) and only ten seats. By 1959 membership had dropped to about 225,000.

From the advent of the Fifth Republic to the death of Maurice Thorez the policy of the PCF was characterized on the one hand by systematic hostility to the de Gaulle regime, denounced as a regime of "personal power" and "monopolies," and on the other hand by attempts toward rapprochement with the government, in the interests of Soviet foreign policy. In October 1959, when the French government invited Khrushchev to France, the first secretary of the Soviet party made a declaration favoring France's recognition of Algeria's right to self-determination. The PCF had at first denounced this recognition as a trick, but it was now declared to be the real thing. Khrushchev visited France on March 23-31, 1960, and returned to Paris on May 14 for the unsuccessful summit conference.

The PCF again turned to violent opposition to the government. At the same time an ideological adjustment was effected. In February 1961 Marcel Servin and Laurent Casanova were removed from the political bureau and central committee on the pretext that they had supported principles favorable to de Gaulle, and also because in October 1960 they had opposed the party's refusal to support some demonstrations organized by students and intellectuals for the National Liberation Front of Algeria. This was a continuation of the conflict which had engaged the party and literary activists since 1956.

At the sixteenth congress of the PCF in May 1961 Waldeck Rochet was named assistant general secretary. The party's approval of the resumption of nuclear testing in the Soviet Union later that year caused disagreements with the leadership of the French Peace Movement, an important PCF front organization. On October 31 *L'Humanité* published Khrushchev's entire address to the twenty-second congress of the Communist Party of the Soviet Union, this time publicly denouncing the "crimes of Stalin," a term which Thorez himself used on November 19. The party leadership faithfully followed the new line from Moscow and when the Sino-Soviet conflict came out in the open, the PCF sided with the Soviet Union—as revealed by Thorez' anti-Chinese interventions at the conference of the eighty-one communist parties meeting in Moscow in November 1960 and in his speech at the twenty-second congress of the Soviet party in 1961.

On February 8, 1962, despite government prohibitions, the PCF organized demonstrations in commemoration of the February 1934 demonstrations; eight people died as a result. Even though the PCF decided to support the referendum ratifying the Evian agreements giving independence to Algeria, it continued its open struggle against the government: large strikes of public utilities and nationalized enterprises were planned for the beginning of June. However, at this point the PCF suddenly found itself in agreement with the government. At a press conference on May 15, 1962, de Gaulle declared that "the destiny of all Europe from the Atlantic to the Urals" depended "on solidarity between France and Germany" and implied that if "a European balance with the Eastern countries" were effected, France would contribute some "solid propositions" for the resolution of the German problems. On May 31 Thorez delivered a speech to the central committee condemning the strikes planned for the following day, and the communist leaders of the CGT, on his orders, managed with difficulty to prevent them. This brief truce with the government was ended by the "shattering declarations of November 1962 on the immediate and unconditional support that the Gaullist government intended to give the United States during the grave crisis in the Caribbean."[8] In the November 1962 legislative elections the communists gained some seats, owing to less general participation of the voters and to a slight increase in votes for their candidates. They won 3,992,431 votes (21.8 percent) and 41 seats out of 465.

By 1963 the PCF was uncompromisingly opposed to the government, but internal party conflicts were marked. Several pro-Chinese groups appeared, but the principal opposition came from the right. In 1962 some old members of the PCF (including Jean Chaintron and Marcel Prenant) had founded an opposition bulletin, *Le Débat communiste*. In April 1963 the congress of the Communist Students' Union (Union des Etudiants Communistes) adopted a draft program which was condemned by PCF leadership and elected a committee favorable to the "Italian theses."

On March 25, 1964, after consultation with Nikolai Podgorny (then a member of the political bureau of the Soviet party), who had come to France to meet him, Thorez gave a new orientation to the internal politics of the PCF: the communists would continue to fight the French regime of personal government and the reactionary character of its economic and social policy, but they would acknowledge that its foreign policy had certain "positive" aspects—recognition of Communist China, proposal for the neutralization of Vietnam, trade with Cuba, etc. Waldeck Rochet presented these ideas to the seventeenth congress of the PCF in May 1964. Thus began a new period, during which the PCF adopted an ambiguous attitude toward the government—opposing it, but in a way that would not obstruct the development of such aspects of its international policy as alienation of the United States and rapprochement with the Soviet Union.

*After Thorez*  Maurice Thorez died on July 11, 1964, on a Soviet ship taking him to Yalta. The choice of his successor apparently presented no problem, since Waldeck Rochet, elected as general secretary in May 1964 by the seventeenth congress, was backed by Moscow. However, the PCF experienced new internal difficulties, caused not so much by pro-Chinese elements as by pressure for more democracy within the party. The intellectuals in particular publicly protested the methods used by the party leadership to end the opposition of the Communist Students' Union. The party's attitude toward the government appeared to be so equivocal that the leftist parties accused it of supporting the reelection of de Gaulle; in fact the PCF made every effort to defeat the socialist candidate Gaston Defferre and announced that it would present a communist candidate if the left parties did not agree to subordinate the nomination of a single candidate to the adoption of a common program. Following a trip by Rochet to the Soviet Union, the party leadership dropped the idea of presenting a communist candidate and decided instead to support the candidacy of moderate leftist François Mitterrand, without insisting on a common program. Thus the communists were able to resume a tactic directed at a new popular front of the left, similar to that of 1934 to 1936. In the November presidential elections Mitterrand received an unexpectedly large number of votes, and a second ballot (December 5, 1965) was necessary to elect de Gaulle. This success strengthened the position within the political bureau of the "young" group, which advocated continued union with the left against the "personal government." The "old" group opposed this policy because it feared that too much opposition to de Gaulle would create difficulties for Soviet diplomacy in its efforts for a rapprochement with France.

On the international level the PCF, whose loyalty to the Soviet Union had never wavered, found itself charged with backing Moscow's attempt to reassemble the parties shaken either by the Chinese split or by the "Italian" ideas on polycentrism. Following the conference of the nineteen parties in Moscow on March 1-15, 1965, it was the PCF that took up the initiative for the conference of the communist parties of the capitalist countries of Europe in Brussels on June 1-3, 1965.

In August 1964 a group excluded from the PCF for pro-Chinese deviations founded a Federation of Marxist-Leninist Circles (Fédération de Cercles Marxistes-Léninistes) and six months later began publication of *L'Humanité nouvelle*, which was at first a monthly and by the end of 1965 was a daily.

## ORGANIZATION AND MEMBERSHIP

The first extraordinary congress of the PCF in May 1921 established organizational rules which were quite similar to those of its parent organization, the SFIO. Not until the Lille congress in 1926 was a new statute adopted, following the general lines of the statute of the Soviet party. The 1936 congress introduced some insignificant changes in the 1926 text; a new statute was adopted by the tenth congress in 1945, but it was revised by the seventeenth congress in 1964, which adopted the present statute.

The internal structure of the party is based on the principle of democratic centralism. The membership is subject to strict party discipline. The cell is the elementary party organization, formed in industrial enterprises or their subdivisions (shop cells), in towns and cities and their subdivisions (local cells), and in rural areas (village cells). Cells are grouped into sections, and sections into federations. Delegates of the federations join in the national congress, which is the supreme authority of the party. The congress elects a central committee and a central control commission for financial affairs. The central committee elects a political bureau, which directs the political affairs of the party between sessions of the central committee, and a secretariat which conducts current party affairs. The central committee also elects a central control commission, which exercises political control and handles violations of party discipline.

The PCF has not published membership figures since 1946, but J. Vermeersch, a member of the political bureau in charge of work among women, reported that women's membership was 49,490 in 1959,[9] and a report to the fifteenth party congress in 1959 announced that women members that year constituted 21.9 percent of the total membership. These two official figures indicate that in 1959 the PCF had around 225,000 members. Available party publications permit calculation of approximate membership changes since 1959. After a slight drop to 215,000 in 1961, membership started to grow slowly and reached an estimated total of 252,000 in 1965.[10]

After the 1964 party congress the political bureau included Maurice Thorez (president), Waldeck Rochet (general secretary), and Gustave Ausart, François Billoux, Jacques Duclos, Etienne Fajon, Georges Frischmann, Roger Garaudy, Raymond Guyot, Paul Laurent, Georges Marchais, Georges Séguy, and Jeannette Thorez-Vermeersch. Alternates were Roland Leroy, Henri Krasucky, René Piquet, and Gaston Plissonnier. Since Thorez' death there have been no significant changes in the leadership.

The number of front organizations at the party's disposal is considerable. The principal group is the CGT, founded in 1895, which managed to escape domination by the PCF in 1921 through a split. The organization born out of this split, the CGTU, rapidly became a satellite of the PCF and as a result was considerably weakened in 1935, when the two organizations were reunified under the aegis of the popular front. The communists quickly occupied leading positions in the reunified CGT, and although they were driven out of the unions in 1939, when Soviet troops entered Poland and the PCF was dissolved, they returned in 1944 and took back some of the directing posts. After the formation of the Cominform it was through the vast movement of insurrectional strikes launched by the CGT that the PCF attempted to grab power. The split in 1947 of the moderate elements, who created the CGT Work Force (CGT Force Ouvrière), broke this attempt but left the communists in full control of the CGT.

The general secretary of the CGT is Benoît Frachon, who has been a member of the PCF political bureau since 1928. Of the fourteen members of the CGT's confederal bureau, seven are avowed communists and members of the directing bodies of the PCF; the other seven are either cryptocommunists or owe their positions to the generosity of the party and are ousted, with no means of resisting, as soon as they try to conduct activities independently of the party. Thus at the time of the 1965 presidential elections Pierre Le Brun was forced to resign from the confederal bureau because he had rallied to the support of de Gaulle.

The 1947 split and the political character the CGT had acquired produced a decline in union membership, from 6 million in 1946 to only a little over 1 million in 1965 (the CGT itself claims 1,700,000). Nevertheless, it remains the strongest of the French trade-union organizations.

The Peace Movement, founded in France in 1948, was very active during the cold war under the presidency of Frédéric Joliot-Curie, a member of the PCF central committee who died in 1957. In 1961 the resumption of nuclear testing in the Soviet Union provided the excuse for the most important of the movement's directors, Emmanuel d'Astier de la Vigerie, to reduce its dependence on the PCF. Since then the Peace Movement has not been active.

Other mass organizations of the PCF are the Union of French Women, headed by Eugénie Cotton, Jeannette Thorez-Vermeersch, and Yvonne Dumont; the National Council of Writers, led by Louis

Aragon; the Association of Democratic Jurists, led by Mme. Joë Nordmann; and the France-USSR Association, headed by General Petit.

PARTY PRESS ORGANS AND RECORDS

The principal press organs with national distribution are the daily *L'Humanité*, founded in 1904 by Jean Jaurès and directed by Etienne Fajon; *France nouvelle*, a weekly founded in 1944 and directed by François Billoux; *Cahiers du communisme*, a monthly founded in 1925 under the title *Cahiers du bolchévisme* and directed by Léo Figuères; *Démocratie nouvelle*, a monthly founded in 1945 and directed by Jacques Duclos; *Economie et politique*, a monthly founded in 1954 and directed by Henri Jourdain; *La Nouvelle critique*, a monthly founded in 1950 and directed by Guy Besse; *Recherches internationales*, a bimonthly founded in 1958 and directed by Jean Kanapa; and *La Pensée*, a bimonthly founded in 1939 and directed by G. Teissier, J. Orcel, G. Cogniot, P. Laberenne, and H. Langevin, with Marcel Cornu as editorial secretary.

The 1964 party statutes can be found in *XVIIe Congrès du Parti communiste français, Paris, 14-17 mai 1964: Rapports, interventions et documents*, a special issue of *Cahiers du communisme*, nos. 6-7, June-July 1964, pp. 484-497. Congress records for the seventeenth congress include the entire contents of this issue.

In addition to the ample literature on the party congresses and central committee meetings, the PCF has published a large number of pamphlets dealing with particular aspects of party work and policies.

CONGRESSES OF THE PCF

Congrès de la scission, December 1920, Tours
1st congress, December 1921, Marseilles
2d congress, October 1922, Paris
3d congress, January 1924, Lyons
4th congress, January 1925, Clichy
5th congress, June 1926, Lille
6th congress, March-April 1929, Saint-Denis
7th congress, March 1932, Paris
8th congress, January 1936, Villeurbanne
9th congress, December 1937, Arles
10th congress, June 1945, Paris
11th congress, June 1947, Strasbourg
12th congress, April 1950, Gennevilliers
13th congress, June 1954, Ivry-sur-Seine
14th congress, July 1956, Le Havre
15th congress, June 1959, Ivry-sur-Seine
16th congress, May 1961, Saint-Denis
17th congress, May 1964, Paris

BIBLIOGRAPHY

Ceyrat, Maurice: *La Trahison permanente: Politique communiste et politique russe*, 3d ed., Paris, Paix et Liberté, n.d.
Fauvet, Jacques (in collaboration with Alain Duhamel): *Histoire du Parti communiste français*, vol. I, *De la guerre à la guerre, 1917-1939*; vol. II, *Vingt-cinq ans de drames, 1939-1965*, Paris, Fayard, 1964-1965.
Ferrat, André: *Histoire du Parti communiste français*, Paris, Bureau d'Editions, 1931.
*Histoire du Parti communiste français*, vol. I, *Des origines à 1940*, Paris, Editions Veridad; vol. II, *De 1940 à la libération*, Paris, Editions Unir; vol. III, *De 1945 à nos jours*, Paris, Editions Unir, n.d.
*Histoire du Parti communiste francais (manuel)*, Paris, Editions Sociales, 1964.
Walter, Gérard: *Histoire du Parti communiste français*, Paris, Somogy, 1948.

CLAUDE HARMEL

1. The Second (Socialist) International.

2. A. Ferrat, *Histoire du Parti communiste français*, Paris, Bureau d'Editions, 1931, p. 130.

3. Parti Républicain Radical et Radical-Socialiste, generally known as Parti Radical.

4. Jacques Fauvet, *Histoire du Parti communiste français*, vol. I, pp. 132-138.

5. *L'Humanité*, May 24, 1933.

6. *L'Humanité*, August 25, 1939.

7. *Journal officiel*, October 21, 1952, annex 4418.

8. Maurice Thorez in *L'Humanité*, March 27, 1964.

9. *L'Humanité*, November 28, 1961.

10. Claude Harmel, "Les Effectifs du PCF de 1959 à 1966," *Est & ouest*, January 16-31, 1967.

# GEORGIA

The roots of the Communist Party of Georgia (Kommunisticheskaia Partiia Gruzii, KPG) go back to the 1890s, when Marxist groups appeared in Georgia following their establishment in the central regions of Russia. The first of them, the Third Group (Mesame-dasi), referring to the third generation of the progressive current in Georgia, was formed in 1893. Its founders included such later communists as M. Tskhakaia, F. Makharadze, and S. Dzhugeli. In 1898 Joseph Stalin (Iosif Dzhugashvili) joined this group.

By the end of the 1890s the development and political activity of the Georgian Marxist groups had led to a merger with the Russian Social Democratic Labor Party, which had just emerged in Russia. Subsequently the social democratic committees created in Georgia split, as did the entire Russian party, into bolsheviks and mensheviks; it was the bolsheviks who later formed the communist party. Other important members of this group were P. Mdivani, A. Enukidze, I. Orakhelashvili, Sh. Eliava, V. Sturua, and A. Dzhaparidze.

Almost all the founders of the Georgian party were later liquidated by Stalin as "enemies of the people." This group included F. Makharadze, P. Mdivani, M. Toroshelidze, A. Enukidze, I. Orakhelashvili, Sh. Eliava, and T. Zhgenti. G. Ordzhonikidze was unable to endure Stalin's purges and took his own life. Lavrentii Beriia, who had begun his communist career during the civil war while he was still a student, withdrew from the ranks of the Georgian party and joined the Soviet party.

## HISTORY

The split between the bolsheviks and the mensheviks in the Georgian committees of the Russian Social Democratic Labor Party occurred without that special brand of intolerance that was observed in the central part of Russia. The only exception was probably Stalin and a small group of his followers. Stalin's activities, however, were of an incidental nature.

The February 1917 revolution caught the bolshevik organizations in Georgia in the midst of a great crisis. They were small and enjoyed little popularity, whereas the mensheviks, whose ranks included many more intellectuals, had won considerable support. As a result, all the revolutionary organs of power in Georgia ended up under menshevik domination. In the period following the February revolution the Georgian bolsheviks did not follow the actions of the bolsheviks in central Russia. Instead of struggling for power in the revolutionary organs, they joined the mensheviks in a common party committee. In December 1917, shortly after the bolsheviks seized power in central Russia, a favorable situation developed in Tiflis for a bolshevik upheaval. Although there were troops in the city that had been propagandized by the bolsheviks, the Georgian bolshevik leaders—P. Mdivani, M. Okudzhava, M. Toroshelidze, K. Tsintsadze, and others—did not consider it feasible to start a civil war in Georgia. They felt that as long as the bolsheviks had won in central Russia, the Georgian mensheviks would sooner or later recognize their government, and that there was therefore no need for Georgians to kill one another. This general consensus, however, did not preclude occasional excesses by individual bolsheviks, such as A. Gegechkori.

Initially the Russian bolshevik leaders, who favored international positions, attributed no special significance to the formation of bolshevik parties according to nationality. The Georgian bolsheviks, in turn, felt no centrifugal forces and did not strive for separation from the unified bolshevik party. As a result, the need to create an independent Georgian communist party did not arise until after the bolshevik takeover in Russia. On May 26, 1918, Georgia had declared itself an independent republic. However, the power in Georgia turned out to be in the hands of the mensheviks, and bolshevik Moscow could not reconcile itself to the existence of a menshevik Georgia, especially when in the spring of 1920 Georgian troops crossed into Transcaucasia. Moscow could not mount an armed occupation of Georgia in violation of its formal position of self-determination of nations, and so, to make the overthrow of the menshevik government and establishment of Soviet power in Georgia appear to be an "internal" affair of the Georgian people, the founding of a bolshevik party in Georgia was announced in May 1920. A temporary party central committee was organized and directed to create a Georgian revolutionary committee, stimulate an uprising in Georgia, and immediately appeal to Soviet Russia for armed assistance.

All the directives from Moscow toward the realization of bolshevik aims were carried out by the political department of the Eleventh Soviet Army, which was then at the borders of Georgia. Grigorii Ordzhonikidze directed the activities of this department. The Georgian government was without adequate armed forces to resist these plans. Nevertheless, it was not until March 1921 that Moscow succeeded in establishing Soviet power in Georgia; in January 1922 the first congress of the Communist Party (Bolshevik) of Georgia [Kommunisticheskaia Partiia (Bolshevikov) Gruzii] was held. The designation bolshevik was preserved in the Georgian party until 1952, when the Soviet party became the Communist Party of the Soviet Union.

After Georgia's takeover by the bolsheviks a "bourgeois-nationalist deviation" arose in the ranks of the Georgian party. Because of the famine in the Volga region and the Ukraine, refugees from those areas headed for Georgia, where food was plentiful. Fearing that the refugees would lay waste to the countryside and force out the indigenous population, the Georgian communists decided to close the border, and a law was passed limiting the settlement of refugees in the republic. Polemics with Moscow on this subject were aggravated by Moscow's plan for the creating of a Soviet Union in which Azerbaidzhan, Armenia, and Georgia would not be independent republics, but would form a Transcaucasian Federation. The Georgian communists interpreted this plan as an affront to Georgian autonomy and voted to affiliate with the Soviet Union only as an independent country. The resistance of the Georgians in Moscow ended with Stalin's removal of P. Mdivani, K. Tsintsadze, S. Kavtaradze, and F. Makharadze from their posts and their exile from Georgia.

The Georgian party also went through a stage of Trotskyist opposition, led by Mamiia Orakhelashvili. This was followed by "rightist" deviations' The party cadres were subjected to attacks from Moscow on a number of occasions, and Beriia was particularly merciless in his dealings. In 1937 more than 150 important Georgian party and government workers were arrested. Over a period of several months 425 of the 644 delegates to the fifth congress of the KPG were also arrested, and some 70 percent of the Georgian delegates to the fifteenth congress of the Soviet party were purged.

After this point the Georgian party was in fact ruled from Moscow. Stalin and Beriia, through their representatives in Georgia, decided all questions, and the party membership was continually harassed by mass arrests, purges, and deportations to forced labor camps. Stalin's death in 1953 and the subsequent arrest and execution of Beriia ended this abuse, and a general "thaw" developed. The Georgian communists welcomed Beriia's fate with great enthusiasm, since they felt that as a Georgian himself, he had betrayed them. Stalin's death was another matter. As a Georgian who had succeeded in ruling a large country, he was considered a national hero, and his death was regarded as a national loss. As a result, the "personality-cult" exposures made by Khrushchev at the twentieth and twenty-second congresses of the Soviet party evoked no enthusiasm among the majority of the Georgian communists and were even taken as a slap at their national dignity. No literature condemning Stalin appeared in Georgia, and his name was preserved in all historical literature. Party publications did occasionally mention the "personality-cult" period, but always in very restrained terms.

Khrushchev's removal in 1964 from the posts of secretary of the central committee of the Soviet party and chairman of the council of ministers of the Soviet Union was received by the Georgian party with satisfaction.

## ORGANIZATION AND MEMBERSHIP

The principle of democratic centralism is strictly observed in the organizational structure of the KPG; all the decisions of its highest organs are binding on the lower organs. The primary party units are organized in rural villages and in shops and factories. By the end of 1965 the party had 9,874 such primary units—2,005 at industrial enterprises as well as at enterprises of the transportation, building, and communication industries—plus 1,643 *kolkhoz* and *sovkhoz* units. These primary units were grouped into fifty district and seven city organizations, which are under the direct jurisdiction of the party's central committee.

Party strength has increased steadily since 1957. In 1957 the total number of members and candidates was 191,439; in 1960 it was 208,584; and in 1963 it was 230,861.[1] At the end of 1965 there were 247,070 members and 12,905 candidates for party membership, a total of 259,975.[2] This constituted 5.5 percent of the entire population of Georgia, the highest percentage of communists in any republic in the Soviet Union except for Russia itself, with 5.1 percent. This growth is the result of Khrushchev's policy aimed at transforming the Communist Party of the Soviet Union into a mass party of the people. Over 40 percent of the new members joining the KPG every year are young people moving up from the party's youth organization. Some 20 percent of KPG members are women.

The social composition of the Georgian party is unusual in that it is dominated by the intelligentsia: the percentage of intellectuals has long remained at 57 percent. Moreover, peasants outnumber workers in the party; party statistics indicated that as of January 1, 1964, 20 percent of the members were workers, whereas *kolkhoz* members accounted for 22 percent[3] (the workers in this case, however, include *sovkhoz* workers, whose orientation differs from that of industrial workers).

The KPG includes communists of seventy-two nationalities, with the predominant role played by Georgians. Of the 918 delegates at its twenty-second congress, for example, 807 were Georgians, 77 were Russians, 32 were Abkhazians, and 15 represented other nationalities.

## RELATION TO SOVIET LEADERSHIP

From the outset the KPG was a component part of the Soviet party. Until 1936 it was controlled by Moscow—at first through the Caucasian committee of the Russian Communist Party and then through the Transcaucasian regional committee of the All-Union Communist Party. Since 1936, when Georgia received the rights of a union republic as part of the Soviet Union, the party has been managed directly by Moscow and has always been loyal to Moscow leadership. Even the objections to the formation of a Transcaucasian Federation were put on the basis that this plan came not from the central committee of the Soviet party, but from certain individuals (Stalin, Ordzhonikidze, S. Kirov, and others).

The Georgian party did not take a direct part in the work of the Comintern and the Cominform. Although M. Tskhakaia claimed to represent the Georgian and Armenian parties at the second Comintern congress in

1920, this was during the Georgian civil war, at the time of Lenin's improvisations, before the party had been founded.

## PARTY PRESS ORGANS

Three daily nespapers are published in Georgia: *Komunisti* (Communist) in Georgian, *Zaria vostoka* (Dawn of the East) in Russian, and *Sovetakan Vrastan* (Soviet Georgia) in Armenian. The theoretical and political journal *Sakartvelos komunisti* (Georgian Communist) is published in Georgian.

## BIBLIOGRAPHY

Beriia, L.: *K voprosu ob istorii bolshevistskikh organizatsii v Zakavkaze* (On the History of Bolshevik Organizations in Transcaucasia), Moscow, Partizdat, 1937.

*Borba za uprochnenie sovetskoi vlasti v Gruzii: Sbornik dokumentov i materialov* (Struggle for the Consolidation of Soviet Power in Georgia: Collection of Documents and Materials), Tbilisi, 1959.

Esaiashvili, V. G. (ed.): *Ocherki istorii Kommunisticheskoi partii Gruzii* (Sketches of the History of the Communist Party of Georgia), part I, *1883-1921*, Tbilisi, 1957.

Gorgiladze, L.M.: *K istorii marksizma v Gruzii* (The History of Marxism in Georgia), Tbilisi, 1956 (in Georgian).

Khachapuridze, G. V.: *Bolsheviki Gruzii v boiakh za pobedu sovetskoi vlasti* (Georgian Bolsheviks in Battles for the Victory of Soviet Rule), Moscow, 1951.

Khachapuridze, G. V.: *Borba gruzinskogo naroda za ustanovlenie sovetskoi vlasti* (The Struggle of the Georgian People for the Establishment of Soviet Rule), 3d ed., Moscow, 1956.

Makharadze, F.: *Sovety i borba za sovetskuiu vlast v Gruzii, 1917-1921* (The Soviets and the Struggle for Soviet Rule in Georgia, 1917-1921), Tiflis, 1928.

*Ocherki istorii Kommunisticheskoi partii Gruzii* (Sketches of the History of the Communist Party of Georgia), part II, 1921-1936, Tbilisi, 1963.

Orakhelashvili, Mamiia: *Zakavkazskie bolshevistskie organizatsii v 1917 godu* (Transcaucasian Bolshevik Organizations in 1917), Tiflis, 1927.

Tskhovrebov, N. Z.: *Ocherk istorii iugoosetinskoi organizatsii Kommunisticheskoi partii Gruzii* (A Historical Sketch of the South Ossetian Organization of the Communist Party of Georgia), Stalinir, Gosizdat Iugo-Osetii, 1961.

PETER P. KRUSCHIN

1. *Bolshaia sovetskaia entsiklopedia: Ezhegodnik*, Moscow, 1957-1965.

2. *Zaria vostoka*, March 3, 1966.

3. *Zaria vostoka*, January 30, 1964.

# GERMANY

German communism may be considered as a social and political movement which at times bore the character of a mass party. Communism eventually found institutional form in a party and a state. But it has never managed wholly to free itself of the traits of the older social democratic movement from which it sprang. Until 1914 the Social Democratic Party of Germany (Sozialdemokratische Partei Deutschlands, SPD) seemed impressive by reason of its imposing organizational unity. Nevertheless, from about 1900 on it contained two opposing groups—the revisionists, to whom E. Bernstein's book *Die*

*Voraussetzungen des Sozialismus und die Aufgaben der Sozialdemokratie* (1899) had given a complete program, and the orthodox Marxists, led ideologically by Karl Kautsky. Following the Russian revolution of 1905, a small but ideologically important radical left broke away from the numerically stronger Marxist center grouped around Kautsky and the SPD leadership. Later on, especially after the dissolution of the Bülow bloc, the radical left took on a more sharply defined identity. As the revisionists put their hopes increasingly in a policy of collaboration with the liberals, and as the contradictions of imperialism became more severe, the apprehensions of the radicals grew apace. All the attempts of the radicals to reform the leadership of the SPD failed, and the party executive took a more severe line against them. The left retaliated, and the battle on both sides became more uncompromising. Admittedly, no member of the left thought of splitting from the party; in fact it had too little unity for such a course.[1]

The weakness of the left became apparent when, under the leadership of Friedrich Ebert and Philipp Scheidemann, the SPD sharply changed its course. On August 4, 1914, it accepted the war policy of the kaiser, who for his part retracted his strictures against the "fellows without a fatherland." The SPD thereby also accepted the status quo in its essentials. When the party leaders enforced this wartime truce with iron discipline, a split became inevitable. On December 12, 1914, only Karl Liebknecht voted against the war credits in the Reichstag. A year later twenty Reichstag members followed his example and another twenty-two walked out of the chamber. In March 1916 the deputies excluded from the parliamentary faction of the SPD united as the Social Democratic Working Partnership (Sozialdemokratische Arbeitsgemeinschaft); from this emerged the Independent Social Democratic Party of Germany (Unabhängige Sozialdemokratische Partei Deutschlands, USPD), which took shape at Gotha in April 1917.

In the meantime Rosa Luxemburg and Karl Liebknecht had gathered the most radical opponents of the war, at first in the International Group (Gruppe Internationale) and later in the Spartacus League (Spartakusbund). The latter, though critical of the USPD, joined it temporarily and broke away completely only after the November 1918 revolution. On December 30, 1918, the Spartacus League and the International Communists of Germany (Internationale Kommunisten Deutschlands), a Bremen faction, formed a new party at a joint congress in Berlin. Contrary to Rosa Luxemburg's wishes, the new party called itself the Communist Party of Germany (Spartacus League) [Kommunistische Partei Deutschlands (Spartakusbund), KPD][2] as an expression of its break with international social democracy and return to the revolutionary Marxism of the 1840s. The KPD was a founding member of the Comintern, formed a few months later, and long remained its most important section outside the Soviet Union.

## HISTORY OF THE KPD

*1919 to 1927* The left majority of the new party believed that victory for the socialist revolution was at hand and rejected participation in the elections for the national assembly —again over the objections of Rosa Luxemburg and Karl Liebknecht. Nevertheless, the party program, drafted by Luxemburg, had as its starting point the concept that the masses "themselves live the entire political and economic life, and guide the same in consciously free self-determination." The socialist revolution, regarded as the first revolution to triumph in the interests of and at the hands of the great majority, "hates and detests murder, and does not necessitate terror"; hence the party would "never take over the power of government except by the clear, unequivocal will of the great majority of the proletarian masses throughout the whole of Germany, and only through the deliberate assent of the masses to the views, aims, and combat methods of the Spartacus League. Its victory will therefore be accomplished only at the end of the revolution." The program stressed, however, that the resistance of the imperialist capitalists, "whose brutality, unconcealed cynicism, and baseness outdid that of all its predecessors," could be broken only with "an iron fist and ruthless energy," and that in the mightiest civil war of history the proletariat must hurl the entire power of the state down upon the heads of the ruling classes "like the hammer of the God Thor."

On January 15, 1919, during the battles against the Ebert government, Luxemburg and Liebknecht were assassinated. The left majority, which determined the party line, led the party from one defeat to another. It was only the profound postwar crisis that gave the KPD new impetus and enabled it to survive as an organization. In the fall of 1919 a right wing crystallized under the leadership of Paul Levi. The ultraleft syndicalist wing broke away and formed the independent Communist Workers' Party of Germany (Kommunistische Arbeiter Partei Deutschlands, KAPD), which soon contracted into a sectarian group. The new, more moderate policy of the KPD led to improved relations with the left wing of the USPD, which in those days had a much wider mass following than the still numerically very small KPD.

In October 1920 the USPD split at the party congress in Halle and its larger left-wing group merged with the KPD at a party congress in Berlin in December 1920. The new party named itself the United Communist Party of Germany (Vereinigte Kommunistische Partei Deutschlands, VKPD), although the "V" was dropped soon afterward. For the first time the communists were able to operate as a mass party in Germany. The new party had nearly 400,000 members, thirty-three daily newspapers, strong positions in the labor unions, and several parliamentary factions both in the Reichstag and in the parliaments of the various states.

The united party gained a certain measure of success through a united front with other labor organizations, a policy carried out with considerable skill by Paul Levi. But in March 1921, contrary to the wishes of Levi and Clara Zetkin, the party leadership tried to organize an uprising in central Germany. This insurrection ended in total defeat, and the party slithered into a serious crisis. Once again, as in 1919 and 1920, the illusionary utopian faith had won out with its insistence that the masses would follow the party as soon as the party issued revolutionary slogans. In the face of the smashing March defeat and pressure from Lenin, the new KPD leaders, Heinrich Brandler, August Thalheimer, and Paul Frölich, had to return to the rightist course of the Comintern's united-front policy at the Jena party congress of 1921. This new tactic coincided with a lessening of inflation in Germany and modest economic recovery throughout the world. The new course remained unchanged even when in 1923 Germany's economy deteriorated catastrophically. Despite all preparations (which in fact were to prove inadequate), there was only one isolated uprising; this occurred in Hamburg in October 1923.

A new turn to the left took place only after Germany's inflation had been brought to a halt in 1923. The shift occurred largely as a spontaneous reaction of party members to the alleged treason of the reformists in the midst of a supposedly revolutionary situation, the assumption being that the leaders should have ventured on a large-scale rising. Because this leftward swing coincided with the beginnings of economic stabilization, it cost the party considerable electoral support. The "left" policy had to be given up in 1925, when massive intervention from Moscow resulted in the defeat and expulsion from the party of the left leadership, including Ruth Fischer, Arkadij Maslow, and others. The left wingers who had broken with Ruth Fischer and remained loyal to the Comintern—Ernst Thälmann, Philipp Dengel, and Franz Dahlem—formed a new central executive in alliance with members of the former centrists and some rightists, including Arthur Ewert, Gerhart Eisler (a brother of Ruth Fischer, her real name being Elfriede Eisler), and later Ernst Meyer and some of the so-called "conciliationists."

There was now talk of a "concentration of

forces," but even in 1927, at the time of the eleventh party congress at Essen, there were at least ten organized factions within and outside the party: (1) the declared Brandler faction, with Paul Böttcher, Jakob Walcher, Robert Siewert, and Rosi Wolfstein (Frölich's wife); (2) the Ernst Meyer faction, known as the "conciliationists"; (3) the party functionaries Arthur Ewert, Wilhelm Pieck, Walter Ulbricht, and Hans Pfeiffer; (4) the Thälmann faction, with Philipp Dengel, Heinz Neumann, Ernst Schneller, Theo Neubauer, Heinrich Süsskind, and Karl Volk; (5) the Chemnitz left faction, led by Paul Bertz, which also had groups in Berlin, and on the middle Rhine; (6) the ultraleft group from the Palatinate, led by Hans Weber; (7) an ultraleft group led by Paul Kötter (the "Wedding left," drawn from a working-class district in Berlin); (8) the left opposition, led by Maslow, Hugo Urbahns, and Ruth Fischer; (9) the ultraleft group of Karl Korsch; and (10) the ultraleft group of Ernst Schwarz.

*1928 to 1933* After 1925 the central executive was headed by Ernst Thälmann, who was now praised in official party terminology as a "professional bolshevik revolutionary." Under his leadership the KPD became more and more dependent on Moscow, and intraparty democracy was progressively eliminated. At its fifth congress in 1924 the Comintern had decided to reorganize the member parties on the basis of "shop nuclei," and above all had decided on a policy of "bolshevization," which was to lead to "Stalinization." The process of *Gleichschaltung* was effected with the expulsion of the Brandler-Thalheimer faction in 1928 and 1929. Since that time no open intraparty opposition has been tolerated.

At first the new leadership tacked along a centrist course, avoiding Brandler's and Ruth Fischer's "exaggerations." This line, which was maintained until 1929, corresponded to the policy followed in those days by Stalin, who was leaning on Bukharin and the rightists in his battle against Trotsky and Zinoviev, without, however, relinquishing the option for a new leftward shift. This was a period of relative stabilization in Germany. Wages rose slowly but steadily, and the number of unemployed workers for the first time dropped to less than 10 percent. During these years even the KPD became relatively "respectable." It concentrated on occasional united-front activities with the SPD (plebiscite for the expropriation of the German princes in 1926) and on work in the labor unions. The chief concentration was on opposition within the various parliaments, on the elections (Thälmann was a presidential candidate in 1925 and 1932), and on the creation of a network of front organizations: the Communist Youth League of Germany (Kommunistischer Jugendverband Deutschlands), International Red Aid, International Workers' Aid, the Red Front Fighters' League, the Red Women's and Girls' League, the Red Youth Front, the Reich League of German Small Holders, the Proletarian Writers' League, and cultural and workers' sport associations. Willy Münzenberg had much success with his Red Trust, which combined newspapers, periodicals, publishing houses, film companies, and theater and other groups sympathetic to the party.

Above all, these organizations made propaganda for the Soviet Union. Before World War I the SPD, under such leaders as August Bebel and Karl Kautsky, had stood only for a verbal variety of Marxist radicalism; in the same way the KPD, for all its Leninist ideology, now functioned in its day-to-day policy as a fairly "loyal" opposition party. Between 1928 and 1929, however, Stalin broke with the rightists (Bukharin, Rykov, and Tomskii) who had supported him in the battle against Trotsky and Zinoviev. The rupture with Bukharin, the leader of the Comintern, immediately led to a struggle with the rightists and the "conciliationists" within the Comintern ranks. The KPD had to move to the left, a policy which appeared all the more plausible as the first storm clouds of the world depression were gathering on the horizon. A new theory of "third-period communism" (see *The Communist International*) postulated that, on the one hand, in the final crisis of world capitalism the masses, increasingly pauperized and radicalized, would automatically be pushed leftward into the communist camp; hence the communists should on no account allow themselves to be left behind. Both the bourgeoisie and the social democrats, on the other hand, were supposed to be progressively shifting to the right. According to the communist argument, a broad-based fascist front was thus being formed; in Germany this front now supposedly extended all the way from Hitler and Ludendorff to the SPD leaders and the Trotskyists. Thus the previous strategy of the "united front from above" would have to be relinquished. War must now be waged against the main enemy, the SPD and the reformist labor unions, which allegedly had become "social fascist." This concept of social fascism, expressed at the sixth Comintern congress in 1928, was linked to certain theoretical formulations dating back to 1923, when the KPD had spoken in a similar fashion of a "reactionary mass."

The communist calculation turned out to be a gross error. The bulk of the bourgeoisie and the petite bourgeoisie, threatened by the depression, moved against the left and to an increasing extent followed Hitler's national socialists. So did a part of the unemployed workers, although some joined the KPD. Those workmen who had managed to keep their jobs clung to the SPD with a growing measure of desperation. Instead of joining forces, the KPD attacked the SPD with increasing bitterness. The KPD was now able to gain substantial electoral successes; the number of its parliamentary seats in the Reichstag rose from two in 1920 to 100 in November 1932 (nearly 17 percent of the votes cast, as against 20.4 percent for the SPD). However, compared to the nazis, the KPD was a colossus with feet of clay; it was so weak that it was unable to organize even a single strike against Hitler's seizure of power.

*1933 to 1945* On February 27, 1933, during the night of the Reichstag fire, Göring ordered the arrest of some 4,000 KPD functionaries. The entire party press was outlawed, the party was deprived of its parliamentary representation, and its legally operating organizations were smashed. For twelve years the KPD was to remain illegal, and the slightest connection with it meant arrest, persecution, penal servitude, concentration camp, torture, or death. Communists formed the bulk of the nazis' political victims; it has been estimated that of the 32,000 people murdered or incarcerated in the region now encompassed by the German Democratic Republic, 55 percent had belonged to the KPD. A number of party leaders, including Thälmann, Schneller, and John Schehr, also fell victim to the Hitler terror, but an even greater number escaped to the Soviet Union and later were liquidated by Stalin; among these were Hans Remmele, Heinz Neumann, Fritz Schulte, H. Schubert, Hugo Eberlein, Leo Flieg, and Hans Kippenberger. Of the twenty-two KPD leaders of the Weimar period who died by violence, four were murdered before 1933, eight were killed by Hitler, and ten were killed by Stalin. As a result of the unheard-of nazi terror and the support of Hitler's regime by the great majority of the population, the party links were broken. Even reorganization into three-member cells availed little. The communist organization in Germany was reduced to a small circle which operated independently of the émigré leadership. Larger resistance groups, such as the so-called Red Chapel (Rote Kapelle), the Georg Schumann group in Leipzig, the Bernhard Bästlein group in Hamburg, the Anton Saefkow group in Berlin, and the Lechleiter group in Mannheim generally had to work in isolation, and most of them were smashed. The few that survived formed the Leipzig National Committee for a Free Germany (Nationalkomitee Freies Deutschland), which was banned by the American occupation authorities on April 28, 1945.

Despite the catastrophe of 1933, the KPD abandoned its ultraleft line only gradually. After the seventh Comintern congress in 1935 the "Brussels conference" of the KPD (which actually took place in the outskirts of Moscow in October 1935) pronounced a new popular-front strategy. The "Bern conference" (in fact held in Paris in January-February 1939) declared its support for the popular front, a new German democratic republic, and the creation of a unified party for the German working class. This new tactic was abandoned, however, with the signing of the Hitler-Stalin pact in August 1939, which, on instructions from Moscow, had to be approved by the central committee of the KPD and Ulbricht. It was only when the Third Reich attacked the Soviet Union in 1941 that the popular-front tactic was resumed and broadened into the policy of a national front. The National Committee for a Free Germany and the German Officers' League, created in the Soviet Union in 1943, were intended to appeal also to nationalist circles; hence they adopted the colors black, white, and red.

*1945 to 1965* In spite of repressions under both Hitler and Stalin, the KPD managed to maintain an illegal skeleton organization within and especially outside Germany and was able to consolidate rapidly after 1945. Above all, the KPD enjoyed the support of the occupying power in the Eastern zone and was one of the four so-called "classical" parties operating in occupied Germany under license. In 1945 all these parties spoke in favor of a new antifascist democratic order, sharply rejecting not only the nazis, but also certain antidemocratic capitalist tendencies which, in their view, had encouraged national socialism before 1933.

As part of its new popular-front policy, the KPD—unlike the SPD—paradoxically avoided a clear commitment to socialism, even though it did not hesitate to make profound changes in the economic order of bourgeois capitalism. The KPD's founding manifesto of June 11, 1945, set forth a radical-democratic "minimal," rather than a full "maximalist," program. It certainly did not mention the party's ultimate goal, the creation of a communist and absolutist one-party regime. The manifesto not only stressed the profound guilt of the Third Reich, it even frankly admitted the KPD's errors in not having understood in time how to ensure antifascist unity. The firm unity of all democratic antifascist parties within one bloc was now declared essential. The Soviet system was not to be forced on Germany; rather, Germany should complete the unfinished task of creating a bourgeois-democratic order within the framework of a parliamentary democratic republic. Only certain properties and enterprises were to be socialized, but otherwise the initiative of private entrepreneurs should be allowed full scope on the basis of private property.

The communists stuck to this theory of the "special German road to socialism" as late as 1946. Anton Ackermann, their ideological spokesman, wrote a much discussed article in the new journal *Einheit*, intended to give theoretical justification to the merger of the SPD and the KPD. He stated that the situation in Germany was unlike that in Russia during 1917, and that socialism would be able to succeed through parliamentary democratic means, without armed revolution, proletarian dictatorship, or rule by Soviets. This was called the "third road to socialism."

In the summer of 1945 conditions were rather favorable for the formation of a united workers' party in Berlin and the Soviet zone of Germany. For the time being, however, the communists' first goal was to rebuild the KPD so that the future unified party would be under their influence. A joint working committee was set up on June 19, 1945, but it was not until fall that the communists made more determined efforts to create a unified party, probably because of the unfavorable election results in Austria and Hungary. In 1945 Kurt Schumacher, the SPD leader in West Germany, was already convinced that the "special German way" was nothing but a tactical device. The communists, for their part, considered the SPD too opportunistic and too bourgeois in its own makeup to enforce socialism ruthlessly against determined resistance from the bourgeoisie. The planned merger was therefore intended to place the SPD firmly under the control of reliable "Marxists."

On October 12 Walter Ulbricht demanded that the KPD and the SPD strengthen their unity of action in future elections. On November 9 Wilhelm Pieck asked for immediate preparations for an organizational merger. On December 20 and 21 the leaders of the two parties met at a joint session, but the social democrats insisted that only an SPD party congress could sanction a merger of the two parties. Pieck and Ulbricht refused to submit the question to a vote of the SPD membership. Under pressure from the KPD and the Soviet occupation authorities, a joint conference of the KPD and the SPD party organizations in the Soviet zone of Germany finally agreed on February 26, 1946, that the merger should take place at a unification congress in April—a decision reached over the opposition of the social democrats in West Berlin and the three Western zones.

This forced merger only increased the mutual distrust between the two parties. Each accused the other of not taking the "third road" seriously. Moreover, the growing disagreement between the Western powers and the Soviet Union, especially over Germany, caused the parties identified with each camp to drift further apart. The agreement of the Great Powers at Potsdam to set up a new noncapitalist, noncommunist "democratic antifascist" Germany proved unworkable. Two Germanys came into existence and blocked the "third road." A bourgeois society was reconstituted in West Germany; in East Germany, a Stalinized "people's democracy" soon replaced socialist democracy.

During 1945 and 1946 the KPD was also licensed in the Western zones. After all attempts at persuading the SPD to merge with the KPD in West Germany had failed, partly because of Schumacher's opposition, a Working Partnership KPD/SED (Arbeitsgemeinschaft KPD/SED) was formed in February 1947, but this broke up in January 1949. In the meantime the KPD had tried to change its name to Socialist People's Party (Sozialistische Volkspartei); the occupation powers, however, would not sanction the change of name, and the KPD had to continue operating in West Germany under its original name.

The KPD had more influence at that point than was apparent from the number of its members. Its electoral strength was partly a result of the revulsion against fascism. The KPD commanded seats in all the provincial parliaments. Until 1947, and to some extent until the spring of 1948, it was also represented in the coalition governments of all the states (*Länder*), except Südwürttenberg-Hohenzollern and Schleswig-Holstein. The KPD had six members (out of 104) in the economic council (*Wirtschaftsrat*) and two (out of sixty-five) in the parliamentary council (*Parlamentarischer Rat*), all of whom voted against the acceptance of the new German constitution. In the first local and state elections, held in 1946, the KPD was still able to secure about 9 percent of the vote. In the elections for the federal parliament (*Bundestag*), however, the party obtained only 5.7 percent of the vote in 1949, and 2.2 percent in 1953.

By 1956 the KPD was represented only in the parliaments of Niedersachsen and Bremen. In the first federal parliament, elected in 1949, the communists with fifteen representatives had been able to operate as a full parliamentary faction. In January 1952, however, with only fourteen representatives, they lost this status (according to German constitutional law only parties commanding at least fifteen members in the federal parliament had the status of a full faction). Subsequent to a motion made by the German federal government on November 22, 1951, the federal constitutional court outlawed the KPD on August 17, 1956. By the end of 1965 the KPD was operating as an underground organization, as it did prior to 1945, but it had not been able to exert any serious influence.

As early as 1948 the KPD had begun to modify its "rightist" line. As the East-West conflict grew more bitter, the party identified itself firmly with the "peace policy" of the Soviet Union. At Moscow's behest it was once more forced to try a "left" offensive against "American imperialism," the "Adenauer regime," and the "treacherous social democracy." The party's program for reunification of Germany was designed to appeal to nationalist circles whom the party tried to recruit for a revolutionary overthrow of the Adenauer regime, which the communists denounced as a satellite of the Western occupation powers. At the same time the party excluded "opportunists" and "Titoists," thereby isolating itself still further.

A new and more moderate policy was begun in 1956, after the twentieth party congress of the Communist Party of the Soviet Union. Walter Fisch even argued that the KPD aimed at changing the existing order by "peaceful and legal means" and enjoined the working-class parties to "make parliament into an effective instrument of the popular will." The program of action issued by the outlawed KPD in 1960 called above all for the defense of democratic rights, including termination of the ban on the KPD. In a speech at the fourth plenum of the central committee, Max Reimann stated:

> The entire development leads toward socialism; the chance for a peaceful transition may be effected while oppositional forces and parties continue to function. Backed by the working class and the broad mass of the people, the socialist government will defend with determination its achievements against counterrevolutionary plots. But this does not necessitate the prohibition and suppression of a parliamentary opposition, as long as the opposition adheres to the laws of the socialist state adopted by the constitution and by the majority of the popular representatives.

Such statements were, of course, intended to facilitate legalization of the outlawed party. However, they may possibly introduce a more democratic phase in the KPD's development.

## ORGANIZATION AND MEMBERSHIP OF THE KPD

The last statute of the KPD in the German Federal Republic, dated May 1963, largely corresponds to that of the East Germany party, as did the previous KPD statutes. The party's organizational structure rests on the principle of "democratic centralism." In a bureaucratic and centralized cadre and cell party such as the outlawed KPD, the eleven-member politburo of the central committee (with sixty members and twenty candidates) and its secretariat are all powerful, although this is not openly admitted. The leaders of the KPD in the German Federal Republic include Max Reimann, Erich Glückauf, Joseph Ledwohn, Jupp Angenforth, Max Schäfer, Otto Niebergall, Oskar Neumann, and Willi Mohn.

The KPD does not rest on local chapters, but on basic units (formerly known as shop nuclei) of a minimum of three members in factories or other places of employment. The party membership has always fluctuated to an extraordinary degree:

Prewar Germany

| 1919 | 107,000 |
| 1920 | 45,000 |
| 1920 | 360,000 |
| 1924 | 150,000 |
| 1929 | 106,000 |
| 1932 | 300,000 |

West Germany

| 1947 | 325,000 |
| 1949 | 215,000 |
| 1956 | 60,000–70,000 |
| 1964 | 6,000–20,000 (est.) |

It is said that in 1950, 57 percent of all members were workers but that the percentage of members organized in shop nuclei had declined from 19 percent to 16.5 percent. Complaints are also heard that the average age of party members is rising. The average age of the politburo members is fifty-four. In Bremen the number of members over fifty is supposedly ten times higher than the number of members between twenty-six and thirty-five. In one part of Hamburg there are reportedly ten members under twenty-five as against eighty-one above the age of sixty. Of the 691 delegates to the Hamburg party congress in 1954, 539 were said to have been workers, sixty employees, forty-three housewives as against nine farmers, five farm laborers, and four members of the middle class. Of the 488 delegates who belonged to labor unions, 163 were members of the Industrial Labor Union Metal (IG Metall) and fifty-seven were members of the Industrial Labor Union Mining (IG Bergbau).

HISTORY OF THE SED

*1946 to 1953* The Socialist Unity Party of Germany (Sozialistische Einheitspartei Deutschlands, SED) was founded at the unification congress held on April 21-22, 1946, in Berlin, but it operated only in the Soviet zone of Germany and in West Berlin. At the time the SED intended to continue the best traditions of both the KPD and the SPD, claiming that the two had "met halfway." The new party's published principles and objectives admitted that the SED aimed at more than achievement of the current democratic demands and intended to create a socialist order. Germany's special position at the time, however, allowed the possibility of a democratic road to socialism; hence the SED would resort to revolutionary means only "if the capitalist class were to abandon the principles of democracy." On this basis the SED succeeded in getting the other political parties in the Soviet zone under its influence. Then, in 1948, it abandoned the "special German road to socialism." After the rupture between Stalin and Tito, Tito was branded as "anti-Soviet." Even Ackermann, the party's ideologist, had to retract the views he had expressed two years earlier and accept the Russian road "as the only possible road to socialism," conceding that it was the same road for all nations, "even though not exactly the same in the sense of a complete analogy."

In 1949 the SED admitted that the existing order in East Germany was not a "people's democracy," but an "antifascist democratic order in which the working class held commanding positions." In the following years, however, it was able to effect a *Gleichschaltung* of all parties and mass organizations, the state machinery, and the economic apparatus. The party also extended its influence into such areas as the judiciary, cultural life, and athletic activities. The SED still hoped to reunify Germany. This, however, had as its precondition the elimination of the Western Allied statutes concerning the Ruhr industrial region and the occupation forces, the liquidation of militarism and nazism, and destruction of the power wielded by capitalist monopolies in the Western zones. The SED also demanded the creation of an all-German government made up of the democratic parties and organizations, the conclusion of a peace treaty, and withdrawal of the occupation forces.

However, the SED was to develop into a party of a new type, a Marxist-Leninist combat party. Such a party, in effect a bolshevized and Stalinized party, would, first of all, have to recognize the leading position of the Soviet Union and the Soviet party; splitters and splinter groups would not be tolerated. After the founding of the German Democratic Republic in 1949, the third party congress of the SED, held in 1950, stated that "the party of Lenin and Stalin . . . enjoys unquestioned authority," but that its development was not yet satisfactory, despite its considerable progress. In 1952 the second party conference renewed the SED's pledge "to the leader of nations, the great Stalin," in an even more forceful manner. New armed forces were to be organized to assure peace. At the same time, socialism was to be "built in a systematic fashion," since the political and economic conditions, as well as the consciousness of the working class, had become ripe for such a course.

*1953 to 1965* After Stalin's death in 1953 the German Democratic Republic shared in the general thaw and experienced some relaxation of pressure ("quiet de-Stalinization"). The uprising of June 17, 1956, against the communist regime was suppressed, but the "new course" did produce some economic liberalization. After Stalin's "cult of personality" was condemned at the Soviet party's twentieth congress, the third conference of the SED in 1956 moved toward an added measure of "liberalization from above," stressing the rights of the workers and of their representatives in the parliament (*Volkskammer*) and in local elective bodies. The conference emphasized the need for a strict observance of socialist legality and for close cooperation of all political parties within the national front, under the sole leadership of the SED. Walter Ulbricht, the party's first secretary, proclaimed the new socialist ethic.

In July 1958 the fifth party congress proclaimed the collectivization of agriculture and resolved to improve and simplify the state machinery. The SED stressed that the main task of the working class, and of all peace lovers, was to prevent atomic rearmament of West Germany and work for the creation of a denuclearized zone. Reunification of Germany was to take place only on the basis of negotiations between equals, and by means of a confederation linking the two German states.

Total collectivization of agriculture was accomplished in 1960, and the Berlin Wall was constructed in 1961. The sixth congress of the SED met in January 1963 to set forth party policy after the achievement of full socialization and the complete blocking off of the German Democratic Republic. De-Stalinization continued, and it was further emphasized at a central committee meeting the following November. The sixth congress adopted the SED's first definitive program, a document of some 160 pages which followed the program of the Soviet party. The program called for an end "of the occupational regime in West Berlin and the transformation of West Berlin into a free city." It demanded "a confederation of the two German states which the free city of Berlin could join" and "comprehensive construction of socialism" in the German Democratic Republic, confidently proclaiming that "the transition from capitalism to socialism is the main content and the fundamental development law of our epoch.... The SED is the party of socialism...."

## ORGANIZATION AND MEMBERSHIP OF THE SED

The SED's first statute, adopted in 1946, embodied the democratic principles and traditions of the workers' parties, as did the constitutions of the other three parties founded in the Soviet zone of Germany. In the beginning the decision-making committees had an equal number of social democrat and communist representatives; Otto Grotewohl and Wilhelm Pieck were joint chairmen. However, the principle of equal representation was violated shortly after the second party congress in September 1947 and was abandoned altogether by the first party conference in January 1949.

The third party congress in July 1950 adopted a new statute, based on an organizational principle more befitting a "party of the new type." Since Stalin's reign "democratic centralism" has been more centralist than democratic. Formally the party organs are elected from below, but in effect the elections consist in confirmation of candidates nominated from above. Decisions of the higher party organs are binding on all lower organs, which must observe strict party discipline. Party unity is the supreme law. Dissident factions are prohibited, and once resolutions have been adopted, they must be defended even by those who voted against them ("corporate discipline").

Any "deviations" that might threaten the party's monolithic unity, either "dogmatism" at one extreme or "revisionism" at the other, are effectively prevented through internal party investigations and purges. By the summer of 1950 Paul Merker, Lex Ende, and other party leaders had already been expelled. Two months later the central committee decided to investigate all party members. After the June 17, 1956, riots, Wilhelm Zaisser, Rudolf Herrnstadt, Max Fechner, and others were disciplined. In February 1958 Karl

Schirdewan, Ernst Wollweber, Fred Oelssner, and others were deprived of their positions. No SED leader, however, has been sentenced to death.

According to the statutes of 1950, 1954, and 1963, the party congress is the highest organ of the party. It elects the central committee and determines the party's program, statute, general political line, and tactics. The 1946 statute provided for an annual party congress, and the 1950 statute provided for a party congress every second year; since the promulgation of the 1954 statute, the congress is to assemble every fourth year. In practice the delegates are selected by the central party machine; hence the congresses always arrive at a unanimous vote, and their resolutions have only a rhetorical character.

At present the central committee meets only every six months. Ostensibly it constitutes the highest party authority during the period between congresses, but at best it serves only as a sounding board for two relatively small supreme committees, the politburo and the secretariat. The politburo elected in 1963 was made up of fourteen members and eight candidates. It meets at least once a week and supervises the political work of the central committee. The eight-member secretariat, headed by Walter Ulbricht as first secretary, controls the execution of party resolutions and the selection of cadres, that is, personnel policy. Not even the central committee, let alone the party congress, ever seems to have annulled a single resolution of the politburo or secretariat. According to the "production principle" laid down in 1961, the machinery of the central committee and its subordinate districts and counties includes bureaus for agriculture, industry, and construction. The lowest party organizations are the 50,000 or more basic units, or cells. There are special party organizations (political administrations) in the army and the railways.

Party membership is granted only after a preliminary qualifying period, and there is no provision for voluntary resignation. Membership is annulled by expulsion, the highest party penalty. Since 1958 membership may also be cancelled.

In addition to Walter Ulbricht, the most important party leaders are Willi Stoph, Albert Norden, Erich Honecker, Paul Verner, Kurt Hager, and Friedrich Ebert. Party membership has been fairly stable. At its formation the SED had 1.3 million members (47.7 percent KPD and 52.3 percent SPD); in June 1948 it had 2 million, in September 1953 1.2 million, and in January 1963 1.65 million. Of the members in 1960, 10 percent were eighteen to twenty-five years old, 30 percent were between twenty-five and fifty, and 60 percent were over fifty. In 1963 the proportion of women was 24 percent and the proportion of workers was about 30 percent. Of the nearly 2,500 delegates at the sixth party congress in 1963, 55.5 percent were workers, 14.9 percent cooperative farmers, 16.2 percent intellectuals, 11.5 percent white-collar workers, and 1.9 percent self-employed persons, students, housewives, and others.

## FUTURE PROSPECTS

*The KPD*   The outlawed KPD is strongly sectarian in character. Its influence in the German Federal Republic is very small, even in major industrial enterprises. Even if the KPD were once again permitted to operate legally, it would be unable to gain much strength unless there were an extended period of relaxation in world policy and in the relations between the two German states. Genuine democratization might perhaps win over disappointed former communists from the ranks of the SPD, but true democratization is likely to be more difficult for the KPD than for the other Western European parties, since the KPD is strongly dependent both ideologically and financially on the SED.

*THE SED*   The SED is the state party of the German Democratic Republic and will retain this position in the foreseeable future. The progressive consolidation of the German Democratic Republic should work in the SED's favor. Its unique position as a second

German state between the more powerful German Federal Republic and the even more powerful Soviet Union implies dependence on a foreign superpower and conflict with the majority of its own people. However, the SED, and especially its leadership under Walter Ulbricht, has shown great skill in meeting the difficulties inherent in this situation. Ulbricht, like Stalin, has destroyed all opponents within and outside the party, while at the same time partially taking over and carrying out their demands. The East German system may lack finality from the standpoint of world history, but it will probably continue for a considerable period, particularly if the SED should effect some modest liberalization. The SED and its regime thus constitute "a permanently provisional arrangement."

## PARTY PRESS ORGANS

*The KPD* Up to 1956, as long as the KPD was legal, it published the daily *Freies Volk* and the ideological monthly *Wissen und Tat*. Since 1956 the underground party has published *Freies Volk* as a weekly and an irregular newssheet, *Informationsdienst*.

*The SED* The official organ of the SED is the daily *Neues Deutschland*, published in East Berlin with a circulation of 800,000. The party's monthly ideological journal is *Einheit*, also published in East Berlin. In West Berlin, where the SED is legal, it publishes *Wahrheit* twice weekly.

## PARTY CONGRESSES AND CONFERENCES

*The KPD* From 1918 to 1946 the KPD held the following congresses and conferences:

1st (constituent) congress, December 1918-January 1919, Berlin
2d congress, October 1919, Heidelberg
3d congress, February 1920, Karlsruhe
4th congress, April 1920, Berlin
5th congress, November 1920, Berlin
6th (unity) congress, December 1920, Berlin
7th congress, August 1921, Jena
8th congress, January-February 1923, Leipzig
9th congress, April 1924, Frankfurt
10th congress, July 1925, Berlin
1st all-party conference, October 1925, Berlin
11th congress, March 1927, Essen
12th congress, June 1929, Berlin
All-German conference, October 1932, Berlin
13th congress ("Brussels conference), October 1935, Moscow
14th congress ("Bern conference"), January-February 1939, Paris
1st conference, March 1946, Berlin
15th congress, April 1946, Berlin

Since the creation in 1946 of the SED the KPD in West Germany and the SED in East Germany have held separate congresses. As the KPD was outlawed in West Germany in 1956, its congresses since then have been held in East Germany.

1st conference, April 1948, Herne
2d conference, March 1949, Solingen
Congress, March 1951, Weimar
Congress, December 1954, Hamburg
Congress, May-June 1957, Bogensee (near Berlin)
Conference, February 1960, Ballenstedt (East Germany)
Congress May 1963, Kleinmachnow (near Berlin)

*The SED* All congresses of the SED have met in East Berlin.

Unification congress, April 1946
2d congress, September 1947
1st conference, January 1949
3d congress, July 1950
2d conference, July 1952
4th congress, March-April 1954
3d conference, March 1956
5th congress, July 1958
6th congress, January 1963

## BIBLIOGRAPHY

*The KPD*

Angress, W. T.: *Stillborn Revolution: The Communist Bid for Power in Germany, 1922-1923*, Princeton, N.J., 1963
Colloti, Enzo (ed.): *Die Kommunistische Partei Deutschlands, 1918-1933: Ein bibliographischer Beitrag*, Milan, 1960.
Fischer, Ruth: *Stalin and German Communism*, Cambridge, Mass., 1948.
Flechtheim, O. K.: *Die KPD in der Weimarer*

*Republik*, Offenbach, 1948; and new ed., Frankfurt, 1969.
*Geschichte der deutschen Arbeiterbewegung*, Berlin, 1966, 8 vols.
Kluth, H.: *Die KPD in der Bundesrepublik*, Cologne, 1959.
*Die Kommunistische Partei Deutschlands Lebt und Kämpft: Dokumente der Kommunistischen Partei Deutschlands, 1956-1962*, Berlin, 1963.
Tjaden, K. H.: *Struktur und Funktion der "KPD-Opposition" (KPD)*, Meisenheim am Glan, 1965.
Weber, H. (ed.): *Der deutsche Kommunismus: Dokumente*, Cologne-Berlin, 1963.
*Zur Geschichte der Kommunistischen Partei Deutschlands: Materialien und Dokumente aus den Jahren 1914-1946*, Berlin, 1955.
*Zur Geschichte des antifaschistischen Widerstandskampfes, 1933-1945: Materialien, Berichte, Dokumente*, Berlin, 1957.

*The SED*

Bundesministerium für Gesamtdeutsche Fragen: *SBZ von A-Z*, 10th ed., Bonn, 1966.
Bundesministerium für Gesantdeutsche Fragen: *SBZ von 1945 bis 1954, SBZ von 1955 bis 1958, SBZ von 1959 bis 1960*, Bonn 1956–.
*Dokumente der SED*, Berlin, 1948–.
Jaenicke, M.: *Der dritte Weg*, Cologne, 1964.
Richert, E.: *Macht ohne Mandat*, Cologne, 1963.
Stern, C.: *Portrait einer bolschewistischen Partei: Entwicklung, Funktion und Situation der SED*, Cologne, 1957.
Thomas, Stefan (ed.): *Das Programm der SED. Das erste Programm der SED. Das vierte Statut der SED. Das nationale Dokument*, Cologne, 1963.
*20 Jahre SED: Zeittafel wichtiger Beratungen und Dokumente*, Berlin, 1966.

OSSIP K. FLECHTHEIM

1. It was not until December 1913 that Rosa Luxemburg, Franz Mehring, and Isetor Karski (Julian Baltazar Marchlewski) began to publish their *Sozialdemokratische Korrespondenz*.

2. Already in March 1918 the Russian Social Democratic Labor Party (Bolshevik) had styled itself the Russian Communist Party (Bolshevik).

# GREAT BRITAIN

Although no fewer than five British revolutionary groups were invited to the founding congress of the Communist International in March 1919, none in fact received news of the congress until after it was over. Unlike most other sections of the Comintern, the British party arose from a fusion of several organizations, and not from a split off the main body of social democracy. Lengthy negotiations spanning a period of almost two and a half years and involving two unity conventions, one at London in August 1920 and the other at Leeds in January 1921, were required before the various contending groups could be fused into a unified party, the Communist Party of Great Britain (CPGB). At every stage of negotiation Comintern influence proved the decisive factor.

The founding groups comprised the British Socialist Party (BSP), the largest group, a lineal descendant of the Social Democratic Federation founded by Hyndman in 1884; the Communist Unity Group, a small split from Britain's De Leonist Socialist Labour Party (SLP); the Communist Party (British section of the Third International), a body which had sprung from Sylvia Pankhurst's prewar women's-suffrage agitation; the Independent Labour Party Left Wing, a minority group which left the Independent Labour Party after its Easter conference in 1921; the rump of the wartime shop stewards' organization of industrial militants; and a number of groupings of a local character. At its founding the CPGB claimed 10,000 members. The actual figure was probably between 3,000 and 5,000.

The party's leader in its first years was Arthur MacManus, a shop stewards' leader of Irish origin, who died in 1924. Originally dominated by the BSP, the party's leadership quickly passed to the industrial militants and former members of the SLP.

The new leadership hinged on the SLP and shop stewards' trio comprised of MacManus, Thomas Bell, and J. T. Murphy, with such other figures as William Gallacher, J. R. Campbell, and William Paul in the immediate background. Albert Inkpin, former secretary of the BSP, acted as party secretary. Palme Dutt, later to become the party's best-known intellectual, first achieved prominence at this time. In the process of consolidation the party lost Pankhurst and some figures later prominent in the labor movement, among them Ellen Wilkinson and Raymond Postgate. Two of the party's first three members of Parliament, Colonel Malone and Walton Newbold, were also lost in the process.

Bell and Inkpin were moved into the background with the onset of the Comintern's "third period" (see *The Communist International*) when the Dutt-Pollitt leadership came to the fore, with Harry Pollitt as party secretary. Murphy, who had been the shop stewards' theorist, was the most able of the early leaders. With Solomon A. Lozovskii and M. P. Tomskii, he was one of the founders of the Red International of Labor Unions. As a member of the Executive Committee of the Comintern, Murphy moved for the expulsion of Leon Trotsky from the Comintern. As a result of the change of leadership in 1929, Murphy was expelled in 1932 on charges of having advocated increased trade with the Soviet Union during a third-period election campaign.

Official communist hagiography treats the CPGB as an essentially British institution. In fact, without the ideological and financial intervention of the Comintern and without the work of its agents in Britain, the party would never have been founded. Until September 1918 the key Russian agent in Britain was Maxim Litvinov, later a Soviet commissar for foreign affairs. Theodore Rothstein, later Soviet ambassador in Persia, took Litvinov's place until the founding of the party in August 1920. Among other Russian socialist émigrés who played a role in the prerevolutionary British socialist movement were Georgii V. Chicherin, later Soviet commissar for foreign affairs, and Ivan Maiskii and Peter Petrov, both later employed in the Soviet diplomatic service. The Comintern representative in 1922 was George Brown (Grusenberg) who later, as Michael Borodin, became Comintern political advisor to Chiang Kai-shek. He was succeeded by Bennet, known elsewhere as A. (sometimes D.) Petrovskii (although his real name was Max Goldfarb).

HISTORY

The immediate postwar years, 1919 and 1920, torn by sharp social contradictions, offered opportunities, since unrepeated, of which the CPGB was unable to take advantage owing to the inability of the quarrelling revolutionary groups to fuse into a single united party.

The fused CPGB of 1920 remained largely social democratic in organization and leadership. The party did not begin to adopt a bolshevik form of organization until after its acceptance of the report of a party commission on organization in October 1922 and was not fully bolshevized until about 1924. The general strike of 1926 and its immediate aftermath allowed the party to reach the highest membership (10,720) of its first fifteen years of existence. The end of the general strike and the subsequent defeat of the miners led to a sharp setback which, accentuated by the adoption of the "class-against-class" policy in 1929, quickly reduced the party to a skeleton of professional functionaries thinly clothed by a small transient membership consisting of unemployed. In the 1920s and 1930s the CPGB gained important success in organizing the unemployed, and its methods were subsequently recommended by the Comintern as a model to other sections.

The rise of Hitler, the war in Spain, and the popular front each allowed the party to make considerable membership advances, notably among the intelligentsia. Thus the social composition of the CPGB changed almost beyond recognition between 1929 and 1936. The about-turn on resistance to fascism which followed the Hitler-Stalin pact of 1939 brought heavy losses among the intelligentsia. Germany's invasion of Russia and the ensuing switch of national press and radio in favor of the Soviets allowed the party to reach its peak membership of 56,000 in 1942 and 1943. The party's calls for a second front, its strike breaking, and its demands for more production won it new allies, albeit among different social elements than in either of the previous decades. The end of the wartime honeymoon in international relations and the opening of the cold war reduced membership rapidly. Following the twentieth congress of the Communist Party of the Soviet Union and the Hungarian revolution, the CPGB experienced the most severe crisis of its existence and lost the larger part of its remaining intellectuals. Membership had fallen to 24,000 by 1958. A limited recovery later allowed the party to approach its former numbers, although with greatly diminished influence.

The CPGB in fact has never at any time come close to its objective of displacing the Labour Party as the political organization of the working class. In the thirteen general elections since its founding, the party has only once exceeded 100,000 votes (102,780 in 1945). In 1964, of thirty-six communist candidates, every one lost his deposit.[1] The prosecution of communist journalist J. R. Campbell and the publication of a Zinoviev letter (almost certainly forged) were contributory causes to the fall of the 1924 Labour government and its subsequent election defeat, but apart from these incidents the CPGB's electoral influence has been minimal.

The Labour Party decides issues by the votes of a majority of affiliated trade unionists and a minority of individual members. Despite repeated endeavors, the CPGB has never been able either to join or to split this federal power structure. As a result, cut off from the basic roots of the working-class movement, the CPGB has never been able to develop a serious rival role of its own.

The party's greatest influence on the course of British political life was exercised in the years 1924 to 1927. In mid-1924 the Trades Union Congress, expressing its dissent with the rigid anticommunism of the Amsterdam Trade Union International, opened direct contact with the Russians (who had split the international trade-union movement by founding the Red International of Labor Unions in 1920). The outcome was an Anglo-Soviet Trade Union Committee, which seemed for a while to offer the Russians the opportunity to reenter the international trade-union movement. This association was valued and utilized by the Soviet and British leaders for conflicting ends. Finally the British leaders, having no further use for the pact as a means of disciplining their own communist opposition, jettisoned the deal in January 1927 once the general strike and its aftermath were safely over.

The outset of the third period in Comintern developments finally brought to an end all hopes of a reconciliation between the British and Soviet trade unions. In the early part of this period the miners, led by A. J. Cook, responded to the coal owners' demands for cuts in their living standards with the slogan "Not a penny off the pay, not a minute on the day." The resulting dispute brought on the general strike of 1926. Cook was not a communist, nor did the party control the miners' executive, but there can be no doubt that the militancy of the party's cadres in the pits played an important role in the development of the struggle. The government thought it necessary to arrest twelve key communist leaders in 1925 in order to limit the party's effectiveness in the expected dispute the following year.

In these years the communist-led Trade Union Minority Movement enabled the party to lay the foundation for its subsequent industrial influence. A. J. Cook was elected the miners' leader as a Minority Movement candidate. The Minority Movement, however, like the party-founded National Left Wing, which sought to lead a struggle inside the Labour Party and achieved considerable influence, was brought to nothing during the ultraleft third period in Comintern policy that followed.

The third period, by reducing the party to a mere cadre of its most determined supporters (membership fell to 1,000-2,000 members), laid the basis for the final Stalinization of the party. As the cadres emerged into the easier atmosphere of the 1930s, they acquired new converts who knew nothing of the original history of the Comintern and were thus to prove largely immune to the Moscow trials and the purges of the 1930s. The party's most popular leader, Harry Pollitt, became general secretary and proletarian figurehead of the party in 1929. The Pollitt-Dutt leadership which emerged set the image of the party for the next decades.

After the ascent of Hitler and the turn of 1935, the CPGB, while never emerging as a challenge to the Labour Party, gained more widespread support, especially among the intelligentsia. The party's antifascist record won it strong support among sections of the Jewish population, and its support for republican Spain added to its credit. There can be little doubt that at this time, through its influence on the climate of public opinion, the party's importance was greater than its numbers suggest. Thus the Left Book Club, heavily under party influence, and with Harold Laski, John Strachey, and Victor Gollancz on the board of editors, was reaching 50,000 readers a month. Yet with only one member of Parliament (William Gallacher) in a house of over 600, with the trades-union-labor alliance intact, the party was unable to emerge as a challenger for power. The leadership nevertheless was able to carry the party through the Soviet purge trials and the GPU activities in Spain without any difficulties with the membership.

The party supported the Hitler-Stalin pact of 1939 as a "dramatic move to halt aggression." When Britain declared war, however, the party, under Pollitt, maintained its former line of resistance to fascism and broke the Comintern front. A few weeks later the line changed and Pollitt was temporarily deposed. As a result, the bulk of the intellectuals left as a body, and many of the sympathizers, Strachey, Gollancz, and Laski among them, broke away as well.

In August 1940, at the height of the nazi invasion danger, the party mounted a people's convention to call for a negotiated peace. Once Germany invaded Russia, the CPGB unhesitatingly expressed its support for the "Churchill government without reservation." Abandoning its former antiwar supporters, the party now experienced the largest expansion in its history, doubling party membership with a 25,000 increase in the first quarter of 1942 alone.

In line with this influx of "Red Army communists," the party made efforts to Anglicize itself and after Yalta became the advocate of a class peace at home after the war to match the international Big Three alliance. Thus the party called for a "new national [coalition] government" to govern after the war. The Labour Party, however, ignored communist advice and won the 1945 election with a massive majority on a policy of its own. An emergent left-wing opposition was steamrollered at the CPGB's 1945 congress. In the immediate postwar years the party maintained a stand of critical support of the Labour Party government.

After the founding of the Cominform the party gave greater support to industrial militancy and turned to a strident nationalism and anti-Americanism, in contrast to its alleged socialist beliefs. Greatly influenced by the success of Rákosi-style "salami socialism" in Eastern Europe, in 1951 the party adopted a new program, the "British road to socialism," which expressly abandoned revolutionary views and called for a parliamentary road to socialism. The new program, however, did not prevent either the continuation of an intensely loyalist attitude to Moscow, extending to even the smallest of issues, or a continuing drain of membership.

The twentieth congress of the Soviet party in 1956 and the Hungarian revolution produced a fundamental revulsion among the membership, and the party experienced the most serious crisis in its history. Pressure from below forced a special congress in April 1957, at which the party leaders emerged triumphant. The result was widespread disillusionment both within and outside the party ranks and a great exodus of members, including some of the best-known intellectual figures.

During the war the CPGB had made important gains in the unions on the basis of its support for the government, the unions' official leadership and its patriotic appeals. It became particularly influential in a number of the largest transport, electricity, and engineering unions. The changed pattern of the postwar years and the party's attacks on its former allies led to a steady loss of support. Following allegations of ballot forging against its leaders, the communist-led electrical union was expelled from the Trades Union Congress and the Labour Party in 1961. When these leaders were subsequently removed from office, the CPGB lost the sole large union remaining under its control.

## ORGANIZATION AND MEMBERSHIP

The organizational structure of the CPGB, based on the standard principle of democratic centralism, extends in pyramid fashion from the party secretary (in 1965 John Gollan) and political committee, down through the central committee and the district committees, to the party branches and party factions in front organizations and in such trade unions as the party has membership of importance.

The composition of the membership was predominantly working class at the party's foundation but is probably now much less so than that of the Labour Party. Since the days of the popular front the party has consistently attracted support from certain middle-class strata at one pole and from industrial militants who join on the basis of a misunderstanding at the other. At present party conrol rests firmly with the hierarchy, without any challenge from either wing. The party no longer enrolls or directly influences a significant number of intellectuals. It has full legal status, although its members are subject to some important security bars as far as employment in civil service and defense-based industries is concerned. A minority of trade unions also restrict the rights of communists to hold office.

Apart from a secondary shift in 1923, one important change of leadership in 1929, and a temporary shift in 1939, the CPGB has been singularly free from the normal pattern of purges and abrupt changes in leadership. The leadership installed in 1929 has remained in power, except for the inevitable changes due to death and retirement, until 1965. Inkpin, the first general secretary, held office from 1920 to 1929, and Pollitt, the second, from 1929 until 1956, shortly before his death. The present general secretary, John Gollan, was groomed for the succession and succeeded without dispute.

The CPGB claims a membership of 33,240, which is probably an overstatement. That a high proportion of the actual membership is relatively inactive is fairly certain. No official geographical allocation is available, but there is no reason to believe that the party's three long-standing concentrations (in London, Scotland, and South Wales) have changed in recent years. The fact that at its 1963 congress the party boasted of its 2,300 members in Glasgow (population 1,050,000) and of its 1,000 members in Birmingham (population 1,100,000) adequately indicates its level of support in the rest of the country.

The party's Young Communist League has fewer than 5,000 members and is overshadowed by both the official Labour Party youth movement and the Trotskyist Young Socialists. Despite recent claims, there is little reason to believe that the party has many members or much influence among students.

The party is surrounded by the usual constellation of front organizations, none of which exercises great influence, often because, as in the case of the World Peace Council, the field has already been preempted by other organizations more genuinely concerned about the issues involved.

## RELATION TO SOVIET LEADERSHIP

The dominant role played by the Comintern in founding the CPGB ensured the party's subsequent ultraloyalist record. The power of the Bell-MacManus-Murphy grouping deteriorated steadily in the years after the adoption of the party commission report in October 1922. The whole executive committee was called to Moscow in June 1923 to discuss differences regarding the report's implementation, and newer members, such as Pollitt and Dutt, were advanced closer to the center of power even though the old leadership had not yet been displaced. The CPGB's only serious leadership crisis arose in 1929, when those reluctant to accept some of the more extreme policies of the Comintern's third period were removed. In an almost clean sweep of the old top leadership, only Murphy temporarily survived, and the Pollitt-Dutt partnership that was to control the party's destiny for the next thirty years was enthroned. The new leadership conducted the about-turn toward the popular front in 1934 and 1935 without a tremor. It failed to protest the execution of its former Comintern advisor, Petrovskii, or the disappearance of his English-born wife, Rose Cohen, during the purges. Nor did it offer a protest at the fate of Borodin after the war. The release from imprisonment in Vorkuta of Len Wincott, the sailor who led the Invergordon naval mutiny of 1931 and later joined the CPBG, was accomplished by noncommunist protests, and not by the action of the party he had joined.

The party's initial support of the war against Hitler in 1939 is believed to have been reversed by the arrival of Dave Springhall, who brought the Comintern line from Moscow. Yet even in this case Pollitt's demotion proved only temporary. A "Chinese" faction now wields some influence among the party's industrial cadres but poses no serious challenge to the leadership. Trotskyist groups formed in the early 1930s, which gained numerous recruits from the party after 1956, have proved unable either to hold members or to emerge as an alternative.

At the present time the party occupies a middle ground in the international communist movement, essentially loyal to the Soviet position, but unwilling to see any open doctrinal and organizational breach with the Chinese. A small pro-Chinese group has split from the party, and there have been some factional struggles within the unions between "Russian" and "Chinese" communists.

## FUTURE PROSPECTS

The CPGB has never grown far beyond the limits of a bureaucratically dominated sect, and as a result the party has remained insulated from the great debates over such issues as unilateralism, which caused serious tensions in the mass organizations of the British labor movement. The CPGB is small enough to be able to lose one set of membership and pick up another at every turn of the political line. While the party can maintain an artificially inflated bureaucracy, it can manipulate this transient membership around its cadres indefinitely. Equally, there is little reason to believe the CPGB can break out of its isolation, a judgment supported by the growth of mass radical movements outside the party's ranks and largely beyond its influence.

Since 1951 the CPGB has given at least lip service to a peaceful and democratic road to socialism. The emergence of Russia as a world power has diminished the party's role as chief defender of the Soviet Union. Stalin's rule shattered the idealized reputation of the Soviet state. In such circumstances it is not at all clear what genuine role the CPGB can perform in future British political life. In its present situation the party's hopes for significant advances, even under a Labour Party government, are unlikely to be fulfilled. The recent decision to change the working-class title of the party's *Daily Worker* (started in January 1930) to the politically neutral *Morning Star*, is an indication of the crisis with which it is faced.

## PARTY PRESS ORGANS AND RECORDS

The party's daily is the *Morning Star,* formerly the *Daily Worker* (1930-1966). The recognized organ of the party on general matters is the *Labour Monthly*, edited by Palme Dutt. The quarterly *Marxism Today* deals with more theoretical and ideological questions.

The CPGB published recently a fifteen-page pamphlet, *Aims & Constitution of the Communist Party of Great Britain*. Furthermore, before each congress the party publishes and distributes documentation on issues to be discussed by the congress; the subsequent *Congress Reports* are devoted almost exclusively to speeches. There is no complete archive of party-congress documents in Britain.

## CONGRESSES OF THE CPGB

1st congress, July-August 1920, London
2d congress, January-February 1921, Leeds
3d congress, April 1921, Manchester
4th congress, March 1922, London
5th congress, October 1922, London
6th congress, May 1924, Manchester
7th congress, May-June 1925, Glasgow
8th congress, October 1926, London
9th congress, October 1927, Salford
10th congress, January 1929, London
11th congress, November-December 1929, Leeds
12th congress, November 1932, London
13th congress, February 1935, Manchester
14th congress, May 1937, London
15th congress, September 1938, Birmingham
16th congress, October 1939, London
17th congress, May-June 1943, London
18th congress, November 1945, London
19th congress, February 1947, London
20th congress, February 1948, London
21st congress, November 1949, Liverpool
22d congress, April 1952. London
23d congress, April 1954, London
24th congress, March-April 1956, London
25th congress, April 1957, London
26th congress, March 1959, London
27th congress, March-April 1961, London
28th congress, April 1963, London
29th congress, November 1965, London

## BIBLIOGRAPHY

Kendall, Walter: *The Revolutionary Movement in Britain, 1900-1921,* London, Weidenfeld & Nicolson, 1959.

Macfarlane, L. J.: *The British Communist Party*, London, McGibbon & Kee, 1956.

Pelling, Henry: *The British Communist Party: A Historical Profile*, London, A. & C. Black, 1958.

WALTER KENDALL

1. Candidates at parliamentary elections who fail to obtain one-eighth of the total vote cast in their constituencies forfeit the deposit of 150 pounds which all candidates must lodge. This law has been enforced since the 1918 election.

# GREECE

As late as 1965 there were two Greek communist parties, both recognized by Moscow. The old party, the Communist Party of Greece (Kommunistikon Komma Ellados, KKE) has been illegal since 1947 but is still in existence abroad. Its leaders and the core of its membership live in the neighboring communist countries. The communists who remained in Greece were able to form a new party in 1951, the United Democratic Left (Eniea Dimokratiki Aristera, EDA). The EDA, the legal organization, is directed by the clandestine KKE, but antagonisms between them have appeared at times.

## HISTORY

*1918 to 1931* The long struggle for liberation from Turkish domination and unification of Greek lands and the predominantly agricultural character of the country did not favor an early creation of a socialist party. Only small socialist groups existed in Athens, Salonika, and Volos before 1917. These groups met in Piraeus on November 18-22, 1918, and founded a political party under the name Socialist Workers' Party of Greece (Socialistikon Ergatikon Komma Ellados, SEKE). This meeting elected the party leaders, N. Demetratos (general secretary), P. Demetratos, M. Sideris, and St. Kokkinos.

Shortly after it was created the SEKE was taken over by probolshevik elements and became in fact a communist party. In 1920 a majority of the membership voted for affiliation with the Comintern and added the word communist to the party's name, in parentheses. In 1924 the graduates of the Communist University for the Peoples of the East in Soviet Russia, known as the KUTV school, began to arrive in Greece. In the same year, at its third (extraordinary) congress, the party changed its name to Communist Party of Greece.

A violent struggle began between the "Greeks" and the "Muscovites," but at the same time the party had its first political success. In the November 1926 parliamentary elections ten KKE candidates were elected. At the third congress, in March 1927, the KUTVists succeeded in ousting the entire leadership elected at the founding meeting in 1918 on charges of social democratic leanings. This internal struggle was complicated by the Macedonian question; Moscow, searching for a port on the Aegean Sea, launched, via the Comintern, the slogan for a "Macedonian state," which would have separated northern Greece from the rest of the country. The KKE adopted this Soviet plan, but some of its cadres opposed it. Although the opponents were expelled from the party, the internal crisis lasted until 1931.

*1931 to 1936* Disturbed by the party's failure, the Comintern decided to intervene. On Comintern orders Nicholas Zachariadis, a KUTVist, assumed leadership of the party on February 1, 1931, and, with a group of younger members, began to apply a new tactic, more flexible, more realistic, and ostensibly more nationalist than before. The internal struggle ceased, and the KKE became a monolithic party. It profited next from Greece's economic and political crisis and gained much ground in becomig an important force for the first time: 8,000 members in 1935 as opposed to 1,500 in 1931, 10,000 copies of its newspaper in circulation as against 2,000, 482 strikes with 183,000 strikers in 1934 as against 41 strikes and 16,000 strikers in 1931.[1]

In the elections of January 26, 1936, no

party in the country received a majority. Ever since the abortive coup of March 1935, Greece had been in a state of chaos. Thus the KKE, with its fifteen deputies (out of 300), found itself master of the situation, since the two large opposing parties had 141 and 143 seats respectively, and could not form a government. The liberal party signed an accord for a popular front with the KKE, and the communists went on the attack. Strikes and revolts shook the country; on May 8-9, 1936, twelve persons were killed and 300 were injured in Salonika; on May 13 there was a general strike. A new general political strike was announed for August 4, with "popular-front government" as the slogan. The same day John Metaxas proclaimed his dictatorship, which lasted until German troops entered Athens in April 1941.

*1936 to 1944* The KKE remained in illegality and undertook no important activity until 1940, when it sided with the Axis and opposed Greece's war against it. It then appealed to the people and the soldiers, asking them to turn their arms on the Greek government and the "British imperialists." After Hitler attacked the Soviet Union the KKE, under the pretext of resistance, formed the National Liberation Front, the People's Liberation Army (Ellenikon Laikon Apelevtherikon Straton, ELAS), and other organizations allegedly as resistance groups against the German occupation. In fact these forces were deployed against the noncommunist resistance organizations and used to exterminate anticommunist elements. In 1943 the KKE launched a true civil war, which ended in the Lebanon agreement of April 1944 with the Greek government in exile and the formation of a coalition government of national unity with strong communist participation.

Despite the Lebanon agreement, the KKE continued to exterminate anticommunist elements, especially in September and October 1944, during the nazi retreat. The government arrived in Athens in October, and on December 3 the communists attempted a coup. The civil war was resumed. Several days later the British responded to the appeal of the Greek government and intervened against the rebels. After thirty-three days of combat, the ELAS retreated; meanwhile, the communists had killed nearly 50,000 people. On February 12, 1945, the revolution ended with the Varkiza agreement, which granted amnesty to the KKE.

*1945 to 1949* The KKE used the Varkiza agreement to reorganize its forces and prepare a new attack. On February 12, 1946, the second plenum of the central committee decided to launch a new revolution in the form of a guerrilla war. The revolution began with an armed attack on March 31, the day of the general elections held under the supervision of the United Nations, in which the KKE refused to participate. The revolution lasted until September 1949 and cost Greece nearly 55,000 dead; 750,000 people lost their homes, and the countryside was destroyed. Since the KKE relied on arms and munitions from the neighboring communist countries, where the party's bases were located, the United Nations took the position that the Greek civil war was in reality an outside attack on the country. On this basis, on March 12, 1947, the United States decided to give aid to the Greek government. This aid permitted Greece to repel the communist attack.

The KKE was outlawed when, on December 24, 1947, it announced the formation of its "government," under the presidency of Markos Vafiadis, military head of the revolt. In November 1948, however, a disagreement developed between the military leadership, under Vafiadis, and the political leadership of the rebels, under Zachariadis. The military leaders insisted that since the KKE could not succeed without the open military intervention of the communist states, the struggle should be continued as a guerrilla war in order to obtain a new arrangement like the Varkiza agreement. The political leaders insisted on the need for organizing the rebels into an army; their view prevailed because they had Moscow's support. Vafiadis was expelled, and Zachariadis assumed direction of the "Democratic Army," while M. Partselidis became "prime minister." In January 1949 the fifth plenum of the central committee set 1949 as the "year of victory" and declared that following victory Macedonia would become "autonomous." But the defeats of the Democratic Army multiplied, and after it was completely routed in the mountains at Vitsi and Grammos in August 1949, its remnants fled to neighboring Yugoslavia, Bulgaria, and Albania.

The communists' defeat can be attributed to the opposition of the Greek people, weary of another war; the nonnational character of the war, underlined by the central committee's resolution on Macedonia at the fifth plenum; the refusal of the working class to participate in the revolt which to the very end never reached the cities; the communists' forceful military conscription of youths, even girls of fifteen; popular reaction to the abduction of 28,000 children to the communist countries; the formation in September 1947 of a national coalition government with the participation of all the Greek parties, which developed into a united anticommunist front; United States aid to the Greek government; the break between Tito and the Cominform, which resulted in the halting of Yugoslav aid to the KKE; and the measures taken by the Greek government and the army, as well as errors on the part of the KKE.

*1949 to 1965* After its defeat in 1949, the clandestine KKE again found itself in internal crisis. In April 1956, in response to a personal appeal to Khrushchev by some cadres of the KKE, Moscow formed an "investigating committee" to study the situation. The study resulted in the dismissal of Zachariadis and the formation of a "collective leadership." However, this leadership was ended by the eighth congress of the KKE in August 1961, which elected Constantine Koliyannis as the party's new first secretary.

The internal disputes among the supporters of Zachariadis, of Vafiadis (revisionists), and of the current leadership were still going on at the end of 1965. Election returns showed the party losing some of its political influence. The rise of a pro-Chinese faction since 1964 has further contributed to a weakening of the party.

ORGANIZATION AND MEMBERSHIP

For a long time the KKE and the EDA have not published membership statistics. The "political refugees" under the KKE's control in the communist countries total 75,000, of which around 20,000 are party members. Within Greece, the EDA had in 1965 nearly 100,000 members, 20 percent of whom were active cadres. Of the 24,000 members in Athens, 11 percent were industrial workers, and 47 percent were clerks, craftsmen, and others; and 13 percent were women. In addition, the communist youth organization Lambrakis has a membership of 20,000.

The KKE is dominated by "professional communists," and the EDA by intellectuals. In general, communism in Greece is more a movement of intellectuals, students, petite bourgeoisie, and young people than of workers. In the 1963 elections 10 percent of the EDA candidates were workers, 11 percent peasants, 23 percent lawyers, 18 percent intellectuals, 14 percent craftsmen, and 12 percent civil servants.

The party's ideological and political influence is much greater than its organized membership. In 1958 the EDA received 940,000 votes, or 24.4 percent of the votes cast. The fact that this influence is not crystallized, however, causes fluctuations: in 1961 the EDA obtained only 14.8 percent of the vote; in 1963 it polled 14.5 percent of the vote and won thirty seats (out of 300); in 1964, it polled 542,865 votes (11.8 percent) and won twenty-two seats.

The communists were hampered after 1949 by the absence of a strong organization. Since 1963 the situation has begun to change. Between 1963 and 1965 the EDA considerably increased its organization and membership and formed a youth organization. In addition, there are nearly fifty communist front organizations, which include the usual associations for friendship with the communist states and committees for peace or for "democracy." The most important is the communist youth organization Lambrakis. There also exists, although on paper only, a National Agrarian Party (Ethiko Agrotiko Komma), which is under strong communist influence.

## RELATION TO SOVIET LEADERSHIP

The KKE has always been loyal to Moscow, and the opponents of Soviet control have never gained decisive influence over the party line. The most important opposition came from the "nationalists," who from 1922 to 1929 were opposed to the Soviet demand for autonomy for northern Greece (part of Macedonia). In 1955 and 1956 Zachariadis also rebelled against Khrushchev; his supporters still refuse to recognize the sixth plenum of April 1956 and condemn Soviet intervention in the internal affairs of the party.

A number of Greek communists were liquidated by Moscow. A. Haitas, general secretary of the KKE in 1928 and its delegate to the Comintern from 1924 to 1926, was imprisoned in Greece in 1929; he escaped to the Soviet Union in 1931 and in 1935 was executed as a "Bukharinist." G. Kolozov, chief of the communist youth organization, was imprisoned in Greece; he escaped to the Soviet Union in 1931, where he was executed in 1935 as a "traitor." G. Karayorgis, editor of the KKE paper *Risospastis* (Radical), member of the party leadership and head of the Democratic Army in southern Greece, fled to Rumania in 1949 and died there in prison.

Both the KKE and the EDA have sided with Moscow in the dispute with Peking, the KKE officially by a resolution of July 1966 and the EDA unofficially by publishing in its press pro-Soviet and anti-Chinese articles. However, an important pro-Chinese faction exists in Greece. Since October 1964 it has published a journal entitled *Anagenissis* (Renaissance), circulated among trade unionists and students. The pro-Chinese group also owns a publishing house which principally publishes translations of Mao's writings.

## PARTY PRESS ORGANS

The KKE publishes the monthly review *Neos Kosmos* (New World) and six papers in the Soviet Union and among Greek displaced persons in other European countries. The EDA publishes two daily newspapers in Athens, *Avgi* (Dawn) under the direction of Leonidas Kyrkos (circulation around 25,000) and *Dimokratiki Allagi* (Democratic Change) under the direction of A. Trikas (circulation 16,000). Its monthly is *Elliniki Aristera* (Greek Left).

## PARTY CONGRESSES

1st congress, SEKE, November 1918, Piraeus
2d congress, SEKE, April 1920, Athens
Extraordinary preelection congress, SEKE, September 1920, Athens
Extraordinary congress, SEKE, October 1922, Athens
Extraordinary preelection congress, SEKE, September 1923, Athens
3d (extraordinary) congress, KKE, November-December 1924, Athens
3d (regular) congress, KKE, March 1927, Athens
4th congress, KKE, December 1928, Athens
5th congress, KKE, March 1934, Athens
6th congress, KKE, December 1935, Athens
7th congress, KKE, October 1945, Athens
8th congress, KKE, August 1961, Bucharest (?)

## BIBLIOGRAPHY

Georgalas, G.: "Anatomie de l'EDA," *Soviétologie,* nos. 5-12, 1960.
Georgalas, G.: "Une brève histoire du KKE," *Soviétologie*, nos. 6-12, 1961; nos. 1, 2, 4, 1962.
Kousoulas, G.: *Revolution and Defeat*, London, Oxford University Press, 1965.
Papaconstantinou, Th.: *Anatomie de la révolution*, Athens, 1951.
Stavrides, E.: *Les coulisses du KKE*, Athens, 1952.
Zachariadis, N.: *Thèses sur l'histoire du KKE*, Athens, Kommunistikon Komma Ellados, 1945.

GEORGES GEORGALAS

1. Report of the KKE to the seventh congress of the Comintern, July-August 1935.

# GUADELOUPE

The origins of the Guadeloupe Communist Party (Parti Communiste Guadeloupéen, PCG) go back no further than the end of World War II. In fact, it was in 1944 that the Guadeloupe Federation of the French Communist Party was founded. On June 7, 1944, the first issue of its weekly organ appeared under the pretentious title *L'Etincelle*.

## HISTORY

The Guadeloupe federation enjoyed considerable success from the very start. In June 1945 it included sixteen sections and 150 cells and had 1,365 members. By December 1946 the number of cells had increased to 180, and membership had grown to 2,000. At the same time, the communists were winning unexpected electoral victories. On November 10, 1946, the three communist candidates polled 16,252 votes (14.2 percent of the registered vote and 45.3 percent of the votes cast), and two were elected—Gerty Archimède, a lawyer, and Rosan Girard, the political director of *L'Etincelle*. These victories were in all likelihood due to the existence since 1944 of a "democratic front," in the midst of which the communists had formed a "Marxist" alliance with the socialists in January 1945, and due also to the presence of communist ministers in the metropolitan French government. Nevertheless, the communists in Guadeloupe held on to their positions after the departure of the communists from the French government on May 5, 1947. In the 1951 and 1956 elections Rosan Girard was the only communist reelected, but the communists maintained their high percentage of votes, obtaining 44 to 46 percent of the votes cast. At the time of the trade-union split in 1949 the communists retained leadership of the Union of CGT Trade Unions (Union des Syndicats CGT), whose general secretary became Amédée Fengarol, and later Nicolas Ludger, both from the political bureau of the Guadeloupe Federation of the French Communist Party.

Although they continued to exert strong influence, the Guadeloupe communists also had their difficulties. In 1950 a delegate from the French party remarked that they were having a hard time distributing 2,000 membership cards, that most of their cells existed in name only, and that attendance at meetings was small. However, when Amédée Fengarol was removed as first secretary because of a disagreement with the French party leadership, he refused to submit to party discipline (Fengarol died on January 11, 1951). The return to violence ordered by the French party resulted in four persons dead and thirteen injured in Le Moule on February 14, 1952, and the communist victory in the Le Moule municipal elections in April 1953 (the entire communist list was elected), which led the colonial administration to annul the election. All this resulted in the renewed vitality of the federation.

Throughout this period the Guadeloupe communists had supported the administration's policy of assimilation, which found concrete expression in the law of March 19, 1946, making Guadeloupe a department of France. During the legislative elections of January 2, 1956, the federation declared that even though it recognized that "the Guadeloupe people [should] be able one day to manage their own affairs in a democratic manner," it stood unequivocally "against any secession, against any adventurist policy of independence which would inevitably lead

[Guadeloupe] from the yoke of French colonialism to the more reactionary, more odious yoke of American racism." The federation thus remained loyal to the "continuation of ties with France" at the price of certain adjustments, particularly "a decentralization which tended to increase in a democratic way the powers of [the] departmental assembly."

In 1956 the worldwide crisis of communism, the start of the war in Algeria, the resignation of Aimé Césaire from the Martinican Communist Party, and the passage by the French parliament of the "basic law" endowing France's colonies in Africa with territorial assemblies and autonomous governments threw the Guadeloupe federation into new conflicts, particularly over the events in Martinique. S. Pierre-Justin, a professor of philosophy, followed the Martinican example and advocated autonomy for Guadeloupe. Another faction, led by Rosan Girard, appealed for patience and rejected autonomy. The French party finally intervened in the conflict. On July 12, 1957, its political bureau decided to approve the transformation of the Martinican Federation of the French Communist Party into an autonomous party and to propose the same solution in Guadeloupe.

On July 18 the Guadeloupe communists fell in line and asked for a statute of autonomy for Guadeloupe and the creation of an autonomous communist party. This "new political orientation"[1] was opposed by those who wanted to remain members of the French party and had to be convinced "that the autonomous struggle of the working class with the aim to achieve socialism must give way to the more general struggle of the Guadeloupe people" against colonialism.[2] It was also opposed by those who, following Césaire's example in Martinique, urged the Guadeloupe communists to go even further and break entirely with the French party to join in a purely Guadeloupe organization.

On March 29-30, 1958, the ninth federal conference, attended by French delegates François Billoux and Georges Thévenin, proclaimed itself the founding congress of the Guadeloupe Communist Party. Membership had grown at that time to 1,500, of whom 1,224 were dues-paying members.[3] The party chose Hégésippe Ibéné, a lawyer, as general secretary and formed three sections: northeast (Serge Pierre-Justin secretary), central (Evremond Gène secretary), and southwest (Gerty Archimède secretary). The new PCG was to have a confederational relationship to the French party and the other two parties which had been formed (the Martinican and Réunion parties). In fact, there was only one joint meeting of these four parties, held in Paris on April 11-15, 1960, but relations between the PCG and the French party have retained a bilateral character.

This new orientation and the change in government in France after May 13, 1958, resulted in a certain setback in voting strength for the communists. The PCG called for a vote against the referendum of September 28, 1958; the party was supported by only 14,422 votes, or 13 percent of the registered voters and 21 percent of the votes cast. In the legislative elections of November 23, the communist candidates received 20,825 votes, or 30.6 percent of the total, and none were elected. The PCG blamed its loss on electoral fraud. Whatever the reason, its electoral results had never been so poor. In both elections, however, the PCG showing was proportionately stronger than those of the French Communist Party and the Martinican Communist Party. In the 1961 municipal elections, the party gained control of a few municipal governments and obtained nine seats in the island's general council. In the 1962 legislative elections it also regained a part of the ground it had lost, although still without a single successful candidate: 27,772 votes, or 36.6 percent.

In reality, although the PCG maintained its external influence during this period, it was weakened by internal conflicts originating in the party's demand for the autonomy of Guadeloupe with ties to France. On the one hand, some militants who had remained loyal to the policy of assimilation were encouraged in their conviction by the increasingly active policy of the French government in the Antilles to the point that they left the party. On the other hand, the PCG's position was attacked both inside and outside party ranks by leftists who preferred the slogan of independence to that of autonomy; most of this group fell under the influence of the pro-Chinese communists.

These internal conflicts produced frequent changes in the PCG leadership. Rosan Girard, who was named general secretary at the second party congress in April 1961, lost his post to Evremond Gène at the third congress in 1964. At the same time he lost his position as political director of the party newspaper to Gerty Archiméde. On October 13, 1963, the political bureau, in defining the tasks of the congress, had demanded that the secretary devote himself "effectively and exclusively to his own role" and that the party leadership see to "the reestablishment of common discipline and collective labor" and deny to everyone, regardless of his position, the right to make decisions outside the collective leadership.

The opposition of the pro-Chinese faction, whose organ was the newspaper *Le Progrès social*, became more active after the formation of the Guadeloupe Front for Autonomy (Front Guadeloupéen pour l'Autonomie) in June 1965. The PCG joined this new organization (stating that it was retaining the independence of its political decisions), but it was unable to take over the leadership. On October 8, 1965, the Guadeloupe Front unanimously adopted the text of a communiqué which took a stand directly opposed to the PCG's position. Advocating independence rather than autonomy, it advised voters to stay away from the polls during the presidential elections.

## RELATION TO SOVIET LEADERSHIP

Since it was founded only in 1958, the PCG was not represented at the first international communist conference in Moscow in November 1957, but it sent delegations to the second conference in November 1960 and to the twenty-second congress of the Communist Party of the Soviet Union in October 1961 (Pierre-Justin and Gène).

## PARTY PRESS ORGAN

The party press organ is the weekly *L'Etincelle*, edited by Gerty Archimède.

## CONGRESSES OF THE PCG

1st (founding) congress, March 1958, Capesterre-de-Guadeloupe
2d congress, April 1961, Pointe-à-Pitre
3d congress, 1964

## BIBLIOGRAPHY

Bagon, H., and S. Pierre-Justin: *Contre l'asphyxie économique de la Guadeloupe: Statut anticolonialiste!*, Paris, 1960.
Ibéné, Hégésippe: *Pour la libération politique et la décolonisation de la Guadeloupe.* (Political report of the second congress of the PCG.) Paris, 1961.
*La Nouvelle revue internationale*, January 1963.
*La Voix du peuple*, October 23, 1964.

CLAUDE HARMEL

1. *L'Etincelle*, August 3, 1957.
2. *L'Etincelle*, August 24, 1957.
3. *L'Etincelle*, April 6, 1958.

# GUATEMALA

The communist movement in Guatemala began in 1923 with the formation of the Socialist Labor Unification (Unificación Obrera Socialista) by a small group of Marxist intellectuals and labor leaders. Some members of this group requested and received help from the Mexican Communist Party in transforming their organization into a full-fledged communist party. The new Communist Party of Guatemala (Partido Comunista de Guatemala, PCG) was recognized in 1924 by the Comintern, which apparently expected it to serve the communists throughout Central America. The party was destroyed in 1932 and recreated in the 1940s. For a discussion of the full circumstances see *Latin America*.

## HISTORY

Between 1944 and 1954 the communists in Guatemala demonstrated how a tiny, dedicated minority could exploit favorable circumstances to become the most influential group in national politics. Those few communists who had survived the repression of 1932 in prison or in exile returned after the revolutions of July and October 1944 to work actively within the new labor, political, and educational organizations created by the Arévalo regime. They were soon joined by communist volunteers from other Latin American countries, who possessed organizational skills unknown to the enthusiastic but inexperienced young men and women catapulted into decision-making posts in the rapidly expanding bureaucracy. The communists infiltrated every new or modified entity that linked the social revolutionary government with the people. Although they formed a secret political group, the Democratic Vanguard (Vanguardia Democrática), in 1947, their chief task was to recruit and indoctrinate the men who were to rise to the top in the revived communist movement in Guatemala. Their prize converts were José Manuel Fortuny, head of the noncommunist Revolutionary Action Party (Partido do Acción Revolucionaria), who recreated the old Communist Party of Guatemala in September 1949, and Víctor Manuel Gutiérrez, head of the labor federation, who established the Revolutionary Workers' Party of Guatemala (Partido Revolucionario Obrero de Guatemala) in June 1950. By December 1952, on instructions from Moscow, the two communist parties had merged and been converted into the legal Guatemalan Labor Party (Partido Guatemalteco del Trabajo, PGT).

Meanwhile the communists had given effective, vociferous support to the candidacy and later to the administration of President Jacobo Arbenz, who relied on them increasingly for counsel and allowed them to assume an ever-larger role in the formation of government policies. Had they not been challenged, the communists might have come to power openly within a few years, but the test came before they were prepared. Although they were excellent manipulators, they proved to have no power base. They had failed to penetrate the armed forces or to arm their urban labor and peasant followers. No one rose to defend the PGT in June 1954, when the regime was toppled, the party outlawed, and its leaders exiled.

During the years of exile the Guatemalan communist leaders carefully reviewed their experience under the Arbenz regime and decided, after the success of the revolution in Cuba, that they had failed for lack of a firm base among the Indian peasantry. Beginning in 1960, with support from Cuba, they launched a small guerrilla movement in the remote regions of the interior and a sporadic terror campaign in the cities. By 1965 two distinct guerrilla groups had been identified: the Rebel Armed Forces (Fuerzas Armadas Rebeldes), led by Major Luis Turcios, and a splinter group, the Thirteenth of November Movement (Movimiento Trece de Noviembre), under the command of Yon Sosa. Their insurgency had little effect on the bulk of the population, but the two forces had defied all efforts by the government to exterminate them. In the urban areas the communists continued to exert influence among students and intellectuals but controlled no significant organizations.

## ORGANIZATION AND MEMBERSHIP

In 1965 United States sources estimated the membership of the Guatemalan party at 1,000.[1] The ability of the Guatemalan communists to maintain active front organizations has varied sharply with the fortunes of the party. It was low in 1965. At its peak in the early 1950s the party operated an elaborate array of interlocking front groups. For a full discussion see *Latin America*.

## RELATION TO SOVIET LEADERSHIP

The PGT has adopted a pro-Soviet attitude, while Yon Sosa's splinter group appears to be sympathetic to the Chinese position in the ideological controversy. For a full discussion see *Latin America*.

## PARTY PRESS ORGANS AND RECORDS

In 1954 the communists lost the extensive publishing facilities previously available to them. Thereafter party documents were usually circulated only within the membership. In the 1960s the clandestine communist organization occasionally issued flysheets exhorting the population to rise against the government, and published one newspaper, *La Verdad*, at irregular intervals.

## CONGRESSES OF THE PGT

There is no information on any congresses by the communist party before 1932. The revived PGT held three congresses between 1949 and 1960. A fourth congress, scheduled for 1965, was postponed.

1st congress, September 1949
2d congress, December 1952
3d congress, May 1960

## BIBLIOGRAPHY

James, Daniel: *Red Design for the Americas: Guatemalan Prelude*, New York, John Day, 1954.
Schlesinger, Jorge: *Revolución comunista*, Guatemala, Editorial Union, 1946.
Schneider, Ronald M.: *Communism in Guatemala, 1944-1954*, New York, Praeger, 1958.
U.S. Department of State: *Intervention of International Communism in Guatemala*, publ. 5556, Washington, U.S. Government Printing Office, August 1954.

See also *Latin America*, refs. 2, 6, 13, 21, 24.

ROLLIE E. POPPINO

1. U.S. Department of State, Bureau of Intelligence and Research, *World Strength of the Communist Party Organizations*, Eighteenth Annual Report, Washington, January 1966, p. 156.

# GUYANA [1]

No official communist party had been formed in Guyana by the end of 1965,[2] but the People's Progressive Party (PPP) is under the leadership of an avowed communist, Cheddi Jagan. On June 25, 1964, Jagan, in testifying before the Commonwealth Commission of Inquiry into the recent riots, said, "I am a communist, in accordance with my own views on communism."[3] Jagan has frequently called himself a socialist, but in a speech in the legislative council on February 27, 1953, he declared, "My idea was to show members of this council that in theory socialism and communism are the same.... According to the people who wrote the textbooks, communism is merely a higher state of society than socialism."[4] In a speech delivered to the PPP annual congress in April 1962, Jagan said, "We must not be divided on the issue of communism. Communism is winning throughout the world—it will win everywhere."[5]

The PPP was formed in January 1950 from the remnants of the Political Affairs Committee and the defunct British Guiana Labour Party. Jagan had returned to British Guiana in 1943 after a seven-year period of study in the United States at Howard University and Northwestern University, where he received a degree in dentistry. He brought with him his wife, Janet Rosenberg, an ardent young American Marxist who had been active in political circles in Chicago and would play a dominant role in the political life of British Guiana. In 1946 the Jagans formed the Political Affairs Committee as a study and action group. Jagan was also active in the Guianese trade-union movement, which was linked with the Caribbean Labor Congress, and was in turn influenced by British communists. One of the officers of the Caribbean Labor Congress was Billy Strachan, a Jamaican who had come to England as a member of the Royal Air Force and then joined the communist party and over the years supplied the Guianese trade-union movement with communist propaganda and textbooks for training the inner circle in the Marxist tradition.

When the PPP was formed, a group within the party known as the "big three"—Sydney King, Rory Westmass, and Martin Carter—felt that the organization should become a genuine communist party, openly committed to Marxist ideology. However, it was decided to give the party a broad base of socialism with a platform of Guianese nationalism and anticolonialism. It was felt that such a program would have a wider electoral appeal, and this proved true.

## HISTORY

In 1953 the PPP won a sweeping victory in the first election to the legislative council, gaining 51 percent of the popular vote of 152,429 and eighteen of the twenty-four seats. This was the first time a political party in British Guiana had enough popular support to become a power in the government. However, the inner circle of the party took the view that under the constitution the real power rested with the governor and refused to cooperate with the governor and the appointed members of the legislature. As a result, the governor suspended the constitution on October 9, 1953, and the PPP ministers were dismissed. For the next four years the country was governed by a nominated legislature and executive. A number of PPP leaders were jailed, publication of the party organ *Thunder* was suspended, and political meetings and demonstrations were banned.

In the White Paper defending the constitutional suspension the British government pointed out the connections between the PPP and international communism, especially the participation of the PPP leaders in the communist-dominated World Federation of Trade Unions. Attention was also drawn to the affiliation of the PPP youth organization, the Pioneer Youth League, with the communist-controlled World Federation of Democratic Youth and the World Peace Council. The British believed in 1953 that the PPP'S objective was to establish a communist-styled satellite regime in Guyana and concluded that on the evidence as a whole there was undoubtedly a very powerful communist influence within the PPP. This conclusion was based on the knowledge that six of the party leaders—the Jagans, Sydney King, Westmass, Carter, and the youth secretary Brindley Benn—"accepted unreservedly the 'classical' doctrines of Marx and Lenin, were enthusiastic supporters of the policies and practices of modern Communist movements, and were contemptuous of social democratic parties, including the British Labour Party."[6]

The vast majority of the party were not communists, but were Indian sugar-plantation workers and rice farmers, with a fair proportion of shopkeepers and civil servants from the Negro and Colored community. Moreover, the PPP was not a party of the proletariat, but comprised a cross section of occupations in the community. The party leaders included Forbes Burnham, a young Negro lawyer, who later differed with the party and broke away in October 1957 to form a new party, the People's National Congress (PNC), which drew its support largely from the Negro community. After Burnham's departure the PPP was predominantly supported by the Indian community on a racial basis. Jagan was the acknowledged leader of the Indian community, and his support came from racial loyalty rather than agreement with either his political philosophy or tactics.

In August 1957 the PPP won another victory in the general election, this time getting 47 percent of the vote. Now Jagan and his ministers maintained a working relationship with the governor and the ex-officio members of the council. Again in 1961 the PPP won its third straight electoral victory and formed the government. The PPP had 93,075 votes (42.57 percent), with twenty seats; the PNC had 89,501 votes (41 percent), with eleven seats; and the United Force (had 35,771 votes (16.43 percent), with four seats.

On February 19, 1962, demonstrations against the government's austerity budget degenerated into large-scale riots, looting, and shooting, during which a part of Georgetown was reduced to shambles in a fire that caused $25 million damage; two were killed, including the superintendent of police, and about fifty were injured in crossfire between the police and demonstrators. The riots were also related to the desire of the opposition parties to defeat the PPP before the country was given independence for fear that once independence was achieved the PPP would abolish democratic procedures and establish a communist dictatorship.

In October 1963 Jagan agreed to have the British impose a solution, and British Colonial Secretary Duncan Sandys declared that proportional representation was to replace representation by a simple majority with new elections in 1964. Although Jagan had agreed to the right of the colonial secretary to impose a solution, the PPP rejected this plan, and the party organ *Thunder* proclaimed in the February-March 1964 issue that "whatever the sacrifices, the Sandys plan must be stopped."

For years the PPP tried to gain control of the British Guiana Trades Union Council by trying to destroy the effectiveness of the Man-Power Citizens' Association, the largest trade union in Guyana, representing the workers in the sugar industry. In the fall of 1963 the Guyana Agriculture Workers' Union was formed, under the direction of the PPP, with the purpose of winning members away from the Man-Power Citizens' Association's voluntary-checkoff system, thus giving the Agricultural Workers' Union a majority of the workers and recognition as the bargaining union. During an eighty-day strike called by the Agricultural Workers' Union in March 1964, there were fifty-eight official reports of murder, 705 buildings set afire, 339 buildings damaged, 584 persons injured, and 10,000 forced to leave their homes because of racial tension between East Indians and Negroes. A total of 1,183 persons were charged with various offenses arising from the violence. These were the tangible results of the strike which ushered in a new chapter of racial strife between the East Indian and Negro communities.

The elections were held on December 7, 1964, under the system of proportional representation, and while the PPP increased its vote from 42 percent in 1961 to 45.8 percent, with twenty-four seats, the PNC maintained its previous strength of 40 percent and obtained twenty-two seats. The PNC then arranged with the United Force, which had received 12.4 percent and seven seats, to form a coalition government, with Forbes Burnham as premier. Jagan at first refused to resign, but under pressure he agreed to allow the new coalition government to function.

Although Jagan had begun the assembly session with twenty-four seats, he lost three because of the defection of party members who became independents. After the elections he maintained a general policy of noncooperation with the government and boycotted the conference in 1965 that provided the constitution for an independent Guyana.

Just over 50 percent of the population of 650,000 is East Indian, and this group has traditionally supported Jagan. The East Indian population is increasing more rapidly than the Negro population, and Jagan thus hoped to gain more votes and an absolute majority in the elections scheduled for October 1968. During this period, however, Forbes Burnham hoped to prove the effectiveness of his economic policies, induce the conflicting racial groups to cooperate in developing the country, and win over the less extreme followers of the PPP. Under Burnham's leadership there have been no serious disturbances, and with the aid of outside financial assistance there has been a significant economic development. Thus Forbes Burnham may well prove to be the statesman Guyana needs.

## RELATION TO SOVIET LEADERSHIP

In recent years scholarships have been provided to send young people to Moscow for study and training. By the end of 1965 the PPP had not sent observers to congresses of the Soviet party or paid tribute to the work of the Soviet leadership and policies.

## PARTY PRESS ORGANS AND RECORDS

The PPP organ *Thunder* has been published in Georgetown since 1960.

For statements of the party's statutes and program see *Constitution of the People's Progressive Party*, ratified and adopted by the first congress, Georgetown, Arcade Printery, 1951 (reprinted and amended in 1962), and the party's 1953, 1957, and 1961 election manifestoes.

## BIBLIOGRAPHY

British Guiana Trades Union Council: *The Communist Martyr Makers: The Account of the Struggle for Free Trade Unionism in British Guiana in 1964* [Georgetown, 1964?].

Jagan, Cheddi: *Forbidden Freedom: The Story of British Guiana*, New York, International Publishers, 1954.

Newman, Peter: *British Guiana*, New York, Oxford University Press, 1964.

People's Progressive Party: *The Great Betrayal*, 2d ed., Georgetown, Arcade Printery, 1956.

People's Progressive Party: *History of the PPP*, Georgetown, New Guiana Company, 1963.

People's Progressive Party: *Independence Now!*, Georgetown Arcade Printery, 1960.

Reno, Philip: *The Ordeal of British Guiana*, New York, Monthly Review Press, 1964.

Sims, Peter: *Trouble in Guyana*, London, Allen & Unwin, 1966.

Smith, Raymond T.: *British Guiana*, New York, Oxford University Press, 1962.

KENNETH M. GLAZIER

1. Known until May 25, 1966, as British Guiana.

2. See the 1968 *Yearbook on International Communist Affairs*, Stanford, Calif., Hoover Institution, 1969.

3. *Daily Chronicle* (Overseas Edition), Georgetown, June 26, 1962, p. 1.

4. *British Guiana Constitutional Commission Report,* 1954, p. 80.

5. *Report of a Commission of Inquiry into Disturbances in British Guiana in February 1962*, p. 71.

6. *Report of the British Constitutional Commission,* 1954 (commonly known as the Robertson report), p. 36.

# HAITI

The communist movement in Latin America has encountered its greatest difficulties in Haiti, where no sector of the population has yet developed a strong sense of political organization. Two attempts to establish workable communist parties failed before 1950. The first party was formed in 1930 by the intellectuals Max Hudicourt and Jacques Roumain and succumbed when these men were exiled later in the year. Roumain died in exile. Hudicourt returned in 1946 to lead one of two revived communist organizations, but his assassination in 1947 marked the end of the movement for at least another dozen years. Under the Duvalier regime, which began in 1957, two clandestine communist parties again appeared.

## HISTORY

Communism has never exerted a significant influence in Haiti, although since at least the 1940s a few Marxist intellectuals have held potentially critical posts in the national bureaucracy. The short-lived communist party of 1930 left no trace, but for a brief period after World War II it appeared that a viable communist organization might develop. Early in 1946, after the fall of the Lescot administration, a clergyman, Félix d'Orléans Juste Constant, founded a new Communist Party of Haiti (Parti Communiste d'Haiti, PCH). Constant was a self-declared Marxist but was unable to obtain the approval of the international movement or the support of the Haitian people. His new party failed to win a single seat in the 1946 elections and disbanded the following year. Shortly after the establishment of the new PCH, a rival communist party was created as the Popular Socialist Party (Parti Socialiste Populaire, PSP), named for and with the approval of the Cuban communist organization. Max Hudicourt was summoned from exile in New York to assume leadership. While the PSP remained one of the smaller parties in the country, it attracted enough voters to elect Hudicourt to the senate and Rossini Pierre-Louis to the chamber of deputies. The party disintegrated rapidly, however, when Hudicourt was killed in 1947, and disappeared altogether under the successive impacts of proscription in 1949 and repression under the Magloire regime after 1950. Those Marxist intellectuals who stayed in Haiti took no part in politics except as supporters of one or another of the noncommunist figures who jockeyed for power during 1956-1958.

A new chapter in the history of the communist movement in Haiti appears to have opened during the Duvalier administration, with the creation for the first time of clandestine communist parties while a strong dictator was in power. Jacques Stephen Alexis, son of the leading Haitian literary figure, is credited with establishing the Party of Popular Accord (Parti d'Entente Populaire, PEP), in 1959, although it did not engage in detectable activities until 1961. In 1961 Roger Gaillard, a former member of the PSP, founded the Cuban-type People's National Liberation Party (Parti Populaire de Libération Nationale, PPLN), which soon claimed to have a nationwide organizational structure. Neither party was able to rally support for an assault on the dictatorship, and by 1965 the PPLN had been badly weakened by police harassment.

## ORGANIZATION AND MEMBERSHIP

No claims or estimates are available to indicate the membership of either the PEP or the PPLN. The Haitian parties appear to follow the usual Latin American communist organizational pattern, although on a greatly reduced scale. Their members are drawn chiefly from the bureaucracy, which is the major employer of intellectuals, and from the weak urban labor movement. For a full discussion of these topics see *Latin America*. There is no information available about front organizations operated by the communist parties in Haiti.

## RELATION TO SOVIET LEADERSHIP

The first PCH did not survive long enough to affiliate with the Comintern, which had been dissolved before the brief flurry of communist activity in Haiti in the 1940s. In February 1946 the PSP was accorded recognition by the international communist movement through the Cuban party, but the PSP itself had largely disappeared before the Cominform was created in 1947. The leaders of both parties in 1965 appeared to have the approval of the Soviet state and party. Neither communist party has issued a formal declaration on the controversy between the Soviet Union and Communist China. Their views are believed to be pro-Soviet.

## PARTY PRESS ORGANS

The PEP issues an irregular internal publication, *Avant-Garde*. The PPLN issued an internal publication, *Libération*, in the early 1960s. It is not known whether this journal survived through 1965.

## PARTY CONGRESSES

There is no indication that any Haitian communist party has held a national congress.

## BIBLIOGRAPHY

See *Latin America*, refs. 2, 13, 24.

ROLLIE E. POPPINO

# HONDURAS

The communist movement in Honduras originated in the late 1920s as an extension of communist activities in Guatemala and El Salvador. Honduran communists have since claimed that the party was first founded in their country in 1927 by Juan Pablo Wainwright, who was also a leader of the party in Guatemala at the time of his execution by the Carías dictatorship in 1932. The original Communist Party of Honduras (Partido Comunista de Honduras, PCH) was one of the parties extinguished in that year as a result of the revolution in El Salvador. See *El Salvador, Guatemala*, and *Latin America*.

## HISTORY

The revival of the communist movement in Honduras began in the 1940s as part of the widespread political ferment that resulted in the overthrow of dictatorships in Guatemala and El Salvador. Its political expression was the clandestine leftist Democratic Revolutionary Party of Honduras (Partido Democrático Revolucionario de Honduras, PDRH), which the communists later claimed to have founded in 1944. In any case, there was enough left-wing activity by 1946 to cause the regime to outlaw the communist movement. The PDRH operated openly after political controls were relaxed in 1948, but in 1953 it was banned and its leaders were exiled. The few communists who escaped arrest and deportation transformed the remnants of the PDRH into a new Communist Party of Honduras in 1954 and gradually built a following among banana-plantation workers around San Pedro Sula and among students and urban laborers in the capital. The formal organization of the PCH was not detected until 1958, when the party held its first congress. Even though the 1957 constitution prohibited communist parties, in the open political climate that prevailed during the administration of President Ramón Villeda Morales (1957-1963) the party enlisted some 2,000 members, to become the largest communist organization in Central America. In 1961 a militant minority, which regards itself as "scientifically Marxist," split off to become the Honduran Revolutionary Party (Partido Revolucionario Hondureño, PRH), while suppression of communist activities by the military junta that toppled the Villeda Morales government caused a further substantial decline in party membership and effectiveness.

## ORGANIZATION AND MEMBERSHIP

United States sources estimated the membership of the PCH in 1965 as 1,000, and that of the splinter PRH as 300.[1] The Honduran party does not control the Communist Youth of Honduras (Juventud Comunista de Honduras), but otherwise appears to follow the usual Latin American communist organizational pattern. For a full discussion see *Latin America*.

## RELATION TO SOVIET LEADERSHIP

The PCH supports the Soviet position in the ideological controversy with Communist China. The PRH has not taken a public stand but generally agrees with the attitude of the parent party. For a discussion of the general relation to Soviet leadership see *Latin America*.

## PARTY PRESS ORGANS

The Honduran communists have limited publications facilities. The PCH issues an irregular weekly newspaper, *Futuro*.

PARTY CONGRESSES

The PCH held its first congress in May 1958. By the end of 1965 there was no indication that a second congress had yet been held.

BIBLIOGRAPHY

James, Daniel: *Red Design for the Americas: Guatemalan Prelude*, New York, John Day, 1954.

See also *Latin America*, refs. 2, 6, 13, 24.

ROLLIE E. POPPINO

1. U.S. Department of State, Bureau of Intelligence and Research, *World Strength of the Communist Party Organizations*, Eighteenth Annual Report, Washington, January 1966, p. 158.

# HUNGARY

The Communist Party of Hungary was first established on March 24, 1918, in Moscow as a section of the Russian Communist Party. The founders were Béla Kun and Tibor Szamuely and a small group of bolshevik-indoctrinated former Hungarian and Slovak militant socialists who were then prisoners of war in Russia. Six months later, acting on Lenin's instructions, Kun's group returned to Hungary and established a communist beachhead there. Aided by various dissident socialist, anarchist, and syndicalist factions, avant-garde artists, and radical intellectuals, Kun founded the Communist Party of Hungary (Kommunisták Magyarországi Pártja, KMP) on November 24, 1918.

HISTORY

*The Hungarian Soviet Republic of 1919* The KMP, born amidst the postwar democratic revolution of 1918 in Hungary, set out to undermine the position of the socialists and the democrats and to seize power through a communist-led social revolution. Communist agitation, propaganda, and recruiting efforts and the vulnerability of socialist ideology to attack from the extreme left, combined with an ill-timed Entente démarche implying further Hungarian territorial losses, resulted in the collapse of Count Mihály Károlyi's democratic republic and the birth of the Hungarian Soviet Republic under a communist-socialist coalition (March 21, 1919). Lack of popular support and foreign military intervention forced the leaders of the new republic (Béla Kun, Jenő Landler, Mátyás Rákosi, József Pogány, György Lukács) to resign and flee to Austria in the first days of August 1919.

The "fugitive bolsheviks" soon reassembled abroad and, as Hungarian sections of foreign communist parties in Vienna, Prague, Berlin, and later Moscow, proceeded to evaluate the lessons of the ill-fated 133-day "proletarian dictatorship" in Hungary. This process degenerated into a twelve-year factional struggle between the followers of Béla Kun, located in Moscow as the KMP's Committee Abroad, and those of Jenő Landler, based in Vienna, Bratislava, and Berlin, who were supported by the remaining underground party cells in Hungary.

*The Interwar Years* Because of these factional strifes and the Horthy regime's effective surveillance and ruthless suppression of all actual and suspected communist activities, the Comintern dissolved the party in the spring of 1922 and permitted its reorganization only in 1925, when the first congress of the KMP met clandestinely in Vienna in August 1925. Earlier that year the communists had succeeded in forming a legal left socialist party, the Hungarian Socialist Workers' Party (Magyar Szocialista Munkáspárt, MSZMP), led by an expelled socialist, István Vági, whose arrest in 1927 also spelled the doom of this thinly disguised communist front organization.

After the sixth Comintern congress in 1928, and especially after the extreme leftist resolutions of the tenth plenum of the Comintern Executive Committee in 1929, the Hungarian communists proved unable to allay socialist fears of communist infiltration of trade unions and factory organizations. Thus during the years of postwar economic difficulties of Hungary, at a time when communism made considerable progress in other European countries, the KMP was unable to increase its membership and influence. It remained isolated both from the industrial proletariat and, because of its maximalist agrarian program, from the poor peasantry. Under these circumstances the party's second congress, held at Aprelevka (a village 130 miles from Moscow) in February-March 1930, had no choice but to resolve to continue its singularly unsuccessful "sectarian" leftist policies in Hungary.

Hungarian exile communists, in addition to or instead of working in the Hungarian party, also participated in various Comintern activities. The more important figures were Béla Kun, member of the Comintern Executive and the Presidium between 1923 and 1937; Mátyás Rákosi, Comintern instructor for the French and Italian parties until his arrest in Hungary in 1925; Jenő Varga, economic expert and official forecaster of impending capitalist crises for the Comintern; Gyula Alpári, editor of *Inprekorr* and later *Rundschau*; and József Pogány, who, as John Pepper, served as a Comintern emissary to the Communist Party of the United States in the 1920s. Several others were involved in the work of the German, Slovak, Rumanian, and Yugoslav party apparatus, and more found employment in the Soviet state and party bureaucracy between the two world wars.

Following the seventh Comintern congress in 1935 the party's underground cadres in Hungary refused to form a popular-front alliance with the group they had up to then called "social-fascist," the social democrats. The Comintern thereupon disbanded all intermediary and top-level party committees in Hungary and transferred the party's headquarters to Prague in the fall of 1936. With this step organized communist activities ceased in Hungary until late 1939, when a series of party instructors (who were immediately arrested) started arriving from Czechoslovakia, France, and Russia in an effort to rally the few hundred (perhaps 1,000) undercover members around slogans of "antifascism," "national independence," and "peace."

Next to the Polish party, the Hungarian party was the hardest hit by the great purges in the Soviet Union. In addition to Béla Kun, who was arrested in June 1937 and shot in November 1939, eighteen former people's commissars of the 1919 Hungarian Soviet Republic and several hundred lesser Hungarian communists were executed or deported to Siberia and Central Asia. Among those who escaped liquidation were Mátyás Rákosi (then in a Hungarian jail and exchanged to the Soviet Union in 1940), Jenő Varga, József Révai, Ernő Gerő, György Lukács, and Imre Nagy.

Although the KMP was at all times numerically very small during the interwar period, communism nevertheless represented to many Hungarian intellectuals a genuine revolutionary cause headed by the Soviet Union and attracted sympathizers among artists, writers, and university students. To the last group belonged many future leaders of the party—László Rajk, Gyula Kállai, Géza Losonczy, Ferenc Donáth, and Tibor Szőnyi, all of whom were to play important roles in the party after 1945. The communists' unrelenting opposition to fascism, irredentism, and national chauvinism also appealed to many middle-class radicals, who had limited outlets for legitimate political participation during the Horthy era.

*Reconstruction of the Party* During World War II the communists made repeated attempts to unite diverse socialist, populist, middle-class radical, and antifascist elements against Nazi Germany within the framework of a loosely united front type of organization. These efforts were interrupted by the dissolution of the Communist International in May 1943, which János Kádár and the party's Budapest-based leaders interpreted as a directive to dissolve the Hungarian party as well. Thus until the Germans invaded Hungary on March 19, 1944, there was again no communist party in Hungary. In response to the German occupation, the communists formed the Peace Party (Béke Párt), which, in cooperation with the Smallholder's Party (Kisgazda Párt), the Social Democratic Party (Szociál Demokrata Párt), and the communist-sponsored Peasant Party (Paraszt Párt), established the National Independence Front (Nemzeti Függetlenségi Front)—the nucleus of the postwar ruling coalition in Hungary.

The postwar reconstruction of the Hungarian Communist Party (Magyar Kommunista Párt, MKP)[1] was led by Mátyás Rákosi and his Moscow associates, Ernő Gerő, Imre Nagy, Mihály Farkas, and József Révai. This group was assisted by the so-called "native" wing of the party, János Kádár, László Rajk, and their group of activists who remained in Hungary during the war. After purging the party of most of the surviving 1919 militants and of the miniscule Trotskyist opposition (led by Aladár Weisshaus), Rákosi then proceeded to elaborate on a strategy designed ultimately to capture power in Hungary. This included a membership drive (at the end of 1944 the party had only 1,240 members in Budapest) and the establishment of party organizations at all levels of state, county, and local bureaucracy, in all factories and workshops, and in the police and the armed forces.

The MKP received 17 percent of the votes cast in Hungary's first free elections held in November 1945. Although the anticommunist Smallholder's Party received a majority of the votes and seats in parliament, in conformance to the conditions of the armistice the MKP participated in the coalition government of Ferenc Nagy. By obtaining the ministry of the interior the communists gained control of the police. The MKP was then able to convince the other opposition parties (Social Democratic Party, Peasant Party) to form a leftist bloc to counteract the Smallholder majority. Rákosi, heading the communist drive against the Smallholders, applied his "salami tactic" designed to divide, isolate, and prevent all noncommunist forces from political support of the government.

The third congress of the MKP in September-October 1946 marked the beginning of a carefully planned and concerted drive for power, highlighted by the nationalization of the larger industrial, commercial, and banking establishments. Ferenc Nagy's government became increasingly powerless because of police terror and its support by Soviet occupation authorities and troops. In May 1947, when Nagy went on a short vacation to Switzerland, he was notified that his return was not desired. In exchange for permission for his son to join him in Switzerland, Nagy resigned on May 29. Indecision and lack of self-confidence among middle-class politicians and the willingness of the socialists and radical peasants to form a leftist bloc with the communists in the spring of 1946 also contributed to Rákosi's successful drive for undivided political power.

In the next elections to parliament in August 1947 the communist-led leftist bloc received 45.3 percent of the votes cast, but the rigging of these elections was obvious. Investigations of alleged plotters against the security of the state led to the dissolution by the government of the Smallholder's Party. In June 1948 the communists and the Soviet occupants forced the Social Democratic Party, by then controlled by its left wing, to unite with the MKP and to form a new "united" party, the Hungarian Workers' Party (Magyar Dolgozók Pártja, MDP), which became the ruling party in communist-dominated Hungary.

*The Period of Stalinism* The period of Stalinism in Hungary began with the arrest, show trial, and execution of László Rajk and his "Titoist friends" in the fall of 1948 and ended in the summer of 1953, when Imre Nagy launched his "new course." During the intervening years Mátyás Rákosi, Stalin's best Hungarian pupil, eliminated all non-Moscow party leaders except a few young zealots and subservient former socialist and radical peasants. János Kádár was also arrested in 1950 (not for Titoism, but for a youthful political indiscretion) and was released only in 1954, along with Hungarian veterans of the Spanish civil war and some unlawfully detained "Rajkists." Stalinist economic policies, particularly the simultaneous launching of ambitious industrialization programs and a ruthless campaign of agricultural collectivization, proved to be both costly and unproductive. Real wages sank to a new low, while agricultural and industrial output failed to keep pace with the basic needs of the population in terms of food, consumer goods, and housing.

After Stalin's death Rákosi, who held simultaneously the posts of first secretary of the party and prime minister, was forced by the presidium of the Communist Party of the Soviet Union to turn over the premiership to Imre Nagy (July 4, 1954). Nagy was another survivor of the "Moscow group," but evaluating the situation in Hungary more realistically, he advocated gradualism in the economic field and moderation in internal politics. Thus he reflected on the Hungarian scene the consumer goods-oriented policies of Malenkov in the Soviet Union. But Nagy's power as prime minister and architect of the "new course" policies was severely limited by the Rákosi-controlled party and police apparatus. Most government-instituted measures of political relaxation and economic de-Stalinization were sabotaged by the party bureaucracy and the police. Malenkov's defeat by Khrushchev in early 1955 permitted Rákosi to make a political comeback which put a temporary end to Nagy's career.

Half a year after his expulsion from the central committee in April 1955, Nagy's friends (released Rajkists, disenchanted young intellectuals, and journalists), demanding the cessation of party control of literature and the arts, launched a counterattack against Rákosi and the party bureaucracy. The "spirit" of the Soviet party's twentieth congress made it impossible to deal effectively with the growing intraparty opposition. The Rákosi group remained on the defensive until late June, when a meeting of the Petőfi Circle, a newly formed debating forum of dissident party and nonparty intellectuals, actually demanded Rákosi's resignation for his complicity in Rajk's execution and the subsequent violations of "socialist legality" committed at his instigation.

The party crisis was resolved at the July 1956 meeting of the central committee, when Mikoyan, the Soviet representative, forced Rákosi's resignation as first secretary and installed another Stalinist, Ernő Gerő, as the party's new leader. Recent evidence suggests that Gerő's appointment was intended as a stop-gap measure prior to the Moscow-desired ascendancy of János Kádár, who was coopted to the politburo at that time.

Events of the next two months, particularly efforts by the recently "rehabilitated" friends of Rajk and supporters of Nagy to apply Moscow's anti-Stalinist policies in Hungary, combined with the gradual deterioration of the party's authority among the membership, made any planned orderly transition of power to Kádár extremely difficult. After Rajk's ceremonial reburial and Nagy's readmission a few days later to the central committee, this transition from orthodox Stalinism to "centrist" moderation became almost impossible. Antagonized by the party's hesitation to take prompt action on the combined grievances of anti-Rákosi dissidents and those of the intellectuals and university students, a peaceful demonstration (as an expression of solidarity with the Polish people, then under strong Russian pressure) was held on October 23, 1956. By nightfall the demonstration had become a revolution, first against the secret police, then against Gerő's communist party, which called in Soviet armored units to suppress what he denounced as "a counterrevolutionary fascist putsch." In fact, the Budapest demonstrations from the very beginning had been led by the industrial proletariat, enlisted soldiers, patriotic policemen, communist-trained students, and national communist intellectuals.

At the end of lengthy debates in the central committee the Kádár-led centrists resolved to support Nagy's leadership of the revolution and, along with other reemerged democratic politicians, they joined the newly formed coalition government under his premiership. The new Nagy government asked for and obtained the withdrawal of Soviet army units from Budapest.

The party, however, could not withstand the mounting pressures to reorganize itself, and at the end of October the central committee declared the dissolution of the MDP and the formation of a new Hungarian Socialist Workers' Party (Magyar Szocialista Munkáspárt, MSZMP). Alarmed by the rapid radicalization of Nagy's policies—actually belated concessions to demands of workers' factory councils and other revolutionary groups—Kádár, Ferenc Münnich, and several others began negotiations with the Soviet party which culminated in the Soviet army's second intervention, the crushing of the revolution, and the formation on November 4, 1956, of a Soviet-sponsored revolutionary worker-peasant government under the leadership of János Kádár.

*The Kádár Regime*   The postrevolution history of the MSZMP may be divided into four more or less distinct periods. The first, between November 1956 and June 1957, was marked (after an initial brief period of equivocation and frustrated government attempts to strike a compromise with the still active writers' and organized workers' groups) by the arrest and imprisonment of Imre Nagy and his associates and thousands of other former leaders and participants of the "October events" in Hungary. The party's shattered unity was also being rebuilt through a policy of wholesale readmission of former members (346,000 by June 1, 1957) who professed faith in and chose to support Kádár's leadership.

The national conference of the MSZMP in June 1957 "scientifically established" the causes of the October revolt and, with considerable moral and economic support from the Soviet Union and Khrushchev personally, set out to rebuild gradually the political and social foundations of one-party rule in Hungary. A year later, bowing to foreign pressure (from the Soviet Union, China, Rumania, Czechoslovakia, and Albania) and internal pressures from the still insecure party bureaucracy, Kádár agreed to take stern measures against the leaders of the "October events." On June 17, 1958, the government announced that Imre Nagy, Pál Maléter, Miklós Gimes, and József Szilágy had been secretly tried and executed. Géza Losonczy died during the investigation, and others were given prison sentences. Similar foreign pressures, particularly the Chinese "great leap" and the alleged Czechoslovak agricultural success, were partly responsible for the party's forced collectivization campaign of 1958-1959, a process that completed the "socialist transformation" of Hungary's politically unreliable countryside.

The third postrevolution period was inaugurated by the seventh congress of the MSZMP in November-December 1959. Party membership had risen to 402,000, with 31.1 percent industrial workers, 27.7 percent "other workers," 9.1 percent intellectuals, 15 percent peasants, and 17.1 percent others. The congress approved a new five-year plan that gave priority to production of consumer goods, housing construction, and the increase of real wages, especially for low-income groups. The ideological platform called for the continuation of the "battle on two fronts" (that is, against revisionism and dogmatism), a policy that is still in effect.

Kádár's new slogan, "He who is not against us is with us," was designed to foster a national unity for the achievement of these goals. As part of the new approach, admission policies to universities, regulations governing small private enterprises, and restrictions on travel abroad were relaxed, and a number of less important political prisoners were released.

The eighth congress of the MSZMP in November 1962 was considerably influenced by the decisions of the Soviet party's twenty-second congress in 1961, especially in the field of ideology and de-Stalinization. Prior to this congress the central committee of the MSZMP had completed its investigations concerning "violations of socialist legality" during the years of "cult of personality" in Hungary and had expelled Mátyás Rákosi (who was living in exile in the Soviet Union), Erno Gerő, Károly Kiss, and several lesser Stalinists from the party. György Marosán, a Kádár supporter and renegade socialist, was also forced to retire. The congress enacted the party's new statutes (containing a preamble that serves as the party's program) and fully endorsed the Soviet party's stand on international relations, including its attitude toward the Chinese Communist Party.

## ORGANIZATION AND MEMBERSHIP

Of the party's 511,000 members in over 17,000 primary organizations in 1965, 21 percent had completed secondary school and about 7.5 percent were graduates of universities and institutions of higher education. The Young Communist League (Kommunista Ifjusági Szövetség Kisz), the party's main source of cadres, had 700,000 members, while its auxiliary, the Young Pioneer League, included 800,000 children.

The statute adopted by the eighth party congress established a tight organizational scheme for the MSZMP which gives the top leadership direct control over all party agencies. The congress, as supreme authority, elects a central committee of eighty-one members and thirty-nine candidates, a presidential council of twenty-one members, and a central control commission. The central committee elects a politburo of thirteen members and eight candidates and a secretariat of six members and establishes several departments and other agencies of the central committee. The "democratic centralism" of Hungarian communism results in the fact that János Kádár was until June 1965 simultaneously first secretary of the party, prime minister of the government, and member of the politburo. The chairman of the presidential council, István Dobi, has only representative duties as formal head of state.

## FUTURE PROSPECTS

Since the last congress of the MSZMP Kádár's control over the party bureaucracy has strengthened considerably. Through the gradual demotion or elimination of conservative and insufficiently trained party elites from the government and local administration, and through the promotion of bright young university-educated cadres, the party has become more businesslike in economic matters and more sophisticated in handling internal politics. Kádár's close association with Khrushchev, especially after the latter's fall in 1964, and his firm opposition to Chinese militancy earned him the toleration and grudging respect of the Hungarian people.

In the broadest sense, the Hungarian party's future prospects will to a large extent be determined by the vicissitudes of east-west relations and the intensity of international tensions over a host of related issues such as German reunification in Europe and the Vietnam war. Hungarian politics will be more directly affected by the outcome of the Sino-Soviet conflict, by the extent of trade, tourism, and cultural exchange with the West, and by the degree of Hungary's economic integration into the Council for Mutual Economic Assistance. The hitherto dormant issue of Hungarian minority in Transylvania and Slovakia must be faced and satisfactorily resolved by the party if it wishes to retain the half-hearted support of the strongly nationalistic Hungarian people.

## PARTY RECORDS

The Institute for Party History of the central committee of the MSZMP as well as individual writers have published several volumes of selected documents covering the history of the party from March 21, 1919, to 1962. Furthermore, the party has published minutes of five congresses held since the June 1948 congress at which the unification with the Hungarian Social Democratic Party was accomplished. Material on the first four congresses is rather scarce. Collections of speeches and writings by party leaders Gyula Alpári, János Kádár, Jenő Landler, and Mátyás Rákosi have appeared in print in the Hungarian language. As the more than twenty Hungarian titles would be of little use to the English-speaking users of the *Handbook,* they can be obtained on request from the Hoover Institution.

## PARTY PRESS

During the short-lived Hungarian Soviet Republic in 1919 the party's main organ was the daily newspaper *Népszava* (Voice of the People). Later communist sympathizers published in Hungary several newspapers as independent progressive organs which in fact followed the communist party line. Among these were *100%* (Budapest, 1927 to 1929) and *Társadalmi szemle* (Social Review, Budapest, 1931 to 1934). In addition, the party at various times published newspapers in Moscow, Vienna, and Prague which were smuggled into Hungary. In 1965 the party's main organ was the daily *Népszabadság* (People's Freedom), with a circulation of about 700,000 issues, and a theoretical-ideological monthly *Társadalmi szemle,* with a circulation of about 35,000 copies.

## PARTY CONGRESSES

1st congress, KMP, August 1925, Vienna
2d congress, KMP, February-March 1930, Aprelevka, Soviet Union
All-Hungarian conference, MKP, May 1945, Budapest
3d congress, MKP, September-October 1946, Budapest
1st congress, MDP, June 1948, Budapest
2d congress, MDP, February-March 1951, Budapest
3d congress, MDP, May 1954, Budapest
7th congress, MSZMP, November-December 1959, Budapest
8th congress, MSZMP, November 1962, Budapest

## BIBLIOGRAPHY

This bibliography lists only the pertinent publications in the English language. (See also "Party Records" above.)

Fejtö, François: "Hungarian Communism," in William E. Griffith (ed.), *Communism in Europe*, vol. I, Cambridge, Mass., MIT Press, 1964.

Kádár, János: *On the Road to Socialism: Selected Speeches and Interviews, 1960-1964*, Budapest, Corvina Press, 1965.

Kádár, János: *Socialist Construction in Hungary: Selected Speeches and Articles, 1957-1961*. Budapest, Corvina Press, 1962.

Kun, Béla: *On the Hungarian Soviet Republic*, Budapest, Kossuth, 1958.

Laski, Melvin J. (ed.): *A White Book: The Hungarian Revolution*, New York, Praeger, 1957.

Tőkés, Rudolf L.: *Béla Kun and the Hungarian Soviet Republic*, New York, Praeger, for the Hoover Institution, 1967.

Váli, Ferenc A.: *Rift and Revolt in Hungary*, Cambridge, Mass., Harvard University Press, 1961.

Zinner, Paul E.: *Revolution in Hungary*, New York, Columbia University Press, 1962.

RUDOLF L. TŐKÉS

1. The party changed names several times: 1918-1943, Communist Party of Hungary (KMP); 1944-1948, Hungarian Communist Party (MKP); 1948-1956, Hungarian Workers' Party (MDP); 1956-1965, Hungarian Socialist Workers' Party (MSZMP).

# ICELAND

Shortly after it was founded in 1916 the Social Democratic Party of Iceland (Althýðuflokkurinn Íslands, AI) was torn by factional strife, and by 1919 the left opposition was advocating radicalization of the party program. Within this opposition group the first communist cell, a small faction which adhered to the Comintern, was founded in 1921. For tactical reasons this cell was advised by the Comintern not to secede from the AI, but to attempt to increase its membership within the general party structure. It was not until 1930, when Iceland experienced the first effects of the European economic depression, that the communists left the AI on the pretext that the social democrats had betrayed the Icelandic proletariat by having entered into compromises with the bourgeoisie. Thus in 1930 the Communist Party of Iceland (Kommúnistaflokkurinn Íslands, KI) was formed with about 800 members.

## HISTORY

The progressing economic crisis enabled the communists to agitate among workers and fishermen and to increase their ranks. By 1937, when the party participated for the first time in the election to the Althing, the Icelandic parliament, it was able to obtain three mandates. This electoral success was due in part to the internal struggle in the AI and the growing communist sympathies of its membership. In mid-1938 the AI's left wing, led by Héðinn Valdimarsson, split off and united with the communists in October. The resulting United Labor-Socialist Party of Iceland (Sameiningarflokkur Althýðu-Sósíalistaflokkurinn, SAS) gained broad popularity at first. However, the Nazi-Soviet collaboration at the outbreak of World War II and the Soviet invasion of Finland brought a considerable decline in SAS membership. The German occupation of Denmark was tacitly accepted by the communists, but when British forces occupied Iceland in January 1940 the communists protested vigorously. This contributed to further losses for the SAS, since the great majority of Icelanders welcomed the British as their savior from nazi occupation. Valdimarsson, rebuked by the SAS leadership for having condemned the Soviet attack on Finland, left the party with a group of followers. The party was again in crisis, but this changed overnight when Hitler invaded the Soviet Union. The SAS now eagerly supported the Allied war effort and regained some of its lost influence. In the 1942 elections its candidates received 16 percent of the vote.

In June 1944 Iceland severed relations with Denmark and became an independent republic. By then the SAS was again very active, and two of its representatives were included in the first coalition government of the new republic. In the elections of 1947, however, the party suffered a considerable loss. As a result of this electoral loss and the coalition's internal difficulties over economic problems, the SAS was dropped from the coalition.

In the early 1950s, with strong support from Moscow, the SAS was able to develop broad propaganda activities and gained influence in the labor unions and among some intellectual circles, chiefly in the capital city of Reykjavik and the towns of Akureyri and Siglufjordur. In the June 1956 parliamentary elections the party polled 15,860 votes (19.2 percent) and won eight seats in the lower house. Again its representatives entered into a coalition government, this time with the Peasant Party (Framsóknarflokkurinn) and the

AI, and the SAS had access to patronage jobs for its members. However, this success was short-lived; events in Hungary in November destroyed much of its popularity, and membership declined. The AI and the Conservative Party (Sjálfstaedisflokkurinn), the strongest parties in Iceland, began to cooperate in the struggle against communist influences in the labor unions. By 1958 the SAS was considerably weakened, and in December of that year it lost its representation in the government. In the June 1959 balloting on an electoral reform the communists received only 15.3 percent of the vote, the lowest since the creation of the republic. In the October 1959 elections their vote increased to 13,621 (16 percent)—still less than in 1956—but owing to the new electoral law they had ten seats.

The conservative-social democratic coalition government formed after the October 1959 elections initiated a broad economic program to improve wages and working conditions. Nevertheless, at the November 1960 convention of the Icelandic Federation of Labor (Althýðusamband Íslands) the communists were able to secure the election of an executive board on which they had the majority. This gave them opportunities to interfere with the government's stabilization program; however, the government's efforts during the first two years were quite successful, and the communists were unable to initiate labor troubles.

After the 1959 electoral defeat the communists attempted to broaden their "front" by enlisting the cooperation of other parties still in opposition to the coalition government. Their approach to the Progressive Party with the proposal of a "popular front" failed, although some local organizations of that party did help them in capturing control of labor-union chapters. They were more successful with the insignificant National Defense Party (Frjáls Thjóð, FT), which had polled only 3.4 percent of the vote in the 1959 elections and which, like the communists, opposed Iceland's membership in the NATO alliance. In November 1962 the thirteenth SAS congress adopted the slogan "Iceland's road to socialism and called for withdrawal from NATO, adoption of neutrality, and the liquidation of American bases in Iceland. In the June 1963 parliamentary elections the communists participated under the guise of the People's Alliance (Althýðubandalagid), an electoral front comprising the SAS, the small FT, and some radical social democratic splinter groups. They obtained 14,274 votes, or 16 percent of the total vote, and nine seats in the lower house. Since then they have been able to maintain and even to strengthen their control of the Icelandic Federation of Labor. The federation was able to obtain considerable wage increases, which in turn caused a growing inflation. Thus in 1965 the government's stabilization program was in danger of faltering without new export possibilities for fish products.

## ORGANIZATION AND MEMBERSHIP

According to Soviet sources, in 1963 the SAS had about 1,500 members in thirty-five party organizations. United States estimates of 1965 membership are somewhat smaller—about 1,000. Every three years the SAS holds a congress, which elects a central committee as the directing body between congresses. The central committee elects its executive committee, which directs the work of the party cells. There is no intermediate organization. The 1963 congress elected Einar Olgeirsson party chairman.

## RELATION TO SOVIET LEADERSHIP

The crisis in the international communist movement resulting from reformist pressures and Peking-inspired opposition against the Moscow leadership had its repercussions in Iceland. In 1963 pro-Peking tendencies found some supporters, who produced factional strife inside the party. Although this situation caused a temporary reduction in communist propaganda and activities, by mid-1964 the pro-Moscow group was able to reestablish full control over the party. It became obvious that Moscow had used every means to eliminate the opposition; Iceland's strategic location was too important to Moscow to risk losing control in the local party. Despite the fact that the SAS is a very weak party in a country with a small population, because of its geographic location and strategic importance, it receives more attention from the Moscow leadership than its size and numbers would justify.

## PARTY PRESS ORGAN

The SAS press organ is the daily *Thjódviljinn* (People's Will), published in Reykjavik, with a circulation of about 10,000.

## BIBLIOGRAPHY

Bellquist, Eric C.: *Political Unrest in Iceland*, Berkeley, Calif., 1932.
Björnsson, B.: *Iceland: A Geographical, Political and Economic Survey*, Reykjavik, 1961.
Fusilier, Raymond: *Les Pays nordiques, Danemark, Finlande, Norvège, Suède, Islande*, Paris, 1965.

WITOLD S. SWORAKOWSKI

# INDIA

Although communist groups had been active in India for several years, the formal establishment of the Communist Party of India (CPI) is probably best set at December 1928. According to the colonial thesis of the sixth Comintern congress in 1928, the Indian communists were directed to form a single independent party and to change their policy of cooperation with "bourgeois nationalism" against British imperial rule to that of a full-scale attack on the Indian National Congress (INC). After some initial hesitation, the newly established party implemented this line.

The CPI also had indigenous roots in India. Numerous individuals, regional groups, and organizations had been active in the communist movement, and some had even been participating in the work of the Comintern. Throughout most of the 1920s Manabendra Nath Roy directed Indian communist activity and interpreted India's affairs to the Comintern. Although he played a major role in determining Comintern policy toward India and strategy for the colonial areas in general (at the second Comintern congress, for example, Roy and Lenin were the main protagonists in the debate on the colonial problem), by 1928 he was in eclipse. The following year he was formally expelled from the Comintern and played no role in the activities of the newly established CPI.

## HISTORY

Less than six months after the CPI was established several communist leaders were arrested for conspiring to overthrow British rule in India. As a result of the Meerut conspiracy trial, thirty-one communist leaders and trade unionists were imprisoned, which virtually wrecked the party's organizational apparatus. In July 1934 the CPI was declared illegal, a curb which was not lifted until 1942.

A far greater obstacle to the CPI were the activities of Gandhi and the INC. Gandhi's famous civil-disobedience campaign in the early 1930s had fired the imagination of the Indian people, and all political activity of any consequence increasingly revolved around the INC. Taking no account of this situation, the Comintern rigidly applied the militant policies adopted at its sixth congress in 1928 and forced the CPI to break off contact with the Indian nationalist movement. Thus, despite increasing radicalization of Indian political life during this period, CPI membership was, according to one estimate, a meager 150 in 1934.

When the Comintern began to soften its leftist line in 1933, the CPI shifted toward active cooperation with the nationalists. With the endorsement of the seventh Comintern congress in 1935, the CPI formed an alliance with the Congress Socialist Party, a Marxist grouping within the INC, which it successfully infiltrated and used to gain access to the INC itself. During this period the CPI also extended its control over substantial segments of peasant, labor, and student organizations. One of the foremost communist leaders, S. A. Dange, was president of the All-India Trade Union Congress, the largest labor organization in the country. Thus during the popular-front period the position of the CPI improved rapidly. In a very brief span of years its membership multiplied many times (reaching 5,000 in 1942), and it built up a tightly knit organizational apparatus and established strong connections with the nationalist movement.

The international complications of World War II placed great strains on the party. Curiously, the impact of Soviet requirements had effects quite the reverse of developments elsewhere. During the period of the Hitler-Stalin pact the communists maintained a strong antiwar and anti-British policy, a position generally in line with that of the INC. However, when the Comintern line switched abruptly after the nazi attack on the Soviet Union, the CPI reversed field. What had until then been an "imperialist war" suddenly became a "people's war," and the party urged full support to the British war effort. Relations with the nationalists were severely strained over this issue when in 1942 the INC launched a campaign demanding that Britain grant India immediate independence. The British response to this "quit India" agitation was to declare the INC illegal and imprison many of its leaders. The communists, however, pledged support to the British, and in return the ban on the CPI was lifted. The CPI now began to operate openly and expand its activities. In June 1943 it held its first congress, and by 1946 party membership had grown to 53,000. The nationalists, however, were extremely embittered by what they considered an act of betrayal by the communists, and in December 1945 they completely broke relations with the CPI.

During the immediate postwar period the CPI, under the general secretaryship of P. C. Joshi, sought respectability rather than revolution and tried to play the role of friend and gentle critic toward the INC. When independence was finally granted by the British in August 1947, the communists rallied behind the Nehru government and adopted a policy of loyal opposition. However, a split developed within the party ranks, and in opposition to Joshi's policy, a radical wing led by B. T. Ranadive called for open insurrection. With the formation of the Cominform in late 1947 and the general hardening of the Soviet line, the CPI also shifted to a more radical policy. At its second congress in February-March 1948 in Calcutta Ranadive replaced Joshi as general secretary, and a strategy of armed struggle was adopted. Taking as his guide the Russian model of revolution based on urban insurrection, Ranadive sought to launch the CPI on a plan for direct seizure of power.

The efforts of the CPI, though violent and disruptive, were abortive. Ranadive's revolutionary strategy had little effect. Furthermore, dissent against his authoritarian style of leadership began to develop within the party. Hostility to both his methods and his policies was especially strong among the communists in Andhra, led by Rajeshwar Rao, who urged the party to emulate not the Russian but the Chinese model of revolution, that is, to focus not on the working class, but on the peasantry. The communists had in fact achieved some success in attempted agrarian revolts both in Andhra and in the Telengana district of Hyderabad. In May 1950, after Moscow had bestowed official approval on the Chinese pattern of revolution, Rao succeeded Ranadive as general secretary, and the CPI shifted its focus from urban to rural areas. However, armed peasant insurrections also failed to produce results, and in late 1950 this policy was also abandoned.

The shift away from an insurrectionary strategy was, in part, the product of failure. Not only was revolutionary militancy unsuccessful in India (and elsewhere in most of Asia), but it cost the communists considerable support. Party membership fell from 89,000 in 1948 to 20,000 in 1950. Furthermore, in light of Nehru's position on the Korean War, Soviet policy toward the Indian government grew increasingly friendly. Finally, the first general elections since independence were scheduled for 1952, and in late 1950 the CPI shelved the strategy of armed struggle in favor of a policy of peaceful competition with the Nehru government. This new line became identified with Ajoy K. Ghosh, who succeeded Rao in October 1951 as general secretary of the party.

The CPI's shift from open hostility to limited support of the Nehru government was accomplished only with considerable internal conflict. While the results of the 1952 elections seemed to vindicate the more militant elements—the CPI scored its greatest victories precisely in those areas where its struggles had been most violent, especially Telengana and Andhra—the moderates sought to return to the role of loyal opposition. The demands of the international environment favored the moderates, for Moscow was increasingly interested in cultivating Nehru as an advocate of neutralism, and perhaps of anti-Western sentiment. At its third congress at Madurai (December 1953-January 1954) the party was badly split between a militant leftist faction unwilling to support either the domestic or foreign policies of the government and a more moderate rightist group urging collaboration with Nehru, especially in his international policies. The more moderate elements prevailed at Madurai, at the party's fourth congress at Palghat in April 1956 and again at its fifth congress in Amritsar in April 1958. Thus, although the CPI continued to adhere to parliamentary tactics and a policy of modified support of the government, a segment within its ranks, led by such radicals as B. T. Ranadive, remained hostile. In general, internal differences regarding proper policy toward the government continued to plague the party.

Although the CPI, and especially its front organizations, were damaged by the 1956 de-Stalinzation campaign and the events in Poland and Hungary, in the following year the party achieved the greatest single success of its history. In April 1957 the CPI won the general elections in Kerala and, under E. M. S. Namboodiripad, head of the party organization in the state, formed a communist government. This success, however, was only temporary; in the summer of 1959, acting in response to widespread antigovernment agitations, the president of India dismissed the Kerala government and proclaimed president's rule, and in February 1960 a coalition of anticommunist parties defeated the CPI in special elections.

While the ouster of the Kerala government reinforced the position of those who doubted the wisdom of parliamentary tactics, ruthless suppression of the uprising in Tibet by Communist China in the spring of 1959 and Chinese pressures along India's Himalayan frontiers in the fall of that year posed further dilemmas for the CPI. There was an open split over the question of attitude toward China: one group was in full support of Nehru's position on the McMahon boundary line; a second group of leftists favored adherence to the requirements of proletarian internationalism and supported Communist China; a third group criticized both India and China and urged that they negotiate. Thus by the beginning of the open phase of the Sino-Soviet dispute the CPI was badly split on several issues.

The sixth party congress, held at Vijayawada in the spring of 1961, was the scene of bitter conflicts over the ideological line to be adopted toward the government and over the party's stand on the growing Sino-Soviet dispute. Moscow's desire to preserve unity, conveyed by Mikhail Suslov, who attended as a representative of the Soviet party, probably helped to avoid an open break. Ghosh's death in January 1962 created yet another source of tension. After much debate, a compromise was reached on the issue of succession: a new position of party chairman was created and given to S. A. Dange, a leading rightist, and E. M. S. Namboodiripad, a centrist (antiright but not pro-Chinese), was made general secretary.

The Chinese attack on India in late 1962 further aggravated tensions within the party. After some delay (signifying heated debate), the national council of the CPI condemned the Chinese aggression. However, three leading leftists resigned from the party secretariat. In response to the Chinese threat the Indian government began a campaign against the left wing of the CPI in November 1962. By January 1963 about 1,000 party members had been arrested. In the wake of this repression organizational splits began to develop within the party. In western Bengal a separate leftist provincial organization was created. Throughout 1963 the situation within the CPI deteriorated. In February Namboodiripad, who had become increasingly anti-rightist, resigned as general secretary. Leftists throughout the country began to set up a rival party organization. After many more months of bitter debate the party finally split. In April 1964 thirty-two members of the CPI national council walked out of its sessions when the rightists refused to consider their demand that Dange resign as party chairman. The split became final in July, when the leftists, in a meeting at Tenali (in Andhra), formed a separate party organization which claimed to be the legitimate Communist Party of India. Thus in the fall of 1964 India was the scene of two seventh party congresses—one convened by the CPI left in Calcutta (in November) and the other by the CPI right in Bombay (in December).

## ORGANIZATION AND MEMBERSHIP

Operating on the traditional bolshevik principle of democratic centralism, the CPI has a five-tiered pyramidal structure. According to its constitution, adopted at an extraordinary congress held in 1958 at Amritsar, Punjab, the party has units at the national, state, district, town (or local), and branch levels. In an apparent effort to Indianize the party, the new constitution changed the name of the basic party unit from cell to branch, the central committee was renamed national council, and the politburo became the central executive committee. Supreme authority is formally vested in the all-India party congress. The national council chooses its general secretary (in 1965 Rajeshwar Rao) and a secretariat.

Party membership has been estimated at approximately 125,000 to 150,000. Its social composition, however, is a matter for speculation, for the CPI has not published detailed information on its membership since the 1940s. On the basis of these earlier data it would seem that while the party leadership has a high proportion of urban middle-class intellectuals, frequently overseas educated, the rank and file include a considerable number of workers, peasants, and students. More recent information indicates a very uneven distribution of CPI strength. The southern Indian element, especially from Andhra and Kerala, seems to dominate, although party strength is also considerable in western Bengal. These estimates of party membership are corroborated by voting statistics. In the 1962 general elections the CPI polled 19.3 percent of the popular vote in Andhra, 25 percent in western Bengal, and 35.5 percent in Kerala. It did not receive more than 8 percent in any other state. In general, then, communist strength in India tends to be regional rather than national. While the party managed to poll over 11 million votes in the general elections (9.9 percent of the total cast), this support seems to be concentrated in a few areas.[1]

It should also be noted that the basis of party strength throughout all of India varies considerably. In Andhra, for example, CPI influence is particularly strong among the

Kamma caste. Here votes for a communist candidate may be as much an expression of caste loyalty as economic discontent, for the communist-dominated Kamma caste represents a more prosperous peasantry (including landlords) than many peasant groups who do not vote communist. Conversely, in Kerala the CPI has drawn its main support from the Ezhavas, a landless low-caste group. Given the strong pull of particularistic and traditional loyalties in India, the CPI seeks to form alliances with caste, tribal, and linguistic groups on the local level. This policy, forced on it by the realities of Indian political life, has been a source of strain on party discipline and unity.

Because of the contradictory claims of both the left and right factions of the divided CPI, their relative strength is not entirely clear. According to the CPI right, it has 107,000 members and its rival only 40,000, The CPI left, however, claims 104,000 party members. The position of the left was seriously weakened when in December 1964, after its Calcutta congress, several hundred of its members were arrested as subversive agents. This move by the government forestalled a major left victory In the March 1965 by-elections to the Kerala legislature the left emerged as the strongest party, having won forty out of 133 seats. However, twenty-nine of the forty elected were and are still "under detention." The CPI right won only three seats.

The CPI left seems strongest in western Bengal, Andhra, and Kerala. Under Namboodiripad as general secretary, it has shunned too close an identification with Peking, and during the Indo-Pakistani war of 1965 it was critical of Chinese support to Pakistan. The CPI left seems increasingly divided between a pro-Chinese and a non-pro-Chinese faction. With many of the former in prison, the latter, headed by Namboodiripad and Jyoti Basu, seems generally in control. The CPI right is now headed by Dange (chairman) and Rajeshwar Rao (again general secretary). Neither wing has been able to capitalize either on the food shortages or on the opposition to United States policy in Vietnam. The Shastri government's performance during the Indo-Pakistani war has won the attention of Indian public opinion and has left little room to maneuver for either branch of the party.

One of the CPI's important sources of political power is its control of a large segment of India's trade unions. The All-India Trade Union Congress, India's second largest labor organization, came under communist control during World War II. Under the leadership of CPI chairman S. A. Dange, the Trade Union Congress claims a membership of over 650,000. A second communist mass organization is the All-India Kisan Sabha, which is used to carry on work among the Indian peasantry. Although it managed at one time to win more than 1 million adherents, its membership has been on the decline. The third mass organization which works closely with the party is the All-India Students' Federation. Whatever influence it may have had, it has steadily lost strength in recent years to its rival, the National Union of Students. A fourth organization, the National Federation of Indian Women, never had much support. In general, while the mass organizaions are weak on the national level, they do tend to have regional strength. Thus in western Bengal all these organizations are strong. The Trade Union Congress is strong in the industrial areas, the Kisan Sabha and the Students' Federation are strong in Andhra, and there are healthy peasant organizations in Kerala.

The front organizations vary, but they are all directed toward India's middle class, and especially the intellectuals. There are three categories of communist fronts in India: the "international-issue" fronts, the professional fronts, and the regional fronts. The international-issue fronts include the Indo-Soviet Cultural Society, the All-India Peace Council (probably the most influential of the front organizations), and the India-China Friendship Association, a body of some influence until 1959. The professional fronts include the All-India Progressive Writers' Association, the Indian People's Theater Association, and the All-India Association of Democratic Lawyers. The various regional fronts, formed to take advantage of the strong sentiments in India favoring single-language states, have been most successful in Andhra, Maharashtra, and western Bengal. In general the success of the front organizations is a useful index of the status of communist influence.

## RELATION TO SOVIET LEADERSHIP

As its history indicates, the CPI has been very sensitive to the shifting demands of the international communist movement. Thus, although it virtually destroyed itself in the process, the party adopted the "class-against-class" slogan of the sixth Comintern congress without much resistance. Similarly, the requirements of Soviet policy during World War II forced the party again to isolate itself from the main currents of Indian nationalism. Sensitive to the obligations of "proletarian internationalism," Indian communists have generally accepted the Soviet lead. The main channel of communication between Moscow and the CPI has usually been the Communist Party of Great Britian. Ever since its inception (and after the expulsion of Roy) the CPI has received instructions from Rajani Palme Dutt, a British communist of Indian extraction, the principal international spokesman on Indian communism. In recent years the party has begun to pay more attention to its own internal requirements. During the Sino-Indian border quarrel of 1962, and especially the Indo-Pakistani war of 1965, international communist considerations seemed to be given less weight by most of the party leadership than the impact of their policy on the CPI's internal position.

## THE SINO-SOVIET DISPUTE

The position taken among Indian communists on the Sino-Soviet split is more a function of internal disputes than of loyalty to the international movement. As already noted, the factional quarrels within the CPI, endemic since Indian independence, broke wide open with the development of the Sino-Soviet dispute. The division of the party into rightist and leftist, nationalist and internationalist groups became increasingly intermeshed with the international communist quarrel. The rightist faction, which favored some degree of cooperation with the Nehru government, gave its support Moscow. Like the Soviet leadership, Dange, Ghosh, and other moderates considered Nehru's policies as frequently progressive and worthy of support. The more militant group regarded Nehru as a reactionary and rejected the notion of any cooperation with his government. Thus when China openly condemned Nehru as an American stooge the radical elements within the party gave their support to Peking. However, while the CPI right tends to be pro-Moscow and the CPI left tends to be pro-Peking, the real source of tension between them is their divergent attitudes toward the congress government. Here the Sino-Soviet rift has merely served to aggravate already existing differences.

## FUTURE PROSPECTS

The future of communism in India seems quite dim. As already suggested, influence is regional rather than national. While the party has considerable strength in Andhra, Kerala, and western Bengal, the government thus far has shown considerable skill in maintaining its control. The CPI's lack of national influence is largely a result of the continuing strength of the INC. Although the influence of the INC was somewhat lessened by the death of Nehru in 1964, it still dominates Indian politics. The split within the CPI in 1964 reflects communist inability to reach agreement on the correct strategy toward the congress government, and the Sino-Soviet dispute merely serves to intensify this quarrel.

## PARTY PRESS ORGANS AND RECORDS

The CPI right publishes a weekly, *New Age*, and a monthly, *New Age*. The organ of the CPI left is *People's Democracy*.

Party statutes are given in *Constitution of the Communist Party of India, Adopted at the Extraordinary Congress, Amritsar, 1958*, Communist Party of India, New Delhi, 1958. For the program of the CPI right see *Draft Programme of the CPI*, Delhi, 1961, and for that of the CPI left see Bhupesh Gupta and P. Ranamurti, *Draft Programme of the CPI*, Delhi, 1961. The best source of party records is the Democratic Research Service, especially their publications *Communist Conspiracy at Madurai*, Bombay, 1954, a collection of documents on the CPI third congress; *Communist Doubletalk at Palghat*, Bombay, 1956, documents on the CPI fourth congress; and *Indian Communist Party Documents, 1930-1956*, Bombay, 1957, a compilation of eighteen key party documents.

## CONGRESSES OF THE CPI

1st congress, May 1943, Bombay
2d congress, February-March 1948, Calcutta
3d congress, December 1953-January 1954, Madurai
4th congress, April 1956, Palghat
5th congress, April 1958, Amritsar
6th congress, April 1961, Vijayawada
7th congress (CPI left), November 1964, Calcutta
7th congress (CPI right), December 1964, Bombay

## BIBLIOGRAPHY

Kautsky, John H.: *Moscow and the Communist Party of India*, Cambridge, Mass., MIT Press, 1956.
Masani, M.R.: *The Communist Party of India: A Short History*, London, D. Verschoyle, 1954.
Overstreet, Gene D., and Marshall Windmiller: *Communism in India*, Berkeley, Calif., University of California Press, 1959.
Scalapino, Robert A. (ed.): *The Communist Revolution in Asia: Tactics, Goals, and Achievements*, Englewood Cliffs, N.J., Prentice-Hall, 1965.

MORTON SCHWARTZ

1. Membership and voting statistics are from the following sources: U.S. Department of State, Bureau of Intelligence and Research, *World Strength of the Communist Party Organizations,* Eighteenth Annual Report, Washington, January 1966, pp. 98-99; W. H. Morris-Jones, *The Government and Politics of India*, London, 1964, pp. 161-168; Ralph Retzlaff, "Revisionism and Dogmatism in the Communist Party of India," in Robert A. Scalapino (ed.), *The Communist Revolution in Asia*, Englewood Cliffs, N.J., 1965, pp. 315-316; Gene D. Overstreet and Marshall Windmiller, *Communism in India*, Berkeley, Calif., 1959, pp. 356-359; Ram Swarup, "Communism in India in the Post-Nehru Period," *Orbis*, vol. 9, no. 4, winter 1966, p. 989.

# INDONESIA

The Communist Party of Indonesia (Partai Komunis Indonesia, PKI) was in mid-1965 not only the oldest communist party in Asia, but also the largest outside the communist bloc. Its origins can be traced back to the arrival in 1913 in the Netherlands East Indies of the Dutch Marxist H. J. F. M. Sneevliet, a young agitator and labor organizer who later became, under the name of Maring, one of the chief architects of Comintern colonial policy. On his initiative, on May 9, 1914, in Semarang, central Java, some sixty social democrats founded the Indies Social Democratic Organization (Indische Sociaal-Democratische Vereniging, ISDV), the precursor of the PKI. Sneevliet and the other European leaders of the ISDV were expelled from Indonesia by the Dutch authorities after December 1918, but in the meantime the organization's Indonesian membership had expanded rapidly owing to growing popular unrest caused by a worsening economic situation, the establishment in 1918 of the Volksraad,[1] and repercussions in the colony of the socialist agitation in Holland. At the ISDV's seventh congress, on May 28, 1920, a resolution was adopted to change the party's name to Communist Party of the Indies (Perserikatan Kommunist di India). The party's first chairman was a young Javanese named Semaun. Thus it came to be the first communist party established in Asia.

Although the party did not affiliate with the Comintern until December 1920, Sneevliet attended the second Comintern congress in July of that year as the Indonesian representative. In Moscow he acted as secretary of the Commission on National and Colonial Questions, which adopted Lenin's theses concerning the necessity in the Far East of cooperation with bourgeois-democratic (revolutionary) nationalism against imperialism, and with the peasant movement against feudalism. Lenin also advocated that while pursuing an alliance with these social forces, the communists should not amalgamate with them but should maintain the independent character of the proletarian movement. At its congress held in Batavia in June 1924 the party changed its name to Communist Party of Indonesia. The party's radical activities led to harsh government repression in 1927, and again in 1948, but became the guiding principles after 1951, when Dwipa Nusantara Aidit assumed leadership.

The first-generation party leadership was basically leftist in nature. Semaun, Alimin, Musso, Tan Malaka, and Raden Darsono, all prominent in the early period, either belonged to the lesser Indonesian nobility or were sons of officials. They were mostly urban and had at least some education; this put them apart from the masses, which at that time had a 95 percent illiteracy rate.

## HISTORY

In 1915 the Indonesian people finally received from their Dutch rulers the right to meet and organize politically, but even this limited freedom from the constraints of the Netherlands Indies constitution of 1854 was subject to limitations "in the interest of public order," to be imposed at the discretion of the colonial government. In December 1925 the PKI leaders decided, at a conference held at Prambanan, that armed revolution was the only possible answer to the Dutch authorities' restrictions on their legal political activities. During the preceding year the PKI had pursued a radical policy, in opposition to the Comintern-advocated united front with the peasantry and the intellectuals, of liquidating the mass organizations under its control and concentrating on purely proletarian action. In May 1925 Stalin himself had warned the PKI against "a deviation to the left, which threatens to alienate the communist party from the masses and to transform it into a sect."

During 1926 a communist underground had been established in Java and Sumatra, and arrangements were made to purchase arms abroad. The PKI at that time had between 9,000 and 10,000 members in eighty branches. The Comintern as well as PKI leaders in exile, such as Tan Malaka, were unable to convince those in control of the party in Indonesia that they were about to engage not in a revolution, but in a disastrous putsch devoid of broad popular support. Armed uprisings took place in west Java in November 1926, and in central Sumatra in January 1927. The repression that followed arrested the growth of the communist movement in Indonesia for almost twenty years: the PKI was banned, 13,000 persons were arrested, a few were executed, 4,500 were sent to prison, 5,000 were placed in preventative detention, and 1,308 were deported to Boven Digul in Dutch New Guinea, where they remained until the outbreak of World War II in the Pacific.

In its official accounts the PKI claims that after a period of decline following the repression of 1927 the party began underground work in 1932 and even formulated an eighteen-point program calling, among other things, for complete independence for Indonesia and for confiscation of the land held by landlords and imperialists and its distribution to the peasants. Musso, one of the exiled party leaders, is reported to have returned clandestinely from Moscow to implement the popular-front policy adopted by the Comintern in August 1935. He was allegedly able to draw the PKI leaders together and form a new central committee. However, he had to leave Indonesia, and as a result, the PKI leaders worked without any firm guiding lines during the crucial period of World War II and the Indonesian struggle for independence from 1945 to 1949.

Japan occupied the Netherlands Indies in March 1942. During the occupation the illegal PKI participated in underground antifascist resistance activities and even accepted some financial aid from the Dutch secret service. However, antifascist ideological beliefs clashed with anticolonial nationalist interests, and some members of the illegal PKI became involved after October 1944 in Marxist anti-Western training programs sponsored by Japanese intelligence services. By July 1945 several hundred Indonesians had graduated from these two-month courses.

On August 17, 1945, only three days after Japan's surrender, the nationalist leader Sukarno declared Indonesia's independence. Following the collapse of Japan the PKI was reestablished openly in October by Mohammad Jusuf, who had not been connected with the earlier PKI. In May 1946, after some futile terrorist activities, leadership of the party was assumed by Sardjono, who had been PKI chairman in 1926, spent sixteen years in exile in New Guinea, and finally worked with the Dutch in Australia after the outbreak of the war in the Pacific. In August Sardjono was joined by Alimin, one of the leaders of the 1926 rebellion who had spent twenty years in exile and had just returned home from a lengthy visit with Mao Tse-tung in Yenan. In the next two years the PKI played only a modest role in both the national independence struggle against the Dutch and the internal struggle for power in the Indonesian republic.

In August 1948 Musso returned again from Moscow and was enthusiastically proclaimed leader of the PKI, replacing Sardjono. He announced a "Gottwald plan" to secure power without resort to major force and pressed the republican leaders to include communists in the cabinet. The republican cabinet of Mohammed Hatta, opposed to Musso's plan, started removing PKI elements from the Indonesian national army. On September 18, during a ceasefire between the Indonesian forces and the Dutch forces attempting to recapture the country, procommunist army officers seized power in the city of Madiun and exhorted communists elsewhere to follow their example. Sukarno appealed by radio to the Indonesian people to choose between Musso's communist party and the Sukarno-Hatta nationalist government. The Siliwangi division of west Java, the Sungkono division of east Java, and the police mobile brigade moved against the 25,000 troops on the communist side. On December 7 army headquarters announced that the rebellion had been quelled and that 35,000 persons, mostly troops, had been arrested. Musso was killed in a skirmish, and almost all the top PKI leaders were captured and imprisoned by the Indonesian army.

On December 19 the Dutch attacked again and took the nationalist capital Jogjakarta in central Java. The overwhelmed Indonesian army withdrew to the mountains, planning to use guerrilla tactics against the Dutch. However, before their retreat they took eleven top leaders of the PKI out of jail and executed them. The PKI had suffered its second major setback and was again discredited for several years. At the beginning of 1952 it claimed only 7,910 members, and even that figure was probably inflated.

In January 1951 a group of younger men— D. N. Aidit (born in 1923), M. H. Lukman (born in 1920), and Njoto (born in 1925)— took control of the politburo. These new leaders concentrated on rebuilding the PKI through united-front tactics as a legitimate mass party seeking power legally within the framework of the political institutions of the country. As a result of this policy, in the next fifteen years the PKI enjoyed spectacular success. In the September 1955 general elections for parliament it obtained 6,176,914 votes, or 16.4 percent of the total, and emerged as a major political force in Indonesian society. Local elections in 1957 revealed that the PKI was in the process of becoming the most powerful party in the country, and concern about a possible communist victory in the forthcoming general elections was a factor in their indefinite postponement, under strong pressure from the army. However, despite army-sponsored efforts to curtail the activities of the party and several attempts in 1960 to have it banned, the communists succeeded in creating a huge mass movement.

The PKI's increasing influence in the 1960s, both in internal matters and in foreign policy, was due partly to its own very vigorous efforts, but also to a coincidence of interests with those of President Sukarno. Its anti-imperialist stand, reinforced by extreme nationalism, paralleled not only Sukarno's feelings, but also the general sentiments of the people, who had bitter memories of their colonial history. It was communist agitation through its labor unions that started Indonesia on the economically disastrous path of expropriating foreign investments in the country. By the end of 1957 Dutch property had been taken over and Dutch citizens expelled from Indonesia. British interests came under attack with Indonesia's "confrontation" policy against Malaysia, and in March 1964 the United States was told by Sukarno to "go to hell with your aid." At about the same time the PKI influence on foreign policy reached a peak and was manifested in such events as the confrontation against Malaysia, Indonesia's withdrawal from the United Nations in January 1965, and the declaration by Sukarno on August 17, 1965, of the Djakarta-Phnom Penh-Peking-Hanoi-Pyongyang axis.

In July 1959 Sukarno formed his own cabinet, responsible to no one but him, and as his power increased, he rewarded the PKI for its staunch support. In March 1962 Aidit and Lukman were appointed ministers without portfolio, and in August 1964 Njoto became a minister attached to the cabinet presidium. In the Indonesian parliament, constituted in June 1960 by Sukarno's appointment, communist party members and sympathizers occupied sixty-four of the 283 seats.

The PKI's spectacular growth can be attributed to a number of factors. The imaginative leadership of the Aidit group, which sought to give the PKI the new image of a peaceful, law-abiding party seeking power through legitimate channels and concerned with the welfare of the masses, was perhaps most important. Although the PKI sided with Peking in the Sino-Soviet debate, its highly nationalist orientation made it invulnerable to attack as a "foreign agent." It also had extremely dynamic party programs, which included two three-year plans, initiated in 1956 and 1960, as well as an ambitious "four-year plan for culture, ideology, and organization" initiated in August 1963.

Perhaps most important to the growth of the PKI was the protection offered by President Sukarno. The communists pandered to Sukarno's political ambitions for himself as a great ideological leader of his nation, and for his nation as the leader of the third world, or as he liked to call it, the "new emerging forces." Indonesian communist propaganda quoted his many pronouncements profusely and reverently, helping to establish the peculiar brand of Indonesian political ideology. In exchange, Sukarno argued vigorously that the Indonesian political system should be based on *nasakom*, the solidaristic cooperation of nationalist, religious, and communist political forces. He also insistently condemned "communist phobia" as un-Indonesian. In an Independence Day address on August 17, 1965, Sukarno appeared to approve the communist policy when he said: "Indonesia clearly states that its revolution is still at the national-democratic stage, although a number of important results have been achieved at this stage. The time will arrive when Indonesia will build socialism—namely, after imperialist capital has been liquidated completely, after the land owned by the landlords is redistributed among the people."

Although popular support for the PKI and

its front organizations proved superficial and weak when it was put to serious test at the end of 1965, earlier that year the party's claimed membership figures were creating an impression of inexorable advances toward the eventual takeover of the Indonesian government. By mid-1964 the PKI was claiming 3 million members, the People's Youth (Pemuda Rakjat) 3 million, the communist-controlled All-Indonesia Central Council of Trade Unions more than 3.5 million, the Indonesian Farmers' Front 8.5 million, and the Women's Movement 1,750,000 members. Taken at face value, these figures meant that almost one-fifth of the total Indonesian population of about 105 million was affiliated with the PKI.

Addressing a mass meeting celebrating the forty-fifth anniversary of the PKI on May 23, 1965, Sukarno himself stated that the party had 3 million members, the youth organization had another 3 million, and there were an additional 20 million sympathizers. He indicated his support of the PKI in urging it "onward, onward, onward, never retreat." Thus by the fall of 1965 it appeared almost inevitable that Indonesia would soon become a communist country. The PKI was at the time making efforts to fill its one remaining need, a paramilitary arm. To this end the communists employed a two-pronged strategy: first, they urged Sukarno to introduce the political-commissar system in the existing four branches of the armed services,[2] in the hope of neutralizing their chief opponent; and second, they pressed for the installation of a "fifth force," to be composed of volunteers.

The armed forces were fighting the commissar system and Sukarno was still hesitating on the fifth-force idea when events took a dramatic and unexpected turn in the early hours of October 1, 1965. On the night of September 30-October 1 six of the most senior general officers of the army, including army minister and commander Lieutenant General Achmad Yani, were abducted and murdered during a coup attempted by communist-influenced army and air force personnel and members of the youth and the women's organizations. Defense minister and armed forces chief of staff General Abdul Haris Nasution narrowly escaped assassination, but under the leadership of Major General Suharto the army neutralized the rebel units without difficulty.

In the changed political atmosphere previously repressed Muslim elements, supported by the army, proceeded toward a ruthless extermination of the communist movement. By January 15, 1966, according to Sukarno, 87,000 communists had been killed. Most observers estimate the total number of communist casualties as considerably higher, probably between 150,000 and 300,000. Most members of the politburo and of the central committee of the PKI, including Aidit, Lukman, and Njoto, were killed or imprisoned. Following massive renunciations of membership, the number of party members dropped very quickly from almost 3 million to an estimted 100,000 to 150,000. Although Sukarno continued to oppose army pressures to outlaw the PKI altogether, local military commanders had banned its activities in at least fifteen of the country's twenty-one provinces by the end of 1965.

Exasperated with the slowness with which the army was moving against the communists in the political sphere and its apparent hesitation to openly confront the president, Indonesian students took to the streets in early 1966. Mass student demonstrations took place in February and March demanding the banning of the PKI, the ouster of all communists and communist sympathizers from parliament and the cabinet, and lowering of prices on essential commodities, especially rice. The offices of the Chinese embassy and consulates were frequent targets, and the students accused the Chinese of complicity in the attempted coup of September 30.

This major and unexpected setback of the PKI is bound to affect the international communist movement in ways which cannot yet be fully assessed. Before the attempted coup the PKI had been the largest communist party outside the Soviet bloc and one of the most influential. Aidit, whose writings had been translated into several languages, was asserting himself as a major figure in the communist world. Had the PKI succeeded in coming to power, Indonesia would have been the third largest communist country in the world and an important independent factor in the international communist movement. Its swift destruction in the last months of 1965 is bound to generate intensive discussions in communist circles on political strategy. It is safe to assume, however, that the PKI will not play a significant overt role in Indonesian political life for some time to come.

## PARTY PRESS ORGANS AND RECORDS

The major newspapers and journals of the PKI before its liquidation in October 1965 were *Harian Rakjat* (People's Daily), with a circulation of 60,000; *Bintang Merah* (Red Flag), a monthly devoted to Marxism-Leninism; *Review of Indonesia*, an English-language version largely for circulation abroad; and *Kehidupan Partai* (Party Life).

Until its downfall in 1965 the PKI had its own very active publishing firm, the Jajasan Pembaruan in Djakarta. In addition, it had numerous printing facilities and bookshops for the sale of its publications, which included most of the major addresses of party leaders and such documents as party and front-organization congress records, programs, and directives. For the party program see *Program Partai Komunis Indonesia disahkan oleh Kongres Nasional ke-VII (Luarbiasa) Partai Komunis Indonesia, 25-30 April 1962*) [Program of the Communist Party of Indonesia Adopted by the Seventh National Congress (Luarbiasa) of the Communist Party of Indonesia (April 25-30, 1962)], Djakarta, 1962. For the party's constitution see *AD-ART (Konstitusi) Partai Komunis Indonesia* (Constitution of the Communist Party of Indonesia), Djakarta, 1962.

## PARTY CONGRESSES

1st congress, May 1920, Semarang
2d congress, June 1924 Batavia (Djakarta)
3d congress, December 1924, Kotagede (near Jogjakarta)
4th congress, January 1947, Soerakarta (Solo)
5th congress, March 1954, Djakarta
6th congress, September 1959, Djakarta
7th congress, April 1962, Djakarta

## BIBLIOGRAPHY

Aidit, Dwipa Nusantara: *Problems of the Indonesian Revolution*, n.p., 1963.
Brackman, Arnold C.: *Indonesian Communism: A History*, New York, Praeger, 1963.
Hindley, Donald: *The Communist Party of Indonesia, 1951-1963*, Berkeley, Calif., University of California Press, 1964.
Van der Kroef, Justus M.: *The Communist Party of Indonesia*, Vancouver, University of British Columbia Press, 1965.
McVey, Ruth T.: *The Rise of Indonesian Communism*, Ithaca, N.Y., Cornell University Press, 1965.
Scalapino, Robert A. (ed.): *The Communist Revolution in Asia*, 2d ed., Englewood Cliffs, N.J., Prentice-Hall, 1969.

GUY PAUKER
EWA PAUKER

1. In 1927 the Volksraad, established as an advisory body, was granted colegislative powers with the Dutch governor general. This body existed until the end of Dutch rule in March 1942.

2. The police force in Indonesia is considered a branch of the armed services.

# THE INTERNATIONAL ASSOCIATION OF DEMOCRATIC LAWYERS

The origins of the International Association of Democratic Lawyers (IADL) have been traced to two conflicting geneses. According to Soviet and East European interpretations, the idea of such an international organization was formulated during the Nuremberg trials in the early part of 1946.[1] On the other hand, Martin Popper, erstwhile executive secretary of the National Lawyers Guild, a left-wing American group and charter member of the IADL, claimed that the foundation was laid as early as during the conference of United Nations legal representatives at San Francisco, that is, in the spring of 1945.[2] The organization, however, that took the first steps toward the creation of the IADL was the French National Judiciary Movement (Mouvement National Judiciaire, MNJ), a group founded under the name National Front of Jurists (Front National des Juristes) during World War II by a communist lawyer, Joë Nordmann. It was in the framework of a convention of the MNJ that an International Congress of Jurists was staged in Paris on October 24-27, 1946, as the first major postwar gathering of that kind.

## HISTORY

The MNJ-sponsored Paris congress attracted 200 delegates from twenty-five countries, representative of a broad cross-section of political alignment. However, already at this first meeting, which was to decide on the nature of the nascent IADL, a developing political orientation was evident. Soviet commentary on the congress noted that

> ... there developed from the beginning of the Congress an influential group: leftist elements of the French delegation, representatives of new democracies, of Republican Spain, Democratic Greece, [and] of the USA: Popper and others. This group, with the support of the Soviet delegation, gained an obvious predominance in the drafting of the resolutions in the committees ... where rightist elements attempted to display considerable activity.[3]

The 1946 meeting decided to hold the IADL's founding congress in Brussels, July 16-19, 1947. A provisional bureau was formed which included a presidium consisting of a president (René Cassin, vice-president of the French Council of State), two secretaries-general (Nordmann and Popper), and six vice-presidents.

Some of the delegates to the Paris meeting had left the IADL in response to initial developments; thus, according to a Soviet report, at the Brussels congress "the delegates represented therefore a more homogeneous group," although "some indirect influence of the liberal and 'non-political' tendencies continued to be felt."[4] The Brussels congress was attended by some 150 delegates from twenty-seven countries. It officially reelected Cassin as president and Nordmann and Popper as secretaries-general of the organization. The congress introduced two elements which were to become major leitmotifs of the IADL: war propaganda and atomic energy as threats to international peace. The United States was accused of war mongering and monopolization of nuclear weapons and its policies were contrasted with the alleged peaceful intentions of the USSR.

Despite the IADL's growing politization, noncommunists continued to give it their guarded support. In August 1947 the organization was given consultative status Category B with the United Nations Economic and Social Council.

The IADL's third congress took place in Prague on September 5-10, 1948. The atmosphere at the congress was to a large extent influenced by the immediately preceding World Congress of Intellectuals for Peace, which had been held in Poland in August (see *The World Council of Peace*). This fact, combined with the Soviet-inspired decision to abolish committee debates and transfer all discussion to plenary sessions, had a calculated effect on minority opinion. According to a Soviet delegate's report, "reactionary elements could not sound off openly; if such [elements] had been at all present in a negligible number among the delegates at the Congress, they would not have dared to stand up alone in front of the mighty collective of democrats."[5] The resolutions adopted by the congress included attacks against domestic developments in the United States; criticisms of the draft of the Declaration prepared by the Committee on Human Rights of the UN; assertions that the United States and British occupational authorities in Germany were not cooperating in the denazification effort; and claims that several Western countries, including the United States, were carrying out propaganda activities in an attempt to "incite aggression against democratic states and peace-loving nations."[6] No criticisms of the Soviet Union or of any other communist state were expressed. Commenting on the congress, a Soviet delegate noted: "The intensifying struggle of two camps, the imperialist and the democratic, leaves less and less space for the adherents of 'the golden middle road.' "[7] The congress reelected Nordmann and Popper as secretaries-general. René Cassin was reelected president, even though he had expressed opposition to some of the resolutions and appeared to be increasingly disenchanted with the developments in the organization.

The IADL's fourth congress took place in Rome on October 28-31, 1949. In the interim period, however, the association was confronted with a number of internal crises, not the least of which was the resignation of its president following a bureau meeting in April 1949. Cassin gave as his reason the IADL's decision to affiliate with what was to become the World Council of Peace and which was then holding its inaugural "Congress for Peace" in Paris. The IADL's policies also affected its national affiliates, with major schisms taking place, particularly in Great Britain, Belgium, and France. By October delegations to the IADL congress were comprised almost in their entirety of communists or fellow-travelers. It was in this context that the decision of the congress to expel its Yugoslav affiliate—a direct result of the Stalin-Tito conflict—was opposed by only one delegation (Yugoslavia), with two abstentions (Great Britain and Republican Spain, on grounds of lacking instructions from their home organizations). The subsequent discussions and resolutions of the congress mirrored the views of the Soviet Union. Nordmann and Popper were once again elected secretaries-general; a left-wing British member of Parliament, Dennis Nowell Pritt, was elected president.

Following the Rome congress, the IADL proceeded to integrate itself fully with the other international communist front organizations. At the same time it became increasingly isolated from noncommunist lawyers, as a result both of its own sectarian policies and of the growing influence of such bodies as the International Bar Association and the World Federation of International Juridical Associations.

The IADL's closest ties appear to have been with the World Council of Peace. The relationship was such that at the IADL council meeting in Budapest in April 1950 it was decided to postpone the fifth IADL congress until the spring of 1951 at the earliest, so that the national sections might assume their full share in the preparation of the World Council of Peace's Second World Peace Congress to be held in the last quarter of 1950. The IADL's complete endorsement of Soviet views extended to the expression of militant opposition to the United Nations intervention in Korea, which it branded as an "unprovoked American intervention in domestic Korean affairs." On July 20, 1950, the UN Economic and Social Council withdrew recognition from the IADL. Nine days later the French government banned the IADL's secretariat-general from its Paris headquarters and prohibited further activity of the association's executive offices from French soil.

The IADL held its fifth congress in East Berlin on September 5-9, 1951. Dominating the discussions was the IADL's apparent desire to capitalize on what it interpreted as United States "criminal aggressive measures" in Korea. In this context the congress approved the suggestion made by Nordmann on behalf of the IADL secretariat to elect an "impartial commission" to "investigate the war crimes committed by the imperialist intervention forces in Korea." This, the first of the IADL's major "commissions of inquiry," arrived in Korea on March 3, 1952. The day before its arrival, however, the Soviet press agency TASS had announced that the commission had been sent to Korea "to investigate and establish the crimes committed by the interventionists," thus deciding in advance the outcome of the inquiry. The commission telegraphed the IADL on March 16 that it had gathered "indisputable evidence" of germ warfare. Its official report presented in mid-April claimed that the facts constituted "an act of aggression committed by the United States, an act of genocide and a particularly odious crime against humanity." Although the commission's report and the subsequent campaign carried out by the IADL were exposed as a fraud, the action set a precedent for the utilization of the IADL which was to be used with increasing frequency in the following years to further communist contentions and propaganda.

The IADL's sixth congress was not held till May 1956. In the intervening years there developed a certain reorientation in the association's interests: a much greater emphasis on establishing ties with the developing areas of the world and, particularly after Stalin's death in 1953, a notable moderation in its political and ideological stance. The IADL also showed a tendency during this period to play down its sponsorship of various endeavors. This was most evident in connection with several international conferences which were initiated and organized by the association; among these were the First [Latin American] Continental Conference of Jurists, Rio de Janeiro, November 1952; the Second Continental Conference of Jurists, Guatemala, October 1953; the International Conference of Lawyers for the Defence of Democratic Liberties, Vienna, January 1954; and the Congress of Asian Democratic Lawyers, Calcutta, January 1955.

The Soviet Union's advocacy of "peaceful coexistence"—a stand that gained momentum from the spring of 1955—was reflected in IADL pronouncements. In some respects the sixth congress, held in Brussels on May 22-25, 1956, was reminiscent, in its courting of Western opinion, of the first congress. While political resolutions mirrored Soviet views and policies, there was an evident effort to reintroduce discussions of a purely legal nature. This tempering of earlier sectarianism was evident in the next two IADL congresses which took place in Sofia, October 1960, and in Budapest, March 1964. The leadership of the association, however, continued relatively unchanged. At the Budapest congress, Nordmann was still secretary-general; Pritt had been appointed honorary president, while the post of president was held by a Frenchman, Pierre Cot, a member of the bureau of the World Council of Peace and a communist sympathizer who was awarded the Lenin Peace Prize in 1963.

Partly as a result of its attenuated political

militancy, new problems faced the IADL in the 1960s. At an Afro-Asian Lawyers' Conference organized by the IADL in Conakry in October 1962, Chinese delegates, with the support of the Japanese IADL vice-president Hirano Yoshitaro, succeeded in outvoting the pro-Soviet delegates. The conference established a permanent secretariat which excluded representation from the Soviet Union. Although the potential for a rival lawyers' organization, dominated by the Chinese, exists, such a group had not been formed by the end of 1965. Instead the Chinese used IADL forums to attack Soviet policy. At the eighth congress in 1964 the Chinese delegation challenged the organizers' "undemocratic attitude" in foisting an "illegal agenda" on the congress to push through the "erroneous line" of the Soviet Union.

## ORGANIZATION AND MEMBERSHIP

Membership in the IADL is open to lawyers' organizations or groups and to individual lawyers. At the IADL's 1964 congress 400 lawyers from sixty-four countries were said to have attended, including delegates from IADL member organizations in sixty-one countries. Lawyers holding membership through organizations or individually are estimated to number about 20,000.

The highest organ of the IADL is the congress, in which each affiliated organization is represented. First held yearly, the congress is now supposed to meet every three years. The congress elects a council, which is supposed to meet yearly and consists of a bureau, a secretariat, and one representative of each affiliated organization and co-opted members.

The IADL claims to be financed by affiliation fees and donations. No details are published.

## PRESS ORGANS

The IADL's organs, published very irregularly, are *Information Bulletin*, which is issued in French and English and supposed to appear quarterly, and *Review of Contemporary Law* (formerly *Law in the Service of Peace*), which should appear every six months but does not always do so. They have been published since 1949.

## CONGRESSES OF THE IADL

1st congress, October 1946, Paris
2d congress, July 1947, Brussels
3d congress, September 1948, Prague
4th congress, October 1949, Rome
5th congress, September 1951, East Berlin
6th congress, May 1956, Brussels
7th congress, October 1960, Sofia
8th congress, March 1964, Budapest

## BIBLIOGRAPHY

Kabes, Vladimir, and Alfons Sergot: *Blueprint of Deception: Character and Record of the International Association of Democratic Lawyers*, The Hague, Mouton & Co., 1957.

International Commission of Jurists: *Under False Colours*, The Hague, International Commission of Jurists, 1955.

MILORAD POPOV

1. See *Sovetskoe gosudarstvo i pravo* (Moscow), no. 11-12, 1946; and *Právní praxe* (Prague), vol. 12, 1948.
2. *Lawyers Guild Review* (New York), no. 4, September-October 1946.
3. *Sovetskoe gosudarstvo i pravo*, no. 11-12, 1946.
4. *Ibid.*, no. 9, 1947.
5. *Ibid.*, no. 11, 1948.
6. *Demokratyczny Przeglad Prawniczy* (Warsaw), no. 9, September 1948.
7. *Izvestiia*, September 19, 1948.

# INTERNATIONAL COMMUNIST FRONT ORGANIZATIONS

Shortly after the March 1919 creation in Moscow of the Communist International as "the party of world revolution," its Executive Committee initiated in many countries the formation of special auxiliary organizations under either open or disguised communist leadership whose purpose was to enroll noncommunists and thus gain broader "civic support" for communist aims and causes. These societies were to be created in countries where active communist parties already existed, and were to be included in international organizations which would coordinate their activities with the operations of the Communist International.

By 1925 there existed five international organizations which belonged to the Communist International and included as their members corresponding organizations outside Russia. In the Soviet Union the corresponding organizations were also members of the "internationals" and, owing to their large number of members, had a considerable influence on these "internationals." The five organizations were:

The Communist Youth International, which emerged from the takeover in November 1919 of the old International Union of Socialist Youth Organizations by German communists.

The Red International of Labor Unions, founded by participants in the second congress of the Communist International in Moscow in July-August 1920.

The Red Sport International, founded by participants at the third congress of the Communist International in Moscow in June-July 1921.

The International Organization for Aid to Revolutionaries, known also as International Red Aid, created in 1922 by the Russian Association of Former Political Prisoners and the Association of Old Bolsheviks, both in Moscow.

The International Peasants' Council, known also as the Peasants' International, founded on the initiative of the Executive Committee of the Communist International in Moscow in October 1923.

(See separate articles on these organizations.)

Two other auxiliary organizations created by the Comintern never developed into "international" organizations because their activities were limited to only a few countries. A worldwide Communist Women's Organization was initiated during the founding congress of the Communist International in 1919, and a "Women's Secretariat" was created in the executive offices of the Communist International. The latter organized several international women's conferences, but was unable to establish a broad network of "member-organizations."

The second "international" that misfired was the Workers' International Relief, founded on the initiative of the Comintern in Berlin in September 1921 with the purpose of starting relief organizations in other countries to aid the famine-stricken workers of Russia. The strongest of these was developed in Germany; a few weaker organizations sprang up in other countries. By 1925, however, when the famine was over, these organizations faded away.

It should be noted that only after the formation of these "internationals" in Moscow did the communists in various countries start broad propaganda in order to create corresponding local organizations which then became members of the "internationals." This entirely Moscow-inspired procedure of the early 1920s which organized international communist organizations "from the top," with member-organizations being formed later, became the prototype for the creation of communist front organizations both before and after World War II. These fronts, directed in each country by the local communist party and supervised by the Communist International, were chiefly concerned with spreading the communist line, more or less disguised, among the noncommunist masses. When Moscow's political aims demanded it, these fronts were quietly liquidated.

Of the five above-mentioned organizations, the first to be closed down was the Peasants' International. Owing to a lack of supporters among peasants, it was quietly dissolved in 1933, and its "activities" transferred to the Red International of Labor Unions. Then, after the seventh congress of the Comintern in 1935 inaugurated the popular-front movement, the existence of these auxiliary organizations became an embarrassment to the Moscow leadership, which was at that time advocating unity in the workers' movement. As a result, after almost two decades the procedure of "boring from within" and subverting noncommunist organizations was officially abandoned. The dissolution of the Red Sport International occurred immediately after the seventh Comintern congress, and by the end of 1937 the Red International of Labor Unions also closed down. In May 1943 the Communist Youth International was dissolved and, at the same time, Stalin liquidated the Communist International as a gesture to Franklin D. Roosevelt and Winston Churchill—as proof of the Soviet Union's intention not to interfere in the future in the internal affairs of foreign countries through Soviet-directed communist organizations.

The only one of these front organizations to survive the prewar popular-front period and the "grand alliance" of World War II was the International Red Aid, which lasted until 1947, when it was exposed in several countries as a Soviet intelligence organization.

In the first postwar months, a period when the Soviet Union was exploiting the wartime friendly attitude of its former allies, Moscow returned to the creation of communist fronts on a much broader scale than before. During the war, in the atmosphere of friendship with the Soviet ally, communist and procommunist movements reached unprecedented strength in many countries. These pro-Soviet elements all over the world were now used to capture existing professional organizations which for all practical purposes became communist fronts of a new type. Communist leadership in these organizations was disguised, and procommunists without party affiliation, or with secret, "underground" party ties, were placed in leading positions. These organizations, which advertised their democratic character, could be identified as communist-directed by their reaction to the communist takeover of Czechoslovakia early in 1948. The cold war, the Korean War, and the Berlin blockade all offered additional occasions for a clear-cut stand on the side either of the Western democracies or of the Soviet bloc. In each case, these new front organizations openly sided with the Soviet Union. Representatives of the noncommunist countries consequently denounced these organizations as communist fronts and left them.

These new communist front organizations are listed below in the sequence in which they were founded:

World Federation of Trade Unions, founded in Paris in September 1945 as a nonpolitical organization.

World Federation of Democratic Youth, founded in London in November 1945 as a nonpolitical organization.

Women's International Democratic Federation, founded in Paris at the end of November 1945 as a result of French communist initiative.

International Organization of Journalists,

founded in Copenhagen in June 1946.

World Federation of Scientific Workers, founded in London in July 1946 as a nonpolitical organization.

International Union of Students, founded in Prague, Czechoslovakia, in August 1946.

International Association of Democratic Lawyers, founded in Paris in October 1946 on French communist initiative.

World Council of Peace, founded in Wroclaw, Poland, in August 1948.

International Federation of Resistance Fighters, founded in Vienna in June 1951.

(See separate articles on these organizations.)

In addition, there are several smaller and less active front organizations which operate independently or as subsidiaries of the above-listed organizations. For instance, the World Federation of Democratic Youth has eight "international committees" and "bureaus" which operate under various innocuous names like "International Bureau of Tourism and Exchanges of Youth." The activities of these fronts reached their climax in the mid-1950s. Khrushchev's policy of peaceful coexistence and the mounting Moscow-Peking tension broke the aggressiveness of these fronts. Particularly the underdeveloped African people rightly concluded that the front organizations, following Moscow's policy of peaceful coexistence, abandoned them in their struggle for emancipation and liberation.

In the early 1960s, Communist China assumed that the vanishing influence of pro-Soviet fronts in Africa created a vacuum which they could fill. Under Peking's tutelage and with Chinese financial support, several "Afro-Asian" fronts were created but they seem to have had little success. The Indonesian events by the end of 1965 played a prominent role in the failure of Peking to gain a foothold in Africa. Also, Chinese attempts to exploit anti-American feelings in Latin America and to replace the diminishing Soviet influence by creating and supporting new fronts seem to have foundered.

The finances of these post-World War II front organizations deserve some attention. Their many congresses, conferences, and festivals, attended by up to several thousand participants, their various "investigating commissions" which traveled all over the world, and other widely advertised mass meetings involved expenditures of tens of millions of dollars. In their published reports these "internationals" mention generally that their finances are based on membership dues and donations of national affiliates. No details of this income are ever included in published reports or in reports given at public meetings. On the other hand, most of the national member organizations, in publications destined for their own membership, complain of financial difficulties and appeal to the membership to pay past due contributions. Some of them complain that they cannot afford adequate staffing of their offices. Their periodical publications appear irregularly because of lack of funds.

Thus arises the enigmatic discrepancy: the member organizations complain of financial difficulties, but their "internationals" lavishly spend millions of dollars alleging that the funds come from these financially unstable member organizations. Thus, from where do these millions of dollars come? This is the well-guarded secret of those who direct the "internationals" of all communist front organizations.

## BIBLIOGRAPHY

Orth, Robert: *International Communist Front Organizations,* Pfaffenhofen/Ilm, Ilmgau Verlag, 1964.

WITOLD S. SWORAKOWSKI

# THE INTERNATIONAL FEDERATION OF RESISTANCE FIGHTERS

The origins of the International Federation of Resistance Fighters (Fédération Internationale des Résistants, FIR) date back to the first International Congress of Former Political Prisoners and Victims of Nazism, held in Warsaw in February 1946. The two principal sponsors of the congress were the Polish government and the French National Federation of Deportees and Internees, Resistance Fighters and Patriots (Fédération Nationale des Déportés et Internés, Résistants et Patriotes, FNDIRP), an organization controlled by the French Communist Party. The congress adopted a resolution calling for the formation of an International Federation of Former Political Prisoners of German Concentration Camps (Fédération Internationale des Anciens Prisonniers Politiques des Camps de Concentration Allemands, FIAPP), whose headquarters were to be in Warsaw. The key positions on the provisional executive committee formed to organize the FIAPP inaugural congress were given to communists. Maurice Lampe, FNDIRP secretary-general and member of the French Communist Party, became president, and Józef Cyrankiewicz, subsequently to become premier in the 1948 communist government of Poland, was given the post of secretary-general.

The official founding congress of the FIAPP took place in Paris, March-April 1947. Representatives from eighteen countries participated: Albania, Belgium, Bulgaria, Belorussia, Czechoslovakia, Denmark, France, Greece, Italy, Luxembourg, the Netherlands, Norway, Poland, Rumania, Soviet Union, Spain (exiles), the Ukraine, and Yugoslavia. The representatives of the Central Committee for the Jews were integrated into the national delegations. Out of the eighteen national groups that participated in the congress only five (Belgium, Denmark, Luxembourg, the Netherlands, and Norway) were not represented by exclusively communist delegations.

## HISTORY

The FIAPP executive committee held its first meeting in Warsaw, July-August 1947. An indication of the political orientation of the organization was its response to the announcement of the Marshall Plan: it would, the FIAPP warned, "lead to the revival of militarism in Germany," and "infringe the sovereignty of the countries of Europe."

The extent of the FIAPP's alignment with Soviet policies, however, was most evident in its reaction to the Stalin-Tito controversy. As early as April 12, 1948, during an FIAPP-sponsored commemoration in Berlin for the victims of fascism, the Soviet delegates publicly urged the Yugoslavs to disassociate themselves from their own government's policies; at the same time, the FIAPP secretariat broke off all contacts with the Yugoslav affiliate. Following the expulsion of Yugoslavia from the Cominform in June 1948, agitation against the FIAPP's Yugoslav affiliate increased considerably. Finally, at a meeting of the FIAPP's international committee in Prague in April 1950, the Yugoslavs were expelled from the organization.

The ouster of the Yugoslavs, in turn, disaffected the few remaining noncommunist FIAPP affiliates. They either broke completely from the FIAPP (as in the case of Norway, Denmark, and Luxembourg) or split on the national level, with only the communist element retaining its alignment with the FIAPP (as in Belgium, France, Italy, Austria, Greece, and the Netherlands). The dissidents created new national organizations, many of which joined in 1950 to form the International Free Federation of Resistance Deportees and Internees (Fédération Internationale Libre des Déportés et des Internés de la Résistance, FILDIR).

At its third congress in June-July 1951 in Vienna, the FIAPP, partly in response to the growing challenge of the FILDIR, decided to broaden its base. It was disbanded at the congress and replaced by a new organization—the FIR, formally the International Federation of Resistance Fighters, Victims and Prisoners of Fascism (Fédération Internationale des Résistants, des Victimes et des Prisonniers du Fascisme). The motivation for the creation of the FIR was best expressed by Aleksandr Gundorov, head of the Soviet delegation:

> The [FIAPP] was founded in the spring of 1947. In the initial period its activities were directed towards the amelioration of the material circumstances in which former political prisoners and hundreds of thousands of widows and orphans found themselves. But, as it became increasingly clear that the American and British imperialists were out to revive fascism and speedily instigate another war, the federation turned its attention to political questions. Its national organizations and members began to participate actively in the peace movement. The threat of another war and the revival of fascism also brought about unity of purpose amongst the former resistance members, who have national organizations in many countries. The aim of our Congress in Vienna was to bring all these anti-fascist forces together.[1]

The leadership of the FIR differed little from that of the FIAPP. Five of the ten-member FIR bureau had been on the FIAPP executive committee; all the members of the bureau were communists. Frédéric Manhés and André Leroy, both from France, were elected president and secretary-general, respectively. Manhés had been honorary president of the FIAPP and Leroy its president. At the outset the FIR headquarters was in Warsaw; it was moved, at the end of 1951, to Vienna. A small secretariat was opened up in Paris.

At the 1951 congress a communist delegate from France, Pierre Villon (alias Roger Ginsberger) had outlined the purpose of the FIR: "The real reason for the existence of the FIR is not to support the rights of former resistance fighters but to carry on a necessary struggle according to the decisions and initiatives of the World Council of Peace."[2] During the following years the FIR steadfastly adhered to the views of the World Council of Peace and its Soviet-controlled leadership, and participated in all its campaigns (see *The World Council of Peace*). The FIR also worked in close collaboration with the International Association of Democratic Lawyers, particularly in organizing protests over the alleged use of bacteriological weapons by United Nations troops in Korea (see *The International Association of Democratic Lawyers*). From 1955, following the inclusion of the Federal Republic of Germany into NATO, FIR propaganda concentrated itself on attacking all West German policies.

Being an all-European organization, the FIR, unlike other international communist front organizations, was not affected by the Sino-Soviet conflict. The only significant disaffection within the organization occurred at the time of the 1956 Hungarian uprising. The FIR's support of the Soviet suppression of that country led to the resignation of one of the organization's secretaries, Luc Somerhausen, a Belgian communist.

## ORGANIZATION AND MEMBERSHIP

Organizations of former partisans and resistance fighters, and of political prisoners and victims of nazism and fascism, can become members of the FIR; individuals are admitted as "associate members." At its fifth congress in December 1965 the FIR claimed a membership of forty-seven organizations in twenty-three countries.

The highest organ of the FIR is the congress, which is supposed to meet every three years. It consists of representatives of the member organizations, who elect a bureau to conduct day-to-day work. The congress also ratifies members who, nominated by national associations, serve together with the bureau on a general council. The general council is supposed to meet at least once a year between meetings of the congress. At the end of 1965 there were 119 members in the general council, of whom forty-nine were also bureau members. In addition to the ordinary members of the bureau, there are a bureau president, twelve vice-presidents, and a secretariat. Elected by the bureau from among its members, the secretariat has a secretary-general, deputy secretary-general, secretary, and treasurer. The bureau president also serves on the secretariat.

Though no details are published, the FIR claims to be financed by affiliation fees, gifts, legacies, and other subventions.

The regular activities of the FIR include the sponsoring of annual rallies at former nazi concentration camps. It also organizes medical conferences to discuss the effects of imprisonment and maltreatment in nazi concentration camps; these have been held in Copenhagen (June 1954), Moscow (June 1957), Liège (March 1961), and Bucharest (June 1964). The FIR's historical commission has organized conferences on the history of the resistance, designed to emphasize the role of communist-led resistance groups and extol the efforts of the Red Army; two major ones were held in Florence (November 1959), and in Warsaw (April 1962). The FIR has also from time to time organized international rallies of resistance fighters, often directing them to a specific subject, such as the October 1963 International Rally Against the Resurgence of Nazism and Fascism, held in Florence.

## PRESS ORGANS

Since mid-1953 the FIR has published a journal in French and German, *Résistance unie (Der Widerstandskämpfer)*, issued ten times a year, and an irregular fortnightly bulletin in French and German, *Service d'Information de la FIR (Informationsdienst der FIR)*. In 1959 the federation started publishing a historical review in French and German, *Cahiers internationaux de la résistance (Internationale Hefte der Widerstandsbewegung)*; scheduled as a quarterly, it has appeared irregularly since 1961.

## CONGRESSES OF THE FIR

1st congress, June-July 1951, Vienna
2d congress, November 1954, Vienna
3d congress (first session) March 1959, Vienna
3d congress (second session) March 1959, Vienna
4th congress, December 1962, Warsaw
5th congress, December 1965, Budapest

## BIBLIOGRAPHY

Heldring, Alexander: *The International Federation of Resistance Movements: History and Background*, The Hague, INTERDOC, 1969.
La Voix Internationale de la Résistance (ed.): *Contre la résistance*, Brussels, n.d.

MILORAD POPOV

1. Alexander Heldring, *The International Federation of Resistance Movements*, The Hague, INTERDOC, 1969, p. 29.
2. *Congrès international des résistants, des victimes et des prisonniers du fascisme*, Vienna, 1951.

# THE INTERNATIONAL ORGANIZATION FOR AID TO REVOLUTIONARIES

The International Organization for Aid to Revolutionaries (Mezhdunarodnaia Organizatsiia Pomoshchi Revoliutsionerom), known as International Red Aid, was founded in Moscow on December 16, 1922, by members of the Association of Old Bolsheviks and the Association of Former Political Prisoners, under the leadership of the Polish communist Julian Marchlewski, a permanent resident of the Soviet Union. Its purpose was to bring material and moral aid to communists incarcerated in "capitalist jails." Member organizations in forty-nine countries operated under various names, such as the Rote Hilfe in Germany and the Labor Defense Council in the United States. In 1928 they allegedly had a total of 7,800,000 members, 3,500,000 of whom were in the Soviet Union.[1] The organization cooperated closely with the Communist International and was under its general direction.

Two international conferences were held in 1924 and 1927. A single international congress was held in Moscow in 1932. In 1923, March 18, the anniversary of the Paris commune, was declared "Red Aid Day" in many countries, with public collections of funds for International Red Aid. During World War II International Red Aid was able to infiltrate many organizations in allied countries which were promoting relief for the victims of nazism and fascism. In 1947, when the organization was exposed as a Soviet front, it was dissolved.

## PRESS ORGAN AND RECORDS

The press organ of International Red Aid was the monthly *Internatsionalnyi maiak* (International Beacon), published in Russian, German, French, and English and sporadically in other languages.

The records of the 1924 conference and the 1932 congress are available, as well as much information on the activities of the member organizations. For a list of all such records see Witold S. Sworakowski, *The Communist International and Its Front Organizations*, Stanford, Calif., Hoover Institution, 1965, part VIII.

## BIBLIOGRAPHY

*5 [Fünf] Jahre Internationale Rote Hilfe*, Berlin, MOPR-Verlag, 1928.
*Ten Years of International Red Aid in Resolutions and Documents, 1922-1932* [Moscow?], International Red Aid, 1932.
Zelt, Johannes: *Und nicht vergessen die Solidarität! Aus der Geschichte der Internationale Roten Hilfe und der Roten Hilfe Deutschlands*, Berlin, Rütten & Loening, 1960.

WITOLD S. SWORAKOWSKI

1. *Sovetskaia istoricheskaia entsiklopediia*, Moscow, 1961, vol. IX, cols. 236-237.

# THE INTERNATIONAL ORGANIZATION OF JOURNALISTS

The International Organization of Journalists (IOJ) was founded at a congress held in Copenhagen in June 1946. The International Federation of Journalists (IFJ), a group in existence since 1926, and the International Federation of Journalists of Allied and Free Countries, founded in December 1941, were both formally disbanded and merged with the IOJ.

## HISTORY

At its founding congress the IOJ included delegates representing journalist organizations of both communist and noncommunist orientation. From the outset, however, communists succeeded in capturing key executive posts. Within a year the organization's ideological alignment had engendered serious differences of opinion, which surfaced at the IOJ's second congress, held in Prague in June 1947. It was at this time, also, that the organization's headquarters were moved from London to the Czechoslovak capital. At the IOJ's executive committee meeting in Budapest, November 16-18, 1948, the adoption of a resolution accusing Western journalists of warmongering precipitated the resignation of the United States representatives. A year later, on October 5, 1949, the president of the IOJ, Archibald Kenyon, a British journalist who had been president of both the IFJ and the International Federation of Journalists of Allied and Free Countries, resigned, claiming that the IOJ had become "a branch office of the Cominform." By 1950, when, in response to the Stalin-Tito conflict, the IOJ expelled its Yugoslav affiliate, all noncommunist organizations had withdrawn their affiliations. Those who left the IOJ refounded the IFJ at a World Congress of Journalists in Brussels in May 1952.

The IOJ held its third congress in Helsinki in September 1950. It elected as its president Jean-Maurice Hermann, secretary-general of the French Journalists' Union, an affiliate of the communist-controlled General Confederation of Labor, and editor-in-chief of *Cahiers internationaux,* a communist monthly published in Paris. By the time of the Helsinki congress the IOJ's partisanship had become so pronounced that it had lost, on July 20, 1950, its Category B consultative status with the United Nations Economic and Social Council.

Until Stalin's death in 1953, IOJ pronouncements and the tenor of its publications were of a highly sectarian nature. The organization was particularly strident in its denuciations of the United Nations intervention in Korea, publishing atrocity stories, including the fraudulent "germ warfare" charges directed against the UN troops. By 1955, however, in line with the new Soviet approach to international relations, the IOJ had developed a more conciliatory stance toward the West. In that year, the IOJ asked the IFJ to cooperate and eventually form a new universal journalists' organization. It called on the IFJ to cosponsor two conferences—one for the Latin American region, to be held in Montevideo, and the other an International Meeting of Journalists, to be held in Europe. The IFJ refused to cooperate in either; the first was abandoned and the second, after many postponements and changes of venue, was held in Finland in June 1956. An offshoot of the meeting in Finland was the creation of an International Committee for Cooperation of

Journalists (ICCJ). In spite of efforts to disguise the IOJ's control of the ICCJ, by the end of 1955 the ICCJ had not succeeded in attracting any significant noncommunist support. In October 1960 in Baden, Austria, it sponsored a second International Meeting of Journalists. Few noncommunists attended, and several delegations walked out in protest against one-sided political resolutions. A third international meeting, held aboard the Soviet liner *Litva*, cruising in the Mediterranean from September 20 to October 3, 1963, was more successful in attracting noncommunist participation, particularly from African and Arab countries. This last meeting, however, was boycotted by the Chinese, the Sino-Soviet conflict having by then extended to the IOJ.

The IOJ's failure to develop ties with Western journalists in the mid-1950s was coupled with its own internal difficulties. The 1956 events in Poland and Hungary appear to have created internal controversies, and it was not until May 1958, when the IOJ held its fourth congress in Bucharest, that the organization fully resumed its activities.

One of the major concerns of the IOJ from 1958 onward appears to have been to develop its ties with journalist groups in the developing areas. Its success was most notable in Africa, where it helped set up a Pan-African Union of Journalists (PAJU), following an All-African Journalists' Conference, held May 19-24, 1961, in Bamako, Mali. While the PAJU is organizationally independent of the IOJ, relations between the two groups have been very close. In Latin America, following a journalists' meeting in Havana in January 1962, the IOJ set up a Commission for Information and Cooperation among Latin American Journalists (CICPLA), with headquarters in Montevideo. Although the CICPLA held a meeting of its "Enlarged Secretariat" in Montevideo on May 23-26, 1964, which called for the convening of a Latin American Journalists' Congress for May 1965, by the end of that year the event had not taken place. The growing rift between Soviet and Cuban interpretations of revolutionary strategy appear to have hindered the IOJ's influence in Latin America, and the CICPLA has remained a relatively ineffective body.

The IOJ's attempts to further its interests in Asia proved abortive. At the fifth IOJ congress in Budapest in August 1962, the Chinese and Indonesian delegations took steps to organize a conference of Afro-Asian journalists, which they scheduled for Bandung in April 1963. Although the IOJ offered its support to the subsequent Afro-Asian Journalists' Conference, its participation at the meeting was limited to the status of "observer." The Bandung Conference proceeded to set up the Afro-Asian Journalists' Association (AAJA), a geographical rival to the IOJ in Africa and Asia. The AAJA was exceptionally active during the next two years, although its attempt to align the PAJU to its cause proved unsuccessful. The abortive communist coup d'état in Indonesia in September 1965 affected the AAJA, whose headquarters were in Djakarta. The organization was still active at the end of 1965, although its center of operations had had to be moved to Peking.

## ORGANIZATION AND MEMBERSHIP

Eligible for membership in the IOJ are national unions and groups of journalists, and also, since the 1950 congress, individuals engaged in journalism. At the end of 1965 the organization claimed to have a membership of about 110,000 from some eighty countries.

The congress is the highest body of the IOJ. Its meetings, which are supposed to take place every four years, are attended by representatives of affiliated organizations or groups and individual members. Individual members and representatives of groups with fewer than twenty members, however, may not vote. The executive committee is elected by the congress; it consists of both officers and ordinary members and meets at least once a year. The bureau (or presidium) consists of the president, secretary general, and vice president, and is responsible for conducting business between meetings of the executive committee. Its members are elected by the congress, and it meets as required. The general secretariat, controlled by the secretary-general, works under the general direction of the bureau. It carries out all administrative work, including finance and publications. At the end of 1965 the president of the IOJ continued to be Jean-Maurice Hermann; the secretary general was Jiří Meisner, from Czechoslovakia.

In the 1960s the IOJ set up a number of journalist training schools in Eastern Europe and Africa to train journalists from developing countries.

An offshoot of the IOJ is the International Photographic Section, an organization set up in Prague in March 1962. Although part of the IOJ, it holds its own meetings, photographic exhibitions, etc., and has its own officers under the chairmanship of Vilem Kropp (Czechoslovakia).

In addition to its congresses, the IOJ has held the following international conferences: Conference of Agricultural Journalists, Plovdiv, Bulgaria, September 1957; International Conference of Reporters, Bucharest, May 1958; International Conference of Sports Editors, Budapest, March 1959; International Conference of Foreign Affairs Editors, Prague, June 1959; Round Table Conference of Eastern and Western Journalists, Warsaw, October 1961; and Conference of Journalists from the Balkans, Bucharest, December 1965.

The IOJ claims to be financed entirely by affiliation fees. No accounts, however, are published.

## PRESS ORGANS

The IOJ publishes a monthly journal, *The Democratic Journalist,* in English, French, Russian, and Spanish. It also issues a fortnightly *Information Bulletin* in the same four languages and, since March 1, 1965, in Arabic.

## CONGRESSES OF THE IOJ

1st congress, June 1946, Copenhagen
2d congress, June 1947, Prague
3d congress, September 1950, Helsinki
4th congress, May 1958, Bucharest
5th congress, August 1962, Budapest

MILORAD POPOV

# THE INTERNATONAL PEASANTS' COUNCIL

The International Peasants' Council (Mezhdunarodnyi Krestianskii Sovet, or Krestianskii Internatsional), usually called the Peasants' International or the Krestintern, was founded at an international peasants' conference in Moscow on October 10-15, 1923, on the initiative of the Comintern. This organization was intended to provide better access to the small farmers and landless farm workers, with the intention of integrating their organizations with communist party work in all countries where peasants formed a sizable proportion of the population. Particular attention was paid to the peasants in Eastern and Central Europe—from the Baltic countries down to Yugoslavia, Bulgaria, and Greece—and in Latin America, where the *campesino* was the target of communist propaganda.

Until the founding of the Peasants' International the communists had been unable to penetrate peasant organizations in Bulgaria, Czechoslovakia, Hungary, Poland, Rumania, and Yugoslavia, where such groups played important roles in the internal politics of their countries. The peasants' parties had met in Prague in 1921 and had created the International Union of Peasants, with its seat in Prague, whose purpose was to coordinate and promote the needs and demands of European peasants. Moscow hoped with the Peasants' International to outbid the International Union. Although the latter was a very loose and weak organization, it outlived the Peasants' International.

A second international peasants' conference met in Moscow in November 1927 to promote the inclusion of the peasants and their political parties in the Comintern's united-front efforts. It did not produce the expected results. The next venture was a widely advertised "first European peasants' congress," held in Berlin on March 26-29, 1930; although the meeting brought a large number of communist peasant representatives to Berlin from about forty countries, its verbose resolutions were never put into practice. With the failure of this last congress, the Peasants' International was quietly dissolved in 1933. Its work among the peasants was turned over to the Red International of Labor Unions, which in turn was dissolved in 1937. Tomasz Dąbal,[1] a Polish communist of peasant origin who had been leader of the Peasants' International, fell under Stalin's purges and was executed.

## PRESS ORGANS AND RECORDS

Official organs of the Peasants' International were the periodicals *Krestianskii Internatsional* (Peasants' International), *Mezhdunarodnyi krestianskii biulleten* (International Peasants' Bulletin), and *Internationale Bauern-Nachrichten*, published in Berlin. All these publications appeared irregularly from 1923 to 1933.

The records of the two conferences were published, and there are a limited number of publications by and about the Peasants' International. For a detailed listing see Witold S. Sworakowski, *The Communist International and Its Front Organizations*, Stanford, Calif., Hoover Institution, 1965, pp. 453-455.

## BIBLIOGRAPHY

Jackson, George D., Jr.: *Comintern and Peasant in East Europe, 1919-1930,* New York, Columbia University Press, 1966.

WITOLD S. SWORAKOWSKI

1. Spelled phonetically in some publications as Dombal.

# THE INTERNATIONAL UNION OF STUDENTS

The origins of the International Union of Students (IUS) date back to December 1941 with the formation—at the initiative of the National Union of Students of England, Wales and Northern Ireland (NUSEWNI)—of an International Council of Students (ICS). Concerned with student problems under wartime conditions, the ICS dissolved itself in the late autumn of 1944 "to make room for a new and better form of international student cooperation" that would correspond to the postwar situation. The ICS called on the NUSEWNI to assist in the creation of the new student organization. In March 1945 the NUSEWNI convened a meeting of Allied nations' student groups, both communist and noncommunist, at which plans for an international student conference were made. Meeting in London in November of that year, the conference established an International Preparatory Committee (IPC) to arrange for a constitutional convention for a new student international. While the majority of the London conference delegates were not communists, the IPC was dominated by communists, and a Soviet proposal to move the IPC headquarters to Prague was accepted. Thus, the Czechoslovak National Student Union (then completely in communist hands) shared the IPC's responsibilities in the preparations for the convention. These preparations included the drafting of statutes and the selection of the credentials committee, both important tasks, since the statutes gave strongly centralized power to the international body's executive committee, while the credentials committee, in turn, had jurisdiction over the granting of delegate status at the convention which was to elect the executive committee.

The founding congress of the IUS took place in August 1946 in Prague. It was attended by some 300 delegates from thirty-eight countries, representing an estimated one and a half million students. Partly as a result of decisions taken by the credentials committee—e.g., the accreditation of the small communist-controlled All-India Students' Federation at the expense of all other Indian student groups, including the 80,000-member All-India Student Congress—the communist element at the congress had a clear majority of delegate votes. Two communists, Josef Grohman (Czechoslovakia) and Tom Madden (Great Britain), were elected president and secretary-general respectively, of the IUS. Communists were also elected to a majority of the executive committee seats.

## HISTORY

Although a sizable number of noncommunists participated in the founding congress of the IUS and many were elected officials, the control over direction and policy exercised by the communist majority on the executive committee and secretariat quickly disillusioned the noncommunist national unions. By 1947 the president of the NUSEWNI was to declare that the IUS had been turned into "the student section of the Cominform." In August of that year the student unions from Austria, Belgium, and Switzerland left the IUS. (The student union from the Netherlands had refused to join the IUS a year earlier, at the founding congress, claiming that the IPC had "already furnished evidence of completely one-sided political influence.")

Despite the IUS's unswerving support of Soviet views and actions, most noncommunist unions continued to favor participation in the international since, with the deterioration of East-West relations, it was one of the few remaining channels for contact between students of opposing camps. By the end of 1950, however, the IUS's seeming indifference to the views of its noncommunist members had resulted in the disaffiliation of nearly all of them. The two events that appear to have been principally responsible for the disaffection were (1) the IUS's failure to protest the February 1948 coup d'état in Czechoslovakia, which had included suppression of the Czechoslovak student leadership (by then no longer controlled by communists), and (2) the expulsion from the IUS two years later of the Yugoslav student union, a direct result of the Stalin-Tito controversy and of Yugoslavia's 1948 ouster from the Cominform.

At the IUS's second congress, in Prague in August 1950, six months after the expulsion of the Yugoslavs, a final attempt was made by the British union to mediate the Yugoslav issue. The response of the IUS came in the form of a strongly worded attack from one of its vice-presidents, Aleksandr Shelepin, who was a leading figure in the international at that time and was to become the head of the Soviet State Security Committee (KGB) eight years later. Referring to the British delegates as "traitors to [their] own people," Shelepin dismissed the request for further discussion of the Yugoslav issue with a Russian proverb: "You can't bow to every sneeze." Shelepin's response reflected the uncompromising attitude that characterized IUS policy at the congress and that was to dominate until Stalin's death in 1953. The partisan stand of the IUS at the second congress was seen most notably in its resolutions on the conflict in Korea: the North Korean forces were praised as promoters of peace while those of the United Nations were branded as "aggressors, headed by the American imperialists." In December 1950 twenty-one national student unions, representing some two million students, met at an International Student Conference in Stockholm. Despite significant opposition to the polarization of the student movement, the International Student Conference and its secretariat—the Co-ordinating Secretariat of National Unions of Students, formed in January 1952—gradually assumed the role of an alternative noncommunist student international.

From the time of the IUS's second congress of 1950 to its third in 1953, the policies of the student organization mirrored those of the Soviet Union to such an extent that even its organizational structure was affected. Thus, following the Soviet-instigated purge and execution of the secretary-general of the Communist Party of Czechoslovakia, Rudolf Slánský in December 1951, the president of the IUS, Grohman, a member of the Czechoslovak party's central committee and supporter of Slánský, was no longer seen at IUS meetings. At the IUS August 1952 council meeting in Bucharest, the Rumanian Bernard Bereanu was elected to the presidency.

With the death of Stalin in March 1953 the IUS moved to reverse its sectarian policies. At its third congress in August of that year the IUS stressed its desire for cooperation with all students, regardless of their individual beliefs. In order to broaden its base the IUS also introduced the concept of associate membership. Finally, responding to a suggestion by Malenkov at a session of the USSR Supreme Soviet of the possible reestablishment of diplomatic relations with Yugoslavia, the IUS announced on the same day—two weeks before the opening of the congress—that it was inviting Yugoslav students to participate.

Between 1953 and 1956, when it held its fourth congress, the IUS continued to play down its political and ideological commitments. It emphasized instead the leit-motifs of "peaceful coexistence" and "national independence," directing them, respectively, to Western student unions and to those of developing countries. It would appear, however, that the effect of the new IUS approach was relatively counterproductive: the student unions in Western Europe and North America continued to be reserved and wary; and many unions in the developing areas saw the shift in IUS policy as being primarily concerned with East-West détente at the expense of anticolonial and national liberation movements.

At its fourth congress in Prague, August-September 1956, the IUS was faced with considerable criticism from left-wing groups in the developing areas, despite the fact that more than a year earlier it had decided to "considerably increase" its anticolonial activities. The principal spokesman for the dissidents was Hu Chi-li, the representative of the All-China Student Federation, who repeatedly stressed the primacy of anticolonialism. Aware of the challenge represented by the Chinese, the IUS increased its scholarships to students from developing areas and organized seminars on colonialism. At the same time, however, it continued to call for "peaceful coexistence" and courted Western student unions with appeals for student unity couched in moderate language. A number of reforms in internal organization proposed by the noncommunists in 1950 were adopted at the 1956 congress.

That this new policy was only a reflection of Soviet interests and not a break with them was evidenced a few months later in the IUS's response to the suppressed Hungarian revolution. In their accounts of the events the IUS publications *World Student News* and *News Service* referred to the insurgents as "armed fascist groups" who wanted to "make Hungary a country of the landlords and the Catholic Church again."

At the same time that the IUS's attitude to the Hungarian crisis alienated many Western student unions, the schism with the left-wing groups from developing areas—partly motivated by the latter's contention of an IUS conciliatory response to "imperialism"—continued to grow, representing an increasingly greater threat to the organization's leadership. At the fifth IUS congress, in Peking in September 1958, political issues were reemphasized, in contrast to the fourth congress, which, in an apparent response to Western student opinion, had included discussion of purely student problems. The IUS leadership's political stands, however, continued to be dictated by the imperatives of Soviet foreign policy with its then advocacy of East-West détente. Thus there developed a bipolarization engendered by political options—peace or anti-imperialism—with the Soviet and East European delegations pitted against those of China and of many of the developing countries of Africa, Asia, and Latin America. Twenty student unions from the latter group, in a demonstration of both unity and independence of the pro-Soviet leadership of the IUS, convened immediatley after the congress a meeting of fifty-seven student organizations from forty-six developing counties to "discuss common problems and seek means and forms of cooperation." While the meeting did not give birth to a rival organization to the IUS, it opened up the possibility of a geographically exclusionary development at the expense of the Soviet Union and its East European allies and over which the Chinese would be likely to have relatively greater control.

By late 1958 there began to appear in IUS publications and in official East European commentaries concerning the IUS references to "differences" in the councils of the organization. Almost entirely, these differences involved the Chinese and revolved around the various facets of the Soviet policy of "peaceful coexistence." At its executive committee meeting in Tunis in 1960, the IUS provided the forum for the first public Moscow-Peking dispute in the presence of noncommunists. For the first time in the history of the international communist movement, the Chinese openly accused the Soviet Union of trying to come to an agreement with the "imperialists."

Although the sixth IUS congress in Baghdad in October 1960 witnessed a certain hardening in the IUS leadership's attitudes toward the West, Sino-Soviet vituperations continued to increase. The seventh congress, held in Leningrad in August 1962, was the scene of an intensification of the polemic.[1] A new plateau in the dispute was not reached, however, till after July 1963, date of the signing of the nuclear test ban treaty between the Soviet Union, Great Britain, and the United States. While the IUS welcomed the treaty, the All-China Student Federation called it "a big fraud to fool students and people of the world," referred to the IUS secretariat's "shameful capitulation to imperialism," and condemned "certain IUS leaders who tail after the Soviet Government in its capitulationist diplomacy."[2] The IUS, in turn, criticized the Chinese for their "demagogic," "harmful," and "irresponsible" statements.

The apogee of the IUS's Sino-Soviet conflict occurred at the eighth congress in Sofia in November-December 1964. By that time the Chinese, together with the Indonesian student union, had already taken steps to create a rival student organization comprising representation from Asia, Africa, and Latin America. Even though a rival body had not been set up by November 1964 (nor established by the end of 1965), Chinese participation at the congress was in the nature of combined disruption and proselytism. The pro-Soviet leadership of the IUS was able to isolate the Chinese, but it was faced with a dilemma. If it continued to allow Chinese participation in its meetings, the conflict could paralyze IUS activities and also spread to other student organizations— e.g., at the congress even the erstwhile automatic support of the Rumanians was beginning to waver. On the other hand, the IUS leadership feared that if it were to expel the Chinese it might be instrumental in the creation of a competing center around which all left-wing disaffected student organizations, particularly those from the developing areas, could rally. At the end of 1965 the IUS was still confronted with the dilemma.

ORGANIZATION AND MEMBERSHIP

Full or associate membership in the IUS is open to national unions of students, or to other student organizations where no national union exists. As its eighth congress in 1964 the IUS claimed a membership of seventy-eight student organizations. Twenty-eight of these, however, were overseas or minority groupings, not representative of the students of their countries. Of the remaining fifty, thirteen full members came from communist countrries, while another twenty-five were from Africa (twelve), Latin America (ten), Asia (two), and Europe (one); and twelve were associate members— four Africans, two Latin Americans, two Asians, and four Europeans. Fifteen of the seventy-eight organizations on the membership list did not participate in the congress and their membership was therefore uncertain.

The congress is the highest body in the IUS. Its meetings are supposed to take place every two years. All affiliated and associated organizations send delegates to the congresses. Observers are invited, but have no voting rights. At Sofia in 1964 some 200 delegates were present. Until its abolition in 1956 there existed an IUS council which met between congresses and was comprised of one delegate from each national student union. The executive committee consists of the president, secretary general, vice presidents, treasurer, secretaries, and "ordinary members." The national student organizations represented are chosen by the congress, but each such organization selects its own representative. Except for a brief period in 1952 when a Rumanian replaced Josef Grohman, the IUS presidency has been held by a Czechoslovak. Although the IUS constitution forbids election to the executive committee of anyone at the time of election whose university courses were completed more than three years before, the longest reigning IUS president was Jiří Pelikan, who, although graduated in 1949, became president in 1953 and did not resign till 1963, when he was replaced by another Czechoslovak, Zbynek Vokrouhlický. The headquarters of the IUS is in Prague.

The IUS claims to be financed by affiliation fees and the sale of its publications, although the scale of the organization's worldwide activities and commitments makes it seem doubtful that these resources would cover all the costs.

The IUS works closely with the World Federation of Democratic Youth, which it assists in running the "World Youth Festivals" and "World Youth Forums" (see *The World Federation of Democratic Youth*). It also regularly supports the activities of the World Council of Peace.

With respect to other international organizations, the IUS enjoyed consultative status with UNESCO from July 1948 until December 1952, when it was relegated to the register (or "Special List"); in June 1962 it was admitted to Category C status, but applications for Category B status have been twice deferred. It has no consultative status with the UN's Economic and Social Council or with any other UN specialized agencies.

PRESS ORGANS

The IUS has published a monthly magazine, *World Student News,* since 1946 and a fortnightly newsheet, *News Service,* since 1950.

CONGRESSES OF THE IUS

1st congress, August 1946, Prague
2d congress, August 1950, Prague
3d congress, August 1953, Warsaw
4th congress, August-September 1956, Prague
5th congress, September 1958, Peking
6th congress, October 1960, Baghdad
7th congress, August 1962, Leningrad
8th congress, November-December 1964, Sofia

BIBLIOGRAPHY

Maanen, Gert van: *The International Student Movement—History and Background,* The Hague, INTERDOC, 1966.
Magnelia, Paul Francis: *The International Union of Students,* Menlo Park, Calif., Peninsula Lithograph Co., 1967. (Doctoral thesis at University of Geneva.)

**MILORAD POPOV**

1. See Frank Griffiths, *Sino-Soviet Conflict at the 7th IUS Congress,* Ottawa, NFCUS, 1962.
2. New China News Agency, August 15, 1963.

# IRAN

Since 1941 communism in Iran has been represented by the Masses Party of Iran (Hezbe Tudeh Iran, known as the Tudeh). Founded in October of that year in the wake of the Soviet-British occupation of Iran, the Tudeh was heir to earlier communist organizations which existed in Iran in the 1920s and 1930s. Its initial founders were Abol Ghassem Assadi, Iraj Eskandari, Morteza Yazdi, Reza Radmanesh, and Reza Rusta. This group was subsequently joined by nineteen other leaders, of whom perhaps the best known were Suleiman Mohsen Eskandari, Abbas Eskandari, Bozorg Alavi, Fereydoun Keshavarz, Nureddin Alamuti, Ardeshir Ovenessian, Khalil Maleki, and Mohammed Bahrami. Of these, Khalil

Maleki broke away from the party in 1948 and proceeded to establish first the Tudeh Socialist League and later (in 1953) a Titoist group called the Third Force.

## HISTORY

It is possible to distinguish four phases in the history of the communist movement in Iran.

*The Baku-Gilan Phase*   Originating among the Iranian workers in Baku under the name of Justice (Adalat), the communist movement spread gradually to Iran toward the end of World War I. Its growth was stimulated by the formation of soviets among the Russian troops in northern Iran in 1917 and 1918. Aided by the Red Army's invasion of Enzeli (Pahlavi), Kuchik Khan's rebellion in Gilan (1917 to 1921) resulted in the proclamation of the Persian Soviet Socialist Republic (the Gilan Republic) on June 4, 1920. Kuchik's cabinet represented a coalition of communists and noncommunists, but ultimate authority rested with an overwhelmingly communist executive committee, among whose members were a Soviet national, Abrahamov, and an Azeri communist, Javad Zadeh, who was to reappear twenty years later in Iran as Jaafar Pishevari. On June 23, 1920, the first congress of the Communist Party of Iran (Hexbe Komunist Iran, HKI) was held in Soviet-occupied Enzeli. The advent of Reza Khan to power in 1921 resulted in the defeat of Kuchik Khan's regime in Gilan and subsequent curbs on communist activity in Iran as a whole. In June 1931 the Iranian parliament (*majlis*) passed a law banning all open or disguised communist organizations

*The Erani Circle*   In the mid-1930s the party was revived by a group of intellectuals (mostly former state scholarship holders in Europe) under the leadership of a physicist, Taghi Erani. The "circle" formed by him was conceived as a Marxist study group, an elite organization. In 1937 fifty-three members of the circle were arrested, and in 1938 they were sentenced to varying prison terms. Erani died in prison.

*World War II*   Following the Soviet-British occupation of Iran in September 1941, the communist movement reappeared as the Tudeh party, an organization avoiding the label "communist" and following, initially, the popular-front tactic with regard to its recruitment. However, its founders and leaders were either former members of the Erani circle (now released from prison) or, in a few cases, veterans of the movement of the 1920s who had returned to Iran with the entry of Soviet troops into the country.

Operating as a legal organization, the Tudeh succeeded in having eight of its candidates seated as deputies in the *majlis* in 1944. In August of that year the party held its first congress in Teheran. Its program called for reforms in a broad nationalist and progressive sense, avoiding all mention of nationalization of the economy or dictatorship of the proletariat. However, the Tudeh did not conceal its advocacy of a close Soviet-Iranian friendship, and in the fall of 1944 it agitated strongly for an oil concession to the Soviet Union. This identification with Soviet interests brought about defections from party ranks.

In September 1945 the Tudeh was replaced in Azerbaijan by a newly established Democratic Party of Iran (Hezbe Demokrate Iran), which broadened its membership to suit local circumstances. On December 12, shielded by the Red Army, the party proclaimed the Autonomous Republic of Azerbaijan. Headed by the veteran fighter Jaafar Pishevari, the rebel government included among its members Salamollah Javid; Mohammed Beria (Biriya), the leader of the street-cleaners' union; and Gholam Danishyan, a Soviet national who had served as political deputy minister of war and commander in chief of the rebel army. In a parallel move Kurdish nationalists, equipped with Soviet arms and uniforms, established their own independent republic at Mahabad with Qazi Mohammed as leader. The two regimes entered into uneasy cooperation with each other under Soviet aegis.

The Azerbaijan revolution materially strengthened the Tudeh influence in Teheran. On August 1, 1946, three portfolios in the

Ghavam Saltaneh cabinet were entrusted to Tudeh leaders Iraj Eskandari, Keshavarz, and Yazdi, while a fellow-traveling aristocrat, Mozaffar Firuz, was appointed minister of labor and propaganda.

Following the inconclusive debates in the U.N. Security Council, the Red Army withdrew from Iran in May 1946, leaving the two autonomous states to their own devices. On December 12 Iranian troops reentered Azerbaijan and put an end to both rebel governments after only a slight resistance. Top leaders of both regimes escaped to the Soviet Union (Pishevari was reported to have died later in an automobile accident in Baku). In a subsequent reshuffle of the Iranian cabinet the Tudeh ministers were deprived of their posts, and communist influence began to wane.

*The National Front* The Tudeh was formally outlawed in February 1949, following an attempt on the life of the shah by a man identified as a Tudeh member. The ensuing government reprisals resulted in the arrest and subsequent escape abroad (in 1950) of nine of its leaders. The party did not reappear in force until the oil crisis of 1951 to 1953. At that time it came out into the open in support of Premier Mohammed Mossadegh's National Front. Its ability to mobilize the masses in the critical days of July 1952 frustrated the shah's attempt to dismiss Mossadegh. The party followed at that time a tactic of united front with any anti-British groups, including the religious followers of Mullah Abol Ghassem Kashani. The proroyalist coup of General Zahedi in August 1953 put an end not only to the Mossadegh regime but also to the growing influence of the Tudeh. The demise of the party was completed with the discovery in 1954 of a communist network in the army (involving 600 officers) which was engaging in espionage for Moscow's benefit. Massive arrests and trials followed.

In the late 1950s Iranian police made occasional discoveries of secret communist printing presses, but in the 1960s there was no evidence of significant party activity inside the country. However, exiled party leaders continued to operate in Europe. Following another attempt on the life of the shah in April 1965, the authorities announced the discovery of an allegedly pro-Chinese group among young engineers graduated from British universities. In August of that year three members of the Tudeh central committee in exile split from its pro-Soviet majority and journeyed to Peking, revealing the existence of a Maoist group of unknown strength within the Iranian communist movement.

The shah's rapprochement with Russia in 1965, exemplified by the Soviet-Iranian steel-plant agreement, posed some serious problems of strategy for the exile Tudeh leadership, who debated privately and in some released statements the effects of such policies on the future of the revolution in Iran.

ORGANIZATION AND MEMBERSHIP

For the first seven years of its existence, until it was outlawed in February 1949, the Tudeh was recognized as a lawful political party. Established initially as an organization encompassing not only communists, but also other leftist and liberal elements, the Tudeh had a fluctuating membership claimed by the party to reach 25,000 in 1944. This claim was based on the attendance of the first party congress in 1944 by 168 delegates, each of whom was said to represent 150 card-carrying members. At all times the Tudeh had an inner core of indoctrinated communists, mostly veterans of pre-World War II days. Because of its clandestine character today, there is no valid basis for estimating its numerical strength. Since 1953 the party has been subjected to close police surveillance, and virtually all its known leaders are presently in exile, mostly in East Germany and other countries of the communist bloc.

During the period of its legal operation in the 1940s the party's leadership consisted of an eleven-man central committee, a nine-man control commission, and a five-man politburo; the first two of these bodies were elected by a congress of party delegates. At the lower echelons the party had provincial and local organizations, with the cell as its basic unit. Party publications during the subsequent clandestine period indicate that this structure, at least in its rudimentary form, has been preserved, inasmuch as references are made to plenum sessions of the central committee (in exile) and to the meetings of the central committee's executive board (probably superseding the earlier politburo). Although the present exile leadership behaves as if it held effective control over the party, conclusive evidence of this control is lacking, and there is a possibility that new and unknown leaders have replaced the old ones in the underground organization in Iran itself. From time to time the Tudeh releases statements reflecting its current stand on national and international issues. Such statements are, as a rule, broadcast by the clandestine radio station Peike Iran, reputedly located in Eastern Europe. Authors of these statements are not identified by name.

The social composition of the Tudeh has varied from phase to phase. Although the inner core of veteran leaders has been predominantly of the intellectual class, during the war there was much recruiting directly among the workers and through the capture of leadership in the labor unions. The ban on the party in 1949 ended its actual or attempted mass character, and the government took strong measures to impose its own control on unions and prevent the communist-dominated World Federation of Trade Unions from establishing a close tie with the Iranian labor movement. On at least two occasions, once in 1945 and again in 1953-1954, the Tudeh tried to penetrate the Iranian officer corps, the second endeavor resulting in substantial recruitment. Since the beginning of the Mossadegh era (1954), considerable emphasis has been placed on party activity among Iranian students, especially the nearly 25,000 studying abroad. Except for a relatively brief period from 1944 to 1946 in the province of Azerbaijan, the party has made no major effort to win over the peasantry, preferring instead to concentrate on the urban and industrial centers of Teheran, Isfahan, Tabriz, Abadan, Pahlavi, Resht, and Meshed.

At the time of intensified party activity (World War II and the oil-crisis period) the Tudeh used some additional organizations as allies or instruments of its policy. During the war and the immediate postwar phase the leadership of the Federation of Iranian Trade Unions was dominated by the Tudeh, while at the peak of the oil crisis, the Association to Fight the Imperialist Oil Monopolies had party ties.

## RELATION TO SOVIET LEADERSHIP

Iran's communist leadership established close links with Moscow in the 1920s, and Kuchik Khan's Gilan government availed itself of political and military Soviet aid. The Iranian delegation was one of the largest at the Baku Congress of the Peoples of the East in September 1920, and the early HKI party was a member of the Comintern. Minutes of the sixth Comintern congress in 1928 indicate active participation of Iranian delegates in the debates on the proposed theses on the revolutionary movement in the colonies and semicolonies. Similarly, strong links existed between the Tudeh (as well as the Azerbaijan democrats) and the Soviet occupation authorities in Iran during and after World War II.

The exile party leadership in the post-Mossadegh era has maintained a close relationship with Moscow, and party delegates attended the congress of eighty-one "fraternal parties" in 1960 as well as the twenty-second and twenty-third Soviet party congresses, at which they affirmed their full loyalty to Moscow in the Sino-Soviet dispute.

## PARTY PRESS ORGANS AND RECORDS

During the Baku period the Iranian Communists published *Bayraghe Adalat* (Banner of Justice) and *Horiyat* (Freedom) in Baku, during the Gilan Republic *Jangal* in Resht, and during the Erani-circle phase *Donya* (The World) in Teheran and *Paykar* (Struggle) in

Berlin. During and after World War II the party published *Siyassat* (Politics), *Rahbar* (The Leader), *Mardom* (The People) and *Razm* (Battle) in Teheran. In the Autonomous Republic of Azerbaijan the party published *Azarbaijan* in Tabriz, and during the postwar period *Mardon* and *Besooyeh Ayandeh* (Toward the Future) in Teheran and *Donya* and *Masaele Hezbi* (Party Issues), probably in East Germany.

The latest texts in Persian under the title "Draft Party Program and Statute Adopted by Seventh Plenum and Unity Conference" (held August 19-29, 1960) appear in *Nashriyeh Hezbi* (Party Publication), September-October 1960. For the English text see Sepehr Zabih, *The Communist Movement in Iran*, Berkeley, Calif., University of California Press, 1966.

## PARTY CONGRESSES

1st congress, HKI, 1920, Enzeli
2d congress, HKI, 1927, Urumia
1st congress, Tudeh, August, 1944, Teheran
2d congress, Tudeh, April 1948, Teheran

## BIBLIOGRAPHY

Alavi, Bozorg: *Kämpfendes Iran*, Berlin, Dietz Verlag, 1955.

Eagleton, William, Jr.: *The Kurdish Republic of 1946*, New York, Oxford University Press, 1963.

Fatemi, Nasrollah Saifpour: *Diplomatic History of Persia, 1917-1923*, New York, Moore, 1952.

Geyer, Dietrich: *Die Sowjetunion und Iran*, Tübingen, Böhlau-Verlag, 1955.

Lenczowski, George: *Russia and the West in Iran, 1918-1948*, Ithaca, N.Y., Cornell University Press, 1949 (supplement 1954).

Pesyan, Najafgholi: *Marg Bud Bazgasht Ham Bud* (There Were Both Death and Retreat), Teheran, 1947.

U.S. House Committee on Foreign Affairs (Subcommittee 5), *Communism in the Near East*, 80th Cong., 1st sess., Washington, 1948.

Zabih, Sepehr: *The Communist Movement in Iran*, Berkeley, Calif., University of California Press, 1966.

GEORGE LENCZOWSKI

# IRAQ

The Communist Party of Iraq (al-Hizb al-Shuyu'i al-'Iraqi, CPI) regards March 1934 as the date of its founding.[1] At that time members of Marxist circles which had been functioning in Iraq for a few years came together to form a Committee to Combat Imperialism and Exploitation, which changed its name in 1935 to Communist Party of Iraq. Among the early communists who figured prominently in the history of the movement in Iraq were Yusuf Salman Yusuf, Zaki Khairi Sa'id, Daud al-Sayigh, and 'Abd al-Qadir Isma'il al-Bustani. The first three were of Christian extraction (Christians are a very small minority in Iraq). Yusuf Salman, better known by his sobriquet of Fahd (the Leopard), became the first secretary general of the party. 'Abd al-Qadir Isma'il was the communist link with a group of socialist politicians known as the People (al-Ahali). The other two, Zaki Khairi and Daud al-Sayigh, were to move to the center of the stage in later years. Soon after founding the party the communists split into tiny factions which remained at odds with each other for years.

## HISTORY

In October 1936 General Bakr Sidqi seized control of the government by a coup. Although he was initially supported by the Ahali group, in March 1937 Sidqi publicly attacked communism, and shortly thereafter the Ahali members of the government resigned. 'Abd al-Qadir Isma'il was sent into exile but kept in touch with the Iraqi communist cells from Damascus, where he later settled.

The most active communist leader inside Iraq was Fahd, who published a clandestine paper called *al-Shararah* (The Spark), and later one called *al-Qa'idah* (The Base). Various factions refused to recognize Fahd's authority, and his chief opponent, Daud al-Sayigh, was read out of the party. In 1944 Fahd formed the CPI's first central committee, said to include two Jews, a Shiite, and a Sabian. In 1945 he drafted the party's national charter, which called for fostering communist groups among the Kurds and other ethnic minorities.

In 1945 Jewish communists in Iraq established an Anti-Zionist League, and in January 1947 *al-Qa'idah* described the United Nations scheme for the partition of Palestine as "an old imperialist proposal."[2] In May, however, Gromyko announced the Soviet Union's support for partition.

The Soviet Union's participation in World War II on the side of Great Britain created an opportunity for accelerated communist growth in Iraq. During the years immediately after the war, however, the government embarked on vigorous anticommunist measures which culminated in the hanging of Fahd and three other party leaders in February 1949. Even in disarray, the communists continued bickering among themselves, and in 1953 the majority drove out a group called Banner of the Workers (Rayat al-Shaghghilah).

In 1957 the opposition parties in Iraq, including the communists, formed an underground united front. This front supported the revolution of July 1958 carried out by General 'Abd al-Karim Qasim and other army officers, although the communist claim that "the working class and the peasants, led by the Communist Party, played the cardinal role"[3] was an exaggeration.

As master of Iraq, Qasim strengthened his position by playing the different interest groups against each other, making particularly wide use of the communists during the first year of his rule. He appointed Ibrahim Kubbah, generally believed to be a communist, as minister of economic affairs. Communists secured other important posts in the government, and by the end of 1958 they had acquired great influence in organizations representing teachers, students, journalists, women, peasants, and other segments of society. Communists or fellow travelers appear to have dominated the Popular Resistance Forces and the Partisans of Peace.

The principal opponents of communism were the Arab nationalists, many of whom wanted Iraq to be closely associated with Egypt and Syria, which had established the United Arab Republic early in 1958 and had outlawed the communist party. The commander of the Mosul garrison in northern Iraq, leading a group of nationalists alarmed at what they regarded as the unchecked growth of communist power, rose against Qasim in March 1959. The help of the communists in suppressing this uprising fortified their position and weakened that of the Arab nationalists.

In July 1959, on the first anniversary of Qasim's revolution, the communists finally overplayed their hand. In the northern town of Kirkuk they joined a Kurdish mob in slaughtering a number of people of the Turcoman ethnic minority. The popular revulsion engendered by this incident cost the party most of its prestige, and from this time on communist strength in the government and in the country at large declined.

In January 1960 Qasim issued a law for the legalization of political parties. Two communist applications were received, one from Zaki Khairi, who had the support of the great majority of the party, and the other from Daud al-Sayigh, who headed a small splinter group. Qasim rejected Khairi's application and approved al-Sayigh's group as the official Communist Party of Iraq.[4] Reports circulated that Qasim had even gone so far as to help al-Sayigh build up his fragile organization and publish his paper *al-Mabda* (The Principle). Khairi's unofficial majority had to content itself with the name Party of People's Unity (Hizb Ittihad al-Sha'b, PPU), borrowed from its newspaper (by then under the editorship of 'Abd al-Qadir Isma'il, who had returned from his long exile in Damascus).

Another party legalized in Iraq at this time was the Democratic Party of Kurdistan (al-Hizb al-Dimuqrati fi Kurdistan), which had been formed five years earlier by Mulla Mustafa al-Barzani, who had cooperated with the Soviets in establishing the evanescent Kurdish Republic of Mahabad on Iranian territory in December 1945 and had afterward sought refuge in the Soviet Union. The new party program drafted in 1960 advocated "friendship and brotherhood" with the communists, but al-Barzani and his followers were more concerned with furthering Kurdish nationalism than with Marxism. Iraqi communists in general had favored greater autonomy for the Kurds within the framework of the republic, but had condemned their excessive nationalist zeal, and al-Barzani's party held by far the stronger position in the competition for the loyalty of the Kurds.

Early in 1961, for the first time, Khairi's illegal PPU came out openly against Qasim, and before the year was out Qasim proceeded by a series of maneuvers to undermine the PPU's control or influence in almost all the organizations in which it had a foothold. The difficulties of the illegal party were increased by internal feuds. Husain Radwi (or Radawi), better known as Salam 'Adil, the leader of the pro-Soviet element, attended the twenty-second congress of the Soviet party in October 1961 as "first secretary of the Communist Party of Iraq." Throughout his regime Qasim continued to work with al-Sayigh's authorized party.

In February 1963 Qasim was overthrown in a coup by army officers and leaders of the Arab Socialist Renaissance Party (Hizb al-Ba'th al-'Arabi al-Ishtiraki, known as the Ba'th), which had been founded in Syria and had spread to the neighboring Arab countries. The chief opposition to this change of government came from the communists, but more out of hostility toward the Ba'th than out of any love for Qasim.[5] In retaliation the new government launched what the communists called the Ba'thist "reign of terror." Salam 'Adil and several other members of the politburo were executed, along with a number of lower-ranking party members.

Another coup in November 1963 gave the military, under Colonel 'Abd al-Salam 'Arif, the upper hand in the government, but the communists continued to complain of harsh treatment throughout 1965. In 1964 the illegal Iraqi party, which had again become the CPI, was represented by Anwar Mustafa and 'Aziz al-Hajj at a meeting in Prague of Marxist theoreticians from various Arab countries. Late that year the party central committee held its first enlarged meeting since the coup of February 1963. The meeting condemned the "factional activities" of the Chinese Communist Party and elected central executive bodies, although no names were published.[6]

The goal of the CPI, as stated in 1964, was to unite all the forces opposed to imperialism —communists, democrats, and Arab and Kurd patriots—to bring about a noncapitalist society as the first stage on the way to true socialism. The party was ready to cooperate with the Arab Socialist Union (al-Ittihad al-'Arabi al-Ishtiraki), the only political organization allowed by the government, on condition that the union abandon its anticommunist conduct. In particular, the CPI supported the demands of the Kurds under al-Barzani, who had been engaged in almost continuous armed conflict with the government since 1961.

PARTY PRESS ORGANS

The party's first national newspaper was *Kifah al-Sha'b* (People's Struggle). The unauthorized PPU published a daily *Ittihad al-Sha'b* (People's Unity).

## BIBLIOGRAPHY

'Abd al-Nasir, Jamal: *Nahnu wal-'Iraq wal-Shuyu 'iyah* (We and Iraq and Communism), Beirut, n.d.

Anonymous: *al-'Iraq wa-A'da al-Wahdah* (Iraq and the Enemies of Unity), Lebanon, 1959.

al-Husri, Khaldun S.: *Haqiqat al-Shuyu'iyin fi al-'Iraq* (The Truth about the Communists in Iraq), n.p., n.d.

al-Jundi, In'am: *Ila Ain Yasir al-Shuyu'iyin bil-'Iraq?* (Where Will the Communists Take Iraq?), Beirut, 1959.

Dann, Uri'el: *Iraq under Qassem: A Political History, 1958-1963*, Jerusalem, 1969.

Khadduri, Majid: *Independent Iraq 1934-1958*, 2d ed., London, 1960.

Khadduri, Majid: *Republican Iraq*, London, 1969.

Laqueur, Walter Z.: *Communism and Nationalism in the Middle East*, 3d ed., London, 1961.

Longrigg, Stephen H.: *'Iraq, 1900 to 1950*, London, 1953.

Longrigg, Stephen H., and Frank Stoakes: *Iraq*, London, 1958.

Rossi, Pierre: *L'Irak des révoltes*, Paris, 1962.

Vernier, Bernard: *L'Irak d'aujourd'hui*, Paris, 1962.

GEORGE RENTZ

1. For earlier trends toward communism in Iraq see the informative chapter by John Batatu in Jaan Pennar (ed.), *Islam and Communism*, New York, 1960.

2. Quoted in Khaldun S. al-Husri, *Haqiqat al-Shuyu-'iyin fi al-'Iraq*, p. 44.

3. M. Salim, in *World Marxist Review* (Prague), vol. 4, no. 10, October 1961, p. 35.

4. Described by M. Salim as "a dummy party consisting of police agents and shady adventurers" in *World Marxist Review* (Prague), vol. 4, no. 10, October 1961, p. 35.

5. A Soviet writer, P. Gevorkyan, called the Ba'th "an extremely reactionary national-chauvinist fascist-type organisation." *International Affairs* (Moscow), vol. 10, no. 1, January 1964, p. 77.

6. *World Marxist Review* (Toronto), vol. 7, no. 11, November 1964, pp. 85-87.

# IRELAND

The Dublin uprising of 1916 marked the beginning of a militant Irish nationalism which, through political action and armed struggle, achieved its aim in 1949: complete separation from England and the establishment of an independent Irish Free State. However, the creation of an Irish Republic after the civil war of 1918-1920 left a part of Northern Ireland (Ulster) in England. Since then the common demand of all political parties in the Irish Republic has been unification of this northern part with the republic. This demand has not been echoed by all Irish political groups in the north; the Irish communists, however, have consistently supported the demand for unification. This stand is designed to place them in a favorable position in the Irish Republic and appeal to nationalist sentiment in Ulster while working toward the traditional communist goal of weakening "capitalist" Great Britain.

## HISTORY

There is no doubt that some militants who fought in the Irish rebellion sympathized with bolshevik slogans. There is adequate proof that this sporadic sympathy was noticed and reciprocated by the Soviet leadership. The Comintern, founded in 1919, was particularly eager to infiltrate the Irish revolutionary organizations. Despite its efforts, however, none of the more prominent Irish revolutionary leaders succumbed to communism. Although the Irish communists proclaimed James Connolly, who had had some communist affiliations in the United States, as their hero and martyr, there is no convincing evidence that Connolly was in fact anything other than an ardent nationalist who had on various occasions preached a hodgepodge of social democratic, Marxist, and reactionary nationalist platitudes. The Irish rebellion is thus a unique example of a revolution in which radical socialist, anarchist, and communist elements were unable to spread their influence.

After great efforts to promote communism in Ireland, Moscow's only achievement was the creation of a few workers' revolutionary groups in Dublin and Belfast, the respective capitals of the Irish Republic and Ulster, and in a few industrial centers. These were local units operating underground, and in the general atmosphere of nationalist secrecy their leaders were able to avoid disclosing their communist character even to members of these groups.

The initiative for the creation of the Communist Party of Ireland (CPI) came directly from Moscow. During the twelfth plenum of the Comintern Executive Committee, held in Moscow on August 27-September 15, 1932, a participant known as Troy presented a report entitled "For a Communist Party of Ireland,"[1] deploring the Cosgrave government's banning of the revolutionary workers' groups, "the future Communist Party of Ireland." Following the plenum's political line that the period of stabilization in the capitalist countries had ended and that an approaching economic crisis would create a new revolutionary situation, Troy insisted that the time had come to create a communist party in Ireland. On June 3-4, 1933, an "inaugural congress" of the CPI issued a verbose manifesto accusing the Irish "capitalist class" of opposing the creation of a unified and truly independent Ireland and claiming that only the Irish working class, backed by the farmers, could carry the national struggle to victory. Finally, it demanded the creation of an Irish workers' and farmers' republic modeled after the Soviet Union.

The CPI operated simultaneously in the southern part of Ireland, at that time semi-independent, and in the northern area tied to England. The party's unity in this respect was meant to underscore its demand for unification of both areas. Despite this simulated nationalism and the care the party took to obscure its ideological adherence to atheism, the CPI was never able to recruit a membership of even 500. The Catholic beliefs and nationalist sentiments of the Irish masses were and still are a strong obstacle to the spread of communism. With such a small membership the party was unable to exert any influence on Irish politics or on local trade unions. Communist claims of influence in the clandestine Irish Republican Army are difficult to substantiate because of the deep secrecy in which this army operated.

In 1940 the government disbanded the CPI in the southern Irish Free State. It continued to operate in Ulster as the Communist Party of Northern Ireland (CPNI), and after the nazi attack on the Soviet Union developed some broad activities in support of British-Soviet friendship. However, the CPNI encountered strong opposition from local organizations of the British Labour Party. Between 1941 and 1945 the communists made great efforts to affiliate with the British Labour Party but met with consistent refusal. During these years the party claimed a great increase in membership, but the only figures presented were that this "increase" amounted to "more than 800 percent" and that the number of branches "had grown to thirty-five."[2]

Next the CPNI joined in the movement to unify the Irish trade unions in Ulster. Unification was accomplished in 1952, but the communists were unable to gain influence in the new organizations. At its eleventh convention in May 1962 the party adopted a new program[3] which, continuing the demand for unification, advocated formation of a progressive Irish government supported by the workers, small farmers, small businessmen, and intellectuals, to assure peaceful coexistence among all nations and socialism for Ireland.

The CPNI was represented at the international communist meetings in Moscow in 1957 and 1960 and approved Moscow's line in the Sino-Soviet conflict.

In 1948, at the time of the final struggle for the separation of the Irish Free State from England, the communists in the south were able to rebuild their organization in the guise of the Irish Workers' League (IWL). In May 1949 the IWL issued an appeal to Irish workers for support in establishing socialism in Ireland. In proposing diplomatic relations with the communist countries and propagating the Soviet slogan of peaceful coexistence, the IWL revealed its communist orientation, and attendance of its representatives at the Moscow meetings of the communist parties in 1957 and 1960 made this official. In March 1962, at the party's fourth conference, it changed its name to Irish Workers' Party (IWP).

## ORGANIZATION AND MEMBERSHIP

In 1965 Andrew Barr was chairman of the executive committee of the CPNI and Hugh Moore was secretary. The IWP was led by Michael O'Ricrdan, secretary of the executive committee. The parties cooperate closely and have a joint coordinating council. The estimated membership of the CPNI in 1965 was 350. The strength of the IWP in the Irish Free State is best indicated by the votes cast for its single candidate in the elections of October 1961 and April 1965: 277 and 183, respectively, or 0.02 and 0.01 percent of the total vote.

## PARTY PRESS ORGANS

The CPNI issues the weekly bulletin *Unity*, and the IWP and CPNI jointly publish the monthly *The Irish Socialist*.

## BIBLIOGRAPHY

*Ireland's Path to Freedom: Manifesto of the Communist Party of Ireland*, introduction by Sean Murray, New York, Workers' Library, 1934.

*Ireland's Path to Socialism*, Belfast, 1963.

MacEoin, Sean P.: *Communism and Ireland*, Cork, Mercier, 1948.

McInerney, M.: *Northern Labour and the Communist Party*, Belfast, CPNI [1943].

*The Next Step in Britain, America and Ireland*, speeches and reports by Gusev, Pollitt, Troy, and Pringle, New York, Workers' Library [1932].

WITOLD S. SWORAKOWSKI

1. "The Next Step in Britian, America and Ireland," *Speeches and Reports: XII Plenum E.C.C.I.*, New York, 1932, pp. 80-[88].

2. M. McInerney, *Northern Labour and the Communist Party*, Belfast [1943], p. [2].

3. *Ireland's Path to Socialism*, Belfast, 1963.

# ISRAEL

In March 1919 the left wing of the Workers of Zion (Pō'alei Zion) organized separate meetings in Palestine. A splinter party was officially founded in September 1920 as the Socialist Workers' Party (Mifleget Pō'alim Sōṣiyalisṭit, MPS). Prominent among its founding members was J. Meyersohn, a Jewish teacher who emigrated in 1920 to the Soviet Union, as did other founders. Some, such as G. Dua and W. Awerbuch, later became active in the Comintern; many were executed in the purges of the 1930s.

After 1921 communist activity reverted back to the Workers of Zion, where leftist groups debated the merits of communism versus zionism. In 1922 one of these groups organized as the Palestinian Communist Party (Palestinische Kommunistische Partei, PKP) and survived splits and purges to become, in October 1948, the Israeli Communist Party (Miflaga Qōmūnistit Isrĕ'elit, known as Maqı).

## HISTORY

The MPS, founded in 1919, disintegrated in 1921 after its May Day demonstrations clashed with those organized by rival Jewish workers, and British authorities subsequently jailed or exiled MPS leaders. The PKP, organized the following year by other leaders, had to contend with a radically antizionist splinter group, the Communist Party of Palestine (Kommunistische Partei fun Palestine). The PKP's strongly antizionist stand provoked repeated purges and brought about the expulsion in 1924 of the Fraction, the front organization of the outlawed MPS, from the General Federation of Labor (ha-Histadrūt ha-Klalīt shel ha-'Ōvdīm ha-'Ivrīm bĕ-Eretz Israel); the Fraction was readmitted only twenty years later.

After the fifth PKP congress in July 1924 efforts at "Arabization" were accelerated, on the orders of Karl Radek (Sobelsohn) of the Comintern. Fear of censure from the Comintern for failure to recruit Arabs further increased antizionist fervor, and zionism was condemned utopian at best and in the interests of British imperialism at worst. Arabization of the PKP was effected by ousting the Jewish leaders, replacing the Yiddish monthly with an Arabic one, and collaborating with certain Arab nationalist groups. This collaboration caused splits in the PKP, particularly in 1929 and 1936, when Arab-Jewish differences erupted in widescale riots.

By 1938 the PKP had become isolated from the main currents of both Jewish and Arab politics in Palestine. It was initially jolted by the Ribbentrop-Molotov agreement but eventually supported it, attacking everyone assisting the British war effort, chiefly the zionists, and praising the Arab states for not breaking relations with Nazi Germany. This led to further cleavages, and from 1939 to 1948 the party worked as two groups, Jewish and Arab. The rift was not bridged even in 1941, after the PKP's about-face following nazi aggression against the Soviet Union and the ensuing legalization of the PKP in Palestine. In 1943 the Arab communists formed an All-Arab League for National Liberation (a title exploiting the Comintern's dissolution). The Arab communists were shocked by the Soviet Union's support for a Jewish state in 1947 and 1948 and split over the issue (nationalists versus supporters of the Soviet line). Jewish communists also split: a small group of "Hebrew communists," mainly students, were considered "Titoist" and were expelled by the old leadership, who controlled the bureaucracy and remained faithful to the Moscow line.

With the establishment of the State of Israel in 1948, the PKP renamed itself the Israeli Communist Party (Maqī). It has operated legally and openly since then but has been hampered by the fact that it is a nonzionist party in a zionist state. It has never entered any coalition cabinet. Maqī's main failure, however, is reflected in its dwindling popularity among Israeli Jews. At first it benefited from Soviet support for the establishment of Israel and from economic dissatisfaction among some new immigrants. However, its lone opposition stand in the 1956 Sinai campaign and the subsequent relative affluence in Israel—including full employment—limited its success in promoting strikes and arousing discontent. Consequently, Maqī has concentrated on seeking support among the Arab minority; its policies and propaganda are noticeably tuned to Arab consumption.

However, in the summer of 1965 another split occurred over the attitude toward zionism, and most of the Arab members left Maqī to form a new party, the New Communist List[1] (Rĕshīma Qōmūnīstīt Ḥadasha, known as Raqah). This rival party has had remarkable success in winning Arab support from Maqī.

## ORGANIZATION AND MEMBERSHIP

The present organization of Maqī appears to resemble the pyramidal pattern in noncommunist states. The fourteenth party congress in 1961[2] reported a membership of 74.3 percent Jews and 25.7 percent Arabs, a considerably higher Arab proportion than in other Israeli parties. Of the total, 83.8 percent had joined since 1948 and 27 percent had joined since 1957, an indication of rapid turnover. Salaried workers and employees comprised 72.9 percent, self-employed (presumably white-collar workers) 20 percent and housewives 7.1 percent. Only 3.2 percent were illiterate. Actual membership statistics are kept secret, despite the fact that Maqī and Raqah are legal and overtly active in Israel. Soviet publications give Maqī membership as "about 30,000,"[3] but this figure has never been verified.

Intellectuals hold leading positions in the Israeli communist movement; Maqī is led by S. Mīqūnīs, an engineer, and M. Sneh, a physician, both Jews; Raqah's leaders include three Arab journalists, E. Tōmā, E. Ḥabībī, and T. Ṭūbī, and a Jewish University graduate, M. Vilner. Although student support for the communists is weak, the youth organization, the Alliance of Communist Youth (Bĕrīth Nō'ar Qōmūnīstī), is important as a source of cadres.

Although communist potential in the overall political arena and trade-union organizations is peripheral, the party has succeeded in enlisting some support from nonaffiliated voters in parliamentary and, to a lesser extent, local elections. In parliamentary elections communists have polled 2.8 to 4.5 percent of the total valid votes and have taken three to six seats in the 120-member parliament (knesset). A special feature has been the electoral support—largely a protest vote—of the Arab minority. Although Arabs constitute a scant one-ninth of the population, Maqī received about one-third of their vote in 1959 and about one-half in 1961. In 1965 Maqī received 13,617 votes (1.1 percent) and one parliament seat and Raqah 27,413 votes (2.3 percent) and three seats.[4] Of these, the Arab communist vote was about two-thirds of the total. This support is also reflected in the 1965 vote for the largest Arab municipality, Nazareth, where the all-Arab vote elected an unprecedented seven municipal councilors out of fifteen.

During the early period of the Palestinian mandate the outlawed MPS often operated through a front organization, the Fraction, in the trade-union elections. During World War II, the main MPS front organization was the V (Victory) League, a body formed to mobilize aid for the Soviet war effort against Germany. There are also various friendship societies with the Soviet Union and other communsit countries, but their impact is very limited, and they have no political influence.

## RELATION TO SOVIET LEADERSHIP

Moscow recognized the PKP as a member party of the Comintern in 1924, and later the party sent students to the Comintern school. However, in 1937 relations with the Comintern were practically severed. Nevertheless, loyalty to Moscow has been a keystone of party policy, and Maqī has adopted all Moscow's decisions, from earliest days to the Vietnam issue. In 1963 a tiny pro-Chinese faction published a few issues of a journal in Mao's favor and was ousted. Maqī vies with Raqaḥ for recognition by Moscow (which has urged them to reunite); however, its attempts to label Raqaḥ as pro-Chinese have failed.

## PARTY PRESS ORGANS AND RECORDS

The main organ of Maqī is the Hebrew daily *Qōl ha-'Am* (Voice of the People) and the newly founded Arabic fortnightly *Ṣawt al-Shaʻb* (Voice of the People). Raqaḥ publishes the Arabic biweekly *al-Ittiḥād* (Union) and the Hebrew weekly *Zō ha-Derekh* (This Is the Way). Maqī-sponsored communist weeklies appear in Yiddish, French, Hungarian, Rumanian, and Bulgarian, and a monthly appears in Polish; all these are aimed at new immigrants. A number of other periodicals appear in Arabic.

The statutes of Maqı, as emended in the fourteenth congress in 1961, are published in the Hebrew report of that congress (pp. 274-284); they are omitted from the Russian translation. They are still valid for Maqī. Raqaḥ is not known to have published its own statutes. Maqī's present program was approved at the fifteenth congress in 1965 and published in Hebrew in *Ha-Vĕʻīda ha-Ḥamesh-ʻesreh* (The Fifteenth Congress), Tel Aviv, 1965 (pp. 173-176). Before the November 1965 elections Maqī and Raqaḥ published their respective platforms in special booklets in Hebrew and Arabic; these were reprinted in their respective organs.

There is no access to Maqī's archives. Decisions of its central committee appear in the party organs in Hebrew or Arabic and in *Information Bulletin, Documents of the Communist and Workers' Parties, Articles and Speeches*, published in Prague. Some statements of communist leaders in Palestine and Israel have been issued as booklets in Hebrew, Yiddish, and Arabic. The main official records, however, are the reports of the party congresses, generally published in Hebrew.

## PARTY CONGRESSES

1st congress, MPS, 1920
2d congress, MPS, 1921
3d congress, PKP, 1922
4th congress, PKP, 1922
5th congress, PKP, July 1924
6th congress, PKP, 1926
7th congress, PKP, 1930
8th congress, PKP, 1944
9th congress, PKP, 1945
10 congress, PKP, 1946
11th congress, Maqı, October 1949, Tel Aviv-Jaffa
12th congress, Maqī, May 1952, Tel Aviv-Jaffa
13th congress, Maqī, May 1957, Tel Aviv-Jaffa
14th congress, Maqī, May-June 1961, Tel Aviv-Jaffa
15th congress, Maqī, August 1965, Tel Aviv-Jaffa

The fifteenth congress, originally scheduled for June 1965, finally collapsed altogether because of the Maqī-Raqaḥ rivalry.

## BIBLIOGRAPHY

Czudnowski, Moshe M., and Jacob M. Landau: *The Israeli Communist Party and the Elections to the Fifth Knesset*, 1961, Stanford, Calif., Hoover Institution, 1965.

Johnston, Scott D.: "Communist Party Politics in Israel," in R. K. Sakai (ed.), *Studies on Asia, 1964*, Lincoln, Neb., University of Nebraska Press, 1964, pp. 105-120.

Landau, Jacob M.: *The Arabs in Israel: A Political Study*, London, Oxford University Press, 1969.

Laqueur, Walter Z.: *Communism and Nationalism in the Middle East*, 3d ed., London, Routledge & Kegan Paul [1961]; previously published under the pseudonym G. Z. Isrĕ'elī in Tel Aviv, probably in 1953.

Lisst, Nahman: "Ṣadaq ha-Qōmīnṭern" (The

Comintern Was Right), series of memoirs in *Qeshet* (The Bow) (Tel Aviv): vol. 5, nos. 2, 4, 1963; vol 6, nos. 2,4, 1964; vol. 7, no. 3, 1965; vol. 8, no. 2, 1966.

JACOB M. LANDAU

1. The split occurred before the November parliamentary elections, and the group adopted the designation "list" because it wanted to appear in a separate list from Maqī.

2. *Ha-Vĕ'īda ha-Arba'-'esreh*, Tel Aviv, 1961, esp. pp. 110-117. This report has been partially translated into Russian as *XIV sezd Kommunisticheskoi-partii Izrailia*, Moscow, 1962.

3. *Bolshaia sovetskaia entsiklopediia: Ezhegodnik 1965*, Moscow, 1965, p. 253.

4. Official results in *Yalqūṭ ha-Pirsūmīm,* no. 1230, November 12, 1965, pp. 311-313.

# ITALY

The Italian Communist Party (Partito Comunista Italiano, PCI) was founded on January 21, 1921, when it seceded from the strife-torn Italian Socialist Party (Partito Socialista Italiano, PSI) at the PSI's seventeenth congress, at Leghorn. The parent organization, which dated from the Genoa congress of 1892, had adopted a contradictory program that led to vacillation between "minimalists," who stressed priority of short-term democratic reform, and left-wing "maximalists," who insisted on long-term goals of revolutionary social change. The years after World War I brought a resurgence of Italian Marxism, because of economic dislocation and the attraction of Lenin's revolution in Russia. In the early fall of 1920 a delegation of Italian maximalists returned from Moscow with the disconcerting announcement that if the PSI wished to gain entry into the Comintern it must rid itself of all "revisionists" and accept unequivocally Lenin's Twenty-one Conditions for Admission. Coming in the wake of abortive sit-down strikes in the metallurgical plants, this news precipitated a crisis within the PSI during which party leaders first approved and then hastily rejected the Twenty-one Conditions. "Revisionists" such as Filippo Turati and Claudio Treves, backed by Bruno Buozzi of the Italian General Confederation of Labor (Confederazione General Italiana del Lavoro), resisted Moscow's blandishments. The largest faction within the PSI, a center group dominated by Pietro Nenni, sought to maintain party unity by paying lip service to both social democratic and maximalist slogans. The PSI's extreme leftist group, who favored acceptance of the Twenty-one Conditions, led the secession at Leghorn.

The first secretary of the PCI was the Neapolitan Amadeo Bordiga, editor of *Il Soviet*. Opposed to collaboration with the socialists, Bordiga also recommended communist abstention from parliamentary struggles and urged instead that power be seized through revolutionary action by the labor unions. Other early PCI leaders included Antonio Graziadei; Giuseppe Tuntar, editor of the Trieste *Lavoratore*; and the Romagnole Nicola Bombacci, who was to become a fascist and Il Duce's partner in death on the shore of Lake Como in 1945.

These extremists were displaced from PCI leadership during the next few years by a cluster of intellectuals headed by Antonio

Gramsci, Palmiro Togliatti, Umberto Terracini, and Angelo Tasca, who founded an influential weekly newspaper *Ordine nuovo* in Turin in May 1919. Impressed by Lenin's use of soviets, Gramsci saw the possibility of making similar use of the new shop committees (*consigli di fabbrica*) emerging in Turin's Fiat plants. The *Ordine nuovo* group took an active part in the backstage maneuvers that accompanied the birth of the PCI in January 1921.

## HISTORY

During the year or so after the PCI's advent Gramsci's *Ordine Nuovo* group won the favor of Grigorii Zinoviev and Nikolai Bukharin in the Comintern. Friendships that Gramsci shrewdly cultivated during eighteen months spent in Moscow after June 1922 served him well in his fight to oust Bordiga from PCI leadership.

While that intraparty contest was shaping up, Mussolini's fascists marched to power in October 1922. Interested chiefly in bringing about the revolutionary overthrow of the "capitalist regime," the PCI at first professed to see very little difference between the blackshirts and the rest of the bourgeoisie. Consequently, it made no serious effort to defend the beleaguered liberal government, despite occasional propagandistic talk about a "united front" with the socialists. In March 1923 at least 2,000 communists were arrested, including such leaders as Bordiga and Ruggiero Grieco, but most were acquitted before the end of the year. Reeling from fascist blows, the PCI lost two-thirds of its members that year; yet in April 1924 it won nineteen seats in the parliament. During the political crisis precipitated by the fascists' assassination in June 1924 of the reformist socialist leader Giacomo Matteotti, the PCI temporarily joined the Aventine secession from parliament but quickly decided to return to its seats and urge action on the barricades.

A major turning point was reached at the third party congress, held in Lyon in January 1926, when the PCI voted overwhelmingly to expel Bordiga from the central committee and to recognize Gramsci as undisputed master. The Lyon theses called on the party to support "piecemeal actions" for improving working conditions, emphasize the "unity" of the working class, stress the fight for "freedom," advocate land for the peasants, and work for the goal of a republican assembly representing committees of workers and peasants.

When Mussolini's "exceptional decrees" clamped down the dictatorship in November 1926, the PCI, which had already adopted a cell-type of organization, went under deep cover. Even so, it suffered heavily. Police arrested Gramsci, Terracini, and other top figures, along with hundreds of the rank and file. Only a handful of leaders escaped, the most noted being Togliatti, who was then on a mission to Moscow. In May 1928 the court handed down sentences of more than twenty years' imprisonment for the party leaders. While he was in prison Gramsci managed to keep notebooks that were to be published after the liberation.[1] Togliatti, who had been *de facto* head of the PCI since Gramsci's arrest, became undisputed chief when Gramsci died on April 27, 1937.

In 1928 Togliatti had defined fascism as an integral phase of capitalist development, "a reactionary movement of the large industrial and agrarian bourgeoisie."[2] During the next six years, in accordance with the instructions of the sixth Comintern congress, the PCI refrained from participating with émigré socialists and others in the Anti-Fascist Concentration organized in Paris. The PCI was being directed from its "foreign center" in Paris, but much of the time it also maintained a covert "internal center" in Milan and occasionally sparked short-lived strikes. Reflecting the increasingly rigid Comintern discipline, in 1929 the PCI expelled the "rightist" Angelo Tasca, and in 1930 it purged "The Three" (Pietro Tresso, Alfonso Leonetti, and Paolo Ravazzoli) for daring to doubt the imminence of a revolutionary situation in Italy. The following summer Ignazio Silone was ousted, and in

1932 others met the same fate. When fascist police crushed the covert internal groups in April 1934, virtually every aspect of communist activity within Italy came to a halt.

A new era began with the announcement in Paris on August 17, 1934, of a "unity-of-action" pact between the PCI and Nenni's PSI. In 1935 the seventh Comintern congress approved this policy and called for an even broader popular front. The Italian version of this was the Italian Popular Union (Unione Popolare Italiana). Formed in March 1937, the Popular Union attracted some 45,000 members in France during the years of the Spanish civil war. In this period it became the strongest émigré Italian antifascist force, outstripping such rival groups as Carlo Rosselli's Justice and Liberty (Giustizia e Liberta). Togliatti represented the Comintern in Spain during much of the Spanish civil war, while Luigi Longo, Giuseppe DiVittorio, and other leaders held key posts in the international brigades. The sudden announcement of the Hitler-Stalin pact of August 23, 1939, caused vast disillusionment among Italian socialists and communists, terminating their Moscow-inspired unity-of-action agreement. Among those who left the party at this point were Romano Cocchi, secretary general of the Popular Union, and Leo Valiani.

When France entered the war in September 1939 many of the antiwar PCI leaders residing in France were arrested. The party had to transfer most of its headquarters to Moscow, where Togliatti arrived in April 1940 and stayed until the spring of 1944. New York became the new center for most PCI publications. After Italy entered the war in June 1940 many of the imprisoned communists (for example, Longo and DiVittorio) were transferred from France to Italian jails, where they remained until the overthrow of Mussolini's regime. Soon after Germany attacked the Soviet Union the PCI joined with the PSI and Rosselli's group in Toulouse in a pact calling for a new "union of the Italian people" (October 1941). Meanwhile, the PCI renewed its activities in Italy and sought to give a political complexion to major strikes in northern industrial cities in March 1943. After Allied forces liberated North Africa, rival conspiracies against Mussolini were fomented by the Italian crown, the army, and dissident fascists; the PCI chose to work with the crown.

When Mussolini was seized on July 25, 1943, the PCI quickly began to reconstruct its party organization and the Italian General Confederation of Labor. When the Germans seized control of northern Italy on September 8, the PCI gave priority to mobilizing armed resistance under the aegis of committees of national liberation. Communist forces, led by Longo and Pietro Secchia, were the largest single contingent in the resistance that lasted until Italy's liberation by Allied forces in April 1945.

Meanwhile, in Allied-held southern Italy, Togliatti had returned from Moscow in April 1944 and had shocked republican-oriented antifascists by ordering the PCI to participate in the hard-pressed government of King Victor Emmanuel III and Marshal Pietro Badoglio. In June, after the liberation of Rome, he switched his support from Badoglio to Ivanoe Bonomi and made it clear that the PCI favored a constituent assembly to decide the monarchical question after the war.

Fully aware of Allied military power, the communists did not try to seize power in Italy in 1945, but instead concentrated on increasing their appeal to the electorate (one out of every five Italians voted communist). When the PCI was eliminated from the government on May 31, 1947, it launched a wave of strikes directed against the centrist government and vigorously opposed both the Marshall Plan and NATO.

Another turning point in PCI history occurred in 1956, when Khrushchev denounced Stalin and suppressed the Hungarian revolution. At this point the party lost 700,000 members and the support of Nenni's PSI. Togliatti spoke out at the eighth party congress that year in favor of the "Italian road to socialism." In 1960 the PCI led demonstrations against the rightist-backed government of Fernando Tambroni, and during the pontificate of John XXIII it sought unsuccessfully to establish a "dialogue" with Italian Catholics, whom the party had already sought to woo by backing the continuation of the Lateran pacts after the war. Togliatti's death on August 21, 1964, marked the end of a generation of uncontested leadership by the Mediterranean maestro of dialectical materialism.

## ORGANIZATION AND MEMBERSHIP

In 1965 the PCI was organized on a pyramidal basis, with some 33,000 cells, 11,222 sections and nuclei, 387 communal committees, 87 municipal committees, 334 zonal committees, 18 regional committees, and 113 federations.

About 70 percent of all the party cells are concentrated in Lombardy, Emilia, Tuscany, and Umbria, and 95 percent of the factory cells are in Lombardy, Piedmont, Liguria, and Emilia. Thus the party has its greatest strength in the industrial north and the agricultural sectors of central Italy, where the outstanding part played by the PCI in the armed resistance of 1943 to 1945 greatly expanded its popular appeal. Since 1945 the party has operated both legally and covertly and has made considerable effort to recruit southern immigrants in the northern industrial cities and in Rome, as well as peasants who have moved down from the mountains into urban centers. It gives special attention to women going into industry and to youth and student groups.

In 1965 the party reported 1,615,296 card-carrying members,[3] a sharp drop from the high point of about 2,500,000 attained between 1948 and 1956. Many of the party's intellectuals left after Khrushchev's denunciation of Stalin and the Hungarian revolution in 1956. Since then PCI membership has declined markedly. The 1965 figure was about 16,000 lower than that of 1964. The decline is especially noticeable in the large cities, in the south, and in the women's organizations.

Despite the drop in party membership, at no time since 1945 has the PCI polled less than 18.3 percent of the popular vote in national elections. In the parliamentary elections of 1963 it received 25.3 percent. By the end of 1964 the number of municipal executive committees run by frontist blocks which included communists had declined from 1,088 to 569, although in conjunction with the Italian Socialist Party of Proletarian Unity (Partito Socialista Italiano di Unità Proletaria, PSIUP), a leftist splinter group that had seceded from Nenni's PSI in 1963, the PCI was able to increase the number of communist-controlled communes from seventy-eight to 334. By 1965 the PCI had lost considerable strength in municipal administrations and had few political allies.[4]

The PCI has made use of mass organizations whenever it could dominate them. Among the most conspicuous are the Italian General Confederation of Labor, the Union of Italian Women, and the National Association of Italian Partisans. During the popular-front era the party promoted the Italian Popular Union. From 1934 to 1939 and again from 1941 to 1956 the PCI enjoyed the collaboration of the PSI. When the PSI joined the Christian Democrats in the government in 1962 the PCI was isolated, except for the small leftist PSIUP.

## RELATION TO SOVIET LEADERSHIP

The PCI owed its origin to the Comintern, and their relationship was always intimate. Togliatti occupied a key position for many years on the Executive Committee of the Comintern, and most of the other major party leaders who avoided fascist arrest were frequent visitors to Moscow. The PCI helped to initiate the popular-front policy adopted in 1935 by the seventh congress of the Comintern. In the conference that met in Warsaw in 1947 to establish the Cominform, the PCI was represented by Luigi Longo, who played a role in that organization throughout its duration.

Khrushchev's criticism of Stalin and suppression of the Hungarian revolution in 1956 were responsible for the Italian communists' first significant questioning of Moscow's omniscience. The CPI lost many of its intellectuals, and since that time there has been increasingly open criticism of some of the Soviet policies. Although Togliatti sided with Moscow on key issues, he did his best to persuade Moscow not to bring its quarrel with Peking to a showdown. Since his death in 1964 the PCI has remained split on this issue, with the majority (led by Giorgio Amendola) supporting the Soviet Union and a minority (led by Pietro Ingrao) favoring China.

## FUTURE PROSPECTS

Although the PCI has become less dogmatic and revolution oriented, it still attracts 1.6 million members and can count on the votes of some 8 million Italians who feel alienated from the present politicoeconomic system. There is little reason to think this will change soon unless there is a major improvement in the standard of living of the workers, greatly augmented opportunities for education and technical training, and a vigorous effort to make Italian parliamentary government both honest and efficient.

## PARTY PRESS ORGANS AND RECORDS

The official daily newspaper is *L'Unità*, founded in 1924 and published in Rome since 1944, with other editions in Milan, Turin, and Genoa. *Lo Stato operaio*, the official monthly devoted to theory and political documentation, has appeared since 1927 and *Rinascita*, another important monthly, has appeared since 1944; both are published in Rome. A weekly, *Vie nuove*, and a daily, *Paese sera*, are also published in Rome.

The present party statutes appear in "Lo Statuto del partito," *VIII congresso nazionale: Atti e risoluzioni*, Rome, Italian Communist Party, 1956; cf. *IX congresso nazionale: Atti e risoluzioni*, Rome, Italian Communist Party, 1960. For the party program see *Tesi per il X congresso del PCI*, Rome, Italian Communist Party, 1962. *Lo Stato operaio* is the chief source for PCI history during the years of clandestine activity. Published in Paris from March 1927 until 1939, in New York from 1940 to 1943, and thereafter in Rome, it is available in fifteen volumes, reprinted in 1966 in Milan by Feltrinelli Editore (which is also reprinting all the major documents of the early history of the PCI).

## CONGRESSES OF THE PCI

1st congress, January 1921, Leghorn
2d congress, March 1922, Rome
3d congress, January 1926, Lyon
4th congress, March-April 1931, Cologne-Dusseldorf
5th congress, December 1945-January 1946, Rome
6th congress, January 1948, Milan
7th congress, April 1951, Rome
8th congress, December 1956, Rome
9th congress, January-February 1960, Rome
10th congress, December 1962, Rome

## BIBLIOGRAPHY

Dallin, Alexander (ed.): *Diversity in International Communism: A Documentary Record, 1961-1963*, New York, Columbia University Press, 1963, pp. 408-475.

Delzell, Charles F.: *Mussolini's Enemies: The Italian Anti-fascist Resistance*, Princeton, N.J., Princeton University Press, 1961.

Galli, Giorgio: "Italian Communism," in William E. Griffith (ed.), *Communism in Europe: Continuity, Change, and the Sino-Soviet Dispute*, vol. I, Cambridge, Mass., MIT Press, 1964, pp. 301-383.

Galli, Giorgio: *Storia del Partito comunista italiano*, Milan, Schwarz, 1958.

Garosci, Aldo: "The Italian Communist Party," in Mario Einaudi (ed.), *Communism in Western Europe*, Ithaca, N.Y., Cornell University Press, 1951, pp. 143-229.

Robotti, Paolo, and Giovanni Germanetto, *Il Comunismo italiano nella seconda guerra mondiale*, Rome, Riuniti, 1963.

Robotti, Paolo, and Giovanni Germanetto, *Trent'anni di lotte dei comunisti italiani*, Rome, Edizioni di Cultura Sociale, 1952.

Spriano, Paolo: *Storia del Partito comunista italiano*, vols. I-III, Turin, Einaudi, 1967-1970.

CHARLES F. DELZELL

1. *Quaderni del carcere*, Turin, 1948-1949.

2. *Lo Stato operaio*, August 10, 1928.

3. *L'Unità*, October 17, 1965.

4. Cf. Marco Cesarini, "Il PCI nel 1965: Un anno mediocre," *Il Mondo* (Rome), vol. 18. no. 2, January 11, 1966.

# JAPAN

The Japan Communist Party (Nihon Kyosanto, JCP) was officially founded on July 15, 1922, although there had been earlier abortive organizational attempts and certain preliminary meetings preceding the July 15 conference. At this time anarchosyndicalist currents were still strong in Japanese radical circles, and several of the party organizers had been a part of the anarchosyndicalist movement. Western-derived radicalism has had a longer history in Japan than in any other East Asian society. Marxism was first introduced into Japan in the late nineteenth century. By the first decade of the twentieth century socialism in a variety of forms had acquired a following among a small but dedicated band of Japanese intellectuals. Initially, Christian social democracy was the predominant form of socialist expression, but after 1905 anarchosyndicalism steadily gained strength—until it was challenged by the Russian revolution and the avant-garde philosophy of Marxism-Leninism.

The most important Japanese communist of the period, Katayama Sen, did not participate directly in the founding of the party. Katayama had gone into exile in 1914 and was introduced to Marxism-Leninism in the United States, primarily through early contacts with S. J. Rutgers and the group of Russian exiles in New York City. By 1919 he had become a part of the American communist movement, and shortly thereafter he went to Moscow, where he served as Asian representative to the Comintern until his death in 1933. Nevertheless, his influence, both upon the Comintern and upon the Japanese communist movement, was limited, He was not regarded as a sophisticated theorist, and his awareness of current Japanese conditions dimmed with the passage of time. Old jealousies and quarrels, moreover, had caused rifts with a number of other party figures that were never truly closed.

The most prominent founders of the JCP were Yamakawa Hitoshi, Sakai Toshihiko, Arahata Kanson, and Tokuda Kyuichi. All were professional radicals, and all, despite some contact with the labor movement, must be considered as belonging to the intellectual class. Japanese communism, from its beginnings to the present, has been dominated by intellectuals, those whom the Marxists would label "petit bourgeois." However, there has also been an enormous turnover, both in the leadership and among the rank and file. Of the four founders mentioned above, only Tokuda remained a party leader until his death in 1953. The others remained with the party only a few years before setting up an independent Marxist movement that served in considerable degree as predecessor to the present Japan Socialist Party (Nihon Shakaito).

## HISTORY

In the period before 1945 the JCP was an illegal organization with extremely limited membership. One tactical issue which divided the early communists was whether to maintain a formal party or to concentrate instead on labor and student movements, thereby avoiding constant police suppression. Thus in 1924, after the first party organization had been smashed, communist leaders decided to dissolve the party, only to have the Shanghai bureau of the Comintern in January 1925 sharply rebuke the "liquidationists" and insist that the party be reestablished. Yamakawa Hitoshi and his followers left the party to maintain an independent Marxist position, one rigorously criticized by the Comintern.

In 1927 Fukumoto Kazuo was also denounced by the international movement. Fukumoto, a bright young theorist trained in Germany, quickly emerged after 1925 as the leader of the JCP and hero of the radical youth. He had insisted that doctrinal purity had to be established and unsound elements weeded out of the party. This position, reinforced by some highly militant tactics, caused the party to move away from the Japanese socialists. However, on July 15, 1927, after lengthy deliberations on the "Japan problem," a Comintern committee issued a thesis severely criticizing "Fukomotoism" as well as "Yamakawaism"; the former was denounced as dogmatism and ultraintellectualism and the latter as liquidationism and social democracy.

After 1927 the Japanese Marxists, both within and outside the JCP, continued to argue whether Japanese capitalism had reached sufficient maturity for proletarian revolution, as Yamakawa's *rono* group insisted, or whether the task of Marxist-Leninists was to complete a bourgeois-democratic revolution and then move on to socialism, as the Comintern-affiliated *koza* group argued. The final program of the pre-1945 era, the so-called "1932 thesis," insisted that the Japanese revolution had to be a two-stage process, that the "feudal remnants," including the emperor system, had to be crushed at all costs, and that revolution could succeed only through violence. It was an exceedingly militant document, but the party scarcely had the power to execute its provisions. By the end of 1928 mass arrests had occurred on three separate occasions, and a series of defections had reduced party ranks.

The JCP was legalized at the conclusion of World War II, and since then its chief concerns have centered on three basic issues: the attitude toward the United States and its policies, the proper form for a Japanese revolution, and the most appropriate tactics for this revolution.

The party was reconstructed in October 1945 by a few old veterans, led by Tokuda Kyuichi, immediately after their release from prison. At first party pronouncements hewed very closely to the doctrines of the 1930s, but with the return of Nosaka Sanzo from Yenan in January 1946, a somewhat revised set of tactics and policies was developed. Making the party "lovable" became a central objective during the years 1946 to 1950, with an essentially "soft" policy toward the United States and strenuous efforts to attract socialist support for united-front activities.

At the outset, the American occupation was defined as a "liberation force," and cooperation with it was decreed. Retaining the concept of the two-stage revolution, based on the thesis that Japan was a highly developed capitalist state with substantial feudal remnants, the JCP held that the necessary bourgeois-democratic revolution had to be completed before proceeding to socialism. That task could be accomplished under the occupation, which itself served as a "progressive bourgeois force." It could lead in eliminating the emperor system, bringing about land reform and improvements in working conditions, and establishing full civil liberties under a democratic constitution. The revolution, moreover, could be attained peacefully, with a reliance on united-front tactics.

Although some modifications were made by the sixth party congress in December 1947, these basic policies remained in effect until January 1950. In many respects they paid handsome dividends. Pursuing "lovable" policies, the JCP had built its membership to some 100,000 by 1947, and in the general elections of 1949 it polled a record vote of nearly 3 million, 10 percent of the total vote, electing thirty-five members to the lower house of the Diet. Cooperation with the occupation authorities in the initial period, moreover, resulted in full freedom of operation, and some party leaders received significant official assignments. Zengakuren, the All-Japan Federation of Student Self-Government Association, which emerged during this period, came under communist control, as did a number of other organizations.

However, the communists failed in their major bid to control the postwar labor movement, with the abortive general strike of February 1, 1947, being the crucial dividing line. Nor were they able to develop a peasant base. The issue of land reform was taken away from them by the far-reaching occupational agrarian reforms. Thus the mass worker-peasant base envisaged by party leaders never materialized, in spite of electoral gains. After 1947, moreover, the American occupation authorities increasingly viewed the communists with suspicion, and while they protected their constitutional rights, they ceased treating them as allies.

Clearly no policy would have been any more successful for the communists in Japan. On January 6, 1950, however, the Cominform ended the "lovable" era by issuing a scorching blast against Nosaka, describing his theories as "antidemocratic and antisocialist." Motivated by internal circumstances, the Soviet leaders demanded that the JCP take a hard line, irrespective of its cost. At a crucial point, moreover, the Chinese communists joined in the criticism of the JCP "Mainstream" leaders, making their capitulation inescapable. This abrupt shift to the left was accompanied by the emergence of intense intraparty factionalism. By accepting Cominform criticism, however, the Nosaka-Tokuda faction managed to survive, and in the process to undertake a counterattack against their opponents within the party.

A new thesis was drafted with extensive Soviet and Chinese assistance, although the conference that approved it was denounced as illegal by one faction of the party. According to the new line, the United States was the foremost "imperialist force" and had brought the Japanese people "only chains and slavery." It was now to be the prime object of attack, with the forces of "Japanese monopoly capitalism" a secondary, albeit important, target. Instead of a bourgeois-democratic revolution, the new objective was a "national-liberation democratic revolution" aimed at establishing a "people's democratic republic." The emphasis was still on building a united front of workers, peasants, and "progressive" bourgeoisie under the leadership of the proletariat, with "peace" and "national liberation" as the basic issues. However, the goal of a peaceful revolution was abandoned, and violence was accepted as an indispensable prerequisite for success. The switch from united-front tactics to guerrilla warfare—the Chinese route—became official party doctrine.

Translating this doctrine into practice, the JCP instituted an era of violence, with the years 1950 to 1952 representing the height of "ultraleft adventurism." The Korean War, of course, was the background against which this panorama unfolded. "Molotov cocktails" were thrown in the streets; attacks against Japanese police stations and some occupation installations were attempted; there was even an effort to establish a Japanese "Yenan" in some mountain villages as bases for guerrilla warfare. The result was catastrophic. In no respects were Japanese conditions similar to those of China in the era before 1949, and the Chinese model simply would not work. Those young terrorists who did not manage to escape to China were captured and given lengthy prison terms. The party rapidly became a symbol for extremism, and any previous links with the masses were rapidly broken. Party membership fell precipitously and election results were disastrous.

By 1951 the JCP had been reduced to only semilegal status; it had already gone largely underground and was engaged in a wide range of illegal activities.

In the midst of failure, factionalism within the party grew more intense. Both the Soviet and the Chinese parties had moved to support the Mainstream leaders after their adjustment to the new international line, but this did not deter the "international faction," which continued to oppose the Nosaka-Tokuda group. For more than five years charges and countercharges were leveled by the warring factions. Many members were purged, and even at the cell level rival elements often existed.

A new era began in 1956, when party leaders admitted "leftist" errors of the past, pledged an end to factional disputes and sought a return to legalism with renewed emphasis on united-front tactics. The Stalinist era had ended, as had the Korean War. Tokuda, moreover, had died in Peking in November 1953. Leadership now passed into new hands, with such men as Miyamoto Kenji and Hakamada Satomi sharing power at the top with Nosaka, who increasingly played the role of senior counsel. Meanwhile, a host of young activists, most of whom had been trained in China from 1950 to 1956, returned to Japan and assumed key positions in the party.

The draft program of 1957, prepared by Miyamoto and Hakamada, had a strong Chinese flavor. It perpetuated the hard line on most key issues, although it supported a shift in tactics. Japan was to be considered a semicolonial nation, and the United States was still to be regarded as the primary enemy. The revolution was now to be a "people's democratic revolution" for national liberation and democracy, based on a broad united front led by the JCP. The use of peaceful or forceful means was to depend on the enemy, but the reactionary forces in power could be counted on to resist violently.

Despite pledges and promises, party factionalism did not end; in fact, new policy differences emerged to sustain the divisions. Miyamoto himself had previously been a leader of the international faction, and his accession to the position of secretary general was widely interpreted as a Chinese-encouraged move to bring about party harmony. Nearly one-third of the party, however, objected to aspects of the 1957 draft program, and its ratification was postponed. A slightly revised program was finally enacted at the eighth party congress in July 1961, but by this time a split had already occurred; Kasuga Shojiro, a key opposition leader within the party, had left with his followers to establish an independent movement. From this point on factionalism within the JCP closely paralleled the Sino-Soviet dispute. The Kasuga line was in essence the current Soviet line; Kasuga played on the basic Khrushchevian themes and directed them against the new Mainstream leaders.

After 1961 every escalation of the Sino-Soviet dispute drastically affected the Japanese party, and this issue became a matter of primary concern. Initially the JCP, in company with other communist parties of Asia, notably those of North Korea and North Vietnam, sought to maintain a strict neutrality between the two communist giants, especially in public, and attempted to minimize the seriousness of the cleavage even in party discussions and to offer its services as mediator. By 1963, however, the JCP was no longer able to sustain this position and found itself compelled to take a stand on a host of issues—Yugoslavia, Albania, the Sino-Indian border conflict, Cuba, and the limited-test-ban-treaty, among others. On all these issues the Mainstream leaders sided with Peking. Moreover, the party became increasingly critical of Khrushchev's tactics within the communist world. A climax was reached in 1963, when party leaders openly accused the Soviet leadership of gross interference in the internal affairs of the JCP, serious policy errors reflecting a "modern revisionist" approach, and abandonment of true Marxist-Leninist principles. Efforts were continued to establish a united front with the communist parties of North Korea, North Vietnam, and Indonesia, all of which were growing more and more hostile to Khrushchev's policies. The change to open and bitter opposition came with the failure of bilateral talks between JCP leaders and Soviet officials in Moscow on March 2-11, 1964. Shortly afterward all pro-Soviet leaders were purged from the party, with Shiga Yoshio and Suzuki Ichiro joining earlier purgees as a reult of their refusal to support the party position against the limited-test-ban treaty. Moscow encouraged the Shiga faction, although it stopped short of giving that group official recognition, and the ensuing exchange of letters between the Soviet and Japanese parties was marked by bitter charges and recriminations.

By the time of the ninth party congress in late November 1964 the JCP had totally estranged itself from the Soviet bloc. The 1964 thesis in essence followed the themes of the 1961 thesis, with increased emphasis on party organization and strong denunciations of past Soviet actions. The cost, however, proved to be heavy. While the ousted pro-Soviet group accounted for no more than 10 percent of the party hierarchy, the split and accompanying events had a serious effect on all front organizations and united-front activities. Gensuikyo, the Japan Council Against Atomic and Hydrogen Bombs, was further torn; the communist faction within Sohyo, the General Council of Trade Unions of Japan, was deeply divided; and the party faced the serious threat of a Soviet-left socialist alliance that would make communist influence over mass organizations impossible. At the end of 1965 the JCP, insisting that it was a "completely independent, sovereign party," was generally pursuing the Peking line on substantive issues—although shortly thereafter it was to quarrel with Mao over his stubborn refusal to accept rapprochement with the Communist Party of the Soviet Union in order to aid North Vietnam.

## ORGANIZATION AND MEMBERSHIP

Until 1945 the JCP was strictly illegal, and its membership never exceeded 1,000 at any time. As a result, its organizational structure was necessarily rudimentary, although it was based entirely on prevailing communist patterns of organization. Before 1945 the party considered itself only a branch of the Comintern, and those who violated or ignored Comintern directives, or were alleged to have done so, were criticized and often purged. Moreover, the continued changes in party policy on orders from Moscow produced sufficient disillusionment to cause many members, particularly young intellectuals, to desert the party. After the JCP was reconstructed in 1945, even though it was not formally a member of the Cominform, it was guided entirely by Moscow until the 1960s.

*Organization* Formally, the supreme party organ is the party congress, which was convened for the ninth time on November 25, 1964. Six of the nine party congresses have been held since 1945, usually attended by 400 to 500 delegates, the great majority of whom are selected by regional and prefectural party conferences. The party congress, which is supposed to meet at least every two years, serves as a platform for party leaders to deliver "progress reports" and provides legal sanction for basic theses and programs. A supplementary organ, the national consultative conference, may be called at the initiative of the central committee and operates as a smaller version of the party congress. It was especially useful from 1950 to 1955, when the party did not have full legality and most of the key leaders were in exile.

In actuality, the real power lies with the central committee, and particularly with the presidium and secretariat, which are formed from that committee. In recent years the central committee has been composed of sixty-six regular and forty-two alternate members. It meets in plenum session at least once every three months, according to party regulations. Most critical decisions, however, are debated and settled within the presidium and secretariat, the two standing bodies of the central committee. Within these organs, in turn, three or four men wield the greatest power. At the end of 1965 Nosaka Sanzo (chairman of the central committee and the presidium), Miyamoto Kenji (secretary general), and Hakamada Satomi (director of the organization bureau) were generally regarded as the key party figures, with Miyamoto gradually attaining top-ranking power. In the JCP, as in other aspects of Japanese politics, however, the collective power of younger subordinate elements must be regarded as important. The "young officers" of the party, most of them exiles in Peking during the Korean War, played a significant role, particularly during the era of Chinese influence.

Party headquarters contains 300 to 600 persons, counting the party publications staff and the various central bureaus of organization, personnel, elections, legislation, budget, youth and students, women, labor, propaganda and education, and others. Without exception, these bureaus have been headed by central committee members, providing the party with an interlocking directorate in some degree. Below the national level there are some forty-six prefectural and 239 district committees, and at the grass-roots level there are over 13,000 cells. In recent years, with younger members assuming an increasingly active headquarters role, there has been much greater emphasis on cadre training and other organizational activities. The party has been moving increasingly from an "ideologue" toward an "activist" orientation, and nowhere has this been more evident than in the organizational field.

*Membership* Despite its ideological and policy problems, the JCP claimed nearly 300,000 members at the time of the tenth national congress in October 1966 (authorities estimate 270,000), a substantial gain over the 150,000 members claimed three years earlier. These gains are attributable mainly to ample finances, dedicated middle-echelon leaders, and the application of a variety of organizational techniques. Party members are predominantly young, with more than 70 percent under the age of forty. A sizable number are students, intellectuals, and government white-collar employees—the "petite bourgeoisie." Workers in industry or mines do not account for more than one-third of the total membership, and agrarian membership is negligible. The party claims, however, that the percentage of worker members is now increasing.

Far from being a party of the proletariat, the JCP has more truly represented a small segment of the intelligentsia. Nearly 15 percent of the party members are university graduates, and an additional 25 percent have had higher education. With rare exceptions, however, the party intellectuals are not leaders in the Japanese intellectual community.

*Electoral Strength* Although the JCP received a record 10 percent of the total vote in the general elections of 1949, its electoral strength in the mid-1960s dropped to only 4 to 5 percent of the total vote in national elections to the Diet. In regional terms, the party was strongest in central Honshu, primarily as a result of the urban concentration in this part of Japan. It was weakest in such rural regions as Hokkaido, Tohoku, and (with the exception of Fukuoka prefecture) Kyushu, indicating that the party lacks appeal in agrarian areas.

The urban vote of the JCP was more than twice as high as its rural vote, and the party made its best showing in industrial centers, polling about 7 percent in such areas. Its greatest concentrated strength lay in the three metropolitan areas of Kyoto, Tokyo, and Osaka, where the communist vote ranges from 8 to 20 percent. Up to 1965 the JCP had been receiving about 6 to 10 percent of the vote from the most heavily industrial areas, 4 to 5 percent from the key mining areas, and 1 to 2 percent from the strongly agrarian sections of the country; the overall urban vote had ranged from 3 to 6 percent and the overall rural vote had fallen within the range of 1 to 3 percent. In 1965 these figrues, especially for the urban vote, rose somewhat.

The "left bloc" of Japanese parties, never united and often labeled the "progressive parties," encompasses the communists, the socialists, the democratic socialists, and some very minor groups. In recent years the socialists polled close to 70 percent of the left-bloc vote, the democratic socialists 16 to 17 percent, and the communists 9.5 to 13 percent. As might be expected, the communists achieved their best results in national elections, making a much weaker showing in prefectural and local contests. By the end of 1965 they had not succeeded in seating a prefectural governor, nor did a party member hold any mayorship in Japan. Except for contests in which the communist candidate was the only opposition, the party had captured less than 1 percent of the 2,688 prefectural assembly seats, less than 3 percent of the city council seats, and only about 1 percent of the town and village council seats.

*Party Finances*   In recent years the JCP has had a substantial income. In 1962, for example, the party reported revenues of nearly 500 million yen ($1,388,888). No Japanese party lists its full revenues and expenditures, and most observers believe that actual communist revenues greatly exceeded this figure. One estimate of true party expenditures for 1963 was 4 billion yen (over $11 million). Whatever the facts, the party has spent lavishly in the course of elections, expanded the scope and nature of its publications, constructed new headquarters, and in other respects given evidence of affluence. At least some of this money came from abroad, primarily from Chinese sources. The sale of Chinese communist publications and contributions from Japanese firms involved in trade with China are two sources of this revenue, although the greater part is undoubtedly from purely indigenous sources.

*Front Organizations*   As might be expected, the party's most prominent front organizations fall into three categories: "peace" groups, student groups, and trade unions. The Japan Peace Committee has been the primary local vehicle, but in recent years Gensuikyo has played a significant role. Begun as a united-front organ in cooperation with religious, socialist, and pacifist groups, it became a purely communist organ after 1962, when the socialists withdrew.

In the field of youth and student activities the Democratic Youth League (Minshu Seinen Domei) is the most recent organization. The party has also waged a fierce battle to recapture control of the student organization Zengakuren. Originally under communist control, Zengakuren was later taken over by an antiparty left element, mislabeled Trotskyists but in reality a group of militant radicals who refused to accept party discipline and whose rather indistinct philosophy contained elements of anarchosyndicalism, Trotskyism, and various other concepts. By 1965 the party had made major gains in reestablishing control over Zengakuren leadership.

Instead of organizing a separate trade-union organization, the communists have preferred to operate as a faction inside Sohyo, which has about 4.2 million members. They have never been able to muster more than one-third of the vote on crucial issues at the national conventions, and their hard-core strength is much less than this. However, they have had substantial influence in some unions, particularly a few of the public-employee unions.

## FUTURE PROSPECTS

The future of communism in Japan probably hinges on the extent to which the JCP is able to infiltrate or form a viable united front with the much more significant left socialists. By itself the party is weak, and despite some recent gains, there is no indication that it can become a major force in Japanese politics without massive outside support. The chances of a sustained, successful united front are less clear. On one hand, left fronts in Japan have a long history of failure, and the socialists are generally wary of intimate relations with the communists as a result of past experiences. Moreover, the left has rarely, if ever, been as extensively fragmented as it is today. Even within the communist movement, innumerable cleavages will continue, with both the Chinese and the Russians deeply involved. On the other hand, both Marxism and anti-Americanism continue to have a powerful hold over the socialists, and such issues as "peace" and "independence" may easily be given a communist orientation, especially if explosive incidents develop to enflame emotions. All things considered, the chances are that the Japanese communists will continue to have an influence on both the tactics and the policies of the broader left in Japan without in any sense dominating the total socialist movement.

## PARTY PRESS ORGANS AND RECORDS

The leading party newspaper is *Akahata* (Red Flag); its monthly theoretical journal is *Zenei* (Vanguard).

Current party bylaws, along with current policies, are contained in *Nihon Kyosanto no Seisaku, 1965* (Policies of the Japanese Communist Party, 1965), Tokyo, Communist Party of Japan, 1965. For recent theses see *Nihon Kyosanto Juyo Rombu Shu* (A Collection of Important Theses of the Japanese Communist Party), vols. I-II, Tokyo, Communist Party of Japan, 1965. The full text of the central committee report to the ninth party congress on November 25, 1964, appears in English in *Translations on International Communist Developments*, no. 691, Joint Publications Research Service, 28,456, Washington, pp. 1-298. Records of all the party congresses may be found in *Zenei* and *Akahata*.

## CONGRESSES AND CONFERENCES OF THE JCP

1st congress (illegal), July 1922, Tokyo
2d congress (illegal), February 1923, Ichikawa
3d congress (illegal), April 1926, Yamagata prefecture
1st national conference, November 1945, Tokyo
4th congress, December 1945, Tokyo
5th congress, February 1946, Tokyo
2d national conference, January 1947, Tokyo
6th congress, December 1947, Tokyo
3d national conference, June 1949, Tokyo
4th national conference (illegal), February 1951, Tokyo
5th national conference (illegal), October 1951, Tokyo
6th national conference, July 1955, Tokyo
7th congress, July-August 1958, Tokyo
8th congress, July 1961, Tokyo
9th congress, November 1964, Tokyo
10th congress, October 1966, Tokyo

## BIBLIOGRAPHY

Baerwald, Hans H.: "The Japanese Communist Party: Yoyogi and Its Rivals," in Robert A. Scalapino (ed.), *The Communist Revolution in Asia: Tactics, Goals, and Achievements*, Englewood Cliffs, N.J., Prentice-Hall, 1965.

Langer, Paul F.: "Independence or Subordination: The Japanese Communist Party between Moscow and Peking," in A. Doak Barnett (ed.), *Communist Strategies in Asia: A Comparative Analysis of Governments and Parties*, New York, Praeger, 1963.

Scalapino, Robert A.: *The Japanese Communist Movement: 1920-1966*, Berkeley, Calif., University of California Press, 1967.

Swearingen, A. Rodger: "Communist Strategy in Japan, 1945-1960," Santa Monica, Calif., Rand Corporation, April 1965.

Swearingen, A. Rodger, and Paul Langer: *Red Flag in Japan: International Communism in Action, 1919-1951*, Cambridge, Mass., Harvard University Press, 1952.

Tsukahira, Toshio G.: *The Postwar Evolution of Communist Strategy in Japan*, Cambridge, Mass., MIT Center for International Studies, September 1954.

ROBERT A. SCALAPINO

# JORDAN

The Amirate of Transjordan was established in 1921 in the region east of the Jordan River as an entity separate from what was to become the British mandate for Palestine in 1922. As ruler of the amirate the British recognized Amir (later King) 'Abd Allah, a son of King Husain of the Hijaz. 'Abd Allah was a lifelong opponent of communism, calling it "a transient creed—a blinding flash which dazzles men's eyes until its true nature and the evil and immorality that lie behind it become known and are rejected."[1]

During the 1930s a small number of communists took part in two abortive attempts to organize workers in Transjordan. In the 1940s the Arab communists of Palestine, operating under the name League of National Liberation ('Usbat al-Tahrir [or al-Taharrur] al-Watani), began to pay more attention to Transjordan, where they stepped up the distribution of communist literature.

## HISTORY

In March 1946 Great Britain recognized the full independence of Transjordan, and in May Amir 'Abd Allah took the title of king. After the establishment of the state of Israel in May 1948, Transjordan absorbed the west bank of the Jordan River, which had been the main base for the Arab communists of Palestine, and immediately enacted anticommunist legislation. Nevertheless, some of the Arab communist leaders, including Fuad Nassar and Rushdi Shahin, chose this country, renamed the following year the Hashemite Kingdom of Jordan, as the new field for their activities. In 1951 Nassar, by birth a Christian from Nazareth, became the first secretary general of the Jordanian communist party, a post he still holds.

The Arab communists were hampered for a time by the Soviet support of zionism. In 1947 the Soviet Union had voted in favor of the United Nations resolution for the creation of a Jewish state and in 1948 had recognized Israel. The following year Moscow at first favored the internationalization of Jerusalem, but before long it reversed this position and has since tended to be pro-Arab and anti-Israel.

In May 1949 Glubb Pasha, the British commander of Jordan's army, the Arab Legion, gave public warning of the potential danger of the spread of communism in the kingdom. In the summer of that year the Jordanian communists began publication of *al-Muqawamah al-Sha'biyah* (Popular Resistance), and the following spring they boycotted the elections. In June 1951 the party changed its name to the Communist Party of Jordan (al-Hizb al-Shuyu'i al-Urdunni). King 'Abd Allah was assassinated in July, and a month later, when the communists participated in the elections under the guise of the Popular Front (al-Jabhah al-Sha'biyah), two of the communist-sponsored candidates, 'Abd al-Qadir al-Salih and Qadri Tuqan, were elected to the parliament. The government reacted by arresting Fuad Nassar in December 1951, and several months later he was sentenced to a long term in jail.

'Abd Allah had been succeeded by his son Talal. Not sufficiently stable to rule, Talal abdicated a year later in favor of his own son, Husain. King Husain's anticommunist stand has been as vigorous and unwavering as his grandfather's. In a speech to the U.N. General Assembly on October 3, 1960, he declared: "We reject communism.... Arab nationalism is too deep-rooted in the love of God, the love of freedom, and the equality of all before God ever to be supplanted by a system which denies the importance of these ideas."[2]

Early in Husain's reign, however, the government's "experiment in democracy" gave the communists more leeway than they had had before. An attempt to check them with a new anticommunist law, passed on December 8, 1953, which also applied to the World Peace Movement, was unsuccessful. The communist organ *al-Jabhah* (The Front), which had appeared in 1952 under the editorship of 'Abd al-Rahman Shuqair, was suppressed in 1954. However, the communists took an energetic part in the elections in October 1954, working with other opposition parties in the National Front ('al-Jabhah al-Wataniyah). They won no seats in parliament, but they succeeded in fomenting riots which required the intervention of the armed forces.

The swing to the left in Jordan approached its apogee in 1956, when three communist-supported candidates won parliamentary seats and Sulaiman al-Nabulsi of the National Front took office as prime minister. Fuad Nassar was released from jail, and the party was allowed to operate legally. In the first months of 1957 King Husain began to move against al-Nabulsi and the trend he represented. In an open letter to the prime minister he said that "no gap must be left to allow the propaganda of communism to ruin our country."[3] In April all political parties were banned, al-Nabulsi was discharged as prime minister, and martial law was proclaimed. Protest demonstrations by the communists were summarily broken up. At the end of 1957 or early in 1958 Nassar and other high-ranking communists fled the country.

Since then Nassar has lived in exile somewhere in Eastern Europe. In November 1960 he represented the Jordanian party at the conference of eighty-one communist parties held in Moscow. In October 1961, in a speech at the twenty-second congress of the Soviet party in Moscow, he said:

> For many years the Jordanian people have lived under the conditions of a black terrorist regime, which has betrayed their interests and sovereignty to American, English, and West German imperialists. The living standard of the people is very low, and the economy is in decline. Oppression and terror reign in the land, directed against all our people and especially against our communist party.... More than 500 members of our party are rotting in prisons and concentration camps....[4]

Nassar appeared in Moscow again in June 1964, accompanied by Farid Sa'id, who was identified by *Pravda* as second secretary of the central committee of the Jordanian party.

The party program, as set forth in *al-Muqawamah al-Sha'biyah* in July 1964, called for speeding up the industrialization of Jordan, the passage of social welfare laws, a policy of neutralism and peaceful coexistence, uprooting foreign influences in the country, freedom for party activity, and a general amnesty. In April 1965 the Jordanian government freed about 1,700 political prisoners and notified its diplomatic missions that the full rights of citizens should be restored to more than 200 "political emigrants." Although Fuad Nassar was specifically mentioned in the second category, no indication has been found that he took advantage of this opportunity to return to Jordan.

## PARTY PRESS ORGANS

In 1965 *al-Muqawamah al-Sha'biyah* (Popular Resistance) was succeeded by *al-Taqaddum* (Progress) as the principal party organ. The party also publishes the periodical *al-Haqiqah* (Truth).

## BIBLIOGRAPHY

'Abdallāh ['Abd Allah]: *My Memoirs Completed*, translated from the Arabic by Harold W. Glidden, Washington, American Council of Learned Societies, 1954.

Abidi, Aqil Hyder Hasan: *Jordan: A Political Study, 1948-1957*, New York, Asia Publishing House, 1965.

Dearden, Ann: *Jordan*, London, Robert Hale, 1958.

Glubb, John Bagot: *A Soldier with the Arabs*, London, Hodder and Stoughton, 1957.

Harris, George L., et al.: *Jordan: Its People; Its Society; Its Culture,* New Haven, Conn., HRAF Press, 1958.

Hussein [Husain]: *Uneasy Lies the Head: The Autobiography of His Majesty, King Hussein I,* New York, Geis-Random House, 1962.

Laqueur, Walter Z.: *Communism and Nationalism in the Middle East*, 3d ed., London, 1961.

Patai, Raphael: *The Kingdom of Jordan*, Princeton, N.J., Princeton University Press, 1958.

GEORGE RENTZ

1. 'Abdallāh ['Abd Allah], *My Memoirs Completed,* translated by Harold W. Glidden, Washington, American Council of Learned Societies. 1954, pp. 70-71.

2. *Official Records of the General Assembly, Fifteenth Session (Part I), Plenary Meetings,* vol. I, Verbatim Records of Meetings, New York, September 20-October 17, 1960, p. 322.

3. King Hussein [Husain], *Uneasy Lies the Head: The Autobiography of His Majesty, King Hussein I,* New York, Geis-Random House, 1962, p. 160.

4. *Pravda*, October 28, 1961.

# KAZAKHSTAN [1]

Until 1917 communist activity in what is now Kazakhstan was weak and insignificant, a part of rather than a major factor in the social unrest of the time. The first Marxist circles began to form at the beginning of the century among the Russian populations of Petropavlovsk, Kokchetav, Uralsk, Akmolinsk, Vernyi, and other towns. After the second congress of the Russian Social Democratic Labor Party in 1903, and especially after 1905, social-democratic groups and organizations became prominent, although they were still small and plagued by factional strife between bolsheviks and mensheviks. During the Stolypin reaction of 1908 to 1912 many of these groups were crushed, but individual members figured in strikes in the Karaganda coal mines, the Spasskii copper mines, the Emba oil fields, and elsewhere.

## HISTORY

After the revolution of February 1917 the bolsheviks joined other extremists in undermining and finally overthrowing the Provisional Government agencies in Kazakhstan and setting up government by soviets. White counterrevolutionary forces imperiled the Soviet regime until Red Army forces led by M. V. Frunze and V. V. Kuibyshev established firm Soviet control. In August 1920 the creation of the Kirgiz (later Kazakh) Autonomous Soviet Socialist Republic was announced.

In June 1921 the first regional (*oblast*) conference of bolsheviks met at Orenburg and completed formation of the Communist Party of Kazakhstan (Kommunisticheskaia Partiia Kazakhstana). From 1921 to 1925 the Kazakhstan communists carried out the resolutions of the tenth (1921) and twelfth (1923) congresses of the Russian Communist Party (Bolshevik) with regard to rebuilding the economy on socialist lines. The land-water reforms of 1921 and 1927 strengthened the new regime by liquidating Russian kulak colonists and the native upper class through confiscation and redistribution of their property.

Kazakhstan became a Soviet state in 1925, and its party became a regional organization of the All-Union Communist Party (Bolshevik). At the time it had over 32,000 members and candidates, 36.5 percent of whom were Kazakhs. Carrying out resolutions of the fourteenth (1925) and fifteenth (1927) congresses of the Soviet party, the Kazakhstan communists took political measures to strengthen Soviet power and led a campaign for industrialization. At the behest of the Soviet party central committee, the sixth regional party conference held in 1927 occupied itself with "unmasking and crushing" nationalist groups, including alleged followers of Ryskulov, Sadvakasov, Bukharin, and Trotsky.

As part of Moscow's First Five-Year Plan, the party instituted collectivization of agriculture in Kazakhstan. Herds and lands belonging to the kulaks were expropriated and distributed among the poorer peasants, who were hastily settled in collective farms. Widespread resistance to this measure took the form of a wholesale slaughter of cattle which crippled animal husbandry for a generation, and over a million Kazakhs died of famine. Responsibility for the failure of collectivization was placed on the Kazakh nationalists, and in March 1935 a number of them, including Kulumbetov, the vice premier of the republic, were executed.

During the five-year plans the Kazakhstan party took a prominent part in directing the economy of the republic. Factories, smelters, railroad lines, and electronic plants were built, and in the rural areas collectivized agriculture finally began to function. Economic improvement permitted a cultural advance, and many new schools and higher educational institutions were opened in an effort to eliminate illiteracy.

Under the 1936 constitution of the Soviet Union Kazakhstan became the Kazakh Soviet Socialist Republic, and in 1937, by decision of the central committee of the All-Union Communist Party (Bolshevik), the regional party was officially named the Communist Party (Bolshevik) of Kazakhstan (Kommunisticheskaia Partiia [Bolsheviki] Kazakhstana). The first party congress, representing 51,440 members and candidates, adopted resolutions on economic and cultural matters, directed party organizations to continue purging their membership, and called for increased watchfulness against hostile elements. The third party congress, held in 1940, reviewed progress in purging the membership and set forth measures for strengthening the economic and defense capacity of the Soviet Union.

During World War II the Kazakhstan party devoted much of its activity to changing the economy to a war footing. More than half the party membership entered the armed forces, and about 70,000 workers, peasants, and intellectuals were accepted as new members. The postwar period was devoted to restoration and development of the economy, in accordance with the fourth Five-Year Plan. Following resolutions of the central committee on ideological questions, the party organizations concentrated on communist education of the population. *The History of the Communist Party of the Soviet Union, Short Course*, and the works of Marx, Lenin, and Stalin were published in the Kazakh language.

Since 1950 the central committee and the party conferences and congresses have been concerned with development of the economy and the transition from socialism to communism. Khrushchev's virgin-lands program more than doubled the cultivated area of the republic, but it caused major crop failures and dustbowl conditions. Livestock production remains unsatisfactory despite party efforts to raise the goals.

On January 1, 1965, the Kazakhstan party claimed 410,716 members and 39,770 candidate members in 13,034 primary organizations.[2]

PARTY PRESS ORGAN

The principal party newspaper is *Kazakhstanskaia pravda* (Kazakhstan Truth), published in Alma-Ata.

## BIBLIOGRAPHY

Abdykalykov, M., and A. Pankratova (eds.): *Istoriia Kazakhskoi SSR s drevneishikh vremen do nashikh dnei* (A History of the Kazakh SSR from Earliest Times to the Present), Alma-Ata, 1943.

Auezov, M. O., et al. (eds.): *Istoriia Kazakhskoi SSR: Epokha sotsializma* (A History of the Kazakh SSR: The Epoch of Socialism), Alma-Ata, 1963.

*Kommunisticheskaia partiia Kazakhstana v dokumentakh i tsifrakh* (The Communist Party of Kazakhstan in Documents and Figures), Alma-Ata, 1960.

*Ocherki istorii Kommunisticheskoi partii Kazakhstana* (Outlines of the History of the Communist Party of Kazakhstan), Alma-Ata, 1963.

Pierce, Richard A.: *Soviet Central Asia: A Bibliography*, part 3, *1917-1966*, Berkeley, Calif., University of California Center for Slavic and East European Studies, 1966.

*Voprosy istorii Kompartii Kazakhstana: Sbornik statei* (Problems in the History of the Communist Party of Kazakhstan: A Collection of Articles), vols. I-III, Alma-Ata, 1963-1965.

RICHARD A. PIERCE

1. See also *Kirgizia, Tadzhikistan, Turkmenistan,* and *Uzbekistan.*

2. *Bolshaia sovetskaia entsiklopediia: Ezhegodnik 1965,* Moscow, 1965.

# KIRGIZIA[1]

The first communist party organizations in Kirgizia, then part of the regions (*oblasts*) of Semirechie and Fergana, took shape in the spring of 1918, following the establishment of Soviet power. On May 1, 1918, the Soviet government proclaimed the Turkestan Autonomous Soviet Socialist Republic a part of the Russian Soviet Federation of Socialist Republics, and in June the first regional congress of bolshevik organizations of Central Asia, including those of Kirgizia, met at Tashkent and created the Communist Party (Bolshevik) of Turkestan. There was virtually no native participation. Russian settlers and recently arrived Soviet occupation troops were represented at this congress.

During the Russian civil war the communists of Kirgizia led the struggle against the forces of Annenkov and Dutov, and the Basmachi.

## HISTORY

In October 1924 the Kara-Kirgiz Autonomous Region was formed. On May 25, 1925, this became the Kirgiz Autonomous Region, and on February 1, 1926, the Kirgiz Autonomous Soviet Socialist Republic. In March 1925 the first regional conference of bolsheviks of Kara-Kirgizia adopted a program for further economic and cultural development and for the strengthening of party and youth organizations. From 1926 to 1929 the party organizations were occupied with the tasks set by the fourteenth congress of the All-Union Communist Party (Bolshevik) for the development of industry, agriculture, animal husbandry, and a land-water reform.

The sixth regional party conference in 1930 reviewed efforts to fulfill resolutions of the sixteenth conference of the Soviet party regarding construction, strenghtening the general party line, increased criticism and self-criticism, and recruitment of workers and agricultural laborers. The Kirgiz party was to increase its membership, "to unmask and crush bourgeois-nationalist and Trotsky-Bukharinist elements," to collectivize agriculture, and to liquidate the kulaks as a class. The seventh regional party conference in 1934 set forth plans for further development of coal production, modernization of agricultural methods, increased turnover of goods, and improvement of communications.

At the end of 1936 the Kirgiz Autonomous Soviet Socialist Republic became the Kirgiz Soviet Socialist Republic, and on April 23, 1937, the Kirgiz regional party was transformed into the Communist Party (Bolshevik) of Kirgizia (Kommunisticheskaia partiia [Bolsheviki] Kirgizii). The first party congress proclaimed plans for further development of industry, agriculture, and culture and achievement of higher living standards, at the same time again calling on the communists of Kirgizia to purge their ranks of "bourgeois-nationalist and Trotskyist-Bukharinist elements." Several thousand natives and Russians, particularly of the educated classes, were arrested during this period and imprisoned or executed.

During World War II the party led efforts to organize the industry of the republic on a wartime basis and to develop animal husbandry, broaden the area under cultivation, and increase the harvest of grain and other basic crops. Since World War II it has continued to carry out directives of the Communist Party of the Soviet Union, mobilizing the population to fulfill the economic plans and to raise cultural levels and living standards.

On January 1, 1965, the party had 77,617 members and 7,014 candidates, in 2,695 primary organizations.[2]

PARTY PRESS ORGAN

The party newspaper is *Sovetskaia Kirgiziia* (Soviet Kirgizia), published in Frunze.

BIBLIOGRAPHY

*Istoriia Kirgizii* (A History of Kirgizia), vol. II, Frunze, 1956.
Pierce, Richard A.: *Soviet Central Asia: A Bibliography*, part 3, *1917-1966*, Berkeley, Calif., Center for Slavic and East European Studies, 1966.
*Rost i regulirovaniia sostava Kommunisticheskoi partii Kirgizii, 1918-1962 gg.: Sbornik dokumentov i materialov* (Growth and Regulation of the Composition of the Communist Party of Kirgizia, 1918-1962: A Collection of Documents and Materials), Frunze, 1963.
*Voprosy istorii Kommunisticheskoi partii Kirgizii: Ezhegodnyi sbornik statei* (Problems of the History of the Communist Party of Kirgizia: An Annual Collection of Articles), vol. I, Frunze, 1962.

RICHARD A. PIERCE

1. See also *Kazakhstan, Tadzhikistan, Turkmenistan,* and *Uzbekistan.*

2. *Bolshaia sovetskaia entsiklopediia: Ezhegodnik 1965,* Moscow, 1965.

# KOREA

The first Korean communist organization was created in Khabarovsk, Siberia, in June 1918, under the name of the Korean People's Socialist Party (Hanin Sahoe-dang). It had the encouragement and blessing of the bolsheviks, who were just beginning to move into that region. Those who took the leadership in this nascent communist movement were exiled nationalists struggling for liberation of Korea from Japanese rule. The principal leader was Yi Tong-hwi, a military patriot who was convinced that the bolsheviks could be induced to fight against Japanese imperialism, or at least give active assistance to the nationalist cause, if the Koreans supported them in their early struggles.

This socialist party seems to have been created as a proof of support for the bolsheviks. Many of the Koreans in Siberia—who in 1918 were estimated to number about 200,000—fought there with the bolsheviks against the White Russians and the Allied Expeditionary Forces, and Yi Tong-hwi was helped with money sent at Lenin's direction. In April 1919 the Korean socialists took the name Korean Communist Party (Koryŏ Kongsan-dang) and moved their headquarters to Vladivostok. Soon afterward the headquarters was moved to Shanghai, where the nationalist Korean provisional government had been set up.

When the bolsheviks failed to move against the Japanese after consolidating their power, the Korean communists, whose organization had been only a nominal one for some years, fell into dissension. The result was that the Comintern instructed them to concentrate on forming a party based in Korea itself. Agents from Vladivostok and young Korean intellectuals recently converted to Marxism in Japanese universities became the nucleus of the new Korean Communist Party (Chosŏn Kongsan-dang, CKD), founded on April 25, 1925, in Seoul.

Most of those at the founding meeting were still in their twenties and were employed as journalists. Some also took part in the labor and youth movements which had begun to take shape in Korea. One of the participants was Pak Hŏn-yŏng, who survived Japanese persecution until 1945 and took a leading role in reconstructing the communist movement after the Japanese surrender. Another was Cho Pong-am, who in 1948 became the first minister of agriculture in the Republic of Korea (South Korea) government, ran for president against Syngman Rhee in 1956, and was executed by the Rhee regime in 1959 for alleged complicity with the North Korean communists.

## HISTORY

Soon after its founding the Korean party ran into a formidable obstacle—the Japanese police. Mass arrests in December 1925, June 1926, and February and July 1928 virtually wiped out the small number of converts. Serious internal dissension also developed, and in December 1928 the Comintern rescinded its recognition of the CKD as a section and ordered the Korean communists to build a strong base among workers and peasants.

In response to the "December theses" of the Comintern, various communist groups inside and outside Korea made serious efforts. The Chinese Communist Party, which absorbed the Korean communists in Manchuria in 1930, sent several agents into Korea through its branches in Manchuria and Shanghai. The Comintern and Profintern dispatched a score of Moscow-trained agents between

1930 and 1935. Most of those sent, however, were intercepted by the Japanese police, and although some did succeed at various times in organizing farmers in the northeastern parts of Korea, these movements, each involving a few hundred persons, were suppressed. By the early 1940s the Japanese had imposed totalitarian control over Korea, and the communist efforts could not be continued.

The Japanese surrender in August 1945 dramatically altered the situation. Particularly in Soviet-occupied North Korea, the building of the communist party became a priority task. Even in American-occupied South Korea the communists enjoyed considerable freedom during at least the first two years. These efforts were accompanied by an intense power struggle among the communists—Pak Hŏn-yŏng and his comrades of the "domestic faction," who had weathered the storms of Japanese persecution in Korea during the previous two decades; Kim Il-sŏng and his followers, who had been a part of the Chinese communist-controlled northeastern anti-Japanese Allied army in Manchuria and engaged in guerrilla warfare against the Japanese there between 1934 and 1941; and the "Yenan returnees" from China, who had collaborated with the Chinese communists in the anti-Japanese struggle. The guerrillas under Kim Il-sŏng's personal command had once numbered 200 to 300 men but had been reduced to a much smaller contingent after their retreat to Siberia in 1941. After recuperation, training, and indoctrination, Kim's group returned to Korea with the Soviet army, which also brought in a number of Koreans born and raised in Siberia. The Yenan returnees were also few in number, although the group had built up a sizable army in Manchuria after the Japanese surrender by enlisting young Korean men who had previously been conscripted into the Japanese army.

In September 1945 the domestic-faction communists, who had already begun the task of rebuilding the CKD, established a party central committee in Seoul. They assumed that this central committee, headed by Pak Hŏn-yŏng, would exercise control over the party throughout Korea, including the local parties in the north, and that the Soviet command would recognize its legitimacy. This assumption was quickly challenged by Kim Il-sŏng, who had returned to North Korea in October with the full backing of the Soviet command in Pyongyang. Kim's position, and hence that of the Soviet command, was that a separate communist organization should be established in the Soviet occupation zone, and that he should head it. Kim insisted on taking full advantage of the presence of the Soviet army in North Korea. The protests of the domestic-faction leaders were to no avail, and at a "conference of the provincial representatives and activists" in October 1945, the North Korean branch of the CKD was created, with Kim Il-sŏng as first secretary. Recruitment was pushed, and on December 17, when the North Korean group was reorganized as the North Korean Communist Party (Puk-Chosŏn Kongsang-dang, PCKD), Kim announced the party strength as 4,500 members. Although Pak Hong-yŏng's domestic faction insisted on calling itself the central committee, the creation of the PCKD in effect limited its power to South Korea. O Ki-sŏp, a strong supporter of Pak in the north, was appointed vice chairman of the PCKD to placate the domestic faction. However, at the third enlarged executive committee meeting of the North Korean communists Kim also announced an internal purge and the establishment of stronger discipline. In the fall and early winter of 1945 new party certificates were issued by the executive committee at Pyongyang, now headed by Kim Il-sŏng; this measure, together with the subsequent purge, rendered the domestic-faction group impotent in North Korea.

Late in August 1946 the PCKD took another major step to expand its forces. The Yenan returnees in North Korea had formed the New People's Party (Shinmin-dang, SD) in March and rapidly expanded its membership, particularly among the intellectuals. The PCKD, in contrast, had emphasized its efforts among the workers and peasants. Naturally the social composition of the two parties had overlapped to some extent. The SD, having a more moderate platform than the communists on such issues as land reform and religion, appealed to important segments of the population, and obviously there was a danger of collision between the two parties. Since the leadership of the SD comprised experienced revolutionaries who enjoyed a considerable popular reputation both as revolutionaries and as intellectuals, the PCKD was in no position to suppress or even demean them. A merger of the two parties, however, offered advantages to both groups.

Between August 28 and 30, therefore, the representatives of the two parties met in a joint conference and agreed to merge as the North Korean Workers' Party (Puk-Chosŏn Nodong-dang, PCND). According to an official source, the membership of the PCKD at the time was 276,000 and that of the SD was 9,000. The announced purpose of the new PCND was to represent and protect "the interest of the working masses of Korea." Kim Il-sŏng declared that anyone engaged in the struggle for democracy and patriotism could join the PCND even if he did not understand Marxism-Leninism. He argued that the main reason for the merger was to unite the strength of the working masses in the struggle for the realization of progressive democracy. Kim Tu-bong, the leader of the Yenan group and a reputed scholar of the Korean language, became the party chairman; Kim Il-sŏng became the vice chairman.

Within a few days—on September 4—the CKD in South Korea took part in a similar merger with the People's Party (Inmin-dang), consisting of moderate social democrats, and the SD, which had only nominal existence in South Korea. The chairmanship of the resulting South Korean Workers' Party (Nam-Chosŏn Nodong-dang, NCND) went to a former nationalist lawyer, Hŏ Hŏn, who had defended communists before Japanese courts. Pak Hŏn-yŏng, the head of the CKD in South Korea, became the vice chairman. The timing and manner of the merger suggest that the developments in South Korea were not totally voluntary.

The communist movement in South Korea suffered considerably from the unfavorable attitude taken by the United States occupation authorities after the discovery of a currency-forgery incident in May 1946. Nevertheless, considerable progress had been made in recruiting members. South Korea was experiencing food shortages resulting from a severe drought in 1946, and the economy as a whole was under severe strain. Political confusion and the delay in implementing reform measures also created opportunities for the communists. The party relied heavily on mass organizations such as the National Conference of Labor Unions, the Federation of Farmers' Unions, the Federation of Youth Organizations, and the Women's League, created during November and December 1945, and controlled by the party through the National United Front, which advocated the establishment of a "progressive and democratic" Korea excluding all "pro-Japanese elements" and "national traitors"—these being so defined as to include all conservative elements. (In North Korea the Democratic National United Front Committee was created on July 22, 1946, several months before its counterpart was established in Seoul.)

Through front organizations the communists in South Korea staged numerous strikes and riots, including the general strikes of September-November 1946, March 22, 1947, and February 7, 1948; the armed riots on Cheju Island, extending from April 1948 into the following year; and the riots against the general elections in May 1948. A regiment of the South Korean army rebelled under communist leadership in the port city of Yosu, precipitating a major crisis for the new regime in Seoul and providing the basic forces for guerrilla operations in the mountains. There is no doubt that the communists had a large following in South Korea. At its peak, the NCND is said to have had 370,000 members.

The American military authorities, and later the Republic of Korea government, formed in South Korea in May 1948, suppressed all manifestations of the radical left, and many of the principal communist leaders went north; Pak Hŏn-yŏng went to Pyongyang and became the vice premier and foreign minister of the Democratic People's Republic, created in North Korea on September 8, 1948. Other communists in the south went underground until the North Korean invasion in June 1950.

Finally, in June 1949, the NCND and the PCND united officially as a single party, the Korean Workers' Party (CND), signaling the final capitulation of the domestic-faction leaders to Kim Il-sŏng. Despite their considerable following, communist leaders in South Korea could no longer effectively counter the argument that the north was in fact the "revolutionary base" for all Korea and that the movement must be placed under a unified command. Kim Il-sŏng became the chairman of the united party, and Pak Hŏn-yŏng the vice chairman. This united communist party, still called the CND, was the best organized and best-disciplined political group in the country in 1949.

It was under these conditions that the communist regime in the north launched the Korean War in June 1950. North Korea not only possessed superior armed forces, but also, according to the statements of Kim Il-sŏng in later years, the Pyongyang regime expected the communist organizations in the south to provide active assistance. The unexpected American and United Nations intervention, particularly General MacArthur's Inchon landing in September 1950, frustrated the original aim of a communist unification of the country. The communist guerrillas in South Korea failed to mobilize the masses to exterminate the government forces from the critical Pusan perimeter in the summer of 1950.

The disastrous outcome of the attempted communist takeover had the usual repercussions within the party. Soon after the 1953 truce Yi Sŭng-yŏp and other leaders of the domestic faction who had held important cabinet and party positions in North Korea were tried and convicted as American spies and for having attempted to overthrow the regime. Pak Hŏn-yŏng, the top man from South Korea, was convicted and executed in 1955. The war also had disastrous effects on the communist movement in South Korea. The South Korean communists and communist sympathizers, having played active roles in assisting the North Korean forces, were too easily identifiable to continue any underground activities. They were therefore forced either to flee to North Korea or to retreat to the mountains and join the guerrilla bands, which were eventually destroyed by the South Korean military and police forces around 1955.

In the meantime the cult of Kim Il-sŏng was pushed in North Korea, and aggressive reconstruction plans were put into effect, including collectivization of farms (completed in 1958) and high-priority development of heavy industries.

The de-Stalinization campaign of 1956 had immediate repercussions in the Korean party. Evidently there were honest differences of opinion regarding the pace of agricultural collectivization and industrial construction, with some elements in the leadership urging a slackening to give respite to the weary populace. The Soviet representatives in North Korea also recommended this course. Another major grievance was over the frenzied cult of Kim Il-sŏng. Khrushchev's report to the twentieth congress of the Communist Party of the Soviet Union thus fell on sympathetic ears in North Korea. Some of the Yenan returnees and the "Soviet-faction men," who had been born and trained in Siberia before 1945, demanded a showdown at the August 1956 plenum of the party's central committee, which had been called to hear the premier's report on his visit to the Soviet Union and Eastern Europe. The Kim Il-sŏng group, however, outmaneuvered and outnumbered the dissidents, and opposition was crushed. Kim defended his leadership as being in accord with the principle of collective leadership and attacked his opponents as "individual heroists" who wished to advance their personal interests above those of the party. The subsequent

1956 purge and another purge of same nature in 1958 effectively eliminated all dissidents.

## ORGANIZATION AND MEMBERSHIP

According to the party bylaws, the "elementary party organization" is the cell, to be organized when there are a minimum of three members in an institution, village, etc. The bylaws also stipulate that the "party is organized under the principle of democratic centralism"; thus a lower party organization must obey the superior organization, and all party organizations must "absolutely obey" the party central committee. The central committee is elected by the party congress, the "supreme organization of the party." To direct its activities between the plenary congresses the central committee elects a political committee. Between the central committee and the cells there are provincial, city, prefectural, and district organizations.

According to the statistics released by the North Korean regime, as of August 1, 1961, the party had 1,311,563 members, including 145,204 candidate members. The party members definitely enjoy special privileges as the "advanced fighters" who protect the interest of the working masses. The preponderance of party members in North Korea is attributable to the nature of the CND. In 1946, when Kim Il-sŏng, merged his party with the heterogeneous elements of the SD, he had argued the need for "a mass party that can consolidate the greatest number of people" and for getting rid of class boundaries in order to "consolidate the entire forces ... of the working masses," including workers, peasants, and intellectuals. In short, the PCND formed at that time supposedly represented a broader spectrum of society than the communist parties elsewhere. A decade later, at the third congress of the CND, Kim Il-sŏng characterized the party in North Korea as a "Marxist-Leninist mass political party." According to the 1960 official statistics, 52 percent of the North Korean population are "workers and office employees" (probably including their families), and 44.4 percent are members of the agricultural cooperatives. No statistics are available regarding the socio-economic background of the party members.

In theory, North Korea is under a "people's dictatorship" or "people's democracy," and the Democratic People's Republic of Korea is the embodiment of this theory. In addition to the CND, other "democratic" parties are presumably functioning in North Korea, such as the Korean Democratic Party and the Heavenly-Way-Religion Youth Fraternal Party. However, members of these parties have been discredited because the vast majority of them proved to be disloyal to the communist regime during the Korean War. Although the names of these parties and of their leaders are still used for propaganda purposes, observers generally agree that the "fraternal parties" do not in fact possess any members.

These phantom political parties and the actual CND and its subsidiary organizations are the participants in the Fatherland United Democratic Front, created in June 1949 and dedicated to the cause of "strengthening the united front under the CND to emancipate South Korea from the enslavement of American imperialism and attain the peaceful unification and complete independence of the fatherland."

The more important mass organizations that serve as the recruiting ground and subsidiary agents of the party in North Korea are the Korean Occupational General League (the equivalent of a general federation of labor unions), with a membership of 1,721,000 in 1962; the Korean Agricultural Workers' League; the Korean Democratic Women's League, with 2,500,000 members; and the Democratic Labor Youth League, with 2,713,000 members—renamed the Socialist Labor Youth League in May 1964 because "the socialist revolution has won an over-all victory [and] the level of the young people's ideological consciousness has been enhanced." The new league is to develop into a "more revolutionary and militant organization."

The aims of these organizations are clearly stated in their respective bylaws. For instance, the Occupational General League is defined as a "belt to joint together the Korean Workers' Party and the working masses [workers and office employees] and become the trustworthy supporting organization of the Korean Workers' Party." The basic duty of the Socialist Labor Youth League is "to unite all young men firmly around the Korean Workers' Party, positively organize and mobilize them for the execution of the great revolutionary tasks of uniting the fatherland and constructing socialism and communism, and raise them to become fully developed communist builders and the trustworthy rear guard of the Korean Workers' Party."

## THE SINO-SOVIET DISPUTE

Evidence indicates that the North Korean communists watched the aggravation of Sino-Soviet relations with discomfort and made some attempts to stop the trend toward a split. Until about 1961, when they were forced to take a clear-cut stand on some of the issues that directly concerned them, they did their best to maintain a neutral stance. The Pyongyang regime in the meantime issued numerous statements that placed supreme value on unity within the communist bloc.

Between 1961 and 1964, however, the Korean communists leaned very heavily toward Peking, supporting it on every major issue. They supported Albania, denounced Nehru, denounced "appeasement" of the United States on the Cuban issue, attacked Tito and the "revisionists," and opposed the conference on world communism in April 1964. Editorials in the party paper *Rodong Shinmun* acrimoniously cited instances of Russian misbehavior both in North Korea and in the international communist movement. The issues that particularly provoked the Korean communists were the Russians' big-power chauvinism, "appeasement of imperialists," and interference in the domestic politics of communist states.

After the demise of Khrushchev in October 1964 the North Korean communists began to tone down their denunciation of the Russians and to take actions suggesting an eventual return to the former neutral stance. The signing of a military-aid pact with the Soviet Union in May 1965, among other things, seems to offer some evidence of reconciliation with Moscow. There are indications, however, that the finger of accusation is still pointed toward Moscow and that Pyongyang is not yet satisfied by whatever conciliatory moves may have come from there. In short, while the CND is pragmatic enough to maintain contacts with the Soviet Union, it is taking the Chinese side on major issues. The North Korean view of international communism is that of an alliance of equals pursuing the same goal by diverse means. Recent behavior suggests that while the CND is not willing to alter its stand on basic issues, it is seeking to reach a *modus vivendi* within the communist camp.

## FUTURE PROSPECTS

The Korean communists have created in North Korea a stringent totalitarian system. In spite of various changes in Eastern Europe, they have pursued their goals with the fanaticism characteristics of first-generation revolutionaries. The present party leaders are also striving to remold the populace under their control into their image of the communist man at high cost to individual dignity and human rights. There is little likelihood that they will diverge from their present course within the foreseeable future.

## PARTY PRESS ORGANS AND RECORDS

*Rodong Shinmun* (Workers' News) is the party's daily, and *Kulloja* (The Worker) is the official monthly.

Party statutes can be found in *Chosŏn Rodong-dang Kyuyak Haesŏl* (Commentary on the Bylaws of the Korean Workers' Party), Tokyo, Hak-u So-bang, 1960, originally published by the party press in Pyongyang and reissued in Tokyo by the Federation of the Koreans in Japan. The best source for current party programs is the *Chosŏn Chung-ang Nyŏn-gam* (Korean Central Yearbook), published annually by the Korean Central News Agency in Pyongyang. The party published the *Documents of the Fourth Congress of the Workers' Party of Korea*, Pyongyang, Foreign Languages Publishing House, 1961. For other congresses see *Kim Il-sŏng Sŏnjip* (Selected Works of Kim Il-sŏng), vols. I-VI, Pyongyang, 1960-1964.

## PARTY CONGRESSES

1st congress, PCND, August 1946
2d congress, PCND, March 1948
3d congress, CND, April 1956
4th congress, CND, September 1961, Pyongyang

## BIBLIOGRAPHY

Lee, Chong-Sik: "Stalinism in the East: Communism in North Korea," in Robert A. Scalapino (ed.), *The Communist Revolution in Asia: Tactics, Goals, and Achievements*, Englewood Cliffs, N.J., 1965.
Lee, Chong-Sik, and Pyoung Hoon Kim: "Korea and the Korean War," in Thomas T. Hammond (ed.), *Soviet Foreign Relations and World Communism: Annotated Bibliography*, Princeton, N.J., 1965, pp. 787-806.
Paige, Glenn D.: "Korea," in Cyril E. Black and T. P. Thornton (eds.), *Communism and Revolution,* Princeton, N.J., 1964.
Paige, Glenn D.: *The Korean People's Democratic Republic*, Stanford, Calif., 1966.
Paige, Glenn D.: "North Korea and the Emulation of Russian and Chinese Behavior," in A. Doak Barnett (ed.), *Communist Strategies in Asia*, New York, 1963.
Scalapino, Robert A.: *North Korea Today*, New York, 1963.
Suh, Dae Sook: *The Korean Communist Movement, 1918-1948*, Princeton, N.J., 1966.
U.S. Department of State: *North Korea: A Case Study in the Techniques of Takeover*, Washington, 1961.

CHONG-SIK LEE

# KRESTINTERN
*See* The International Peasants' Council

# LAOS

Communist activity in Laos is relatively well known under the cover of two front organizations—one political in character, the Laotian Patriotic Front (Neo Lao Hak Xat, NLHX), and the other a military organization, the Laotian Fighting Units (Pathet Lao). However, little is known about the activities of the communist party itself, the Laotian People's Party (Pasachone Lao, PL).

Communist activity in Laos has always been closely linked to the communist movement in Vietnam, before independence as well as since. Early Laotian communists joined groups formed by Ho Chi Minh and his collaborators, and they were among the first members of the Communist Party of Indochina (Dong Duong Cong San Dang), founded in 1930. When this party was dissolved in 1945, the general "restructuring" of the Vietnamese communist movement affected Laos as well. But once again, it was in Vietnam that the movement took shape, with regard both to communist activity and to the first front organization.

## HISTORY

The Laotian party had its origins in 1945-1946 in a communist cell in Hanoi, under the close surveillance of the Vietnamese party. Kaysone Phomvihan, a law student from Hanoi, soon became the leader of the group. By the end of 1946 he had passed into the ranks of the Viet Minh and was sent to Laos to establish the first liaison with the Laotian communist movement.

The Vietnamese party was also instrumental in setting up front activity in Laos. Prince Souphanouvong returned to Laos in 1945 with instructions from the Viet Minh to organize a national-liberation movement in Laos on the Vietnamese pattern. On his arrival he founded the Association for the Independence of Laos. The group was nationalist in character, but its lack of success forced a change of tactics. Instead of creating a movement for liberation and independence out of thin air, the association decided that it could more effectively infiltrate the existing organization of Free Laos (Lao Issara), set up communist cells within it, and give it a procommunist orientation. As minister of foreign affairs of the Free Laos government, Souphanouvong traveled to Hanoi in 1945 and made official contact with the Viet Minh. However, in 1947-1948 the Free Laos government began to break up as a result of nationalist opposition to communist aims, and in May 1949 Souphanouvong was relieved of his duties as foreign minister. The communiqué of the council of ministers on May 16, 1949, accused the prince of having "sent Chinese mercenaries to fight in Upper Laos."

Six months later Souphanouvong met with Ho Chi Minh, established still closer ties with the Viet Minh, and joined the Laotian communist units directed by Kaysone Phomvihan to form the Free Laos Front (Neo Lao Issara). In late 1950 he returned to Sam Neua province to form regional committees designed to be the nuclei of the "popular government." In the provincial capital he proclaimed the installation of a provisional government and a national assembly, but this façade had little political and military backing, and Souphanouvong was forced to flee with his partisans to North Vietnam.

A few years later, with generous aid from the Viet Minh, a reduced number of Laotian communists once again succeeded in gaining a foothold in the country. In 1953 North Vietnamese troops invaded Laos, and the Pathet Lao, military units formed by Prince Souphanouvong's partisans, established "free territory" in the provinces of Phong Saly and Sam Neua. The prince proclaimed to his troops that "the liberation of Sam Neua was also the result of the fraternal unity between the Neo Lao Issara and Vietnam, of the unconditional aid of the people of Vietnam. These people have a very strict discipline and a high spirit of internationalism. In the name of the Laotian people, I welcome them and express my gratitude to them."[1]

Sam Neua became the military headquarters of the Pathet Lao, and a government and national assembly were set up. A successful counteroffensive was soon launched by the French colonial government, however, and the prince and his partisans once again took refuge with the Vietnamese communists, who added diplomatic support to their political and military assistance. At the opening of the Geneva conference in 1954, Pham Van Dong, the foreign minister of the Democratic Republic of Vietnam (North Vietnam), insisted that a delegation of the "Laotian patriotic fighting units" be admitted to the talks. In

1954, the Free Laos Front was renamed the Laotian Patriotic Front (NLHX). The NLHX held its first congress in January 1956 in Sam Neua and elected Prince Souphanouvong president.

Several months earlier, in 1955, the party itself had held its first congress. Kaysone Phomvihan became general secretary, a post he still held at the end of 1965, although he alternated his time between Laos and North Vietnam. Thus in the space of a few months parallel structures were set up: the Laotian party, with its underground apparatus, and the NLHX, the so-called "national movement."

The NLHX scored a political success when it was granted legal status by the Vientiane agreement of 1957 and its representatives entered the coalition government formed by Prince Souvanna Phouma in November 1957. However, this was to be only a temporary phase. In May 1959 the Pathet Lao refused to agree to incorporation of its fighting units—estimated at 2,000 strong—into the Royal Laotian Army, and the two communist-controlled provinces entered the dispute. In August 1960 a coup against the Vientiane government, organized by Captain Kong-Lê and supported by the Pathet Lao at the outset, overthrew the regime. The Pathet Lao forces, with aid from other communist countries, scored a considerable success, and skirmishes on the Plaine des Jarres continued until the Geneva agreements in July 1962 managed to set up a new cease-fire, short-lived though it was.

Since that time politics in Laos in general and the tactics of the communist and procommunist forces in particular have become more and more closely linked to events in Vietnam.

## RELATION TO SOVIET LEADERSHIP

The Laotian party has never attended the world meetings of the communist parties. It is not among the signatories to the texts adopted at the world communist meetings of November 1957 and November 1960 in Moscow, and there is no record of its presence either among the foreign delegations at the congresses of the Soviet party or among some thirty Marxist-Leninist delegations meeting in Tirana in 1966 during the fifth congress of the Albanian party. Its very close ties with North Vietnam would indicate an alignment with Hanoi in the Sino-Soviet dispute.

## PARTY CONGRESSES

1st congress, PL, 1955
1st congress, NLHX, January 1956, Sam Neua
2d congress, NLHX, April 1964

## BIBLIOGRAPHY

Dommen, Arthur J.: *Conflict in Laos: The Politics of Neutralization*, New York, Praeger, 1964.
Fall, Bernard B.: "The Pathet Lao: A 'Liberation' Army," in Robert A. Scalapino (ed.), *The Communist Revolution in Asia: Tactics, Goals, and Achievements*, Englewood Cliffs, N.J., Prentice-Hall, 1965.
Halpern, Abraham M., and H. B. Fredman: *Communist Strategy in Laos*, Santa Monica, Calif., Rand Corporation, November 15, 1960.

BRANKO LAZITCH

1. *Est & ouest*, no. 333, January 1-15, 1965, p. 20.

# LATIN AMERICA[1]

Communist parties or groups were created in every country in Latin America between 1918 and 1942. The majority have had a continuous, if often precarious, existence from the date of their founding, but several have been repressed and reestablished two or three times. The present communist parties of Bolivia, Guatemala, Haiti, and Honduras were founded between 1949 and 1959. Although there have often been rival communist organizations competing within a single country, it is only since 1959 that communist parties have existed simultaneously in all twenty of the Latin American republics.

## ORIGINS

Thirteen of the national communist parties are now known as communist, but only two—those of Brazil and Paraguay—have always been openly identified as such. The communist parties of Argentina, Chile, Mexico, and Uruguay owe their origin to socialist parties that existed before 1917, while those of Colombia, Ecuador, Panama, and Peru grew out of socialist or workers' parties established in the 1920s. The party in El Salvador masqueraded for several years as a branch of International Red Aid. During the Comintern's third period (see *The Communist International*), from 1928 to 1935, all Latin American member parties were obliged to declare themselves communist, but since the era of the popular front, a variety of other names has again been employed. The Venezuelan party was frequently overshadowed by front parties in the 1930s and 1940s, and after 1943 the word "communist" was dropped from the name of the Soviet-approved party in Costa Rica, Cuba, the Dominican Republic, Guatemala, Haiti, Panama, and, for a time, Colombia. The postwar communist parties of Bolivia and Honduras began as splinter groups of self-proclaimed "revolutionary" parties. The Socialist Party of Nicaragua (Partido Socialista de Nicaragua), founded in 1937, is the only orthodox Marxist-Leninist party in Latin America that has never been known formally as communist. In Mexico the Socialist People's Party (Partido Popular Socialista), which also eschews the communist tag, appears to be an approved front party.[2]

*Early Founders* The early communist leaders in Latin America were rebels who claimed to speak in the name of the masses. They were young when they became communists, many less than twenty and few over thirty years of age. With considerable enthusiasm and limited effectiveness they had participated in socialist, anarchist, anarchosyndicalist, or indigenous political parties, trade unions, and revolutionary movements in their respective countries or elsewhere in the hemisphere. The originators of some of the later parties first joined the international communist movement during periods of exile in neighboring Latin American republics or the United States. Their objective was to overthrow or transform the traditional order in which wealth and political power were the monopoly of a small upper class.

Although the early communists presented themselves as representatives of the proletariat, very few were actually from the working class. In a region where formal education was the privilege of the few, and where literacy alone was usually enough to distinguish the individual from the common herd, nearly all the party leaders had been to school and many had university training. By today's standards they were members of the middle and lower middle classes, and their appeals were most effective among other members of these social strata. In this respect the communists were not unlike the leaders of noncommunist protest groups throughout Latin America, who relied heavily on the written word and the experiences of "more advanced" foreign peoples in their political programs and propaganda. They differed from other proponents of radical change in looking to the example of the Russian revolution, to the writings of Lenin, and later to the accomplishments of the Soviet Union for inspiration, a blueprint for revolution, and a model for a new political system in Latin America. The overwhelming majority of the perennial communist leaders in Latin America, including virtually all the party founders who remained active in the communist movement, have been consistently loyal and subservient to the Soviet Union, regularly placing its interests before those of their nation and frequently over the immediate interests of their own party.

While the above characteristics are common to the generality of Latin American communist leadership since 1918, there have been significant differences in the backgrounds and personalities of the men who established the Latin American parties. Foreigners, although few in number, deserve special mention. They include the Indian nationalist M. N. Roy and Linn Gale, Charles Phillips, and Bertram D. Wolfe of the United States. Wolfe arrived in Mexico more or less by chance to play an instrumental role in the origin and early development of the Mexican Communist Party (Partido Comunista Mexicano). Comintern agents also figured prominently among the foreign contingent in Latin America. Katayama Sen from Japan and Luis Fraina of the United States counseled the young party in Mexico and recommended the establishment of communist organizations in El Salvador and Guatemala in the early 1920s. A few years later another communist from the United States, Joseph Zack Kornfedder, served as the Comintern's representative in northern South America. Kornfedder presided over the conversion of the Colombian Socialist Revolutionary Party (Partido Socialista Revolucionario) into the Communist Party of Colombia (Partido Comunista de Colombia) in 1930 and maintained liaison with Venezuelan exiles who merged incipient communist groups into the Communist Party of Venezuela (Partido Comunista de Venezuela) in 1931. Other communists from the United States and various parts of Europe held positions in the Caribbean and South American Bureaus of the Comintern, advising existing parties and contributing to the formation of new ones, between 1928 and 1935. However, non-Latin American agents of the international communist movement have appeared only rarely in regional or national communist party councils in the past thirty years. The principal exception occurred in the Dominican Republic, where the Dominican Communist Party (Partido Comunista Dominicano) was inspired in 1942 by exiles from Spain.

From the beginning of the communist movement in Latin America the vast majority of party leaders have been citizens of the republic in which their party operated. But even here the leadership has reflected a relatively broad variety of origins, training, and experience. A small group, of which Victorio Codovilla of the Communist Party of Argentina (Partido Comunista de la Argentina) is the most notable example, were immigrants. A much larger group were the descendants of immigrants, as evidenced in such names as Rodney Arismendi of Uruguay, Obdulio Barthe and Oscar Creydt of Paraguay, Aurelio Fortoul of Venezuela, Rodolfo Ghioldi of Argentina, Luis Corvalán Leppe and Elías Lafertte of Chile, Pedro Saad of Ecuador, Gilberto Vieira White of Colombia, and Juan Pablo Wainwright of Honduras.

*Composition of Early Parties* More significant than the national or ethnic origins of the communist spokesmen, however, were their professional and occupational backgrounds. Some, like Julio Antonio Mella, a founder of the Communist Party of Cuba (Partido Comunista de Cuba), were university student leaders before becoming communists. Still more were former university students, who therefore regarded themselves and were accepted by their contemporaries as intellectuals. Every Latin American communist party includes such intellectuals among its founders and continuing leaders. Typical of this group were Jacques Roumain and Max Hudicourt, co-founders of the first Communist Party of Haiti (Parti Communiste d'Haiti), Obdulio Barthe, who helped to create the Paraguayan Communist Party (Partido Comunista Paraguayo), and Manuel Mora Valverde, originator and long-time leader of the Communist Party of Costa Rica (Partido Comunista de Costa Rica) and its successor, the Popular Vanguard Party (Partido Vanguardia Popular). Outstanding among the intellectuals was José Carlos Mariátegui, perhaps the only original Marxist theoretician of Latin America, who is claimed by both socialists and communists in Peru as the founder of their parties. In Chile a somewhat comparable position is occupied by Luis Emilio Recabarren, a labor journalist who created the Socialist Workers' Party (Partido Obrero Socialista) in 1912 and converted it into the Communist Party of Chile (Partido Comunista de Chile) ten years later. Also included in the category of communist party intellectuals are newsmen such as Astrogildo Pereira, a founder and one-time secretary general of the Communist Party of Brazil (Partido Comunista do Brasil), schoolteachers such as Ricardo Fonseca of Chile, and physicians such as Ricardo Paredes, a founder of the Ecuadorean Socialist Party (Partido Socialista Ecuatoriano) who later transformed its left wing into the Communist Party of Ecuador (Partido Comunista del Ecuador).

Recabarren and Paredes also belong in the group of trade-union leaders who figured conspicuously among the originators of most of the Latin American communist parties. Others in this category include Carlos Baliño, cofounder of the Cuban communist movement, Elías Lafertte, long prominent among the top leadership of the Chilean party, and Eugenio Gómez, a founder and for thirty years secretary general of the Communist Party of Uruguay (Partido Comunista del Uruguay). In view of the rudimentary stage of development of organized labor in Latin America at the time of the founding of the communist parties, it is not surprising that relatively few communist labor leaders were true representatives of the working class. It is significant, however, that only a minute percentage of the sons of laborers who entered the party rose to important posts within the Latin American communist movement. The select group of party leaders drawn from the working class, which included men such as the Chilean Lafertte and the Cuban Blas Roca (Francisco Calderío), was relatively larger in countries where upward social mobility was a common occurrence.

A further indication of the origins and early direction of the Latin American communist movement may be discerned from the professional, occupational, and social groups that were excluded or at best poorly represented in the membership of the young communist parties. These parties all described themselves as the vanguard of the workers and peasants. Without exception the description was largely erroneous. Even though the landless rural populace—the "peasantry," in communist terminology—accounted for up to 90 percent of the population when the first parties were created, it appears that no peasants were included among the founders of any communist party in Latin America in the 1920s or 1930s. The Mexican party organized a few "peasant" battalions for the civil war in 1923, but elsewhere the wage-earning plantation-labor force was the only agricultural group then of interest to the communists, and this primarily in the Caribbean area on estates owned and managed by foreign firms. Like virtually all other political parties throughout Latin America at the time, the early communist parties were predominantly urban oriented. The communists were concerned above all with the proletariat, which in their view was limited to transport workers, miners, and laborers in the few manufacturing and processing industries. They did not initially seek recruits among laborers or white-collar workers in the service industries or the bureaucracy, which accounted for the bulk of the urban wage earners in Latin America. Members of the regular armed forces were also omitted from the communist parties in their early years, and the communists were generally unsuccessful when they later sought to build a following among soldiers and sailors. Nonetheless, some veterans of the 1910 revolution were drawn to the party in Mexico for a short time in the 1920s, and substantial numbers of his former comrades in revolution were brought into the Brazilian party by the ex-army captain Luiz Carlos Prestes after 1934. A few Latin American parties, however, appear to have attracted experienced revolutionaries with no fixed military ties or affiliations. Undoubtedly the most flamboyant of these was the professional soldier of fortune Juan Pablo Wainwright, who was active in the communist movement in El Salvador and Guatemala before 1932 and is claimed as a founder of the first Communist Party of Honduras (Partido Comunista de Honduras).

*Defections* The communist parties of Latin America have always been characterized by a continuous, and at times heavy and rapid, turnover in membership. This process has been more pronounced among the rank and file, although over the years it has also included a substantial segment of party leaders. Some of the founders of each of the Latin American parties later broke with the communist movement or were expelled as a result of disenchantment or unwillingness to accept a sudden reversal of the party line. Understandably, the casualty rate among founding members was usually highest during the first few years of the party's existence, but occasional expulsions of once-venerated charter members and long-time party dignitaries have been recorded in each decade since 1920.

The disaffected party founders fall into one or more of several categories, according to the circumstances under which they left the party and their subsequent importance in national politics. The great majority appear either to have abandoned politics altogether or to have played only a modest role in other organizations after leaving the communist movement. The following examples are typical. José C. Valadés, the first theoretician of the Mexican party, who had dropped out of sight by 1923, seems to have withdrawn from the party voluntarily. Antonio Canelas, who joined the Communist Party of Brazil in its first year, resigned two years later after representing Brazil at the fourth Comintern congress in Moscow, where he quarreled with the then-powerful Leon Trotsky. Canelas continued active but inconspicuous in left-wing labor circles in Brazil for several years. José F. Penelón, one of the original Argentine communists, broke with Codovilla's leadership in 1928 to form his own dissident party. His Workers' Concentration Party (Partido Concentración Obrera) survived for over a quarter of a century but never exerted significant influence in Argentine politics.

Several party founders were expelled for personal or political misconduct. This group includes Guillermo Hernández Rodríguez, the first secretary general of the Colombian party, who was expelled in 1932 for unspecified indiscretions. Francisco Henríquez, one of the founders of the Dominican party, was expelled in 1946 on charges of "deviationism." Ricardo A. Martínez, a Venezuelan communist labor leader who had been a Comintern agent before the founding of the Venezuelan party, was expelled from his party in 1951 for advocating "appeasement" of the Pérez Jiménez dictatorship. Another whose public career ended with his separation from the communist movement was Eugenio Gómez, a leader of the Uruguayan party from its inception until his expulsion in 1955. Gomez was a victim of long-smoldering factionalism that was fanned into open opposition by resentment over the party's poor showing at the polls. In 1956, when the anti-Stalin campaign was publicized in Latin America, he was further denounced for having tried to establish a "personality cult" among Uruguayan communists.

A few who participated in the formation of communist parties in Latin America later became effective opponents of communism. The most successful of these was Rómulo Betancourt of Venezuela. As a political exile in Costa Rica in the 1920s, Betancourt cooperated with Manuel Mora Valverde in organizing the communist party in that country. Within a few years, however, he became disillusioned with communism as a solution for Latin America's political ills. Returning to Venezuela, he eventually formed the noncommunist leftist Democratic Action (Acción Democrática), a party with which he held power for nearly three years after World War II and again from 1959 to 1964. Less well known is Manuel Hidalgo of Chile, who represented the communist party in congress in the 1920s. He broke with the Comintern-approved leadership in the early 1930s, headed a Trotskyist group for a time, and finally joined the socialist party, which he represented in congress for many years. The most notorious ex-communist in Latin America is Eudocio Ravines, a founder of the Peruvian Communist Party (Partido Comunista Peruano) and Comintern agent whose faith in communism was shattered by the Hitler-Stalin pact of 1939. Ravines became the outstanding propagandist against communism in Latin America after his expulsion from the Peruvian party in 1942.

## HISTORY

The history of the communist movement in Latin America can be recounted in terms of the political evolution of the twenty republics since 1918, but it is more meaningful when considered as an aspect of Soviet communist expansion in the twentieth century. The Latin American parties long constituted little more than servile extensions of the international communist movement directed from Moscow. Without exception, they were inspired by the example of the Communist Party of the Soviet Union. Few had an adequate national or regional basis to justify their separate existence. Their exclusive ideology was Marxism-Leninism as interpreted by the head of the Soviet state, and those rare communists who suggested that the party should interpret Marxism for itself in the light of Latin America's unique heritage were driven out of the movement as heretics. Moreover, from the founding of the first communist party in the western hemisphere until the establishment of Cuba as a "socialist republic," the Latin American parties were generally ineffective political instruments, incapable of seizing power by force and too alien to the views of the electorate to achieve this objective at the polls. The great majority were still in this position in 1965. Even in Guatemala, where the communists had seemed close to victory in 1954, their presence evaporated with the first hostile act. This chronic condition resulted at least as much from the policies and misconceptions of Soviet leaders as from the deficiencies and limitations of the communists in Latin America.

From the beginning Soviet leaders placed a low priority on Latin America. In view of their basic assumptions about the nature of the world and of the world revolution, it could hardly have been otherwise. Their first concern was for the security of the Soviet Union. Beyond the frontier the communist parties in the heavily industrialized countries of the West and in the teeming European colonies in Asia commanded their close attention. They tended to equate Latin America with "the colonies," but obviously regarded it as a relatively unimportant and unpromising area. It was apparently inconceivable to Stalin, and perhaps to Lenin as well, that the United States would permit the emergence of a communist government in the western hemisphere. In any case, although the Soviet Union occasionally probed beyond the Atlantic, it did not seriously attempt to extend its influence to Latin America until after the death of Stalin. As a result, throughout most of their existence the Latin American parties have been relegated to a minor position in the international communist hierarchy and have usually been obliged to employ tactics designed for other peoples and other situations.

The successive heads of the Soviet state were concerned chiefly that the leaders of

Latin American communist parties exhibit unquestioned loyalty to the Soviet Union. These circumstances effectively discouraged initiative and imagination in the Latin American communist movement. Only during the Stalin-Trotsky power struggle, and more recently with the Sino-Soviet dispute, did an appreciable number of Latin American communists publicly criticize Soviet direction of world communism. And even in their infrequent moments of dissent, the communists in Latin America showed that they were more closely attuned to situations affecting the Soviet Union than to problems of their own area. Thus each phase in the history of the communist movement in Latin America more nearly corresponds to a trend in Soviet domestic or foreign affairs than to developments within the hemisphere. This history may be divided into at least eight unequal spans, each of which witnessed the creation of communist parties subjected to new demands and opportunities determined largely by events abroad.

*The Birth of the Movement: 1918 to 1922* The first period was one of euphoria following the news of the Russian revolution. During these years five parties were formed, four of them from existing socialist parties and the fifth from a convergence of dissident anarchist groups. Thus, by and large, the early communists in Latin America were already familiar with Marxism and were prepared to accept Soviet assertions that the victory of the bolsheviks marked the beginning of the world revolution and the road to communism. It is more than coincidence that four parties— those of Chile, Argentina, Uruguay, and Brazil—appeared in countries that had received large contingents of immigrants from Europe, where labor organizations were beginning to assume political significance, and where a generally open political system had been established. The fifth party was formed in Mexico, where these conditions did not prevail, although an incipient labor movement had begun to attract notice. There, however, a decade of violent social revoltuion had produced a climate conducive to the spread of radical doctrines.

The oldest communist organization in the western hemisphere is the Communist Party of Argentina, which was founded in January 1918 as the International Socialist Party (Partido Socialista Internacional) by dissidents from the established socialist party. The Argentine party claims to have been a charter member of the Comintern, represented at the first Comintern congress by the Italian Socialist Party (which in fact failed to arrive at the congress). (See *The Communist International*.) It took the communist name in December 1920. Shortly after the founding of the Comintern the Mexican Communist Party was formed, in September 1919. In fact, two dissident factions of the young and ineffectual socialist party organized self-avowed "communist" groups at about the same time and competed for recognition by the Comintern. The M. N. Roy faction, which was affiliated with the Comintern in 1920, survived to become the Soviet-approved party in Mexico. Throughout 1920 the socialist party in Uruguay debated the issue of affiliation with the Comintern. The rank and file generally favored the proposal, but most party leaders objected to Lenin's Twenty-one Conditions. The question was resolved at the party congress in April 1921, when the great majority of the delegates voted to adhere to the Comintern and to adopt the name Communist Party of Uruguay. The minority withdrew to form a new socialist party.

A similar debate took place among Chilean socialists in 1920 and 1921. Here the top party leaders were willing to accept the Twenty-one Conditions but delayed action until their subordinates were convinced of the advantages of membership in the international movement. The party's congress in December 1921-January 1922 voted unanimously to join the Comintern as the Communist Party of Chile. The Socialist Workers' Party in Chile was thus the only such party in Latin America to transfer intact to the international communist movement. The communists in Brazil were the first in Latin America to create an entirely new party. The few socialists appear to have played no role in the formation of the Communist Party of Brazil in March 1922.

Rather, the early communists were intellectuals, journalists, and workers who had been active in underground anarchist groups within the labor movement in various parts of the country. Only one of the party founders, moreover, had previously been in contact with communist organizations in Uruguay and Europe.

The emergence of these small communist parties passed unnoticed in their respective countries. At its inception the Brazilian party had fewer than 100 members, and it grew slowly. The Mexican party was probably even smaller in its early years and seems to have attracted little public attention until it supported the Obregón regime during the 1923 revolt. In Argentina, Chile, and Uruguay, where the communists had inherited an established political organization, they continued to participate in elections, regularly placing a representative or two in national provincial legislatures, but their influence on national politics was minimal. The Mexican and Brazilian parties made little effort to use parliamentary methods until after 1926, when the Comintern called for the formation of worker-peasant blocs to engage in electoral campaigns. The five parties directed their major efforts toward the labor movement, with marginal success. The Brazilian communists were outlawed in July 1922 under a sweeping decree banning all subversive activities, but the other parties continued to enjoy full legal status during most of the 1920s.

*Expansion and Flexibility: 1923 to 1928* During the second stage in Latin America communist or communist-oriented parties and groups appeared in nine republics. Three of these adopted the communist name when they were formed or shortly thereafter, while the others were disguised under various labels. Generally, the second-stage parties were even smaller and faced more serious handicaps than their predecessors. The chief obstacle in each of the nine countries was the existence and long tradition of highly authoritarian regimes opposed to the establishment of labor unions and intolerant of radical political groups. Thus the new parties were illegal and subject to persecution from the beginning. These difficulties were partially offset, however, by the guidance and material aid available from the Comintern and the neighboring communist parties in Latin America.

The Mexican party assisted in the formation of two, and possibly three, new communist groups in Central America. Agents from Mexico took part in the conversion of the young Socialist Labor Unification (Unificación Obrera Socialista) into the Communist Party of Guatemala (Partido Comunista de Guatemala), which affiliated with the Comintern in 1924. The following year Mexican and Guatemalan communists cooperated in organizing a communist group in El Salvador, and in 1927 they may well have aided Juan Pablo Wainwright of Honduras in creating a small communist apparatus in his native country. The Salvadoran and Honduran groups were apparently conceived as sections of a future Communist Party of Central America. In any case, they operated entirely within the labor movement and a variety of international communist front organizations until after the regional party concept was abandoned about 1929.

While a nebulous communist movement was coalescing in Central America, formal communist parties were established in Cuba and Paraguay. In August 1925 the so-called Communist Group of Havana (Agrupación Comunista de La Habana), which dated from 1923, merged with a number of Marxist labor and study groups to form the Communist Party of Cuba under the leadership of Carlos Baliño and Julio Antonio Mella. The Cuban party was admitted into the Comintern in 1928, and despite police harassment and the death of its leaders, it survived to become an influential force in the labor movement. The Paraguayan party was organized in 1928 and affiliated with the Comintern that same year. The new organization was made up of a few ex-anarchist labor agitators and a small coterie of young intellectuals. From the outset the party was handicapped by strong police controls, although it was not formally outlawed until 1936. In contrast to the Cuban party, it exerted little attraction among Paraguayan workers and never achieved a significant position in national politics.

Elsewhere in Latin America during the second period the new communist groups operated within other parties in order to avoid repression. A small handful of self-styled communists were included in the miniscule Laborite (Laborista) party founded in Panama in 1926. This ineffective nucleus was unable either to gain control of the cover party or to persuade its leaders to seek admission into the Comintern. Also in 1926, left-wing elements, including some who advocated immediate adherence to the Comintern, established the Ecuadorean Socialist Party and the Socialist Revolutionary Party in Colombia. These parties were accepted into the Comintern with one-half vote each in 1928, even though they did not adopt the communist name at that time. In Peru the men who later formed the communist party were first drawn into the American Popular Revolutionary Alliance (Alianza Popular Revolucionaria Americana, APRA), a movement established in Mexico by Haya de la Torre in 1924, and then split off in 1928 to create the Peruvian Socialist Party (Partido Socialista Peruano), under the leadership of José Carlos Mariátegui. Mariátegui died before deciding whether to affiliate his party with the Comintern.

*Sectarian Isolationism: 1929 to 1934* The third stage of communism in Latin America coincides with the third period of the Communist International, when Marxist-Leninists everywhere were instructed to identify themselves openly as communists, to establish exclusively communist-led labor and mass organizations, and to cease cooperation with "bourgeois" and "leftist-reformist" parties in their efforts to seize the leadership of the proletarian revolution. Since the effectiveness of the communist parties in fact depended largely on successful collaboration with other political groups—in the labor movement above all—faithful execution of these instructions led to schisms in every party and greatly weakened the position of the communists throughout Latin America. Misinterpretation of the new instructions could bring even more serious consequences, as in Mexico, where in 1929 the party was proscribed by the government and its leadership was purged on orders from the Comintern following its cooperation with other dissident elements in an abortive revolt. The Uruguayan party was the only one in all of Latin America to retain legal status and substantial freedom of operation during these years.

The third period opened with two regional congresses—at Montevideo in May and at Buenos Aires in June 1929—which provided an indication of the growth of the communist movement in Latin America during the preceding decade. The first of these was a communist labor congress attended by representatives of the Comintern and by delegates and observers from fifteen Latin American republics: Argentina, Bolivia, Brazil, Colombia, Costa Rica, Cuba, Ecuador, El Salvador, Guatemala, Mexico, Panama, Paraguay, Peru, Uruguay, and Venezuela. With the exception of Costa Rica, all these countries were also represented at the second congress, a political meeting in which the new international communist line, as determined at the sixth Comintern congress, was explained to the delegates. The Chilean party, which had been suppressed by the Ibáñez dictatorship, was unable to send delegates to either gathering, nor were the Honduran communists represented at either Montevideo or Buenos Aires. Bolivia and Venezuela were represented even though there was neither a communist party nor a front group in either country. Nonetheless, the regional congresses demonstrated that there were communist organizations or spokesmen active in seventeen of the twenty republics by mid-1929.

The Comintern directives left no doubt that in countries where the communists operated within other parties they should either transform these parties into avowed communist organizations or break away to create their own communist party. In response to the new line, the leaders of the Peruvian Socialist Party changed its name to Peruvian Communist Party and requested admission to the Comintern in 1930. In that same year the Panamanian communists withdrew from the Laborite party to establish the Communist Party of Panama (Partido Comunista del Panamá), and in Colombia the communists inherited the remnants of the disintegrating Socialist Revolutionary Party, which they converted into the Communist Party of Colombia. In Ecuador the transition of the socialist party into the Communist Party of Ecuador required about two years and was completed in 1931.

Meanwhile new communist parties were founded in Costa Rica, Haiti, and Venezuela. The Communist Party of Costa Rica was established in 1929 by Manuel Mora Valverde, then a young intellectual, who still dominated his party in 1965. Although technically illegal, the party enjoyed freedom of action for nearly two decades as the only spokesman of the lower class in Costa Rica. It joined the Comintern in 1935. In striking contrast, the tiny Communist Party of Haiti, formed in mid-1930, was suppressed almost immediately. Its two founders, Max Hudicourt and Jacques Roumain, were exiled before the end of the year, leaving the party leaderless and impotent, and it was formally banned in 1936. The first Venezuelan communists were exiles who joined the movement abroad. One of these, Aurelio Fortoul Briceño, returned to Caracas, where he organized the Communist Party of Venezuela in March 1931. It consisted of fewer than thirty students and workers from clandestine Marxist study circles, which were now converted into communist cells. Within two months the new party came to the attention of the Gómez dictatorship and its leaders were jailed. The party survived to affiliate with the Comintern in 1935, but it did not prosper until after the death of Gómez at the end of that year.

During the third period the previously established communist groups in Central America were virtually extinguished as the result of an uprising in January 1932, led by the communists in El Salvador. The Salvadoran party, which had begun to penetrate the army rank and file and to organize a small rural following, had been permitted to participate openly in local elections, but it was awarded no seats. Denied a parliamentary role by the dictatorship and prohibited by the Comintern from cooperating with other political forces, the communists called upon their comrades in Guatemala and Honduras for assistance in an assault on the regime. After victory in El Salvador the revolution was to be carried to the rest of Central America. One of the requests was intercepted by Guatemalan authorities, who alerted neighboring governments. Consequently, rebel units within the army were disarmed, and when the revolt broke out among the peasantry it was ruthlessly suppressed. This first communist attempt to seize power by violence in Latin America cost more than 20,000 lives. Most of the Salvadoran communists were killed, and the few who escaped to Guatemala were imprisoned. A similar fate befell communist leaders in Guatemala and Honduras. For all practical purposes, the communist movement ceased to exist in these three countries for the next dozen years.

*The Decade of Cooperation: 1935 to 1945*
This era of the popular front represented a complete reversal of the international communist line. The objective was now to promote the broadest possible alliance of center and leftist parties for the urgent task of defeating the nazi-fascist threat. Throughout Latin America ineffective communist labor, student, and front organizations were dissolved and their members were advised to join groups led by other "democratic" parties. The communists also contributed to the formation of areawide labor and front bodies, in which they participated as only one of numerous "antifascist" elements. In the late 1930s,

for the first time in several countries the communist party achieved a degree of national prominence.

In Chile and Cuba, where the popular-front strategy was most successful, the communists worked closely with administration parties in alliances that survived the Russo-German entente between August 1939 and June 1941. Elsewhere in Latin America many of the recent communist gains were lost during the period of the Hitler-Stalin pact, as the party turned on its erstwhile allies, denounced the "imperialist" war, and attempted, usually apathetically, to collaborate with the pseudonazi parties of the area.

The communists were extricated from this untenable position by the German attack on the Soviet Union and by the subsequent involvement of the Latin American nations in the war against the Axis. Even though war in the Soviet Union in effect freed the Latin American communists to devise their own strategy and tactics, there was remarkable uniformity in their continuing response to the international situation. Everywhere the party line was again reversed to encourage the unity of all political groups in support of the war, which was now described as a struggle of democratic peoples against fascist tyranny. During the remaining years of World War II the communists went far beyond the limits of the popular front in cooperating with political parties of every hue. Wherever the party was permitted freedom of action its membership increased.

The experience of the Latin American communists in 1935, particularly in Brazil and Chile, suggests that the popular-front strategy was initially regarded as an experiment which did not necessarily preclude the use of force. In Brazil the communists appear to have anticipated the popular-front approach in June 1934, when they adopted the line then known as the "united national front," calling for unity of all "anti-imperialist, antifascist" groups in an electoral campaign to establish a national revolutionary government. This campaign, exploiting the grievances of the depression era, led in March 1935 to the formation of the broad National Liberation Alliance, which soon became the principal communist front in Brazil, although only about 1 percent of its members were communists. The alliance, in effect a popular front, assumed real political prominence in April 1935, when Luiz Carlos Prestes returned from a protracted stay in the Soviet Union to become its honorary president and guiding spirit. With the counsel of four Comintern agents, Prestes quickly moved it to the left. In July, when he demanded "all power" for the alliance and hinted at revolution if the demand were refused, the National Liberation Alliance was outlawed. Most of the noncommunists immediately abandoned the organization, thus eliminating any possibility that it might come to power by peaceful means. The communists then plotted to seize the government by force. Their plan, based on communist cadres within the army and presumed widespread revolutionary ferment among the people, provided for simultaneous uprising in various parts of the country to spark a popular upheaval in which the communists would take power in the name of the National Liberation Alliance. The plan failed, in part because the barracks revolts that broke out in Natal and Recife on November 24 and in Rio de Janeiro on November 27, 1935, were uncoordinated, but primarily because of apathy among the civilian population. The rebels were quickly contained by loyal army forces, the National Liberation Alliance was destroyed, and Prestes, the Comintern agents, and many communist party leaders were sentenced to long prison terms. The Brazilian party did not recover from the failure of its revolution for another decade, and the Latin American communists generally abandoned revolution as a political method for the next twenty years.

At about the same time in Chile the communists were demonstrating the effectiveness of parliamentary means in achieving the goals indicated by the Comintern. Early in 1935 Comintern agent Eudocio Ravines was sent to Chile to work for the formation of a popular front which would include not only the communist party, the socialists, and small left-of-center groups, but also the large center Radical Party (Partido Radical). This grouping, extended to embrace the communist labor federation as well, was formally constituted as the Popular Front in March 1936. Within a year it proved to be the largest political bloc in the country, winning ten seats in the senate and sixty-six in the chamber of deputies in the congressional elections. One senator and seven of the deputies were communists. Although outnumbered by both radicals and socialists, the communists held the balance of power within the Popular Front. Their support for Pedro Aguirre Cerda was therefore decisive in his selection as the Popular Front candidate in the presidential elections in 1937, and his narrow victory at the polls raised communist prestige to a new high in Chile. Even after the signing of the Hitler-Stalin pact, when the communists became increasingly critical of their "antifascist" allies, the radicals continued to regard communist participation in the Popular Front as essential to the administration. The socialists protested, however, and finally withdrew early in 1941. The Popular Front was then dissolved, but the left-wing parties continued to cooperate informally with the radical regime. After the Japanese attack on Pearl Harbor the communists persudaded the socialists to revive the Popular Front, which was renamed the Democratic Alliance. This arrangement continued for the remainder of the war years, contributing to a steady growth in the size and influence of the communist party.

One of the most successful communist ventures during the popular-front era and World War II was in the field of inter-American labor relations. This was the Confederation of Latin American Workers (Confederación de Trabajadores de América Latina), founded in 1938 under the leadership of Vicente Lombardo Toledano, then head of Mexico's main labor body. The desirability of such a confederation had long been recognized by trade-union officials of differing political persuasions throughout the hemisphere. The confederation began as a legitimate labor central, supported by the major national labor confederations of Argentina, Chile, Colombia, Cuba, Ecuador, Mexico, Peru, and Venezuela. From the outset, however, communist labor leaders were prominent in it, and their influence increased during the war years, when communist labor activities were encouraged or tolerated by most of the Latin American governments. Local or national labor entities from fourteen countries had affiliated with the confederation by 1944, when the communists gained control of most of the top offices. The communist takeover appears to have been manipulated by Lombardo Toledano. He had been removed from control of the Confederation of Mexican Workers (Confederación de Trabajadores Mexicanas) in 1940 and thereafter had worked closely with communists in the Confederation of Latin American Workers. Even after this international body became a communist front it remained for some time the only important regional labor organization in Latin America.

During this decade when cooperation was the most prominent feature of Latin American communist strategy, three new Marxist parties were formed, one during the popular-front period, one during the period of the Hitler-Stalin pact, and one during World War II. The first of these was the Socialist Party of Nicaragua, which was communist in all but name. It was founded in 1937 by a minority faction of the workers' party opposed to the election of Anastasio Somoza as president of the republic. After two years of relative freedom of operation, the party was formally banned and its leaders were exiled. During the war years the communists were permitted to return and to assume an influential role in the labor movement in exchange for support of the Somoza regime, even though the anticommunist laws remained on the books. The Nicaraguan party is the only Latin American communist party that has never been known officially as communist.

The Bolivian Party of the Revolutionary Left (Partido de la Izquierda Revolucionaria), created early in 1940 when ideological distinctions between the extreme right and extreme left were deliberately blurred, was a communist party only to the extent that it provided an organization in which Stalinists could participate. Its members were all political radicals, but few appear to have had clearly defined doctrines or ideological convictions. With all its weaknesses, however, it served for a decade as the chief link between the international communist movement and those Bolivians who regarded themselves as communists.

Until 1942 the Dominican Republic was the only country in Latin America in which no local communist group had ever formed. In that year, under the influence of communist exiles from the Spanish civil war and Dominican students who had become communists abroad, a Dominican communist party was formed in Ciudad Trujillo. Its members were drawn chiefly from students at the national university. Although it was illegal, it nonetheless cooperated with and was tolerated by the Trujillo dictatorship until the end of the war. In 1945 the party's leaders were exiled and its activities suppressed. The following year, when Trujillo staged "democratic" national elections, the communists were invited to return. They registered the party legally as the Dominican Popular Socialist Party (Partido Socialista Popular Dominicano) and launched a vigorous recruitment campaign. In 1947 the party was again outlawed and its leaders were expelled from the country, to lead a purely exile organization for the next fifteen years.

The wartime policy followed by the Nicaraguan and Dominican parties was typical of that employed by communists in most of Latin America. For the moment everything else was secondary to the war effort. It was far preferable to tolerate an oppressive regime than to permit work stoppages or political upheavals that would reduce the flow of vital raw materials from Latin America to the war industries of the Allied powers. The communists registered some impressive gains in the labor field during this period because they could be relied upon to prevent strikes or to break those called by noncommunist labor leaders. In the political field the communists generally took no part in the protests and revolts against authoritarian regimes that broke out in 1944 and 1945. (The principal exception was the communist party in Ecuador, which obtained legal status and a temporary cabinet position by siding with the popular revolution that brought Valasco Ibarra to power in 1944.)

Several parties went to the extreme of abandoning the communist name (as did the party in the United States) in an effort to demonstrate that they were really the national, independent, democratic parties they now claimed to be. The Nicaraguan communists, already known as socialists, kept their misleading label. Within a year after the dissolution of the Comintern four parties adopted new, noncommunist names: the Costa Rican party became the Popular Vanguard Party; the Panamanian party became the Party of the People (Partido del Pueblo); the Cuban communists, who had experimented with a variety of names, settled on Popular Socialist Party (Partido Socialista Popular); and the Colombian communists registered their organization as the Social Democratic Party (Partido Social Democrático). This trend continued after the war. In 1946 both the Dominican party and one of the revived communist groups in Haiti, following the Cuban model, identified themselves as Popular Socialist Party (Parti Socialiste Populaire). The adoption of the name Labor Party (Partido Guatemalteco del Trabajo) by the Guatemalan communists in 1952 occurred under different circumstances but had the same objective—to imply the party's independence from Moscow. In Colombia the party resumed its former name in 1947, and in Cuba the Popular Socialist Party was absorbed into the administration party in 1961, but all the other wartime and postwar names have been retained.

*The Era of Good Feeling: 1945 to 1947* During the two years following World War II communist fortunes in Latin America reached their highest point. Overall party membership—in excess of 375,000 by the beginning of 1947—was larger and more evenly distributed than at any other time. The party was legal or enjoyed freedom of operation, at least briefly, in all but three countries, and in one of these, Guatemala, restraints on the political rights of individual communists had been lifted. In El Salvador the party had been allowed to reform during a frenzied six-month period of open political activity after the overthrow of the Martínez government in 1944 but was driven underground again before the end of the year. Only in Honduras was there neither a communist organization nor discernible communist activity after 1945.

This situation was the result of a fortuitous combination of circumstances for which the Latin American communists could claim only partial credit. The wartime spirit of friendship and tolerance among the Allies had not yet cooled. The prestige of the Soviet Union was high following the success of Soviet arms against German military might. The communist world power was regarded as a distant, democratic giant disposed to cooperate to preserve peace through the new United Nations. Soviet propaganda, and therefore the Latin American communist line as well, stressed the importance of continued close relations with the Western democracies and was silent on the subject of world revolution. Thus, for the time being, the identification of the Latin American communist parties with Moscow was an asset rather than a liability, even though during 1946 and 1947 nearly every prominent communist leader was obliged to declare publicly that he owed his first allegiance to the Soviet Union.

At the same time, within Latin America the communists were reaping the benefits of their wartime policies and of the change in political fashions throughout much of the area in the immediate postwar years. They were widely accepted at face value as reasonable, democratic nationalists who should have as much right as other democrats to espouse their views and to seek power at the polls. They were favored in this respect by the restoration of open, representative government or the marked relaxation of authoritarian controls in more than half the Latin American republics at the end of the war. Ultimately, the communist parties had an enhanced appeal and influence in direct proportion to their apparent political moderation.

Although the communists were not in power anywhere in Latin America, they demonstrated substantial political strength in half a dozen or more countries between 1945 and 1947. In Ecuador, where a communist had been included in the national executive junta for a short time in 1944, another party member served in the national cabinet until early in 1945. The Argentine party, outlawed since 1930, regained legal status and polled over 65,000 votes for various communist candidates in the congressional elections of 1945. The revived Brazilian party astounded all observers by polling more than half a million votes in the elections of 1945 and 1947 to place about eighty candidates in national and state legislatures. Next in voter appeal were the Cuban communists, who had been close to the Batista regime since 1939 and included in the cabinet in 1943. They polled over 120,000 votes to elect three senators and seven congressmen and win a firm place in the administration bloc under President Grau San Martín from 1944 to 1947. In the late 1940s their vote approached 160,000 before the party's strength began to erode. In Chile, where the communists had cooperated with radical administrations for nearly a decade, three party members were appointed to the cabinet in 1946. Within five months party membership rose to 50,000. The Uruguayan party polled over 33,000 votes, double its previous high, to elect its first senator and five congressmen in 1946. In Peru the communists benefited from the willingness of the government to relax the longstanding ban on revolutionary parties in the 1945 elections. Thinly disguised as the Socialist Vanguard, they took part in the congressional race, electing several candidates to the lower house. The Venezuelan party, operating legally for the first time, amassed over 50,000 votes to elect two members to the constituent assembly in 1946. Elsewhere in Latin America communist electoral strength was less impressive, but it was still usually enough to alarm moderate and conservative party leaders.

In the postwar period the Latin American communists took advantage of opportunities to revive some long-defunct parties and to raise the level of proficiency of others. This two-pronged campaign was evident in Haiti and Mexico by 1947. The communist revival in Haiti proved to be premature, but the establishment of an effective communist organization in Mexico was at least a qualified success. Two rival Haitian communist parties appeared shortly after the overthrow of the Lescot regime early in 1946. The first, founded by an obscure Protestant clergyman, took the name Communist Party of Haiti. It was avowedly Marxist but apparently was not sufficiently orthodox to merit Soviet approval. It attracted few members, disbanded voluntarily in 1947, and was formally outlawed in 1948. The second, known as the Popular Socialist Party, was the heir of the original Haitian communist party of 1930. One of the founders of that party, Max Hudicourt, returned from exile to lead the new organization, which quickly secured the blessing of the international movement. The party seemed to have a promising future when Hudicourt was elected to the senate and another popular socialist candidate was elected to the lower house in 1946, but it did not long survive the assassination of Hudicourt in 1947. The party was proscribed in November 1949, and the communist movement disappeared from Haiti for the second time in two decades.

In Mexico there were also two communist parties, both small, legal, and ineffectual. These were the long-established Mexican Communist Party and the dissident Mexican Worker-Peasant Party (Partido Obrero-Campesino Mexicano), which had split off from the parent body in 1940. Neither could attract enough members to participate in national elections or to raise a significant protest against their exclusion from the polls. Here the problem was resolved by creating the new procommunist People's Party (Partido Popular) under the leadership of Vicente Lombardo Toledano in 1948. The People's Party added the word "socialist" to its title in 1960 and absorbed the Mexican Worker-Peasant Party in 1963, but otherwise retained its original organization and orientation. In domestic politics it was more willing than the communist party to cooperate with the administration, but in international affairs it consistently echoed the approved Soviet line. This "reasonable" approach to internal matters enabled the People's Party to win at least ten times as many members as the orthodox and dissident communist parties combined, and thus to serve as a more effective vehicle for the Marxist point of view in Mexico. While not formally a part of the world communist apparatus, the People's Party in practice bears most of the propaganda burden of the international communist movement in Mexico.

*The Cold War and the End of the Stalin Era: 1947 to 1955* The onset of the cold war in 1947 brought another drastic reversal of communist fortunes in most of Latin America. Nearly all the favorable conditions that had prevailed in the preceding period ceased to exist. The flood tide of democratic government that had begun to run in Latin America in 1944 ebbed in 1947 and 1948, and in the next seven years authoritarian regimes were restored or reaffirmed in twelve of the twenty republics. Elsewhere during these years the democratic governments of five countries recognized the potential danger of the communist movement and either outlawed the party entirely or denied it access to the polls. By 1955 the communist party was legal in only six Latin American republics—Argentina, Bolivia, Colombia, Ecuador, Mexico, and Uruguay—and even in these countries noncommunist political forces again competed vigorously with communists for control of labor, student, and other organizations after 1947. The communist-led Confederation of Latin American Workers lost most of its major national affiliates during these years.

The impact of the cold war on the Latin American parties was not as disastrous as the third-period line had been, for they managed to survive in all countries except Haiti and the Dominican Republic. Where the ban on communist activites was lightly enforced, as in Brazil and Costa Rica, proscription meant merely that party meetings were not held publicly and that communist candidates for elective office were obliged to run on the tickets of other parties. Nonetheless, generally throughout the area the communists lost the respectability and much of the influence they had built up since 1935. This situation was reflected in the decline in party membership, which fell below 200,000 in all of Latin America in the early 1950s.

The communists would surely have suffered some loss of influence and following in any event as a result of the political trend to the right in much of Latin America after 1947. The deterioration of their position, however, was owing primarily to the shift in Soviet policy and actions and to their own vociferous endorsement and dissemination of the new international communist line. For over a decade Latin American communists had publicly ignored the theoretical concept of inevitable proletarian revolution and had usually opposed the use of violence as a political weapon. Now, in response to indications from the Soviet Union, they resumed a militant revolutionary stance. From the beginning of the cold war until after the death of Stalin in 1953 they called for "antifeudal, anti-imperialist" revolutions to overthrow "dictatorships in the service of imperialism." Such revolutions were to create "democratic governments of the people" in which the communist party would play the leading role. Except in Argentina where Great Britain was denounced as the "imperialist oppressor," the Latin American communists sustained a vehement and vituperative propaganda attack on "Yankee imperialism," insisting that only by violence could the "yoke of United States colonialism" be overthrown. Nowhere, however, were the communists strong enough to initiate the uprisings they advocated, and in Bolivia and Colombia, where they participated as minor elements in revolutionary activities begun by noncommunists, their appeal encountered widespread public apathy. Many of the communist charges against the United States—which were widely accepted as fact—were made more convincingly by other opposition groups. While resentment against "Yankee imperialism" could easily be aroused, there was little popular support for communism in Latin America. By adopting an extreme line that they were not able to convert into political action, the communists made it difficult for sincere democrats to defend the party's right to operate openly and at the same time facilitated the task of dictators seeking a plausible excuse to ban all political opposition.

Despite the serious obstacles faced by the communist movement in most of Latin America, its situation improved in three countries during the last years of the Stalin era. In Bolivia an orthodox communist party was formed for the first time, and in Guatemala and Honduras the communists returned to the political scene after an absence of more than ten years. In Bolivia through the 1940s the amorphous Party of the Revolutionary Left remained the only political organization acceptable to Bolivian Marxist-Leninists, even though it was not officially part of the world communist movement. A self-styled, proadministration communist party, formed about 1943, failed to win the approval of Stalinists and disappeared when its founder was assassinated in 1946. The first formal Communist Party of Bolivia (Partido Comunista de Bolivia) was established in late 1949 or early 1950 by dissidents who split off from the Party of the Revolutionary Left. A second group of defectors from the same party entered the Communist Party of Bolivia in 1951. The new, clandestine communist party was small and was composed chiefly of intellectuals and men associated with the urban labor movement. It acquired legal status more or less automatically in 1952, when the noncommunist National Revolutionary Movement (Movimiento Revolucionario Nacional) seized power by force. Although the communists thereafter enjoyed complete freedom of operation, they could not compete effectively against the administration for the loyalty of the tin miners and peasants, who constituted the bulk of the Bolivian lower class. In this situation, in which the regime of the National Revolutionary Movement was carrying out a sweeping social revolution, the communist program held virtually no attraction for the populace.

In contrast to the Bolivian experience, the communists in Guatemala rose from total obscurity to a position of near power within a single decade. Their unprecedented success stemmed largely from identification with an on-going social revolution. The opportunity they exploited began with the revolutions of 1944, which ended a long series of dictatorships and gave the republic an open political climate for the first time. Almost immediately a few communist exiles, who had acquired valuable organizational skills abroad, started filtering back into Guatemala to penetrate noncommunist revolutionary parties and the newly organized labor movement. During the Arévalo administration (1945 to 1950) they continued to work unobtrusively, infiltrating as many political and mass organizations as possible. Not until the Arbenz campaign for the presidency in 1950 did the communists seek to attract some public attention to themselves, and only after the orientation of the Arbenz regime was unmistakably clear did they emerge entirely into the open.

The first Guatemalan communist organization, the Democratic Vanguard (Vanguardia Democrática), had been established in 1947 as a secret faction within the largest administration party. In 1949 it was transformed into the Communist Party of Guatemala but remained entirely underground for about a year. It was essentially a political vehicle. A parallel labor arm was established openly in mid-1950 as the Revolutionary Workers' Party of Guatemala (Partido Revolucionario Obrero de Guatemala). On orders from Moscow the two merged late in 1951, and in December 1952 the combined party was registered legally as the Guatemalan Labor Party. By this time the communists held decision-making positions in organized labor, in the national school system, in some peasant bodies, and in several noncommunist parties that had been grouped into a pro-Arbenz National Democratic Front during the presidential campaign. Subsequently the communist-dominated executive board of the front became Arbenz' "kitchen cabinet" and principal source of counsel on national policies. For the last year and a half of the Arbenz administration the communist party was the most influential political force in Guatemala.

This position, however, was not as powerful as it appeared. While the communists were able to shape some national policies, particularly in the field of foreign relations, and could manipulate much of the political apparatus of the regime, they had failed to build a strong and cohesive popular following outside the capital or to establish a base of support within the armed forces. This was clearly demonstrated by the sudden collapse of the entire communist structure in 1954. Neither workers, peasants, nor soldiers would fight to prevent the overthrow of Arbenz and his communist allies by Castillo Armas' invasion army. This lesson was not lost on the communists when they attempted to reestablish themselves as a revolutionary force in Guatemala after 1960 (see *Guatemala*).

Communists seeking to revive the party in Honduras in the 1940s were obliged to work under much less favorable conditions. At the height of the era of good feeling in 1946 a slight indication of leftist political activity had led to the issuing of an anticommunist decree and renewed repression by the Carías dictatorship. Only after the revolution of 1948 were political controls relaxed somewhat. The communists then penetrated, and eventually dominated, the new Democratic Revolutionary Party of Honduras (Partido

Democrático Revolucionario de Honduras). They operated within this front party until 1953, when it was outlawed and most of its leaders were exiled. Spokesmen for the Honduran movement have since claimed that the present Communist Party of Honduras was created in 1954 by a few survivors of the old party who remained active in Tegucigalpa and among plantation workers on the north coast. There was no evidence of organized party activity, however, until 1958, when the first communist party congress was held in Honduras.

*Peaceful Coexistence and the Cuban Revolution: 1955 to 1960* The mid-1950s marked another turning point for the communist movement in Latin America. The post-Stalin policies of the Soviet state and party, a new trend toward representative government in Latin America, and the success of the revolution in Cuba combined to permit the communists to adopt a more flexible line and to give them confidence that the long-delayed day of victory was at hand. At the same time such apparently damaging blows to Soviet and international communist prestige as the Hungarian revolt, the Pasternak affair, and the Chinese invasion of Tibet provoked little sustained reaction in Latin America to injure the image of reasonableness and respectability now presented by the communists.

The improved climate for communist activities in the second half of the decade resulted in part from a considerable enhancement in Soviet prestige among the governments and noncommunist political groups in much of Latin America. Even while the problem of the post-Stalin succession was being worked out, the Soviet Union launched its campaign to establish regular and substantial trade with the republics of Latin America. The Soviet Union and the communist states of Eastern Europe would exchange a variety of industrial products, plants, machinery, and petroleum for the unsaleable surplus raw materials of Latin America. The Soviet economic offensive did not develop significantly except in Argentina, Brazil, Uruguay, and, after 1960, Cuba. However, its appeal to producers and exporters throughout Latin America was strong, for it seemed to offer an unlimited potential market to supplement the existing ones in the United States and Western Europe. The anti-Stalin campaign and the thaw in the cold war also served to give many noncommunists a more favorable impression of the Soviet Union. These developments seemed to indicate that the Soviet Union was moving toward open, responsible government and that its leaders were concerned more with improving the lot of the Soviet people under communism than with imposing communist governments on foreign peoples. These convictions were strengthened by the launching of the first Soviet sputnik in 1957, a clear demonstration that the Soviet Union was equal or superior to the United States in the technological and military fields. Henceforth it was argued by communists and noncommunists alike that it did not behoove small Latin American republics to ignore the economic and military power of the Soviet Union, no matter how distasteful its form of government might be.

Within the Latin American communist parties these events had an even stronger impact. The communists were jubilant over Soviet accomplishments in outer space and found the economic offensive a highly attractive propaganda theme, acceptable to many who rejected the party's political line. In the late 1950s communist propaganda focused increasingly on Soviet trade-and-aid overtures, stressing that it was not necessary to install communist or procommunist governments in Latin America in order to benefit from trade with the socialist camp. Appealing to ultranationalists throughout the region, the communists insisted that here was a way to use the plantation, ranch, and mine products the United States would not buy to achieve economic independence from the United States.

These examples of Soviet prowess directly affected relations between communists and other political groups, but it was the anti-

Stalin campaign that ultimately exerted the greatest influence on intraparty relationships and contributed to the growing self-confidence of party members. Khrushchev's denunciation of the former Soviet dictator did not lead in Latin America to the wholesale removal of the long-entrenched party leaders and cliques who dominated more than half the communist parties in the area. In fact, of the dozen perennial party leaders identified with Stalin and Stalinist methods, only Eugenio Gómez of Uruguay, who was deposed before the anti-Stalin campaign began, and Dionisio Encina of Mexico, demoted in 1960, lost their positions during this period. Nevertheless, late in 1956, after the initial shock had passed and the views of communist elder statemen in Europe and Asia had been published, nearly all the Latin American communist parties indulged in extensive discussion of the "cult of the personality." In later years there was some bitter criticism of the hypocritical manner in which the anti-Stalin issue was handled by the old leadership in several parties, but at the time the discussion apparently increased the feeling of personal participation by rank-and file members in the party's decision-making process. The often heated debates within the communist parties seem also to have helped persuade some leaders of Christian democat, socialist, and other left-wing parties that the communists were becoming more democratic, and therefore more acceptable as allies.

The communists appeared less objectionable as potential allies on other grounds as well. The new Soviet policies and the thaw in the cold war enabled the Latin American communists quietly to abandon the extreme line they had been obliged to espouse during the last years of the Stalin era. No longer were they committed to the advocacy of revolution under the leadership of the communist party as the road to political power for the masses. In most of Latin America, where the previous line had been counterproductive, the communists now emphasized that it was possible to achieve socialism—which remained their ultimate goal—by a variety of evolutionary means. In Latin America the most promising route was through a "democratic front of national liberation," which might well come to power by election. Moreover, the communists expressed complete willingness to accept a subordinate role in alliances with other "progressive" parties. The "nonviolent" line was most successful in Chile, where the communists had enlisted the cooperation of the socialists and minor leftist parties in a protracted propaganda campaign that resulted in restoration of the party's legal status in 1958 and the creation of a formal electoral coaltion, the Popular Action Front, between the communist party and its noncommunist partners. Elsewhere efforts to legalize the communist party or to register thinly disguised front parties consistently failed, although the communist party regained legal status in the wake of coups or revolutions in three countries.

Paradoxically, as the communists were moving away from their policy of revolution, the noncommunist left and center in much of Latin America were becoming increasingly prone to employ violence for political ends. Generally the stronger the regime in power, the greater the willingness of the noncommunist opposition to accept communist support in overthrowing it. The trend was again toward open, representative governments, but experience showed that only force or the threat of force could topple an entrenched dictatorship. This was borne out in the elimination of authoritarian regimes in Argentina in 1955, Peru in 1956, Colombia in 1957, Venezuela in 1958, and Cuba in 1959. In Argentina and Colombia revolt by the army paved the way for the return of civilian rule, while in Peru strong pressure led the dictatorship to transfer power to an elected successor. In these countries communist support for revolution was neither desired nor necessary. The Argentine and Peruvian communists profited little from the change in government, and the real situation of the Colombian party remained substantially unaltered even though the blanket repeal of decrees of the dictatorship restored its legal status.

In Venezuela, however, the communist party was welcomed by the Democratic Action, the Christian socialist Independent Political Electoral Organization Committee, and the Republican Democratic Union as an equal partner in the revolutionary coalition that plotted and executed the overthrow of the Pérez Jiménez dictatorship in January 1958. Here the communist party not only recovered its legal standing, but more important, emerged from the revolution as a completely respectable element of the Venezuelan body politic. It participated in the drafting of a new electoral code and constitution and in the elections that followed proved to be the second strongest party in the capital and the fourth largest in the country as a whole. By using violent tactics the Venezuelan communists seemed to have achieved everything that the Soviet line insisted could be attained by peaceful means. The dichotomy between policy and action was explained away by party leaders, who rationalized that the revolution had been a necessary step to establish the conditions in which the parliamentary route to power might be pursued.

The resurgence of the Cuban party, which identified itself with the Castro movement in the waning months of the revolution against Batista, was even more spectacular. The communist Popular Socialist Party was the only political party to continue after the fall of the dictatorship and thus enjoyed an enormous advantage among the groups seeking to influence the course of the Castro regime. The victory of the Cuban revolution thrilled and inspired democrats and revolutionaries throughout Latin America. No dictatorship now seemed impregnable. Cuba had provided an infallible recipe for successful revolution, and the ingredients were readily available. All that was needed, it seemed, was a small band of determined, well-organized guerrillas and the promise of agrarian reform to win over the peasant masses. The young communists in particular found Castro's example irresistible and were quick to claim that this must be the party's road to socialism in Latin America. Some of them took part in the Cuban-based assaults on Nicaragua, Panama, the Dominican Republic, and Haiti in 1959 and seem not to have been deterred by the prompt defeat of these adventures, which demonstrated that the Cuban model could not be applied indiscriminately in the Caribbean area. Generally the party leaders continued to follow a more cautious line, in keeping with the propaganda pronouncements of the Khrushchev regime; thus the Cuban revolution sowed seeds of discord within the Latin American communist parties which were to be reaped in the 1960s.

In practice the leaders of individual communist parties in Latin America have always enjoyed a considerable degree of authority to interpret some aspects of the international line in the light of their own resources and political conditions in their own countries. Since no two parties faced exactly the same situation, there was never complete uniformity of approach in the twenty republics. In the 1950s, however, the Soviet Union attempted to coordinate Latin American communist party activities more closely than at any time since the seventh Comintern congress in 1935. Beginning with the nineteenth congress of the Soviet party in 1952, and at frequent intervals after the death of Stalin, leaders of the communist movement were brought together at international meetings in Moscow to hear the full Soviet arguments on each ideological debate and shift in global strategy, and more important, confer with Soviet leaders on special tactics to be employed in Latin America. In 1952 delegates from twelve Latin American parties met in Moscow. Eighteen parties were represented at the twentieth Soviet party congress in 1956 and at the ceremonies commemorating the fortieth anniversary of the Russian revolution in 1957. At the twenty-first congress in 1959 the Latin American parties were urged to work more closely with one another and to hold their own congresses more frequently.

Communist delegations from all twenty

Latin American countries attended the Moscow meeting of communist and workers' parties in 1960. This unprecedented meeting of all Latin American communist parties in Moscow suggested that for the first time there was a communist party in each of the Latin American republics simultaneously. In actuality, the Dominican party was still an exile organization in 1960, and several of the weaker parties were usually represented by exiles at world communist conclaves. However, during this period a new communist organization was formed in Haiti, marking the third such attempt in as many decades. This new party, the tiny, clandestine Party of Popular Accord (Parti d'Entente Populaire) founded in 1959 by Jacques Stephen Alexis, was so small and unobtrusive that it appears to have escaped detection by the Duvalier regime until 1961. Its chief significance lay in its potential as the nucleus of a viable communist party.

*The Sino-Soviet Dispute and the Cuban Socialist Republic: 1960 to 1965* The major trends that had begun to appear in Latin America in the period 1955 to 1960 continued in intensified form after 1960. No communist party in the area escaped the internal and external repercussions of the Sino-Soviet dispute and the open establishment of Cuba as a "socialist republic." In Latin America the ideological rift was inseparably linked with the Cuban issue. On the whole the entrenched party leaderships tended to support the Soviet position in the verbal conflict with the Chinese, but at the cost of a split in party ranks. By the end of 1965 twelve parties, including Castro's organization in Cuba, were formally aligned with the Soviet Union, as were the Moscow-approved factions in six others. The views of the Haitian communists were not known, and the Venezuelan communist leaders, still seeking to heal a three-way breach in the party, had taken no public stand.

In Latin America, as elsewhere, the debate was couched in ideological terms, but here the communists were concerned primarily with the practical matter of tactics to be used in the quest for power. After the fall of Khrushchev the Latin American parties were permitted to choose whichever tactics seemed appropriate to their particular circumstances, provided they did not deny the theoretical possibility of a peaceful road to socialism. However, even this qualification was unacceptable to the extremists, who insisted the party could achieve its goal only by revolution. Occasionally, as in Brazil, the most militant advocates of the violent line were "old" communists, but by and large, the split was between the cautious old-guard leaders, accustomed to unquestioning acceptance of Soviet views, and the bold, impatient younger party members. Some of the latter maintained that the Chinese example should be followed in Latin America, but the majority did not distinguish neatly between the Chinese and Cuban models in responding pragmatically to increased opportunities for political violence.

Regardless of their views on the Sino-Soviet dispute, the chief asset enjoyed by the communists for a time after 1960 was optimism. Revolutionaries of all political persuasions were convinced that the success of the Cuban revolution, the awakening political consciousness of the rural populace, and the assistance available to left-wing governments from the Soviet Union and other communist states guaranteed that the trend to the left could not be checked in Latin America. They differed only on the techniques and time required to achieve victory. Not only was the left confident of victory, but many elements of the center and right also agreed that Castro communism represented the wave of the future. From Mexico to Argentina, parties patterned after the Cuban Twenty-sixth of July movement appeared, disposed to contest for power with ballots or rifles. Even in Haiti, with a new People's Party of National Liberation (Parti Populaire de Libération Nationale), founded by a former popular socialist in 1961, and the Dominican Republic with its Fourteenth of June party, named in commemoration of the Cuban assault on the country in 1959, some opposition forces were caught up in the euphoria of the moment. The bandwagon psychology was also evident in Chile, where the communist party hewed closely to the parliamentary road to win more than 250,000 votes in the 1961 municipal elections and over 285,000 in the congressional contest in 1965.

The existence of militant Castroist groups in most of the Latin American republics between 1960 and 1965 did in fact greatly enhance the opportunities for communists to cooperate with the noncommunist left in "wars of national liberation" where electoral coalitions were not feasible. In some countries—Argentina, Brazil, Mexico, and Peru, for example—the attempts by Castroists and communists to convert real or presumed peasant unrest into guerrilla warfare were suppressed by the government. However, in others— Guatemala and Venezuela, in particular—the survival of guerrilla bands dedicated to the overthrow of the existing political order permitted the communist dissidents to test their hypotheses about the "national liberation front" and, perhaps, to develop a solid rural following for the first time.

By the same token, the existence or threat of guerrilla warfare in many republics alerted the governments of the hemisphere to the seriousness of the danger posed by Castro-communist groups. Official reactions were intensified by the bald attempt of the Soviet Union to introduce nuclear weapons into Cuba in 1962. Largely as a result of these developments, the ban on communist activities was renewed in five countries—Argentina, the Dominican Republic, Ecuador, Guatemala, and Venezuela—and more rigorously enforced in most of the other republics. The Castro-communist threat was used, moreover, as partial justification for the overthrow of the government by the armed forces in El Salvador in 1961, Argentina in 1962, the Dominican Republic, Ecuador, Guatemala, and Honduras in 1963, and Brazil in 1964, and for intervention by the Inter-American Peace Force in the civil war in the Dominican Republic in 1965. All in all, by the end of 1965, the opportunities for the communists to exploit sociopolitical unrest in Latin American had been significantly reduced.

## ORGANIZATION AND MEMBERSHIP

*Organization* The communist parties in Latin America, by and large, have a more disciplined organization than do other political parties in the area. This is unquestionably their greatest asset, and has at times allowed them to exert influence out of all proportion to their size, to operate overtly or clandestinely, or both, according to immediate circumstances, to expand or contract rapidly in membership, and above all to endure extended periods of repression. The degree of influence or success at the polls attained by an individual communist party has generally been in direct relation to the effectiveness of its internal discipline.

In Latin America, as elsewhere, there is a vast discrepancy between what the communist party is and what its leaders and members allege, and perhaps believe it to be. The communists invariably describe their party as a monolith functioning under the twin principles of democratic centralism and collective leadership, in which policy decisions are debated and determined at the grass-roots level and passed upward to leaders freely selected by the membership at each level. In practice nearly the reverse is true, with decisions binding on all members ordinarily being made at the top and transmitted downward through a rigid chain of command. No longer are explicit directives regularly or frequently imposed on the larger parties by Soviet or other foreign communist party leaders, although the weaker parties in Latin America no doubt still receive guidance from their more successful colleagues in neighboring republics. The Cuban party now appears to have considerable responsibility in this regard. However, whether policy directives emanate from abroad or are formulated by local party officers on the basis of guidelines in international communist news media, the general membership has little opportunity to modify or reject them. Under these circumstances the communist parties are usually able to respond to new situations more quickly than their rivals, but the inability of the party leaders to tolerate serious disagreement—or any challenge to their authority—has made factionalism a chronic problem throughout the Latin American communist movement.

The communist parties in Latin America follow in greater or lesser detail the organizational pattern of the Communist Party of the Soviet Union, based on the principle of "democratic centralism." The pyramidal structure of the party organizations is almost identical everywhere, with the national leadership at the apex and local cells as the broad base. The number, order, and nomenclature of the intervening levels vary from country to country but are always specified in the statutes of the respective parties. The smaller and weaker parties may have only national, state, municipal, and local echelons, while others, particularly those in the larger republics, have up to seven or eight levels of command, including regional, district, zonal, or departmental organizations distributed geographically, and perhaps one or more professional or occupational commands with nationwide jurisdiction; party units among transportation workers are frequently organized on the latter basis. Regardless of the number of intermediate echelons between the cell and the central committee, all have the same parallel apparatus—a conference, or assemlby, and an executive committee. The conference meets periodically to resolve questions submitted by higher authorities and to elect delegates to conferences at the next higher level of the party, while the executive committee handles routine party business within its jurisdiction, including supervision of subordinate echelons.

The vertical structure of the communist party rarely changes and tends to remain intact when the party is suppressed. However, the size and number of units that may exist at each level below the central committee are quite flexible. Thus, as necessity or opportunity dictates, the party is equally able to survive a staggering loss of members or to absorb thousands of recruits within a brief span of time. This is the great organizational strength of communism in Latin America.

By statute the national congress—sometimes known as the national convention, and in Cuba as the national assembly—is the highest party authority. It is to be convoked by the central committee at regular two- or three-year intervals, following a series of conferences at lower levels, in which documents drawn up or authorized by the central committee are discussed and delegates are elected from among party militants. In practice, however, it is usually impossible or inadvisable for underground parties to hold the periodic congresses, and even those parties with legal status or comparative freedom of action have often failed to observe the statutory regulation. For example, the Brazilian party did not hold a congress between 1929 and 1954; the twelfth congress of the Argentine party in 1963 was its first in nearly seventeen years; the Paraguayan party has still held only two national congresses, even though the call for its third was issued in 1955. This widespread situation appears to have aroused serious criticism at the conference of the twenty Latin American parties in Moscow in November 1960. In contrast to the general practice, some parties have been able to meet at fairly regular intervals, as evidenced by the fact that the Uruguayan communists convoked their eighteenth congress in 1962, the Mexicans their fourteenth in 1963, and the Chileans their thirteenth in 1965.

The stipulated functions of the national congress are (1) to determine current political tactics; (2) to review, and if necessary revise, the program and statutes; (3) to hear and approve reports of the central committee; and (4) to elect the members and alternate members of that body. In many parties the national congress also serves as the agency that disciplines members who have opposed the party leaders. Ordinarily, however, the congress automatically approves the actions and proposals of the top leadership, for the central committee seldom convokes a party congress unless it can assure the selection of amenable delegates.

Even more manageable is the national conference, which is often used as a substitute for the national congress, particularly in clandestine parties, for the purpose of weighing political problems that must be resolved immediately. The national conference has the advantage of having fewer members, handpicked by the central committee, who can meet on short notice and are therefore less likely than the cumbersome national congress to attract undesired attention.

Between meetings the authority of the party congress is delegated largely to the central committee, known in some parties as the national committee. The central committee includes all the top party leaders and often the principal secondary figures, in most instances militants of at least ten years' standing. Alternate members may be men younger in years and experience, who have revealed strong leadership potential at the middle levels of the party. The central committee is responsible for executing decisions of the national congress, for regulating the number and order of subordinate units, and for supervising party finances, observation of the program and statutes, operation of the press and propaganda apparatus, and indoctrination of the membership. Where the party is legal, the central committee also selects the party's candidates for national public office. In such parties the central committee usually meets two or three times yearly, as stipulated in the statutes. Elsewhere, plenary meetings of the central committee occur irregularly and may, if the party is severely repressed, take the place of the national congress or conference.

The executive arm of the central committee is the executive bureau—known variously as the presidium, political commission, and executive committee—which is charged by statute with the direction of all party functions between sessions of the central committee. This body, drawn from the central committee, is made up of old-line communists, almost invariably long and close associates of the secretary general. The executive bureau usually dominates the central committee, in whose name it makes key decisions and prepares documents for use within the party or for publication. It also supplies from its membership the individuals who comprise the secretariat, where real authority resides in nearly all the Latin American communist parties. The secretariat varies in size according to the size and condition of the party, but it always includes the secretary general and his most trusted aides. Although it is technically a staff responsible for the daily routine operations of the party, the secretariat is in fact the chief executive organ, with *de facto* power to direct party activities, to alter tactics, and to create, shift, or abolish subordinate units within the party. Ordinarily the decisions and actions of the secretariat are not challenged by the executive bureau, the central committee, or the party congress.

With rare exceptions, the strongest figure and highest official in the party structure is the secretary general, who is elected by the party congress and is a member of the central committee, the executive bureau, and the secretariat. The party statutes are brief and noncommittal with respect to his duties and responsibilities, for his authority derives primarily from the trust shown in him by the Soviet leadership. No secretary general who loses this trust can long retain his office, although on occasion a party head acceptable to Moscow may be replaced by another pro-Soviet leader. Victorio Codovilla of Argentina is one of the few Latin American communists who is content to dominate his party from a post in the executive bureau while allowing a figurehead to serve as secretary general. In some parties the highest office is that of party president. Where it exists, however, it is purely an honorary post which in no way restricts the jurisdiction and authority of the secretary general.

The party cell, which is often known appropriately as the base organization, is the grass roots of the Latin American communist movement. It is here that new members are recruited, finances are collected, and contacts are made or maintained with friends and sympathizers of the party. And it is here that the rank and file receive indoctrination, training, and current assignments. Every communist, no matter how lofty his position in the party, is generally expected to be a cell member and to participate in its weekly or biweekly meetings. Each cell has a conference, which ordinarily includes the entire membership, and a secretariat of three to seven officers. When it outgrows this limit it is usually subdivided. Cells are formed both in places of employment and in residential areas, at the convenience of the party. In most instances cells are authorized by and are responsible to the party committee at the next higher level. However, among certain groups, such as factory workers, special cells may be formed under the direct authority and jurisdiction of a regional committee or the central committee. In public and professional organizations where party cells do not exist, communists are expected to create smaller units known as party factions, or fractions, which have most of the recruitment and propaganda functions of cells. Party factions are usually converted into cells when enough new members have been recruited.

*Social Composition*  No two Latin American communist parties are identical in social composition, but the movement as a whole is remarkably uniform. The communist parties, like all other Latin American political parties, are overwhelmingly urban. With rare exceptions, the top leaders are of middle-class origin or have risen to middle-class status. At least half the current party leaders first entered the communist movement as university students. Women are found in every party and are included in the leadership of most, although they constitute only a small percentage of the total leadership. The Argentine party has the greatest number of women, about 30 percent in the Buenos Aires area and perhaps 15 percent overall. The great bulk of the membership in nearly every party is drawn from the lower middle class and the upper rungs of the working class, although in some of the smaller countries artisans make up a substantial portion of the total. In no case does the rural lower class contribute more than a tiny percentage of the rank and file and a statistically insignificant portion of the party leadership.

As the self-declared vanguard of the proletariat, which seeks to awaken the political consciousness of the workers and lead them to political power, the communist movement directs its chief appeal to the working class in Latin America. Communists have competed vigorously for positions of leadership in the labor movement, often taking the initiative in establishing trade unions and federations among unorganized workers. After the first few years, when many communists insisted the party should be *for* but not *of* the proletariat, recruitment was conducted most heavily, and with varying results, among wage earners, particularly factory, transport, mine, and plantation workers. The parties have also concentrated upon employees in such strategic sectors as the food and service industries, communications, and entertainment, and these areas have consistently supplied a disproportionate share of the total party membership. It is probable that wage earners of all categories now constitute an absolute majority in the Latin American communist movement as a whole. Working-class members, however, appear to be the least stable element, more prone to become bored with party activities, to shirk assigned tasks, and to abandon the movement when the party's legal status or freedom of operations is curtailed.

Prior to the Cuban revolution the Latin American communist leadership, with its predominantly urban background and outlook, was neither concerned for nor able to communicate effectively with the rural populace, despite the fact that the parties invariably claimed to represent both peasants and workers. After 1959, alerted to the political potential of the rural masses, communists in most countries overcame their prejudices enough to launch a concerted drive to win a rural following. However, they have had relatively little success in building the party in the countryside, for the agents assigned to this task have been city dwellers temporarily operating in an alien environment. By and large, rural Latin America has yet to produce its own political leaders, and where such men have arisen—as in Bolivia and Venezuela—they have been attracted chiefly to noncommunist parties.

Since the communist movement began in Latin America the party leaders and press in every country have reiterated the standard Marxist-Leninist fulminations against the bourgeoisie, yet nearly every party in the area draws most of its leaders and fervent militants from the despised middle class. Numerically the most important such element within the party comprises while-collar employees in commercial firms, schoolteachers, bank workers, and bureaucrats with modest salaries, as well as a smaller proportion of self-employed craftsmen and small shopkeepers. Throughout Latin America the social status, but not necessarily the income, of such persons is considerably higher than that of even skilled laborers.

The intellectual elite of artists, writers, professionals, and higher-level bureaucrats, which supplies the top leadership of all political parties in Latin America, makes up a select sector of the middle class that is a prime target of communist recruitment efforts. This element tends to be deeply concerned with questions of social justice, economic development, and national sovereignty, and because of its distinguished position in society it is uniquely qualified to convey its views to the electorate. The community of intellectuals accounts for at least half the communist party leaders in Latin America, a significant percentage of the new members recruited into the party, and a larger number of sympathizers who support communist causes and lend the prestige of their names to the communist movement. Such men as the Mexican painters Diego Rivera and David Alfaro Siqueiros, the Brazilian writer Jorge Amado, and the poets Nicolás Guillén of Cuba and Pablo Neruda of Chile have, through their long identification with communism, contributed prestige and respectability to the communist movement in much of Latin America.

Youth and students are another important and highly susceptible target of communist propaganda in all of Latin America. Nearly every communist party maintains a youth organization that is technically separate from the formal party structure but is in fact closely coordinated with it. The members are not required to be communists, but they are instructed in Marxist-Leninist doctrine and are encouraged to enter the party at the age of eighteen. Where the parties are well developed, the youth organization is a significant source of new members. The communists also seek to penetrate and control student organizations in the universities and secondary schools. Although students in Latin America generally come from upper- and middle-class families, they do not ordinarily share their parents' political views at this stage. As a group they tend to be ultranationalistic, extremely sensitive to social and economic injustice, impatient for change, and quick to seize upon ready-made formulas that promise easy, immediate solutions to national problems. They are equally prone to take direct political action to achieve their objectives. At the same time, students are widely respected as an elite group and are thus usually protected against the consequences of rash actions. Relatively few Latin American students actually become communists, but the communist youth and student organizations remain large enough to serve as effective adjuncts to the party in most countries, and as a reservoir of potential communist party leaders.

The social composition of the party is of continuing concern to Latin American communist leaders. In those parties that enjoy legal status or comparative freedom of action, reports on the class origins and occupations of the members are frequently submitted to the national congress, conference, or plenary session of the central committee. Such reports are seldom complete, however, and in the case of the underground parties they either remain closely guarded secrets or are published only in the most general terms. It is unusual, moreover, for the national or international communist press to publish comparable data for different Latin American parties in any single year. Nonetheless, a few examples taken from the decade 1954 to 1964 suggest the degree of similarity and something of the differences between the various communist parties in Latin America.

One of the most thorough analyses of party membership was a review of the occupations and professions of delegates to the fourth congress of the Communist Party of Brazil in November 1954. All the delegates were party leaders or militants of more than two years' standing. Nearly half, 48 percent, were workers, predominantly from large business enterprises; only 4 percent were described as peasants; 16 percent were identified as merchants, a category that embraced the entire range of small shopkeepers and self-employed artisans; 10.7 percent were former students; 8 percent were government employees; 8 percent were former members of the armed forces, divided equally between officers and enlisted men; and 5.3 percent were drawn from other activities. Of the total, fewer than 10 percent were women, and 16 percent were officers in labor unions or other mass organizations. These proportions are probably still generally valid for the Brazilian party, and except for the inclusion of former military personnel, appear to be reasonably typical of the larger communist parties of Latin America.

In 1963 the Colombian party reported briefly on the class composition of one of its district committees. Of the twenty-one members, nine were identified as workers and trade-union officials, seven were party functionaries, four were intellectuals, and one was a handicraftsman. The party in El Salvador, at its fifth congress in February 1964, did not provide specific numbers or percentages but noted that from the beginning most of its members had come from workers in the handicrafts sector. Only now was the party attempting to build a broader base by recruiting more members from the industrial and agricultural proletariat.

*Political Status* The political status of the Latin American communist parties ranges across a broad spectrum, from complete and unrestricted legality to nearly total suppression. This situation has prevailed since the founding of the first parties. At no time were all existing communist parties banned concurrently, yet only one, the Uruguayan party, has never been formally proscribed. All the others have alternated between shorter or longer periods of legality and varying degrees of repression. In 1965 the communist parties in the respective Latin American republics could be divided roughly into the following categories:

In power: CUBA

Legal, unrestricted: CHILE, URUGUAY

Legal but barred by law from presenting candidates for public office on its own ticket: ARGENTINA, BOLIVA, COLOMBIA, MEXICO

Illegal but in fact usually barred only from presenting its own candidates for public office: COSTA RICA, PERU

Illegal, active, and subject to repression: BRAZIL, ECUADOR, EL SALVADOR, HONDURAS, NICARAGUA, PANAMA

Illegal, engaged in armed revolt: DOMINICAN REPUBLIC, GUATEMALA, VENEZUELA

Illegal, severely repressed: HAITI, PARAGUAY

The Venezuelan party enjoys a further distinction in that its legal status was "suspended" rather than canceled in 1962.

*Party Strength* The Latin American communist parties vary even more in numerical strength than in political status, ranging from several tens of thousands to only a few dozen members. This diversity has been characteristic of the movement in Latin America from the beginning. However, the precise number of party members active throughout the area at any one time has never been known, chiefly because the communists themselves have been both unable and unwilling to provide such information. Each party has experienced periods of rapid expansion and decline and is subject to a more or less continuous turnover in membership, with the result that it is constantly fluctuating in size. At best, party leaders can only approximate the number of their followers at a given moment, and even when a reasonably accurate estimate is available within the party, it is seldom publicized.

There are two sound and apparently opposed justifications for this policy of secrecy. The communist movement is tolerated in much of Latin America because it represents only a small segment of the politically active population. In these circumstances the authorities tend to feel that the communists are too few to be taken seriously. Thus effusive public statements about the party's size or rate of growth might well provoke repressive action by the government. At the same time, the communists have learned that it behooves them to be less than precise about their numbers when seeking political alliances, for potential allies are disposed to regard the party as larger than it is in fact.

On occasion, particularly when a party has legal status and is engaged in a major recruitment drive, it may publish highly exaggerated membership claims, both to raise the morale of current members and to make the party seem more attractive to potential recruits. The Argentine party, for example, which had no more than 70,000 members in 1965, claimed to have passed the 100,000 rank in its 1963-1964 recruitment campaign. Conversely, a party that suffers a rapid, drastic loss of members, as in the case of the Brazilian party in the 1960s, may continue for some time to claim an earlier, higher figure. In any event, the number of party members is always less significant than their militancy. Each party has discovered that when its freedom of action is restored, it can recover many of its former members and quickly resume operations on a larger scale.

Despite the fact that there are no membership statistics universally accepted as accurate and authoritative, both communist and noncommunist sources agree closely on the magnitude of the communist movement in Latin America. The Latin American Institute of the Academy of Sciences of the Soviet Union asserts that the combined membership of the communist parties in Latin America (incuding the Caribbean islands and the Guianas) was over 250,000 in 1963 and over 300,000 in 1965. This source gives only the total figure.[3] Estimates by United States sources suggest that the overall communist party membership in the twenty Latin American republics ranged from 235,000 to 260,000 in 1963 and from 275,000 to 295,000 in 1965. Front parties and splinter groups accounted for up to 50,000 additional communists in both years. Nearly 90 percent of all Latin American communists were found in seven parties—those of Argentina, Brazil, Chile, Colombia, Cuba, Uruguay, and Venezuela. The only large front party was the Socialist People's Party in Mexico.

*Front Organizations* From the beginning a proliferation of front organizations has been characteristic of the communist movement in Latin America. This is a technique employed deliberately to create the impression of widespread, spontaneous, and growing enthusiasm for the issues and objectives currently propounded by the local communist party. The communists use two basic types of front organizations, in addition to labor, youth, and student bodies, which they seek to penetrate and manipulate. One of these is the special-interest front, built around women's organizations, professional societies, cultural associations, and the like, dedicated to securing some legitimate objective or aspiration of the group; the communists soon go beyond such limited goals to engage the front in political propaganda. The other type is the contrived front group, supposedly nonpolitical and created to foster a particular propaganda theme or objective of the local party or the world communist movement. A few fronts are preserved as regular features of the party's propaganda apparatus, to be emphasized periodically even though they may be ineffectual. For example, there has been at least one "peace" front in each republic since the late 1940s. This and similar women's, students', youth, journalists', teachers', and lawyers' fronts are affiliated with the appropriate international communist front body.

Most of the major fronts would probably exist regardless of communist involvement in them, but the contrived fronts, and some presumably mass-based front groups, are in fact paper organizations with limited membership and little or no resonance among the public they claim to represent. In the postwar years such organizations were formed to protest "the high cost of living," to defend "national sovereignty" against "Yankee imperialism," and to promote "nationalization of large landholdings," "nationalization of natural resources," "expropriation of foreign-owned utilities and industries," and "defense of the Cuban revolution." The sheer number of these organizations serves in large measure to compensate for their individual weaknesses and to further the illusion the communists seek to project.

The Latin American communist parties use all their front groups as echo chambers to magnify and distort the volume of popular support for the themes each one emphasizes. Nominally these front organizations are separate, autonomous entities, but in fact the key positions in substantially all fronts within each country are held by the same small clique of disguised communists, fellow travelers, and sympathizers. Wherever possible, this leadership is supplemented by useful innocents to provide a façade masking the front's links with the party. The leaders and ranking members of supposedly unrelated groups sign each other's petitions, echo each other's slogans, and attend each other's public meetings. This has been a consistent pattern since the formation of the first communist fronts in the area and has involved ever larger numbers of organizations since World War II.[4] In more than half the republics the communists also maintain binational "cultural" centers and friendship societies designed to improve local attitudes toward individual communist regimes. These cultural centers serve as points of dissemination for propaganda publications prepared abroad and fellowship and travel grants to Latin Americans invited to visit the socialist camp. The only significant political party which serves as a communist front in Latin American is the Socialist People's Party in Mexico.

RELATION TO SOVIET LEADERSHIP

Between 1920 and 1935 nearly every prominent Latin American communist took part in at least one meeting of the Comintern, the Profintern, or other prewar world communist fronts in Moscow. These men all appear to have been awed and inspired by their association with the leaders of the international movement. The Russians and Europeans who dominated the international bodies, however, consistently looked upon Latin America as a secondary area and considered most of the Latin American communists as unsophisticated and unreliable. Under these circumstances, the first originator of a Latin American party to become a trusted Comintern agent was M. N. Roy of India, who represented Mexico at the second Comintern congress in 1920. Roy, however, merely used his Mexican experience and affiliation to prove his value to the Comintern, which thereafter employed him almost entirely in Asia; he never returned to Latin America.

In time a few Latin American communists earned the respect and confidence of the Soviet leadership and came to be relied upon to advise the Comintern on Latin American affairs, to represent the Latin American movement in Moscow, and to serve as direct links between international headquarters and the local parties. The principal figure in this group was the Argentine Victorio Codovilla, who was a member of the Latin American secretariat formed in Moscow in 1927 and treasurer of its South American Bureau, which was moved to Buenos Aires the following year. Other

Latin Americans highly regarded by the Comintern during the 1930s were Rodolfo Ghioldi of Argentina, Eudocio Ravines and Julio Portocarrero of Peru, Ricardo Martínez of Venezuela, and Julio Antonio Mella of Cuba. Ghioldi frequently served as a Comintern spokesman to parties in neighboring South American republics. Ravines was carrying out Comintern directives when he formed the Peruvian Communist Party. Portocarrero and Martínez were employed chiefly as advisors on labor matters, and Mella was a Comintern agent in Mexico at the time of his assassination in 1929.

In the mid-1930s the group was expanded to include Luiz Carlos Prestes of Brazil and Blas Roca of Cuba. In 1935 the Latin American representatives on the Executive Committee of the Comintern were Prestes, with full membership, and Roca and Ghioldi as alternate members. In that year, Ravines, with Ricardo Martínez, went to Chile to direct the formation of the Popular Front, while Ghioldi accompanied Prestes to Brazil, where they were imprisoned following the failure of the communist-led revolt. Codovilla spent several years after 1930 in the Soviet Union and then served as a Comintern agent in Spain during the Spanish civil war, as did Ravines for a time before defecting from the communist movement. On his return to Latin America in 1940, Codovilla apparently carried Comintern instructions for a purge of the Mexican party. Such activities were halted in 1941 by the German invasion of the Soviet Union, which severed communications indefinitely between the Comintern and its key personnel in Latin America. The formal dissolution of the Comintern in 1943 simply acknowledged the *de facto* situation.

In addition to the few top communists who served as trusted lieutenants, a fairly large number of middle-level communist officials from Latin America were also attracted to the Comintern and affiliated bodies in the Soviet Union, where they received employment, indoctrination, and a safe haven during times of persecution at home. In the postwar years the Latin American functionaries of the Cominform, the worldwide front organizations, and related agencies of the international communist bureaucracy appear to have been drawn primarily from this group. The full number and identity of the Latin Americans employed in the Soviet Union and Eastern Europe for shorter or longer periods are not known, since for the most part they occupied obscure positions as students, research assistants, clerks, translators, editors, or technicians of one kind or another. Moreover, it was usually not politic for them to publicize their recent connection with the Soviet Union or Soviet bloc when they returned home.

One Latin American communist whose situation enabled him to reveal some of the details of his prolonged stay in the Soviet Union was Octávio Brandão of Brazil. An early admirer of the Russian revolution and the first communist elected to the legislative assembly in Rio de Janeiro, Brandão was exiled to Germany by the revolutionary government in 1931. That same year he made his way to Moscow, where he remained until 1946. After nearly two years spent in "work and study," he was employed as a "scientific collaborator" in the Institute of World Economy and Politics. In 1935 he pioneered Portuguese-language propaganda broadcasts on Radio Moscow and continued for a decade to broadcast regularly over shortwave radio to Brazil and Portugal. In the course of his long residence in the Soviet capital he also gave public lectures on the history and literature of his homeland. While Brandão's duties brought him to public attention, and therefore make his case somewhat unique, in many respects his experiences were comparable to those of other Latin Americans who held subordinate posts in the international communist propaganda apparatus during periods of enforced or voluntary exile.

THE SINO-SOVIET DISPUTE

The Sino-Soviet dispute made some contribution to the splits in a number of Latin American parties in the 1960s. In Brazil a dissident pro-Chinese group led by men long prominent in the Brazilian Communist Party (Partido Comunista Brasileiro) formed the rival Communist Party of Brazil (Partido Comunista do Brasil) in 1961. In Chile individual pro-Peking members of the communist party were expelled, but there was no indication that they had formed a separate communist organization by 1965. A small pro-Chinese group split off from the Communist Party of Colombia in 1964 and organized the Communist Party of Colombia, Marxist-Leninist (Partido Comunista de Colombia, Marxista-Leninista).

Other dissidents drifted into various Castroist parties and fronts rather than create rival communist parties. The communist party in Ecuador has traditionally been split into two principal factions, based in Guayaquil and Quito. After 1963 each of these was further divided by conflicting personal animosities and ambitions; some of the Quito communists expressed pro-Chinese sentiments but made no effort to form a separate communist party. A unique situation existed in Honduras, where the small, dissident Honduran Revolutionary Party (Partido Revolucionario Hondureño), which split from the Communist Party of Honduras in 1961, agreed with the pro-Castro, pro-Soviet line of the parent organization. A small Bolshevik Communist Party of Mexico (Partido Comunista Bolchevique de México), organized by dissident communists and other leftists in 1963, was avowedly pro-Chinese.

In Panama the communist Party of the People is formally pro-Soviet, but its university-student following, which comprises much of the membership and potential leadership of the party, was about equally divided between pro-Peking and pro-Moscow factions in the mid-1960s. The Paraguayan Communist Party in 1963 lost a splinter group which established a pro-Chinese Paraguayan Leninist Communist Party (Partido Comunista Leninista Paraguayo) that proved to be even less effective than the pro-Soviet parent party. In January 1964 the Peruvian Communist Party split into rival pro-Moscow and pro-Peking factions, each of which retained the original party name and claimed to be the authentic representative of the communist movement in Peru. In Venezuela internal factionalism along Soviet and Chinese lines was not yet strong enough in 1965 to produce an organizational split in the party but was sufficient to force communist leaders to preserve a precarious neutrality in the ideological dispute.

The propaganda war between Communist China and the Soviet Union thus tended to weaken the Latin American communist parties somewhat, but nowhere did a majority of any party swing to a pro-Chinese position. At the end of 1965 Moscow's primacy in the communist movement in Latin America was being challenged, but it was not in jeopardy.

## BIBLIOGRAPHY

The titles cited here are works on Latin America in general. Works on communist parties in specific countries are cited in the bibliographies for those countries. The periodicals in the following list contain articles in which spokesmen of the twenty republics published interpretations and factual accounts of the origins and development of the communist movement in Latin America or in which non-communists comment on this movement.

1. Alba, Victor: *Historia del comunismo en América Latina*, Mexico City, Ediciones Occidentales, 1954.
2. Alexander, Robert J.: *Communism in Latin America*, New Brunswick, N.J., Rutgers University Press, 1957.
3. Alexander, Robert J.: *Organized Labor in Latin America*, New York, Free Press, 1965.
4. Allen, Robert Loring: *Soviet Influence in Latin America: The Role of Economic Relations*, Washington, Public Affairs Press, 1959.
5. Arismendi, R.: *Problemy latinsko-amerikanskoi revoliutsii* (Problems of the Latin American Revolution) (translated from Spanish), Moscow, 1964.
6. Basaldua, Pedro de: *La Garra comunista en América Latina*, Buenos Aires, Asociación Argentina por la Libertad de la Cultura [1962].

7. Beals, Carleton: *Glass Houses: Ten Years of Free Lancing*, New York, Lippincott, 1938.
8. Brandão, Octavio: *Os intelectuais progressistas*, Rio de Janeiro, Organização Simões Editôra, 1956.
9. Dillon, Dorothy: *International Communism and Latin America: Perspectives and Prospects*, Latin American Monograph 19, Gainsville, Fla., University of Florida Press, 1962.
10. Halperin, Ernst: *Castro and Latin American Communism*, Cambridge, Mass., MIT Center for International Studies, May 1963.
11. Kirkpatrick, Evron M. (ed.): *Target the World*, New York, Macmillan, 1956.
12. Kirkpatrick, Evron M. (ed.): *Year of Crisis: Communist Propaganda Activities in 1956*, New York, Macmillan, 1957.
13. Poppino, Rollie E.: *International Communism in Latin America: A History of the Movement, 1917-1963*, New York, Free Press, 1964.
14. *Programnye dokumenty kommunisticheskikh i rabochikh partii stran Ameriki* (Documents on the Programs of the Communist and Workers' Parties of the Countries of America), Moscow, 1962.
15. Ravines, Eudocio: *The Yenan Way*, New York, Scribner, 1951.
16. Schlesinger, Jorge: *Revolución comunista*, Guatemala City, Editorial Unión, 1946.
17. U.S. Department of State: *The Sino-Soviet Economic Offensive in the Less Developed Countries*, Publication 6632, Washington, May 1958.
18. U.S. Department of State, Bureau of Intelligence and Research: *World Strength of the Communist Party Organizations*, Annual Reports, Washington, 1956-1966.
19. U.S. Senate: "Soviet Bloc-Latin American Relations and Their Implications for United States Foreign Policy," *United States-Latin American Relations*, Washington, February 1960.

*PERIODICALS*

20. *Communist International* (in English, Russian, French, and German; some issues in Spanish and Chinese), 1919-1943.
21. *For a Lasting Peace, for a People's Democracy* (published in Belgrade, later in Bucharest), vols. 1-10, 1947-1956.
22. *International Press Correspondence* (Vienna, Berlin, London), vols. 1-18, 1921-1938.
23. *Problems of Communism* (U.S. Information Agency, Washington), vols. 1-14, 1952-1965.
24. *World Marxist Review: Problems of Peace and Socialism* (London and Toronto), vols. 1-8, 1958-1965.

ROLLIE E. POPPINO

1. See articles on individual Latin American countries.

2. For full particulars about the various names employed by individual Latin American communist parties see the respective country articles.

3. For membership estimates of the individual communist parties see the articles on the respective countries.

4. The articles on particular Latin American countries contain more detailed information on local front organizations.

# LATVIA

The origins of the Communist Party of Latvia (Latvijas Komunistiskā Partija, LKP) are closely related to events in the Baltic area during World War I and the few months following its conclusion. Latvian social democratic organizations had existed since the end of the 1890s. During the 1904-1905 revolution in Russia the Latvian Social Democratic Workers' Party (Latviešu Sociāldemokratiskā Strādnieku Partija, LSDSP) played a leading role in the Baltic area. It collaborated with the Russian Social Democratic Labor Party but was closer to its menshevik wing than to Lenin's bolshevik faction. Not until the fourth congress of the LSDSP, held in Brussels in January-February 1914, did the bolsheviks win a slim majority and capture the central committee of the party. Although the party was at that time quite insignificant in membership (about 3,500), the bolshevik success at Brussels later took on great importance.

## HISTORY

After the Russian revolution of 1917 the bolshevik-dominated LSDSP was able to infiltrate the Latvian Riflemen's Brigades, formed in 1915, and the newly formed councils of soldiers, workers, and landless peasants. A special Latvian bolshevik military organization in Petrograd brought the Riflemen's Brigades to Lenin's side during the October coup that established bolshevik power in Russia. On December 31, 1917, a soviet in northern Latvia, organized by Latvian bolsheviks and headed by Fricis Roziņš (Āzis), proclaimed Latvia an autonomous unit of the Russian Socialist Federal Soviet Republic. However, bolshevik rule in Latvia lasted only until mid-February of 1918, when the Germans occupied the entire country.

At this point Latvian bolshevik activities were transferred to Russia. On March 24, 1918, the Soviet Russian government created a Latvian commissariat within the framework of the Commissariat of Nationality Affairs under Stalin's leadership (see *The Communist International*). The main purpose of this Latvian commissariat was to work for the return of Latvia as a communist-dominated country into communist-dominated Russia.

In the meantime, after the collapse of the German Empire, on November 18, 1918, a coalition of Latvian bourgeois and socialist parties had met in Riga to proclaim the independence of the Latvian Republic. A small procommunist "Spartacus" organization in Latvia, opposed to the proclamation of independence, did not play an important role. However, it received support from the "government of Soviet Latvia," which was created in Moscow on December 17, 1918, from among members of the Latvian commissariat, with Pēteris Stučka (known later in the Soviet Union as Piotr Shtuchka) as its head. This "government" was recognized by Soviet Russia on December 22, 1918, the day the Red Army invaded Latvian soil. After the occupation of Riga by the Red Army (January 3, 1919) the Moscow-created government ruled for about five months over most of Latvia, including the capital city of Riga. By June 1919 the Red Army and the Latvian communist government were forced to abandon Riga, but they were able to hold the easternmost province of Latgale until the first days of 1920.

The LSDSP was not invited to attend the founding congress of the Comintern. However, on the day this congress closed, March 6, 1919, the Latvian bolsheviks announced in Moscow that the LSDSP was changing its name to Communist (Bolshevik) Party of Latvia (Latvijas Komunistiskā Partija, LKP) and joined the Comintern. Thus the maneuverings of a group of salaried functionaries of the Soviet Commissariat of Nationality Affairs, acting in complete isolation from the membership of the LSDSP and using it only as an object of bolshevik policy, culminated in the creation of the Communist Party of Latvia. At the time of its creation the new party had little influence on developments in those parts of Latvia which still remained uner the occupation and administration of the Red Army.

With the bolsheviks and Soviet Russia refusing to recognize the independence of Latvia, the remnants of the bolshevik cells in Latvia, now organizational units of the LKP, started subversive activities against the Latvian state and army. In January 1920, when the remnants of the Red Army were expelled from Latvian soil, the Soviet Latvian government, seated now in Pskov, transferred its powers to the central committee of the LKP. Its Bureau Abroad, seated in Moscow, thus became the directing body of the party. In Latvia itself the party went underground. At that time it had eighty-three cells in Latvia, with 630 members and about 1,000 sympathizers. Almost the entire membership consisted of industrial workers, with a thin sprinkling of intellectuals and professionals.

From Russia the Bureau organized subversive activities in Latvia, trained agitators and party functionaries, and provided the underground movement with political literature and money. Two Latvian communist presses in Russia produced the literature, Spartaks from 1920 to 1923 and Prometējs from 1923 to 1927.

Attempts to organize strikes and labor disturbances in different parts of Latvia generally brought very few results, and the masses remained predominantly under the influence of the nationalist and social democratic parties. Moreover, during the 1920s the party was weakened by internal strife. The political line in Moscow dictated that Trotskyists and "right wingers" be purged. These activities were followed by a strong wave of opposition to legal operation through front organizations, as approved by the twentieth party conference in 1922. In 1932 and 1933 the opposition group, led by A. Strautnieks (Citrons), was expelled from the party. This coincided with a move to broaden party activities, with particular attention to agitation among the rural proletariat. A partial strike of the Latvian merchant marine in June 1933 was the most spectacular achievement. In 1934 membership in the LKP (which had by now dropped the designation bolshevik) had reached an all-time high of 1,150.

In the third and fourth legislative elections communist candidates, running on various tickets won six and seven seats, respectively, in the 100-seat Saeima, the Latvian parliament. A splinter group of the LSDSP, the Independent Socialist Party of Latvia, had supported the communists in the 1928 elections, and attempts to create a broader "popular front" in Latvia were finally being met with some success, when in mid-1934 the political situation suddenly changed radically and the government eliminated all opposition.

The coup by Kārlis Ulmanis and his nationalist regime brought about strong measures against communism. Some communists were arrested, and others fled to the Soviet Union. The LKP membership declined to about 600 in 1936 and 200 in 1938. Meanwhile the purges in the Soviet Union in the mid-1930s and later decimated those Latvian communists who had taken refuge in the "fatherland of the proletariat." The Bureau Abroad was liquidated in July 1936 and replaced by a provisional secretariat of the LKP. Stučka and most of the other Latvian communist leaders residing in the Soviet Union were arrested and later executed.

When the Soviet army occupied Latvia on June 17, 1940, there were only 400 Latvian communists in a country of 2 million inhabitants. The LKP was legalized on June 21 and became instrumental in converting Latvia into a soviet republic. On October 8, 1940, the Latvian party, now consisting of 1,000 members, became a branch of the Communist Party of the Soviet Union. The last leading Latvian communists were Jānis Kalnberziņš (Zaķis), Žānis Spure, and Fricis Deglavs. In December 1940 the LKP held its last (ninth) congress and replaced its central committee by a bureau.

## ORGANIZATION AND MEMBERSHIP

The basic unit of the LKP was the cell (three to ten members), supported by groups of sympathizers. Several cells formed a district organization, which in turn formed provincial organizations. The provincial organizations were governed by committees. Owing to the clandestine nature of party work in Latvia, the membership was rather small, ranging from a few hundred to the all-time high of 1,150 in 1934.

A prominent role was played by party sympathizers and several front organizations. The most active front group was the communist youth organization, which changed its name several times between March 1919 and July 1940. Like the LKP, its membership was also small (with an all-time high of 910 in 1937). An illegal communist Red Cross organization that aided imprisoned party members from 1920 to 1924 was replaced by a Latvian branch of International Red Aid. For a while its legal front organization was the Human Rights Association, which enrolled 4,500 members in fourteen local chapters. Communist activities in trade unions resulted in their control of the Central Association of Trade Unions in Riga from 1919 until 1928.

## PARTY PRESS ORGANS

The official organ of the LKP was the newspaper *Cīņa* (Struggle), but owing to the clandestine operation of the party it appeared very irregularly. Many other illegal and legal communist newspapers appeared in Latvia, but none for any long period.

## CONGRESSES OF THE LKP

Only two party congresses were held during the years of Latvia's independence: the seventh in February 1923, and the eighth in January-February 1931, both in Moscow. The numeration was continued from congresses of the LSDSP. A number of plenary meetings of the central committee and party conferences were also held from 1920 to 1939.

## BIBLIOGRAPHY

Freivalds, Osvalds: *Latviešu polītiskās partiijas, 60 gados* (The Latvian Political Parties, Sixty Years), Copenhagen, Imanta, 1961.

Kalniņš, Bruno: *Latvijas sociāldemokratijas, piecdesmit gadi* (The Latvian Social Democracy, Fifty Years), Stockholm, LSDSP Ārzemju Komiteja, 1956.

Miške, V. (ed.): *Latvijas komunistiskās partijas vēstures apcerējumi* (The Latvian Communist Party: Historical Sketches), vols. I and II, Riga, Latvijas Valsts Izdevniecība, 1961, 1965.

Šteimanis, J.: *Latvijas komunistiskās partijas taktika cīņa par padomju varas atjaunošanu, 1920-1940* (The LKP's Tactics in the Struggle for the Restoration of Soviet Power, 1920-1940), Riga, Liesma, 1965.

Strazdiņš, Kārlis (ed.): *Latvijas PSR vēsture* (History of the Latvian Soviet Socialist Republic), vol. III, Riga, Latvijas PSR Zinātņu Akademijas Izdevniecība, 1959.

EDGAR ANDERSON

# LEBANON AND SYRIA

With the collapse of the Ottoman Empire at the end of World War I there emerged in Greater Syria (Syria, Lebanon, and Palestine) a nationalist movement and an educated elite to give it expression, free of the constraints imposed by Turkish repressive policies. In this period of relative freedom (1919 and 1920) barriers to communication evaporated and new contacts were made with socialist currents in Europe. As a result, traditional nationalist concerns were expanded to include an interest in the economic condition of the poor—of special importance in Lebanon, where famine and economic depression had affected thousands during the war.

It was at this time that communist thought first penetrated intellectual circles in Lebanon and Syria. What particularly distinguished the development of communism in the Arab world was that, unlike most communist movements in Europe, it did not emerge from a split in the ranks of the workers' movement or the socialist parties. Rather, it started with an undiluted communist orientation inspired by the bolshevik revolution in Russia.

Among the more obvious characteristics of the new bolshevik party in Greater Syria were the lack of a concrete plan and a vagueness about objectives and methodology. Organized in cells and ideological groups, the early communists did not adhere to pure Marxist doctrine, nor did they clearly pursue a Leninist line. They were concerned primarily with equality among the classes, the eradication of poverty, and improvement of the lot of workers. This ambiguity of purpose reflected a number of contradictions. Arab communists were simultaneously religiously and socialist-materialistically oriented. They praised the achievements of the Soviet Union and took them as a model, while at the same time they attacked its government and policies and applauded its enemies. They never, however, abandoned the essentially socialist character of their movement, and they continued to attack capitalism in all its forms and at every possible opportunity. They called for justice and equality, the rights of the working classes, and socialization of the means of production. The term "comrade" (*rafiq*) was from the beginning a commonplace in Arab communist circles.

## HISTORY

Although communism was at first anything but a popular movement in the Arab world, an attempt was made in 1922 to broaden its appeal. On September 22, 1922, the first issue of the semiweekly *al-Sahafi al-Ta'ih* (The Wandering Journalist) appeared in Zahle, Lebanon. This paper carried the bolshevik banner in its early issues and first called for the establishment of a communist party in Syria and Lebanon. At the same time Yusuf Yazbak and Salah Mahfuz, both Lebanese, of bolshevik orientation, were also calling for the founding of a communist party in Syria and Lebanon.

The early communist movement in Lebanon and Syria was animated more by romantic idealism than by political activism. The Third International symbolized the beginning of an era, and those early enthusiasts went so far as to use the year of the Comintern's founding to begin a new calendar in their private and personal correspondence. Doctrinal rather than substantive local problems absorbed most of their energies, and the movement remained aloof from the political life of the community. Ironically, it was this very detachment from local politics that was later to place the movement on a stronger and more viable foundation.

In the early months of 1923 new recruits to the socialist cause—among them Nicola Harb, Fu'ad Shamali, and Margaret Sam'an—wrote openly and freely in an ever-widening circle of notable Arabic journals. Also in 1923, the first labor union was established in Zahle with the assent of the Lebanese government. A second labor union was organized the same year in Bikfayya by Fu'ad Shamali, who had recently been expelled from Egypt by the British for his bolshevik activities.

In November 1924 Fu'ad Shamali, Yusuf Yazbak, and Joseph Berger of the Palestine Bolshevik Party met in Bikfayya to discuss the prospects for founding a bolshevik party in Syria and Lebanon. At a second meeting a few days later in Hadath, a suburb of Beirut, they were joined by others. Progress was limited, however, by a general disapproval of Berger's proposal that the new party be a satellite of the one in Palestine. This point was resolved at a third meeting, also in Hadath, and the bolshevik party was founded as the Lebanese People's Party (Hizb al-Sha'b al-Lubnani). Liaison between the Lebanese party and its Palestinian counterpart began immediately and was carefully maintained by Berger; Eliahu Teper, a Lithuanian; and Abu Ziyam, a long-time bolshevik and friend of Lenin in Switzerland sent to organize the movement in the Arab countries. They were joined by Nakhman Litvinsky, a Russian Jew. It was allegedly through Abu Ziyam that the Lebanese communists requested the Palestinian party to reject the Balfour Declaration for a separate state of Israel. The Palestinian party agreed and issued a bulletin in which for the first time Jewish communists rejected the Balfour Declaration and thus denounced the plan for a Jewish national home in Palestine.

By April 1925 the Lebanese party was enjoying unprecedented strength and popularity. It was granted a license to hold a public May Day celebration which was a great success. Encouraged by these events, Yusuf Yazbak left his job at the Beirut Port to devote full attention to party activities. He began publication in Beirut of an Arabic party weekly, *al-Insaniyah* (Humanity), but its open espousal of communist doctrine proved too much for the French authorities, who closed it down after the fifth issue. The British government had for the same reason already prevented the paper from entering Egypt. Fearing arrest, Yazbak fled to Paris, where he joined the staff of *L'Humanité* and provided the first contact with the French party.

During the summer of 1925 the Lebanese communists made contact with Armenian communists in Beirut, who had established the Spartacus Party, headed by Artine Madoyan. Soon afterward the two parties formed a temporary joint committee. At this juncture various parts of Syria were in full revolution against French mandate rule, and one of the first decisions taken by the Lebanese party was to support the Syrian nationalists. In December 1925 the first regional Lebanese party congress appointed a permanent central committee. However, the congress was followed by a series of arrests, and Yazbak, Madoyan, and an 'Ali Nasir al-Din were tried by a military court and sent into exile, where they remained until the end of the revolt in 1928.

Between 1928 and 1932 the party organization was revived under Fu'ad Shamali. This transfer of leadership from Yazbak was understood to symbolize the Lebanese party's new posture of more action and less theorizing. Communist influence spread out from Beirut into some rural districts and such cities as Damascus and Tripoli. In 1930 Khalid Bakdash, son of a prominent Kurdish family in Syria and a former member of the Nationalist Bloc (al-Kutlah al-Wataniyah), joined the party in Damascus. The eighteen-year-old Bakdash was sent to Moscow for two years to study Marxist ideology, and upon his return he became Shamali's strongest rival, accusing him of being an agent of the French police. With the support of Madoyan from Beirut and Rafiq Rida from Tripoli, Bakdash succeeded in ousting Shamali in 1952 and replaced him as party first secretary. Faraj Allah al-Halu and Nicola Shawi joined the trio to form the new party leadership.

The communists made unsuccessful attempts in the early 1930s to publish *Sawt al-'Ummal* (The Workers' Voice) as a legal party organ. *Al-Fajr al-Ahmar al-Dami* (Blood Red Dawn) appeared for a few months in 1930 and 1931 before its suppression by the police; a party publication in Armenian appeared during the same period. The following year the communists in Beirut succeeded in fomenting the first workers' strikes and street demonstrations. During the next four years the party passed through a period of ideological reorientation. Important communist literature was translated on an unprecedented scale. Bakdash produced the first Arabic translation of the *Communist Manifesto* and some of Stalin's works and began publication of an Arabic literary journal, *al-Tali'ah* (The Vanguard). In 1932 a new party had emerged in Beirut, the Syrian Social Nationalist Party (commonly known by its French name, Parti Populaire Syrien), under the dynamic leadership of its founder Antun Sa'adah. The two parties, ideologically poles apart, became locked in a continuous strife which had the effect of compelling both parties to clarify their objectives and revamp their activities, in effect, recasting themselves into a strong organization.

By 1936 the years of organizational experience had begun to yield rewards. Strong communist roots had developed in a number of labor unions. The cause of the workers was further championed, and the motto "freedom and bread" had become a popular slogan. For the first time national unity was emphasized over internationalism. The emergence of the Popular Front in France had put the Syrian and Lebanese communists in better favor with the mandate authorities, and financial aid and directives were dispatched from Paris in abundance. In 1938 Rida, a member of the central committee, was sent to France as the party representative, and from his office at the French party headquarters in Paris he worked closely with the leadership of the French party in matters relating to communist affairs in the Near East and North Africa.

In 1937 the communists participated for the first time in Lebanese elections but did not win any seats. In May of that year the first issue of *Sawt al-Sha'b* (Voice of the People), the official party organ, appeared. Financially, the party had never enjoyed greater prosperity, as evidenced by the quantity and quality of literature it put out as well as the general increase in party activities. Membership in Syria and Lebanon was reported to have risen from 200 to 2,000.

In September 1939, when France entered the war, the party was banned, and *Sawt al-Sha'b* ceased publication. In 1940 and 1941 a number of party leaders, including al-Halu, were arrested and sentenced to jail, where they remained during most of World War II. With the Soviet Union's entry into the war on the side of the Allies—an event which raised the morale of the world communist movement in general—the communists in Syria and Lebanon began cautiously to reappear in the open and to tailor their policy and program to Soviet foreign policy. In December 1941 a League for Struggle Against Nazism and Fascism in Syria and Lebanon, formed in Beirut and headed by Antun Thabit, began publication of the literary journal *al-Tariq* (The Way). The following month *Sawt al-Sha'b* reappeared in Beirut. Four communists participated in the 1943 Lebanese elections, although the leading communist, al-Halu, polled only a little more than 9,000 votes.

On January 2, 1944, a party congress, held in Beirut, concluded its deliberations with the motto "a free homeland and a prosperous people." In addition to drafting a national charter, the congress drew up a set of bylaws stressing the national, rather than the international, character of the party and resolved to introduce "moderate democratic reform" and emphasize "national solidarity." At this congress it was also decided to divide the party into separate Syrian and Lebanese parties, but with joint leadership and a single central committee. However, in July of that year the Soviet Union recognized the independence of Syria and Lebanon, and by a decision of the central committee the Lebanese Communist Party (al-Hizb al-Shuyu'i al-Lubnani) and the Syrian Communist Party (al-Hizb al-Shuyu'i al-Suri) emerged as closely coordinated but as wholly independent parties. Faraj Allah al-Halu was appointed president of the Lebanese party and Khalid Bakdash president of the Syrian party. A Soviet embassy was established in Beirut, providing a convenient official link with the Kremlin.

In 1946 French mandate rule was terminated in Syria and Lebanon, and seemingly overnight France's traditional political influence was shattered in the area. The result was an even further, and more permanent, shift toward Moscow and away from the old connections with the communist parties of Tel Aviv and Paris. The first meeting of the Lebanon and Syrian party central committees, held in Beirut on February 24, issued a joint statement calling for the unconditional, immediate, and complete evacuation of the British and French troops that had been stationed there and made it clear that they would construe any continuation of Anglo-French influence as imperialism. The statement specifically referred to Soviet friendship with the people of Syria and Lebanon as well as to the Soviet support of the two countries at the United Nations.

Toward the end of 1946, while al-Halu was on a trip to Europe, Nicola Shawi succeeded him as party president. During the next two years, as the Palestine problem developed into a heated issue, the communists in Syria and Lebanon issued several statements clarifying their stand on zionism, which they strongly condemned as an imperialist and capitalist movement supported by Britain and the United States.

Early in 1947 they renewed their attacks on the Syrian social nationalists and the Muslim Brotherhood. In Lebanon, although all four communist candidates again lost in the 1947 elections, they gained a larger number of votes than in previous campaigns. Similarly, in Syria's elections the same year none of the three communist candidates scored sufficient votes for victory. At this time the Lebanese party actually befriended leaders in government and politics, including some with whom they had serious ideological differences. However, when the Soviet Union came out in favor of a Jewish state at the United Nations in November 1947 and subsequently recognized the State of Israel, the communists in Lebanon were exposed to such severe repercussions that the Lebanese party was dissolved in January 1948. Internal conflicts within the Syrian party over the Palestine issue led some prominent communists to quit the party, and in March 1949 stern measures taken by the new military dictatorship of Husni al-Za'im drove the Syrian party underground. Even though both parties were formally underground, they appeared in the open at various times without undergoing government repression, as long as they abstained from overt subversive or antigovernment activities.

During the late 1940s and the early 1950s the front organization Partisans for Peace staged a number of demonstrations in both Syria and Lebanon and distributed the periodical *al-Salam* (Peace) and numerous pamphlets.

The overthrow of Syrian president Adib al-Shishakli in February 1954 ushered in a period of renewed activity, and the communists in Syria and Lebanon made special efforts to increase party membership and attract supporters. In the general relaxation of communist militancy that followed Stalin's death they succeeded in penetrating the nationalist movement in Syria and called for a "common front" of all "enemies of feudalism, reaction, and imperialism." This appeal was intended to elicit the cooperation of the Arab socialists and nationalists, who had thus far been extremely anticommunist. To win student support they called for the right of students to be involved in the political affairs of the country.

At the time of the September 1954 elections in Syria the party was not legally recognized by the government. Khalid Bakdash campaigned on the National Unionist ticket and became the first communist representative to occupy a seat in the parliament of any Arab country. His electoral strength had jumped from 16 percent in 1943 to about 75 percent in 1954, and this new showing at the polls emboldened him to demand that the bourgeoisie immediately be uprooted in Syria and the rest of the Arab world and replaced by the proletariat. In Damascus a new communist newspaper, *al-Nur* (The Light), sprang up, allegedly with generous financial support from the Soviet Union, as was the case with *Sawt al-Sha'b* in Beirut. In Beirut the Arabic weekly *al-Akhbar* (The News), which eventually became a more authoritative organ of the party, was joined by the clandestine *Nidal al-Sha'b* (People's Struggle), mainly for distribution in Syria. In 1960 the communist daily *al-Nida'* (The Call) appeared in Beirut.

In Lebanon the communist candidates lost by large margins in both the 1951 and the 1964 elections. Thus no communist party member has ever been seated in the Lebanese parliament. However, since 1952 the Lebanese communists have enjoyed considerable freedom in carrying on their activities. Apart from a clash with the police in 1953, no party activity has required government interference. During the 1958 Lebanese crisis the communists opposed President Chamoun's government and pro-Western policies, especially the acceptance of the Eisenhower Doctrine, which had been signed on March 16, 1957. The party did not deny that its members were active both in the United National Front, organized in April 1957 in opposition to Chamoun's policies, and in the civil strife of 1958.

During the negotiations for the union of Egypt and Syria in January 1958 the Syrian communists issued a bulletin supporting the proposed merger. However, Khalid Bakdash's departure from the country on the eve of the Syrian parliament's special session to ratify the union hardly indicated satisfaction with the outcome. In July of that year the Iraqi revolution opened new vistas for the Arab communists. Bakdash returned immediately to Damascus with a proposal for a loose confederation between Syria and Egypt instead of the existing federal union. During the resulting severe government campaign against the communists Bakdash took refuge in Eastern Europe, supposedly Czechoslovakia, and was still there at the end of 1965. A number of prominent Syrian communists sought political asylum in Iraq. During the years that followed the communists remaining in Syria were obliged to go underground.

## ORGANIZATION AND MEMBERSHIP

*Lebanon* In 1965 the command of the Lebanese party consisted of Nicola Shawi, Hasan Quraitim, and Artine Madoyan. Faraj Allah al-Halu, the party's leader for many years and later its president, disappeared and is alleged to have been tortured to death in a Syrian prison at the time when Syria was part of the United Arab Republic.

It is difficult to determine the actual strength of the Lebanese party. The figure 40,000 was given for the total membership at one time, but this cannot be substantiated. The number of card-carrying members is believed to be considerably smaller. Other estimates placed total membership at 8,000 to 10,000 over a decade ago. It is known, however, that various ethnic groups in Lebanon, mainly the Kurds and the Armenians, account for a higher percentage of party members than the rest of the Lebanese community. Jewish communists have not played a leading role in the Lebanese party, as they have in other communist parties in the region. Furthermore, the majority of party members are not from the lower classes, but rather from the middle and upper classes, with a remarkably high percentage of professional and literary men and young intellectuals. It is reported that members regularly contribute 10 percent of their income to the support of the party. Organizations which support and work with the party in Lebanon are the Partisans of Peace, the Society for Cultural Cooperation between Lebanon and the Soviet Union, Friends of the Soviet Union, Farabi's Center, and the Center of New Thought. Allegedly, the party's main current objectives are not to establish a socialist or communist system in Lebanon, but rather to check foreign influence and Western designs on the country and to introduce reforms on the basis of democratic principles. Because of Lebanon's special situation, the party supports Lebanese independence rather than unity with the other Arab states.

*Syria* Khalid Bakdash has remained leader and first secretary of the Syrian party and was in 1965 the leading communist personality in the Arab world. The strength of the Syrian party has often been overestimated, mainly because of the charisma of its leader. Like the Lebanese party, it has drawn most of its support from professionals and young intellectuals rather than from the peasants, the poor, and the working masses.

The major opponent of the Syrian party has always been the more popular and powerful Ba'th Arab Socialist Party (Hizb al-Ba'th al-'Arabi al-Ishtiraki), influenced by Marxist ideology and carrying the motto "unity, freedom, and socialism." The parliamentary strength of the Ba'thists has been greatly augmented by their influence in the army and among students. Cooperation between the two parties has been at best symbolic and superficial, and mostly for the purpose of combating common enemies.

## PARTY PRESS ORGANS

The Lebanese party publishes two newspapers in Beirut, the daily *al-Nida'* (The Call) and the weekly *al-Akhbar* (The News), in addition to its monthly *al-Waqt* (Time).

In Syria the party apparently has no regular press organ, but occasionally puts out newssheets and bulletins.

## BIBLIOGRAPHY

'Aflaq, Michel: *Fī Sabīl al-Ba'th* (On the Path of the Ba'th), Beirut, Dār al-Talī'ah, 1963.

Ayub, Sami: *al-Hizb al-Shuyu'i fi Suriyah wa Lubnan, 1922-1958* (The Communist Party in Syria and Lebanon, 1922-1958), Beirut, Dar al-Hurriyah lil-Tiba'ah wal-Nashr, 1959.

Bolton, A. R. C.: *Soviet Middle East Studies (Syria and Lebanon)*, Chatham House Memoranda, London, Royal Institute of International Affairs, June 1959.

George, Lucien, and Toufic Mokdessi: *Les Partis libanais en 1959,* Beirut, Editions "L'Orient-al-Jaridah," 1959.

Hamadi, Sa'dun: *Nahnu wal-Shuyu'iyah fi al-Azmah al-Hadirah* (We and Communism in the Present Crisis), Cairo, al-Dar al-Qawniyah lil-Tiba'ah wal-Nashr, 1961.

Laqueur, Walter Z.: *Communism and Nationalism in the Middle East*, 2d ed., New York, Praeger, 1957.

Qal'aji, Qadri: *Tajribat 'Arabi fi al-Hizb al-Shuyu'i* (An Arab's Experiment with the Communist Party), Beirut, Dar al-Kitab al-'Arabi, n.d.

Seale, Patrick: *The Struggle for Syria: A Study of Post-war Arab Politics, 1945-1958,* Royal Institute of International Affairs, London, Oxford University Press, 1965.

Suleiman, Michael W.: "The Lebanese Communist Party," *Middle Eastern Studies* (London), vol. 3, no. 2, January 1967.

Wahbi, Ibrahim: *al-Mu'amarah al-Jadidah . . . Hilal Khasib Shuyu'i* (The New Plot . . . a Communist Fertile Crescent), Cairo, Dar al-Qahirah lil-Tiba'ah, 1959.

al-Zayn, Mustafa: *Khams Sanawat ma'a al-Shuyu'iyah* (Five Years with Communism), Beirut, 1959.

MICHEL G. NABTI

# LESOTHO

Lesotho, formerly known as Basutoland, is a poverty-stricken mountainous enclave within the Republic of South Africa; communist organization in the country thus owed a good deal to South African inspiration. In 1928 the Communist Party of South Africa established contacts with the Commoners' Party (Lekhotla la Bafo), a small organization led by the brothers Maphutseng and Josiel Lefela. The Lefela brothers sympathized to some extent with communist aspirations but wielded little influence in the country at large. Communists subsequently attempted to infiltrate the Basutoland National Congress, later known as the Basutoland Congress Party (BCP). In the 1960 elections this group emerged as a strong political force, but its orientation remained pan-African, not communist. Toward the end of 1961 communist leaders in the territory therefore opened an all-out attack on Ntsu Mokhehle, the party president, himself a former member of the Lekhotla la Bafo. Opponents of communism argued that the communists were attempting to establish a stronghold in a remote and inaccessible region from which they could hardly be subsequently evicted, and which would serve as a base for revolutionary activities in a wider South African setting. The communists, however, failed in their attempt to take over the BCP and accordingly decided to build up their party as an independent political force.

## HISTORY

The Communist Party of Lesotho (CPL) was founded in November 1961. At its inaugural congress, held on May 5, 1962, the new party elected a central committee, with John Motloheloa as its general secretary, and resolved to establish party offices in various parts of the territory and to initiate a party bulletin to be called *Mosebetsi* (The Worker). The party claimed that over the last thirty years individual communists had already made a valuable contribution to the people's struggle against imperialism as members of either the Lekhotla la Bafo or the BCP. Led by the CPL, the united people of Lesotho could defeat imperialism, create a national democratic state, and advance on a noncapitalist path to socialism and eventually to communism. These aims could be achieved—in the opinion of the party leadership—even within an area entirely surrounded by a hostile South Africa because of the favorable international conditions and the existence of a powerful socialist system, and with aid from the struggling working class in the imperialist countries and the national liberation movements of Asia, Africa, and Latin America. The CPL pledged itself to the fight against British imperialism and its ally, white South African imperialism. It considered that the flow of migratory labor from Lesotho to the Republic of South Africa had brought about disastrous social and economic consequences in Lesotho, but had also given rise to the emergence of a class-conscious working class trained in the harsh conditions of South African wage labor. The party resolved to create the closest fraternal relations with the international working class, and especially with progressive organizations in the Republic of South Africa.

The CPL demanded destruction of colonialism and the creation of a united national front of workers, peasants, professionals and businessmen, and chiefs and commoners which would aim at an independent, self-governing, democratic Lesotho. It advocated the dictatorship of the proletariat and urged changes that would lead to socialism and finally to communism. It proposed extensive land reforms, including cooperatives and collectives under democratic administration, the mechanization of farming operations, and other agricultural improvements, and suggested the immediate nationalization of all labor recruitment. In the field of international relations, the party asked for South African recognition of Lesotho's independence, and also for the return of territories belonging to former Basutoland and wrongfully included in the Republic of South Africa. The CPL was, and remains, pro-Soviet in its orientation.

The communists managed to make some progress in the local trade-union movement, especially within the Basutoland Workers' Union, a body affiliated with the Basutoland Congress of Trade Unions. In 1962 the Workers' Union supported the CPL's call for the creation of a national liberation front consisting of all patriotic parties, organizations, and individuals united on a minimum program of action. The communists were opposed in the trade union field, however, by the BCP, which in 1961 formed the Basutoland Federation of Labor, dedicated to pan-Africanism. The BCP also took stern measures to combat communism in the political field, and in 1961 it prohibited its members from belonging to other political organizations.

The CPL met with considerable difficulty in attracting recruits. In a special interview in 1963 Motloheloa stated that his party did not have a very large membership and that it wished to build up a hard core of devoted communists, mainly in the lowlands, which had a greater population density. He stated that while intellectuals were helping in party organization and propaganda, the rank and file in an agricultural country such as this consisted mainly of peasants. By the end of 1965 the CPL had failed to gain much influence or to secure any representation in the Basutoland national assembly.[1]

The CPL gave political support to the Marema-Tlou Freedom Party (MFP), an oppositional group composed both of traditionalists and modernizers and led by Seth Mokotoko. In the 1965 election the CPL did not contest any seats; the MFP gained four seats. The MFP was also reported to have secured some financial assistance from the Soviet Union, but it was in no sense a communist organization. Pro-Chinese sentiments were expressed within the ranks of the radical BCP, which had allegedly received some aid from Peking, but again, the BCP could in no way be considered as a Marxist-Leninist body.

In 1965 the leader of the CPL was Jacob Kena; John Motloheloa was general secretary.

## PARTY PRESS ORGAN AND RECORDS

The CPL puts out the journal *Tokoloholo*, published in Maseru.

The party program is given in *Communism in Basutoland*, Maseru [1962] (typescript in possession of the Hoover Institution, Stanford, California).

## BIBLIOGRAPHY

Roux, Edward: *Time Longer than Rope: A History of the Black Man's Struggle for Freedom in South Africa*, London, Gollancz, 1948.

Segal, Ronald: *African Profiles*, Baltimore, Penguin Books, 1963.

LEWIS H. GANN

1. U.S. Department of State, Bureau of Intelligence and Research, *World Strength of Communist Party Organizations*, Eighteenth Annual Report, Washington, January 1966, p. 114, gives an estimated strength of less than 100.

# LITHUANIA

The Lithuanian Communist Party (Lietuvos Komunistu Partija, LKP), founded in 1918, descends from the Lithuanian Social Democratic Party and the Social Democratic Party of the Kingdom of Poland and Lithuania, but it was a direct outgrowth of the October revolution in Russia. Radical elements in Lithuania had long tended toward Lenin's programs, and World War I had brought them even closer. In the spring and summer of 1917, in Petrograd, the bolshevik party drew new recruits from Lithuanians returning from abroad and from the many Lithuanian war refugees in Russia.

The first two decades of the communist movement in Lithuania were dominated by Zigmas Aleksa-Angarietis, who returned in 1917 from Siberia, and Vincas Mickevičius-Kapsukas, who had spent the war years first in Scotland and then in the United States. Kapsukas represented the Lithuanian bolsheviks at the sixth congress of the Russian party and headed the central bureau of Lithuanian sections of the Russian party, organized in October 1917; he was Lithuanian commissar in Stalin's Commissariat of Nationality Affairs, and spoke on the Lithuanian question at the Brest-Litovsk peace negotiations. Angarietis served as Kapsukas's deputy and directed the Lithuanian communist press.

In the spring of 1918 the Soviet leadership decided that it was expedient to organize separate parties for the various minority nationalities of Russia. The Lithuanian bolsheviks objected to this decision but in the end grudgingly executed it.

In Lithuania itself, then still under German occupation, a group of socialists headed by Pranas Eidukevičius and aided by agents from Moscow formed the Social Democratic Workers' Party of Lithuania and Belorussia in July 1918. At its first "party conference" this group renamed itself the Communist Party of Lithuania and Belorussia (Lietuvos ir Belorusijos Komunistu Partija, LBKP). Eidukevičius then traveled to Moscow to effect a formal union with Kapsukas's central bureau. The party was explicitly responsible to the central committee of the Russian Communist Party (Bolshevik).

## HISTORY

The collapse of Imperial Germany in the fall of 1918 marked the beginning of a new era for the Lithuanian communists. The first congress of the LBKP gathered secretly in Vilna on October 1-3, 1918, attended by thirty-four delegates representing some 800 party members. In the absence of Kapsukas and Angarietis, Eidukevičius directed the meeting. The major topic of discussion was the organization of party work throughout Lithuania. In November Kapsukas and Angarietis came secretly to Vilna, and on December 8 they prepared a manifesto proclaiming the establishment of a provisional revolutionary Lithuanian workers' and peasants' government. After Moscow had reviewed the text, the manifesto was published on December 16 in Vilna.

A Lithuanian nationalist government had been set up in Vilna in November 1918, but it was unable to organize its own defense. When the German forces left Vilna in January 1919, the nationalist government moved westward to Kaunas, where it was sustained by German aid.

On December 15, 1918, while the greatly demoralized German army was still holding Vilna, a soviet had been developed there by representatives of several radical parties. The Vilna soviet, however, soon came into conflict with the LBKP leadership, and on December 22 it refused to recognize the government which the communists had proclaimed.

The LBKP had chosen to bide its time. Angarietis stated openly that it had been the task of the party simply to prepare the way for the Red Army. After the German army evacuated Vilna and bolshevik troops entered the city on the evening of January 5-6, 1919, a soviet government headed by Kapsukas and Angarietis moved in to establish its authority. Recalcitrant soviets were suppressed. Until new, more reliable soviets could be elected, military revolutionary committees chosen by the party took power. Even these, however, eventually proved unreliable; the government found the Lithuanian peasantry, who desired an immediate land reform, unalterably opposed to its agrarian policy of keeping the large estates intact.

The communists also faced a certain confusion implicit in the very name Communist Party of Lithuania and Belorussia. A separate Belorussian party and government had now come into being, and Moscow was even plagued by a territorial conflict between the two communist states. As a result, in view of the weakness and the instability of the Lithuanian soviet regime, Moscow decided to merge the two parties and their governments. The first congress of soviets of Lithuania, meeting on February 18-23, 1919, endorsed the merger. The second conference of the LBKP had already approved the action, and the second (united) congress of the LBKP, on March 4-6, 1919, consummated the union. Kapsukas was named prime minister of the new state, although he and Angarietis were the only Lithuanians in the central organs of the new unified party.

When Vilna fell to Polish forces in April 1919, the LBKP central committee retreated first to Minsk and then to Smolensk. A bureau for illegal work, located in Daugavpils and headed by Angarietis, took over the task of coordinating the work of communist groups still in Lithuania (including Vilna). In August 1919 a central bureau was established in Kaunas. The party now posed as its basic goal the infiltration of Lithuanian trade unions, and during the next year party members played an active role in labor unrest and in the Lithuanian soldiers' rebellion of February 1920.

The Soviet advance into Poland in the summer of 1920 briefly offered new hope to the Lithuanian communists. After Soviet troops had occupied Vilna on July 14, the communists proceeded with preparations for a revolution in Lithuania. However, the defeat of Soviet forces at Warsaw and their retreat from Vilna forced abandonment of these plans.

By the end of 1920 frontiers in Eastern Europe had stabilized, and Lithuanian communism moved into a new phase. In September a meeting of the LBKP central committee had decided that the two parties should again separate. Accordingly, a separate Lithuanian party came into being, directed by a central bureau, later renamed the central committee, to be located in Kaunas. The party's Bureau Abroad in Moscow, which was nominally responsible to the central committee and was itself headed by Angarietis, remained in Russia as the official link between the LKP central bureau and the central committee of the parent Russian party.

As an underground organization the LKP suffered varying fortune. The failure of the 1919-1920 revolution in Lithuania discouraged many followers, and arrests took a heavy toll. In 1920 the communists formed a youth organization, the Lithuanian Communist Youth League (Lietuvos Komunistinio Jaunimo Sajunga), but it was unable to hold a conference until August 1922. In 1921 the Comintern censured the LKP leadership for resorting to calls for the use of terror. The party also had to resolve inner conflicts, as when a party faction in Moscow, opposed to Kapsukas and Angarietis briefly gained control in 1920-1921 of the still-existing central bureau of Lithuanian sections of the central committee of the Russian party.

When the third congress of the LKP met in Königsberg on October 24, 1921, the chief subject for discussion by the twelve delegates was the "crisis" in the party. The congress approved a purge of party ranks and called for struggle against both "petit-bourgeois tendencies" from within and "opportunistic and counterrevolutionary organizations" from without. The congress condemned the Lithuanian soviet government's agrarian policies of 1919, asserting that the estates should have been divided up immediately and that the party should have recruited more support among smallholders. The congress also adopted new party statutes especially adapted to conditions of illegal work in Lithuania.

On October 29 German police broke up the congress and arrested most of the participants; according to some accounts, the imprisoned delegates met by chance in prison and formally closed the congress on November 24. At the request of the Soviet government, the German police did not deport the prisoners to Lithuania, but instead allowed them to travel to Russia. The news of the arrests brought more confusion in the party ranks and for the moment the organization in Lithuania was held together mainly through the efforts of the one member of the party secretariat still in Kaunas, Karolis Požela.

In 1922 and 1923 the party underwent further reorganization as the central committee, following the Russian model, organized a politburo and an organization bureau. The three-man politburo consisted of Kapsukas, Angarietis, and a man to be named by the Comintern (in February 1923 a Russian, V. Knorin, took this post).

The party membership lists sharply reflected these various changes. The LKP claimed 863 members in April 1920 and 1,300 by December 1920. By the middle of 1922 the party listed only 211 active members. In July 1923 it claimed 186 members out of jail and 112 in jail and in December 241 members out of jail and 236 in jail. These figures were also affected by the transfer in 1922 of the Vilna regional organizations from the LKP to the Polish party and by the addition in 1923 of communist organizations in the Memelland.

Despite these vicissitudes, the party continued to be active. In 1922 the communists participated in elections to the first Lithuanian parliament, under the name Labor Group (Darbo Kuopa); they received 51,441 votes and won five seats. The communist deputies participated actively in parliamentary debates, and they were part of the coalition that defeated the Christian democrat-dominated Galvanauskas cabinet in March 1923. However, in the elections for the new parliament in May 1923 the communist slate received only 34,365 votes and won no seats.

Official government policy in these years was dominated by the protracted dispute with Poland over the possession of Vilna. The LKP took an extremely nationalist position on this issue, opposing any reconciliation with Poland and advocating close ties with Soviet Russia.

The fourth congress of the LKP, held in Moscow on July 17-21, 1924, was attended by eleven delegates, representing 800 members. The struggle for power in the Russian party had already begun, and the Lithuanian leaders aligned themselves with the prevailing currents in Moscow in attacking Trotsky. Kapsukas and Angarietis went on to play roles in the Comintern. The fifth, sixth, and seventh Comintern congresses elected Angarietis to the International Control Commission, and from 1926 to 1935 he served as its secretary.

In Lithuania itself the party enjoyed its period of greatest freedom in 1926, under the populist-social-democratic coalition government. However, in December of that year Lithuanian military leaders seized power and installed a dictatorship headed by Antanas Smetona, who ruled as Lithuania's president until 1940. The new regime claimed to have acted to block a bolshevik coup, and to emphasize this claim it arrested and executed four leading communists, including Karolis Požela and Kazys Giedrys (the latter had been the Lithuanian delegate to the founding congress of the Comintern in 1919).

Despite this repression, until 1934 the LKP followed Moscow's basic line in refusing to cooperate with other parties against the dictatorship. In 1935 the party switched to the Comintern's program of a popular front of all democratic parties. However, its efforts were now hampered by Stalin's purges. Kapsukas died in Russia of tuberculosis in February 1935, but Angarietis fell victim to the purge and vanished. A new party leadership was arranged by Moscow, and in 1936 Antanas Sniečkus was named first secretary of the LKP. It was not until 1939, with the incorporation of the Vilna territory into the Lithuanian state, that party membership passed the 1,000 mark.

After the Soviet Union's ultimatum to Lithuania in June 1940 the LKP took the lead in organizing elections for a new parliament. At first the LKP insisted that Lithuania was to remain an independent state, but two or three days before the parliament convened it officially advocated incorporation of Lithuania into the Soviet Union as a constituent republic. Since the country was now essentially under the control of Soviet troops, first admitted in October 1939 and reinforced in June 1940, the parliament had no choice but to follow these directions and request admission into the Soviet Union. In August 1940 the Soviet Union formally admitted Lithuania, and in October 1940 the LKP was incorporated into the All-Union Communist Party (Bolshevik).

In 1940 and 1941 Stalin completed his purge of the LKP. During the German occupation of Lithuania from 1941 to 1944, partisan units provided a major source for the reestablishment of the party, which numbered some 6,000 members at the end of the war. In 1949 the party reported 25,000 members; in 1952, 27,469; in 1959, 41,574; and in 1964, 69,522.

During World War II the Lithuanian intellectuals and the nation's leadership were decimated by death, exile, and emigration. By 1950 a new group of intellectuals was beginning to graduate from the university and win the recognition of the regime. After Stalin's death in March 1953, Beriia's brief hold on power had a great impact in Lithuania because of the new emphasis on "national cadres." Russians thereafter played a greatly reduced role in public governmental and party affairs.

For the most part the LKP has shared the history of the Soviet party since World War II, with two striking exceptions. On the one hand, the periodic campaigns against vestiges of "bourgeois nationalism" testify to problems in maintaining the idea of monolithic Soviet unity within this national party. On the other hand, Antanas Sniečkus, who first entered the party secretariat in 1926, has remained as party secretary throughout the changes which followed Stalin's death and Khrushchev's ouster.

BIBLIOGRAPHY

*40 metu* (Forty Years), Vilna, 1958.
*Lietuvos Komunistu Partijos atsisaukimai* (Appeals of the Lithuanian Communist Party), vols. I and II, Vilna, 1962.
*LKP istorijos klausimai* (Problems of History of the LKP), Vilna, n.d.
Lopajevas, S.: *Lietuvos Komunistu Partijos idejinis ir organizacinis stiprejimas* (Ideological and Organizational Development of the Communist Party of Lithuania), Vilna, 1964.
*Proletarine revoliucija Lietuvoje* (Proletarian Revolution in Lithuania), Vilna, 1960.
Šarmaitis, R. (ed.): *Revoliucinis judejimas Lietuvoje* (The Revolutionary Movement in Lithuania), Vilna, 1957.
Senn, Alfred Erich: *The Emergence of Modern Lithuania*, New York, 1959.
Vardys, V. Stanley: *Lithuania under the Soviets*, New York, 1965.
Žiugžda, J., et al.: *Už socialistine Lietuva* (For a Socialist Lithuania), Vilna, 1960.

ALFRED ERICH SENN

# LUXEMBOURG

At its congress in January 1921 the Luxembourg Social Democratic Party (Parti Social-Démocrate Luxembourgeois, PSDL) was called upon to decide whether to join the Cominern, with the decision to be based on Lenin's Twenty-one Conditions for Admission. The vote of the congress was 67 to 21 to join, but with reservations. A disappointed minority who had sought unconditional adherence left the congress and on the same day (January 2, 1921) founded the Communist Party of Luxembourg (Parti Communiste du Luxembourg, PCL), with Zenon Bernard as president.

## HISTORY

In March 1921, two months after it was founded, the PCL launched a widespread strike movement, notably in the metallurgy and mining industries, during which the country witnessed occupation of its factories and heated encounters with its police. For several years the principal communist activity in Luxembourg was this kind of a social struggle. At the time of the third congress of the Comintern in 1921 the PCL numbered around 500 members, and in the elections of 1922 it received only 1 percent of the vote.

In the years 1925 to 1928 the PCL grew progressively weaker, owing to the opposition of Trotskyist elements to the official political line imposed by the Comintern. In the years which followed the country's economic crisis—a period marked by united-front tactics—the PCL regained some of the ground it had lost. In 1931 it received 5.6 percent of the vote, and in the 1934 elections the first communist deputy was elected to parliament.

During World War II the Grand Duchy of Luxembourg was annexed by the Third Reich. It was not, however, until after the German attack on the Soviet Union that the PCL began clandestine resistance activities. Several party leaders, including Zenon Bernard, were arrested and executed. The PCL enjoyed its greatest influence during and after the liberation. The legislative elections of 1945 gave the party nearly 14 percent of the total vote. It now participated in the coalition government; in June 1946 Dominique Urbany, the party's general secretary, became minister of public health, a post which he occupied until March 1947.

In the elections of 1948 and 1951, however, communist support dropped to 10 percent, and in 1954 to less than 9 percent. Of the seven seats (out of fifty-two) the communists had won in 1945, they retained only three in 1954. Party membership had dropped from 5,000 in 1945 to 1,500 in 1950, and by 1954 to 700 or 800, with the influence mainly in the industrial southern region of the country. This decline was due principally to the return to normal of the political and economic life of Luxembourg, where democratic traditions had always been particularly strong.

Neither de-Stalinization nor the later Sino-Soviet conflict had much effect on the PCL. Only a few intellectuals and leaders of the National Movement for Peace, created after the Stockholm peace appeal in March 1950, left the party or its satellite organizations. Despite the reaction stirred up in 1956 by the Hungarian revolution, mainly among the communist trade unionists, the PCL even showed some small recovery and minor electoral successes. In the municipal elections of October

1957 the communists polled 1,200 votes and increased their representation by one seat (to a total of thirteen out of 181). In the 1959 legislative elections, under a unity-of-action agreement with the socialists, the PCL refrained from running its own candidates in the northern electoral district, enabling the socialists to recover a seat lost in the central district and preventing the Christian socialists from obtaining an absolute majority. The PCL retained its three seats and gained nearly 15,000 votes.

Finally, in the national elections of June 7, 1964, the communists received more than 330,000 votes (12.47 percent), as opposed to 220,000 in 1959, and more seats in parliament (five out of fifty-six).[1] The results of this election returned the PCL to a position that it had not held for fifteen years. Expressing satisfaction at the 110,000-vote increase for the party, the party organ *Zeitung vum Letzeburger Vollek*, declared that "the success of the socialists and communists in the legislative elections of June 7 reveals an important push toward the left." At this point the PCL again offered the socialists a unity-of-action program, a proposal which they rejected, since they had joined the Christian socialists in forming the government.

## ORGANIZATION AND MEMBERSHIP

Although membership of the PCL at the end of 1965 was only around 1,000, the party does play a role in the industrialized regions in the south of the country and retains some positions in the capital.

There are a number of movements and organizations affiliated with the PCL, such as the Free Association of Luxembourg Workers and the Union of Democratic Women of Luxembourg, an association affiliated with the International Federation of Democratic Women. Several other movements, such as the Luxembourg Democratic Youth (Jeunesse Démocratique Luxembourgeoise), the Awakening of the Resistance, and the National Movement for Peace, cooperate closely with the PCL. The Free Association of Luxembourg Workers, affiliated with the World Federation of Trade Unions, had nearly 7,000 members from 1945 to 1950, but it has progressively lost influence to the socialist and Christian socialist trade-union centrals. In 1955 Joseph Michiels, one of the association directors and a member of the PCL central committee, founded an autonomous railwaymen's union and a year later was excluded from the party.

## RELATION TO SOVIET LEADERSHIP

Still the most important of the three communist parties of Benelux, the PCL faithfully follows the Moscow line. In the fall of 1963 a party delegation led by Dominique Urbany went to the Soviet Union for meetings with the top leaders of the Soviet party. Urbany's subsequent report to the PCL central committee exposed in detail "the errors of the leadership of the Chinese Communist Party and its secessionist activities, which have hurt the unity of the international communist movement," and clarified the PCL's position, which "is characterized by its loyalty to Marxism-Leninism, to the decisions of the Moscow conference." His report was adopted unanimously by the central committee.

## PARTY PRESS ORGANS

The PCL publishes several newspapers. The official party organ is the daily *Zeitung vum Letzeburger Vollek* (News of the Luxembourg People), whose circulation exceeded 5,000 in 1945 and was around 1,500 in 1965. *Wochenzeitung* (Weekly Newspaper), sold in the streets by party militants, summarizes principal news events of the week. Other periodicals are *Der Frien Arbechter* (The Free Worker), organ of the Free Association of Luxembourg Workers; *Zeitschrift für Information über die Sowjet Union* (Soviet Union Information Sheet); and *Femmes luxembourgeoises* (Luxembourg Women), the journal of the Union of Democratic Women of Luxembourg.

## CONGRESSES OF THE PCL

1st congress, January 1921, Differdange
2d congress, May 1921, Zenningen-Esch
Extraordinary congress, February 1922, Esch
3d congress, January 1931, Luxembourg
4th congress, 1934, Dudelange
5th congress, March 1937, Rumelange
6th congress, February 1938, Wiltz
7th congress, June 1939, Dudelange
8th congress, April 1945, Esch
9th congress, March 1946, Esch
10th congress, April 1947, Petange
11th congress, March 1948, Differdange
12th congress, December 1949, Belvaux
13th congress, April 1952, Niederkorn
14th congress, January 1956, Kayl
15th congress, December 1958, Rumelange
16th congress, December 1960, Differdange
17th congress, April 1964, Differdange
18th congress, April 1965, Luxembourg

## BIBLIOGRAPHY

Kill, Jean: "Le Luxembourg: Illusions et réalité," *La Nouvelle revue internationale*, December 1966.

Lazitch, Branko: *Les Partis communistes d'Europe, 1919-1955*, Paris, Les Iles d'Or, 1956.

NICOLAS LANG

1. The electoral system of the Grand Duchy of Luxembourg grants each voter as many votes as there are deputies to be elected in each district; thus the number of votes is higher than the number of actual voters.

# MALAGASY REPUBLIC

Although communist activity in Madagascar has had a considerable history, for a long period there was no Malagasy communist party as such. The communists acted through infiltration of mass organizations, to avoid both repressions and adverse public opinion. Even after the Malagasy Communist Party (Parti Communiste Malgache, PCM) was formed in 1958, it engaged in no overt activity. Shortly afterward it entered the Peking orbit.

## HISTORY

Before 1939 the communists made several efforts to establish themselves on Madagascar, but their activities, led by Paul Dussac, were quite irregular and limited. In May 1929 they participated in the violent demonstrations in Tananarive in front of the palace of the governor general. In 1933 a Malagasy section of International Red Aid was created. In 1936, at the time of the popular-front government in France, a large number of trade-union organizations affiliated with the French General Confederation of Labor (CGT), whose activity was primarily political. They also succeeded in creating a large number of cells in the villages (as revealed in 1939, when the dissolution of the French Communist Party permitted the authorities to seize the party archives from the known communist militants). However, perhaps because of the repression by Governor General Léon Cayla, they were unable to form a Malagasy federation of the French Communist Party.

After World War II communist activity was resumed under the direction of French party functionaries, who were sent to Madagascar from Paris. Pierre Boiteau, who had first been sent to Madagascar in 1932, created a communist study group in Tananarive in 1945 or

1946. Two communist newspapers also appeared on the island, *En action* in French and *Tenimiera* in Malagasy. The CGT trade unions, dominated by the communists in Madagascar, as they were in France, became firmly established in Tananarive and in the island's ports, principally Tamatave and Diégo-Suarez.

After the insurrection fomented by the nationalists and supported by the communists in March 1947, French party delegates arrived to organize communist activity on the island—Raymond Lombardo in 1947 and 1948, Jacques Arnault in 1948 and 1949, Pierre Boiteau in 1949, Raymond Barbé in 1949, Marcel Egretaud in 1950, and Gaston Donnat in 1952. As French communist members of the Assembly of the French Union, these delegates were protected by parliamentary immunity. It was not until 1954 that the Malagasy communists were judged sufficiently numerous and well trained to assume leadership of their own movement.

The communists assumed leadership of the CGT-affiliated unions and in 1956 formed the Union of Trade Unions of the Workers of Madagascar (Firaisan'ny Sendika Eran'i Madagasikara), which was directly affiliated with the communist-dominated World Federation of Trade Unions. Following an expression of solidarity with the victims of the March 1947 revolt, in 1951 they created the Solidarity Committee of Madagascar. Also, despite the fact that until 1954 they were opposed to independence, they made attempts to infiltrate nationalist organizations.

In 1953 the communists formed the first semiclandestine organization, the Malagasy Union (Fivondronana Malagasy, or Union des Malgaches), with a bureau composed of French party member Zèle Rasoanoro, Gisèle Rabesahala and Henri Rakotobé representing the Solidarity Committee of Madagascar, and Ralaierijaona and Albert Rasafinjohany representing the Workers of Madagascar. At the end of 1956 the Malagasy Union, which had brought some noncommunist nationalists into its ranks, was transformed into the Union of the Malagasy People (Union du Peuple Malgache, UPM). Under this name it won considerable success in the municipal elections of November 1956 (an absolute majority in Diégo-Suarez and an important minority in Tananarive and Tamatave) and in the provincial elections of March 1957 (twenty-six out of 240 seats).

The UPM also participated in the National Congress of Independence, organized in May 1958 to unify the various nationalist movements. However, the Malagasy Social Democratic Party (Parti Socialiste Démocratique Malgache), led by President Philibert Tsiranana, refused to join a congress in which communists participated, and the resulting coalition party, the Congress Party for the Independence of Madagascar (Ankotonny Kongreiny Fahaleovantenan Madagasikara, AKFM, or Parti du Congrès de l'Indépendance de Madagascar), did not include a single communist in its leadership. Nevertheless, the communists did form a solid nucleus inside the party, and in 1959 they managed to install Gisèle Rabesahala in charge of the organizational bureau of the new party.[1]

The PCM, formally founded in 1958, held its first congress in Tananarive on March 18-20, 1960, and appointed René Anselme Randrianja first secretary. In all likelihood the creation of the PCM was the work of communist Malagasy militants who had acted on their own initiative and then sought recognition of their organization by the Soviet and French parties. Randrianja traveled to Moscow in November 1960, but according to his report to the central committee on April 24, 1961, he was unable "to participate in the conference of the communist parties—the formalities not having been completed." In Paris a permanent delegation of the PCM was said to have launched ties with the French and Italian parties. In 1961 the congress of the French Communist Party received a message (as it had in 1954, 1956, and 1959) from the editorial committee of the daily *Imongo Vaovao*, which included Gisèle Rabesahala and Rasaholy. In 1964, however, it was the AKFM that sent such a message, indicating a powerful communist faction in that organization. It became evident that the French party had supported those Malagasy communists who had adhered to the tactic of infiltration of noncommunist organizations.

In April 1961 Randrianja had fixed the work of the "strengthening of the party" in five stages: spontaneous circles, an organized party, the struggle for power, liberated zones, and a general counteroffensive. He specified that "it is necessary to move to the second [stage]." The fourth stage, liberated zones, betrayed the influence of the Chinese communists. Randrianja had paid a long visit to China after his trip to Moscow, and there he established more solid ties than he had with Moscow. When the Sino-Soviet conflict broke out into the open, the PCM sided with Peking, However, the communist faction within the AKFM has remained pro-Soviet, and despite the fact that it is not organized as a formal party, it is the more important of the two communist groups.

## BIBLIOGRAPHY

Albertini, G.: "Le Communisme à Madagascar," *Est & ouest*, April 16-30, 1957.
Albertini, G.: "Le Communisme à Madagascar en 1960," *Est & ouest*, April 1-15, 1960.
Albertini, G.: "Les Communistes et les elections à Madagascar," *Est & ouest*, November 1-15, 1960.
Albertini, G.: "Bilan d'activité du P. C. Malgache," *Est & ouest*, November 1-15, 1961.
Boiteau, Pierre: *Contribution à l'histoire de la nation malgache*, Paris, 1958.
Boiteau, Pierre: "Où en est Madagascar?" *Démocratie nouvelle*, December 1961.

CLAUDE HARMEL

1. The AKFM had seventy sections in October 1959, according to Gisèle Rabesahala *(France-nouvelle*, October 22, 1959).

# MALAYSIA AND SINGAPORE

The Federation of Malaysia, created in September 1963, included the former British protectorate of Malaya and the former British colonies of Singapore, Sarawak, and British North Borneo (Sabah). Singapore withdrew from the Federation in August 1965. Thus for historical reasons three separate communist movements exist in Malaysia. The Communist Party of Malaya (CPM), operating from the Thai side of the Thai-Malayan border, nominally directs communist activity both on the peninsula and in Singapore, although the evidence indicates that the movement in Singapore is, in practice, virtually autonomous. The Sarawak movement has no organizational ties with the CPM, since neither side recognizes the existence of Malaysia. There may or may not be a Borneo communist party, centered in Sarawak. However, a communist organization, the Sarawak Advanced Youths' Association, does function actively there.

Apparently the Indonesian communist Tan Malaka first brought Malaya to the attention of the Comintern. However, from its inception the communist movement in Malaya had close ties with the Chinese Communist Party; a Chinese party representative, Fu Ta Ching, arrived in Singapore in 1925 and was reportedly the first agent to operate in the colony. Prior to the Kuomintang-communist split in China in 1927 communist activity in Malaya had been channeled through local

Kuomintang organs, and it was therefore temporarily disrupted by the break. In 1928, however, the South Seas (Nanyang) Communist Party was organized at Singapore to direct organizational activities among overseas Chinese for most of Southeast Asia. In April 1930 this party was superseded by the CPM, active chiefly in Malaya and Thailand; theoretically, it lost its Chinese character and became multiracial at this time.

The initial period of activity of the CPM was short lived. Joseph Ducroux, a French party official sent to Singapore at the time of the reorganization, was apprehended in 1931. With his arrest the entire party apparatus in the Far East was exposed, and most of it was eliminated shortly thereafter. Following the reorganization of the Comintern apparatus in Shanghai in 1933, an agent named Ling was sent to revitalize the CPM. The central committee was convened, and new bylaws were adopted on March 6, 1934. The labor and youth affiliates, dating originally from 1926, were also revived, and in spite of continued efforts at repression by the British government, the party entered one of the most active periods of its existence. Around 1937 Loi Teck, reportedly a Vietnamese, appeared in Malaya and emerged as secretary of the party.

Although there was some minor communist activity in Borneo during the war with Japan, the present movement dates roughly from the formation of the Sarawak Overseas Democratic Youth League in October 1951. It engaged in a number of student strikes and other acts against the government, but when an emergency was proclaimed briefly in 1952, many of its leaders fled or were deported. In 1954 the work of communist indoctrination was taken over by the Sarawak Liberation League, which in turn was replaced by the Sarawak Advanced Youths' Association. Moves to establish a Communist Party of Borneo were made in 1958 and 1959, but there is no evidence that it was actually set up (the Sarawak government designates the Advanced Youths' Association as the "clandestine communist organization").

A number of persons involved in the communist underground have been arrested, and a few of these have been deported or sent to China. None has been specifically identified, however, as a founding member or ranking official of the communist organization.

## HISTORY

*Malaya and Singapore* The organizational thrust in the 1920s came from the Chinese communists. After the revitalization of the party in the mid-1930s, it became actively engaged in labor agitation through its general workers' organization. In Selangor in 1935 communist-led workers actually succeeded briefly in seizing a coal mine and setting up a soviet.

Anti-Japanese activity among the Malayan Chinese dated from the Japanese invasion of Manchuria in 1931, with the communists attempting from an early date to capture the movement. After 1935 the Malayan communists functioned in and frequently dominated various national liberation and anti-Japanese associations in accordance with the Comintern's united-front policy. However, the CPM abandoned efforts to obstruct the British war effort in September 1940, nine months before the Soviet Union was invaded—on orders of the Chinese Communist Party rather than the Comintern.

The following year the party organized an extensive resistance network, with which the British agreed to cooperate only after the Japanese landings in December 1941. Throughout the Pacific war the communist-led Malayan People's Anti-Japanese Army and its civilian arm continued to resist the Japanese, and although its prewar leaders were virtually wiped out early in the war, the CPM emerged at war's end as the only organized political force in Malaya. However, the party leadership did not make decisive moves to consolidate communist strength at this time; in fact in 1947 Loi Teck vanished with the party's funds in the face of an impending investigation. During a period of legality from

1945 to 1948 the party attempted chiefly to strengthen its mass base through open front activities, and at this time there was a real effort to unite the ethnic groups in radical movements such as the Malayan Democratic Union.

In 1948, in keeping with the Cominform instructions (the Calcutta directive), the legal struggle was abandoned in favor of armed struggle. On June 18 the government proclaimed a state of emergency which was not officially ended until 1960. The Malayan National Liberation Army, successor to the People's Anti-Japanese Army, relied heavily on Mao Tse-tung's works on strategy to defeat the British. In the outcome, at a tremendous cost to the British, the war was not a success for the communists, who by 1951 were forced to resort to persuasive tactics in an attempt to rebuild popular support. Increasingly hard pressed, the army remnants shifted northward during 1953 and 1954, finally digging in above the Thai border. In 1955 and 1957 the CPM secretary general Chen Ping tried unsuccessfully to negotiate an end to hostilities. From the border region, where the CPM hierarchy enjoys relative security and has apparently scored successes among the Malays, the party continues to issue directives and manifestos. However, its influence in Malaysia is negligible.

Although Singapore was not the scene of armed insurrection in the postwar period, it did experience substantial unrest, much of it fomented by communists in the labor movement and in Chinese middle schools. The chief target of communist activity in the 1950s was the British colonial administration, with agitation for a merger with Malaya rather than direct independence (preservation of Chinese language and culture was also an immediate issue).

Although its Singapore town committee was destroyed in 1951, the CPM continued to maintain extensive underground activities through the decade; the extent of these is attested to both by captured documents and by the testimony of defectors. However, with increasingly close police surveillance, the party relied more and more on open front activities. By 1965, except for isolated instances, evidence of actual party connections had disappeared from Singapore.

*Sarawak* The communist appeal in Sarawak was initially to youths in Chinese middle schools, but by 1958 there was a shift to trade-union activity. The need for political organization led the Sarawak Advanced Youths' Association to direct its attention in 1959 to infiltrating the Sarawak United Peoples' Party. By 1960 they undertook, without much initial success, to organize the Sarawak farmers.

The Malaysia issue brought a direct clash between the communist movement and the government. Having failed to prevent Malaysia's formation, the organization subsequently turned to terrorist tactics and to collaboration with Indonesian forces in an effort to disrupt it. In late 1964 the government moved to resettle large numbers of Chinese from the Indonesian border to protect them and guard against subversion. However, after Singapore's expulsion from Malaysia in August 1965, there was a renewed wave of anti-Malaysia activity in Sarawak.

## ORGANIZATION AND MEMBERSHIP

*Malaya* The present structure of the CPM dates from the reorganization of 1955, although the constriction of the party's sphere of activity has resulted in practice in elimination of organs that are unnecessary or unable to function. Since the CPM did not have a mass base in Malaya in 1965, its organization was comparable only with the higher echelons of parties elsewhere. In 1955 a Chinese, Chen Ping, was confirmed as secretary general; a Malay, Musa Ahmad, as chairman; and an Indian, Balan, as vice chairman. Except for Balan, who was then under detention and later renounced communism, these men still occupied their posts in 1965.

The central committee was probably made

up of no more than ten men, and some of those with prior experience in China may be serving there now. The political bureau, apparently the only functioning organ of the central committee, consisted of the secretary general and no more than two or three associates. A Department of Malay Work, charged with activities among the Malay populace, has been quite active in recent years; however, its counterpart for activities among the Indian populace is no longer in existence.

The party's military arm, the Malayan National Liberation Army, consisted in 1965 of three regiments: the eighth in the west, the twelfth in the center, and the tenth in the east. The last composed of Malays backed up by Chinese cadres, served as the Department of Malay Work. Of three regional bureaus, only the northern bureau remained; it was later replaced by two border committees—the Kelantan-Perak committee on the eastern extremity of the border and the Penang-Kedah committee on the western extremity.

Official sources fixed the number of known communists (called "charted terrorists") in the Thai border region at 500 to 600. This figure, however, did not include the Thais and Malays in the region, chiefly farmers, who supported them.

In addition, there were a number of underground front organizations on the peninsula, with membership estimated at about 500. Under police vigilance, these are broken up or dissolved, but are frequently reformed. The Malayan Races Liberation League, for example, was originally formed in Pontian, underwent a number of disruptions in Malaysia, moved for a time to Indonesia, and after the September 30, 1965, coup there shifted to Peking.

*Singapore* The party organization has for some time been in a state of flux. Direction of the movement apparently derives from the underground, which, for the sake of safety, has operated from the Indonesian Riau islands, with infiltrations into Singapore from time to time. Although there has been virtually no contact between the underground and the sizable united front in Singapore, repressive actions against the front organizations themselves led to a shift from mass action by 1964. Underground auxiliary organizations were reportedly set up, on functional lines, to direct aboveground activity.

It would appear that 250 to 400 persons comprise what the Malaysian minister of internal security has termed the "well-established network of underground cadres in Singapore," although there are certainly several times as many communist activists serving in the open front.

Support for the movement in Singapore has come from labor, from students in the Chinese middle schools, and from Chinese farmers. There has also been support from intellectuals, far more than on the peninsula. Both in trade-union and in intellectual circles, in the years after the war the Chinese were joined by fairly substantial numbers of Indians and Eurasians, but the rate of defection among non-Chinese has been extremely high.

*Sarawak* Official sources indicate that the communist organization in Sarawak adheres to the classic pyramidal structure based on democratic centralism. From cells, it moves upward to branches, to district committees, to area and town committees, to divisional committees, and to the central committee at the top. Departments of work, peasantry, students, and political work are under the central committee, which is directed by a political bureau and an organization bureau.

As in Singapore, Chinese middle-school students play a major role in the Sarawak organization. It also draws heavily on urban Chinese labor and Chinese farmers. Government sources cited 1,000 to 2,000 active communists in Sarawak in the mid-1960s, although far higher figures have been given for those who support the movement in varying degrees.

*Front Organizations* Since communist parties in Malaysia were legal only for a brief period at the end of World War II in the Pacific, participation in leftist fronts has been significant. In Malaya communist activity has been channeled through the socialist front. In Singapore the communists made use of the People's Action Party before it split over the Malaysia issue in 1961. Thereafter the Socialist Front (Barisan Sosialis) in Singapore and the People's Party (Rakyat) in Malaya were the chief instruments of political action. In Sarawak, the Sarawak United People's Front has served this function.

In the labor field the fronts have been numerous but short lived, particularly in Singapore. The Singapore Trade Unions Liaison Secretariat succeeded the Singapore Association of Trade Unions, liquidated by government action in late 1963. In Sarawak the labor fronts have been local organizations such as the First Division Trade Unions Congress. In addition, in Singapore and Sarawak numerous cultural associations and student and alumni groups (such as the Nanyang University Guild of Graduates) have been used as open fronts, with some, such as the Sarawak Farmers' Association, set up specifically for this purpose.

## RELATION TO SOVIET LEADERSHIP

The CPM became a member of the Comintern in 1934, and prior to the Sino-Soviet split it generally adhered to policies laid down in Moscow even when they were not suited to the Malayan situation (such as the Calcutta directive of 1948). However, the ethnic, linguistic, and emotional ties with China create a dependence on the Chinese movement which at times has made the Malaysian parties appear as little more than appendages of the Chinese Communist Party. There is some evidence that in recent years the CPM's foreign policy has been literally made in Peking. Certainly in the Sino-Soviet dispute the Malaysian communists have done no more than add their slight weight to that of the Chinese communists, since Malaysia's position has simply reflected that of Peking.

## FUTURE PROSPECTS

Two events, occurring within less than two months of each other in the latter half of 1965, had an important bearing on the communist movement in Malaysia. The first of these was the withdrawal of Singapore from the Federation of Malaysia, and the second was the anti-Sukarno coup in Indonesia, which greatly diminished Indonesia's ability and willingness to continue her opposition to Malaysia. Communism is a far greater challenge in a Singapore that is politically independent but not economically self-sustaining than to one integrated in a greater Malaysia. Also, Singapore's withdrawal increased the chances that Malaysia could be disrupted from the Borneo side. However, the coup and its aftermath dealt a major blow to Malaysian communists by virtually eliminating Indonesia as a base for subversive activity against Singapore and Malaysia. The stepped-up campaign of subversion in Thailand by the Chinese also has implications for the CPM, with its Thai base.

Internally, the future of communism in Malaysia will be determined largely by the state's ability to solve its communal problems and make major adjustments in the economy. Externally, it is tied to the successes and failures of the Chinese People's Republic in Southeast Asia.

## PARTY PRESS ORGANS AND RECORDS

There is no single source of official documents of the CPM or the communist organization in Sarawak. The New China News Agency, the Cominform weekly, and various publications of Malaysian governments have published programs, directives, and manifestos from time to time; the *Malayan Monitor*, published in London, has consistently published CPM documents in recent years. Most documents, however, are among the confiscated papers in the Malaysian government's files, and their contents have been made known to some of the authors of the secondary works cited in the bibliography.

## PARTY CONGRESSES

The CPM had apparently not held a congress as such by the end of 1965. All major decisions were ratified by "enlarged" or "expanded" conferences of the central committee.

## BIBLIOGRAPHY

Brimmell, J. H.: *Communism in Southeast Asia: A Political Analysis*, London, Oxford University Press, 1959.
*Communism and the Farmers*, Kuching, Government of Sarawak, 1961.
*The Communist Threat in Singapore*, Singapore Legislative Assembly, Cmd. 33, Singapore, 1957.
*The Communist Threat to the Federation of Malaya*, Federation of Malaya Legislative Council Paper 23, Kuala Lumpur, 1959.
*The Danger and Where It Lies*, Kuala Lumpur, Federation of Malaya Information Services, 1957.
*The Danger Within*, Kuching, Sarawak Information Service, 1963.
Hanrahan, Gene Z.: *The Communist Struggle in Malaya*, New York, Institute of Pacific Relations, 1954.
Pye, Lucian W.: *Guerrilla Communism in Malaya: Its Social and Political Meaning*, Princeton, N.J., Princeton University Press, 1956.
Starner, Frances L.: "Communism in Malaysia: A Multifront Struggle," in Robert A. Scalapino (ed.), *The Communist Revolution in Asia*, Englewood Cliffs, N.J., Prentice-Hall, 1965.
*Subversion in Sarawak*, Council Negri Sessional Paper 3, Kuching, 1960.

FRANCES L. STARNER

# MARTINIQUE

Officially, the Martinican Communist Party (Parti Communiste Martiniquais, PCM) has existed only since 1957. The communist movement in Martinique, however, is thirty-five or forty years older. In 1918 some left socialists had founded a group that they called The Friends of Jean Jaurès. In 1923 this organization became the Jean Jaurès Communist Group, and in 1925 it became a section of the French Communist Party. By 1937 the Martinican section had around 100 members, and although it exerted little influence, one of its members, Démétrius Bissol, was successful that year in his candidacy for counselor general of Fort de France, the island's capital city. The section was dissolved in September 1939 along with the French Communist Party.

## HISTORY

In 1944 the communists reorganized and made rapid progress. In 1945 the Martinican communist federation included three sections with forty-two cells and 983 members; by 1946 there were eight sections, with ninety cells and 2,900 members. Communists won control of six municipalities in 1945, and communist candidates received nearly 63 percent of the votes cast in the legislative elections of 1946, 1951, and 1956. Two of the island's three deputies to the French national assembly were communists—the poet Aimé Césaire (theoretician of Negro culture) and Démétrius Bissol. The Martinican communists were then defending a policy of "assimilation"—that is, application of the French law of March 19, 1946, that gave Martinique the same rights as the metropolitan French departments.

The decline began in 1956, when Aimé Césaire resigned from the party. In a letter to Maurice Thorez in October 1956 he reproached the French communists for their "reluctance to begin de-Stalinization" and for their conception of communism, which tended to "put the black people at the service of Marxism and communism." Césaire founded a new organization, the Martinican People's Party (Parti Populaire Martiniquais, PPM), into which he led many of the Martinican communists. The primary point in the PPM's program was independence for Martinique.

In the face of this competition, and in compliance with a general order (which was applied also in other areas; see *Algeria, Guadeloupe*, and *Réunion*), the French party decided, with Moscow's consent, to transform its Martinican federation into an autonomous communist party. On September 22, 1957, the twelfth communist federal conference of Martinique, also attended by a large delegation of French communists headed by Marcel Servin, member of the political bureau and secretary for organizational matters of the French party, was transformed into the first congress of the Martinican Communist Party. Servin declared to the congress: "The political bureau of the French party has had long, fraternal discussions with your delegation, composed of comrades Sylvestre and Bissol. . . . An agreement has been reached . . . as to orientation and organization structure of the communists in Martinique." Nevertheless, it was agreed that the new PCM would remain under the guidance of and in a confederational relationship with the French Communist Party. Camille Sylvestre became the PCM's general secretary.

It is not known whether the confederational relationship thus envisioned was actually created. On April 11-15, 1960, a joint meeting of the communist parties of Guadeloupe, Réunion, and Martinique (represented by Armand Nicolas, PCM secretary) was held in Paris, but there was no mention of confederation in the final communiqué. It is believed that the relations between the PCM and the French Communist Party have retained their bilateral character.

On becoming autonomous, the Martinican party changed its policy. Instead of calling for application of the 1946 law on assimilation, the PCM now demanded "administration of Martinique's affairs by the people of Martinique"—in other words, autonomy. Independence was excluded, for the moment at least. Actually, the French party would have liked the PCM to advocate independence, but a large number of Martinican communists were fearful of local opposition to demands for an independence that the population feared. Even this modified new orientation cost the Martinican communists the majority of their electoral following. From 36,915 votes in 1956 (38 percent of the registered voters and 62.5 percent of the votes cast), the communist vote in the legislative elections fell to 11,338 in 1958 (8 and 19 percent, respectively), and to 10,510 in 1962 (7 and 21 percent, respectively). At the same time, Césaire's PPM also saw its electoral support drop to 22,384 votes in 1958, and 13,670 in 1962.

In order to put their new policy in action the Martinican communists attempted to form a "broad Martinican anticolonialist front." This effort did not meet with large success at first, especially since the constitutional revision in 1958 had changed the character of French policy. But the communists were able to exploit the spontaneous riots which broke out in Fort de France on December 20-23, 1959, after a traffic accident resulting in three deaths and dozens of injuries. The PCM announced: "In the course of these events, our party has played a decisive role. . . . It has boldly aligned itself with the masses through its press, its tracts, its meetings. . . ."[1]

Following these events, the PCM published a draft statute on February 24, 1960, which advocated transformation of Martinique into a federated state. In April it successfully organized a roundtable discussion in which nearly all of Martinique's parties participated. This group adopted a program considerably different from that of the PCM, but the communists supported it as a means of acting on behalf of the other signatories.

After its second congress on July 30-31, 1960, the PCM succeeded in establishing a Front for the Defense of Public Liberties (Front pour la Défense des Libertés Publiques). In addition to the Martinican trade-union confederation (whose secretary Walter Guitteaud was a member of the PCM political bureau) and the usual communist mass organizations, the front included the PPM, the United Socialist Party (Parti Socialiste Unitaire), and the General Association of Students of Martinique, which had been formed in 1957, chiefly by Martinican students in France, and was a member of the International Union of Students. Through this front the communists instigated and exploited new public disturbances (three died and twenty-five were injured in Lamentin on March 23, 1961), which resulted in prosecution of some PCM militants and seizure of the party newspaper *Justice*. For its part, the students' association (whose *grand rassemblement* planned for August 1961 at Fort de France had been banned by order of the prefecture) formed in September 1962 at Fort de France an Organization of Anticolonialist Youth of Martinique, headed largely by militants from the Union of Martinican Communist Youth (Union de la Jeunesse Communiste Martiniquaise). The organization's activity gave grounds for legal action and a trial which began on November 25, 1963; of the eighteen accused, seven were members of the PCM.

At its third congress, on December 27-29, 1963, the PCM claimed to have over 2,000 members, grouped in twenty-two sections. It conducted a central school for the indoctrination of its cadres. Armand Nicolas had been chosen general secretary of the party after Camille Sylvestre's death in December 1962.

The third congress confirmed the party's policy of autonomy and proclaimed the PCM's loyalty to the Communist Party of the Soviet Union.

New riots causing one death and forty injuries in October 1965 led to new prosecutions of PCM militants and the arrest of Guy Dufond, member of the central committee.

## RELATION TO SOVIET LEADERSHIP

The PCM was not represented at the international communist conference of November 1957 in Moscow (the party had just been founded), but delegations attended the conference of the eighty-one communist parties in Moscow in November 1960, as well as the twenty-second congress of the Soviet party in October 1961 (Camille Sylvestre and Armand Nicolas). In the Sino-Soviet conflict, the party has upheld the position of the Soviet Union.

## PARTY PRESS ORGANS

Besides *Justice*, the PCM publishes a theoretical review entitled *Action*.

## CONGRESSES OF THE PCM

1st congress, September 22, 1957
2d congress, July 30-31, 1960
3d congress, December 27-29, 1963

## BIBLIOGRAPHY

Césaire, Aimé: In *France-observateur*, October 25, 1956.
Le Cornec, Michel: "Le Parti communiste martiniquais," *Est & ouest*, no. 300, May 16-31, 1963.
Nicolas, Armand: In *La Nouvelle revue internationale*, January 1963.
*La nouvelle revue internationale*, April 1964.
Servin, Marcel: In *Cahiers du communisme*, November 1947.

CLAUDE HARMEL

1. Armand Nicolas, in *Cahiers du communisme*, January 1961.

# MEXICO

The communist movement in Mexico owes its origin largely to the efforts of foreign radicals at the close of World War I, who splintered the small socialist party and created rival communist organizations in September 1919. The faction led by Indian nationalist Manabendra Nath Roy and sponsored by the Russian agent Michael Borodin was represented at the second Comintern congress, received the approval of the international movement, and has remained the official Mexican Communist Party (Partido Comunista Mexicano, PCM). Among the Mexican leaders of the party in its early years were José C. Valadés, Jesús Bernal, Rafael Carrillo, and, after 1923, the artists Diego Rivera, David Alfaro Siquieros, and Javier Guerrero. For the first decade, however, foreigners continued to dominate the party leadership. These included Charles Phillips, Bertram D. Wolfe, Katayama Sen, and Alfred Stirner. Since 1940 there have always been at least two communist parties or front parties in Mexico.

## HISTORY

The history of the communist movement in Mexico has been one of perennial frustration, because the appeal of communism cannot compete with the heritage of the Mexican revolution and because the Mexican communist parties have never been able to compete effectively against the huge administration party, known since 1945 as the Institutional Revolutionary Party (Partido Revolucionario Institucional). The PCM began its existence as a legal organization and retained legal status until 1929, when it was outlawed for its part in an abortive revolt against the government. The proscription was lifted in 1935, and thereafter the party enjoyed full legality and freedom of operation, except that it was not able to meet the membership requirements for registration of its candidates to public office in national elections.

The Mexican communists were among the first in Latin America to develop a rural following, particularly in the Vera Cruz area in the 1920s and in the Laguna region after 1935. Dionisio Encina, who became secretary general of the PCM in 1940, and Valentin Campa and Hernan Laborde, who formed the dissident Mexican Worker-Peasant Party (Partido Obrero-Campesino Mexicano, POCM) in that year, were active in the latter area. From the outset the communists were also active among transport workers and miners, who formed the bulk of the members of the regional labor federation in the 1920s and of the government-controlled Confederation of Mexican Workers (Confederación de Trabajadores Mexicanos) founded in 1936. Intellectuals and teachers in the public schools at all levels, as well as secondary school and university students, have constituted another continuing source of members and sympathizers of the various communist and procommunist parties in Mexico.

Communist influence was highest in the middle years of the Cardenas administration (1934 to 1940), when Vincente Lombardo Toledano headed the Mexican labor confederation and formed the hemispherewide Confederation of Latin American Workers, while the party followed the popular-front line of full cooperation with the government. These favorable circumstances were ended by a series of misfortunes that befell the party in 1939 and 1940. The Hitler-Stalin pact and the continuing pressure from the Soviet Union for the elimination of Leon Trotsky contributed to factionalism that split the party; the implication of communists in Trotsky's murder and, more significantly, the election of Avila Camacho as president of Mexico destroyed communist prestige in the eyes of the government. The communists were forced to operate on the fringes of national politics, even though they offered to cooperate again after the Soviet Union entered the war.

To offset the ineffectiveness of the orthodox party, in 1948 Lombardo Toledano created the broad, left-wing People's Party (Partido Popular), which followed the Soviet line on international matters and a practical policy of reasonable cooperation with the regime on domestic matters, thus attracting a substantial membership and a measure of influence on the administration. In 1960 this party added the world "socialist" to its name, to become the Socialist People's Party (Partido Popular Socialista, PPS), and in 1963 it absorbed the small POCM.

The PCM attributed its weakness to faulty leadership. At its thirteenth national congress in 1960 Dionisio Encina was removed from his post of secretary general, and a triumvirate, including David Alfaro Siqueiros and Arnaldo Martínez Verdugo, was installed as executive. In December 1963 Martínez Verdugo was given full responsibility as secretary general. Neither the experiment with the triumvirate nor the return to the traditional executive appears to have had any discernible impact on the prestige or efficiency of the party. The People's Electoral Front, which the PCM organized with other extreme left groups in 1963 as a device for participating in the 1964 elections, failed to win enough adherents to register as a party. Pro-Chinese dissidents expelled by the PCM in 1963 created their own Bolshevik Communist Party of Mexico (Partido Comunista Bolchevique de Mexico, PCBM), which further splintered the Mexican communist movement.

## ORGANIZATION AND MEMBERSHIP

In the mid-1960s United States sources estimated the membership of the PCM as 5,000 and that of the pro-Chinese PCBM as 200 to 300. The broad leftist PPS had an estimated membership of 38,000, and the coalition People's Electoral Front an estimated membership of 8,000 to 10,000.[1]

The Mexican communists are among the few in Latin America who have made consistent use of front parties. The PPS is by far the most important front party in the hemisphere. In addition, the communists frequently seek to cooperate with noncommunist parties and groups in temporary fronts, such as the People's Electoral Front. For further discussion see *Latin America*.

## RELATION TO SOVIET LEADERSHIP

The Mexican party was the second in Latin American to affiliate with the Comintern, and it was more closely supervised by the Comintern than any other Latin American party until 1929. In that year, under the direction of Diego Rivera, the PCM incurred the wrath of the Soviet leaders by participating with "bourgeois" parties in a revolt against the government. Mexican party leaders were purged, and for more than a decade Rivera was identified with the Trotskyist wing of the communist movement in Mexico. In 1940 the Comintern ordered another purge of the PCM, for reasons that have never been satisfactorily explained but appear to have stemmed from the party's failure to carry out Soviet directives to assassinate Leon Trotsky, then in exile in Mexico. The purge order was conveyed by Victorio Codovilla of Argentina, who attended the extraordinary congress at which party leaders Valentin Campa and Hernan Laborde were expelled. Other representatives of the Comintern and of the Communist Party of the U.S.A. were also present. For a discussion of other aspects of relations between the Mexican communists and the Moscow-directed international movement see *Latin America*.

The PCM and the PPS support the Soviet position in the ideological controversy with Communist China. The PCBM tends to sympathize with the Chinese position.

## PARTY PRESS ORGANS AND RECORDS

The official newspaper of the PCM is *La Voz de México*. The PPS issues a semimonthly theoretical journal, *Avante*, and an irregular newspaper, *El Día*.

## CONGRESSES OF THE PCM

The Mexican party has held congresses, sometimes called conventions, more often than most of the Latin American parties. All party congresses have been held in Mexico City.

1st congress, December 1921
2d congress, 1923
3d congress, April 1925
4th congress, May 1926
5th congress, 1927
6th congress, January 1937
7th congress, January-February 1939
Extraordinary congress, March 1940
8th congress, May 1941
9th congress, March 1944
10th congress, November-December 1947
11th congress, December 1950
12th congress, September 1954
13th congress, May 1960
14th congress, December 1963

## BIBLIOGRAPHY

Halperin, Ernst: *Communism in Mexico*, Cambridge, Mass., MIT Center for International Studies, January 1963.

Schmitt, Karl M.: *Communism in Mexico*, Austin, Tex., University of Texas Press, 1965.

Wolfe, Bertram D.: *The Fabulous Life of Diego Rivera*, New York, Stein and Day, 1963.

See also *Latin America*, refs. 1, 2, 3, 6, 7, 13, 24.

ROLLIE E. POPPINO

1. U.S. Department of State, Bureau of Intelligence and Research, *World Strength of the Communist Party Organizations*, Seventeenth Annual Report, Washington, January 1965, p. 137; Eighteenth Annual Report, Washington, January 1966, p. 160.

# MONGOLIA
*See* Outer Mongolia

# MOROCCO

During the "Rif war" of Morocco in 1924 and 1925 the French Communist Party first took on the true appearance of a revolutionary party, both through the methods it employed to weaken the French military effort and through the decisiveness with which it took up the cause for Abd el-Krim and the Moroccan rebels. Speaking before the French chamber of deputies on May 27, 1925, Jacques Doriot said: "My party is for the military evacuation of Morocco; my party is for the formula 'Morocco for the Moroccans.' . . . The Moroccans are sufficiently enlightened to find the course of their destinies by themselves." Although this stand disposed certain Moroccan nationalists to accept communist support, it made little contribution to the development of communism in Morocco itself. No Moroccan socialist organization had been represented at the congress of Tours, at which the French Communist Party was born (December 1920). Hence the communist movement in Morocco did not start with an organized group, as in the other French territories. During the entire interwar period, however, the socialists proved to be very active in Morocco, and it was to them that the nationalists turned for support. In July 1932 the first issue of *el-Maghreb* (The West), a review inspired by the Moroccan nationalists, appeared in Paris. Its editor was Robert Jean-Longuet, great grandson of Karl Marx and son of one of the important French socialist leaders. When the nationalist group that had inspired this review presented its "program of Moroccan reforms," it counted on metropolitan French supporters, including the communist lawyer André Berthon. The French Communist Party thus managed to insert itself into this movement, although in an episodic, marginal way. A third obstacle, but not the least in importance, was the fact that the authorities, who had been put on guard by communist activities during the Moroccan war, banned "communist associations," so that the few followers that the French party had in the protectorate were unable to meet except in secrecy. This underground activity did not get very far. It took the advent of the popular-front government in Paris to lift the ban.

The "Moroccan region" of the French Communist Party did not exist legally, therefore, until 1936. Its headquarters was at Casablanca, and its secretary was Léon Sultan, a Jewish lawyer. It published a weekly organ, *Clarté*. Although the Moroccan party never had more than a small number of members, mostly intellectuals, it was not exempted from internal quarrels. In 1937 a group of its members of Spanish origin with anarchist tendencies separated from the official organization and attempted to form a separate communist party with no ties to the French party. The government dissolution of the French Communist Party in September 1939 put an end to this dispute.

## HISTORY

In July 1943 the communists reappeared in the open in Morocco. This time they formed an autonomous organization, the Moroccan Communist Party (Parti Communiste Marocain, PCM), whose first congress was held three years later, on April 5-7, 1946. The general secretary of the new party was Léon Sultan; after Sultan's death in February 1945 the post went to Ali Yata. At the same time, the Moroccan General Union of CGT Trade Unions (Union Générale des Syndicats CGT) was revived, with the directing bureau composed mostly of communists. Its membership quickly grew to 30,000. In 1945 the party itself counted around 10,000 members, 80 percent of whom were Europeans. Its weekly newspaper *Espoir*, directed by Abd es-Slam Bourquia, had around 2,500 subscribers at the beginning of 1946. In the elections to the French constituent assembly on October 21, 1945, the communist ticket received 17,609 votes, or 25.6 percent of the total, and one candidate was elected (Pierre Parent). The next year the electoral results were not as good: 12,902 votes, 17.5 percent of the total votes cast, and no candidates elected. The PCM nevertheless enjoyed a considerable influence, at least in European circles.

This influence declined as the communists drew closer to the nationalists and adopted their program. For several years the PCM program had not included a demand for independence. On August 3, 1946, the party finally issued a manifesto advocating abrogation of the protectorate treaty and the evacuation of French troops. On August 28 a delegation from the PCM political bureau was granted an official audience by the sultan, thereby confirming its character as a Moroccan organization. At that time the majority of the party leaders were Moroccans; the party's French membership had begun to diminish by the end of the war and disappeared almost completely after the publication of the 1946 manifesto and the elimination of communists from the French government on May 5, 1947. At that time the PCM had scarcely any members other than Moroccan workers who had returned from France, where they had been members of the French party (as was the case with Ali Yata himself). Moreover, party membership was constantly falling; it dropped from 6,000 in 1948 (2,500 Europeans, 3,000 Moroccans, and 500 Jews) to 3,700 in 1950 (1,000 Europeans). Its principal strength came from the influence it exerted on the trade-union association, three-fourths of whose members were Moroccans.

When the Moroccan party had adopted the slogan of independence, it sought an alliance with the nationalists, especially with the Independence Party (Hizb el-Istiqlal), and proposed the formation of a national front. However, the PCM was unable to overcome nationalist distrust, despite its zealous efforts to infiltrate the nationalist movement. When the Moroccan National Front was created on April 9, 1951, by the "Tangiers pact" between Istiqlal and three other nationalist groups, the PCM was formally excluded; article 7 of the pact expressly stipulated that a united front with the Moroccan communists was unacceptable.

The similarity of their declarations and activities has often led to the belief that the PCM and Istiqlal were in collusion. Although the communists sought to further this confusion, the nationalist leaders saw to it that the communists did not profit from any of the mutual contacts to which they consented. In fact, they took advantage of such contacts themselves to draw members away from the communist party and especially to penetrate the trade unions belonging to the CGT-affiliated General Union, the only authorized labor organization in Morocco. They were successful in their efforts. After taking a dominant role in the editorship of the trade-union organ *L'Action syndicale*, the nationalists gained access in October 1950 to the directing posts of the General Union itself. In 1952 its directing bureau included four members from Istiqlal, two from the PCM (Mamoun Alaoui and Haddaoui ben Mohammed ben Lahoucine), and four from the French Communist Party. The nationalists were in a position to leave the General Union and take with them the majority of the unionists. In 1955 the Moroccan Labor Union (Union Marocaine du Travail) was founded. Despite these general results, there were, of course, some nationalists who came under the communist influence—either that of the PCM or that of the international communist movement.

From 1946 to 1952 the PCM continued to lose strength. Its newspaper *Clarté* soon began to appear only irregularly. By removing from its program and activities everything that might be subject to criticism from the nationalists, it lost its reason for existence in the eyes of those who were not familiar with the communists' real intentions and who preferred to follow Istiqlal. In addition, repressions deprived the PCM of its best militants; communists of European origin were forced to return to France, and Ali Yata was deported in June 1948. He tried to avoid deportation but was finally arrested in July 1950, sentenced to ten months in prison, and arrested again in Algiers in September 1952. His successor, Abd Allah Layachi, member of the political bureau, was arrested shortly afterward. Finally, after the clashes during demonstrations organized to protest the murder of Tunisian unionist Ferhat Achet (see *Tunisia*), the PCM was outlawed in December 1952. At that time it had about 2,000 members, 700 of whom were Europeans and 1,300 Moroccans.

The communists continued activity clandestinely but were able only to distribute a few tracts or duplicated issues of *Espoir* and, in October 1953, a brochure protesting the deposing of the sultan. The official expulsion from Morocco of the PCM's last European leaders and the difficulties of underground existence reduced the party to just a few handfuls of militants.

The proclamation of Morocco's independence on March 2, 1956, gave the PCM a chance to resume legal existence and activity, or at least to attempt to do so. Since the ban had been imposed by the French authorities, the PCM took the position that the ban had ended with the protectorate. At the same time, anxious to forestall any repressive measures by the new government, they loudly made known that they had supported the nationalist movement. They also declared that, being good patriots and respecting national traditions, they were not opposed to the continuation of a monarchy (a constitutional monarchy), and they again set out to outbid the nationalists. This was especially true when the Mauritanian question came up. The PCM insisted that Mauritania's independence was only formal and would hamper her development, and that reunification with Morocco would permit her to move toward progress. The communists expressed indignation over the "hesitations of the national bourgeoisie" in a matter of "the liberation of a part of the Moroccan territory."[1]

This conciliatory policy did not succeed in dispelling the mistrust which the party's ideology and its ties with the international communist movement had aroused among the nationalists. In September 1959 the government dissolved the PCM, both because of its hostility at that point toward the monarchy and because of its opposition to Muslim religious institutions. The party appealed, but the court in Rabat upheld the dissolution in February 1960.[2] In May 1964 the Moroccan supreme court declared that the communist party was "opposed to the present regime of Morocco and to the fundamental principles of Islam."

Upon his succession in February 1961, Hassan II offered the agriculture portfolio to the communist Hadi Messouak, but on a personal basis rather than as a representative of the PCM. The party leaders, in an open letter to the king which was widely distributed throughout the country, stated that the party had "decided on the nonparticipation of comrade Messouak in the government, not because it fears the responsibilities, but to avoid the further division of the nationalist forces."[3] With this demonstration of common cause, the communists hoped to infiltrate the National Union of People's Forces (Union Nationale des Forces Populaires), a group founded by Mehdi ben Barka, Abd er-Rahim Bouabid, and others who had separated from Istiqlal in November 1959.

In May 1960 the Moroccan communists founded a theoretically independent newspaper, *el-Moukafih* (The Struggler), with Ali Yata as director and Abd Allah Layachi as editor. Both were arrested on October 25, 1963, together with Abd es-Slam Bourquia, director of the review *el-Madabi* (The Principle), for having taken an antinationalist stand during the Algerian-Tunisian battles of 1963; they were temporarily released in January 1964. *El-Moukafih* was outlawed by a decree of October 31, 1964, when it changed from a weekly to a daily (since 1962 it had included a supplement in French).

On April 26, 1965, Ali Yata addressed to the king a "draft of an immediate program for national recovery and democratic and social progress," taking care not to reveal that the text was issued by the PCM.[4]

### RELATION TO SOVIET LEADERSHIP

The PCM was represented at the Moscow conferences of November 1957 and November 1960, as well as at the twenty-second congress of the Communist Party of the Soviet Union in October 1961 and the congresses of the French Communist Party. In the Sino-Soviet conflict the PCM supports the Soviet line.

### PARTY PRESS ORGANS

The PCM, operating underground, no longer published a press organ in 1965.

CONGRESSES OF THE PCM

The PCM held its first congress in April 1946. The date of its second congress is unknown.

BIBLIOGRAPHY

Julien, Charles-André: *L'Afrique du nord en marche*, Paris, Julliard, 1952.
Moroccan Communist Party: *Le Parti communiste marocain: Lutte pour son existence légale* (documents pertaining to the party's legal proceedings appealing the government's dissolution of the party), 1960-1964.

Rézette, Robert: *Les Partis politiques marocains*, Paris, Armand Colin, 1955.

CLAUDE HARMEL

1. Mohammed Essaoui, in *La Nouvelle revue internationale*, January 1961.

2. See *Le Parti communiste marocain: Lutte pour son existence légale* (a collection of documents pertaining to the trial, edited by a group of jurists—prepared in fact by the PCM itself), 1960-1964.

3. *La Nouvelle revue internationale*, May 1961.

4. *Bulletin d'information* (Prague), no. 25, 1965.

# NEPAL

The autocratic Rana regime that ruled Nepal until 1950 effectively banned organized political activity in the country. In the period after World War II a core group of anti-Rana Nepali political exiles became increasingly active in India. Most of them affiliated with the Indian National Congress, particularly its socialist wing, but a number joined the Indian Communist Party. This latter group first sought to work with noncommunist political groups, such as the Nepali National Congress (NNP). In accordance with the decisions reached at the 1948 Cominform meeting in Calcutta, however, they established a separate organization. The Communist Party of Nepal (Nepal Kamyunist Party, CPN) was founded in Calcutta on September 15, 1949, by a small group led by Pushpa Lal. A few other Nepali communists, including Man Mohan Adhikari, did not attend the inaugural session but were associated with the party from the beginning. However, several leaders who later became prominent, such as Keshar Jang Rayamajhi, did not join until the party transferred its activities to Nepal after the 1950 revolution. This difference in the date of joining the party has been one critical factor in subsequent leadership struggles.

HISTORY

The CPN was able to operate openly in Nepal only after the 1950 revolution, led by the rival NNP, had overthrown the Rana regime and legalized political activity. The party immediately joined the opposition and formed tactical alliances with other anti-NNP political groups. For its alleged complicity in an attempted coup in February 1952, the CPN was again outlawed. With the failure of a united-front policy, the party adopted an extremist "go-it-alone" program at its first all-party congress in 1954. This proved to be a serious miscalculation. The second all-party congress in 1955 adopted a more moderate program over the strong opposition of the leftist faction led by Pushpa Lal. The new program brought immediate benefits, as the party was granted legal status in 1956.

The split in the party leadership, particularly over the monarchy issue, continued to plague the CPN. King Mahendra's abolition of the parliamentary system in 1960 caused a major crisis in the party. Pushpa Lal and a small group of followers fled to India, where they called for the overthrow of the royal regime. The rest of the party, led by Keshar Jang Rayamajhi, formally disbanded as ordered by the government and offered to cooperate in setting up a new political system. However, the party structure was in fact kept intact, and the CPN continued to operate more or less openly, if illegally. Attempts to negotiate the differences between the two factions in 1961 were unsuccessful; in May 1962 the Pushpa Lal group held an "all-party" conference in Banaras (India) and set up a separate organization. The CPN central committee then expelled Pushpa Lal and several of his followers. denouncing them as "deviationists." The split has continued up to the present, in spite of repeated efforts by both Nepali communists and other communist parties to bring the two factions together.

## ORGANIZATION AND MEMBERSHIP

The Nepali party is organized in the typical pyramidal pattern, from local cells at the base to the politburo at the top, with district committees, provincial committees, and a central committee at intermediate stages. The party leadership and cadre are composed mostly of intellectuals, students, and professional men from high- or middle-caste communities in this Hindu kingdom. Some lower-caste members from hill tribes or factory-worker communities were drawn into the movement by the Peasants' Organization and the unions on the Darjeeling tea estates or in Nepal's first industries, but none have as yet assumed much prominence in the party.

Data on the CPN are difficult to obtain, particularly for the period after December 1960. Although substantial changes in the organizational structure had been proposed and reportedly approved by the central committee in 1960, they had never been adopted by a party congress. The constitution adopted at the 1954 all-party congress in Kathmandu appeared still to be in force at the end of 1965.

There are no official membership figures for either the Rayamajhi faction in Nepal or Pushpa Lal's dissident group in India. According to unofficial estimates, the Pushpa Lal faction has 300 to 500 members in India, as well as a smaller number of supporters working underground in Nepal. The Rayamajhi faction reportedly is somewhat larger, but probably has at most 1,000 active members.

The king's ban on political activity extended to all organizations within Nepal, whatever their ostensible character. There were therefore no organizations in 1965 that could strictly be classified as fronts for the CPN. However, communists were making strenuous and partially successful efforts to infiltrate a number of the organizations which were allowed to function, such as the officially sponsored student, peasant, and workers' organizations, and the semiofficial Nepal-China and Nepali-Soviet friendship associations. Their efforts since 1961 to establish "nonpolitical" organizations (such as the Intellectuals' Forum created in 1965), either alone or in cooperation with other political groups, have been less rewarding. Communists have also been active in some communal cultural organizations, particularly within the important Newari community in Kathmandu valley.

## RELATION TO SOVIET LEADERSHIP

The basic reaction of both factions of the CPN to the Sino-Soviet dispute was one of acute embarrassment, and strenuous efforts have been made to remain as unaligned as circumstances permit. None of the major party leaders had taken an explicit pro-Soviet or pro-Chinese position by 1965, although their general predilections are evident in some of their policy statements. The Rayamajhi group, for instance, sided (somewhat vaguely) with the Soviet Union on the test-ban treaty and on the Soviet interpretation of "peaceful co-existence." Rayamajhi himself visited the Soviet Union on several occasions and was reportedly dependent on the Russian embassy for financial support. Pushpa Lal has often been described as pro-Chinese, but this may be misleading, at least in relation to the Sino-Soviet dispute. One of his principal supporters (and rivals), Tulsi Lal Amatya, however, has long been an ardent Maoist and reportedly heads a staunchly pro-Chinese group within the leftist faction of the CPN. It is apparent that the Sino-Soviet dispute was at most a contributory factor in the division of the Nepali party, and not a major cause. However, as the dispute between the two giants of the communist world grows more bitter and becomes polarized, it may prove to be a serious obstacle to future reunification of the party.

## FUTURE PROSPECTS

The past record of the CPN would seem to discourage predictions of success for the party in the coming decade, at least if this is to be achieved on its own integral strength rather than through external assistance. Badly divided over both tactical and ideological questions and rent by personal feuds at the leadership level, the party has yet to demonstrate the capacity to assume a dynamic role in Nepali political developments.

## PARTY PRESS ORGANS AND RECORDS

The CPN has published several journals since 1951. The most important of these were *Mashal* (Torch) and *Navayug* (New Age), both of which disappeared after December 1960. In 1965 the weekly *Samiksha* (Inquiry) was considered to be the unofficial voice of the Rayamajhi faction of the party.

The party program adopted at the second all-party conference in November 1955 had not been legally amended or changed and presumably was still in force in 1965: *Nepal Kamyunist Party ko Rajnaitik Prastab Dwitiya Kanpherens ma Swikrit* (Political Resolution Adopted at the Second All-Party Conference), Kathmandu, Sharada Press, 1955. The second all-party congress (May-June 1957) debated changes in this program proposed by the central committee, but reportedly failed to approve them. The conference held by the Pushpa Lal faction of the CPN in Banaras in May 1962 adopted a "short-term program"; see "Communist Volte Face," *Nepal Today*, vol. 2, no. 19, September 1, 1963, p. 178.

## CONFERENCES AND CONGRESSES OF THE CPN

1st conference, September 1951, Kathmandu
1st congress, January 1954, Kathmandu
2d conference, November 1955, Kathmandu
2d congress, May-June 1957, Kathmandu

The third all-party congress was first scheduled for November 1958, postponed first to February 1960, and then again to February 1961. The royal coup of December 1960 intruded before the congress could be held, and the party was officially disbanded in Nepal. The Pushpa Lal faction of the party held what it termed an *adhibeshan* (general conference) of the party in Banaras in May 1962, but it is unclear whether this was considered to be the third all-party congress. In any case, the Rayamajhi faction of the party would not recognize it as such.

## BIBLIOGRAPHY

Gupta, Amirudha: *Politics in Nepal: A Study of Post-Rana Political Developments and Party Politics*, Bombay, Allied Publishers, 1964.
Joshi, Bhuwan Lal, and Leo E. Rose: *Democratic Innovations in Nepal: A Case Study of Political Acculturation*, Berkeley, Calif., University of California Press, 1967.
Rose, Leo E.: "Communism under High Atmospheric Conditions: The Party in Nepal," in Robert A. Scalapino (ed.), *The Communist Revolution in Asia*, Englewood Cliffs, N.J., Prentice-Hall, 1965, pp. 243-272.

LEO E. ROSE

# THE NETHERLANDS

The Netherlands is one of the few countries in Western Europe where communism had a foundation, albeit very restricted, both in theory and in practice, even before the victory of the bolshevik revolution in Russia and the formation of the Third International. The theoretical basis lay in the "Dutch school of Marxism," and the practical basis lay in the leftist Socialist Democratic Workers' Party (Sociaal-demokratische Arbeiders-partij, SDAP). But in spite of this double root, communism in the Netherlands never really succeeded in becoming a large movement of the masses.

The Dutch school of Marxism in the years before the Russian revolution included three prominent personalities: Hermann Gorter, poet and publicist; Anton Pannekoek, professor of astronomy; and Henriette Roland-Holst, woman of letters—all three keenly interested in theoretical studies of Marxism. The left-socialist movement, on the other hand, took official form on formation in 1909 of the dissenting SDAP, which had at its disposal the organ *De Tribune*, whose two editors in chief, W. Van Ravensteyn and D. Wijnkoop, were elected deputies at the end of 1917.

The "theoreticians" and the "practicians," joined in the same party since 1909, took a pacifist and internationalist position during World War I. Henriette Roland-Holst was delegate and spokesman for this line at the international socialist conference at Zimmerald in September 1915. The party did not rally to the Zimmerwald left, but in the course of the war a rapprochement took shape between this left, led by Lenin, and the Dutch Marxist left. When Lenin seized power in Russia, Hermann Gorter was among his enthusiastic supporters.

## HISTORY

The transformation of the dissenting SDAP into the Communist Party of Holland (Communistische Partij van Holland), effected on November 16-17, 1918, gave birth to an organization which adhered in 1919 to the Comintern but whose membership remained very weak. On April 1, 1919, the party counted forty-nine local sections, with 1,799 members in all. Two of the most important sections were Amsterdam, with 342 members, and Rotterdam, with 162 members. By May 1920, according to official reports, the party had a membership of 2,431.

Conflicts soon arose between two opposing tendencies within the party, as well as between the party and the Comintern. The conflict within the party found the theoreticians Gorter and Pannekoek in opposition to the parliamentarians van Ravensteyn and Wijnkoop on the question of tactics, starting with the problem of communist participation in trade-union and parliamentary work, which Gorter and Pannekoek condemned. When the Comintern's emissary Rutgers came to Amsterdam at the end of 1919 to set up the West European Bureau of the Comintern, the division between these two currents erupted in February 1920 during the only international conference organized by this bureau. Throughout 1920 the Comintern, and even Lenin personally, intervened in the affairs of the Dutch party. The Amsterdam branch of the bureau was dissolved, and Lenin, in his book *Left-Wing Communism: An Infantile Disease*, criticized the line which Gorter and Pannekoek advocated. That same year the leaders of the two opposing tendencies of Dutch communism went to Moscow; Wijnkoop participated in the second congress of the Comintern and dissociated himself from the ultraleftist line, while Gorter went to Moscow to defend, in vain, his point of view, which he publicized at the same time as Pannekoek in printed brochures. The result was that Gorter and Pannekoek left the party and in 1921 became masters of thought on leftist communism, while the leadership of the Dutch party was left in the hands of Ravensteyn and Wijnkoop.

In 1922 new opposition to the Ravensteyn-Wijnkoop leadership developed within the party, but this time the opposition found support in Moscow, and during the second plenum of the enlarged Executive Committee of the Comintern, in June 1922, a commission went to work to resolve the Dutch question. When H. J. F. M. Sneevliet (who had been known as Maring when he was a Comintern emissary to China) returned to the Netherlands in the fall of 1923, the opposition found an authoritative spokesman at its disposal.

At the party congress held in April 1924 in Rotterdam the official party leadership easily prevailed over the opposition, and in June-July 1924 Wijnkoop, delegate to the fifth Comintern congress in Moscow, was elected a member of its Executive Committee. However, the opposition, aided by the Comintern, gained ground, and at the party congress in May 1925 the resolution calling for straight application of the directives of the Comintern Executive Committee received 706 votes, while the official leadership's position received 975 votes. This loss of influence for the Ravensteyn-Wijnkoop leadership became more pronounced, and at the next congress in May 1926 they were excluded as "rightists." Leadership of the party passed to the opposition; however, the following year the Comintern excluded Sneevliet and his supporters as "elements of the extreme left and Trotskyists." Henriette Roland-Holst also broke with the party in 1927 and later dissociated herself from communism.

Both the Wijnkoop and Sneevliet factions tried to found communist organizations independent of Moscow. Wijnkoop had retained some influence, and he took with him the majority of the Rotterdam organization. In the municipal elections he drew more votes than the communist candidates and was elected deputy in 1929. Sneevliet initiated a Trotskyist movement which elected him deputy to the Dutch parliament.

These splits and purges, during which the Dutch party had lost most of its early leaders—with the exception of Wijnkoop, who returned to the party in 1930—were characterized by the Comintern as "a crisis provoked by the development of bolshevization and the transformation into a communist party of a party which previously had been nothing more than a leftist social democratic party." Although the party congress in April 1928 was styled a "congress of consolidation," at the congress in February 1930, following the Comintern campaign against "the opportunist deviation," the old leadership was thrown aside and a new, young leadership was named, with Paul de Groot as general secretary.

In 1929, before its last purge, the Dutch party had had an official membership of 1,100 members and had polled 37,662 votes in the parliamentary elections. With the new team in charge, it began the job of recovery, and on the eve of the seventh Comintern congress in 1935 the party, now renamed the Communist Party of the Netherlands (Communistische Partij van Nederland, CPN), expressed satisfaction with its achievements: 6,000 members registered and 118,354 votes received in the parliamentary elections of 1933, with four communist deputies elected and two mandates won in Indonesia. Nevertheless, the communist party was clearly outdistanced by the socialist party, which won 25.7 percent of the votes cast in the 1937 elections, while the communists won only 3.35 percent.

The party continued to follow the zigzag line of Comintern policy, from the popular front in 1935 to the tactic of defeatism developed after the Hitler-Stalin pact in 1939, to the antifascist and patriotic struggle in 1941. When the CPN became active in the resistance against German occupation, it gained a certain moral and political authority which offered a direct advantage in the liberation of the country but was a handicap in the long run. The advantage lay in the fact that the CPN was able to profit from its participation in the resistance movement and from Soviet military victories in Europe to attain its highest point in numerical and political strength. In 1946 the official membership figure was 53,000; in the parliamentary elections of the same year the party received 502,963 votes (10.5 percent of the total vote) and ten seats in parliament. The socialists, however, received 28.1 percent of the votes in the same elections. The communists were not given a chance to enter the coalition government.

The disadvantage of the CPN's sudden spurt of growth was that responsible posts fell to militants who had no party education and no knowledge of Soviet and Stalinist communism, and who were unable to conceal first their astonishment and later their opposition to the events which were to unfold in the communist world. These new militants were later condemned by the official leadership as "agents provocateurs" introduced by the class enemy. As the party spokesman explained it in 1959:

> When at the end of 1942 and in 1943 it became evident that Hitler would be crushed by the Soviet Union, the Nazis and the bourgeois governments which had emigrated to London after the occupation of their countries made every effort to undermine the growing influence of the communists in these countries. In 1943, the Gestapo managed to deliver a blow on the leadership of the communist party, then clandestine. Some individuals more devoted to the Intelligence Service than to the Dutch people profited from this to grab the leadership.[1]

With the aggravation of the "personality cult" of Stalin and the onset of the cold war, the CPN began to lose the position it had won after liberation. Membership fell considerably and rapidly; in 1950, according to official data, there were 33,000 members, but estimates showed only 25,000 in 1952. In parliamentary elections the percentage of communist votes fell proportionately; in 1948 the CPN received 7.74 percent of the total votes cast, in 1952 6.16 percent, and in 1965 4.7 percent. Membership in the communist-controlled Unity Trade Union Central (Eenheid Vak Centrale) also showed a steady drop, and of the 175,000 registered members in 1946, estimates gave no more than 30,000 in 1953.

At the twentieth congress of the Communist Party of the Soviet Union in February 1956 Paul de Groot headed the Dutch delegation, and like several other communist leaders in Western Europe, he insisted on avoiding an open and free discussion on the effects of the "personality cult" both in the Soviet party and in the Dutch party. At the eighteenth congress of the CPN in October 1956 he affirmed that a discussion on the personality cult was useless, inasmuch as it had never existed in the CPN.

In addition to the problem of de-Stalinization itself, a tactical problem arose during this period. At its twentieth congress the Soviet party had inaugurated a policy of the "extended hand" and of unity of action with the socialist parties and trade unions; as a result, it became necessary to liquidate the moribund communist trade-union organization and return to the socialist Dutch Trade Union Federation. The communist trade-union group refused to comply with this decision, and the ensuing struggle both in the trade unions and in the party ended, in April 1958, in the exclusion from the party of Gerben Wagenaar, deputy and president of the CPN; Bertus Brandsen, communist deputy; Fritz Reuter, president of the communist trade-union group and member of the political bureau of the CPN; and Herben Grootzak, communist deputy. Four of the seven communist deputies in the Dutch parliament revolted against the Moscow-imposed political line. In May 1958 the dissenting members launched a monthly review, *De Brug* (The Bridge), labeled revisionist by the official leadership.

When the official party leadership, headed by de Groot, accelerated preparations for the nineteenth party congress, which convened in December 1958, the dissidents published an open letter severely criticizing the line taken by de Groot and demanding that the congress name a commission—to exclude any member of the central committee—to examine the party's policy from 1939 to 1945, on the one hand, and from 1946 to 1958, on the other. The party congress did not do so; de Groot dominated the decisions (which were accepted unanimously), and the dissidents were invited to resign their elective positions as members of parliament and municipal counselors. Paul de Groot was reelected general secretary of the party and was still in the top party post at the end of 1965. In September 1962 the plenum of the central committee did away with the office of general secretary, formed a secretariat of the central committee, and gave de Groot the title of president of the party.

In the legislative elections of March 1959 the official communists and the dissident communists came face to face; the former polled 144,371 votes (2.41 percent of the total) and obtained three deputies (out of 150), and the latter received 34,917 votes (0.58 percent) and no seats in parliament. In the elections of May 1963 the CPN scarcely improved its position, gathering 173,457 votes (2.77 percent) and four seats in parliament. Party membership remained equally modest.

On January 31, 1960, the communist trade-union organization decided to dissolve and urged its members to adhere to the socialist trade-union group, a decision the party announced as "a real step toward unity."

## ORGANIZATION AND MEMBERSHIP

The Dutch party has followed the general scheme of the Comintern, with the political bureau and the general secretary at the top. Factory cells were formed at the time of bolshevization in 1925 and 1926. The CPN operates according to the principle of democratic centralism, prohibiting the existence of factions within the party. After de-Stalinization it established the position of president and abolished the post of general secretary.

The party has enjoyed relatively strong support among the workers of Rotterdam and especially Amsterdam. Since the election of Paul de Groot as general secretary in 1930, it has avoided giving leadership to the intellectuals.

In the absence of official figures, estimates gave the CPN around 15,000 members in 1960. At a national party conference held in Amsterdam on December 15-16, 1962, Henk Hoekstra, secretary of the central committee, expressed satisfaction—for the first time in a long while—at the increase in membership, but without giving the total figure: "In the course of the last eighteen months, the party has registered 1,683 new members, 700 of which joined last year. Today, we again have more than 7,000 members in Amsterdam or as many as before the counterrevolutionary uprising in Hungary."

## RELATION TO SOVIET LEADERSHIP

The deterioration in relations between Moscow and Peking and the internal conflicts of the CPN leaders have created a peculiar situation in the Dutch party. As Moscow insisted on the condemnation of Peking, the Dutch communists became increasingly silent and moved toward a form of neutrality in the conflict. Finally, when the pro-Soviet parties of "capitalist" Europe—nineteen parties in all—met in Brussels on June 1-3, 1965, the Dutch delegation attended but under various pretexts refused to sign the conference documents.

A pro-Chinese group is evidenced by the existence of the Marxist-Leninist Center of Holland, particularly active in Rotterdam and Amsterdam. Chris Petersen and N. Schzevel are leaders of the pro-Chinese faction in Rotterdam and Chris Bischot heads the Amsterdam group. The pro-Chinese communists attack the Soviet party as well as certain leaders of the CPN, but they no longer offer their own candidates in legislative or other elections.

## PARTY PRESS ORGANS

The CPN's main organ is the daily *De Waarheid* (Truth) edited by Wim van het Ship, with a circulation of about 20,000 copies. The party's monthly *Politiek en Cultuur* (Politics and Culture) is devoted to "theory and practice of Marxism-Leninism." The pro-Chinese group publishes *De Rode Tribune* (Red Tribune) in Rotterdam and *De Rode Vlag* (Red Flag) in Amsterdam. Both appear irregularly.

## CONGRESSES OF THE CPN

14th congress, December 1947, Amsterdam
15th congress, February 1950, Rotterdam
16th congress, November 1952, Amsterdam
17th congress, April 1955, Amsterdam
18th congress, October 1956, Amsterdam
19th congress, December 1958, Amsterdam
20th congress, May 1961, Amsterdam
21st congress, March 1964, Amsterdam

## BIBLIOGRAPHY

*L'Activité de l'I.C. du Ve au VIe congrès*, Paris, Bureau d'Editions, 1928.
*Die Kommunistische Internationale vor dem VII Weltkongress*, Moscow-Leningrad, 1935.
Kool, Frits: "Communism in Holland: A Study in Futility," *Problems of Communism*, no. 5, September-October 1960.
Van Ravensteyn, W.: *De Wording van het Communisme in Nederland, 1907-1925*. Amsterdam, 1949.

BRANKO LAZITCH

1. Marcus Bakker (secretary of the central committee of the CPM). in *Les Problèmes de la paix et du socialisme* (édition française), no. 7, March 1959, p. 121.

# NEW ZEALAND

The Communist Party of New Zealand (CPNZ) traces its origin to a number of Marxist study clubs which were formed during World War I, mainly in the small mining townships of the west coast of the South Island. At Christmas 1918 these groups combined into a New Zealand Marxian Association, and the following year they sent their secretary T. W. Feary and two other members across the Pacific to obtain up-to-date information on Russian developments, which the strict government censorship prevented from being reported locally. In San Francisco and Vancouver Feary obtained copies of Lenin's speech *Soviets at Work* and of John Reed's *Ten Days That Shook the World*, which he was able to smuggle back into New Zealand.

*Soviets at Work* was promptly reprinted in New Zealand, and under the impact of the new revolutionary ideas, the Marxist students decided to disband their association and replace it by a Marxist political party, the Communist Party of New Zealand. The founding conference took place in Wellington at Easter 1921; the first secretary of the new CPNZ was E. J. Dyer of Wellington. Branches were formed in the main towns and in the west coast mining settlements. In 1923 a communist candidate participated for the first time in an election and polled the respectable total of 2,128 votes for the Dunedin city council. In August 1924 the first issue of a communist journal appeared in New Zealand, the *Communist*, published in Auckland.

## HISTORY

Although nominally part of a national organization, the communist party branches in New Zealand were virtually independent of each other and differed in their political approach. An attempt at more centralized direction was made at a conference at Christmas 1924, attended by Australian delegates, which decided to make the New Zealand party a section of the Communist Party of Australia. However, the Auckland group insisted on maintaining its separate existence, and unity was not restored until 1926, when Norman Jeffrey, a leading Australian communist, spent six months in New Zealand on an organizing mission. A new monthly national journal, the *Workers' Vanguard*, began publication at Blackball, on the west coast, in April 1926, and at the end of that year the national headquarters of the party was also transferred to Blackball. Soon afterward the party resumed its independence from Australia. It was granted the right to affiliate with the Comintern, and in 1928 the New Zealand delegate R. F. Griffin attended the sixth Comintern congress in Moscow.

Although small in numbers (total membership was below 100), in 1928 the CPNZ dominated the Miners' Union and exerted considerable influence in the Seamen's Union. In the following year, however, the miners' leaders seceded and the party's influence on the west coast collapsed. The national headquarters returned to Wellington, and with it went the *Workers' Vanguard*, soon to be renamed the *Red Worker*.

In the early 1930s the CPNZ concentrated its efforts among the unemployed, whose numbers grew rapidly as the worldwide economic depression deepened. Bitter strikes, demonstrations, and riots took place in New Zealand cities, and repressive legislation, frequent police raids, and severe prison sentences failed to curb the steady growth of communist influence.

In 1933 F. E. Freeman, freshly returned from Moscow, took over the party leadership. The CPNZ sponsored a number of subsidiary organizations, including a short-lived Youth Communist League, a Working Women's Movement, and the Friends of the Soviet Union, each with its own monthly journal. A Movement Against War and Fascism was active for a time, and as prosperity gradually returned, formerly unemployed party members were able to gain influence once more in the trade unions. For the first time, too, communist ideas found an echo in the universities, and the party gained a number of intellectual supporters. In November 1933 the monthly *Red Worker* was succeeded by the *Workers' Weekly*, and in December a theoretical journal was added, the *New Zealand Labour Monthly*, later renamed the *New Zealand Communist Review*.

At the seventh congress of the Comintern in 1935 the New Zealand delegate Leo Sim (known as Andrews) was able to report that party membership had increased sixfold since affiliation in 1928. Circulation of the party's journal had grown from 2,500 to 6,000 in the same period. Ideologically, however, the CPNZ was ill equipped to follow the new popular-front course laid down for the world communist movement. In the general elections of 1935, which brought a labor government to power, the communist slogan was "neither reaction nor labour." The party conference that year admitted "sectarian" mistakes and replaced Freeman by Sim, but it required the personal intervention of L. Sharkey, the Australian communist leader, before the CPNZ wholeheartedly accepted the new Comintern policy. In 1938 the national headquarters was transferred to Auckland, where it has remained. A new weekly journal, the *People's Voice*, was launched there in July 1939.

The outbreak of war once again brought the CPNZ into conflict with the authorities, and although the party remained legal, its journal was suppressed. After the German attack on the Soviet Union, however, New Zealand communists eagerly supported the war effort, and in 1945 and 1946 the party reached the peak of its influence, with a membership of 2,000 and a weekly circulation of the *People's Voice* exceeding 14,000. Since then the decline in communist strength in New Zealand has been continual, aggravated in particular by the Hungarian events of 1956 and the Sino-Soviet dispute.

## ORGANIZATION AND MEMBERSHIP

Membership in the New Zealand party is a closely guarded secret but has been estimated at 300 to 400, mostly in the Auckland area. Circulation of the weekly *People's Voice* is below 5,000. Members are organized in branches on an area or industrial basis, and where several branches exist in a locality, they are combined in a district organization, which holds annual district conferences. In 1965 the CPNZ had district committees in Auckland, Wellington, and Christchurch. The highest party authority is the national conference, which is required to meet at least once every three years. This conference elects a national committee, which in turn appoints a political committee and a still smaller national secretariat, consisting of full-time party workers. This last body, located in Auckland, is the real seat of power in the party.

The membership of the CPNZ is predominantly urban working class and lower middle class. The number of intellectuals who remained in the party after 1956 is negligible, and in a recent statement in parliament the prime minister claimed that there was only one known communist student in New Zealand universities. Very few Maoris have ever joined the CPNZ, and the party as a whole is aging because of the slow influx of young recruits.

Electoral support for communist candidates is negligible. The party has participated in parliamentary elections regularly since the end of World War II, but from a peak of just over 3 percent of the vote in 1946, its support had fallen by 1965 to below 1 percent or an average of 100 to 150 communist votes in electorates exceeding 15,000 voters. In the trade unions, too, the party's influence has declined steadily in the postwar years.

## RELATION TO SOVIET LEADERSHIP

In 1956 S. W. Scott, the party's leading theoretician and former general secretary, defected with a following of about 100 members, including the bulk of the party's intellectuals. The "Scott affair," and particularly Scott's later political development, helped to predispose New Zealand party leaders toward the Chinese viewpoint in the subsequent Sino-Soviet conflict. Around 1960 V. G. Wilcox, the party's general secretary, and other national leaders began taking China's side in the ideological dispute, and by 1963 they had won over a majority of the party membership. The pro-Russian minority, which included the party's former national chairman G. E. Jackson, resigned in stages from late 1964 on.

Inevitably the split in the communist ranks must affect all organizations in which communists have been active. For example, a dissident group supports the New Zealand-Soviet Union Society, while the CPNZ will presumably continue its interest in the China Friendship Society. It is less clear how women's, youth, and peace groups will be affected by communist denunciations of revisionists as traitors, saboteurs, and subverters with whom it is impossible to work in a united front. Communist approval of Chinese nuclear tests makes cooperation in peace groups difficult, just as the party's opposition to a negotiated settlement in Vietnam endangers its standing in the peace-for-Vietnam committees.

The CPNZ is one of the few original communist parties which supports Peking, and as the only such party from a white "Western" country, it is an immense asset to the Chinese.

Wilcox, whose name is unknown to the bulk of his own countrymen, has become a household word in Communist China. Received on his frequent visits to Peking in a style befitting a head of state, his writings are studied in Chinese schools and are given worldwide distribution by the Chinese propaganda machine. As China's most faithful ally, next to the Albanians, the CPNZ is thus able to play a part on the international scene out of all proportion to its domestic importance.

Barring a major economic disaster, the prospects of both the CPNZ and the dissident pro-Soviet group are very slight in New Zealand itself. Their importance on the international plane is as active participants in the ideological dispute which has split the international communist movement, and until this split is formalized the CPNZ remains the recognized party for New Zealand, assured of a place at any future world communist meeting.

PARTY PRESS ORGANS AND RECORDS

The CPNZ publishes the *People's Voice*, a weekly, and the *New Zealand Communist Review*, a monthly, both in Auckland.

The party program is contained in *New Zealand's Road to Socialism*, Auckland, Communist Party of New Zealand, 1955. For party statutes see the CPNZ *Constitution*, Auckland, 1957. Conference reports have never been published separately but are reported in varying detail in the communist press.

BIBLIOGRAPHY

Brookes, R. H.: "The CPNZ and the Sino-Soviet Split," *Political Science* (Wellington), vol. 17, no. 2, September 1965.
Roth, H.: "The Communist Vote in New Zealand," *Political Science*, vol. 17, no. 2, September 1965.
Roth H.: "Fragmentation on the Left," *Comment* (Wellington), no. 27, June 1966.
Scott, S. W.: *Rebel in a Wrong Cause*, Auckland, Collins, 1960.

HERBERT ROTH

# NICARAGUA

The Socialist Party of Nicaragua (Partido Socialista de Nicaragua, PSN) is the only communist party in Latin America created during the popular-front period, and the only one that has never borne the communist name openly. It was founded in 1937 by a small group of communists who had previously operated within the Nicaraguan Workers' Party (Partido de Trabajadores Nicaragüenses, PTN). The first secretary general of the communist party was the journalist Francisco Hernández Segura.

HISTORY

The Nicaraguan communists are perhaps the most anonymous of any such group in Latin America. The party has been illegal during most of its existence, has never enjoyed unrestricted freedom of operation, and has never been able to operate effectively against the government, dominated since 1936 by the Somoza family.

For about two years the PSN functioned openly in the labor movement and among intellectuals and university students in the cities. It was suppressed and its leaders were exiled in 1939, but it was allowed to resume activities during the wartime and postwar era of good feeling. The party gained control of the new labor confederation and participated in the 1947 elections, despite the fact that it had been formally proscribed by decree in 1945.

With the advent of the cold war, both the PSN and the labor confederation were banned, and thereafter the communists could function only underground. Inspired by the success of the Castro revolution, some Nicaraguan communists took part in the Cuban-based attack on their homeland in 1959, and others sought to develop a sustained guerrilla force in the coastal jungles. Both efforts failed. In 1965 the Nicaraguan communists were still waiting for a dramatic change in the political situation to improve their position.

### ORGANIZATION AND MEMBERSHIP

United States sources estimated PSN membership in 1965 as about 200.[1] The party maintains the usual labor, student, and general-purpose front groups. For a full discussion see *Latin America*.

### RELATION TO SOVIET LEADERSHIP

The leadership of the PSN supports the Soviet position in the ideological dispute with Communist China. For a full discussion of the PSN's relationship to the international communist movement see *Latin America*.

### PARTY PRESS ORGAN

The Nicaraguan party has limited publication facilities. It issues a semiclandestine weekly newspaper, *Orientación popular*.

### PARTY CONGRESSES

Little information is available on the dates and frequency of communist party congresses in Nicaragua. The ninth congress met late in 1964.

### BIBLIOGRAPHY

See *Latin America*, refs. 2, 6, 13, 24.

ROLLIE E. POPPINO

1. U.S. Department of State, Bureau of Intelligence and Research, *World Strength of the Communist Party Organizations*, Eighteenth Annual Report, January 1966, p. 162.

# NIGER REPUBLIC

The present Independence Party (Sawaba, in the Djerma language) was founded in 1951 by Djibo Bakary, a schoolteacher born in 1922. Bakary, who was secretary of the Niger Progressive Party (Parti Progressiste Nigérien, PPN), the Niger section of the African Democratic Rally (Rassemblement Démocratique Africain, RDA) refused to follow Félix Houphouët-Boigny and the principal leaders of the RDA when they broke their original ties with the French Communist Party. The other sections which broke away at that point were the Union of Cameroon Peoples and the Senegalese Democratic Union, from which the African Independence Party later developed (see *Senegal* and *Cameroon*). With one part of the PPN, Bakary created the Niger Democratic Union (Union Démocratique

Nigérienne, UDN) in 1951. The new UDN was supported by the trade unions of Niger. Bakary was also the secretary of the trade-union organization and remained in close touch with the French Communist Party (Bakary attended its thirteenth congress in 1954).

In 1956 the UDN became the Niger section of the African Socialist Movement (Mouvement Socialiste Africain, MSA), founded shortly before by Lamine Gueye, then mayor of Dakar. It was on the MSA ticket that Bakary and his followers entered the elections to the territorial assembly and won the majority of the votes. Bakary was appointed vice president of the executive council—that is, head of the government (the president was the governor nominated by France). Among his ministers was the communist Abdoulaye Diallo, vice president of the World Federation of Trade Unions from 1949 to 1957.

At the time of the referendum of September 1958, in which French-speaking African countries had the choice of remaining constitutionally linked to France or of becoming independent, Bakary campaigned against passage (as did Sékou Touré of Guinea), but he was defeated and forced to leave office. He refused to follow the leaders of the MSA into the Parti du Regroupement Africain, founded by Léopold Senghor of Senegal, and to demonstrate his independence renamed his party Sawaba. With notable assistance from the trade unions he then launched a violent opposition campaign. In October 1959 the government decreed the dissolution of Sawaba. Djibo Bakary went underground and supposedly took refuge in Ghana and then in East Berlin.

Sawaba, reduced to a handful of militants, held a joint meeting with the revolutionary committee of the Cameroon and Senegalese communist parties in November 1962.[1] It seemed then that Sawaba was oriented in favor of the Communist Party of the Soviet Union, but afterward it came under the influence of the Chinese Communist Party. Sawaba was responsible for the grenade attempt against Diori Hamani, president of Niger, on April 13, 1963. On September 27, 1964, its political bureau issued an appeal to the Niger people to take up arms and put an end to the "antinational and antidemocratic regime imposed by foreign forces." Guerrilla forces were trained in Algeria, Ghana, and Communist China. Acting in the name of Sawaba, in October and November 1964 they entered Niger territory from Ghana and attempted to stir up the populace; they were annihilated.

Since then, Sawaba seems to have come back under pro-Soviet influence. By 1965 it claimed to be directing the "struggle against neocolonialsim and imperialism for better coordination of the armed and political struggle of the Niger people,"[2] and was maintaining "contacts with the revolutionary forces of Africa which declare themselves for scientific socialism."

BIBLIOGRAPHY

Morillon, J. P.: "La Tentative insurrectionelle du Sawaba," *Est & ouest*, no. 342, May 16-31, 1965.
"Un Nouveau parti communiste: Le Sawaba," *Est & ouest*, no. 291, January 1-15, 1963.

CLAUDE HARMEL

1. *L'Humanité*, December 7, 1962.

2. *La Nouvelle revue internationale,* February 1966.

# NIGERIA

Nigeria, Africa's most populous country, became independent in 1960. The local adherents of Marxism-Leninism had played only a very small part in the struggle, but they considered that the political transformation must lead to intensification of the class struggle and new efforts to liberate Nigeria from the "yoke of imperialism and feudalism." Communist sympathizers and radicals rallied to the Nigerian Youth Congress, founded in 1960 by Tunji Otegbeye. The Youth Congress supported pan-African unity, as advocated by Nigeria's Kwame Nkrumah and Guinea's Sékou Touré, and condemned the activities of Western European and American "imperialists and neocolonialists" in Africa. It also censured American economic assistance as an "instrument of the Pentagon" that might involve its recipients in "nuclear death." Nigerian communists also gained influence in the Nigerian Trade Union Congress, which elected a new leadership in August 1963 and called for joint action of all trade unions, regardless of ideological orientation, in demanding a national minimum wage, control of prices and rentals, and abolition of the daily-pay system. The Trade Union Congress succeeded in setting up a joint action committee which included the United Labour Congress and other trade-union bodies.

On September 27, 1963, there was a general strike; according to Tunji Otegbeye, this was intended not merely as a protest for higher wages, but also to express mass discontent with a government that mainly represented the interests of capitalists, feudalists, and high officials. The government came to terms with the strikers, and the joint action committee subsequently broke up, despite strong opposition from the Trade Union Congress.

## HISTORY

In terms of the general procedure in African countries which had "fallen into the hands of a reactionary national bourgeoisie," Nigerian Marxists set as their immediate goal the creation of a united front of all progressive forces to lead the fight for a national-democratic revolution. Depending on local circumstances, they might engage in an armed struggle, but care must be taken that any such strategy had popular support; a party which prematurely took to arms would find itself isolated, and hence doomed to destruction. Accordingly, in August 1963[1] they set up the Socialist Workers' and Farmers' Party (SWFP) of Nigeria, a legal party founded on the principles of "scientific socialism" and aimed at a national-democratic, and eventually a socialist, Nigeria.

Otegbeye proclaimed that the preceding three years of independence had shown that the interests of the toiling masses did not coincide with those of feudalists, tribal chiefs, capitalists, and the allies of capitalism, and that many of the noncommunist political groups of Nigeria consisted of reactionaries and opportunists who opposed the Nigerian "revolution." The "revolution," however, was strongly support by the Action Group, which had freed itself of most feudal and colonialist interests and was being led by progressive bourgeoisie and intellectuals. Otegbeye also viewed the National Council of Nigeria and the Cameroons as an alliance of widely disparate class interests. As such, the progressive forces within it should be supported, and, if necessary, the reationary tendencies of its leaders unmasked. He argued that the battle for full independence and socialism could assume many different forms, from parliamentary struggle to armed insurrection, and that revolutionary methods would depend on the means used by the ruling classes, which in the case of Africa included the monopoly capitalists of Europe and America.

The first congress of the SWFP, held on December 18-20, 1965, in Lagos, was attended by all Marxist groups and "democratic" organizations in the country, including the Nigerian Congress of Trade Unions, the Nigerian Youth Congress, and the People's Party of Nigeria, comprising 135 delegates in all. The congress elected a central committee of seventeen members, with Uche Omo as president and Tunji Otegbeye as general secretary.

The SWFP proclaimed itself to be a party of Nigerian workers, peasants, and progressive intellectuals with the goal of a socialist Nigeria to be achieved by means of a national-democratic revolution, according to the immutable principles of Marxism-Leninism. In order to strengthen ties with foreign workers and labor movements, the party, assisted by sympathetic trade unions, established the Patrice Lumumba Institute of Political Science. However, the trade-union movement in Nigeria itself was not unified, and the communists influenced only some of the groups. Some unions supported the Nigerian Trade Union Congress and the Labor Unity Front. Both these organizations stood for "complete economic liberation" of the country and for a socialist orientation. The Nigerian Trade Union Congress was a member of both the All-African Trade Union Federation and the communist-directed World Federation of Trade Unions.

The SWFP was pro-Soviet in orientation, and its emergence was welcomed in Eastern Europe. Nevertheless, it was unable to make any impact on Nigerian politics or to affect the bitter ethnic and regional conflicts that plagued the country.

## ORGANIZATION AND MEMBERSHIP

The SWFP was organized on the principle of democratic centralism and collective leadership. Its actual strength, however, is difficult to ascertain. According to Soviet sources, in December 1965 the party had 22,000 members and eighty-three local organizations,[2] while United States estimates placed membership at less than 1,000.[3] The party itself claimed a membership of 16,000, distributed in fifty-six branches. In the federal elections of December 1964 the SWFP received 23,000 votes, but in the Lagos city council elections of November 1965 it received only 733 of 100,000 votes cast.

## PARTY PRESS ORGANS

In 1965 the SWFP was publishing the regular journal *Advance*. The Nigerian Labour Party, a splinter group which broke away from the SWFP in 1964, was issuing *Labour Vanguard*.

## BIBLIOGRAPHY

Goodluck, W. O.: "Nigeria and Marxism," *The African Communist*, no. 19, October-December 1964, pp. 49-59.

"Nigeria: Agitation im volkreichsten Land Afrikas," *Ost-Probleme*, no. 3, February 12, 1965, pp. 85-87.

LEWIS H. GANN

1. *World Marxist Review*, November 1965, pp. 81-82.

2. *Agitator*, no. 6, 1966, p. 60.

3. U.S. Department of State, Bureau of Intelligence and Research, *World Strength of the Communist Party Organizations*, Eighteenth Annual Report, January 1966, p. 127.

# NORTH KOREA
*See* Korea

# NORTH VIETNAM
*See* Vietnam

# NORTHERN IRELAND
*See* Ireland

# NORWAY

On November 4, 1923, after the Norwegian Labor Party (Norsk Arbeiderparti, NAP) had voted to withdraw from the Comintern, a minority which considered itself the legal continuation of the party formed the Communist Party of Norway (Norges Kommunistiske Parti, NKP). The NKP was strongest in the first few months of its existence. Thirteen of the twenty-eight labor members of the parliament supported the NKP, as did the majority of the NAP's youth organization. The 1923 election gave the communists 59,401 votes (or 6.10 percent) and six representatives to the parliament.

## HISTORY

From the time it was founded until the outbreak of World War II, the NKP steadily lost electoral strength and members, With its own rather radical position, the NAP had managed to retain the majority of the workers. In fact, the new youth organization of the NAP even called itself the Left Communist Youth Organization. Several intellectuals left the NKP after inner party splits and exclusions. Like other members of the Comintern, the NKP became an instrument of Soviet interests, as illustrated by its support of the Ribbentrop-Molotov pact and the Finnish winter war of 1939-1940. As a result, by the beginning of 1940 the NKP was unable to muster even 1 percent of the vote.

The NKP's support for the shifting political lines of Soviet foreign policy also caused confusion within the party, and when Germany attacked Norway on April 9, 1940, the party papers failed to criticize the aggressors—an attitude that was disastrous to the image of the party. It was only with the German attack on the Soviet Union on June 22, 1941, that what remained of the party started to build up underground cells and a resistance movement. A key role was played by Peder Furubotn, who had been secretary general of the party in the 1920s and had already been in conflict with Moscow before the war. Furubotn was the only underground Norwegian leader operating under his real name. This, in addition to the fact that his underground movement favored a more active war policy, contributed to the communists' increase in popularity. Another important factor was the fact that the Soviet Union was Norway's ally in the fight against Germany, and Soviet troops participated in the liberation of Finnmark, the northern part of the country.

The NKP's new popularity after the war was demonstrated in the parliamentary elections in 1945; it received 176,535 votes (or 11.89 percent) and won eleven seats, the best the Norwegian communists have done in any election. The main paper of the NKP, *Friheten*, which had been published illegally during the war, now reached a circulation of more than 100,000, which was high indeed by Norwegian standards.

Most of the prestige and popularity that the communists enjoyed in 1945 was lost, however, when the cold war again placed the NKP in the position of apologist for Soviet policy, both in Soviet home affairs and in foreign policy. The NKP's endorsement of the Soviet takeover in Czechoslovakia in February 1948 further alienated popular sentiment. In the elections of 1949 the vote for communist candidates fell to 102,722 (or 5.48 percent), and in the next election in 1953 it dropped to 90,432 (or 5.08 percent).

Moreover, purges and inner party conflicts gave the NKP the appearance of a conspiratorial and suspect group. Furubotn, who had again been made secretary general in 1946, was expelled from the party, together with many followers, in the autumn of 1949, and a violent campaign depicted him as a "Titoist" and "imperialist." Although Furubotn continued long after his purge to express his personal loyalty to Moscow and Stalin, the general anti-Tito campaign in which he had been deposed had been reinforced in his case by personal factors. His lack of discipline and heavy drinking had been noted both at home and in Moscow, and his administrative practices made him many personal enemies.

However, some of Furnbotn's followers stayed together after the purge and later played a more important role than the NKP or even the new leftist Socialist People's Party (Sosialistisk Folkeparti) in the campaign against Norway's participation in the Common Market and against nuclear arms in the early 1960s. Furnbotn's influence continued, but chiefly in an indirect and symbolic sense.

The NKP's continued decline was given further momentum by the de-Stalinization campaign in the Soviet Union. Khrushchev's speech at the twentieth congress of the Soviet party in 1956 came as a complete surprise to the NKP leadership; even the Norwegian delegates in Moscow had not been informed beforehand. Besides irritating and confusing the Norwegian communists, Khrushchev's de-Stalinization campaign raised the delicate question of rehabilitation. The NKP became one of the very few European communist parties not to offer rehabilitation to former "Titoists." Later in 1956 the NKP was shocked by the Soviet intervention in Hungary. The party leaders and press supported the Soviet position, and after some confusion and hesitation, many young intellectuals left the NKP in protest.

The Sino-Soviet conflict further added to the split and confusion in the party, but at the same time it gave the communists a new opportunity for a comeback into Norwegian politics. After the end of 1961, when they first commented upon the Sino-Soviet conflict, the party leaders avoided taking stands but did so in such a way that they irritated the

Russians without really pleasing the Chinese. As in Rumania, this attitude was intended to demonstrate the NKP's independence of Moscow and a more national line. This new line was further evidenced by the party daily's criticism of the new Soviet leadership for the way in which Khrushchev had been ousted.

However, the new national policy and the party's attempts to form electoral coalitions with the NAP were of no avail. Similarly, a change of leadership—the younger Reidar Larsen succeeded Emil Lövlien as party chairman at the 1965 party congress—failed to give the NKP a new image. Before and during the party congress there was a strong discussion of both the Sino-Soviet conflict and the NKP's Norwegian policy, but the young party members felt more and more uneasy within the party. The Norwegian Communist Youth Organization (Norsk Kommunistiske Ungdomslag) took a more independent stand than its parent party, and after some clashes with the older generation, a number of young members left the party or withdrew from active political work. An additional obstacle for the communists was the fact that the Norwegian socialists had a sufficiently leftist policy that they appealed to the same groups of voters. This explains to a certain degree the difference from developments in Sweden where the communists had never had to compete with a left-socialist party.

In the elections of 1965 the vote for communist candidates had dropped to 28,002 (or 1.4 percent).

## PARTY PRESS ORGAN

The NKP's press organ *Friheten* (Freedom) was being published in 1965 as a daily.

## CONGRESSES OF THE NKP

1st congress, November 1923
2d congress, May 1925
3d congress, February 1929
4th congress, March 1932
5th congress, April 1936
6th congress, June 1946
7th congress, February 1950
[Extra] congress, February 1950
8th congress, March 1953
9th congress, March 1957
10th congress, March 1961
11th congress, March 1965

## BIBLIOGRAPHY

Johansen, Jahn Otto: "Norway," in William E. Griffith (ed.), *Communism in Europe*, vol. II, Cambridge, Mass., MIT Press, 1966, pp. 321-369.

Kommunistische Internationale: *Die kommunistischen Parteien Skandinaviens und die Kommunistische Internationale*, Hamburg, Hoym, 1923.

*Norges Kommunistiske Partis historie* (History of the Communist Party of Norway), vol. I, Oslo, Communist Party of Norway, 1963.

Sparring, Åke (ed.): *Kommunismen i Norden og krisen i den verdenkommunistiske bevaegelse* (Communism in the Nordic Countries and the Crisis in the International Movement), Copenhagen, Fremad, 1966.

JAHN OTTO JOHANSEN

# OUTER MONGOLIA

Early in this century Outer Mongolia was still a feudal and theocratic country, ruled by the Living Buddha Bogdo Gegen and isolated from twentieth-century civilization. The majority of the population was nomadic and illiterate. When the Russian civil war gradually spread eastward over Siberia in 1919, a group of Russian communists in Urga (now Ulan Bator) organized a secret revolutionary committee to supply arms and ammunition to Russian communist guerrillas who were active at the borders between Mongolia and Siberia. For the Mongol *arat* (the lowest-class nomad) who witnessed these activities, this was the first exposure to the ideas of the Russian revolution.

At that point the international status of Outer Mongolia was very complex. In 1911 the Outer Mongolian princes had declared their independence, with the Living Buddha of Urga as ruler. However, neither China nor Russia had recognized this independence, and in 1915 a tripartite treaty of Kiakhta signed by Russia, China, and Outer Mongolia recognized the country's autonomy under Chinese sovereignty. Following establishment of a Soviet government in Russia, and this government's cancellation of all czarist treaties concerning Outer Mongolia, the Chinese government strengthened its "guard" in the capital, Urga. In November 1919 China annulled Outer Mongolia's autonomy on the pretext that this was favored by some Outer Mongolian princes and lamas. However, this unilateral step was not approved by the Outer Mongolian government and Diet, and opposition to Chinese rule spread fast. This renewed desire for independence was encouraged by the Soviet government's declaration in support of self-determination and independence for Outer Mongolia.

This independence movement, later called a "liberation movement from feudalism and imperialism," was led by two groups, one organized in late 1918 by Suhe Bator and the other started by Choibalsan in 1919. Suhe Bator, who was from an *arat* family, had been a professional officer of the Mongolian Autonomous Army and may have been introduced to bolshevism by a Russian instruction officer in his regiment. The Chinese occupation forced Suhe Bator to retire from the military service, and in 1918 he organized the first revolutionary cell in Mongolia. Choibalsan was also from the *arat* class. Late in 1914 he had won a scholarship from the Mongolian foreign office to study in Irkutsk, where he observed the process of the Russian revolution and became convinced of the necessity for revolution in his own country. With the assistance of Russian revolutionists in Urga, he started a semicommunist movement and held several meetings.

These two leaders first met in the fall of 1919. They agreed to unite their groups and immediately initiated propaganda among the *arat* against the Chinese warlords and their collaborators, the Mongol feudal lords. When General Chu Shu-chêng, Chinese commandant in Urga, was ordered to dissolve the autonomous government, he imposed a heavy tax on the *arat* to support his army in Outer Mongolia. In June 1920 Suhe Bator proposed a unified revolutionary organization with the support of Choibalsan, and each led a separate delegation to Russia to seek assistance in restoring Mongolian autonomy under Bogdo Gegen. However, the White Russian army, led by Baron Ungern-Sternberg, had penetrated into Mongolia on the pretext of liberating it from the Chinese occupation, and in February 1921, after severe battles with the Chinese occupation force, Ungern-Sternberg set up his own puppet government in Urga. At this point Sukhe-Bator and Choibalsan, who were in Irkutsk, sent their missions to Moscow to confer with Lenin and Stalin on the organization of a Mongolian People's Party (Mongol Ardyn Nam, MAN) and a united front of the *arat* and princes against the White Russian and Chinese armies.

HISTORY

On March 1-3, 1921, the Mongolian party held its first congress in Kiakhta, a town on the Russian side of the Russian-Mongolian border. Twenty-six delegates, including members of the *arat* class and a small number of lamas and officials, attended, under the chairmanship of Suhe Bator. The congress called for a party statute and a military organization, clearly establishing the new party as a communist-oriented guerrilla type of organization, and adopted guidelines for the liberation of Mongolia from foreign intervention.

On March 19, 1921, the Mongolian communists set up a provisional government in Maimaicheng (now Altan Burak) and appealed to the nationalistic feudal princes to join the liberation movement. In collaboration with the Soviet army, a cavalry brigade and several independent battalions organized by Suhe Bator finally liberated Urga from Ungern-Sternberg on July 6, and on July 10 they officially proclaimed the formation of a people's revolutionary government. Suhe Bator was appointed war minister and Choibalsan vice war minister. The government itself was a kind of constitutional monarchy; Bogdo Gegen was retained as head of state, with some restrictions, and the government asked for cooperation from some lamas and princes during the transition period, because it considered the organization of a national front against foreign intervention necessary.

After the death of Bogdo Gegen in 1924, the third party congress of August 1924 adopted a resolution for the formation of a people's republic and changed the party's name to the Mongolian People's Revolutionary Party (Mongol Ardyn Khuvagalt Nam, MAKN). The congress also set the goal of a Mongolian revolution based directly on the *arat* and middle classes, and further strengthening of ties with the Soviet Union was emphasized. The next year the fourth party congress resolved that with the assistance of the proletariat in advanced countries Mongolia was to be transformed to the Soviet system without passing through capitalistic development; it would then achieve communism through certain stages of development.

In actuality, the "remaining vestiges" of feudalism and theocracy had not been liquidated completely. Princes, lamas, and the general public resisted this radical policy, and right-wing spokesmen such as Danzan gradually rose in the party, advocating pan-Mongolism and coexistence with the lama system. At the seventh party congress in 1928 the antagonism between these groups was brought to a head, and the left wing gained control of the party. After the eighth congress in early 1930 the party adopted the drastic policy of confiscation of the livestock of princes, lamas, and rich nomads; the collectivization of the nomads; the development of antireligious campaigns and forced secularization of lower-class lamas; and a ban on private commerce.

This line of "war communism," which was simply an imitation of agricultural collectivization in the Soviet Union, disregarded the differences of developing stages between Russia and Outer Mongolia. Princes and lamas protested confiscation of their livestock; forcibly collectivized nomads sabotaged the program and killed their livestock; the antireligious campaigns drove many Mongols to the side of the lamas. During the ensuing revolts many people took refuge in China and Manchuria. In June 1932 the party's central committee and central control committee were forced to retract their policy. Extreme radicals such as Chija and Budalho were expelled, and a softer line was adopted to provide for a gradual noncapitalistic transformation of the country. The ninth party congress of 1934 confirmed the new policy, and the nation's economy began to recover.

After the Japanese penetration into Manchuria in 1931 a nationalist group in Mongolia, led by Premier Gendan and War Minister Demid, had organized an antirevolutionary movement which intended to collaborate with Japan in liquidating Soviet influence. Between 1937 and 1939 these leaders and their followers were executed, and the communists established a complete dictatorship under Choibalsan, with further ties with the Soviet Union. "Feudal" elements were purged from the party membership and gradually the party became filled with members from the "proletariat"—*arat* who had given up their nomadic life for industrial occupations.

The eleventh party congress in 1949 adopted a new statute which proclaimed that Outer Mongolia had already entered the socialist stage, specified that the party was to be guided by Marxism-Leninism, and resolved that it was to maintain relations with the Cominform.

The death of Choibalsan, the "Stalin of Mongolia," in January 1952 was immediately followed by a power struggle between Tsedenbal, premier of the republic, and Damba, party first secretary. In March 1959 Damba was purged from the party. After the twenty-second congress of the Communist Party of the Soviet Union in 1961, when the waves of de-Stalinization reached Outer Mongolia, Choibalsan became the scapegoat. His name was removed from all public buildings except those in the city of Choibalsan.

## ORGANIZATION AND MEMBERSHIP

The party congress, the supreme party organ, is supposed to be held every three years, with delegates elected by cells, party committees in local organizations, and the armed forces. Members of the central committee also participate in the congresses. The central committee and central control committee are elected by the congress. The central committee elects a politbureau and a secretariat. To coordinate activities at the lower levels small assemblies are called every eighteen months by the party committees.

Social composition of the party membership is about 25 percent factory workers, 42 percent intellectuals and 33 percent *arat*. The total membership in 1965 was given as 48,000, including candidates.

## RELATION TO SOVIET LEADERSHIP

Outer Mongolia is geographically a buffer state between the Soviet Union and China. Politically, however, the country has been a satellite of the Soviet Union since the founding of the Mongolian People's Republic. Without Soviet assistance and protection, Outer Mongolia could not have survived as a sovereign country.

After Choibalsan's death in 1952 a rather intimate politicoeconomic relationship developed between Outer Mongolia and Communist China, and in May 1960 the two countries signed a treaty of friendship and mutual assistance. When the Sino-Soviet dispute was intensified, Outer Mongolia at first remained neutral. However, on the Albania issue in 1961 it took a stand in favor of the Soviet Union, and since then it has not changed position. The Mongolian party has always sent a delegate to the world communist party meetings in Moscow, and Mongolia participates in the Comecon as an observer.

## PARTY PRESS ORGANS AND RECORDS

The Mongolian party publishes the daily *Unen* (Truth) and the monthly *Namyn Amdral* (Party Life).

Party statutes are published in *Mongol Ardyn Khuvagalt Namyn Program ba Durem* (Statutes of the Mongolian People's Revolutionary Party), Ulan Bator, 1957. Congress reports appear in *Sezd Mongolskoi narodno-revoliutsionnoi partii* (Congress of the Mongolian People's Revolutionary Party), published in Russian in Ulan Bator.

## PARTY CONGRESSES

All congresses except the first, which was held in Kiakhta, have met in Ulan Bator.

1st congress, MAN, March 1-3, 1921
2d congress, MAN, July 18-August 18, 1923

3d congress, MAN, August 4-24, 1924
4th congress, MAKN, September 23-October 2, 1925
5th congress, MAKN, September 26-October 4, 1926
6th congress, MAKN, September 22-October 4, 1927
7th congress, MAKN, October 23-December 10, 1928
8th congress, MAKN, February 21-April 3, 1930
9th congress, MAKN, September 28-October 5, 1934
10th congress, MAKN, March 20-April 5, 1940
11th congress, MAKN, December 7-23, 1947
12th congress, MAKN, November 19-24, 1954
13th congress, MAKN, March 17-22, 1958
14th congress, MAKN, July 3-7, 1961

BIBLIOGRAPHY

Akademiia Nauk SSSR, Institut Narodov Azii: *Mongolskaia Narodnaia Respublika 1921-1961*, (The Mongolian People's Republic, 1921-1961), Moscow, Izd. vostochnoi lit., 1961.
Friters, G. M.: *Outer Mongolia and Its International Position*, Baltimore, Johns Hopkins Press, 1949.
Lattimore, Owen: *Nomads and Commissars*, New York, Oxford University Press, 1962.
Rupen, Robert A.: *The Mongolian People's Republic*, Stanford, Calif., Hoover Institution, 1965.
Rupen, Robert A.: *Mongols of the Twentieth Century*, Bloomington, Ind., Indiana University Press, 1962.
Tsedenbal, Iu.: *Izbrannye stati i rechi* (Collected Essays and Speeches), Moscow, Gos. izdat. polit. lit., 1962.
Vasilev, V. L.: *Sorok let narodnoi revoliutsii v Mongolii* (Forty Years of the People's Revolution in Mongolia), Moscow, Znanie, 1961.

TAMOTSU TAKASE

# PAKISTAN

Soon after the creation of the independent states of India and Pakistan in 1947 the communist movement in this area proceeded with the same sort of reorganization. Separation was accomplished first on the trade-union level; in January 1948 a Trade Union Federation of Pakistan was founded, with its seat in Lahore, and immediately declared its affiliation with the communist-dominated World Federation of Trade Unions. In February a Conference of the Youth and Students of South East Asia Fighting for Freedom and Independence was held in Calcutta on the initiative of the World Federation of Democratic Youth and the International Union of Students. This conference, attended by the student and youth delegations of India and Pakistan, as well as representatives of the workers' and peasants' groups was intended to align the communist movement in this region with the new policy decreed for world communism. The resolution passed by the conference denounced the "fictional independence" of India and Pakistan and called for revolutionary struggle.

Immediately after the close of the youth conference the second congress of the Communist Party of India met. In March 1948 the Communist Party of Pakistan (CPP) held its founding congress and elected a central committee; Sajjad Sahher became general secretary.

## HISTORY

The Pakistani party was burdened from the outset with the same obligation as the other parties throughout Southeast Asia. Violent insurgent action was the order of the day, and communists in India, Burma, Indonesia, Malaysia, and elsewhere were trying to transform this theory into action in 1948. The communists in Pakistan followed suit. The attempt was concentrated in East Pakistan, where geographic and political conditions, especially the possibility of contact with the Indian and Burmese communists, led the weak communist cadres to believe that such action stood a chance of success.

The plan was to arouse the peasantry against the landowners and then transform the peasants' movement into a communist-led insurrection similar to those in Burma and Malaysia. This movement had started with expropriation of the large land holdings, and in 1950 it took the form of an armed insurrection in the district of Mymensingh. The local governments of numerous villages were suppressed and "popular governments" were installed. When the Pakistani army intervened and quelled the insurrection, several communist leaders fled to the Garo Hills of India.

The communist leaders did not yet believe themselves totally defeated, nor did they yet consider the tactic of violence to be ineffective; they continued the same policy through 1950 and 1951. In March 1951 the government of Pakistan announced discovery of a plot hatched by communist leaders and a small group of officers, which came to be known as the "Rawalpindi plot." Police action resulted in the arrest of several superior officers, as well as the arrest of Sajjad Sahher a month later. Feros Din Mansour assumed the functions of general secretary, and in June the party announced a draft program advocating a "popular-democratic revolution" as the next step for Pakistan.

The failure of violence obliged the communists to consider other tactics, such as political action, both legal and illegal. The objective of a popular-democratic revolution was modified to the creation of a broad national front directed against the "imperialists and their lackeys." In contrast to the insurgent activity in East Pakistan, the communists in West Pakistan concentrated on legal activity. In the labor field they scored some success with the workers of Lahore and the dockers of Karachi. The Partisans of Peace also made its appearance and in May 1952 held its second national conference in Lahore. This movement was active in all the international propaganda activities of this period—the Stockholm peace appeal, the five-power pact, and various groups opposing the atomic bomb, alleged bacteriological warfare in Korea, etc.

The Pakistani party also attemtped to organize an underground apparatus, but the authorities reacted with increasing firmness. When disturbances broke out in Karachi in January 1953, the government placed the blame on the communists and proceeded to arrest party members. That same month a special tribunal convicted fourteen defendants, including Akhbar Khan, of trying to overthrow the government in alliance with the communists and of trying to set up a "progressive" regime in the country.

The showdown between the government and the communists finally came around 1954. In the elections for the legislative assembly of East Pakistan, the Muslim League, in power for seven years, won only ten seats out of 309, while the opposition United Front, supported by the communists, won 223 seats. The Cominform enthusiastically proclaimed that "the Constituent Assembly elections in East Pakistan ... demonstrated that the popular masses resolutely reject the policy of intrigue with the U.S. aggressors and do not want to become cannon fodder for the sake of the profits of U.S. imperialists."[1] Pakistani authorities reacted by outlawing the party. This measure was taken first in East Pakistan, when Governor General Iskander Mirza published a special communiqué on July 6, 1954, announcing the outlawing of the CPP following police operations during which more than 1,000 party members and sympathizers had been arrested. The ban was then extended to the entire country, and even the trade unions under communist influence were affected by the legislation.

In ensuing years the communists sought legal outlets under various guises, such as the strongly leftist National Awami Party, founded in July 1957 by Maulana Bhashani. However, the military coup of 1958 interrupted this activity for a time; the government of Ayub Khan also arrested Bhashani, and his party did not participate in elections until 1965, in alliance with other opposition parties.

The communists continued their attempts to combine clandestine and legal activities and to find new legal outlets. However, they encountered opposition from the authorities in both areas. Hasan Nasir, one of the prominent party leaders, was arrested several times for communist activities and released after a time in prison. He was arrested again in August 1960 and transferred from the prison in Karachi to the Lahore fortress, where he died on November 13. According to the police version, he committed suicide; the communists claimed that he was tortured to death.[2] The national-front tactic was more effective, and the formation of a National Democratic Front with Hussein Suhrawardy, former prime minister and leader of the Awami party, was hailed by the communists: "The establishment of the National Democratic Front, which unites all the opposition groups, all the former political leaders removed by Ayubkhan [sic] from leading positions in political life, shows that the social base of the present rulers has become narrower and their positions weaker."[3]

Meanwhile, the communists also concentrated on building up their own political strength, particularly among workers and students. Among both these groups they were more successful in East Pakistan than in West Pakistan. Communist students were very active at Dacca University; intermittent strikes were provoked, and in 1962 communists even managed to organize mass demonstrations in the large cities of East Pakistan.

## RELATION TO SOVIET LEADERSHIP

The CPP has been conspicuous by its absence from all the important international communist meetings. It has never been discussed in the official organ of the Cominform or in the Prague review *Problèmes de la paix et du socialisme*. There was no Pakistani delegation at the 1957 world conference of communist parties, attended by both Nikita Khrushchev and Mao Tse-tung, or at the subsequent conference in November 1960.

## BIBLIOGRAPHY

Callard, Keith: *Pakistan: A Political Study*, New York, Macmillan, 1957.
Callard, Keith, and Richard S. Wheeler: "Pakistan," in George McTurnan Kahin (ed.), *Major Governments of Asia*, 2d ed., Ithaca, N.Y., Cornell University Press, 1963, pp. 419-532.
Gankovsky, Yurii V., and Liudmila R. Gordon-Polonskaya: *A History of Pakistan*, Moscow, Nauka, 1964.

BRANKO LAZITCH

1. *For a Lasting Peace, for a People's Democracy*, April 16, 1954, p. 4.

2. *World Marxist Review*, December 1961, pp. 100-101.

3. *La Nouvelle revue internationale*, July 1963, p. 158.

# PANAMA

The communist movement in Panama began with the creation of the leftist Laborite Party (Partido Laborista) about 1926. This small party provided a vehicle for the few Panamanian communists until, on instructions from Moscow, they broke away to form the Communist Party of Panama (Partido Comunista del Panamá, PCP) in 1930. Among the early communist leaders were Eliseo Echévez and Cristóbal Segundo. The latter was the party's candidate for presidency of the republic in 1947.

## HISTORY

The communists enjoyed full legality and freedom of operation in Panama until 1953. For a time during and after World War II they gained a strong position in the organized labor movement, but they were unable to compete effectively against the socialists and demagogic politicians of various personalist parties or to attract enough votes to elect any candidates to public office. In a vain attempt to increase its popular appeal, the party adopted its present name, Party of the People (Partido del Pueblo, PP), in 1944.

Proscription of the party in 1953 reduced its already limited appeal to employees of the government and of the Canal Zone. Thereafter its following was restricted chiefly to students and working-class employees of private concerns. The communists were not even able to take an active part in the Cuban-based attack on the country in 1959. In 1964 they demonstrated a brief ability to exert influence out of proportion to their numbers by cooperating with ultranationalists and other extremists during the anti-United States rioting. However, they were unable to sustain public interest or promote significant violence once the crisis had passed. In 1965 the party retained a strong position only among a few vociferous university student groups.

## ORGANIZATION AND MEMBERSHIP

The Panamanian party has never been large; by 1963 membership had fallen to about 150 members. In 1964, in the wake of the anti-United States rioting in Panama City and the Canal Zone, the party grew to perhaps 500 members, but it quickly declined. United States sources estimated party membership in 1965 as about 300.[1] For a full discussion of party strength see *Latin America*.

## RELATION TO SOVIET LEADERSHIP

The Panamanian party did not affiliate with the Comintern until the 1930s. For a discussion of other aspects of relations with the international movement see *Latin America*.

The party has adopted a pro-Soviet position in the ideological dispute with Communist China, but one of the communist-influenced student groups, the Reform Unity Movement, has endorsed the Chinese views.

## PARTY PRESS ORGAN

The Panamanian party sporadically issues the clandestine newspaper *El Mazo*.

## PARTY CONGRESSES

1st congress, PCP, December 1943, Panama City.
2d congress, PP, 1948, Panama City
3d congress, PP, March-April 1951, Panama City

Since it was outlawed in 1953 the party appears to have employed plenary and expanded sessions of the central committee, held in secrecy, at approximately one-year intervals, as a substitute for the national congress.

BIBLIOGRAPHY

See *Latin America*, refs. 1, 2, 6, 13, 24.

ROLLIE E. POPPINO

1. U.S. Department of State, Bureau of Intelligence and Research, *World Strength of the Communist Party Organizations*, Eighteenth Annual Report, Washington, January 1966, p. 163.

# PARAGUAY

The Paraguayan Communist Party (Partido Comunista Paraguayo, PCP) was founded in 1928 by a small group of self-styled Marxist intellectuals and former anarchists from the labor movement in Asunción. Obdulio Barthe and Oscar Creydt, still active in 1965, were among the early leaders of the new party.

## HISTORY

The Paraguayan party has never enjoyed complete freedom of operation and has not been able to exert significant influence in national affairs. It has been formally proscribed since 1936. Since before the founding of the party the country has been ruled by a series of rigorously anticommunist dictatorships; hence the communists have been allowed to work freely only during the brief interludes between regimes. Their high point occurred during the mid-1940s, when the party had some 8,000 members and a strong position in the national labor confederation. With the imposition of a new authoritarian government, however, the party was again repressed, and its leaders were imprisoned or sent into exile. The effective strength of the party has steadily declined since that period, although the continual deportation of communists who were recruited, trained, and raised to positions of importance within the clandestine party has resulted in the buildup of a largely inactive but substantial communist reserve in Uruguay and Argentina, ready to resume operations in Paraguay when the political situation permits.

The exile party sought to launch a Cuban-style guerrilla "war of national liberation" in late 1959 and early 1960, but it was quickly routed by the Paraguayan army. This defeat appears to have contributed to a factionalism that resulted in at least two open splits in the party in the 1960s. In mid-1963 a pro-Chinese minority broke away to form the Paraguayan Leninist Communist Party (Partido Comunista Leninista Paraguayo, PCLP). In 1965 a faction under the leadership of Obdulio Barthe called for the ouster of the party's secretary general, Oscar Creydt, on grounds of inactivity and personalism and styled itself a commission for reorganization of the party.

## ORGANIZATION AND MEMBERSHIP

United States sources estimated that in 1965 there were about 500 communists within Paraguay and perhaps 4,500 in exile, chiefly in Argentina and Uruguay.[1] For a full discussion see *Latin America*.

### RELATION TO SOVIET LEADERSHIP

For a discussion of the Paraguayan communists' role in the international communist movement see *Latin America*.

The PCP is pro-Soviet and the PCLP has taken a pro-Chinese stand in the Sino-Soviet dispute. Both parties, however, advocate the use of violence as the proper road to socialism in Paraguay.

### PARTY PRESS ORGANS

The PCP issues an irregular clandestine newspaper, *Unidad paraguaya*. During the 1960s it also published a journal, *Adelante*, more or less monthly.

### CONGRESSES OF THE PCP

Only two congresses had been held by 1965, the first in June 1941 and the second in 1949. The summons for a third congress was issued in 1955, but a decade later it had not yet met. In these circumstances, according to the Barthe group, the party had been without a statute since at least 1955.

### BIBLIOGRAPHY

See *Latin America*, refs. 1, 3, 6, 13, 24.

ROLLIE E. POPPINO

1. U.S. Department of State, Bureau of Intelligence and Research, *World Strength of the Communist Party Organizations*, Eighteenth Annual Report, Washington, January 1966, p. 176.

# THE PEASANTS' INTERNATIONAL
*See* The International Peasants' Council

# PERU

The impact of the Russian revolution and the rise of the Comintern produced two irreconcilable political organizations in the community of young intellectuals in Peru. The first of these was the American Popular Revolutionary Alliance (Alianza Popular Revolucionaria Americana, APRA), founded in Mexico by the Peruvian Victor Raúl Haya de la Torre in 1924. The second was the Peruvian Communist Party (Partido Comunista Peruano, PCP). At the outset nearly all the self-styled Marxist revolutionaries in Peru were drawn to the APRA, but in 1928, when it became apparent that Haya de la Torre was determined to follow his own ideological path, a small group broke away to form the Peruvian Socialist Party (Partido Socialista Peruano, PSP).

Outstanding among the leaders of the PSP was José Carlos Mariátegui, perhaps the only original Marxist theoretician of Latin America. In a series of brilliant essays Mariátegui held that the teachings of Marx should be adapted to the unique politicocultural reality of Peru and other predominantly Indian countries of Latin America. The PSP was represented at the Latin American communist congresses in Montevideo and Buenos Aires in 1929, where this thesis was denounced. Mariátegui died in May 1930, before accepting or rejecting Lenin's Twenty-one Conditions for Admission to the Comintern. Later that year several of his disciples, including Eudocio Ravines and Julio Portocarrero, converted the PSP into the Peruvian Communist Party, which was accepted as a member of the Comintern. In the 1940s Ravines and Portocarrero were expelled from the party.

## HISTORY

The PCP has never realized its potential as one of the stronger communist organizations in Latin America. Although it has been technically illegal since 1933, the PCP has enjoyed considerable *de facto* freedom of operation at various times, because it was usually regarded by the ruling groups as less dangerous than Haya de la Torre's large, militantly anticommunist APRA, which advocated sweeping social reform. Under these circumstances the communists were allowed to develop a strong following among university students and industrial workers in Lima and in the southern half of the country. During World War II and the immediate postwar "era of good feeling" the party attained a membership of about 30,000 and control of much of the organized labor movement. Even during the authoritarian Odría regime of 1948 to 1956, while the communist party as such was being suppressed, a communist labor leader, Juan P. Luna, was elected to the senate, and several of his associates served in the chamber of deputies. Nonetheless, the repression of the party after 1948, and the emergence of numerous rival extremist organizations after 1959, caused a gradual but uninterrupted decline in active membership.

A persistent weakness of the communist movement in Peru is factionalism, both within the party and within the Peruvian left as a whole. The impact of the Cuban revolution exacerbated this weakness. The heightened urgency for social change contributed in 1963 to the election of President Belaúnde Terry, whom the communists supported and sought to influence; however, it also split the left into various factions divided over personalities and tactics. Among the more vociferous of these was the Castroist Movement of the Revolutionary Left (Movimiento de la Izquierda Revolucionaria), which tried to launch a guerrilla movement in 1965, provoking the regime to restrict the activities of all left-wing groups, including the communists.

The Sino-Soviet dispute had even more deleterious effects within the PCP, splitting the central committee wide open. Raúl Acosta Sálas, the party's secretary general, and Jorge del Prado, former secretary general, supported the Soviet view, while José Sotomayor Perez and Saturnino Paredes Macedo of the central committee endorsed the Chinese position. In January 1964 the latter group "expelled" the pro-Soviet faction and set itself up as the authentic Peruvian Communist Party. Thus in 1965 there were two communist parties of the same name, each claiming to speak for all Peruvian communists, and each neutralizing the other's efforts.

## ORGANIZATION AND MEMBERSHIP

United States sources estimated the membership of the Peruvian communist parties in 1965 as about 5,000, with about 25,000 sympathizers.[1] For a full discussion of party strength see *Latin America*.

## RELATION TO SOVIET LEADERSHIP

For a discussion of the relationship of the Peruvian party and of Eudocio Ravines to the Moscow-directed international movement see *Latin America*.

## PARTY PRESS ORGAN

The PCP newspaper *Unidad* appears at frequent but irregular intervals.

## CONGRESSES AND CONFERENCES OF THE PCP

1st congress, 1942
2d congress, May 1946
3d congress, August 1948
2d conference, February 1956
3d conference, 1960
4th congress, August-September 1962
4th conference, August 1964

The first national conference was probably held before 1946.

## BIBLIOGRAPHY

Mariátegui, José Carlos: *Siete ensayos de interpretación de la realidad peruana*, 2d ed., Lima, 1943.

Partido Comunista Peruano: *Que es el Partido comunista peruano y que se propone*, Lima, Comisión Nacional de Educación del Partido Comunista Peruano, 1961.

See also *Latin America*, refs. 1, 2, 6, 13, 15, 24.

ROLLIE E. POPPINO

1. U.S. Department of State, Bureau of Intelligence and Research, *World Strength of the Communist Party Organizations*, Eighteenth Annual Report, Washington, January 1966, p. 178.

# THE PHILIPPINES

The communist movement in the Philippines originated in the strong peasant and trade-union movements which appeared shortly after World War I. Jacinto Manahan, allegedly one of the earliest Filipino communists, organized the Union of Filipino Tenants in 1919. This organization soon expanded to include agricultural laborers in its membership, and in 1924 it assumed the name National Union of Peasants in the Philippines. It quickly became the basis for continuing communist activity among the peasantry, especially in the central provinces of Bulacan and Neuva Ecija. In 1942 the Union of Peasants was absorbed into the Hukbalahap resistance movement.

With the notable exception of Manahan, the early communist organizers were urban-oriented intellectuals and labor leaders, assisted and encouraged in their efforts by representatives of other communist parties. In 1924, at the invitation of William Janequette of the United States, a delegation of Filipino labor leaders attended the Comintern-sponsored Conference of the Transport Workers of the Pacific, held in Canton (China). The five-man delegation was led by Domingo Ponce, who returned to Manila and founded a small "secretariat" under the direction of the Comintern. Janequette remained in Manila to render assistance.

Tan Malaka, the Indonesian Comintern agent, was in Manila from 1925 to 1927 and became quite popular with many Filipino political, labor, and academic leaders. Among his associates was Crisanto Evangelista, a fiery labor leader who became a key figure in founding the communist party. Evangelista was president of the printers' union, active in the leadership of the Congress of Filipino Workers, and well known in radical circles. When the Congress of Filipino Workers held its first convention in 1928, Evangelista and his supporters persuaded that organization to affiliate with the Red International of Labor Unions and establish its own political party, the Workers' Party (Partido Obrero). After setting up the party under his own leadership,

Evangelista and another Filipino communist, Cirilio Bognot, left for Moscow, where they were joined by Manahan, who was there at the invitation of the Peasants' International. All three attended the sixth Comintern congress in 1928.

On his return to Manila Evangelista delivered a series of controversial public lectures at the University of the Philippines. His radical views alarmed government officials and triggered a strong negative reaction in the press. He also came under attack by his more conservative colleagues in the Congress of Filipino Workers. When Evangelista and his supporters failed to gain control of this organization, they seceded from it to create their own, the Congress of the Sons of Sweat of the Philippines. The new group was founded on May 5, 1930, and at its first convention, on August 26, the assembled delegates moved to become the Communist Party of the Philippines (Partido Komunista ñg Pilipinas, PKP). A committee was formed to write a statute, a political bureau and a central committee were elected, and a party organ, *Titis* (Spark), was founded. The creation of the PKP was announced on November 7, 1930, in the Plaza Moriones, Manila.

## HISTORY

Two years after the PKP was founded, following violent peasant riots in which the Philippine communists were involved, the supreme court declared it illegal, and many of the party leaders were imprisoned. United States communists were active in their behalf, and one of them, James Allen, was influential in persuading President Manuel Quezon to pardon the prisoners and allow the party legal status in 1938. This protection and guidance by the United States party was, in fact, in accordance with a Comintern directive of 1923 and was maintained until the eve of the Japanese attack on Manila.

When the PKP reappeared in the open in 1938, it merged with the recently created Socialist Party of the Philippines (Partido Socialista ñg Pilipinas) and the Chinese Bureau, a branch of the Communist Party of China. The united party kept the name Partido Komunista ñg Pilipinas, but abandoned its former policies of violence. In line with the Comintern's popular-front tactics, the PKP now established antifascist front organizations and attempted to effect an anti-Japanese economic boycott.

In anticipation of Japanese invasion and occupation, by October 1941 the communists had begun organizing a guerrilla resistance movement. In March 1942 they established the People's Anti-Japanese Army (Hukbong Bayan Labon sa Hapon, Hukbalahap), whose members became known as Huks. Edgar Snow's *Red Star over China* and a military treatise by Chu Teh apparently provided early guidelines for organization and training, and later a colonel from the Chinese communist Eighth Route Army served as instructor in tactics and as advisor.

During the Japanese occupation of the Philippines the Hukbalahap rendered signal service as a resistance organization. In the central provinces of Luzon it was successful in mobilizing the peasantry and establishing political and administrative hegemony. After the defeat of Japan it continued to exercise control in these areas through provincial and town officials appointed without the sanction of the central government. In the immediate postwar years the Hukbalahap attempted to create a political organization and elect its own candidates to local and national office. To this end it founded a National Peasants' Union and a new labor federation, the Congress of Labor Organization. The Hukbalahap also adopted the name People's Liberation Army (Hukbong Mapagpalaya ñg Bayan) and refused government offers to negotiate the surrender of its arms. As a consequence, President Manuel Roxas in 1948 issued an executive order outlawing both the National Peasants' Union and the People's Liberation Army. Efforts by President Quirino to reconcile these organizations with the government also failed.

In 1946 the PKP had founded the Democratic Alliance as a front to enable its candidates to participate in the national election. Six communist candidates were successful in the election, but they were barred from taking office on charges of fraud and corruption. The party immediately undertook intensive insurgent activity against the central government, although there was evidence of intense rivalry in the party leadership and bitter struggles over party policies.

In January 1950 the PKP political bureau declared that a revolutionary situation existed in the Philippines and made plans to seize power from the government by May 1952. In the interim the territorial base of the People's Liberation Army was to be expanded through guerilla warfare, mass support was to be rallied through the labor organizations, and the political order was to be weakened through infiltration of the central government. When these conditions had been fulfilled a general uprising was to be launched to seize control of the government. In October 1950, however, the secretary of defense, Ramon Magsaysay, conducted raids on party headquarters in Manila and the residences of the leading political bureau members and seized documents disclosing the PKP's plans. Magsaysay embarked on a strong campaign against the insurgents, and by combined tactics of clemency and force of arms, he scored a resounding success. Party membership declined, recruitment dropped, and many party leaders were killed, captured, or surrendered. By 1952, the year the PKP had planned to triumph, communist strength had dwindled by 60 percent. In 1957 an antisubversion law was passed, and the PKP, with its allied organizations, was outlawed for the third time.

These reverses did not serve to change the communist goal of overthrowing the Philippine government. There is evidence that by 1965 the communists were involved in regrouping and reestablishing their influence. Particularly in central Luzon, they had undertaken intensive recruitment of cadres for subversive activities and had taken advantage of local chaotic and depressed conditions to step up their terrorist activities.

## ORGANIZATION AND MEMBERSHIP

The organizational structure of the PKP has undergone many changes since its creation. According to recent information,[1] the party is organized on four levels—national, provincial, city or district, and cell. Theoretically, the national congress is the highest authority and is composed of elected delegates from the lower levels of the party hierarchy on the basis of uniform representation. When the national congress is not in session, the central committee assumes its powers. Real power, however, resides in a three-man secretariat, which has replaced the political bureau.

A number of subordinate organizations report to the secretariat. The members of an advisory group, in charge of party activities in peasant, labor, youth, and student organizations, are responsible for coordinating the united front of the party in their respective areas. The secretariat cadre is charged with transmitting secretariat directives to various subordinate groups. The political intelligence bureau, the PKP's espionage branch, provides the secretariat with information about the "enemy" and about party members.

The People's Liberation Army, the insurgent arm of the party, is also directed by the secretariat. Membership is usually divided into regular, combat-support, or service-support units. Regulars are full-time armed members of the party. Combat-support members, also armed, may be farmers during the daylight hours and insurgents at night. Service-support members are charged with organizing new recruits. Widely distributed throughout the *barrios* of central Luzon, these members are also responsible for raising money and for courier duty.

## RELATION TO SOVIET LEADERSHIP

In the period prior to World War II Philippine communists participated in Comintern-sponsored labor organizations and conferences outside the Philippines. Both of the party's mass organizations, the National Union of Peasants and the Congress of the Sons of Sweat, were affiliated with the Comintern through the Profintern and Peasants' International. The first public declarations of party officials proclaimed the PKP a branch of the Comintern, with identical aims and ideals. On occasion party officials journeyed to the Soviet Union.

During World War II communications with Western communist parties and organizations were disrupted, and their influence waned. However, Chinese influence and prestige increased. The Hukbalahap gradually assumed the organizational structure and tactics of the Chinese People's Liberation Army, and in 1946 it assumed the name People's Liberation Army. Nevertheless, the PKP's relationship to foreign communist parties was obscure and has remained so. Although Marxist theory appears to predominate among the remaining party leaders, there is little or no substantial evidence of cooperation with or support from either the People's Republic of China or the Soviet Union.

BIBLIOGRAPHY

Brimmell, J. H.: *Communism in Southeast Asia: A Political Analysis*, London, Oxford University Press, 1959.
Lava, José: *Milestones in the History of the CPP,* Manila [1950].
McLane, Charles B.: *Soviet Strategies in Southeast Asia: An Exploration of Eastern Policy under Lenin and Stalin*, Princeton, N.J., Princeton University Press, 1966.
Scaff, Alvin H.: *The Philippine Answer to Communism*, Stanford, Calif., Stanford University Press, 1955.
Taruc, Luis: *Born of the People*, New York, International Publishers, 1953.

CLAUDE A. BUSS

1. *The Challenge of Central Luzon*, report of the Committee on National Defense and Security, submitted at the Second Regular Session, Sixth Congress of the Philippines, May 1967.

# POLAND

From its first organized efforts in the 1830s Polish socialism contained an element of protest against the political suppression and economic exploitation of the Poles by the three partition powers, Prussia, Russia, and Austria. The nationalist sentiments generated at this stage among Polish workers and peasants culminated nearly a century later in their support for an independent Polish state and their opposition to the bolshevik concept of internationalism.

The communist movement in Poland had its origin in two socialist organizations, the Polish Socialist Party (Polska Partja Socjalistyczna, PPS), founded in Paris in November 1892 at a convention of representatives of socialist organizations in Poland, and the Social Democracy of the Kingdom of Poland (Socjal-Demokracja Królestwa Polskiego, SDKP), founded in the spring of 1893 by a dissident group from the Paris convention. The program of the PPS was a blend of Marxist doctrine and nationalist aspirations, with the goal of an independent Polish socialist state. The SDKP, under the leadership of Julian Marchlewski, Rosa Luxemburg, and Adolf

Warski (Warszawski), based its program on the Marxist slogan that "workers have no country" and opposed the demands for an independent Poland. Furthermore, the PPS aimed at spreading its activities throughout all three partition areas of Poland and refused to be tied to the Russian social-democratic organization. This policy was strongly opposed by Rosa Luxemburg and the SDKP on the premise that any unification of the Polish workers in the three areas would remove them from the working-class movements in Germany, Russia, and Austria, and thus weaken the revolutionary stimulus in these countries. This theory by definition excluded Polish independence. The PPS claimed that the SDKP's acceptance of the partitions was not only betrayal of the Polish cause, but was also contrary to Marx's demand that Poland be reconstructed as an independent state. The SDKP, in turn, accused the PPS of "social patriotism" and nationalism.

The PPS remained faithful to its program and refused to enter into any permanent relationship with the Russian social democrats. It did cooperate with them in the struggle against Russian autocracy, but a group of PPS members who objected to the terrorist activities of the PPS fighting squads, under the leadership of Józef Piłsudski, proclaimed itself a separate party in 1906, the PPS-Left (PPS-Lewica, PPS-L). In the meantime, a workers' party in Vilna, led by Feliks Dzierzyński, had joined the SDKP, and in 1900 the party had renamed itself the Social Democracy of the Kingdom of Poland and Lithuania (Socjal-Demokracja Królestwa Polskiego i Litwy, SDKPL). The SDKPL became affiliated with the Russian party in 1906 and was involved in the bolshevik-menshevik struggle.

In 1915 Russian authorities, retreating before the advancing German and Austrian armies, evacuated about 2 million workers and peasants from Poland into Russia. These evacuees included numerous members of the PPS, SDKPL, and PPS-L. After the overthrow of the czarist regime in March 1917, these party members revived their organizations and developed extensive political propaganda among the evacuees and refugees. The SDKPL and the PPS-L openly sympathized with the Russian bolsheviks, and when the Provisional Government of Russia was in turn overthrown by the bolsheviks in November 1917, their close cooperation became formalized. Both parties played leading roles in the Polish commissariat, created as part of Stalin's Commissariat of Nationality Affairs, and both were ordered to prepare a bolshevik revolution in Poland.

The military collapse of Germany and Austria-Hungary opened the way for the restoration of an independent Polish state, to comprise the former partition areas held by Russia, Germany, and Austria. On November 14, 1918, representatives of the PPS joined a coalition government with centrist and leftist peasant parties. The new government announced a program of broad social reform, promised land to the peasants, and called for elections to a constituent assembly. The SDKPL and PPS-L, hoping to obtain armed support from Soviet Russia, ignored the resurrected Polish state and refused to participate in the left-centrist coalition. Both parties announced they would continue to struggle for a "social revolution" in Poland which would introduce a Soviet-style dictatorship of the proletariat and would place the country under Moscow's control as a federated soviet republic. During these turbulent days sporadic workers' councils (*rady robotnicze*) sprang up in industrial centers and some villages. The SDKPL and PPS-L played a considerable part in establishing these councils, but a large number of them arose on local initiative, under the leadership of leftist peasant and socialist elements.

The enthusiasm with which the Poles greeted the rebirth of an independent Polish state placed the SDKPL and PPS-L (with a combined active membership of about 5,000) in a precarious position. In this political atmosphere, an earlier plan for the unification of the SDKPL and PPS-L matured. On December 16, 1918, after prolonged negotiations, this fusion was accomplished, and the creation of a Communist Workers' Party of Poland (Komunistyczna Partja Robotnicza Polski, KPRP) was announced.

## HISTORY

*1918 to 1938*  In the program adopted at the unification congress the new KPRP asserted its belief in the forthcoming world revolution and rather nebulously outlined its immediate tasks as destruction of capitalism and its subservient institutions, introduction of the dictatorship of the "proletariat of towns and villages," and nationalization of industry, commerce, and land. The KPRP immediately embarked on a broad program of antigovernment propaganda and street demonstrations, which had only a small following and little success. In January 1919 the KPRP abstained from participation in elections to the constituent assembly. That same month the government decreed the registration of all social and political organizations with the local administrative authorities. Compliance with this decree would have allowed the KPRP to operate legally, but it would also have implied recognition of the Polish state. The party chose to place itself outside the law and went underground, where it remained until it was dissolved by the Comintern in 1938.

In February 1919, on the heels of the retreating Germans, the Soviet Red Army, with five weak Polish "red regiments" in its ranks, began its advance "toward the Vistula River and Warsaw."[1] The KPRP and some Jewish radical groups welcomed the "armed assistance of the Russian proletariat" and sabotaged Polish defense measures. On August 2, 1920, at the peak of the Red Army's advance into Poland, Soviet authorities in Bialystok created a provisional revolutionary committee for Poland, which was to prepare for the establishment of a Polish soviet republic, with the KPRP as the ruling party. The Red Army was defeated at the gates of Warsaw in mid-August and retreated from Poland. The Polish-Soviet peace treaty at Riga on March 18, 1921, put an end to Moscow's hopes that a sovietized Poland would form a bridge to revolutionary Germany. Lenin gave up his immediate design for world revolution and turned to the consolidation of Soviet power inside Russia. At the same time, he scolded the Polish communists for their "Luxemburgist error" of refusing to recognize the independent Polish state as an expression of the national self-determination which he and his party advocated.

The aftermath of the war offered the KPRP fertile ground for propaganda and recruitment. Splinter groups from Polish and Jewish workers' and peasants' parties joined the KPRP. Some defectors from the PPS gave the party a seat in the constituent assembly (Stanisław Łancucki) and a future leader (Jerzy Sochacki [Czeszejko]). Henryk Henrykowski (Saul Amsterdam), who came from a Jewish group, played a leading role in Polish communism until World War II and in communist-dominated Poland after 1945. In 1922 the KPRP participated in the parliamentary elections through a front, the Union of Urban and Rural Proletariats, receiving 130,000 votes and two seats out of 444.

The KPRP, at that time still isolated from the Polish proletariat, only reluctantly accepted the Comintern's united-front-from-below plan to detach the workers' masses from their social-democratic leaders. At the third party conference in April 1922 a newly elected leadership—Adolf Warski, Max Walecki (Horwitz), and Wera Kostrzewa (Maria Koszucka), all proponents of more moderate party tactics—adjusted the party's activities to the new line.

The second KPRP congress was held in Moscow in August 1923. With Lenin deathly ill, Zinoviev was directing the Comintern in close cooperation with Stalin. The struggle between Stalin and Trotsky for Lenin's mantle was not yet in the open, and the KPRP was loyally following Comintern instructions. Internal difficulties in Poland raised great hopes, and Comintern and Soviet support, especially lavish financial subsidies, strengthened the Polish party at a time when Moscow was preparing in great secrecy for a communist uprising in Germany.

The revolt in Hamburg in October 1923 was followed in early November by bloody riots in Cracow. For a short time it seemed that the revolutionary wave of 1918 could be revived in Poland and Germany, but in both cases the governments suppressed the rebellions. The communist-inspired Hamburg revolt resulted in a dispute between the Communist Party of Germany and the Comintern. The leaders of the KPRP sided with the German party and expressed concern that the controversy between Stalin and Trotsky might produce a split in the Soviet party; a reply from Moscow, signed by Stalin, rebuked them. A few Polish communists in Moscow, better informed on the situation than their comrades in Poland, attacked the KPRP leadership as opportunistic and unable to lead the party along revolutionary paths.

By the time of the fifth Comintern congress in June-July 1924 the Stalin-Trotsky controversy had become a violent struggle. A special commission, under Stalin's chairmanship, was appointed to deal with the "Polish question." It deposed the entire Polish leadership, and the leftist opposition, headed by Julian Leński (Leszczyński), Leon Purman, and L. Domski (Henryk Stein, also known as Kaminski), was installed in Moscow. This high-handed interference by the Comintern in the internal affairs of one of its sections became a precedent for similar dismissals and appointments by Stalin in other parties.

In March 1925 the third KPRP congress was held in Minsk, on Soviet soil, with Stalin as a member of its honorary presidium. The congress "approved" the decisions of the Polish commission at the fifth Comintern congress by electing the new leadership appointed in Moscow. It also adopted the Comintern's decision to reorganize and bolshevize the party and voted for a more revolutionary course in party activities. Finally, the party was renamed the Communist Party of Poland (Komunistyczna Partja Polski, KKP), without the word "workers," as an expression of its intention to pay more attention to the peasants, "the proletarian allies of the workers."

Even before their confirmation by the third party congress the new leaders had initiated a wave of sabotage, riots, and assassinations. Four of the terrorists were caught, convicted in court, and executed; two others were killed in a fight with the police. This reprisal was attacked by other communist parties and their front organizations as repression by "white" Poland, but the government was able to bring terror and subversion to a halt, and in May 1925 nearly all the members of the KPP central committee were arrested. Domski, who had managed to avoid arrest, became the new party leader. Shortly afterward, however, he and his central committee also fell from Moscow's graces. A new Polish commission of the Comintern, under Stalin's chairmanship, convened hastily in Moscow in July 1925 to censure Domski and his central committee and summarily dismissed them. With most of the Moscow-subservient communists in jail, Stalin was forced to reinstate the "rightist" Warski to leadership.

The fourth party conference held in Moscow in December 1925 rubber-stamped Stalin's decisions on the new leadership and elaborated a new program which heavily stressed the agrarian and peasant problem. This was aimed at broadening communist activities in Poland from the narrow base of industrial workers (where the PPS and Christian democrats enjoyed more success and influence) to the landless peasants and smallholders. The growing economic crisis in Poland seemed to favor these plans. Warski utilized his position in the parliament to advocate a rapprochement with the Soviet Union in order to secure the Russian market for industrial and agricultural exports. At a meeting of the Comintern in March 1926 Zinoviev pointed to Poland as the next possibility for revolution.

In March and April 1926 riots of the unemployed occurred in major Polish cities. At the May Day celebration in Warsaw clashes between socialist and communist demonstrators left workers dead or wounded. The government seemed unable to control the situation. On May 12 Marshal Józef Piłsudski staged a coup, and in the ensuing street battles the communists sided with his antigovernment forces. The KPP hoped, of course, that the outcome would be a civil war in which the communists would assume leadership of the worker and peasant masses, but sudden termination of the strife and the parliament's legalization of the Piłsudski regime frustrated these plans. The fighting had scarcely stopped on Warsaw's streets when Moscow denounced the new Piłsudski government as fascist, and the KPP found itself in the awkward position of having helped in the advent of this "fascist government."

Warski and his leadership were denounced by Moscow for the "May error," although it later became apparent that their participation had been highly recommended by the Comintern representative in Warsaw at that time. The issue was debated at a session of the Polish commission of the Comintern Executive Committee in January 1927. The commission found the KPP political line correct, and Warski remained at the helm of the party. The fourth congress of the KPP, held in Moscow in September, again affirmed, after some tempestuous discussions, that the Warski and the Leński factions had been equally responsible for aiding the rise of the Piłsudski government.

Warski and his group had managed to survive the "May-error" storm and the kaleidoscopic changes in the Comintern from 1925 to 1929 chiefly because, despite the strong anticommunist measures enacted by the Piłsudski government, the communists had been able to extend their influence greatly among the Polish masses. Although party membership never exceeded 20,000,[2] the KPP had succeeded in organizing sizable front organizations and securing the indirect aid of disgruntled intellectuals. In the March 1928 elections the communists, running on various tickets, received 830,000 votes (7 percent of the total vote) and won seven seats in the lower house, with Warski heading the parliamentary faction. This was an achievement which Moscow could not ignore.

However, at the sixth Comintern congress during July-September 1928 the quarrel between the two Polish factions was renewed. A new Polish commission held prolonged hearings which culminated in an open letter from the Comintern Executive Committee emphasizing the party's insufficient efforts in defense of the Soviet Union and the need for party unity. Furthermore, Warski and Kostrzewa had committed a further error at the congress in supporting Bukharin. After Bukharin's replacement by Molotov as Comintern chairman the March 1929 session of the Comintern Presidium dismissed both Warski and Kostrzewa from the KPP leadership. The "left" group with Leński, Amsterdam, Purman, and Alfred Lampe was installed in April 1929 as the new leadership.

The growing economic crisis from 1928 to 1933 created favorable conditions for the communists. However, the struggles between the rightist and leftist factions and between the Stalinist and Trotskyist factions absorbed most of the party's attention. Moreover, the Comintern's erratic policy during the years of Hitler's rise in Germany contributed to uncoordinated and often chaotic changes in the KPP's policies under Leński's Moscow-subservient leadership. Finally, the party's subversive and disruptive political line toward the Polish state precipitated effective reprisals by the government, followed by growing numbers of defections and loss of public support. By 1935 party membership had dropped to an all-time low of about 10,000, the leadership was conspiring abroad, with only little contact with the membership, and the party was again isolated, as it had been in 1920 and 1921.

The fifth party congress met in Russia in September 1930 and passed resolutions which never became effective. Following the seventh congress of the Comintern during July-August 1935, the KPP (whose leadership now resided in Prague and enjoyed the fruits of the Beneš-Stalin friendship) attempted to initiate a popular front in Poland. Both the PPS and the peasant parties, although strongly opposed to the "government of the colonels," rejected the communist overtures. The KPP was unable to break through its isolation and political impotence, and its only contribution to the cause of international communism in the last years of its existence was the recruitment of some 500 volunteers from Poland and among the Polish émigrés in France and Belgium to serve in the International Brigade in Spain.

In 1938 the Executive Committee of the Comintern dissolved the KPP on the charge that it was thoroughly infiltrated by agents of the Polish secret police and counterintelligence. Almost all party leaders and members residing in Russia were arrested and were either executed or deported to forced-labor camps in Siberia. Only one important Polish communist survived this purge: Alfred Lampe, who was ill and hospitalized at the time.

*1939 to 1948* When Nazi Germany overran Poland in September 1939, all political prisoners were released, including the Polish communists, who were mainly local or provincial party officials of lesser importance. Two of them, Władysław Gomułka and Bolesław Bierut (Rutkowski), later assumed prominent roles in the new Polish party.

During the first two years of the nazi occupation the Polish communists, still without a national organization, were apparently inactive. The Germans abstained from persecuting them, and even offered certain favors. In Moscow, shortly after the German invasion of the Soviet Union in June 1941, a small group of Polish communist refugees began to meet in the offices of the Comintern. Both Bierut (who managed to escape to Soviet-occupied Lwów) and Lampe played leading roles in this group, which decided, with the Comintern's blessings, to revive the Polish party. To offset the old KPP's image in Poland of being a Soviet agency, the revived party was to be named the Polish Workers' Party (Polska Partja Robotnicza, PPR). At the end of December 1941 six members of the Moscow group were parachuted into German-occupied Poland, where they remained under strict Comintern discipline. At a secret meeting in Warsaw, on January 5, 1942, these six, together with a few local old party members, "founded" the PPR on Polish soil.

Marceli Nowotko, one of the six from Moscow, assumed leadership of the new party, and when he was killed in November 1942, he was replaced by Paweł Finder, from the same group. Gomułka, in the meantime, had risen to a position of importance in the new PPR and recommended that it arrive at an understanding with the Polish resistance movement loyal to the exile government in London. Negotiations to this end broke up when the Soviet Union severed relations with the London Poles in April 1943. In November Finder was arrested by the Gestapo. Radio communications with Moscow had been temporarily interrupted, and Gomułka succeeded him in the top post without Moscow's knowledge.

The PPR developed its own military organization, the People's Guard, which in January 1944 was renamed the People's Army. Neither the PPR nor its armed units gained popularity among the Poles. Postwar Polish communist publications estimate the PPR membership in July 1944 as 20,000, but it was probably less than half this number. The party's attempts to convince the Poles that it was not communist in nature, but "truly democratic," were not successful, and the Polish masses remained faithful to the underground organizations directed by the Polish exile government in London and its clandestine resistance, the Home Army.

Meanwhile, after the defeat of the Germans at Stalingrad, Moscow began to formulate its own plans for a communist Poland following its occupation by the Red Army. After severing diplomatic relations with the London Poles, in May 1943 the Soviet government began to organize its own "Polish army." In June communist and leftist refugees from Poland were encouraged to establish a

Union of Polish Patriots (Związek Patriotów Polskich) in Moscow as a political superstructure for this army. In reality this union was a front for the Moscow group of the PPR. When Soviet troops advanced into Poland during July 1944, the Union of Polish Patriots installed itself at Lublin as the Polish Committee of National Liberation, with semigovernmental powers. In January 1945, despite protests by the United States and Great Britain, this committee was recognized by the Soviet Union as the provisional government of Poland, with Bierut as premier and Gomułka as vice premier.

Supported by the Soviet occupation army and secret police, the PPR, which formed the backbone of both the committee and the provisional government, began the ruthless elimination of all social and political elements opposing communist domination. PPR "operational groups," composed of three to ten trusted party members, followed on the heels of the Red Army and supported by the Soviet secret police, started to introduce the "new order." Sporadic armed opposition cost the communists over 8,000 lives,[3] and estimates of the number of persons killed in resisting Poland's "liberation" by the Red Army range from 80,000 to 200,000.

At the Yalta conference in February 1945 the Western powers were maneuvered into recognizing the communist-dominated provisional regime as the basis for a new Polish "government of national unity." Despite its democratic façade, the coalition government continued to implement typical Soviet patterns of political and social engineering. After manipulated elections in January 1947 gave the communists a majority in the parliament, all opposition to sovietization of the country was broken, and a new, "monolithic" communist government was installed. The PPS, the most dangerous competitor for the allegiance of the Polish workers, had earlier been maneuvered into a united front for electoral purposes. In December 1948 it was forced into complete fusion with the PPR to form the new Polish United Workers' Party (Polska Zjednoczona Partia Robotnicza, PZPR), the current ruling communist party of Poland.

*1949 to 1965* Bierut, the Moscow-imposed head of state, and Gomułka, who had been party general secretary since 1945, had increasingly disagreed over the extent to which Moscow should control Poland's affairs, particularly its economy. In November 1949 Gomułka was stripped of his post and membership in the central committee, and in August he was arrested and imprisoned. During the next four years the Bierut regime liquidated the political opposition and nationalized the entire economy, although it failed to collectivize the peasantry.

Stalin's death in 1953 was followed by a "thaw," both in the Soviet Union and in Poland. Khrushchev's de-Stalinization campaign was accompanied by demands in Poland for liberalization of the regime. Defections of high state and party officials disclosed the internal weaknesses of the governing party and the growing contempt of the younger generation for communism. The outcome was the 1956 crisis in Poland. Bierut died in March and was succeeded by Edward Ochab, who, despite a lengthy wartime residence in Moscow, was not a "Muscovite." The June riots in Poznań manifested the rising tide of popular discontent and the sympathies of the army with the dissatisfied masses. At the October plenum of the central committee the Muscovite faction lost its control despite Khrushchev's personal intervention at Warsaw. Gormułka, who had been freed from jail in 1954 and reinstated to party membership, once more assumed leadership. During the "Polish October," he was hailed by the man in the street for his victory over the Muscovites and for taking the "Polish road to socialism."

After initial success resulting from his reluctance to follow the Moscow line blindly, Gomułka by 1961 returned to Bierut's old pattern of internal and foreign policy. Those who had expected Gomułka to avenge his Moscow-inspired purge by loosening Poland's dependence on the Soviet Union did not understand his aims and policies. Although Gomułka wanted Moscow to refrain from interfering in Polish internal affairs, he had no intention of jeopardizing the PZPR's power in Poland by disrupting relations with the Soviet Union. The ambiguous attitude of the Western powers toward Poland's western frontier, the Oder-Neisse line, and their acceptance of the incorporation of Poland's eastern provinces into the Soviet Union, had made the western frontier a condition of survival for Poland. Thus as long as this frontier was not definitely settled Poland was forced to maintain close ties with the Soviet Union, which supported its frontier claims. For the same reason Poland consistently supported the Soviet Union in international affairs and in its conflict with China.

After 1963 economic difficulties, growing unemployment, tensions between the state and the Catholic church, and new reprisals against intellectuals and writers who were demanding further liberalization of internal affairs brought about a new deterioration of relations between the communist bureaucracy and the broad masses. The rehabilitation of the former Home Army and the access of many of its old members to a veterans' organization, the Union of Fighters for Freedom and Democracy (Związek Bojowników o Wolność i Demokrację), popularly known as Zbowid, created a new source of hope for the masses and a possible outlet for their dissent. This organization, led by Mieczysław Moczar, had been founded during the heyday of Stalinisim in Poland and had changed sides during the "Polish October." When Moczar assumed leadership, free of any obligations to Moscow, it became a fast-growing faction within the PZPR. General Moczar, ten years Gomułka's junior, was mentioned in 1965 as a possible successor to the ailing party chief.

## ORGANIZATION AND MEMBERSHIP

The organization of the PZPR follows the basic communist pattern of democratic centralism. The primary party organization is the cell, formed in factories, shops, offices, or villages. The work of several cells in towns and cities is directed by local committees, which in turn report to county and province committees; these elect officials, including secretaries who are the county and provincial executives.

The highest authority is the party congress, which is supposed to convene every four years and elects a central committee, a central control commission, and a central audit commission. Between congresses the central committee directs party activities and policies. From among its members it elects a politburo and a secretariat. The twelve-member politburo is the *de facto* collective leadership of the party. The secretariat is the executive organ of the politburo and central committee. All the important members of the council of ministers in 1965 were members of the central committee, and some even belonged to the politburo, creating an interlocking personal union between the party and the government.

In November 1945, nine months after the United States and Great Britian accepted Stalin's "solution" for Poland at Yalta, the PPR had only 6,568 "party activists," the core of a regime imposed on a nation of 25 million. Of this number, only 1,951 (29.6 percent) were old KPP members (all that remained alive after the Moscow purges and wartime losses), and 216 (3.3 percent) were former members of the prewar communist youth organization. Of the remainder, 2,142 activists (32.5 percent) had joined the party during its illegal period under German occupation, and 2,259 (34.6 percent) had joined after the communist takeover. Party membership grew from an alleged 20,000 in July 1944 to 225,000 in November 1945 but was soon greatly reduced by a purge of "opportunists" and "unreliable elements." Although the PPR had a predominantly working-class membership in these early years, party members in large industrial firms constituted only 1.1 to 9.0 percent of the work crews.[4] The combined PZPR began in December 1948 with a total membership of 1,500,000. By the end of

1964, although Poland's population had increased at least 25 percent, party membershp had grown only to 1,614,237, or about 7.7 percent.[5] Despite great efforts to increase membership among the peasants, their party enrollment dropped from 28.2 percent in 1945 (before the land reform) to about 11 percent in 1964, when collectivization was almost completely liquidated. Membership of factory workers decreased from 62.2 percent in 1945 to 40 percent in 1964. Membership of white-collar workers and intellectuals showed an increase, from 9.6 percent in 1945 to about 44 percent in 1964; however, all white-collar workers and most intellectuals are on the state payroll.

Although the PZPR includes only 9 percent of the adult population of Poland, it has a decisive influence on state affairs. Almost all the cabinet posts and the more importnat ministerial and provincial, county, and local administrative positions are occupied by party members, who account for the growing number of white-collar workers in party statistics. The system of government in the Polish People's Republic is in fact a dictatorship of a one-party bureaucracy operating behind a constitutional façade. The constitution of 1952, which defines Poland as a "people's democratic state," does not even mention the PZPR. In 1965 the first secretary of the PZPR central committee, Gomułka, was the undisputed leader of the party.

## PARTY PRESS ORGANS AND RECORDS

In Poland the entire press is state licensed and, except for one Catholic weekly, party controlled. The press organs of the PZPR are the daily *Trybuna Ludu* (People's Tribune), published in Warsaw, and the monthly *Nowe Drogi* (New Roads). The quarterly *Z Pola Walki* (From the Battlefield) contains contributions on the history of communism in Poland.

The party publishes stenographic records of its congresses and of some of its central committee meetings. The texts of the latest party statute are contained in *Statut Polskiej Zjednoczonej Partii Robotniczej uchwalony przez II Zjazd PZPR* (Statute of the Polish United Workers' Party Adopted at the Second Congress of the PZPR), Toruń, 1956.

## PARTY CONGRESSES

1st congress, KPRP, December 16, 1918, Warsaw
2d congress, KPRP, August 1923, Moscow
3d congress, KPRP (KPP), March 1925, Minsk
4th congress, KPP, September 1927, Moscow
5th congress, KPP, September 1930, Moscow
6th congress, KPP, November 1932, Moscow
1st congress, PPR, December 1945, Katowice
2d congress, PPR (1st congress, PZPR), December 1948, Warsaw
2d congress, PZPR, March 1954, Warsaw
3d congress, PZPR, March 1959, Warsaw
4th congress, PZPR, June 1964, Warsaw

## BIBLIOGRAPHY

Dziewanowski, M. K.: *The Communist Party of Poland: An Outline of History*, Cambridge, Mass., 1959.

Gomułka, Władysław: *Artykuły i przemówienia* (Articles and Speeches), 2 vols., Warsaw, 1962.

Kołomejczyk, Norbert: *PPR, 1944-1945: Studia nad rozwojem organizacyjnym partii* (PPR, 1944-1945: Studies on the Organizational Development of the Party), Warsaw, 1965.

Kowalski, Józef: *Zarys historii polskiego ruchu robotniczego w latach 1918-1939* (Outline of a History of the Polish Workers' Movement in the Years 1918-1939), 2d ed., Warsaw, 1962.

*KPP: Uchwały i rezolucje* (KPP: Resolutions), 3 vols., Warsaw, 1953-1956.

Reguła, Jan (J. Demant): *Historja Komunistycznej Partji Polski w świetle faktów i dokumentów* (History of the KPP: Facts and Documents), 2d ed., Warsaw, 1934.

Staar, Richard F.: *Poland, 1944-1962: The Sovietization of a Captive People*, Baton Rouge, La., Louisiana State University Press, 1962.

Stehle, Hansjakob: *The Independent Satellite: Society and Politics in Poland since*

*1945*, New York, Praeger, 1965.

WITOLD S. SWORAKOWSKI

1. *Grazhdanskaia voina*, vol. III, Moscow, 1930, pp. 152-156.

2. According to party historian Tadeusz Daniszewski, in an article in *Nowe Drogi*, November-December 1948, p. 148.

3. Norbert Kołomejczyk, *PPR, 1944-1945*, Warsaw, 1965, p. 120.

4. Kołomejczyk, *op. cit.*, pp. 275-296, table 7.

5. *Trybuna Ludu*, December 21, 1948. Some claims in party newspapers that membership had grown to 1,725,000 by July 1965 seem to be exaggerated.

# PORTUGAL

The Portuguese Communist Party (Partido Comunista Português, PCP) was founded in February 1921 as a splinter group of the Portuguese Socialist Party (Partido Socialista Português, PSP), which had been launched nearly a half century earlier. Almost from its inception the PSP had been divided by ideological differences between the left Marxists, who argued for a seizure of power, and the right "possibilists," who took a moderate approach; both factions had put up separate candidates in the 1892 elections and had divided over the the extent to which socialists should support the republican campaign to end the monarchy. The republicans came into power with the 1910 revolution, and from 1919 to 1921 three socialists served as cabinet ministers, despite socialist opposition to participation in bourgeois-republican governments. This conciliatory behavior, the rapidly growing anarchosyndicalist sentiment among industrial workers in trade unions, and the success of revolutionary Marxists in Russia provoked dissident socialists to form the PCP.

Nearly all the prominent PCP leaders suffered persecution or imprisonment, especially under the military dictatorship established in 1926. Among them were Bento Gonçalves, who was secretary general until his death in September 1942; Alvaro Cunhal, who was imprisoned from 1950 to 1960 and was secretary general in 1965; and Soeiro Pereira Gomes, a writer and member of the central committee until his death in 1949.

## HISTORY

Left-wing politics declined quickly under the military regime that came to power in 1926. The PCP, like the PSP, was declared illegal, its offices were closed, and its leaders were arrested and imprisoned or exiled. Socialist strength dwindled to a few thousand members in the early 1930s, and the anarchist-led General Federation of Labor (Confederação Geral do Trabalho) also declined rapidly. The PCP membership had dropped to little more than fifty members in Lisbon and Oporto by 1928. A year later, however, the party reorganized, and with support from anarchosyndicalists, it gained strength, especially among intellectuals and students, through several political groups, including the Federation of Communist Youth (Federação das Juventudes Comunistas).

Since the early 1930s the PCP has demonstrated persistent opposition to the Salazar regime. Communists were active in a series of strikes called by dock workers during 1931 and 1932 and in demonstrations against unemployment. Communists joined anarchists and socialists in protesting the 1933 labor statute that banned strikes and the old trade unions; however, the mass strike of January 1934 was crushed by army troops.

In 1936, following the resolution of the seventh Comintern congress, the communists promoted cooperation with the liberal and socialist opposition in an attempt to establish a clandestine popular front—a policy the PCP was still pursuing in 1965. In 1941 the party again reorganized and allegedly supported a student's strike in Lisbon and a textile workers' strike in Covilhã. It led a strike of Lisbon dock workers in October and November 1942 and Lisbon workers in July and August 1943. In 1943 the clandestine PCP held its first congress and promoted a united front, the National Antifascist Unity Movement. At the end of World War II, it participated in the broad Democratic Unity Movement (Movimento de Unidade Democrática, MUD). After boycotting the 1945 elections for the national assembly, the Democratic Unity Movement nominated General José Maria Norton de Matos as candidate for the presidential elections in 1949. He withdrew, however, after dissension arose between the movement's old republicans on the right and its supporters on the left, including the PCP—which at this point may have changed its policy slightly in accordance with the hard line of the Cominform directives of 1947. Communist influence appears to have been great in the Young Democratic Unity Movement (MUD Juvenil), which was founded in April 1946 and supported the leftist groups in the parent body. In 1954 the left wing of the Democratic Unity Movement, which a year earlier had renamed itself the National Democratic Movement, demanded self-determination for Goa, a Portuguese colony in India. Demonstrations in support of this appeal were suppressed, and widespread arrests led to the trial of fifty-two defendants in Oporto in 1956 and 1957.

Meanwhile, the PCP claimed credit for fomenting strikes by Lisbon workers during April 1947 and by Alentejo peasants in July 1947, in February 1952, and again a year later. The Portuguese government alleged that the communists had participated in other disturbances, including strikes by Oporto textile workers in May 1954 and farm workers in July 1954, a demonstration by fishermen for higher wages in May 1955, and a student demonstration in early 1957.

In 1957 the fifth congress of the PCP established a party program similar to those of other European communist parties, except for emphasis on a unified action front to oust by peaceful means the dictatorship of António de Oliveira Salazar. Like other Portuguese opposition groups, the PCP demanded political amnesty and dissolution of the secret police. Unlike other opposition groups, however, the communists called for self-determination for the Portuguese colonies. In the international sphere they advocated Portuguese neutrality in the cold war, as well as a cessation of United States economic influence and military control over bases in the Azores.

During the 1958 campaign for the presidency the PCP first supported the left-wing socialist Arlindo Vicente. However, it later joined with other opposition forces to support General Humberto Delgado. Despite police harassment and election irregularities, Delgado was conceded nearly 23 percent of the vote against Salazar's candidate Americo Tomas. His campaign provided a serious challenge to the dictatorship and marked a turning point in Portuguese politics. Allowed nearly a month in which to campaign publicly, Delgado addressed his moderate demands to hundreds of thousands of Portuguese throughout the country. His defeat in June was followed by demonstrations and the distribution of manifestos against the government. In March 1959 there was an attempted coup by army officers and civilians. Occasional workers' and students' demonstrations took place in 1960. In January 1961 the luxury liner *Santa Maria* was seized by Henrique Galvão, a former colonial officer and

Salazar supporter. An abortive attack on the Beja army barracks took place in January 1962, and by March large student demonstrations had begun.

Although communist participation in these events was probably minimal, the PCP remained active, and in 1962 it joined with other opposition groups to establish the Patriotic National Liberation Front (Frente Patriótica de Liberação Nacional) in Algiers. In addition to the PCP, this broad coalition included the leftist Revolutionary Action Movement, an outgrowth of the 1962 student disorders comprising the Catholic and socialist youth, and the Republican Resistance Movement, a loose coalition of republicans and liberals in Portugal and in exile. Its six-man executive committee consisted of one communist, Pedro Ramos de Almeida; representatives of the other two leftist groups; and three independents, including Manuel Sertório, a social democrat and one of the opposition's leading theoreticians. At its second congress the Liberation Front elected Delgado as president. Delgado, a noncommunist, found himself at odds with the nonmilitant strategy of communists and social democrats alike and formed his own Portuguese National Liberation Front (Frente de Liberação Nacional Português), which remained in existence until his mysterious assassination in early 1965. Paradoxically, Delgado's revolutionary perspective coincided with that of a pro-Chinese group that had defected from the PCP in 1964.

In August-September 1965 the sixth congress of the PCP advocated "the unity of the democratic and patriotic forces to overthrow the fascist dictatorship." The current transition to socialist revolution was the "national-democratic revolution," which would "guarantee political freedom, abolish the rule of the finance oligarchy, defend the interests of the people, and effect a series of reforms. . . . Doing away with imperialist domination over other peoples it will ensure the sovereignty, territorial integrity, and genuine independence of the country." Specifically, the party's objectives included the establishment of a democratic system, elimination of monopoly rule and the guarantee of economic development, agrarian reform and a better standard of living for the working classes, recognition of independence for the colonies, and the pursuit of peace and friendship with all nations. To carry out these objectives the PCP condemned "putschist, terrorist, and adventurous trends, on the one hand, and legalistic trends and constitutional illusions, on the other." Furthermore, the program stated that unless conditions ripened into a revolutionary situation, political changes would be brought about by peaceful means. Emphasis would be placed on expanding the underground organizations and publishing propaganda to ensure working-class unity and an alliance with the peasantry to fight for higher wages, the guaranteed eight-hour day, and other fundamental reforms. The overthrow of the dictatorship would be followed by the establishment of a provisional government in which the PCP would participate, but would not condition its participation on acceptance of its program.

The political potential of the PCP is difficult to assess, although it undoubtedly is the best-organized opposition group in Portugal and benefits from the government's tendency to blame communists for all opposition, thereby enhancing and publicizing party activities.

## ORGANIZATION AND MEMBERSHIP

According to its statutes, the PCP is based on the principles of democratic centralism and is organized on a territorial basis, with the central committee coordinating the activities of provincial, regional, subregional, local, zonal, and sectoral organizations. The central committee also elects a secretary general and a political committee of the secretariat and directs party activities between congresses. The congress, the supreme party body, studies and amends reports of the central committee, adopts resolutions, and approves and modifies the party's program and statutes. The basic party unit is the cell, which is found "in factories, offices, ships, ports, shops, administrations, schools, barracks, and the like." A large cell is divided into nuclei, and all cells are responsible to their respective assemblies. Further, the party establishes groups to control the activity of communists in such mass organizations as *casas do povo* (for rural workers), *casas dos pescadores* (for fishermen), cooperatives, recreational and sporting clubs, and cultural institutions.

Because of its illegal status, the PCP operates underground within Portugal. Its membership, roughly estimated as 2,000, consists mainly of urban industrial workers and some fishermen concentrated in and near Lisbon and Oporto and a smaller number of rural farm laborers, principally from Alentejo province. The party also includes a minority of middle-class groups and is supported by numerous intellectuals and students. Exiled party members are active in Algeria, Brazil, France, and Portuguese Africa. Several PCP leaders reside in Moscow or elsewhere in Eastern Europe.

The tactics of the PCP have traditionally been those of participation with other political groupings, and in 1929 and 1930 the party established or participated in a number of front organizations, including the Inter-Syndical Commission, the Revolutionary Naval Organization, International Red Aid, the Soviet Friendship League, the League Against War and Fascism, and the Academic Defense Groups. It attempted to establish a "popular front" in 1936 and participated in the National Antifascist Unity Movement in 1943, the Democratic Unity Movement in 1945, the Young Democratic Unity Movement in 1946, and the National Democratic Movement in 1954. In 1958 the PCP supported Delgado's National Independence Movement, and in 1963 it established the Patriotic National Liberation Front, as well as some scattered associated "patriotic action groups."

The PCP also encouraged organizational activity in the Portuguese colonies, especially in Africa. In Angola three autonomous clandestine front organizations existed in 1948: the Angolan Federal Committee of the PCP, the Youth Commission for the Struggle Against Colonial Imperialism in Angola, and Black Angola. In 1952 these groups reportedly joined in a Council for Liberation of Angola, and in October 1955 an Angolan communist party was established. In 1956 the Angolan party and several other organizations reportedly established the Peoples' Movement for the Liberation of Angola (Movimento Popular para a Liberação de Angola), which led an uprising in Luanda in February 1961. This group, however, later emerged as a nationalist Angolan organization relatively disassociated from the PCP and other Portuguese opposition groups. The Portuguese government has also mentioned communist influence in Mozambique and Portuguese Guinea.

RELATION TO SOVIET LEADERSHIP

The PCP adhered closely to Comintern policies, and following the resolution of the seventh congress of the Comintern it attempted to establish a semilegal popular front in 1936. Probably influenced by the hard-line Cominform resolutions of 1947 and 1948, the PCP appears to have provoked dissension in the Portuguese opposition during the 1949 presidential campaign.

The PCP has consistently supported Moscow and has issued several statements affirming its position. In early 1964 a dissident pro-Chinese faction defected and then divided into two movements, the "open" People's Action Front and the "closed" Marxist-Leninist Committee, believed to have links with the student movement in Portugal. The former group, led by Carlos Lança, with headquarters in Paris, may also have been behind the pro-Peking Portuguese Revolutionary Liberation Group, which for a short time published the bulletin *Revolução portuguesa*. The People's Action Front published *Revolução popular* from March to September 1964.

## PARTY PRESS ORGANS AND RECORDS

*O Proletário* was published legally until 1931. After that time the monthly *Avante* regularly appeared clandestinely as the principal PCP organ. In 1965 the party was publishing clandestinely and irregularly *O Militante* for activists, *O Camponês* (since 1946) for the rural peasantry, *O Têxtil* for textile workers, *O Corticeiro* for cork workers, and *O Marinheiro vermelho* for the merchant marine.

The draft proposals of the party statute appear in *Foreign Radio Broadcasts,* February 28, 1964, pp. W1-W9. For the party's program see "Program of the Portuguese Communist Party Adopted by the Sixth Congress of the PCP, September 1965, Abridged," in *Information Bulletin* (supplement to *World Marxist Review*), vol. 67, March 11, 1966, pp. 7-27. Official records are not available, and information about congresses and activities can be found in the party organs and manifestoes, which are distributed in very limited quantity. Little information exists on the party's formation or its reorganization in 1929 and 1941.

## CONGRESSES OF THE PCP

1st congress, November 1923, Lisbon
2d congress, May 1926, Lisbon
3d congress, November 1943
4th congress, July 1946
5th congress, September 1957
6th congress, August-September 1965

## BIBLIOGRAPHY

César, Amândio: *Angola, 1961*, Lisbon, Verbo, 1961 (esp. pp. 93-109).

Cunhal, Alvarez: *A questão agrária en Portugal*, Rio de Janeiro, Editora Civilização Brasileira, 1968.

Fryer, Peter, and Patricia McGowan Pinheiro: *Oldest Ally: A Portrait of Salazar*, London, Dennis Dobson, 1961 (esp. pp. 203-218).

International Union of Students: *The Case against Salazar: Report on Portugal*, Prague, n.d.

Portuguese Communist Party: *Piatyi sezd Portugalskoi kommunisticheskoi partii* (Fifth Congress of the Portuguese Communist Party), Moscow, 1959.

Rêgo, Victor da Cunha, and João M. Tito de Morais: *A Resistência em Portugal: Crónicas*, São Paulo, Editora Felman-Rêgo [1962].

RONALD H. CHILCOTE

# THE PROFINTERN
*See* The Red International of Labor Unions

# THE RED INTERNATIONAL OF LABOR UNIONS

In July 1920, while the second congress of the Communist International was deliberating in Moscow, some of the delegates met separately with representatives of the All-Russian Council of Trade Unions and established themselves as an "international conference of revolutionary trade unions." This conference turned to the Comintern congress with a request for support of the creation of a Red International of Labor Unions (Krasnyi Internatsional Profsoiuzov), generally known as the Profintern. After a report by Karl Radek, the Comintern welcomed the initiative and promised its support. Thus was engineered the founding of a new "international" organization.

There were a few communist-dominated trade-union chapters in some European countries, but they belonged to large unions that were predominantly socialist in orientation. The communists had just begun to form their own factions in these unions and were attempting to gain the support of leftist elements and the old anarchosyndicalist opposition. Their efforts to capture or split local chapters were met with stern reprisals by the socialist union leadership. Some communist-dominated locals were expelled, and individual members advocating the communist line were excluded from local chapters. At the time of the Moscow conference no country had a nationwide communist labor organization, despite the claims of the delegates that they represented the "red labor unions" of some forty countries.

This sudden creation of an international communist labor organization in Moscow had been prompted by the Socialist International's revival of the prewar Amsterdam-based International of Trade Unions (known as the Amsterdam International). The communist leadership in Moscow realized that if the Amsterdam International were to develop a broader activity, it would strengthen social-democratic parties everywhere and impede the spread of communism among the workers. Their hope was that the new Profintern would enable them to oppose the Amsterdam International by disrupting and splitting the existing labor unions.

## HISTORY

The Moscow conference elected an International Council of Revolutionary Trade and Industrial Unions, which was charged with calling the founding congress of the Profintern on July 3-19, 1921. This first congress, which coincided with the third Comintern congress, adopted a statute and program and defined its relationship to the Comintern. Both documents established the Profintern's task as organization of the workers' masses around the world for the overthrow of capitalism and the creation of "socialist governments." From the reports, speeches, and resolutions it was clear that "socialist" in fact meant "communist," but the Profintern consistently used the former term, apparently in the hope that socialism would be more acceptable to the working masses than communism. The program stressed as the main objective of the Profintern the struggle against the "reactionary" International Labor Bureau of the League of Nations and the Amsterdam International. The Profintern's second congress, which met during the fourth Comintern congress, accepted and elaborated the united-front tactic of the Communist International and worked out instructions for organizing factory committees, which were to be the starting place for united-front action.

The third congress met in July 1924, just after the close of the fifth Comintern congress. The main topics under consideration were the planning of an international campaign to promote a united trade-union organization in every country and the elaboration of a strike strategy. The "united front from above" was still pursued as the means of creating such a worldwide organization. Whereas the Comintern had abandoned this tactic at its fifth congress, the Profintern was evidently instructed to continue it in the trade-union area.

The fourth congress of the Profintern, held in Moscow in March-April 1928, which preceded the sixth Comintern congress by three months, was devoted to development of the trade-union movement in underdeveloped and colonial countries. A year later these deliberations bore fruit, with the creation in May of the communist-inspired Latin American Federation of Trade Unions and in August of the Pacific Secretariat of Trade Unions, opening the way for communist trade-union work in the Far East.

The fifth congress, held in August 1930, adopted long resolutions concerning the world economic crisis, the fight against unemployment, and the demand that communist trade unionists "go to the masses." The congress also adopted the recommendations of a special conference on strike strategy, which had been held in January 1929 in Strassburg, near Berlin. After this congress the Profintern was very active in promoting strikes and workers' demonstrations in various countries, but as the seventh congress of the Comintern approached, and groundwork for the popular-front strategy was laid, the Profintern's activities started to fade away. During the popular-front period of "proletarian unity" members of communist trade unions were ordered to disband their chapters and join the socialist unions in order to promote the new communist objectives from within the old socialist unions. One by one the member unions of the Profintern began to disappear, and the existence of the Profintern itself became embarrassing to Moscow. At the end of 1937 the Profintern announced its liquidation.

## ORGANIZATION AND MEMBERSHIP

The Profintern was tied to the Comintern by organizational and personal bonds, thus assuring its loyalty. Alfred Rosmer and Pierre Sémard of France, Georgi Dimitrov of Bulgaria, Fritz Heckert and Walter Ulbricht of Germany, and Grigorii Zinoviev, Aleksandr Lozovskii (Solomon Abramovich Dridzo), and Osip Piatnitskii of Russia continually appeared on the roster of activities of both organizations. Lozovskii, as general secretary of the Profintern, served as liaison with the Comintern. The day-to-day work of the Profintern was directed by a central council and an executive bureau, which met between congresses.

The sections of the Profintern consisted of associations of red trade unions in some countries and communist minority factions from noncommunist unions in countries that had no such associations. However, these general membership requirements were applied with great flexibility. In 1929, shortly after its fourth congress, the Profintern comprised 46 countries: nineteen of these countries had a central association of communist labor unions; nine countries had existing central organizations which had to forego formal membership but followed the political line of the Profintern; and eighteen countries had "revolutionary minorities" in socialist-dominated trade unions.[1] The numerical strength of these members is unknown.

## PRESS ORGANS AND RECORDS

The central council of the Profintern published its official monthly organ in Russian, German, and French: *Krasnyi internatsional profsoiuzov* (Red International of Labor Unions), *Die Rote Gewerkschafts-Internationale*, and *L'Internationale syndicale rouge*. All editions began publication in 1921. The German and French editions ceased to appear in 1933; the Russian edition continued until

1936. In addition, short-lived periodicals and bulletins appeared at various times and in various places.

The stenographic records of all five congresses of the Profintern were published in Russian, and some were translated into French, German, and Italian. Reports on the activities of the central council between the first four congresses were also published in Russian, with some translated into French and German. In addition, the reports and speeches delivered at the congresses and central council meetings were published in several languages. For a detailed listing see Witold S. Sworakowski, *The Communist International and Its Front Organizations: A Research Guide and Checklist of Holdings in American and European Libraries*, Stanford, Calif., Hoover Institution, 1965, pp. 381-401.

PROFINTERN CONGRESSES

1st congress, July 19, 1921, Moscow
2d congress, November 19-December 2, 1922, Moscow
3d congress, July 8-22, 1924, Moscow
4th congress, March 17-April 3, 1928, Moscow
5th congress, August 15-30, 1930, Moscow

BIBLIOGRAPHY

Galsen, S.: *Komintern i Profintern* (The Comintern and the Profintern), Moscow, 1926.
Lozowskii, A.: *Mirovoe professionalnoe dvizhenie: Spravochnik Profinterna* (The World Trade-Union Movement: A Reference Book on the Profintern), Moscow, Goz. izd-vo., 1926-1927.
Olberg, Paul: *Die Rote Gewerkschafts-Internationale und die europäische Gewerkschaftsbewegung,* Stuttgart, 1930.
Zelikman, M. (ed.): *Malaia entsiklopediia po mezhdunarodnomu profdvizheniiu* (Small Encyclopedia on the International Trade-Union Movement), Moscow, Izd., Profinterna, 1927.

WITOLD S. SWORAKOWSKI

1. A. Tivel and K. Kheimo (comps.), *10 let Kominterna v resheniiakh i tsifrakh: Spravochnik po istorii Kominterna*, Moscow, Gos. izd-vo, 1929, p. 367.

# THE RED SPORT INTERNATIONAL

The Red Sport International (Krasnyi Sportivnyi Internatsional), generally known as the Sportintern, was founded in Moscow during the third congress of the Comintern in July 1921. Its purpose was "the unification of all proletarians active in sports with the purpose of winning them over for the class struggle."[1] Workers' sport teams were used in some countries as the recruiting grounds for the local communist party's "security guards," who protected communist meetings and demonstrations from attacks of opponents and were also used to break up the meetings and demonstrations of anticommunist groups.

The "red sport teams" collaborated closely with local communist youth organizations belonging to the Communist Youth International, whose general secretary, Willy Münzenberg, played an important role in the founding of the Sportintern.

The first, third, and fourth congresses of the Sportintern were held almost simultaneously with the third, fifth, and sixth congresses of the Comintern. The Sportintern was apparently given special attention by the fifth and sixth Comintern congresses, which held special consultative meetings concerning Sportintern matters. Delegates of the Sportintern participated in these two Comintern congresses with consultative votes.

The Sportintern was dissolved after the seventh Comintern congress in 1935, when most communist front organizations became a liability in the Soviet Union's bid for "proletarian unity" in the struggle against Italian and German fascism.

Although the official organ *Der Internationale Arbeiter-Sport* was published in Berlin and the second Sportintern congress met in Berlin in July 1922, no German sport organizations were affiliated with it. In 1929 the Sportintern organizations included about 2 million members from the Soviet Union, about 100,000 from Czechoslovakia, 25,000 from Norway, 12,000 from France, 6,000 from Sweden, 2,500 from Argentina, and 2,000 from Uruguay.

ORGANIZATION AND MEMBERSHIP

The Sportintern was a "section" of the Communist International. Its own congresses elected an Executive Committee, and the day-to-day work was directed by a Secretariat.

SPORTINTERN CONGRESSES

1st congress, July 1921, Moscow
2d congress, July 1922, Berlin
3d congress, October 1924, Moscow
4th congress, August 1928, Moscow

Dates of any later congresses are unknown.

BIBLIOGRAPHY

Tivel, A., and M. Kheimo (eds.): *10 [desiat] let Kominterna v resheniiakh i tsifrakh: Spravochnik po istorii Kominterna* (Ten Years of the Comintern in Decisions and Figures: A Reference Book on the History of the Comintern), Moscow, Gos. izd-vo, 1929.

WITOLD S. SWORAKOWSKI

1. A. Tivel and M. Kheimo (eds.), *10 let Kominterna v resheniiakh i tsifrakh: Spravochnik po istorii Kominterna,* Moscow, Gosizdat, 1929, p. 388.

# REPUBLIC OF SOUTH AFRICA
*See* South Africa

# REUNION

Before World War II there was no communist organization in Réunion. In 1936 several leftists, including Auguste Mondon and Raymond Vergès, had formed a small popular-front group, but it was short lived. In 1945 some of these same men founded the Republican Committee for Democratic and Social Action (Comité Républicain d'Action Démocratique et Sociale), on whose ticket Vergès, mayor of Saint-Denis, and Léon Lepervanche. mayor of Le Port, were elected to the French constituent assembly. On their arrival in Paris Vergès joined the French Communist Party and Lepervanche joined the progressivist group. They were both reelected on November 10, 1946, with 51, 572 votes, or 55.2 percent of the votes cast. Meanwhile, they had founded a small newspaper, *Le Communiste*, whose title they changed shortly after to the less explicit *Témoignages*.

At this point the French party began to send delegates to the island: Hubert Ruffé, member of the central committee (1947), Louis Odru (1948), and finally Raymond Barbé (1949), who got the Réunion party on its feet as a member federation of the French Communist Party. In 1949 the post of secretary was filled by a lawyer from Saint-Denis, Claudine Lewkowicz Samarito, who stressed the violent character of the party's activity. As early as the May 1946 elections (in which the French communist candidates were defeated), Paul Vergès had shot and killed the popular-democratic candidate who was running against his father, Raymond Vergès.[1] Réunion communists increased their violent demonstrations in compliance with the general line the French party had taken since October 1947, but to an extent unknown in metropolitan France. Nevertheless, the party still defended the policy of "departmentalization" (see *Martinique*). Party leaders claimed around 10,000 members.

In 1950, when Claudine Samarito was convicted for provocation of the shooting in 1946, the party began a rapid decline and fell into internal quarrels. The Creoles criticized the policy of violence, which they said was inspired by French communists, and Claudine Samarito, on whom blame was laid, resigned as secretary of the federation and returned to France. Recovery of the party was effected by Paul Vergès. Although legal proceedings brought against him after the assassination were not completed, Vergès was authorized to return to Réunion, where the colonial bureau of the French party made him federal secretary in 1954. He succeeded in being elected deputy on January 2, 1956, along with Raymond Mondon; together they received 52 percent of the total vote, giving the communists eleven general counselors (out of thirty-six) and seven mayors on the island.

In 1958, however, the Réunion communist movement began a new decline as a result of the change in regime in France (it lost its two seats in the legislative elections of November 1958) and also as a result of the radical transformation of its program and structure. It had abandoned the policy of assimilation (that is, "departmentalization") and had taken up the demand for autonomy within the framework of a union with France. In compliance with the directives of the French party, on May 17-18, 1959, the sixth party conference, which was attended by Léon Feix, head of the French party's colonial bureau, changed the Réunion member federation to the Réunion Communist Party (Parti Communiste Réunionnais, PCR), with Paul Vergès as secretary (see *Martinique*). This transformation was opposed by some militants (such as

Lepervanche), and resulted in the defection of a large group of minor civil servants (principally schoolteachers, until then the majority of the party's cadres), who feared that autonomy would result in lower salaries. Finally, the PCR was henceforth to orient its propaganda toward the African and Malabar ethnic groups in Réunion.

The PCR was represented by Paul Vergès and Gervais Baret at the Moscow conference of the eighty-one communist parties in November 1960, at the twenty-second congress of the Communist Party of the Soviet Union in October 1961, and at the 1959, 1961, and 1964 congresses of the French Communist Party.

The mass organizations of the PCR are the Departmental Union of the General Confederation of Labor (Union Départementale de la CGT), whose general secretary is Raymond Hoarau, the Democratic Organization of Réunion Youth (Organisation Démocratique de la Jeunesse Réunionnaise), the Union of Réunion Women, and the People's Réunion Relief.

The PCR was unsuccessful in electing any deputies in the legislative elections of November 1962, and by 1965 it had lost more than half its seats in the general council and on city councils. In March 1963 Paul Vergès was accused of attacking the integrity of the national territory. After being sentenced to three months in prison in March 1964 for violation of the laws governing the press, he escaped and was still in hiding in 1965.

It is possible that Paul Vergès was at one time sympathetic to the theses of the Chinese Communist Party (like his brother Jacques Vergès, who broke with the French party for that reason), but he very quickly returned to the Soviet camp, and the PCR affirmed its "loyalty" to the Soviet party.

PARTY PRESS ORGAN

The PCR publishes *Témoignages*, which began in the 1940s as *Le Communiste*.

BIBLIOGRAPHY

*Est & ouest*, no. 159, October 1-15, 1956; no. 250, January 16-31, 1961; no. 307, October 16-31, 1963.

Le Cornec, Michel: "La Politique actuelle du Parti communiste réunionnaise," *Est & ouest*, no. 309, November 16-30, 1963.

CLAUDE HARMEL

1. *Le Monde*, May 30, 1946.

# RUMANIA

The Rumanian Communist Party (Partidul Comunist Român, PCR), originally a splinter group of the Rumanian Social Democratic Party (Partidul Social Democrat Român, PSDR), was founded on May 13, 1921. The circumstances under which the party was established are still obscure. It is generally believed that the split was engineered by extremist groups of the PSDR seeking affiliation with the Comintern and by the Rumanian police seeking destruction of the PSDR. The founders of the PCR included the hard core of Wallachian and Moldavian "maximalists" and the leaders of the PSDR regional organizations from Bessarabia, Transylvania, and the Dobrudja. The power elite consisted initially of A. Constantinescu, A. Dobrogeanu-Gherea, Gh. Cristescu, M. G. Bujor, Boris Ştefanov, Marcel and Ana Pauker, Bela Brainer, Petre Borilă, Pavel Cacenco, Elek Koblos, and B. Donchev. Apparently none of these persons had been trained in the Soviet Union or had been associated with the early bolshevik movement, although contacts with the Russian leadership are known to have occurred. The political fate of the Rumanian leadership, however, was directly linked with the activities of the Russian party.

After the PCR was banned in 1923 the majority of its founders either continued their activities clandestinely in Rumania or joined the Rumanian Bureau of the Russian organization in Moscow. All, with the exception of Ana Pauker and Petre Borilă, failed to survive the period of illegality, succumbing either of natural causes or, as in the case of Marcel Pauker, in Russia during the Stalinist purges of the 1930s. Ana Pauker and Borilă returned to Rumania at the end of World War II to assume commanding positions, first in the reconstituted PCR and after 1948 in the renamed Rumanian Workers' Party (Partidul Muncitoresc Român, PMR). Borilă alone withstood the postwar purges and in 1965 still occupied a leading position in the party, which that year resumed the name Rumanian Communist Party.

## HISTORY

The history of the PCR prior to its "legalization" in 1944 is generally unknown. The basic information available on the party's activities after 1923 is unreliable, and any survey of its history during those years is subject to revision as materials are released by the current leadership. It is known, however, that the PCR blindly followed the dictates of Moscow throughout the interwar years and that its influence in international communist affairs and Rumanian internal politics was negligible. The party was directed by the Soviet leaders through members of the Rumanian Bureau in Moscow and international officials of the Comintern.

The constant purges of the Rumanian leadership, usually on Stalin's orders, attest to the party's subservience to Moscow, but not necessarily to its impotence. The liquidation of Dobrogeanu-Gherea and Marcel Pauker during the Stalinist purges in 1934 was, in fact, a reflection of apprehension over the potential strength of the intellectuals in the Rumanian party. Similarly, the Kremlin viewed with great disfavor any independent appraisal of Rumanian conditions by Rumanian communists not belonging to the Moscow coterie headed by Ana Pauker. The *de facto* disavowal of the railwaymen's rebellion, headed by Gheorghiu-Dej (the Griviţa strike of 1933) and of the activities of the younger Rumanian cadres (Grigori Preoteasă, Lucreţiu Pătrăşcanu, and other contemporary communist intellectuals) is indicative of Stalin's apprehension over possible reconciliation of Rumanian nationalism and communist reform programs.

Soviet policies lessened the effectiveness of the antifascist front functioning in the late 1930s. In particular, the Ribbentrop-Molotov agreement and the Soviet Union's annexation in 1940 of Bessarabia and northern Bucovina destroyed whatever support the native communists had been able to secure from the disaffected Rumanian peasants and workers.

The incarceration by 1941 of most of the Rumanian party leaders, except for those who escaped to Russia, increased the growing antagonism between the contingent of the party in Rumania and the privileged members of the Rumanian Bureau in Moscow. The postwar struggle between the "Rumanians" and the "Muscovites" (and the current Russo-Rumanian controversies themselves) may indeed be traced to an awareness of the Kremlin's plans to assume command of Rumanian affairs at the end of the war directly through the Red Army, the Tudor Vladimirescu division of Rumanian "volunteers," and Stalin's most trusted agents, Ana Pauker and Vasile Luca. In the immediate postwar years, however, the

Rumanian contingent, headed by Gheorghiu-Dej, skillfully pursued a policy of subservience and apparent agreement with Stalin's plans for Rumania. In this manner Gheorghiu-Dej was able to secure the Kremlin's consent for his election as secretary general in 1945 and reelection to the same office in 1948. Continuing subservience to Moscow and concurrent exploitation of the weaknesses of his opponents in the Moscow group permitted Gheorghiu-Dej to emerge victorious in the internal struggle for power with Pauker and Luca and obtain Stalin's blessing in the spring of 1952.

Gheorghiu-Dej's Stalinism was, however, less tolerable to Khrushchev, and in the ensuing struggle for political survival, Gheorghiu-Dej and his associates assumed more and more the role of champions of national communism and defenders of Rumania's independence from Russia. In 1955 the second party congress laid down the fundamental plans for the "socialist construction of Rumania" for the benefit of the Rumanian people, in accordance with Stalin's national principles. These plans were restated at the third congress in 1960.

The PCR's independent position in international affairs and its defiance of Russian policies considered contrary to Rumanian interests have cast communist Rumania in the role of the "France of the East." Whether the party will be able to continue such a course depends on the evolution of East-West and Sino-Soviet relations and on the Kremlin's ability to exert meaningful pressure on the Rumanian leadership. In the absence of any internal opposition to the Ceaușescu regime that could be exploited by Moscow, and under unfavorable international circumstances, the Soviet Union's retaliatory power appeared to be limited in 1965.

## ORGANIZATION AND MEMBERSHIP

The PCR is a tightly knit organization, efficiently ruled by the executive committee and the secretary general, who in 1965 was Nicolae Ceaușescu. Massive purges among the rank and file between 1948 and 1950 and 1957 and 1958 cleansed the party of "fascists," "revisionists," and "right-wing deviationists"—all identifiable with factions opposed to the "national Stalinism" of the late secretary general Gheorghe Gheorghiu-Dej and his immediate associates. Purges among the top echelons have been less drastic than in other Eastern European countries. The principal victims of Gheorghiu-Dej's team were Lucrețiu Pătrășcanu, the wartime leader of the organization; Ana Pauker, Vasile Luca, and Teohari Georgescu, the so-called "Muscovite group," which was removed from power in 1952; and Iosif Chisinevski and Miron Constantinescu, accused of "Khrushchevism" in 1957.

According to the statute adopted in 1965 the PCR is organized on the principles of democratic centralism, and "on the territorial and place-of-production basis." Except in urban centers, the basic party organizations are subordinate to the district organizations, which in turn are subordinate to the regional organizations whose ultimate subordination is to the party's central committee. In urban centers the basic party organizations report to the district and regional urban organizations and eventually to the central committee.

The supreme organ of the PCR is the party congress, which ordinarily should meet once in every four years. The central committee elects the executive committee, the permanent presidium, the secretary general, and the secretariat, the ultimte repositiories of party power.

Nicolae Ceaușescu, the party's secretary general, reported to the fourth party congress in July 1965 that membership was approximately 1,450,000, including candidate members. Of these, 630,000 (or 44 percent) were workers, 500,000 (34 percent) peasants, 145,000 (10 percent) intellectuals, and the rest unaccounted for in terms of social composition. The percentage of women members was given as 21 percent. On the basis of national origin, 87 percent of the members were

Rumanian, 9 percent Hungarian, and the rest German, Serbian, and other nationalities. Sixty-four percent of the members were under forty years of age.[1]

The younger cadres are recruited largely from among members and alumni of the Communist Youth Union (Uniunea Tineretului Comunist), whose membership in 1965 was approximately 2,250,000. Of these, 336,000 already belonged to the PCR. Unlike the parent organization, peasants outnumbered workers (720,000 and 670,000, respectively) in the youth group. The rest of the membership consisted of 600,000 students, 114,000 engineers and intellectuals, and 150,000 persons defying group classification.

The party's reliance on front organizations decreased as it consolidated its power and proceeded with national and social reconciliation. Of the many organizations functioning in the 1940s and 1950s, the only one deemed important by 1965 was the People's Democratic Front (Frontul Democrației Populare), the umbrella for elections to the national assembly and regional and local government bodies.

## RELATION TO SOVIET LEADERSHIP

The success of the PCR's independent stand is ascribable to masterful exploitation of the political opportunities provided by Khrushchev's policies of peaceful coexistence, the Hungarian revolution, and the Sino-Soviet conflict. "Peaceful coexistence" provided opportunities for economic contacts with the West and a corollary lessening of economic dependence on Moscow. The Hungarian events of 1956 made the Kremlin more tolerant of Rumanian Stalinism, thus assuring the continuation of the Gheorghiu-Dej regime at a crucial moment in communist history. The Rumanians' trump card, however, was the Sino-Soviet conflict. Since 1954 the party has sought and Peking has provided leverage against the Kremlin. The loosening of Rumania's economic, political, and military ties with the Soviet bloc must be accounted for primarily in terms of Gheorghiu-Dej's reliance on China and its doctrines on the nature of the socialist camp.

The assumption of the role of intermediary in the Sino-Soviet conflict since 1963 has considerably strengthened Bucharest's position in relation to Moscow, not because of any visible successes as "honest broker," but because of the Kremlin's unwillingness to break with Peking and its corollary inability to arrest the growing anti-Russian "independent course" in Rumania. As a consequence, the Rumanian leadership appears convinced that under current international conditions its ultimate goal, identified as the execution of the country's historic legacy of an independent and prosperous Rumania, will soon be achieved.

## PARTY PRESS ORGANS AND RECORDS

The leading party newspaper is *Scînteia*; the official journal is *Lupta de clasa*.

The party statute appears in *Statutul Partidului Comunist Român* (Statute of the Rumanian Communist Party), Bucharest, Editura Politică, 1965. The program of the party appears in Nicolae Ceaușescu, *Raport la cel de al IX-lea Congres at Partidului Comunist Român*, Bucharest, Editura Politica, 1965, pp. 18-56. Party records and other sources relating to the history of the PCR are generally unavailable for the period preceding 1944. A few minor compendia of documents (*Documente din istoria Partidului Comunist din România*) provide only limited data relevant to the period of illegality; they contain materials on the five party congresses held during that period. Complete records of the postwar congresses are published in the Rumanian press and special collections in mongraphic form.

## PARTY CONGRESSES

1st congress, PCR, May 1921
2d congress, PCR, 1922
3d congress, PCR, September 1924
4th congress, PCR, 1928
5th congress, PCR, 1932
6th congress, PCR (1st congress, PMR), 1948

7th congress, PCR (2d congress, PMR), December 1955

8th congress, PCR (3d congress, PMR), June 1960

9th congress, PCR (4th congress, PMR), July 1965

BIBLIOGRAPHY

Fischer-Galati, Stephen: *The New Romania; From People's Democracy to Socialist Republic*, Cambridge, Mass., MIT Press, 1967.

Ionescu, Ghiţa: *Communism in Rumania, 1944-1962*, London, Oxford University Press, 1964.

STEPHEN FISCHER-GALATI

1. Nicolae Ceauşescu, *Raport la cel de al IX-lea Congres al Partidului Comunist Român*, Bucharest, Editura Politica, 1965, pp. 64-65.

# SAN MARINO

In this minuscule republic, under Italian protectorate, the San Marino Communist Party (Partito Communista de San Marino, PCSM) was reorganized at the end of World War II and immediately enjoyed strong political influence, as did the Italian Communist Party in all the surrounding regions of Italy. A coalition of the PCSM and the San Marino Socialist Party (Partito Socialist di San Marino, PSSM) governed without interruption from 1945 to 1957. The parliament, composed of sixty deputies elected by universal suffrage, was until March 1957 in the hands of the socialist-communist majority, which held thirty-five seats, nineteen of which belonged to the PCSM.

In April 1957, however, a socialist faction split from the PSSM and broke the coalition. In September, on the eve of the election of the republic's executive diumvirate, the opposition found itself in the majority, with thirty-five deputies in the parliament. On election day, September 19, the governing socialist-communist diumvirate instructed the police to forbid the opposition deputies access to the parliament and proclaimed its dissolution. The Italian government intervened, and the socialist-communist diumvirate was forced to give way on October 14 to a government formed by their opposition.

In the next elections, in September 1959, the democratic coalition won the majority of seats, and the socialist-communist coalition remained in the minority, with only twenty-four deputies (out of a total of sixty), sixteen of whom were communists. In the 1964 elections the PCSM received 3,058 votes out of a total of 12,928 votes cast, or 24.11 percent, and was still represented as a minority party in the parliament, with fourteen seats.

After 1959 the PCSM ceased to play an important local role, but it continued to figure as one of the parties recognized by the international communist movement. In this capacity a party delegation had participated in the world conference of communist parties meeting in Moscow in November 1957, and the manifesto for peace, signed by sixty-four "sister parties" from all over the world, included the signature of the PCSM representative. The PCSM was also represented in 1959 at the first conference of the communist parties of "capitalist" Europe, and in November 1960 at Moscow at the conference of eighty-one communist parties. The twenty-second congress of the Communist Party of the Soviet Union in October 1961 was attended by a PCSM delegation led by the general secretary, Ermenegildo Gasperoni. At the end of 1965 the PCSM's position in the Sino-Soviet dispute was pro-Soviet.

## ORGANIZATION AND MEMBERSHIP

Party membership in 1965 was estimated as around 960 (out of a total population of 17,000). The central committee included nearly fifty members, and the ten-member top leadership was headed by Gasperoni.

The party had at its disposal two subsidiary organizations, the Federation of Communist Women and the Federation of Communist Youth, directed by Gastone Pasolini. It also owned the Casa del Popolo, headquarters for the party organization.

## PARTY PRESS ORGAN

The organ of the PCM in 1965 was the monthly *La Scintilla*.

## CONGRESSES OF THE PCSM

5th congress, March 1955
6th congress, March 1961

## BIBLIOGRAPHY

"L'Affaire de Saint-Marin," *Est & ouest*, no. 184, December 1-15, 1957.

BRANKO LAZITCH

# SENEGAL

The first Senegalese to come in contact with the ideas of Marxism-Leninism were expatriate soldiers and students. Conscription, introduced in Senegal by the French, aroused much opposition among local chiefs as well as the population at large. During World War I the heavy losses among the *poilus* on the Western front led to profound bitterness and discouragement among black and white fighting men alike; and after the war was over, the French Communist Party attempted to carry on its work in the masses through the men in uniform. In addition, a handful of Senegalese students and intellectuals in France became familiar with communist concepts. They included such men as Lamine Senghor, a relative of Léopold Sédar Senghor, the well-known Senegalese poet and statesman. Lamine Senghor helped to found the Defense League of the Black Race, which maintained close ties with the French party.

During the popular-front government of the later 1930s a number of French communist teachers, clerks, and foremen secured employment in West Africa and thereby obtained the opportunity to propagate their party's interpretation of world events. Communist concepts, however, did not make much impact until the end of World War II. The French party's participation in the tripartite government at Paris from 1945 to 1947 gave the communists propaganda facilities in West Africa equal to those enjoyed by the socialists and Christian democrats. Marxist-Leninist ideas were disseminated in West Africa by communist study groups, which had been established at Dakar and other French West African cities as early as 1943. In addition, the communist-controlled French General Confederation of Labor helped to spread among African workers in Dakar and elsewhere the basic theoretical propositions of Marxism and popularize the program of the French Communist Party.

In the political sphere communists exercised some influence through the African Democratic Rally (Rassemblement Africain Démocratique, RDA), a mass organization founded in 1946 to serve French West and Equatorial Africa. The RDA enjoyed the support of the French party, but in 1950 the movement led by Ivory Coast's Félix Houphouët-Boigny, a landowner of Baoulé origin, broke with the communists. After the referendum of September 1958, whereby General de Gaulle permitted French-speaking Africa to decide on its constitutional destiny, the RDA broke up. The referendum brought into the open a split between the advocates of Africa's continued constitutional links with France and those who wanted African independence. The African Independence Party (Parti Africain de l'Indépendance, PAI), formed in 1957 and led by Majhemout Diop and Oumar Diallo, was the first French West African party to demand immediate independence from France. In 1960 Senegal became independent.

The PAI held its first congress in 1962 to discuss whether it should remain federal in character, operating throughout the territories of former French Black Africa, or whether it should limit its activities to Senegal. It had been founded at a time when the French-initiated West African and Equatorial African Federations were still in existence; this had been reflected in the party's organizational structure. The congress decided that since the federal regime was no longer in existence, the party's original organization had outlived its usefulness and the PAI should now operate as a Senegalese organization. The minimum program called for full political and economic independence, and to this end the PAI was to join a United Independence Front and rally all progressive forces to build a national democracy which would sever all ties from France, liquidate all French bases and military pacts with France, and reorganize the national economy. The goal was a socialist society, to be achieved through socialization of the basic means of production and distribution, industrialization, cooperative farming, mechanization of agriculture, and economic planning. The PAI was orthodox Marxist-Leninist in character and the French Communist Party expressed complete solidarity with the views of its Senegalese sister party.

After riots during the municipal elections at Saint Louis, the PAI was banned later in 1962 but apparently continued illegal work both within and outside the borders of Senegal. In January 1965, however, the progovernment Senegalese Progressive Union (Union Progressiste Sénégalaise) issued a communiqué stating that members of the PAI who were taking refuge in Bamako (Mali) would shortly be expelled by the Mali authorities. In June a special tribunal in Dakar convicted twenty-seven persons of attempting to reorganize the banned party and of plotting against the security of the state. According to Radio Dakar, four leaders of the former PAI had recruited men in Senegal and in 1963 had sent thirty young men to Bamako. In January 1964 a group had reportedly gone to Cuba for training in guerrilla warfare and sabotage and had eight months later returned to Bamako, where two units had been formed to carry out partisan operations in Senegal. Some of these insurgents were caught by farmers and handed over to the authorities. The special tribunal sentenced the accused to terms of imprisonment ranging from ten to twelve years. The Senegal national assembly subsequently passed new and more stringent sedition laws.

By 1965 the PAI's adherents seemed to be confined largely to university circles and to expatriates in Mali, and its effective strength was accordingly small.

ORGANIZATION AND MEMBERSHIP

The functions of secretariat and politbureau were performed in the PAI by a single body elected by the central committee, which also appointed members responsible for party publications. According to the *World Marxist*

*Review*, the party's general secretary was Majhemout Diop.

Party sources gave the composition of delegates to its first congress in 1962 as 43 percent functionaries, 20 percent factory workers, 3 percent peasants, 7 percent students, 20 percent teachers, 3 percent engineers and technicians, and 3 percent office workers; 7 percent were illiterate, 30 percent had an elementary schooling, 15 percent had a secondary education, and 48 percent had a higher education. The great majority was less than thirty-five years old.[1] The party's leadership was accordingly youthful in composition, and by African standards it contained a high percentage of intellectuals, deriving its main strength from white-collar professionals, to a lesser degree from factory workers, and very little from farmers. In 1965 the PAI's general composition was reported as 35 percent peasants, 35 percent intellectuals, and 30 percent workers,[2] but it is not known to what extent these statistics were politically motivated.

The party congress of 1962 decided to organize a students' organization and a youth and women's organization to be affiliated to the United Independence Front; these were to take the place of its former mass organizations. The party was also reported to have illegal trade-union groups.

## PARTY PRESS ORGANS AND RECORDS

*La Lutte: Organe du Parti africain de l'indépendance* was issued irregularly for a time from 1958 on. In 1962 the party decided to publish *Momsarer* as a theoretical journal.

The program and resolutions of the first party congress of 1962 are summarized in *World Marxist Review*, vol. 6, no. 1, January 1963, pp. 51-52. Party activities are discussed in the monthly *Africa Research Bulletin*, published in Exeter (England).

## BIBLIOGRAPHY

Decraene, Philippe: *Tableau des partis politiques de l'Afrique au sud du Sahara*, Paris, Fondation Nationale des Sciences Politiques, 1963.

Diop, Majhemout: *Contribution à l'étude des problèmes politiques en Afrique*, Paris, Présence Africaine, 1958.

Foltz, William J.: *From French West Africa to the Mali Federation*, New Haven, Conn., Yale University Press, 1965.

Foltz, William J.: "Senegal," in James S. Coleman and Carl G. Rosberg, Jr. (eds.), *Political Parties and National Integration in Tropical Africa*, Berkeley, Calif., University of California Press, 1964.

Gauthier, Gustave: *Le Bolshevisme aux colonies et l'impérialisme rouge*, Paris, Librairie de la Revue Française, 1930.

Gavrilov, N.: *National Liberation Movements in West Africa*, Moscow, Progress Publishers [1965].

Hodgkin, Thomas: *African Political Parties: An Introductory Guide*, Harmondsworth, Middlesex, Penguin Books, 1961.

Ly, Abdoulaye: *Sur le nationalisme dans l'Ouest-Africain*, Publications du Parti du Regroupement Africain, no. 1, Dakar, 1959.

Morgenthau, Ruth (Schachter): *Political Parties in French-speaking West Africa*, Oxford, Clarendon Press, 1964.

LEWIS H. GANN

1. *World Marxist Review*, vol. 6, no. 1, January 1963, p. 50.

2. *World Marxist Review*, vol. 9, no. 2, February 1966, p. 62.

# SINGAPORE
*See* Malaysia and Singapore

# SLOVAKIA
*See* Czechoslovakia

# SOUTH AFRICA

During most of the nineteenth century the great majority of South Africans of all colors depended on farming for their livelihood. The discovery of diamonds and gold in the second half of the century, however, brought revolutionary changes to the country's economy. South Africa became a major exporter of minerals, and mining in turn provided a base for other associated industries. In the first stages of the South African mining revolution, the country had to import a large number of skilled workmen from overseas. The bulk of South Africa's early "aristocracy of labor" thus consisted of British immigrants who organized themselves into trade unions on the British pattern.

In 1907 William H. Andrews, a Leicester fitter, and other English-speaking workmen took the lead in forming the South African Labour Party, which, like its British counterpart, was the political wing of the trade-union movement. In 1914 this party split over the question of support for the war. Sidney Percival Bunting, a lawyer descended from a distinguished English family with a Wesleyan background, spoke for the pacifist faction and in September 1914 formed the War on War League, which stood for international socialist solidarity to oppose the war. The bulk of the party, however, rallied to "king and country." In 1915 the league was dissolved, and on September 22 it was replaced by a minuscule party, the International Socialist League of South Africa (ISL), headed by Andrews, the former chairman of the labor party and a Marxist.

The ISL welcomed the bolshevik revolution in Russia but remained numerically small. It was further split on the question of native policy, with Bunting and David Ivon Jones, the ISL secretary, heading the "negrophilist" faction. In 1920 Jones left for Europe, where he became friendly with Karl Radek and subsequently attended the Comintern congress in Moscow. On July 29, 1921, at a congress at Cape Town, the ISL joined with the Industrial Socialist League of Cape Town, the Marxist Club of Durban, and some other bodies to form the Communist Party of South Africa (CPSA), which, as the first communist party in Africa, affiliated with the Comintern. Andrews became the party's secretary, while Jones stayed on in Russia, where he subsequently died of natural causes.

## HISTORY

*1922 to 1925* During its first years the CPSA drew the bulk of its members from English-speaking workers and professionals, with a sprinkling of Jewish members trained in the revolutionary traditions of czarist Russia. In 1922 the white miners on the Witwatersrand, fearing that their employers would lower wages for skilled labor by employing black men to work for less, embarked on an armed revolt. The workers were split into three sections. Some adhered to the South African Industrial Federation, whose reformist leadership was largely swept aside during the insurrection. A second group, led by the Council of Action, received communist support and during the final stages of the revolt had its headquarters in the CPSA offices in Johannesburg. The largest and most militant group, however, consisted of Afrikaners, who now formed the bulk of the non-African labor force on the Rand. They were organized on semimilitary lines as "commandos," and for a time armed white workers controlled most of the Rand under the slogan "Workers of the world unite and fight for a white South Africa." This war cry oddly expressed the conflicting ideals held by the rebels.[1]

Many European soldiers in the government's citizens' force sympathized with the rebels, and toward the end of February practically the whole of the South African government's permanent force had to be sent to the Rand. The black Africans, who were sometimes subjected to violence from the insurgents, stood aloof from the struggle. In the end the South African government suppressed the insurrection after heavy fighting, and three prominent white leaders were hanged.

The CPSA, however, survived the outbreak, though internal divisions continued. Andrews stood above all for the interests of white workers, while Bunting represented the pro-African wing. In 1924 the communists supported the nationalist-labor "pact," an alliance between Afrikaans farmers and white workmen. The new "pact government," headed by General J. B. M. Hertzog, stood for a policy of segregation and for a "civilized" labor program. This policy met with strong opposition from negrophilist Europeans, mainly of middle-class background, and at a CPSA conference in December 1924 the pro-African section obtained control. Andrews resigned from his post as secretary early in 1925 and subsequently devoted himself to white South African trade-union affairs. Leadership of the party remained with Bunting, who was much more willing to make concessions to Africans.

*1925 to 1935* As a result of the CPSA's new policy, many European workmen left, and the party's white support derived mainly from professionals and intellectuals. The party tried to broaden its base by joining the African-controlled Industrial and Commercial Workers' Union, the first significant African labor organization, and by founding trade unions of its own. However, in 1926 the labor organization expelled its communist members. The African labor force, split into different ethnic segments and largely migratory in nature, was difficult to organize. The communists had some early successes in the trucking, textile, mattress-making, and similar trades, but they could make no impact on the great army of African farm workers and miners. Appeals to African voters in the reserves also brought few results, partly because of police interference and partly because of the party's harsh attitude toward the African petite bourgeoisie. This class comprised most of the politically conscious Africans, but they were subjected to heavy attack by the communists unless they identified themselves specifically with the CPSA.

The communists also tried to establish links with the African National Congress, which had been founded in 1912 as the South African Native National Congress with a very moderate program. They received some cooperation from its president J. T. Gumede, but in 1930 he lost his position to a rival. The CPSA's most reliable recruits came from a small group of African workers who joined the party directly and were trained in its night school; among them was Moses M. Kotane, subsequently one of the party's leading theoreticians.

Until 1927 the CPSA was left largely to its own devices, but from then on it was expected to fall more into line with directives from Moscow. In 1927 J. A. La Guma, a Coloured communist trade unionist, conferred with Bukharin in Moscow. They agreed that the South African struggle was primarily an anti-imperialist one, that South Africa was a semicolony of British finance capitalists who had left a share of their superprofits to their "South African allies." The goal of revolutionary struggle in South Africa was to overthrow the British and Boer "imperialists" and set up a democratic independent native republic. The following year Bunting opposed this position before the sixth congress of the Comintern and before the Anglo-American Secretariat, which included "Black Africa" within its scope. He argued that CPSA had only 1,750 members, of whom 1,600 were African blacks, and that for further growth it needed white support as well. However, he was unable to sway the Moscow line, which also had the support of a minority group led by Douglas Wolton, an English-born schoolteacher, and La Guma. The CPSA thus had to accept the Moscow-backed slogan of "a South African native republic as a stage toward a workers' and peasants' government, with full protection and equal rights for all national minorities."[2]

At the same time the CPSA was subjected to rigid bolshevization. Directives from Moscow replaced empirical methods of trial and error, and in 1929 the League of African Rights, a front organization with a studiously moderate program, had to be terminated on receipt of a cable from Moscow. In 1930 Douglas Wolton became secretary of the CPSA. The "social-democratic" method of electing officials disappeared and the new executive committee had to be voted for as a bloc. Wolton condemned the Buntingists, their alleged chauvinism, and their doctrine of "South African exceptionalism." Between 1931 and 1932 Bunting, Andrews, Solly Sachs (secretary of the Garment Workers' Union), La Guma, and others were expelled from the party, and by 1933 splits and expulsions had reduced the membership to no more than 150, most of whom were Europeans. The "bolshevizers" sustained a serious blow when Wolton defected to England in 1933, and Lazar Bach, a Lithuanian Jew and Wolton's principal associate, was left to continue the struggle against "right wingers," assisted by Louis Joffe, the party's financial secretary. There were further expulsions in 1935, and even Kotane was temporarily lost to the party. Bach went to Moscow, where he also became involved in a purge and was never heard of again.

*1935 to 1950* In 1935 the CPSA switched to the popular-front policy, conforming to the new Comintern line of alliances with other "progressive" forces against fascism in defense of the Soviet Union. As early as 1933 the South African communists had begun to use more moderate language regarding the African petite bourgeoisie. Antireligious propaganda was stopped; sometimes the party formed a united front with European clergymen. There was agitation against African civil and economic disabilities. The party made bids for joint action of the white and black unemployed and tried to make gains in the trade-union field. Joffe became secretary of a front organization, the Anti-Fascist League. In 1935 the party gained some Indian converts, and communists subsequently joined the Natal Indian Congress, where the procommunist faction became known as the "national bloc." In 1937 the National Liberation League was founded as a Coloured body, largely under communist inspiration. In 1938 it became part of the Non-European United Front of South Africa, but the communists could not overcome the factional tendencies in non-European politics, and their influence remained limited.

The popular-front period also witnessed a change in the party leadership. In 1937 Andrews was welcomed in Moscow; he rejoined the CPSA in 1938 and became chairman of its central committee. In 1939 Kotane, who had also been readmitted to the party, became its general secretary, a position he retained until the CPSA was officially dissolved in 1950.

The conclusion of the Ribbentrop-Molotov agreement once again led to a change in policy. South Africa's entry into the war as Britian's ally was condemned by both the communists and the Afrikaner nationalists. After some initial reluctance, the black African National Congress approved South Africa's policy. However, some communists, such as La Guma, broke party discipline on the war question, and the party once again found itself both isolated and divided.

The German invasion of the Soviet Union in 1941 brought another switch in policy. The CPSA now supported the "people's war" and put forth the slogan "arm the non-European soldiers." As a result, the communists made some progress in the trade-union field, and in 1942 a new Council of Non-European Trade Unions came into being at Johannesburg. By 1945 it claimed to represent some 168,000 workers, organized in 119 unions, some of them communist controlled, some Trotskyist, and others independent. The communists secured the election of J. B. Marks, secretary of the African Mine Workers' Union and a communist, as chairman of the council. However, this did not give them control of the organization, nor were they able to overcome its basic weaknesses. Nonunion men continued to form the great majority of the labor force. Non-European unions remained subject to political splits, personal factionalism, and police interference; their membership often fluctuated and their organization and financial framework commonly left much to be desired. In 1946, for instance, the African Mine Workers' Union staged a strike, but it was mismanaged by the communist leadership. Within a few days the strike was broken, and fifty people associated with the union and the party were sentenced to fines or short jail sentences. Among them were Y. M. Dadoo, an Indian communist; and Brian Bunting, son of S. P. Bunting.

The party nevertheless made some progress in the political field. In 1948 Sam Kahn, a communist lawyer, was returned to parliament as a native representative. In 1949 Fred Carneson won a seat in the provincial council of the Cape as a native representative, and a few other communists succeeded in obtaining seats on the Johannesburg and Cape Town city councils. The South African Nationalist Party, which had been voted into office in 1948 on a program of apartheid and Afrikaner nationalism, accordingly made preparations to outlaw the CPSA. On June 20, 1950, a few days before the suppression-of-communism act was to come into effect, Kahn announced the party's dissolution. This tactic created certain legal complications for the government, but the authorities tightened their legislation, and in July the CPSA was declared an unlawful organization.

*1950 to 1965* Soon after the CPSA was banned, the communists decided to refashion their movement as a clandestine body. In 1953 they reorganized as the South African Communist Party (SACP), which operated underground. Details of its founding and leadership were not published. The SACP attempted to build up its influence in the basic industries through the creation of shop units, but it had only limited success. It also made a major effort through the various South African congresses. These political bodies, organized according to racial group, were demanding a radical political and social transformation of South Africa and the liquidation of apartheid in all its forms. They joined to form the Congress Alliance, which in effect was controlled by the SACP.

The communists attained considerable influence in the South African Indian Congress; they gained control over the executive committee of the Congress of Democrats, an alliance of liberal and left-wing Europeans formed in 1952; and they obtained strong influence in the South African People's Congress, a Coloured organization. The Indian Congress had no more than a few thousand members, and the European and Coloured congresses had no more than a few hundred each, many of them intellectuals. However, the communists also made their weight felt in the African National Congress, a much larger body with a more variegated membership. Its leaders themselves differed considerably over how far to cooperate with the communists. The youth league of this congress, for instance, at first strongly opposed such collaboration. However, after 1950 many youth leaders reevaluated this position, partly as the result of the government's repressive policy, and communist influence gained greater weight in the congress movement. For instance, a communist, J. B. Marks, was elected president of the Transvaal Congress and simultaneously became vice president of the Transvaal Peace Council.[3] The congresses then set up coordinating committees on which all associated bodies were represented equally, enabling the smaller organizations to exercise an influence quite out of proportion to their membership.

In June 1955 a "congress of the people" was held at Kliptown, where some 3,000 delegates from various parts of South Africa directly represented some 200,000 people, just over 1½ percent of South Africa's population.[4] The Kliptown congress adopted a "freedom charter," which was accepted by the African National Congress only after bitter internal struggles between the "charterists" and the "Africanists." The charter proclaimed that "South Africa belongs to all who live in it, black and white," and that government must be based on the will of the people, a formulation closer to the Buntingist position than the "native-republic" slogan of the late 1920s. The charter called for many reforms of the bourgeois liberal kind and for nationalization of the mineral wealth, the banks, and the monopoly industries in South Africa, with all other industries to be controlled for the wellbeing of the people.[5] According to Kotane, these socialist clauses had been introduced as a first step toward a people's republic.[6]

However, the communists could not prevent a split in the African National Congress. In 1956 the government arraigned its leaders and allies, as well as a number of Africanists, on charges of treason; after a trial lasting four years, all were acquitted by a South African court, but the African National Congress was outlawed. The Africanists, who wished to rely on the African people alone in the freedom struggle, broke away, and in 1959 they formed the Pan-Africanist Congress as an independent organization.

South African communists subsequently formed the Socialist League of Africa. In the early 1960s this body published *Spark*, which followed the orthodox communist line in condemning American, British, and West German "neocolonialism" and supporting Soviet policy. In the Sino-Soviet dispute it observed friendly neutrality toward both parties but backed a plea for the restoration of socialist unity made by the Communist Party of Great Britain early in 1963. The principal figures associated with *Spark*, which was banned in 1963, were Brian Bunting, previously editor of *New Age*; Govan A. M. Mbeki, an African lecturer who was subsequently imprisoned on charges of attempting to overthrow the South African government by violence; M. P. Naicker; and Ruth First.

Throughout the 1950s the communists had been anxious to conceal their connection with the Congress Alliance and similar bodies, but in 1960 they began to claim extensive successes and devote much attention to propaganda. They also intensified their hold over the clandestine cadres of the African National Congress. In 1961 the SACP decided on a policy of industrial sabotage and armed resistance. Together with the African National Congress, it created an independent combat organization, Spear of the Nation (Umkonto we Sizwe). On paper this organization had an elaborate structure, with a national high command and subordinate regional commands. The regional commands were to train saboteurs and select targets. The organization as a whole operated on the cell system. It was, however, unable to gain any significant successes and was soon broken by South African security organs.

The South African government similarly disrupted the underground organizations of the African National Congress and SACP. Industrial sabotage had no effect on South Africa's rapidly expanding economy, and the party remained incapable of creating effective mass support for its policy. Nevertheless, in a joint communiqué with the Communist Party of Great Britain, the SACP stated in 1965 that "the decision of the liberation movement to prepare for the armed overthrow of the white-supremacy state remains basically correct, irrespective of the success or failure of any particular plan or operation."[7]

By 1965 the SACP was largely an émigré organization and suffered from the weaknesses common to such bodies. It was small in numbers (probably a few hundred at the most),[8] and there was good evidence of police penetration. Most of its members appeared to be intellectuals, "officers without an army," who by reason of their ethnic or class background or their personal inclinations were not suited to the task of penetrating the country's armed forces, security services, or administration, all of which remained loyal to the authorities. The SACP nevertheless retained some significance. Its strategy aimed at a protracted struggle; the leadership looked for results in the more distant future, when the country's internal contradictions would become more acute. According to some reports, activists were being instructed no longer to seek safety in exile in order to build up cadres and contacts overseas, but to continue the underground struggle in South Africa, at the risk of being caught and sentenced to long terms of imprisonment.

## ORGANIZATION AND MEMBERSHIP

In 1965 the local leadership of the SACP was a matter of conjecture. Marks later became officially known as party chairman. The important task of reporting to the *World Marxist Review* on the fortieth anniversary of the SACP in 1961 was entrusted to a P. Tlalé. A. Lerumo contributed much to the party's theoretical work. Abram Louis Fischer, acting chairman of the central committee, jumped bail early in 1965 and went underground. The precise role played during this period by other South Africans, including émigrés such as Kotane, Joe Slovo, Ruth First, Brian Bunting, and others, was not published, but the party leadership was aging.

In the trade-union field, the South African Congress of Trade Unions, founded in 1955, operated as an affiliate both of the All-African Trade Union Federation and of the communist-dominated World Federation of Trade Unions.[9] Its general secretary, Mark Williams-Shope, demanded a policy of antifascist unity and of increased pressure on the government so as to isolate the South African regime and hasten its downfall.[10] The Congress of Trade Unions claimed 50,000 members, but its practical importance was small.

## RELATION TO SOVIET LEADERSHIP

The SACP has generally followed a pro-Soviet line. It supported the Soviet position over Albania and Cuba. However, it came closer to the Chinese viewpoint over India. *The African Communist* carried many references to the Chinese experience and its relevance to Africa and expressed regret over the substitution of negotiations for militant struggles for freedom in East Africa. At the occasion of its fortieth anniversary in 1961 the SACP received "warm and fraternal greetings" from the Chinese party. In later statements, however, the SACP adopted a firm pro-Soviet stand.

## PARTY PRESS ORGANS AND RECORDS

In September 1915 the communists brought out a weekly, *International*, which was incorporated by the *South African Worker* in June 1926. By 1929 this journal was appearing only irregularly, and in April 1930 it was reorganized as the official party organ *Umsebenzi*, which was published until about March 1938. Intermittent publications included the *Young Worker*, a bulletin of the Young Communist League of South Africa published for a time in 1924; *Maraphanga*, which came out in 1932; *Inkululeko*; and *Arbeider en arm Boer: Afrikaanse Maandblad van die Kommunistiese Party van Suid Afrika*, published during 1935 in Afrikaans as a monthly.

In February 1937 *The Guardian* was started as a weekly. It was banned in May 1952 and was succeeded by *The Clarion*, and then by *New Age*, also as a weekly, edited by Brian Bunting. *New Age* was subsequently banned and replaced by *Spark*, also edited by Bunting. *Spark* was restarted as a regular journal in July 1962 and continued publication as a weekly until March 1963, when it was banned.

In the fall of 1959 the clandestine SACP began to put out *The African Communist*, which in 1965 was being published in London as a quarterly.

The party's program, adopted in 1963, is reproduced in full as "The Road to South African Freedom: Programme of the South African Communist Party," *The African Communist*, vol. 2, no. 2, January-March 1963, pp. 24-70.

## BIBLIOGRAPHY

Benson, Mary: *The African Patriots: The Story of the African National Congress of South Africa*, London, Faber & Faber, 1963.

Brzezinski, Zbigniew (ed.): *Africa and the Communist World*, Stanford, Calif., Stanford University Press for the Hoover Institution, 1963.

Carter, Gwendolen M.: *The Politics of Inequality: South Africa since 1948*, New York, Praeger, 1958.

Cope, R. K.: *Comrade Bill: The Life and Times of W. H. Andrews, Workers' Leader*, Cape Town, Stewart, 1943.

Feit, Ewald: *South Africa: The Dynamics of the African National Congress*, London, Oxford University Press, 1962.

Kotane, Moses M.: *South Africa's Way Forward*, Cape Town, Competent Printing and Publishing, 1954.

Mtolo, Bruno Sipiwe: *Umkonto we Sizwe: The Road to the Left*, Durban, Drakensberg, 1966.

Roux, Edward: *S. P. Bunting: A Political Biography*, Cape Town, African Bookman, 1944.

Roux, Edward: *Time Longer than Rope: A History of the Black Man's Struggle for Freedom in South Africa*, 2d ed., Madison, Wisc., University of Wisconsin Press, 1964.

Vermaak, Chris: *Braam Fischer: The Man with the Two Faces*, Johannesburg, 1966.

LEWIS H. GANN

1. Edward Roux, *Time Longer than Rope: A History of the Black Man's Struggle for Freedom in South Africa*, Madison, Wisc., University of Wisconsin Press, 1966, p. 148.

2. Edward Roux, *S. P. Bunting: A Political Biography*, Cape Town, African Bookman, 1944, p. 103.

3. See A. Lerumo, "After Forty Years: An Important Anniversary," *The African Communist*, no. 7, September 1961, pp. 62-82, for names and details concerning the part played by the communists in various congresses and trade unions.

4. Ewald Feit, *South Africa: The Dynamics of the African National Congress*, London, Oxford University Press, 1962, p. 32.

5. The charter is reproduced in Gwendolen M. Carter, *The Politics of Inequality: South Africa since 1948*, New York, Praeger, 1958, pp. 486-490.

6. Feit, *op. cit.*, pp. 15-16.

7. "Joint Communique of Joint Meetings of Communist Party of Great Britain and South African Communist Party," *The African Communist*, no. 23, 1965, p. 103.

8. U.S. Department of State, Bureau of Intelligence and Research, *World Strength of the Communist Party Organizations*, Eighteenth Annual Report, Washington, January 1966, p. 131, gives the estimated strength as 100.

9. See *World Marxist Review*, vol 9, no. 2, February 1966, p. 69.

10. See the interview with Mark Williams-Shope in *World Marxist Review*, vol. 7, no. 6, June 1964, pp. 85-88.

# SOUTH KOREA
*See* Korea

# SOUTH VIETNAM
*See* Vietnam

# SOVIET UNION
*See* Union of Soviet Socialist Republics

# SPAIN

The Spanish communist movement emanated from a dissident revolutionary wing of the Spanish Socialist Labor Party (Partido Socialista Obrero Español, PSOE), founded in 1879, and from two labor organizations—the socialist-oriented General Workers' Union (Unión General de Trabajadores) and the anarcho-syndicalist National Labor Confederation (Confederación Nacional del Trabajo), established in 1888 and 1911, respectively. On April 15, 1920, the Federation of Socialist Youth (Federación de Juventudes Socialistas) convened in Madrid, denounced the "reformist" majority of the PSOE, and named itself the Spanish Communist Party (Partido Comunista Español, PCE). Among the new party's founders were A. Buendia, Vicente Arroyo, Rafael Millá, and Ramón Merino García, who were named to the party's central committee at its first congress in March 1921, and Merino García, Juan Andrade Rodríguez, and Gabriel León Trilla, who later defected or were purged from the party.

A second split in the PSOE occurred in July 1920, when a majority voted to send a delegation to attend the second congress of the Comintern. The PSOE refused to accept Lenin's Twenty-one Conditions for Admission, and a group of socialists broke away to form the Spanish Communist Labor Party (Partido Comunista Obrero Espanol, PCOE). On April 13, 1921, this group issued a manifesto of intention which included the signatures of Antonio García Quejido, a founder of the General Workers' Union and a member of the PSOE executive committee, and Oscar Pérez Solís, who later was named secretary general of the PCOE but abandoned the party. The PCOE immediately established ties with the Comintern. The socialist youth organization changed its name to Federation of Communist Youth of Spain (Federación de Juventudes Comunistas de España) and also joined the Comintern. On November 7, 1921, the two communist parties united as the Communist Party of Spain (Partido Comunista de España, PCE); the youth organization affiliated with the new PCE. Other important activists were José Bullejos, who had followed Pérez Solís as PCOE secretary general, and Barcelona leaders Andrés Nin Pérez, who left the PCE in 1932 to establish the Trotskyist Communist Left (Izquierda Comunista), and Joaquín Maurín Julía, who founded the Peasant Workers' Bloc (Bloque Obrero Campesino). These two organizations were merged to form the Workers' Party of Marxist Unification (Partido Obrero de Unificación Marxista, POUM).

## HISTORY

The first congress of the PCE, held on March 15, 1922, focused on the problem of uniting the labor movement. Despite opposition and factionalism among the eighty-odd delegations in attendance, the congress approved a policy of establishing a united front with the General Workers' Union and the National Labor Confederation. Antonio García Quejido was named secretary general. In the summer of 1922 the PCE invited the PSOE and both labor groups to join in a united front to protest workers' grievances, demand an amnesty for political prisoners, and call for an end to Spanish military activity in Morocco. This bid was opposed by the PSOE and the General Workers' Union, which promptly expelled twenty-nine communist-led unions. Nevertheless, the PCE supported workers' strikes in Asturias and the Basque provinces throughout 1922 and 1923.

At its second congress, which began July 8, 1923, the party again called for unity among the working classes and advocated a united front. Not until Miguel Primo de Rivera established his military dictatorship in September did the PCE policy win support. On September 13, the PCE and the Madrid section of the National Labor Confederation joined to form the Action Committee Against War and Dictatorship. The dictatorship moved against the party in December, alleging a conspiracy involving communists in Spain and Portugal. Large numbers of suspects were arrested, and a year later the PCE was banned altogether. With the government repression, many of the socialists and anarchosyndicalists who had participated in the party's formation defected. Other activists, including Nin, Maurín, and Bullejos, joined the PCE ranks at this time, but their loss at a later time considerably weakened the party's strength and effectiveness. The party also suffered later from the deaths of such leaders as García Quejido and Virginia Gonzalez.

Repressions by the Primo de Rivera dictatorship forced the party to hold its third congress in Paris in August 1929. The congress resolved that socialism could come to Spain "only through the bourgeois-democratic revolution," and that there was a need for an alliance of workers, peasants, and others to destroy the landed aristocracy and the monarchy. The dictatorship fell in January 1930, and two months later the PCE held a national conference in Bilbao which reaffirmed the resolutions of the third congress. Despite a semblance of unity, the party suffered from factionalism, first in Catalonia and later within the central committee. After unsuccessful attempts to get the Comintern to adopt a more flexible policy, Nin and Maurín, two of the best-known leaders, were denounced as Trotskyists and left the party. In October 1932 Bullejos, Manuel Adame, and Gabriel León Trilla were expelled for their hard-line revolutionary views against electoral alliances, an issue which traditionally had plagued the party. Their expulsion came after the proclamation of the republic, the waging of a series of strikes in Seville, and the PCE's fourth congress, which convened in Seville on March 17, 1932.

The fourth congress represented the beginning of party reorganization under the leadership of José Díaz. As before, the PCE advocated cooperation with other leftist forces in the formation of an antifascist front (although at the same time the Comintern and its affiliated parties were denouncing socialists and anarchists as fascists). The front policy was reconfirmed in a plenary session of the central committee in April 1933, and a front was established which included the PCE, the Federation of Communist Youth, the Unity General Confederation of Labor (Confederación General del Trabajo Unitaria), the Tobacco Workers' Federation, the Federal Party (Partido Federal), and the Socialist Radical Left (Izquierda Radical Socialista).

According to the PCE official party history, in the 1933 electoral campaign communists joined some socialists and republicans in Málaga to form what the PCE proclaimed as "the first popular front" in Spain; one communist, Cayetano Bolívar, was elected as deputy. The victory of the rightist parties assured their entrenchment in the republican government during the next two years, a period marked by the rise of the fascist right under José Antonio Primo de Rivera and by leftist-provoked strikes and agitation, notably in Asturias, where in October 1934 the PCE participated in a miners' uprising.

The PCE again called upon the socialists to cooperate in a united front but finally accepted a counterproposal to participate in the socialist-led Workers' Alliance (Alianza Obrera). At the same time the PCE called for amnesty for political prisoners, unity among workers, and the establishment of an antifascist popular front. In March 1935 a National Committee of Aid to Prisoners was formed, with the participation of the PCE, socialists, and a large number of less important groups. In the summer of 1935 the Comintern launched its popular-front program, in which all liberal and leftist forces were to join against the threat of fascism. By the end of the year a rapprochement was achieved between revolutionary socialists and communists, and on January 15, 1936, a popular-front pact was signed in which the Republican Left (Izquierda Republicana), the Republican Union (Unión Republicana), and the Catalan Left (Catalán Esquerra) aligned with the PCE and PSOE to demand a return to the religious, educational, and regional policies of the first two years of the republic, land reform, and amnesty for political prisoners. According to the pact, the socialists and communists would support a government composed of republicans for the purpose of fulfilling the announced "bourgeois-democratic program." Electoral victory was achieved on February 16, with sixteen communists elected to the parliament.

With the emergence of the popular front the PCE was strengthened by the amalgamation in April 1936 of the socialist and communist youth into the Unified Socialist Youth (Juventudes Socialistas Unificadas), under the leadership of Santiago Carrillo and Fernando Claudín, and by the fusion in July of four Catalan parties into the Catalonian Unified Socialist Party (Partido Socialista Unificado de Cataluña, PSUC). The communists continued to exert little influence on the General Workers' Union and the National Labor Confederation, however. When the civil war broke out in mid-July, the PCE continued to advocate cooperation between middle-class liberals and the working class. In reality, however, it opposed local collectivist revolutions and made itself the champion of the petit-bourgeois property owners. The party ranks grew with the added support of petite bourgeoisie, government functionaries, army officers, and young intellectuals. The PCE's distinct middle-class orientation and subservience to Moscow's interest in maintaining the status quo in Spain paradoxically made the communists a real threat to revolutionaries interested in restructuring and reforming Spanish society.

By March 1937, five years after the formation of the POUM by Nin and Maurín, the PCE had declared open war on that organization, which it condemned as an "agent of fascism." In June the PCE was apparently responsible for the arrest of more than 1,000 POUM members, many of whom, including Nin, were assassinated or deported to the Soviet Union.

The popular front and the civil war delayed the PCE's fifth congress, but four plenary sessions of its central committee were held during 1937 and 1938. The first session, held on March 5-8, 1937, concerned itself with the problem of uniting socialists and communists. A month later the PCE central committee and the PSOE executive committee formed a joint national committee, which proposed the immediate establishment of provincial committees throughout Spain. The second session, held on June 18-20 in Valencia, dealt with the possibility of forming a united party of the proletariat. The third plenary session met in Valencia on November 13-15, and the fourth was held in Madrid on May 23-25, 1938.

With the intervention of the Soviet Union on the side of the loyalists, the activity of Soviet and Comintern representatives increased considerably. The communists, Spanish and foreign alike, assumed a more active role in government and military affairs. On September 4, 1936, two communists, Vicente Uribe and Jesús Hernández, joined the first cabinet of socialist Francisco Largo Caballero. Influence in the foreign-affairs ministry was substantial, and the communists also exerted control over censorship. While their participation in the cabinets of Largo Caballero and his successor Juan Negrín was minimal, communist supporters were influential in the lower government echelons and were especially influential in military affairs. One of the most important party units, the famous fifth regiment, numbering about 70,000, about half of whom were communists, was disbanded and reorganized into "mixed brigades," led for the most part by communists.

In early 1939 the republic controlled a large section of central Spain, including Madrid, and several hundred thousand troops. Premier Negrín and his top military advisors agreed that they could not hope to defend the republic without the support of England and France and in view of the apparent failure of negotiating a peace with General Francisco Franco, leader of the opposing nationalist forces. With communist backing, however, Negrín called for continued resistance. On March 5 the noncommunist commanders revolted, and Negrín and his government fled to Algiers. The new government was immediately challenged by communist resistance, which was put down at the cost of several hundred lives. The government attempted further negotiations with the nationalist forces, hoping in particular to achieve a guarantee against political reprisals. However, the nationalist forces gained unconditional victory on April 1, 1939.

After the civil war communists were severely persecuted, and many were executed. The PCE continued clandestine activities in Spain, and in manifestoes of August 1941 and September 1942 it called for a national union of all Spaniards, with a program acceptable to both rightist and leftist opposition, to overturn the Franco dictatorship and lead to elections. Party newspapers and propaganda were continued underground. In 1945 Jesús Monzón, a leader of Spanish communist exiles in France, objected to the policy of seeking antifascist unity in the opposition. However, the PCE central committee accused him of opportunism, and a plenary session in December affirmed the policy of cooperation with certain segments of the opposition.

In early 1946 the PCE joined the Alliance of Democractic Forces (Alianza de Fuerzas Democráticas), established two years earlier by right-wing socialists, anarchists, and republicans, and also agreed to participate in the exile republican government in Mexico. Santiago Carrillo served in the exile government until the summer of 1947, when the PCE withdrew, partially in response to the cold war and directives of the Cominform. At the same time the PSOE, adopting an anticommunist position, also abandoned the exile government, and from France the ruling socialist government banned the PCE exile press. Nevertheless, throughout 1947 communists participated in labor agitation in the metallurgical factories of Madrid, in the textile factories of Catalonia, in Guipúzcoa, and elsewhere. Communists in Viscaya claimed credit for a strike in Bilbao on May 1. Labor unrest continued, and on March 4, 1951, a PSUC manifesto led two days later to a strike in Barcelona.

On November 1-5, 1954, the PCE finally held its fifth congress and issued a new appeal for a national antifascist front to overthrow the Franco government, to be followed by a coalition government that would implement a series of reforms in education, agriculture, and industry. The congress also approved a new party statute based on the principle of "democratic centralism" and named Dolores Ibarruri secretary general.

In June 1955 the PCE sponsored a national workers' congress, which called for a minimum wage and the right to strike. A year later, at the second postwar plenary session of the central committee, the PCE proposed a policy of "national reconciliation" to unite all Spaniards in the struggle for civil liberties. In September 1957 a third plenary session proposed further labor agitation, and communists participated in strikes in Asturias during March 1958 and a one-day national strike on June 18, 1959.

A sixth party congress met on January 28-31, 1960. The PCE affirmed its adherence to the peaceful-coexistence policy of the Soviet Union, substantially revised its party program, and ratified the policy of national reconciliation, calling upon the opposition to discuss means of challenging the dictatorship. Dolores Ibarruri was named party chairman and Santiago Carrillo secretary general.

In November 1962, after widespread labor unrest had swept Asturias, the communist Julián Grimau García was arrested by Spanish police and was executed in April 1963; the incident received widespread attention in the international press. A few months later the PCE was beset by factionalism over the Sino-Soviet dispute, and on August 4 a pro-Chinese group was ousted. The pro-Peking group associated itself with a small anarchist movement, the Iberian Federation of Libertarian Youth (Federación Ibérica de Juventud Libertaria). In 1965 Fernando Claudín of the PCE central committee was also expelled for revisionism and pro-Peking views.

During 1964 and 1965 the party attempted to take advantage of labor unrest in Asturias and elsewhere, student disorders in Madrid, and Catholic demonstrations in Barcelona. One party statement advocated "amnesty for all political prisoners and émigrés, recognition of the right to strike, trade-union freedoms, freedom of the press, speech, and association, freedom of conscience, and universal suffrage." Another pragmatic PCE view acknowledged that "the Catholics are our main allies today in the struggle against Franco."

## ORGANIZATION AND MEMBERSHIP

According to its 1954 statute, the underground PCE is organized on the basis of democratic centralism. It is directed by a central committee, which elects a president and a secretary general and coordinates party activities in the provincial, regional, subregional, local, zonal, and sectoral organizations. The party congress, the highest authority, studies and amends reports of the central committee, adopts resolutions, and approves the party statutes and program. The basic unit, the cell, is found in all sectors of Spanish society.

PCE membership, roughly estimated as about 5,000 in 1965, is drawn generally from manual workers and intellectuals in Spanish urban areas—Madrid, Barcelona, and Bilbao in particular—and from exiles abroad, especially in Paris and Toulouse. Many top leaders and some members are in the Soviet Union, Eastern Europe, North Africa, and Latin America.

In its early stage the party included only a small number of intellectuals and labor leaders. Despite factionalism, it was able to increase its membership from 1,000 in early 1931 to a reported 20,000 in October 1934 and some 35,000 by February 1936. By March 1936, shortly before the start of the civil war, membership had reached more than 300,000, drawn chiefly from industrial and agricultural workers as well as peasants, with a lesser representation from the middle class and intellectuals. After the demise of the republic in 1939 support waned owing to the party's illegal status and the suppression by the Franco government.

Since its inception the PCE has attempted with only moderate success to establish alliances with other parties and organizations. In September 1923 it sponsored the Action Committee Against War and Dictatorship. With the rise of fascism in Europe, in 1933 it established the Antifascist Front, women's committees against war and fascism, and a "popular front" in Málaga. In 1934 it participated in the Workers' Alliance and in 1935 established with other parties, the National Committee of Aid to Prisoners. In the summer of 1935 the party called for an antifascist bloc and achieved this objective with the popular-front pact of January 1936.

During the civil war the PCE sponsored a large number of organizations, including International Red Aid, the Girls' Union, the Antifascist Women, the Cultural Militias, the Friends of the Soviet Union, the Alliance of Antifascist Intellectuals, and the Young Mothers' Union, while the fifth regiment was an important PCE-controlled battlefront unit during the Spanish civil war. After World War II the party joined the Alliance of Democratic Forces and the republican government exiled in Mexico. During the 1950s the PCE advocated first a national antifascist front and later a policy of "national reconciliation" involving all opposition movements. In the 1960s the PCE was believed to be involved in the Iberian Revolutionary Liberation Directorate.

## RELATION TO SOVIET LEADERSHIP

In December 1919 the Federation of Socialist Youth voted to join the Comintern, and a few months later it evolved into the first PCE, which sent a delegation to the second congress of the Comintern in Moscow. Angel Pestaña also attended the second Comintern congress as a representative of the National Labor Confederation. A Spaniard was named to the Comintern Executive Committee after Lenin announced that "the second successful proletarian revolution" would take place in Spain. In April 1921 the rival PCOE also adhered to the Comintern, as did the Federation of Communist Youth. By the third Comintern congress the two Spanish communist parties had formed the new united PCE and accepted the Comintern tactic of attempting to establish a united front with labor and other organizations. In 1936 the Soviet Union announced its intention to intervene in the civil war, and Comintern agents assumed a major role in this struggle. Except for occasional dissidence resulting in expulsion or defection, the PCE leadership continued to give its unqualified support to Moscow.

The dispute between China and the Soviet Union provoked an open split in late 1963, resulting in the establishment of two separate pro-Peking organizations, the Revolutionary Communist Party (Partido Comunista Revolucionario) and the "Spanish Marxist-Leninist" faction. The pro-Chinese groups probably have no more than several hundred members in all, many of whom are young militants. The expulsion of Fernando Claudín in 1965 was a result of his revolutionary views "upheld by the Chinese comrades." At the same time another faction in the PCE was reportedly advocating greater independence from Moscow.

## PARTY PRESS ORGANS AND RECORDS

The clandestine publication *Mundo obrero*, the leading PCE organ, was first issued in August 1930. Its predecessor was *La Antorcha*, first issued in 1921. Other party organs first issued in the 1920s were *Aurora roja* in Asturias, *Bandera roja* in the Basque provinces, and *El Comunista balear* in Mallorca. During the republic and the civil-war periods the party issued numerous legal and illegal periodicals. After the war it clandestinely distributed *Verdad* in Valencia, *Unidad* in Málaga, *El Obrero* in the Canary Islands, and *Nuestra palabra* in the Baleares Islands.

A full text of the party statute, approved at the PCE's fifth congress in November 1954, can be found in *V Congreso del Partido comunista de España: Informe del comité central, presentado por su Secretario general Dolores Ibarruri*, Nice, 1954. The party program, approved at the central committee's plenary session of December 1945 in Toulouse and revised at the fifth congress, is published in *For a Lasting Peace, for a People's Democracy*, December 24, 1954. Official records are unavailable except for sporadic party statements printed usually in Eastern Europe or the Soviet Union.

## CONGRESSES OF THE PCE

1st congress, March 1922, Madrid
2d congress, July 1923, Madrid
3d congress, August 1929, Paris
4th congress, March 1932, Seville
5th congress, November 1954
6th congress, January 1960

## BIBLIOGRAPHY

Bolloten, Burnett: *The Grand Camouflage: The Communist Conspiracy in the Spanish Civil War*, New York, Praeger, 1961.

Carrillo, Santiago: *La Situación en el movimiento comunista y obrero internacional* [Santiago, Chile], Communist Party of Spain, 1963.

Cattell, David T.: *Communism and the Spanish Civil War*, Berkeley, Calif., University of California Press, 1955.

Comín Colomer, Eduardo: *Historia del Partido comunista de España, abril 1920-febrero 1936: Del nacimiento a la mayoría de edad*, Madrid, O.I.D., 1963.

*Deberes del pueblo español en la presente situación internacional y nacional*, Montevideo, España Democrática, 1961.

*Historia del Partido comunista de España: Versión abreviada*, Paris, Editions Sociales, 1960.

Ibarruri, Delores: *El único camino*, Paris, Editions Sociales, 1962.

*Plenum TSK Kommunisticheskoi partii Ispanii, avgust 1956 goda* (Plenum of the Central Committee of the Communist Party of Spain, August 1956), Moscow, 1957.

*VI zjazd Komunistycznej partii Hiszpanii, Marzec, 1960* (Sixth Congress of the Communist Party of Spain, March 1960), Warsaw, Książka i Wiedza, 1960.

RONALD H. CHILCOTE

# THE SPORTINTERN

*See* The Red Sport International

# SUBSAHARAN AFRICA[1]

The Chinese and Soviet blocs have stepped up their campaigns to influence the new leaders of Africa and to present communist experience as the most efficient and progressive example for all young nations to follow. But their policies have differed. Soviet strategists in the 1950s and the 1960s did not want to foment revolution everywhere in Africa, since there were relatively few communist parties there. Their aim was rather to discredit capitalism, imperialism, and neocolonialism; to deny the West trade and access to Africa's mineral wealth; to shut out the Western Alliance from bases in Africa; in sum, to draw as many African states as possible into the neutralist camp and out of the Western political and economic sphere.

For the Chinese communists the underdeveloped world has been an arena in which they hoped to prove their interpretation of Marxism-Leninism to be the correct one and thus win leadership of the world communist movement. In addition, they have urged wars of national liberation and the defeat of capitalism and imperialism while at the same time seeking to discredit the Soviet Union's policy of "peaceful coexistence."

## HISTORY OF COMMUNIST INTEREST IN AFRICA

Colonialism, long an important doctrinal issue within the world communist movement, has also provided an effective communist ideological weapon to attack capitalism. Lenin's book *Imperialism: The Highest Stage of Capitalism* (published first in 1917, reissued in French and German in 1920), has been one of the most influential anticolonial tracts ever written. Its theses have found favor among Marxists and non-Marxists alike, among African nationalists and colonial officials, Europeans and Asians.

Lenin wrote his book because he was faced with the problem of how to account for the continued vitality of capitalism and the improving conditions of the working class when Marx had predicted their imminent decline. Lenin's explanation was simple: imperialist expansion and profits from colonies had temporarily saved capitalism. Borrowing from the British writer J. A. Hobson (*Imperialism: A Study,* 1902), Lenin asserted that imperialism represented the most advanced stage of finance capitalism. Financiers in search of new investments, he said, had promoted European seizure of colonies where investors might earn higher profits than at home, and where land and labor could be obtained more cheaply than in the metropolitan countries. Imperialism exacted excessive investor profits and led to brutal exploitation of the indigenous peoples in Africa, Asia, and Latin America, and ultimately colonial rivalries produced World War I. Only by ending imperialism could capitalism be destroyed and its wars avoided. When the Western bourgeoisie could no longer bribe the metropolitan "aristocracy of labor" by paying high wages derived from excess colonial profits, Europe would fall to communism. Lenin's anti-imperialism arguments have continued to dominate the debate on colonialism and to influence African attitudes toward capitalism, imperialism, and the West.

Yet the Communist International between 1919 and 1943 was little concerned with Africa. A communist party was founded in South Africa in 1921 and a "League Against Imperialism" was formed in Brussels in 1927, but for the most part Moscow left it up to the communist parties in Western Europe to infiltrate the European colonial territories and mandates. When the need for European allies against Hitler led Stalin to abandon the interests of African nationalists in the 1930s, many Negro intellectuals became disillusioned with communism as a solution for African problems and broke with the movement.

SOVIET INTERESTS IN AFRICA

Since World War II communism's African policy has gone through two major phases spanning two distinct time periods: 1945 to 1955, and 1955 to the present. During the first period, Stalin's interest in the colonial struggle was only marginal. He used colonialism to embarrass the West in the United Nations, and he tried to divide the Allies by claiming the United States was bent on an economic takeover of Africa. Beyond that, he felt communism would triumph in Africa when capitalism was defeated in Europe. Stalin's insistence that only the working class could lead the struggle for independence and only the communist party could direct the working-class liberation movement was doomed to frustration in Africa, where there were few wage workers and even fewer communists. Control of Africa's communist parties remained in the hands of Europeans; and although communist study groups were organized for Africans from about 1943 onward and African students in Europe were approached by communists, still no disciplined black communist cadre emerged.

The second phase of communist activity in Africa grew out of the Bandung Conference of 1955. Moscow saw then that if it was to expand its influence in Asia and Africa it had to come to terms with the rising nationalist, anticolonialist movements of independence, most of them led by noncommunists. Moreover, because the African states were moving toward independence by nonrevolutionary methods the Soviet leadership had to change its stance concerning the African bourgeoisie. After the 1956 congress of the Communist Party of the Soviet Union which admitted that national independence in Africa could be achieved under the leadership of the bourgeoisie, noncommunist leaders like Kwame Nkrumah (Gold Coast-Ghana) and William V. S. Tubman (Liberia), whom the communists had once called "lackeys of imperialism," were styled friends and great leaders.

After Bandung the communists also shifted their emphasis from organizing Africans through the communist parties of Western Europe to the creation of indigenous organizations in Africa itself. Pro-Soviet Marxist-Leninist parties in Basutoland (now Lesotho), Nigeria, Senegal, South Africa, and the Sudan all stressed the need for a broad-based alliance that would include the national bourgeoisie as well as the peasant and working classes. They called for a national democratic revolution and relegated the achievement of socialism to a more distant future. Communists of the pro-Moscow persuasion tended to play down the need for armed struggles except in South Africa, Rhodesia, and the Portuguese colonies, where they insisted on national wars of liberation. The West still was continually attacked and accused of gross exploitation; nationalist movements were encouraged and immediate independence was demanded.

By 1965, however, Soviet leaders had begun to return to a more orthodox communist approach. They began to attack African assertions that there was no basis for a class struggle within the framework of indigenous African society. They also criticized the assumption that African socialism must follow its own lines of development rather than cleave to the scientific socialism of the Soviet Union.

White rule continued only in Southern Africa. Africa, however, continued to be a backward continent. Soviet theoreticians now blamed the shortcomings of the new Africa on what they called "neocolonialism"; in other words, they developed a doctrine which brought the Leninist interpretation of imperialism up to date. In the Soviet view, the newly independent countries were only formally independent: they remained in economic serfdom, still exploited and dominated by Western capitalists. This interpretation of Africa's poverty helped to explain the absence of revolutionary activism in the West. Continued colonial profits had once again prolonged the survival of capitalism. The doctrine also invalidated in advance any political concessions made by Western powers to their African dependencies and undermined the legitimacy of the more conservative African leaders while enhancing the prestige of the more "progressive" ones.

The long-term African policy of the Kremlin has envisioned an eventual communist takeover of the entire continent as part of the avowed scheme for world communization. But short-term Soviet strategy has revolved around the cold war, the immediate aims being to deny the West access to African minerals and to military and naval bases, to gain the adherence of young people, and to keep as many African states as possible in the neutralist camp.

The Soviet leaders have been somewhat ambivalent in their African policy. To some extent they have fostered instability—in their support for national liberation movements, for example, and in their efforts to inflame racial passions against white Africa. However, because most African leaders resent acts which encourage wars or revolutions in black-held areas, the communists have found it expedient since the advent of African independence to play down their image as revolution makers. Soviet interference in African internal politics in some areas, such as the Congo, Guinea, and Kenya, led to several diplomatic disasters; more recently, Soviet militancy has increased only when Moscow interests have been challenged by Chinese communists in key areas such as Somalia.

In recent years the Soviets have not particularly stressed the leadership role of the working class or of communist parties. Communists loyal to Moscow instead infiltrated nationalist movements and trade unions and concentrated on building up a network of agents and supporters. The channels and techniques used to extend Soviet influence in Africa have been similar to those used elsewhere.

Local peace movements, cultural fronts and youth leagues, women's associations, scholarship programs for study in the Soviet Union or elsewhere in Eastern Europe, student exchanges, technical and diplomatic missions, all have provided opportunities for infiltration and subversion. Training of African cadres has been stepped up in East Berlin, Prague, Warsaw, Budapest, and Moscow.

African youth and trade-union leaders have taken courses ranging from six months to two years at training centers in Eastern Europe. In 1965 the best known of these centers was the Central Komsomol School, which opened in Moscow in 1961. Some of Ghana's Young Pioneers were trained there, and the school also received leaders from Kenya, Tanzania, Mali, Rhodesia, and South West Africa. The Institute for Economic Studies in Prague trained African political cadres. In East Germany, the Free German Youth ran the Wilhelm-Pieck Institute in Bernau, near Berlin, for youth cadres from Ghana, Guinea, Nigeria, and other African countries. Trade unionists attended the Fritz-Heckert-Gewerkschaftsschule, also at Bernau. Other centers included the Karl Marx University and the Max Gerber Institute at Leipzig and the School for Ideological Training for Africans near Bautzen. Warsaw also had a training center for African students.

In 1958 a school for guerrilla fighters opened at Prague, and Bulgaria was reported to have a similar camp near Sofia. However, China seemed to be doing more training of guerrillas, at least up to 1963. Some members of the Movement for the Liberation of Angola were trained in China, and Mulele of the Congo (Kinshasa) reportedly was trained there, possibly in 1960 or 1961, as was the Mozambican Luca Fernandez. Chinese courses were thorough; they included sabotage, guerrilla warfare, and fortifications as well as political studies. In Africa itself colleges to train labor leaders were set up with Soviet assistance in Conakry (Guinea) and Bamako (Mali). A political training school, the Lumumba Institute, was established in Nairobi in 1964, but the Kenya government closed it in 1965.

The familiar communist tactic of working through front groups was also applied in Africa. The major international fronts, such as the World Federation of Trade Unions, the World Federation of Democratic Youth, the World Peace Council, and the International Union of Students, were too patently communist-dominated to gain wide acceptance in Africa. Hence Soviet representatives more recently have concentrated on infiltrating nationalist and pan-African movements such as the All-African Trade Union Congress. By 1965 Russian and Chinese experts also were involved with the Afro-Asian Peoples' Solidarity Organization.

Cultural exchanges and lavish treatment for African visitors in the Soviet Union have further linked African countries to the Soviet bloc. In June 1965 the first group of 228 students from forty-seven African countries graduated from Moscow's Friendship University (sometimes called Lumumba University), which attempts to convert African students to communism as well as to teach such subjects as medicine, agriculture, and science. By the end of 1965 more than 750 Africans from thirty-four countries were studying there, with the largest number from Nigeria, Kenya, and Ghana.

Economic aid also has served as an important political tool. Soviet aid has been channeled to influence the subjective attitudes of the African elite and to create a network of relationships that will expand economic bridgeheads. The goal is to induce African leaders to follow the domestic economic methods and models of the Soviet Union.

In support of all Soviet activity in Africa, propaganda has flowed freely from Zanzibar and Dar es Salaam, from Guinea and Congo (Brazzaville), and (before Nkrumah's ouster) from Ghana, to discredit the West and to heighten political and ethnic tensions. The Soviets have steadily tried to identify themselves with African values and culture, to say the kinds of things Africans want to hear—for example, that African backwardness is due to European exploitation and that Africa was a progressive place before the Europeans arrived and ruined everything.

After the French pulled out of Guinea in 1958, Guinea for a time became the main focus of Soviet interest in Subsaharan Africa. Although Guinean leader Sékou Touré is a Marxist, he first sought aid from the West. When he was refused he turned to the East, and by 1961 twelve communist countries were represented in Guinea. The Soviet bloc tried to make Guinea a showplace of communism and a base for subversion against neighboring states. Over $100 million was poured in, and a stadium, radio station, and printing plant were built. At one time there were more than 1,500 Soviet-bloc technicians in Guinea. To many observers Touré appeared to be ruling a communist state; however, when the Soviet ambassador Daniel Solod was implicated in disorders caused by students and trade unionists in 1961, Touré asked him to leave.

In 1960 both the Chinese and the Russians supported Lumumba and Gizenga in the Congo. China sent money, but its arms were held up in the Sudan; the Soviet Union sent military equipment of all kinds. However, when Lumumba was overthrown and Colonel Mobutu expelled all Soviet representatives, Moscow's interest in the Congo declined appreciably. In fact so disillusioned was the Soviet Union by the Congo debacle that it gave little or no help to Congolese radicals and in effect drove them into the hands of the Chinese. In 1962 more than a hundred Congolese were reported to be in China. Of the Congolese rebels who borrowed ideas and weapons from Communist China after Lumumba's ouster, the most important was Pierre Mulele. Mulele may have set up a guerrilla training camp near Brazzaville; it is certain that Chinese arms and aid enabled him to launch a rebellion in 1964 in the Kwilu province of Congo (Kinshasa). Although Mulele's rebellion was contained, others broke out. Gaston Soumialot, aided by the Chinese in Burundi, and Christophe Gbenye from Congo (Brazzaville) both launched later attacks against the central government. The most serious rebellion broke out in the eastern region around Stanleyville (now Kisangani) in 1964. Some Soviet arms came in through Egypt and the Sudan, but Moscow appears to have supported the rebels only after it appeared the Chinese would dominate the movements. These rebellions, also defeated, harmed Chinese and Soviet interests in many African countries, particularly in Kenya.

Many African political leaders have come to expect subversion from Soviet missions. Hastings Banda, head of Malawi, has vigorously denounced communist interference. Julius Nyerere of Tanzania has warned the Chinese not to meddle in the internal affairs of African states. And Kenya leader Jomo Kenyatta acted quickly to curb his vice president, Oginga Odinga, when Odinga used communist money and arms in an attempt to build up a political organization of his own. Odinga got Moscow to establish the Lumumba Institute in Nairobi in 1964; from there students were secretly sent to China and the Soviet Union for military training. Odinga clashed with Kenyatta when a Chinese pamphlet was uncovered which advocated the overthrow of the government of Kenya. Odinga's office was raided, and Soviet arms were found. Kenyatta thereupon ordered a Soviet military shipment sent back to the Soviet Union and asked the Soviet military mission to leave the country. He also closed the Lumumba Institute, dissolved two trade-union groups to get rid of communist sympathizers, and issued a pointed warning against the "dangers of imperialism from the East." Moscow was badly disillusioned. The Chinese continued to finance Odinga and to call for world revolution, however—with the result that by late 1965 some Soviet and Chinese embassy staff and newsmen had been expelled from Kenya and Odinga was effectively neutralized.

Nevertheless, some African political leaders impatient for progress and economic development viewed communism as the most promising system to increase productivity rapidly. Many Marxist assumptions have been accepted by Africans educated in Europe, including the idea that since the Soviet Union and Communist China are newly developed countries their economic and political models are more relevant to the demands of Africa than are models derived earlier in the West. Moreover the demonstrated effectiveness of communist parties in forging one-party states and maintaining power has favorably impressed first-generation political leaders, who often seek sweeping solutions to national problems.

Communism sometimes has had a strong psychological appeal. Communists champion nationalist movements; they usually praise precolonial society; they offer a vision of a more perfect world to be quickly attained. To Africans searching for new moral values as well as new political and economic models, the West has often seemed divided and equivocating while the communists have confidently promised a total system for organization and development.

But the Russians have labored under many limitations. Africans are jealous of their independence, and established African leaders naturally fear inroads into their power and dread revolutionary takeovers. Many have been alienated by the materialism of communist philosophy, and to some the doctrine of the class struggle as the key to history seems inapplicable to African traditional society. In 1965 the Soviets still lacked experience with Africa's peoples and languages and there were few trained communists in Africa to run communist parties. The lack of disciplined cadres meant the Soviets could neither control nor trust the indigenous movements. As a consequence, an unplanned variety of African socialist and communist parties was developing. Moreover, Soviet personnel in Africa had not entirely escaped the charges commonly leveled at their capitalist counterparts. Segregated living arrangements, excessive drinking, and ill-concealed Soviet contempt for African workers had led to accusations of racism. The failure of communist countries to solve their own agrarian problems has been damaging to their image in agrarian Africa. Moreover, the

Soviet and African economies complement each other only to a very limited extent, and by 1965 a barter system for exchanging Russian goods for African primary products had not been too successful. Some African leaders felt they were losing by these arrangements: Soviet goods often appeared inferior to Western goods, and African countries were sending to the Soviet Union crops they could have exchanged elsewhere for hard currency.

In 1965 there was still a large gap between Soviet promises and Soviet performances; less than a third of what was promised had been delivered. Between 1956 and 1960 the Soviet bloc spent $266 million in Africa, while France alone in the same period spent $703 million. Nevertheless, Soviet aid was used shrewdly. The Kremlin knew what it wanted to do with its aid program: increase Soviet prestige and influence, gain trade and markets, and keep the Americans and the Chinese out. The United States, not so single-minded but far more lavish in its expenditures, used aid for a variety of purposes that often proved contradictory. Thus in some respects the Soviet Union has realized more political and economic benefits from its relatively small African investments in the 1950s and 1960s.

CHINESE INTERESTS IN AFRICA

After 1961 the People's Republic of China intensified its efforts to win influence in Africa, which it considered one of the centers of the anti-imperialist struggle. By the mid-1960s Chinese communists were waging a battle in Africa for leadership of the world communist movement. Through people's wars of liberation (in the rural areas), the imperialist powers (of the urban areas), now led by the United States, were to be divided, distracted, and defeated. In the fall of 1965 Marshal Lin Piao set forth the new strategy: "Everything is divisible. And so is the colossus of United States imperialism. It can be split up and defeated. The peoples of Asia, Africa, Latin America and other regions can destroy it piece by piece, some striking at its head and others at its feet."[2]

By training revolutionaries, shipping arms, spreading revolutionary propaganda, and sponsoring national-liberation fronts, China hoped to produce chaos in Africa—and at small cost to itself. Bribes and pressures, diplomatic representation, and aid programs were designed to win friends in Africa and to present China as the model for revolution and development. China's approach to Africa has generally been pragmatic. Africa had few communist parties, and those that did exist tended to be pro-Soviet. Thus, to gain a foothold in Africa China was willing until recently to support noncommunist nationalist groups provided they were radically disposed. This policy resulted in some strange expedients, such as Chinese assistance to the anticommunist Pan-African Congress in South Africa and even an alliance with the Tutsi aristocracy in their efforts to displace the peasant-based government of Rwanda.

Because of their limited resources, the Chinese communists decided to establish a few training bases in strategically situated African countries from which they could launch wars of national liberation. The two most successful footholds were in Burundi and Congo (Brazzaville). Burundi, a minuscule country on the eastern border of Congo (Kinshasa), became independent in 1962 and recognized Communist China in 1963. Clearly the Chinese viewed Burundi as a stepping stone to the unstable Congo, and by 1964 there were more than twenty Chinese diplomats in Usumbura, the capital (Britain had three representatives, and the Soviet Union had four). A top official of the New China News Agency, Kao Liang, headed the operations, and through the Chinese embassy in Usumbura arms and money were sent into the Congo to support rebel groups. When the major rebellion broke out in 1964, Chinese support for the insurgents became even more overt. Arms came openly through Tanganyika and secretly across Kenya and Uganda to rebels in Stanleyville; the Stanleyville rebels were finally defeated in 1964 by Congolese troops spearheaded by white mercenaries. Soon after the premier of Burundi, Pierre Ngendandumwe, was assassinated on January 15, 1965, a Chinese arms cache was discovered in Usumbura. Burundi broke relations with the Chinese and expelled them on February 2, 1965.

Congo (Brazzaville) recognized Communist China in 1964. After the Youlou government fell in 1963 the Congolese labor leader Massemba-Débat had moved increasingly to the left, and when the Chinese were expelled from Burundi they turned their attention to Brazzaville. Colonel Kan Mai headed a fifty-man mission there, and training camps and staging areas for infiltration and subversion were reported by several observers. General Wang Ping, an expert on guerrilla warfare, arrived in June 1965, and Kao Liang moved to Brazzaville to head the New China News Agency office there. Chinese aid to Massemba-Débat was reported to equal that from France in 1965—$5 million—and a $20 million loan was promised to develop small-scale industries. To counter Chinese influence, in 1965 the Soviet Union increased its aid program considerably. Meanwhile Chinese officials advised the government, set up a powerful radio station, and helped to organize the paramilitary youth groups known as the Jeunesse; they also partially financed and ran the pro-Chinese party newspaper *Dipanda*.

Congo (Brazzaville) thus appeared to be the main Chinese base in Africa in 1965, with Zanzibar possibly the second most active center. Chinese communist influence over rebel leaders and disgruntled exiles was also strong in Dar es Salaam, Tanzania. In addition, the Chinese had sent small aid missions to several other countries, notably Guinea, Ghana, Mali, Niger, and Tanzania. Guerrilla training camps were reported in Guinea, Ghana, and Zanzibar. Students, journalists, and politicians were offered scholarships, financial aid, and trips to China. Radio and newspapers were subsidized to follow a pro-Chinese line.

During the first half of the 1960s Chinese delegates toured the continent through diplomatic channels. The Chinese embassies in Africa were reported second in size only to those of the United States. These diplomatic posts were used for infiltration, espionage, and intelligence gathering. For the masses there were movies, radio broadcasts, and a variety of magazines (*Peking Review, China Reconstructs,* and *People's Pictorial*) to foster the image of Chinese industriousness, wealth, and economic advancement. Pulp magazines and translations of the works of Mao were widely distributed, and China was broadcasting more hours in more languages to Africa than either the United States or Great Britain.

Guerrilla-training and propaganda programs were supplemented by real aid and trade programs. Countries were carefully selected for the most effective use of the limited Chinese resources. Ghana, Guinea, and Mali—the more radical states—received the most aid before 1964. After 1964 more aid was offered to less politically stable states, or those in which crisis situations, current and future, might be exploited. On this basis Tanzania was offered $44 million and help in building a railroad to Zambia; Kenya was offered $18 million; and Somalia $23 million and arms shipments. The amount of this aid actually received was probably no more than 30 percent.

Guerrilla training and arms shipments to rebels seeking to unseat African governments or to seize control of the areas still dominated by whites (Rhodesia, South Africa, Angola, Mozambique, and Portuguese Guinea) have given Communist China a chance to gain influence in Africa. Such leaders as Nkrumah, Touré, and Nyerere have insisted that Africa will not be free until all remnants of colonialism are destroyed. They have offered their countries as bases for freedom fighters—a situation the Chinese have been eager to exploit. However, China's revolutionary style and encouragement of wars of national liberation have upset the many Africans who want peace, and Chou En-lai's observation in Somalia in 1964 that "Africa is ripe for revolution" was not well received. Subsequent military coups in several countries showed

Chou to be right, but none of these revolutions had benefited the Chinese by the end of 1965.

On the contrary, Communist China had lost influence in the Central African Republic, Upper Volta, Dahomey, and Ghana. Diplomatic relations had been broken in Dahomey and the Central African Republic, and Chinese diplomats and staff had been expelled from all four countries. African leaders began to associate the Chinese presence with subversion and with a radical and militant rhetoric that was disruptive of relations with other states and with the Eastern and Western blocs. Such setbacks in Africa, as well as in Latin America and Indonesia, have caused Peking to reassess its entire strategy in colonial areas.[3] In general the new African states are more interested in stability and economic development than wars of national liberation, except in the areas still under white domination, and China is less equipped for economic aid and nation building than either the Soviet Union or the West. Moreover, China's professed adherence to a policy of nonalignment and peaceful intentions in Africa has been belied by the militant rhetoric and aggressive actions of the Chinese communists. Peking's meddling in the internal affairs of independent nations and the efforts of Chinese communists to turn meetings and conferences into anit-American demonstrations have led the leaders of the Ivory Coast, the Malagasy Republic, Malawi, and Niger to protest that China's only interest in Africa is in gaining support for its own policies and programs.

It is too soon to assess the consequences of Peking's new and more limited policy in Africa. However, in spite of past mistakes, lack of resources, the language barrier, and vast cultural differences, Mao's precept that political power springs from the barrel of a gun may yet have results in South Africa, Rhodesia, Angola, Mozambique, and Portuguese Guinea, where the Chinese can appeal to minority groups or rural radicals incensed at the privileges of indigenous white-collar groups, the "profiteers of decolonization."

THE SINO-SOVIET DISPUTE

By the mid-1960s Africa had become an important theater for the worldwide struggle for leadership of the communist movement. Moscow was still stressing a policy of "peaceful coexistence" and hoped to win Africa over by aid and by example. Where necessary the Soviet Union would support wars of national liberation or supply arms or seek to disrupt governments. In general, however, Moscow was relying on subversion, the eventual growth of indigenous communist cadres, and the linkage of African and Soviet economies to bring about gradual communization in Africa.

The Chinese, in theory at least, were insisting on the primacy of armed struggle. This is not to say that they would not use peaceful means. The evidence shows, however, that they were doing more training of guerrillas and supplying of arms than the Soviet bloc. After their defeat in the Congo in 1960 and 1961 the Russians appeared reluctant to give arms to insurrectionary or nationalist groups; for several years they gave money but not arms to the Somalian communists. However, Chinese militancy confronted Moscow with the dilemma of either aiding national-liberation and irredentist movements—at the risk of clashing with the United States and losing the good will of many African governments—or letting Peking become the champion of revolution in Africa. In 1964 the Soviet Union escalated its arms shipments and was sending weapons to Congo rebels, to Somalia, and to Zanzibar.

The Somali Republic affords a specific example of the Sino-Soviet rivalry for political influence in Africa. The Somalis are a warlike nomadic people living mainly in the northeast part of Africa (the Horn) but also spread throughout parts of Ethiopia, northern Kenya, and the French Territory of the Afars and the Issas (formerly French Somaliland). The drive to unite all Somalis is a paramount political issue in the African Horn. In June 1960 the Chinese sent to Somalia one of their most able Arabic specialists, Chang Yueh, to head a staff of forty—the biggest diplomatic representation in the country. Neither the Soviet Union nor the West was eager to arm Somalia. However, when the Somalian prime minister Shermarke visited Peking and signed an economic agreement with China early in 1963, the Soviet Union felt forced to counter the growing Chinese influence, even at the risk of jeopardizing its relations with Ethiopia and Kenya. In the competition for influence the Soviet Union put up $60 million to China's $24 million and offered eighty scholarships to China's eight. By 1965 the Russians were training and equipping Somalia's army and building port facilities at Berbera. Having failed in the Congo and Ghana and given up on Ethiopia, they may well have made Somalia their major base in Africa.

Another example of rival communist activity is Tanzania. Numerous exiled African movements from Southern Africa have set up offices in Dar es Salaam and planned guerrilla activities in such areas as Mozambique and Rhodesia. Both Soviet and Chinese officials were seeking to win influence with these groups in the 1960s, and by 1965 Tanzania had received 11,000 tons of communist arms.[4]

Both communist blocs also shared interests in Zanzibar. The Chinese and the East Germans were training the army, the Russians were supplying weapons, and aid projects were being run by all groups. The main link to Peking was the leftist Abdul Rahman Mohammed (Babu), who was on the editorial staff of *Revolution*, a pro-Chinese magazine, and was correspondent for the New China News Agency in Zanzibar.

## FUTURE PROSPECTS

There were few communist parties in Africa in 1965, and fewer still that were allowed to operate aboveground. The Chinese and Soviet aid and exchange programs and their schools for trade unionists and guerrilla fighters had undoubtedly produced some results, but there was as yet little evidence of trained, disciplined indigenous cadres ready to carry forward the gospel of Marx.

Attempts to determine who was a communist, or even procommunist, presented major difficulties, and Chinese and Soviet leaders were no doubt as confused as leaders in the West about the political ideology of most African politicians. Some leaders were using communist techniques to gain and hold power and call for agrarian reform, centralized planning, a one-party dictatorship, and a program to indoctrinate the people—as were many clearly noncommunist radical nationalists. Even those who appeared to consider themselves communists manipulated the communist ideology in a way that made it difficult to label them as such in the usual sense. Nationalism and pan-Africanism were as important as Marxism in their ideologies. They belonged to all kinds of groups. Their strength and influence varied from party to party. Their eventual alignment, whether with Peking, Moscow, or the West, and their future role in the internal politics of the continent were impossible to foresee.

In 1965 there were orthodox communist parties in the Republic of South Africa, Lesotho, the Sudan, Nigeria, and Senegal and procommunist parties in Cameroon, Madagascar, and Zanzibar. In Ghana before the fall of Nkrumah one wing of the Convention People's Party was procommunist (some members were orthodox Marxist-Leninists). In the Niger Republic a procommunist party, Sawaba, was reported to have been organized, but it went underground and its leader, Djibo Bakary, is believed to have fled to Ghana and then to East Berlin.

There were also a few paracommunist parties which shared many, but not all, of the Soviet views. They followed a Marxist ideology and relied on a strong party organization based on democratic centralism. They viewed the party as the vanguard of a socialist society based on police-state control and centralized planning. Parties in Ghana (until recently), Guinea, and Mali would fall into this category.

Communists are hard to identify in the various national-liberation movements and fronts, but it seems clear that in 1965 they were working with and using various nationalist groups from South Africa, Rhodesia, Mozambique, and Angola. A communist party was founded in Angola in 1955, formed a national front in 1959, and was involved with one wing of the Angolan rebellion, the Movement for the Liberation of Angola (see *Portugal*). In Mozambique they worked with another united front known as Frelimo. The Soviet bloc and China have both supported and trained cadres for guerrilla warfare, but the loyalty of these cadres to the communist cause is difficult to assess.

The African states have clearly exploited both the East-West rivalry and the Sino-Soviet rivalry to their own benefit. However, Chinese efforts to discredit Soviet communism have some grim implications for peaceful development in Africa. The Soviet Union, although committed for the moment to "peaceful coexistence," may be driven to do more to promote revolution and wars of national liberation in Africa in order to retain leadership of the world communist movement. Because some African politicians will accept aid and arms from any quarter to achieve their own goal—be it reuniting all Somalis, overthrowing Mobutu in the Congo, or bringing black men to power in Southern Africa—there is a real possibility that Africa faces a prolonged period of civil wars, nationalist revolutions, and border conflicts. Given the weakness of the newly established African governments, these are circumstances that could be exploited by well-disciplined and well-organized communist cadres.

Nevertheless, African communists are not as well read, trained, or disciplined as their counterparts in other areas of the world. Moreover, in view of the variety of political viewpoints in Africa and the desire of Africans to remain free of domination by East and West alike, the Leninist arguments against imperialism put forth by an African politician may indicate no more than a personal reaffirmation of independence from the former colonial powers in Africa and a commitment to socialist planning. The same opportunism that leads African statesmen to accept the aid they need from any source also leads them to modify all alien ideologies to suit their own needs. Similarly, most of Africa's left-wing groups can properly be regarded as essentially nationalist. Prudent Western policy should distinguish these groups from the orthodox communist parties on the African scene, and should attempt by constructive means to draw them out of the Sino-Soviet orbit in order to secure Africa's chances for independent development in the future. Neither capitalism nor communism is likely to be recognizable after it has been Africanized.

BIBLIOGRAPHY

Attwood, William: *The Reds and the Blacks: A Personal Adventure*, New York, Harper and Row, 1967.

Brzezinski, Zbigniew K. (ed.): *Africa and the Communist World*, Stanford, Calif., Stanford University Press, 1963.

Chadwick, Andrea: "China-Africa and ACD," a working paper for the Arms Control and Disarmament Project, Stanford, Calif., Hoover Institution, 1966.

Cooley, John: *East Wind over Africa: Red China's African Offensive*, New York, Walker, 1965.

Crozier, Brian: "The Struggle for the Third World," *International Affairs*, vol. 40, July 1964, pp. 440-452.

Goldman, Marshall I.: *Soviet Foreign Aid*, New York, Praeger, 1967.

Goncharov, L.: "New Forms of Colonialism in Africa," *Journal of Modern African Studies*, vol. 1, December 1963, pp. 467-474.

Hammell, Sven (ed.): *The Soviet Bloc, China and Africa*, Uppsala, Scandinavian Institute of African Studies, 1964.

Laqueur, Walter: "Communism and Nationalism in Tropical Africa," *Foreign Affairs*, vol. 39, July 1961, pp. 610-621.

Morison, David: "The Africa of Moscow and Peking: A Review Article," *African Af-*

*fairs,* October 1967, pp. 343-347.
Morison, David: *The U.S.S.R. and Africa,* London, Oxford University Press, 1964.
Sawyer, Carole A.: *Communist Trade with Developing Countries, 1955-1965.* Praeger Special Studies Series, New York, Praeger, 1966.
Scalapino, Robert A.: "Sino-Soviet Competition in Africa," *Foreign Affairs,* vol. 42, July 1964, pp. 640-654.

PETER DUIGNAN

1. See also *Cameroon, Lesotho, Malagasy Republic, Niger Republic, Nigeria, South Africa, Senegal,* and *The Sudan.*

2. Lin Piao, in *Peking Review,* September 3, 1965.

3. See the 1966 *Yearbook on International Communist Affairs,* Stanford, Calif., Hoover Institution, 1967.

4. *New York Times,* March 15, 1965.

# THE SUDAN

The original adherents of Marxism-Leninism in the Sudan were primarily students and intellectuals. In 1946 communists began to form Marxist circles within bourgeois organizations that aimed at national independence. A year later they formed a political party of their own, the Sudan Movement for National Liberation (al-Harakah al-Sudaniyah lil-Tahrir al-Qawni), with 'Abd al-Khaliq Mahjub as its general secretary. Within this movement the communists operated as a distinct organization known as the Sudanese Communist Party (al-Hizb al-Shuyu'i al-Sudani). The entire movement was outlawed shortly afterward and had to continue its work underground. In 1952 communists and other leftists joined the Anti-imperialist Front, which operated under communist leadership. Between 1953 and 1958 the front had one representative in the legislature. Its political power was, however, greater in the urban areas than indicated by its parliamentary strength. It acquired a considerable voice in the councils of the Trade Union Federation, the Sudan Railway Workers' Union (the largest union in the country), the Sudan Gezira Board Tenants' Union, and various women's and youth organizations.

## HISTORY

In 1956 the Sudan achieved independence, and Isma'il al-Azhari became prime minister. However, two years later a military coup led by Lieutenant General Ibrahim 'Abbud deposed him. 'Abbud banned many communist-controlled organizations, and the communists returned to clandestine activities. At the same time the party, according to its secretary general, aimed at expanding its base from a cadre organization to a mass party. It also put up numerous candidates for local government elections, and some were successful. In October 1964 'Abbud's military dictatorship was overthrown, and the following month he resigned as chief of state and supreme commander. Power passed into the hands of a United National Front, which contained a number of communists and communist sympathizers and aimed at the liquidation of all forms of colonialism and "neocolonialism." It also opposed the separatist movements in the southern provinces, arguing that an independent south would fall victim to the greed of neocolonialists. The front considered that the Sudan was destined to play a key role in the unity of the Arab-African campaign against the imperialists, a campaign which in turn was linked to the efforts made by international socialist and workers' movements.

In 1964 the communist party began to function as a legal organization and obtained recruits not only among students and the small working class, but also among the peasantry. It elected eleven members to the national assembly, and in a key election at Omdurman South the combined forces of the noncommunist groups only barely succeeded in holding their own against the communist candidate. However, the communists ran afoul of their Islamic allies over religious and other issues. On November 15, 1965, the Sudanese constitutent assembly accordingly approved a proposal to dissolve the communist party and any other organization whose principles allowed atheism and abused things sacred to the citizens. The party's centers were closed, its publications were suspended, and the communist members were expelled from parliament, except for three who had been elected with communist support to represent various associations.

By 1965 the Sudanese communists had proved their ability to work underground and could be expected to continue their activities, especially among the intellectuals, unemployed workers, and the poorer sections of the peasantry. However, they also faced the difficult task of guiding the "clerico-chauvinism of the backward [Islamic] masses into progressive channels." This task could be accomplished only by finding a *modus vivendi* with Islam. The party also had to cope with the problem of the south, where territorial separatism made a strong appeal to the pagan and Christian majority, and where revolutionary guerrilla operations were actually in progress. In 1965 Aggrey Jaden, an exiled African rebel leader, denounced Russia, China, and the United Arab Republic for supporting Arab imperialism in the south. Jaden did not receive any support for his activities from the Organization of African Unity, but his movement raised problems for the southern borderland of Muslim Africa that no communist party could afford to ignore.

## ORGANIZATION AND MEMBERSHIP

The Sudanese party organized its adherents into cells, known as "struggle units." These were grouped into circles, which in turn were organized on provincial lines. The party was directed by the central committee, which in theory was elected by periodic national congresses. Direct political activity was carried out by a political bureau and an organization office.

In 1965 the party's general secretary was Abd al-Khaliq Mahjub. Two other important figures, both members of the central committee, were Hasan Zarruj, editor of *al-Maydan,* and al-Tajjib Tijani. Party strength was estimated at some 11,000 members and active sympathizers. Precise figures were not available, but the Sudanese party was one of the largest communist parties in Africa.

The Federation of Sudanese Trade Unions, formed in 1949, was affiliated with both the All-African Trade Union Federation and the communist-directed World Federation of Trade Unions. In 1965 it supposedly had a membership of about 300,000. According to the charter adopted at its fifth congress in October 1965, its goal is a national-democratic government that would put an end to imperialist domination of the Sudan's economy and direct development along socialist lines. The federation's general secretary was Shafi Ahmed el Sheikh.

At the end of 1964 several peasant and agricultural workers' organizations united to form a Tenants' Union, with a reported membership of about 250,000. Shortly after its founding, the Tenants' Union signed a joint charter with the Federation of Sudanese Trade Unions, calling on all political parties and organizations in the country to work for socialism.

## RELATION TO SOVIET LEADERSHIP

Early in 1965 Mahjub stated that his party should seek a specifically Sudanese road to socialism, with a policy based on the social realities of the Sudan and the experience of the masses in the battle against the military dictatorship. The party had approved the Moscow resolutions of 1960, but it nevertheless had occasion to criticize the Soviet party at a time when Moscow considered that 'Abbud's military dictatorship was carrying out a national task. Party leaders similarly disagreed with Chou En-lai, who had argued in 1963 that 'Abbud was adopting an anti-imperialist and progressive position. They were obliged to take action against party members who were influenced by Chinese ideology and denied the need for a Sudanese road to socialism, and in August 1964 a number of left-wing "deviationists" were expelled.[1]

By 1965 the Sudanese party had apparently split into two factions, with the pro-Soviet group gaining a clear victory. The head of the pro-Chinese splinter group, Ahmad Muhammad al-Khayr, took refuge in Peking, from where he was reputedly supporting the southern rebels, not for ideological purposes but to prolong the civil war.[2]

## PARTY PRESS ORGAN

The party journal in 1965 was *al-Maydan* (The Forum).

## BIBLIOGRAPHY

Fawzi, Saad ed Din: *The Labour Movement in the Sudan, 1946-1955*, London, Oxford University Press, 1957.

*Ost-Probleme*, no. 3, February 12, 1965, pp. 83-84.

Segal, Ronald: *Political Africa: A Who's Who of Personalities and Parties*, in collaboration with Catherine Hoskyns and Rosalynde Ainslie, New York, Praeger, 1961.

LEWIS H. GANN

1. Interview with *L'Unità*, January 5-6, 1965. quoted with comments in *Ost-Probleme*, no. 3, February 12, 1965, p. 84.

2. *Africa* (Madrid), no. 289, January 1966, p. 47; no. 291, March 1966, p. 41.

# SWEDEN

The communist movement in Sweden grew out of the Social Democratic Left Party of Sweden (Sveriges Socialdemokratiska Vänsterparti, SSVP), founded in May 1917. The SSVP developed as a result of a split in the old Social Democratic Labor Party (Socialdemokratiska Arbetarparti, SAP) when a radical minority, under the leadership of Zeth Höglund, left to form a party of its own. The new SSVP declared its solidarity with the Russian bolsheviks and joined the Comintern in July 1919. Otto Grimlund, who had represented the Swedish party at the founding congress of the Comintern in Petrograd in March 1919, was one of the most active organizers of the Swedish left. In 1965 he had no party affiliation and was living as a landowner on the island of Gotland. Other early leaders were the poet Ture Nerman (later one of the most critical anticommunists), mayor Carl Lindhagen, author Frederick Ström (the first Soviet consul in Stockholm), editor Karl Kilbom, and journalist Ivar Wennerström. In subsequent years all of them left the communist movement and returned to the old SAP.

At the fourth congress of the SSVP in 1921 a majority accepted Lenin's Twenty-one Conditions for Admission, changed the name of the party to Communist Party of Sweden (Sveriges Kommunistiska Parti, SKP), and became a section of the Comintern. The minority of the SSVP, under the direction of Lindhagen and Wennerström, kept the former party name and two years later rejoined the old SAP. The first chairman of the SKP was Zeth Höglund, who held this position until 1924. In 1926 he too returned to the SAP.

## HISTORY

The relationship of the SKP to the Comintern remained a topic of constant conflict within the party. The party chairman, Höglund, did not wish to submit blindly to Moscow's leadership, and in 1924, for a second time, he and his supporters left to form a separate Left Socialist Party (Socialistiska Vänsterparti). However, in 1926 this party was dissolved, and Höglund returned with his adherents to the old SAP. Kilbom directed the SKP during the next three years.

A third split took place in 1929, when Kilbom no longer wished to propagate in Sweden the revolutionary slogans of the Comintern and sought a rapprochement with the SAP. The Comintern condemned his moderate policy and switched its support to a group led by Hugo Sillén and Sven Linderot—despite the fact that Kilbom's supporters constituted a majority. As a result of this split, from 1929 to 1934 Sweden had two communist parties, the minority party affiliated with the Comintern and the majority party opposed to it. In 1934, however, Kilbom renamed his party the Socialist Party (Socialistiska Parti) and moved away from the communist orientation. In 1937 he and many of his supporters returned to the old SAP.

After this third split the SKP was very weak and no longer had a representative in the Swedish parliament. In the 1932 elections it received two seats out of 230 in the lower house; in the following election, in 1936, this number rose to five. Then, as a result of the Hitler-Stalin pact of 1939 and the Finnish-Russian winter campaign of 1939 and 1940, when the SKP took a strong position against Finland, the number of communist representatives dropped back to three. The party was unable to obtain any representation in the upper house.

The communists received new impetus from the Soviet Union's struggle against Hitler during World War II, and the 1944 elections brought them fifteen seats, the highest number they ever obtained. After the war the Stalinist terror and the suppression of the Baltic and Eastern European states resulted in a strong negative influence, and the number of communist representatives fell to eight in 1948 and to five in 1952. They kept these five seats until 1962. There was a corresponding decline in the percentage of communist votes, from 11.2 percent in 1944 to 6.3 percent in 1948 and to only 4.5 percent in 1960, although later there was a slight increase.

In 1953 a fourth split occurred. A radical and strongly Stalinist splinter group led by Seth Persson accused the SKP of reformism and formed its own party, the Communist Workers' Federation of Sweden (Sveriges Kommunistiska Arbetarförbund); only a small minority followed Persson. This organization later adopted a pro-Chinese stand, but it was without significance and played no part in the political life of Sweden.

The anti-Stalin campaign in the Soviet Union and the Soviet intervention in Hungary in 1956 contributed further to the party's difficulties. These events and the later split in world communism produced strong dissatisfaction with the old Stalin-line party leadership. An increasingly strong opposition demanded that the SKP follow a policy independent of Moscow and adapted to the national interests of the Swedish people. Transition to a peaceful and parliamentary road in the struggle for socialism was also requested. Although these problems had been discussed by the party for many years, no solution was worked out.

In this context, grave conflicts developed at the twentieth party congress in January 1964. The old pro-Stalin (and later pro-Khrushchev) Hilding Hagberg was replaced as party chairman by C. H. Hermansson, an academically trained and national-oriented moderate. The congress also decided on a revision of the party program and statutes. A special commission was given the task of carrying out these changes before the next party congress, but it soon split up into dogmatic and revisionist groups.

## ORGANIZATION AND MEMBERSHIP

The basic unit of the SKP is the cell in local labor unions, and the community clubs in rural areas. The cells and clubs of a city form local workers' communes (if only one community club exists in a locality, it forms the workers' commune). In 1965 there were 511 of these workers' communes. The next organizational step is the party district, generally identical to the electoral district.

The highest level is the party executive, whose members are elected by the party congresses supposedly held every three years. The twentieth party congress in 1964 was attended by 387 delegates, who were elected at district conferences.

The communist party has always been legal in Sweden. Membership figures are rarely published, but membership is known to have decreased steadily over the last twenty years. In 1944 it was 58,056; by 1965 it had dropped to 22,987.[1] The SKP has greatest strength in northern Sweden (chiefly Norrbotten province) and around Stockholm and in Göteborg. The communists have strong followings among the miners, the forestry workers, the construction workers of central Sweden, and the shipbuilding workers of Göteborg. Although official data are not available, it has been established that about 80 percent of the membership is from the working class. Farmers, whose number is relatively small in Sweden, account for only a small proportion. During the postwar years a fairly large number of radical intellectuals with academic backgrounds joined the party; among these was Hermansson.

The great majority of party members are between the ages of forty and seventy. The very weak communist youth organization, the Democratic Youth (Demokratisk Ungdom), plays only an insignificant role in the recruitment of new members. Recruitment for the SKP is conducted at places of work or through student organizations which are closely related to the communists. However, the Democratic Youth itself is very small; in 1965 it had only 6,500 members. More important as a front organization is the left socialist student organization Clarté, with branches in all Swedish university towns. It is, in fact, under communist leadership and has considerable influence in radical circles of Swedish students, but is now pro-Chinese.

## RELATION TO SOVIET LEADERSHIP

Hermansson's chairmanship began the new orientation of the SKP. The party was now "going to take its own road to socialism in Sweden," and this road was to be "peaceful and parliamentarian." The party refused to continue taking stands according to direction from Moscow; it has even stated that it did not intend to establish socialism according to the Soviet or Eastern European model. Parliamentary democracy was recently recognized, and fairly free political discussion is tolerated in the communist press. The new policy is more left socialist than communist in character, and since 1964 Hermansson has maintained direct contact with the left socialist parties of Denmark and Norway. He has declared that the SKP may soon change its name and call itself the Left Socialist Party. Hermansson has spoken out strongly on Swedish television against the conviction of the Soviet authors Siniavskii and Daniel.

The SKP also demonstrated its independence from Moscow by strong criticism of the methods of Khrushchev's removal in 1964. On the occasion of the twenty-third party congress of the Communist Party of the Soviet Union in Moscow the SKP did not send its party chairman, but rather a little-known party secretary. The SKP has repeatedly taken a stand against United States policy and action in Vietnam. In a recently published book, *Vänsterns Väg* (The Way of the Left), Hermansson renewed the old efforts of the SKP to force the SAP to "give up its present tactics" and "to turn to a concentrated struggle against large capitalism."

At the end of 1965 the SKP was divided into three factions: the "dogmatists," with some followers among the older workers who could not forget the old Stalin days; the "centrists" around Hermansson, who followed his new line; and the "democrats," who rejected traditional communist tactics and wanted to be left socialists. An open struggle among these factions may produce a new split and further weakening of the party.

The SKP maintains a neutral position in the Soviet-Chinese conflict. Although the Swedish communists reject the dogmatic Stalinist ideology of the Chinese Communist Party, they do not wish to take sides in the conflict. A small pro-Chinese group exists in Göteborg under the direction of the old Stalinists K. Senander and N. Holmberg. It has little influence in the party, although it has attracted a few young local intellectuals.

## FUTURE PROSPECTS

The new independent policy under Hermansson's leadership brought the SKP some gains in the national assembly elections of 1964. Hermansson was successful at least in stemming the decline and marking a slight electoral gain; the percentage of communist votes rose from 4.5 percent in 1960 to 5.2 percent in 1964. Since then, the moderate and nationalist line of the SKP has gained new supporters, and the skillful party president has even gained some slight popularity among noncommunist voters. Future prospects will depend, of course, on Hermansson's ability to dominate the dissenting factions of the party.

## PARTY PRESS ORGANS AND RECORDS

The main organ of the SKP was in 1965 *Ny Dag* (New Day), a weekly published in Stockholm. *Norskens Flamman* (Northern Lights) was published in Boden in northern Sweden. *Arbetaren* (The Worker) was being published as a weekly in Göteborg.

For statutes of the party see *SKP Stadgar* (SKP Statutes), Stockholm, 1966 (draft). The SKP program is contained in *Sveriges Väg till Socialismen: Sveriges Kommunistiska Partis Program* (Sweden's Road to Socialism: Program of the SKP), Stockholm, 1953. See also *Programförklaring* (Draft Program), 1961, for a new program published in 1966.

## PARTY CONGRESSES

With the exception of the thirteenth congress, held in Göteborg, all meetings were held in Stockholm.

1st congress, SSVP, May 1917
2d congress, SSVP, 1918
3d congress, SSVP, June 1919
4th congress, SKP, March 1921
5th congress, SKP, May 1923
6th congress, SKP, 1924
7th congress, SKP, June 1927
8th congress, SKP, December 1929
9th congress, SKP, February 1933
10th congress, SKP, May 1937
11th congress, SKP, April 1939
12th congress, SKP, May 1944
13th congress, SKP, May 1946
14th congress, SKP, May 1948
15th congress, SKP, March 1951
16th congress, SKP, April 1953
17th congress, SKP, December 1955
18th congress, SKP, December 1957
19th congress, SKP, January 1961
20th congress, SKP, January 1964

## BIBLIOGRAPHY

Hastad, Elis: *Det Moderna Partiväsendets Organisation* (The Organization of the Modern Party System), Stockholm, 1949.

Hermansson, C. H.: *Vänsterns Väg* (Way of the Left), Stockholm, Rabén & Sjogren, 1965.

Rydenfelt, Sven: *Kommunismen i Sverige* (Communism in Sweden), Kristianstad, 1954.

Sparring, Åke (ed.): *Kommunismen i Norden* (Communism in the Nordic Countries), Stockholm, Aldus, 1965.

Sparring, Åke: *Revisionismen i Sveriges Kommunistiska Parti* (Revisionism in the Communist Party of Sweden), Stockholm, Aldus, 1966.

Sparring, Åke (ed.): *Röd Opposition* (Red Opposition), Stockholm, Aldus, 1965.

BRUNO KALNINS

1. Information from the secretariat of the SAP.

# SWITZERLAND

At the end of 1965 there were two parties in Switzerland which by their ideology had to be recognized as communist parties: an older party, under the name Labor Party of Switzerland (Partei der Arbeit der Schweiz, PdAS), and a more recently established Swiss Communist Party (Parti Communiste Suisse, PCS),[1] which follows the leadership of Mao Tse-tung and is not recognized by Moscow. The PdAS is a direct descendant of the old Communist Party of Switzerland (Kommunistische Partei der Schweiz, KPS), which was founded in 1921 and outlawed by the Swiss government in November 1940.

The PdAS was formed on October 14-15, 1944, in Zurich, by the unification of the Federation of Labor Parties (Föderation der Parteien der Arbeit, FPdA) and the Social Democratic Party, Opposition (Sozialdemokratische Partei, Opposition, SPO). Although the PdAS was a revival of the former KPS, because of political conditions in Switzerland during the war the new party at first denied its communist character and refrained from advocating such communist aims as class struggle and dictatorship of the proletariat. Only after the ban against radical political movements and parties was lifted by the Swiss authorities in March 1945 did the PdAS reveal its communist alignment.

The initiators and founders of the PdAS were Léon Nicole and Karl Hofmaier, both with long records in the extreme leftist and communist movements, and both later purged from the party. The Moscow-trained Hofmaier had been secretary of the KPS from 1936 until its dissolution by the Swiss government on November 26, 1940. Later, in cooperation with Nicole, he became cofounder of the PdAS and its general secretary. In December 1946 he was forced to resign from this position because of irregularities in the management of party finances, and in July 1947 he was expelled from the party.

Nicole had been a leader of the Swiss Social Democratic Party (Sozialdemokratische Partei der Schweiz, SPS; Parti Socialiste Suisse), in the French-speaking part of Switzerland since the 1930s. The French-speaking Swiss socialists had traditionally been more radical than the German- and Italian-speaking socialists, and when the Geneva canton outlawed the KPS in June 1937, Nicole permitted communists to join his regional SPS organization and revealed his own procommunist leanings. In January 1939 he was censured for this by the party leadership. In March 1939 he went, with Hofmaier, to the Soviet Union and after his return became openly procommunist. When he undertook a campaign defending the Molotov-Ribbentrop agreement of August 1939, the SPS expelled him from its ranks. He created the Swiss Socialist Federation (Fédération Socialiste Suisse, FSS), which started strong antinazi and antifascist propaganda and was able to win considerable influence in the western cantons of Switzerland. In June 1941, when Germany invaded the Soviet Union, the FSS was banned by the Swiss government, and Nicole and his organization went underground. Through clever electoral manipulations, and thanks to a changed political atmosphere in Switzerland, Nicole (again in cooperation with Hofmaier) was able in May 1944 to organize a conference of local labor groups, which in turn formed the FPdA. Thus, under a changed name and with its communist nature hidden, a legal communist organization was reestablished in Switzerland. Nicole became its president. Before long, however, he fell victim to Moscow's interference in internal party affairs. Overconfident because of his long social-democratic leadership, he disregarded some changes in Moscow's peace policy and was toppled from the chairmanship in February 1952 by a group loyal to Moscow led by Edgar Woog and Jean Vincent. In December he was stripped of party membership. In March 1954 Nicole and some 500 followers founded another new communist organization, the Progressive Party (Parti Progressiste), which developed some activities in Geneva, Zurich, and a few other localities. In 1955 Nicole withdrew from political activities because of ill health; he died in June 1965.

The personal histories of both Nicole and Hofmaier explain many details of the history of the party.

## HISTORY

*The KPS* During World War I Switzerland was torn by growing labor unrest, and by 1917 violent clashes between the demonstrating workers and the police had left dead and wounded on both sides. The SPS was divided into three factions. The right wing, under Hermann Greulich, approved credits for the preparation of the army for the defense of Switzerland's neutrality; this group advocated a peaceful settlement of all workers' grievances. The left wing, under Fritz Platten, had the support and guidance of exiled radical socialists residing in Switzerland, such as Lenin, Henri Guilbeaux, and Willy Münzenberg; this group favored social revolution and the overthrow of the Swiss bourgeois government, demanded immediate suppression of all military preparations in Switzerland, and incited the Swiss workers to violence against the government and its police. The center group, led by Robert Grimm, had the largest following; this group vacillated between the two extreme wings, aware of the progressive radicalization of the workers' masses and of the necessity to improve their material and work conditions. It went along with some of the demands of the left in order not to lose the masses, but it refused to follow the precepts of the foreign radicals.

The Russian revolution of March 1917 had a great impact on the Swiss working masses and encouraged their hope that direct action might produce the results desired. The overthrow of the Russian Provisional Government and the victory of Lenin's bolsheviks in October incited violent demonstrations on November 15 and 17 in Zurich. During 1918, as the abyss between the right and the left in the SPS widened, Grimm and his center group were ready to make compromises in order to prevent a split in the party. However, Jakob Herzog, a member of the left who was expelled from the SPS for breaking party discipline, founded a local communist organization in Zurich in October 1918. Early in 1919 he managed to organize affiliated groups in a few other localities.

In March 1919 the founding congress of the Communist International was held in Petrograd, and Platten represented the SPS left wing, but without a mandate from the party. When the party congress in August 1919 voted to affiliate with the Comintern, Grimm voted with the left because he believed that by joining the Comintern he would be able to influence its policies. However, in a referendum the party membership rejected affiliation by a great majority. The Comintern's adoption in July-August 1920 of Lenin's Twenty-one Conditions for Admission produced a storm of protest among the right faction and also met with disapproval from the center group. The left accepted the conditions and favored affiliation. When the question of joining the Comintern came once more before an extraordinary congress of the party in December 1920, the motion was defeated by the joint vote of the right and the center. The left walked out of the congress, and the split in the party became a fact. The decision of the congress was again submitted to a referendum in January 1921. The 25,475 votes against and the 8,777 in favor of affiliation with the Comintern showed the real strength of the communists in Switzerland in early 1921.

At a meeting in Zurich on March 5-6, 1921, the left wing of the SPS and Herzog's group (by then about 800 members) united to form the first Communist Party of Switzerland, which became a "section of the Communist International." The delegates to this congress represented 6,356 members of both groups. Franz Welti became chairman of the new KPS, and Platten, Herzog, and Jules Humbert-Droz were the most prominent members of the executive committee. The founding congress elected a program committee, and the program adopted by the second congress, held in Basel on June 3-5, 1922, demanded the crushing of the bourgeoisie, a dictatorship of the proletariat, and the creation of a Swiss Soviet federation. However, the demands for social and economic changes were less radical than those introduced by the bolsheviks in Russia. This restrained program was certainly intended to avoid antagonizing moderate Swiss workers.

Following its second congress the KPS began activities designed to disrupt Swiss society. An antireligious movement was started, and widespread demoralizing propaganda was developed. The struggle against the SPS was initiated by the promotion of a "united front from below," which had negligible results. The third party congress, held on December 13-14, 1924, introduced a reorganization of the lowest echelon of the party. Shop cells and small local cells replaced the old local organizations. The communists also attempted to organize several front organizations, but Switzerland proved to be the wrong place for such activities.

The fifth congress, held in Basel on June 7-9, 1930, accepted the Moscow-ordered "bolshevization" of the party. The first purges of "opportunists" produced some protest and defections among the intellectuals. These measures of Stalinization did not produce an increase of the party's strength and influence. Membership remained quite stationary at about 12,000. The communists also attempted to form opposition groups in the trade unions. They had little success, although a few trade-union groups were loudly proclaimed as the "revolutionary trade-union opposition" and joined the Red International of Labor Unions. The Communist Youth Organization of Switzerland (Kommunistischer Jugendverband der Schweiz), which had been founded before the KPS, melted from its initial membership of about 4,000 in 1919 to less than 2,000 in the middle 1930s.

The seventh congress of the Comintern in 1935 proclaimed the new tactic known as the popular-front policy and directed all the communist parties to dissolve communist-directed organizations and encourage their membership to join corresponding socialist organizations. Accordingly the communist trade unions and other front organizations in Switzerland were dissolved before the sixth congress of the KPS held in Zurich on May 30-June 1, 1936. At the congress the communists extended an invitation to the SPS to join in a common antifascist front but their offer was rejected. The communists now created new "joint committees" and organizations with the aim of attracting broader strata of Swiss citizens for the fight against nazism, fascism, war, or all three; because of the general attitude of the Swiss, these efforts had some success. However, the new tactic was recognized by many Swiss communists as a device to engage Swiss citizens in actions designed to aid Soviet foreign-policy objectives. As a result, this policy, in conjunction with the purge trials in the Soviet Union, antagonized many members and produced a mass exodus from the party. By 1938 the KPS had little more than 1,000 members.

Even earlier, however, in 1937, Swiss civic

leaders had correctly evaluated this tactic as a transformation of the communist party into an agency of the Soviet government. On this basis some cantons had already started to outlaw the KPS (Geneva in June 1937). Although the party lost membership, its press became more vociferous than before. At the start of the war the antifascist and anti-German tune of the communist press and of the remnants of the party became embarrassing to the Swiss policy of neutrality, as did the pronazi press. To avoid political complications the Swiss government issued a decree on August 6, 1940, prohibiting the acitivities of both pronazi and communist organizations, followed by a second decree on November 26, 1940, outlawing the KPS and its fronts. Even earlier, one by one, the communist press organs had been liquidated by government order.

In the French-speaking cantons the communists joined Nicole's federation. In other parts of the country they went underground. After the German invasion of the Soviet Union their underground efforts concentrated on antinazi propaganda and activities. Because pro-German sympathies in Switzerland were quite strong during the first years of the war, a peculiar situation developed in which Swiss antinazi circles tolerated disguised communist support to maintain Swiss neutrality. After the battle of Stalingrad (February 1943), when it became obvious that Germany was losing the war and the nazi threat to Switzerland began to lessen, the internal situation of the country changed. As Allied and especially Soviet victories multiplied, the communists began to prepare in 1944 for the open revival of their activities.

*The PdAS* The PdAS arose in October 1944 from the unification of the SPO and Nicole's FPdA. The SPO had been started in 1940 as loose opposition factions in local chapters of the SPS. At first these factions were negligible, and although party leadership disapproved of them, it refrained from disciplinary measures because it did not wish to force a split in the party. The oppositionists, for their part, did not leave the party; they expected that with a steadily growing following they would be able to capture it. But in May and June 1944 the boldness of the opposition groups exceeded the patience of the social-democratic leadership. Several local opposition leaders were expelled from the party, and the split became unavoidable. In July the SPO groups held a conference at Olten and voted to unite with Nicole's FPdA.

The FPdA was the outcome of the success of local illegal communist groups in the western cantons during local elections. In 1943 and 1944 Nicole had initiated the political tactic of presenting at local elections "workers' lists," which included candidates who were almost unknown to the voters and had no political past to betray them as communists. These candidates received unexpectedly large numbers of votes and seats on the basis of radical programs and then created local "labor parties." In May 1944 Nicole called a conference of these local parties, which created a federation with Nicole as president and Hofmaier as secretary. By October the situation had become ripe for the revival of the communist party as the PdAS. Hiding its real communist character until the Swiss government lifted the ban against communist activities in March 1945, the party prepared its cadres and party organizations. When the communists reappeared from illegality, they identified the PdAS as the successor to the old KPS.

In the first few postwar years the PdAS was quite successful among the workers. The second and third party congresses (October 1945 and November-December 1946) were dedicated to the reconstruction of the party and its influence among the workers, but at the third congress Hofmaier was ousted from the post of general secretary and replaced by Edgar Woog. In the 1947 parliamentary elections the communist lists received almost 50,000 votes (5.1 percent). This was the peak of communist strength in Switzerland. After 1947 the party, rigidly following the Moscow political line and emphasizing its communist character, began to lose membership and following. The fourth congress, in June 1949, was held in an atmosphere of mass desertion of the membership. The congress adopted the party's first program, which included minimum and maximum demands. Although it proclaimed revolutionary aims, these aims were to be obtained gradually and by peaceful means. The party was obviously in retreat.

After the fourth congress an internal struggle developed between Nicole and the newly elected general secretary Woog. At an all-Swiss conference held in February 1952 the Moscow-supported Woog succeeded in ousting Nicole from the party presidency. Under Woog's leadership the PdAS increasingly became a tool of Soviet foreign policy. The internal struggle which culminated in Nicole's expulsion from the party did not end with this purge. De-Stalinization was another object of internal contention, only to be followed by conflicts between the pro-Moscow majority led by Woog and a pro-Peking faction. These rifts produced the walkout of a small group of radicals from the French-speaking areas from the party in 1963. Since then the PdAS has solidly supported the Moscow leadership, and Woog has traveled to Moscow several times to participate in the conclaves of world communism. In the October 27, 1963, elections to the lower house of parliament, the party still received 21,000 votes and four seats, but the votes were cast in the western, French-speaking cantons, where developments since 1963 have weakened the party.

*The PCS* When the Sino-Soviet dispute reached wide proportions and created repercussions in other communist parties, a group of radicals from the French-speaking area left the PdAS and on September 1, 1963, founded the PCS. The leader of this group was Gérard Bulliard from Vevey, and his residence became the new party headquarters. It was apparently a small group, whose main activity was publication of the irregularly appearing mimeographed *L'Etincelle*, which reflected a pro-Chinese and pro-Albanian stand. As small as the PCS was, it had its internal difficulties. A group led by Nils Andersson (a Swedish citizen married to a Swiss woman) and Lucien Mathys advocated a more militant pro-Chinese line and were expelled by the PCS central committee on June 16, 1964, on the charge that they wanted to monopolize the pro-Chinese orientation and the sale of Peking publications in Switzerland. Andersson's group, which used the names Romansch Federation of Swiss Communists (Fédération Romande des Communistes Suisses) and Organization of Marxist-Leninists of Switzerland (Organisation des Marxistes-Léninistes de Suisse), established a "Lenin center" at Lausanne and published a newssheet entitled *Octobre*.

The PCS held its first "national congress" in Vevey on September 5-6, 1964, at which a new program was adopted and the statute was revised. Another congress was called for September 1965 but was never mentioned in later issues of *L'Etincelle*. The party seems to have had a very slow start. Until 1965 its press organ appeared irregularly and perpetually complained of lack of funds. Apparently in mid-1965 it was able to secure some funds and started to develop much broader activities. By the end of the year it had twelve branches in the larger cities, with a foothold in the German-speaking area. Total membership at the end of 1965 was estimated as about 400.

Bulliard was also able to create a few front organizations for the PCS: a youth organization called the Groups of Swiss Progressive Youth (Groupes de Jeunesses Progressistes Suisses) and led by John Sauter; a women's organization first known as Progressive Women and then Democratic Women, led by Gertrude Oulevay-Busset; and a trade union under the impressive title General Federation of Workers of Switzerland (Fédération Générale des Travailleurs de Suisse). This last group, under Buiiliard's leadership, announced the publication of its organ *L'Etoile syndicale*.

Finally, on October 4, 1964, a meeting was held in Geneva to "revive" the Communist Party of Spain in Switzerland. As this party was using the postal box of the PCS as its mailing address, and as Bulliard played some role in the meeting, it can be assumed that this new Spanish party has also accepted the pro-Chinese orientation. It has announced publication of the organ *Vanguardia obrera*.

Bulliard initiated a collaboration of the other pro-Chinese communist organizations in Western Europe. He was aided by the pro-Chinese Movement of Progressive Workers of Belgium, led by Julien Frisque (although he was on bad terms with the pro-Chinese Belgian Communist Party—Marxist-Leninist, led by Jacques Grippa). On August 7-8, 1965, representatives of pro-Chinese communists in Italy, Spain, France, West Germany, Belgium, and Switzerland met in Luxembourg and decided to create a "revolutionary international" as a coordinating center. A program and statute were drafted, and a second meeting was to initiate the activities of the new international. The same representatives held a second meeting in Paris on November 27-28, 1965, but they abandoned the plan for the international and instead created a Committee for an International Revolutionary Front. Bulliard was secretary of this committee and apparently obtained funds for travel and propaganda.

## ORGANIZATION AND MEMBERSHIP

The PdAS, like the pre-1940 KPS, is organized on the principle of democratic centralism, although in the party's first years this structure was adjusted to Swiss political and administrative conditions. Party cells are combined into local sections, which form cantonal organizations; these in turn elect delegates to the national congress (*Parteitag*), held every three years. The congress elects a central committee of fifty-one members, which in turn elects the seventeen-member executive (*Parteileitung*) and an eight-member politburo. The most important leader in the politburo is the general secretary; in 1965 this post was held by Edgar Woog.

Shortly after its founding in October 1944 the party secretary Karl Hofmaier announced that the PdAS had "about 10,000 members." The following year he reported to the second congress that the party had twenty-two cantonal organizations comprising 229 local sections, with a total of 19,692 members. The report to the third party congress at the end of 1946 mentioned only nineteen cantonal organizations, with a total membership of "around 15,000," signaling the beginning of the party's decline. This gradual decline was accelerated in 1956 by reaction of the membership to the Hungarian revolt. In 1965 estimates by Swiss sources set membership at no more than 7,000.

Election results for the lower house of the Swiss parliament showed a similar drop. In the elections of 1947 the communists obtained almost 50,000 votes (5.1 percent of the total) and seven mandates. In the elections of October 27, 1963, they received only 21,008 votes (2.2 percent of the total); the socialist vote of 225,201 (26.7 percent) in this election is a good indication of how small the communist following was among Swiss workers. The communists had some strength and influence in five western French-speaking cantons and in the cities of Basel and Zurich in the German-speaking area, but in other cantons their strength was negligible.

In the mid-1960s about two-thirds of the party members were industrial workers, with public-utilities employees and craftsmen the next largest group, and a sprinkling of intellectuals and white-collar employees. A growing number of the members are old-age pensioners and renters. In recent years the PdAS has tried to gain a foothold among the foreign workers who are employed in increasing numbers in Switzerland, but these attempts have been thwarted by the authorities, who want to keep foreigners out of Swiss politics.

The Swiss communists attempted both before and after World War II to establish front organizations. Although they were able to create a number of organizations, particularly after 1945, the average Swiss citizen was politically too well informed for such infiltration tactics, and all but two of these fronts had short life spans. The two exceptions were the Communist Youth Organization and the Swiss Friends of the Soviet Union. The youth group arose in the early 1920s from a split in the socialist youth organization. It never had more than 2,000 members, but was still active in 1965 with a reduced membership of some 500. The Swiss Friends of the Soviet Union has always been the stamping ground of the intellectual "parlor pinks." In 1965 it had several local branches and was organizing conducted travel tours to the Soviet Union. Pacifist, cultural, and economic fronts (the last under the guise of promoting trade with the Soviet bloc) have appeared and disappeared during the last fifteen years in accordance with the demands of Soviet foreign policy. All have been quite vociferous at the time of their founding and have faded out when they were exposed as communist or pro-Soviet fronts, only to reappear under another name. The communists have also tried to establish their own trade unions, but such efforts have always been countered by the strong response of the socialist-dominated trade unions and the SPS itself.

## PARTY PRESS ORGANS

Until it was outlawed in 1940 the old KPS published two weeklies, *Vorwärts* in Basel and *Voix ouvrière* in Geneva. Both papers were revived by the PdAS late in 1944, and early in 1945 both became dailies. In 1946 and 1947 *Vorwärts* increased its circulation to 18,000 but later started to lose ground; it went back to a weekly and dropped to a recent circulation of about 6,000. The fate of *Voix ouvrière* was similar: by 1965 its circulation was about 5,000.

In April 1945 the PdAS began to publish a theoretical monthly in German and French, *Sozialismus* and *Socialisme*, respectively, but neither survived for long. An Italian-language publication *Falce e martello*, published before the war, was not revived after 1944. About a dozen other early publications had ephemeral existences.

In 1965 the Peking-oriented PCS was publishing the mimeographed monthly *L'Etincelle*, with an unknown circulation (supposedly around 700). The other Peking-oriented group, led by Nils Andersson, published the monthly *Octobre*. Both appeared quite irregularly.

## PARTY CONGRESSES

1st congress, KPS, March 5-6, 1921, Zurich
2d congress, KPS, June 3-5, 1922, Basel
3d congress, KPS, December 13-14, 1924
4th congress, KPS, April 16-18, 1927
5th congress, KPS, June 7-9, 1930, Basel
6th congress, KPS, May 30-June 1, 1936, Zurich
7th congress, KPS, May 28-29, 1939, Zurich
1st (founding) congress, PdAS, October 14-15, 1944, Zurich
2d congress, PdAS, October 7, 1945, Geneva
3d congress, PdAS, November 30-December 1, 1946, Zurich
4th congress, PdAS, June 14-15, 1949
All-Swiss conference, PdAS, February 24, 1952
5th congress, PdAS, June 1-2, 1952, Zurich
6th congress, PdAS, 1955
7th congress, PdAS, May 16-18, 1959, Geneva

Founding meeting, PCS, September 1, 1963, Vevey
1st congress, PCS, September 5-6, 1964, Vevey

A second congress of the PCS was called for September 1965, but it is unknown whether it actually took place.

## BIBLIOGRAPHY

Bodenmann, Marino: *Zum 40. Jahrestag der Gründung der Kommunistischen Partei der Schweiz*, Zurich, Verlag der Partei der Arbeit, 1961.

Bretscher, W., and E. Steinmann: *Die sozialistische Bewegung in der Schweiz, 1848-1920*, Bern, G. Iseli, 1923.

Egger, Heinz: *Die Entstehung der Kommunistischen Partei und des Kommunistischen Jugendverbandes der Schweiz*, Zurich, Genossenschaft Literaturvertrieb, 1951.

*Kommunismus in der Schweiz: Skizze über*

*seine Anfänge, Geschichte und Gegenwart*, Lausanne and Bern, Aktion Freier Staatsbürger [1954].

*Was will die Partei der Arbeit der Schweiz?* [report about the first congress of the PdAS, October 14-15, 1944], Zurich, Verlag der Partei der Arbeit [1944].

WITOLD S. SWORAKOWSKI

1. Switzerland has a population which speaks German, French, Italian, and Romansch. None of these nationality groups forms a majority in the country as a whole, and each language is official in the cantons in which the respective nationality forms a majority. Thus all political parties in Switzerland have official names in all four languages. As most of the publications of the Swiss communists are in German, the German names and their abbreviations are used here for all parties except those that are active only in the French-speaking cantons.

# SYRIA
*See* Lebanon and Syria

# TADZHIKISTAN[1]

The revolution of October 1917 brought Soviet power to the northern part of what is now Tadzhikistan, then part of the Fergana region (*oblast*) of the governor generalship of Turkestan. In 1918 this region became part of the Turkestan Autonomous Soviet Socialist Republic, and the bolshevik party organizations of those areas entered the Communist Party of Turkestan. The southern territories of the present Tadzhik republic remained under the rule of the emir of Bukhara until the fall of 1920, when detachments of the Red Army, accompanied by a small number of Bukharan communists, overthrew the emir and organized the Bukharan People's Soviet Republic.

Defeat in the summer of 1922 of the main forces of native opposition, the *basmachi*, made it possible to begin economic and cultural reconstruction. In 1924, as part of the national territorial delimitation of Central Asia, the Bukharan republic was liquidated and most of its territory was placed within the new Uzbek Soviet Socialist Republic. On October 14 the Tadzhik Autonomous Soviet Socialist Republic was formed within the Uzbek Soviet Socialist Republic. Party organs were formed at the same time.

Following policies set by the All-Union Communist Party (Bolshevik), the communist organizations of Tadzhikistan led the population through completion of various economic and cultural tasks. The first regional party conference, on October 20-27, 1927, announced plans for dealing with economic questions, strengthening the soviets, improving the youth organization, and conducting political education of the population.

On October 25, 1929, the central committee of the All-Union Communist Party proclaimed the Tadzhik Autonomous Soviet Socialist Republic a union republic and at the same time decreed transformation of the Tadzhik regional party organization into the Communist Party of Tadzhikistan (Kommunisticheskaia Partiia Tadzhikistana, KPT). The first congress of the KPT, on June 6-15, 1930, following directives of the central committee, devoted its attention to industrialization, collectivization of agriculture, trade unions, education, and other aspects of the first Five-Year Plan, as well as the elimination of alleged Trotskyists, Bukharinists, and bourgeois nationalists.

The second congress of the KPT, on January 7-14, 1934, directed party organizations to mobilize for the elimination of bourgeois nationalists and planned an increase in the harvest of cotton and other agricultural products, expansion of irrigation, further development of industry and trade, the strengthening of soviets, trade unions, and youth organizations, and increased antireligious propaganda. The third congress, held on August 16-27, 1937, during the great purges, noted progress in the liquidation of hostile elements and successes in industry and agriculture and set forth plans for increasing the harvest of grain and cotton, development of livestock raising, and road building.

During World War II the KPT rallied the population for defense of the Soviet Union, and at the call of the party many communists and nonparty people alike volunteered for the armed services. After the war the KPT, following guidelines set by the central committee of the All-Union Communist Party, led the struggle for fulfillment of the fourth Five-Year Plan (1946 to 1950). Since that time the KPT has continued its role as an adjunct of the Communist Party of the Soviet Union.

On January 1, 1965, the KPT had 61,039 members and 6,585 candidates in 2,655 primary organizations.[2]

## PARTY PRESS ORGANS

The principal party organs are the newspaper *Kommunist Tadzhikistana* (in Russian) and the journal *Kommunisti Todzhikistona* (in Tadzhik), both published in Dushanbe.

## BIBLIOGRAPHY

Irkaev, M. L.: *Ocherk istorii sovetskogo Tadzhikistana, 1917-1957* (An Outline of the History of Soviet Tadzhikistan, 1917-1957), Stalinabad, 1957.

*Istoriia tadzhikskogo naroda* (A History of the Tadzhik People), vol. III, parts 1 and 2, Moscow, 1964-1965.

Pierce, Richard A.: *Soviet Central Asia: A Bibliography*, part 3, *1917-1966*, Berkeley, Calif., University of California Center for Slavic and East European Studies, 1966.

RICHARD A. PIERCE

1. See also *Kazakhstan, Kirgizia, Turkmenistan*, and *Uzbekistan*.

2. *Bolshaia sovetskaia entsiklopediia: Ezhegodnik, 1965*, Moscow, 1965.

# THAILAND

Communist activity in Thailand goes back to 1929 or 1930, when the Comintern press first mentioned communist organizations there. At one of the last meetings of the seventh Comintern congress in 1935 Rachi spoke on behalf of the communists of Siam. The first repressive measures by local authorities against the communists also date from this period, and in the following years the communist movement saw little development.

## HISTORY

It was not until 1942, in the generally favorable climate of the antifascist alliance, that the Communist Party of Thailand (CPT) was officially formed. It was later recognized as a section of the Comintern, one of the last parties to join before the Comintern's dissolution in 1943. In the first years of its existence the CPT was able to operate legally and concentrated on forming front organizations. A Trade Union Federation was created in 1944 in Bangkok and was expanded in 1947 into a nationwide National Trade Union Federation. From its very beginning the party had to operate simultaneously among two ethnic groups—the Thai population and the Chinese colony; the latter's numerical, economic, and political importance was to increase continuously in the years to come.

The party structure and its directing organs, established at the founding congress in 1942, were not revealed publicly until 1946, and then only in part. During the 1946 parliamentary elections, Prasad Sabsunthorn, a former student of the University of Bangkok and lecturer at Chulalongkorn University, won a seat on the democratic list. Once in parliament, he introduced a law to abrogate the anticommunist legislation of 1933. It was not until November of that year that it became known that he was the general secretary of the communist party. Soon thereafter the party held its first public meeting in Bangkok and began to publish a weekly, *Masses*.

Following a military coup in November 1947, the first repressive measures were taken against the so-called progressive press and trade unions, although the CPT was not forced underground. In light of events in the Far East (the capture of China by the communists, the war in Indochina, the Korean War, and insurrections in other Asian countries), the communists modified their tactics, putting primary importance on the struggle against "American imperialism" by political and insurrectional methods. In October 1950 the party issued an appeal for the formation of a Unified National Democratic Front, with its objective the struggle for peace and democracy to "liberate the country from the yoke of foreign imperialists." The same year the National Committee for Peace, three of whose members also sat on the World Peace Council, was very active in organizing the campaign against American intervention in Korea.

At the second party congress, in early 1952, the new general secretary, Prasong Vongvivat, reported on the "mobilization of the masses" in the struggle for independence and democracy. The new party program applied the "theory of Marxism-Leninism to the concrete conditions in Thailand."[1] A new central committee was elected, with former general secretary Prasad Sabsunthorn as one of the members.

In November, however, the authorities decided to deal severely with the communists. A number of leftists and extremist militants were arrested, and the CPT was outlawed. Numerous party militants went underground or fled to Communist China. Sabsunthorn, who had gone to an international conference in China in October 1952, remained there until 1955. The government repression resulted in heavy losses in the party ranks and posed many difficult political and technical problems. When the party organized an underground printing house in Bangkok, the authorities discovered its location and seized many party documents and propaganda materials. Spachai, a militant communist, was executed in 1960; two former deputies, Krong Chandawong and Togohan Sutimat, suspected of communist activities, were executed in May 1961; in January 1962 Ruam Wongphan, a former teacher and chief of the underground apparatus of the party, and his lieutenant, Ret Savros, were arrested and executed in April.

Throughout these years the communists continued to call for a national front. In October 1960 the central committee issued an appeal to "all patriots and democrats, prominent personalities, parties and groups" to "overthrow the treacherous dictatorship of Sarit Dhanarat, oust the aggressive forces of American imperialism and form a government that would conduct a policy of genuine independence, neutrality, peace and democracy."[2]

Meanwhile, however, the CPT began to supplement its underground political activity with terrorist and insurgent activities, depending on aid from neighboring countries (primarily Communist China). In 1960 Thai communists who had taken refuge in Yunnan province in China formed the organization Free Thailand and underwent political and military training along Chinese communist patterns. In November the procommunist Thai refugees in Laos formed an association of exiles which a communiqué of the Thai ministry of the interior accused of fomenting disturbances in the northeastern part of the country with the cooperation of subversive elements in the interior. The party itself, and especially its exile leaders in Communist China, encouraged these insurrectionary activities. Two organizations created in China—the Thailand Independence Movement, formed in November 1964, and the Thailand Patriotic Front, formed in January 1965—supported insurrectionary activities in Thailand.

The Thai communists continued to concentrate on the organization of guerrilla units, with the intention of creating "free" pockets in Thai territory. Most attention was devoted to the northeastern border area, where economic, health, and educational conditions, poor communications, and proximity to communist-held regions of Laos created a favorable situation for communist propaganda and subversion. Peking found Thailand a natural test area for Mao's theory of "people's wars" conducted from communist-controlled bases. Some 40,000 North Vietnamese, who took refuge in Thailand after the French defeat, reinforced the local Thai converts to communism. Subversion and terrorism in central Thailand were organized in communist training camps in the northeast. China, the Pathet Lao in neighboring Laos, and North Vietnam supported communist activities and provided "advanced training" to Thai activists. The Peking-based Thailand Independence Movement was directing the "people's war of national liberation" in Thailand under the formal leadership of two Thai communist exiles in Peking, Phayom Chulanonda and Mongkhon Na Nakhorn. In the southern part of Thailand, bordering with Malaya, there was also a small but well-organized group of Malay guerrillas, who fled from their country when a concentrated action of the Malay government liquidated communist subversion in Malaya.

In the early 1960s the Thai government had started to improve economic and other conditions in the northeastern area, particularly in the villages, but progress was slow. In December 1965 it created a Communist Suppression Operations Command, under military leadership and with broad collaboration of civilian administrative elements, which was charged with the location and elimination of communist strongholds.

## RELATION TO SOVIET LEADERSHIP

The CPT was represented at the world conferences of communist parties in Moscow in November 1957 and in November 1960, when its spokesman was one of the first to align his party with the Chinese camp. Since then this alignment with China has not wavered, and ties with Moscow have been broken.

## PARTY PRESS ORGAN

The party issued the weekly *Masses* from 1946 until 1952, when it was prohibited by the government. After 1952 illegally published issues appeared irregularly.

## CONGRESSES OF THE CPT

1st (founding) congress, 1942
2d congress, 1952
3d congress, 1961

BRANKO LAZITCH

1. *For a Lasting Peace, for a People's Democracy*, June 27, 1952, p. 3.

2. *World Marxist Review*, December 1960, p. 64.

# TUNISIA

When the French Communist Party emerged at the congress of Tours on December 30, 1920, the Tunisian section of the parent socialist party could count no more than a few hundred members, principally "civil servants from the metropolis who lived there in often particularly unfavorable conditions."[1] Six of the nine Tunisian delegates voted in favor of the French party's affiliation with the Comintern; thus the Tunisian Federation of the French Communist Party (Fédération Tunisienne du Parti Communiste Français) was formed. The leadership of Robert Louzon, a mining engineer who had attended the school of revolutionary syndicalism, and the small personal fortune which he placed at the disposal of the party, gave the Tunisian communists a solid start. Their propaganda was directed primarily toward the native population; the party newspaper *L'Avenir social* had an Arabic-language edition.

## HISTORY

Communist activities in Tunisia were severely repressed by the French colonial authorities. Louzon's party newspaper was outlawed many times (it reappeared each time with a new title), and the Arabic edition was finally banned altogether. In April 1922, during the visit of Alexandre Millerand, president of the French republic, the authorities proceeded with preventive arrests of Louzon, el-Kéfi, and others, and on May 20 the Executive Committee of the Comintern issued an appeal referring to the "uprising of the Muslim masses" (see *Algeria*).

The first wave of repression did not severely hamper the Tunisian communists, who were aided by the moderate nationalists of the old liberal Constitution Party (Hizb el-Destour), known as the Destour. However, communist growth was brought to an abrupt halt in 1925, when, on instructions from the French party, the Tunisian communists led a violent campaign against the "Rif war" in Morocco. The campaign resulted in trials, convictions, and the expulsion of the principal communist leaders.[2] In October 1924, in conjunction with the nationalists, the communists had set up the autonomous Tunisian General Confederation of Labor (Confédération Générale du Travail Tunisienne), with Mohammed ben Ali as secretary. This organization was open to all workers but had hardly any members other than native Tunisians. During the violent strikes of 1924 and 1925, to which the nationalists and communists tried to attach political significance, the Tunisian laborers employed forceful means of preventing European workers from resuming work. The government responded with legal action for plotting against the security of the state; the principal strike leaders (including the communist J. P. Finidori, director of *L'Avenir social*), were arrested and deported, and the Confederation of Labor was dissolved.

Political unrest in Tunisia subsided after the failure of these riots. Moreover, the Destour nationalists had become increasingly distrustful of the communsits, who had tried to turn the trade-union action to their own ends. Finally, an internal crisis in the French Communist Party brought on the resignation or expulsion of such trade-union militants as Louzon and Finidori, who had played important roles in the Tunisian communist movement. All these factors led to a noticeable slackening of activity, and by the end of 1928 the Tunisian party was reduced to only a few members.[3]

Early in 1929 the French Communist Party resolved to "exert all the efforts toward the reconstitution of [its] organization [in Tunisia] by orienting all its work toward the formation of a Tunisian section of the Comintern." The Tunisian labor confederation was to be reconstituted, but meanwhile in order to reach that goal, systematic work would be conducted in the Tunisian branch of the French reformist General Confederation of Labor (CGT). The intention was clear: the Tunisian branch of the CGT was to be infiltrated by communists.[4]

This program was given impetus in the early 1930s by Ali Djerad's leadership of the reconstituted Tunisian party and by the nationalist agitation that preceded Habib Bourguiba's creation of the Neo-Destour Party (Hizb el-Destour el-Djedid) in March 1934. In compliance with basic directives that had been issued by the fifth congress of the French Communist Party, held in 1926, the Tunisian communists tried to cooperate with the nationalist movement and to achieve their own goals through it while retaining their autonomy as an organization. To this end the Tunisian Federation of the French Communist Party was reorganized in 1934 into an autonomous party, the Communist Party of Tunisia (Parti Communiste de Tunisie, PCT), with the Moscow-trained Ali Djerad as general secretary.

The new PCT was unsuccessful in forming an alliance with Bourguiba's new party. As before, the nationalists were suspicious of communist support, and the French party's current policy of appealing to French nationalism conflicted with any appeals the PCT might make to Tunisian nationalism. In fact, with the growing wave of antifascism, the Tunisian communists soon began to accuse the nationalists of receiving financial aid from Mussolini. In the trade-union field as well, the Union of Tunisian Trade Unions (Union des Syndicats Tunisiens), which was affiliated with the now communist-dominated CGT in metropolitan France, found itself in disagreement with the Tunisian General Confederation of Labor, which had been reorganized under the sponsorship of the Neo-Destour.

In September 1939 the PCT was dissolved along with the French Communist Party. There was no communist underground activity in Tunisia until the German invasion of the Soviet Union in 1941, and even then it was limited to clandestine distribution of several issues of *L'Avenir social*. In May 1943, when the Axis troops evacuated Tunisia, the PCT resumed legal activities; its secretary was still Ali Djerad and its organ *L'avenir social*.

However, even after the war the PCT was unable to make headway against Bourguiba's vigorous nationalist movement, which had the support of the Arab League and Western public opinion, particularly in the United States.

The Tunisian communists were critical of the demand for independence. At the tenth congress of the French party, Nizard, the PCT representative, recalled that his party had not ceased for "one instant from standing at the side of its sister party in France," and that it had been "the only Tunisian political organization to be complimented by General Juin for its struggle against the nazi occupation." He expressed amazement that the French colonial authorities continued to restrict the activity of the Tunisian communists and at the same time encouraged parties which, "under the pretext of independence," were opposing continued ties with the French people.[5]

At this time, however, the Tunisian trade unionists rebelled against domination by the communist party and broke with the CGT to form the independent General Union of Tunisian Workers (Union Générale des Travailleurs Tunisiens). This new organization had a wide appeal among Tunisian union members, despite the PCT's attempts to compete by transforming its own trade-union organization into an autonomous Union of Trade Unions of the Workers of Tunisia (Union Syndicale des Travailleurs de Tunisie). The independent Union of Tunisian Workers was directed by Ferhat Achet, a firm anticommunist, and on orders from the Neo-Destour it joined the anticommunist International Confederation of Free Trade Unions in 1951. Achet was killed on December 6, 1952, by persons who still have not been identified.

In 1947, when the communists in metropolitan France left the French government, the PCT renewed its efforts for an alliance with the Neo-Destour Party and its trade-union organization; this tactical maneuver failed. In 1950, under the aegis of the peace movement, a partial agreement was reached to hold joint public meetings, but at the first joint meeting, on October 2, the nationalists and communists came to blows. On January 25, 1952, the communists issued a call to the Tunisian people for national union and for a "Tunisian national front." Their proposal remained unanswered, and in 1953 Mohammed en-Nafaa, the PCT's new general secretary, complained that the nationalist leaders were resisting the PCT's efforts for union and the creation of an anti-imperialist national front because they hoped to gain the support of the United States.[6]

The PCT continued to proclaim its adherence to the cause of independence, as confirmed by the dispatch in 1952 and 1953 of three memoranda to the United Nations demanding the abrogation of the French protectorate, but it was still unable to allay the suspicions of nationalist leaders. The trade-union leaders in particular were careful to keep their distance from the PCT. At that time the French authorities were repressing Tunisian nationalist and communist militants without distinction, and the nationalists were concerned that world opinion might be that the communists had succeeded in infiltrating the Destour and its trade union. Toward the end of this period of nationalist struggle for independence, as terrorist acts increased and guerrilla operations developed, the communists were able to establish cooperation with the lower echelons of some local nationalist extremists, despite directives to the contrary from the Neo-Destour leadership. However, independence came too quickly for the communists to exploit this sporadic cooperation and claim any contribution to having won independence.

Despite the PCT's repeated avowals since the early 1950s of adherence to the cause of independence, and even though French communists had been ordered "to work for the defeat of the French army" in Tunisia,[7] the leadership of the international communist movement was very reserved, and at times hostile, toward nationalist movements with neutralist tendencies, especially if they appeared to be pro-Western. This attitude did not change until 1955, and at that time Tunisia's independence (which was to become official in March 1956) was already assured. The PCT thus had played only a marginal role in Tunisia's struggle for independence, and had not yet managed to make a place for itself among the forces which would govern the new nation.

In 1955 the communists campaigned against the statute of internal autonomy granted to Tunisia by the French government, denouncing "certain Destourian leaders" for having accepted negotiations with the French government "without first demanding the cessation of all repressions, the lifting of the martial law, and the liberation of the prisoners." The fifth PCT congress in May 1956 confirmed this line of hostility toward the Neo-Destour. By the end of 1957, however, the party's orientation had shifted; in his report to the sixth congress en-Nafaa went so far as to speak of a "renewal of the political conceptions" of the party. The PCT was at this point the only authorized opposition party and wished not only to retain the advantages of legality, but through apparently loyal cooperation to obtain a place in the new regime. Accordingly, the PCT called for national unity and declared itself ready to support the new authorities in their policies of national independence and economic development, without relinquishing its own autonomy and its right to criticize. The communist trade-union organization had already moved to dissolve on September 2, 1956, and its members, on an individual basis, had entered the General Union of Tunisian Workers, which was now becoming the official trade-union organization.

The communists worked hard at this new policy of support. On March 9, 1958, they indignantly condemned the plot of Salah ben Youssef and "the criminal acts which he was hoping to perpetrate," and in July 1961, together with the French communists, they supported the struggle which put an end to the French presence in Bizerte. However, their diligence failed to overcome the nationalist government's hostility, and the final resolution of the seventh PCT congress, held in March 1962, protested the suspicion in which the party was held and complained that its legality was "purely formal."[8] The resolution pointed out in another connection that the Neo-Destour leaders, "after having long defended the principles of free enterprise," had come over "to the idea of planned economy" and were even speaking of socialism, but that "the term 'socialism' is used for the effect it has on the masses, and not for its real meaning. 'Destourian socialism' is not socialism ... [and] is destined to check the revolutionary ardor of the masses."[9] The resolution closed with a reiteration of the CPT's objectives (dictatorship of the proletariat and collective ownership of the means of production) and a moderate condemnation of the policy pursued by the Neo-Destour government.

Following this congress communist criticism of the government became still sharper, especially on the subject of its economic policy, and the PCT attracted the open hostility of the Destourians. When a plot against Bourguiba was uncovered in December 1962, the communists published a communiqué condemning "the criminal attempt of political assassination" and repudiating "the conspiratorial methods as being foreign to communist concepts," but they were unable to avoid reprisals. The party organ *et-Talia* was suspended on December 30, 1962; the party was outlawed on January 8, 1963, and some of its leaders (including Mohammed Harmel on March 9) were arrested and imprisoned for several months.

The PCT continued clandestinely, but its activity was limited to a few declarations and the distribution of a few underground publications. In 1965 Mohammed en-Nafaa requested, on an individual basis—"as a citizen, and without prejudging the return of the Tunisian Communist Party to legality"— authorization to publish a newspaper to be called *Dialogues*, which, although outwardly independent in orientation, would play the role of a party organ. This authorization was refused.[10] In the elections to the constituent assembly in March 1965 the PCT offered candidates in only one district and received 7,352 votes; a coalition headed by Bourguiba's party received 597,763 votes and won all the seats.

## ORGANIZATION AND MEMBERSHIP

At the end of 1965 the PCT was led by a two-member secretariat, with Mohammed en-Nafaa as general secretary and Mohammed Harmel as secretary; a six-member political bureau which included en-Nafaa, Harmel, Taoufik Joumni, Khemaïs el-Kaabi, Abd Allah el-Meisi, and Abd el-Hamid ben Mustapha; and a central committee of fifteen. Membership was estimated to be less than 1,000.

## RELATION TO SOVIET LEADERSHIP

The PCT was represented at the international communist conferences in Moscow in November 1957 and November 1960, as well as at the twenty-second congress of the Communist Party of the Soviet Union in October 1961. Following this congress, it sided with the Soviet party in the Sino-Soviet conflict.

## PARTY PRESS ORGANS

The party organ *L'Avenir social* was first published in 1920 and subsequently appeared under a variety of names. As the Arabic daily *et-Talia* (Vanguard), edited by Mohammed el-Hadj Djarrad, it ceased publication at the end of 1962.

## CONGRESSES OF THE CPT

1st congress, 1934 or 1935
5th congress, May 1956
6th congress, December 1957
7th congress, March 1962

## BIBLIOGRAPHY

Julien, Charles-André: *L'Afrique du nord en marche*, Paris, Julliard, 1952.

Le Tourneau, Roger: *Evolution politique de l'Afrique du nord musulmane, 1920-1962*, Paris, Armand Colin, 1962.

CLAUDE HARMEL

1. *Parti Socialiste, 18e congrès national tenue à Tours: Compte rendu sténographique*, Paris, 1921, p. 116.

2. French administrators were authorized to expel or deport to France Frenchmen who disturbed the peace in France's overseas possessions. Such measures were sometimes applied to organizers who had been sent abroad by the French Communist Party.

3. André Ferrat, in *Cahiers du bolshévisme*, October 1, 1954.

4. *VIe congrès national du Parti communiste français: Manifeste, thèses et résolutions*, Paris, Bureau d'Editions, 1929, p. 42.

5. *L'Humanité*, June 30, 1945.

6. *Alger-républicain*, December 26, 1953.

7. From a notebook taken from Jacques Duclos at the time of his arrest during the demonstration against General Matthew Ridgway (May 28, 1952), containing notes taken during the meetings of the party secretariat and political bureau (perhaps with a view toward drawing up official minutes). Fragments of the notebook appear in various places, notably in document no. 4415 of the National Assembly, 1952 session, *Annexe au procès-verbal de la séance du 21 octobre 1952, demande en autorisation de pursuites contre cinq membres de l'Assemblée Nationale*, pp. 29, 85.

8. *La Nouvelle revue internationale*, July 1962.

9. *France-nouvelle*, May 16-22, 1962.

10. *Bulletin d'information* (Prague), no. 24(54), 1965.

11. *Pravda*, January 15, 1962.

# TURKEY

The Turkish Communist Party (Türkiye Komünist Partisi, TKP) emerged from the confluence of three separate communist movements. The first of these was an émigré movement headed by Mustafa Subhi, who formed an Executive Committee of Turkish Socialist-Communists at a conference of "Turkish left socialists" which he had convened in Moscow on July 22, 1918. This organization changed its name to the Turkish Communist Party (Türkiye Komünist Fırkası), probably in June 1920, after moving its headquarters to Baku. Subhi, who had been converted to communism as a prisoner in Russia during World War I, drew his adherents mainly from among other Turkish prisoners of war. Most of the party leaders, including Subhi, were killed in January 1921 in Trabzon while they were returning from Baku to Turkey. The others were eventually absorbed by the communist movement in Turkey.

The first communist group in Turkey itself was organized in Istanbul in October 1918 by Gensberg and Serafim Maximos, who, as members of the minority communities, drew members largely from among the non-Turkish population. This group, whose name remains unknown, disbanded in February 1919; it was succeeded in September 1919 by the Turkish Workers' and Peasants' Socialist Party (Türkiye Işcive Cliftci Sosyalist Fırkaşı), organized by the future communist leaders Şefik Hüsnü Deymer and Ethem Nejat. Although this was a Marxist-socialist rather than a specifically communist party, it soon collected all communist-oriented elements in Istanbul. With the Entente military occupation of Istanbul in March 1920, the party was forced to suspend activity. Those of its leaders who did not flee to Anatolia then founded a Turkish communist party, the forerunner of the present party, which was first called Türkiye Komünist Fırkası, or TKF, and later became the TKP. The early party was a clandestine conspiratorial band, allegedly quite independent of Subhi's party in Baku. Its original central committee included Sadrettin Celâl Antel and Şefik Hüsnü Deymer. Antel left the party after his release from jail in 1926; Deymer remained the foremost communist leader in Turkey until his death in 1959.

A third communist party, the People's Communist Party of Turkey (Türkiye Halk İştirakiyun Fırkası, THIF), was organized in Ankara in December 1920 by Veterinary Major Hacıoğlu Salih and Nâzım, a deputy from Tokat. This party was an outgrowth of the "Green Army," an anti-imperialist body originally formed with approval of the Ankara government to attract Soviet support. After the THIF was suppressed for the last time in October 1922, its members joined the group in Istanbul. Nâzım's fate is unknown; Hacıoğlu Salih was purged from the party in 1927 and eventually made his way to the Soviet Union, where he apparently died in one of Stalin's concentration camps.

## HISTORY

The communist movement appeared on the Turkish scene as a force in competition with Atatürk's nationalist movement. Even before the formal creation of the THIF, Soviet and local communist agitators had attempted to organize a Populist Group (Halk Zümresi) in the newly formed Ankara parliament in the summer of 1920. At the same time some of the chief leaders of the partisan bands which had sprung up spontaneously to resist the Greek invasion, and which formed the mainstay of the military forces at Ankara's disposal, fell under communist influence. In Eskişehir, under the protection of Ethem the Circassian, Turkish communists began publishing their own daily, *Seyyarei Yeni Dünya* (Partisans of the New World), at the end of August 1920.

In an effort to bring this burgeoning communist movement under his control, Atatürk formed his own "official" communist party in October 1920. Shortly thereafter he dispatched his newly organized regular army troops to bring the rebellious Ethem to heel. The Ankara government also used the occasion to close *Seyyarei Yeni Dünya* and to round up the main Anatolian communist leaders, and Atatürk dissolved his "official" party as well. When Mustafa Subhi chose this moment to move his party headquarters from Baku to Anatolia, he and his comrades were killed en route to Ankara.

The imprisoned communist leaders were granted amnesty in September 1921, at the insistence of Soviet Russia, which was then supplying Ankara with much-needed arms and ammunition. By the following spring the THIF had returned to open activity in close relations with the Soviet embassy. It began publication of *Yeni Hayat* (New Life), a periodical which became increasingly critical of the government. However, after the final Turkish victory over the Greeks in September 1922, the Ankara government no longer saw any need to tolerate such Anatolian communist activity. The Kemalist authorities moved to suppress the THIF in October 1922, and those leaders who had not already left the country were arrested.

The TKF in Istanbul presented a somewhat different face. Here the communists at first devoted their main attention to anti-Entente agitation and to theoretical explanations of Marxism in their organ *Kurtuhuş* (Liberation), transferred from Berlin and published from October 1919 until the British military occupation in March 1920. In the burst of activity that followed the formal organization of the party, in June 1921 the Istanbul communists launched a new monthly, *Aydınlık* (Light) (modeled on Henri Barbusse's *Clarté*), which appeared more or less regularly until 1925 and became considerably more radical after the Kemalist victory in Anatolia. Despite the fact that they had supported Atatürk in the 1923 elections, the leaders of the TKF were arrested in May of that year. They were acquitted on grounds that the treason law had not been validly promulgated in Istanbul and were permitted relatively free activity for the next two years.

The Istanbul party concentrated its attention on youth and workers, and several Istanbul unions came under communist influence at this point. Although the strike of the Ottoman Printers' Union in September 1923 helped to popularize the communist cause, efforts to unite the various unions in Istanbul under a communist-dominated confederation failed, as even the communist-led unions could not submerge their ethnic and craft rivalries. In response to Comintern criticism, the party began to issue special worker supplements of *Aydınlık* in the last half of 1924, and early the next year it began publication of a weekly, *Orak Çekiç* (Hammer and Sickle), which paid particular attention to labor matters.

The communists were careful to back Atatürk in the political controversies attending the birth of the Progressive Republican Party (Terakkiperver Cumhuriyet Fırkası) at the end of 1924, and especially opposed the reactionary Kurdish revolt that broke out in February 1925. However, their growing militancy evidently alarmed the Kemalists, who used the famous law for the maintenance of order to close both *Aydınlık* and *Orak Çekiç* on March 5, 1925. When the communists persisted in disseminating May Day propaganda and even sought to use the organ *Yoldaş* (Comrade) in Bursa, the government arrested the chief party leaders, except for Şefik Hüsnü Deymer and Nâzım Hikmet, who escaped and took refuge abroad. Since then the communist party has been illegal in Turkey.

The amnesty which accompanied the introduction of a Western-style penal code in

1926 allowed the hard core of the communist leadership to resume student and labor activities. This work was not perceptively slowed when new arrests in 1927 led to merely token sentences. In the face of this communist determination, the government again rounded up party members, this time imposing more severe penalties. Moreover, Atatürk spoke out on August 5, 1929, for the first time equating communism with treason. In response, the party's 1931 program called for a direct assault on the Kemalist government, which it condemned root and branch. The party also attacked the syncretic efforts of a group of former communists who, through the periodical *Kadro* (Cadre), from 1932 to 1935 sought to enrich Kemalism with selected borrowings from Soviet experience.

By the mid-1930s the Turkish communists began to see the need for a change in tactics. They now assumed a more conciliatory attitude toward the government, seeking to woo the "progressive" wing of Atatürk's party. This shift led them to concentrate on extending their influence into key institutions of the elite, especially in infiltrating literary and artistic circles as well as building cells in the Turkish military establishment. As part of their propaganda campaign they began to publish pamphlets, magazines, and newspapers espousing Marxist ideas. In 1938 the government discovered a communist cell in the naval academy; the following year Nâzım Hikmet was sentenced to thirty years at hard labor for organizing cells on the cruiser *Yavuz*.

World War II posed new problems. Encouraged by the Germans, a group of Turkish pan-Turanists now emerged in strong opposition to the Soviet Union and sought to root out all traces of the communist organization. In order to resist these attacks more effectively, the Turkish communists tried to set up front organizations which could operate legally to exploit antifascist sentiment, especially among the youth. Thus during the war the TKP tried to form a Progressive Youth League, a Democratic National Unity Front, and a Progressive Democrats Front. These organizations made almost no headway in winning over the elite, for by 1944 the Soviet Union had already adopted a hostile attitude toward Turkey. Soviet demands for control of the Straits and for cession of territory in eastern Turkey in 1946 turned public opinion all the more sharply against the communists.

Nonetheless, Şefik Hüsnü Deymer, now at the party's helm, attempted to use the increased political freedom after the war to form a Turkish Socialist Workers' and Peasants' Party (Türkiye Sosyalist Emekçi ve Köylü Partisi) as a legal front. The Istanbul martial-law commander banned this party on December 16, 1946, in a move to suppress all communist-oriented organizations, including several labor organizations, the Turkish Socialist Party (Türkiye Sosyalist Partisi), and some press organs. In this atmosphere, although the TKP continued efforts in Ankara and Istanbul universities to form front organizations and capitalize on the world peace movement, the main focus of activity perforce shifted abroad. The most important of the émigré fronts formed at this time was the League of Progressive Young Turks, based in Paris. Its main leaders were arrested in an extensive roundup of communist suspects in 1951, however, and during the decade of Democratic Party rule prior to 1960 the TKP remained strictly repressed in Turkey.

With the death of Stalin in 1953 the Soviet Union dropped its claims on Turkish territory, setting the stage for a relaxation in Turkish-Soviet hostility. Moreover, after the 1960 military coup the political climate inside Turkey permitted significantly more experimentation and the emergence of a much broader range of views. Despite this presumably more favorable atmosphere for communist activity, the party remained deep underground, and by 1965 there was still no reliable information on its activity in Turkey.

## ORGANIZATION AND MEMBERSHIP

The TKP is evidently organized in interlocking clandestine cells, culminating in a central committee which in 1951 (the latest date for which any reasonably reliable information is available) had some eight identified members. Even before the party was banned in 1925 it was subjected to frequent repression by the government. In recent years all overt activity in the name of the TKP has been carried on exclusively from outside Turkey. Yakup Demir (Zeki Baştımar) was first secretary of the party in 1965.

Elements of Turkey's educated elite have played a dominant role in the party leadership since its founding. Prominent writers and artists, such as Nâzım Hikmet, Turkey's foremost poet of the twentieth century, have figured importantly in the party. Turkish communists have set much store on wooing students and have also sought to enlist members of the Turkish military establishment.

Over the years the party has undergone several purges. After the third Comintern congress in 1921 the Balkan Communist Federation, which was then authorized to direct the Turkish party, conducted a purge in an effort to clarify the confusion engendered by the party's diverse origins. Similarly, after the arrest of most of the party leaders in 1925, Deymer purged all those who refused to accept his leadership. Subsequent activity has been shrouded in deep secrecy, and no information is available on any later purges.

The party has published no membership figures since its claim in 1924 of 600 members. In March 1959 the French journal *Est & ouest*, which specializes in the study of the world communist movement, estimated that the Turkish party had no more than 3,000 members. More recently a Turkish student of the communist movement accepted this figure as still the maximum probable communist strength in Turkey.[1] Neither source, however, indicates on what basis the estimate was made. The conservatively oriented peasantry, which comprises some 70 percent of Turkey's population, remains highly antipathetic to communism.

In 1965 there were no parties or other organizations either in Turkey or abroad which could be identified with reasonable certainty as fronts for the TKP.

RELATION TO SOVIET LEADERSHIP

Until after the sixth congress of the Comintern, Turkish communists played an active part in Comintern affairs. Mustafa Subhi attended the first congress representing himself, as the Turkish party had not yet been recognized by the Comintern. A Turkish representative was elected to the International Control Commission at the fifth Comintern congress. Representatives of both the Istanbul and Ankara parties attended the third and fourth Comintern congresses. However, the Turkish communists were strongly attacked by Manuilskii at the fifth congress for "nationalist deviations," and Comintern interest declined after the party was banned in 1925. The sixth congress in 1928 was the last Comintern gathering at which the Turkish party was represented.

Nevertheless, the TKP has closely followed Moscow's lead, especially since 1925, and Deymer's efforts to impose the Comintern line in the period immediately following the arrests of the party's main leaders led to the defection of some of its most prominent theoreticians—Şevket Süreyya Aydemir and Vedat Nedim Tör, sometime secretary general of the party. Since this time the Turkish party has been closely controlled by elements responsive to Moscow. In fact, all but one of the eight identified central committee members of the party in 1951 had received training in the Soviet Union at some point during their careers. Yakup Demir has attended Soviet party congresses and has contributed to such Soviet publications as the *World Marxist Review*.

The TKP has consistently supported Moscow in the Sino-Soviet dispute. On August 27, 1963, the exile central committee held a special meeting to proclaim its unreserved endorsement of Moscow's open letter of July 14, 1963, to the Chinese party. This pronouncement, which set the Turkish party's line thereafter, hailed the nuclear-test-ban treaty as a victory for the policy of peaceful coexistence and castigated the Chinese communists for seeking to provoke war. In connection with a meeting of nineteen communist and workers' parties in Moscow in March 1965, the Turkish party reiterated this stand, calling for restoration of unity of the international communist movement under the leadership of the Communist Party of the Soviet Union.

## PARTY PRESS ORGANS AND RECORDS

Party pronouncements appear in special supplements of *Yeni Çağ* (New Age), the Turkish-language edition of *World Marxist Review*, published in Prague. The clandestine radio, Bizim Radyo, located behind the Iron Curtain, broadcasts statements in the name of the party from time to time. No party organs are published inside Turkey.

No party program is known to have been published since 1931.

## PARTY CONGRESSES

1st congress, TKF, September 1920, Baku
2d congress, THIF, August 1922, Ankara
3d congress, TKP, 1926, Vienna
4th congress, TKP, 1933

No information is available on any subsequent party congresses.

## BIBLIOGRAPHY

Darendelioğlu, İlhan E.: *Türkiyede Komünist Hareketleri* (Communist Movements in Turkey), 2d ed., vol. I, Istanbul, Tan Matbaası, 1962; vol. II, Çınar Matbaası, Istanbul, 1963.

Harris, George S.: *The Origins of Communism in Turkey*, Stanford, Calif., Hoover Institution, 1967.

Kandemir, Feridun: *Atatürk'ün Kurdugu Komünist Partisi ve Sonrası* (The Communist Party Established by Ataturk and Its Sequel), Istanbul [1966].

Kornienko, R. P.: *Rabochee dvizhenie v Turtsii* (The Workers' Movement in Turkey), Moscow, 1965; published in English as *The Labor Movement in Turkey*, Washington, Joint Publications Research Service, 1967.

Laqueur, Walter Z.: *Communism and Nationalism in the Middle East*, New York, Praeger, 1956.

Sayılgan, Aclan: *Solun 94 Yılı, 1871-1965* (94 Years of the Left, 1871-1965), [Ankara, 1967].

Tevetoğlu, Fethi: *Türkiye'de Sosyalist ve Komünist Faâliyetler, 1910-1960* (Socialist and Communist Activities in Turkey, 1910-1960), Ankara, Ayyıldız Matbaası, 1967.

Tunçay, Mete: *Türkiye'de Sol Akımlar, 1908-1925* (Left Currents in Turkey, 1908-1925), Ankara, Sevinç Matbaası, 1967.

GEORGE S. HARRIS

1. Enver Esenkova, "Le communisme en Turquie," *Est & ouest*, no. 326, September 16-30, 1964, pp. 14-21.

# TURKMENISTAN [1]

The Communist Party of Turkmenistan (Kommunisticheskaia Partiia Turkmenistana, KPT) is a section of the Communist Party of the Soviet Union, closely linked to it in history and policy. The first social-democratic circles in Turkmenistan, and then the region (*oblast*) of Transcaspia, arose in about 1902 in Kizyl-Arvat, Ashkhabad, and other towns along the Transcaspian railroad. From 1905 to 1907 these groups entered the Turkestan section of the Russian Social Democratic Labor Party, which had been formed in Tashkent. The social democrats led strikes, formed fighting units, and conducted propaganda work among the military. In November 1905 they organized a railroad strike in Turkestan and in June 1906 instigated an abortive armed uprising of workers and soldiers in Ashkabad. During the "Stolypin reaction" (1907 to 1910) most of the social-democratic and other radical organizations were crushed, but new ones formed afterward. A bolshevik, I. T. Fioletov, led a strike in the oil fields of Cheleken.

After the revolution of February 1917 the bolsheviks of Transcaspia led the struggle of extremist elements to unseat the local Provisional Government organs. In December 1917 and January 1918 they established Soviet power, but they were forced underground in July 1918, when socialist revolutionaries and other opposition groups seized control of Transcaspia. A small British force helped to hold back detachments sent by the Tashkent soviet, but after it retired the Ashkhabad government was driven out, and in February 1920 Transcaspia was again under Soviet rule. In August 1920 the first regional party conference met in Ashkhabad and formed party organizations for the rest of the region. In October 1924 the Turkmen Soviet Socialist Republic was established.

From 1921 to 1925 the Turkmenian communists led in rebuilding the economy. The land and water reforms begun in 1921 and completed in 1927 attracted the support of the peasants and hired laborers and discouraged the middle-class and wealthy natives. This aided the communists in crushing the native *basmachi* resistance and strengthened Soviet rule in the villages. From 1930 to 1934, under the guidance of central party organs, agriculture was collectivized and the remnants of opposition elements were liquidated.

During World War II the party organized the transformation of the economy to a wartime footing. Many party members joined the armed forces, and the party admitted 20,561 workers, collective farmers, and intellectuals to its ranks. After the war the party central committee and the congresses directed their attention to the restoration and further development of the economy and to ideological work.

On January 1, 1965, the KPT had 53,638 members and 3,568 candidates, in 2,501 primary organizations.[2]

## PARTY PRESS ORGANS

The main party organs are the newspaper *Turkmenskaia iskra* (Turkmenian Spark) and the journal *Kommunist Turkmenistana* (Communist of Turkmenistan), both published in Russian, in Ashkhabad.

## BIBLIOGRAPHY

*Istoriia Turkmenskoi SSR* (History of the Turkmenian SSR), vol. II, part 2, Ashkhabad, 1957.

Khudaiberdyev, Ia.: *Obrazovanie Kommunisticheskoi partii Turkmenistana* (Formation of the Communist Party of Turkmenistan), Ashkhabad, 1964.

Melkumov, V. G.: *Ocherk istorii partorgani-*

zatsii Turkmenskoi oblasti Turkestanskoi ASSR, 1920-1924 (An Outline of the History of Party Organization of the Turkmenian Region of the Turkestan ASSR, 1920-1924), Ashkhabad, 1959.

Pierce, Richard A.: *Soviet Central Asia: A Bibliography*, part 3, *1917-1966*, Berkeley, Calif., University of California Center for Slavic and East European Studies, 1966.

Shikhmuradov, O. O., and A. A. Rosliakov (eds.): *Ocherki istorii Kommunisticheskoi partii Turkmenistana* (Outlines of the History of the Communist Party of Turkmenistan), Ashkhabad, 1961.

*Voprosy istorii Kommunisticheskoi partii Turkmenistana* (Problems of the History of the Communist Party of Turkmenistan), Ashkhabad, 1963.

RICHARD A. PIERCE

1. See also *Kazakhstan, Kirgizia, Tadzhikistan*, and *Uzbekistan*.

2. *Bolshaia sovetskaia entsiklopediia: Ezhegodnik, 1965*, Moscow, 1965.

# THE UKRAINE

The Communist Party of the Ukraine (Komunistychna Partiia Ukrainy, KPU) had its origins in several small Marxist groups that sprang up in the larger Ukrainian cities in the 1890s. These groups consisted chiefly of members of the Russian and Jewish minorities, who had little in common with the Ukrainian national movement. The groups also had few mutual ties, although the Kiev and Yekaterinoslav (Dnepropetrovsk) groups did develop into Unions for the Struggle for the Emancipation of the Working Class. In August 1897 an illicit Russian-language newspaper, *Rabochaia gazeta* (Workers' Newspaper), appeared in Kiev. The two unions and the newspaper were represented at the founding congress of the Russian Social Democratic Labor Party in Minsk; the Kiev newspaper became the new party's organ but was soon closed by the police.

A few Ukrainians participated in Lenin's bolshevik movement. Among them were Mykola Skrypnyk and Hryhoriy Petrovsky; the latter served as one of six bolshevik deputies in the fourth Duma (1912 to 1914), where he was especially critical of the czarist regime's oppressive nationality policies toward the Ukrainians. Although bolshevik groups existed in such cities as Odessa, Yekaterinoslav, Mykolaiv, Luhansk, Kharkov, and Kiev, there was no all-Ukrainian bolshevik organization.

## HISTORY

*1917 to 1919* In 1917 the bolsheviks in the Ukraine found themselves confronted with a Ukrainian national movement which they conveniently termed "bourgeois," but which some bolsheviks wished to recognize. Although most of the Ukrainian bolsheviks were in the industrial eastern Ukraine, those in Kiev were aware of the nationalist appeal exercised by the Ukrainian Central Council (Ukrainska Tsentralna Rada) and favored limited collaboration with it. A meeting of bolsheviks of the "right-bank" Ukraine (west of the Dnieper), held in Kiev during December 1917, failed to establish a unified party. Their weakness in Kiev prompted the bolsheviks to go to Kharkov, where they proclaimed a Ukrainian soviet (*radianska*) government on

December 25 in the hope of giving their campaign against the anticommunist Central Council the appearance of a civil war.

This Ukrainian communist regime, supported by Lenin's army, succeeded in holding Kiev for two weeks in February 1918, but it soon had to take refuge in Russia. During the retreat a conference was held in Taganrog on April 19-20, 1918, and a majority, led by Skrypnyk, decided to establish an independent Communist Party (Bolshevik) of the Ukraine [Komunistychna Partiia (Bilshovykiv) Ukrainy], which was to be related to the Russian party only in the Comintern. The new party held its first congress in exile in Moscow on July 5-12, 1918; under Russian pressure it rescinded the Taganrog decision and declared itself to be an autonomous part of the Russian Communist Party (Bolshevik). Two groups of exiles were in conflict—those in Yekaterinoslav, led by E. I. Kviring, and those in Kiev, led by Volodymyr Zatonsky. Although the Kiev faction eventually proved to be closer to Ukrainian realities, Kviring's group triumphed at the second party congress, held in Moscow in October 1918; it excluded the Kiev bolsheviks from the central committee and elected to it the Georgian Stalin.

At the third party congress, held in Kharkov in March 1919 after the military reoccupation of part of the Ukraine by Lenin's armies, the Kiev group took control of the central committee. However, dependence on the Russian military prompted a resolution giving the Ukrainian party the status of a regional organization within the Russian party.[1] However, the alien and Russian character of the Ukrainian communist regime, its unrepresentative membership, and its lack of appreciation of Ukrainian needs led to a drastic revision of policy. The KPU had to retreat to Russia again—this time in the face of Denikin's offensive, which was facilitiated by Ukrainian peasant uprisings and a renewed right-bank military campaign by the anticommunist Ukrainian People's Republic, led by Simon Petliura. By December 1919 the KPU and the Russian party were forced to adopt a policy that would bring the KPU closer to the peasant masses and to recognize the Ukrainian language and culture.

*1920 to 1932* The KPU was somewhat strengthened in March 1920 by the absorption of the Ukrainian left socialist revolutionaries, or *borotbisty*, but its continued dependence on Moscow was evident; V. M. Molotov served as party first secretary from November 1920 until February 1921, when he was succeeded by Kviring. In 1922 the Ukrainian communists led by Skrypnyk and Rakovskii opposed Stalin and advocated the establishment of a confederation of independent soviet republics in lieu of a Soviet Union. At the seventh party conference in April 1923 the KPU's Russian membership had to accept a demand—voiced by M. V. Frunze on behalf of the Russian Communist Party—that the urban proletariat, schools, and the party and state apparatus be Ukrainized, although at this time only 24 percent of the KPU membership was Ukrainian. Dissatisfaction with the pace at which Ukrainian demands were being fulfilled led to the removal of Kviring from the general secretaryship in May 1925. He was succeeded by Lazar Kaganovich, who was instructed by Stalin to proceed with Ukrainization. By December 1925, 40 percent of the party membership (which numbered 98,000 members and 69,000 candidate members) was Ukrainian.

The steady growth of Ukrainian national cadres and the outspokenness of some of the intellectuals prompted concern on Stalin's part about possible development along lines detrimental to Moscow's interests. On April 16, 1926, Stalin sent a letter to the KPU central committee criticizing the writer Mykola Khvylovy and Oleksander Shumsky, a former socialist revolutionary who was commissar of education, for their Ukrainian nationalism. Although Shumsky and Khvylovy had to admit their "errors," they were supported by the Communist Party of the Western Ukraine (under Polish rule), which was censured by the KPU central committee on June 7, 1927, for "Shumskyist deviation." However, Ukrainization continued under

Skrypnyk, the new commissar of education; by June 1930, 52.6 percent of the party membership was Ukrainian.

*1933 to 1938* Moscow's demands for increased grain deliveries and intensified collectivization led to a mass famine in the Ukraine in which millions perished, and in January 1933 Stalin designated an outsider, Pavel P. Postyshev, as KPU second secretary. S. V. Kosior, who had succeeded Kaganovich in August 1928, remained as first secretary, but with very circumscribed powers. Postyshev arrived with instructions from Stalin to purge the party and was accompanied by thousands of Russian officials to serve as replacements. A mass repression of Ukrainian intellectuals and cultural workers followed. Khvylovy committed suicide on May 13, 1933. Skrypnyk committed suicide on July 7, after Postyshev attacked him for protecting nationalists. The Ukrainians were told that the danger of Russian chauvinism had been replaced by the greater danger of Ukrainian nationalism.

Stalin was duly elected a member of the KPU central committee at the twelfth congress in January 1934, but only thirty-eight of the seventy-five previous central committee members were reelected. Although the capital was moved to Kiev, the persecution of alleged nationalists continued, and various "conspiratorial organizations" were discovered by Postyshev. Postyshev was summarily removed by Stalin in March 1937. At the thirteenth congress in May-June 1937 only thirty-six of the 115 previous central committee members were reelected, and Stalin appointed Nikita Khrushchev, first secretary of the Moscow party organization, to succeed Kosior as KPU first secretary. The Ukrainian central committee objected, and the premier of the Ukrainian Soviet Socialist Republic, Panas Liubchenko, committed suicide on August 29, 1937. Khrushchev was nevertheless installed on January 27, 1938, and arrived with a retinue of officials and a new chief of police, A. I. Uspensky. Khrushchev proceeded to denounce "Ukrainian bourgeois nationalism," demand more intensive purges, and advocate policies of Russification. The central committee elected at the fourteenth KPU congress in June 1938 contained only one member and two candidate members from the central committee elected the previous year; fifty-nine of the sixty members and twenty-five of the twenty-seven candidate members who had dared to oppose Khrushchev's appointment had been replaced.

*1939 to 1953* The annexation of the Western Ukraine (Eastern Galicia and Volhynia) in September 1939 presented the party with the task of absorbing a recalcitrant population. The rapid nazi invasion of 1941 compelled the KPU leadership and most of the membership to flee; M. Burmystenko, Khrushchev's lieutenant, was killed during the conflict. As Soviet forces assumed the offensive after 1943, the KPU was confronted with a devastated country and a Western Ukraine which was seething with unrest; the nationalist underground had to be combated with armed force. Famine conditions and renewed attacks on "bourgeois nationalists" made it necessary for Khrushchev to relinquish the first secretaryship to Kaganovich from March to December 1947; Khrushchev continued to serve as head of the Ukrainian government. In January 1949 the sixteenth congress elected a central committee of seventy-seven members and forty-six candidate members, of whom only twenty-two were holdovers from the 1940 congress. In December 1949 Khrushchev was appointed Moscow regional committee *(obkom)* secretary and was replaced as KPU first secretary by another Russian, Leonid G. Melnikov.

One of Melnikov's first acts was to visit the Western Ukraine, where he demanded more intensive propaganda and a strengthening of the collective-farm apparatus. During 1951 he launched a campaign against "bourgeois nationalism" in the arts and literature and prompted the Russian chauvinism which was characteristic of Stalin's last years. Following

Stalin's death in March 1953, Melnikov was removed from his post early in June and was accused of "gross errors in the selection of cadres and the conduct of the party's nationality policy." More specifically, he was charged with introducing Russian into Western Ukrainian higher education as the language of instruction. His successor, Aleksei I. Kirichenko, was the first Ukrainian in the KPU's history to hold the post of first secretary.

*1953 to 1965*   Kirichenko remained at the head of the KPU until December 1957, when he became a central committee secretary in Moscow. In July 1955 he became a full member of the Soviet party politburo—the first Ukrainian to be included in that body since Chubar had been purged in 1938—but he was removed in 1960. Kirichenko was succeeded from December 1957 to June 1963 as KPU first secretary by Nikolai Podgorny (Mykola Pidhorny), who also succeeded him as a full member of the Soviet politburo in May 1960 and headed the Ukrainian delegation to the United Nations General Assembly in that year. In July 1963, when Podgorny became a secretary in Moscow, Piotr Iu. Shelest became KPU first secretary; in November 1964, following the ouster of Khrushchev, Shelest also became a full member of the Soviet party politburo.

## ORGANIZATION AND MEMBERSHIP

The KPU is a branch of the Communist Party of the Soviet Union and corresponds to it in organization. It consists of twenty-five regional party organizations; as of January 1965 it also had 112 city party organizations, eighty urban district organizations, and 379 rural district organizations. The KPU congress, which is supposed to convene every four years, elects a central committee of 130 members and seventy-five candidate members. The presidium has eleven members and five candidate members.

In 1965 the KPU had 1,977,119 members and 145,697 candidate members and nearly 54,000 primary party organizations. Workers and collective farmers were said to comprise 56.7 percent of its membership; the remainder were salaried workers and others.[2] Women constituted 18.1 percent of the membership. The age distribution of the membership in 1965 was 7.3 percent under twenty-six, 15.9 percent twenty-six to thirty, 31.3 percent thirty-one to forty, 25.1 percent forty-one to fifty, and 20.4 percent over fifty. Distribution by education was 15.9 percent with higher education, 35.7 percent with secondary and incomplete higher education, 29.1 percent with incomplete secondary education, 18.6 percent with elementary education, and 0.7 percent with incomplete elementary edcation. Ethnic composition of the party as of January 1, 1965, was as shown below.

| Ethnic group | Number | % party membership | % population |
|---|---|---|---|
| Ukrainians | 1,174,518 | 64.2 | 76.8 |
| Russians | 492,046 | 26.9 | 16.9 |
| Jews | 97,421 | 5.3 | 2.0 |
| Belorussians | 23,692 | 1.3 | 0.7 |
| Poles | 7,571 | 0.4 | 0.9 |
| Bulgars | 4,972 | 0.3 | 0.5 |
| Moldavians | 4,708 | 0.2 | 0.6 |
| Others | 24,710 | 1.4 | 1.6 |

SOURCE: *Ukrainska radianska entsyklopedia*, vol. XVII, Kiev, 1965, pp. 68, 201.

The KPU has undergone numerous purges. In 1921, 22.5 percent of the membership was expelled. Between 1933 and 1938 more than 162,000 members (35 percent) were expelled, and many were executed. Among the purged leaders were V. P. Zatonsky, S. V. Kosior, M. M. Khataevych, A. A. Khvylia, O. H. Shlikhter, and M. M. Popov. After 1956 a number of executed leaders of the KPU were posthumously rehabilitated. Skrypnyk, who had committed suicide, was only partially rehabilitated.

## PARTY PRESS ORGANS AND RECORDS

The KPU publishes the daily *Radianska Ukrai-*

*na* (Soviet Ukraine) in Ukrainian and a Russian-language daily, *Pravda Ukrainy* (Truth of the Ukraine). Its journal is *Komunist Ukrainy* (Communist of the Ukraine), published in Ukrainian and Russian editions.

Documents are available in *Komunistychna partiia Ukrainy v rezoliutsiiakh i rishenniakh zizdiv i konferentsii, 1918-1956* (The Communist Party of the Ukraine in Resolutions and Decisions of the Congresses and Conferences, 1918-1956), Kiev, Politvydav Ukrainy, 1958. Extensive secondary literature dealing with the KPU congresses is cited in *Ukrainska radianska entsyklopediia* (Ukrainian Soviet Encyclopedia), vol. XVII, Kiev, 1965, p. 201. Materials and memoirs for the earlier congresses as well as stenographic reports for subsequent congresses are available.

## CONGRESSES OF THE KPU

1st congress, July 1918, Moscow
2d congress, October 1918, Moscow
3d congress, March 1919, Kharkov
4th conference, March 1920, Kharkov
5th conference, November 1920, Kharkov
6th conference, December 1921, Kharkov
7th conference, April 1923, Kharkov
8th conference, May 1924, Kharkov
9th congress, December 1925, Kharkov
10th congress, November 1927, Kharkov
11th congress, June 1930, Kharkov
12th congress, January 1934, Kharkov
13th congress, May-June 1937, Kiev
14th congress, June 1938, Kiev
15th congress, May 1940, Kiev
16th congress, January 1949, Kiev
17th congress, September 1952, Kiev
18th congress, March 1954, Kiev
19th congress, January 1956, Kiev
20th (extraordinary) congress, January 1959, Kiev
21st congress February 1960, Kiev
22d congress, September 1961, Kiev
23d congress, March 1966, Kiev

## BIBLIOGRAPHY

Adams, Arthur R.: *Bolsheviks in the Ukraine: The Second Campaign, 1918-1919,* New Haven, Conn., Yale University Press, 1963.

Armstrong, John A.: *The Soviet Bureaucratic Elite: A Case Study of the Ukrainian Apparatus,* New York, Praeger, 1959.

Bilinsky, Yaroslav: *The Second Soviet Republic: The Ukraine after World War II,* New Brunswick, N. J., Rutgers University Press, 1964.

Borys, Jurij: *The Russian Communist Party and the Sovietization of Ukraine,* Stockholm, 1960.

Dmytryshyn, Basil: *Moscow and the Ukraine, 1918-1953,* New York, Bookman, 1956.

Holubnychy, Vsevolod: "Outline History of the Communist Party of the Ukraine," *Ukrainian Review* (Munich), no. 6, 1958.

Kostiuk, Hryhory: *Stalinist Rule in the Ukraine: A Study of the Decade of Mass Terror, 1929-1939,* New York, Praeger, 1961.

Lawrynenko, Jurij: *Ukrainian Communism and Soviet Russian Policy toward the Ukraine: An Annotated Bibliography, 1917-1953,* New York, Research Program on the USSR, 1953.

Luckyj, George S. N.: *Literary Politics in the Soviet Ukraine, 1917-1934,* New York, Columbia University Press, 1956.

Majstrenko, Iwan: *Borotbism: A Chapter in the History of Ukrainian Communism,* New York, Research Program on the USSR, 1954.

*Narysy istorii Komunistychnoi partii Ukrainy* (Outline of the History of the Communist Party of the Ukraine), 2d ed., Kiev, Politvydav Ukrainy, 1964.

Sullivant, Robert S.: *Soviet Politics in the Ukraine, 1917-1957,* New York, Columbia University Press, 1962.

JOHN S. RESHETAR, JR.

1. Hence the next five conclaves of the KPU were termed conferences rather than congresses; the term "congress" was readopted in 1925 at the ninth congress.

2. *Radianska Ukraina,* March 16, 1966.

# UNION OF SOVIET SOCIALIST REPUBLICS

The Communist Party of the Soviet Union (Kommunisticheskaia Partiia Sovetskogo Soiuza, CPSU) emerged from the Russian Social Democratic Labor Party (Rossiiskaia Sotsialdemokraticheskaia Rabochaia Partiia, RSDRP), which held its first congress in Minsk in March 1898. A Russian Marxist émigré group, the Emancipation of Labor, founded in Geneva in 1883 by Georgii Plekhanov, had little direct influence on developments in the Russian Empire. Russian Marxists rejected the views of the populists, who advocated an agrarian socialism based on the peasant commune. The Marxists contended that the Russian Empire would have to experience capitalism and develop a new politicoeconomic order based on a rising industrial proletariat. However, the social democratic movement was primarily the work of intellectuals and professionals. Among these was Vladimir Ilyich Ulianov, who adopted the pen name Lenin.

Following his admission to legal practice in 1892, Lenin opposed the populists and became active in Marxist study groups and in the St. Petersburg Union for the Struggle for the Emancipation of the Working Class. His arrest in 1895 and subsequent exile to Siberia, as well as the failure of the first congress of the RSDRP, prompted him to advocate the organization of a centralized conspiratorial party of tested professional revolutionaries subject to iron discipline. He also launched an attack on the "economists," a Russian Marxist group whose members he accused of advocating economic reformism at the expense of political struggle. In 1900, aided by Plekhanov, Martov, Axelrod, and other Marxists, Lenin, in voluntary exile in Western Europe, began to publish a newspaper *Iskra* (The Spark) to propagate his views on party organization and to recruit followers. He also explained his plan in *Chto delat?* (What Is to Be Done? ), published in 1902.

Lenin's extremist views prompted a division among social democrats in 1903 and 1904 into the bolshevik (majority) and menshevik (minority) factions. The walkout of seven delegates at the party's second congress in 1903 gave Lenin and his followers a slight majority and the "majoritarian" label, which they monopolized thereafter. Initially the disagreement centered on a narrow (Leninist) definition of party membership qualifications versus a broader formula advocated by the mensheviks, and on a centralist organization in contrast to a federal scheme that would have protected the rights of non-Russian party groups within the Russian Empire. The mensheviks, led by L. Martov (Julius Tsederbaum) and at times by Plekhanov, boycotted a purely bolshevik third congress of the party convened by Lenin in London in April-May 1905.

A "unity" congress held in Stockholm in April-May 1906 resulted in the defeat of Lenin's bolsheviks and placed the mensheviks in temporary control of the party. The dispute continued and was intensified when the mensheviks condemned the bolshevik practice of conducting armed robberies ("expropriations") in Russia to finance their factional activities. There was also disagreement over the land issue: the bolsheviks favored nationalization, while the mensheviks advocated "municipalization." Some mensheviks advocated a mass party with a broad working-class membership, while Lenin continued to champion the cause of an elite party. The two factions disagreed on the policy to be adopted toward bourgeois liberal parties and the Duma, the czarist legislative assembly with limited powers. The mensheviks favored participation in Duma elections and entry into electoral alliances with some liberal parties, but only in certain constituencies. Lenin opposed such alliances. The two factions disagreed over the speed at which the revolution was developing and the role of violence: the mensheviks saw the need for a longer period of bourgeois rule, while Lenin demanded a speedup and use of insurrectionary methods. Their disagreements were usually over tactics, methods, and timing, rather than ultimate goals, and were differences of degree.

Efforts to reunite the two factions in 1909 and 1910 failed; each published its own newspaper and had its own funds. The breach became irreparable in January 1912, when Lenin convoked a bolshevik conference in Prague which in effect established a separate Russian Social Democratic Labor Party (Bolshevik) with its own central committee and newspaper, *Pravda*, founded in April 1912. Among Lenin's principal lieutenants were his wife Nadezhda Krupskaia, his successor Joseph V. Stalin (Iosif Dzhugashvili); Lev Kamenev, Grigorii Zinoviev, and a czarist police spy, Roman Malinovskii.

The executive of the Second (Socialist) International, of which both Russian factions were members, attempted to bring about the reunification of the party, but encountered Lenin's decided opposition to any arrangement short of capitulation by the mensheviks. In 1914 a special commission of the International investigated the causes of the split and prepared a resolution to be presented to the forthcoming August congress. This resolution condemned Lenin's splitting tactics and recommended unification of the party. The outbreak of World War I prevented the convening of the congress in Vienna in August 1914 and saved Lenin from public censure.

When the inefficiency and despair caused by Imperial Russia's protracted involvement in World War I led to the fall of the monarchy in February 1917, Lenin returned from exile in Switzerland. The bolsheviks embarked upon a program of promoting demoralization and disaffection in the armed forces, in opposition to the Russian Provisional Government's attempt to continue the increasingly unpopular war against the Central Powers, through newspapers published at great expense by the party for distribution among the troops. Peasant unrest and seizure of the land contributed to the breakdown of authority, from which the bolsheviks benefited. While depriving the Provisional Government of armed support by neutralizing or winning over the capital's garrison, Lenin organized the Red Guards, a paramilitary force with which his party was able to seize power in Petrograd on November 6-7, 1917.

In March 1918 the seventh congress renamed the party the Russian Communist Party (Bolshevik) [ Rossiiskaia Kommunisticheskaia Partiia (Bolshevikov), RKP(B)]. In December 1925, following the establishment of the Soviet Union, it became the All-Union Communist Party (Bolshevik) [Vsesoiuznaia Kommunisticheskaia Partiia (Bolshevikov), VKP(B)]. In October 1952 the reference to bolshevism was abandoned when the present name, Communist Party of the Soviet Union (CPSU), was adopted.

## HISTORY

*Leninist Rule: 1918 to 1922* Following the establishment of bolshevik rule in Petrograd and Moscow, it was still necessary to combat the regime's Russian and non-Russian opponents for three years in what has been called a "civil war." Party membership in late 1917 was approximately 240,000 out of a total population of about 150 million; by 1920 it had risen to 431,400. In order to preserve his weak regime Lenin sought a peace treaty with the Central Powers at any cost. This aroused the opposition of a group of "left communists," which included Nikolai Bukharin, Karl Radek, Aleksandra Kollontai, Emilian Iaroslavskii, and Mikhail Pokrovskii. Lenin defeated this group at the seventh congress in March 1918 and succeeded in obtaining approval of the Brest-Litovsk treaty. This treaty also brought an end to the collaboration of the left socialist revolutionaries with the bolsheviks and the withdrawal of three socialist revolutionaries from the Soviet government.

Lenin adopted other drastic measures to retain power, including terror and the establishment of a secret-police apparatus, recruitment of a new army, and the hiring of czarist army officers and "bourgeois" technical specialists. Food was requisitioned from peasants, rationing was imposed, and labor was conscripted as the party adopted a policy of "war communism."

Certain of Lenin's policies resulted in opposition from various groups of communists. Advocates of independent trade unions were defeated at the ninth congress in March-April 1920, when it was decided that the union leadership would be subordinate to the party. As the party became increasingly bureaucratized and came to rely on the appointment rather than the election of officials, a "democratic-centralist" opposition emerged, under the leadership of Sapronov, and was defeated by Lenin. The "workers' opposition," led by Aleksandr Shliapnikov and Aleksandra Kollontai, objected to the increasingly nonproletarian nature of the party membership and contended that it had ceased to be a workers' party. This opposition also criticized the bureaucratization of the party and Lenin's policy of hiring technicians and specialists who had served the czarist regime. Lenin countered with a resolution, adopted by the tenth congress in March 1921, outlawing all factions and threatening oppositionists with expulsion.

The bankruptcy of the policy of "war communism" was evident in the breakdown of the economy and in strikes and famine; a mutiny at the Kronstadt naval base also had to be suppressed at the time of the tenth congress. In March 1921 Lenin launched a limited retreat in adopting the New Economic Policy (NEP), which permitted dwarf "capitalism" in the form of small enterprises and retail trade; peasants were allowed to sell the surplus that remained after they paid a tax in kind. These limited incentives made possible a restoration of the economy. However, economic concessions were accompanied by a tightening of party controls and the emergence of a powerful secretariat. In 1918 the secretariat had been in the hands of Yakov Sverdlov. A subsequent three-man secretariat headed by Nikolai Krestinskii was replaced in 1921 by V. M. Molotov, who was given the title of responsible secretary. In April 1922 Stalin became general secretary and reorganized the party's administrative apparatus. On May 26, 1922, Lenin had the first of three strokes; in December he became an invalid as a result of the second stroke, and his ability to control the party came to an end.

*Collective Leadership and Stalin's Rise: 1923 to 1927* During Lenin's illness the triumvirate of Stalin, Kamenev, and Zinoviev assumed control. Relations between Lenin and Stalin deteriorated during December 1922; in January 1923, in a codicil to his testament, Lenin advised that Stalin be removed from the general secretaryship. The triumvirate suppressed the testament and assured Stalin's survival. Fear of Leon Trotsky, who was organizer of the Red Army and was regarded as a potential Bonaparte, held the triumvirate together. A personal conflict between Trotsky and Zinoviev also benefited Stalin, who assumed the pose of a "moderate" who could consolidate Zinoviev's position. As Stalin began to acquire excessive power, his colleagues entered into an alliance with Trotsky in 1926.

Stalin claimed to be the interpreter and faithful executor of Leninism after Lenin's death in January 1924 and took pains to justify his policies with quotations from Lenin's writings. He denounced "Trotskyism" and had Trotsky removed from his post as war commissar in January 1925. Stalin, unlike his opponents, had the advantage of not having quarrelled with Lenin prior to the establishment of the bolshevik regime. He succeeded in enlarging the central committee with his followers and using it to counter politburo opposition. He also enlarged and strengthened the secretariat and was able to control personnel and place his followers in key posts in the party apparatus. In addition, by controlling the administration of local party organizations, Stalin was able to have his followers elected as delegates to party congresses.

Stalin advocated the "building of socialism in one country" (with less emphasis on the promotion of communist activities in foreign countries), while his opponents advocated termination of the New Economic Policy. Stalin initially defeated the left opposition by defending the policy (including additional concessions to the peasantry) as a Leninist policy and thus winning the support of the politburo right wing, which consisted of Nikolai Bukharin, Aleksei Rykov, and Mikhail Tomskii. Stalin had argued that socialism could be built in the Soviet Union only with peasant support. By 1926 he had demoted Kamenev to candidate membership in the politburo and had promoted three of his lieutenants (Molotov, Voroshilov, and Kalinin) to full membership. Zinoviev was removed from his position as chief of the Leningrad party organization in February 1926 and was expelled from the politburo in July. Trotsky and Kamenev were removed from the politburo in October. During 1927 the left opposition attempted to discredit Stalin, but without success, and took to holding clandestine meetings. Zinoviev and Trotsky were expelled from the central committee in October; when anti-Stalin demonstrations took place on November 7, 1927, they were expelled from the party. The fifteenth congress, the first held without any debate, met in December 1927, and Stalin's followers duly upheld the general secretary and expelled from the party nearly a hundred opposition leaders.

*Consolidation of Stalin's Dictatorship: 1928 to 1934* In the new quadrumvirate Stalin's influence was even greater than it had been in the triumvirate. Although the support of the right was necessary to enable Stalin to defeat the left, he was able to dispense with it relatively rapidly. Bukharin, Rykov, and Tomskii had been deceived into thinking Stalin had adopted their moderate policy of slower industrialization, to be financed by agricultural production increased through incentives to peasant farmers. By April 1928 Stalin was advocating the establishment of large collective and state farms as a result of reduced deliveries of grain by the peasants to the state. The peasants would not sell because of low agricultural prices, lack of confidence in the currency, and a shortage of manufactured goods. By October 1928 Stalin began to speak of the danger of a right opposition. While denying that disagreement had split the politburo, Stalin threatened to remove those who would not accept his plans for rapid industrialization carried out at great cost with mass deprivation.

The right was weak in the politburo, with only three members out of nine, although it had some strength within the leadership of the Moscow city organization. In April 1929 Stalin launched an attack on the right, and especially on Bukharin, who was accused of advocating a pro-kulak policy and the transformation of village "capitalism" into socialism. Bukharin was removed from the politburo in November 1929, Tomskii in July 1930, and Rykov in December 1930; Rykov also surrendered the premiership to Molotov. Stalin proceeded with the abandonment of the New Economic Policy. He even succeeded in attracting some of Trotsky's supporters with the adoption of a "leftist" course. Trotsky was expelled from the country in January 1929, after having spent the preceding year in enforced exile in Kazakhstan.

The economic goals set by Stalin involved the establishment of a brutal dictatorship and the use of terror against a sullen and resistant population. No exception was made for the party membership. The sixteenth congress, held in June-July 1930, witnessed the abject recantations of some of the leaders of the defeated right, but there were complaints that the opposition was insincere and was playing for time in order to renew its plotting under more favorable circumstances. The elimination of alleged rightists from key positions continued for several years. Stalin's personal secretariat grew in power and developed close relations with the secret police, although the seventeenth congress, in January-February 1934, gave the appearance of compromise and reconciliation. However, this was misleading, and the "congress of victors" was in reality the congress of the doomed, since approximately ninety-eight of the 139 members and candidate members (70 percent) of the central committee elected by this congress were to be executed on Stalin's orders during the coming years. Of the 1,966 delegates to the congress itself, 56 percent were subsequently arrested as counterrevolutionaries.

*The Purges: 1935 to 1939* Mass arrests of party members were precipitated by the mysterious assassination on December 1, 1934, of Sergei M. Kirov, who had succeeded Zinoviev as leader of the Leningrad party organization and had also been a member of the politburo and secretariat. Circumstantial evidence points to the likelihood of Stalin's involvement in the assassination. In any case, he used it as a pretext for unleashing a reign of terror, especially against the remnants of the left opposition. The adoption in 1936 of what was termed the world's most "democratic" constitution did not preclude the staging of the Moscow show trials in August 1936, January 1937, and March 1938. Prominent old bolsheviks who now opposed the Stalin regime, such as Kamenev, Zinoviev, Bukharin, Rykov, and Krestinskii, were executed. None of the defendants was acquitted, and all were linked to the exiled Trotsky by the prosecutor, the ex-menshevik Andrei Vyshinskii.

In March 1937 Stalin asserted that the class enemy was becoming more dangerous as he grew weaker; hence the need for ever-greater vigilance. Such politburo members as Jan Rudzutak, Vlas Chubar, and Stanislav Kosior were removed in 1938 and were subsequently executed; Grigorii Ordzhonikidze was apparently compelled to commit suicide. Mikoyan, elected to the politburo in February 1935, was to survive until his retirement in 1965. The purges finally ground to a halt by the end of 1938. The eighteenth congress met in March 1939—two years later than the party statutes provided—and Stalin conceded that "serious errors" had been made during the purges. Andrei Zhdanov, Leningrad party leader, and Nikita Khrushchev, head of the Ukrainian party organization, were made full members of the politburo. Stalin's regime, weakened by extensive blood purging, now sought to avoid, or at least postpone, involvement in the growing international conflict as the war clouds gathered on the horizon.

*War and Crisis: 1940 to 1945* The Soviet-Nazi nonaggression pact of August 23, 1939, postponed Soviet involvement in the war and made possible extensive territorial gains. It also shocked many communists who had accepted at face value the antinazi pronouncements of Soviet diplomats and publicists and were unprepared for this piece of Stalinist *Realpolitik*. Stalin's personal dictatorship continued to eclipse the party, and as a result of the war, the general secretary also took the post of premier and assumed the title of generalissimo. The politburo declined in importance as the central committee ceased to meet. Instead, command was concentrated in the state defense committee, made up of Stalin and his principal lieutenants. Foremost among these were Georgii Malenkov, who was in charge of the secretariat's cadres department, and Lavrentii Beriia, head of the secret police. Party and government merged on an unprecedented scale. The heavy casualties suffered by the party were compensated for by the mass admission of new members, especially soldiers and officers. Membership increased from 3.8 million in 1941 to 5.7 million by late 1944, but the party maintained tight control over the armed forces and reimposed more rigid controls upon the civilian population.

*The "Cult of Personality" and the Iron Curtain: 1946 to 1952* At the close of World War II Stalin placed seven East European communist parties in power, while reducing contacts between the Soviet Union and the noncommunist world to a bare minimum. He also ordered a campaign against ideologically deviant writers and intellectuals, while promoting a new species of Russian chauvinism. Zhdanov supervised the drive for ideological vigilance and purity and soon became a rival to Malenkov, who had become a full member of the politburo in 1946 along with Beriia. Zhdanov's death in 1948 was followed by the appointment of Nikolai Bulganin to the politburo; in 1948 Aleksei Kosygin also became a full member, replacing Nikolai Voznesenskii, a Zhdanov protégé who was removed from the politburo in 1949 and executed (probably for advocating less restrictive economic policies of which Stalin did not approve).

Stalin ruled arbitrarily and was obsessed by enemies. He did not convene the politburo with any regularity, but divided it into smaller committees for particular problems. The adulation of Stalin's person knew no bounds. He was hailed as a "genius," as the "Lenin of today," and as the inspirer and organizer of the regime's achievements; he dictated style in art, music, and architecture and told professors of linguistics, genetics, and economics how to teach their subjects. In October 1952, at the nineteenth congress (which was ten years overdue), he abandoned the "bolshevik" label, renamed the politburo the presidium, and increased its voting membership to twenty-five. In all likelihood he was preparing to dispense with certain of his older lieutenants and replace them with younger men in a new full-scale purge.

*"Collective Leadership": 1953 to 1957*

Stalin's death on March 5, 1953, brought an era to an end and necessitated a distribution of the dead dictator's powers among his uneasy heirs. Khrushchev became the leading figure in the secretariat, to which he had been transferred in December 1949 after having ruled the Communist Party of the Ukraine for nearly twelve years. He adopted the title of first secretary, and Beriia resumed control of the secret police as minister of the interior. Malenkov became chairman of the council of ministers but had to relinquish his secretariat position. The presidium-politburo membership was reduced to its pre-October 1952 size of ten members. The collective leadership soon faced a crisis. In June 1953 Beriia was removed from his post and executed—as were a number of his aides—presumably because he was a threat to the other members of the politburo. Foreign Minister Molotov's influence increased in the leadership. A new power struggle in February 1955 led to the removal of Malenkov from the premiership on charges of various "errors," but primrily because of disagreement with Khrushchev over the rate of development of heavy industry (and consumer-goods production) and over foreign policy. Bulganin succeeded to the premiership and collaborated with Khrushchev for more than two years. Molotov was accused of an "ideological error" in September 1955 and was compelled to resign as foreign minister in June 1956, after having opposed various policy decisions.

The twentieth party congress in February 1956 elected a new central committee, in which Khrushchev had much support. A lengthy "secret speech" on the "cult of the person and its consequences" was delivered to the congress by Khrushchev on the night of February 24-25. Khrushchev hoped to use the anti-Stalin campaign to compromise certain of his associates by making it appear that they had been closer to Stalin than he; the speech was also a means of assuring doubters that he did not aspire to Stalin's powers and that there would be no repetition of the "cult of personality." It was, moreover, convenient to blame Stalin for all the regime's excesses and failures. Lenin's testament and various documents relating to his negative views on Stalin in 1923 were later released to the Soviet public. Khrushchev attempted to argue that Stalin had many accomplishments, but that he had departed from "Leninist norms of party life" in 1934, following the assassination of Kirov. The criticism of Stalin was confined largely to the excesses he had perpetrated against party members, and the statement actually approved his cruel treatment of left and right oppositionists, "kulaks," and non-Russian "bourgeois nationalists." Stalin's only crime from Khrushchev's perspective was that he had destroyed loyal Stalinists.

The secret speech was an additonal source of disagreement within the leadership, especially since it contributed to the rebellions in Hungary and in Poland in the autumn of 1956 and caused doubt and disillusionment both in the "communist orbit" and in communist parties all over the world. Other issues causing disagreement were Khrushchev's ambitious and speculative program of cultivating the virgin and fallow lands of western Siberia and Kazakhstan, various of his foreign-policy undertakings, and his scheme for economic reorganization. The lines for a showdown were drawn in the spring of 1957, when Khrushchev demanded establishment of more than 100 regional economic councils and the dissolution of many economic ministries in Moscow—a move which would also strengthen his position and weaken that of his critics within the leadership.

In June 1957 an effort was made to remove Khrushchev from his position as first secretary at a politburo meeting at which he was outvoted. Khrushchev refused to resign and instead hastily convened a meeting of the central committee in which he defeated the majority of seven politburo members who had voted to oust him. He termed his opponents the "antiparty group" and identified its leaders as "Malenkov, Molotov, Kaganovich, and Shepilov [the former foreign minister], who joined them." They were removed from the central committee; subsequently Pervukhin and Saburov were also ousted, and Voroshilov and Bulganin were later identified as having been associated with the "antiparty group."

*Khrushchev's Ascendancy: 1958 to 1964*
Not content with the part of party first secretary, Khrushchev also became chairman of the council of ministers on March 27, 1958. He brought into the politburo-presidium a number of new members, including Yekaterina Furtseva (the first woman to serve in that body), Aleksei Kirichenko, Mikhail Suslov, Otto Kuusinen (who was seventy-five at the time of his promotion), Leonid Brezhnev, and Nikolai Podgorny. He relied heavily upon Mikoyan. Khrushchev developed a distinctive style of rule. He traveled throughout the Soviet Union and made numerous trips abroad, attracting much attention with his various pronouncements and colorful language. Having reduced the powers of the secret police in relation to the party, he was unable to use Stalin's repressive measures against his opponents, but instead employed castigation and humiliation after first ousting or demoting them.

Khrushchev revived the central committee, convening it in plenary session two or more times each year. He increased its size, using it in the power struggle against his opponents and rewarding followers with membership in it. He added 4.5 million new members to the party between 1956 and 1964, increasing the percentage recruited from among factory workers and peasants. He continued the campaign against Stalin's memory and the so-called antiparty group. At the twenty-second party congress, in October 1961, Khrushchev had Stalin's body removed from the Lenin-Stalin mausoleum and interred in a grave near the Kremlin wall. The congress also adopted new statutes and a lengthy party program to replace the obsolete document of 1919. In November 1963 he divided most regional (*oblast*) party administrations into separate industrial and agricultural organizations and reduced the powers of the prominent men who had served as first secretaries of the unified regional committees (*obkoms*). This measure antagonized the largest single group of central committee members, the *obkom* secretaries. He also reduced the status of central committee members by inviting many nonmembers to attend particular plenary sessions.

On October 14, 1964, the central committee summarily removed Khrushchev from his posts of first secretary and premier in a carefully planned coup organized by his former lieutenants while he was on vacation. This time Khrushchev was not able to win the support of the central committee, as he had in June 1957. Although his ouster was originally explained in terms of age and health, it soon became apparent that there were other reasons: his various ineffective reorganizations and "hare-brained schemes," his failure to solve the chronic agricultural problem, and objections to his volubility and personal style. He was criticized for hasty decisions and improvisation and for alleged violation of "Leninist norms of party life" (which Khrushchev had claimed to have restored) and of the "collective-leadership" principle. Thus Khrushchev joined Stalin as a leader in ill repute.

*A New "Collective Leadership": 1964-1965* Khrushchev was replaced by an oligarchy led by Leonid Brezhnev, the new general secretary, and Aleksei Kosygin, the new head of government. It also included Mikhail Suslov, Aleksandr Shelepin, Nikolai Podgorny, and Dmitri Polianskii. One of the first acts of the new leadership was to rescind the November 1962 division of the regional committees and reestablish the single first secretary and unified apparatus in each region. Khrushchev's economic reforms were also abandoned as economic regions were dissolved and numerous new ministries were established. The new leadership proceeded with caution, but promised a rise in the living standards, more consumer goods, and increased automobile production (foreign models to be assembled in the Soviet Union).

## ORGANIZATION AND MEMBERSHIP

The CPSU is organized on the basis of "democratic centralism," which in theory provides for the election of higher party bodies by lower bodies, but also makes all decisions of superior bodies binding upon subordinate organizations. At the base of the party are the "primary party organizations," of which there were 312,000 in 1965. These operate in all Soviet enterprises, institutions, military units, collective and state farms, and government offices and departments in which there are at least three party members. The organization of party units on the functional principle is limited to the lowest level. All other party bodies are based on the territorial principle.

All primary party organizations within a rural or urban district (*raion*) are subordinated to the district committee (*raikom*), elected at a district party conference to which the primary party organizations send representatives. The district party organizations are in turn subordinated to an *oblast* or regional organization, which also has a committee (the *obkom*) elected at the regional conference. Each *obkom* in the Russian Soviet Federated Socialist Republic is directly subordinated to the CPSU secretariat in Moscow. Of the fourteen other union republics within the Soviet Union, the larger ones (the Ukraine, Belorussia, Kazakhstan, and Uzbekistan) are divided into *oblasts*; the smaller union republics do not have *oblasts*, but have a central committee (in lieu of the *obkom*) to which the district and city party organizations are subordinate. Republic central committees are elected at republic party congresses. In the larger non-Russian republics subdivided into *oblasts*, the *obkom* is subordinate to the republic central committee, which is in turn subordinate to the CPSU central committee and secretariat in Moscow. The Russian Republic has no separate party organization and central committee, since Russians are in a dominant position in the CPSU central committee and Moscow is the capital both of the Soviet Union and of the Russian Soviet Federated Socialist Republic.

The regional party conferences and union republic party congresses elect delegates to the CPSU congress, which is supposed to be held every four years. Although party statutes define the congress as the "supreme organ," in practice its functions are limited to electing the central committee and central auditing commission and to hearing and approving the reports of both bodies. The congress adopts and amends the party program and statutes and approves the party line on domestic and foreign policy. It also attracts representatives from foreign communist parties, who address the conclave. The large number of voting delegates (more than 4,400 since 1961) and the infrequency of congresses have made it necessary to have a smaller body to approve policy measures.

The CPSU central committee, with 195 voting members in 1965, is elected at each regular party congress and "directs all party activities and local party bodies." It meets in plenary session at least twice a year, and all important policy decisions are made in its name. It elects a political bureau (politburo) of ten to twelve voting members, which probably meets weekly and makes all important decisions. A secretariat, elected by the central committee, directs the party apparatus, controls its personnel, and checks on the fulfillment of decisions. The party is headed by the general secretary, who is also the leading member of the politburo. In 1965 Leonid I. Brezhnev held this post.

The Soviet party is the world's oldest communist party and the second largest (it is second in membership to the Chinese Communist Party). In late 1965 its membership exceeded 11.6 million, and in addition, it had about 800,000 candidate members. Approximately 2.5 million of the members were women. In social composition membership was comprised of workers, 37.8 percent; collective farmers, 16.2 percent; and salaried employees and others, 46.0 perccent. Length of membership broke down as follows: less than ten years, 47.1 percent; ten to thirty years, 47.3 percent; and more than thirty years, 5.6 percent. The party was composed of the following age groups: under twenty-six, 6.2 percent; twenty-six to forty, 46.8 percent; forty-one to fifty, 24.9 percent; and over fifty, 22.1 percent. The educational attainment of members was as follows: higher and incomplete higher education, 18.2 percent; secondary education, 30.9 percent; incomplete secondary schooling, 27.5 percent; and elementary schooling, 23.4 percent.[2]

The regional distribution of party membership is uneven. In 1965 the city of Moscow alone had more than 770,000 members; an additional 385,000 were in the Moscow *oblast*. Leningrad and its region had more than 460,000 members. Regions having more than 200,000 members were Rostov, Gorky, Krasnodar, and Sverdlovsk. As of January 1, 1965, the ethnic composition of the 11,758,200 members and candidates of the CPSU was as shown in the table below.

| Nationality | Number | % party membership | % population (1959 census) |
|---|---|---|---|
| Russians | 7,335,200 | 62.40 | 54.5 |
| Ukrainians | 1,813,400 | 15.43 | 18.0 |
| Belo-russians | 386,000 | 3.28 | 3.8 |
| Uzbeks | 193,600 | 1.64 | 2.9 |
| Kazakhs | 181,300 | 1.54 | 1.7 |
| Georgians | 194,300 | 1.65 | 1.3 |
| Armenians | 187,900 | 1.60 | 1.4 |
| Azerbaidzhanians | 141,900 | 1.20 | 1.4 |
| Lithuanians | 61,500 | 0.52 | 1.1 |
| Moldavians | 40,300 | 0.34 | 1.1 |
| Latvians | 44,300 | 0.38 | 0.7 |
| Tadzhiks | 41,900 | 0.35 | 0.7 |
| Kirghiz | 35,000 | 0.29 | 0.5 |
| Turkmenians | 32,400 | 0.28 | 0.5 |
| Estonians | 33,900 | 0.28 | 0.5 |
| Others | 1,035,300 | 8.80 | 9.9 |

SOURCE: Based on "KPSS v tsifrakh (1961-1964 gody)," *Partiinaia zhizn*, May 1965, no. 10, p. 12.

The CPSU has experienced numerous purges. In 1919 Lenin expelled approximately half the membership, and in 1921 nearly 170,000 members were expelled. These purges involved disillusioned communists, oppositionists, careerists, and former members of other parties. The next large-scale purge occurred in 1927, with the expulsion of the left opposition. The right opposition was purged in 1933. The review and issuance of new party documents in 1936 facilitated the expulsion of more than 1.5 million of the 3.5 million members in the 1930s.

Prominent party officials purged since the 1920s include Trotsky, Kamenev, Zinoviev, Radek, Preobrazhenskii, and Rakovskii (left opposition); Bukharin, Rykov, and Uglanov (right opposition); Syrtsov, Lominadze, Enukidze, Iagoda (head of the secret police from 1934 to 1936), and Ezhov (Iagoda's successor and executor of the 1937 and 1938 blood purges). In 1950 politburo member Nikolai Voznesenskii was executed, and following Stalin's death, Beriia and his aides were executed. Foremost among those purged by Khrushchev were the members of the "antiparty group" and politburo members Aleksei Kirichenko and N. I. Belaev. Khrushchev himself was purged (although with a pension) in 1964, as was his son-in-law, the journalist Adzhubei.

The principal auxiliary organization of the CPSU is the All-Union Leninist Communist Union of Youth (Vsesoiuznyi Leninskii Kommunisticheskii Soiuz Molodezhi), known as the Komsomol, which had a membership of 23 million in 1965; it accepts members of ages fourteen to twenty-six.

*Relationship to Comintern and Cominform*
The Communist International was founded in Petrograd in March 1919 on Lenin's initiative and with little outside support, since there were only a few communist parties in existence at that time. It rapidly became an instrument of Soviet foreign policy designed to develop support for its undertakings and defend its interests. The Comintern was dissolved in May 1943, as it outlived its organizational usefulness.

After World War II, Soviet initiative led to the establishment of the Communist Information Bureau (Cominform) in September 1947. Although the organization was founded in Poland and the headquarters were located in Belgrade and later in Bucharest, the Cominform was at all times under Soviet domination. It was dissolved in April 1956.

For additional information on these two organizations and on other international communist front organizations see *The Communist International, The Communist Information Bureau, The Red International of Labor Unions, The International Peasants' Council, The Communist Youth International, International Red Aid,* and *The Red Sport International.*

THE SINO-SOVIET DISPUTE

The conflict between China and the Soviet Union, which broke into the open in 1961, was of much older origin. Peking's claims on Chinese territory which had been taken over by the Russian czarist regime were set forth in a map published in China in 1954. The Chinese communist leaders raised the question in meetings with Soviet leaders in 1954 and again in 1957, but the Soviet Union refused to honor their claims. The animosity was heightened when the CPSU, and Khrushchev in particular, made unilateral decisions in 1956 which affected the entire communist movement and were subsequently unacceptable to the Chinese Communist Party. These included the decision to denigrate Stalin posthumously and Khrushchev's pronouncements on various roads to socialism (including a parliamentary road) and on the role of violence in world politics and in future communist strategy. Basic to the controversy was the question of whether the Russian or the Chinese revolution would be regarded as the model for communist strategy in Asia and Africa. Moscow's decision to resume relations with Yugoslavia and to accept it as a socialist country served as a source of conflict and gave Peking a means of obliquely denouncing Soviet "revisionism." The absence in the Soviet leadership of a figure possessing a reputation as a theoretician comparable to that of Stalin or Mao also contributed to the dispute. Khrushchev had weakened the Soviet position by conceding in January 1959 that all parties are "equal and independent." He also decided to criticize the Chinese effort to find a short cut to communism by means of agrarian communes.

Moscow's reluctance to assume risks and utilize its nuclear arsenal in support of Peking's foreign-policy aims (such as the seizure of Taiwan) and in pressing the Western powers in Berlin in 1959 and 1960 also contributed to the controversy. Khrushchev's visit to the United States in September 1959 did not meet with Peking's approval; Moscow responded by not supporting Peking's territorial demands against India. In June 1960 in Bucharest Khrushchev sharply attacked Peking's views on foreign policy in response to a Chinese effort in April to criticize Soviet foreign policy as "anti-Leninist." The November 1960 Moscow meeting of eighty-one communist parties resulted in a break between the Albanian party and the CPSU in which Peking supported the Albanians. The issue of whether or not the decisions of the twentieth congress of the CPSU were binding upon all other parties was the principal matter in dispute.

The Soviet decision to employ economic pressure in 1959 and 1960 against Peking failed to bring the Chinese to heel. It did enable Peking to assert that Moscow had violated numerous economic agreements. The CPSU refused to underwrite the rapid industrialization of China or even provide famine relief in 1960 and 1961. As early as 1956 Soviet economic credits had ceased, and Peking had to repay outstanding debts by decreased imports from and increased exports to the Soviet Union.

The conflict was made public by Khrushchev at the twenty-second party congress in October 1961, when he openly attacked Albania after refusing to invite the Albanian party to Moscow; Chou En-lai criticized this tactic and defended the Albanians. The decision to remove Stalin's body from the mausoleum did not meet with Chinese or Albanian approval. With the controversy in the open, Peking could also employ fewer restraints. The Cuban missile crisis of October 1962 and the withdrawal of Soviet missiles and bombers provided Peking with another opportunity to criticize Moscow's alleged willingness to purchase peace at any price. The signing of the nuclear-test-ban treaty in Moscow on August 5, 1963, was denounced by Peking as a "Soviet-American alliance."

Bitter exchanges occurred in June and July 1963 and in February and March 1964. The Russians accused the Chinese of "Trotskyism" and "nationalism," while Peking asserted that Moscow had betrayed Leninism. Khrushchev's advocacy of a conference of communist parties to expel China from the communist movement may have been a factor in his abrupt removal from office. Although Moscow has been able to retain the support of a majority of the world's communist parties, this has not appreciably enhanced its ability to resolve the dispute with Peking.

## FUTURE PROSPECTS

A party which has been in power as long as the CPSU faces serious problems of hypertrophy and corruption. Its unprecedented size alone means that the quality of which it once boasted is likely to have been sacrificed to quantity. It is a far cry from Lenin's elite organization and is highly vulnerable to mass cynicism and careerism. The Soviet party has yet to develop a stable method of changing leaders and of empowering its principal spokesman adequately while creating effective institutional safeguards to prevent abuse of authority. If the dictates of dogma die hard, it may have difficulty in discarding the myth of unanimity and granting genuine recognition to functional and ethnic groups within its ranks and leadership. Among the most serious problems facing the CPSU are those of providing an adequate food supply for its subjects, attempting to combine state ownership with a system of effective incentives, and making available a sufficient quantity of consumer goods of adequate quality. It must live with the human desire for freedom of expression and of conscience. The party must attempt to retain its claim to moral primacy in a communist world in which example rather than fiat is likely to prevail. The nature of its answer to the question "what is communism?" will probably determine its ultimate fate.

## PARTY PRESS ORGANS AND RECORDS

The central committee publishes the daily *Pravda* (Truth), the semimonthly journal *Partiinaia zhizn* (Party Life), and the theoretical and political journal *Kommunist*, which appears in eighteen issues a year, being semimonthly and monthly in alternating months.

The text of the CPSU statutes and the party program adopted in October 1961 can be found in *XXII Sezd KPSS: Stenograficheskii otchet* (Twenty-second Congress of the CPUS: Stenographic Report), vol. III, Moscow, Gospolitizdat, 1962, pp. 229-355. Amendments adopted by the twenty-third congress are in *Pravda*, April 9, 1966, p. 4. An official English translation of the program has been published by Foreign Languages Publishing House in Moscow; see also Jan F. Triska (ed.), *Soviet Communism: Programs and Rules*, San Francisco, Chandler, 1962.

Russian stenographic reports of nearly all CPSU congresses except the first are available in volume form in various editions (with the exception of the nineteenth congress, which was recorded only in the Soviet press). The records of the nineteenth, twentieth, twenty-first, and twenty-second congresses are available in English translation in the four volumes of *Current Soviet Policies*, edited by Leo Gruliow. Basic documents are to be found in *KPSS v rezoliutsiiakh i resheniiakh sezdov, konferentsii i plenumov TsK, 1898-1960* (The CPSU in Resolutions and Decisons of [Its] Congresses, Conferences and Plenums of the Central Committees, 1898-1960), 7th ed., Moscow, Gospolitizdat, 1953-1960.

## PARTY CONGRESSES AND CONFERENCES

1st congress of the RSDRP, March 1898, Minsk
2d congress of the RSDRP, July-August 1903, Brussels-London
3d congress of the RSDRP, April-May 1905, London
1st conference of the RSDRP, December 1905, Tampere (Finland)
4th (unity) congress of the RSDRP, April-May 1906, Stockholm
2d conference of the RSDRP, November 1906, Tampere (Finland)
5th congress of the RSDRP, May-June 1907, London
3d conference of the RSDRP, August 1907, Kotka (Finland)
4th conference of the RSDRP, November 1907, Helsinki (Finland)
5th all-Russian conference of the RSDRP, January 1908, Paris
6th all-Russian conference of the RSDRP, January 1912, Prague
7th all-Russian conference of the RSDRP, May 1917, St. Petersburg
6th congress of the RSDRP(B), August 1917, Petrograd
7th congress of the RKP(B), March 1918, Petrograd
8th congress of the RKP(B), March 1919, Moscow
8th all-Russian conference of the RKP(B), December 1919, Moscow
9th congress of the RKP(B), March-April 1920, Moscow
9th all-Russian conference of the RKP(B), September 1920, Moscow
10th congress of the RKP(B), March 1921, Moscow
10th all-Russian conference of the RKP(B), May 1921, Moscow
11th all-Russian conference of the RKP(B), December 1921, Moscow
11th congress of the RKP(B), March-April 1922, Moscow
12th all-Russian conference of the RKP(B), August 1922, Moscow
12th congress of the RKP(B), April 1923, Moscow
13th conference of the RKP(B), January 1924, Moscow
13th congress of the RKP(B), May 1924, Moscow
14th conference of the RKP(B), April 1925, Moscow
14th congress of the VKP(B), December 1925, Moscow
15th conference of the VKP(B), October-November 1926, Moscow
15th congress of the VKP(B), December 1927, Moscow
16th conference of the VKP(B), April 1929, Moscow
16th congress of the VKP(B), June-July 1930, Moscow

17th conference of the VKP(B), January-February 1932, Moscow

17th congress of the VKP(B), January-February 1934, Moscow

18th congress of the VKP(B), March 1939, Moscow

18th conference of the VKP(B), February 1941, Moscow

19th congress of the CPSU, October 1952, Moscow

20th congress of the CPSU, February 1956, Moscow

21st (extraordinary) congress of the CPSU, January-February 1959, Moscow

22d congress of the CPSU, October 1961, Moscow

BIBLIOGRAPHY

Armstrong, John A.: *The Politics of Totalitarianism*, New York, Random House, 1961.

Avtorkhanov, Abdurakhman: *The Communist Party Apparatus*, Chicago, Regnery, 1966.

Conquest, Robert: *Power and Policy in the USSR*, New York, St. Martin's Press, 1961.

Daniels, Robert V.: *The Conscience of the Revolution: Communist Opposition in Soviet Russia*, Cambridge, Mass., Harvard University Press, 1960.

Fainsod, Merle: *How Russia Is Ruled*, rev. ed., Cambridge, Mass., Harvard University Press, 1963.

Fischer, Louis: *The Life of Lenin*, New York, Harper and Row, 1964.

Linden, Carl A.: *Khrushchev and the Soviet Leadership, 1957-1964*, Baltimore, Md., Johns Hopkins Press, 1965.

Randall, Francis B.: *Stalin's Russia*, New York, Free Press, 1965.

Reshetar, John S., Jr.: *A Concise History of the Communist Party of the Soviet Union*, rev. ed., New York, Praeger, 1964.

Schapiro, Leonard: *The Communist Party of the Soviet Union*, New York, Random House, 1960.

Schueller, George: *The Politburo*, Stanford, Calif., Stanford University Press, 1951.

*Sovetskaia istoricheskaia entsiklopediia* (Soviet Historical Encyclopedia), vol. VII, Moscow, 1965, pp. 713-722 (a bibliography).

Ulam, Adam B.: *The Bolsheviks*, New York, Macmillan, 1965.

Wolfe, Bertram D.: *Three Who Made a Revolution*, New York, Dial Press, 1948.

JOHN S. RESHETAR, JR.

1. See also *Armenia, Belorussia, Estonia, Georgia, Kazakhstan, Kirgizia, Latvia, Lithuania, Tadzhikistan, Turkmenistan, The Ukraine,* and *Uzbekistan.*

2. Statistics are from *Pravda*, March 30, 1966, p. 8, and April 1, 1966, p. 6.

# UNITED ARAB REPUBLIC

The period immediately following World War I was one of tension and turbulence in Egypt. Egyptian nationalists had become increasingly resentful of British control, and their sentiments were fostered and guided by the Delegation Party (Hizb al-Wafd), under the leadership of Sa'd Zaghlul. While nationalism was developing a broad popular base, socialism of the European variety appealed to a handful of intellectuals, who began forming study groups and revolutionary cells. Salamah Musa, a Copt, relates in his autobiography how he was influenced by socialist doctrines, particularly those of the Fabians, during his stay in France and England just before the war.[1]

In or about 1920[2] Salamah Musa, a Dr. al-'Inani, Muhammad 'Abd Allah 'Inan, and Husni al-'Urabi formed the Socialist Party of Egypt (al-Hizb al-Ishtiraki al-Misri) in Cairo. Husni al-'Urabi became impatient with the pace in Cairo and moved to Alexandria, taking with him the party's files and enough of the younger members to wreck the Cairo group.

In Alexandria Husni al-'Urabi cast his lot with a small band of self-styled socialists who, if not already communists, were well on the way to becoming such. This group was led by Joseph Rosenthal, a jeweler, who was allegedly a bolshevik agent disguised as a White Russian refugee.[3] Yehiel Kossai, a Ukrainian Jew also known as Weiss, who later became a leading Soviet expert on the Middle East under the pen name Avigdor, married a daughter of Rosenthal's on one of his visits to Egypt.[4] According to the Italian archives, the chief bolshevik emissary until his arrest and deportation by the Egyptian authorities in 1921 was a Circassian who called himself Zaki Sa'id.[5] The Soviet Association for the Liberation of Egypt, based in Baku, and the Executive Committee of the Comintern kept in close touch with the probolshevik elements in Egypt.

Husni al-'Urabi was welcomed by the Rosenthal group, which at the time consisted almost entirely of representatives of minority communities (Jews, Greeks, Armenians, etc.). One of the few other Arabs was the lawyer Antun Marun, a Christian, who later became the first secretary general of the Communist Party of Egypt (al-Hizb al-Shuyu'i al-Misri).

## HISTORY

The Rosenthal group, which had also named itself the Socialist Party of Egypt, issued a manifesto on December 22, 1921, to "the manual and brain workers of the world," denouncing "British militarists and imperialists" and calling for Egyptian independence. After referring to the "Egyptian intellectual proletariat," the manifesto declared, "We, the proletariat... are organising our forces in the Trade Unions.... Let the intellectuals go to the peasants to create a united political and economic front."[6] The group was in fact far more intellectual than proletarian.

In 1922 the Alexandria socialists decided to seek affiliation with the Comintern. Rosenthal himself opposed the move and was read out of the party. Husni al-'Urabi attended the fourth Comintern congress in Moscow in November-December 1922 as a delegate with a consultative vote. He stated to the congress that the Egyptian party had "attracted 1,000 members to its ranks" since being "legally established" in August 1922. He convinced the Comintern's investigating commission that his party was "a substantial revolutionary movement in conformity with the Communist International," but affiliation was postponed until the party expelled "certain undesirable elements," tried to unite with any other communists in Egypt, accepted the Twenty-one Conditions for Admission to the

Comintern, and changed its name to Communist Party of Egypt.[7]

When the fifth Comintern congress assembled in June-July 1924, the Egyptian party was a recognized section, but an impotent one. In March 1923 the secretary general, Antun Marun, and some members of the central committee had been arrested. In January 1924 the Wafd nationalists had taken over the government, with Zaghlul as prime minister, and mass arrests of communists had followed. Indian and British delegates to the fifth Comintern congress lamented the fact that the whole Egyptian central committee was behind bars. The communist leaders were eventually tried and given relatively mild sentences, although Marun died before his release from jail. The Zaghlul government did not go so far as to outlaw the communist party, which regained some of its strength and for the first time began publishing a paper in Arabic, *al-Hisab* (The Account). The government of Ahmad Ziwar, who succeeded Zaghlul in November 1924, delivered the *coup de grâce*. In June 1925 Ziwar suppressed *al-Hisab* and arrested its editor Jaboux and a dozen other communist leaders, including Rosenthal's daughter Charlotte, all of whom were held in jail for months without trial. So ended what has been called the "prehistoric period" of Egyptian communism, which, as far as can be determined, had no direct link with later developments.

The following fifteen years or so were a bleak period for communism in Egypt. The Comintern from time to time spoke of the Egyptian party even though no properly organized party existed and the devotees of Marxism, still drawn largely from the minorities, apparently never numbered more than a few score. Between 1925 and 1932 the Comintern tried without success to bring the party back to life by working through Soviet commercial representatives in Egypt, one of whom, Ignaz Semenyuk, was an American citizen. In 1929 and 1930 the Comintern Executive Committee fruitlessly proposed a federation of the communist parties of Egypt, Palestine, Syria, and other Arab countries.[8]

The communist organ *Internationale Presse Korrespondenz* in May 1932 stated that "as a result of the temporary weakness of the labor movement in Egypt, police provocateurs and petit-bourgeois adventurers succeeded in disorganizing the activity of the Egyptian Communist Party, detaching it from the workers, and alienating it from the revolutionary mass struggle." The principal share of the blame for disrupting the party was placed on an Egyptian member, Muhammad 'Abd al-'Aziz, who was branded a police spy. In 1934 a Syrian communist, Mahmud Wahib Malik, was sent to Egypt to help the party, but his efforts resulted in the arrest of almost all the forty militants then comprising the cadre.

The entry of the Soviet Union into World War II and its victories from Stalingrad on facilitated the rebirth of communism in Egypt. During the winter of 1941-1942 Marxist study groups began to function again in Cairo and Alexandria. Since then, "more than twenty different groups, frequently changing their names and the names of their publications, have taken part in the competition to become the only true Egyptian Communist Party."[9]

Among the tiny factions appearing in the earliest stage of this new era, the two most prominent were the Egyptian National Liberation Movement (Mouvement Egyptien de Libération Nationale), founded by Henry Curiel (alias Yunus), a Jewish bookdealer in Cairo, and the Iskra (al-Shararah), founded by Hillel Schwarz. The influence of minority elements was again revealed when Marcel Israel led a secession from the Iskra. Curiel was persuasive in preaching the Marxist gospel among workers, as was the Muslim deputy Mustafa Musa, who was believed to have support from the Soviet diplomatic mission in forming a National Committee of Workers and Students, which included communists, Wafdists, and other nationalists. In February and March 1946 students and workers clashed with the Egyptian authorities and the British, giving the new communist movement the first opportunity to show its revolutionary mettle.

Between 1941 and 1946 the Egyptian

communists were also active in political and cultural centers such as the House of Scientific Research, the Committee for Publication of Modern Culture, and Etudes. The Marxist press at this time included *al-Fajr al-Jadid* (New Dawn), *Umm Durman* (named for a large city in the Sudan), and *al-Tali'ah* (Vanguard).

In May 1947 Curiel and Schwarz merged their communist organizations in a none-too-stable alliance called the Democratic National Liberation Movement (Mouvement Démocratique de Libération Nationale, MDLN). Almost immediately the whole communist movement in Egypt was confronted with a crisis when the Soviet Union announced its support for the United Nations proposal to partition Palestine into separate Arab and Jewish states. Although a few Jewish communists proclaimed their opposition to zionism, Curiel and other extreme leftists defended the Soviet policy. This may be taken as the beginning of the end for Jewish leadership of Egyptian communism. When martial law was declared at the outset of the Palestinian war in May 1948, the communist leaders were hauled off to concentration camps, where they lived at close quarters with the leaders of other parties, who later collaborated with them on occasion (socialists, Muslim Brothers, etc.).

The rising tide of anti-British feeling in the winter of 1951-1952 gave the communists new opportunities. They were involved in the burning of Cairo on "Black Saturday," January 26, 1952, although 'Abd al-Nasir's charge that they were primarily responsible must be viewed with caution, as the evidence indicates that their role was a minor one. The communists played a secondary part in the revolution of July 1952 which dethroned King Faruq, Lieutenant Colonel Yusuf Sadiq, a communist associated with the MDLN, and Major Khalid Muhyi al-Din, at least a fellow traveler, were among the Free Officers who carried out the revolution, but were not particularly influential. The leader of the Free Officers, Lieutenant Colonel Gamal 'Abd al-Nasir, was friendly with Judge Ahmad Fuad, a member of the MDLN, but he was not attracted by Marxism, with its hostility toward religion.

In August 1952 'Abd al-Nasir's new revolutionary government clashed for the first time with the communists in connection with an uprising of textile workers at Kafr al-Dawar, near Alexandria. Early in 1953 Sadiq gave up his place in the government and went off to Paris. Early in 1954 Muhyi al-Din left for Europe.

Inspired by the spirit of the Bandung Conference in 1955, the Egyptian government gave the communists considerable leeway for a few years. The most influential journal for the airing of Marxist views was *al-Masa'* (Evening), edited by Muhyi al-Din, who had returned to Egypt in the summer of 1956. The communist movement in Egypt continued, however, to be rent by internal dissension. In 1956 the Italian Communist Party acted as intermediary in securing the election of a central committee for Egypt, but at least three Egyptian factions balked at participating. In February 1958 a number of branches or "tendencies" came together in what was called the Unified (Second) Communist Party of Egypt (al-Hizb al-Shuyu'i al-Misri al-Muwahhad), but this union fell apart only six months or so later.

The upsurge of communism in Syria during the months just before its union with Egypt in February 1958 and the communist strength revealed in Iraq shortly after the Qasim regime came to power in July alerted President 'Abd al-Nasir and his government to the threat the communists might pose in Egypt. Beginning in the summer of 1958, many Egyptian communists were arrested and lodged in jails or concentration camps. When the eighty-one communist parties met in Moscow in November 1960, there was no Egyptian party representative among them. In November 1963 Laqueur stated, "The situation is utterly confused; nobody knows into how many factions the communist movement in Egypt is split at present. . . . Egypt is now the only country of comparable size without an officially recognized communist party."[10] Nevertheless, an organization calling itself the Communist Party of Egypt announced in the spring of 1965 that it had decided to dissolve itself.

## PARTY PRESS ORGANS

From 1941 to 1946 the Egyptian communists published *al-Fajr al-Jadid* (New Dawn), *Umm Durman* (named for a city in the Sudan), and *al-Tali'ah* (Vanguard). In 1956 Muhyi al-Din began publication of the journal *al-Masa'* (Evening).

## BIBLIOGRAPHY

Abdel-Malek, Anouar (Anwar 'Abd al-Malik): *Egypte: Société militaire*, rev. ed., Paris, 1962; published in English as *Egypt: Military Society: The Army Regime, the Left, and Social Change under Nasser*, translated by Charles Lam Markmann, New York, 1968.

Abu Jaber, Kamel S.: "Salamah Musa: Precursor of Arab Socialism," *The Middle East Journal*, vol. 20, no. 2, spring 1966, pp. 196-206.

Filesi, Teobaldo: *Comunismo e nazionalismo in Africa*, Rome, 1958.

Hamrell, Sven, and C. G. Widstrand (eds.): *The Soviet Bloc, China and Africa*, Uppsala, 1964.

Kirk, George: *The Middle East in the War*, rev. ed., London, 1953.

Lacouture, Jean, and Simonne Lacouture: *Egypt in Transition*, translated by Francis Scarfe, London, 1958.

Laqueur, Walter Z.: *Communism and Nationalism in the Middle East*, 2d ed., London, 1957.

Laqueur, Walter Z.: *The Soviet Union and the Middle East*, London, 1959.

Little, Tom: *Egypt*, London, 1958.

Musa, Salamah: *Tarbiyat Salamah Musa* (The Education of Salamah Musa), Cairo, 1958; English translation by L. O. Schuman, Leiden, 1961.

Qal'aji, Qadri: *Tajribat 'Arabi fi al-Hizb al-Shuyu'i* (The Experience of an Arab in the Communist Party), Beirut, n.d.

Riad, Hassan (Hasan Riyad): *L'Egypte nassérienne*, Paris, 1964.

Vatikiotis, P. J.: *The Modern History of Egypt*, New York, 1969.

GEORGE RENTZ

1. Salamah Musa, *Tarbiyat Salamah Musa*, Cairo, 1958, pp. 62 ff; published in English as L. O. Schuman, *The Education of Salamah Musa*, Leiden, 1961.

2. Musa, *op. cit.*, gives the date as 1920 on p. 165 and as 1921 on p. 268.

3. Qadri Qal'aji, *Tajribat 'Arabi fi al-Hizb al-Shuyu'i*, Beirut, p. 21. Qal'aji is an ex-communist.

4. Walter Z. Laqueur, *The Soviet Union and the Middle East*, London, 1959, p. 83. See pp. 82-85 for details on other Jewish bolsheviks concerned with Egyptian affairs, such as Nahum Nadab (Leshchinsky) and Y. Barzilai (Berger).

5. Teobaldo Filesi, *Comunismo e nazionalismo in Africa*, Rome, 1958, pp. 115-116. Filesi says that the Egyptian police learned that Zaki Sa'id's real name was 'Ali Zaki Yuta.

6. From the English version of the manifesto published by *The Labour Monthly* (London), vol. 2, no. 3, March 1922, pp. 267-269.

7. *Fourth Congress of the Communist International, Abridged Report*, London, n.d., p. 217, 287.

8. Jane Degras (ed.), *The Communist International, 1919-1943: Documents*, vol. III, London, 1965, pp. 78, 83.

9. Walter Z. Laqueur, *Communism and Nationalism in the Middle East*, 2d ed., London, 1957, p. 42. See also Jean and Simonne Lacouture, *Egypt in Transition*, translated by Francis Scarfe, London, 1958, p. 263.

10. Walter Z. Laqueur, in Sven Hamrell and C. G. Widstrand (eds.), *The Soviet Bloc, China and Africa*, Uppsala, 1964, pp. 64, 70.

# UNITED KINGDOM

*See* Great Britain *and* Ireland

# UNITED STATES OF AMERICA

During the period of revolutionary ferment inspired by the bolshevik revolution of October 1917 a left wing in the Socialist Party of America (SPA) sought to take over the existing party or split off to form a separate communist party. The split came in September 1919, but differences among the nascent communists caused them to form two parties that month instead of one. At simultaneous conventions in Chicago one group organized the Communist Party of America (CPA), with Charles E. Ruthenberg as national secretary and Luis C Fraina as international secretary and another group set up the Communist Labor Party (CLP), with Alfred Wagenknecht as executive secretary and John Reed as an international delegate. Reed died in Moscow in 1920, and Fraina (later better known as Lewis Corey) dropped out in 1922.

Both new parties were driven underground by government repression early in 1920 (the Palmer raids), and for the next three years the American communists were mainly preoccupied with their own internecine struggles. Efforts at unification were followed by more splits. A United Communist Party was formed in May 1920; another Communist Party of America was set up in May 1921 and split into two parties with the same name in January 1922. Before this split the underground party had set up an open, legal instrument, the Workers Party of America (WPA), in December 1921. A month after the split the other underground party followed suit with another ostensibly legal party, the United Toilers of America.

In April 1923 the communists emerged from underground and joined forces in the legal WPA; in 1925 this party became the Workers (Communist) Party of America and in 1929 the Communist Party of the United States of America (CPUSA), a section of the Communist International. Its most important organizational figure was Ruthenberg, who served as general secretary from 1922 until his death in 1927. Other major early leaders were Max Bedacht, Alexander Bittleman, Earl Browder, James P. Cannon, William Z. Foster, Benjamin Gitlow, and Jay Lovestone.

## HISTORY

*1923 to 1929* The united communist party was plagued from the outset by a factional struggle between Ruthenberg's followers and a group headed by Foster. When Foster's faction developed a majority at the party's fourth convention in 1925, the official Comintern representative, S. I. Gusev, unilaterally reversed the vote by reading a cable from Moscow which gave the leadership to the Ruthenberg faction. Ruthenberg died in March 1927, and Jay Lovestone succeeded him as head of both the party and their faction. However, two years later, after winning an overwhelming majority at the sixth party convention, Lovestone's group fell into disfavor in Moscow. Considered important enough to merit Stalin's personal intercession, Lovestone and his closest associates, including Benjamin Gitlow and Bertram D. Wolfe, were expelled in June 1929. This shakeup coincided with the downfall in the Soviet party and the Comintern of Nikolai Bukharin, with whom Lovestone had been closely identified. Lovestone proceeded to organize a Communist Party (Majority Group), in memory of his former majority. This party, later renamed the Communist Party of the United States of America (Opposition) and then the Independent Labor League of America, was disbanded in 1940.

James P. Cannon, who had been won over to Trotsky's views at the Comintern's sixth congress in 1928, was expelled from the party later that year. In May 1929, with about 100 followers, including Max Shachtman and Martin Abern, he founded the Communist League of America (Opposition), a forerunner of the Socialist Workers Party (SWP). During most of the 1930s Cannon's group was known as the "left opposition" and Lovestone's as the "right opposition."

*1930 to 1934* By 1930, as the economic depression entrenched itself, Earl Browder began to emerge as the top leader of the CPUSA, although he was not formally named general secretary until the eighth party convention in Cleveland, in 1934. At this point American communism was characterized mainly by its extreme leftism, in line with the Comintern's "third-period" policy which anticipated imminent revolution (see *The Communist International*). The tactic of infiltration of the trade unions gave way once more to "dual unionism." The previous position of equality for Negroes was replaced by the slogan of "the right of self-determination of the Negroes in the Black Belt," defined as those contiguous areas in the southern states with a Negro majority. All rival radical parties and groups, especially the SPA, were reviled as "social fascists." When Franklin D. Roosevelt was elected to the presidency in 1932, his New Deal was equated with Hitler's nazism and Mussolini's fascism. Among the most important communist campaigns in these years were the nationwide unemployment demonstrations on March 6, 1930, the successful defense, begun in 1931, of nine Negro boys (eight of whom had been sentenced to death) in Scottsboro, Alabama, the "bonus march" of World War I veterans in July 1932 (the leadership of which the communists soon lost), and organizing efforts in trade unions, student movements, and farming areas.

*1935 to 1940* The popular-front policy initiated at the seventh Comintern congress in the summer of 1935 entailed a drastic change of attitude toward the Roosevelt administration. After the 1936 presidential election the communists ardently supported Roosevelt, with some reservations. They invited the SPA to enter into a united front, but this effort was short lived, partly because the socialists temporarily admitted the Trotskyists into their ranks in 1936. The campaign for self-determination for Negroes was muted, although it was not officially dropped until November 1943 (it was briefly resurrected from 1956 to 1958). Browder put forward the slogan that "communism is twentieth-century Americanism" and sought to identify American communism with the Jeffersonian tradition. However, this "Americanization" was largely limited to domestic matters. In foreign affairs Moscow's lead was always followed enthusiastically and automatically. The purge trials in the Soviet Union were dutifully defended and provoked little perturbation among the general membership, except for protests from some intellectuals on the fringe.

The next great change of line came in 1939, after the German-Soviet pact of August 23 and the outbreak of war on September 1. After some initial confusion, the CPUSA came out against the "imperialist war." This position implied a complete reversal of attitude toward the Roosevelt administration, which was now attacked as implicitly prowar.

In general the reformist popular-front line was replaced by a more militant "anticapitalist" line. A number of strikes were instigated or supported, but some of the party's front organizations, which had flourished during the 1930s, were unable to survive this period of relative communist extremism and isolation.

The government responded promptly to the new party line. In 1940 Browder was sentenced to four years in prison on an old passport violation. The Smith act, which made a crime of "teaching and advocating the overthrow of the United States government by force and violence," was passed in June 1940 and used the following year to prosecute the Trotskyist leadership, including Cannon and Farrell Dobbs; it was later used to prosecute the communist leadership. The Voorhis act of October 1940 forced the party to go through the motions, at a special convention the following month, of disaffiliating itself from the Comintern, though this was basically a matter of form to comply with the law. The available figures indicate that the party may have lost 15 to 20 percent of its prewar membership in this period, although it managed to hold onto most of its hard-won strength.

*1941 to 1945* For most Americans the turning point in World War II was the Japanese attack on Pearl Harbor in December 1941; for the American communists, however, it was the German attack on the Soviet Union on June 22, 1941. In a single day the communist line changed from a militantly antiwar to a militantly prowar position. The chief demand became the opening of a second front in the West to ease the German pressure on the Soviet army in the East. The CPUSA came out for "national unity," a "no-strike" pledge, and unconditional support of the Roosevelt administration—in short, a total reversal of its previous stand. The new communist line brought some tangible rewards. President Roosevelt pardoned Browder in May 1942, and most restrictions were lifted on communist political activity.

After his release from prison Browder developed a new political line which virtually presupposed an indefinite truce with capitalism. In a major statement in 1944 he interpreted the Roosevelt-Churchill-Stalin agreement of December 1943 as a guarantee of indefinite "peaceful coexistence and collaboration," from which he drew far-reaching domestic and international conclusions.[1] As a practical consequence of Browder's new line, in May 1944 the CPUSA was transformed into the Communist Political Association (CPA), with the implication that it was to be mainly an educational organization with basically reformist objectives. Browder's title was changed from general secretary to president, and the lower units became clubs instead of branches.

With the exception of William Z. Foster and Samuel A. Darcy (who was expelled in 1944), the top leadership solidly supported Browder's theories and actions. American communism registered its maximum membership early in 1944, a total of 80,000, and Foster claimed a rate of over 4,000 new members a week.

At this pinnacle of its fortunes the CPUSA was suddenly and unexpectedly plunged into internal crisis. In April 1945 the French communist leader Jacques Duclos published an article in *Cahiers du communisme* sharply criticizing the new Browder line, and especially the change from communist party to communist political association. When this article reached New York in May, Foster, Browder's chief rival in the top leadership, took immediate advantage of the opportunity. In a matter of days Browder's power evaporated. He was repudiated at a special convention on July 16-28, which reestablished the party as the CPUSA, and was formally expelled in February 1946.

*1945 to 1948* Browder was succeeded as general secretary by Eugene Dennis, one of his former lieutenants; the chief authority in the party, however, was wielded by Foster as national chairman. The new party line shifted sharply to the left; from almost unconditional support of United States foreign and domestic policy, it swung over to almost unconditional opposition. At first Browder's expulsion set the party back perhaps as many as 25,000 members, but it soon forged ahead again and claimed about 73,000 members at the end of 1946.

The drop in membership to a reported 60,000 in August 1948 signaled the onset of the great decline in communist strength in the Untied States. The CPUSA's support in the 1948 presidential campaign of the Progressive Party and its candidate Henry A. Wallace, the former secretary of agriculture, represented the high point of communist influence in a national election. However, it was a costly gamble; Wallace's disappointing vote of little over 1 million hardly compensated the communists for their split with those liberals who had refused to support Wallace and with the union leaders who had opposed the third party.

*1949 to 1956* After the Progressive Party fiasco of 1948 American communism went into a precipitous decline. Increasing government repression resulted in the conviction in October 1949 of eleven top communist leaders, including Dennis, for violation of the Smith act. Convictions of other lesser communist leaders followed. Of the several cases involving pro-Soviet espionage, the trial in 1950 of Alger Hiss, a former state department official, on charges made by Whittaker Chambers, received the widest publicity. In February 1950 Senator Joseph R. McCarthy launched a violent anticommunist campaign based on various "lists" of alleged communists in the state department and elsewhere; the McCarthy campaign raged for the next five years before it finally overreached itself. The subversive-activities control act (McCarran act), requiring both the party and individual members to register, was also passed in 1950. In defense against these threats and reverses the party expelled hundreds of members, weeded out thousands, and ordered a portion of its leadership to go underground.

By the beginning of 1956 party membership had dropped to only about 20,000.

*1956 to 1960* The increasing disintegration and demoralization of American communism was transformed into another full-fledged party crisis in 1956 as a result of Khrushchev's "secret speech" on Stalin's "cult of personality" at the twentieth congress of the Soviet party, the near revolt in Poland, and the historic uprising in Hungary. All the pent-up tensions and discontents in the American party burst out in a factional struggle of unprecedented proportions. A predominantly younger group, headed by John Gates, then editor of the *Daily Worker,* rose up against the old-line leadership, represented by Foster, and to a lesser extent by Dennis. At first the Gates faction, highly critical of the Stalinist heritage and swayed by the Polish and Hungarian developments, seemed to have a majority of what was left of the party behind it. However, partly because they were often outmaneuvered and partly because their supporters prematurely resigned en masse, Gates and his followers gradually lost out. Most of the leaders of this group resigned in 1957, and Gates himself left the party in January 1958.

Gates estimated the party membership at this time as less than 7,000; only about 3,000 were officially registered a few months later, probably because the party's general disarray deterred some members from registering. Nevertheless, it may be estimated that at least one-half, and perhaps three-quarters, of the 20,000 still in the party at the beginning of 1956 had dropped out by 1958. This continuing decline, together with Dennis' illness, produced a partial shakeup in the top leadership. At the seventeenth party convention in December 1959 Eugene Dennis was replaced as general secretary by Gus Hall, the former Midwest party secretary. The convention elected a national committee of sixty, including Foster as chairman emeritus, Dennis as chairman, Claude Lightfoot and Elizabeth Gurley Flynn as vice chairmen, and Benjamin

J. Davis as national secretary. The passing of the older generation of American communists was marked by the early deaths of four of these five—Foster at the age of eighty and Dennis at fifty-six in 1961, and Davis at sixty and Flynn at seventy-four in 1964.

*1961 to 1965* In June 1961 the Supreme Court upheld a ruling by the subversive-activities control board requiring the CPUSA to register with the board in compliance with the McCarran act of 1950. In order to protect itself and its members from prosecution for failing to register, the party virtually ceased to operate openly in its own name. For example, although party publications continued to appear, they referred to General Secretary Hall as merely the "leading communist spokesman."

Nevertheless, all left-wing groups began to make some gains during the 1960s. Protests against United States participation in the Vietnam war and the beginnings of unrest on university campuses, particularly on the West Coast, gave birth to a number of radical student movements. In 1961 a pro-Chinese faction was expelled from the CPUSA and held its first convention as the Progressive Labor Party (PLP) in April 1965, with an estimated following of about 1,000. The PLP was headed by Milt Rosen, Mort Scheer, and Fred Jerome. An offshoot of the PLP, the May Second Movement, originated in an anti-Vietnam war demonstration in New York on May 2, 1964. Two other minuscule offshoots of the CPUSA, with a pro-Stalinist and pro-Maoist slant, were the Provisional Organizing Committee for a Marxist-Leninist Communist Party, headed by Armando Roman, and the Communist Party of the United States of America, Marxist-Leninist, formed in September 1965, with Michael I. Laski as general secretary.

The Trotskyist SWP, headed in the 1960s by James P. Cannon and Farrell Dobbs, also became more active, and party sources claim that in 1965 it was equal in "effective strength" to the CPUSA. Three small groups have split off from the SWP: the Spartacists, headed by Jim Robertson, the American Committee for the Fourth International (see *The Fourth Internatinal*), headed by Tim Wohlforth, and the Workers World Party, headed by Sam Ballan and Vincent Copeland.

In November 1965 another Supreme Court decision ruled against the individual-registration provision of the McCarran act, in effect making the entire act unenforceable. The CPUSA immediately announced that the decision "gives ua a new freedom in the country" and made known the intention of issuing a new party program, holding an open national convention, and running candidates in forthcoming elections.[2] These steps indicated the beginning of a new, more dynamic stage in the party's activity. At this point party spokesmen claimed that the CPUSA represented the largest single organized revolutionary group in the country. Nevertheless, its actual gains in membership have been relatively modest, and its future will probably depend on the extent to which it succeeds in allying itself with and gaining recruits from the more varied and amorphous "new-left" movement of the 1960s.

## ORGANIZATION AND MEMBERSHIP

*Organization* The first communist parties of 1919 were largely modeled after the organizational structure of the SPA. Although Soviet-influenced changes in organization were made in the next five years, a typically communist structure was not put through until 1925, when the party was reorganized on the basis of democratic centralism. The top leadership was set up as a central executive committee (changed in 1929 to a central committee), a general secretary, a political committee (changed in 1929 to a political bureau), a secretariat, a central control commission, and departments of agitation and propaganda, organization, trade unions, women, agrarian affairs, Negro affairs, and sports. At the next level the party was divided into districts, subdistricts, sections, subsections, and city organizations. The basic party units were the factory and street nuclei, called cells or simply units. Communist caucuses in noncommunist organizations were called fractions.

During the popular-front period attempts were made to Americanize the party. By 1938 the small street units had been replaced by large neighborhood branches, shop units had been sharply curtailed in number and importance, and fractions in trade unions had been formally abolished (though not always in practice).

A party statement in November 1965 indicated that there had been no basic changes in structure. The party hierarchy consisted of a national convention, a national committee, an executive committee (secretariat), and regional, district, state, section, and club committees, with the local clubs set up on an electoral-subdivision, neighborhood, town, shop, or industry basis.[3]

*Membership* The two communist parties that were formed in September 1919 started with a total membership estimated at about 40,000. However, within a few months government repression and underground pressures had reduced this number to about 10,000. The basic membership hovered around this figure throughout the 1920s, with a probable high of 13,000 in 1924, during the period of the farmer-labor movement, and a drop by 1925 to a probable 7,500. The CPUSA entered the depression with an officially reported membership of only 7,500 in early 1930, but it made substantial gains during the 1930s; by 1939 membership had risen to perhaps 75,000.[4] Even at half Foster's 1928 claim of twenty sympathizers for every party member, there were possibly 1 million who more or less followed the party line during the 1930s.

Membership reached an all-time high in 1944, but this achievement was short lived. As a result of Browder's fall from power in 1945, increasing differences with the unions, and the official anticommunist campaign of the early 1950s, by 1956 it had dropped to about 20,000. The events of 1956 and the ensuing factional struggles reduced the party to fewer than 7,000 members at the beginning of 1958. Despite some gains during the 1960s, in November 1965 the party reported only 10,000 members.

*Social Composition* At its inception the American communist movement was made up mainly of semiautonomous foreign-language federations taken over from the SPA. From 1919 to 1921 Russian immigrants made up the single largest contingent, and from 1922 to 1925 the Finnish section predominated, with almost 50 percent of the total membership. The foreign-language federations were formally disbanded in 1925, but until the 1930s the American party consisted chiefly of English-speaking leaders and a predominantly immigrant rank and file. It was not until 1936 that the party was able to boast a native-born majority.

Since the foreign-languge federations were made up chiefly of industrial workers, the American party began with a largely proletarian composition. An "industrial registration" taken in 1924-1925 indicated that about 75 percent of the party members belonged to the working class, about 15 percent were housewives, and no more than 10 percent came from middle-class and professional ranks. In 1928 metal workers gave way to needle-trades workers as the single largest occupational group in the party (21 percent). After 1930 most recruiting took place among the unemployed; they represented 60 percent of the membership in 1933. With the advent of the popular front the party was able to attract a much larger professional and middle-class following, and by 1941 a party report classified 44 percent as professional and white-collar workers. During the same period the concentration of party members in New York City had risen from 22.5 percent in 1934 to about 50 percent in 1938.

*Front Organizations* Some of the communist auxiliary organizations formed in the early 1920s aimed at mass membership; others were little more than letterhead organizations. The largest of these early organizations was the Friends of Soviet Russia, which was founded in August 1921, underwent numerous name changes, and continued into the 1930s as the Friends of the Soviet Union. Typical organizations of the 1930s were the International Workers Order, the American League Against War and Fascism (later the American League for Peace and Democracy), the League of American Writers, and—in alliance with other leftist groups—the American Student Union, the American Youth Congress (which became communist dominated soon after it was formed), the National Negro Congress, and the Workers Alliance. Membership in these organizations ranged from a few thousand to several million, depending on whether affiliated groups with their own large memberships were counted.

Whereas the fronts of the 1920s were so tightly controlled that they were virtually appendages of the party, those that flourished after 1935 were given far more leeway in both program and organization setup. Nevertheless, many of them perished as a result of the party's abrupt changes of line at the beginning of World War II. The American League for Peace and Democracy was dissolved in 1940, and its successor, the American Peace Mobilization, was given up in 1941. The League of American Writers was also abandoned in 1941; in 1942 the American Youth Congress was disbanded, and the National Negro Congress and its offshoots went into decline.

In 1948 the communists concentrated their efforts in Wallace's Progressive Party, but the severe government repression of the 1950s brought an end to most front activity for a decade. In 1960 the New York School for Marxist Studies was founded, and in June 1964 the W.E.B. DuBois Clubs were set up on a national scale as independent youth associations with a "socialist" orientation and apparently welcomed communists as members.

## TRADE-UNION AND POLITICAL ACTIVITY

*The Trade Unions* The first wave of American communists were opposed to the American Federation of Labor (AFL); some were in favor of the Industrial Workers of the World (IWW); all favored a new, revolutionary trade-union center, or the policy of "dual unionism." Lenin's *Left-Wing Communism: An Infantile Disease*, written in the spring of 1920, persuaded them to try working within the AFL, and in 1921 they managed to win over William Z. Foster, an unorthodox syndicalist who had formed the Trade Union Educational League in November 1920. This organization affiliated with the Red International of Trade Unions (Profintern) and served as the party's trade-union medium throughout the 1920s. It made considerable headway in 1922 and 1923, as long as the communists were allied in the farmer-labor movement with the AFL's progressive wing, led by John Fitzpatrick, president of the Chicago Federation of Labor; it declined precipitously as soon as this alliance was broken in July 1923.

One manifestation of the leftist turn of 1929 was the resurrection of dual unionism. For this purpose the Trade Union Educational League was transformed into the Trade Union Unity League on September 1, 1929, again with Foster as general secretary. The league claimed that it led 200,000 workers in strikes in 1933, in the depths of the depression, but it never succeeded in gaining a real foothold in the major industries. In 1935 the new popular-front line was reflected in the repudiation of dual unionism, and the league was disbanded. At first the communists tried to entrench themselves again in the AFL, but by 1936 they decided that prospects were more promising in the newly organized Congress of Industrial Organizations (CIO), founded by John L. Lewis. During the next three years they were able to win control of about ten CIO unions, including the National Maritime Union, the United Office and Professional Workers Union, the Mine, Mill and Smelter Workers Union, the International Longshoremen's and Warehousemen's Union, the United Electrical, Radio and Machine Workers, the Fur and Leather Workers Union, and the American Communications Association.

The party's support of the administration's

no-strike pledge in 1941 brought the communists into sharp conflict with John L. Lewis, then president of the United Mine Workers of America, especially during the miners' strike in 1943. Nevertheless, in 1944 an estimated 20 to 25 percent of all CIO members belonged to unions led by communists or those close to them, and the party could count on one-third of the votes of the CIO executive board.[5]

The communists began to slip badly in the CIO in 1946, when an anticommunist group led by Walter Reuther won control of the United Auto Workers Union. The Taft-Hartley act of 1947, requiring union officials to file affidavits that they were not communists, resulted in further losses. A split with the CIO leadership, headed by Philip Murray, over the communist-supported third-party movement in 1948 was widened by the party's opposition to the Marshall Plan. The following year the CIO broke decisively with the communists; in 1949 it expelled the communist-dominated United Electrical, Radio and Machine Workers, and in 1950 it expelled all the remaining communist-controlled unions.

*Politics* The first communist parties refrained on principle from all political or electoral activity. The earliest effort to run a communist candidate, in the guise of a Workers League, took place in New York City in November 1921, but the candidate, Benjamin Gitlow, was ruled off the ballot. Another minor attempt was made in 1922 with state candidates in four states and local candidates in six others.

The party entered the national political arena for the first time in 1923 in connection with the farmer-labor movement. This "united front" miscarried, however, and in 1924 the communists put up their own candidates, William Z. Foster for president and Benjamin Gitlow for vice president; their vote was only 33,000. The same candidates ran in 1928 and received 48,228 votes. The 1932 ticket of Foster and James W. Ford, an outstanding Negro leader, received 103,000 votes. Browder and Ford ran in 1936, but their campaign put more stress on the defeat of the Republican candidate, Alfred M. Landon, than on support for themselves. As a result, in a year when the communists might have gotten a substantial vote, they threw the bulk of their support to Roosevelt and polled only 80,181 votes. Browder and Ford also ran in 1940, but their unpopular antiwar line cut their vote to only 46,251.

Although 1940 was the last year that the CPUSA ran its own candidates for national office, the communists made marked electoral gains on the local level after restrictions were lifted in 1942 and reached the high point of their national influence in the third-party movement of the 1948 presidential campaign.

RELATION TO SOVIET LEADERSHIP

The American communists were represented only by proxy at the founding congress of the Comintern in 1919, but official delegates were present at the second congress in 1920 and at all subsequent congresses and plenums. From 1920 on, the Comintern largely determined both the policy and the leadership of the American party. John Pepper (József Pogány), a Hungarian, came to the United States with a Comintern delegation in the summer of 1922 and remained as the party's chief mentor until the spring of 1924 (he spent a shorter, less influential period in the United States in 1928). An official Comintern representative, S. I. Gusev, played a decisive role in the Ruthenberg-Foster conflict in 1925. Other Comintern representatives sent to the United States on various missions during the next decade included the Germans Arthur Ewert (1927) and Philipp Dengel, the British Harry Pollitt (1929), and the Russian Boris Mikhailov (1930). Another German, Gerhart Eisler (known in the United States as Edwards), arrived in the early 1930s and played a major role in the top leadership for about three years. Contingents of American communists were trained in the Lenin School in Moscow from its inception in 1926, the party maintained an official representative in Moscow, and American communists were employed on Comintern missions to other countries.

The CPUSA continued to lean heavily on direction from abroad. Throughout the 1930s the party followed Moscow's line enthusiastically, and even Stalin's zigzag policy regarding the war was implemented immediately and without question. In 1945 when the American communists acted with dispatch to depose Browder, under whom they had reached their highest point in numbers and influence, it was again in response to a signal from abroad—this time ostensibly from France.

The CPUSA has unconditionally supported the Soviet Union in its disputes with Communist China. The party was not represented at the 1960 world conference of communist parties but sent a delegation to the twenty-second congress of the Communist Party of the Soviet Union in 1961. The PLP and other splinter groups have taken a pro-Chinese stand, as have to some extent the SWP, its youth group Young Socialist Alliance, and the SWP splinter groups.

## PARTY PRESS ORGANS AND RECORDS

Among the first communist periodicals in 1919 and 1920 were the CLP's *Communist Labor*, published in New York, and *The Toiler*, published in Cleveland, and the CPA's *The Communist*. *The Toiler* was transferred to New York in October 1921, changed its name to *The Worker*, a weekly, in February 1922, and became the *Daily Worker* in January 1924, with *The Worker* as a separate Sunday issue. The *Daily Worker* ceased publication on January 12, 1958, during the party's decline in that period; only the Sunday *The Worker* survived.

The theoretical organ of the party derived from *The Liberator*, originally a cultural and political magazine founded by Max Eastman in 1918 and taken over by the party as its monthly in 1922. *The Liberator*, *The Labor Herald* (organ of the Trade Union Educational League), and *Soviet Russia Pictorial* (organ of the Friends of Soviet Russia) were combined as *The Workers Monthly* in November 1924. It was renamed *The Communist* in 1927, and in 1944, during the short-lived interlude of the Communist Political Association, it adopted the name *Political Affairs*.

In the intellectual field, *The New Masses* was founded in 1927 as a broadly based radical monthly, but it was soon dominated by its communist editors and made to follow the party line. It became a weekly in 1934, during the party's upsurge, merged with the cultural magazine *Mainstream* to become *Masses & Mainstream* in 1947, during the party's downward course, and ceased publication in 1957, at the party's low point. The present cultural publication is *American Dialog*, founded in 1964 and edited by Joseph North, a former editor of *The New Masses*.

The communist organ in the Jewish language, *Freiheit*, which became *Morning Freiheit*, began publication in April 1922. In 1938 the West Coast organ *People's World* was started in San Francisco. Dozens of other journals have been issued off and on by various party divisions and mass organizations, but few survived the debacle of the 1950s.

Among the publications which have expressed pro-Chinese sentiments are the SWP's weekly *The Militant*, first issued in 1928; its monthly *International Socialist Review*, which began in 1934 as *New International* and then became *Fourth International*; and *The Young Socialist*, which was put out by the SWP's youth group. Publications of the more recent pro-Chinese splinter and literary groups include the PLP's monthly *Progressive Labor* and its weeklies *Challenge*, issued in New York, and *Spark*, issued in Berkeley, California. *Hammer and Steel* was put out by another CPUSA offshoot; a "nonparty" publication which for some time supported the Chinese cause is *Monthly Review*; the weekly *National Guardian* began as a journalistic follower of the official communist line but then adopted a more leftist position.

The CPUSA publishes books through International Publishers in New York, founded in 1924, and issues pamphlets through the more recent New Outlook Publishers. The official party history is William Z. Foster, *History of the Communist Party of the United States*, New York, International Publishers, 1952. For the party's new statute and program see the 1966 *Yearbook on International Communist Affairs*, Stanford, Calif., Hoover Institution, 1967.

## PARTY CONVENTIONS

Founding convention, CPA, September 1919, Chicago
Founding convention, CLP, September 1919, Chicago
Unity convention, May 1921, Woodstock, New York
Founding convention, WPA, December 1921, New York
2d convention, illegal CPA, August 1922, Bridgman, Michigan
2d convention, WPA, December 1922, New York
3d convention, illegal CPA, April 1923, New York
3d convention, WPA, December 1923, New York
4th convention, WPA, August 1925, Chicago
5th convention, W(C)PA, August 31–September 7, 1927, New York
6th convention, W(C)PA, March 1929, New York
7th convention, CPUSA, June 1930, New York
8th convention, CPUSA, April 1934, Cleveland
9th convention, CPUSA, June 1936, New York
10th convention, CPUSA, May 1938, New York
11th convention, CPUSA, May 30, 1940, New York
Special convention to disaffiliate from Comintern, CPUSA, November 1940, New York
12th convention, CPUSA (CPA), May 1944, New York
13th convention, CPA (CPUSA), July 1945, New York
14th convention, CPUSA, August 1948, New York
15th convention, CPUSA, December 28, 1950, New York
16th convention, CPUSA, February 1957, New York
17th convention, CPUSA, December 1959, New York

## BIBLIOGRAPHY

Aaron, Daniel: *Writers on the Left*, New York, Harcourt, Brace, 1961.
Cannon, James P.: *The First Ten Years of American Communism*, New York, Lyle Stuart, 1962.
Draper, Theodore: *American Communism and Soviet Russia*, New York, Viking, 1960.
Draper, Theodore: *The Roots of American Communism*, New York, Viking, 1957.
Foster, W.Z.: *History of the Communist Party of the United States*, New York, International Publishers, 1952.
Glazer, Nathan: *The Social Basis of American Communism*, New York, Harcourt, Brace, 1961.
Gitlow, Benjamin: *I Confess*, New York, Dutton, 1940.
Howe, Irving, and Lewis Coser: *The American Communist Party*, Boston, Beacon, 1957.
Iverson, Robert W.: *The Communists and the Schools*, New York, Harcourt, Brace, 1959.
Kampelman, Max M.: *The Communist Party vs. the C.I.O.*, New York, Praeger, 1957.
Latham, Earl: *The Communist Controversy in Washington*, Cambridge, Mass., Harvard University Press, 1966.
Meyer, Frank S.: *The Moulding of Communists*, New York, Harcourt, Brace, 1961.
Oneal, James, and G. A. Werner: *American Communism*, rev. ed., New York, Dutton, 1947.
Roy, Ralph Lord: *Communism and the Churches*, New York, Harcourt, Brace, 1961.
Saposs, David J.: *Communism in American Politics*, Washington, Public Affairs Press, 1960.
Shannon, David A.: *The Decline of American Communism*, New York, Harcourt, Brace, 1959.
Voros, Sandor: *American Commissar*, Philadelphia, Chilton, 1961.
Warren, Frank A. III: *Liberals and Communism*, Bloomington, Ind., Indiana University Press, 1966.

THEODORE DRAPER

1. Earl Browder, *Teheran: Our Path in Peace and War*, New York, 1944.

2. For a report of the eighteenth party convention and the new party program see the 1966 *Yearbook on International Communist Affairs*, Stanford, Calif., Hoover Institution, 1967.

3. *The Worker*, November 14, 1965.

4. Browder claimed a total membership of 100,000 (which probably included the Young Communist League), of whom 72 percent paid dues. This claim has often been cited as the all-time high in American communist membership, but the communists themselves do not seem to have taken it seriously. The official party history states that membership "reached its maximum of some 80,000 members" at the beginning of 1944 (William Z. Foster, *History of the Communist Party of the United States*, New York, International Publishers, 1952, p. 421).

5. David A. Shannon, *The Decline of American Communism*, New York, Harcourt, Brace, 1959, p. 3.

# URUGUAY

The communist movement in Uruguay began in 1919, when members of the Socialist Party of Uruguay (Partido Socialista del Uruguay, PSU) first called for affiliation with the Comintern. The proposal was debated for about two years, for the top leaders were unwilling to accept Lenin's Twenty-one Conditions for Admission to the Comintern. By October 1920 a substantial majority of the delegates to the eighth party congress was prepared to join, but the socialist leadership still resisted. In April 1921, at an extraordinary congress of the PSU, the majority, led by Eugenio Gómez, voted to adhere to the Comintern and to adopt the name Communist Party of Uruguay (Partido Comunista del Uruguay, PCU). The PCU has since claimed October 1920 as the date of its founding. Other founders were R. Ramirez, J. Arevalo, F. Pintas, and J. Blanco. Gómez later left the party.

## HISTORY

The CPU is the only communist organization in Latin America that has never been proscribed. Moreover, except for a time during the Terra administration in the mid-1930s, it has enjoyed complete freedom of operation as a legitimate element of the Uruguayan body politic. The party has invariably participated in the electoral process, and has regularly been represented in the national congress. Nonetheless, it has not been able to develop a major following and has seldom exerted more than marginal influence on national affairs. The major handicap faced by the Uruguayan communists is the fact that the country had begun to take on many of the attributes of a welfare state before the party was founded, and it remained under the control of the center-left Colorado Party until the late 1950s. In these circumstances the usual communist appeal to the underprivileged was dulled.

The CPU has always been most effective when it has been allowed to cooperate with the administration and with the influential PSU, as during the war and in the immediate postwar period, when the CPU reached its greatest membership and prestige. In the early 1960s economic recession and a vaguely expressed popular discontent with the policies of the regime again permitted the communists to cooperate closely with socialists in the labor field, enabling them to regain a substantial part of the membership lost during the 1950s.

In the summer of 1962 the PCU was able to organize the Leftist Liberation Front (Frente Izquierda de Liberación), popularly known by its acronym Fidel; it included the PCU, dissatisfied splinter groups from other parties, and some left-oriented groups of students and intellectuals. In the November 1962 elections the Fidel obtained almost twice as many votes as the communists had obtained alone in 1958, giving them one seat in the senate and three seats in the chamber of deputies. The Uruguayan party was one of the few in Latin America whose prospects seemed to be brightening in 1965.

The PCU has taken a firm pro-Soviet stand on the Sino-Soviet ideological dispute.

## ORGANIZATION AND MEMBERSHIP

United States sources estimated the membership of the PCU in 1965 as about 10,000.[1] The Uruguayan communists have maintained one of the most elaborate and complex batteries of front organizations in Latin America. For a full discussion see *Latin America*.

## PARTY PRESS ORGANS AND RECORDS

The PCU publishes the daily *El Popular* and a monthly theoretical review, *Estudios*. The party has an active press and publications program and serves as a reprint and distribution center for documents and propaganda of the international communist movement. Party documents are usually available to the public, either as separate pamphlets or as articles in *Estudios*.

## PARTY CONGRESSES

The Uruguayan communists include the regular and extraordinary congresses of the original PSU in the listing of their party congresses. This accounts for the apparent inconsistency in the enumeration of congresses in the early 1920s.

8th congress, PSU, September 1920
6th extraordinary congress, PSU, April 1921
7th extraordinary congress, PCU, July 1921
8th extraordinary congress, PCU, October 1923
9th congress, PCU, December 1924
10th congress, PCU, July 1927
11th congress, PCU, 1930
12th congress, PCU, January 1938
13th congress, PCU, March 1940
Extraordinary congress, PCU, August 1941
14th congress, PCU, April 1944
15th congress, PCU, May 1950
16th congress, PCU, August-September 1955
17th congress, PCU, August 1958
18th congress, PCU, June-July 1962

## BIBLIOGRAPHY

Gómez, Eugenio: *Historia del Partido comunista del Uruguay (Hasta el año 1951)*, Montevideo, Editorial Elite, 1961.

See also *Latin America*, refs. 1, 2, 6, 13, 15, 24.

ROLLIE E. POPPINO

1. U.S. Department of State, Bureau of Intelligence and Research, *World Strength of the Communist Party Organizations*, Eighteenth Annual Report, Washington, January 1966, p. 180.

# UZBEKISTAN[1]

The Communist Party of Uzbekistan (Kommunisticheskaia Partiia Uzbekistana, KPU) is a branch of the Communist Party of the Soviet Union and is subordinate to it in all matters.

The first Marxist circles in Uzbekistan, then part of the governor generalship of Turkestan, arose after 1902 in Tashkent, Samarkand, Novyi Margelan (Fergana), Kokand, and other towns, chiefly along the railroad lines. The Russian population, particularly the railroad workers and intellectuals, was the main source of membership. Virtually no natives took part.

In 1903, after the second congress of the Russian Social Democratic Labor Party, the Marxist circles in Tashkent united under the Tashkent social democratic organization, and from 1905 to 1907 social democratic organizations formed in other towns. Small in numbers and torn by factional strife, they had only a contributory role in the social unrest of that time. By the end of 1906 the government had crushed or dispersed most of the social democratic and other radical organizations in the region, forcing members to act in isolation.

After the revolution of February 1917 the bolsheviks gained in number and influence and played an increasingly prominent role in the radical fringe in the Tashkent soviet, eventually gaining control of the organization. On November 1-12, 1917, an uprising of workers and soldiers in Tashkent toppled the local organs of the Provisional Government, placed the soviet in control, and extended its authority to other towns. On November 20 the Turkestan regional soviet was renamed the Council of Peoples' Commissars (*sovnarkom*) of the Turkestan Region (*oblast*) with the bolshevik F. I. Kolesov, a railroad worker, as chairman.

The new regime, led by the bolsheviks, struggled with economic crisis as well as with native nationalists and White opposition elements. The so-called Kokand Autonomy, organized in Kokand on November 28, 1917, by the fourth extraordinary Muslim congress as a rival to the Tashkent government, was liquidated in February 1918. The subsequent reign of terror initiated in Tashkent and elsewhere was countered by a guerrilla movement, the *basmachi*, formed among the natives. In March, the liberal Young Bukharan Party invited a force of Red Guards, led by Kolesov, to overthrow the emir of Bukhara. This force was repulsed, and the Young Bukharans fled to Soviet territory, where they formed the Bukharan Communist Party. In July 1918 a counterrevolutionary government of socialist revolutionaries and other opposition groups formed in Transcaspia. Supported for some months by a small British force, this threat to communist domination was liquidated only after the British force retired in February 1920.

On April 30, 1918, the fifth congress of soviets of Turkestan proclaimed the Turkestan Autonomous Soviet Socialist Republic. In June the first regional congress of communists founded the Communist Party (Bolshevik) of Turkestan. This organization was composed primarily of Russians, intent on maintaining Russian supremacy in the region. Doctrinal deviations, and especially the "Great Russian chauvinism" of the Turkestan communists, forced the Moscow government to send a "Turkestan commission" to the scene in 1919 and the central committee of the Russian party to form a Turkestan bureau (*Turkbiuro*) in 1920, and its successor the Central Asian bureau (*Sredazbiuro*) in 1922, to settle matters in the region.

The Red Army liquidated opposing White forces in the Kirgiz (Kazakh) steppe in 1919 and those in Turkmenia and other Central Asian regions in 1920. Soviet forces from Tashkent overthrew the Khivan and Bukharan khanates and proclaimed the Khoresmian People's Soviet Republic. At the end of May a Khoresmian Communist Party was set up. By fall the Bukharan People's Soviet Republic was proclaimed. The Young Khivans and Young Bukharans were gradually frozen out of their respective communist parties, and in May 1922 the Moscow politburo approved a merger of the parties of both republics with the Russian Communist Party. A drastic purge then reduced the membership of both parties to "reliable elements."

On October 27, 1924, as a result of the national-territorial delimitation of republics of Central Asia, the Bukharan and Khivan territories were merged with parts of the Samarkand, Syr-Darya, and Fergana regions (*oblasti*) to form the Uzbek Soviet Socialist Republic. In February 1925 the first congress of the KPU met, attended by M. I. Kalinin, the head of the Soviet state.

The second party congress, in November 1925, approved the decision of the Russian communist party to put through land and water reforms which strengthened the communist regime by depriving opposition elements of their economic base. The KPU had a major share in collectivization in Uzbekistan, and major errors were committed. Between 1930 and 1934 more than 40,000 kulak holdings were forcibly liquidated and their possessors summarily shot or deported.

The fourth congress, in February 1929, reviewed efforts to implement resolutions of the fifteenth congress of the Soviet party for collectivization and industrialization. The congress set forth measures for expanding national cadres (that is, representatives of the native population in industry and government), attracting workers and hired laborers into the party, and improving the work of soviet, party, economic, and youth organizations. Resolutions were also adopted for increased criticism and self-criticism, emancipation of women, and the struggle against "bourgeois nationalism."

The great purges of 1935 to 1937 were particularly drastic in Uzbekistan. Faizullah Khodzhaev, prime minister of the republic, and Ikramov, first secretary of the party, were accused of organizing a nationalist plot with British aid, and both were executed.

During World War II the KPU rallied the population in support of the Soviet Union's war effort. Industry and agriculture were placed on a wartime footing. Since that time the KPU has continued its role as executor of the resolutions of the central committee, the conferences, plenary sessions, and congresses of the Communist Party of Soviet Union, Uzbekistan has become the main cotton base of the Soviet Union and has developed an industry of considerable importance.

On January 1, 1965, the KPU had 288,358 members and 25,921 candidates in 9,266 primary organizations.[2]

## PARTY PRESS ORGANS

The main party organs are the newspaper *Pravda vostoka* (Truth of the East), published in Russian, and the periodical *Uzbekiston kommunisti* (Uzbekistan Communist), published in Uzbek.

## BIBLIOGRAPHY

*Istoriia Uzbekskoi SSR* (History of the Uzbek SSR), vol. II, Tashkent, 1957.

Park, Alexander G.: *Bolshevism in Turkestan, 1917-1927*, New York, 1957.

Pierce, Richard A.: *Soviet Central Asia: A Bibliography*, Part 3, *1917-1966*, Berkeley, Calif., University of California Center for Slavic and East European Studies, 1966.

Safarov, G. I.: *Kolonialnaia revoliutsiia: Opyt Turkestana* (Colonial Revolution: The Experience of Turkestan), Moscow, 1921.

Vakhabov, M. G., et al.: *Ocherki istorii Kommunisticheskoi partii Uzbekistana* (Outlines of the History of the Communist Party of Uzbekistan), Tashkent, 1964.

# VENEZUELA

The communist movement in Venezuela originated during the 1920s among exiles who became communists in neighboring Latin American countries, the United States, or Europe. One of these, Ricardo Martínez, was an officer of the Comintern's Latin American secretariat several years before a communist party was formed in Venezuela. Another, Aurelio Fortoul Briceño, who slipped into the country early in 1931 to transform a few spontaneous Marxist "study groups" into organized cells, became the founder of the Communist Party of Venezuela (Partido Comunista de Venezuela, PCV). The founding date of the party was March 6, 1931. Others who rose to prominence in the party were Jesús Faría, Elroy Torres, and the brothers Gustavo and Eduardo Machado.

## HISTORY

The PCV has had perhaps as varied and accidented a history as any communist party in Latin America without achieving political power. Its survival during the first five years is eloquent testimony to the ingenuity and will power of the few party members who escaped exile or imprisonment by the most repressive regime of the day. After the death of dictator-president Juan Vicente Gómez in 1935 the party was able to develop a regular organizational structure and a cadre of leaders, but for nearly a decade it operated chiefly through a succession of front parties and coalitions. With the 1945 coup that brought the Democratic Action party (Acción Democrática, AD) to power the PCV gained legal status but split into squabbling factions. It remained divided until 1952, when it was outlawed by the Pérez Jiménez dictatorship.

The Venezuelan communists reached their zenith after the overthrow of Pérez Jiménez in January 1958, through a four-party coalition in which they had played a prominent role. Communists helped to draft the new electoral law, which restored the party's legality, and polled over 160,000 votes, demonstrating that they had become respectable as well. In the next two years PCV membership rose to at least 30,000; the party gained a commanding position in organized labor and came to control much of the nation's news media. It was unable, however, to reach an understanding with the AD or to repress the militant left that insisted on following the Cuban example as the road to power. By 1962 the PCV was again fragmented, and in May of that year its legal status was again suspended. In September 1963 its secretary general Jesús Faría and several other party militants were arrested.

In 1965 it appeared that only the total defeat of the party's extremist revolutionary arm, the Armed Forces of National Liberation, or a change in government would permit the communists to regroup in order to exert an influence in proportion to their numbers.

## ORGANIZATION AND MEMBERSHIP

United States sources estimated the membership of the PCV in 1965 at about 20,000.[1] For a full discussion see *Latin America*.

## RELATION TO SOVIET LEADERSHIP

The PCV was admitted to full membership in the Comintern in 1935. For other aspects of the Venezuelan communists' relation to the international communist movement see *Latin America*.

The leaders of the badly fragmented communist movement in Venezuela have maintained a neutral attitude toward the ideological controversy between the Soviet Union and Communist China.

## PARTY PRESS ORGANS

The official party newspaper was *Tribuna popular*, and the theoretical journal was *Principios*. However the PCV has issued only occasional flysheets and clandestine publications for distribution among the party members since its substantial press and publications apparatus was destroyed by the suspension of its legal status in 1962.

## CONGRESSES AND CONFERENCES OF THE PCV

The PCV has frequently employed national conferences or enlarged sessions of the central committee in lieu of national party congresses.

1st national conference, August 1937, Maracaibo
1st (unity) congress, November-December 1946, Carácas
2d congress, August 1948, Carácas
6th national conference, April 1951, Yaracuy state
3d congress, March 1961, Carácas

## BIBLIOGRAPHY

See *Latin America*, refs. 1, 3, 6, 13, 15, 24.

ROLLIE E. POPPINO

1. U.S. Department of State, Bureau of Intelligence and Research, *World Strength of the Communist Party Organizations*, Eighteenth Annual Report, Washington, January 1966.

# VIETNAM

During the mid-1920s two fundamental, partly underground, revolutionary tendencies evolved in Vietnam. Under one name or another they occasionally united, but more often they contested for leadership of the struggle against the French, who had imposed their power on all the states of Indochina by the late 1880s. In 1965 these two tendencies were embodied in the communist Democratic Republic of Vietnam and the nationalist, anti-communist Republic of Vietnam, struggling against a communist rebellion and invasion.

The arrest of Phan Boi Chau in June 1925 and the death of Phan Chau Trinh in March 1926 ended the first period of Vietnamese nationalism, which for forty years had tried to find some means of reasserting the individuality of Vietnamese life and diminishing, if not removing, French imperialist power. In 1927 the nationalists organized as the Vietnam Nationalist Party (Viet Nam Quoc Dan Dang, VNQDD). Their party was modeled after the Kuomintang and frequently supported by it. During January and February 1930 various communist groups, such as the Canton-based Vietnam Revolutionary Youth League (Viet Nam Cach Menh Thanh Nien Dong Chi Hoi) and the Indochina Communist Alliance (Dong Duong Cong San Lien Doan), were fused in Hong Kong under the leadership of the Comintern agent later known as Ho Chi Minh.[1] Ho had joined the French Communist Party in 1920, had been assigned to assist the Comintern agent Borodin in China from 1924 to 1927, and has been in charge of communist affairs in Indochina ever since. Shortly after it was founded Ho's new party took the name Communist Party of Indochina (Dong Duong Cong San Dang).[2] It was re-formed in 1941 as the League for the Independence of Vietnam (Viet Nam Doc Lap Dong Minh Hoi), popularly known as the Viet Minh; according to Ho Chi Minh, since March 1951 it has been called the Vietnam Workers' Party (Dang Lao Dong).

## HISTORY

The revolutionary nationalists (VNQDD) initially based their public operations on a publishing business in Hanoi and clandestinely enrolled and trained members for action against the French colonial authorities. The French security police—a most efficient organization between the wars—discovered and arrested some of the members in 1929, following the assassination of a French labor recruiter. This in turn led to plans for an uprising which was to be joined by nationalist-oriented Vietnamese troops in the French army stationed at Lao Kay. The insurrection was scheduled for February 10, 1930, probably by its young student leader, Nguyen Thai Hoc. A meeting of Vietnamese soldiers against their French officers took place that night at Yen Bay, but the plans miscarried and the French police and armed forces quickly suppressed the mutineers. Hoc and others charged with complicity in the insurrection were arrested and executed, and the remnants of the Nationalist Party fled to Canton and Yunnan.

This unsuccessful nationalist uprising was followed by a communist effort in September 1930. Ho's communist party, with headquarters at Haiphong, organized a series of demonstrations and strikes, sacked public buildings, and, with some 6,000 peasants, marched on Vinh. Two "soviets" were set up in nearby areas. Landowners were killed, and their estates in Ha Tinh and Nghe An provinces were divided. At that point the communists were operating under the "hard-line" revolutionary policy enunciated by the sixth Comintern congress of 1928.

The French responded vigorously with troops, planes, and first-class military materiel to quell the uprising. Ten thousand civilian casualties were reported, with another 10,000 arrested and confined to penal islands and other prisons. French security police penetrated the communist cadres and wrecked their organization. Ho Chi Minh escaped, but he was arrested by British police in June 1931 and was tried in Hong Kong. In January 1933 he was allowed to leave Hong Kong, and for a time he disappeared from public view; he is reported to have gone first to Shanghai and then to Moscow.

The next few years were relatively quiet. Nationalist and communist activity shifted from Tonkin (Hanoi) to Cochinchina (Saigon). Ho's communist party reappeared in 1933, under the leadership of Tran Van Giau, a Moscow trainee, as part of La Lutte (also the name of its publication), a united front with the Trotskyists and unaffiliated nationalists. In the Saigon municipal elections of 1933 La Lutte succeeded in electing two representatives. It also helped to organize aboveground rural societies and an Indochinese democratic front. In the Saigon council elections of 1935 and 1937 La Lutte elected four and three representatives, respectively.

La Lutte had been led from the start by Ta Thu Thau, the Cochinchinese leader of the Trotskyist Fourth International who was subsequently assassinated by the Stalinists. Hence it was the Trotskyists, uncompromising in policy, who were winning increasing support from the people during the popular-front period of 1935 to 1939, as evidenced by their electoral successes. In the April 1939 elections for the colonial council of Cochinchina, Ta Thu Thau and two of his comrades received 80 percent of all votes cast, defeating three constitutionalists, two Stalinists, and several independent representatives in the balloting. In September 1939 the French authorities successfully squelched the Trotskyist faction by a series of raids and mass arrests. After the Nazi-Soviet pact of 1939 the Stalinists militantly refused to support the war effort, and under Tran Van Giau they organized an uprising in the Mekong delta on November 22, 1940. Once again French troops and aircraft crushed the communists in a two-week action. The French Communist Party was also pursuing Moscow's policy regarding the war effort, and its followers among the French colonialists in Indochina were jailed whenever possible.

The French colony in Vietnam, which numbered some 40,000, was unwilling to make any concessions to bona-fide Vietnamese nationalists, even in the face of Japanese armed forces poised in China and known to have designs on Indochina. By agreement with the French, Japanese troops moved into Indochina in September 1940. Vichy France made its peace with Japan in 1940, through Pétain and Admiral Decoux in Vietnam. In return for Japanese recognition of French sovereignty over Indochina, the Japanese were given air bases in Tonkin, the right to garrison these with troops, and other troop-transit rights.

After 1941 Vietnamese nationalists and communists alike were suppressed or imprisoned or otherwise subject to punishment. Those who escaped took refuge in China. In May 1941, in Kwangsi province near the Vietnamese border city of Cao Bang, the Viet Minh, under Ho Chi Minh, held its first congress. The nationalists also reorganized at about this time. With the aid of the Kuomintang, émigré sections of the old nationalist party, who had fled to Canton and Yunnan after the abortive rebellion of 1930, formed factions of the VNQDD and Vietnam Nationalist Party (Dai Viet Quoc Dan Dang, popularly known as the Dai Viet).

The Kuomintang, suspicious of Ho, caused his arrest in early 1942. However, when the Viet Minh, operating from China with Allied support, offered to supply intelligence and to fight against Vichy France and the Japanese, the Kuomintang set aside its distrust of the communists to the extent of arranging in October 1942 for the organization of a new Vietnamese united front called the Vietnam Revolutionary League (Viet Nam Cach Menh Dong Minh Hoi), which the Viet Minh promptly joined. This league, which was a nationalist coalition of the Dai Viet and other nationalist elements still supporting Prince Cuong De, the monarchical pretender residing in Japan, failed to deliver what the Kuomintang expected, and Ho asked for his release from jail to make it work better. In February 1943 the Kuomintang installed him as the League's chief officer, a post he held for fourteen months.

During this period Ho kept his own organization, the Viet Minh, intact and at work. Two of his most trusted lieutenants were left in charge of it; Vo Nguyen Giap, who had received guerrilla training under Maoist tutelage in China, directed the Viet Minh post in the south. These arrangements enabled Ho, while receiving United States and other Allied aid, to lead the Viet Minh in the so-called "August revolution" and on September 2, 1945, proclaim the independent Democratic Republic of Vietnam.[3] Claiming to be a nationalist whose guerrilla warfare against the Japanese had received acknowledgment in the form of Allied aid, Ho called for Vietnamese independence in the "liberated zone" in the Cao Bang-Lang Son area, contiguous to China.

The Viet Minh's charges in early 1945 that the Bao Dai regime was a Japanese puppet found support among those Vietnamese who had lost respect for him during the years in which as emperor he had in fact been a French puppet. Thus the military and political struggles of the Viet Minh against French power in Vietnam were reinforced not only by the Soviet and Chinese communists, but by the aspirations of Vietnamese nationalists to be through with all outside masters.[4] From 1945 until 1954, aided by a flow of both Soviet and Chinese supplies and direct military assistance across the China-Vietnam border, Ho and General Vo Nguyen Giap waged guerrilla warfare against the French for control of the countryside. Although the French held the cities and fortified areas until their defeat at Dien Bien Phu in 1954, through negotiations with Ho in 1946 they had recognized the Democratic Republic of Vietnam as a "free state . . . belong[ing] to the Indochinese Federation and to the French Union," thereby giving some legitimacy to the communist assertions of statehood and independence. The French had expected that Annam and Cochinchina, the other "colonial" administrative areas in the territory of Vietnam, would also become members of this federation. In 1949 they had combined Annam and Cochinchina as the "state of Vietnam," and appointed Bao Dai, the former emperor, as "head of state." The southern boundary of the Democratic Republic of Vietnam had not been fixed; it was to be determined by the military and political outcome of the French-Indochinese war. However, before the cease-fire took place the state of Vietnam signed a treaty of independence with France, and it was left to the Geneva conference of 1954 to partition Vietnam at the seventeenth parallel.

The Geneva conference gave international recognition to Ho Chi Minh's sovereignty in North Vietnam, which had been won on the slogan of Doc Lap or national independence. However, the official Geneva Declaration, containing the 1956 "elections clause," was not signed by any state at the conference and was explicitly rejected by South Vietnam. The state of Vietnam required recognition of its sovereignty over all of Vietnam as a precondition of internationally supervised elections with no partition. The Democratic Republic of Vietnam made similar claims as its precondition. The cease-fire agreement itself was signed only by France and the Democratic Republic of Vietnam.

The specific intent of the Geneva agreements of 1954 was to end armed conflict in the Indochinese peninsula. The general goal of the Western powers was to halt further communist expansion by providing favorable conditions for the development of the newly independent states of Cambodia, Laos, and Vietnam into politically and economically stable countries. Nevertheless, at Geneva the communists gained a solid base stretching from Moscow to Hanoi, with territorial salients in Laos contiguous to China and North Vietnam.

In the meantime, South Vietnam was in confusion and near to chaos. On June 4, 1954, while the Geneva conference was in session, France and South Vietnam had signed two treaties of independence and association, creating the new state of Vietnam. Bao Dai, who had apparently sold the vice and gambling concessions in the Saigon-Cholon area at a considerable profit and was spending his time in France, offered the premiership to Ngo Dinh Diem, a nationalist who for the past twenty years had opposed both the French and the communists. Diem replaced Bao Dai's cousin, Prince Buu Loc, as premier and on July 7 formed an independent government in Saigon.

Diem was faced with the task of governing a newly sovereign state, the borders of which had just been redrawn and the parts of which had previously been responsible to a variety of domestic and external jurisdictions. The removal of the former French government apparatus in Cochinchina (a colony) and part of Annam (a protectorate) left him with virtually no civil administration. Moreover, the Geneva cease-fire agreement, which Diem's government had not signed but had accepted in principle, was implemented only in stages. The French did not complete evacuation of Hanoi and Haiphong until May 1955, and the transfers of population (refugees) ended in July 1956.

In February 1955 North Vietnam had asked Diem's government to resume "normal relations." In accordance with the unsigned Geneva Declaration, consultations with respect to the elections to be held in 1956 were to begin in July 1955. However, Diem refused to participate in such discussions. His position, made clear at the Geneva conference itself, was that the Geneva Declaration had not been signed by any government of South Vietnam (or, for that matter, by any other state at the Geneva conference), and hence his government was not bound by it. Furthermore, he was skeptical about the likelihood of free elections in the north under a communist regime. When North Vietnam protested to the Anglo-Soviet cochairmen at Geneva, Gromyko urged proper implementation but did little else. On the whole, it appears that none of the principal participants had really expected the elections to take place, but their failure served the cause of communist propaganda.

More important was the problem created in South Vietnam by the Viet Cong San, that is, the communists, or Viet Cong, as they came to be known. A significant number of Viet Minh cadres, perhaps 5,000 to 10,000, had been picked to remain in South Vietnam after the exchange of regular troops and prisoners, especially in the mountainous area along the Laotian and Cambodian borders, the coastal area immediately south of the seventeenth parallel, and the Mekong delta. This communist network, made up of southerners trained by the Viet Minh as well as northern infiltrees working among the "legitimate" refugees, infiltrated the government apparatus, the police, and the armed forces and set up guerrilla bases in the rural areas.

In July 1955 Diem's government, alarmed by the deterioration of security in the northern provinces of Quang Nam and Quang Tri, close to the dividing line, set up a campaign of denunciation of communist subversion which had at its command "all military, administrative, and technical services." Between July 1955 and May 1956 the campaign claimed to have taken more than 15,000 North Vietnamese agents, uncovered more than 700 caches of arms and ammunition, and captured seventy-five tons of "documents" containing instructions and directives allegedly from the "eighth Congress of the Viet Minh Communist Party (North), held in August 1955."

Hanoi countered with complaints to the Geneva-created International Commission for Supervision and Control in Vietnam that the Diem government was "illegally" arresting "former" resistance fighters, creating "concentration camps," and arresting members of the Movement for Defense of Peace, a front organization created by North Vietnam's Fatherland Front. Although Hanoi disclaimed any connection with rebel activities in South Vietnam, the preciseness of detail in its complaints indicates that its agents had in fact been at the scene of most of these incidents. By any account of actual events in 1955 and 1956, Diem's government was already confronted with determined political and military attacks on the Republic of Vietnam.

The Democratic Republic of Vietnam was having its own problems in 1956. It had just lost the battle over the Geneva Declaration elections. It had not only failed to solve its recurrent rice shortage, but this year the failure had led to a well-publicized peasant uprising against the regime. It had become economically dependent on the Soviet Union and Communist China. Nevertheless, Hanoi was determined to engage in protracted Maoist-style warfare—the long war and the short campaigns. In 1956 and 1957 the Viet Cong began a stepped-up campaign of terror, extortion, assassination, and guerrilla activities in the villages of South Vietnam. Such activities were always directed against the local village officials, the civil guards and self-defense corpsmen, teachers, and especially officials sent out from the capital as local administrators of one kind or another. When the Viet Cong killed an unpopular government official the local population approved; when they killed a popular one, it served as a warning. In the relatively isolated villages, remote from any defense, or with only intermittent police and security aid, acquiescence to the resident Viet Cong power became a matter of survival.

By mid-1959 Viet Cong activities accounted for the death of fifteen to twenty provincial government officials a month, with many particularly brutal cases reported. In May 1961 President Kennedy estimated that 4,000 low-level officials had been killed in the preceding twelve months, and the figures mounted in subsequent years. As many as 14,000 provincial and local officials, police, teachers, and related personnel are said to have been assassinated by the Viet Cong during Diem's regime.

In addition to terrorist activities, the Viet Cong directed extensive propaganda against the evils of the central government, which had never been popular among the villagers, and held forth the promise of land, free of any returning landlord or other proprietor. In some instances the communists provided public-health and other facilities. However, in general, the only support they were able to elicit from the villagers was passive opposition to the government forces in the hope of avoiding further terrorization.

In 1959 the central committee of Ho's party, now known as the Lao Dong, stepped up its offensive, calling for national unification by "all appropriate means." The military pace was quickened, and in Sepetember 1960 the third party congress resolved "to carry out the socialist revolution in North Vietnam" and "to liberate South Vietnam from the ruling yoke of United States imperialists . . . in order to achieve national unity and complete independence and freedom throughout the country." Ho Chi Minh addressed the congress on the need to "step up the socialist revolution in the north and . . . the national-democratic people's revolution in the south." This, of course, was the familiar communist strategy of the two-stage revolution: first a national-democratic revolution and then a socialist revolution.

On December 20, 1960, the creation of a "united front" of "national and democratic forces," Mat Tran Dan Toc Giai Phong Mien Nam, or the National Front for the Liberation of South Vietnam (NFLSV) was announced. Its manifesto, broadcast by Radio Hanoi on January 29, 1961, and again on February 11, outlined a ten-point program for the overthrow of the Saigon government, implicitly through armed revolution, and the formation of a "broad national-democratic coalition administration" to "negotiate" with the Democratic Republic of Vietnam on "reunification."

Viet Cong activities in South Vietnam continued to increase and were repelled with the assistance of increasing United States reinforcements. Saigon's difficulties were augmented by the problems surrounding the Diem family, which culminated in a coup against them in November 1963. During this and the subsequent period regular units of the North Vietnamese army appeared in the battles in South Vietnam, and by February 1965 United States military combat and support units, later joined by troops from Australia, the Republic of China, the Republic of Korea, New Zealand, the Philippines, and Thailand, entered the war.

In 1965 both the Soviet Union and Communist China were assisting North Vietnam in its effort to sustain the war. The Soviet Union was supplying heavy machinery, fighter planes, ground-to-air missiles, and other weapons. The Chinese were providing military goods, as well as military and civilian technicians. Both have exacted payment from North Vietnam.

## ORGANIZATION AND MEMBERSHIP

Although Ho Chi Minh was the paramount leader of the Vietnamese party, he did not stand alone in the apparatus of the Lao Dong. He held together a strong leadership group which, as to be expected, was full of personal and political rivalries. When the party was renamed in 1951, its politburo included Ho Chi Minh and twelve other members, at least four of whom were powerful enough to be considered in their own right and as possible successors to Ho: Le Duan, first secretary and youngest leader in the party; Pham Van Dong, premier of the Democratic Republic of Vietnam and close associate of Ho; Vo Nguyen Giap, deputy premier, minister of defense, commander of the people's army, and hero of Dien Bien Phu; and Truong Chinh, leader of the pro-Peking faction within the party.

The party leadership is composed chiefly of intellectuals. Some, such as Pham Van Dong, are from aristocratic families whose members served in the senior ranks of the mandarinate. Others are from peasant families that were able to provide their sons with education; Giap, for example, has a doctorate in political economy. Although peasants and urban workers make up the general party membership, the upper-echelon leaders and the members of the fronts and the military—the "linking cadres," who are active in one or more of the party and front organizations—have had some degree of westernized education and can be said to represent intellectuals and middle-class elements.

According to its official records, in 1960 the party had 500,000 members, increased from 20,000 in 1946.[5] A 1953 party study indicates that of 1,855 key positions, at least 1,365 were held by intellectuals and descendants of the bourgeoisie, while only 351 and 139, respectively, were held by peasants and workers.[6] No comparable data are available for later years, but there is little reason to suppose that these proportions have substantially changed.

The Viet Cong military activities in South Vietnam are directed by the high command of the People's Army of Vietnam, under close supervision of the party apparatus in Hanoi. The Central Research Agency, a separate intelligence branch with headquarters in Hanoi, is directed by a committee which in 1965 included Premier Pham Van Dong and Defense Minister Vo Nguyen Giap. Its principal function is to expedite the war effort.

The National Liberation Front of South Vietnam, the more common name for the NFLSV, headed in 1965 by Nguyen Huu Tho, is directed by its central committee through a Committee for Supervision of the South. The highlands and coastal zones and the south and southwestern provinces, including the Mekong delta, are administered by a separate executive committee operating in Hanoi, whose activities include propaganda, training, subversion, and upkeep of military bases. The NFLSV comprises a variety of organized units from each significant segment of Vietnamese society—soldiers, peasants, youths, workers, women, and intellectuals. Its structure parallels the Lao Dong's political and military organization, including the fiction that it represents groups and parties other than the communists.

In December 1961 a new organization, the People's Revolutionary Party (Dang Nhan Dan Cach Mang), was formed to play the role of a separate South Vietnamese communist party to lend currency to the fiction that the communists in the south are independent of those in the north.

## THE SINO-SOVIET DISPUTE

The Democratic Republic of Vietnam, dependent on aid from both Communist China and the Soviet Union, has attempted to steer a cautious path in the Moscow-Peking rift. In 1961, when the Chinese Communist delegation walked out of the twenty-second congress of the Communist Party of the Soviet Union, Ho also left the meeting, but he remained in the Soviet Union to keep relations cemented. On his return to Hanoi he praised Albania, thus "clearing the slate" with Peking.

## BIBLIOGRAPHY

Fall, Bernard B.: *Le Viet Minh...,  1945-1960*, Paris, Armand Colin, 1960.

Hoang Van Chi: *From Colonialism to Communism*, New York, Praeger, 1964.

Honey, P. J.: *Communism in North Vietnam: Its Role in the Sino-Soviet Dispute*, Cambridge, Mass., MIT Press. 1963.

Le Thanh Khoi: *Le Viet-Nam*, Paris, Editions de Minuit, 1955.

Pike, Douglas: *Vietcong: The Organization and Techniques of the National Liberation Front of South Viet-Nam*, Cambridge, Mass., MIT Press, 1966.

Rathansky, Rima: *Documents of the August 1945 Revolution: Revolution in Viet Nam*, translated by C. Kiriloff, Canberra, Australian National University, Research School of Pacific Studies, Department of International Relations, 1963 (mimeographed).

Tanham, George K.: *Communist Revolutionary Warfare: The Vietminh in Indochina*, New York, Praeger, 1961.

Thompson, Sir Robert: *Defeating Communist Insurgency: The Lessons of Malaya and Vietnam*, New York, Praeger, 1966.

Trager, Frank N. (ed.): *Marxism in Southeast Asia*, Stanford, Calif., Stanford University Press, 1959 (esp. the chapter by I. Milton Sacks).

Trager, Frank N. (ed.): *Why Viet Nam?*, New York, Praeger, 1966.

FRANK N. TRAGER

1. Until about 1942 Ho Chi Minh (He Who is Enlightened), whose name appears to have been Nguyen Tat (or That) Than (Nguyen Who Will Succeed), frequently used such aliases as Nguyen Ai Quoc (Nguyen the Patriot) or Hong Qui Vit (Hong Who Is Alive).

2. Ho Chi Minh, *Selected Works*, vol. IV, Hanoi, Foreign Languages Publishing House, 1962, p. 431. The party celebrates January 6, 1930, as its founding date. It was then called the Vietnam Communist Party but according to Sacks its admission to the Comintern in 1931 as a "national section" was conditional on this change, effected in October 1930. See I. Milton Sacks, in *Marxism in Southeast Asia*, ed. by Frank N. Trager, Stanford, Calif., Stanford University Press, 1959, pp. 123, 318.

3. *Documents of the August 1945 Revolution: Revolution in Viet Nam*, translated from the Russian by C. Kiriloff and edited by Rima Rathansky, Canberra, Australian National University, Research School of Pacific Studies, Department of International Relations, 1963 (mimeographed).

4. See Frank N. Trager, *Why Viet Nam?*, New York, Praeger, 1966, chaps. 3 and 4, for the war years and the Geneva "settlement" of 1954.

5. *Third National Congress of the Viet Nam Workers' Party*, Hanoi, Foreign Languages Publishing House, 1960.

6. Bernard Fall, *Le Viet-Minh...1945-1960*, Paris, Armand Colin, 1960, p. 173.

# THE WARSAW TREATY ORGANIZATION[1]

An alliance signed in Warsaw on May 14, 1955, by the Soviet Union, Albania, Bulgaria, Czechoslovakia, the German Democratic Republic, Hungary, Poland, and Rumania created the Warsaw Treaty Organization (WTO) as a joint political and military organ for the "collective security" of the East European communist bloc. The contracting parties agreed to consult "in all important international questions that affect their common interests" and to establish a joint command of their armed forces.

Political considerations affecting the WTO are handled by the organization's Political Consultative Committee. The irregularly convened sessions of the committee are attended by representatives from two distinct levels of government: most meetings are attended by foreign ministers or their deputies who analyze current affairs and resolve minor questions; "summit meetings," attended by the chiefs of governments, the first secretaries of the respective communist parties, and the ministers of the armed forces, gather occasionally when major decisions must be made. The presence of party secretaries at high-level WTO meetings is a unique feature in communist international relations. In practice, the decisions of summit meetings of the WTO Political Consultative Committee are imposed by the Soviet Union. Hence the meetings serve chiefly to convey Soviet views and policies to the governments of communist-ruled states and to present to the outside world a façade of unanimity of action in the communist bloc.

Since October 1961, when at the twenty-second congress of the Communist Party of the Soviet Union Khrushchev denounced the leadership of the Albanian party for its pro-Peking attitudes, Albania has been only a "paper member" of the WTO. It has declined to participate in all subsequent meetings, but nevertheless has not been expelled from the organization.

The principal military roles of the WTO consist in mapping joint strategy, standardizing armaments and supplies, and directing joint maneuvers. Maneuvers involving military units from several member states were held in October 1963 in East Germany, in August 1964 in Bulgaria, and in October 1965 again in East Germany. In 1965 Soviet Marshal Ivan I. Iakubovskii was commander in chief of all WTO forces and Soviet General Mikhail I. Kazakov was chief of staff. The ministers of armed forces of the member states are deputies to the commander in chief, and for liaison purposes the commander in chief has his own representatives in the command of each allied army. In 1965 the estimated strength of the joint armed forces of the WTO was about 2 million men (including only those Soviet forces stationed in East Germany, Hungary, and Poland).

An English translation of the Warsaw treaty appears in the *United Nations Treaty Series*, vol. 219, part I, p. 24ff., and in Ruth C. Lawson (ed.), *International Regional Organizations*, New York, 1962, pp. 206-210. For more detailed information on the WTO see:

Meissner, Boris (ed.): *Der Warschauer Pakt: Dokumentensammlung*, Cologne, Wissenschaft und Politik, 1962.

Staar, Richard F.: *The Communist Regimes in Eastern Europe: An Introduction*, Stanford, Calif., Hoover Institution, 1967 (chapter on WTO).

WITOLD S. SWORAKOWSKI

1. The Warsaw Treaty Organization is mentioned in several articles in this *Handbook*. Although the WTO is not an organization of communist parties but rather an organization of communist-led states, this short note explaining its character is added as a convenience to the reader.

# THE WOMEN'S INTERNATIONAL DEMOCRATIC FEDERATION

The Women's International Democratic Federation (WIDF) was founded on December 1, 1945, at a Congress of Women sponsored by the communist-controlled Union of French Women (Union des Femmes Françaises, UFF). The women's organizations that participated in the congress came from some forty different countries; nearly all, however, were communist controlled. Thus, from the outset, the WIDF has been dominated by communists; no noncommunist women's organizations of any importance have joined the federation.

## HISTORY

Partly as a result of its homogeneous nature, and partly because of its general membership's (as opposed to its leadership's) primary concern with nonpolitical matters, the WIDF has not been confronted with any major dissensions within its ranks. Thus, the WIDF's 1949 ouster of its Yugoslav affiliate—an action taken in response to Yugoslavia's expulsion from the Cominform in 1948—did not result in any significant disaffection from the federation's membership.

In its furthering of Soviet interests, and with little potential for internal dissent, the WIDF has been free to operate with relative impunity. It has had close relations with most of the other international communist front organizations, particularly with the World Council of Peace (WCP). The WIDF's president from its inception has been Eugénie Cotton, president of the UFF and a member of the WCP presidential committee. The WIDF has also cooperated frequently with the World Federation of Democratic Youth over the defense of children and with the World Federation of Trade Unions over the rights of women workers. It was in conjunction with a campaign mainly coordinated by the WCP that the WIDF sent an International Investigating Commission to Korea in May 1951, at the invitation of the North Korean ministry of propaganda, to study "the atrocities committed by the aggressors." The commission produced a report accusing the United Nations forces of atrocities, which the WIDF later published as a pamphlet entitled *We Accuse*. A year later, in May 1952, the WIDF sent its then vice president, Monica Felton, to Korea to support the "germ warfare" charges that were being directed at the United Nations troops, principally by the WCP and the International Association of Democratic Lawyers. Mrs. Felton claimed to have seen "full proof" that bacteriological warfare was being waged against the Chinese and North Koreans.

The WIDF supported the WCP in campaigns against nuclear tests but, like the WCP, protested only against those carried out by the United States, Great Britain, and France. In this context, the WIDF organized an International Assembly of Women for Disarmament in December 1959 in Küngälv, Sweden, and in March 1962 held a similar gathering in Vienna.

The WIDF has tended to set up a number of subsidiary organizations and committees. One of the first to be set up, in February 1947, was the Permanent Committee for Women's Questions in Colonial Territories. This committee sent commissions of inquiry to Southeast Asia in 1948 and to North Africa in 1949, and sponsored a conference in Bamako, Mali, in January 1962. In 1951 the WIDF created an International Committee for the Defense of Children; in April of the following year this committee organized in Vienna an International Conference for the Defense of Children. A Permanent International Committee of Mothers was set up at a WIDF-sponsored World Congress of Mothers, held in July 1955 in Lausanne. This group appeared to take over the functions of the Committee for the Defense of Children; it held further meetings in February 1956 (Geneva), April 1957 (Lausanne), and February 1958 (Sofia). By 1959 it seemed to have become defunct. In April 1960 in Copenhagen the WIDF sponsored an International Assembly of Women, which created an International Liaison Bureau. The bureau, which has headquarters in Copenhagen and a secretariat in Brussels, is mainly concerned with establishing contact with other women's organizations and securing support for the WIDF. In November 1962 it organized a World Forum on Children's Education, held in Brussels. One of the WIDF's most active subsidiary organizations is the International Solidarity Committee with South Vietnam, set up to mobilize support for communist forces in the Vietnam conflict. First proposed by the WIDF bureau in December 1963, the committee was founded in July 1964. It originally consisted of forty-six members from twenty-nine countries but has since expanded its representation.

The WIDF has had little success in organizing regional activities in the developing countries, and by the end of 1965 its only significant meeting outside Europe had been a Seminar on Mother and Child in Africa, held in Bamako, Mali, in August 1965. As a possible consequence, the Sino-Soviet conflict erupted in the WIDF later than in other front organizations. It was not until its fifth congress in Moscow on June 24-29, 1963, that the WIDF was faced with the Chinese delegates' disruptive activities, which several times brought the proceedings to a standstill. Similar attempts were made by the Chinese to disrupt meetings at WIDF council sessions in Sofia, October 1964, and in Salzburg, October 1965. At the Moscow congress the Chinese were supported by delegations from Albania, Brazil, Indonesia, Japan, North Korea, Mozambique, Nepal, Venezuela, Vietnam, and Zanzibar. Although there appeared to have been attempts by the Chinese to set up a rival organization to the WIDF, by the end of 1965 no such group had emerged. Partly in response to the Chinese challenge, the WIDF at its Moscow congress elected a number of high-level communist party officials to its leadership, among the most prominent being the chairman of the Communist Party of Spain, Dolores Ibarruri ("La Pasionaria" of civil war days), who became honorary vice president.

## ORGANIZATION AND MEMBERSHIP

Membership is open to women's organizations, groups of women, and in exceptional cases, individuals. The WIDF claims to have eighty-three affiliated organizations, contact with groups in many other countries, and a total membership of over 200 million. Originally headquartered in Paris, the WIDF was expelled by the French government in January 1951 and has since operated from East Berlin.

The highest WIDF organ, the congress, is supposed to meet every four years. Comprised of representatives of affiliated organizations plus some individual members, it elects the WIDF president and council. The council meets annually and controls activities between congresses. Each affiliated organization must have at least one representative on the council, the total number of members being fixed by the congress. The council elects the WIDF bureau and secretariat. The bureau, consisting of the president, vice presidents, secretary-general, and ordinary members, meets at least twice a year. It is assisted by the secretariat, comprising a secretary-general, various secretaries, and a treasurer. Until 1958, the WIDF also had an executive committee of some thirty members. This body was abolished at the fourth WIDF congress.

The WIDF held consultative status B with UNESCO from July 1948 to November 1952, at which time it was relegated to the register (or "Special List"). The federation was granted Category C status in 1962. From 1947 to 1954 the WIDF held Category B status with the United Nations Economic and Social Council; in 1954, however, it was deprived of all status—a situation which still obtained at the end of 1965.

## PRESS ORGAN

The only regular publication of the WIDF is *Women of the Whole World*, published monthly from 1951 through 1965 and quarterly since January 1966.

## CONGRESSES OF THE WIDF

1st (founding) congress, November-December 1945, Paris
2d congress, December 1948, Budapest
3d congress, June 1953, Copenhagen
4th congress, June 1958, Vienna
5th congress, June 1963, Moscow

MILORAD POPOV

# THE WORLD COUNCIL OF PEACE

The "world peace" movement headed by the World Council of Peace (WCP) dates from August 1948 when a "World Congress of Intellectuals for Peace" in Wroclaw, Poland, set up an organization called the International Liaison Committee of Intellectuals for Peace, headed by the French communist scientist, Professor Frédéric Joliot-Curie. This committee, together with the Women's International Democratic Federation, sponsored a First World Congress of Peace Partisans, in Paris on April 20-25, 1949. (Part of the meeting had to be held in Prague because the French government refused visas to a number of delegates from the Soviet Union and Eastern Europe.) The Paris gathering alone was attended by 2,000 delegates from seventy-five countries; it launched a World Committee of Partisans for Peace, which in November 1950, at a Second World Peace Congress in Warsaw, was renamed the World Peace Council. Originally based in Paris, the World Peace Council was expelled in 1951 by the French government. It moved first to Prague and then, in 1954, to Vienna. When the occupation forces withdrew and Austria regained independence, the World Council of Peace (this name having been adopted meanwhile) was permitted to remain on the condition that it would observe Austrian laws. On February 2, 1957, the Austrian ministry of the interior announced that the WCP had been banned and its offices closed because it "interfered in the internal affairs of countries with which Austria has good and friendly relations" and its activities were "directed against the interest of the Austrian State." Though invited back to Prague, the WCP remained in Austria and continued its operations from the same address under the cover of an ostensibly new organization, the International Institute for Peace.

## HISTORY

The WCP has been more successful than other communist front organizations in winning noncommunist support. From the beginning it attracted a number of neutralists, internationalists, pacifists, and left-wing socialists. The diversity of its membership has, however, led to difficulties, and its officers have had more trouble than those in other front organizations in keeping the membership on line with Soviet policy. Nonetheless, the WCP has occupied a central position in communist propaganda since 1949, when the Cominform designated the peace movement as the "pivot of the entire activity of the Communist parties and democratic organizations."[1]

The WCP's main activity has been to organize worldwide campaigns, often involving the mass collection of signatures to support appeals. The first of these was formulated at a meeting of the Partisans for Peace, held in Stockholm on March 15-19, 1950. The so-called Stockholm Appeal demanded prohibition of the atomic bomb; asked that the government which first used it be treated as a war criminal; and, finally, demanded strict international control to ensure that the ban was carried out. The Appeal, which reflected Soviet concern with the United States nuclear superiority, was allegedly signed by 482,482,198 persons. In February of the following year, at the first council meeting of the newly formed World Peace Council held in East Berlin, another

Appeal was launched in support of a campaign calling for a Five-Power Conference (United States, Soviet Union, Great Britain, France, and Communist China) to settle disputes, including the Korean War. At the end of the year it was claimed that 612,522,504 signatures had been collected.

The WCP's campaigns against the United Nations intervention in Korea became increasingly strident following a meeting of the organization's executive bureau in Oslo in March 1952. At the initiative of Chinese representatives an investigative commission was sent to Korea to substantiate claims that United Nations troops were engaging in bacteriological warfare. This WCP-initiated venture, which received the full support of other front organizations and was broadly publicized, did not include participation of such bodies as the International Red Cross or the World Health Organization, their offers to assist in the investigation having been rejected. The commission's *Report on Germ Warfare in Korea* (1952) asserted that UN troops had indeed used "bacteriological weapons." Both the report and the subsequent campaign were finally exposed when after the Korean armistice former prisoners returned and related how "confessions" of germ warfare had been forced out of them by torture.

In December 1952 in Vienna the WCP sponsored a World Congress of Peoples for Peace. Attended by 1,904 delegates from eighty-five countries, the congress was advertised as a nonpartisan affair, not confined to the WCP's affiliates. Although assurances were given that free discussion would prevail, the congress turned out to be undisguisedly communist-controlled. It failed so badly that Pierre Cot, a communist-sympathizer and leader of both the peace organization and the International Association of Democratic Lawyers, stated afterwards that the WCP would have to adopt new methods and speak a new language if it were to be successful.[2]

During 1953 and 1954 the WCP was primarily concerned with expressing opposition to the presence of Western military bases in foreign countries, and with campaigning against the European Defense Community and West German rearmament.

In June 1954 in Stockholm, the WCP held a carefully camouflaged Meeting for the Relaxation of International Tensions. This took place with very little publicity, unlike other WCP meetings, and succeeded in attracting a number of noncommunists, many from developing nations. The Stockholm meeting was followed in April 1955 by a Conference of Asian Nations for the Relaxation of International Tensions, held in Delhi. This second meeting founded an Asian Peoples' Solidarity Committee, which at a conference in Cairo in 1958, was to be incorporated into a broader Afro-Asian Peoples' Solidarity Committee, an organization which by 1963 was to provide a milieu for considerable Sino-Soviet conflict.

At its meeting in Vienna in January 1955 the WCP presidential committee issued another Appeal, similar to the 1950 Stockholm Appeal. By the end of the year the WCP announced that it had collected 655,963,811 signatures. But by mid-1955 notable changes occurred in WCP pronouncements, reflecting the new stance of "peaceful coexistence" advocated by the Soviet Union. An attenuation in WCP's attacks against the West was evident during the World Assembly for Peace, held in Helsinki on June 22-29, 1955, which was attended by 1,647 delegates.

The first major instance of dissension within the WCP leadership occurred a year later, at the time of the 1956 Hungarian uprising. Following the suppression of the revolt by the Soviet military, the WCP executive bureau held a meeting in Helsinki on November 18-19. A statement subsequently issued stated that "serious differences" existed both in the WCP and in the national peace movements and that it was "impossible to formulate an agreed evaluation of events."

The WCP held its fifth major gathering—the Congress for Disarmament and International Cooperation—in Stockholm, on July 16-22, 1958. It was attended by 1,264 delegates from seventy-eight countries. While no reference was made to Hungary, the congress was the occasion for repeated criticism of Anglo-French intervention in the 1956 Suez crisis and for general condemnations of alleged Western neocolonialism in the developing countries. The Stockholm meeting was the first one over which Joliot-Curie no longer presided; the French scientist was to die in August of that year. At a council meeting in Stockholm on May 8-13, 1959, the post of president was replaced by a twenty-four-member presidential committee, with Professor John D. Bernal (Great Britain) as its chairman.

In the latter part of 1961 the WCP was confronted with two-pronged criticism. Following the resumption of Soviet nuclear testing, the WCP expressed its "regret that the Soviet Government has, however reluctantly, found it necessary to resume testing." The peace movement attempted to justify the tests on the grounds that they were made necessary by alleged Western threats to use force over Berlin. The WCP's partisanship—in March 1960 it had declared that it would "accept no excuses for resuming" tests—was criticized by several of its national affiliates, including the Japanese, Italian, and Austrian. Another challenge to the WCP leadership became evident at a council meeting in Stockholm on December 16-19 of the same year. The Chinese delegation criticized the WCP for advocating disarmament as the only way to achieve peace, and claimed that developing countries should, in fact, increase their military strength in order to combat imperialism. This Chinese thesis was reiterated repeatedly at subsequent WCP meetings: the World Congress for Disarmament and Peace, Moscow, July 9-14, 1962; the presidential committee meeting, Malmö, Sweden, March 2-3, 1963; the council meeting, Warsaw, November 28-December 2, 1963; the presidential committee meeting, Budapest, April 25-27, 1964; and the World Congress for Peace, National Independence and General Disarmament, Helsinki, July 10-15, 1965. In addition to expressing their opinions, the Chinese often disrupted the proceedings, in some instances bringing them to a complete standstill. They did not, however, attend the November 1965 presidential committee meeting, held in Budapest. There were indications in 1962 that the Chinese were attempting to revive the 1952 WCP-founded Peace Liaison Committee for the Asian and Pacific Regions (PLCAPR) as a rival to its parent body. By the end of 1965, however, the PLCAPR had limited itself to issuing occasional statements in support of Chinese policy.

## ORGANIZATION AND MEMBERSHIP

The WCP is organized on a national basis. No figure of the total number of members has ever been given, but in 1965 National Peace Committees from more than eighty countries were affiliated.

Since its inception the WCP has on a number of occasions changed its organizational structure. With John Bernal's retirement in July 1965 from the post of chairman of the presidential committee, further organizational modifications were adopted for consideration; by the end of the year, however, no decisions had been made. The leading body of the WCP in 1965 was its twenty-four-member presidential committee; it met at least twice a year and set policy. The presidential committee was assisted by a six-member permanent secretariat. The WCP's council, comprising individual "peace fighters," leaders of National Peace Committees, and representatives of other front organizations, had a membership of some 500. The council is supposed to meet at least once every two years—from 1951 through

1965 it met thirteen times. The WCP also had an executive bureau, consisting of the presidential committee, the secretariat, and about seventy ordinary members; its latest meeting took place in 1960. The exact organizational function of the WCP-organized mass congresses is difficult to ascertain.

The WCP has never had consultative status with the United Nations or with any of its agencies.

A subsidiary organization of the WCP is the Vienna-based International Institute for Peace (IIP), set up in 1957 to provide a legal cover for the WCP's secretariat and thus circumvent its expulsion. In 1965 it was headed by the Reverend James G. Endicott of Canada, a member of the WCP presidential committee. The organs of the IIP are the general assembly, which is supposed to meet at least once every three years; the executive committee, meeting every six months; the presidium, which is the governing body of the IIP and consists of the president, secretary, and treasurer; and the technical secretariat.

## PRESS ORGANS

Up to 1965 the WCP published a monthly journal, *Horizons*, which was issued from Paris, in thirteen languages. At the end of 1965 the only regular publication of the WCP was the monthly *Bulletin of the World Council of Peace*, published in Vienna in English, French, German, Russian, and Spanish. The IIP's Department of Reference and Research issues three publications: Series 1—*Current Documents and Papers*; Series 2—*Current Articles, Interviews and Statements*; and Series 3—*Nuclear Energy—Documentation on Its Military or Peaceful Use*. Series 1 and 2 are supposed to appear at least once a month in English, French, German, and Spanish, and Series 3 every two months in English and French.

## CONGRESSES OF THE WCP

First World Congress of Peace Partisans, April 1949, Paris

Second World Peace Congress, November 1950, Warsaw

World Congress of Peoples for Peace, December 1952, Vienna

World Assembly for Peace, June 1955, Helsinki

Congress for Disarmament and International Cooperation, July 1958, Stockholm

World Congress for Disarmament and Peace, July 1962, Moscow

World Congress for Peace, National Independence, and General Disarmament, July 1965, Helsinki

MILORAD POPOV

1. "Resolution of the Information Bureau of the Communist Parties," *For a Lasting Peace, for a People's Democracy*, November 29, 1949, p 1.
2. *Défense de la paix* (Paris), no. 20, January 1953, p. 6.

# THE WORLD FEDERATION OF DEMOCRATIC YOUTH

The origins of the World Federation of Democratic Youth (WFDY) date back to the late fall of 1941, when a number of youth groups, many of whose members had moved to Great Britain from continental Europe in response to German occupation of their homelands, formed an International Youth Council. In November of the following year the council held a conference at which it officially transformed itself into the World Youth Council (WYC). While the WYC assumed a number of technical functions, such as relief work, its primary purpose was political—to further the struggle against the Axis powers. The Soviet Union evidenced considerable interest in the developments within the WYC, and it would appear that its influence within the organization's leadership was significant, with five of the WYC's seven-member executive committee being communists or communist sympathizers. In November 1945 the WYC sponsored a World Youth Conference in London, which was attended by 437 delegates and 148 observers from sixty-three countries, representing an estimated 30 million persons. The WYC was disbanded at the conference, making way for the new World Federation of Democratic Youth. Although youths of varied political persuasions attended the WFDY's founding conference, communists were elected to most of the federation's key executive positions.

## HISTORY

With the deterioration of East-West relations in 1947, the WFDY assumed an increasingly hostile attitude toward any opposition to Soviet views and policies. One of the first major demonstrations of its ideological alignment was the First World Youth Festival, which it organized jointly with the International Union of Students. The festival, held in Prague on July 20-August 17, 1947 and attended by some 20,000 persons from sixty-seven countries, was the occasion for highly invective propaganda against Western countries, particularly the United States. During the following two years the WFDY's sectarian stance hardened even further, resulting in the disaffiliation of most of the WFDY noncommunist membership. In August 1949 youth organizations from thirty-seven countries founded the independent World Assembly of Youth (WAY). At the same time, the WFDY held its second congress in Budapest, scheduling it to coincide with the Second World Youth Festival on August 14-28, which was also held in the Hungarian capital. The festival, boycotted by most noncommunist organizations, was, according to WFDY claims, attended by some 10,000 youths from eighty countries. It distributed *The Manifesto for Peace*, adopted at the WFDY congress, which condemned the "warlike preparations" of the capitalist countries," led by the American "imperialists," attacked NATO and the Marshall Plan, alleged violation of democratic freedom in "imperialist" countries, and appealed to youth to support the "invincible army of peace partisans headed by the mighty Soviet Union."

Conforming to its pro-Soviet alignment, and in response to the 1948 expulsion of Yugoslavia from the Cominform, the WFDY in January 1950 expelled its Yugoslav affiliates, describing the latter as "traitors to the cause of peace and democracy, and deserters to the camp of the imperialist warmongers." A final occasion for the WFDY to proselytize its sectarian views—before Stalin's death and the consequent modification in the Soviet stance—was the Third World Youth Festival, held in East Berlin on August 5-19, 1951. At an estimated cost of 50 million dollars, the festival gathered together some 26,000 young people from 104 countries. The two dominating themes at the festival were the communist victory in China and attacks against the United Nations intervention in Korea.

Stalin's death in March 1953 had a tempering effect on the WFDY's anti-Western militancy. In the summer of that year, the federation held its third congress (July 25-30) and sponsored the Fourth World Youth Festival (August 2-16), both held in Bucharest. The festival was attended by 29,000 youths from 111 countries, at an estimated cost of between 50 and 75 million dollars. The WFDY ceased demanding complete support from noncommunist organizations and suggested "limited support" on specific "nonpartisan" issues. Compared with former years, there were fewer direct and vituperative attacks on the West by delegations from communist countries. These attacks were left instead to communists in delegations from colonial or neutral states. The Soviet Union's continuing interest in retaining the WFDY's allegiance, however, was indicated by the appointment to the post of the federation's first vice president of Aleksandr Shelepin, who five years later was to become the head of the Soviet Committee for State Security. Elected president of the WFDY was Enrico Berlinguer, who in the 1960s was to become a leader of the Italian Communist Party.

The fifth youth festival was organized in Warsaw in July-August 1955. Attended by 30,000 youths from 115 countries, it reflected—in its deemphasis of ideological issues—the line of "peaceful coexistence" then favored by the Soviet Union.

In January 1951 the WFDY had been expelled from its headquarters in Paris and had moved to Budapest. During the Hungarian uprising in 1956 it moved its headquarters temporarily to Prague. The events in Hungary engendered the only occasion in the 1950s for a minor difference of opinion within the WFDY's leadership. In a statement issued on December 6, 1956, the WFDY regretted "the tragic events" in Hungary, indicating that there had been "differences of opinion over their interpretation."

The WFDY's fourth congress and the Sixth World Youth Festival were both held in the summer of 1957 in the Soviet Union. The Moscow festival and the Kiev congress were oriented primarily toward attracting the support of young people from developing areas. This concern of the WFDY had been evident as early as February 1948, when the federation had sponsored a South-East Asia Youth Conference in Calcutta. The WFDY, however, had tended to concentrate its activities in Latin America, organizing conferences in Cuba (March 1947), Mexico City (August 1948), and Sao Paulo (February 1955). The major theme that dominated the Moscow festival was that of anticolonialism, and delegates from developing areas were given preferential treatment, such as special accommodations. The festival attracted 35,000 participants; it was to be the last youth festival to be relatively free of controversy. In 1959 and 1962 the WFDY held gatherings in noncommunist European countries—Austria and Finland, respectively. These gatherings, with a lowered participation of 18,000 (Vienna) and 10,800 (Helsinki), offered an opportunity for significant noncommunist dissenting opinion.

By the mid-1960s the WFDY was confronted with two-pronged opposition from the Chinese and the Cubans. The Sino-Soviet conflict was evident in the WFDY as early as 1960; it did not develop into a major issue, however, until 1963. At an international seminar on colonialism, held in Algiers in April 1963, the Chinese delegation attacked the Soviet policy of "peaceful coexistence" and called for greater support for the revolutionary "national liberation" movements. Having failed to obtain significant support for their views, the Chinese walked out of the meeting. In August of that year, at a meeting of the WFDY secretariat, the Chinese criticized the federation's support for the Nuclear Test Ban Treaty, noted that the WFDY's leadership was not representative of youth but composed of "paid Soviet agents," and, again, left the meeting. The main support for the Chinese came from the Indonesians; thus, a WFDY executive committee meeting held in Djakarta in January 1964 had to be canceled because the Indonesians, encouraged by the Chinese, insisted on excluding certain delegates. Although attempts were made by the Chinese to create a rival international youth movement, by the end of 1965 such an organization had not been founded. Chinese opposition to the WFDY was increasingly evidenced in the form of boycotts of WFDY meetings and conferences.

Cuban opposition to the WFDY developed from 1964 and had motivations somewhat similar to those of the Chinese, with accusations directed against the WFDY's lack of "revolutionary fervor." Cuban criticisms undercut much of the federation's work in Latin America. Apart from a Latin American Youth Congress held in Havana in July-August 1960, the WFDY succeeded in holding only one other major gathering in Latin America—a Latin American Youth Conference, held in Santiago, Chile, in March 1964. Since 1964 the WFDY has confined its Latin American activities to issuing periodical statements of solidarity with the youth of Latin America.

ORGANIZATION AND MEMBERSHIP

According to the constitution of the WFDY, all youth organizations and other organizations which contribute to the safeguarding or to the activities of young persons are eligible for membership. In 1965, the secretary-general the WFDY, Francis Le Gal, claimed that "organizations in over 100 countries, representing over 100 million youths" had joined the federation's ranks.[1] The assembly (until August 1957 known as the congress) is the highest body of the WFDY, and all affiliated organizations are represented at its meetings, which are supposed to take place every three years. The assembly elects an executive committee, which is supposed to meet at least twice a year and which comprises some fifty-five members, including the WFDY's officers. The latter are represented in the bureau, which is under the direction of the executive committee. The bureau meets when necessary and is responsible for the day-to-day work of the WFDY; it is assisted by a secretariat, with secretaries in charge of (1) regional commissions for Europe, Asia, Africa, North America and Australia, Latin America, and the Middle East, and (2) special departments for International Solidarity, Peace and National Independence, Youth Rights, Press and Information, Relations with International Organizations, and Finance and Administration.

The WFDY has a number of subsidiary organizations:

The International Committee of Children's and Adolescents' Movements, founded in 1957 and claiming affiliated organizations in twenty-five countries.

The International Bureau of Tourism and Exchanges of Youth, set up in March 1960, which claims to have full members in thirteen countries and a number of corresponding members. Describing its work in an interview published by the Czechoslovak Youth Union organ, *Mlada Fronta*, November 2, 1965, Ryszard Tyrluk (Poland), director of the bureau, stated: "Some youth organizations cannot or do not want to cooperate with WFDY directly and the first steps for bringing them in touch with the international progressive youth movement lead through this very department."

The International Sports Committee for Youth, established in March 1960. Apart from organizing events in connection with the World Youth Festivals the committee has not been very active.

The International Committee of Solidarity with South Vietnam, set up in February 1963. Its aim is to further the cause of the "democratic" forces in the Vietnam conflict.

The WFDY works in close cooperation with the International Union of Students, with which it cosponsors the World Youth Festivals. It also regularly participates in the activities of the World Council of Peace, and has regular contact with the World Federation of Trade Unions, particularly on questions regarding young workers.

The WFDY lost its consultative standing with UNESCO in 1950; in 1965 it obtained Category C status.

## PRESS ORGANS

The principal organ of the WFDY is *World Youth*, a magazine that has been published since 1946. Until 1963 it appeared monthly in English, French, Russian, Spanish, Chinese, Hungarian, and Rumanian, and bimonthly in Arabic and Swedish. In 1963 it appeared monthly only in Hungarian, Polish, Rumanian, and Russian, and bimonthly in German, English, French, and Swedish. At the end of 1963 the Hungarian, Polish, Rumanian, and Russian editions were completely discontinued, and the magazine continued to appear only quarterly in the remaining languages. *WFDY News* is a monthly newssheet published in English, French, and Spanish editions. The WFDY publishes an annual *WFDY Diary* which reports details of its activities.

## CONGRESSES AND ASSEMBLIES OF THE WFDY

1st (founding) congress, November 1945, London
2d congress, September 1949, Budapest
3d congress, July 1953, Bucharest
4th congress, August 1957, Kiev
5th assembly, August 1959, Prague
6th assembly, August 1962, Warsaw

## BIBLIOGRAPHY

Independent Research Service: *The Background of the 9th World Youth Festival*, New York, IRS, 1965.

Institute for International Youth Affairs: *The Youth Fronts: 1946-1966*, New York, IIYA, 1966.

MILORAD POPOV

1. *World Youth*, no. 3-4, 1965.

# THE WORLD FEDERATION OF SCIENTIFIC WORKERS

The World Federation of Scientific Workers (WFSW) was founded at the initiative of the British Association of Scientific Workers. Eighteen organizations of scientists from fourteen countries were represented at the inaugural conference held in London on July 20-21, 1946. Although communists and their sympathizers took over the leadership of the WFSW shortly after its inception, the federation, in contrast to other international communist front organizations, succeeded in retaining the affiliation of many of its noncommunist members. Soviet scientists were not represented in the WFSW until 1952.

HISTORY

The first president of the WFSW, who remained in that post until his death in 1958, was Professor Frédéric Joliot-Curie, a Nobel Prize winner and member of the central committee of the French Communist Party. In view of Joliot-Curie's simultaneous presidency of the World Council of Peace (WCP), the views and policies of the WCP were reflected by the WFSW. With its headquarters in London, the WFSW's pronouncements have generally been couched in relatively moderate language; this has not, however, precluded a steadfast support of Soviet views and contentions. Thus, in one of its first dramatically partisan actions and in response to Yugoslavia's 1948 expulsion from the Cominform, the WFSW expelled its Yugoslav affiliate in 1949. In contrast to reactions to similar ousters in other front organizations, this action did not precipitate mass resignations of the WFSW's noncommunist members. Noncommunist members also seemed to acquiesce to the WFSW's militant involvement during the Korean War in the campaign waged against the United Nations intervention. One of the actions of the WFSW was to send an "International Scientific Commission" to China and Korea, which subsequently published "scientific proof" of the Chinese allegations that UN forces were waging bacteriological warfare. It was later found that the allegations had been based on faked photographs and forced "confessions" by prisoners. During the period from 1947 to Stalin's death in 1953—years in which the WFSW followed its most ideologically sectarian course—only three noncommunist national affiliates left the federation: the Netherlands, New Zealand, and South Africa, all in 1951.

One of the leit-motifs in WFSW policy has been its repeated warnings about the dangers of nuclear weapons in general and of nuclear tests in particular. Its protests have invariably been directed against the United States, Great Britain, and France, never against the Soviet Union. Although an attempt was made in September 1961 by Professor Cecil F. Powell, president of the WFSW and successor to Joliot-Curie, to protest against the Soviet Union's resumption of atmospheric testing, his action was rescinded by the WFSW, which emphasized that Powell had only expressed his personal opinion. The WFSW created in 1957 a Nuclear Hazards Committee, which worked closely with the WCP's Vienna-based International Institute for Peace; by the end of 1965, however, the committee appeared to have ceased functioning.

In the early 1960s the WFSW was confronted with criticism from both the right and the left. Its partisan intervention in foreign affairs had finally elicited a significant response, particularly from the non-communist elements in its British and French affiliates. In 1962, these affiliates threatened to leave the WFSW if statements continued to be issued without their agreement. Since that time the WFSW leadership has tended to be more cautious for fear of losing its only important affiliates in the West. The WSFW was also faced with a growing challenge from its Chinese affiliates. Already evident in 1959-1960, the Sino-Soviet conflict in the WFSW increased progressively. By 1962 the Chinese delegates were disrupting WFSW meetings by challenging the agenda, putting up resolutions condemning both United States and Soviet policy, and seeking support for their views among the delegates from Africa and Asia. Relations worsened after the signing in the summer of 1963 of the Nuclear Test Ban Treaty, which the WFSW supported but the Chinese opposed. In September of that year the Chinese opened a "Peking Center of the WFSW," claiming that it was in implementation of a resolution passed by the WFSW executive council in September 1962 authorizing an Asian regional center. The Peking Center was set up without the knowledge of the WFSW headquarters and as a rival to it. The claim that it was an Asian branch of the WFSW was exposed when the Chinese invited Africans, Latin Americans, and other non-Asians to its first meeting. At the end of 1965 the Chinese were still sending delegates to WFSW meetings; the only major activity of the Peking Center was the convening in August 1964 of an International Scientific Symposium in Peking.

## ORGANIZATION AND MEMBERSHIP

Membership in the WFSW is open to organizations of scientific workers or to individual scientists in countries where no affiliated organization exists. The federation does not publish exact membership figures; by the end of 1965, however, it was claiming about 300,000 members. The WFSW has affiliated organizations in twenty-three countries, and individual members in a further twenty-four. The only large noncommunist affiliation is that of the British Association of Scientific Workers, which in 1965 had a membership of some 17,000.

The governing body of the WFSW is the general assembly, which meets every two or three years. Between these meetings an executive council is responsible for leading the work of the federation. Since regular meetings even of the executive council are difficult to arrange, its powers are delegated to the bureau, which meets more frequently. The executive council, according to the WFSW constitution, consists of twenty-seven members, of whom seventeen, including the elected officers, are chosen on an individual basis and ten are regional representatives. The executive council is elected by the assembly, except for its regional members, who are elected by their respective regions. The WFSW bureau comprises the president, vice president, treasurer, and chairman and vice chairman of the executive council; the chairman of the editorial board of WFSW publications; and the heads of the regional centers. In addition there are seven appointed officers—the secretary-general, assistant secretary-general, and five honorary assistant secretaries—who participate in the work of the bureau but have no voting rights. They are responsible for a major part of the WFSW's organizational work and operate from an office in Paris.

In 1965 the WFSW obtained consultative status Category B with UNESCO (it had previously held Category C); it has no status with the United Nations Economic and Social Council.

## PRESS ORGANS

*Scientific World* is the official organ of the WFSW and is issued quarterly in English, French, German, Russian, Chinese, and

Spanish; it was first published in January 1957. The *WFSW Bulletin* is issued irregularly to members only, in English, French, German, Russian, and Chinese; it has appeared since April 1953, and since the 1960s has been used to report official WFSW statements and meetings.

The WFSW has issued in several languages a series of booklets under the general heading *Science and Mankind*. In addition to publishing special reports on its assemblies, the federation has published a number of pamphlets—e.g., *Unmeasured Hazards*, which, issued in 1956 and since then translated into twelve languages, deals with the dangers of atomic radiation.

GENERAL ASSEMBLIES OF THE WFSW

1st assembly, July 1946, London
2d assembly, September 1948, Dobris (Czechoslovakia)
3d assembly, April 1951, Paris and Prague
4th assembly, September 1953, Budapest
5th assembly, September 1955, East Berlin
6th assembly, August-September 1957, Helsinki
7th assembly, September 1959, Warsaw
8th assembly, September 1962, Moscow
9th assembly, September 1965, Budapest

The WFSW has organized several international symposiums in conjunction with its general assemblies, among which have been those on "Science and Planning" and "The Training of Students of Science and Technology" (Helsinki, 1957); "Science and the Development of the Economy and Welfare of Mankind" (Warsaw, 1959); "Higher Scientific and Technological Education" (Moscow, 1962); and "Problems of the Advancement of Science in Developing Countries and the Role of International Scientific Cooperation" (Budapest, 1965). In the last three, particular attention was paid to the way in which science could help newly developing countries. In contrast to the assemblies, the symposiums have tended to limit themselves to scientific discussions and have attracted many scientists unconnected with the WFSW.

MILORAD POPOV

# THE WORLD FEDERATION OF TRADE UNIONS

The genesis of the World Federation of Trade Unions (WFTU) can be traced to an initiative by the British Trades Union Congress (TUC), which in November 1943 issued invitations to a World Trade Union Conference, to lay the foundations for postwar international trade-union unity. The conference was held in London on February 6-17, 1945, and was attended by representatives of fifty-three trade-union organizations. It appointed a forty-one-member preparatory committee, headed by Louis Saillant, secretary-general of the French communist-controlled General Confederation of Labor (Confédération Générale du Travail, CGT), to organize the establishment of a permanent international trade-union body. At a subsequent international trade-union conference, held in Paris on September 2-October 8, the WFTU was founded. The conference was attended by sixty-five trade-union organizations, representing some 66 million workers. Sir Walter Citrine, secretary of the TUC, was elected president. The post of secretary-general, however, went to the procommunist Louis Saillant, and the direction of the

WFTU's department of press and information was given to a Soviet nominee. Moreover, under strong Soviet pressure, the headquarters of the WFTU were located in Paris, placing the administrative machinery of the federation in close proximity to the communist-dominated CGT.

## HISTORY

Although differences between communist and noncommunist elements within the WFTU leadership did not come to a head until the summer of 1947, controversy was evident as early as 1946, when the WFTU secretariat made unsuccessful attempts to involve the federation in Germany and Japan, while opposing any suggestion of assistance to trade unions in the countries of Eastern Europe which were in process of succumbing to Soviet control. Within the WFTU's executive bureau communists and noncommunists appear to have been relatively evenly divided, giving the communist-dominated secretariat considerable freedom of action to further its political goals.

The Marshall Plan of 1947 and the subsequent European Recovery Program (ERP) fostered the first major conflict within the WFTU. Although the majority of European trade unions had responded favorably to the ERP, the WFTU secretariat's *Information Bulletin* issued without authority from the WFTU executive a series of attacks against the ERP; moreover, it accused the TUC, the American Congress of Industrial Organizations (CIO), and other noncommunist trade unions of being "agents of American imperialism" and "betrayers of trade unionunity." Attempts by noncommunist unions to organize open discussion of the Marshall Plan were repeatedly stalled by the secretary-general.

The communist coup d'état in Czechoslovakia in February 1948 and the initiation of the Berlin blockade in July of the same year created further dissension within the WFTU leadership. In October the general council of the TUC recommended that the WFTU temporarily suspend all its operations because it could no longer reach any agreement on what the TUC called "real trade-union tasks." It also stated that if this recommendation were not accepted the TUC would be compelled to withdraw from the WFTU. A month later, at its convention in Portland, Oregon, the CIO took similar action. At the final joint session of the WFTU's executive bureau, which met in Paris on January 17-21, 1949, Arthur Deakin (who had succeeded Citrine as WFTU president and chairman of the TUC) formally presented the TUC proposal. When the executive bureau refused to endorse the recommended course of action, the TUC and the CIO withdrew from the WFTU. In the following months, trade-union representatives from ten countries—Australia, Austria, Belgium, Denmark, Ireland, the Netherlands, New Zealand, Norway, Sweden, and Switzerland—also disaffiliated from the WFTU. Since in the meantime the trade-union movements in Italy and France had themselves split into communist and noncommunist groups—with only the communist groups remaining in the WFTU—by mid-1949 the federation was representative only of communist and procommunist trade unions. Reporting on the WFTU schism to the congress of the TUC in September 1949, Arthur Deakin noted: "We started with an honest intention, but we were not dealing with honest men." At a conference in London on November 28-December 7, 1949, a new International Confederation of Free Trade Unions (ICFTU) was formed, in which trade unions from fifty-three countries were participants, representing some 48 million workers.

The WFTU held its second congress in Milan on June 29-July 8, 1949. Although at the time of the January break it had had a combined membership of 76,072,560, at the Milan congress the WFTU claimed 71,786,515 members—a drop of less than 4½ million, even though the great majority of the 48 million trade unionists who formed the ICFTU were former members of the

WFTU. It would appear that the Milan figure was arrived at by arbitrarily raising the Soviet and East European membership and by the addition of the newly formed East German trade unions, with a claimed membership of 5 million. The 1949 congress also attempted to broaden the base of the WFTU by setting up a number of Trade Unions Internationals (TUIs) representing workers of similar or connected trades or crafts, thus recruiting local unions which did not, through their national centers, belong to the WFTU. The founding of the TUIs was also in response to the fact that the existing International Trade Secretariats (most of which were set up before World War II) had refused to cooperate with the WFTU and aligned themselves with the noncommunists following the schism in the federation. The Milan congress reelected Louis Saillant as secretary-general; Guiseppe DiVittorio, member of the Italian Communist Party's central committee and secretary-general of the communist-controlled Italian General Confederation of Labor (Confederazione Generale Italiana del Lavoro, CGIL), was elected president.

From 1949 to 1953 the WFTU reflected the Stalinist views and policies of the Soviet Union. For a while it appeared to be primarily concerned with opposition to the ERP. Following the establishment of a special International Fund at the Milan congress, the WFTU's activities extended to providing financial support to communist-led strikes directed against the implementation of ERP assistance. The WFTU's anti-ERP campaign, however, proved to be somewhat narrow in scope; moreover, it had the disadvantage of being purely negative and only applicable to Western Europe. The WFTU gradually reoriented its activities, giving priority to the campaigns organized by the World Council of Peace (WCP). The WCP's "Peace Appeal" (Stockholm Appeal) of March 1950 was broadly publicized by the WFTU, whose executive bureau urged all WFTU-affiliated unions to participate in their respective national peace committees and to "mobilize [themselves] as distributing agencies for the journals, literature and leaflets of the Peace Movement groups." The WFTU was particularly active in propagandizing the allegations of the WCP and other communist organizations that United Nations troops had waged bacteriological warfare during the Korean conflict. The WFTU's Soviet orientation extended also to its own ranks; thus, following Yugoslavia's expulsion from the Cominform in 1948, the WFTU in 1950 expelled its Yugoslav affiliates, branding them as "traitors" and "agents of the Fascist Tito clique."

The WFTU's sectarian policies during this period resulted in its expulsion on January 24, 1951, from France for subversive activities. The WFTU headquarters were moved to the Soviet-occupied sector of Vienna, but, following Austria's independence, the federation was once again expelled, on February 4, 1956, on the grounds that it had failed to live up to its statutes and that its operations had endangered Austrian neutrality. The WFTU headquarters then moved to Prague.

Although WFTU pronouncements were tempered after Stalin's death in 1953 and the subsequent attenuation of Soviet attacks against the West, the federation continued to focus its attention primarily on political as opposed to trade-union issues. Thus, in 1954 and 1955 its limited trade-union activities were eclipsed by a concerted opposition to the creation of a European Defense Community (EDC). The WFTU organized several conferences during this time in protest against the EDC, coupling this theme with attacks against West German rearmament. The WFTU's political alignment with the Soviet Union was also evident during the 1956 uprising in Hungary, which it branded as a "counterrevolution led by Fascist groups."

The WFTU showed an early concern for furthering its interests in the developing countries. However, its efforts, which were considerably increased as of the mid-1950s, had shown only limited success by the end of 1965. The WFTU's only functioning regional bureau was the Workers' Confederation of Latin America (Confederación de Trabajadores de America Latina, CTAL), which was founded in 1938 and became a WFTU bureau in 1949. It was run by Vincente Lombardo Toledano, a WFTU vice president. By January 1964, the CTAL had become so ineffective that it was disbanded. Since then the WFTU has attempted to replace it with a new trade-union center for Latin America, ostensibly autonomous but in practice under WFTU control. Discussions regarding a new center had taken place periodically as early as 1961. A meeting held to launch it, in Brasilia in January 1964, was abortive, but a continuing organization, the Permanent Congress for the Trade Union Unity of Latin American Workers, was set up.

In Africa, instead of urging African trade unions to join it, the WFTU encouraged them to support the concept of a Pan-African trade-union organization. In May 1961, the WFTU assisted in the setting up of the All-African Trade Union Federation (AATUF); it supplied funds and offered a number of WFTU-trained Africans to run the organization. The establishment of the headquarters in Accra, however, enabled Ghana's President Nkrumah to use the AATUF to further his Pan-African ambitions, and its trade-union functions became a secondary consideration. Africa has figured substantially in the WFTU's intensified training programs. Meetings organized by the federation in Africa, however, have been mainly of solidarity committees. Before 1964 the WFTU was involved in few meetings in the Middle East, but in January of that year it cooperated with the International Confederation of Arab Trade Unions in setting up an International Trade Union Committee for Solidarity with the Workers and People of Aden and subsequently increased its activities in the Middle East considerably. By the end of 1965, however, it had not registered any significant breakthrough.

The WFTU's inroad into Asia has been severely handicapped by the Sino-Soviet conflict, which erupted within the federation at a meeting of its general council in Peking May 30-June 9, 1960, when the head of the Chinese delegation, Liu Chang-sheng, expressed severe criticism of the resolutions adopted by the twenty-first congress of the Communist Party of the Soviet Union. Relations deteriorated further at the WFTU's fifth congress in Moscow on December 4-15, 1961; and on a number of subsequent occasions the Chinese disrupted WFTU meetings. An attempt by the Chinese, with the support of the Indonesian trade unions, to create a rival Afro-Asian organization proved unsuccessful. Although a call was issued in 1962 for an Afro-Asian Workers' Conference, its venue was postponed several times, and, following the 1965 abortive communist coup d'état in Indonesia, the idea appears to have been dropped.

At the end of 1965 there appeared to be developing a growing dissatisfaction among members of a minority group lead by the Italian CGIL. This element was increasingly critical of the WFTU's centralism and called for greater regional autonomy for WFTU affiliate activities. It also criticized the federation's continuing attacks against the European Economic Community (EEC), seeing them as counter-productive, since the EEC was an established fact and had been accepted by most West European workers.

ORGANIZATION AND MEMBERSHIP

According to its constitution, membership in the WFTU is open only to national trade-union centers, but in practice many splinter groups from noncommunist countries have been accepted because most of the national centers belong to the ICFTU. In 1965 the WFTU claimed a membership of about 140 million, although over 90 percent of this total were from communist countries—60 percent from the Soviet Union alone.

The congress is the highest authority of the WFTU and is supposed to be held every four years. Each affiliated organization sends delegates, the number varying according to its membership. The congress elects the subsidiary bodies, which include the general council, executive committee, secretariat, and executive bureau. The general council is supposed to meet every two years. In 1965 it consisted of 165 members, comprising eighty-six full and seventy-nine deputy members, nominated by affiliated organizations. Because of its size the general council is not a policy-making body as such. The executive committee meets twice a year. In 1965 it consisted of seventy-six regular and deputy members representing thirty-seven countries and the TUIs plus the members of the secretariat; its main function has been to confirm decisions already taken by the executive bureau. The latter consists of the secretary-general, assistant secretary-general, and (in 1965) eight secretaries. Its functions are divided among several departments: Press and Information; Relations with National Centers; Trade Unions Internationals; Economic and Social Questions (including the UN); and Administration and Finance. At the end of 1965 the president of the WFTU was Renato Bitossi, a communist senator from Italy; Louis Saillant was still secretary-general.

Most of the TUIs of the WFTU were set up in 1949-1950. They include the following: Agricultural and Forestry Workers' TUI (headquartered in Prague); Building, Wood and Building Materials Industries' TUI (Helsinki); Chemical, Oil and Allied Workers' TUI (Budapest); Commercial, Office and Bank Workers' TUI (Prague); Food, Tobacco and Beverage Industries and Hotel, Café and Restaurant Workers' TUI (Sofia); Metal and Engineering Industries' TUI (Prague); Miners' TUI (Prague); Public and Allied Employees' TUI (East Berlin); Textile, Clothing, Leather and Fur Workers' TUI (Prague); Transport, Port and Fishery Workers' TUI (Prague); and World Federation of Teachers' Unions (Prague).

The TUIs claim a combined membership of more than 100 million, but this is mostly a part of, and not additional to, the membership of the parent body—the WFTU.

In the late 1950s the WFTU started setting up an increasing number of subsidiary bodies to deal with special questions. These organizations proved particularly useful in nonaligned countries or in achieving collaboration with noncommunist trade unionists, since the WFTU's control of them was often disguised. Among the most prominent were:

The Trade Union Coordination and Action Committee of Common Market Countries; proposed in July 1958, it held its first meeting in Paris in September 1958. Primarily represented by trade unions from Italy, France, and Luxembourg, the committee in January 1963 set up a liaison office in Brussels for contacts with the EEC. In the same year it was superseded by a broader World Trade Union Committee for Consultation and United Action Against Monopolies.

International Trade Union Committee of Solidarity with the Algerian Workers and People, founded in Cairo in September 1958. In 1962 it claimed to represent thirty-eight trade-union organizations of all continents. Although it was reported that it would not be wound up after Algerian independence, in 1965 it no longer appeared to be active.

International Trade Union and Legal Commission for the Defense and Extension of Trade Union Rights and the Protection of Victims of Repression Against Trade Unions; its first meeting was held in March 1961 in Prague.

International Trade Union Committee for Solidarity with the Workers and People of South Africa, established in July 1961.

International Trade Union Commission of Study and Inquiry on East and West Germany, established in October 1963. It was supposed to comprise three representatives from the WFTU, three from the ICFTU, and two from neutral trade-union centers, but the ICFTU has not cooperated in it.

Committee for Solidarity with Workers and People of South Vietnam; its inaugural meeting was held in Hanoi in October 1963.

The WFTU is the only international communist front organization to enjoy Category A status with the United Nations Economic and Social Council, the International Labor Organization, the Food and Agriculture Organization, and the United Nations Educational, Scientific and Cultural Organization.

## PRESS ORGANS

The major organs of the WFTU are *World Trade Union Movement*, a magazine appearing in Russian, English, French, German, Spanish, Rumanian, and Japanese, and usually issued every two months; *Trade Union Press* (until 1959 known as *World Trade Union News*), published fortnightly, also in several languages; and *News in Brief*, a monthly bulletin published in English, French, Spanish, and Russian. Each TUI publishes its own bulletin.

Every four years the WFTU publishes its *Report to Congress*, covering the four years between congresses.

## CONGRESSES OF THE WFTU

1st congress, October 1945, Paris
2d congress, June-July 1949, Milan
3d congress, October 1953, Vienna
4th congress, October 1957, Leipzig
5th congress, December 1961, Moscow
6th congress, October 1965, Warsaw

## BIBLIOGRAPHY

Donahue, George R.: *Focus on a Communist Front*, London, Phoenix House, 1958.

Peyneli, Anne: *La Fédération syndicale mondiale: Propagande politique ou progrès social?* Les Cahiers africains, no. 14, Brussels, n.d.

MILORAD POPOV

# YUGOSLAVIA

Yugoslav communism came into being in the wake of the bolshevik victory in Russia and Lenin's decision to found the Comintern. The pre-1914 Yugoslav social democracy was in shambles after the end of the war, and several radical groups decided to break all ties with the Second International and establish a new revolutionary party. A peculiarity in the Yugoslav case was the role played by a group of former Austro-Hungarian soldiers, both Serbs and Croats, who were prisoners of war in Russia and after the bolshevik revolution had formed a Yugoslav communist group in Russia. This group laid plans for a "revolutionary government" to be established in Yugoslavia after the end of the war, and on November 20, 1918, the central committee of the Yugoslav section of the Russian Communist Party (Bolshevik) started home from Russia.[1]

On March 2, 1919, in greatest secrecy, some thirty persons from the various regions met in Srem (Vojvodina), led by Nikola Grulović and Lazar Vukićević, members of the politburo of the Yugoslav section of the Russian Communist Party. The Yugoslav Communist Revolutionary League of Pelagićevci (Jugoslavenski Komunistički Revolucionarni Savez Pelagićevaca), named after the old socialist tribune Vaso Pelagić, was created at this meeting, with a program revolving around the central theme of a "single Yugoslav soviet socialist republic." This was the first organized group of communists in Yugoslavia.[2] The strategic plan of the league was twofold: to continue to act clandestinely as a distinct group, but to send delegates openly to the forthcoming congress of unification of Yugoslav revolutionary socialists in order to influence its policy.

The congress of unification convened in Belgrade on April 20-23, 1919, and was attended by 431 delegates from across the newly created kingdom of Serbs, Croats, and Slovenes. Two main currents dominated the congress: the centrists, or "socialist revolutionaries," as they called themselves (in distinction from the "rightist" social democrats, who boycotted or were not allowed to take part in the congress), and the leftist, or communist, followers of the Russian bolsheviks (with the Pelagićevci league as a separate group in their midst). These two groups clashed on many issues but succeeded in making a compromise reflected in the name of the new party founded at the congress, the Socialist Workers' Party of Yugoslavia (Communist) [Socijalistička Radnička Partija, Jugoslavije (Komunista), SRPJ(K)]. The new party's "platform of unification" and practical program of action" were also a mixture of Austro-German orthodox Marxism and revolutionary bolshevism. The congress denounced the Second International and declared the new party's adherence to the Third International. A leftist, Filip Filipović, was elected the party's main secretary, and a Pelagićevac, Vladimir Čopić, became its technical (organizational) secretary.

The centrist-leftist unity did not last long, and the internal balance of power within the new party quickly shifted to the left. Thus when the second party congress convened in Vukovar on June 20-24, 1920, the 374 delegates took part in an ideological and political confrontation which ended with a full-fledged leftist victory. The name of the party was changed to Communist Party of Yugoslavia (Komunistička Partija Jugoslavije, KPJ), and its leadership was henceforth in communist hands with Filipović and Sima Marković as secretaries. The centrists tried for a while to organize an opposition within the party but were expelled from it in December 1920.

All these earliest party leaders—Filipović, Čopić, and Marković—perished in the Soviet Union, where they had sought asylum, during the Stalin purges of the 1930s.

After the Vukovar congress the name of the party remained unchanged until November 2-7, 1952, when the sixth congress adopted the name League of Communists of Yugoslavia (Savez Komunista Jugoslavije, LCY).

## HISTORY

*1920 to 1929* The years 1919 and 1920 represented the golden age of Yugoslav communism in the interwar period. At one point the party had over 60,000 members, and the trade unions it controlled had 300,000 adherents. At the election for the constituent assembly on November 28, 1920, the party polled 198,736 votes (12.4 percent) and gained fifty-eight seats out of 419. The Yugoslav party was considered one of the most promising Comintern sections.

The KPJ's revolutionary propaganda and a series of strikes and demonstrations which it fomented or supported caused the government to take stern measures, and on December 30, 1920, the government issued an *obznana* (announcement) notifying the country that all communist organizations, meetings, and propaganda were prohibited and party offices were closed. The communist deputies in the assembly were not affected by these measures, but they were cut off from the party rank and file. The entire party was paralyzed, and its leaders were divided on the problem of how to react. Then in the summer of 1921 an attempt on the life of Prince Regent Alexander by a former Pelagićevac and the assassination of Milorad Drašković, the minister of the interior and author of the *obznana*, by a member of the secret communist terrorist group Red Justice induced parliament to issue on August 1 a "law on protection of the state" which banned the communist party altogether. It was forced underground and remained in illegality until the dismemberment of Yugoslavia during World War II.

These blows against the KPJ were very effective; by the end of 1921 the party leadership had disintegrated (some abandoned communism, some withdrew from political life altogether, some were imprisoned, some escaped abroad, and others continued the illegal struggle in a variety of new forms), and the rank and file melted away. The party's demise would have been complete had it not been for the survival of communism in Russia.

These difficulties were compounded by the emergence of factional struggles, both inside and outside the country. Clashes of personalities first and then a conflict over the party attitude toward the national question in Yugoslavia prevented the restoration of party unity and led the Comintern to intervene and actually impose its own tutelage on the party. The national question was indeed a hard one for the Yugoslav communists. The Vukovar congress had solemnly subscribed to the principle of Yugoslav national unity, and in 1923 Marković published two theoretical works arguing that national unification could only help the unfolding of a pure class struggle, while national bickerings would hinder it. The same year the Comintern criticized Marković's views, and the reversal of the Vukovar standpoint was spelled out at the fifth Comintern congress in 1924. One paragraph of the congress's resolution on the national question in Yugoslavia stated that "the general slogan about the right of peoples to self-determination, on which the KPJ insists, must express the demand for separation of Croatia, Slovenia, and Macedonia from Yugoslavia and their transformation into independent republics." This inept slogan did not help the party in its efforts to recapture its lost influence, while the feuding factions failed to achieve the unity of leadership.

*1929 to 1941* In a supreme effort to heal intraparty feuds, the Comintern sent "Comrade Ercoli" (Palmiro Togliatti) to deliver a harsh speech at the fourth KPJ congress, which took place in Dresden at the beginning of November 1928 and was attended by only twenty-two persons. Togliatti's attacks were directed at the party's intellectual leaders, particularly Sima Marković. The congress unreservedly hailed the decisions of the sixth congress of the Comintern (July-September 1928) and elected a completely new party leadership dominated by those who had already been trained in the Comintern's political schools. Jovan Mališić-Martinović was nominated political secretary and Djuro Djaković organizational secretary.

In February 1929 the new party leaders decided to stage an armed insurrection against the authoritarian regime of King Alexander. The decision was taken in application of the new "class-against-class" tactic of the Comintern. A more ruinous policy could hardly have been devised. A real armed insurrection never took place, but the meager party cadres were pitted against and largely destroyed by the Yugoslav police. Six secretaries of the party's youth organization and Djuro Djaković, among others, perished. Twenty years later Tito called the entire endeavor "stupid and irresponsible" and blamed Martinović for causing the "decimation of the small number of party members." The indictment was justifiable, but the culprit was wrongly chosen. Martinović was hardly a man to decide party policy; if anyone had been responsible it was the Comintern. In fact, the Comintern found Martinović expendable, and in 1930 he was replaced as secretary-general by Anton Mavrak. A new central committee was appointed, only to be dismissed by the Comintern two years later for not showing any progress. At that time, in 1932, the party membership reached its lowest figure ever, 200 members.[3] Another party leadership was designated, with Milan Gorkić (Josip Čižinski), a Comintern functionary, as secretary general.

Under Gorkić's leadership, the KPJ began a slow climb toward recovery. At the party's clandestine fourth conference, held in Ljubljana in December 1934, some progress was recorded. The popular-front line adopted by the seventh Comintern congress (July-August 1935) considerably helped the Yugoslav party. Echoing the new Comintern course, the KPJ politburo announced that the claim to secession of any part of Yugoslavia should be abandoned. In August 1936 the party began to dispatch volunteers to the civil war in Spain; 560 Yugoslav party members fought in units of the International Brigades, and those who survived gained military and revolutionary experience which they used to advantage during World War II in Yugoslavia's partisan warfare.

The popular-front recovery of the KPJ during the middle 1930s unfolded under strange conditions. In the Soviet Union Stalin's purges claimed not only the initial Yugoslav party leaders, but the entire team of Comintern-appointed secretaries. Martinović, Mavrak, Gorkić, and scores of others who had sought refuge in the Soviet Union or were there attending Comintern schools perished at the hands of Soviet police. At one time the Yugoslav party was on the verge of being officially dissolved. The Comintern's Georgi Dimitrov personally intervened and decided to give a last chance to Josip Broz (Walter, as he was known at that time in Comintern circles) to try to revamp what seemed to be a hopelessly divided and inefficient party. Actually, Broz was handpicked by the Comintern as the only trustworthy Yugoslav communist. To merit such confidence and to emerge as the sole and undisputed leader of the party he had to prove his fitness in the deadly game which Milovan Djilas described in the following way: "There was no one to stand behind the Yugoslavs [during the purges]; rather, they dug graves for one another in their race for power in the party and in their zeal to prove their devotion to Stalin and to Leninism."[4]

After his nomination in the fall of 1937 as secretary general, Josip Broz, subsequently called Tito, did a great deal to revive the party. His new leadership included several young and able professional revolutionaries in their twenties, among them Aleksandar Ranković, Edvard Kardelj, and Milovan Djilas. He transferred the center of the party's action to Yugoslavia and thoroughly cleansed it of "alien and vacillating elements." He was indeed the only interwar KPJ leader who succeeded in "bolshevizing" the party. He himself stressed, in an article written in the fall of 1939, that the KPJ "is proceeding along the same road taken by the heroic bolshevik party of the Soviet Union, learning from its experience as described in the *History of the All-Union Communist Party (Bolsheviks)*."

Tito's leadership finally gave the Comintern an effective and disciplined section in Yugoslavia. The party followed faithfully all the twists and turns of Stalin's foreign policy; it was militantly antifascist before the Hitler-Stalin pact of August 1939 and became "defeatist" afterward. In domestic politics it emerged as strictly a cadre party, whose membership rose steadily,[5] but which nevertheless remained until the outbreak of the war in Yugoslavia more a militant sect than a powerful movement. It achieved considerable success in organizing cells in high schools and universities (the University of Belgrade was its stronghold) but failed in its efforts to create a large antifascist popular front with other oppositional parties. Similarly, communist influence among the peasantry and in larger industrial centers was marginal, and infiltration of the army and the state administration was negligible.

*The "People's Liberation Struggle"* Two events totally altered the KPJ's dim prospects. The first was the dismemberment of Yugoslavia in April 1941 by Nazi Germany and its allies; the collapse of the Yugoslav state and its replacement by foreign occupations and domestic chaos enhanced the operative possibilities of the communists, whose cells had remained intact throughout the country. Comintern discipline still dictated passivity, but the KPJ was eager for action. The second and decisive event was Germany's attack on the Soviet Union on June 22, 1941. Immediately after receipt that same day of a Comintern telegram asking for help, the central committee issued a proclamation emphatically pledging unconditional support of the Soviet Union. On July 1 another telegram from the Comintern called for partisan warfare, and on July 4 the central committee issued a call for a general armed uprising.

From the very beginning of the uprising the KPJ concentrated in its hands both the conduct of military operations and the direction of political developments. The prewar party military committees, transformed into leading centers for the new "people's liberation partisan detachments," were directed by members of the party politburo. Tito himself became military commander of the partisan detachments of Yugoslavia. The "people's liberation struggle" had two fundamental purposes in the eyes of the party leadership: one, with international significance, was "to support through an armed uprising the first country of socialism"; the other, essentially internal, was to transform the national war of liberation into a socialist revolution.[6] The KPJ was finally in a position to implement the lessons learned during its Comintern apprenticeship: "Calling people to arms and securing its leading role in the people's uprising," wrote Aleksandar Ranković in 1942, "our party has honorably paid its debt to the people, has justified the obligations assumed at the seventh congress of the Communist International."

The outward image that the party presented after July 1941 to Yugoslavia, and later to the rest of the world, was quite different. The KPJ's real revolutionary aims were hidden behind official appeals to all the patriots and all the Yugoslav nationalities to join a common antifascist front. The people's liberation struggle was projected above all as genuinely democratic and genuinely Yugoslav. "The National Liberation Movement of Yugoslavia is in its essence an all-peoples', national, and democratic one," stated a declaration signed on August 8, 1944, by Tito as the president of the National Committee of Yugoslavia (in fact a partisans' self-appointed government, established in 1943 as rival to the royal government in exile, stationed in London). "We are, therefore, underlining once more that the leadership of the National Liberation Movement in Yugoslavia concerns itself with the only and most important aim—the struggle against the invader and his aides and creation of a democratic, federative Yugoslavia, and not establishment of communism, as some of our enemies claim."[7] Tito himself recognized this solemn war promise as only a political strategem, for he was to say four years later: "This statement was, of course, a correct one at that time."

The people's liberation struggle unfolded with many ups and downs. Cooperation between the communist-led partisans and the first resistance movement in Yugoslavia, launched in May 1941 by the pro-Western *četniks* under Colonel Draža Mihajlović, ended in the fall of the same year, and the ensuing battle became a merciless civil war. At several points the partisan forces were on the verge of collapse and used such extreme measures as the establishment of "proletarian shock brigades" in combating their foreign and domestic enemies. The Comintern itself, anxious to preserve the antinazi alliance, objected to such radical moves, at odds with its own moderating and struggle-by-stages counsel. Moreover, while, according to Tito in November 1942, "profound faith in the strength and might of the Soviet Union, in the strength and might of the Red Army, sustained us [the partisans] while we were overcoming all the difficulties we endured during these past eighteen months,"[8] the partisans did not actually receive Soviet military aid until the spring of 1944. However, for strictly military reasons the Western Allies had been supplying the partisans abundantly with war materiel since May 1943. At the end, the entry of the Soviet Red Army into Yugoslavia and the fact that British and American troops were absent settled the issue of the civil war in favor of the partisans and permitted the KPJ to capture political power in Belgrade in the fall of 1944.

*The Tito-Stalin Conflict* Of the 12,000 party members with which the KPJ entered the people's liberation struggle, 9,000 perished during the war, but the struggle also served as a reservoir of new members. According to official data, the party membership at the end of the war was 141,066.[9] This was the primary unit which took upon itself the total transformation of the country.

In domestic affairs the party moved quickly to renege on its war promises of a postwar democratic order. A joint government with some representatives of prewar democratic parties who had returned from London (Ivan Šubašić, Milan Grol, Juraj Šutej), established in March 1945, did not last more than five months; in August they were maneuvered into resigning. On November 29 the Federal People's Republic of Yugoslavia was proclaimed and the monarchy was abolished without the formality of the promised plebiscite. The People's Front (Narodni Front), under the complete control of the KPJ, was used to eliminate other political figures or groups which showed any inclination toward political independence. Along with these measures, there was a complete reorganization of both the state apparatus and the army. By 1948 two-thirds of the federal and republican employees were party members, and Tito announced at the fifth congress of the KPJ in 1948 that "over 94 percent of the commanding cadre of our army are communists whom our party educated during the war or before it." This also applied to the state security, whose carefully selected members were organizing a huge control system over the lives of all citizens, including party members.

Stern measures of economic collectivization followed the political regimentation of the country. A law in December 1946 on nationalization of private enterprises transferred economic initiative to the state; the law on agrarian reform of August 23, 1945, amended every subsequent three years, dealt, in Tito's words, "the first hard blow to the capitalist elements in the villages," and laid the foundation of socialist ownership in agriculture. The first Five-Year Plan of economic development, adopted in April 1947, represented a full-fledged transition to a rigidly planned economy whose fundamental target was the building up of heavy industry.

Yugoslavia's new constitution, passed on January 31, 1946, had as a conspicuous model the Stalin constitution of 1936. A few months earlier, in June 1945, Edvard Kardelj had confided to the Soviet ambassador to Yugoslavia that Yugoslav-Soviet relations "should be based on the prospect of Yugoslavia becoming in the future a constituent part of the U.S.S.R."[10] Yugoslav foreign policy was also bursting with intransigence and militancy. Even before the end of the war in Europe Tito had attempted to seize and to hold Trieste by force; in 1946 two American military planes had been shot down; Yugoslavia was actively helping the communist rebels in Greece, and the Yugoslav representatives at the founding meeting of the Cominform, in September 1947 in Poland, hailed the radicalism of their own party as a paragon of revolutionary virtue. A self-confident party, intoxicated by its revolutionary success, was imposing a reckless tempo on the country and was rightfully considered the most aggressive communist party in the world.

This self-propelled militancy, at odds with Moscow's plans and timetable, angered Stalin, who opposed every communist move not initiated or approved by himself. After a secret exchange of letters between the Soviet and Yugoslav central committees, Stalin decided to settle accounts with Tito by expelling the KPJ from the Cominform on June 28, 1948. The Soviet act of excommunication was extremely harsh in substance and offensive in form. It condemned the Yugoslav communists for "betraying the cause of international solidarity of the working people" and for taking up "a position of nationalism." It castigated the party leaders for "boundless ambition, arrogance, and conceit," for their deviations in domestic and foreign policy, and for their "anti-Soviet stand . . . borrowed from the arsenal of counterrevolutionary Trotskyism." It appealed to the "healthy elements" within the party to replace Tito and his henchmen.[11]

On his side, at the fifth KPJ congress, held a month after the excommunication, Tito refuted "the monstrous accusations of our party and its leadership" but promised that "we shall work with all our might to mend the relations between our party and the [Soviet party]." This was the last KPJ congress at which the chanting "Stalin-Tito" drowned Tito's words.

For several months after the fifth congress domestic radicalism, particularly in the economic field, was increased to prove to Moscow that its accusations were unjustified. However, the increased hostility of the Soviet Union and other communist states, which threatened to isolate Yugoslavia economically, placed Tito in a dilemma: he had either to capitulate to Stalin, which would mean loss of power and perhaps of life, or to turn for economic help and political protection to the vilified West. The United States in particular was the power able—and willing—to help him to survive. "Titoism" was thus born not out of Tito's rebellion against Stalin, but out of his self-defense against Stalin's onslaught.

*Titoism* Conflict with Stalin forced the KPJ leadership to abandon many features of socioeconomic life that had simply been copied from the Soviet prototype. The most important departures from what was now reprovingly called "bureaucratic centralism" were introduced in the economic sphere. Titoism can largely be identified with these innovations: ". . . worker-management of enterprises, decentralized planning and control of an economic system that is relatively competitive and free (although not private) and socialist at the same time, and decollectivized, privately owned agriculture."[12] This process began on July 2, 1950, with the enactment of a law on workers' councils which, at least in theory, transferred to the elected workers' representatives general responsibility for operation of enterprises, including the determination of production norms, remuneration of personnel, and distribution of investments and surpluses. Since then Tito's new economic system has undergone numerous changes, the most significant of which was the introduction on July 24, 1965, of a general economic reform designed to spur economic activity and to eliminate persistent weaknesses.

The economic de-Stalinization of Yugoslavia was accompanied by other reforms: constitutional alterations culminating in a new 1963 constitution with its specific federalist features and rearrangements of the executive-legislative relationship; administrative reforms emphasizing the autonomy of communes, considered thenceforth to be the basic units of a decentralized social life; and abandonment of party dictates in the realm of cultural and artistic life, such as the previously imposed "socialist realism." Similarly, estrangement from the communist East opened Yugoslavia to the West in terms of easy travel, the exchange of public information and printed matter, and cultural and scholarly contacts.

De-Stalinization in Yugoslavia was to a large extent determined by the acuity of the Stalin-Tito conflict. From the middle of 1949 to the time of Stalin's death in March 1953 the conflict reached extraordinary proportions. Nearly 500 pages of a "white book" published in 1951 by th Yugoslav ministry of foreign affairs were devoted to examples of political and economic forms of aggressive pressure against Yugoslavia by the government of the Soviet Union and East European countries. On the Titoist side, thousands of the Yugoslav "Cominformists" were arrested and maltreated in jails (particularly in a concentration camp on a barren Adriatic island).

The sixth party congress in November 1952 turned into a huge anti-Stalinist demonstration. In his report to the congress Tito accused Stalin of every imaginable crime and declared that even Hitler would envy the methods Stalin had used to liquidate entire ethnic groups in the Soviet Union. The villain of the congress was the "imperialist, bureaucratic, antisocialist" Soviet Union. This was an inverse echo of Malenkov's declaration a few weeks earlier, at the nineteenth congress of the Communist Party of the Soviet Union, that Yugoslavia had already been converted into an American colony.

Stalin's death brought a halt to the fury of Soviet-Yugoslav mutual vilifications. Stalin's heirs realized that his blind resentment of Tito had been pushing Yugoslavia into the hands of NATO. Two years and three months after Stalin's death Khrushchev made a "Canossa" trip to Yugoslavia, with a plea to forgive and forget. As a price for reconciliation, Khrushchev subscribed to one of the basic tenets of Titoism, the concept that "questions of internal organization, or differences in social systems and in forms of socialist development, are solely the concern of the individual countries."[13] Tito's eagerness for reconciliation was expressed in a letter to the twentieth congress of the Soviet party in February 1956, in which he praised the "tremendous triumphs" achieved in the Soviet Union and hailed the "Leninist consistency, firmness, and tenacity" of the Russian communists.

Despite another flare-up in Yugoslav-Soviet relations in 1958 and 1959 (the "second dispute"), which never reached the proportions of the Tito-Stalin animosity, Stalin's successors, and then Brezhnev after Khrushchev, made their accommodation to Tito. A joint statement issued on July 1, 1965, stressed the "identity and great similarity of [Soviet-Yugoslav] views" on international issues. Confident that his domestic power was no longer threatened from the East, and put in the same category of "revisionists" as the Soviets by the Chinese communists, Tito was adding his branch of communism—domestic independence and alignment with the Soviet Union on major international issues—to the diversified post-Stalin communist world.

In one essential respect, both while resisting Stalin and after his death, the Yugoslav party was not willing to make a change: it refused to relinquish its monopoly of political power. The case of Milovan Djilas epitomized this point. Djilas' political itinerary oscillated from idolatry of Stalin before and during the war to extreme revulsion for his former idol after 1948, but his new anti-Stalinism was carried further than that of his colleagues in the party leadership. In a series of articles in the party press organ *Borba* (Struggle) at the end of 1953, Djilas argued that the old KPJ was obsolete because of its Stalinist roots, and that the new LCY should go even beyond Leninism and "gradually take on the character of a strong, ideological, widely diffused nucleus, [and eventually] lose its party character."[14] A year later, on December 24, 1954, after he had been demoted from all state and party functions and had voluntarily resigned from the LCY, Djilas appealed for the "formation of a new democratic socialist party and thus for a two-party system."[15] These views—and another direct attack on the morality and mentality of LCY leaders and their wives—were bitterly assailed at a plenary meeting of the LCY central committee in January 1954, when Tito warned his listeners: "If we were to permit this [unrestricted spreading of Djilas' ideas], within one year our socialist reality would cease to exist."[16] The basic document of Titoism—the program adopted by the LCY at its seventh congress in April 1958—was explicit in stating that "the communists will continue the struggle for keeping key positions of state authority in firm revolutionary hands."

While maintaining the one-party political regime, Yugoslav communists have continued with socioeconomic experimentation. This continual and contradictory process (three divergent economic reforms were introduced between 1960 and 1965), which has changed the material and psychological outlook of the country, inevitably has affected the role and the nature of the party. While it opposes genuine political liberalization, the LCY has lost its ideological and moral unity. This phenomenon, which Milovan Djilas prophesied, was depicted with extraordinary frankness in mid-1962 in a memorandum of the LCY executive committee addressed to the leading organs and members of the league:

> We are daily confronted with numerous manifestations in economic and political life (violation of the rights of working people, bureaucracy on all levels and in new forms, smothering of democracy, failure to fulfill responsibility for the safety of working people on work, and so on).... The trend [exists] toward more and more frequent manifestations of ideological attitudes alien and contrary to the views of the League of Communists. This is reflected in the intensified manifestations of chauvinism, nationalism, particularism, of various bureaucratic and petit bourgeois-liberal concepts.... By their conduct [some individuals] are active in diverse negative directions, in the direction of ideological dilution, disunity, and disintegration of our socialist community.[17]

## ORGANIZATIONS AND MEMBERSHIP

At the eighth party congress in Belgrade on December 7-13, 1964, a detailed survey of the LCY's organization and modes of action provided the following information. The party is organized on the principle of democratic centralism. It is a highly structured hierarchical organization, enjoying the monopoly of political power in the country. Its basic units are set up in industrial and other self-managing and work organizations, in local communities, in villages, in the Yugoslav People's Army, and elsewhere as the need arises. The LCY's vertical structure progresses from the commune, through the district, the province, and the six socialist republics, to the level of Socialist Federal Republic of Yugoslavia. Organs of the lower leading bodies (commune, district, province) are the conference, committee, control commission, and audit commission; at the two upper levels (the six republics and the federation itself) they are the congress, central committee, control commission, and audit commission.

The highest organ is the party congress, which is supposed to be convened every four years by the central committee. The congress adopts the party program and the statutes and amends them, determines policy, and elects the central committee and the control and audit commissions. In the interval between congresses the LCY is run by the central committee, which elects the executive committee and the secretary general. The executive committee directs party work between central committee meetings. The central committee elected at the eighth congress had 155 members, the executive committee nineteen, the control commission twenty-five, and the audit commission fifteen. Josip Broz Tito was reelected secretary general, and Edvard Kardelj, Aleksandar Ranković, and Veljko Vlahović were elected secretaries of the central committee.

In 1964 the LCY had 35,280 basic units, although many of them had very limited membership (for example, 5,623 of the units had fewer than ten members, and some 960 fewer than six members). The largest number of basic units was in the industrial and commerical enterprises (36.7 percent); the next largest number were rural units, which had sharply declined (from 46.8 percent in 1957 to 35.2 percent in 1964).

Membership statistics indicated social composition in 1964 was 36.2 percent workers, 7.9 percent agricultural producers (peasants), 38.4 percent office employees, 3.5 percent students, 5.6 percent military, and 8.4 percent others. The official report of the central committee submitted to the eighth congress complained that "the inadequate proportion of workers and agricultural producers in the total membership of the league is a great handicap to the development of its social structure. The proportion of workers in the league organizations in the enterprises dropped from 70.4 percent in 1961 to 67 percent in 1964. The proportion of [peasants] in the rural organizations dropped from 38 percent in 1961 to 34.5 percent in 1964." Another significant feature of the statistics is that "of all the workers employed in the socialized sector of the economy, only about 15 percent are members of the League of Communists, while the proportion of other employees in this sector is 39 percent, and of student members 20.8 percent."

Of the many mass organizations in Yugoslavia, three represent the most important fields of activity for the LCY. The largest of these is the Socialist Alliance of the Working People of Yugoslavia, formerly the People's Front. The Socialist Alliance, which had 8,126,204 members by the end of 1965, serves the purpose of "rallying the broadest strata of the working people and mobilizing them for political action." It also represents "a most powerful level of the influence of communists on the shaping of public opinion." The leadership of the Socialist Alliance includes, along with some noncommunists, the highest functionaries of the LCY. The Confederation of Yugoslav Trade Unions, with 2,754,000 members by the end of 1963, also acts in accordance with LCY policy. Finally, the Youth League of Yugoslavia (Savez Omladine Jugoslavije), with 1,807,000 members, provides socialist education for youth and offers to the LCY an important reservoir of future party members.

By the end of 1965 the membership of the LCY had reached 1,046,202. This figure can be broken down as follows: 437,034 from Serbia, 221,594 from Croatia, 71,128 from Slovenia, 132,696 from Bosnia and Herzegovina, 68,972 from Macedonia, 35,284 from Montenegro, and 79,394 in the army.[18]

## FUTURE PROSPECTS

With the roots of Yugoslav communism as thin as they were, and with Tito's rule over the party and the country so filled with dramatic changes of ideological orientation and practical policies, it is small wonder that the present Titoist "center," or status quo, is assailed from various sides in a world that wants change in the East no less than in the West. Tito may confidently assume that during his lifetime (he was born in 1892) he will be able to maintain the formal unity of his party and country, but his death may lead to developments no more predictable than were those of the three decades of turbulent party history with him at the helm.

## PARTY PRESS ORGANS AND RECORDS

The official organ of the LCY is the newspaper *Komunist*, which has appeared weekly since May 1, 1957; before that date it was a monthly political review. It has four editions (Serbo-Croatian, in both Cyrillic and Latin script, Slovenian, and Macedonian), and its circulation in 1964 was 230,000. A monthly theoretical review, *Socijalizam*, was launched in 1958 and had a circulation of 20,000 copies in 1965. The daily *Borba* (Struggle), present organ of the Socialist Alliance of the Working People of Yugoslavia, also reflects the LCY's official political line.

The full English text of the LCY statutes may be found in *Practice and Theory of Socialist Development in Yugoslavia*, Eighth Congress of the League of Communists of Yugoslavia, Belgrade, 1965, pp. 261-276. The party program, adopted at the seventh congress in April 1958, appears in the same work and was also published separately by All Nations Press, New York, 1958.

While full documentary reports of prewar party congresses do not exist in book form, the materials of the four postwar congresses in separate volumes were published shortly after each congress.

## PARTY CONGRESSES AND CONFERENCES

1st (unification) congress, SRPJ(K), April 1919, Belgrade
2d congress, KPJ, June 1920, Vukovar
1st all-Yugoslav conference, July 1922, Vienna
2d all-Yugoslav conference, May 1923, Vienna
3d all-Yugoslav conference, January 1924, Belgrade
3d congress, KPJ, May 1926, Vienna

4th congress, KPJ, November 1928, Dresden
4th all-Yugoslav conference, December 1934, Ljubljana
5th all-Yugoslav conference, October 1940, Zagreb
5th congress, KPJ, July 1948, Belgrade
6th congress, LCY, November 1952, Zagreb
7th congress, LCY, April 1958, Ljubljana
8th congress, LCY, December 1964, Belgrade

BIBLIOGRAPHY

Avakumović, Ivan: *History of the Communist Party of Yugoslavia*, vol. I, Aberdeen, 1964.

Bass, Robert Hugo, and Elizabeth Marbury (eds.): *The Soviet-Yugoslav Controversy, 1948-58: A Documentary Record*, New York, 1959.

Colaković, Rodoljub (ed.): *Pregled istorije Saveza komunista Jugoslavije* (Survey of the History of the League of Communists of Yugoslavia), Belgrade, 1963.

Djilas, Milovan: *Anatomy of a Moral: The Political Essays of Milovan Djilas*, New York, 1959.

Hoffman, George W. and Fred Warner Neal: *Yugoslavia and The New Communism*, New York, 1962.

*Political Report of the Central Committee of the Communist Party of Yugoslavia*, Report to the 5th congress of the KPJ by Josip Broz Tito, Belgrade, 1949.

*Yugoslavia's Way: The Program of the League of Communists of Yugoslavia*, New York, 1958.

MILORAD M. DRACHKOVITCH

1. Nikola Grulovič, *Jugosloveni u ratu i Oktobarskoj revoluciji*, Belgrade, 1962, p. 282.

2. Danilo Knezevič et al. (eds.), *Četrdeset godina: Zbornik sećanja aktivista jugoslovenskog revolucionarnog radnickog pokreta*, vol. I, Belgrade, 1945, pp. 41-49.

3. Jovan Marjanović, *Potsetnik iz istorije Komunisticke partije Jugoslavije*, Belgrade, 1953, p. 43.

4. Milovan Djilas, *Conversations with Stalin*, New York, 1962, p. 34.

5. The KPJ had 1,500 members at the end of 1937, 6,000 in November 1940, 8,000 in May 1941, and 12,000 in July 1941. Marjanović, *op. cit.*, pp. 56, 64; Moma Marković and Ivan Laća, *Organizacioni razvitak Komunističke partije Jugoslavije*, Belgrade, 1953, pp. 69, 80, 83. These figures do not include the membership of the Alliance of the Communist Youth of Yugoslavia, which in September 1940 had 18,000 members and in July 1941, 30,000. *Report of the Central Committee of the Communist Party of Yugoslavia on the Organization Work of the CPY* [KPJ], Report to the 5th congress of the KPJ, by Aleksander Ranković, Belgrade, 1948, pp. 26, 32.

6. *Yugoslavia's Way: The Program of the League of Communists of Yugoslavia*, New York, 1958, pp. 94-103.

7. *Political Report of the Central Committee of the Communist Party of Yugoslavia*, Report to the 5th congress of the KPJ, by Josip Broz Tito, Belgrade, 1948, p. 117.

8. Vladimir Dedijer, *Dnevnik*, vol. I, Belgrade, 1945, p. 360.

9. Rodoljub Čolaković (ed.), *Pregled istorije Saveza komunista Jugoslavije*, Belgrade, 1963, p. 454.

10. *The Soviet-Yugoslav Dispute: Text of the Published Correspondence*, London, 1948, p. 37.

11. Robert H. Bass and Elizabeth Marbury (eds.), *The Soviet-Yugoslav Controversy, 1948-58: A Documentary Record*, New York, 1959, pp. 41-46.

12. George W. Hoffman and Fred Warner Neal, *Yugoslavia and the New Communism*, New York, 1962, p. 212.

13. This statement is taken from the so-called Belgrade declaration, signed by Khrushchev and Tito on June 2, 1955. It was reaffirmed a year later in Moscow, and again in the official communiqué following the Khrushchev-Tito meeting in Rumania early in August 1957.

14. Milovan Djilas, *Anatomy of a Moral: The Political Essays of Milovan Djilas*, New York, 1959, p. 137.

15. *New York Times*, international edition, December 25, 1954.

16. *Komunist* (Belgrade), January-February 1954, pp. 8-9.

17. *Komunist*, June 14, 1962.

18. *Komunist*, April 28, 1966.

# APPENDIX

## LIST OF COMMUNIST PARTIES BY COUNTRY, WITH NAME CHANGES, 1918-1965

Prepared by Witold S. Sworakowski

*Note:* An asterisk indicates that the party was active at the end of 1965.

### ALBANIA
| | |
|---|---|
| 1928 | Albanian communist group founded in Moscow. |
| 1941 | Albanian Communist Party founded. |
| 1948* | Adopted name Albanian Party of Labor. |

### ALGERIA
| | |
|---|---|
| 1920 | At Tours congress of French Socialist Party its Algerian Federation voted to join Comintern and become Federation of French Communist Party. |
| 1935 | Federation transformed into Communist Party of Algeria. |
| 1936-62 | Adopted name Algerian Communist Party; repeatedly outlawed and reinstated. |
| 1965 | Had disintegrated. |

### ANGOLA
| | |
|---|---|
| 1965* | Angolan Communist Party founded; operated underground and in exile. |

### ARGENTINA
| | |
|---|---|
| 1918 Jan. | International Socialist Party founded (probolshevik). |
| 1918 Dec. | Changed name to Communist Party of Argentina. |
| 1963 | Outlawed. |
| 1964* | Reappeared under same name. |

### ARMENIA
| | |
|---|---|
| 1920 | Communist Party of Armenia founded. |
| 1922* | Became pseudo-autonomous part of Russian Communist Party (Bolshevik). |

### AUSTRALIA
| | |
|---|---|
| 1920 | Communist Party of Australia founded. |
| 1922 | Changed name to United Communist Party of Australia. |
| 1922-44 | Adopted name Communist Party of Australia, Section of the Communist International. |
| 1944-51 | Changed name to Australian Communist Party. |
| 1951* | Returned to name Communist Party of Australia. |

### AUSTRIA
| | |
|---|---|
| 1918 | Communist Party of German Austria founded. |

## AUSTRIA (continued)

| | |
|---|---|
| 1919 | Changed name to Communist Party of Austria. |
| 1933 | Dissolved by government; went underground. |
| 1945* | Reemerged into legality. |

## BELGIUM

| | |
|---|---|
| 1921 | Communist Party of Belgium founded. |
| 1940-45 | During German occupation illegal, underground. |
| 1945* | Reappeared after war. |
| 1962* | Belgian Communist Party, Marxist-Leninist founded (pro-Chinese). |

## BELORUSSIA

| | |
|---|---|
| 1918* | Communist Party of Belorussia founded as part of Russian Communist Party (Bolshevik). |

## BOLIVIA

| | |
|---|---|
| 1938* | Revolutionary Workers' Party founded (Trotskyist). |
| 1940 | Party of the Revolutionary Left (PIR) founded; disintegrated in early 1950s. |
| 1950* | Communist Party of Bolivia founded by dissidents from PIR. |
| 1952* | PIR revived. |

## BRAZIL

| | |
|---|---|
| 1922 | Communist Party of Brazil founded. |
| 1960* | Changed name to Brazilian Communist Party. |
| 1961* | Communist Party of Brazil founded (pro-Chinese). |

## BULGARIA

| | |
|---|---|
| 1903 | Workers' Social Democratic Party (Narrow Socialists) founded. |
| 1919 | Renamed Bulgarian Communist Party. |
| 1924 | Dissolved by government. |
| 1927 | Reappeared as legal Workers' Party. |
| 1934 | Dissolved by government; continued illegally as Bulgarian Workers' Party (Communist). |
| 1948* | After seizure of power reappeared in the open and changed name to Bulgarian Communist Party. |

## BURMA

| | |
|---|---|
| 1939? | Burma Communist Party founded (date uncertain). |
| 1946 | Split in Burma Communist Party results in founding of Communist Party of Burma (former called "white flags," latter "red flags"). |
| 1965* | Both parties active underground, pro-Chinese. |

## CAMBODIA

| | |
|---|---|
| 1930 | Communist Party of Indochina founded, active in Cambodia. |

## CAMBODIA (continued)

| | |
|---|---|
| 1951 | People's Party of Khmer founded, active underground. |
| 1955 | Part of this party appeared as legal Masses Party. |
| 1960-62* | Repressions against communist underground indicated that People's Party of Khmer still active. |

## CAMEROON

| | |
|---|---|
| 1947 | Cameroon People's Union founded, affiliated with African Democratic Rally. |
| 1955 | Dissolved by government; went underground. |
| 1960 | Dissolution repealed; party revived. |
| 1961* | Split into pro-Soviet and pro-Chinese factions. |

## CANADA

| | |
|---|---|
| 1921 | Communist Party of Canada founded as illegal party. |
| 1922-24 | Workers' Party of Canada active as legal branch of Communist Party of Canada. |
| 1924-31 | Communist Party of Canada legalized. |
| 1931-34 | Government repressions forced party underground. |
| 1934-40 | Returned to legal activities. |
| 1940 | Banned by government. |
| 1943 | Revived as Labor Progressive Party. |
| 1946* | Returned to name Communist Party of Canada. |
| 1947* | Split in party produced Progressive Workers' Movement (pro-Chinese). |

## CEYLON

| | |
|---|---|
| 1935 | Ceylon Equality Party founded; shortly thereafter came under Trotsky's influence. |
| 1942 | Dissolved by government. |
| 1943 | Ceylon Communist Party founded (Stalinist). |
| 1946 | Ceylon Equality Party revived (Trotskyist). |
| 1964* | Changed name to Revolutionary Ceylon Equality Party. |
| 1964* | Ceylon Communist Party split into pro-Soviet and pro-Chinese factions. |

## CHILE

| | |
|---|---|
| 1912 | Socialist Workers' Party founded. |
| 1922 | Changed name to Communist Party of Chile. |
| 1948-52 | Outlawed by government. |
| 1952* | Returned to legal operations. |

## CHINA (pre-1949)

| | |
|---|---|
| 1921 | Chinese Communist Party founded; never outlawed, but persecuted by warlords. |

518　APPENDIX

## CHINA, PEOPLE'S REPUBLIC OF

| | |
|---|---|
| 1949* | Chinese Communist Party became ruling party. |

## CHINA, REPUBLIC OF (Taiwan)

| | |
|---|---|
| 1965* | Remnants of Chinese Communist Party allegedly active underground. |

## COLOMBIA

| | |
|---|---|
| 1926 | Socialist Revolutionary Party founded; joined Comintern in 1928. |
| 1930 | Changed name to Communist Party of Colombia. |
| 1944 | Adopted name Social Democratic Party of Colombia. |
| 1947* | Returned to name Communist Party of Colombia. |
| 1964* | Communist Party of Colombia, Marxist-Leninist founded (pro-Chinese). |

## COSTA RICA

| | |
|---|---|
| 1929 | Communist Party of Costa Rica founded. |
| 1943* | Changed name to Popular Vanguard Party. |

## CUBA

| | |
|---|---|
| 1923 | Communist Group of Havana founded. |
| 1925 | Adopted name Communist Party of Cuba. |
| 1935 | Went underground. |
| 1937 | Communist front Revolutionary Union Party founded. |
| 1938 | Communist Party of Cuba legalized. |
| 1940 | Communist Party of Cuba and Revolutionary Union Party merged to form Revolutionary Union Communist Party. |
| 1944 | Changed name to Popular Socialist Party (PSP). |
| 1953 | PSP outlawed. |
| 1959 | After Castro's takeover PSP again legal. |
| 1960-64 | Integration of PSP and Twenty-sixth of July movement. |
| 1964 | United Party of the Socialist Revolution formed. |
| 1965* | Changed name to Communist Party of Cuba. |

## CYPRUS

| | |
|---|---|
| 1926 | Communist Party of Cyprus founded. |
| 1931 | Outlawed by British authorities. |
| 1935-36 | Disintegrated in Cyprus; London group remained active. |
| 1941 | Reappeared in Cyprus as Reform Party of the Working People. |
| 1955-59 | Party illegal; operated underground. |
| 1959* | After Cyprus became independent, party again legalized. |

## CZECHOSLOVAKIA

| | |
|---|---|
| 1920-21 | Several communist groups formed in Czechoslovakia. |
| 1921 | Communist Party of Czechoslovakia founded. |
| 1938-45 | Outlawed, first by Czechoslovak government, later by German occupation authorities. |
| 1945* | Communist Party of Czechoslovakia revived. |

## DENMARK

| | |
|---|---|
| 1920 | Danish Communist Party founded. |
| 1940-45 | Underground during German occupation. |
| 1945* | Reappeared as legal party. |
| 1964* | Split in party produces pro-Chinese Communist Working Circle. |

## DOMINICAN REPUBLIC

| | |
|---|---|
| 1939 | Spanish civil war refugees formed communist group. |
| 1942 | Dominican Communist Party founded clandestinely. |
| 1945 | Repressions against party; leaders exiled. |
| 1946 | Party reestablished legally as Dominican Popular Socialist Party. |
| 1947 | Outlawed; leaders exiled; party disintegrated. |
| 1961 | Communists established legal front Dominican Popular Movement; outlawed same year. |
| 1965* | During April coup members of front identified themselves as members of Dominican Communist Party. |

## ECUADOR

| | |
|---|---|
| 1928 | Left faction of Ecuadorean Socialist Party joined Comintern. |
| 1931 | Established itself as Communist Party of Ecuador; operated clandestinely. |
| 1944 | During May revolution achieved legal status. |
| 1963* | Outlawed, but continued underground operations. |

**EGYPT** (see United Arab Republic)

## EL SALVADOR

| | |
|---|---|
| Mid-1920s | Communist Party of El Salvador began as part of proposed Communist Party of Central America (Salvadoran communists later claimed their party formed in 1930). |
| 1965* | Operated as small underground group. |

## ESTONIA

| | |
|---|---|
| 1917 | Estonian Section of Russian bolshevik party founded in Russia. |
| 1920 | Estonian Communist Party founded; remained illegal until 1940. |
| 1940* | After Soviet occupation revived as legal party and incorporated as Section into Communist Party of the Soviet Union. |

## FINLAND

| | |
|---|---|
| 1918 | Finnish Communist Party founded in Moscow; illegal in Finland but active underground. |
| 1920 May | Socialist Workers' Party founded in Finland as legal communist front; outlawed shortly afterward. |
| 1920 June | Finnish Socialist Workers' Party founded as new legal communist front. |
| 1939-40 | In Soviet-occupied part of Finland (Terijoki), Finnish Communist Party acted for short time as ruling party. |
| 1944* | Legalization of Finnish Communist Party. |

## FRANCE

| | |
|---|---|
| 1921 | French Communist Party founded. |
| 1939-44 | Outlawed, first by French government, later by German occupation authorities; in 1943 party declared allegiance to de Gaulle's Free France. |
| 1944* | Revived activities in France. |
| 1964* | Group of party members excluded from party for pro-Chinese deviation founded Federation of Marxist-Leninist Circles. |

## GEORGIA

| | |
|---|---|
| 1920 | Bolshevik Party of Georgia founded when Georgia independent. |
| 1921* | Communist Party (Bolshevik) of Georgia founded after occupation of Georgia by Soviet army; became section of Communist Party of the Soviet Union; dropped designation "Bolshevik" in 1952. |

## GERMANY

| | |
|---|---|
| 1918 | Communist Party of Germany (Spartacus League)—KPD—founded; designation "Spartacus League" soon dropped. |
| 1919 | Split in party produced new Communist Workers' Party of Germany; dissolved shortly thereafter. |
| 1920 | Left wing of Independent Social Democratic Party of Germany merged with KPD to form United Communist Party of Germany; designation "United" soon dropped. |
| 1933-45 | KPD outlawed; operated underground and abroad. |
| 1945 | KPD revived in East Germany under Soviet occupation and in West Germany under Allied occupation. |
| 1946* | Socialist Unity Party of Germany resulted from merger of KPD and Social Democratic Party of Germany in East Germany. |
| 1956* | KPD in West Germany outlawed; went underground. |

## GREAT BRITAIN

| | |
|---|---|
| 1920* | Communist Party of Great Britain founded; never changed name; never outlawed. |

## GREECE

| | |
|---|---|
| 1918 | Socialist Workers' Party of Greece founded. |
| 1920 | Majority voted affiliation with Comintern and added "Communist" to name of party in parentheses. |
| 1924 | Changed name to Communist Party of Greece. |
| 1936-44 | Outlawed, first by Greek government, later by German occupation authorities; went underground; organized armed resistance against Axis forces. |
| 1944 Apr. | "Lebanon agreement" with exile government. |
| 1944 Oct. | After German withdrawal party reappeared as legal party. |
| 1947 | Outlawed by government; went underground; emigré centers of party continued activities. |
| 1951* | United Democratic Left founded as legal political party directed by clandestine Communist Party of Greece. |
| 1964* | Pro-Chinese faction of Communist Party of Greece started publication of journal. |

## GUADELOUPE

| | |
|---|---|
| 1944 | Guadeloupe Federation of French Communist Party founded. |
| 1958* | Adopted name Guadeloupe Communist Party. |

## GUATEMALA

| | |
|---|---|
| 1923 | Socialist Labor Unification founded. |
| 1924 | Changed name to Communist Party of Guatemala. |
| 1932-47 | Destroyed by government repression; remnants went underground or abroad. |
| 1947 | Democratic Vanguard formed as secret communist political group. |
| 1949 | Communist Party of Guatemala revived. |
| 1950 | Revolutionary Workers' Party of Guatemala founded as second communist party. |
| 1952 | Both parties united as Guatemalan Labor Party. |
| 1954* | New party outlawed; leaders exiled; underground party elements, supported by Cuba, organized guerrilla movement. |

## GUYANA

| | |
|---|---|
| 1950* | People's Progressive Party founded; although formally not a communist party, its leadership adhered to communist ideology, its domestic policy and international alignment indicated communist character. |

## HAITI

| | |
|---|---|
| 1930 | Communist Party of Haiti founded; disintegrated shortly afterward. |
| 1946 | Communist Party of Haiti founded again; disbanded in 1947. |
| 1947 | Popular Socialist Party founded; modeled after Cuban party. |

## HAITI (continued)

| | |
|---|---|
| 1949-50 | Completely destroyed by government repressions. |
| 1959* | Party of Popular Accord founded as legal communist party. |
| 1961* | People's National Liberation Party founded as successor to Popular Socialist Party; modeled after Cuban party. |

## HONDURAS

| | |
|---|---|
| 1927 | Communist Party of Honduras founded. |
| 1932 | Destroyed by government repressions. |
| 1944 | Democratic Revolutionary Party of Honduras founded as clandestine party. |
| 1948-53 | Operated openly; banned in 1953. |
| 1954 | Communist Party of Honduras revived; clandestine up to 1958, then open activities until military coup in 1963. |
| 1961* | Split in party produced Honduran Revolutionary Party as rival party; underground since 1963. |
| 1963* | Communist Party of Honduras forced underground by government repressions. |

## HUNGARY

| | |
|---|---|
| 1918 Mar. | Communist Party of Hungary founded in Moscow as section of Russian Communist Party. |
| 1918 Nov. | Communist Party of Hungary founded in Hungary; became ruling party in Hungarian Soviet Republic, Mar.-Aug. 1919. |
| 1919 | Became illegal after collapse of Hungarian Soviet Republic; continued underground and abroad. |
| 1922 | Dissolved by Comintern. |
| 1925 | Reorganized abroad; in Hungary active underground. |
| 1936 | Comintern disbanded intermediary and top-level party units in Hungary and moved party headquarters to Prague. |
| 1944 | Part reestablished as Hungarian Communist Party. |
| 1948 | Merged with Social Democratic Party to form Hungarian Workers' Party. |
| 1956* | This party reorganized and changed name to Hungarian Socialist Workers' Party. |

## ICELAND

| | |
|---|---|
| 1921 | Small faction of Social Democratic Party of Iceland affiliated with Comintern but ordered not to secede. |
| 1930* | Communist Party of Iceland founded after secession from Social Democratic Party. |
| 1938* | Left wing split off from Social Democratic Party and united with Communist Party of Iceland to form United Labor-Socialist Party of Iceland. |

## INDIA

| | |
|---|---|
| 1928 | Communist Party of India founded. |
| 1934-42 | Declared illegal; active underground. |
| 1942 | Legalized as a result of its pledge to support British war effort. |
| 1964 | Split in party; left faction formed separate organization claiming to be legitimate Communist Party of India; had pro-Chinese tendencies. |
| 1965* | Two parties with name Communist Party of India operated simultaneously. |

## INDONESIA

| | |
|---|---|
| 1914 | Marxist-oriented Indies Social Democratic Organization founded. |
| 1920 | Adopted name Communist Party of the Indies. |
| 1924 | Changed name to Communist Party of Indonesia. |
| 1927 | Banned by Dutch government. |
| 1932 | Started underground work. |
| 1942-45 | Underground struggle against Japanese occupation. |
| 1945 | Reestablished as open party; joined rebellion against Dutch. |
| 1949 | Indonesian independence brings legalization of party. |
| 1965 | Unsuccessful coup followed by stern repressions; party outlawed. |

## IRAN

| | |
|---|---|
| 1920 | First congress of Communist Party of Iran in Soviet-occupied territory. |
| 1931 | Iranian parliament passed law banning communist organizations; party went underground; leaders in exile. |
| 1941 | Communist movement reappeared as Masses Party of Iran, known also as Tudeh, operating in the open. |
| 1945 | In Azerbaijan province Tudeh replaced by Democratic Party of Iran as ruling party in Soviet Republic of Azerbaijan. |
| 1949 | Tudeh outlawed following attempt on life of Shah by party member. |
| 1951-53 | Operated in the open during Mossadegh regime. |
| 1954* | Again outlawed and repressed; went underground in Iran; groups abroad continued activities. |

## IRAQ

| | |
|---|---|
| 1934 | Committee to Combat Imperialism and Exploitation founded. |
| 1935 | Changed name to Communist Party of Iraq. |
| 1949 | Forced underground by government repressions. |
| 1958 | Brought into open activities by Qasim coup, but still not legal. |
| 1960 | Two communist parties legalized: Communist Party of Iraq and Party of People's Unity. |
| 1963* | Ba'th coup followed by "reign of terror" against communists; communists went underground; leadership of Communist Party of Iraq active abroad. |

## IRELAND

| | |
|---|---|
| 1933 | Communist Party of Ireland founded for Northern and Southern Ireland. |
| 1940* | Disbanded in southern Irish Free State by government; continued in Ulster under name Communist Party of Northern Ireland. |
| 1948 | Irish Workers' League founded in south. |
| 1962* | This party changed name to Irish Workers' Party. |

## ISRAEL

| | |
|---|---|
| 1919 | Workers of Zion founded. |
| 1920 | Splinter party—Socialist Workers' Party—founded; disintegrated in 1921. |
| 1922 | Palestinian Communist Party founded. |
| (?) | Communist Party of Palestine, radical antizionist splinter group of Palestinian Communist Party, active for short time (date uncertain). |
| 1939-48 | Palestinian Communist Party operated in separate Jewish and Arab groups. |
| 1943 | Arab communists formed All-Arab League for National Liberation. |
| 1948* | Palestinian Communist Party adopted name Israeli Communist Party (Maqī). |
| 1965* | Most Arabs left Maqī; formed party named New Communist List. |

## ITALY

| | |
|---|---|
| 1921 | Split in Italian Socialist Party resulted in founding of Italian Communist Party. |
| 1923-26 | Forced underground by fascist government repressions; leadership moved to France. |
| 1939 | Party headquarters moved from France to USSR. |
| 1945* | Party began operating both legally and covertly. |
| 1964 | Pro-Chinese faction emerged in party. |

## JAPAN

| | |
|---|---|
| 1922 | Japan Communist Party founded as illegal party. |
| 1945 | Legalized. |
| 1951 | Reduced to semilegal status by repressions; activities mostly underground. |
| 1956* | New leadership returned party to legal activities. |

## JORDAN

| | |
|---|---|
| 1951 | Communist Party of Jordan founded. |
| 1957* | Went underground when all political parties outlawed; leaders active abroad. |

## KAZAKHSTAN

| | |
|---|---|
| 1921 | Communist Party of Kazakhstan founded. |
| 1925* | Became regional organization of All-Union Communist Party (Bolshevik). |

## KIRGIZIA

| | |
|---|---|
| 1918 | Communist Party (Bolshevik) of Turkestan founded, with minimal participation of natives. |
| 1937* | Renamed Communist Party (Bolshevik) of Kirgizia; later dropped designation "Bolshevik." |

## KOREA (pre-1945)

| | |
|---|---|
| 1918 | Korean People's Socialist Party founded in Khabarovsk, Soviet Russia. |
| 1919 | Changed name to Korean Communist Party and moved headquarters to Vladivostok. |
| 1925 | Korean Communist Party founded in Seoul as illegal organization; decimated by Japanese government repressions; went underground. |
| 1930 | Chinese Communist Party absorbed Korean communists in Manchuria. |

## KOREA, DEMOCRATIC PEOPLE'S REPUBLIC OF (North)

| | |
|---|---|
| 1945 Oct. | Korean Communist Party legalized by Soviet occupation authorities. |
| 1945 Dec. | Name changed to North Korean Communist Party. |
| 1946 Mar. | Yenan returnees from New People's Party. |
| 1946 Aug. | These two parties merged, forming North Korean Workers' Party. |
| 1949* | This party and South Korean Workers' Party united to form Korean Workers' Party—ruling party in North Korea. |

## KOREA, REPUBLIC OF (South)

| | |
|---|---|
| 1945 Oct. | Korean Communist Party legalized by American occupation authorities. |
| 1946 | Merged with People's Party to form South Korean Workers' Party. |
| 1948 | Activities suppressed by government; went underground. |
| 1949* | United with North Korean Workers' Party to form Korean Workers' Party; active underground. |

## LAOS

| | |
|---|---|
| 1930 | Communist Party of Indochina founded; active in Laos; dissolved in 1945. |

## LAOS (continued)

1944-45 — Various local communist cells created for support of Laotian and Vietnamese guerrilla units operating on Laotian territory; Pathet Lao emerged as Laotian communist guerrilla unit.

1955* — Laotian People's Party held first congress; operated in the open in areas held by Pathet Lao and underground in other parts of Laos.

## LATVIA

1919 — Some elements of Latvian Social Democratic Workers' Party in Moscow founded Communist (Bolshevik) Party of Latvia; until 1940 party operated underground in Latvia.

1940 June — After occupation of Latvia by Soviet troops party came into the open.

1940 Oct.* — Incorporated as branch of All-Union Communist Party (Bolshevik); had dropped designation "Bolshevik."

## LEBANON

1924 — Lebanese People's Party founded.

1944* — Lebanese Communist Party emerged from division of Lebanese People's Party into separate Lebanese and Syrian parties.

## LESOTHO

1961* — Communist Party of Lesotho founded; operated as legal party.

## LITHUANIA

1918 — Social Democratic Workers' Party of Lithuania and Belorussia founded under German occupation; shortly renamed itself Communist Party of Lithuania and Belorussia.

1919 — Took refuge in Soviet Russia after Polish troops took Vilna.

1920 — Lithuanian Communist Party emerged as separate party with headquarters in Soviet Russia; in Lithuania operated underground until 1940.

1922 — Regional organization of Lithuanian Communist Party in Vilna transferred to Communist Party of Poland.

1940* — Lithuanian Communist Party came into the open after occupation of Lithuania by Soviet troops; shortly thereafter incorporated into All-Union Communist Party (Bolshevik).

## LUXEMBOURG

1921 — Split in Luxembourg Social Democratic Party resulted in founding of Communist Party of Luxembourg.

1940-45 — Went underground during German occupation; started armed resistance after German invasion of USSR.

1945* — Reappeared in the open after war; never changed name.

## MALAGASY REPUBLIC

1953 — Malagasy Union founded.

## MALAGASY (continued)
| | |
|---|---|
| 1956* | Adopted name Union of Malagasy People. |
| 1958* | Malagasy Communist Party founded (pro-Chinese). |

## MALAYA and SINGAPORE
| | |
|---|---|
| 1928 | South Seas Communist Party founded. |
| 1930* | Changed name to Communist Party of Malaya. |

## MARTINIQUE
| | |
|---|---|
| 1923 | Jean Jaures Communist Group founded. |
| 1925 | Became section of French Communist Party. |
| 1939 | Dissolved by French government. |
| 1944 | Revived as Martinican federation of French Communist Party. |
| 1957* | Became Martinican Communist Party. |

## MEXICO
| | |
|---|---|
| 1919 | Several communist groups founded. |
| 1920* | Mexican Communist Party founded. |
| 1940 | Dissidents founded Mexican Peasant-Worker Party. |
| 1948 | People's Party became pro-Soviet front party (led by Toledano). |
| 1960* | This party changed name to Socialist People's Party; in 1963 absorbed Mexican Peasant-Worker Party. |
| 1963* | Pro-Chinese members expelled from Mexican Communist Party founded Bolshevik Communist Party of Mexico. |

## MOROCCO
| | |
|---|---|
| 1936 | "Moroccan region" of French Communist Party founded. |
| 1939 | Dissolved by French authorities. |
| 1943 | Revived as Moroccan Communist Party. |
| 1952 | Outlawed; went underground. |
| 1956 | Legality restored when Morocco became independent. |
| 1959* | Dissolved by government; operated underground. |

## NEPAL
| | |
|---|---|
| 1949 | Communist Party of Nepal founded in Calcutta. |
| 1950 | Operated openly in Nepal. |
| 1952 | Outlawed. |
| 1956 | Granted legal status. |
| 1960* | Formally disbanded as ordered by government; operated more or less openly, but illegally. |
| 1962* | Dissident exiles in Banares (India) set up separate party organization. |

### NETHERLANDS

| | |
|---|---|
| 1918 | Communist Party of Holland founded. |
| 1935 | Renamed Communist Party of the Netherlands. |
| 1940-45 | Went underground during German occupation; conducted armed resistance after German invasion of USSR. |
| 1945* | Revived after war. |
| 1960?* | Marxist-Leninist Center of Holland founded (pro-Chinese). |

### NEW ZEALAND

| | |
|---|---|
| 1921 | Communist Party of New Zealand founded. |
| 1924 | Became section of Communist Party of Australia. |
| 1926* | Communist Party of New Zealand against independent organization; in mid-1960s supported Peking. |

### NICARAGUA

| | |
|---|---|
| 1937 | Socialist Party of Nicaragua founded. |
| 1939-45 | Suppressed by government; leaders exiled; then party allowed to resume activities during war. |
| 1945* | Outlawed; at first continued operating openly, then went underground. |

### NIGER REPUBLIC

| | |
|---|---|
| 1951 | Niger Democratic Union founded. |
| 1958* | Changed name to Independence Party (Sawaba). |

### NIGERIA

| | |
|---|---|
| 1963* | Socialist Workers' and Farmers' Party founded. |

### NORWAY

| | |
|---|---|
| 1923 | Split in Norwegian Labor Party resulted in founding of Communist Party of Norway. |
| 1940-45 | Went underground during German occupation; started armed resistance after German invasion of USSR. |
| 1945* | Revived after war. |

### OUTER MONGOLIA

| | |
|---|---|
| 1921 | Mongolian People's Party held first congress in Kiakhta, Soviet Russia. |
| 1924* | Changed name to Mongolian People's Revolutionary Party. |

### PAKISTAN

| | |
|---|---|
| 1928 | Communist Party of Pakistan founded. |
| 1954* | Outlawed; up to end of 1965 remained illegal, but was active underground. |

### PALESTINE (see Israel)

## PANAMA

| | |
|---|---|
| 1930 | Communist Party of Panama founded. |
| 1944 | Changed name to Party of the People. |
| 1953* | Outlawed; operated underground. |

## PARAGUAY

| | |
|---|---|
| 1928 | Paraguayan Communist Party founded. |
| 1936* | Outlawed; communists allowed to work freely during brief interludes between regimes. |
| 1963* | Paraguayan Leninist Communist Party founded (pro-Chinese); operated illegally. |

## PERU

| | |
|---|---|
| 1928 | Peruvian Socialist Party founded. |
| 1930 | Renamed Peruvian Communist Party. |
| 1948-56 | Suppressed; subsequently declined. |
| 1963* | Movement of the Revolutionary Left founded (Castroist). |
| 1964* | Pro-Chinese dissidents "expelled" pro-Soviet faction, thus creating two parties with same name—Peruvian Communist Party; both active illegally at end of 1965. |

## PHILIPPINES

| | |
|---|---|
| 1919 | Communist-influenced Union of Filipino Tenants (since 1924 National Union of Peasants in the Philippines) organized; absorbed into Huk resistance movement in 1942. |
| 1930 | Communist Party of the Philippines founded. |
| 1932 | Declared illegal by supreme court. |
| 1938 | Legal status restored; merged with Socialist Party and Chinese Bureau (branch of Chinese Communist Party). |
| 1941 | Organized guerrilla forces known as Huks (later People's Liberation Army) in anticipation of Japanese occupation. |
| 1948 | Huks outlawed; went underground. |
| 1957* | Communist Party of the Philippines and allied organizations again outlawed; never returned to legality; operated underground. |

## POLAND

| | |
|---|---|
| 1918 | Communist Workers' Party of Poland founded; refused to ask for legalization; operated underground. |
| 1925 | Changed name to Communist Party of Poland. |
| 1938 | Disbanded by Comintern. |
| 1941 | Revived in Moscow as Polish Workers' Party. |
| 1942 | Polish Workers' Party "founded" in Warsaw. |
| 1948* | After merger with Polish Socialist Party renamed Polish United Workers' Party. |

## PORTUGAL

| | |
|---|---|
| 1921* | Portuguese Communist Party founded; outlawed several times but never changed name. |
| 1964* | Pro-Chinese dissidents formed "open" People's Action Front and "closed" Marxist-Leninist Committee. |
| 1964* | Portuguese emigrés in Paris founded pro-Chinese Portuguese Revolutionary Liberation Group. |

## RÉUNION

| | |
|---|---|
| 1949 | Réunion member federation of French Communist Party founded. |
| 1959* | Changed name to Réunion Communist Party. |

## RUMANIA

| | |
|---|---|
| 1921 | Rumanian Communist Party founded; operated underground until 1944; later legal. |
| 1948 | Changed name to Rumanian Workers' Party. |
| 1965* | Returned to name Rumanian Communist Party. |

## SAN MARINO

| | |
|---|---|
| 1945* | San Marino Communist Party founded; never changed name; never outlawed. |

## SARAWAK

| | |
|---|---|
| 1959* | Sarawak United People's Party founded—legal front for communist underground organizations; no communist party created. |

## SENEGAL

| | |
|---|---|
| 1957 | African Independence Party founded as first French West African party to demand immediate African independence from France. |
| 1962* | Began operating as Senegalese party only; banned same year; continued underground activities both at home and abroad. |

## SINGAPORE (see Malaya)

## SLOVAKIA

| | |
|---|---|
| 1938-44 | Communist Party of Slovakia founded after Slovakia declared independence; operated underground during war; in 1944 organized uprising against German occupants. |
| 1945* | Came into the open as autonomous part of Communist Party of Czechoslovakia after occupation by Soviet troops. |

## SOUTH AFRICA

| | |
|---|---|
| 1921 | Communist Party of Africa founded. |
| 1950 | Dissolved itself just before being officially outlawed. |
| 1953* | South African Communist Party founded as illegal, underground party; suppressed by government; by 1965 largely emigré organization. |

## SPAIN

| | |
|---|---|
| 1920 Apr. | Federation of Socialist Youth adopted name Spanish Communist Party. |
| 1920 July | Secessionists from Spanish Socialist Labor Party founded Spanish Communist Labor Party. |
| 1921 | Above two parties merged as Communist Party of Spain; outlawed several times and forced underground, but never changed name. |
| 1932 | Trotskyist group—Communist Left—established by dissenters from party; merged with Peasant Workers' Bloc to form Trotskyist party—Workers' Party of Marxist Unification (POUM); operated underground. |
| 1964* | Split in Communist Party of Spain resulted in establishment of two pro-Peking organizations: Revolutionary Communist Party and "Spanish-Marxist-Leninist" faction. |
| 1965* | Communist Party of Spain illegal in Spain; operated underground with leadership abroad; remnants of POUM also active underground. |

## SUDAN

| | |
|---|---|
| 1947 | Sudanese Communist Party founded; operated semilegally and legally; mostly underground. |
| 1965* | Split into pro-Soviet and pro-Chinese factions; both operated underground. |

## SWEDEN

| | |
|---|---|
| 1919 | Social Democratic Left Party of Sweden joined Comintern. |
| 1921* | Changed name to Communist Party of Sweden. |
| 1929-34 | Split in party produced two communist parties operating simultaneously under same name; Comintern recognized minority group; majority group abandoned communist orientation. |
| 1953* | New split produced Communist Workers' Federation of Sweden; later turned pro-Chinese. |

## SWITZERLAND

| | |
|---|---|
| 1921 | Communist Party of Switzerland founded. |
| 1940 | Outlawed. |
| 1944* | Revived as Labor Party of Switzerland; active since then. |
| 1954 | Progressive Party founded by Nicole, who had been expelled from Labor Party. |
| 1963* | Splinter group from Labor Party founded pro-Chinese Swiss Communist Party. |
| 1964* | Expelled members of Swiss Communist Party created Romansch Federation of Swiss Communists and Organization of Marxist-Leninists of Switzerland, both pro-Chinese. |

## SYRIA

| | |
|---|---|
| 1944* | Syrian Communist Party emerged from division of Lebanese People's Party into separate Lebanese and Syrian parties; illegal; operated underground. |

## TADZHIKISTAN

| | |
|---|---|
| 1918 | Communist Party of Turkestan founded. |
| 1924 | Regional communist organizations tied to Russian Communist Party (Bolshevik) when Tadzhikistan became autonomous SSR. |
| 1929* | Regional party organization transformed into adjunct of All-Union Communist Party (Bolshevik) when Tadzhikistan proclaimed union republic. |

## THAILAND

| | |
|---|---|
| 1942 | Communist Party of Thailand founded. |
| 1952* | Outlawed; operated underground. |

## TUNISIA

| | |
|---|---|
| 1920 | Tunisian Federation of French Communist Party founded. |
| 1934 | Became Communist Party of Tunisia. |
| 1939 | Dissolved by French authorities. |
| 1943 | Resumed legal activities. |
| 1963* | Outlawed by Tunisian authorities; continued operating clandestinely. |

## TURKEY

| | |
|---|---|
| 1918 | Executive Committee of Turkish Socialist-Communists established in Moscow; in 1920 moved to Baku; changed name to Turkish Communist Party; eventually absorbed by communist movement in Turkey. |
| 1919 | Turkish Workers' and Peasants' Party founded in Istanbul; suspended activities in 1920 after Istanbul occupied by Allied forces. |
| 1920 | Turkish Communist Party founded in Istanbul; illegal, acted underground. |
| 1920 Dec. | People's Communist Party of Turkey founded in Ankara, with government approval; suppressed in 1922; members joined Turkish Communist Party in Istanbul. |
| 1946 | Turkish Socialist Workers' and Peasants' Party formed as legal front; banned in Dec. 1946. |
| 1965* | Turkish Communist Party continued to operate underground. |

## TURKMENISTAN

| | |
|---|---|
| 1920* | Communist Party of Turkmenistan founded as section of Russian Communist Party (Bolshevik). |

APPENDIX 533

## UKRAINE

| | |
|---|---|
| 1918 Apr. | Communist Party (Bolshevik) of the Ukraine founded, independent from Russian Communist Party (Bolshevik). |
| 1918 July | Became autonomous part of Russian party. |
| 1919* | Became regional organization within Russian party; later dropped designation "Bolshevik." |

## UNION OF SOVIET SOCIALIST REPUBLICS[1]

| | |
|---|---|
| 1903-4 | Russian Social Democratic Labor Party split into "bolshevik" and "menshevik" factions. |
| 1918 | After becoming ruling party of Russia, "bolshevik" faction adopted name Russian Communist Party (Bolshevik). |
| 1925 | Changed name to All-Union Communist Party (Bolshevik). |
| 1952* | Changed name to Communist Party of the Soviet Union. |

## UNITED ARAB REPUBLIC

| | |
|---|---|
| 1921 | Communist Party of Egypt founded. |
| 1923-25 | Suppressed by British authorities; disintegrated. |
| 1947 | Communist front Democratic National Liberation Movement founded. |
| 1948 | Front ceased activities; leaders arrested; movement disintegrated. |
| 1958 | Unified (Second) Communist Party of Egypt founded. |
| 1965 | Dissolved itself. |

## UNITED STATES OF AMERICA

| | |
|---|---|
| 1919 | Two parties founded simultaneously: Communist Party of America and Communist Labor Party; both driven underground in early 1920 by government repressions. |
| 1920 | United Communist Party founded. |
| 1921 May | Another Communist Party of America founded; in Jan. 1922 split into two parties with same name. |
| 1921 Dec. | Before split, underground Communist Party of America set up open, legal Workers' Party of America. |
| 1922 Feb. | Underground Communist Labor Party set up open, legal party—United Toilers of America. |
| 1923 | Communists emerged from underground and joined forces in legal Workers' Party of America. |
| 1925 | This party became Workers' (Communist) Party of America. |

1. See also Armenia, Belorussia, Estonia, Georgia, Kazakhstan, Kirgizia, Latvia, Lithuania, Tadzhikistan, Turkmenistan, Ukraine, and Uzbekistan.

## UNITED STATES OF AMERICA (continued)

| | |
|---|---|
| 1926 | Changed name to Communist Party of the United States of America. |
| 1944 | Changed name to Communist Political Association. |
| 1945* | Returned to name Communist Party of the United States of America (CPUSA). |

*Communist opposition parties:*

| | |
|---|---|
| 1928* | After expulsion from CPUSA for echoing Trotsky's views, James P. Cannon founded Communist League of America (Opposition), known as "left opposition." From this party Socialist Workers' Party later developed; in 1965 still militant Trotskyist party. Three groups split off from Socialist Workers' Party: Spartacists, American Committee for the Fourth International, and Workers' World Party. |
| 1929-40 | After expulsion from CPUSA for falling into Moscow's disfavor, Jay Lovestone and associates founded Communist Party (Majority Group), known as "right opposition"; party later changed name to Communist Party of the United States of America (Opposition), then to Independent Labor League of America; disbanded in 1940. |
| 1961* | Pro-Chinese faction expelled from CPUSA founded Progressive Labor Party; in 1965 held first convention. |
| 1965* | Two small offshoots from CPUSA established themselves as Provisional Organizing Committee for a Marxist-Leninist Party (with pro-Stalinist slant) and Communist Party of the United States, Marxist-Leninist (with pro-Chinese tendencies). |

## URUGUAY

| | |
|---|---|
| 1920* | Communist Party of Uruguay founded; never changed name; never outlawed. |

## UZBEKISTAN (including Bukhara and Khiva)

| | |
|---|---|
| 1918 May? | Bukharan Communist Party founded in Soviet Russian territory. |
| 1918 June | Communist Party (Bolshevik) of Turkestan founded with predominantly Russian membership. |
| 1920 | Khoresmian Communist Party founded in Khiva. |
| 1922 | Bukharan and Khoresmian parties merged with Russian Communist Party (Bolshevik). |
| 1925* | Communist Party of Uzbekistan founded as section of Russian party. |

## VENEZUELA

| | |
|---|---|
| 1931* | Communist Party of Venezuela founded; outlawed on several occasions, but never changed name. |

## VIETNAM

| | |
|---|---|
| 1930 | Communist Party of Indochina founded in Hong Kong by merger of various communist groups. |
| 1941 | Re-formed as League for the Independence of Vietnam (known as Viet Minh). |
| 1951 | Changed name to Vietnam Workers' Party. |
| 1954* | After partition of Vietnam, Viet Minh was communist party in North Vietnam, whereas Viet Cong San (better known as Viet Cong) was underground communist party in South Vietnam. |

## YUGOSLAVIA

| | |
|---|---|
| 1918 | Yugoslav section of Russian Communist Party (Bolshevik) founded in Soviet Russia. |
| 1919 Mar. | Yugoslav Communist Revolutionary League of Pelagićevci founded in Srem, Yugoslavia. |
| 1919 Apr. | Socialist Workers' Party of Yugoslavia (Communist) founded. |
| 1920 | Changed name to Communist Party of Yugoslavia; operated underground until 1945, when it became ruling party. |
| 1952* | Changed name to League of Communists of Yugoslavia. |

# INDEX OF PERSONS

Aaltonen, Aimo, 128, 129
Aarons, L., 20
Abbas, Ferhat, 9, 10
'Abbud, Ibrahim, 412, 413, 414
'Abd al-'Aziz, Muhammad, 459
'Abd Allah, Amir, King of Transjordan, 251
'Abd al-Nasir, Gamal, 460
'Abd al-Qadir Isma'il, *see* Isma'il al-Bustani, 'Abd al-Qadir
Abd el-Kader, Hadj Ali, 7
Abd el-Krim, 138, 326
Abd er-Rahmane, Djemard, 9
Abern, Martin, 463
Abrahamov, 226
Achet, Ferhat, 431
Ackermann, Anton, 156, 159
Acosta Sálas, Raúl, 357
Adame, Manuel, 396
Adenauer, Konrad, 158
Adhikari, Man Mohan, 330
'Adil, Salam (*pseud. of* Husain Radwi [Radawi]), 231
Adzhubei, Aleksei I., 454
Afana, Osende, 56
Aguirre Cerda, Pedro, 276
Aidit, Dwipa Nusantara, 201-4 *passim*
Alamuti, Nureddin, 225
Alaoui, Mamoun, 329
Alaverdian, Stepan, 15
Alavi, Bozorg, 225
Aleksa-Angarietis, Zigmas, *see* Angarietis, Zigmas Aleksa-
Alexander, King of Yugoslavia, 505
Alexis, Jacques Stephen, 183, 285
Alimin (Indonesian), 201, 202
Allen, James, 359
Almeida, Juan, 103
Alpári, Gyula, 186, 191
Alvarez, A., 14
Amado, Jorge, 290
Amatya, Tulsi Lal, 332
Amazonas, João, 41
Amendola, Giorgio, 242
Amsterdam, Saul (*pseud.* Henryk Henrykowski), 363, 365
Ananun, 16
Andersson, Nils, 422, 424
Andrade Rodríguez, Juan, 395
Andressen, Nigol, 124
Andrews, *see* Sim, Leo
Andrews, William H., 388-91 *passim*
Anev, Svetko, 45
Angarietis, Zigmas Aleksa-, 308-11 *passim*
Angenforth, Jupp, 158
Annenkov, Boris V., 255
Antel, Sadrettin Celâl, 434
Anvelt, Jaan, 123, 124
Apfelbaum, *see* Zinoviev, Grigorii F
Appel, Gotfred, 117
Apresoft, 72
Aragon, Louis, 146-47
Arahata Kanson, 243

Arbenz, Jacobo, 177, 281
Archimède, Gerty, 174, 175, 176
Arevalo, J., 472
Arévalo, Juan José, 177, 281
'Arif, 'Abd al-Salam, 231
Arismendi, Rodney, 267
Ariyaratne, M. G. W., 60
Arnault, Jacques, 315
Arroyo, Vicente, 395
Assadi, Abol Ghassem, 225
Assalé, Charles, 54
Atabegian, 16
Atatürk, Kemal, 434, 435, 436
Aung San, 48, 49
Ausart, Gustave, 146
Avigdor, *see* Kossai, Yehiel
Avila Camacho, Manuel, 325
Awerbuch, W., 235
Axelrod, B. P., 445
Aydemir, Şevket Süreyya, 437
Ayub Khan, Mohammad, 353
al-Azhari, Isma'il, 412
Āzis, *see* Roziņś, Fricis

Ba Hein, 48
Ba Maw, 48
Ba Nyein, 49
Ba Tin, *see* Goshal, H.
Babu, *see* Mohammed, Abdul Rahman
Bach, Lazar, 390
Bacílek, Karol, 110, 112
Badoglio, Pietro, 240
Bahrami, Mohammed, 225
Bakary, Djibo, 341, 342, 410
Bakdash, Khalid, 301-5 *passim*
Baker, C., 18
Bakulin, 72
Bakunin, Mikhail, 98
Balan, 318
Baliño, Carlos, 98, 99, 268, 272
Ballan, Sam, 466
Banda, Hastings, 406
Bandaranaike, S. W. R. D., 61
Bandaranaike, Sirimavo, 61
Bao Dai, 479, 480
Barata, Agildo, 41
Barbé, Henri, 138, 139
Barbé, Raymond, 315, 379
Barbusse, Henri, 435
Baret, Gervais, 380
Barr, Andrew, 234
Barthe, Obdulio, 267, 268, 355, 356
Barthel, *see* Chaintron, Jean
al-Barzani, Mulla Mustafa, 231
Baştımar, Zeki, *see* Demir, Yakup
Bästlein, Bernhard, 155
Basu, Jyoti, 198
Batista, Fulgencio, 100-104 *passim*, 278, 284
  coup of Mar. 1952, 101
  and Communist Party of Cuba, 100
  outlaws communist party, 102
Bauer, Otto, 22
Beasley, J., 19

## INDEX OF PERSONS

Bebel, August, 154
Becerra, Gustavo, 120
Bedacht, Max, 462
Beelen, René, 33, 35
Belaev, N. I., 454
Belaúnde Terry, Fernando, 357
Belishova, Liri, 5
Bell, Thomas, 164, 168
Ben Ali, Mohammed, 430
Ben Barka, Mehdi, 329
Ben Bella, Ahmed, 11
Ben Lahoucine, Haddaoui ben Mohammed, 328
Ben Mustapha, Abd al-Hammid, 433
Beneš, Eduard, 110, 111
Benn, Brindley, 180
Bennet, A. J., see Goldfarb, Max
Ben Youssef, Salah, 432
Bereanu, Bernard, 222
Berger, Joseph, 301
Beria (Biriya), Mohammed, 226
Beriia, Lavrentii P., 72, 148, 149, 311, 449, 450
  executed, 450
Berlinguer, Enrico, 493
Bernal, Jesús, 324
Bernal, John D., 490
Bernard, Zenon, 312
Berton, André, 327
Bertz, Paul, 154
Besse, Guy, 147
Betancourt, Rómulo, 95, 270
Bhashani, Maulana, 353
Bierut, Bolesław (pseud. Rutkowski), 366, 367
Billoux, François, 139, 141, 142, 146, 147, 175
Biriya, Mohammed, see Beria Mohammed
Bischot, Chris, 337
Bissol, Démétrius, 321
Bitossi, Renato, 502
Bittleman, Alexander, 462
Blagoev, Dimitŭr, 42-43
Blanco, Hugh, 134
Blanco, J., 472
Bliukher, V. K., see Blücher, V. K.
Blücher, V. K (pseud. Galen), 72
Blum, Léon, 136, 140, 141
Bogdo Gegen, 349
Bognot, Cirilio, 359
Boiteau, Pierre, 314, 315
Bolívar, Cayetano, 397
Bombacci, Nicola, 238
Bonomi, Ivanoe, 240
Bordiga, Amadeo, 238, 239
Borilă, Petre, 381
Borodin, Michael (pseud. of Mikhail M. Grusenberg; also known as George Brown), 72, 164, 168, 324, 478
  Comintern representative in Great Britain, 164
  political advisor to Chiang Kai-shek, 72
Borreman, Jean, 33
Bosch, Juan, 118
Boshnjaku, Kostandin, 3
Böttcher, Paul, 154
Bouabid, Abd er-Rahim, 329

Bouhali, Larbi, 11, 12
Boukhort, Ben Ali, 8
Bourguiba, Habib, 430, 432, 433
Bourquia, Abd es-Slam, 327, 329
Bowman, 18
Brainer, Bela, 381
Brandão, Octavio, 40, 294
Brandler, Heinrich, 71, 153, 154
Brandsen, Bertus, 335
Braun, Otto (pseuds. Li T'e; Albert Wagner), 71
Brezhnev, Leonid I., 129, 130, 451, 452, 453, 510
Browder, Earl, 71, 85, 101, 462-70 passim, 472n4
Brown, George, see Borodin, Michael
Broz, Josip, see Tito
Bubnik, Josef, 109
Buck, T., 56, 57
Budalho, 349
Budennyi, S. M., 81
Buendia, A., 395
Bujor, M. G., 381
Bukharin, Nikolai, 84, 85, 154, 239, 254, 365, 390, 446, 448, 449, 454, 463
Bulganin, Nikolai, 450, 451
Bullejos, José, 396
Bulliard, Gérard, 422, 423
Bülow, Bernhard von, 152
Bunting, Brian, 392, 393, 394
Bunting, Sidney Percival, 388-91 passim
Buozzi, Bruno, 240
Burmystenko, M., 442
Burnelle, Ernest, 33, 34, 35
Burnham, Forbes, 180, 181
al-Bustani, 'Abd al-Qadir Isma'il, see Isma'il al-Bustani, 'Abd al-Qadir
Buu Loc, Prince, 480

Caballero, Paul, 9
Cacenco, Pavel, 381
Cachin, Marcel, 136, 137
Calderío, Francisco, see Roca, Blas
Campa, Valentin, 324, 325
Campbell, J. R., 164, 165
Canelas, Antonio, 269
Cannon, James P., 132, 462-66 passim
Cardenas, Lázaro, 324
Carías, Tiburcio, 184, 281
Carneson, Fred, 391
Carrillo, Rafael, 324
Carrillo, Santiago, 397, 398, 399
Carter, Martin, 179, 180
Casanova, Laurent, 143-44
Cassin, René, 206, 207
Castello Branco, Humberto, 41
Castillo Armas, Carlos, 281
Castro, Fidel, 102, 103, 104, 105n3, 284, 285, 286, 341
  attack on Moncada barracks (1953), 102
  criticizes communism, 102
  general secretary of Cuban party, 103
Castro, Raúl, 103, 104
Cayla, Léon, 314
Ceaușescu, Nicolae, 382
Célor, Pierre, 139

Čepička, Alexei, 112
Césaire, Aimé, 175, 321, 322
Chaintron, Jean (*pseud*. Barthel), 8, 144
Chambers, Whittaker, 465
Chamoun, Camille, 304
Chang Kuo-t'ao, 66, 72
Chang Tso-lin, 66
Chang Yueh, 410
Chankov, 45
Chau, Phan Boi, 477
Chemodanov, V. T., 94
Ch'en Ch'i-yu, 71
Chen Ping, 318
Ch'en Po-ta, 69
Ch'en Shao-yü, *see* Wang Ming
Ch'en Tu-hsiu, 66, 72
Ch'en Yi, 66, 69
Ch'en Yün, 69
Cheng Chen, 72
Chervenkov, Vŭlko, 43-46 *passim*
Chi Fang, 71
Chiang Kai-shek, 67, 164
Chibás, Eduardo, 101
Chicherin, Georgii V., 92, 164
Chija, 349
Chinh, Truong, 483
Chisinevski, Iosif, 382
Chit Maung, 49
Cho Pong-am, 257
Choibalsan, 348, 349, 350
Chou En-lai, 66, 68, 69, 408, 409, 414, 455
Chou Yang, 71
Chouadria, Mohammed, 9
Christiansen, Ernst, 115
Ch'ü Ch'iu-pai, 66, 72
Chu Teh, 67, 69, 359
Ch'u T'u-nan, 71
Chubar, Vlas, 443, 449
Churchill, Sir Winston, 166, 211, 464
Citrine, Sir Walter, 498, 499
Citrons, *see* Strautnieks, A.
Čižinski, Josip, *see* Gorkić, Milan
Claudín, Fernando, 397, 399, 400
Clementis, Vladimír (Vlado), 77, 111, 114, 115n4, 155
  executed 111
Cocchi, Romano, 240
Codovilla, Victorio, 13, 14, 267, 269, 288, 293, 294, 325
Cogniot, G., 147
Cohen, Rose, 168
Coninck, Albert de, 35
Connolly, James, 232
Constant, Félix d'Orléans Juste, 182
Constantinescu, A., 381
Constantinescu, Miron, 382
Cook, A. J., 165, 166
Copeland, Vincent, 466
Čopić, Vladimir, 504
Corey, Lewis, *see* Fraina, Luis C.
Cornu, Marcel, 147
Corvalán Leppe, Luis, 267
Cosgrave, William T., 233
Cot, Pierre, 208, 489
Cotton, Eugénie, 146, 486

Creydt, Oscar, 267, 355
Cristescu, Gh., 381
Croizat, Ambroise, 141, 142
Cuenca, Abel, 121
Cunhal, Alvaro, 370
Cuong De, Prince, 479
Curiel, Henry (*pseud*. Yunus), 459, 460
Custance, Florence A., 56
Cyrankiewicz, Józef, 213
Czeszejiko, *see* Sochacki, Jerzy

Dąbal (Dombal), Tomasz, 220
  executed in USSR, 220
Dadoo, Y. M., 391
Dahlem, Franz, 153
Damba, 350
Dange, S. A., 49, 195-99 *passim*
Daniel, Iuli, 416
Danishyan, Gholam, 226
Danzan, 349
Darcy, Samuel A., 464
Darsono, Raden, 201
D'Astier de la Vigerie, Emmanuel, 146
Davis, Benjamin J., 465-66
Deakin, Arthur, 499
Decoux, Jean, 479
Defferre, Gaston, 145
De Gaulle, Charles, 141-46 *passim*, 385
Deglavs, Fricis, 299
De Groot, Paul, 334, 335, 336
Dejaze, 33
Dekanozov, V. G., 72
Delgado, Humberto, 371, 372, 373
Demetratos, N., 170
Demetratos, P., 170
Demetriades, Chrysis O., 107
Demid, 350
Demir, Yakup (*pseud*. of Zeki Baştımar), 437
Denford, H. L., 18
Dengel, Philipp, 153, 154, 469
Denikin, A. I., 81, 441
Dennis, Eugene, 464, 465, 466
Deutscher, Isaac, 133
Deymer, Şefik Hüsnü, 434-37 *passim*
Diallo, Abdoulaye, 342
Diallo, Oumar, 386
Díaz, José 397
Diem, Ngo Dinh, 480, 481, 482
Dimitrov, Georgi, 29, 30, 43, 44, 46, 85, 86, 87, 140, 376, 506
  plans for Balkan federation, 30
al-Din, 'Ali Nasir, 301
al-Din, Khalid Muhyi, *see* Muhyi al-Din, Khalid
Diop, Majhemout, 386, 387
DiVittorio, Giuseppe, 240, 500
Dixon, R., 20
Djaković, Djuro, 505
Djarrad, Mohammed el-Hadj, 433
Djerad, Ali, 430
Djilas, Milovan, 506, 510, 511
  dispute with Tito, 510
Dobbs, Farrell, 464, 466
Dobi, István, 190
Dobrogeanu-Gherea, A., 381
Dolanský, Jaromír, 109, 110

Dombal, Tomasz, *see* Dąbal, Tomasz
Domski, L. (*pseud. of* Henryk Stein; *also known as* Kaminski), 364
Donáth, Ferenc, 186
Donchev, B., 381
Dong, Pham Van, 483
Donnat, Gaston, 54, 315
Doriot, Jacques, 8, 138, 326
Dorticós, Osvaldo, 103, 104
Doucoudray, Felix, 118
Doucoudray, Juan, 118
Drašković, Milbrad, 505
  assassinated by communists, 505
Dridzo, Solomon Abramovich, *see* Lozovskii, Alexander
Dua, G., 235
Duan, Le, 483
Dubček, Alexander, 112
Duclos, Jacques, 101, 146, 147, 433n7, 464
Ducroux, Joseph, 317
Dufond, Guy, 323
Dumont, Yvonne, 146
Dunois, Amedée, 137
Ďuriš, Július, 110, 112
Dussac, Paul, 314
Dutov, Ataman, 255
Dutt, Rajani Palme, 164-69 *passim*, 199
Duvalier, François D., 182, 285
Dyer, E. J., 337
Dzhaparidze, A., 148
Dzhugashvili, Iosif, *see* Stalin, Joseph
Dzhugeli, S., 148
Dzierzyński, Feliks, 362

Earsman, W. P., 18
Eastman, Max, 470
Eberlein, Hugo, 80, 155
Ebert, Friedrich, 152, 153, 161
Echévez, Eliseo, 354
Edwards, *see* Eisler, Gerhart
Egretaud, Marcel, 315
Eidukevičius, Pranas, 308
Eisler, Elfriede, *see* Fischer, Ruth
Eisler, Gerhart (*pseud.* Edwards), 71, 153, 469
Eliava, Sh., 148
Encina, Dionisio, 283, 324, 325
Ende, Lex, 160
Endicott, James G., 491
Engels, Friedrich, 98
Enukidze, Avel S., 148, 454
Erani, Taghi, 226
Ercoli, *see* Togliatti, Palmiro
Erzenkian (Armenian), 16
Escalante, Aníbal, 99, 100, 103
Escalante, César, 99
Eskandari, Abbas, 225
Eskandari, Iraj, 225, 227
Eskandari, Suleiman Mohsen, 225
Evä, K. M., 125
Evangelista, Cristanto, 358, 359
Ewert, Arthur, 154, 469

"Fahd," *see* Yusuf, Yusuf Salman
Fajon, Etienne, 146, 147
Faría, Jesús, 476

Farkas, Mihály, 187
Faruq, King of Egypt, 460
Faure, Paul, 136
Fayet, Pierre, 9, 10
Feary, T. W., 337
Fechner, Max, 160
Feix, Léon, 379
Felton, Monica, 486
Fengarol, Amédée, 174
Ferlini, Juan, 13
Fernandez, Luca, 404
Fiala, Gottlieb, 25
Fierlinger, Zdeněk, 110
Figl, Leopold, 25
Figueres, José, 95
Figuères, Léo, 147
Filipović, Filip, 504
Finder, Paweł, 366
Fines, Ernest, 54
Finidori, J. P., 430
Fioletov, I. T., 439
Firman, Mikhail, *see* Mif, Pavel
First, Ruth, 392, 393
Fisch, Walter, 158
Fischer, Abram Louis, 393
Fischer, Ruth (*pseud. of* Elfriede Eisler), 85, 153, 154
Fitzpatrick, John, 468
Flieg, Leo, 155
Flores Magon, Enrique, 99
Flynn, Elizabeth Gurley, 465, 466
Fomin, V. V., 37
Fonseca, Ricardo, 268
Ford, James W., 469
Fortoul Briceño, Aurelio, 267, 274, 476
Fortuny, José Manuel, 177
Foster, William Z., 85, 462-70 *passim*
Frachon, Benoît, 139, 146
Fraina, Luis C. (*pseud.* Lewis Corey), 267, 462
Franco, Francisco, 398, 399, 400
Franco Ornes, Pericles, 118
Frank, Pierre, 134, 135
Freeman, F. E., 338
Frischmann, Georges, 146
Frisque, Julien, 423
Frölich, Paul, 153
Frölich, Mrs. Paul, *see* Wolfstein, Rosi
Frondizi, Arturo, 14
Frossard, André Louis, 136, 137
Frunze, M. V., 37, 253, 441
Fu Ta Ching, 317
Fuad, Ahmad, 460
Fucik, Július, 110
Fukumoto Kazuo, 244
Fürnberg, Friedl, 26
Furtseva, Yekaterina, 451
Furubotn, Peder, 346

Gaillard, Roger, 183
Gaitán, Jorge, 75
Gale, Linn, 267
Galen, *see* Blücher, V. K.
Gallacher, William, 85, 164, 166
Galvanauskas, 310
Galvão, Henrique, 371
Gandhi, Mahatma, 194

## INDEX OF PERSONS 541

Garaudy, Roger, 146
García, Guillermo, 103
García Agüero, Salvador, 99, 101
García Quejido, Antonio, 396
Garden, J. S., 18, 19
Gasperoni, Ermenegildo, 385
Gates, John, 465
Gaulle, Charles de, *see* De Gaulle, Charles
Gbenye, Christophe, 405
Gegechkori, A., 148
Gendan, 350
Gène, Evremond, 175, 176
Gensberg, 434
Georgescu, Teohari, 382
Gerő, Ernő, 186–90, *passim*
Gheorghiu-Dej, Gheorghe, 381, 382, 383
Ghioldi, Rodolfo, 13, 267, 294
Ghosh, Ajoy K., 196, 197, 199
Ghukasian, Ghukas, 15
Giap, Vo Nguyen, 480, 483
Giau, Tran Van, 478, 479
Giedrys, Kazys, 310
Gikalo, N. E., 37
Gimes, Miklós, 189
Ginsberger, Roger, *see* Villon, Pierre
Girard, Rosan, 174, 175, 176
Girault, Suzanne, 84, 85, 138
Gitlow, Benjamin, 85, 462, 463, 469
Gizenga, Antoine, 405
Glineur, Henri, 33
Glubb, Sir John B. (Glubb Pasha), 251
Glückauf, Erich, 158
Goldfarb, Max (*pseuds*. A. [*sometimes* D.] Petrovskii, A. J. Bennet), 164, 168
Gollan, John, 167
Gollancz, Victor, 166
Gómez, Eugenio, 268, 269, 283, 472
Gómez, Juan Vicente, 274, 476
Gomułka, Władysław, 77, 366-69, *passim*
  arrested by communist government, 367
Gonçalves, Bento, 370
Gonzalez, Virginia, 396
Goonewardena, Leslie, 59, 60
Göring, Hermann, 155
Gorkić, Milan (*pseud. of* Josip Čižinski), 506
Gorky, Maxim, 79
Gorter, Hermann, 333
Goshal, H. (*pseud*. Ba Tin), 49
Gottwald, Klement, 85, 109, 110, 111, 112, 115n4
Goulart, João, 41
Govidnan, 60
Grabois, Mauricio, 41
Gramsci, Antonio, 238-39
Grau San Martín, Ramón, 100, 101, 278
Graves, J., 19
Graziadei, Antonio, 238
Grenier, Fernand, 141
Greulich, Hermann, 419
Grieco, Ruggiero, 239
Griffin, R. F., 338
Grimau García, Julián, 399
Grimlund, Otto, 414
Grimm, Robert, 419
Grippa, Jacques, 35, 423
  forms pro-Chinese communist party, 35

Grivas, George, 107
Grobart, Fabio (*pseud. of* Yunger Semjovich), 98, 99
Grohman, Josef, 221, 222, 224
Grol, Milan, 508
Gromyko, Andrei A., 230, 481
Grootzak, Herben, 335
Grotewohl, Otto, 160
Grulović, Nikola, 503
Grusenberg, Mikhail M., *see* Borodin, Michael
Guerrero, Javier, 324
Guevara, Ernesto Che, 103
Gueye, Lamine, 342
Guilbeaux, Henri, 419
Guillén, Nicolás, 290
Guinqouin, 142
Guitteaud, Walter, 323
Gumede, J. T., 390
Gunasekara, A., 60
Gunasekera, Vernon, 59
Gunawardena, D. P. R., *see* Gunawardena, Philip
Gunawardena, Philip (D.P.R.), 59, 60, 61
Gunawardena, Robert, 61
Gunawardhena, Theja, 63
Gundorov, Aleksandr, 214
Gusev, S. I., 462, 469
Gutiérrez, Víctor Manuel, 177
Guyot, Raymond, 139, 140, 146
Guzenko, Igor, 57
Gylling, E., 129

Habībī, E., 236
Hadj, Messali, 8, 10, 11
Hadj Ali, Bachir, 11, 12
Hagberg, Hilding, 415
Hager, Kurt, 161
Haitas, A., 173
al-Hajj, 'Azīz, 231
Hakamada Satomi, 246, 248
Haken, Josef, 109
Haladzed, N. M., 37
Hall, Gus, 465, 466
al-Halu, Faraj Allah, 301-4 *passim*
Hansen, Joseph, 134, 135
Harb, Nicola, 301
Harmel, Mohammed, 433
Hart, Armando, 103
Haruthiunian, S., 16
Hassan II, King of Morocco, 329
Hatta, Mohammed, 202
Haya de la Torre, Víctor Raúl, 273, 356
Healy, Gerry, 134
Heckert, Fritz, 376
Heidermann, Hans, 124
Hellberg, Sigvald, 115
Hendrych, Jiří, 110
Henríquez, Francisco, 118, 269
Henrykowski, Henryk, *see* Amsterdam, Saul
Hermann, Jean-Maurice, 217, 219
Hermansson, C. H., 415, 416-17
Hernández, Jesús, 398
Hernández Martínez, Maximiliano, *see* Martínez, Maximiliano Hernández
Hernández Rodríguez, Guillermo, 74, 269
Hernández Segura, Francisco, 340
Herrnstadt, Rudolf, 160

Hertzog, J. B. M., 389
Herzog, Jakob, 419, 420
Hidalgo, Manuel, 270
Hikmet, Nâzım, 435, 436, 437
Hill, E., 20
Hirano Yoshitaro, 209
Hiss, Alger, 465
Hitler, Adolf, 23, 85-89 *passim*, 155, 156, 165, 166, 335, 365, 403, 415, 463, 510
 communists concede error re, 86, 156, 193
 influence abroad, 23
Hla Kyway, 49
Ho Chi Minh, 51, 52, 264, 478-83 *passim*
Hŏ Hŏn, 259
Ho Hsiang-ning, Mme., 71
Ho Lung, 69
Ho Meng-hsiung, 67
Hoarau, Raymond, 380
Hobson, J. A., 402
Hoc, Nguyen Thai, 478
Hodinová, Anežka, 115n4
Hoekstra, Henk, 336
Hofmaier, Karl, 418, 419, 421, 423
Höglund, Zeth, 414, 415
Holmberg, N., 417
Honecker, Erich, 161
Horthy, Miklós, 185, 187
Horwitz, Max, *see* Walecki, Max
Houphouët-Boigny, Félix, 341, 386
Hoxha, Enver, 3, 4, 5
Hsiang Chung-fa, 66, 72
Hsiu Yen, 72
Hsü Hsiang-ch'ien, 69
Hsü Te-hung, 71
Hu Chi-li, 223
Huang K'o-ch'eng, 69
Hudicourt, Max, 182, 268, 274, 279
Hůla, Břetislav, 108
Humbert-Droz, Jules, 420
Husain, King of Jordan, 251, 252
Husák, Gustav, 111
Hyndman, H. M., 163

Iagoda, G. G., 454
Iakubovskii, Ivan I., 485
Iaroslavskii, Emilian, 446
Ibáñez, Carlos, 273
Ibarra, Valasco, 277
Ibarruri, Dolores, 85, 399, 487
Ibéné, Hégésippe, 175
Ibn 'Abd Allah, Talal, *see* Talal, King
Ibn Talal, Husain, *see* Husain, King
Ikramov, 475
Iliev, Petŭr, 44
'Inan, Muhammad 'Abd Allah, 458
al-'Inani (Egyptian), 458
Ingrao, Pietro, 242
Inkpin, Albert, 164, 167
Isma'il al-Bustani, 'Abd al-Qadir, 229, 230, 231
Israel, Marcel, 459
Iudin, P. F., 77

Jaboux, 459
Jackson, G. E., 339
Jacquemotte, Joseph, 31, 32, 33
 disappearance in 1936, 32, 33

Jaden, Aggrey, 413
Jagan, Cheddi, 179, 180, 181
Jagan, Mrs. Cheddi, *see* Rosenberg, Janet
Jakova, Tuk, 5
Jalak, Kristjan, 124
Janequette, William, 358
Janhunen, Matti, 128
Janoušek, A., 109
Jao Shu-shih, 69
Jaurès, Jean, 136, 147
Javid, Salamollah, 226
Jean-Longuet, Robert, 327
Jeffrey, N., 18, 338
Jensen, Alfred, 116
Jerome, Fred, 466
Jespersen, Knud, 116
Jílek, Bohumil, 109, 110
Jõeäär, Aleksander, 124
Joffe, Adolf, 67
Joffe, Louis, 390
John XXII, Pope, 241
Johnson, F., 20
Joliot-Curie, Frédéric, 146, 488, 490, 496
Jones, C., 20
Jones, David Ivon, 388, 389
Joshi, P. C., 195
Joumni, Taoufik, 433
Jourdain, Henri, 147
Juin, Alphonse, 431
Julien, Charles André, 7
Jürman, Johannes, 124
Just, Stephen, 134
Jusuf, Mohammad, 202

el-Kaabi, Khemaïs, 433
Kádár, János, 187-91 *passim*
Kaganovich, Lazar, 441, 442, 451
Kahn, Sam, 391
Kalinin, Mikhail I., 122, 448, 475
Kállai, Gyula, 186
Kalnberziņš, Jānis (*pseud.* Zaķis), 299
Kamenev, Lev, 131, 446-49 *passim*, 454
Kaminski, *see* Domski, L.
Kamphan, Khieu, 53
Kan Mai, 408
Kanapa, Jean, 147
K'ang Sheng, 69, 72
Kao Kang, 69
Kao Liang, 407, 408
Kapsukas, Vincas Mickevičius-, 37, 308-11 *passim*
Karakhan, L., 71
Karayorgis, G., 173
Kardelj, Edvard, 506, 508, 511
Károlyi, Mihály, 185
Karpov, 72
Karski, Isetor, *see* Marchlewski, Julian
Kashani, Abol Ghassem, 227
Kasian, Sarkis, 15
Kasuga Shojiro, 246
Katayama Sen, 243, 267, 324
Kautsky, Karl, 152, 154
Kavanagh, J., 19
Kavtaradze, S., 149
Kaysone Phomvihan, 264, 265
Kazakov, Mikhail I., 485

## INDEX OF PERSONS

Marinello, Juan, 100, 101
Maring, *see* Sneevliet, H. J. F. M.
Marinov, Ivan, 44
Marković, Sima, 504, 505, 506
Marks, J. B., 391, 392
Mármol, Miguel, 121
Marosán, György, 190
Marrane, Georges, 142
Marshall, George C., 67
Martí, Augustín P., 121
Martínez, Maximiliano Hernández, 121, 278
Martínez, Ricardo A., 269, 294, 476
Martínez Verdugo, Arnaldo, 325
Martínex Villena, Rubén, 99
Martna, Mihkel, 123
Martov, L. (*pseud. of* Julius Tsederbaum), 445
Marty, André, 9, 139, 141, 142
Marun, Antun, 458, 459
Marx, Karl, 98, 128, 136, 180, 254, 327, 356, 362, 402, 410
Masaryk, Thomas, 108
Masherov, P. M., 37
Maslow, Arkadij, 153, 154
Massemba-Débat, Alphonse, 408
Mathys, Lucien, 422
Matip, Mayi, 55
Matos, Hubert, 102
Matteotti, Giacomo, 239
Maurín Julía, Joaquín, 396, 397
Mavrak, Anton, 505, 506
Maximos, Serafim, 434
Mazurov, K. T., 37
Mbeki, Govan A. M., 392
Mdivani, P., 148, 149
Mehring, Franz, 163n1
el-Meisi, Abd Allah, 433
Meisner, Jiří, 219
Mella, Julio Antonio, 98, 99, 105n1, 267, 272, 294
Melnikov, Leonid G., 442
Mendès-France, Pierre, 143
Mendieta, Carlos, 100
Meravian, Askanaz, 15
Merino García, Ramón, 395
Merker, Paul, 160
Messouak, Hadi, 329
Metaxas, John, 171
Meyer, Ernst, 153, 154
Meyersohn, J., 235
Miasnikov, A. F., 37
Michiels, Joseph, 313
Mickevičius-Kapsukas, Vincas, *see* Kapsukas, Vincas Mickevičius-
Mif, Pavel (*pseud. of* Mikhail Firman), 66, 71
Mihajlović, Draža, 507
Mikhailov, Boris, 469
Mikoyan, Anastas I., 16, 50, 103, 188, 449, 451
Miles J. B., 19
Millá, Rafael, 395
Millerand, Alexandre, 429
Minh, Son Ngoc, 52
Mīqūnīs, S., 236
Miro Cardona, José, 102

Mirza, Iskander, 352
Mitterrand, François, 145
Miyamoto Kenji, 246, 247-48
Mobutu, Joseph, 405, 411
Moczar, Mieczysław, 368
Mohammed, Abdul Rahman (*pseud.* Babu), 410
Mohammed, Moktari, 9
Mohn, Willi, 158
Mokhehle, Ntsu, 306
Mokotoko, Seth, 307
Mollet, Guy, 142
Molotov, Viacheslav, 84, 85, 365, 441, 447, 448, 450, 451
Monatte, Pierre, 136, 138
Mondon, Auguste, 379
Mondon, Raymond, 379
Mongkhon Na Nakhorn, 428
Monje Molina, Mario, 39
Monmousseau, Gaston, 136
Monzón, Jesús, 398
Moore, Herbert, *see* Wicks, H. M.
Moore, Hugh, 234
Mora Valverde, Manuel, 95, 268, 274
Moriarty, W., 56
Mornard, Jacques, 132
Mossadegh, Mohammed, 227, 228
Motloheloa, John, 306, 307
Moumié, Félix, 54, 55
Moxon, H., 19
Mugoša, Dušan, 4
Muhri, Franz, 26
Muhyi al-Din, Khalid, 460
Mulele, Pierre, 404, 405
Muna, Alois, 108, 110
Münnich, Ferenc, 189
Münzenberg, Willy, 92, 93, 94, 154, 377, 419
  dies under mysterious circumstances, 94
Muraviev, Konstantin, 44
Murphy, J. T., 164, 168
Murray, Philip, 469
Murto, Yrjö, 128
Musa, Mustafa, 459
Musa, Salamah, 458
Musa Ahmad, 318
Musso, 49, 201, 202
Mussolini, Benito, 23, 82, 238, 239, 240, 430, 463
Mustafa, Anwar, 231
Mya, Thakin, 48

al-Nabulsi, Sulaiman, 252
en-Nafaa, Mohammed, 431, 432, 433
Nagy, Ferenc, 187
Nagy, Imre, 186-89 *passim*
Naicker, M. P., 392
Namboodiripad, E. M. S., 196, 197, 198
Nan Han-chen, 71
Nasir, Hasan, 353
Nassar, Fuad, 251, 252
Nasser, Gamal Abdel, *see* 'Abd al-Nasir, Gamal
Nasution, Abdul Haris, 204
Nâzım, 434
Ne Win, 47, 48, 50

Nearing, Scott, 59
Negrín, Juan, 398
Nehru, Jawaharlal, 195, 196, 199, 262
Nejat, Ethem, 434, 435
Nejedlý, Zdeněk, 115-4
Nenni, Pietro, 238, 240, 241
Nerman, Ture, 414
Neruda, Pablo, 290
Neubauer, Theo, 154
Neumann, Heinz, 71, 154, 155
Neumann, Oskar, 158
Newbold, Walton, 164
Ngendandumwe, Pierre, 407
Ngom, Jacques, 55
Nicolas, Armand, 322, 323
Nicole, Léon, 418-22 passim
Niebergall, Otto, 158
Nieh Jung-chen, 69
Nielsen, Einar, 115
Nim, Hu, 53
Nin Pérez, Andrés, 396, 397, 398
Nizard (Tunisian), 431
Njoto, 202, 203, 204
Nkrumah, Kwame, 343, 403, 405, 408, 410, 501
Noli, Fan, 3
Norden, Albert, 161
Nordmann, Joë, 206, 207, 208
Nordmann, Mme. Joë, 147
North, Joseph, 470
Norton de Matos, José Maria, 371
Nosaka Sanzo, 244-47 passim
Nosek, Václav, 155n4
Noulens, Hilaire, see Ruegg, Paul
Novomeský, Laco, 111
Novotný, Antonín, 110, 112, 114
Nový, Vilém, 111
Nowotko, Marceli, 366
Nu, U, 48, 49
Nyerere, Julius, 406, 408

Obregón, Alvaro, 272
Ochab, Edward, 367
Odinga, Oginga, 406
Odría, Manuel, 357
Odru, Louis, 379
Oelssner, Fred, 161
O Ki-sŏp, 258
Okudzhava, M., 148
Olgeirsson, Einar, 193
Omo, Uche, 344
Orakhelashvili, Ivan (Mamiia) D., 148, 149
Orcel, J., 147
Ordoqui, Joaquín, 99, 103
Ordzhonikidze, Grigorii, 148, 149, 150, 449
O'Riordan, Michael, 234
O'Shea, C., 20
Osoha, Jan, 110
Otegbeye, Tunji, 343, 344
Ouandié, Ernest, 54, 55
Oulevay-Busset, Gertrude, 422
Ouyanjak, 72
Ouzegane, Amar, 8, 9
Ovenessian, Ardeshir, 225
Overstraeten, Edouard van, 31, 32

Pablo, Michel (*pseud. of* Michael Raptis), 133
Pahlavi, Mohammed Reza, Shah of Iran, 226, 227
Pak Hŏn-yŏng, 257-60 passim
Pankhurst, Sylvia, 163, 164
Pannekoek, Anton, 333
Panov, 45
Papaioannou, Ezekias, 106
Paredes, Ricardo, 119, 268
Paredes Macedo, Saturnino, 357
Parent, Pierre, 327
Partselidis, M., 172
Pasolini, Gastone, 385
Pasternak, Boris, 282
Paterson, Fred, 19
Patolichev, N. S., 37
Pătrășcanu, Lucrețiu, 381, 382
Pauker, Ana, 381, 382
Pauker, Marcel, 381
Paul, Marcel, 141
Paul, William, 164
Pekkala, Mauno, 128
Pelagić, Vaso, 504
Pelikán, Jiří, 225
Peña, Lázaro, 99, 100
Peña Vilaboa, José, 99
Penelón, José F., 13, 269
P'eng Te-huai, 69, 72
Pepper, John, *see* Pogány, József
Pereira, Astrogildo, 40, 268
Pereira Gomes, Soeiro, 370
Perera, N. M., 59, 60, 62
Pérez, José Miguel, 99
Pérez Jiménez, Marcos, 269, 284, 476
Pérez Solís, Oscar, 396
Perón, Juan D., 13
Persson, Seth, 415
Pervukhin, M. G., 451
Pessi, Ville, 128, 129
Pestaña, Angel, 400
Pétain, Henri Philippe, 9, 479
Petersen, Chris, 336
Petit, Ernest, 105
Petliura, Simon, 441
Petrov, Peter, 164
  defection and spy affair, 19
Petrovskii, A. (*sometimes* D.), *see* Goldfarb, Max
Petrovsky, Hryhoriy, 440
Pfeiffer, Hans, 154
Pham Van Dong, 264
Phayom Chulanonda, 428
Phillips, Charles, 267, 324
Piatnitskii, Osip, 376
Pidhorny, Mykola, *see* Podgorny, Nikolai
Pieck, Wilhelm, 85, 87, 154, 157, 160
Pierre-Justin, Serge, 175, 176
Pierre-Louis, Rossini, 182
Piłsudski, Józef, 362, 365
Pintas, F., 472
Piquet, René, 146
Pishevari, Jaafar (*pseud. of* Javad Zadeh), 226, 227
Platten, Fritz, 80, 419, 420
Plekhanov, Georgii V., 43, 445
Plissionier, Gaston, 146

Po Ku, 72
Podgorny, Nikolai (Mykola Pidhorny), 144, 443, 451, 452
Pogány, József (*pseud*. John Pepper), 185, 186, 469
Pokrovskii, Mikhail, 446
Polianskii, Dmitri, 452
Pollitt, Harry, 85, 164-68 *passim*, 469
Pomar, Pedro, 41
Ponce, Domingo, 358
Ponomarenko, P. K., 37
Ponomarev, Boris N., 129
Pöögelmann, Hans, 123, 125
Popov, M. M., 443
Popović, Miladin, 4
Popper, Martin, 206, 207
Portocarrero, Julio, 294, 357
Posadas, Juan, 134, 135
Pospelov, Piotr, 116
Postgate, Raymond, 164
Postyshev, Pavel P., 442
Powell, Cecil F., 496
Požela, Karolis, 310
Prado, Jorge del, 357
Prasad Sabsunthorn, 427, 428
Prasong Vongvivat, 427
Prenant, Marcel, 141, 144
Preobrazhenskii, E. A., 454
Preoteasă, Grigori, 381
Prestes, Luiz Carlos, 40, 41, 269, 275, 294
Primo de Rivera, Miguel, 396, 397
Prío Socarrás, Carlos, 101
Pritt, Dennis Nowell, 207, 208
Purman, Leon, 364, 365
Pushpa Lal, 331, 332


Qasım, 'Abd al-Karim, 230, 231, 461
Qazi Mohammed, 226
Quezon, Manuel, 359
Quirino, Elpidio, 359
Quraitim, Hasan, 304


Rabchinskii, Ivan, 123
Rabesahala, Gisèle, 315
Rachi, 427
Radawi, Husain, *see* 'Adil, Salam
Radek, Karl (*pseud*. of Tobiach Sobelsohn), 80, 81, 235, 375, 388, 446, 454
Radmanesh, Reza, 225
Radwi (Radawi), Husain, *see* 'Adil, Salam
Rahja, Jukka, 125
Rajk, László, 77, 186, 187, 188
Rákosi, Mátyás, 166, 185-91 *passim*
Rakotobé, Henri, 315
Rakovskii, Khristian G., 80, 441, 454
Ralaierijaona, 315
Ramadier, Paul, 142
Ramanathan, K., 60
Ramirez, R., 472
Ramos de Almeida, Pedro, 372
Ranadive, B. T., 195, 196
Randrianja, René Anselme, 315, 316
Ranković, Aleksandar, 77, 506, 507, 511

Rao, Rajeshwar, 195-98 *passim*
Raptis, Michael, *see* Pablo, Michel
Rasafinjohany, Albert, 315
Rasaholy, 315
Rasoanoro, Zèle, 315
Rästas, Otto, 124
Ratos, M., 134
Ravazzoli, Paolo, 239
Ravensteyn, W. van, 333, 334
Ravines, Eudocio, 270, 275, 294, 357
Rayamagjhi, Keshar Jang, 330, 331, 332
Recabarren, Luis Emilio, 64, 269
Reed, John, 337, 462
Reimann, Max, 158
Reinstein, Boris, 80
Relecom, Xavier, 32, 33
Remmele, Hans, 155
Renner, Karl, 22, 24
Ret Savros, 428
Reuter, Fritz, 335
Reuther, Walter, 469
Révai, József, 186, 187
Reza Khan, *see* Pahlavi, Mohammed Reza
Rhee, Syngman, 257
Rida, Rafiq, 301, 302
Ridgway, Matthew, 142, 433n7
Rivera, Diego, 290, 324, 325
Robertson, Jim, 466
Roca, Blas (*pseud*. of Francisco Calderío), 99, 101, 103, 268, 294
Rochet, Waldeck, 144, 145, 146
Rodríguez, Carlos Rafael, 99, 100, 103
Rodríguez, Marcos, 103
Roig y San Martín, Enrique, 98
Rojas, Ursinio, 99
Roland-Holst, Henriette, 333, 334
Roman, Armando, 466
Roosevelt, Franklin D., 211, 463, 464, 469
Rosen, Milt, 466
Rosenberg, Janet (Mrs. Cheddi Jagan), 179, 180
Rosenthal, Charlotte, 459
Rosenthal, Joseph, 458, 459
Rosmer, Alfred, 138, 376
Ross, H., 18
Rosselli, Carlo, 240
Rothstein, Theodore, 164
Roumain, Jacques, 182, 268, 274
Roxas, Manuel, 359
Roy, Manabendra Nath, 71, 194, 199, 267, 271, 293, 324
  expelled from Comintern, 194
Roziņš, Fricis (*pseud*. Āzis), 297
Ruam Wongphan, 428
Rudzutak, Jan, 449
Ruegg, Paul (*pseud*. Hilaire Noulens), 71
Ruffé, Hubert, 379
Rürman, A., 124
Rusta, Reza, 225
Rutgers, S. J., 243, 333
Ruthenberg, Charles E., 462, 469
Rutkowski, *see* Bierut, Bolesław
Ruus, Neeme, 124
Rykov, Aleksei, 85, 154, 448, 449, 454
Ryskulov, 254
Ryti, Risto, 127

## INDEX OF PERSONS

Saad, Pedro, 120, 267
Sa'adah, Antun, 302
Saarinen, Arne, 129
Saburov, M. Z., 451
Sachs, Solly, 390,
Sadiq, Yusuf, 460
Sadvakasov, 254
Saefkow, Anton, 155
Sahher, Sajjad, 350, 351
Sa'id, Farid, 252
Sa'id, Zaki, 458
Saillant, Louis, 498, 500, 502
Sakai Toshihiko, 243
Sakŭzov, Yanko, 42
Saladrigas, Carlos, 101
Salazar, António de Oliveira, 371, 372
al-Salih, 'Abd al-Qadir, 251
Salih, Hacioglu, 434
Salsberg, J. B., 57, 58
Saltaneh, Ghavam, 227
Sam'an, Margaret, 301
Samarakkody, Edmund, 60, 62
Samarito, Claudine Lewkowicz, 379
Sandys, Duncan, 180
Sanmugathasan, Nagalingam N., 62, 63
Sapronov, Timofei, 446
Sardjono, 202
Sarit Dhanarat, 428
Sauter, John, 422
al-Sayigh, Daud, 229, 230, 231
Schäfer, Max, 158
Scharf, Erwin, 26
Scheer, Mort, 466
Scheidemann, Philipp, 152
Schiavro, 7
Schirdewan, Karl, 160-61
Schneller, Ernst, 154, 155
Schubert, H., 155
Schulte, Fritz, 155
Schumacher, Kurt, 156, 157
Schumann, Georg, 155
Schwarz, Ernst, 154
Schwarz, Hillel, 459, 460
Schzevel, N., 336
Scocozza, Benito, 117
Scott, Jack, 58
Scott, S. W., 339
Secchia, Pietro, 240
Segundo, Cristóbal, 354
Séguy, Georges, 146
Sellier, Louis, 137, 138, 139
Sémard, Pierre, 138, 139, 376
Semaun, 201
Semenyuk, Ignaz, 459
Semjovich, Yunger, see Grobart, Fabio
Senanayake, D. S., 61
Senanayake, Dudley, 61
Senander, K., 417
Senghor, Lamine, 385
Senghor, Léopold Sédar, 385
Sertório, Manuel, 372
Servin, Marcel, 143, 322
Severo Aguirre, Manuel Luzardo, 99
Shachtman, Max, 132, 133, 463
Shahin, Rushdi, 251
Shamali, Fu'ad, 301
Sharangovich (Belorussian), 37

Sharkey, L., 338
Sharkey, L. L., 19, 20
Shastri, Lal Bahadur, 198
Shatskin, Lazar, 92
Shaumian, Stepan, 15
Shawi, Nicole, 302, 303, 304
Shehu, Mehmet, 4, 5
el Sheikh, Shafi Ahmed, 413
Shelepin, Aleksandr, 222, 452, 493
Shelest, Piotr Iu., 443
Shepilov, Dmitri T., 451
Shermarke, Abdi Rashid, 410
Shiga Yoshio, 247
al-Shishakli, Adib, 303
Shliapnikov, Aleksandr, 447
Shlikhter, O. H., 443
Shtuchka, Piotr, see Stučka, Pēteris
Shumsky, Oleksander, 441
Shuqair, 'Abd al-Rahman, 252
Sideris, M., 170
Siewert, Robert, 154
Sihanouk, Norodom, 52, 53
Sillén, Hugo, 415
Silone, Ignazio, 239
Silva, Colvin R. de, 59, 60
Sim, Leo (*pseud*. Andrews), 338
Simonoff, Peter, 18
Siniavskii, Andrei, 416
Siqueiros, David Alfaro, 290, 324, 325
Siroký, Viliam, 109, 110, 112
Sirola, Yrjö, 80, 125, 126
Skrypnyk, Mykola, 440-43 *passim*
Slánský, Rudolf, 77, 109, 111, 114, 115n4, 222
   executed, 111, 114, 222
Slaughter, Cliff, 134
Slovo, Joe, 393
Šmeral, Bohumil, 108, 109
Smetona, Antanas, 310
Šmidke, Karol, 111
Smith, C., 18
Sneevliet, H. J. F. M. (*pseud*. Maring), 71, 200, 201, 334
Sneh, M., 236
Sniečkus, Antanas, 311
Snow, Edgar, 359
Sobelsohn, Tobiach, see Radek, Karl
Sochacki, Jerzy (*pseud*. Czeszejiko), 363
Soe, Thakin, 47-50 *passim*
Solod, Daniel, 405
Solomon, 61
Somerhausen, Luc, 214
Sommerling, Arnold, 124, 125
Somoza, Anastasio, 276, 341
Sotomayor Perez, José, 357
Soumialot, Gaston, 405
Souphanouvong, Prince, 264, 265
Souvanna Phouma, Prince, 265
Souvarine, Boris, 132, 137, 138
Spachai, 428
Spahiu, Bedri, 5
Spandarian, Suren, 15
Spector, Maurice, 56
Spiru, Nako, 4
Sportisse, Alice, 9, 10
Springhall, Dave, 168
Spure, Žānis, 299

INDEX OF PERSONS 549

Stalin, Joseph (*pseud. of* Iosif Dzhugashvili), 20, 27, 31, 33, 34, 37, 40, 41, 45, 57, 59, 68, 71, 72, 77-88 *passim*, 91n1, 94, 110, 111, 112, 124, 129, 131, 132, 133, 139, 140, 143, 144, 148, 149-50, 154, 156, 159, 160, 162, 168, 188, 201, 208, 211, 213, 217, 222, 241, 254, 269, 270, 271, 280-84 *passim*, 297, 302, 303, 310, 311, 335, 346, 349, 362, 363, 364, 367, 368, 381, 382, 403, 417, 436, 441, 442, 443, 446-55 *passim*, 463, 464, 465, 470, 493, 496, 500, 504-10 *passim*
  concedes "serious errors" during purges, 449
  "crimes of Stalin" (Thorez), 144
  his demotion advised by Lenin, 449, 450
  his "socialism in one country," 448
  and Hitler, 87, 155, 449
  power struggle with Trotsky, 31, 40, 84, 131, 154, 271, 364, 447, 448
  returns exiled German communists to Nazi Germany, 87
  and Tito, 508, 509, 510
Stambolyiski, Alexandŭr, 43
Ştefanov, Boris, 381
Stein, Henryk, *see* Domski, L.
Stirner, Alfred, 324
Stolypin, P. A., 253, 439
Stoph, Willi, 161
Strachan, Billy, 179
Strachey, John, 166
Strautnieks, A. (*pseud.* Citrons), 298
Strobl, Franz, 28
Ström, Frederick, 414
Stučka, Pēteris (*known also as* Piotr Shtuchka), 297, 298
Sturua, V., 148
Suan, Son, 53
Šubašić, Ivan, 508
Subhi, Mustafa, 434, 435, 437
Suharto, T. N. J., 204
Suhe Bator, 348, 349
Suhrawardy, Hussein, 353
Sukarno, 202, 203, 204
Sultan, Léon, 327
Sun Yat-sen, 67, 71
Suslov, Mikhail A., 129, 197, 451, 452
Süsskind, Heinrich, 154
Šutej, Juraj, 508
Suzuki Ichiro, 247
Sverdlov, Yakov, 79, 447
Šverma, Jan, 115n4
Svoboda, Ludvík, 111
Sylvestre, Camille, 322, 323
Syrtsov, S. I., 454
Szamuely, Tibor, 185
Szilágy, József, 189
Szőnyi, Tibor, 186


Talal, King of Jordan, 251
Tambroni, Fernando, 241
Tampoe, Bela, 62
T'an Chen-lin, 69
Tan Malaka, 201, 316
T'an P'ing-shan, 71, 72

Tanner, Väinö, 127
T'ao Chu, 69
Tasca, Angelo, 239
Tashko, Koço, 5
Teissier, G., 147
Tejera, Diego Vicente, 98
Teng Hsiao-p'ing, 69
Teper, Eliahu, 301
Terfve, Jean, 33
Terpeshev (Bulgarian), 45
Terra, Gabriel, 472
Terracini, Umberto, 239
Thabit, Antun, 302
Thalheimer, August, 71, 153
Thälmann, Ernst, 153, 154, 155
Than Tun, Thakin, 47-50 *passim*
Thau, Ta Thu, 478, 479
Thein Pe, *see* Thein Pe Myint
Thein Pe Myint (*formerly* Thein Pe), 47-50 *passim*
Thero, U. Sarankara, 60
Thévenin, Georges, 175
Tho, Nguyen Huu, 483
Thomas, A., 18
Thorez, Maurice, 8, 85, 138-46 *passim*, 322
Thorez-Vermeesch, Jeannette, *see* Vermeesch, Jeannette
Tijani, al-Tajjib, 413
Tillon, Charles, 141, 142
Tito (*pseud. of* Josip Broz; *also known as* Walter), 5, 44, 77, 78, 159, 172, 213, 217, 222, 262, 346, 506-12 *passim*
Tlalé, P., 393
Togliatti, Palmiro (*pseud.* Ercoli), 72, 85, 87, 239-42 *passim*
Togohan Sutimat, 428
Tokuda Kyuichi, 243-46 *passim*
Toledano, Vincente Lombardo, 501
Tolstikov, V. S., 130
Tōmā, E., 236
Tomann, Karl, 22, 27
Tomas, Americo, 371
Tomp, Jaan, 124
Tomskii, Mikhail P., 154, 164, 448
Tör, Vedat Nedim, 437
Toroshelidze, M., 148
Torres, Elroy, 476
Torres Giraldo, Ignacio, 74
Touré, Sékou, 342, 343, 405, 408
Treint, Albert, 84, 85, 137, 138, 139
Tresso, Pietro, 239
Treves, Claudio, 238
Trikas, A., 173
Trinh, Phan Chau, 477
Trotsky, Leon, 31, 40, 60, 79, 81, 82, 84, 85, 91n3, 94, 131, 132, 133, 136, 154, 164, 254, 269, 271, 311, 324, 325, 363, 364, 447, 448, 449, 454, 463
  assassinated by GPU agent, 132, 133, 325
  deported to Turkey, 131, 448
  expelled from Comintern, 164
  expelled from CPSU, 131, 448
Troy, 233
Trujillo, Rafael Leónidas, 118, 277
Truman, Harry S, 67
Tsedenbal, 350
Tsederbaum, Julius, *see* Martov, L.

## INDEX OF PERSONS

Tsintsadze, K., 148, 149
Tsiranana, Philibert, 315
Tu Ho-hsin, 72
Tubert, Paul, 9
Tūbī, T., 236
Tubman, William V. S., 403
Tung Pi-wu, 69
Tuntar, Giuseppe, 238
Tuominen, Arvo, 129
Tuominen, Erkki, 129
Tuqan, Qadri, 251
Turati, Filippo, 238
Turcios, Luis, 178
Tyrluk, Ryszard, 494

U Nu, *see* Nu, U
U Tze-pu, 130
Ubico, Jorge, 121
Uglanov, Nikolai A., 454
Ulbricht, Walter, 85, 87, 154, 156, 157, 160, 161, 162, 376
Ulianov, Dmitri, 122
Ulianov, Vladimir Ilyich, *see* Lenin, V. I.
Ulmanis, Kārlis, 298
Um Nyobé, Ruben, 54, 55
Ungern-Sternberg, Alexander von, 348, 349
al-'Urabi, Husni, 458
Urbahns, Hugo, 154
Urbany, Dominique, 312, 313
Uribe, Vicente, 398
Urrutia, Manuel, 102
Uspensky, A. I., 442

Vafiadis, Markos, 171, 172
Vági, István, 186
Vaillant-Couturier, Paul, 137
Vakman, Richard, 123, 124
Valadés, José C., 269, 325
Valdés, Ramiro, 103
Valdimarsson, Héðinn, 192
Valiani, Leo, 240
Valle, Sergio del, 103
Van het Ship, Wim, 337
Varga, Jenő, 186
Varga, M., 134
Vargas, Getulio, 40
Varona, Antonio de, 101
Velasco Ibarra, José, 120
Veluchamy (Ceylonese), 60
Vera y Vera, Alfredo, 120
Vergès, Jacques, 380
Vergès, Paul, 379, 380
Vergès, Raymond, 379
Vermeesch, Jeannette (Mme. Maurice Thorez), 146
Verner, Paul, 161
Vicente, Arlindo, 371
Victor Emmanuel III, King of Italy, 240
Videla, González, 64
Vieira White, Eduardo, 75
Vieira White, Gilberto, 267
Vilar, César, 99, 101
Villeda Morales, Ramón, 184
Villon, Pierre (*pseud*. Roger Ginsberger), 214

Vilner, M., 236
Vincent, Jean, 419
Viollette, Maurice, 7
Vivó, Jorge, 99
Vladimirescu, Tudor, 381
Vlahović, Veljko, 511
Voitinsky, G., 66, 71
Vokrouhlický, Zbyněk, 225
Volk, Karl, 154
Voroshilov, K. E., 448, 451
Voznesenskii, Nikolai, 450, 454
  executed, 450
Vujovich, Voja, 84
Vukićević, Lazar, 503
Vyshinskii, Andrei, 449

Wagenaar, Gerben, 335
Wagenknecht, Alfred, 462
Wagner, Albert, *see* Braun, Otto
Wainwright, Juan Pablo, 184, 267, 269, 272
Walcher, Jakob, 154
Walecki, Max (*pseud.* of Max Horwitz), 363
Wallace, Henry A., 465, 468
Walter, *see* Tito
Wang Ming (*pseud.* of Ch'en Shao-yü), 66, 72
Wang Ming-chai, 66
Wang Ping, 408
Warski, Adolf (*pseud.* of Warszawski), 361-65 *passim*
Warszawski, *see* Warski, Adolf
Weber, Hans, 154
Weiss, *see* Kossai, Yehiel
Weisshaus, Aladár, 187
Welti, Franz, 420
Wennerström, Ivar, 414, 415
Westmass, Rory, 179, 180
Wickremasinghe, A. S., 59, 60, 63
Wicks, H. M. (*pseud.* Herbert Moore), 19
Wijnkoop, David, 85, 333-34
Wilcox, V. G., 339, 340
Wilkinson, Ellen, 164
William II, Kaiser, 152
Williams-Shope, Mark, 393
Wincott, Len, 168
Winster, Lord, 106
Wohlforth, Tim, 134, 466
Wolfe, Bertram D., 267, 324, 463
Wolfstein, Rosi (Mrs. Paul Frölich), 154
Wollweber, Ernst, 161
Wolton, Douglas, 390
Woog, Edgar, 419-23 *passim*

Xoxe, Koçi, 4, 5

Yamakawa Hitoshi, 243, 244
Yang Ming-hsüan, 71
Yani, Achmad, 204
Yasodis, D. P., 60
Yata, Ali, 327, 328, 329
Yazbak, Yusuf, 300, 301
Yazdi, Morteza, 225, 227
Yeh Chien-ying, 69
Yi Sŭng-yŏp, 260
Yi Tong-hwi, 257
Yon Sosa, Marco Antonio, 178
Youlou, Abbé Fulbert, 408

Yugov, Anton, 45
Yunus, *see* Curiel, Henry
Yuon, Hou, 53
Yusuf, Yusuf Salman ("Fahd"), 229, 230

Zachariadis, Nicholas, 170-73 *passim*
Zadeh, Javad, *see* Pishevari, Jaafar
Zaghlul, Sa'd, 458, 459
Zahedi, Gen., 227
al-Za'im, Husni, 303
Zaisser, Wilhelm, 160
Zaķis, *see* Kalnberziņš, Jānis
Zápotocký, Antonín, 108, 109, 110, 112

Zarruj, Hasan, 413
Zatonsky, Volodymyr, 441, 443
Zetkin, Clara, 153
Zhdanov, Andrei, 77, 449, 450
Zhgenti, T., 148
Zhivkov, Todor, 44-45, 46
Ziartides, Andreas, 106
Zinoviev, Grigorii E. (*pseud.* Apfelbaum), 31, 79-84 *passim*, 131, 136, 154, 165, 239, 363, 364, 376, 446-49 *passim*, 454
Ziwar, Ahmad, 459
Ziyam, Abu, 301
Zogu, Ahmed, 3, 4

# INDEX OF SUBJECTS

**Note:** The following abbreviations are generally used, except where their use would be inappropriate (as at the beginning of an entry or in the names of certain organizations):

>com; coms   communist; communists
>CP; CPs   communist party; communist parties
>CPSU   Communist Party of the Soviet Union
>f.   founded
>pro-Ch   pro-Chinese
>Tr   Trotskyist

Page numbers for major articles on a subject appear in boldface type.

Since almost all communist parties at one time or another were outlawed, an entry for "Outlawing of CPs" has not been included.

Afghanistan, 71
Africa, 85
  Chinese interests in, 407-9
  com cooperation with nationalist parties in, 403, 405, 407, 411
  Soviet interests in, 402-7
  *See also* Subsaharan Africa *and individual countries*
African Democratic Rally (Rassemblement Démocratique Africain, RDA):
  breaks with coms (1950), 341, 386
  connected with French CP, 54, 386
  disintegrates, 386
  excludes communist affiliates, 54
African Independence Party (com, 1957, French West Africa; since 1960, Senegal), 341, 342, 386, 387
African Socialist Movement (com), 342
African states: oppose and denounce Soviet and Chinese interference in internal affairs, 404, 405, 406
Afro-Asian Journalists' Association, 218
Afro-Asian Peoples' Solidarity Committee (in China), 63, 71, 405, 489
Albania, **3-6**, 130, 172, 262, 350, 393, 422, 483, 484, 487
  relations with Comecon, 96, 97; with USSR, 4, 5, 455
Albanian CP, **3-6**, 340, 455, 485
Algeria, **7-12**, 373
  independence and French CP, 143, 144
  Niger coms' guerrilla training in, 342
  Portuguese coms active in, 373
  war in, 175
Algerian CP, **8-12**
All-African Trade Union Federation (*formerly* Congress), 344, 393, 405, 413, 501
All-Arab League for National Liberation (com, Palestine), 235, 251
All-China Student Federation, 223, 224
All-India Student Congress, 221
All-India Students' Federation, 221
All-Union Communist Party (Bolshevik) (1925-52), 255, 425, 446, 448-50. *See also* Communist Party of Soviet Union
All-Union Leninist Communist Union of Youth (Komsomol), 454

Allied Expeditionary Forces in Siberia, 257
American Committee for the Fourth International (Tr), 466
American Popular Revolutionary Alliance (APRA, Peru), 356, 357
Amnesty for coms:
  Estonia (1938), 124
  France (1945), 141
  Greece (1945), 171
  Turkey (1926), 435
  USA (1942), 464
Anarchists, 22, 98, 99, 137, 355
Anglo-Soviet Trade Union Committee, 84, 165
Angola, 373, 404, 408, 409. *See also* Portuguese colonies
Angolan CP, 373, 411
Anti-American propaganda:
  by com international front organizations, 207, 208, 214, 492, 496, 497
  by CPs, 10, 55, 77, 101, 142, 166, 193, 212, 250, 280, 352
Anticolonialism, 179
Anticommunism: as state crime in Cuba, 102
Anticommunist actions and demonstrations against local CPs:
  Australia, 19
  Cameroon, 55
  Czechoslovakia, 112
  France, 143
  Iceland, 193
  India (Kerala), 196
  Indonesia, 203-4
  Iraq, 230-31
  Thailand, 428
  Turkey, 436
Anticommunist elements eliminated in com-dominated areas and states:
  Armenia, 16
  Bulgaria, 44
  Uzbekistan, 475
Anticommunist laws and measures:
  Australia, 19
  Austria, 23
  Brazil, 40
  Cambodia, 53
  Finland, 127
  Greece, 171-72

554  INDEX OF SUBJECTS

Anticommunist laws & measures (*continued*):
   Honduras, 134, 281
   Iran, 226
   Iraq, 230
   Jordan, 251, 252
   Nicaragua, 276
   South Africa, 391
   Thailand, 427
   USA:
      McCarran act, 465, 466
      Smith act, 464, 465
      Taft-Hartley act, 469
      Voorhis act, 464
Anticommunist movements and organizations:
   Algeria, 8
   Australia, 19
   Finland, 127
   Iraq, 231
   USA, 469
Anticommunist uprisings in com-dominated states:
   East Germany (1956), 159
   Hungary (1956), 188, 189
   North Vietnam (1956), 481
   Poland (1956), 367
   USSR (1921), 447
"Antifascist" fronts and activities promoting com aims in:
   Albania, 4, 5
   Bulgaria, 44
   Burma, 48
   Great Britain, 166
   Hungary, 186
   Indonesia, 202
   Spain, 397, 400
   Yugoslavia, 506-7
Anti-Zionist League founded by Jewish coms, 230
Antizionist propaganda by Palestinian coms, 235
Arab coms:
   denounce Soviet recognition of Israel, 303, 460
   vs. nationalists, 7, 9, 230, 431
Arab League, 430
Arab Socialist Renaissance Party (Ba'th):
   in Iraq, 305
   in Syria, 231
Arab Socialist Union (Iraq), 231
Argentina, 13-15, 134, 266, 271, 272, 276-83 *passim*, 286, 355
Armenia, 15-18
Armenian Republic (1918-20), 16
Armenians in Lebanon, 301, 304
Armenkom, 16
Arms for com guerrillas and rebels from:
   China, 504-10 *passim*
   USSR, 405-10 *passim*
Arrest of CP members in com-ruled states:
   Czechoslovakia, 111
   Hungary, 188, 189
   North Korea, 260
   Poland, 367
   USSR, 149, 254, 256, 449

Asia-Africa Society (in China), 71
Assassination attempts by coms against:
   Alexander, Prince Regent of Yugoslavia (1921), 505
   Shah of Iran (1949 and 1965), 227
   Sihanouk, Thailand (1960), 52
Assassinations by coms of high government officials and army officers:
   Indonesia (1965), 204
   Yugoslavia (1921), 505
Assassinations by coms of opponents of communism:
   Indonesia, 204
   Poland, 367
   Spain, 398
   Vietnam, 478
   Yugoslavia, 505
Assassinations of com leaders by unknown assassins:
   Belgium, 33
   Cuba, 99
   Germany, 153
   Tunisia, 431
Australia, **18-21**, 499
   Petrov spy affair, 19
   troops in Vietnam, 482
Australian CP, *see* Communist Party of Australia
Austria, **22-29**, 93, 156, 185, 499
   com uprisings: (1919), 23; (1950), 25
   international com fronts outlawed and expelled, 488, 491, 500
   Schutzbund uprising (1934), 23-24
Austrian Soviet of Workers' and Soldiers' Deputies in RSFSR (1918), 22, 27
Azerbaijan, Autonomous Republic of (com), 226-27
Azores Island, 371

Baleares Islands, 400, 401
Balkan Communist Federation, 3, **29-30**, 105
   directs com movement in Turkey, 437
Balkan federation, Dimitrov plan for, 44
Balkan Socialist Federation, 29, 105
Bandung Conference (1955), 68, 218, 403, 460
*Basmachi* (in Soviet Central Asia), 425, 439, 474
Basutoland, *see* Lesotho
Ba'th, *see* Arab Socialist Renaissance Party
Bavarian Soviet Republic (1919), 22, 81
Belgian CP, Marxist-Leninist (pro-Chi), 35, 423
Belgium, **31-36**, 132, 499
Belorussia, **37-39**, 452
Berlin blockade (1948), 211, 499
Bolivia, **39-40**, 266, 276, 279, 280, 281, 291
Bolshevik CP of Mexico (f. 1963), 295. *See also* Mexican CP
Bolshevik revolution in Russia (1917):
   its influence on start of com movement in other countries, 3, 18, 22, 40, 92, 98, 115, 149, 238, 243, 267, 271, 297, 300, 308, 348, 356, 370, 388, 419, 425, 462, 503

INDEX OF SUBJECTS 555

Bolshevik revolution (*continued*):
  10th anniversary celebrations, 119
"Bolshevization" of CPs:
  France, 138
  Germany, 154
  Great Britain, 164
  Netherlands, 336
  South Africa, 390
  Switzerland, 420
  Yugoslavia, 506
Borneo, *see* Malaysia; Sabah; Sarawak
*Borotbisty, see* Ukrainian Left Social Revolutionary Party
Brazil, **40-42**, 266, 271, 275, 282, 286, 291, 437
  com revolt fails (1935), 40, 275
  Portuguese exiled coms active in, 373
Brazilian CP, **40-42**, 266-72 *passim*, 278, 280, 287, 295
Bremen, com group in, 152, 157, 158
British Guiana, *see* Guyana
"British road to socialism," 166
"Browderism," 49, 101
Brussels meeting of 19 European CPs (1965), 145, 336
Bukhara, 425, 474, 475
  com attack repulsed (1918), 474
  Soviet Army invades (1920), 425, 475
Bukharan CP, 474
Bukharan People's Soviet Republic (1920), 425, 475
"Bukharinists" purged, 173, 256, 426
Bulgaria, 29, 30, **42-47**, 96, 172, 220, 484, 485
  com uprising fails (1923), 43, 83
Bulgarian CP, **42-47**, 76, 83
Burma, 47-51
Burma CP, 47-51, 352
Burundi, Chinese in:
  aid com rebellion, 405
  diplomats expelled, 408
  establish com training base, 407


Cambodia, **51-53**, 71, 480, 481
Cameroon, **54-56**, 343
Cameroon Peoples' Union (com), **54-56**, 341, 342
Canada, **56-58**
Canary Islands, 401
Canton com uprising and commune, 67
Caribbean Labor Congress, 179
Catholic church:
  opposes Franco rule in Spain, 399
  persecution under com rule, 111, 368
Central African Republic: expels Chinese diplomats, 409
Central America, 184. *See also* Latin America *and individual countries*
Ceylon, **59-64**
Ceylon CP, 61-64
Ceylon Equality Party (LSSP; com, Tr), **59-64**
  and Fourth International: affiliated with, 60; expelled from, 134

Chile, **64-65**, 266, 271, 272, 275, 278, 283, 291
China (pre-1949), 66-74 *passim*, 83, 89, 348, 349. *See also* China, People's Republic of; China, Republic of
China, People's Republic of, **66-74**, 130
  aids North Vietnam, 482
  and Africa, 342, 402-10 *passim*
  and Albania, 5, 73
  confrontation with USSR:
    in Africa, 404, 409, 410
    in international front organizations, 209, 212, 223, 487, 490, 493-94, 497, 501
  diplomatic missions used for espionage, 408
  discredits CPSU, 411
  expands influence at USSR's expense, 212
  invades Tibet, 282
  *See also* China (pre-1949); Sino-Soviet conflict
China, Republic of (Taiwan), 66-74 *passim*, 455. *See also* China (pre-1949)
Chinese CP, **66-74**, 231, 320, 334, 359, 454-55
  absorbs Korean coms in Manchuria, 257
  Bureau in Philippines, 359
  dominates CP of Malaya, 316, 317
Chinese-Indian border incidents, 69, 72, 196, 197
Chinese interference in internal political affairs in:
  Kenya, 406
  Malawi, 406
  Tanzania, 406
Chinese People's Liberation Army (*formerly* Chinese Red Army), 67, 68, 361
Chinese Soviet Republic in Juichin (Kiangsi province), 67
"Class against class" tactic, 84-85, 86, 138, 164, 199, 505
"Cold war," 77, 211, 279, 283, 335, 341, 346, 371, 398, 404
Colombia, **74-76**, 266, 267, 269, 273-80 *passim*, 283, 291, 295
Comecon, *see* Council for Mutual Economic Assistance
Cominform, *see* Communist Information Bureau
Comintern, *see* Communist International
Commissariat of Nationality Affairs, *see* Russian Soviet Federated Socialist Republic, Commissariat . . .
Commission for Information and Cooperation among Latin American Journalists, 218
Committee for an International Revolutionary Front (Switzerland, com, pro-Ch), 423
Committee of Turkish Socialist-Communists (f. Moscow 1918), *see* Turkish CP
Common Market, *see* European Economic Community
Communism, widest spread of (1944-47), 166, 230, 277, 335, 339, 421, 464, 467

Communist armed resistance during World War II against:
  Germany, 4, 32, 43, 111, 116, 141, 155, 171, 240, 311, 312, 335, 346, 366, 431, 507
  Japan, 48, 202, 317, 359
Communist cadre training, see Training of com cadres
Communist coups against com governments:
  Bulgaria (1965), 45
  Hungary (1965), 189
Communist governments, collapsed, see Soviet Republics, collapsed
Communist guerrilla (insurrectional, partisan) warfare against home government:
  Algeria, 11
  Bulgaria, 44
  Cambodia, 52
  Cameroon, 55-56
  China, 67
  Cuba, 102
  Greece, 171
  Guatemala, 178
  Indonesia, 202
  Japan, 245
  Korea, 258
  Latin America, 286
  Niger, 342
  Paraguay, 355
  Peru, 357
  Philippines, 359-61
  Senegal, 386
  Thailand, 428
  Tunisia, 431
  Vietnam (South), 481
  Yugoslavia, 507
  See also Communist uprisings, revolts, and coups
Communist Information Bureau (Cominform), 19, 20, 27, 46, 49, 76-78, 117, 142, 146, 166, 183, 195, 217, 241, 245, 247, 350, 352, 353, 371, 373, 398, 454, 486, 488, 492, 496, 500, 508
  Calcutta meeting (1948), 318, 330
  dissolution (1956), 77, 454
  expels Yugoslavia (1948), 77, 508
  membership, 4, 76
  "policy of revolution, armed struggle, and national liberation," 49, 318
Communist-inspired and -led strikes:
  Cuba, 99
  Czechoslovakia, 110
  France, 142
  Greece, 171
  Guyana, 181
  Japan, 245
  Korea (South), 259
  Latvia, 298
  Lebanon, 302
  Luxembourg, 302
  Pakistan, 353
  Portugal, 371
  Spain, 396-99 passim
  USA, 464

  Vietnam (South), 478
  Yugoslavia, 504
Communist International (Comintern; Third International), 7, 13, 18, 20, 27-32 passim, 35, 43, 46, 57-60 passim, 64-67 passim, 74, 77, 78-92, 93, 95, 100, 105, 115, 117, 119, 122, 125-29 passim, 136-40 passim, 150-55 passim, 163-70 passim, 177, 192-95 passim, 199, 201, 210, 211, 216, 219, 233, 235, 238-44 passim, 257, 271-77 passim, 285, 293, 294, 297-300 passim, 309-12 passim, 316, 317, 320, 325, 333-38 passim, 345, 354, 356, 380, 395-402 passim, 414, 419, 427-30 passim, 435, 437, 441, 454, 458, 459, 463, 464, 472, 476, 503-7 passim
  agents, instructors, and representatives in CPs of:
    Australia, 19
    Belgium, 32
    Chile, 64, 65
    China, 66, 71-72 (list), 334
    France, 137
    Germany, 86
    Great Britain, 59, 164, 168
    Hungary, 186
    Indonesia, 203
    Korea, 257
    Latin America, 267-70 passim, 275
    Malaya, 317
    Mexico, 324
    Netherlands, 333
    Philippines, 358
    Poland, 365
    Spain, 294, 398, 400
    USA, 462, 469 (list)
    Vietnam, 478
  "Bolshevization" of CPs (see "Bolshevization" of CPs)
  Bureaus abroad:
    Far Eastern, 66, 71, 72, 89; Shanghai branch, 71, 89, 244, 317
    Latin American, 65, 89, 293
    Manila "secretariat," 358
    Western European, 71, 88, 126, 333
  combats social democracy, 80-86 passim, 127, 155
  commission act as policy-making bodies and disciplinary courts, 83, 244, 334, 364, 365
  concedes mistakes, 86, 193
  conflicts with Communist Youth International, 92-93
  conflicts with CPs of:
    China, 67, 72
    France, 137
    Germany, 83
    Great Britain, 168
    Indonesia, 201
    Netherlands, 334
    Poland, 364, 365
    South Africa, 390
    Spain, 396

Communist International (*continued*)
  conflicts with CPs of (*continued*):
    Sweden, 415
    USA, 462, 463
  congresses:
    1st (1919), 80, 126, 310, 414, 419, 437, 469
    2d (1920), 80-82, 201, 375, 395, 400, 469
    3d (1921), 82, 375, 377, 400, 437
    4th (1922), 82-83, 137, 375, 437, 458
    5th (1924), 83-84, 138, 364, 375, 377, 378, 437, 459, 505
    6th (1928), 84-87, 186, 194, 195, 199, 228, 359, 365, 376, 377-78, 390, 437, 463, 478, 505
    7th (1936), 43, 87-88, 140, 186, 285, 371, 373, 376, 378, 420, 427, 507
  decisions opposed by CPs, 7, 67, 109, 166, 168, 170, 173, 186, 201, 334, 390, 396, 415
  dismisses old and appoints new party leaders in:
    France, 139
    Poland, 364-65
    Sweden, 415
    USA, 469
    Yugoslavia, 505-6
  dissolution (May 1943), 88, 187, 211, 294, 427, 454
  dissolves CPs of:
    Hungary (1922 and 1936), 186
    Korea (recognition withdrawn,1928), 257
    Poland (1938), 363, 366
  dissolves its front organizations, 93, 211, 220, 235, 277, 373, 378
  financial aid to CPs, 164, 272
  foreign coms in high positions in, 41, 72, 109, 126, 129, 186, 228, 293, 294, 334, 400, 437
  "general staff of world revolution," 78, 88
  hoax of founding of, 80
  inspires uprising and revolts in:
    Estonia, 124, 125
    Germany, 83, 84, 153
    Yugoslavia, 505
  interference in internal party affairs of CPs in:
    Australia, 19
    Austria, 27
    Belgium, 31
    Chile, 65
    China, 67
    Colombia, 74
    Cuba, 99
    Czechoslovakia, 109
    Estonia, 124
    Finland, 129
    France, 138-39
    Germany, 153
    Greece, 170, 173
    Israel, 235
    Netherlands, 333, 334
    Poland, 363-64, 365
    Rumania, 381
    USA, 85, 462, 463
    Yugoslavia, 505
  interference in internal party affairs voted inadmissible by its 7th congress, 87
  overrules majority in CPs and supports minority in:
    Poland, 364
    Sweden, 415
    USA, 462, 463
  "party of world revolution," 210
  periodization of development of world com movement, 84
    "third period," 65, 84, 100, 155, 164-68 *passim*, 266, 273, 280, 463
  press organs, 89
  records, 90
  school in Moscow, 33, 237, 469
  Secretariats in Moscow:
    Anglo-American (also South African), 390
    Caribbean, 267
    *Ländersekretariats*, 88
    Latin American, 393, 476
    South American, 267
    Women's Secretariat, 210
  theses on national and colonial questions, 7, 85, 194, 201, 228
  "world communist party" as goal, 81, 132
Communist Labor Congress, Montevideo (1929), 273
Communist Labor Party (USA), 462
Communist leaders, expatriated, residing in Moscow, 80, 81, 85, 125, 126, 129, 140, 202, 227, 239, 275, 298, 399
Communist League of America (Opposition) (Tr), 463. *See also* Socialist Workers Party
Communist Left (Spain), 396
Communist ministers in coalition governments:
  Austria, 24, 25
  Belgium, 32
  Bulgaria, and overthrow of non-com government, 44
  Chile, 64, 278
  Cuba, 100
  Czechoslovakia, and overthrow of non-com government, 111
  Denmark, 116
  Ecuador, 120, 277, 278
  Finland, 128
  France, 141, 142, 174
  Germany, 157
  Greece, 171
  Hungary, and overthrow of non-com government, 187
  Iceland, 192
  Indonesia, 203
  Iran, 226-27
  Iraq, 230
  Luxembourg, 312
  Morocco, 329
  Niger, 342
  Poland, and overthrow of non-com government, 367

558  INDEX OF SUBJECTS

Communist ministers in coalition governments (*continued*):
  San Marino, 384
  Spain, 398
  Yugoslavia, 508
Communist parties, disintegration of:
  Algeria, 11
  Cameroon, 55
  Cyprus, 106
  Haiti, 182
  South Africa, 393
  United Arab Republic, 459, 460
  USA, 465
  Yugoslavia, 505
Communist parties, underground (illegal activities):
  Argentina, 13
  Austria, 23, 24
  Belgium, 32
  Brazil, 40
  Bulgaria, 43
  Burma, 48
  Cameroon, 55
  Canada, 56
  Cuba, 100
  Cyprus, 106
  Czechoslovakia, 111
  Denmark, 116
  Estonia, 124
  Finland, 126-30 *passim*
  Germany, 155, 157
  Greece, 171
  Indonesia, 202
  Iran, 227
  Iraq, 230
  Italy, 239
  Japan, 243, 245, 247
  Korea (South), 260
  Laos, 265
  Latin America, 291 (list)
  Latvia, 298
  Lebanon, 302, 303
  Lithuania, 309
  Malaya, 317-20
  Nicaragua, 341
  Niger, 342
  Norway, 346
  Pakistan, 352, 353
  Poland, 363
  Portugal, 371, 373
  Rumania, 381
  South Africa, 391
  Spain, 399
  Sudan, 413
  Switzerland, 428
  Syria, 303, 304
  Thailand, 428
  Tunisia, 430
  Turkey, 435, 436
  USA, 462, 465, 477
  Yugoslavia, 505
Communist parties defending and supporting USSR, 34, 138-42 *passim*, 145, 168, 226, 390, 463, 507

Communist parties founded in Soviet Russia:
  Albanian, 3
  Czechoslovak, 108
  Finnish, 125
  Hungarian, 185
  Iranian, 226
  Korean, 257
  Latvian, 297-98
  Polish, 366
  Turkish, 434
  Yugoslav, 503
Communist parties incorporated as branches of CPSU:
  Armenian, 16
  Estonian, 124
  Kazakh, 254
  Khoresmian, 475
  Latvian, 299
  Lithuanian, 311
  Ukrainian, 441, 443
Communist parties manifesting independence from Moscow:
  Norway, 347
  Rumania, 382, 383
  Spain, 400
  Sweden, 415, 416
  Ukraine (1918), 441
  Yugoslavia, 508-9
Communist parties objecting to Moscow interference into internal party affairs:
  Japan, 246
  Korea, 262
  Spain, 396
  Yugoslavia, 509-10
Communist party activities directed by exiled leadership, 55, 56, 118, 186, 201, 228, 230, 239, 277, 298, 330, 331, 355, 365, 393, 436, 437
Communist party members, arrest of, *see* Arrest of CP members in com-ruled states
Communist Party of:
  Albania (*see* Albanian CP)
  Algeria (*see* Algerian CP)
  America (f. Sept. 1919), 56, 462 (*see also* Communist Party of United States)
  America (f. May 1920), 462 (*see also* Communist Party of United States)
  America (Majority Group), 463 (*see also* Communist Party of United States [Opposition])
  Argentina, **13-15**, 266-72 *passim*, 278, 283, 287, 289, 291
  Armenia, **15-18**
  Australia, **18-21**, 338
  Austria, **22-29**, 80
  Belgium, **31-36**
  Belorussia, **36-38**
  Bolivia, **39-40**, 266, 276, 279, 280, 281, 291
  Brazil (f. 1922) (*see* Brazilian CP)
  Brazil (f. 1961; pro-Ch), 295 (*see also* Brazilian CP)
  Bulgaria (*see* Bulgarian CP)

# INDEX OF SUBJECTS

Communist Party of (*continued*):
  Burma (*see* Burma CP)
  Cambodia (*see* People's Party of Khmer)
  Cameroon (*see* Cameroon Peoples' Union)
  Canada, **56-58**
  Central America, 121, 272
  Ceylon (*see* Ceylon Equality Party)
  Chile, **64-65**, 266, 267, 268, 271-75 *passim*, 287, 291
  China (*see* Chinese CP)
  Colombia, 74-76, 266, 267, 269, 273, 274, 277, 280, 283, 291, 295
  Colombia, Marxist-Leninist (pro-Ch), 74, 295
  Costa Rica (*see* Popular Vanguard Party of Costa Rica)
  Cuba, **98-105**, 177, 182, 183, 266, 267-68, 271, 275-78 *passim*, 284-87 *passim*, 291
  Cyprus, **105-8**
  Czechoslovakia, 76, 83, **108-15**
  Denmark (*see* Danish CP)
  Dominican Republic (*see* Dominican CP)
  Ecuador, **119-20**, 266, 267, 268, 273, 274, 277, 291, 295
  Egypt, 458, 459 (*see also* Unified [Second] CP of Egypt)
  El Salvador, **121-22**, 266-71 *passim*, 274, 278, 291
  Estonia (*see* Estonian CP)
  Finland (*see* Finnish CP)
  France (*see* French CP)
  Georgia, **148-51**
  German Austria (*see* Communist Party of Austria)
  Germany, 80, 85, 86, 87, **151-63**, 364
    and Hitler's rise to power, 85-87
    leaders executed in USSR, 155
    sides with Nazis in opposing socialists in Prussia, 86
    (*see also* Socialist Unity Party of Germany)
  Great Britain, **163-69**, 179, 199, 393, 394
  Greece, 30, 105, **170-73**
  Guadeloupe (*see* Guadeloupe CP)
  Guatemala (*see* Guatemalan Labor Party)
  Haiti, 182, 268, 274, 279
  Holland (*see* Communist Party of Netherlands)
  Honduras, **184-85**, 266-74 *passim*, 281, 282, 291, 295
  Hungary, 76, **185-91**
  Iceland (*see* United Labor-Socialist Party of Iceland)
  India, 49, 61, **194-200**, 330, 351, 352
    as transmitter of Soviet policies to Southern Asia, 49
  Indies (*see* Communist Party of Indonesia)
  Indochina, 51, 478
  Indonesia, **200-205**, 334, 352, 358
  Iran (*see* Tudeh)
  Iraq, **229-32**, 460
  Ireland, **232-34**
  Israel (*see* Israeli CP)
  Italy (*see* Italian CP)
  Japan (*see* Japan CP)
  Jordan, **251-53**
  Kazakhstan, **253-55**
  Kirgizia, **255-56**
  Korea (*see* Korean Workers' Party)
  Laos (*see* Laotian People's Party)
  Latvia, 80, **297-99**, 309
    Bureau abroad (Soviet Russia), 80, 298
  Lebanon (*see* Lebanese CP)
  Lesotho, **306-7**
  Lithuania (*see* Lithuanian CP)
  Luxembourg, **312-14**
  Malagasy (*see* Malagasy CP)
  Malaya, **316-21**, 352
  Martinique (*see* Martinican CP)
  Mexico (*see* Mexican CP)
  Morocco (*see* Moroccan CP)
  Nepal, **330-32**
  Netherlands, **333-37**
  New Zealand, **337-40**
  Nicaragua (*see* Socialist Party of Nicaragua)
  Niger Republic (*see* Independence Party [Sawaba])
  Nigeria (*see* Socialist Workers' and Farmers' Party of Nigeria)
  North Ireland, 233-34 (*see also* Communist Party of Ireland)
  Norway, 80, **345-47**
  Outer Mongolia (*see* Mongolian People's Revolutionary Party)
  Pakistan, **351-53**
  Palestine (*see* Israeli CP)
  Panama (*see* Party of the People of Panama)
  Paraguay (*see* Paraguayan CP)
  Peru (*see* Peruvian CP)
  Philippines, **358-61**
  Poland (1925-38), 76, 80, **361-70**
    created as Communist Workers' Party of Poland (1918-25), 363-64
    dissolved by Comintern (1938), 366
    reactivated as Polish Workers' Party (1942), 366
    renamed Polish United Workers' Party (1948), 367
  Portugal (*see* Portuguese CP)
  Réunion (*see* Réunion CP)
  Rumania (*see* Rumanian CP)
  San Marino (*see* San Marino CP)
  Senegal (*see* African Independence Party)
  Slovakia, 110, 111
  South Africa, 306, **388-91** (*see also* South African CP)
  Soviet Union (*formerly* Russian CP [Bolshevik] and All-Union Communist Party [Bolshevik]), 76, 109, 124, 131, 145, 158, 270, 287, 311, 381, 425, 426, 438, **445-57**, 474, 475
    congresses: 20th (1956), 165, 188, 450, 455; 21st (1959), 501; 22d (1961), 5, 12, 35, 190, 350, 380, 385, 433, 451, 470, 483, 485
    "Left Opposition" (Tr), 131, 448
    national and social composition, 453
    national bureaus and sections, 381, 450, 452, 474, 503-4

560   INDEX OF SUBJECTS

Communist Party of (*continued*):
  Spain, **395-401**, 487
    emerges in Geneva (1964) as pro-Ch group, 422-23
  Sudan (*see* Sudanese CP)
  Sweden, 80, **414-18**
  Switzerland (*see* Labor Party of Switzerland)
  Syria (*see* Syrian CP)
  Tadzhikstan **425-26**
  Thailand, **427-29**
  Tunisia, **429-33**
  Turkestan, 255, 425, 474
  Turkey (*see* Turkish CP)
  Turkmenistan, **439-40**
  Ukraine, **440-44**, 450
    national and social composition, 443
  United Arab Republic (*see* Unified [Second] CP of Egypt)
  United States, 56, 83, 359, **462-72**
    Comintern deposes leadership, 85
    Comintern representatives in, 186, 462, 469
    Comintern's mediator in Cuba, 101
    disaffiliates from Comintern, 464
    McCarran act (1950) drives party underground, 465, 466
    renamed temporarily Communist Political Association, 464
  United States (Opposition) (*known as* "right opposition"), 463 (*see also* Independent Labor League of America)
  United States of America, Marxist-Leninist (pro-Ch), 466
  Uruguay, 266-73 *passim*, 278, 287, 291, **472-74**
  Uzbekistan, **474-76**
  Venezuela, 266-69 *passim*, 274, 278, 284, 291, **476-77**
  Vietnam (North) (*see* Vietnam Workers' Party)
  Vietnam (South) (*see* People's Revolutionary Party)
  Western Ukraine, 441
  Yugoslavia, 30, 76, 84, **503-9**
    expelled from Cominform, 77
    its revisionism attacked by Fourth International, 135
    (*see also* League of Communists of Yugoslavia)
Communist Political Association (USA), 464. See also Communist Party of United States
Communist political congress, Buenos Aires (1929), 273
Communist riots and violence, 23, 32, 43, 110, 138, 139, 142, 144, 174, 180, 181, 245, 259, 298, 302, 322, 323, 328, 352-53, 363, 364, 379, 399, 478, 504
Communist Students' Union (France), 144, 145
Communist terrorist activities, 10, 43, 178, 364, 505

Communist University for the Peoples of the East, in USSR, 170
Communist uprisings, revolts, and coups:
  failed:
    Algeria (1965), 12
    Austria (1919), 22-23; (1934), 23, 24; (1950), 25
    Brazil (1935), 40, 375
    Bulgaria (1923), 43, 83
    Burma (1948), 49
    China (1927-28; Shanghai, Hunan, Nanchang, Canton), 67
    Congo-Kinshasa (1964), 405, 406, 407
    Dominican Republic (1965), 118
    El Salvador (1932), 121, 274
    Estonia (1924), 124, 125
    Germany (1921), 81, 153; (1923), 83, 84, 153, 364
    Greece (1936), 171; (1944), 171; (1946-49), 171, 508
    India (1949), 196
    Indonesia (1926), 201; (1948), 202; (1965), 204
    Iran (1917), 226; (1946), 226, 227
    Lithuania (1920), 309
    Mexico (1929), 324, 325
    Niger (1964), 342
    Pakistan (1950), 352
    Paraguay (1959-60), 355
    Spain (1934), 397
    Vietnam (1930), 478, 479; (1940), 479
  planned but prevented:
    Cambodia (1960), 52
    Finland (1948), 128
    Nepal (1952), 330
    Pakistan (1951), 352
    Yugoslavia (1929), 505
  successful:
    Czechoslovakia (1948), 108, 111, 113, 116
    Vietnam (North) (1945), 479
    Yugoslavia (1941-44), 507, 508
  *See also* Communist guerrilla . . . warfare
Communist Workers' Federation of Sweden (pro-Ch), 415
Communist Workers' Party of Poland (1918-25), 363-64
Communist Workers' Party of Sweden (pro-Ch), 415
Communist Working Circle (Denmark, pro-Ch), 117
Communist Youth International, 89, 90, **92-94**, 126, 377
  conflict with Comintern, 93
  dissolution by Comintern, 93, 211
Communist Youth League (Cuba), 99
Communists, amnesty for, *see* Amnesty for coms
Communists, executed, *see* Execution of coms . . . ; Execution of foreign coms . . . ; Execution of prominent coms . . . ; Execution of prominent party leaders . . .
Communists, exiled, 106, 177, 184, 201, 239-40, 298, 301, 304, 330, 342,

INDEX OF SUBJECTS 561

Communists, exiled (*continued*):
　355, 370, 373, 386, 393, 428, 436, 479
Communists, expelled, *see* Expulsion of founders and prominent members of CPs
Communists, foreign, disappearance in Russia
　Austrian, 24
　British, 168
　Estonian, 124
　Lithuanian, 311
　South African, 390
　Turkish, 434
Communists in representative assemblies of non-com-ruled states (incl. election results):
　Algeria, 10
　Australia, 19
　Austria, 25
　Argentina, 278
　Belgium, 31-35 *passim*
　Brazil, 40
　Bulgaria, 43
　Cameroon, 55
　Canada, 57
　Ceylon, 61
　Chile, 64
　Colombia, 75
　Cuba, 100, 101, 103, 278
　Cyprus, 106
　Czechoslovakia, 109-12 *passim*
　Denmark, 116
　Ecuador, 120
　Estonia, 124
　Finland, 126, 127, 128
　France, 137-44 *passim*
　Germany, 153, 155, 157
　Great Britain, 164, 165, 166
　Greece, 170-73 *passim*
　Guadeloupe, 174, 175
　Guyana, 179, 180, 181
　Haiti, 182, 279
　Hungary, 187
　Iceland, 192, 193
　India, 196, 197, 200n1
　Indonesia, 203
　Iran, 226
　Israel, 236
　Italy, 239-42 *passim*
　Japan, 245, 248
　Latin America, 276, 286
　Latvia, 298
　Lebanon, 302
　Lithuania, 310, 311
　Luxembourg, 312, 313
　Malagasy, 315
　Martinique, 321, 322
　Morocco, 327
　Netherlands, 334, 335, 336
　New Zealand, 337, 339
　Niger, 342
　Norway, 345, 346, 347
　Pakistan, 352, 353
　Peru, 278, 357
　Philippines, 360
　Poland, 363, 365, 367
　Réunion, 379, 380
　Rumania, 382
　San Marino, 384
　South Africa, 391
　Spain, 397
　Sudan, 413
　Sweden, 415
　Switzerland, 421, 422, 423
　Syria, 304
　Thailand, 427
　Tunisia, 432
　USA (presidential elections), 463, 465, 469
　Uruguay, 278, 472, 473
　Venezuela, 278, 416
　Yugoslavia, 504
Communists opposing independence of:
　Algeria, 7, 9
　Cyprus, 106, 107
　Guadeloupe, 174
　India, 195
　Madagascar, 315
　Poland, 362
　Tunisia, 431, 432
　Ukraine, 440
Communists serving Soviet espionage:
　in Australia, 19
　in Canada, 57
　in Iran, 227
　in USA, 465
Confederation of Latin American Workers (f. 1938; *also known as* Workers' Confederation of Latin America), 75, 276, 279, 324
　disbanded in 1964, 501
Conference of Transport Workers of the Pacific, Canton (1924), 358
Conference on Strike Strategy, Strassburg near Berlin (1929), 376
Congo-Brazzaville, 71, 407, 408
　com rebellion, 405
Congo-Kinshasa, 404, 407, 409, 411
　coms trained in China, 405
　expels Soviet representatives, 405
Congress of Industrial Organizations (CIO, in USA): withdraws from World Federation of Trade Unions (1949), 499
Congress of the Peoples of the East, Baku (1920), 228
Congress of the Sons of Sweat of the Philippines, *see* Communist Party of Philippines
Congresses and meetings of foreign CPs, in Russia
　Latvian, 299
　Lithuanian, 310
　Outer Mongolian, 349
　Polish, 363, 364, 365
　Ukrainian, 441
Costa Rica, **95-96**, 266, 274, 291
Council for Mutual Economic Assistance (Comecon), 5, 46, 78, **96-98**, 190, 350
Cuba, **98-105**, 118, 144, 177, 182, 183,

Cuba (*continued*):
  266-72 *passim*, 275-78 *passim*, 283, 286, 287, 291, 386, 393, 455, 494
  base for attacks against other Latin American countries, 284, 341, 354
Cyprus, **105-8**
Czechoslovak National Student Union, 221, 222
Czechoslovakia, 77, 83, 93, 96, 97, **108-15**, 220, 484, 492
  com takeover (1948), 108, 111, 499

Dahomey, 409
Danish CP, **115-18**
Defections and resignations of prominent members from CPs:
  Australia, 13
  Belgium, 34
  Brazil, 41
  Colombia, 74
  Denmark, 115, 116, 117
  Finland, 129
  France, 137, 139
  Iran, 226
  Italy, 240
  Japan, 244, 247
  Latin America, 269-70
  Luxembourg, 312
  Malaya, 317
  Martinique, 322
  Netherlands, 334
  New Zealand, 339
  Norway, 346, 347
  Poland, 365, 367
  Portugal, 372, 373
  Réunion, 380
  South Africa, 389, 390
  Spain, 396
  Sweden, 414, 415
  Switzerland, 420, 422
  Syria, 303
  Turkey, 437
  USA, 465
Democratic National Liberation Movement (com, Egypt), 460
Democratic Party of Iran (com, Iranian Azerbaijan), 226
Democratic Party of Kurdistan (com, Mahabad [1945]; revived in Iraq [1960]), 231
Democratic Revolutionary Party, *see* Communist Party of Honduras
Denmark, 93, **115-18**, 499
Deportations to forced labor camps in USSR:
  British coms visiting USSR, 168
  Georgian CP members, 149
  Hungarian CP members, 186
  Polish CP members, 366
  Spanish Trotskyites, 398
De-Stalinization, 5, 26, 34, 72, 112, 114, 116, 143, 160, 188, 190, 196, 260, 312, 322, 335, 336, 346, 350, 367, 415, 422
  economic, in Yugoslavia, 509
  sabotaged in Hungary, 188

Djakarta-Phnom Penh-Peking-Hanoi-Pyongyang axis, 203
Dominican CP, **118-19**, 266-69 *passim*, 277, 280, 291
Dominican Popular Movement, *see* Dominican CP
Dominican Popular Socialist Party, *see* Dominican CP
Dominican Republic, **118-19**, 266, 277, 291
  Cuba-based assault on (1959), 284
  Inter-American Peace Force intervention during civil war (1965), 286
Du Bois Clubs (W. E. B. Du Bois Clubs, USA), 468

East Germany, *see* Germany, Democratic Republic of
Ecuador, **119-20**, 266, 276-79 *passim*, 286, 291
Egypt, *see* United Arab Republic
Egyptian National Liberation Movement (com), 459
El Salvador, **121-22**, 184, 266-71 *passim*, 278, 286, 291
  com uprising fails, 274
Election of coms to representative assemblies, *see* Communists in representative assemblies . . .
England, *see* Great Britain
Estonia, 79, **122-25**
Estonian Soviet Republic (1918), 79, 123
Ethiopia, 409, 410
Ethnic composition of CPs in:
  Rumania, 382-83
  USSR, 453
  Yugoslavia, 512
European Defense Community, *see* North Atlantic Treaty Organization
European Economic Community (Common Market), 346, 501
European Recovery Program, *see* Marshall Plan
Evian agreement (independence of Algeria, 1962), 11, 144
Execution of coms by non-com governments in:
  Cambodia, 52
  China (pre-1949), 66, 67, 71
  Czechoslovakia, 110 (by Germans)
  Estonia, 124
  France, 140, 141 (by Germans)
  Honduras, 184
  Indonesia, 201-4 *passim*
  Iraq, 230, 231
  Korea (South), 257
  Lithuania, 310
  Luxembourg, 312 (by Germans)
  Poland, 364
  Spain, 398, 399
  Thailand, 428
Execution of dissenters in com-dominated states:
  Outer Mongolia (1931), 350
  Poland (1944-45), 367

Execution of foreign coms in USSR:
  Austrian, 24
  Bulgarian, 94
  Finnish, 129
  German, 155 (list)
  Greek, 173
  Hungarian, 186
  Israeli, 235
  Latvian, 298
  Lithuanian, 311
  Polish, 220, 366
  Rumanian, 381
  Yugoslavian, 504, 506
Execution of prominent coms by com governments in:
  Bulgaria, 44-47 passim
  Czechoslovakia, 77, 111, 114
  Hungary, 77, 188, 189
Execution of prominent party leaders in USSR:
  Armenians, 16
  Belorussians, 37
  Georgians, 148, 149
  heads of Soviet Secret Police, 149, 454
  Kazakhs, 254
  Kirgiz, 256
  "Old Bolsheviks," 449
  Russians, 94, 168, 449, 450
  Ukrainians, 443
  Uzbeks, 475
Exiled coms, see Communist, exiled
Expulsion of founders and prominent members of CPs:
  by Comintern, 83, 84, 85, 194
  by CPs, 18, 19, 28, 32, 33, 56, 66, 69, 74, 83, 110, 111, 132, 137, 138, 139, 145, 153, 154, 160, 161, 164, 168-71 passim, 269, 298, 313, 325, 334, 335, 346, 357, 390, 396, 418, 419, 443, 463, 464, 504

Factional strife and power struggle in CPs:
  Albania, 4
  Argentina, 13
  Bulgaria, 44
  Burma, 48
  Egypt, 460
  France, 139
  Germany, 154
  Hungary, 185
  Iceland, 193
  Iraq, 229, 231
  Japan, 246
  Korea, 258
  Latin America, 287
  Lithuania, 298
  Netherlands, 333
  Norway, 346
  Outer Mongolia, 350
  Paraguay, 355
  Peru, 357
  Philippines, 360
  Poland, 364, 365
  Portugal, 370, 373
  Réunion, 379

  South Africa, 389
  Spain, 396, 399
  Sweden, 417
  Switzerland, 421
  Ukraine, 441
  USA, 462, 465
  Venezuela, 476
  Yugoslavia, 505
Famine:
  in Russia (1921-22), 149, 447
    Kazakhstan (1929-30), 254
    Ukraine (1932), 442
  in China (1960, 1961), 455
Fascism, "black" fascism, 82, 85, 117, 127, 139, 155, 166, 239
Federation of Communist Youth of Portugal, 370
Federation of Communist Youth of Spain, 396, 397
Federation of Former Political Prisoners of German Concentration Camps, see International Federation of Resistance Fighters
Fergana (oblast in Soviet Central Asia), 255
FIDEL, see Leftist Liberation Front
"Fifth regiment" of Spanish loyalists, 398, 400
Finances of CPs, 27, 249
Financial support, Chinese, of CPs in:
  Congo-Brazzaville, 403
  Congo-Kinshasa, 405, 407
  Kenya, 407
  Lesotho, 307
Financial support, Soviet, of CPs in:
  Kenya, 406
  Lesotho, 307
  Somalia, 409
  Syria, 304
Finland, 80, 123, **125-31**
  "Red government" (1918), 79, 125-26
  Soviet invasion (1939), 116, 127; (1941), 127, 192
  Terijoki government (1939), 126-29 passim
Finnish CP, **125-31**
Finnish Soviet Republic (Terijoki, 1939), 126-29 passim
Food and Agriculture Organization, 503
Forced labor camps in USSR, see Deportations . . .
Foreign com visitors to USSR, disappearance of, see Communists, foreign, disappearance in USSR
Formosa, see China, Republic of
Fourth International (Tr), **131-35**
  acts in defense of USSR, 132, 133
  affiliation of parties, 60, 62
  founding congress, 132
  international centers (1965), 134
  and Sino-Soviet split, 135
  split at 4th congress (1953), 134
  unification congress, Rome (1963), 134
  "world party of the socialist revolution" as goal, 132
  and Yugoslavia, 135

## INDEX OF SUBJECTS

France, 83, 84, 132, 134, **136-47**, 398, 480, 496
  economic aid to African states, 407, 408
  expels international com front organizations, 208, 487, 488, 493, 500
  Portuguese exiled coms active in, 373
  Spanish exiled coms active in, 398
Freemasons, *see* Masons
French CP, 10, 77, 78, **136-47**, 322, 326, 385, 429, 478, 479, 496
  activities in colonies and territories:
    Algeria, 7-12 *passim*
    Cameroon, 54, 55
    Guadeloupe, 174, 175
    Malagasy, 314, 315
    Martinique, 321
    Morocco, 326
    Niger, 341
    Réunion, 379
    Senegal, 385
    Tunisia, 429, 433n2
    Vietnam, 478, 479
  activities in defense of USSR, 140
  and African Democratic Rally, 54, 341
  agents in CP of Malaya, 317
  Colonial Bureau, 379
  and de Gaulle, 141-45 *passim*
  disapproves acts of individual terrorism, 10
  and founding of Comintern, 80
  loyalty to USSR, 142-45 *passim*
  purges in, 138, 139
  starts "class-against-class" tactic, 138
  starts popular-front tactic, 139
French Equatorial Africa, former, 386. *See also* Subsaharan Africa *and individual countries*
French Territory of the Afars and the Issas (*former* French Somaliland), 409
French West Africa, former, 386. *See also* Subsaharan Africa *and individual countries*
Friendship University, Moscow (*formerly* Lumumba University), 405
Fritz-Heckert-Gewerkschaftsschule, Bernau: East German training Center for African coms, 404

General Confederation of Labor (CGT, France), 11, 54, 136, 139-42 *passim*, 146, 314, 315, 327, 385, 430, 431, 498
General Confederation of Labor Work Force (CGT Force Ouvrière, France), 146
"General staff of world revolution" (Comintern), 78, 88
Geneva conference and declaration concerning Indochina (1954), 52, 68, 480, 481
Georgia, **148-51**
  declares independence (1918), 149
  occupation by Soviet Army, 149
German invasion of:
  Austria (1938), 24
  Denmark (1940), 192
  Hungary (1944), 187
  Poland (1939), 366
  *See also* German invasion of USSR
German invasion of USSR (1941):
  effect on Fourth International, 132
  general impact on CPs, 88
  influence on CP tactics in:
    Argentina, 13
    Belgium, 32
    Bulgaria, 43
    Canada, 57
    Ceylon, 60
    Colombia, 75
    Denmark, 116
    France, 141
    Germany, 156
    Great Britain, 166
    Greece, 171
    Iceland, 192
    India, 195
    Italy, 240
    Latin America, 275
    Mexico, 325
    New Zealand, 339
    Norway, 346
    Poland, 366
    South Africa, 391
    Sweden, 415
    Switzerland, 419, 421
    Tunisia, 430
    Ukraine, 442
    USA, 464
    Yugoslavia, 507
German Officers' League (in USSR), 156
"German road to socialism," 156-59 *passim*
German-Soviet relations:
  exchange of Dimitrov, 86
  friendship (1939-41), 87
  military cooperation (after 1922), 86
  USSR returns German com exiles, 87
Germany, 81-87 *passim*, 93, 125, 127, 132, 133, **151-63**, 214, 342, 363, 364, 499. *See also* Germany, Democratic Republic of; Germany, Federal Republic of
Germany, Democratic Republic of, 96, 97, 157-62 *passim*, 227, 484, 485. *See also* Germany
Germany, Federal Republic of, 161, 214. *See also* Germany
Ghana (*former* Gold Coast), 403, 405, 408-11 *passim*
  coms trained in USSR and satellites, 404
  expels Chinese diplomats, 409
  guerrilla warfare training for Niger coms, 342
Gilan (Soviet) Republic (Persia, 1920-21), 226
Goa, 371. *See also* Portuguese colonies
Gold Coast, *see* Ghana
Great Britain, 83, 84, 132-35 *passim*, **163-69**, 179, 194, 195, 199, 280, 398, 492, 496, 498
  intervention in Greece (1944), 171

Great Britain (*continued*):
  occupation of Iceland opposed by local coms, 192
"Great leap forward" (China), 68
Greece, 29, 30, 105, 106, 107, 132, **170-73**
  British intervention (1944), 171
  com uprising (1946), 171, 508
Guadeloupe, **174-76**
Guadeloupe CP, **174-76**, 322
Guatemala, 121, **177-78**, 184, 266, 269, 270, 274, 278-81 *passim*, 286, 291
Guatemalan Labor Party (com), 121, **177-78**, 266-71 *passim*, 274, 277, 281
Guinea, 342, 343, 404, 405, 408, 411
  coms trained in East Germany, 404
  expels Soviet diplomats, 404, 405
  training college for labor leaders in, 404
Guyana (*former* British Guiana), **179-82**
Guzenko affair in Canada, 57

Haiti, 182-83, 266, 268, 274, 279, 291
  Cuba-based assault on (1959), 284, 285
Hitler-Stalin pact (Ribbentrop-Molotov pact, 1939), 87, 94, 449
  influence on CPs in:
    Argentina, 13
    Ceylon, 59
    Chile, 64
    Colombia, 75
    Denmark, 116
    France, 140
    Germany, 156
    Great Britain, 165, 166
    Iceland, 192
    Italy, 240
    Latin America, 275
    Mexico, 324
    Netherlands, 335
    Norway, 345
    Palestine, 235
    Rumania, 381
    Slovakia, 110
    South Africa, 391
    Sweden, 415
    Switzerland, 418
    USA, 463
    Vietnam, 479
    Yugoslavia, 506
Hoax of founding of Comintern, 80
Holland, *see* Netherlands
Honduran Revolutionary Party (com), 184. *See also* Communist Party of Honduras
Honduras, **184-85**, 266, 267, 272-74 *passim*, 281, 282, 291, 295
Huks, *see* People's Liberation Army ("Huks," Philippines)
Hunan com uprising, 67
Hungarian 1956 rebellion and Soviet intervention:
  execution of rebellion leaders, 189
  influence on other CPs, 5, 20, 26, 34, 44, 72, 96, 112, 116, 143, 165, 167, 193, 196, 214, 224, 240, 282, 312, 339, 346, 383, 415, 423, 451, 465, 489, 493, 500
Hungary, 22, 23, 79, 81, 93, 96, 156, **185-91**, 220, 484
  Hungarian Red Army units enter Slovakia, 109
  Hungarian Soviet Republic (1919), 22, 79, 81, 93, 109

Iceland, **192-94**
  British occupation protested by local coms, 192
  "road to socialism," 193
Independence Party (Sawaba; com, Niger), **341-42**, 410
Independent Labor League of America (com), 463
India, **194-200**, 351, 393, 455
  Chinese border violations (1962), 197, 199
  Chinese territorial claims, 196, 455
  war with Pakistan (1965), 198, 199
Indochina, 477, 478, 479
  uprising against French rule (1946), 10, 142, 480
Indochina Communist Alliance (Canton, China), 478
Indoctrination of foreign coms in USSR, *see* Training of com cadres
Indonesia (*former* Netherlands Indies), **200-205**, 487, 494
  army cooperates with Sarawak coms, 318
  pro-Peking coup (1965), 69, 73, 212, 218, 320, 501
Infiltration of European coms into colonial Africa, 402
Infiltration tactic applied by CPs:
  failures:
    Hungary (1930s), 186
    Ireland, 233
    Morocco, 328
    Sarawak, 318
  successes:
    Guatemala, 177
    India, 195
    Malagasy, 315, 316
    Turkey, 436, 437
    USA, trade unions (1930s), 481
    Vietnam, 481
Intellectuals:
  disillusionment with coms in Africa, 403
  important role in com movement, 290, 324, 327, 338, 355, 369, 370, 387, 393, 399, 412, 420, 436, 437, 441, 458, 483, 488, 506
Inter-American Peace Force: intervention in Dominican Republic, 286
International Association of Democratic Lawyers, **206-9**, 212, 486, 489
  excludes Soviet representative from permanent secretariat, 209
  expels Yugoslav affiliate, 207
International Bank for Economic Cooperation, Moscow (Comecon bank), 97
International Bar Association (non-com), 208
International Brigades (Spanish civil war), 32, 110, 240, 398, 506

International Bureau of Tourism and Exchanges of Youth, 212, 294
International Committee for Cooperation of Journalists, 217-18
International Committee of Fourth International (London), 133, 135
International com front organizations, **210-12**
   expelled from non-com states, 487, 488, 493, 500
   non-com affiliates withdraw from, 487, 488, 492, 499
   *See also specific organizations*
International Communist League (Tr), 132
International Communists of Germany (Bremen), 152
International Council of Students, 221
International Confederation of Arab Trade Unions, 501
International Confederation of Free Trade Unions (non-com), 431, 499
International Federation of Journalists, 217
International Federation of Resistance Fighters, 212, **213-15**
International Institute for Peace, 488, 491, 496. *See also* World Council of Peace
International Labor Organization, 503
International Organization for Aid to Revolutionaries (International Red Aid), 89, 121, 154, 210, 211, **216**, 299
   branches:
     El Salvador, 121, 266
     Lithuania, 299
     Malagasy, 314
     Portugal, 373
     Spain, 400
   exposed as Soviet intelligence organization, 211
International Organization of Journalists, 211, **217-19**
"International Party of Communists" (Trotsky's description of Comintern), 81
International Peasants' Council (Krestintern; Peasants' International), 90, 210, 211, **219-20**, 320, 359, 361
International Red Aid, *see* International Organization for Aid to Revolutionaries
International Red Cross, 489
International Secretariat of Fourth International (Argentina), 134, 135
International Socialist Party, *see* CP of Argentina
"International Soviet Republic," as goal of Comintern, 78, 80, 81
International Union of Peasants (non-com), 220
International Union of Socialist Youth Organizations, 92
International Union of Students, 212, **221-26**, 323, 351, 405, 492
International Workers' Aid (Germany), 154
Iran, **225-29**
   Gilan (Soviet) Republic (1920-21), 226

Iraq, **229-232**, 460
   revolution (1958), 304
Ireland, **232-34**, 499
Irish Workers' League (com, Free State), 234. *See also* Communist Party of Ireland
Iskra [group] (com, Egypt), 459
Islamic religious elements oppose communism, 413
Israel, **235-38**, 251, 301
Israeli CP (*formerly* Palestinian CP), **235-38**, 251, 301
   "arabization" of, 235
   opposes Sinai campaign (1956), 236
   rejects Balfour Declaration, 301
   splits over USSR support for Jewish state, 235
Italian CP, 76, 77, **238-43**, 315, 460, 493, 500
   failed attempt of "dialogue" with church, 241
   influence in San Marino, 384
   "Italian line" (*also* "Italian theses," "Italian road to socialism"), 20, 21, 144, 145, 240
Italy, 81-84 *passim*, 93, 132, **238-43**
Ivory Coast: Chinese interference into internal affairs of, 409

Japan, **243-50**, 350, 359, 464, 487, 499
   occupation of: Burma, 48; Philippines, 359
   Outer Mongolian coup to replace Soviet influence with that of (1931), 350
Japan CP, **243-50**
   financially supported by China, 249
Jews, 213, 304, 458
   in Egypt: Jewish coms oppose Zionism, 460
   in Iraq: Jewish coms establish Anti-Zionist League (1945), 230
   mistreatment in com-ruled states, 57
   in Poland: radical Jewish groups welcome Soviet invasion (1919), 363
   support CPs, 166, 363, 389
   *See also* Israel
Jordan, **252-53**

Kara-Kirgiz Autonomous Region, 255
Karen (ethnic group in Burma), 49
Kazakhstan, **253-55**, 452
Kenya, 404-10 *passim*
   Chinese representatives expelled, 406
   coms trained in USSR, 404
   Odinga com conspiracy liquidated, 406
   Soviet representatives expelled, 405
Kerala (India) com government (1957-59), 196
Khivan khanate: overthrown by Soviet invasion (1920), 475
Khoresmian CP, 475
Khoresmian People's Soviet Republic (1920), 475
Kirgiz Autonomous Soviet Socialist Republic (1920), 253
Kirgizia, **255-56**

# INDEX OF SUBJECTS

Kokand Autonomy (1917), 474
Komsomol, *see* All-Union Leninist Communist Union of Youth
Korea, **257-63**. *See also* Korea, Democratic People's Republic of; Korea, Republic of; Korean War
Korea, Democratic People's Republic of (North Korea), 97, **257-63**, 487. *See also* Korea
Korea, Republic of (South Korea), 257-61 *passim*
  troops in Vietnam, 482
  *See also* Korea
Korean CP, 257. *See also* Korean Workers' Party
Korean War, 68, 196, 222, 260, 427, 496
Korean Workers' Party (1949 merger of North and South Korean workers' parties), **257-63**
  Korean coms in Manchuria absorbed by Chinese CP, 257
Krestintern, *see* International Peasants' Council
Kronstadt uprising against Soviet rule (1921), 81, 447
Kuomintang, 66, 67, 73, 84, 316, 317, 477, 479
Kurdish Soviet Republic (Mahabad), 226, 227, 231
Kurds, 226, 230, 304
  revolt in Turkey (1925), 435

Labor Defense Council (USA), 216
Labor Party of Switzerland (*former* CP of Switzerland), 80, **418-25**
Labor Progressive Party, *see* Communist Party of Canada
Labour Party (Great Britain), 163-67 *passim*, 180
*Ländersekretariats* in Comintern, 88
Laos, 51, 52, **263-65**, 480, 481
Laotian People's Party, **263-65**
Lapuan Movement (anti-com, Finland), 127
Latin America, 182, 183, 212, 218, 220, **266-96**, 493, 494
Latin American CPs:
  and Castro's takeover in Cuba, 270, 282, 285-86
  com armed revolts, 274, 275
  conferences in Buenos Aires and Montevideo (1929), 357
  defections, 269-70
  front organizations, 292
  legal status (1965), 291
  meetings in Moscow (1950s and 1960), 284, 287
  membership, 292
  organization, 286-89
  origins, 266, 271
  and Sino-Soviet conflict, 285, 294
  social composition, 289-90
  strength, 291
  youth and students in, 291
Latin American Federation of Trade Unions, 376

Latvia, 79, **297-99**
  autonomous part of RSFSR (1917), 297
  Latvian Soviet Republic (1918), 79, 297, 298
    government seated in Russia (1919-20), 297, 298
  Soviet army invades (1918), 297
League Against Imperialism (Brussels), 402
League for the Independence of Vietnam (Viet Minh; com), 478
League of Communists of Yugoslavia, 503-13. *See also* Communist Party of Yugoslavia
League of Nations, 80, 110
Lebanese CP, **300-5**
Lebanese People's Party, *see* Lebanese CP
Lebanon, **300-5**
"Left Opposition" (Tr) in CPSU:
  in Russia, 131, 448
  outside Russia, 132
Leftist Liberation Front (FIDEL; com, Uruguay), 473
Lenin Peace Prize, 209
Lenin School, Moscow, 33, 237, 469
Lesotho (*former* Basutoland), **306-7**, 403, 410
Liberia, 403
"Litbel," *see* Lithuanian-Belorussian Soviet Socialist Republic
Lithuania, 79, **308-11**
Lithuanian-Belorussian Soviet Socialist Republic ("Litbel," 1919), 37, 308-9
Lithuanian CP, **308-11**
  "Bureau Abroad" in Moscow, 309
  founding in Russia (1920), 309
  role in "soldiers' rebellion" (1920), 309
"Long March" (China, 1934-35), 67
Lumumba Institute, Nairobi, 406
Lumumba University, *see* Friendship University, Moscow
Luxembourg, **312-14**

Macedonian question, 30, 170-73 *passim*
Madagascar, *see* Malagasy Republic
Malagasy CP, **314-16**
Malagasy Republic (Madagascar), **314-16**, 410
  Chinese interference in internal affairs of, 409
Malagasy Union, *see* Malagasy CP
Malawi: Chinese and Soviet interference in internal affairs of, 406, 409
Malaya, **316-21**
Malaysia, **316-21**
Mali, 71, 386, 404, 411
  college for labor leaders, Bamakao, 404
  coms trained in USSR, 404
  Senegal com refugees in, 386
Manchuria, 67, 69, 349
Maori (tribe in New Zealand), 339
Marshall Plan (European Recovery Program), 77, 96, 142, 213, 240, 469, 492, 499
Martinican CP, 175, **321-23**
Martinique, **321-23**

Marxist-Leninist Center of Holland (com), 336
Marxist-Leninist Committee (com, pro-Ch, Portugal), 373
Masons:
 Chinese, 71
 expelled from French CP, 137
Mass killings of:
 coms in: El Salvador (1932), 274; Indonesia (1965), 204
 opponents of communism in: Poland (1945-46), 367; Greece (1944), 171
Masses Party of Iran, see Tudeh
Mauritania, 329
Mexican CP, 121, 177, 266-73 passim, 279, 287, 291, 295, 324-26
Mexican Worker-Peasant Party (com), 279. See also Mexican CP
Mexico, 266, 267, 271, 273, 276, 279, 286, 324-26
 seat of Spanish republican exile government with com participation, 398, 400
Molotov-Ribbentrop pact, see Hitler-Stalin pact
Moncada barracks incident (Santiago de Cuba), 102
Mongolia, see Outer Mongolia
Mongolian People's Party, see Mongolian People's Revolutionary Party
Mongolian People's Republic, see Outer Mongolia
Mongolian People's Revolutionary Party (com), 348-51
Moroccan CP, 326-30
Morocco, 326-30
 war (1924-25), 7, 137, 326, 396, 429
Moscow conference of CPS (1957), 12, 28, 53, 75, 95, 120, 176, 234, 323, 329, 353, 384, 429, 433
Moscow conference of 81 "fraternal parties" (1960), 5, 12, 20, 28, 35, 53, 55, 75, 95, 117, 120, 144, 176, 228, 234, 252, 285, 323, 329, 353, 380, 384, 429, 433, 455
Moscow economic conference (1948), 96
Moscow meeting of leaders of 19 CPs (1965), 104, 145, 438
Moscow meetings of Latin American CP leaders (1950s and 1960), 283, 287
Movement of Progressive Workers of Belgium (com, pro-Ch), 423
Movement of the Revolutionary Left, see Peruvian CP
Mozambique, 373, 404, 408-11 passim, 487. See also Portuguese colonies
Muslim Brotherhood, 303

Nanchang com uprising, 67
National Front for the Liberation of South Vietnam (National Liberation Front of South Vietnam), 482, 483
National Lawyers Guild (USA), 206
National Liberation Front of South Vietnam, see National Front for the Liberation of South Vietnam

National Peasants' Union (Philippines), 359, 361
National Socialist German Workers' Party (NSDAP), 85, 86, 155
 its push to power aided by com struggle against socialists, 85, 155
Nationalist trends in CPs, 41, 141, 166, 167, 179, 195, 203, 226, 382, 383
"Natives vs. Muscovites" in CPs of:
 Greece, 170
 Hungary, 187, 188
 Korea, 258, 260
 Poland, 364, 367
 Rumania, 381, 382
NATO, see North Atlantic Treaty Organization
Negro intellectuals in Africa: disillusionment with coms, 403
Negroes in USA, 463
Neocolonialism, 403, 412, 490
Nepal, 71, 330-32, 487
Netherlands, 83, 333-37, 496, 499
Netherlands Indies, see Indonesia
Neutralist policy advocated by CPs, 193, 402, 404
New China News Agency: disguise for Chinese illegal operations in Africa, 407, 408
New Communist List (Israel), 236
New Economic Policy (NEP), 81, 447, 448
"New Left" in USA, 466
New People's Party (com, Korea), 259
New York School for Marxist Studies, 468
New Zealand, 337-40, 496, 499
 troops in Vietnam, 482
Nicaragua, 340-41
 Cuba-based attack on (1959), 284, 341
Niger Democratic Union, see Independence Party
Niger Republic, 341-42, 408, 409, 410
Nigeria, 343-44, 403, 404, 405, 410
North Atlantic Treaty Organization (NATO), 10, 78, 116, 193, 214, 240, 489, 492, 500, 510
North Korea, see Korea, Democratic People's Republic of
North Korean CP, 258. See also Korean Worker's Party
North Korean Workers' Party (com), 259. See also Korean Workers' Party
North Vietnam, see Vietnam, Democratic Republic of
Northern Ireland, 233-34. See also Ireland
Norway, 83, 93, 345-47

October revolution in Russia, see Bolshevik revolution in Russia
Organization of Marxists-Leninists of Switzerland (pro-Ch), 422
Outer Mongolia, 97, 348-51
 nationalist coup against Soviet domination fails, 350

Pacific Secretariat of Trade Unions (1929), 376

INDEX OF SUBJECTS 569

Pakistan, 71, **351-53**
   war with India (1965), 198, 199
Palestine, *see* Israel
Palestinian CP, *see* Israeli CP
Palestinian question: divides Arab coms, 460
Pan-African Union of Journalists, 218
Pan-Africanism, 306, 307, 343, 501
Panama, 266, 273, 284, 291, **354-55**
Paraguay, 266, 272, **355-56**
Paraguayan CP, 266, 267, 268, 271, 287, 291, 295, **355-56**
Paraguayan Leninist CP (pro-Ch), 295, 355
Parliamentary elections, *see* Communists in representative assemblies . . .
Party of People of Panama (com), 266, 273, 274, 277, 291, 295, **354-55**
Party of People's Unity, *see* Party of Popular Accord
Party of Popular Accord (com, Haiti), 182-83, 266, 279, 285, 291
Party of Revolutionary Left (com), 280. *See also* Communist Party of Bolivia
Pasabala (Burmese anti-Japanese front organization), 48, 49
Patrice Lumumba Institute of Political Science (Lagos, Nigeria), 344
"Peaceful coexistence" line, 27-28, 72, 208, 212, 222, 223, 234, 282, 332, 383, 399, 402, 409, 411, 438, 464, 489, 493
Peasant Workers' Bloc (com, Spain), 396
Peasants' International, *see* International Peasants' Council
People's Action Front (com, pro-Ch, Portugal), 373
People's Anti-Japanese Army ("Huks," Philippines), 359. *See also* People's Liberation Army ("Huks," Philippines)
People's CP of Turkey, *see* Turkish CP
People's Liberation Army (China), *see* Chinese Red Army
People's Liberation Army ("Huks," Philippines), **359-61**
People's National Liberation Party (com, Haiti), 183. *See also* Party of Popular Accord
People's Party of Khmer (com, Cambodia), **51-53**
People's Progressive Party (com, Guyana), **179-82**
People's Revolutionary Party (com, South Vietnam), 483
People's Revolutionary Party of Tuva (com), 89, 92n19
People's Socialist Party (Mexico), 325
Permanent Congress for Trade Union Unity of Latin American Workers, 501
Persian Soviet Socialist Republic (Gilan Republic, 1920-21), 226
Peru, 266, 268, 276, 283, 286, 291, **356-57**
Peruvian CP, 266-70 *passim*, 273, 274, 278, 283, 291, 295, **356-57**
Peruvian Socialist Party, *see* Peruvian CP
Pescadores Islands, 68

Philippines, **358-61**
   bureau of Chinese CP in, 359
   troops in Vietnam, 482
Poale Zion, 109, 235
Poland, 76-80 *passim*, 86, 93, 96, 97, 112, 132, 189, 213, 214, 220, **361-70**, 484
Polish Commissariat in Russia (1918), *see* Russian Soviet Federated Socialist Republic: Commissariat of Nationality Affairs
Polish October rebellion (1956), 367, 368
   impact on other CPs, 5, 72, 96, 113, 143, 189, 196, 451, 465
Polish Socialist Party-Left, 362
Polish United Workers' Party (com, 1942-48), **361-70**. *See also* Communist Party of Soviet Union
Polish Workers' Party, *see* Polish United Workers' Party
Political training of foreign coms, *see* Training of com cadres
"Polycentrism," 87, 145
Popular-front tactics adopted by CPs, 4, 13, 32, 43, 56, 59, 60, 64-68 *passim*, 71, 74, 86-87, 94, 105, 110, 127, 156, 165, 168, 171, 186, 193, 195, 202, 226, 240, 274, 302, 310, 324, 327, 338, 359, 365, 367, 371, 373, 385, 390, 391, 397, 400, 420, 463, 467, 468, 479, 506
   Dimitrov report on, 87
   initiated in France, 86-87, 139-40
   "popular front of the left" in France (1965), 145
Popular-front tactics and policies adopted by coms in:
   Albania, 4
   Argentina, 13
   Belgium, 32
   Bulgaria, 43
   Canada, 56
   Ceylon, 59, 60
   Chile, 64, 65, 276
   China, 67, 68, 71
   Colombia, 74
   Comintern, 87, 211
   Cyprus, 105
   Czechoslovakia, 110
   Finland, 127
   France, 86-87, 139-40, 145, 302, 327, 385; by Italians in, 240
   front organizations, 94, 211
   Germany, 156
   Great Britain, 165, 168
   Greece, 171
   Hungary, 186
   Iceland, 193
   India, 195
   Indonesia, 202
   Iran, 226
   Latin America, 274
   Lithuania, 310
   Mexico, 324
   Netherlands, 334

INDEX OF SUBJECTS

Popular-front tactics adopted by coms in (*continued*):
  New Zealand, 338
  Philippines, 359
  Poland, 366
  Portugal, 371, 373
  South Africa, 390, 391
  Spain, 397, 400
  Switzerland, 420
  USA, 463, 467, 468
  Vietnam, 479
  Yugoslavia, 506
Popular Socialist Party of Cuba, *see* Communist Party of Cuba
Popular Socialist Party of Haiti (com), 182, 277, 291. *See also* Party of Popular Accord
Popular Vanguard Party of Costa Rica (com), **95-96**, 266, 268, 274, 277, 280, 291
Portugal, **370-74**, 396
Portuguese colonies, 373, 403. *See also* Angola; Goa; Mozambique; Portuguese Guinea
Portuguese CP, **370-74**
  activities in Portuguese colonies, 373
Portuguese Guinea, 373, 408, 409. *See also* Portuguese colonies
Portuguese Revolutionary Liberation Group (com, pro-Ch), 373
Power seizure by CPs, *see* Seizure of power by CPs
Prisoners of war in Russia, *see* War prisoners and refugees in Russia ...
Pro-Chinese "International," *see* Committee for an International Revolutionary Front
Profintern, *see* Red International of Labor Unions
Progressive Labor Party (com, pro-Ch, USA), 466
Progressive Party (com, Switzerland), 419
Provisional Organizing Committee for a Marxist-Leninist Communist Party (pro-Ch, USA), 466
Provisional revolutionary committee for Poland (com, Bialystok, 1920), 363
Purges and trials of coms in USSR:
  influence on other CPs, 166, 186, 420, 448, 449, 451, 453, 454
  list of purged, 457, 475
Purges in CPs and international com organizations:
  Albania, 4, 5
  Armenia, 16
  Australia, 18, 19, 20
  Austria, 23
  Belgium, 33
  Bulgaria, 44, 45, 46
  Canada, 57, 58
  China, 66, 69
  Comintern, 83, 84, 85
  Communist Youth International, 94
  Cyprus, 106
  Czechoslovakia, 110, 111
  Estonia, 124
  Finland, 129, 130
  France, 138, 139, 142, 145
  Georgia, 149
  Greece, 170
  Italy, 239
  Japan, 246, 247
  Korea (North), 258, 260
  Latvia, 298
  Lithuania, 309
  Mexico, 325
  Netherlands, 334, 335
  Norway, 346
  Outer Mongolia, 349, 350
  Palestine, 235
  Poland, 364
  Rumania, 381, 382
  Tadzhikstan, 426
  Turkey, 434, 437
  Ukraine, 442, 443
  USA, 465, 466
  Yugoslavia, 504, 506
Purges in USSR of foreign coms who fled homeland persecutions, 84, 87, 298, 311, 366, 368, 390
Purges of founders and prominent members of CPs and international com organizations:
  China, 66
  Comintern, 85
  Communist Youth International, 94
  Czechoslovakia, 110, 111
  Estonia, 124
  France, 138
  Greece, 171, 172, 173
  Hungary, 190
  Italy, 239
  Japan, 247
  Lithuania, 298
  Netherlands, 334, 335
  Poland, 367
  Rumania, 382
  USA, 463, 464
Purges of pro-Soviet elements from CPs:
  Albania, 5
  Japan, 247
  Yugoslavia, 509

Queensland, 19
Quemoy (island), 68, 72

Radio broadcasts:
  com propaganda to Turkey, 438
  from China and USSR to Africa, 408
  from Moscow by foreign coms, 294
Rajk (László) affair (Hungary), 188
Rassemblement Démocratique Africain, *see* African Democratic Rally
Red Aid, *see* International Organization for Aid to Revolutionaries
Red Army, Soviet, intervention to impose com regimes, 25, 37, 44, 81, 110, 111, 123, 253, 258, 425, 447, 485
  Armenia (1920), 16
  Bukhara (1920), 425

INDEX OF SUBJECTS 571

Czechoslovakia (1948), 108
Estonia (1918), 123; (1940), 124
Finland (1918), 125; (1939), 127
Georgia (1921), 149
Iran (1918 and 1945), 226
Latvia (1919), 297; (1940), 298
Lithuania (1919), 309; (1940), 311
Poland (1919-20), 363; (1939), 367
Ukraine (1918 and 1920), 441
"Red Flag" coms (Burma), 48
Red International of Labor Unions
    (Profintern), 81, 82, 89, 90, 126,
    137, 164, 165, 210, 220, 257, 293,
    358, 361, **375-77**, 420, 468
  dissolved by Comintern (1937), 211, 376
"Red regiments" formed in Soviet Russia
    (1918), 79
  Czechs in, 108
  Estonians in, 123
  Poles in, 363
Red Sport International (Sportintern), 210,
    211, **377-78**
Reichstag fire, Berlin (1933), 85, 86, 155
Repressions against coms and CPs:
  Algeria, 7, 12
  Argentina, 13
  Austria, 24
  Balkan countries, 83
  Belgium, 31
  Brazil, 40, 41, 275
  Cambodia, 52-53
  Cameroon, 54
  Canada, 56, 57
  Cuba, 99, 101
  Dominican Republic, 118
  El Salvador, 121
  France, 138
  Germany, 155, 156
  Guatemala, 177
  Haiti, 182
  Honduras, 281
  Hungary, 186
  Indonesia, 201
  Iran, 226
  Italy, 239
  Japan, 244, 245
  Latin America, 274, 275, 291
  Malaya (by British), 317
  Morocco, 328
  Pakistan, 352
  Paraguay, 355
  Poland, 364
  Portugal, 370, 371
  Spain, 398
  Thailand, 427
  Tunisia, 429, 430
  USA, 462, 465, 466, 467
  Vietnam, 479
  Yugoslavia, 504
Repressions against non-coms in com-dominated states:
  Armenia, 16
  Bulgaria, 45
  China (People's Republic of), 68
  Czechoslovakia, 111, 112

Germany (East), 160
Hungary, 187, 188
Poland, 508
Ukraine, 442
Yugoslavia, 508
Republic of South Africa, *see* South Africa
Réunion, **379-80**
Réunion CP, 175, 322, **379-80**
Revisionism and revisionists in CPs, 57, 72,
    112, 160, 172, 193, 262, 336, 510
Revolutionary Ceylon Equality Party
    (com), 62
Revolutionary CP (pro-Ch, Spain), 400
Revolutionary Union Party of Cuba, *see*
    Communist Party of Cuba
Revolutionary Workers' Party of Bolivia
    (Tr, later pro-Ch), *see* CP of Bolivia
Revolutionary Workers' Party of Guatemala,
    *see* Guatemalan Labor Party
Rhodesia, 403, 408-11 *passim*
  coms trained in USSR, 404
Ribbentrop-Molotov pact, *see* Hitler-Stalin
    pact
Rif war, *see* Morocco
Romansch Federation of Swiss Communists
    (pro-Ch), 422
Rote Hilfe (Germany), 216
Rumania, 29, 30, 76, 93, 96, 109, 220, 347,
    **380-84**, 484
  antagonized by Soviet annexations of
    1940, 381
Rumanian Bureau of Russian CP, Moscow,
    381
Rumanian CP, 30, 76, **380-84**
Rumanian Workers' Party, *see* Rumanian CP
Russia, *see* Union of Soviet Socialist
    Republics
Russian CP (Bolshevik) (1918-25), 446-47.
    *See also* Communist Party of Soviet
    Union
Russian revolution (Nov. 1917), *see* Bolshevik revolution in Russia
Russian Social Democratic Labor Party, 16,
    36, 148, 253, 297, 439, 440, 445,
    474
  Northern Baltic Organization of, 123
  Northwestern regional organization of, 37
  Tallinn Committee of, 122
  *See also* Communist Party of Soviet Union
Russian Social Democratic Labor Party
    (Bolshevik), 37, 79, 148, 446
  Estonian section of, 123
  *See also* Communist Party of Soviet Union
Russian Soviet Federated Socialist Republic,
    79, 80, 81, 297, 452
  Commissariat of Foreign Affairs, 80, 92
  Commissariat of Nationality Affairs, 79
  national commissariats:
    Estonian, 123
    Finnish, 80
    Latvian, 297, 298
    Lithuanian, 308
    Polish, 362
Russians heading non-Russian CPs in USSR:
  in Belorussia, 37

## INDEX OF SUBJECTS

Russians heading non-Russian CPs in USSR (*continued*):
   in Lithuania, 310
   in Ukraine, 441, 442, 443
Russification of non-Russian ethnic areas by Soviet government:
   Belorussia, 37
   Ukraine, 441, 443
Rwanda, 407

Sabah (North Borneo), 316
San Marino, **384-85**
San Marino CP, **384-85**
Sarawak, 316-21 *passim*
Sarawak Advanced Youths' Association, *see* Communist Party of Malaya
Sarawak Liberation League, *see* Communist Party of Malaya
Sarawak Overseas Democratic Youth League, *see* Communist Party of Malaya
Scholarships for Africans for studies in Moscow, 181, 404-8 *passim*
School for Ideological Training for Africans, Bautzen, East Germany, 404
Schools for African guerrilla fighters in Prague and Bulgaria, 404
Schutzbund (Austria), 23, 24, 27, 87
   exiles in USSR executed, 24
Second-and-a-Half International, *see* Vienna Socialist Union
Second International, *see* Socialist (Second) International
Seizure of power by CPs in:
   Albania, 4
   Armenia (1920), 16
   Bulgaria, 44
   Czechoslovakia, 108, 111, 116, 211, 222
   Estonia (1917-18), 123
   Hungary, 187
   Poland, 366-67
   Rumania, 381-82
   Yugoslavia, 508
Semirechie (*oblast* in Soviet Central Asia), 255
Senegal, 341, 342, **385-87**, 403, 410
Senegalese Democratic Union (com), 341
Serbia, 29. *See also* Yugoslavia
Shanghai:
   com uprising (1927), 67
   massacre of coms (1927), 67
Singapore, **316-321**
Sinkiang, 67
Sino-Soviet border incidents, 69
Sino-Soviet conflict, 12, 14, 39, 46, 50, 55, 65, 95, 107, 119, 122, 130, 144, 168, 183, 184, 190, 203, 228, 234, 294, 312, 313, 323, 329, 341-44 *passim*, 350, 368, 380, 385, 393, 433, 437, 454-55, 473
   and Africa, 404, 409-10
   background, 454
   Chinese accused of Trotskyism, 455
   Chinese attitude, 72-73
   Chinese territorial demands, 455
   consequences in Comecon, 97
   and Fourth International, 135
   influence on international front organizations, 209, 223-24, 484, 487, 490
   and Latin America, 294-95
   Rumanian attempt to mediate, 383
   Soviet attitude, 454-55
   *See also* Sino-Soviet conflict, influence on other CPs
Sino-Soviet conflict, influence on other CPs:
   CPs remain neutral:
      Cuba, 104
      Norway, 346-47
      Rumania, 383
      South Africa, 392
      Venezuela, 295, 477
   CPs split, pro-Ch parties formed:
      Australia, 20, 73
      Belgium, 34-36
      Brazil, 41, 73, 295
      Canada, 58
      Ceylon, 62-63
      Colombia, 73, 74-75, 295
      Denmark, 117
      France, 73, 145
      Mexico, 73, 295, 325
      Netherlands, 336-37
      Paraguay, 73, 295, 355
      Peru, 73, 295, 357
      Portugal, 373
      Spain, 73, 399-400
      Switzerland, 73, 422
      USA, 466, 470
   CPs switch allegiance to Peking:
      Albania, 5, 73
      Indonesia, 73, 203
      Japan, 73, 246-47
      Korea, 73, 262
      Laos, 73, 265
      Malagasy, 314, 316
      Malaysia, 73, 316, 320
      New Zealand, 73, 339-40
      Thailand, 73, 429
      Vietnam, 73, 483
   CPs with pro-Ch factions:
      Austria, 28, 73
      Cameroon, 55-56
      Ecuador, 73, 295
      Great Britain, 168
      Greece, 173
      Guadeloupe, 176
      Guatemala, 178
      India, 73, 199
      Iran, 227
      Israel, 237
      Italy, 242
      Lebanon, 73
      Nepal, 331-32
      Panama, 354
      Sudan, 414
      Sweden, 415, 417
Slovakia, 109-112
   Slovak Soviet Republic (1919), 79, 81, 109
   uprising (1944), 111
Social composition of CPs in:
   Armenia, 17

Social composition of CPs in (*continued*):
  Bulgaria, 45
  Czechoslovakia, 113
  Germany, 158-59
  Poland, 368-69
  Rumania, 382
  USSR, 453
  USA, 467
  Yugoslavia, 511
Social Democracy of Kingdom of Poland and Lithuania, 361, 362
Social Democratic Left Party of Sweden, 414
Social Democratic Party of Colombia, *see* Communist Party of Colombia
"Social fascists," 155, 186, 463
Social Revolutionary Party of Colombia, *see* Communist Party of Colombia
Socialist Federal Republic of Yugoslavia, *see* Yugoslavia
Socialist International, *see* Socialist (Second) International
Socialist League of South Africa (com), 392. *See also* South African CP
Socialist Party of America, 462, 463
Socialist Party of Nicaragua (com), 266, 276, 277, **340-41**
Socialist Party of Philippines, *see* Communist Party of Philippines
Socialist People's Party of Mexico, 266. *See also* Mexican CP
Socialist (Second) International, 78, 79, 82, 92, 446, 503, 504
  Lenin's disruptive activities in, 22, 79, 446
Socialist Unity Party (com, East Germany), 159-61
Socialist Workers' and Farmers' Party of Nigeria (com), **343-44**
Socialist Workers Party (Tr, USA), 463, 466
  adheres to Fourth International, 132
  pro-Ch stand, 470
Socialist Workers' Party of Chile, *see* Communist Party of Chile
Socialist Workers' Party of Yugoslavia (com), 504. *See also* League of Communists of Yugoslavia
Socialist Youth International, *see* International Union of Socialist Youth Organizations
Somali Republic (Somalia), 408-11 *passim*
  Soviet-Chinese rivalry in, 404, 410
South Africa, 306, **388-94**, 402, 407-11 *passim*, 496
South African CP, **391-94**. *See also* Communist Party of Africa
South Korea, *see* Korea, Republic of
South Korean Workers' Party (com), 259. *See also* Korean Workers' Party
South Seas CP, *see* Communist Party of Malaya
South West Africa: coms trained in USSR, 404
Soviet advice to and support of CPs, 24, 25, 49, 117, 129, 141, 143, 187, 188, 189, 192, 197, 228
Soviet aggression against Finland: influence on foreign CPs, 116, 127, 133, 345, 415
Soviet and East European instructors for armies of African states, 406, 410
Soviet and Soviet bloc economic aid to African states, 407
  Congo-Brazzaville, 408
  Guinea, 405
  Somalia, 410
Soviet Association for the Liberation of Egypt (Baku, USSR), 458
Soviet diplomatic and consular officials aiding foreign CPs:
  Africa, 404
  Australia, 18
  China, 67, 71
  Egypt, 459
Soviet financial support to CPs, 79, 332, 363
Soviet government interference in internal political affairs:
  Albania, 5
  Algeria, 12
  Asian countries, 49
  Bulgaria, 44
  Canada, 57
  China, 67, 71
  Congo, 404
  Czechoslovakia, 112
  France, 77
  Greece, 173
  Guinea, 404, 405
  Hungary, 188
  India, 197
  Italy, 77
  Kenya, 406
  Malawi, 406
  Poland, 367-68
  Rumania, 382
  Switzerland, 419
  Ukraine, 441-42
  Yugoslavia, 77, 508-9
Soviet intelligence:
  uses Comintern emissaries, 89
  uses International Red Aid, 211
Soviet military interventions to secure com regimes:
  Bukhara, 475
  Estonia, 123-24
  Hungary, 187, 189
  Latvia, 297
  Lithuania, 309
  Ukraine, 441
Soviet persecution of Ukrainian nationalists, 441-42
Soviet republics and governments, collapse of:
  Azerbaijan (Iran, 1946), 226, 227
  Bavaria (1919), 22, 81
  Estonia (1919), 79, 123
  Finland (1918), 79, 125; (1939), 126-29 *passim*
  Hungary (1919), 22, 23, 79, 81, 109, 185
  Iran (Gilan, 1920), 226

## INDEX OF SUBJECTS

Soviet republics and governments, collapse of (*continued*):
   Juichin (Kiangsi province, 1931-34), 67
   Kurdish Republic (Iran, 1946), 226, 227
   Latvia (1919), 79, 297
   Lithuania (1919), 79, 308-9
   Poland (1920), 79, 363
   Slovakia (1919), 79, 81, 109
Soviet-sponsored Polish army in USSR (1943), 366
Soviet strategy in Africa, 402-7 *passim*
Soviet Union, see Union of Soviet Socialist Republics
Soviet-Yugoslav rupture, 4, 77, 78, 172, 207, 213, 222, 454, 486, 509-11
Spain, 87, 93, 110, 240, 395-401, 506
   civil war (1936-39), 32, 110, 118, 165, 188, 240, 294, 397-400 *passim*, 506
   refugees in Dominican Republic set up exile com organizations, 118
Spanish com exiles in:
   Eastern Europe, 399
   France, 393, 399
   North Africa, 399
   USSR, 399
Spanish CP, 395. See also Communist Party of Spain
Spanish Communist Workers' Party, 395. See also Communist Party of Spain
"Spanish Marxist-Leninist" faction (com, pro-Ch), 400
Spardak (Armenian com youth organization), 15
Spartacists (Tr, USA), 466
"Spartacus" (Latvia), 297
Spartacus Party (com, Armenian, in Beirut, Lebanon), 301
Spartakus Bund (Germany), 152
Sportintern, see Red Sport International
Stockholm peace appeal (1950), 142, 352, 488, 500
Subsaharan Africa, **402-12**
Sudan, 403-6 *passim*, 410, **412-14**
Sudanese CP, **412-14**
   Islamic opposition causes dissolution (1965), 413
Sweden, 80, 93, **414-18**, 486
Swiss CP (f. 1963, pro-Ch), 418, 422, 424
Swiss Social Democratic Party: membership referendum rejects affiliation with Comintern, 419-20
Switzerland, 79, 80, 93, 132, **418-25**
Syria, 71, 300-305, 460
Syrian CP, 302-5, 460

Tadzhikistan **425-26**
Taiwan, see China, Republic of
Tanganyika, 407. See also Tanzania
Tannu Tuva, 89, 92 (n. 19)
Tanzania, 71, 406, 408
   coms trained in USSR, 404
   See also Tanganyika
Terijoki government, see Finnish Soviet Republic

Thailand, 320, **427-29**
   CP of Malaya active in, 317, 428
   troops in Vietnam, 482
Thailand Independence Movement (in China), 428
Thailand Patriotic Front (in China), 428
Third International, see Communist International
Tibet, 68, 282
   uprising against Chinese domination (1959), 69, 196
"Titoists" expelled and liquidated by CPs, 45, 46, 77, 158, 159, 226, 346, 367
Trade Union Educational League (USA), 468
Trade Union Federation of Pakistan (com), 351
Trade Union International (Amsterdam), 165
Trades Union Congress (TUC, Great Britain), 498
   withdraws from World Federation of Trade Unions (1949), 499
Training of com cadres:
   African:
     by Chinese, 342, 403-8 *passim*
     in Cuba, 386
     in Eastern Europe, 404-5
     in USSR, 404-5
   Asian, by Chinese, 50, 246, 428, 479
   in USSR, 3, 22, 23, 33, 40, 109, 171, 301, 338, 430, 437, 469, 478, 505
Training of Indonesian coms by Japanese intelligence (1944), 202
Transcaucasian Federation, 150
Trials of coms in non-com states:
   Cambodia, 53
   Pakistan, 352
   Portugal, 371
   Senegal, 386
   Tunisia, 429
   USA, 464, 465
Trials of coms in USSR, see Purges and trials in USSR
Trotskyism, 85, 94, 447, 449, 455, 509. See also Fourth International; Trotskyists
Trotskyists, 16, 21, 37, 39, 59-62, 66, 72, 84, 85, 94, **131-135**, 138, 149, 155, 167, 168, 187, 256, 270, 298, 312, 325, 334, 364, 365, 391, 396, 398, 426, 463, 478-79
   factions in CPs, 84, 139, 149, 168, 187, 325, 364, 365
   ministers in Ceylon government, 62
   parties in USA, 463
   in Spain, assassinated or deported to USSR, 398
   support USSR, 132-33
Tudeh (Masses Party of Iran, com), **225-29**
Tudor Vladimirescu division (Rumania), 381
Tunisia, **429-33**
Turkestan, 69, 255, 425
Turkestan Autonomous Soviet Republic, 255, 474
Turkey, **434-38**

Turkey (*continued*):
  communism treated as treason, 436
  radio com propaganda broadcast to, 438
Turkish CP, **434-38**
Turkish Socialist Workers' and Peasants' Party (legal com front), 436
Turkish Workers' and Peasants' Socialist Party (com), 434. *See also* Turkish CP
Turkmenistan, **439-40**
Tuva, *see* Tannu Tuva
Twenty-sixth of July movement (Cuba), 102, 285

Uganda, 407
Ukraine, 81, **440-44**, 452
  coms advocate confederation of independent soviet republics instead of Soviet Union (1922), 441
  peasant uprising against Soviet occupation (1919), 441
Ukrainian Left Socialist Revolutionary Party (*borotbisty*), 441. *See also* Communist Party of Ukraine
Ukrainian People's Republic (1919-20): opposes Soviet domination, 441
UNESCO, *see* United Nations Educational, Scientific and Cultural Organization
Unified (Second) CP of Egypt, 460
Union of Cameroon Peoples, *see* Cameroon Peoples' Union
Union of Malagasy People, *see* Malagasy CP
Union of Polish Patriots (Moscow, 1943), 367
Union of Soviet Socialist Republics, 5, 12, 16, 17, 20, 24, 30, 32, 37, 40, 43, 44, 45, 49, 55, 57, 65, 67, 71, 72, 73, 76-88 *passim*, 93, 96, 104, 108-16 *passim*, 123-32 *passim*, 138, 140, 142, 145, 154, 155, 158, 162, 207, 210-11, 267, 270, 278, 280, 282, 284, 298-303 *passim*, 324, 325, 346, 348, 366, 367, 368, 382, 403-6 *passim*, 409, 410, 413, 420, 436, **445-57**, 475, 484, 485, 493, 507, 510
  accused by Africans of racism, 406
  "anti-party group" in, 451
  and Hitler, 87, 155, 449 (*see also* Hitler-Stalin pact)
  intervenes in Spanish civil war, 398, 400
  and Outer Mongolia, 348, 350
  and the Straits, 436
  *See also* Russian Soviet Federated Socialist Republic *and individual Soviet* republics; Sino-Soviet conflict; Soviet . . .
United Arab Republic, 230, 301, 304, 406, 413, 456, **458-61**
United CP of America, 56, 462. *See also* Communist Party of United States
United CP of Australia, *see* Communist Party of Australia
United Democratic Left (com, Greece), 170. *See also* Communist Party of Greece

"United front from above," 61, 82, 84, 87, 155, 376
"United front from below," 82, 84, 85, 127, 139, 363, 420
United Kingdom, *see* Great Britain; Northern Ireland
United Labor-Socialist Party of Iceland (com), **192-94**
United Nations, 171, 203, 206, 208, 214, 217, 222, 230, 278, 303, 403, 431, 486, 493, 496, 500
  Committee on Human Rights, 207
  Economic and Social Council, 207, 208, 217, 225, 487, 497, 503
  Security Council, 227
United Nations Educational, Scientific and Cultural Organization (UNESCO), 225, 487, 495, 497, 503
United Party of Socialist Revolution, *see* Communist Party of Cuba
United States of America, 77, 96, 99, 100, 132, 145, 179, 198, 203, 207, 208, 217, 244, 280, 371, 403, 430, 431, 455, **462-72**, 509
  Comintern agents in, 462, 469
  economic aid to African states, 407
  seat of Fourth International, 132
  supports Greece against com attack, 171, 172
  Supreme Court decision on McCarran act, 466
United Toilers of America (com), 463. *See also* Communist Party of United States
Unity Confederation of Labor (CGTU, France), 7, 136-39 *passim*, 146
Upper Volta, 409
  expels Chinese diplomats, 409
Uprisings and rebellions against com regimes:
  East Germany (1956), 159
  Hungary (1956), 189
  Outer Mongolia (1937-39), 350
  Poland (1956), 367
  Tibet (1959), 69, 196
Uprisings, revolts, and coups by coms, *see* Communist uprisings, revolts, and coups
Uruguay, 266-73 *passim*, 278, 279, 282, 287, 291, 355, **472-73**
Uzbekistan (Uzbek Soviet Socialist Republic), 425, 452, **474-76**

Venezuela, 266-69 *passim*, 274, 276, 278, 283-86 *passim*, 291, 295, **476-77**, 487
Vienna Socialist Union (Second-and-a-Half International), 82
Viet Cong (com, South Vietnam), 481, 482
Viet Minh, *see* League for the Independence of Vietnam
Vietnam, 46, 190, **477-84**. See also Vietnam, Democratic Republic of; Vietnam, Republic of

Vietnam, Democratic Republic of (North Vietnam), 51, 52, 97, 428, 477, **479-84**, 487. *See also* Vietnam
Vietnam, Republic of (South Vietnam), 477, 480-84 *passim*, 495. *See also* Vietnam
Vietnam Revolutionary Youth League (Canton, China), 478
Vietnam war, 46, 190, 482
Vietnam Workers' Party (com), 51, **477-84**
Violence, com, *see* Assassination attempts . . . ; Assassinations by coms . . . ; Communist riots and violence; Communist uprisings, revolts, and coups

"War communism," 81, 447
War prisoners and refugees in Russia trained to spread communism abroad, 79, 362, 434, 503
   Austrians, 22
   Austro-Hungarians, 27, 503
   Croatians, 503
   Czechs, 108
   Hungarians, 185
   Poles, 362
   Serbians, 503
   Slovaks, 185
   Turks, 434
Wars of national liberation, 402, 403, 407, 408, 409, 428
Warsaw Pact, *see* Warsaw Treaty Organization
Warsaw Treaty Organization (Warsaw Pact), 5, 46, 78, **484-85**
West Germany, *see* Germany, Federal Republic of
"White Flag" coms (Burma), 48
Wilhelm-Pieck Institute, East Berlin, 404
Women's International Democratic Federation, 211, **485-87**, 488
   expelled by French government, 487
   expels Yugoslav affiliate, 486
Workers (Communist) Party of America, 462
Workers' Confederation of Latin America, *see* Confederation of Latin American Workers
Workers' International Relief, 210
Workers League (Tr, USA), 134
Workers of Zion, *see* Poale Zion
Workers' Party, *see* Bulgarian CP
Workers Party of America (com), 462
Workers' Party of Marxist Unification (Tr, Spain), 396, 397, 398
   members assassinated or deported to USSR during Spanish civil war, 398
   *See also* Communist Party of Spain
Workers World Party (Tr, USA), 466
World Assembly of Youth, 492
"World communist party," as goal of Comintern, 81, 132
World Congress of Intellectuals for Peace, 207, 488
World Council of Peace (formerly World Peace Council), 168, 180, 207, 208, 209, 212, 214, 225, 405, 427, 486, **488-91**, 495, 496, 500
   banned from Austria (1957), 488, 491
   expelled from France (1951), 488
   *See also* Stockholm peace appeal
World Federation of Democratic Youth, 211, 212, 225, 351, 405, 486, **492-95**
   abandoned by non-com affiliates, 492
   denounced by Chinese as "paid Soviet agents", 494
   expelled from France, 493
   expels Yugoslav affiliates, 492
World Federation of International Juridical Associations, 208
World Federation of Scientific Workers, 212, **496-98**
   expels Yugoslav affiliates, 496
   "Peking Center," 497
World Federation of Trade Unions, 180, 211, 228, 313, 315, 342, 344, 351, 393, 405, 413, 486, **498-503**
   CIO (USA) and TUC (Great Britain) withdraw from, 499
   expelled from Austria and France, 500
   expels Yugoslav affiliate, 500
   gives financial aid to com-inspired strikes, 500
   Latin American bureau, 501
World Health Organization, 489
"World party of the socialist revolution," as goal of Fourth International, 132
World Peace Council, *see* World Council of Peace
World revolution, 278, 404
   Soviet goal, 79, 271, 363
   Soviet government's subsidy for, 79

Yalta conference (1945), 367
"Yenan returnees" in Korea, 258
Young Communist International, *see* Communist Youth International
Yugoslav Communist Revolutionary League of Pelagićevci, 504
Yugoslavia, 30, 77, 112, 172, 207, 220, **503-13**
   and Albania, 4
   and Comecon, 97
   expelled from Cominform, 47, 172, 213, 222, 486
   expelled from international com front organizations, 207, 213, 222, 486, 493, 496, 500
   USSR resumes relations with, 78, 454

Zambia, 408
Zanzibar, 405, 408, 409, 410, 487
Zionism, 111, 303
   Jewish coms in Egypt oppose, 460
   Soviet support (1946-47), 251
   *See also* Israel
Zveno (Bulgarian military league), 44